P9-ECN-503

PEARSON

ALWAYS LEARNING

Hugh D. Young • Roger A. Freedman •
Contributions by A. Lewis Ford

Sears and Zemansky's University Physics

with Modern Physics

Technology Update
Volume A

Fourth Custom Edition for the University of British Columbia

Taken from:
*Sears and Zemansky's University Physics with Modern Physics:
Technology Update*, Thirteenth Edition
by Hugh D. Young and Roger A. Freedman
with Contributions by A. Lewis Ford

Cover Art: "Steam Locomotive" courtesy of Richard A. Cooke III/Getty Images; "Steelworks" courtesy of Shutterstock.

Taken from:

Sears and Zemansky's University Physics with Modern Physics: Technology Update, Thirteenth Edition
by Hugh D. Young and Roger A. Freedman
with Contributions by A. Lewis Ford
Copyright © 2014, 2012, 2008 by Pearson Education, Inc.
San Francisco, California 94111

All rights reserved. No part of this book may be reproduced, in any form or by any means, without permission in writing from the publisher.

This special edition published in cooperation with Pearson Learning Solutions.

All trademarks, service marks, registered trademarks, and registered service marks are the property of their respective owners and are used herein for identification purposes only.

Pearson Learning Solutions, 501 Boylston Street, Suite 900, Boston, MA 02116
A Pearson Education Company
www.pearsoned.com

Printed in Canada

1 2 3 4 5 6 7 8 9 10 XXXX 17 16 15 14 13

000200010271795935

BK/MB

ISBN 10: 1-269-42315-0
ISBN 13: 978-1-269-42315-1

DETAILED CONTENTS

SEARS AND ZEMANSKY'S

UNIVERSITY PHYSICS

WITH MODERN PHYSICS

TECHNOLOGY UPDATE

HUGH D. YOUNG
CARNEGIE MELLON
UNIVERSITY

ROGER A. FREEDMAN
UNIVERSITY
OF CALIFORNIA,
SANTA BARBARA

CONTRIBUTING AUTHOR
A. LEWIS FORD
TEXAS A&M UNIVERSITY

6

WORK AND KINETIC ENERGY

? After finding a piece of breakfast cereal on the floor, this ant picked it up and carried it away. As the ant was lifting the piece of cereal, did the *cereal* do work on the *ant*?

Suppose you try to find the speed of an arrow that has been shot from a bow. You apply Newton's laws and all the problem-solving techniques that we've learned, but you run across a major stumbling block: After the archer releases the arrow, the bow string exerts a *varying* force that depends on the arrow's position. As a result, the simple methods that we've learned aren't enough to calculate the speed. Never fear; we aren't by any means finished with mechanics, and there are other methods for dealing with such problems.

The new method that we're about to introduce uses the ideas of *work* and *energy*. The importance of the energy idea stems from the *principle of conservation of energy*: Energy is a quantity that can be converted from one form to another but cannot be created or destroyed. In an automobile engine, chemical energy stored in the fuel is converted partially to the energy of the automobile's motion and partially to thermal energy. In a microwave oven, electromagnetic energy obtained from your power company is converted to thermal energy of the food being cooked. In these and all other processes, the *total* energy—the sum of all energy present in all different forms—remains the same. No exception has ever been found.

We'll use the energy idea throughout the rest of this book to study a tremendous range of physical phenomena. This idea will help you understand why a sweater keeps you warm, how a camera's flash unit can produce a short burst of light, and the meaning of Einstein's famous equation $E = mc^2$.

In this chapter, though, our concentration will be on mechanics. We'll learn about one important form of energy called *kinetic energy*, or energy of motion, and how it relates to the concept of *work*. We'll also consider *power*, which is the time rate of doing work. In Chapter 7 we'll expand the ideas of work and kinetic energy into a deeper understanding of the concepts of energy and the conservation of energy.

6.1 Work

You'd probably agree that it's hard work to pull a heavy sofa across the room, to lift a stack of encyclopedias from the floor to a high shelf, or to push a stalled car off the road. Indeed, all of these examples agree with the everyday meaning of *work*—any activity that requires muscular or mental effort.

In physics, work has a much more precise definition. By making use of this definition we'll find that in any motion, no matter how complicated, the total work done on a particle by all forces that act on it equals the change in its *kinetic energy*—a quantity that's related to the particle's speed. This relationship holds even when the forces acting on the particle aren't constant, a situation that can be difficult or impossible to handle with the techniques you learned in Chapters 4 and 5. The ideas of work and kinetic energy enable us to solve problems in mechanics that we could not have attempted before.

In this section we'll see how work is defined and how to calculate work in a variety of situations involving *constant* forces. Even though we already know how to solve problems in which the forces are constant, the idea of work is still useful in such problems. Later in this chapter we'll relate work and kinetic energy, and then apply these ideas to problems in which the forces are *not* constant.

The three examples of work described above—pulling a sofa, lifting encyclopedias, and pushing a car—have something in common. In each case you do work by exerting a *force* on a body while that body *moves* from one place to another—that is, undergoes a *displacement* (Fig. 6.1). You do more work if the force is greater (you push harder on the car) or if the displacement is greater (you push the car farther down the road).

The physicist's definition of work is based on these observations. Consider a body that undergoes a displacement of magnitude s along a straight line. (For now, we'll assume that any body we discuss can be treated as a particle so that we can ignore any rotation or changes in shape of the body.) While the body moves, a constant force $\vec{F}$ acts on it in the same direction as the displacement $\vec{s}$ (Fig. 6.2). We define the **work** W done by this constant force under these circumstances as the product of the force magnitude F and the displacement magnitude s:

$$W = Fs \quad \text{(constant force in direction of straight-line displacement)} \quad (6.1)$$

The work done on the body is greater if either the force F or the displacement s is greater, in agreement with our observations above.

CAUTION **Work = W, weight = w** Don't confuse uppercase W (work) with lowercase w (weight). Though the symbols are similar, work and weight are different quantities. ▌

The SI unit of work is the **joule** (abbreviated J, pronounced "jool," and named in honor of the 19th-century English physicist James Prescott Joule). From Eq. (6.1) we see that in any system of units, the unit of work is the unit of force multiplied by the unit of distance. In SI units the unit of force is the newton and the unit of distance is the meter, so 1 joule is equivalent to 1 *newton-meter* (N·m):

$$1 \text{ joule} = (1 \text{ newton})(1 \text{ meter}) \quad \text{or} \quad 1 \text{ J} = 1 \text{ N·m}$$

In the British system the unit of force is the pound (lb), the unit of distance is the foot (ft), and the unit of work is the *foot-pound* (ft·lb). The following conversions are useful:

$$1 \text{ J} = 0.7376 \text{ ft·lb} \qquad 1 \text{ ft·lb} = 1.356 \text{ J}$$

As an illustration of Eq. (6.1), think of a person pushing a stalled car. If he pushes the car through a displacement $\vec{s}$ with a constant force $\vec{F}$ in the direction

6.1 These people are doing work as they push on the stalled car because they exert a force on the car as it moves.

6.2 The work done by a constant force acting in the same direction as the displacement.

If a body moves through a displacement $\vec{s}$ while a constant force $\vec{F}$ acts on it in the same direction ...

... the work done by the force on the body is $W = Fs$.

Application Work and Muscle Fibers
Our ability to do work with our bodies comes from our skeletal muscles. The fiberlike cells of skeletal muscle, shown in this micrograph, have the ability to shorten, causing the muscle as a whole to contract and to exert force on the tendons to which it attaches. Muscle can exert a force of about 0.3 N per square millimeter of cross-sectional area: The greater the cross-sectional area, the more fibers the muscle has and the more force it can exert when it contracts.

6.3 The work done by a constant force acting at an angle to the displacement.

Car moves through displacement $\vec{s}$ while a constant force $\vec{F}$ acts on it at an angle ϕ to the displacement.

$F_\perp$ does *no* work on car.
$F_\perp = F\sin\phi$

Only $F_\parallel$ does work on car:
$W = F_\parallel s = (F\cos\phi)s$
$= Fs\cos\phi$

$F_\parallel = F\cos\phi$

$\vec{s}$

ActivPhysics 5.1: Work Calculations

of motion, the amount of work he does on the car is given by Eq. (6.1): $W = Fs$. But what if the person pushes at an angle ϕ to the car's displacement (Fig. 6.3)? Then $\vec{F}$ has a component $F_\parallel = F\cos\phi$ in the direction of the displacement and a component $F_\perp = F\sin\phi$ that acts perpendicular to the displacement. (Other forces must act on the car so that it moves along $\vec{s}$, not in the direction of $\vec{F}$. We're interested only in the work that the person does, however, so we'll consider only the force he exerts.) In this case only the parallel component $F_\parallel$ is effective in moving the car, so we define the work as the product of this force component and the magnitude of the displacement. Hence $W = F_\parallel s = (F\cos\phi)s$, or

$$W = Fs\cos\phi \quad \text{(constant force, straight-line displacement)} \quad (6.2)$$

We are assuming that F and ϕ are constant during the displacement. If $\phi = 0$, so that $\vec{F}$ and $\vec{s}$ are in the same direction, then $\cos\phi = 1$ and we are back to Eq. (6.1).

Equation (6.2) has the form of the *scalar product* of two vectors, which we introduced in Section 1.10: $\vec{A} \cdot \vec{B} = AB\cos\phi$. You may want to review that definition. Hence we can write Eq. (6.2) more compactly as

$$W = \vec{F} \cdot \vec{s} \quad \text{(constant force, straight-line displacement)} \quad (6.3)$$

CAUTION **Work is a scalar** Here's an essential point: Work is a *scalar* quantity, even though it's calculated by using two vector quantities (force and displacement). A 5-N force toward the east acting on a body that moves 6 m to the east does exactly the same amount of work as a 5-N force toward the north acting on a body that moves 6 m to the north.

Example 6.1 **Work done by a constant force**

(a) Steve exerts a steady force of magnitude 210 N (about 47 lb) on the stalled car in Fig. 6.3 as he pushes it a distance of 18 m. The car also has a flat tire, so to make the car track straight Steve must push at an angle of 30° to the direction of motion. How much work does Steve do? (b) In a helpful mood, Steve pushes a second stalled car with a steady force $\vec{F} = (160\ \text{N})\hat{\imath} - (40\ \text{N})\hat{\jmath}$. The displacement of the car is $\vec{s} = (14\ \text{m})\hat{\imath} + (11\ \text{m})\hat{\jmath}$. How much work does Steve do in this case?

SOLUTION

IDENTIFY and SET UP: In both parts (a) and (b), the target variable is the work W done by Steve. In each case the force is constant and the displacement is along a straight line, so we can use Eq. (6.2) or (6.3). The angle between $\vec{F}$ and $\vec{s}$ is given in part (a), so we can apply Eq. (6.2) directly. In part (b) both $\vec{F}$ and $\vec{s}$ are given in terms

of components, so it's best to calculate the scalar product using Eq. (1.21): $\vec{A} \cdot \vec{B} = A_x B_x + A_y B_y + A_z B_z$.

EXECUTE: (a) From Eq. (6.2),

$$W = Fs\cos\phi = (210\ \text{N})(18\ \text{m})\cos 30° = 3.3 \times 10^3\ \text{J}$$

(b) The components of $\vec{F}$ are $F_x = 160\ \text{N}$ and $F_y = -40\ \text{N}$, and the components of $\vec{s}$ are $x = 14\ \text{m}$ and $y = 11\ \text{m}$. (There are no z-components for either vector.) Hence, using Eqs. (1.21) and (6.3), we have

$$W = \vec{F} \cdot \vec{s} = F_x x + F_y y$$
$$= (160\ \text{N})(14\ \text{m}) + (-40\ \text{N})(11\ \text{m})$$
$$= 1.8 \times 10^3\ \text{J}$$

EVALUATE: In each case the work that Steve does is more than 1000 J. This shows that 1 joule is a rather small amount of work.

6.4 A constant force $\vec{F}$ can do positive, negative, or zero work depending on the angle between $\vec{F}$ and the displacement $\vec{s}$.

Direction of Force (or Force Component)	Situation	Force Diagram
(a) **Force $\vec{F}$ has a component in direction of displacement:** $W = F_{\parallel}s = (F\cos\phi)s$ Work is *positive*.		
(b) **Force $\vec{F}$ has a component opposite to direction of displacement:** $W = F_{\parallel}s = (F\cos\phi)s$ Work is *negative* (because $F\cos\phi$ is negative for $90° < \phi < 180°$).		
(c) **Force $\vec{F}$ (or force component $F_{\perp}$) is perpendicular to direction of displacement:** The force (or force component) does *no* work on the object.		

Work: Positive, Negative, or Zero

In Example 6.1 the work done in pushing the cars was positive. But it's important to understand that work can also be negative or zero. This is the essential way in which work as defined in physics differs from the "everyday" definition of work. When the force has a component in the *same direction* as the displacement (ϕ between zero and 90°), $\cos\phi$ in Eq. (6.2) is positive and the work W is *positive* (Fig. 6.4a). When the force has a component *opposite* to the displacement (ϕ between 90° and 180°), $\cos\phi$ is negative and the work is *negative* (Fig. 6.4b). When the force is *perpendicular* to the displacement, $\phi = 90°$ and the work done by the force is *zero* (Fig. 6.4c). The cases of zero work and negative work bear closer examination, so let's look at some examples.

There are many situations in which forces act but do zero work. You might think it's "hard work" to hold a barbell motionless in the air for 5 minutes (Fig. 6.5). But in fact, you aren't doing any work at all on the barbell because there is no displacement. You get tired because the components of muscle fibers in your arm do work as they continually contract and relax. This is work done by one part of the arm exerting force on another part, however, *not* on the barbell. (We'll say more in Section 6.2 about work done by one part of a body on another part.) Even when you walk with constant velocity on a level floor while carrying a book, you still do no work on it. The book has a displacement, but the (vertical) supporting force that you exert on the book has no component in the direction of the (horizontal) motion. Then $\phi = 90°$ in Eq. (6.2), and $\cos\phi = 0$. When a body slides along a surface, the work done on the body by the normal force is zero; and when a ball on a string moves in uniform circular motion, the work done on the ball by the tension in the string is also zero. In both cases the work is zero because the force has no component in the direction of motion.

What does it really mean to do *negative* work? The answer comes from Newton's third law of motion. When a weightlifter lowers a barbell as in Fig. 6.6a, his hands and the barbell move together with the same displacement $\vec{s}$. The barbell exerts a force $\vec{F}_{\text{barbell on hands}}$ on his hands in the same direction as the hands' displacement, so the work done by the *barbell* on his *hands* is positive (Fig. 6.6b). But by Newton's third law the weightlifter's hands exert an equal and opposite force $\vec{F}_{\text{hands on barbell}} = -\vec{F}_{\text{barbell on hands}}$ on the barbell (Fig. 6.6c). This force, which keeps the barbell from crashing to the floor, acts opposite to the barbell's displacement. Thus the work done by his *hands* on the *barbell* is negative.

6.5 A weightlifter does no work on a barbell as long as he holds it stationary.

····The weightlifter exerts an upward force on the barbell ...

... but because the barbell is stationary (its displacement is zero), he does no work on it.

6.6 This weightlifter's hands do negative work on a barbell as the barbell does positive work on his hands.

(a) A weightlifter lowers a barbell to the floor.

(b) The barbell does *positive* work on the weightlifter's hands.

The force of the barbell on the weightlifter's hands is in the *same* direction as the hands' displacement.

(c) The weightlifter's hands do *negative* work on the barbell.

The force of the weightlifter's hands on the barbell is *opposite* to the barbell's displacement.

Because the weightlifter's hands and the barbell have the same displacement, the work that his hands do on the barbell is just the negative of the work that the barbell does on his hands. In general, when one body does negative work on a second body, the second body does an equal amount of *positive* work on the first body.

CAUTION **Keep track of who's doing the work** We always speak of work done *on* a particular body *by* a specific force. Always be sure to specify exactly what force is doing the work you are talking about. When you lift a book, you exert an upward force on the book and the book's displacement is upward, so the work done by the lifting force on the book is positive. But the work done by the *gravitational* force (weight) on a book being lifted is *negative* because the downward gravitational force is opposite to the upward displacement.

Total Work

How do we calculate work when *several* forces act on a body? One way is to use Eq. (6.2) or (6.3) to compute the work done by each separate force. Then, because work is a scalar quantity, the *total* work W_{tot} done on the body by all the forces is the algebraic sum of the quantities of work done by the individual forces. An alternative way to find the total work W_{tot} is to compute the vector sum of the forces (that is, the net force) and then use this vector sum as $\vec{F}$ in Eq. (6.2) or (6.3). The following example illustrates both of these techniques.

Example 6.2 **Work done by several forces**

A farmer hitches her tractor to a sled loaded with firewood and pulls it a distance of 20 m along level ground (Fig. 6.7a). The total weight of sled and load is 14,700 N. The tractor exerts a constant 5000-N force at an angle of 36.9° above the horizontal. A 3500-N friction force opposes the sled's motion. Find the work done by each force acting on the sled and the total work done by all the forces.

SOLUTION

IDENTIFY AND SET UP: Each force is constant and the sled's displacement is along a straight line, so we can calculate the work using the ideas of this section. We'll find the total work in two ways: (1) by adding the work done on the sled by each force and (2) by finding the work done by the net force on the sled. We first draw a free-body diagram showing all of the forces acting on the sled, and we choose a coordinate system (Fig. 6.7b). For each force—weight, normal force, force of the tractor, and friction force—we know the angle between the displacement (in the positive *x*-direction) and the force. Hence we can use Eq. (6.2) to calculate the work each force does.

As in Chapter 5, we'll find the net force by adding the components of the four forces. Newton's second law tells us that because the sled's motion is purely horizontal, the net force can have only a horizontal component.

EXECUTE: (1) The work W_w done by the weight is zero because its direction is perpendicular to the displacement (compare Fig. 6.4c). For the same reason, the work W_n done by the normal force is also zero. (Note that we don't need to calculate the magnitude *n* to conclude this.) So $W_w = W_n = 0$.

That leaves the work W_T done by the force F_T exerted by the tractor and the work W_f done by the friction force *f*. From Eq. (6.2),

$$W_T = F_T s \cos \phi = (5000 \text{ N})(20 \text{ m})(0.800) = 80,000 \text{ N} \cdot \text{m}$$
$$= 80 \text{ kJ}$$

The friction force $\vec{f}$ is opposite to the displacement, so for this force $\phi = 180°$ and $\cos \phi = -1$. Again from Eq. (6.2),

$$W_f = f s \cos 180° = (3500 \text{ N})(20 \text{ m})(-1) = -70,000 \text{ N} \cdot \text{m}$$
$$= -70 \text{ kJ}$$

6.7 Calculating the work done on a sled of firewood being pulled by a tractor.

(a)

(b) Free-body diagram for sled

The total work W_{tot} done on the sled by all forces is the *algebraic* sum of the work done by the individual forces:

$$W_{tot} = W_w + W_n + W_T + W_f = 0 + 0 + 80 \text{ kJ} + (-70 \text{ kJ})$$
$$= 10 \text{ kJ}$$

(2) In the second approach, we first find the *vector* sum of all the forces (the net force) and then use it to compute the total work. The vector sum is best found by using components. From Fig. 6.7b,

$$\sum F_x = F_T \cos\phi + (-f) = (5000 \text{ N}) \cos 36.9° - 3500 \text{ N}$$
$$= 500 \text{ N}$$

$$\sum F_y = F_T \sin\phi + n + (-w)$$
$$= (5000 \text{ N}) \sin 36.9° + n - 14{,}700 \text{ N}$$

We don't need the second equation; we know that the y-component of force is perpendicular to the displacement, so it does no work. Besides, there is no y-component of acceleration, so $\sum F_y$ must be zero anyway. The total work is therefore the work done by the total x-component:

$$W_{tot} = \left(\sum \vec{F}\right) \cdot \vec{s} = \left(\sum F_x\right)s = (500 \text{ N})(20 \text{ m}) = 10{,}000 \text{ J}$$
$$= 10 \text{ kJ}$$

EVALUATE: We get the same result for W_{tot} with either method, as we should. Note also that the net force in the x-direction is *not* zero, and so the sled must accelerate as it moves. In Section 6.2 we'll return to this example and see how to use the concept of work to explore the sled's changes of speed.

Test Your Understanding of Section 6.1   An electron moves in a straight line toward the east with a constant speed of 8×10^7 m/s. It has electric, magnetic, and gravitational forces acting on it. During a 1-m displacement, the total work done on the electron is (i) positive; (ii) negative; (iii) zero; (iv) not enough information given to decide.

6.2 Kinetic Energy and the Work–Energy Theorem

The total work done on a body by external forces is related to the body's displacement—that is, to changes in its position. But the total work is also related to changes in the *speed* of the body. To see this, consider Fig. 6.8, which shows three examples of a block sliding on a frictionless table. The forces acting on the block are its weight $\vec{w}$, the normal force $\vec{n}$, and the force $\vec{F}$ exerted on it by the hand.

In Fig. 6.8a the net force on the block is in the direction of its motion. From Newton's second law, this means that the block speeds up; from Eq. (6.1), this also means that the total work W_{tot} done on the block is positive. The total work is *negative* in Fig. 6.8b because the net force opposes the displacement; in this case the block slows down. The net force is zero in Fig. 6.8c, so the speed of the block stays the same and the total work done on the block is zero. We can conclude that *when a particle undergoes a displacement, it speeds up if $W_{tot} > 0$, slows down if $W_{tot} < 0$, and maintains the same speed if $W_{tot} = 0$.*

Let's make these observations more quantitative. Consider a particle with mass m moving along the x-axis under the action of a constant net force with magnitude F directed along the positive x-axis (Fig. 6.9). The particle's acceleration is constant and given by Newton's second law, $F = ma_x$. Suppose the speed changes from v_1 to v_2 while the particle undergoes a displacement $s = x_2 - x_1$

PhET: The Ramp

6.8 The relationship between the total work done on a body and how the body's speed changes.

(a)

A block slides to the right on a frictionless surface.

If you push to the right on the moving block, the net force on the block is to the right.

- The total work done on the block during a displacement $\vec{s}$ is positive: $W_{tot} > 0$.
- The block speeds up.

(b)

If you push to the left on the moving block, the net force on the block is to the left.

- The total work done on the block during a displacement $\vec{s}$ is negative: $W_{tot} < 0$.
- The block slows down.

(c)

If you push straight down on the moving block, the net force on the block is zero.

- The total work done on the block during a displacement $\vec{s}$ is zero: $W_{tot} = 0$.
- The block's speed stays the same.

6.9 A constant net force $\vec{F}$ does work on a moving body.

from point x_1 to x_2. Using a constant-acceleration equation, Eq. (2.13), and replacing v_{0x} by v_1, v_x by v_2, and $(x - x_0)$ by s, we have

$$v_2^2 = v_1^2 + 2a_x s$$
$$a_x = \frac{v_2^2 - v_1^2}{2s}$$

When we multiply this equation by m and equate ma_x to the net force F, we find

$$F = ma_x = m\frac{v_2^2 - v_1^2}{2s} \qquad \text{and}$$

$$Fs = \tfrac{1}{2}mv_2^2 - \tfrac{1}{2}mv_1^2 \qquad (6.4)$$

The product Fs is the work done by the net force F and thus is equal to the total work W_{tot} done by all the forces acting on the particle. The quantity $\tfrac{1}{2}mv^2$ is called the **kinetic energy** K of the particle:

6.10 Comparing the kinetic energy $K = \tfrac{1}{2}mv^2$ of different bodies.

$$K = \tfrac{1}{2}mv^2 \qquad \text{(definition of kinetic energy)} \qquad (6.5)$$

Like work, the kinetic energy of a particle is a scalar quantity; it depends on only the particle's mass and speed, not its direction of motion (Fig. 6.10). A car (viewed as a particle) has the same kinetic energy when going north at 10 m/s as when going east at 10 m/s. Kinetic energy can never be negative, and it is zero only when the particle is at rest.

Same mass, same speed, different directions of motion: *same* kinetic energy

We can now interpret Eq. (6.4) in terms of work and kinetic energy. The first term on the right side of Eq. (6.4) is $K_2 = \tfrac{1}{2}mv_2^2$, the final kinetic energy of the particle (that is, after the displacement). The second term is the initial kinetic energy, $K_1 = \tfrac{1}{2}mv_1^2$, and the difference between these terms is the *change* in kinetic energy. So Eq. (6.4) says:

Twice the mass, same speed: *twice* the kinetic energy

The work done by the net force on a particle equals the change in the particle's kinetic energy:

$$W_{tot} = K_2 - K_1 = \Delta K \qquad \text{(work–energy theorem)} \qquad (6.6)$$

Same mass, twice the speed: *four times* the kinetic energy

This result is the **work–energy theorem.**

The work–energy theorem agrees with our observations about the block in Fig. 6.8. When W_{tot} is *positive,* the kinetic energy *increases* (the final kinetic energy K_2 is greater than the initial kinetic energy K_1) and the particle is going faster at the end of the displacement than at the beginning. When W_{tot} is *negative,* the kinetic energy *decreases* (K_2 is less than K_1) and the speed is less after the displacement. When $W_{tot} = 0$, the kinetic energy stays the same ($K_1 = K_2$) and the speed is unchanged. Note that the work–energy theorem by itself tells us only about changes in *speed,* not velocity, since the kinetic energy doesn't depend on the direction of motion.

From Eq. (6.4) or Eq. (6.6), kinetic energy and work must have the same units. Hence the joule is the SI unit of both work and kinetic energy (and, as we will see later, of all kinds of energy). To verify this, note that in SI units the quantity $K = \frac{1}{2}mv^2$ has units $kg \cdot (m/s)^2$ or $kg \cdot m^2/s^2$; we recall that $1\ N = 1\ kg \cdot m/s^2$, so

$$1\ J = 1\ N \cdot m = 1\ (kg \cdot m/s^2) \cdot m = 1\ kg \cdot m^2/s^2$$

In the British system the unit of kinetic energy and of work is

$$1\ ft \cdot lb = 1\ ft \cdot slug \cdot ft/s^2 = 1\ slug \cdot ft^2/s^2$$

Because we used Newton's laws in deriving the work–energy theorem, we can use this theorem only in an inertial frame of reference. Note also that the work–energy theorem is valid in *any* inertial frame, but the values of W_{tot} and $K_2 - K_1$ may differ from one inertial frame to another (because the displacement and speed of a body may be different in different frames).

We've derived the work–energy theorem for the special case of straight-line motion with constant forces, and in the following examples we'll apply it to this special case only. We'll find in the next section that the theorem is valid in general, even when the forces are not constant and the particle's trajectory is curved.

Problem-Solving Strategy 6.1 **Work and Kinetic Energy**

IDENTIFY *the relevant concepts:* The work–energy theorem, $W_{tot} = K_2 - K_1$, is extremely useful when you want to relate a body's speed v_1 at one point in its motion to its speed v_2 at a different point. (It's less useful for problems that involve the *time* it takes a body to go from point 1 to point 2 because the work–energy theorem doesn't involve time at all. For such problems it's usually best to use the relationships among time, position, velocity, and acceleration described in Chapters 2 and 3.)

SET UP *the problem* using the following steps:
1. Identify the initial and final positions of the body, and draw a free-body diagram showing all the forces that act on the body.
2. Choose a coordinate system. (If the motion is along a straight line, it's usually easiest to have both the initial and final positions lie along one of the axes.)
3. List the unknown and known quantities, and decide which unknowns are your target variables. The target variable may be the body's initial or final speed, the magnitude of one of the forces acting on the body, or the body's displacement.

EXECUTE *the solution:* Calculate the work W done by each force. If the force is constant and the displacement is a straight line, you can use Eq. (6.2) or Eq. (6.3). (Later in this chapter we'll see how to handle varying forces and curved trajectories.) Be sure to check signs; W must be positive if the force has a component in the direction of the displacement, negative if the force has a component opposite to the displacement, and zero if the force and displacement are perpendicular.

Add the amounts of work done by each force to find the total work W_{tot}. Sometimes it's easier to calculate the vector sum of the forces (the net force) and then find the work done by the net force; this value is also equal to W_{tot}.

Write expressions for the initial and final kinetic energies, K_1 and K_2. Note that kinetic energy involves *mass,* not *weight*; if you are given the body's weight, use $w = mg$ to find the mass.

Finally, use Eq. (6.6), $W_{tot} = K_2 - K_1$, and Eq. (6.5), $K = \frac{1}{2}mv^2$, to solve for the target variable. Remember that the right-hand side of Eq. (6.6) represents the change of the body's kinetic energy between points 1 and 2; that is, it is the *final* kinetic energy minus the *initial* kinetic energy, never the other way around. (If you can predict the sign of W_{tot}, you can predict whether the body speeds up or slows down.)

EVALUATE *your answer:* Check whether your answer makes sense. Remember that kinetic energy $K = \frac{1}{2}mv^2$ can never be negative. If you come up with a negative value of K, perhaps you interchanged the initial and final kinetic energies in $W_{tot} = K_2 - K_1$ or made a sign error in one of the work calculations.

Example 6.3 Using work and energy to calculate speed

Let's look again at the sled in Fig. 6.7 and our results from Example 6.2. Suppose the sled's initial speed v_1 is 2.0 m/s. What is the speed of the sled after it moves 20 m?

SOLUTION

IDENTIFY and SET UP: We'll use the work–energy theorem, Eq. (6.6), $W_{tot} = K_2 - K_1$, since we are given the initial speed $v_1 = 2.0$ m/s and want to find the final speed v_2. Figure 6.11 shows our sketch of the situation. The motion is in the positive x-direction. In Example 6.2 we calculated the total work done by all the forces: $W_{tot} = 10$ kJ. Hence the kinetic energy of the sled and its load must increase by 10 kJ, and the speed of the sled must also increase.

EXECUTE: To write expressions for the initial and final kinetic energies, we need the mass of the sled and load. The combined *weight* is 14,700 N, so the mass is

$$m = \frac{w}{g} = \frac{14,700 \text{ N}}{9.8 \text{ m/s}^2} = 1500 \text{ kg}$$

Then the initial kinetic energy K_1 is

$$K_1 = \tfrac{1}{2}mv_1^2 = \tfrac{1}{2}(1500 \text{ kg})(2.0 \text{ m/s})^2 = 3000 \text{ kg} \cdot \text{m}^2/\text{s}^2$$
$$= 3000 \text{ J}$$

6.11 Our sketch for this problem.

The final kinetic energy K_2 is

$$K_2 = \tfrac{1}{2}mv_2^2 = \tfrac{1}{2}(1500 \text{ kg})v_2^2$$

The work–energy theorem, Eq. (6.6), gives

$$K_2 = K_1 + W_{tot} = 3000 \text{ J} + 10,000 \text{ J} = 13,000 \text{ J}$$

Setting these two expressions for K_2 equal, substituting 1 J = 1 kg $\cdot$ m^2/s^2, and solving for the final speed v_2, we find

$$v_2 = 4.2 \text{ m/s}$$

EVALUATE: The total work is positive, so the kinetic energy increases ($K_2 > K_1$) and the speed increases ($v_2 > v_1$).

This problem can also be solved without the work–energy theorem. We can find the acceleration from $\Sigma \vec{F} = m\vec{a}$ and then use the equations of motion for constant acceleration to find v_2. Since the acceleration is along the x-axis,

$$a = a_x = \frac{\Sigma F_x}{m} = \frac{500 \text{ N}}{1500 \text{ kg}} = 0.333 \text{ m/s}^2$$

Then, using Eq. (2.13),

$$v_2^2 = v_1^2 + 2as = (2.0 \text{ m/s})^2 + 2(0.333 \text{ m/s}^2)(20 \text{ m})$$
$$= 17.3 \text{ m}^2/\text{s}^2$$
$$v_2 = 4.2 \text{ m/s}$$

This is the same result we obtained with the work–energy approach, but there we avoided the intermediate step of finding the acceleration. You will find several other examples in this chapter and the next that *can* be done without using energy considerations but that are easier when energy methods are used. When a problem can be done by two methods, doing it by both methods (as we did here) is a good way to check your work.

Example 6.4 Forces on a hammerhead

The 200-kg steel hammerhead of a pile driver is lifted 3.00 m above the top of a vertical I-beam being driven into the ground (Fig. 6.12a). The hammerhead is then dropped, driving the I-beam 7.4 cm deeper into the ground. The vertical guide rails exert a constant 60-N friction force on the hammerhead. Use the work–energy theorem to find (a) the speed of the hammerhead just as it hits the I-beam and (b) the average force the hammerhead exerts on the I-beam. Ignore the effects of the air.

SOLUTION

IDENTIFY: We'll use the work–energy theorem to relate the hammerhead's speed at different locations and the forces acting on it. There are *three* locations of interest: point 1, where the hammerhead starts from rest; point 2, where it first contacts the I-beam; and point 3, where the hammerhead and I-beam come to a halt (Fig. 6.12a). The two target variables are the hammerhead's speed at point 2 and the average force the hammerhead exerts between points 2 and 3. Hence we'll apply the work–energy theorem

twice: once for the motion from 1 to 2, and once for the motion from 2 to 3.

SET UP: Figure 6.12b shows the vertical forces on the hammerhead as it falls from point 1 to point 2. (We can ignore any horizontal forces that may be present because they do no work as the hammerhead moves vertically.) For this part of the motion, our target variable is the hammerhead's final speed v_2.

Figure 6.12c shows the vertical forces on the hammerhead during the motion from point 2 to point 3. In addition to the forces shown in Fig. 6.12b, the I-beam exerts an upward normal force of magnitude n on the hammerhead. This force actually varies as the hammerhead comes to a halt, but for simplicity we'll treat n as a constant. Hence n represents the *average* value of this upward force during the motion. Our target variable for this part of the motion is the force that the *hammerhead* exerts on the I-beam; it is the reaction force to the normal force exerted by the I-beam, so by Newton's third law its magnitude is also n.

EXECUTE: (a) From point 1 to point 2, the vertical forces are the downward weight $w = mg = (200 \text{ kg})(9.8 \text{ m/s}^2) = 1960 \text{ N}$ and the upward friction force $f = 60 \text{ N}$. Thus the net downward force is $w - f = 1900 \text{ N}$. The displacement of the hammerhead from point 1 to point 2 is downward and equal to $s_{12} = 3.00 \text{ m}$. The total work done on the hammerhead between point 1 and point 2 is then

$$W_{\text{tot}} = (w - f)s_{12} = (1900 \text{ N})(3.00 \text{ m}) = 5700 \text{ J}$$

At point 1 the hammerhead is at rest, so its initial kinetic energy K_1 is zero. Hence the kinetic energy K_2 at point 2 equals the total work done on the hammerhead between points 1 and 2:

$$W_{\text{tot}} = K_2 - K_1 = K_2 - 0 = \tfrac{1}{2}mv_2^2 - 0$$

$$v_2 = \sqrt{\frac{2W_{\text{tot}}}{m}} = \sqrt{\frac{2(5700 \text{ J})}{200 \text{ kg}}} = 7.55 \text{ m/s}$$

This is the hammerhead's speed at point 2, just as it hits the I-beam.

(b) As the hammerhead moves downward from point 2 to point 3, its displacement is $s_{23} = 7.4 \text{ cm} = 0.074 \text{ m}$ and the net downward force acting on it is $w - f - n$ (Fig. 6.12c). The total work done on the hammerhead during this displacement is

$$W_{\text{tot}} = (w - f - n)s_{23}$$

The initial kinetic energy for this part of the motion is K_2, which from part (a) equals 5700 J. The final kinetic energy is $K_3 = 0$ (the hammerhead ends at rest). From the work–energy theorem,

$$W_{\text{tot}} = (w - f - n)s_{23} = K_3 - K_2$$

$$n = w - f - \frac{K_3 - K_2}{s_{23}}$$

$$= 1960 \text{ N} - 60 \text{ N} - \frac{0 \text{ J} - 5700 \text{ J}}{0.074 \text{ m}} = 79,000 \text{ N}$$

The downward force that the hammerhead exerts on the I-beam has this same magnitude, 79,000 N (about 9 tons)—more than 40 times the weight of the hammerhead.

EVALUATE: The net change in the hammerhead's kinetic energy from point 1 to point 3 is zero; a relatively small net force does positive work over a large distance, and then a much larger net force does negative work over a much smaller distance. The same thing happens if you speed up your car gradually and then drive it into a brick wall. The very large force needed to reduce the kinetic energy to zero over a short distance is what does the damage to your car—and possibly to you.

6.12 (a) A pile driver pounds an I-beam into the ground. (b), (c) Free-body diagrams. Vector lengths are not to scale.

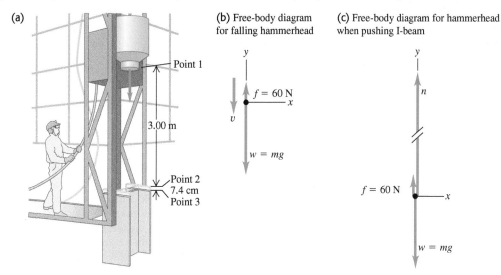

The Meaning of Kinetic Energy

Example 6.4 gives insight into the physical meaning of kinetic energy. The hammerhead is dropped from rest, and its kinetic energy when it hits the I-beam equals the total work done on it up to that point by the net force. This result is true in general: To accelerate a particle of mass m from rest (zero kinetic energy)

6.13 When a billiards player hits a cue ball at rest, the ball's kinetic energy after being hit is equal to the work that was done on it by the cue. The greater the force exerted by the cue and the greater the distance the ball moves while in contact with it, the greater the ball's kinetic energy.

up to a speed , the total work done on it must equal the change in kinetic energy from zero to $K = \frac{1}{2}mv^2$:

$$W_{\text{tot}} = K - 0 = K$$

So *the kinetic energy of a particle is equal to the total work that was done to accelerate it from rest to its present speed* (Fig. 6.13). The definition $K = \frac{1}{2}mv^2$, Eq. (6.5), wasn't chosen at random; it's the *only* definition that agrees with this interpretation of kinetic energy.

In the second part of Example 6.4 the kinetic energy of the hammerhead did work on the I-beam and drove it into the ground. This gives us another interpretation of kinetic energy: *The kinetic energy of a particle is equal to the total work that particle can do in the process of being brought to rest.* This is why you pull your hand and arm backward when you catch a ball. As the ball comes to rest, it does an amount of work (force times distance) on your hand equal to the ball's initial kinetic energy. By pulling your hand back, you maximize the distance over which the force acts and so minimize the force on your hand.

Conceptual Example 6.5 | **Comparing kinetic energies**

Two iceboats like the one in Example 5.6 (Section 5.2) hold a race on a frictionless horizontal lake (Fig. 6.14). The two iceboats have masses m and $2m$. The iceboats have identical sails, so the wind exerts the same constant force $\vec{F}$ on each iceboat. They start from rest and cross the finish line a distance s away. Which iceboat crosses the finish line with greater kinetic energy?

SOLUTION

If you use the definition of kinetic energy, $K = \frac{1}{2}mv^2$, Eq. (6.5), the answer to this problem isn't obvious. The iceboat of mass $2m$ has greater mass, so you might guess that it has greater kinetic energy at the finish line. But the lighter iceboat, of mass m, has greater acceleration and crosses the finish line with a greater speed, so you might guess that *this* iceboat has the greater kinetic energy. How can we decide?

The key is to remember that *the kinetic energy of a particle is equal to the total work done to accelerate it from rest.* Both iceboats travel the same distance s from rest, and only the horizontal force F in the direction of motion does work on either iceboat. Hence the total work done between the starting line and the finish line is the *same* for each iceboat, $W_{\text{tot}} = Fs$. At the finish line, each iceboat has a kinetic energy equal to the work W_{tot} done on it, because each iceboat started from rest. So both iceboats have the *same* kinetic energy at the finish line!

6.14 A race between iceboats.

You might think this is a "trick" question, but it isn't. If you really understand the meanings of quantities such as kinetic energy, you can solve problems more easily and with better insight.

Notice that we didn't need to know anything about how much time each iceboat took to reach the finish line. This is because the work–energy theorem makes no direct reference to time, only to displacement. In fact the iceboat of mass m has greater acceleration and so takes less time to reach the finish line than does the iceboat of mass $2m$.

Work and Kinetic Energy in Composite Systems

In this section we've been careful to apply the work–energy theorem only to bodies that we can represent as *particles*—that is, as moving point masses. New subtleties appear for more complex systems that have to be represented as many particles with different motions. We can't go into these subtleties in detail in this chapter, but here's an example.

Suppose a boy stands on frictionless roller skates on a level surface, facing a rigid wall (Fig. 6.15). He pushes against the wall, which makes him move to the right. The forces acting on him are his weight $\vec{w}$, the upward normal forces $\vec{n}_1$ and $\vec{n}_2$ exerted by the ground on his skates, and the horizontal force $\vec{F}$ exerted on him by the wall. There is no vertical displacement, so $\vec{w}$, $\vec{n}_1$, and $\vec{n}_2$ do no work. Force $\vec{F}$ accelerates him to the right, but the parts of his body where that force is applied (the boy's hands) do not move while the force acts. Thus the force $\vec{F}$ also does no work. Where, then, does the boy's kinetic energy come from?

The explanation is that it's not adequate to represent the boy as a single point mass. Different parts of the boy's body have different motions; his hands remain stationary against the wall while his torso is moving away from the wall. The various parts of his body interact with each other, and one part can exert forces and do work on another part. Therefore the *total* kinetic energy of this *composite* system of body parts can change, even though no work is done by forces applied by bodies (such as the wall) that are outside the system. In Chapter 8 we'll consider further the motion of a collection of particles that interact with each other. We'll discover that just as for the boy in this example, the total kinetic energy of such a system can change even when no work is done on any part of the system by anything outside it.

Test Your Understanding of Section 6.2 Rank the following bodies in order of their kinetic energy, from least to greatest. (i) a 2.0-kg body moving at 5.0 m/s; (ii) a 1.0-kg body that initially was at rest and then had 30 J of work done on it; (iii) a 1.0-kg body that initially was moving at 4.0 m/s and then had 20 J of work done on it; (iv) a 2.0-kg body that initially was moving at 10 m/s and then did 80 J of work on another body. ❙

6.3 Work and Energy with Varying Forces

So far in this chapter we've considered work done by *constant forces* only. But what happens when you stretch a spring? The more you stretch it, the harder you have to pull, so the force you exert is *not* constant as the spring is stretched. We've also restricted our discussion to *straight-line* motion. There are many situations in which a body moves along a curved path and is acted on by a force that varies in magnitude, direction, or both. We need to be able to compute the work done by the force in these more general cases. Fortunately, we'll find that the work–energy theorem holds true even when varying forces are considered and when the body's path is not straight.

Work Done by a Varying Force, Straight-Line Motion

To add only one complication at a time, let's consider straight-line motion along the x-axis with a force whose x-component F_x may change as the body moves. (A real-life example is driving a car along a straight road with stop signs, so the driver has to alternately step on the gas and apply the brakes.) Suppose a particle moves along the x-axis from point x_1 to x_2 (Fig. 6.16a). Figure 6.16b is a graph of the x-component of force as a function of the particle's coordinate x. To find the work done by this force, we divide the total displacement into small segments Δx_a, Δx_b, and so on (Fig. 6.16c). We approximate the work done by the force during segment Δx_a as the average x-component of force F_{ax} in that segment multiplied by the x-displacement Δx_a. We do this for each segment and then add the results for all the segments. The work done by the force in the total displacement from x_1 to x_2 is approximately

$$W = F_{ax}\Delta x_a + F_{bx}\Delta x_b + \cdots$$

6.15 The external forces acting on a skater pushing off a wall. The work done by these forces is zero, but the skater's kinetic energy changes nonetheless.

6.16 Calculating the work done by a varying force F_x in the x-direction as a particle moves from x_1 to x_2.

(a) Particle moving from x_1 to x_2 in response to a changing force in the x-direction

(b)

(c)

PhET: Molecular Motors
PhET: Stretching DNA

In the limit that the number of segments becomes very large and the width of each becomes very small, this sum becomes the *integral* of F_x from x_1 to x_2:

$$W = \int_{x_1}^{x_2} F_x \, dx \qquad \text{(varying x-component of force,}\atop\text{straight-line displacement)} \qquad (6.7)$$

Note that $F_{ax} \Delta x_a$ represents the *area* of the first vertical strip in Fig. 6.16c and that the integral in Eq. (6.7) represents the area under the curve of Fig. 6.16b between x_1 and x_2. *On a graph of force as a function of position, the total work done by the force is represented by the area under the curve between the initial and final positions.* An alternative interpretation of Eq. (6.7) is that the work W equals the average force that acts over the entire displacement, multiplied by the displacement.

In the special case that F_x, the x-component of the force, is constant, it may be taken outside the integral in Eq. (6.7):

$$W = \int_{x_1}^{x_2} F_x \, dx = F_x \int_{x_1}^{x_2} dx = F_x(x_2 - x_1) \qquad \text{(constant force)}$$

But $x_2 - x_1 = s$, the total displacement of the particle. So in the case of a constant force F, Eq. (6.7) says that $W = Fs$, in agreement with Eq. (6.1). The interpretation of work as the area under the curve of F_x as a function of x also holds for a constant force; $W = Fs$ is the area of a rectangle of height F and width s (Fig. 6.17).

Now let's apply these ideas to the stretched spring. To keep a spring stretched beyond its unstretched length by an amount x, we have to apply a force of equal magnitude at each end (Fig. 6.18). If the elongation x is not too great, the force we apply to the right-hand end has an x-component directly proportional to x:

$$F_x = kx \qquad \text{(force required to stretch a spring)} \qquad (6.8)$$

6.17 The work done by a constant force F in the x-direction as a particle moves from x_1 to x_2.

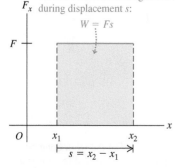

The rectangular area under the graph represents the work done by the constant force of magnitude F during displacement s:

$$W = Fs$$

6.18 The force needed to stretch an ideal spring is proportional to the spring's elongation: $F_x = kx$.

where k is a constant called the **force constant** (or spring constant) of the spring. The units of k are force divided by distance: N/m in SI units and lb/ft in British units. A floppy toy spring such as a Slinky™ has a force constant of about 1 N/m; for the much stiffer springs in an automobile's suspension, k is about 10^5 N/m. The observation that force is directly proportional to elongation for elongations that are not too great was made by Robert Hooke in 1678 and is known as **Hooke's law.** It really shouldn't be called a "law," since it's a statement about a specific device and not a fundamental law of nature. Real springs don't always obey Eq. (6.8) precisely, but it's still a useful idealized model. We'll discuss Hooke's law more fully in Chapter 11.

To stretch a spring, we must do work. We apply equal and opposite forces to the ends of the spring and gradually increase the forces. We hold the left end stationary, so the force we apply at this end does no work. The force at the moving end *does* do work. Figure 6.19 is a graph of F_x as a function of x, the elongation of the spring. The work done by this force when the elongation goes from zero to a maximum value X is

6.19 Calculating the work done to stretch a spring by a length X.

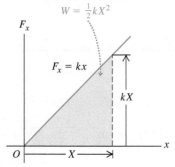

The area under the graph represents the work done on the spring as the spring is stretched from $x = 0$ to a maximum value X:

$$W = \tfrac{1}{2}kX^2$$

$$W = \int_{0}^{X} F_x \, dx = \int_{0}^{X} kx \, dx = \tfrac{1}{2}kX^2 \qquad (6.9)$$

We can also obtain this result graphically. The area of the shaded triangle in Fig. 6.19, representing the total work done by the force, is equal to half the product of the base and altitude, or

$$W = \tfrac{1}{2}(X)(kX) = \tfrac{1}{2}kX^2$$

This equation also says that the work is the *average* force $kX/2$ multiplied by the total displacement X. We see that the total work is proportional to the *square* of the final elongation X. To stretch an ideal spring by 2 cm, you must do four times as much work as is needed to stretch it by 1 cm.

Equation (6.9) assumes that the spring was originally unstretched. If initially the spring is already stretched a distance x_1, the work we must do to stretch it to a greater elongation x_2 (Fig. 6.20a) is

$$W = \int_{x_1}^{x_2} F_x \, dx = \int_{x_1}^{x_2} kx \, dx = \tfrac{1}{2}kx_2^2 - \tfrac{1}{2}kx_1^2 \qquad (6.10)$$

You should use your knowledge of geometry to convince yourself that the trapezoidal area under the graph in Fig. 6.20b is given by the expression in Eq. (6.10).

If the spring has spaces between the coils when it is unstretched, then it can also be compressed, and Hooke's law holds for compression as well as stretching. In this case the force and displacement are in the opposite directions from those shown in Fig. 6.18, and so F_x and x in Eq. (6.8) are both negative. Since both F_x and x are reversed, the force again is in the same direction as the displacement, and the work done by F_x is again positive. So the total work is still given by Eq. (6.9) or (6.10), even when X is negative or either or both of x_1 and x_2 are negative.

CAUTION **Work done *on* a spring vs. work done *by* a spring** Note that Eq. (6.10) gives the work that *you* must do *on* a spring to change its length. For example, if you stretch a spring that's originally relaxed, then $x_1 = 0$, $x_2 > 0$, and $W > 0$: The force you apply to one end of the spring is in the same direction as the displacement, and the work you do is positive. By contrast, the work that the *spring* does on whatever it's attached to is given by the *negative* of Eq. (6.10). Thus, as you pull on the spring, the spring does negative work on you. Paying careful attention to the sign of work will eliminate confusion later on!

6.20 Calculating the work done to stretch a spring from one extension to a greater one.

(a) Stretching a spring from elongation x_1 to elongation x_2

(b) Force-versus-distance graph

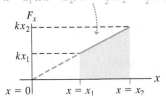

The trapezoidal area under the graph represents the work done on the spring to stretch it from $x = x_1$ to $x = x_2$: $W = \tfrac{1}{2}kx_2^2 - \tfrac{1}{2}kx_1^2$

Example 6.6 **Work done on a spring scale**

A woman weighing 600 N steps on a bathroom scale that contains a stiff spring (Fig. 6.21). In equilibrium, the spring is compressed 1.0 cm under her weight. Find the force constant of the spring and the total work done on it during the compression.

SOLUTION

IDENTIFY and SET UP: In equilibrium the upward force exerted by the spring balances the downward force of the woman's weight. We'll use this principle and Eq. (6.8) to determine the force constant k, and we'll use Eq. (6.10) to calculate the work W that the

6.21 Compressing a spring in a bathroom scale.

Because of our choice of axis, both the force component and displacement are negative. The work *on* the spring is positive.

$+x$

$F_x < 0$

-1.0 cm

woman does on the spring to compress it. We take positive values of x to correspond to elongation (upward in Fig. 6.21), so that the displacement of the end of the spring (x) and the x-component of the force that the woman exerts on it (F_x) are both negative. The applied force and the displacement are in the same direction, so the work done on the spring will be positive.

EXECUTE: The top of the spring is displaced by $x = -1.0$ cm $= -0.010$ m, and the woman exerts a force $F_x = -600$ N on the spring. From Eq. (6.8) the force constant is then

$$k = \frac{F_x}{x} = \frac{-600 \text{ N}}{-0.010 \text{ m}} = 6.0 \times 10^4 \text{ N/m}$$

Then, using $x_1 = 0$ and $x_2 = -0.010$ m in Eq. (6.10), we have

$$W = \tfrac{1}{2}kx_2^2 - \tfrac{1}{2}kx_1^2$$

$$= \tfrac{1}{2}(6.0 \times 10^4 \text{ N/m})(-0.010 \text{ m})^2 - 0 = 3.0 \text{ J}$$

EVALUATE: The work done is positive, as expected. Our arbitrary choice of the positive direction has no effect on the answer for W. You can test this by taking the positive x-direction to be downward, corresponding to compression. Do you get the same values for k and W as we found here?

Application Tendons Are Nonideal Springs

Muscles exert forces via the tendons that attach them to bones. A tendon consists of long, stiff, elastic collagen fibers. The graph shows how the tendon from the hind leg of a wallaby (a small kangaroo) stretches in response to an applied force. The tendon does not exhibit the simple, straight-line behavior of an ideal spring, so the work it does has to be found by integration [Eq. (6.7)]. Note that the tendon exerts less force while relaxing than while stretching. As a result, the relaxing tendon does only about 93% of the work that was done to stretch it.

Work–Energy Theorem for Straight-Line Motion, Varying Forces

In Section 6.2 we derived the work–energy theorem, $W_{tot} = K_2 - K_1$, for the special case of straight-line motion with a constant net force. We can now prove that this theorem is true even when the force varies with position. As in Section 6.2, let's consider a particle that undergoes a displacement x while being acted on by a net force with x-component F_x, which we now allow to vary. Just as in Fig. 6.16, we divide the total displacement x into a large number of small segments Δx. We can apply the work–energy theorem, Eq. (6.6), to each segment because the value of F_x in each small segment is approximately constant. The change in kinetic energy in segment Δx_a is equal to the work $F_{ax}\Delta x_a$, and so on. The total change of kinetic energy is the sum of the changes in the individual segments, and thus is equal to the total work done on the particle during the entire displacement. So $W_{tot} = \Delta K$ holds for varying forces as well as for constant ones.

Here's an alternative derivation of the work–energy theorem for a force that may vary with position. It involves making a change of variable from x to v_x in the work integral. As a preliminary, we note that the acceleration a of the particle can be expressed in various ways, using $a_x = dv_x/dt$, $v_x = dx/dt$, and the chain rule for derivatives:

$$a_x = \frac{dv_x}{dt} = \frac{dv_x}{dx}\frac{dx}{dt} = v_x\frac{dv_x}{dx} \qquad (6.11)$$

From this result, Eq. (6.7) tells us that the total work done by the *net* force F_x is

$$W_{tot} = \int_{x_1}^{x_2} F_x\,dx = \int_{x_1}^{x_2} ma_x\,dx = \int_{x_1}^{x_2} mv_x\frac{dv_x}{dx}\,dx \qquad (6.12)$$

Now $(dv_x/dx)dx$ is the change in velocity dv_x during the displacement dx, so in Eq. (6.12) we can substitute dv_x for $(dv_x/dx)\,dx$. This changes the integration variable from x to v_x, so we change the limits from x_1 and x_2 to the corresponding x-velocities v_1 and v_2 at these points. This gives us

$$W_{tot} = \int_{v_1}^{v_2} mv_x\,dv_x$$

The integral of $v_x\,dv_x$ is just $v_x^2/2$. Substituting the upper and lower limits, we finally find

$$W_{tot} = \tfrac{1}{2}mv_2^2 - \tfrac{1}{2}mv_1^2 \qquad (6.13)$$

This is the same as Eq. (6.6), so the work–energy theorem is valid even without the assumption that the net force is constant.

Example 6.7 **Motion with a varying force**

An air-track glider of mass 0.100 kg is attached to the end of a horizontal air track by a spring with force constant 20.0 N/m (Fig. 6.22a). Initially the spring is unstretched and the glider is moving at 1.50 m/s to the right. Find the maximum distance d that the glider moves to the right (a) if the air track is turned on, so that there is no friction, and (b) if the air is turned off, so that there is kinetic friction with coefficient $\mu_k = 0.47$.

SOLUTION

IDENTIFY and SET UP: The force exerted by the spring is not constant, so we *cannot* use the constant-acceleration formulas of Chapter 2 to solve this problem. Instead, we'll use the work–energy theorem, since the total work done involves the distance moved (our target variable). In Figs. 6.22b and 6.22c we choose the positive x-direction to be to the right (in the direction of the glider's motion). We take $x = 0$ at the glider's initial position (where the spring is unstretched) and $x = d$ (the target variable) at the position where the glider stops. The motion is purely horizontal, so only the horizontal forces do work. Note that Eq. (6.10) gives the work done by the *glider* on the *spring* as it stretches; to use the work–energy theorem we need the work done by the *spring* on the *glider*, which is the negative of Eq. (6.10). We expect the glider to move farther without friction than with friction.

Force exerted by tendon (N)

Maximum tendon extension

Tendon being stretched

Tendon relaxing

Extension (mm)

6.22 (a) A glider attached to an air track by a spring. (b), (c) Our free-body diagrams.

(a)

(b) No friction

(c) With friction

EXECUTE: (a) Equation (6.10) says that as the glider moves from $x_1 = 0$ to $x_2 = d$, it does an amount of work $W = \frac{1}{2}kd^2 - \frac{1}{2}k(0)^2 = \frac{1}{2}kd^2$ on the spring. The amount of work that the *spring* does on the *glider* is the negative of this, $-\frac{1}{2}kd^2$. The spring stretches until the glider comes instantaneously to rest, so the final kinetic energy K_2 is zero. The initial kinetic energy is $\frac{1}{2}mv_1^2$, where $v_1 = 1.50$ m/s is the glider's initial speed. From the work–energy theorem,

$$-\tfrac{1}{2}kd^2 = 0 - \tfrac{1}{2}mv_1^2$$

We solve for the distance d the glider moves:

$$d = v_1\sqrt{\frac{m}{k}} = (1.50 \text{ m/s})\sqrt{\frac{0.100 \text{ kg}}{20.0 \text{ N/m}}}$$
$$= 0.106 \text{ m} = 10.6 \text{ cm}$$

The stretched spring subsequently pulls the glider back to the left, so the glider is at rest only instantaneously.

(b) If the air is turned off, we must include the work done by the kinetic friction force. The normal force n is equal in magnitude to the weight of the glider, since the track is horizontal and there are no other vertical forces. Hence the kinetic friction force has constant magnitude $f_k = \mu_k n = \mu_k mg$. The friction force is directed opposite to the displacement, so the work done by friction is

$$W_{\text{fric}} = f_k d \cos 180° = -f_k d = -\mu_k mg d$$

The total work is the sum of W_{fric} and the work done by the spring, $-\frac{1}{2}kd^2$. The work–energy theorem then says that

$$-\mu_k mg d - \tfrac{1}{2}kd^2 = 0 - \tfrac{1}{2}mv_1^2 \qquad \text{or}$$
$$\tfrac{1}{2}kd^2 + \mu_k mg d - \tfrac{1}{2}mv_1^2 = 0$$

This is a quadratic equation for d. The solutions are

$$d = -\frac{\mu_k mg}{k} \pm \sqrt{\left(\frac{\mu_k mg}{k}\right)^2 + \frac{mv_1^2}{k}}$$

We have

$$\frac{\mu_k mg}{k} = \frac{(0.47)(0.100 \text{ kg})(9.80 \text{ m/s}^2)}{20.0 \text{ N/m}} = 0.02303 \text{ m}$$

$$\frac{mv_1^2}{k} = \frac{(0.100 \text{ kg})(1.50 \text{ m/s})^2}{20.0 \text{ N/m}} = 0.01125 \text{ m}^2$$

so

$$d = -(0.02303 \text{ m}) \pm \sqrt{(0.02303 \text{ m})^2 + 0.01125 \text{ m}^2}$$
$$= 0.086 \text{ m} \quad \text{or} \quad -0.132 \text{ m}$$

The quantity d is a positive displacement, so only the positive value of d makes sense. Thus with friction the glider moves a distance $d = 0.086$ m = 8.6 cm.

EVALUATE: Note that if we set $\mu_k = 0$, our algebraic solution for d in part (b) reduces to $d = v_1\sqrt{m/k}$, the zero-friction result from part (a). With friction, the glider goes a shorter distance. Again the glider stops instantaneously, and again the spring force pulls it toward the left; whether it moves or not depends on how great the *static* friction force is. How large would the coefficient of static friction μ_s have to be to keep the glider from springing back to the left?

Work–Energy Theorem for Motion Along a Curve

We can generalize our definition of work further to include a force that varies in direction as well as magnitude, and a displacement that lies along a curved path. Figure 6.23a shows a particle moving from P_1 to P_2 along a curve. We divide the curve between these points into many infinitesimal vector displacements, and we call a typical one of these $d\vec{l}$. Each $d\vec{l}$ is tangent to the path at its position. Let $\vec{F}$ be the force at a typical point along the path, and let ϕ be the angle between $\vec{F}$ and $d\vec{l}$ at this point. Then the small element of work dW done on the particle during the displacement $d\vec{l}$ may be written as

$$dW = F \cos \phi \, dl = F_{\parallel} \, dl = \vec{F} \cdot d\vec{l}$$

where $F_{\parallel} = F \cos \phi$ is the component of $\vec{F}$ in the direction parallel to $d\vec{l}$ (Fig. 6.23b). The total work done by $\vec{F}$ on the particle as it moves from P_1 to P_2 is then

$$W = \int_{P_1}^{P_2} F \cos \phi \, dl = \int_{P_1}^{P_2} F_{\parallel} \, dl = \int_{P_1}^{P_2} \vec{F} \cdot d\vec{l} \qquad \begin{array}{l}\text{(work done on} \\ \text{a curved path)}\end{array} \quad \text{(6.14)}$$

6.23 A particle moves along a curved path from point P_1 to P_2, acted on by a force $\vec{F}$ that varies in magnitude and direction.

(a)

During an infinitesimal displacement $d\vec{l}$, the force $\vec{F}$ does work dW on the particle:
$$dW = \vec{F} \cdot d\vec{l} = F \cos\phi \, dl$$

(b)

Only the component of $\vec{F}$ parallel to the displacement, $F_\parallel = F\cos\phi$, contributes to the work done by $\vec{F}$.

We can now show that the work–energy theorem, Eq. (6.6), holds true even with varying forces and a displacement along a curved path. The force $\vec{F}$ is essentially constant over any given infinitesimal segment $d\vec{l}$ of the path, so we can apply the work–energy theorem for straight-line motion to that segment. Thus the change in the particle's kinetic energy K over that segment equals the work $dW = F_\parallel \, dl = \vec{F} \cdot d\vec{l}$ done on the particle. Adding up these infinitesimal quantities of work from all the segments along the whole path gives the total work done, Eq. (6.14), which equals the total change in kinetic energy over the whole path. So $W_{\text{tot}} = \Delta K = K_2 - K_1$ is true *in general,* no matter what the path and no matter what the character of the forces. This can be proved more rigorously by using steps like those in Eqs. (6.11) through (6.13).

Note that only the component of the net force parallel to the path, $F_\parallel$, does work on the particle, so only this component can change the speed and kinetic energy of the particle. The component perpendicular to the path, $F_\perp = F\sin\phi$, has no effect on the particle's speed; it acts only to change the particle's direction.

The integral in Eq. (6.14) is called a *line integral.* To evaluate this integral in a specific problem, we need some sort of detailed description of the path and of the way in which $\vec{F}$ varies along the path. We usually express the line integral in terms of some scalar variable, as in the following example.

Example 6.8 | **Motion on a curved path**

At a family picnic you are appointed to push your obnoxious cousin Throckmorton in a swing (Fig. 6.24a). His weight is w, the length of the chains is R, and you push Throcky until the chains make an angle θ_0 with the vertical. To do this, you exert a varying horizontal force $\vec{F}$ that starts at zero and gradually increases just enough that Throcky and the swing move very slowly and remain very nearly in equilibrium throughout the process. What is the total work done on Throcky by all forces? What is the work done by the tension T in the chains? What is the work you do by exerting the force $\vec{F}$? (Neglect the weight of the chains and seat.)

SOLUTION

IDENTIFY and SET UP: The motion is along a curve, so we'll use Eq. (6.14) to calculate the work done by the net force, by the tension force, and by the force $\vec{F}$. Figure 6.24b shows our free-body diagram and coordinate system for some arbitrary point in Throcky's motion. We have replaced the sum of the tensions in the two chains with a single tension T.

EXECUTE: There are two ways to find the total work done during the motion: (1) by calculating the work done by each force and then adding those quantities, and (2) by calculating the work done by the net force. The second approach is far easier here because Throcky is in equilibrium at every point. Hence the net force on him is zero, the integral of the net force in Eq. (6.14) is zero, and the total work done on him is zero.

It's also easy to find the work done by the chain tension T because this force is perpendicular to the direction of motion at all points along the path. Hence at all points the angle between the chain tension and the displacement vector $d\vec{l}$ is 90° and the scalar product in Eq. (6.14) is zero. Thus the chain tension does zero work.

6.24 (a) Pushing cousin Throckmorton in a swing. (b) Our free-body diagram.

(a)

(b) Free-body diagram for Throckmorton (neglecting the weight of the chains and seat)

To compute the work done by $\vec{F}$, we need to know how this force varies with the angle θ. The net force on Throcky is zero, so $\Sigma F_x = 0$ and $\Sigma F_y = 0$. From Fig. 6.24b,

$$\sum F_x = F + (-T\sin\theta) = 0$$
$$\sum F_y = T\cos\theta + (-w) = 0$$

By eliminating T from these two equations, we obtain the magnitude $F = w\tan\theta$.

The point where $\vec{F}$ is applied moves through the arc s (Fig. 6.24a). The arc length s equals the radius R of the circular path multiplied by the length θ (in radians), so $s = R\theta$. Therefore the displacement $d\vec{l}$ corresponding to a small change of angle $d\theta$ has a magnitude $dl = ds = R\, d\theta$. The work done by $\vec{F}$ is then

$$W = \int \vec{F} \cdot d\vec{l} = \int F\cos\theta \, ds$$

Now we express F and ds in terms of the angle θ, whose value increases from 0 to θ_0:

$$W = \int_0^{\theta_0} (w\tan\theta)\cos\theta\,(R\,d\theta) = wR\int_0^{\theta_0} \sin\theta\,d\theta$$

$$= wR(1 - \cos\theta_0)$$

EVALUATE: If $\theta_0 = 0$, there is no displacement; then $\cos\theta_0 = 1$ and $W = 0$, as we should expect. If $\theta_0 = 90°$, then $\cos\theta_0 = 0$ and $W = wR$. In that case the work you do is the same as if you had lifted Throcky straight up a distance R with a force equal to his weight w. In fact (as you may wish to confirm), the quantity $R(1 - \cos\theta_0)$ is the increase in his height above the ground during the displacement, so for any value of θ_0 the work done by the force $\vec{F}$ is the change in height multiplied by the weight. This is an example of a more general result that we'll prove in Section 7.1.

We can check our results by writing the forces and the infinitesimal displacement $d\vec{l}$ in terms of their x- and y-components. Figure 6.24a shows that $d\vec{l}$ has a magnitude of ds, an x-component of $ds\cos\theta$, and a y-component of $ds\sin\theta$. Hence $d\vec{l} = \hat{\imath}\, ds\cos\theta + \hat{\jmath}\, ds\sin\theta$. Similarly, we can write the three forces as

$$\vec{T} = \hat{\imath}(-T\sin\theta) + \hat{\jmath}T\cos\theta$$
$$\vec{w} = \hat{\jmath}(-w)$$
$$\vec{F} = \hat{\imath}F$$

We use Eq. (1.21) to calculate the scalar product of each of these forces with $d\vec{l}$:

$$\vec{T}\cdot d\vec{l} = (-T\sin\theta)(ds\cos\theta) + (T\cos\theta)(ds\sin\theta) = 0$$
$$\vec{w}\cdot d\vec{l} = (-w)(ds\sin\theta) = -w\,\sin\theta\,ds$$
$$\vec{F}\cdot d\vec{l} = F(ds\cos\theta) = F\cos\theta\,ds$$

Since $\vec{T}\cdot d\vec{l} = 0$, the integral of this quantity is zero and the work done by the chain tension is zero, just as we found above. Using $ds = R\,d\theta$, we find the work done by the force of gravity is

$$\int \vec{w}\cdot d\vec{l} = \int (-w\sin\theta)R\,d\theta = -wR\int_0^{\theta_0}\sin\theta\,d\theta$$

$$= -wR(1 - \cos\theta_0)$$

Gravity does negative work because this force pulls down while Throcky moves upward. Finally, the work done by the force $\vec{F}$ is the same integral $\int\vec{F}\cdot d\vec{l} = \int F\cos\theta\,ds$ that we calculated above. The method of components is often the most convenient way to calculate scalar products, so use it when it makes your life easier!

Test Your Understanding of Section 6.3 In Example 5.20 (Section 5.4) we examined a conical pendulum. The speed of the pendulum bob remains constant as it travels around the circle shown in Fig. 5.32a. (a) Over one complete circle, how much work does the tension force F do on the bob? (i) a positive amount; (ii) a negative amount; (iii) zero. (b) Over one complete circle, how much work does the weight do on the bob? (i) a positive amount; (ii) a negative amount; (iii) zero.

6.4 Power

The definition of work makes no reference to the passage of time. If you lift a barbell weighing 100 N through a vertical distance of 1.0 m at constant velocity, you do $(100\text{ N})(1.0\text{ m}) = 100\text{ J}$ of work whether it takes you 1 second, 1 hour, or 1 year to do it. But often we need to know how quickly work is done. We describe this in terms of *power*. In ordinary conversation the word "power" is often synonymous with "energy" or "force." In physics we use a much more precise definition: **Power** is the time *rate* at which work is done. Like work and energy, power is a scalar quantity.

When a quantity of work ΔW is done during a time interval Δt, the average work done per unit time or **average power** P_{av} is defined to be

$$P_{av} = \frac{\Delta W}{\Delta t} \qquad \text{(average power)} \qquad (6.15)$$

The rate at which work is done might not be constant. We can define **instantaneous power** P as the quotient in Eq. (6.15) as Δt approaches zero:

$$P = \lim_{\Delta t \to 0} \frac{\Delta W}{\Delta t} = \frac{dW}{dt} \qquad \text{(instantaneous power)} \qquad (6.16)$$

The SI unit of power is the **watt** (W), named for the English inventor James Watt. One watt equals 1 joule per second: $1\text{ W} = 1\text{ J/s}$ (Fig. 6.25). The kilowatt

6.25 The same amount of work is done in both of these situations, but the power (the rate at which work is done) is different.

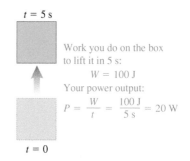

Work you do on the box to lift it in 5 s:
$W = 100\text{ J}$
Your power output:
$P = \dfrac{W}{t} = \dfrac{100\text{ J}}{5\text{ s}} = 20\text{ W}$

Work you do on the same box to lift it the same distance in 1 s:
$W = 100\text{ J}$
Your power output:
$P = \dfrac{W}{t} = \dfrac{100\text{ J}}{1\text{ s}} = 100\text{ W}$

6.26 The value of the horsepower derives from experiments by James Watt, who measured that a horse could do 33,000 foot-pounds of work per minute in lifting coal from a coal pit.

$(1 \text{ kW} = 10^3 \text{ W})$ and the megawatt $(1 \text{ MW} = 10^6 \text{ W})$ are also commonly used. In the British system, work is expressed in foot-pounds, and the unit of power is the foot-pound per second. A larger unit called the *horsepower* (hp) is also used (Fig. 6.26):

$$1 \text{ hp} = 550 \text{ ft} \cdot \text{lb/s} = 33{,}000 \text{ ft} \cdot \text{lb/min}$$

That is, a 1-hp motor running at full load does 33,000 ft·lb of work every minute. A useful conversion factor is

$$1 \text{ hp} = 746 \text{ W} = 0.746 \text{ kW}$$

The watt is a familiar unit of *electrical* power; a 100-W light bulb converts 100 J of electrical energy into light and heat each second. But there's nothing inherently electrical about a watt. A light bulb could be rated in horsepower, and an engine can be rated in kilowatts.

The *kilowatt-hour* (kW·h) is the usual commercial unit of electrical energy. One kilowatt-hour is the total work done in 1 hour (3600 s) when the power is 1 kilowatt (10^3 J/s), so

$$1 \text{ kW} \cdot \text{h} = (10^3 \text{ J/s})(3600 \text{ s}) = 3.6 \times 10^6 \text{ J} = 3.6 \text{ MJ}$$

The kilowatt-hour is a unit of *work* or *energy,* not power.

In mechanics we can also express power in terms of force and velocity. Suppose that a force $\vec{F}$ acts on a body while it undergoes a vector displacement $\Delta \vec{s}$. If $F_\parallel$ is the component of $\vec{F}$ tangent to the path (parallel to $\Delta \vec{s}$), then the work done by the force is $\Delta W = F_\parallel \Delta s$. The average power is

$$P_{av} = \frac{F_\parallel \Delta s}{\Delta t} = F_\parallel \frac{\Delta s}{\Delta t} = F_\parallel v_{av} \qquad (6.17)$$

Instantaneous power P is the limit of this expression as $\Delta t \to 0$:

$$P = F_\parallel v \qquad (6.18)$$

where v is the magnitude of the instantaneous velocity. We can also express Eq. (6.18) in terms of the scalar product:

$$P = \vec{F} \cdot \vec{v} \qquad \begin{array}{l}\text{(instantaneous rate at which}\\ \text{force } \vec{F} \text{ does work on a particle)}\end{array} \qquad (6.19)$$

Example 6.9 **Force and power**

Each of the four jet engines on an Airbus A380 airliner develops a thrust (a forward force on the airliner) of 322,000 N (72,000 lb). When the airplane is flying at 250 m/s (900 km/h, or roughly 560 mi/h), what horsepower does each engine develop?

SOLUTION

IDENTIFY, SET UP and EXECUTE: Our target variable is the instantaneous power P, which is the rate at which the thrust does work. We use Eq. (6.18). The thrust is in the direction of motion, so $F_\parallel$ is just equal to the thrust. At $v = 250$ m/s, the power developed by each engine is

$$P = F_\parallel v = (3.22 \times 10^5 \text{ N})(250 \text{ m/s}) = 8.05 \times 10^7 \text{ W}$$

$$= (8.05 \times 10^7 \text{ W}) \frac{1 \text{ hp}}{746 \text{ W}} = 108{,}000 \text{ hp}$$

EVALUATE: The speed of modern airliners is directly related to the power of their engines (Fig. 6.27). The largest propeller-driven airliners of the 1950s had engines that developed about 3400 hp

6.27 (a) Propeller-driven and (b) jet airliners.

(a)

(b)

$(2.5 \times 10^6 \text{ W})$, giving them maximum speeds of about 600 km/h (370 mi/h). Each engine on an Airbus A380 develops more than 30 times more power, enabling it to fly at about 900 km/h (560 mi/h) and to carry a much heavier load.

If the engines are at maximum thrust while the airliner is at rest on the ground so that $v = 0$, the engines develop *zero* power. Force and power are not the same thing!

Example 6.10 A "power climb"

A 50.0-kg marathon runner runs up the stairs to the top of Chicago's 443-m-tall Willis Tower, the tallest building in the United States (Fig. 6.28). To lift herself to the top in 15.0 minutes, what must be her average power output? Express your answer in watts, in kilowatts, and in horsepower.

SOLUTION

IDENTIFY and SET UP: We'll treat the runner as a particle of mass m. Her average power output P_{av} must be enough to lift her at constant speed against gravity.

We can find P_{av} in two ways: (1) by determining how much work she must do and dividing that quantity by the elapsed time, as in Eq. (6.15), or (2) by calculating the average upward force she must exert (in the direction of the climb) and multiplying that quantity by her upward velocity, as in Eq. (6.17).

EXECUTE: (1) As in Example 6.8, lifting a mass m against gravity requires an amount of work equal to the weight mg multiplied by the height h it is lifted. Hence the work the runner must do is

$$W = mgh = (50.0 \text{ kg})(9.80 \text{ m/s}^2)(443 \text{ m})$$
$$= 2.17 \times 10^5 \text{ J}$$

She does this work in a time 15.0 min = 900 s, so from Eq. (6.15) the average power is

$$P_{av} = \frac{2.17 \times 10^5 \text{J}}{900 \text{ s}} = 241 \text{ W} = 0.241 \text{ kW} = 0.323 \text{ hp}$$

(2) The force exerted is vertical and the average vertical component of velocity is $(443 \text{ m})/(900 \text{ s}) = 0.492$ m/s, so from Eq. (6.17) the average power is

6.28 How much power is required to run up the stairs of Chicago's Willis Tower in 15 minutes?

$$P_{av} = F_{\parallel}v_{av} = (mg)v_{av}$$
$$= (50.0 \text{ kg})(9.80 \text{ m/s}^2)(0.492 \text{ m/s}) = 241 \text{ W}$$

which is the same result as before.

EVALUATE: The runner's *total* power output will be several times greater than 241 W. The reason is that the runner isn't really a particle but a collection of parts that exert forces on each other and do work, such as the work done to inhale and exhale and to make her arms and legs swing. What we've calculated is only the part of her power output that lifts her to the top of the building.

Test Your Understanding of Section 6.4 The air surrounding an airplane in flight exerts a drag force that acts opposite to the airplane's motion. When the Airbus A380 in Example 6.9 is flying in a straight line at a constant altitude at a constant 250 m/s, what is the rate at which the drag force does work on it? (i) 432,000 hp; (ii) 108,000 hp; (iii) 0; (iv) −108,000 hp; (v) −432,000 hp.

Work done by a force: When a constant force $\vec{F}$ acts on a particle that undergoes a straight-line displacement $\vec{s}$, the work done by the force on the particle is defined to be the scalar product of $\vec{F}$ and $\vec{s}$. The unit of work in SI units is 1 joule = 1 newton-meter $(1\ \text{J} = 1\ \text{N} \cdot \text{m})$. Work is a scalar quantity; it can be positive or negative, but it has no direction in space. (See Examples 6.1 and 6.2.)

$$W = \vec{F} \cdot \vec{s} = Fs\cos\phi \quad \text{(6.2), (6.3)}$$
$$\phi = \text{angle between } \vec{F} \text{ and } \vec{s}$$

Kinetic energy: The kinetic energy K of a particle equals the amount of work required to accelerate the particle from rest to speed v. It is also equal to the amount of work the particle can do in the process of being brought to rest. Kinetic energy is a scalar that has no direction in space; it is always positive or zero. Its units are the same as the units of work: $1\ \text{J} = 1\ \text{N} \cdot \text{m} = 1\ \text{kg} \cdot \text{m}^2/\text{s}^2$.

$$K = \tfrac{1}{2}mv^2 \quad \text{(6.5)}$$

Doubling m doubles K.

Doubling v quadruples K.

The work–energy theorem: When forces act on a particle while it undergoes a displacement, the particle's kinetic energy changes by an amount equal to the total work done on the particle by all the forces. This relationship, called the work–energy theorem, is valid whether the forces are constant or varying and whether the particle moves along a straight or curved path. It is applicable only to bodies that can be treated as particles. (See Examples 6.3–6.5.)

$$W_{\text{tot}} = K_2 - K_1 = \Delta K \quad \text{(6.6)}$$

$W_{\text{tot}} = $ Total work done on particle along path

$K_1 = \tfrac{1}{2}mv_1^2$

$K_2 = \tfrac{1}{2}mv_2^2 = K_1 + W_{\text{tot}}$

Work done by a varying force or on a curved path: When a force varies during a straight-line displacement, the work done by the force is given by an integral, Eq. (6.7). (See Examples 6.6 and 6.7.) When a particle follows a curved path, the work done on it by a force $\vec{F}$ is given by an integral that involves the angle ϕ between the force and the displacement. This expression is valid even if the force magnitude and the angle ϕ vary during the displacement. (See Example 6.8.)

$$W = \int_{x_1}^{x_2} F_x\, dx \quad \text{(6.7)}$$

$$W = \int_{P_1}^{P_2} F\cos\phi\, dl = \int_{P_1}^{P_2} F_{\parallel}\, dl$$

$$= \int_{P_1}^{P_2} \vec{F} \cdot d\vec{l} \quad \text{(6.14)}$$

Area = Work done by force during displacement

Power: Power is the time rate of doing work. The average power P_{av} is the amount of work ΔW done in time Δt divided by that time. The instantaneous power is the limit of the average power as Δt goes to zero. When a force $\vec{F}$ acts on a particle moving with velocity $\vec{v}$, the instantaneous power (the rate at which the force does work) is the scalar product of $\vec{F}$ and $\vec{v}$. Like work and kinetic energy, power is a scalar quantity. The SI unit of power is 1 watt = 1 joule/second $(1\ \text{W} = 1\ \text{J/s})$. (See Examples 6.9 and 6.10.)

$$P_{\text{av}} = \frac{\Delta W}{\Delta t} \quad \text{(6.15)}$$

$$P = \lim_{\Delta t \to 0} \frac{\Delta W}{\Delta t} = \frac{dW}{dt} \quad \text{(6.16)}$$

$$P = \vec{F} \cdot \vec{v} \quad \text{(6.19)}$$

Consider a hanging spring of negligible mass that does *not* obey Hooke's law. When the spring is extended by a distance x, the force exerted by the spring has magnitude αx^2, where α is a positive constant. The spring is not extended when a block of mass m is attached to it. The block is then released, stretching the spring as it falls (Fig. 6.29). (a) How fast is the block moving when it has fallen a distance x_1? (b) At what rate does the spring do work on the block at this point? (c) Find the maximum distance x_2 that the spring stretches. (d) Will the block *remain* at the point found in part (c)?

6.29 The block is attached to a spring that does not obey Hooke's law.

SOLUTION GUIDE

 See MasteringPhysics® study area for a Video Tutor solution.

IDENTIFY and SET UP

1. The spring force in this problem isn't constant, so you have to use the work–energy theorem. You'll also need to use Eq. (6.7) to find the work done by the spring over a given displacement.
2. Draw a free-body diagram for the block, including your choice of coordinate axes. Note that x represents how far the spring is *stretched,* so choose the positive x-axis accordingly. On your coordinate axis, label the points $x = x_1$ and $x = x_2$.
3. Make a list of the unknown quantities, and decide which of these are the target variables.

EXECUTE

4. Calculate the work done on the block by the spring as the block falls an arbitrary distance x. (The integral isn't a difficult one. Use Appendix B if you need a reminder.) Is the work done by the spring positive, negative, or zero?

5. Calculate the work done on the block by any other forces as the block falls an arbitrary distance x. Is this work positive, negative, or zero?
6. Use the work–energy theorem to find the target variables. (You'll also need to use an equation for power.) *Hint:* When the spring is at its maximum stretch, what is the speed of the block?
7. To answer part (d), consider the *net* force that acts on the block when it is at the point found in part (c).

EVALUATE

8. We learned in Chapter 2 that after an object dropped from rest has fallen freely a distance x_1, its speed is $\sqrt{2gx_1}$. Use this to decide whether your answer in part (a) makes sense. In addition, ask yourself whether the algebraic sign of your answer in part (b) makes sense.
9. Find the value of x where the net force on the block would be zero. How does this compare to your result for x_2? Is this consistent with your answer in part (d)?

Problems   For instructor-assigned homework, go to MasteringPhysics®.

•, ••, •••: Problems of increasing difficulty. **CP:** Cumulative problems incorporating material from earlier chapters. **CALC:** Problems requiring calculus. **BIO:** Biosciences problems.

DISCUSSION QUESTIONS

Q6.1 The sign of many physical quantities depends on the choice of coordinates. For example, a_y for free-fall motion can be negative or positive, depending on whether we choose upward or downward as positive. Is the same thing true of work? In other words, can we make positive work negative by a different choice of coordinates? Explain.

Q6.2 An elevator is hoisted by its cables at constant speed. Is the total work done on the elevator positive, negative, or zero? Explain.

Q6.3 A rope tied to a body is pulled, causing the body to accelerate. But according to Newton's third law, the body pulls back on the rope with an equal and opposite force. Is the total work done then zero? If so, how can the body's kinetic energy change? Explain.

Q6.4 If it takes total work W to give an object a speed v and kinetic energy K, starting from rest, what will be the object's speed (in terms of v) and kinetic energy (in terms of K) if we do twice as much work on it, again starting from rest?

Q6.5 If there is a net nonzero force on a moving object, is it possible for the total work done on the object to be zero? Explain, with an example that illustrates your answer.

Q6.6 In Example 5.5 (Section 5.1), how does the work done on the bucket by the tension in the cable compare to the work done on the cart by the tension in the cable?

Q6.7 In the conical pendulum in Example 5.20 (Section 5.4), which of the forces do work on the bob while it is swinging?

Q6.8 For the cases shown in Fig. Q6.8, the object is released from rest at the top and feels no friction or air resistance. In

Figure **Q6.8**

(a) m h

(b) m h

(c) $2m$ h

which (if any) cases will the mass have (i) the greatest speed at the bottom and (ii) the most work done on it by the time it reaches the bottom?

Q6.9 A force $\vec{F}$ is in the x-direction and has a magnitude that depends on x. Sketch a possible graph of F versus x such that the force does zero work on an object that moves from x_1 to x_2, even though the force magnitude is not zero at all x in this range.

Q6.10 Does the kinetic energy of a car change more when it speeds up from 10 to 15 m/s or from 15 to 20 m/s? Explain.

Q6.11 A falling brick has a mass of 1.5 kg and is moving straight downward with a speed of 5.0 m/s. A 1.5-kg physics book is sliding across the floor with a speed of 5.0 m/s. A 1.5-kg melon is traveling with a horizontal velocity component 3.0 m/s to the right and a vertical component 4.0 m/s upward. Do these objects all have the same velocity? Do these objects all have the same kinetic energy? For each question, give the reasoning behind your answer.

Q6.12 Can the *total* work done on an object during a displacement be negative? Explain. If the total work is negative, can its magnitude be larger than the initial kinetic energy of the object? Explain.

Q6.13 A net force acts on an object and accelerates it from rest to a speed v_1. In doing so, the force does an amount of work W_1. By what factor must the work done on the object be increased to produce three times the final speed, with the object again starting from rest?

Q6.14 A truck speeding down the highway has a lot of kinetic energy relative to a stopped state trooper, but no kinetic energy relative to the truck driver. In these two frames of reference, is the same amount of work required to stop the truck? Explain.

Q6.15 You are holding a briefcase by the handle, with your arm straight down by your side. Does the force your hand exerts do work on the briefcase when (a) you walk at a constant speed down a horizontal hallway and (b) you ride an escalator from the first to second floor of a building? In each case justify your answer.

Q6.16 When a book slides along a tabletop, the force of friction does negative work on it. Can friction ever do *positive* work? Explain. (*Hint:* Think of a box in the back of an accelerating truck.)

Q6.17 Time yourself while running up a flight of steps, and compute the average rate at which you do work against the force of gravity. Express your answer in watts and in horsepower.

Q6.18 Fractured Physics. Many terms from physics are badly misused in everyday language. In each case, explain the errors involved. (a) A *strong* person is called *powerful*. What is wrong with this use of *power*? (b) When a worker carries a bag of concrete along a level construction site, people say he did a lot of *work*. Did he?

Q6.19 An advertisement for a portable electrical generating unit claims that the unit's diesel engine produces 28,000 hp to drive an electrical generator that produces 30 MW of electrical power. Is this possible? Explain.

Q6.20 A car speeds up while the engine delivers constant power. Is the acceleration greater at the beginning of this process or at the end? Explain.

Q6.21 Consider a graph of instantaneous power versus time, with the vertical P-axis starting at $P = 0$. What is the physical significance of the area under the P-versus-t curve between vertical lines at t_1 and

t_2? How could you find the average power from the graph? Draw a P-versus-t curve that consists of two straight-line sections and for which the peak power is equal to twice the average power.

Q6.22 A nonzero net force acts on an object. Is it possible for any of the following quantities to be constant: (a) the particle's speed; (b) the particle's velocity; (c) the particle's kinetic energy?

Q6.23 When a certain force is applied to an ideal spring, the spring stretches a distance x from its unstretched length and does work W. If instead twice the force is applied, what distance (in terms of x) does the spring stretch from its unstretched length, and how much work (in terms of W) is required to stretch it this distance?

Q6.24 If work W is required to stretch a spring a distance x from its unstretched length, what work (in terms of W) is required to stretch the spring an *additional* distance x?

EXERCISES

Section 6.1 Work

6.1 • You push your physics book 1.50 m along a horizontal tabletop with a horizontal push of 2.40 N while the opposing force of friction is 0.600 N. How much work does each of the following forces do on the book: (a) your 2.40-N push, (b) the friction force, (c) the normal force from the tabletop, and (d) gravity? (e) What is the net work done on the book?

6.2 • A tow truck pulls a car 5.00 km along a horizontal roadway using a cable having a tension of 850 N. (a) How much work does the cable do on the car if it pulls horizontally? If it pulls at 35.0° above the horizontal? (b) How much work does the cable do on the tow truck in both cases of part (a)? (c) How much work does gravity do on the car in part (a)?

6.3 • A factory worker pushes a 30.0-kg crate a distance of 4.5 m along a level floor at constant velocity by pushing horizontally on it. The coefficient of kinetic friction between the crate and the floor is 0.25. (a) What magnitude of force must the worker apply? (b) How much work is done on the crate by this force? (c) How much work is done on the crate by friction? (d) How much work is done on the crate by the normal force? By gravity? (e) What is the total work done on the crate?

6.4 •• Suppose the worker in Exercise 6.3 pushes downward at an angle of 30° below the horizontal. (a) What magnitude of force must the worker apply to move the crate at constant velocity? (b) How much work is done on the crate by this force when the crate is pushed a distance of 4.5 m? (c) How much work is done on the crate by friction during this displacement? (d) How much work is done on the crate by the normal force? By gravity? (e) What is the total work done on the crate?

6.5 •• A 75.0-kg painter climbs a ladder that is 2.75 m long leaning against a vertical wall. The ladder makes a 30.0° angle with the wall. (a) How much work does gravity do on the painter? (b) Does the answer to part (a) depend on whether the painter climbs at constant speed or accelerates up the ladder?

6.6 •• Two tugboats pull a disabled supertanker. Each tug exerts a constant force of 1.80×10^6 N, one 14° west of north and the other 14° east of north, as they pull the tanker 0.75 km toward the north. What is the total work they do on the supertanker?

6.7 • Two blocks are connected by a very light string passing over a massless and frictionless pulley (Fig. E6.7). Traveling at constant speed, the 20.0-N block moves 75.0 cm to the right and the 12.0-N block moves 75.0 cm downward. During this process, how much work is done (a) on the 12.0-N block by (i) gravity and (ii) the tension in the string? (b) On the 20.0-N block by (i) gravity,

(ii) the tension in the string, (iii) friction, and (iv) the normal force? (c) Find the total work done on each block.

Figure **E6.7**

6.8 •• A loaded grocery cart is rolling across a parking lot in a strong wind. You apply a constant force $\vec{F} = (30 \text{ N})\hat{\imath} - (40 \text{ N})\hat{\jmath}$ to the cart as it undergoes a displacement $\vec{s} = (-9.0 \text{ m})\hat{\imath} - (3.0 \text{ m})\hat{\jmath}$. How much work does the force you apply do on the grocery cart?

6.9 • A 0.800-kg ball is tied to the end of a string 1.60 m long and swung in a vertical circle. (a) During one complete circle, starting anywhere, calculate the total work done on the ball by (i) the tension in the string and (ii) gravity. (b) Repeat part (a) for motion along the semicircle from the lowest to the highest point on the path.

6.10 •• An 8.00-kg package in a mail-sorting room slides 2.00 m down a chute that is inclined at 53.0° below the horizontal. The coefficient of kinetic friction between the package and the chute's surface is 0.40. Calculate the work done on the package by (a) friction, (b) gravity, and (c) the normal force. (d) What is the net work done on the package?

6.11 •• A boxed 10.0-kg computer monitor is dragged by friction 5.50 m up along the moving surface of a conveyor belt inclined at an angle of 36.9° above the horizontal. If the monitor's speed is a constant 2.10 cm/s, how much work is done on the monitor by (a) friction, (b) gravity, and (c) the normal force of the conveyor belt?

6.12 •• You apply a constant force $\vec{F} = (-68.0 \text{ N})\hat{\imath} + (36.0 \text{ N})\hat{\jmath}$ to a 380-kg car as the car travels 48.0 m in a direction that is 240.0° counterclockwise from the $+x$-axis. How much work does the force you apply do on the car?

Section 6.2 Kinetic Energy and the Work–Energy Theorem

6.13 •• **Animal Energy.** BIO Adult cheetahs, the fastest of the great cats, have a mass of about 70 kg and have been clocked running at up to 72 mph (32 m/s). (a) How many joules of kinetic energy does such a swift cheetah have? (b) By what factor would its kinetic energy change if its speed were doubled?

6.14 •• A 1.50-kg book is sliding along a rough horizontal surface. At point A it is moving at 3.21 m/s, and at point B it has slowed to 1.25 m/s. (a) How much work was done on the book between A and B? (b) If -0.750 J of work is done on the book from B to C, how fast is it moving at point C? (c) How fast would it be moving at C if $+0.750$ J of work were done on it from B to C?

6.15 • **Meteor Crater.** About 50,000 years ago, a meteor crashed into the earth near present-day Flagstaff, Arizona. Measurements from 2005 estimate that this meteor had a mass of about 1.4×10^8 kg (around 150,000 tons) and hit the ground at a speed of 12 km/s. (a) How much kinetic energy did this meteor deliver to the ground? (b) How does this energy compare to the energy released by a 1.0-megaton nuclear bomb? (A megaton bomb releases the same amount of energy as a million tons of TNT, and 1.0 ton of TNT releases 4.184×10^9 J of energy.)

6.16 • **Some Typical Kinetic Energies.** (a) In the Bohr model of the atom, the ground-state electron in hydrogen has an orbital speed of 2190 km/s. What is its kinetic energy? (Consult Appendix F.)

(b) If you drop a 1.0-kg weight (about 2 lb) from a height of 1.0 m, how many joules of kinetic energy will it have when it reaches the ground? (c) Is it reasonable that a 30-kg child could run fast enough to have 100 J of kinetic energy?

6.17 •• In Fig. E6.7 assume that there is no friction force on the 20.0-N block that sits on the tabletop. The pulley is light and frictionless. (a) Calculate the tension T in the light string that connects the blocks. (b) For a displacement in which the 12.0-N block descends 1.20 m, calculate the total work done on (i) the 20.0-N block and (ii) the 12.0-N block. (c) For the displacement in part (b), calculate the total work done on the system of the two blocks. How does your answer compare to the work done on the 12.0-N block by gravity? (d) If the system is released from rest, what is the speed of the 12.0-N block when it has descended 1.20 m?

6.18 • A 4.80-kg watermelon is dropped from rest from the roof of a 25.0-m-tall building and feels no appreciable air resistance. (a) Calculate the work done by gravity on the watermelon during its displacement from the roof to the ground. (b) Just before it strikes the ground, what is the watermelon's (i) kinetic energy and (ii) speed? (c) Which of the answers in parts (a) and (b) would be *different* if there were appreciable air resistance?

6.19 •• Use the work–energy theorem to solve each of these problems. You can use Newton's laws to check your answers. Neglect air resistance in all cases. (a) A branch falls from the top of a 95.0-m-tall redwood tree, starting from rest. How fast is it moving when it reaches the ground? (b) A volcano ejects a boulder directly upward 525 m into the air. How fast was the boulder moving just as it left the volcano? (c) A skier moving at 5.00 m/s encounters a long, rough horizontal patch of snow having coefficient of kinetic friction 0.220 with her skis. How far does she travel on this patch before stopping? (d) Suppose the rough patch in part (c) was only 2.90 m long? How fast would the skier be moving when she reached the end of the patch? (e) At the base of a frictionless icy hill that rises at 25.0° above the horizontal, a toboggan has a speed of 12.0 m/s toward the hill. How high vertically above the base will it go before stopping?

6.20 •• You throw a 20-N rock vertically into the air from ground level. You observe that when it is 15.0 m above the ground, it is traveling at 25.0 m/s upward. Use the work–energy theorem to find (a) the rock's speed just as it left the ground and (b) its maximum height.

6.21 •• You are a member of an Alpine Rescue Team. You must project a box of supplies up an incline of constant slope angle α so that it reaches a stranded skier who is a vertical distance h above the bottom of the incline. The incline is slippery, but there is some friction present, with kinetic friction coefficient μ_k. Use the work–energy theorem to calculate the minimum speed you must give the box at the bottom of the incline so that it will reach the skier. Express your answer in terms of g, h, μ_k, and α.

6.22 •• A mass m slides down a smooth inclined plane from an initial vertical height h, making an angle α with the horizontal. (a) The work done by a force is the sum of the work done by the components of the force. Consider the components of gravity parallel and perpendicular to the surface of the plane. Calculate the work done on the mass by each of the components, and use these results to show that the work done by gravity is exactly the same as if the mass had fallen straight down through the air from a height h. (b) Use the work–energy theorem to prove that the speed of the mass at the bottom of the incline is the same as if it had been dropped from height h, independent of the angle α of the incline. Explain how this speed can be independent of the slope angle. (c) Use the results of part (b) to find the speed of a rock that slides down an icy frictionless hill, starting from rest 15.0 m above the bottom.

6.23 • A sled with mass 8.00 kg moves in a straight line on a frictionless horizontal surface. At one point in its path, its speed is 4.00 m/s; after it has traveled 2.50 m beyond this point, its speed is 6.00 m/s. Use the work–energy theorem to find the force acting on the sled, assuming that this force is constant and that it acts in the direction of the sled's motion.

6.24 •• A soccer ball with mass 0.420 kg is initially moving with speed 2.00 m/s. A soccer player kicks the ball, exerting a constant force of magnitude 40.0 N in the same direction as the ball's motion. Over what distance must the player's foot be in contact with the ball to increase the ball's speed to 6.00 m/s?

6.25 • A 12-pack of Omni-Cola (mass 4.30 kg) is initially at rest on a horizontal floor. It is then pushed in a straight line for 1.20 m by a trained dog that exerts a horizontal force with magnitude 36.0 N. Use the work–energy theorem to find the final speed of the 12-pack if (a) there is no friction between the 12-pack and the floor, and (b) the coefficient of kinetic friction between the 12-pack and the floor is 0.30.

6.26 • A batter hits a baseball with mass 0.145 kg straight upward with an initial speed of 25.0 m/s. (a) How much work has gravity done on the baseball when it reaches a height of 20.0 m above the bat? (b) Use the work–energy theorem to calculate the speed of the baseball at a height of 20.0 m above the bat. You can ignore air resistance. (c) Does the answer to part (b) depend on whether the baseball is moving upward or downward at a height of 20.0 m? Explain.

6.27 • A little red wagon with mass 7.00 kg moves in a straight line on a frictionless horizontal surface. It has an initial speed of 4.00 m/s and then is pushed 3.0 m in the direction of the initial velocity by a force with a magnitude of 10.0 N. (a) Use the work–energy theorem to calculate the wagon's final speed. (b) Calculate the acceleration produced by the force. Use this acceleration in the kinematic relationships of Chapter 2 to calculate the wagon's final speed. Compare this result to that calculated in part (a).

6.28 •• A block of ice with mass 2.00 kg slides 0.750 m down an inclined plane that slopes downward at an angle of 36.9° below the horizontal. If the block of ice starts from rest, what is its final speed? You can ignore friction.

6.29 • **Stopping Distance.** A car is traveling on a level road with speed v_0 at the instant when the brakes lock, so that the tires slide rather than roll. (a) Use the work–energy theorem to calculate the minimum stopping distance of the car in terms of v_0, g, and the coefficient of kinetic friction μ_k between the tires and the road. (b) By what factor would the minimum stopping distance change if (i) the coefficient of kinetic friction were doubled, or (ii) the initial speed were doubled, or (iii) both the coefficient of kinetic friction and the initial speed were doubled?

6.30 •• A 30.0-kg crate is initially moving with a velocity that has magnitude 3.90 m/s in a direction 37.0° west of north. How much work must be done on the crate to change its velocity to 5.62 m/s in a direction 63.0° south of east?

Section 6.3 Work and Energy with Varying Forces

6.31 • **BIO Heart Repair.** A surgeon is using material from a donated heart to repair a patient's damaged aorta and needs to know the elastic characteristics of this aortal material. Tests performed on a 16.0-cm strip of the donated aorta reveal that it stretches 3.75 cm when a 1.50-N pull is exerted on it. (a) What is the force constant of this strip of aortal material? (b) If the maximum distance it will be able to stretch when it replaces the aorta in the damaged heart is 1.14 cm, what is the greatest force it will be able to exert there?

6.32 •• To stretch a spring 3.00 cm from its unstretched length, 12.0 J of work must be done. (a) What is the force constant of this spring? (b) What magnitude force is needed to stretch the spring 3.00 cm from its unstretched length? (c) How much work must be done to compress this spring 4.00 cm from its unstretched length, and what force is needed to compress it this distance?

6.33 • Three identical 6.40-kg masses are hung by three identical springs, as shown in Fig. E6.33. Each spring has a force constant of 7.80 kN/m and was 12.0 cm long before any masses were attached to it. (a) Draw a free-body diagram of each mass. (b) How long is each spring when hanging as shown? (*Hint:* First isolate only the bottom mass. Then treat the bottom two masses as a system. Finally, treat all three masses as a system.)

Figure **E6.33**

6.34 • A child applies a force $\vec{F}$ parallel to the x-axis to a 10.0-kg sled moving on the frozen surface of a small pond. As the child controls the speed of the sled, the x-component of the force she applies varies with the x-coordinate of the sled as shown in Fig. E6.34. Calculate the work done by the force $\vec{F}$ when the sled moves (a) from x = 0 to x = 8.0 m; (b) from x = 8.0 m to x = 12.0 m; (c) from x = 0 to 12.0 m.

Figure **E6.34**

6.35 •• Suppose the sled in Exercise 6.34 is initially at rest at x = 0. Use the work–energy theorem to find the speed of the sled at (a) x = 8.0 m and (b) x = 12.0 m. You can ignore friction between the sled and the surface of the pond.

6.36 • A 2.0-kg box and a 3.0-kg box on a perfectly smooth horizontal floor have a spring of force constant 250 N/m compressed between them. If the initial compression of the spring is 6.0 cm, find the acceleration of each box the instant after they are released. Be sure to include free-body diagrams of each box as part of your solution.

6.37 •• A 6.0-kg box moving at 3.0 m/s on a horizontal, frictionless surface runs into a light spring of force constant 75 N/cm. Use the work–energy theorem to find the maximum compression of the spring.

6.38 •• **Leg Presses.** As part of your daily workout, you lie on your back and push with your feet against a platform attached to two stiff springs arranged side by side so that they are parallel to each other. When you push the platform, you compress the springs. You do 80.0 J of work when you compress the springs 0.200 m from their uncompressed length. (a) What magnitude of force must you apply to hold the platform in this position? (b) How much *additional* work must you do to move the platform 0.200 m *farther*, and what maximum force must you apply?

6.39 •• (a) In Example 6.7 (Section 6.3) it was calculated that with the air track turned off, the glider travels 8.6 cm before it stops instantaneously. How large would the coefficient of static friction μ_s have to be to keep the glider from springing back to the left? (b) If the coefficient of static friction between the glider and the track is $\mu_s = 0.60$, what is the maximum initial speed v_1 that the glider can be given and still remain at rest after it stops instantaneously? With the air track turned off, the coefficient of kinetic friction is $\mu_k = 0.47$.

6.40 • A 4.00-kg block of ice is placed against a horizontal spring that has force constant $k = 200$ N/m and is compressed 0.025 m. The spring is released and accelerates the block along a horizontal surface. You can ignore friction and the mass of the spring. (a) Calculate the work done on the block by the spring during the motion of the block from its initial position to where the spring has returned to its uncompressed length. (b) What is the speed of the block after it leaves the spring?

6.41 • A force $\vec{F}$ is applied to a 2.0-kg radio-controlled model car parallel to the x-axis as it moves along a straight track. The x-component of the force varies with the x-coordinate of the car as shown in Fig. E6.41. Calculate the work done by the force $\vec{F}$ when the car moves from (a) $x = 0$ to $x = 3.0$ m; (b) $x = 3.0$ m to $x = 4.0$ m; (c) $x = 4.0$ m to $x = 7.0$ m; (d) $x = 0$ to $x = 7.0$ m; (e) $x = 7.0$ m to $x = 2.0$ m.

Figure **E6.41**

6.42 • Suppose the 2.0-kg model car in Exercise 6.41 is initially at rest at $x = 0$ and $\vec{F}$ is the net force acting on it. Use the work–energy theorem to find the speed of the car at (a) $x = 3.0$ m; (b) $x = 4.0$ m; (c) $x = 7.0$ m.

6.43 •• At a waterpark, sleds with riders are sent along a slippery, horizontal surface by the release of a large compressed spring. The spring with force constant $k = 40.0$ N/cm and negligible mass rests on the frictionless horizontal surface. One end is in contact with a stationary wall. A sled and rider with total mass 70.0 kg are pushed against the other end, compressing the spring 0.375 m. The sled is then released with zero initial velocity. What is the sled's speed when the spring (a) returns to its uncompressed length and (b) is still compressed 0.200 m?

6.44 • **Half of a Spring.** (a) Suppose you cut a massless ideal spring in half. If the full spring had a force constant k, what is the force constant of each half, in terms of k? (*Hint:* Think of the original spring as two equal halves, each producing the same force as the entire spring. Do you see why the forces must be equal?) (b) If you cut the spring into three equal segments instead, what is the force constant of each one, in terms of k?

6.45 •• A small glider is placed against a compressed spring at the bottom of an air track that slopes upward at an angle of 40.0° above the horizontal. The glider has mass 0.0900 kg. The spring has $k = 640$ N/m and negligible mass. When the spring is released, the glider travels a maximum distance of 1.80 m along the air track before sliding back down. Before reaching this maximum distance, the glider loses contact with the spring. (a) What distance was the spring originally compressed? (b) When the glider has traveled along the air track 0.80 m from its initial position against the compressed spring, is it still in contact with the spring? What is the kinetic energy of the glider at this point?

6.46 •• An ingenious bricklayer builds a device for shooting bricks up to the top of the wall where he is working. He places a brick on a vertical compressed spring with force constant $k = 450$ N/m and negligible mass. When the spring is released, the brick is propelled upward. If the brick has mass 1.80 kg and is to reach a maximum height of 3.6 m above its initial position on the compressed spring, what distance must the bricklayer compress the spring initially? (The brick loses contact with the spring when the spring returns to its uncompressed length. Why?)

6.47 •• **CALC** A force in the $+x$-direction with magnitude $F(x) = 18.0$ N $- (0.530$ N/m$)x$ is applied to a 6.00-kg box that is sitting on the horizontal, frictionless surface of a frozen lake. $F(x)$ is the only horizontal force on the box. If the box is initially at rest at $x = 0$, what is its speed after it has traveled 14.0 m?

Section 6.4 Power

6.48 •• A crate on a motorized cart starts from rest and moves with a constant eastward acceleration of $a = 2.80$ m/s². A worker assists the cart by pushing on the crate with a force that is eastward and has magnitude that depends on time according to $F(t) = (5.40$ N/s$)t$. What is the instantaneous power supplied by this force at $t = 5.00$ s?

6.49 • How many joules of energy does a 100-watt light bulb use per hour? How fast would a 70-kg person have to run to have that amount of kinetic energy?

6.50 •• **BIO** **Should You Walk or Run?** It is 5.0 km from your home to the physics lab. As part of your physical fitness program, you could run that distance at 10 km/h (which uses up energy at the rate of 700 W), or you could walk it leisurely at 3.0 km/h (which uses energy at 290 W). Which choice would burn more energy, and how much energy (in joules) would it burn? Why is it that the more intense exercise actually burns up less energy than the less intense exercise?

6.51 •• **Magnetar.** On December 27, 2004, astronomers observed the greatest flash of light ever recorded from outside the solar system. It came from the highly magnetic neutron star SGR 1806-20 (a *magnetar*). During 0.20 s, this star released as much energy as our sun does in 250,000 years. If P is the average power output of our sun, what was the average power output (in terms of P) of this magnetar?

6.52 •• A 20.0-kg rock is sliding on a rough, horizontal surface at 8.00 m/s and eventually stops due to friction. The coefficient of kinetic friction between the rock and the surface is 0.200. What average power is produced by friction as the rock stops?

6.53 • A tandem (two-person) bicycle team must overcome a force of 165 N to maintain a speed of 9.00 m/s. Find the power required per rider, assuming that each contributes equally. Express your answer in watts and in horsepower.

6.54 •• When its 75-kW (100-hp) engine is generating full power, a small single-engine airplane with mass 700 kg gains altitude at a rate of 2.5 m/s (150 m/min, or 500 ft/min). What fraction of the engine power is being used to make the airplane climb? (The remainder is used to overcome the effects of air resistance and of inefficiencies in the propeller and engine.)

6.55 •• **Working Like a Horse.** Your job is to lift 30-kg crates a vertical distance of 0.90 m from the ground onto the bed of a truck. (a) How many crates would you have to load onto the truck in 1 minute for the average power output you use to lift the crates to equal 0.50 hp? (b) How many crates for an average power output of 100 W?

6.56 •• An elevator has mass 600 kg, not including passengers. The elevator is designed to ascend, at constant speed, a vertical distance of 20.0 m (five floors) in 16.0 s, and it is driven by a motor that can provide up to 40 hp to the elevator. What is the maximum number of passengers that can ride in the elevator? Assume that an average passenger has mass 65.0 kg.

6.57 •• A ski tow operates on a 15.0° slope of length 300 m. The rope moves at 12.0 km/h and provides power for 50 riders at one time, with an average mass per rider of 70.0 kg. Estimate the power required to operate the tow.

6.58 •• The aircraft carrier *John F. Kennedy* has mass 7.4×10^7 kg. When its engines are developing their full power of 280,000 hp, the *John F. Kennedy* travels at its top speed of 35 knots (65 km/h). If 70% of the power output of the engines is applied to pushing the ship through the water, what is the magnitude of the force of water resistance that opposes the carrier's motion at this speed?

6.59 • BIO A typical flying insect applies an average force equal to twice its weight during each downward stroke while hovering. Take the mass of the insect to be 10 g, and assume the wings move an average downward distance of 1.0 cm during each stroke. Assuming 100 downward strokes per second, estimate the average power output of the insect.

PROBLEMS

6.60 ••• CALC A balky cow is leaving the barn as you try harder and harder to push her back in. In coordinates with the origin at the barn door, the cow walks from $x = 0$ to $x = 6.9$ m as you apply a force with x-component $F_x = -[20.0 \text{ N} + (3.0 \text{ N/m})x]$. How much work does the force you apply do on the cow during this displacement?

6.61 •• CALC **Rotating Bar.** A thin, uniform 12.0-kg bar that is 2.00 m long rotates uniformly about a pivot at one end, making 5.00 complete revolutions every 3.00 seconds. What is the kinetic energy of this bar? (*Hint:* Different points in the bar have different speeds. Break the bar up into infinitesimal segments of mass dm and integrate to add up the kinetic energies of all these segments.)

6.62 •• **A Near-Earth Asteroid.** On April 13, 2029 (Friday the 13th!), the asteroid 99942 Apophis will pass within 18,600 mi of the earth—about $\frac{1}{13}$ the distance to the moon! It has a density of 2600 kg/m³, can be modeled as a sphere 320 m in diameter, and will be traveling at 12.6 km/s. (a) If, due to a small disturbance in its orbit, the asteroid were to hit the earth, how much kinetic energy would it deliver? (b) The largest nuclear bomb ever tested by the United States was the "Castle/Bravo" bomb, having a yield of 15 megatons of TNT. (A megaton of TNT releases 4.184×10^{15} J of energy.) How many Castle/Bravo bombs would be equivalent to the energy of Apophis?

6.63 • A luggage handler pulls a 20.0-kg suitcase up a ramp inclined at 25.0° above the horizontal by a force $\vec{F}$ of magnitude 140 N that acts parallel to the ramp. The coefficient of kinetic friction between the ramp and the incline is $\mu_k = 0.300$. If the suitcase travels 3.80 m along the ramp, calculate (a) the work done on the suitcase by the force $\vec{F}$; (b) the work done on the suitcase by the gravitational force; (c) the work done on the suitcase by the normal force; (d) the work done on the suitcase by the friction force; (e) the total work done on the suitcase. (f) If the speed of the suitcase is zero at the bottom of the ramp, what is its speed after it has traveled 3.80 m along the ramp?

6.64 • BIO **Chin-Ups.** While doing a chin-up, a man lifts his body 0.40 m. (a) How much work must the man do per kilogram of body mass? (b) The muscles involved in doing a chin-up can generate about 70 J of work per kilogram of muscle mass. If the man can

just barely do a 0.40-m chin-up, what percentage of his body's mass do these muscles constitute? (For comparison, the *total* percentage of muscle in a typical 70-kg man with 14% body fat is about 43%.) (c) Repeat part (b) for the man's young son, who has arms half as long as his father's but whose muscles can also generate 70 J of work per kilogram of muscle mass. (d) Adults and children have about the same percentage of muscle in their bodies. Explain why children can commonly do chin-ups more easily than their fathers.

6.65 ••• CP A 20.0-kg crate sits at rest at the bottom of a 15.0-m-long ramp that is inclined at 34.0° above the horizontal. A constant horizontal force of 290 N is applied to the crate to push it up the ramp. While the crate is moving, the ramp exerts a constant frictional force on it that has magnitude 65.0 N. (a) What is the total work done on the crate during its motion from the bottom to the top of the ramp? (b) How much time does it take the crate to travel to the top of the ramp?

6.66 ••• Consider the blocks in Exercise 6.7 as they move 75.0 cm. Find the total work done on each one (a) if there is no friction between the table and the 20.0-N block, and (b) if $\mu_s = 0.500$ and $\mu_k = 0.325$ between the table and the 20.0-N block.

6.67 • The space shuttle, with mass 86,400 kg, is in a circular orbit of radius 6.66×10^6 m around the earth. It takes 90.1 min for the shuttle to complete each orbit. On a repair mission, the shuttle is cautiously moving 1.00 m closer to a disabled satellite every 3.00 s. Calculate the shuttle's kinetic energy (a) relative to the earth and (b) relative to the satellite.

6.68 •• A 5.00-kg package slides 1.50 m down a long ramp that is inclined at 24.0° below the horizontal. The coefficient of kinetic friction between the package and the ramp is $\mu_k = 0.310$. Calculate (a) the work done on the package by friction; (b) the work done on the package by gravity; (c) the work done on the package by the normal force; (d) the total work done on the package. (e) If the package has a speed of 2.20 m/s at the top of the ramp, what is its speed after sliding 1.50 m down the ramp?

6.69 •• CP BIO **Whiplash Injuries.** When a car is hit from behind, its passengers undergo sudden forward acceleration, which can cause a severe neck injury known as *whiplash*. During normal acceleration, the neck muscles play a large role in accelerating the head so that the bones are not injured. But during a very sudden acceleration, the muscles do not react immediately because they are flexible, so most of the accelerating force is provided by the neck bones. Experimental tests have shown that these bones will fracture if they absorb more than 8.0 J of energy. (a) If a car waiting at a stoplight is rear-ended in a collision that lasts for 10.0 ms, what is the greatest speed this car and its driver can reach without breaking neck bones if the driver's head has a mass of 5.0 kg (which is about right for a 70-kg person)? Express your answer in m/s and in mph. (b) What is the acceleration of the passengers during the collision in part (a), and how large a force is acting to accelerate their heads? Express the acceleration in m/s² and in g's.

6.70 •• CALC A net force along the x-axis that has x-component $F_x = -12.0 \text{ N} + (0.300 \text{ N/m}^2)x^2$ is applied to a 5.00-kg object that is initially at the origin and moving in the $-x$-direction with a speed of 6.00 m/s. What is the speed of the object when it reaches the point $x = 5.00$ m?

6.71 • CALC An object is attracted toward the origin with a force given by $F_x = -k/x^2$. (Gravitational and electrical forces have this distance dependence.) (a) Calculate the work done by the force F_x when the object moves in the x-direction from x_1 to x_2. If $x_2 > x_1$, is the work done by F_x positive or negative? (b) The only other force acting on the object is a force that you exert with your hand to move the object slowly from x_1 to x_2. How much work do you do? If $x_2 > x_1$, is the work you do positive or negative? (c) Explain the similarities and differences between your answers to parts (a) and (b).

6.72 ••• **CALC** The gravitational pull of the earth on an object is inversely proportional to the square of the distance of the object from the center of the earth. At the earth's surface this force is equal to the object's normal weight mg, where $g = 9.8$ m/s^2, and at large distances, the force is zero. If a 20,000-kg asteroid falls to earth from a very great distance away, what will be its minimum speed as it strikes the earth's surface, and how much kinetic energy will it impart to our planet? You can ignore the effects of the earth's atmosphere.

6.73 • **CALC** **Varying Coefficient of Friction.** A box is sliding with a speed of 4.50 m/s on a horizontal surface when, at point P, it encounters a rough section. On the rough section, the coefficient of friction is not constant, but starts at 0.100 at P and increases linearly with distance past P, reaching a value of 0.600 at 12.5 m past point P. (a) Use the work–energy theorem to find how far this box slides before stopping. (b) What is the coefficient of friction at the stopping point? (c) How far would the box have slid if the friction coefficient didn't increase but instead had the constant value of 0.100?

6.74 •• **CALC** Consider a spring that does not obey Hooke's law very faithfully. One end of the spring is fixed. To keep the spring stretched or compressed an amount x, a force along the x-axis with x-component $F_x = kx - bx^2 + cx^3$ must be applied to the free end. Here $k = 100$ N/m, $b = 700$ N/m^2, and $c = 12,000$ N/m^3. Note that $x > 0$ when the spring is stretched and $x < 0$ when it is compressed. (a) How much work must be done to stretch this spring by 0.050 m from its unstretched length? (b) How much work must be done to *compress* this spring by 0.050 m from its unstretched length? (c) Is it easier to stretch or compress this spring? Explain why in terms of the dependence of F_x on x. (Many real springs behave qualitatively in the same way.)

6.75 •• **CP** A small block with a mass of 0.0900 kg is attached to a cord passing through a hole in a frictionless, horizontal surface (Fig. P6.75). The block is originally revolving at a distance of 0.40 m from the hole with a speed of 0.70 m/s. The cord is then pulled from below, shortening the radius of the circle in which the block revolves to 0.10 m. At this new distance, the speed of the block is observed to be 2.80 m/s. (a) What is the tension in the cord in the original situation when the block has speed $v = 0.70$ m/s? (b) What is the tension in the cord in the final situation when the block has speed $v = 2.80$ m/s? (c) How much work was done by the person who pulled on the cord?

Figure **P6.75**

6.76 •• **CALC** **Proton Bombardment.** A proton with mass 1.67×10^{-27} kg is propelled at an initial speed of 3.00×10^5 m/s directly toward a uranium nucleus 5.00 m away. The proton is repelled by the uranium nucleus with a force of magnitude $F = \alpha/x^2$, where x is the separation between the two objects and $\alpha = 2.12 \times 10^{-26}$ N·m^2. Assume that the uranium nucleus remains at rest. (a) What is the speed of the proton when it is 8.00×10^{-10} m from the uranium nucleus? (b) As the proton approaches the uranium nucleus, the repulsive force slows down the proton until it comes momentarily to rest, after which the proton moves away from the uranium nucleus. How close to the uranium nucleus does the proton get? (c) What is the speed of the proton when it is again 5.00 m away from the uranium nucleus?

6.77 •• **CP CALC** A block of ice with mass 4.00 kg is initially at rest on a frictionless, horizontal surface. A worker then applies a horizontal force $\vec{F}$ to it. As a result, the block moves along the x-axis such that its position as a function of time is given by $x(t) = \alpha t^2 + \beta t^3$, where $\alpha = 0.200$ m/s^2 and $\beta = 0.0200$ m/s^3. (a) Calculate the velocity of the object when $t = 4.00$ s. (b) Calculate the magnitude of $\vec{F}$ when $t = 4.00$ s. (c) Calculate the work done by the force $\vec{F}$ during the first 4.00 s of the motion.

6.78 •• You and your bicycle have combined mass 80.0 kg. When you reach the base of a bridge, you are traveling along the road at 5.00 m/s (Fig. P6.78). At the top of the bridge, you have climbed a vertical distance of 5.20 m and have slowed to 1.50 m/s. You can ignore work done by friction and any inefficiency in the bike or your legs. (a) What is the total work done on you and your bicycle when you go from the base to the top of the bridge? (b) How much work have you done with the force you apply to the pedals?

Figure **P6.78**

$m = 80.0$ kg

5.20 m

6.79 •• You are asked to design spring bumpers for the walls of a parking garage. A freely rolling 1200-kg car moving at 0.65 m/s is to compress the spring no more than 0.090 m before stopping. What should be the force constant of the spring? Assume that the spring has negligible mass.

6.80 •• The spring of a spring gun has force constant $k = 400$ N/m and negligible mass. The spring is compressed 6.00 cm, and a ball with mass 0.0300 kg is placed in the horizontal barrel against the compressed spring. The spring is then released, and the ball is propelled out the barrel of the gun. The barrel is 6.00 cm long, so the ball leaves the barrel at the same point that it loses contact with the spring. The gun is held so the barrel is horizontal. (a) Calculate the speed with which the ball leaves the barrel if you can ignore friction. (b) Calculate the speed of the ball as it leaves the barrel if a constant resisting force of 6.00 N acts on the ball as it moves along the barrel. (c) For the situation in part (b), at what position along the barrel does the ball have the greatest speed, and what is that speed? (In this case, the maximum speed does not occur at the end of the barrel.)

6.81 ••• A 2.50-kg textbook is forced against a horizontal spring of negligible mass and force constant 250 N/m, compressing the spring a distance of 0.250 m. When released, the textbook slides on a horizontal tabletop with coefficient of kinetic friction

$\mu_k = 0.30$. Use the work–energy theorem to find how far the textbook moves from its initial position before coming to rest.

6.82 ••• **Pushing a Cat.** Your cat "Ms." (mass 7.00 kg) is trying to make it to the top of a frictionless ramp 2.00 m long and inclined upward at 30.0° above the horizontal. Since the poor cat can't get any traction on the ramp, you push her up the entire length of the ramp by exerting a constant 100-N force parallel to the ramp. If Ms. takes a running start so that she is moving at 2.40 m/s at the bottom of the ramp, what is her speed when she reaches the top of the incline? Use the work–energy theorem.

6.83 •• **Crash Barrier.** A student proposes a design for an automobile crash barrier in which a 1700-kg sport utility vehicle moving at 20.0 m/s crashes into a spring of negligible mass that slows it to a stop. So that the passengers are not injured, the acceleration of the vehicle as it slows can be no greater than 5.00g. (a) Find the required spring constant k, and find the distance the spring will compress in slowing the vehicle to a stop. In your calculation, disregard any deformation or crumpling of the vehicle and the friction between the vehicle and the ground. (b) What disadvantages are there to this design?

6.84 ••• A physics professor is pushed up a ramp inclined upward at 30.0° above the horizontal as he sits in his desk chair that slides on frictionless rollers. The combined mass of the professor and chair is 85.0 kg. He is pushed 2.50 m along the incline by a group of students who together exert a constant horizontal force of 600 N. The professor's speed at the bottom of the ramp is 2.00 m/s. Use the work–energy theorem to find his speed at the top of the ramp.

6.85 • A 5.00-kg block is moving at $v_0 = 6.00$ m/s along a frictionless, horizontal surface toward a spring with force constant $k = 500$ N/m that is attached to a wall (Fig. P6.85). The spring has negligible mass. (a) Find the maximum distance the spring will be compressed. (b) If the spring is to compress by no more than 0.150 m, what should be the maximum value of v_0?

Figure **P6.85**

$k = 500$ N/m

$v_0 = 6.00$ m/s

5.00 kg

6.86 •• Consider the system shown in Fig. P6.86. The rope and pulley have negligible mass, and the pulley is frictionless. The coefficient of kinetic friction between the 8.00-kg block and the tabletop is $\mu_k = 0.250$. The blocks are released from rest. Use energy methods to calculate the speed of the 6.00-kg block after it has descended 1.50 m.

Figure **P6.86**

8.00 kg

6.00 kg

6.87 •• Consider the system shown in Fig. P6.86. The rope and pulley have negligible mass, and the pulley is frictionless. Initially the 6.00-kg block is moving downward and the 8.00-kg block is moving to the right, both with a speed of 0.900 m/s. The blocks come to rest after moving 2.00 m. Use the work–energy theorem to calculate the coefficient of kinetic friction between the 8.00-kg block and the tabletop.

6.88 ••• **CALC Bow and Arrow.** Figure P6.88 shows how the force exerted by the string of a compound bow on an arrow varies as a function of how far back the arrow is pulled (the draw length). Assume that the same force is exerted on the arrow as it moves forward after being released. Full draw for this bow is at a draw length of 75.0 cm. If the bow shoots a 0.0250-kg arrow from full draw, what is the speed of the arrow as it leaves the bow?

Figure **P6.88**

6.89 •• On an essentially frictionless, horizontal ice rink, a skater moving at 3.0 m/s encounters a rough patch that reduces her speed to 1.65 m/s due to a friction force that is 25% of her weight. Use the work–energy theorem to find the length of this rough patch.

6.90 • **Rescue.** Your friend (mass 65.0 kg) is standing on the ice in the middle of a frozen pond. There is very little friction between her feet and the ice, so she is unable to walk. Fortunately, a light rope is tied around her waist and you stand on the bank holding the other end. You pull on the rope for 3.00 s and accelerate your friend from rest to a speed of 6.00 m/s while you remain at rest. What is the average power supplied by the force you applied?

6.91 •• A pump is required to lift 800 kg of water (about 210 gallons) per minute from a well 14.0 m deep and eject it with a speed of 18.0 m/s. (a) How much work is done per minute in lifting the water? (b) How much work is done in giving the water the kinetic energy it has when ejected? (c) What must be the power output of the pump?

6.92 •• **BIO** All birds, independent of their size, must maintain a power output of 10–25 watts per kilogram of body mass in order to fly by flapping their wings. (a) The Andean giant hummingbird *(Patagona gigas)* has mass 70 g and flaps its wings 10 times per second while hovering. Estimate the amount of work done by such a hummingbird in each wingbeat. (b) A 70-kg athlete can maintain a power output of 1.4 kW for no more than a few seconds; the *steady* power output of a typical athlete is only 500 W or so. Is it possible for a human-powered aircraft to fly for extended periods by flapping its wings? Explain.

6.93 ••• A physics student spends part of her day walking between classes or for recreation, during which time she expends energy at an average rate of 280 W. The remainder of the day she is sitting in class, studying, or resting; during these activities, she expends energy at an average rate of 100 W. If she expends a total of 1.1×10^7 J of energy in a 24-hour day, how much of the day did she spend walking?

6.94 ••• The Grand Coulee Dam is 1270 m long and 170 m high. The electrical power output from generators at its base is approximately 2000 MW. How many cubic meters of water must flow from the top of the dam per second to produce this amount of power if 92% of the work done on the water by gravity is converted to electrical energy? (Each cubic meter of water has a mass of 1000 kg.)

6.95 • **BIO** **Power of the Human Heart.** The human heart is a powerful and extremely reliable pump. Each day it takes in and discharges about 7500 L of blood. Assume that the work done by the heart is equal to the work required to lift this amount of blood a height equal to that of the average American woman (1.63 m). The density (mass per unit volume) of blood is 1.05×10^3 kg/m^3. (a) How much work does the heart do in a day? (b) What is the heart's power output in watts?

6.96 ••• Six diesel units in series can provide 13.4 MW of power to the lead car of a freight train. The diesel units have total mass 1.10×10^6 kg. The average car in the train has mass 8.2×10^4 kg and requires a horizontal pull of 2.8 kN to move at a constant 27 m/s on level tracks. (a) How many cars can be in the train under these conditions? (b) This would leave no power for accelerating or climbing hills. Show that the extra force needed to accelerate the train is about the same for a 0.10-m/s^2 acceleration or a 1.0% slope (slope angle α = arctan 0.010). (c) With the 1.0% slope, show that an extra 2.9 MW of power is needed to maintain the 27-m/s speed of the diesel units. (d) With 2.9 MW less power available, how many cars can the six diesel units pull up a 1.0% slope at a constant 27 m/s?

6.97 • It takes a force of 53 kN on the lead car of a 16-car passenger train with mass 9.1×10^5 kg to pull it at a constant 45 m/s (101 mi/h) on level tracks. (a) What power must the locomotive provide to the lead car? (b) How much more power to the lead car than calculated in part (a) would be needed to give the train an acceleration of 1.5 m/s^2, at the instant that the train has a speed of 45 m/s on level tracks? (c) How much more power to the lead car than that calculated in part (a) would be needed to move the train up a 1.5% grade (slope angle α = arctan 0.015) at a constant 45 m/s?

6.98 • **CALC** An object has several forces acting on it. One of these forces is $\vec{F} = axy\hat{\imath}$, a force in the x-direction whose magnitude depends on the position of the object, with α = 2.50 N/m^2. Calculate the work done on the object by this force for the following displacements of the object: (a) The object starts at the point x = 0, y = 3.00 m and moves parallel to the x-axis to the point x = 2.00 m, y = 3.00 m. (b) The object starts at the point x = 2.00 m, y = 0 and moves in the y-direction to the point x = 2.00 m, y = 3.00 m. (c) The object starts at the origin and moves on the line y = 1.5x to the point x = 2.00 m, y = 3.00 m.

6.99 •• **Cycling.** For a touring bicyclist the drag coefficient $C(f_{air} = \frac{1}{2}CA\rho v^2)$ is 1.00, the frontal area A is 0.463 m^2, and the coefficient of rolling friction is 0.0045. The rider has mass 50.0 kg, and her bike has mass 12.0 kg. (a) To maintain a speed of 12.0 m/s (about 27 mi/h) on a level road, what must the rider's power output to the rear wheel be? (b) For racing, the same rider uses a different bike with coefficient of rolling friction 0.0030 and mass 9.00 kg. She also crouches down, reducing her drag coefficient to 0.88 and reducing her frontal area to 0.366 m^2. What must her power output to the rear wheel be then to maintain a speed of 12.0 m/s? (c) For the situation in part (b), what power output is required to maintain a speed of 6.0 m/s? Note the great drop in power requirement when the speed is only halved. (For more on aerodynamic speed limitations for a wide variety of human-powered vehicles, see "The Aerodynamics of Human-Powered Land Vehicles," *Scientific American,* December 1983.)

6.100 •• **Automotive Power I.** A truck engine transmits 28.0 kW (37.5 hp) to the driving wheels when the truck is traveling at a constant velocity of magnitude 60.0 km/h (37.3 mi/h) on a level

road. (a) What is the resisting force acting on the truck? (b) Assume that 65% of the resisting force is due to rolling friction and the remainder is due to air resistance. If the force of rolling friction is independent of speed, and the force of air resistance is proportional to the square of the speed, what power will drive the truck at 30.0 km/h? At 120.0 km/h? Give your answers in kilowatts and in horsepower.

6.101 •• **Automotive Power II.** (a) If 8.00 hp are required to drive a 1800-kg automobile at 60.0 km/h on a level road, what is the total retarding force due to friction, air resistance, and so on? (b) What power is necessary to drive the car at 60.0 km/h up a 10.0% grade (a hill rising 10.0 m vertically in 100.0 m horizontally)? (c) What power is necessary to drive the car at 60.0 km/h *down* a 1.00% grade? (d) Down what percent grade would the car coast at 60.0 km/h?

CHALLENGE PROBLEMS

6.102 ••• **CALC** On a winter day in Maine, a warehouse worker is shoving boxes up a rough plank inclined at an angle α above the horizontal. The plank is partially covered with ice, with more ice near the bottom of the plank than near the top, so that the coefficient of friction increases with the distance x along the plank: $\mu = Ax$, where A is a positive constant and the bottom of the plank is at x = 0. (For this plank the coefficients of kinetic and static friction are equal: $\mu_k = \mu_s = \mu$.) The worker shoves a box up the plank so that it leaves the bottom of the plank moving at speed v_0. Show that when the box first comes to rest, it will remain at rest if

$$v_0^2 \geq \frac{3g \sin^2\alpha}{A \cos\alpha}$$

6.103 ••• **CALC** **A Spring with Mass.** We usually ignore the kinetic energy of the moving coils of a spring, but let's try to get a reasonable approximation to this. Consider a spring of mass M, equilibrium length L_0, and spring constant k. The work done to stretch or compress the spring by a distance L is $\frac{1}{2}kX^2$, where $X = L - L_0$. Consider a spring, as described above, that has one end fixed and the other end moving with speed v. Assume that the speed of points along the length of the spring varies linearly with distance l from the fixed end. Assume also that the mass M of the spring is distributed uniformly along the length of the spring. (a) Calculate the kinetic energy of the spring in terms of M and v. (*Hint:* Divide the spring into pieces of length dl; find the speed of each piece in terms of l, v, and L; find the mass of each piece in terms of dl, M, and L; and integrate from 0 to L. The result is *not* $\frac{1}{2}Mv^2$, since not all of the spring moves with the same speed.) In a spring gun, a spring of mass 0.243 kg and force constant 3200 N/m is compressed 2.50 cm from its unstretched length. When the trigger is pulled, the spring pushes horizontally on a 0.053-kg ball. The work done by friction is negligible. Calculate the ball's speed when the spring reaches its uncompressed length (b) ignoring the mass of the spring and (c) including, using the results of part (a), the mass of the spring. (d) In part (c), what is the final kinetic energy of the ball and of the spring?

6.104 ••• **CALC** An airplane in flight is subject to an air resistance force proportional to the square of its speed v. But there is an additional resistive force because the airplane has wings. Air flowing over the wings is pushed down and slightly forward, so from Newton's third law the air exerts a force on the wings and airplane that is up and slightly backward (Fig. P6.104). The upward force is the lift force that keeps the airplane aloft, and the backward force is called *induced drag*. At flying speeds, induced drag is inversely proportional to v^2, so that the total air resistance force can be expressed by $F_{air} = \alpha v^2 + \beta/v^2$, where α and β are positive constants that depend on the shape and size of the airplane and the density of the air. For a Cessna 150, a small single-engine airplane, $\alpha = 0.30 \text{ N} \cdot \text{s}^2/\text{m}^2$ and $\beta = 3.5 \times 10^5 \text{ N} \cdot \text{m}^2/\text{s}^2$. In steady flight, the engine must provide a forward force that exactly balances the air resistance force. (a) Calculate the speed (in km/h) at which this airplane will have the maximum *range* (that is, travel the greatest distance) for a given quantity of fuel. (b) Calculate the speed (in km/h) for which the airplane will have the maximum *endurance* (that is, remain in the air the longest time).

Figure **P6.104**

Induced drag

Lift   Force of air on wings

Answers

Chapter Opening Question ?

The answer is yes. As the ant was exerting an upward force on the piece of cereal, the cereal was exerting a downward force of the same magnitude on the ant (due to Newton's third law). However, because the ant's body had an upward displacement, the work that the cereal did on the ant was *negative* (see Section 6.1).

Test Your Understanding Questions

6.1 Answer: (iii) The electron has constant velocity, so its acceleration is zero and (by Newton's second law) the net force on the electron is also zero. Therefore the total work done by all the forces (equal to the work done by the net force) must be zero as well. The individual forces may do nonzero work, but that's not what the question asks.

6.2 Answer: (iv), (i), (iii), (ii) Body (i) has kinetic energy $K = \frac{1}{2}mv^2 = \frac{1}{2}(2.0 \text{ kg})(5.0 \text{ m/s})^2 = 25 \text{ J}$. Body (ii) had zero kinetic energy initially and then had 30 J of work done it, so its final kinetic energy is $K_2 = K_1 + W = 0 + 30 \text{ J} = 30 \text{ J}$. Body (iii) had initial kinetic energy $K_1 = \frac{1}{2}mv_1^2 = \frac{1}{2}(1.0 \text{ kg})(4.0 \text{ m/s})^2 = 8.0 \text{ J}$ and then had 20 J of work done on it, so its final kinetic energy is $K_2 = K_1 + W = 8.0 \text{ J} + 20 \text{ J} = 28 \text{ J}$. Body (iv) had initial kinetic energy $K_1 = \frac{1}{2}mv_1^2 = \frac{1}{2}(2.0 \text{ kg})(10 \text{ m/s})^2 = 100 \text{ J}$; when it did 80 J of work on another body, the other body did -80 J of work on body (iv), so the final kinetic energy of body (iv) is $K_2 = K_1 + W = 100 \text{ J} + (-80 \text{ J}) = 20 \text{ J}$.

6.3 Answers: (a) (iii), (b) (iii) At any point during the pendulum bob's motion, the tension force and the weight both act perpendicular to the motion—that is, perpendicular to an infinitesimal displacement $d\vec{l}$ of the bob. (In Fig. 5.32b, the displacement $d\vec{l}$ would be directed outward from the plane of the free-body diagram.) Hence for either force the scalar product inside the integral in Eq. (6.14) is $\vec{F} \cdot d\vec{l} = 0$, and the work done along any part of the circular path (including a complete circle) is $W = \int \vec{F} \cdot d\vec{l} = 0$.

6.4 Answer: (v) The airliner has a constant horizontal velocity, so the net horizontal force on it must be zero. Hence the backward drag force must have the same magnitude as the forward force due to the combined thrust of the four engines. This means that the drag force must do *negative* work on the airplane at the same rate that the combined thrust force does *positive* work. The combined thrust does work at a rate of $4(108{,}000 \text{ hp}) = 432{,}000 \text{ hp}$, so the drag force must do work at a rate of $-432{,}000 \text{ hp}$.

Bridging Problem

Answers: **(a)** $v_1 = \sqrt{\dfrac{2}{m}\left(mgx_1 - \dfrac{1}{3}\alpha x_1^3\right)} = \sqrt{2gx_1 - \dfrac{2\alpha x_1^3}{3m}}$

(b) $P = -F_{\text{spring}-1}v_1 = -\alpha x_1^2 \sqrt{2gx_1 - \dfrac{2\alpha x_1^3}{3m}}$

(c) $x_2 = \sqrt{\dfrac{3mg}{\alpha}}$ **(d)** No

POTENTIAL ENERGY AND ENERGY CONSERVATION

7

? As this mallard glides in to a landing, it descends along a straight-line path at a constant speed. Does the mallard's mechanical energy increase, decrease, or stay the same during the glide? If it increases, where does the added energy come from? If it decreases, where does the lost energy go?

LEARNING GOALS

By studying this chapter, you will learn:

• How to use the concept of gravitational potential energy in problems that involve vertical motion.

• How to use the concept of elastic potential energy in problems that involve a moving body attached to a stretched or compressed spring.

• The distinction between conservative and nonconservative forces, and how to solve problems in which both kinds of forces act on a moving body.

• How to calculate the properties of a conservative force if you know the corresponding potential-energy function.

• How to use energy diagrams to understand the motion of an object moving in a straight line under the influence of a conservative force.

When a diver jumps off a high board into a swimming pool, he hits the water moving pretty fast, with a lot of kinetic energy. Where does that energy come from? The answer we learned in Chapter 6 was that the gravitational force (his weight) does work on the diver as he falls. The diver's kinetic energy—energy associated with his *motion*—increases by an amount equal to the work done.

However, there is a very useful alternative way to think about work and kinetic energy. This new approach is based on the concept of *potential energy,* which is energy associated with the *position* of a system rather than its motion. In this approach, there is *gravitational potential energy* even while the diver is standing on the high board. Energy is not added to the earth–diver system as the diver falls, but rather a storehouse of energy is *transformed* from one form (potential energy) to another (kinetic energy) as he falls. In this chapter we'll see how the work–energy theorem explains this transformation.

If the diver bounces on the end of the board before he jumps, the bent board stores a second kind of potential energy called *elastic potential energy*. We'll discuss elastic potential energy of simple systems such as a stretched or compressed spring. (An important third kind of potential energy is associated with the positions of electrically charged particles relative to each other. We'll encounter this potential energy in Chapter 23.)

We will prove that in some cases the sum of a system's kinetic and potential energy, called the *total mechanical energy* of the system, is constant during the motion of the system. This will lead us to the general statement of the *law of conservation of energy,* one of the most fundamental and far-reaching principles in all of science.

7.1 Gravitational Potential Energy

7.1 As a basketball descends, gravitational potential energy is converted to kinetic energy and the basketball's speed increases.

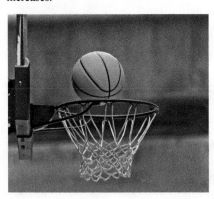

We learned in Chapter 6 that a particle gains or loses kinetic energy because it interacts with other objects that exert forces on it. During any interaction, the change in a particle's kinetic energy is equal to the total work done on the particle by the forces that act on it.

In many situations it seems as though energy has been stored in a system, to be recovered later. For example, you must do work to lift a heavy stone over your head. It seems reasonable that in hoisting the stone into the air you are storing energy in the system, energy that is later converted into kinetic energy when you let the stone fall.

This example points to the idea of an energy associated with the *position* of bodies in a system. This kind of energy is a measure of the *potential* or *possibility* for work to be done; when a stone is raised into the air, there is a potential for work to be done on it by the gravitational force, but only if the stone is allowed to fall to the ground. For this reason, energy associated with position is called **potential energy.** Our discussion suggests that there is potential energy associated with a body's weight and its height above the ground. We call this *gravitational potential energy* (Fig. 7.1).

We now have *two* ways to describe what happens when a body falls without air resistance. One way is to say that gravitational potential energy decreases and the falling body's kinetic energy increases. The other way, which we learned in Chapter 6, is that a falling body's kinetic energy increases because the force of the earth's gravity (the body's weight) does work on the body. Later in this section we'll use the work–energy theorem to show that these two descriptions are equivalent.

7.2 When a body moves vertically from an initial height y_1 to a final height y_2, the gravitational force $\vec{w}$ does work and the gravitational potential energy changes.

To begin with, however, let's derive the expression for gravitational potential energy. Suppose a body with mass m moves along the (vertical) y-axis, as in Fig. 7.2. The forces acting on it are its weight, with magnitude $w = mg$, and possibly some other forces; we call the vector sum (resultant) of all the other forces $\vec{F}_{\text{other}}$. We'll assume that the body stays close enough to the earth's surface that the weight is constant. (We'll find in Chapter 13 that weight decreases with altitude.) We want to find the work done by the weight when the body moves downward from a height y_1 above the origin to a lower height y_2 (Fig. 7.2a). The weight and displacement are in the same direction, so the work W_{grav} done on the body by its weight is positive;

(a) A body moves downward

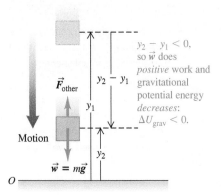

$y_2 - y_1 < 0$, so $\vec{w}$ does *positive* work and gravitational potential energy *decreases*: $\Delta U_{\text{grav}} < 0$.

$$W_{\text{grav}} = Fs = w(y_1 - y_2) = mgy_1 - mgy_2 \qquad (7.1)$$

This expression also gives the correct work when the body moves *upward* and y_2 is greater than y_1 (Fig. 7.2b). In that case the quantity $(y_1 - y_2)$ is negative, and W_{grav} is negative because the weight and displacement are opposite in direction.

Equation (7.1) shows that we can express W_{grav} in terms of the values of the quantity mgy at the beginning and end of the displacement. This quantity, the product of the weight mg and the height y above the origin of coordinates, is called the **gravitational potential energy,** U_{grav}:

$$U_{\text{grav}} = mgy \qquad \text{(gravitational potential energy)} \qquad (7.2)$$

(b) A body moves upward

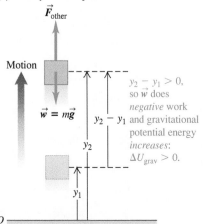

$y_2 - y_1 > 0$, so $\vec{w}$ does *negative* work and gravitational potential energy *increases*: $\Delta U_{\text{grav}} > 0$.

Its initial value is $U_{\text{grav},1} = mgy_1$ and its final value is $U_{\text{grav},2} = mgy_2$. The change in U_{grav} is the final value minus the initial value, or $\Delta U_{\text{grav}} = U_{\text{grav},2} - U_{\text{grav},1}$. We can express the work W_{grav} done by the gravitational force during the displacement from y_1 to y_2 as

$$W_{\text{grav}} = U_{\text{grav},1} - U_{\text{grav},2} = -(U_{\text{grav},2} - U_{\text{grav},1}) = -\Delta U_{\text{grav}} \qquad (7.3)$$

The negative sign in front of ΔU_{grav} is *essential*. When the body moves up, y increases, the work done by the gravitational force is negative, and the gravitational potential energy increases ($\Delta U_{grav} > 0$). When the body moves down, y decreases, the gravitational force does positive work, and the gravitational potential energy decreases ($\Delta U_{grav} < 0$). It's like drawing money out of the bank (decreasing U_{grav}) and spending it (doing positive work). The unit of potential energy is the joule (J), the same unit as is used for work.

CAUTION **To what body does gravitational potential energy "belong"?** It is *not* correct to call $U_{grav} = mgy$ the "gravitational potential energy of the body." The reason is that gravitational potential energy U_{grav} is a *shared* property of the body and the earth. The value of U_{grav} increases if the earth stays fixed and the body moves upward, away from the earth; it also increases if the body stays fixed and the earth is moved away from it. Notice that the formula $U_{grav} = mgy$ involves characteristics of both the body (its mass m) and the earth (the value of g). ▮

Conservation of Mechanical Energy (Gravitational Forces Only)

To see what gravitational potential energy is good for, suppose the body's weight is the *only* force acting on it, so $\vec{F}_{other} = 0$. The body is then falling freely with no air resistance and can be moving either up or down. Let its speed at point y_1 be v_1 and let its speed at y_2 be v_2. The work–energy theorem, Eq. (6.6), says that the total work done on the body equals the change in the body's kinetic energy: $W_{tot} = \Delta K = K_2 - K_1$. If gravity is the only force that acts, then from Eq. (7.3), $W_{tot} = W_{grav} = -\Delta U_{grav} = U_{grav,1} - U_{grav,2}$. Putting these together, we get

$$\Delta K = -\Delta U_{grav} \quad \text{or} \quad K_2 - K_1 = U_{grav,1} - U_{grav,2}$$

which we can rewrite as

$$K_1 + U_{grav,1} = K_2 + U_{grav,2} \quad \text{(if only gravity does work)} \quad (7.4)$$

or

$$\tfrac{1}{2}mv_1^2 + mgy_1 = \tfrac{1}{2}mv_2^2 + mgy_2 \quad \text{(if only gravity does work)} \quad (7.5)$$

The sum $K + U_{grav}$ of kinetic and potential energy is called E, the **total mechanical energy of the system.** By "system" we mean the body of mass m and the earth considered together, because gravitational potential energy U is a shared property of both bodies. Then $E_1 = K_1 + U_{grav,1}$ is the total mechanical energy at y_1 and $E_2 = K_2 + U_{grav,2}$ is the total mechanical energy at y_2. Equation (7.4) says that when the body's weight is the only force doing work on it, $E_1 = E_2$. That is, E is constant; it has the same value at y_1 and y_2. But since the positions y_1 and y_2 are arbitrary points in the motion of the body, the total mechanical energy E has the same value at *all* points during the motion:

$$E = K + U_{grav} = \text{constant} \quad \text{(if only gravity does work)}$$

A quantity that always has the same value is called a *conserved* quantity. *When only the force of gravity does work, the total mechanical energy is constant—that is, it is conserved* (Fig. 7.3). This is our first example of the **conservation of mechanical energy.**

When we throw a ball into the air, its speed decreases on the way up as kinetic energy is converted to potential energy; $\Delta K < 0$ and $\Delta U_{grav} > 0$. On the way back down, potential energy is converted back to kinetic energy and the ball's speed increases; $\Delta K > 0$ and $\Delta U_{grav} < 0$. But the *total* mechanical energy (kinetic plus potential) is the same at every point in the motion, provided that no force other than gravity does work on the ball (that is, air resistance must be negligible). It's still true that the gravitational force does work on the body as it

Application Which Egg Has More Mechanical Energy?
The mechanical energy of each of these identical eggs has the *same* value. The mechanical energy for an egg at rest atop the stone is purely gravitational potential energy. For the falling egg, the gravitational potential energy decreases as the egg descends and the egg's kinetic energy increases. If there is negligible air resistance, the mechanical energy of the falling egg remains constant.

Video Tutor Demo

ActivPhysics 5.2: Upward-Moving Elevator Stops
ActivPhysics 5.3: Stopping a Downward-Moving Elevator
ActivPhysics 5.6: Skier Speed

7.3 While this athlete is in midair, only gravity does work on him (if we neglect the minor effects of air resistance). Mechanical energy E—the sum of kinetic and gravitational potential energy—is conserved.

Moving up:
- K decreases.
- U_{grav} increases.
- $E = K + U_{grav}$ stays the same.

Moving down:
- K increases.
- U_{grav} decreases.
- $E = K + U_{grav}$ stays the same.

$\vec{w} = m\vec{g}$

moves up or down, but we no longer have to calculate work directly; keeping track of changes in the value of U_{grav} takes care of this completely.

CAUTION **Choose "zero height" to be wherever you like** When working with gravitational potential energy, we may choose any height to be $y = 0$. If we shift the origin for y, the values of y_1 and y_2 change, as do the values of $U_{grav,1}$ and $U_{grav,2}$. But this shift has no effect on the *difference* in height $y_2 - y_1$ or on the *difference* in gravitational potential energy $U_{grav,2} - U_{grav,1} = mg(y_2 - y_1)$. As the following example shows, the physically significant quantity is not the value of U_{grav} at a particular point, but only the *difference* in U_{grav} between two points. So we can define U_{grav} to be zero at whatever point we choose without affecting the physics. ▮

| **Example 7.1** | **Height of a baseball from energy conservation** |

You throw a 0.145-kg baseball straight up, giving it an initial velocity of magnitude 20.0 m/s. Find how high it goes, ignoring air resistance.

SOLUTION

IDENTIFY and SET UP: After the ball leaves your hand, only gravity does work on it. Hence mechanical energy is conserved, and we can use Eqs. (7.4) and (7.5). We take point 1 to be where the ball leaves your hand and point 2 to be where it reaches its maximum height. As in Fig. 7.2, we take the positive y-direction to be upward. The ball's speed at point 1 is $v_1 = 20.0$ m/s; at its maximum height it is instantaneously at rest, so $v_2 = 0$. We take the origin at point 1, so $y_1 = 0$ (Fig. 7.4). Our target variable, the distance the ball moves vertically between the two points, is the displacement $y_2 - y_1 = y_2 - 0 = y_2$.

EXECUTE: We have $y_1 = 0$, $U_{grav,1} = mgy_1 = 0$, and $K_2 = \frac{1}{2}mv_2^2 = 0$. Then Eq. (7.4), $K_1 + U_{grav,1} = K_2 + U_{grav,2}$, becomes

$$K_1 = U_{grav,2}$$

As the energy bar graphs in Fig. 7.4 show, this equation says that the kinetic energy of the ball at point 1 is completely converted to gravitational potential energy at point 2. We substitute $K_1 = \frac{1}{2}mv_1^2$ and $U_{grav,2} = mgy_2$ and solve for y_2:

$$\frac{1}{2}mv_1^2 = mgy_2$$

$$y_2 = \frac{v_1^2}{2g} = \frac{(20.0 \text{ m/s})^2}{2(9.80 \text{ m/s}^2)} = 20.4 \text{ m}$$

7.4 After a baseball leaves your hand, mechanical energy $E = K + U$ is conserved.

$v_2 = 0$

After the ball leaves your hand, the only force acting on it is gravity ...

$v_1 = 20.0$ m/s
$m = 0.145$ kg

$y_1 = 0$

Energy at y_2

zero

$E = K + U_{grav}$

... so the mechanical energy $E = K + U$ stays constant.

Energy at y_1

zero

$E = K + U_{grav}$

EVALUATE: As a check on our work, use the given value of v_1 and our result for y_2 to calculate the kinetic energy at point 1 and the gravitational potential energy at point 2. You should find that these are equal: $K_1 = \frac{1}{2}mv_1^2 = 29.0$ J and $U_{grav,2} = mgy_2 = 29.0$ J. Note also that we could have found the result $y_2 = v_1^2/2g$ using Eq. (2.13).

What if we put the origin somewhere else? For example, what if we put it 5.0 m below point 1, so that $y_1 = 5.0$ m? Then the total mechanical energy at point 1 is part kinetic and part potential; at point 2 it's still purely potential because $v_2 = 0$. You'll find that this choice of origin yields $y_2 = 25.4$ m, but again $y_2 - y_1 = 20.4$ m. In problems like this, you are free to choose the height at which $U_{grav} = 0$. The physics doesn't depend on your choice, so don't agonize over it.

When Forces Other Than Gravity Do Work

If other forces act on the body in addition to its weight, then $\vec{F}_{other}$ in Fig. 7.2 is *not* zero. For the pile driver described in Example 6.4 (Section 6.2), the force applied by the hoisting cable and the friction with the vertical guide rails are examples of forces that might be included in $\vec{F}_{other}$. The gravitational work W_{grav} is still given by Eq. (7.3), but the total work W_{tot} is then the sum of W_{grav} and the work done by $\vec{F}_{other}$. We will call this additional work W_{other}, so the total work done by all forces is $W_{tot} = W_{grav} + W_{other}$. Equating this to the change in kinetic energy, we have

$$W_{other} + W_{grav} = K_2 - K_1 \qquad (7.6)$$

Also, from Eq. (7.3), $W_{grav} = U_{grav,1} - U_{grav,2}$, so

$$W_{other} + U_{grav,1} - U_{grav,2} = K_2 - K_1$$

which we can rearrange in the form

$$K_1 + U_{grav,1} + W_{other} = K_2 + U_{grav,2} \qquad \text{(if forces other than gravity do work)} \qquad (7.7)$$

Finally, using the appropriate expressions for the various energy terms, we obtain

$$\tfrac{1}{2}mv_1^2 + mgy_1 + W_{other} = \tfrac{1}{2}mv_2^2 + mgy_2 \qquad \text{(if forces other than gravity do work)} \qquad (7.8)$$

The meaning of Eqs. (7.7) and (7.8) is this: *The work done by all forces other than the gravitational force equals the change in the total mechanical energy $E = K + U_{grav}$ of the system, where U_{grav} is the gravitational potential energy.* When W_{other} is positive, E increases and $K_2 + U_{grav,2}$ is greater than $K_1 + U_{grav,1}$. When W_{other} is negative, E decreases (Fig. 7.5). In the special case in which no forces other than the body's weight do work, $W_{other} = 0$. The total mechanical energy is then constant, and we are back to Eq. (7.4) or (7.5).

7.5 As this skydiver moves downward, the upward force of air resistance does negative work W_{other} on him. Hence the total mechanical energy $E = K + U$ decreases: The skydiver's speed and kinetic energy K stay the same, while the gravitational potential energy U decreases.

Problem-Solving Strategy 7.1 **Problems Using Mechanical Energy I**

IDENTIFY *the relevant concepts:* Decide whether the problem should be solved by energy methods, by using $\Sigma\vec{F} = m\vec{a}$ directly, or by a combination of these. The energy approach is best when the problem involves varying forces or motion along a curved path (discussed later in this section). If the problem involves elapsed time, the energy approach is usually *not* the best choice because it doesn't involve time directly.

SET UP *the problem* using the following steps:
1. When using the energy approach, first identify the initial and final states (the positions and velocities) of the bodies in question. Use the subscript 1 for the initial state and the subscript 2 for the final state. Draw sketches showing these states.
2. Define a coordinate system, and choose the level at which $y = 0$. Choose the positive y-direction to be upward, as is assumed in Eq. (7.1) and in the equations that follow from it.
3. Identify any forces that do work on each body and that *cannot* be described in terms of potential energy. (So far, this means

any forces other than gravity. In Section 7.2 we'll see that the work done by an ideal spring can also be expressed as a change in potential energy.) Sketch a free-body diagram for each body.
4. List the unknown and known quantities, including the coordinates and velocities at each point. Identify the target variables.

EXECUTE *the solution:* Write expressions for the initial and final kinetic and potential energies K_1, K_2, $U_{grav,1}$, and $U_{grav,2}$. If no other forces do work, use Eq. (7.4). If there are other forces that do work, use Eq. (7.7). Draw bar graphs showing the initial and final values of K, $U_{grav,1}$, and $E = K + U_{grav}$. Then solve to find your target variables.

EVALUATE *your answer:* Check whether your answer makes physical sense. Remember that the gravitational work is included in ΔU_{grav}, so do not include it in W_{other}.

Example 7.2 | **Work and energy in throwing a baseball**

In Example 7.1 suppose your hand moves upward by 0.50 m while you are throwing the ball. The ball leaves your hand with an upward velocity of 20.0 m/s. (a) Find the magnitude of the force (assumed constant) that your hand exerts on the ball. (b) Find the speed of the ball at a point 15.0 m above the point where it leaves your hand. Ignore air resistance.

SOLUTION

IDENTIFY and SET UP: In Example 7.1 only gravity did work. Here we must include the nongravitational, "other" work done by your hand. Figure 7.6 shows a diagram of the situation, including a free-body diagram for the ball while it is being thrown. We let point 1 be where your hand begins to move, point 2 be where the ball leaves your hand, and point 3 be where the ball is 15.0 m above point 2. The nongravitational force $\vec{F}$ of your hand acts only between points 1 and 2. Using the same coordinate system as in Example 7.1, we have $y_1 = -0.50$ m, $y_2 = 0$, and $y_3 = 15.0$ m. The ball starts at rest at point 1, so $v_1 = 0$, and the ball's speed as it leaves your hand is $v_2 = 20.0$ m/s. Our target variables are (a) the magnitude F of the force of your hand and (b) the ball's velocity v_{3y} at point 3.

EXECUTE: (a) To determine F, we'll first use Eq. (7.7) to calculate the work W_{other} done by this force. We have

$$K_1 = 0$$
$$U_{\text{grav},1} = mgy_1 = (0.145 \text{ kg})(9.80 \text{ m/s}^2)(-0.50 \text{ m}) = -0.71 \text{ J}$$

7.6 (a) Applying energy ideas to a ball thrown vertically upward. (b) Free-body diagram for the ball as you throw it.

(a)

v_3 = 15.0 m

After the ball leaves your hand, the only force acting on it is gravity ...

$v_2 = 20.0$ m/s

As you throw the ball, you do positive work W_{other} on it ...

$v_1 = 0$

$y_2 = 0$

0.50 m

$y_1 = -0.50$ m

... so the total mechanical energy $E = K + U$ stays constant.

$E = K + U_{\text{grav}}$

... so the total mechanical energy E increases.

zero

$E = K + U_{\text{grav}}$

zero

$E = K + U_{\text{grav}}$

(b)

y

F

x

w

$$K_2 = \tfrac{1}{2}mv_2^2 = \tfrac{1}{2}(0.145 \text{ kg})(20.0 \text{ m/s})^2 = 29.0 \text{ J}$$
$$U_{\text{grav},2} = mgy_2 = (0.145 \text{ kg})(9.80 \text{ m/s}^2)(0) = 0$$

(Don't worry that $U_{\text{grav},1}$ is less than zero; all that matters is the *difference* in potential energy from one point to another.) From Eq. (7.7),

$$K_1 + U_{\text{grav},1} + W_{\text{other}} = K_2 + U_{\text{grav},2}$$
$$W_{\text{other}} = (K_2 - K_1) + (U_{\text{grav},2} - U_{\text{grav},1})$$
$$= (29.0 \text{ J} - 0) + [0 - (-0.71 \text{ J})] = 29.7 \text{ J}$$

But since $\vec{F}$ is constant and upward, the work done by $\vec{F}$ equals the force magnitude times the displacement: $W_{\text{other}} = F(y_2 - y_1)$. So

$$F = \frac{W_{\text{other}}}{y_2 - y_1} = \frac{29.7 \text{ J}}{0.50 \text{ m}} = 59 \text{ N}$$

This is more than 40 times the weight of the ball (1.42 N).

(b) To find v_{3y}, note that between points 2 and 3 only gravity acts on the ball. So between these points mechanical energy is conserved and $W_{\text{other}} = 0$. From Eq. (7.4), we can solve for K_3 and from that solve for v_{3y}:

$$K_2 + U_{\text{grav},2} = K_3 + U_{\text{grav},3}$$
$$U_{\text{grav},3} = mgy_3 = (0.145 \text{ kg})(9.80 \text{ m/s}^2)(15.0 \text{ m}) = 21.3 \text{ J}$$
$$K_3 = (K_2 + U_{\text{grav},2}) - U_{\text{grav},3}$$
$$= (29.0 \text{ J} + 0 \text{ J}) - 21.3 \text{ J} = 7.7 \text{ J}$$

Since $K_3 = \tfrac{1}{2}mv_{3y}^2$, we find

$$v_{3y} = \pm\sqrt{\frac{2K_3}{m}} = \pm\sqrt{\frac{2(7.7 \text{ J})}{0.145 \text{ kg}}} = \pm 10 \text{ m/s}$$

The plus-or-minus sign reminds us that the ball passes point 3 on the way up and again on the way down. The total mechanical energy E is constant and equal to $K_2 + U_{\text{grav},2} = 29.0$ J while the ball is in free fall, and the potential energy at point 3 is $U_{\text{grav},3} = mgy_3 = 21.3$ J whether the ball is moving up or down. So at point 3, the ball's kinetic energy K_3 (and therefore its speed) don't depend on the direction the ball is moving. The velocity v_{3y} is positive ($+10$ m/s) when the ball is moving up and negative (-10 m/s) when it is moving down; the speed v_3 is 10 m/s in either case.

EVALUATE: In Example 7.1 we found that the ball reaches a maximum height $y = 20.4$ m. At that point all of the kinetic energy it had when it left your hand at $y = 0$ has been converted to gravitational potential energy. At $y = 15.0$ m, the ball is about three-fourths of the way to its maximum height, so about three-fourths of its mechanical energy should be in the form of potential energy. (The energy bar graphs in Fig. 7.6a show this.) Can you show that this is true from our results for K_3 and $U_{\text{grav},3}$?

Gravitational Potential Energy for Motion Along a Curved Path

In our first two examples the body moved along a straight vertical line. What happens when the path is slanted or curved (Fig. 7.7a)? The body is acted on by the gravitational force $\vec{w} = m\vec{g}$ and possibly by other forces whose resultant we call $\vec{F}_{\text{other}}$. To find the work done by the gravitational force during this displacement, we divide the path into small segments $\Delta\vec{s}$; Fig. 7.7b shows a typical segment. The work done by the gravitational force over this segment is the scalar product of the force and the displacement. In terms of unit vectors, the force is $\vec{w} = m\vec{g} = -mg\hat{\jmath}$ and the displacement is $\Delta\vec{s} = \Delta x\hat{\imath} + \Delta y\hat{\jmath}$, so the work done by the gravitational force is

$$\vec{w} \cdot \Delta\vec{s} = -mg\hat{\jmath} \cdot (\Delta x\hat{\imath} + \Delta y\hat{\jmath}) = -mg\Delta y$$

The work done by gravity is the same as though the body had been displaced vertically a distance Δy, with no horizontal displacement. This is true for every segment, so the *total* work done by the gravitational force is $-mg$ multiplied by the *total* vertical displacement $(y_2 - y_1)$:

$$W_{\text{grav}} = -mg(y_2 - y_1) = mgy_1 - mgy_2 = U_{\text{grav},1} - U_{\text{grav},2}$$

This is the same as Eq. (7.1) or (7.3), in which we assumed a purely vertical path. So even if the path a body follows between two points is curved, the total work done by the gravitational force depends only on the difference in height between the two points of the path. This work is unaffected by any horizontal motion that may occur. So *we can use the same expression for gravitational potential energy whether the body's path is curved or straight.*

7.7 Calculating the change in gravitational potential energy for a displacement along a curved path.

(a)

(b)

The work done by the gravitational force depends only on the vertical component of displacement Δy.

In this case Δy is negative.

Conceptual Example 7.3 **Energy in projectile motion**

A batter hits two identical baseballs with the same initial speed and from the same initial height but at different initial angles. Prove that both balls have the same speed at any height h if air resistance can be neglected.

SOLUTION

The only force acting on each ball after it is hit is its weight. Hence the total mechanical energy for each ball is constant. Figure 7.8 shows the trajectories of two balls batted at the same height with the same initial speed, and thus the same total mechanical energy, but with different initial angles. At all points at the same height the potential energy is the same. Thus the kinetic energy at this height must be the same for both balls, and the speeds are the same.

7.8 For the same initial speed and initial height, the speed of a projectile at a given elevation h is always the same, neglecting air resistance.

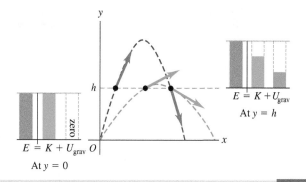

$E = K + U_{\text{grav}}$
At $y = h$

zero

$E = K + U_{\text{grav}}$
At $y = 0$

Example 7.4 **Speed at the bottom of a vertical circle**

Your cousin Throckmorton skateboards from rest down a curved, frictionless ramp. If we treat Throcky and his skateboard as a particle, he moves through a quarter-circle with radius $R = 3.00$ m (Fig. 7.9). Throcky and his skateboard have a total mass of 25.0 kg. (a) Find his speed at the bottom of the ramp. (b) Find the normal force that acts on him at the bottom of the curve.

SOLUTION

IDENTIFY: We can't use the constant-acceleration equations of Chapter 2 because Throcky's acceleration isn't constant; the slope decreases as he descends. Instead, we'll use the energy approach. Throcky moves along a circular arc, so we'll also use what we learned about circular motion in Section 5.4.

SET UP: The only forces on Throcky are his weight and the normal force $\vec{n}$ exerted by the ramp (Fig. 7.9b). Although $\vec{n}$ acts all along the path, it does zero work because $\vec{n}$ is perpendicular to Throcky's displacement at every point. Hence $W_{\text{other}} = 0$ and mechanical energy is conserved. We take point 1 at the starting point and point 2 at the bottom of the ramp, and we let $y = 0$ be at the bottom of the ramp (Fig. 7.9a). We take the positive y-direction upward; then $y_1 = R$ and $y_2 = 0$. Throcky starts at rest at the top, so $v_1 = 0$. In part (a) our target variable is his speed v_2 at the bottom; in part (b) the target variable is the magnitude n of the normal force at point 2. To find n, we'll use Newton's second law and the relation $a = v^2/R$.

Continued

EXECUTE: (a) The various energy quantities are

$$K_1 = 0 \qquad U_{\text{grav},1} = mgR$$
$$K_2 = \tfrac{1}{2}mv_2^2 \qquad U_{\text{grav},2} = 0$$

From conservation of mechanical energy, Eq. (7.4),

$$K_1 + U_{\text{grav},1} = K_2 + U_{\text{grav},2}$$
$$0 + mgR = \tfrac{1}{2}mv_2^2 + 0$$
$$v_2 = \sqrt{2gR}$$
$$= \sqrt{2(9.80 \text{ m/s}^2)(3.00 \text{ m})} = 7.67 \text{ m/s}$$

This answer doesn't depend on the ramp being circular; Throcky will have the same speed $v_2 = \sqrt{2gR}$ at the bottom of any ramp of height R, no matter what its shape.

(b) To find n at point 2 using Newton's second law, we need the free-body diagram at that point (Fig. 7.9b). At point 2, Throcky is moving at speed $v_2 = \sqrt{2gR}$ in a circle of radius R; his acceleration is toward the center of the circle and has magnitude

$$a_{\text{rad}} = \frac{v_2^2}{R} = \frac{2gR}{R} = 2g$$

The y-component of Newton's second law is

$$\sum F_y = n + (-w) = ma_{\text{rad}} = 2mg$$
$$n = w + 2mg = 3mg$$
$$= 3(25.0 \text{ kg})(9.80 \text{ m/s}^2) = 735 \text{ N}$$

At point 2 the normal force is three times Throcky's weight. This result doesn't depend on the radius R of the ramp. We saw in Examples 5.9 and 5.23 that the magnitude of n is the *apparent weight*, so at the bottom of the *curved part* of the ramp Throcky feels as though he weighs three times his true weight mg. But when he reaches the *horizontal* part of the ramp, immediately to the right of point 2, the normal force decreases to $w = mg$ and thereafter Throcky feels his true weight again. Can you see why?

EVALUATE: This example shows a general rule about the role of forces in problems in which we use energy techniques: What matters is not simply whether a force *acts*, but whether that force *does work*. If the force does no work, like the normal force $\vec{n}$ here, then it does not appear in Eqs. (7.4) and (7.7).

7.9 (a) Throcky skateboarding down a frictionless circular ramp. The total mechanical energy is constant. (b) Free-body diagrams for Throcky and his skateboard at various points on the ramp.

Example 7.5 A vertical circle with friction

Suppose that the ramp of Example 7.4 is not frictionless, and that Throcky's speed at the bottom is only 6.00 m/s, not the 7.67 m/s we found there. What work was done on him by the friction force?

SOLUTION

IDENTIFY and SET UP: Figure 7.10 shows that again the normal force does no work, but now there is a friction force $\vec{f}$ that *does* do work W_f. Hence the nongravitational work W_{other} done on Throcky between points 1 and 2 is equal to W_f and is not zero. We use the same coordinate system and the same initial and final points as in Example 7.4. Our target variable is $W_f = W_{\text{other}}$, which we'll find using Eq. (7.7).

EXECUTE: The energy quantities are

$$K_1 = 0$$
$$U_{\text{grav},1} = mgR = (25.0 \text{ kg})(9.80 \text{ m/s}^2)(3.00 \text{ m}) = 735 \text{ J}$$
$$K_2 = \tfrac{1}{2}mv_2^2 = \tfrac{1}{2}(25.0 \text{ kg})(6.00 \text{ m/s})^2 = 450 \text{ J}$$
$$U_{\text{grav},2} = 0$$

7.10 Energy bar graphs and free-body diagrams for Throcky skateboarding down a ramp with friction.

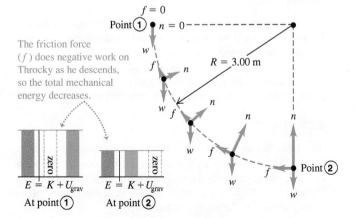

From Eq. (7.7),

$$W_f = W_{\text{other}} = K_2 + U_{\text{grav},2} - K_1 - U_{\text{grav},1}$$
$$= 450 \text{ J} + 0 - 0 - 735 \text{ J} = -285 \text{ J}$$

The work done by the friction force is −285 J, and the total mechanical energy *decreases* by 285 J.

EVALUATE: Our result for W_f is negative. Can you see from the free-body diagrams in Fig. 7.10 why this must be so?

It would be very difficult to apply Newton's second law, $\sum \vec{F} = m\vec{a}$, directly to this problem because the normal and friction forces and the acceleration are continuously changing in both magnitude and direction as Throcky descends. The energy approach, by contrast, relates the motions at the top and bottom of the ramp without involving the details of the motion in between.

Example 7.6 An inclined plane with friction

We want to slide a 12-kg crate up a 2.5-m-long ramp inclined at 30°. A worker, ignoring friction, calculates that he can do this by giving it an initial speed of 5.0 m/s at the bottom and letting it go. But friction is *not* negligible; the crate slides only 1.6 m up the ramp, stops, and slides back down (Fig. 7.11a). (a) Find the magnitude of the friction force acting on the crate, assuming that it is constant. (b) How fast is the crate moving when it reaches the bottom of the ramp?

SOLUTION

IDENTIFY and SET UP: The friction force does work on the crate as it slides. The first part of the motion is from point 1, at the bottom of the ramp, to point 2, where the crate stops instantaneously ($v_2 = 0$). In the second part of the motion, the crate returns to the bottom of the ramp, which we'll also call point 3 (Fig. 7.11a). We take the positive *y*-direction upward. We take $y = 0$ (and hence $U_{\text{grav}} = 0$) to be at ground level (point 1), so that $y_1 = 0$, $y_2 = (1.6 \text{ m})\sin 30° = 0.80 \text{ m}$, and $y_3 = 0$. We are given $v_1 = 5.0 \text{ m/s}$. In part (a) our target variable is f, the magnitude of the friction force as the crate slides up; as in Example 7.2, we'll find this using the energy approach. In part (b) our target variable is v_3, the crate's speed at the bottom of the ramp. We'll calculate the work done by friction as the crate slides back down, then use the energy approach to find v_3.

7.11 (a) A crate slides partway up the ramp, stops, and slides back down. (b) Energy bar graphs for points 1, 2, and 3.

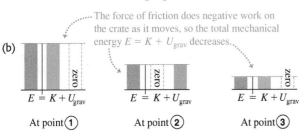

EXECUTE: (a) The energy quantities are

$$K_1 = \tfrac{1}{2}(12 \text{ kg})(5.0 \text{ m/s})^2 = 150 \text{ J}$$
$$U_{\text{grav},1} = 0$$
$$K_2 = 0$$
$$U_{\text{grav},2} = (12 \text{ kg})(9.8 \text{ m/s}^2)(0.80 \text{ m}) = 94 \text{ J}$$
$$W_{\text{other}} = -fs$$

Here $s = 1.6$ m. Using Eq. (7.7), we find

$$K_1 + U_{\text{grav},1} + W_{\text{other}} = K_2 + U_{\text{grav},2}$$
$$W_{\text{other}} = -fs = (K_2 + U_{\text{grav},2}) - (K_1 + U_{\text{grav},1})$$
$$= (0 + 94 \text{ J}) - (150 \text{ J} + 0) = -56 \text{ J} = -fs$$
$$f = \frac{W_{\text{other}}}{s} = \frac{56 \text{ J}}{1.6 \text{ m}} = 35 \text{ N}$$

The friction force of 35 N, acting over 1.6 m, causes the mechanical energy of the crate to decrease from 150 J to 94 J (Fig. 7.11b).

(b) As the crate moves from point 2 to point 3, the work done by friction has the same negative value as from point 1 to point 2. (The friction force and the displacement both reverse direction but have the same magnitudes.) The total work done by friction between points 1 and 3 is therefore

$$W_{\text{other}} = W_{\text{fric}} = -2fs = -2(56 \text{ J}) = -112 \text{ J}$$

From part (a), $K_1 = 150$ J and $U_{\text{grav},1} = 0$. Equation (7.7) then gives

$$K_1 + U_{\text{grav},1} + W_{\text{other}} = K_3 + U_{\text{grav},3}$$
$$K_3 = K_1 + U_{\text{grav},1} - U_{\text{grav},3} + W_{\text{other}}$$
$$= 150 \text{ J} + 0 - 0 + (-112 \text{ J}) = 38 \text{ J}$$

The crate returns to the bottom of the ramp with only 38 J of the original 150 J of mechanical energy (Fig. 7.11b). Since $K_3 = \tfrac{1}{2}mv_3^2$,

$$v_3 = \sqrt{\frac{2K_3}{m}} = \sqrt{\frac{2(38 \text{ J})}{12 \text{ kg}}} = 2.5 \text{ m/s}$$

EVALUATE: Energy was lost due to friction, so the crate's speed $v_3 = 2.5$ m/s when it returns to the bottom of the ramp is less than the speed $v_1 = 5.0$ m/s at which it left that point. In part (b) we applied Eq. (7.7) to points 1 and 3, considering the round trip as a whole. Alternatively, we could have considered the second part of the motion by itself and applied Eq. (7.7) to points 2 and 3. Try it; do you get the same result for v_3?

(MP)

Test Your Understanding of Section 7.1 The figure shows two different frictionless ramps. The heights y_1 and y_2 are the same for both ramps. If a block of mass m is released from rest at the left-hand end of each ramp, which block arrives at the right-hand end with the greater speed? (i) block I; (ii) block II; (iii) the speed is the same for both blocks.

7.2 Elastic Potential Energy

7.12 The Achilles tendon, which runs along the back of the ankle to the heel bone, acts like a natural spring. When it stretches and then relaxes, this tendon stores and then releases elastic potential energy. This spring action reduces the amount of work your leg muscles must do as you run.

(MP)

ActivPhysics 5.4: Inverse Bungee Jumper
ActivPhysics 5.5: Spring-Launched Bowler

There are many situations in which we encounter potential energy that is not gravitational in nature. One example is a rubber-band slingshot. Work is done on the rubber band by the force that stretches it, and that work is stored in the rubber band until you let it go. Then the rubber band gives kinetic energy to the projectile.

This is the same pattern we saw with the pile driver in Section 7.1: Do work on the system to store energy, which can later be converted to kinetic energy. We'll describe the process of storing energy in a deformable body such as a spring or rubber band in terms of *elastic potential energy* (Fig. 7.12). A body is called *elastic* if it returns to its original shape and size after being deformed.

To be specific, we'll consider storing energy in an ideal spring, like the ones we discussed in Section 6.3. To keep such an ideal spring stretched by a distance x, we must exert a force $F = kx$, where k is the force constant of the spring. The ideal spring is a useful idealization because many elastic bodies show this same direct proportionality between force $\vec{F}$ and displacement x, provided that x is sufficiently small.

Let's proceed just as we did for gravitational potential energy. We begin with the work done by the elastic (spring) force and then combine this with the work–energy theorem. The difference is that gravitational potential energy is a shared property of a body and the earth, but elastic potential energy is stored just in the spring (or other deformable body).

Figure 7.13 shows the ideal spring from Fig. 6.18, with its left end held stationary and its right end attached to a block with mass m that can move along the x-axis. In Fig. 7.13a the body is at $x = 0$ when the spring is neither stretched nor compressed. We move the block to one side, thereby stretching or compressing the spring, and then let it go. As the block moves from one position x_1 to another position x_2, how much work does the elastic (spring) force do on the block?

We found in Section 6.3 that the work we must do *on* the spring to move one end from an elongation x_1 to a different elongation x_2 is

$$W = \tfrac{1}{2}kx_2^2 - \tfrac{1}{2}kx_1^2 \qquad \text{(work done } on \text{ a spring)}$$

where k is the force constant of the spring. If we stretch the spring farther, we do positive work on the spring; if we let the spring relax while holding one end, we do negative work on it. We also saw that this expression for work is still correct if the spring is compressed, not stretched, so that x_1 or x_2 or both are negative. Now we need to find the work done *by* the spring. From Newton's third law the two quantities of work are just negatives of each other. Changing the signs in this equation, we find that in a displacement from x_1 to x_2 the spring does an amount of work W_{el} given by

$$W_{el} = \tfrac{1}{2}kx_1^2 - \tfrac{1}{2}kx_2^2 \qquad \text{(work done } by \text{ a spring)}$$

The subscript "el" stands for *elastic*. When x_1 and x_2 are both positive and $x_2 > x_1$ (Fig. 7.13b), the spring does negative work on the block, which moves in the $+x$-direction while the spring pulls on it in the $-x$-direction. The spring stretches farther, and the block slows down. When x_1 and x_2 are both positive and $x_2 < x_1$ (Fig. 7.13c), the spring does positive work as it relaxes and the block speeds up. If the spring can be compressed as well as stretched, x_1 or x_2 or both may be negative, but the expression for W_{el} is still valid. In Fig. 7.13d, both x_1 and x_2 are negative, but x_2 is less negative than x_1; the compressed spring does positive work as it relaxes, speeding the block up.

Just as for gravitational work, we can express the work done by the spring in terms of a given quantity at the beginning and end of the displacement. This quantity is $\frac{1}{2}kx^2$, and we define it to be the **elastic potential energy:**

$$U_{el} = \tfrac{1}{2}kx^2 \qquad \text{(elastic potential energy)} \qquad (7.9)$$

Figure 7.14 is a graph of Eq. (7.9). The unit of U_{el} is the joule (J), the unit used for *all* energy and work quantities; to see this from Eq. (7.9), recall that the units of k are N/m and that $1 \text{ N} \cdot \text{m} = 1 \text{ J}$.

We can use Eq. (7.9) to express the work W_{el} done on the block by the elastic force in terms of the change in elastic potential energy:

$$W_{el} = \tfrac{1}{2}kx_1{}^2 - \tfrac{1}{2}kx_2{}^2 = U_{el,1} - U_{el,2} = -\Delta U_{el} \qquad (7.10)$$

When a stretched spring is stretched farther, as in Fig. 7.13b, W_{el} is negative and U_{el} *increases;* a greater amount of elastic potential energy is stored in the spring. When a stretched spring relaxes, as in Fig. 7.13c, x decreases, W_{el} is positive, and U_{el} *decreases;* the spring loses elastic potential energy. Negative values of x refer to a compressed spring. But, as Fig. 7.14 shows, U_{el} is positive for both positive and negative x, and Eqs. (7.9) and (7.10) are valid for both cases. The more a spring is compressed *or* stretched, the greater its elastic potential energy.

CAUTION **Gravitational potential energy vs. elastic potential energy** An important difference between gravitational potential energy $U_{grav} = mgy$ and elastic potential energy $U_{el} = \frac{1}{2}kx^2$ is that we do *not* have the freedom to choose $x = 0$ to be wherever we wish. To be consistent with Eq. (7.9), $x = 0$ *must* be the position at which the spring is neither stretched nor compressed. At that position, its elastic potential energy and the force that it exerts are both zero. █

The work–energy theorem says that $W_{tot} = K_2 - K_1$, no matter what kind of forces are acting on a body. If the elastic force is the *only* force that does work on the body, then

$$W_{tot} = W_{el} = U_{el,1} - U_{el,2}$$

The work–energy theorem, $W_{tot} = K_2 - K_1$, then gives us

$$K_1 + U_{el,1} = K_2 + U_{el,2} \qquad \text{(if only the elastic force does work)} \qquad (7.11)$$

Here U_{el} is given by Eq. (7.9), so

$$\tfrac{1}{2}mv_1{}^2 + \tfrac{1}{2}kx_1{}^2 = \tfrac{1}{2}mv_2{}^2 + \tfrac{1}{2}kx_2{}^2 \qquad \begin{array}{l}\text{(if only the elastic}\\ \text{force does work)}\end{array} \qquad (7.12)$$

In this case the total mechanical energy $E = K + U_{el}$—the sum of kinetic and *elastic* potential energy—is *conserved*. An example of this is the motion of the

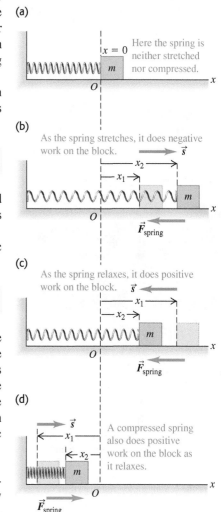

7.13 Calculating the work done by a spring attached to a block on a horizontal surface. The quantity x is the extension or compression of the spring.

(a)

Here the spring is neither stretched nor compressed.

$x = 0$

(b)

As the spring stretches, it does negative work on the block.

(c)

As the spring relaxes, it does positive work on the block.

(d)

A compressed spring also does positive work on the block as it relaxes.

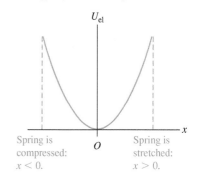

7.14 The graph of elastic potential energy for an ideal spring is a parabola: $U_{el} = \frac{1}{2}kx^2$, where x is the extension or compression of the spring. Elastic potential energy U_{el} is never negative.

U_{el}

Spring is compressed: $x < 0$.

Spring is stretched: $x > 0$.

Application Elastic Potential Energy of a Cheetah
When a cheetah gallops, its back flexes and extends by an exceptional amount. Flexion of the back stretches elastic tendons and muscles along the top of the spine and also compresses the spine, storing mechanical energy. When the cheetah launches into its next bound, this energy helps to extend the spine, enabling the cheetah to run more efficiently.

Difference in nose-to-tail length

7.15 Trampoline jumping involves an interplay among kinetic energy, gravitational potential energy, and elastic potential energy. Due to air resistance and frictional forces within the trampoline, mechanical energy is not conserved. That's why the bouncing eventually stops unless the jumper does work with his or her legs to compensate for the lost energy.

block in Fig. 7.13, provided the horizontal surface is frictionless so that no force does work other than that exerted by the spring.

For Eq. (7.12) to be strictly correct, the ideal spring that we've been discussing must also be *massless*. If the spring has a mass, it also has kinetic energy as the coils of the spring move back and forth. We can neglect the kinetic energy of the spring if its mass is much less than the mass m of the body attached to the spring. For instance, a typical automobile has a mass of 1200 kg or more. The springs in its suspension have masses of only a few kilograms, so their mass can be neglected if we want to study how a car bounces on its suspension.

Situations with Both Gravitational and Elastic Potential Energy

Equations (7.11) and (7.12) are valid when the only potential energy in the system is elastic potential energy. What happens when we have *both* gravitational and elastic forces, such as a block attached to the lower end of a vertically hanging spring? And what if work is also done by other forces that *cannot* be described in terms of potential energy, such as the force of air resistance on a moving block? Then the total work is the sum of the work done by the gravitational force (W_{grav}), the work done by the elastic force (W_{el}), and the work done by other forces (W_{other}): $W_{tot} = W_{grav} + W_{el} + W_{other}$. Then the work–energy theorem gives

$$W_{grav} + W_{el} + W_{other} = K_2 - K_1$$

The work done by the gravitational force is $W_{grav} = U_{grav,1} - U_{grav,2}$ and the work done by the spring is $W_{el} = U_{el,1} - U_{el,2}$. Hence we can rewrite the work–energy theorem for this most general case as

$$K_1 + U_{grav,1} + U_{el,1} + W_{other} = K_2 + U_{grav,2} + U_{el,2} \quad \text{(valid in general)} \quad (7.13)$$

or, equivalently,

$$K_1 + U_1 + W_{other} = K_2 + U_2 \quad \text{(valid in general)} \quad (7.14)$$

where $U = U_{grav} + U_{el} = mgy + \frac{1}{2}kx^2$ is the *sum* of gravitational potential energy and elastic potential energy. For short, we call U simply "the potential energy."

Equation (7.14) is *the most general statement* of the relationship among kinetic energy, potential energy, and work done by other forces. It says:

> **The work done by all forces other than the gravitational force or elastic force equals the change in the total mechanical energy $E = K + U$ of the system, where $U = U_{grav} + U_{el}$ is the sum of the gravitational potential energy and the elastic potential energy.**

The "system" is made up of the body of mass m, the earth with which it interacts through the gravitational force, and the spring of force constant k.

If W_{other} is positive, $E = K + U$ increases; if W_{other} is negative, E decreases. If the gravitational and elastic forces are the *only* forces that do work on the body, then $W_{other} = 0$ and the total mechanical energy (including both gravitational and elastic potential energy) is conserved. (You should compare Eq. (7.14) to Eqs. (7.7) and (7.8), which describe situations in which there is gravitational potential energy but no elastic potential energy.)

Trampoline jumping (Fig. 7.15) involves transformations among kinetic energy, elastic potential energy, and gravitational potential energy. As the jumper descends through the air from the high point of the bounce, gravitational potential energy U_{grav} decreases and kinetic energy K increases. Once the jumper touches the trampoline, some of the mechanical energy goes into elastic potential energy U_{el} stored in the trampoline's springs. Beyond a certain point the jumper's speed and kinetic energy K decrease while U_{grav} continues to decrease and U_{el} continues to increase. At the low point the jumper comes to a momentary halt ($K = 0$) at the lowest point of the trajectory (U_{grav} is minimum) and the springs are maximally stretched (U_{el} is maximum). The springs then convert their energy back into K and U_{grav}, propelling the jumper upward.

Problem-Solving Strategy 7.2 | **Problems Using Mechanical Energy II**

Problem-Solving Strategy 7.1 (Section 7.1) is equally useful in solving problems that involve elastic forces as well as gravitational forces. The only new wrinkle is that the potential energy U now includes the elastic potential energy $U_{el} = \frac{1}{2}kx^2$, where x is the dis-

placement of the spring *from its unstretched length*. The work done by the gravitational and elastic forces is accounted for by their potential energies; the work done by other forces, W_{other}, must still be included separately.

Example 7.7 | **Motion with elastic potential energy**

A glider with mass $m = 0.200$ kg sits on a frictionless horizontal air track, connected to a spring with force constant $k = 5.00$ N/m. You pull on the glider, stretching the spring 0.100 m, and release it from rest. The glider moves back toward its equilibrium position ($x = 0$). What is its x-velocity when $x = 0.080$ m?

SOLUTION

IDENTIFY and SET UP: As the glider starts to move, elastic potential energy is converted to kinetic energy. The glider remains at the same height throughout the motion, so gravitational potential energy is not a factor and $U = U_{el} = \frac{1}{2}kx^2$. Figure 7.16 shows our sketches. Only the spring force does work on the glider, so $W_{other} = 0$ and we may use Eq. (7.11). We designate the point

where the glider is released as point 1 (that is, $x_1 = 0.100$ m) and $x_2 = 0.080$ m as point 2. We are given $v_{1x} = 0$; our target variable is v_{2x}.

EXECUTE: The energy quantities are

$$K_1 = \frac{1}{2}mv_{1x}^2 = \frac{1}{2}(0.200 \text{ kg})(0)^2 = 0$$
$$U_1 = \frac{1}{2}kx_1^2 = \frac{1}{2}(5.00 \text{ N/m})(0.100 \text{ m})^2 = 0.0250 \text{ J}$$
$$K_2 = \frac{1}{2}mv_{2x}^2$$
$$U_2 = \frac{1}{2}kx_2^2 = \frac{1}{2}(5.00 \text{ N/m})(0.080 \text{ m})^2 = 0.0160 \text{ J}$$

We use Eq. (7.11) to solve for K_2 and then find v_{2x}:

$$K_2 = K_1 + U_1 - U_2 = 0 + 0.0250 \text{ J} - 0.0160 \text{ J} = 0.0090 \text{ J}$$
$$v_{2x} = \pm\sqrt{\frac{2K_2}{m}} = \pm\sqrt{\frac{2(0.0090 \text{ J})}{0.200 \text{ kg}}} = \pm 0.30 \text{ m/s}$$

We choose the negative root because the glider is moving in the $-x$-direction. Our answer is $v_{2x} = -0.30$ m/s.

EVALUATE: Eventually the spring will reverse the glider's motion, pushing it back in the $+x$-direction (see Fig. 7.13d). The solution $v_{2x} = +0.30$ m/s tells us that when the glider passes through $x = 0.080$ m on this return trip, its speed will be 0.30 m/s, just as when it passed through this point while moving to the left.

7.16 Our sketches and energy bar graphs for this problem.

Example 7.8 | **Motion with elastic potential energy and work done by other forces**

Suppose the glider in Example 7.7 is initially at rest at $x = 0$, with the spring unstretched. You then push on the glider with a constant force $\vec{F}$ (magnitude 0.610 N) in the $+x$-direction. What is the glider's velocity when it has moved to $x = 0.100$ m?

SOLUTION

IDENTIFY and SET UP: Although the force $\vec{F}$ you apply is constant, the spring force isn't, so the acceleration of the glider won't be constant. Total mechanical energy is not conserved because of

Continued

the work done by the force $\vec{F}$, so we must use the generalized energy relationship given by Eq. (7.13). As in Example 7.7, we ignore gravitational potential energy because the glider's height doesn't change. Hence we again have $U = U_{el} = \frac{1}{2}kx^2$. This time, we let point 1 be at $x_1 = 0$, where the velocity is $v_{1x} = 0$, and let point 2 be at $x = 0.100$ m. The glider's displacement is then $\Delta x = x_2 - x_1 = 0.100$ m. Our target variable is v_{2x}, the velocity at point 2.

EXECUTE: The force $\vec{F}$ is constant and in the same direction as the displacement, so the work done by this force is $F\Delta x$. Then the energy quantities are

$$K_1 = 0$$
$$U_1 = \frac{1}{2}kx_1^2 = 0$$
$$K_2 = \frac{1}{2}mv_{2x}^2$$
$$U_2 = \frac{1}{2}kx_2^2 = \frac{1}{2}(5.00 \text{ N/m})(0.100 \text{ m})^2 = 0.0250 \text{ J}$$
$$W_{other} = F\Delta x = (0.610 \text{ N})(0.100 \text{ m}) = 0.0610 \text{ J}$$

The initial total mechanical energy is zero; the work done by $\vec{F}$ increases the total mechanical energy to 0.0610 J, of which $U_2 = 0.0250$ J is elastic potential energy. The remainder is kinetic energy. From Eq. (7.13),

$$K_1 + U_1 + W_{other} = K_2 + U_2$$
$$K_2 = K_1 + U_1 + W_{other} - U_2$$

$$= 0 + 0 + 0.0610 \text{ J} - 0.0250 \text{ J} = 0.0360 \text{ J}$$
$$v_{2x} = \sqrt{\frac{2K_2}{m}} = \sqrt{\frac{2(0.0360 \text{ J})}{0.200 \text{ kg}}} = 0.60 \text{ m/s}$$

We choose the positive square root because the glider is moving in the $+x$-direction.

EVALUATE: To test our answer, think what would be different if we disconnected the glider from the spring. Then only $\vec{F}$ would do work, there would be zero elastic potential energy at all times, and Eq. (7.13) would give us

$$K_2 = K_1 + W_{other} = 0 + 0.0610 \text{ J}$$
$$v_{2x} = \sqrt{\frac{2K_2}{m}} = \sqrt{\frac{2(0.0610 \text{ J})}{0.200 \text{ kg}}} = 0.78 \text{ m/s}$$

Our answer $v_{2x} = 0.60$ m/s is less than 0.78 m/s because the spring does negative work on the glider as it stretches (see Fig. 7.13b).

If you stop pushing on the glider when it reaches $x = 0.100$ m, only the spring force does work on it thereafter. Hence for $x > 0.100$ m, the total mechanical energy $E = K + U = 0.0610$ J is constant. As the spring continues to stretch, the glider slows down and the kinetic energy K decreases as the potential energy increases. The glider comes to rest at some point $x = x_3$, at which the kinetic energy is zero and the potential energy $U = U_{el} = \frac{1}{2}kx_3^2$ equals the total mechanical energy 0.0610 J. Can you show that $x_3 = 0.156$ m? (It moves an additional 0.056 m after you stop pushing.) If there is no friction, will the glider remain at rest?

Example 7.9   **Motion with gravitational, elastic, and friction forces**

A 2000-kg (19,600-N) elevator with broken cables in a test rig is falling at 4.00 m/s when it contacts a cushioning spring at the bottom of the shaft. The spring is intended to stop the elevator, compressing 2.00 m as it does so (Fig. 7.17). During the motion a safety clamp applies a constant 17,000-N frictional force to the elevator. What is the necessary force constant k for the spring?

7.17 The fall of an elevator is stopped by a spring and by a constant friction force.

SOLUTION

IDENTIFY and SET UP: We'll use the energy approach to determine k, which appears in the expression for elastic potential energy. This problem involves *both* gravitational and elastic potential energy. Total mechanical energy is not conserved because the friction force does negative work W_{other} on the elevator. We'll therefore use the most general form of the energy relationship, Eq. (7.13). We take point 1 as the position of the bottom of the elevator when it contacts the spring, and point 2 as its position when it stops. We choose the origin to be at point 1, so $y_1 = 0$ and $y_2 = -2.00$ m. With this choice the coordinate of the upper end of the spring after contact is the same as the coordinate of the elevator, so the elastic potential energy at any point between points 1 and 2 is $U_{el} = \frac{1}{2}ky^2$. The gravitational potential energy is $U_{grav} = mgy$ as usual. We know the initial and final speeds of the elevator and the magnitude of the friction force, so the only unknown is the force constant k (our target variable).

EXECUTE: The elevator's initial speed is $v_1 = 4.00$ m/s, so its initial kinetic energy is

$$K_1 = \frac{1}{2}mv_1^2 = \frac{1}{2}(2000 \text{ kg})(4.00 \text{ m/s})^2 = 16,000 \text{ J}$$

The elevator stops at point 2, so $K_2 = 0$. At point 1 the potential energy $U_1 = U_{grav} + U_{el}$ is zero; U_{grav} is zero because $y_1 = 0$, and $U_{el} = 0$ because the spring is uncompressed. At point 2 there is both gravitational and elastic potential energy, so

$$U_2 = mgy_2 + \frac{1}{2}ky_2^2$$

The gravitational potential energy at point 2 is

$$mgy_2 = (2000 \text{ kg})(9.80 \text{ m/s}^2)(-2.00 \text{ m}) = -39,200 \text{ J}$$

The "other" force is the constant 17,000-N friction force. It acts opposite to the 2.00-m displacement, so

$$W_{\text{other}} = -(17,000 \text{ N})(2.00 \text{ m}) = -34,000 \text{ J}$$

We put these terms into Eq. (7.14), $K_1 + U_1 + W_{\text{other}} = K_2 + U_2$:

$$K_1 + 0 + W_{\text{other}} = 0 + (mgy_2 + \tfrac{1}{2}ky_2^2)$$

$$k = \frac{2(K_1 + W_{\text{other}} - mgy_2)}{y_2^2}$$

$$= \frac{2[16,000 \text{ J} + (-34,000 \text{ J}) - (-39,200 \text{ J})]}{(-2.00 \text{ m})^2}$$

$$= 1.06 \times 10^4 \text{ N/m}$$

This is about one-tenth the force constant of a spring in an automobile suspension.

EVALUATE: There might seem to be a paradox here. The elastic potential energy at point 2 is

$$\tfrac{1}{2}ky_2^2 = \tfrac{1}{2}(1.06 \times 10^4 \text{ N/m})(-2.00 \text{ m})^2 = 21,200 \text{ J}$$

This is *more* than the total mechanical energy at point 1:

$$E_1 = K_1 + U_1 = 16,000 \text{ J} + 0 = 16,000 \text{ J}$$

But the friction force *decreased* the mechanical energy of the system by 34,000 J between points 1 and 2. Did energy appear from nowhere? No. At point 2, which is below the origin, there is also *negative* gravitational potential energy $mgy_2 = -39,200 \text{ J}$. The total mechanical energy at point 2 is therefore not 21,200 J but rather

$$E_2 = K_2 + U_2 = 0 + \tfrac{1}{2}ky_2^2 + mgy_2$$

$$= 0 + 21,200 \text{ J} + (-39,200 \text{ J}) = -18,000 \text{ J}$$

This is just the initial mechanical energy of 16,000 J minus 34,000 J lost to friction.

Will the elevator stay at the bottom of the shaft? At point 2 the compressed spring exerts an upward force of magnitude $F_{\text{spring}} = (1.06 \times 10^4 \text{ N/m})(2.00 \text{ m}) = 21,200 \text{ N}$, while the downward force of gravity is only $w = mg = (2000 \text{ kg})(9.80 \text{ m/s}^2) = 19,600 \text{ N}$. If there were no friction, there would be a net upward force of $21,200 \text{ N} - 19,600 \text{ N} = 1600 \text{ N}$, and the elevator would rebound. But the safety clamp can exert a kinetic friction force of 17,000 N, and it can presumably exert a maximum static friction force greater than that. Hence the clamp will keep the elevator from rebounding.

Test Your Understanding of Section 7.2 Consider the situation in Example 7.9 at the instant when the elevator is still moving downward and the spring is compressed by 1.00 m. Which of the energy bar graphs in the figure most accurately shows the kinetic energy K, gravitational potential energy U_{grav}, and elastic potential energy U_{el} at this instant?

7.3 Conservative and Nonconservative Forces

In our discussions of potential energy we have talked about "storing" kinetic energy by converting it to potential energy. We always have in mind that later we may retrieve it again as kinetic energy. For example, when you throw a ball up in the air, it slows down as kinetic energy is converted to gravitational potential energy. But on the way down, the conversion is reversed, and the ball speeds up as potential energy is converted back to kinetic energy. If there is no air resistance, the ball is moving just as fast when you catch it as when you threw it.

Another example is a glider moving on a frictionless horizontal air track that runs into a spring bumper at the end of the track. The glider stops as it compresses the spring and then bounces back. If there is no friction, the glider ends up with the same speed and kinetic energy it had before the collision. Again, there is a two-way conversion from kinetic to potential energy and back. In both cases we can define a potential-energy function so that the total mechanical energy, kinetic plus potential, is constant or *conserved* during the motion.

Conservative Forces

A force that offers this opportunity of two-way conversion between kinetic and potential energies is called a **conservative force.** We have seen two examples of

7.18 The work done by a conservative force such as gravity depends only on the end points of a path, not on the specific path taken between those points.

Because the gravitational force is conservative, the work it does is the same for all three paths.

Initial position

Final position

PhET: The Ramp

conservative forces: the gravitational force and the spring force. (Later in this book we will study another conservative force, the electric force between charged objects.) An essential feature of conservative forces is that their work is always *reversible*. Anything that we deposit in the energy "bank" can later be withdrawn without loss. Another important aspect of conservative forces is that a body may move from point 1 to point 2 by various paths, but the work done by a conservative force is the same for all of these paths (Fig. 7.18). Thus, if a body stays close to the surface of the earth, the gravitational force $m\vec{g}$ is independent of height, and the work done by this force depends only on the change in height. If the body moves around a closed path, ending at the same point where it started, the *total* work done by the gravitational force is always zero.

The work done by a conservative force *always* has four properties:

1. It can be expressed as the difference between the initial and final values of a *potential-energy* function.
2. It is reversible.
3. It is independent of the path of the body and depends only on the starting and ending points.
4. When the starting and ending points are the same, the total work is zero.

When the *only* forces that do work are conservative forces, the total mechanical energy $E = K + U$ is constant.

Nonconservative Forces

Not all forces are conservative. Consider the friction force acting on the crate sliding on a ramp in Example 7.6 (Section 7.1). When the body slides up and then back down to the starting point, the total work done on it by the friction force is *not* zero. When the direction of motion reverses, so does the friction force, and friction does *negative* work in *both* directions. When a car with its brakes locked skids across the pavement with decreasing speed (and decreasing kinetic energy), the lost kinetic energy cannot be recovered by reversing the motion or in any other way, and mechanical energy is *not* conserved. There is *no* potential-energy function for the friction force.

In the same way, the force of fluid resistance (see Section 5.3) is not conservative. If you throw a ball up in the air, air resistance does negative work on the ball while it's rising *and* while it's descending. The ball returns to your hand with less speed and less kinetic energy than when it left, and there is no way to get back the lost mechanical energy.

A force that is not conservative is called a **nonconservative force.** The work done by a nonconservative force *cannot* be represented by a potential-energy function. Some nonconservative forces, like kinetic friction or fluid resistance, cause mechanical energy to be lost or dissipated; a force of this kind is called a **dissipative force.** There are also nonconservative forces that *increase* mechanical energy. The fragments of an exploding firecracker fly off with very large kinetic energy, thanks to a chemical reaction of gunpowder with oxygen. The forces unleashed by this reaction are nonconservative because the process is not reversible. (The fragments never spontaneously reassemble themselves into a complete firecracker!)

Example 7.10 Frictional work depends on the path

You are rearranging your furniture and wish to move a 40.0-kg futon 2.50 m across the room. A heavy coffee table, which you don't want to move, blocks this straight-line path. Instead, you slide the futon along a dogleg path; the doglegs are 2.00 m and 1.50 m long. How much more work must you do to push the futon along the dogleg path than along the straight-line path? The coefficient of kinetic friction is $\mu_k = 0.200$.

SOLUTION

IDENTIFY and SET UP: Here both you and friction do work on the futon, so we must use the energy relationship that includes "other" forces. We'll use this relationship to find a connection between the work that *you* do and the work that *friction* does. Figure 7.19 shows our sketch. The futon is at rest at both point 1 and point 2, so

7.19 Our sketch for this problem.

$K_1 = K_2 = 0$. There is no elastic potential energy (there are no springs), and the gravitational potential energy does not change because the futon moves only horizontally, so $U_1 = U_2$. From Eq. (7.14) it follows that $W_{other} = 0$. That "other" work done on the futon is the sum of the positive work you do, W_{you}, and the negative work done by friction, W_{fric}. Since the sum of these is zero, we have

$$W_{you} = -W_{fric}$$

Thus we'll calculate the work done by friction to determine W_{you}.

EXECUTE: The floor is horizontal, so the normal force on the futon equals its weight mg and the magnitude of the friction force is $f_k = \mu_k n = \mu_k mg$. The work you do over each path is then

$$\begin{aligned} W_{you} &= -W_{fric} = -(-f_k s) = +\mu_k mgs \\ &= (0.200)(40.0\text{ kg})(9.80\text{ m/s}^2)(2.50\text{ m}) \\ &= 196\text{ J} \quad \text{(straight-line path)} \\ W_{you} &= -W_{fric} = +\mu_k mgs \\ &= (0.200)(40.0\text{ kg})(9.80\text{ m/s}^2)(2.00\text{ m} + 1.50\text{ m}) \\ &= 274\text{ J} \quad \text{(dogleg path)} \end{aligned}$$

The extra work you must do is $274\text{ J} - 196\text{ J} = 78\text{ J}$.

EVALUATE: Friction does different amounts of work on the futon, -196 J and -274 J, on these different paths between points 1 and 2. Hence friction is a *nonconservative* force.

Example 7.11 Conservative or nonconservative?

In a region of space the force on an electron is $\vec{F} = Cx\hat{\jmath}$, where C is a positive constant. The electron moves around a square loop in the xy-plane (Fig. 7.20). Calculate the work done on the electron by the force $\vec{F}$ during a counterclockwise trip around the square. Is this force conservative or nonconservative?

SOLUTION

IDENTIFY and SET UP: The force $\vec{F}$ is not constant, and in general it is not in the same direction as the displacement. To calculate the work done by $\vec{F}$, we'll use the general expression for work, Eq. (6.14):

$$W = \int_{P_1}^{P_2} \vec{F} \cdot d\vec{l}$$

where $d\vec{l}$ is an infinitesimal displacement. We'll calculate the work done on each leg of the square separately, and add the results to find the work done on the round trip. If this round-trip work is zero, force $\vec{F}$ is conservative and can be represented by a potential-energy function.

7.20 An electron moving around a square loop while being acted on by the force $\vec{F} = Cx\hat{\jmath}$.

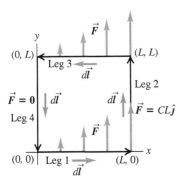

EXECUTE: On the first leg, from $(0, 0)$ to $(L, 0)$, the force is everywhere perpendicular to the displacement. So $\vec{F} \cdot d\vec{l} = 0$, and the work done on the first leg is $W_1 = 0$. The force has the same value $\vec{F} = CL\hat{\jmath}$ everywhere on the second leg, from $(L, 0)$ to (L, L). The displacement on this leg is in the $+y$-direction, so $d\vec{l} = dy\hat{\jmath}$ and

$$\vec{F} \cdot d\vec{l} = CL\hat{\jmath} \cdot dy\hat{\jmath} = CL\,dy$$

The work done on the second leg is then

$$W_2 = \int_{(L, 0)}^{(L, L)} \vec{F} \cdot d\vec{l} = \int_{y=0}^{y=L} CL\,dy = CL \int_0^L dy = CL^2$$

On the third leg, from (L, L) to $(0, L)$, $\vec{F}$ is again perpendicular to the displacement and so $W_3 = 0$. The force is zero on the final leg, from $(0, L)$ to $(0, 0)$, so $W_4 = 0$. The work done by $\vec{F}$ on the round trip is therefore

$$W = W_1 + W_2 + W_3 + W_4 = 0 + CL^2 + 0 + 0 = CL^2$$

The starting and ending points are the same, but the total work done by $\vec{F}$ is not zero. This is a *nonconservative* force; it *cannot* be represented by a potential-energy function.

EVALUATE: Because W is positive, the mechanical energy *increases* as the electron goes around the loop. This is not a mathematical curiosity; it's a much-simplified description of what happens in an electrical generating plant. There, a loop of wire is moved through a magnetic field, which gives rise to a nonconservative force similar to the one here. Electrons in the wire gain energy as they move around the loop, and this energy is carried via transmission lines to the consumer. (We'll discuss how this works in Chapter 29.)

If the electron went *clockwise* around the loop, $\vec{F}$ would be unaffected but the direction of each infinitesimal displacement $d\vec{l}$ would be reversed. Thus the sign of work would also reverse, and the work for a clockwise round trip would be $W = -CL^2$. This is a different behavior than the nonconservative friction force. The work done by friction on a body that slides in any direction over a stationary surface is always negative (see Example 7.6 in Section 7.1).

The Law of Conservation of Energy

Nonconservative forces cannot be represented in terms of potential energy. But we can describe the effects of these forces in terms of kinds of energy other than kinetic and potential energy. When a car with locked brakes skids to a stop, the tires and the road surface both become hotter. The energy associated with this change in the state of the materials is called **internal energy.** Raising the temperature of a body increases its internal energy; lowering the body's temperature decreases its internal energy.

To see the significance of internal energy, let's consider a block sliding on a rough surface. Friction does *negative* work on the block as it slides, and the change in internal energy of the block and surface (both of which get hotter) is *positive.* Careful experiments show that the increase in the internal energy is *exactly* equal to the absolute value of the work done by friction. In other words,

$$\Delta U_{int} = -W_{other}$$

where ΔU_{int} is the change in internal energy. If we substitute this into Eq. (7.7) or (7.14), we find

$$K_1 + U_1 - \Delta U_{int} = K_2 + U_2$$

Writing $\Delta K = K_2 - K_1$ and $\Delta U = U_2 - U_1$, we can finally express this as

$$\Delta K + \Delta U + \Delta U_{int} = 0 \qquad \text{(law of conservation of energy)} \qquad (7.15)$$

This remarkable statement is the general form of the **law of conservation of energy.** In a given process, the kinetic energy, potential energy, and internal energy of a system may all change. But the *sum* of those changes is always zero. If there is a decrease in one form of energy, it is made up for by an increase in the other forms (Fig. 7.21). When we expand our definition of energy to include internal energy, Eq. (7.15) says: *Energy is never created or destroyed; it only changes form.* No exception to this rule has ever been found.

The concept of work has been banished from Eq. (7.15); instead, it suggests that we think purely in terms of the conversion of energy from one form to another. For example, when you throw a baseball straight up, you convert a portion of the internal energy of your molecules to kinetic energy of the baseball. This is converted to gravitational potential energy as the ball climbs and back to kinetic energy as the ball falls. If there is air resistance, part of the energy is used to heat up the air and the ball and increase their internal energy. Energy is converted back to the kinetic form as the ball falls. If you catch the ball in your hand, whatever energy was not lost to the air once again becomes internal energy; the ball and your hand are now warmer than they were at the beginning.

In Chapters 19 and 20, we will study the relationship of internal energy to temperature changes, heat, and work. This is the heart of the area of physics called *thermodynamics.*

7.21 When 1 liter of gasoline is burned in an automotive engine, it releases 3.3×10^7 J of internal energy. Hence $\Delta U_{int} = -3.3 \times 10^7$ J, where the minus sign means that the amount of energy stored in the gasoline has decreased. This energy can be converted to kinetic energy (making the car go faster) or to potential energy (enabling the car to climb uphill).

Conceptual Example 7.12 **Work done by friction**

Let's return to Example 7.5 (Section 7.1), in which Throcky skateboards down a curved ramp. He starts with zero kinetic energy and 735 J of potential energy, and at the bottom he has 450 J of kinetic energy and zero potential energy; hence $\Delta K = +450$ J and $\Delta U = -735$ J. The work $W_{other} = W_{fric}$ done by the friction forces is -285 J, so the change in internal energy is $\Delta U_{int} = -W_{other} = +285$ J. The skateboard wheels and bearings and the ramp all get a little warmer. In accordance with Eq. (7.15), the sum of the energy changes equals zero:

$$\Delta K + \Delta U + \Delta U_{int} = +450\,\text{J} + (-735\,\text{J}) + 285\,\text{J} = 0$$

The total energy of the system (including internal, nonmechanical forms of energy) is conserved.

Test Your Understanding of Section 7.3 In a hydroelectric generating station, falling water is used to drive turbines ("water wheels"), which in turn run electric generators. Compared to the amount of gravitational potential energy released by the falling water, how much electrical energy is produced? (i) the same; (ii) more; (iii) less.

7.4 Force and Potential Energy

For the two kinds of conservative forces (gravitational and elastic) we have studied, we started with a description of the behavior of the *force* and derived from that an expression for the *potential energy*. For example, for a body with mass m in a uniform gravitational field, the gravitational force is $F_y = -mg$. We found that the corresponding potential energy is $U(y) = mgy$. To stretch an ideal spring by a distance x, we exert a force equal to $+kx$. By Newton's third law the force that an ideal spring exerts on a body is opposite this, or $F_x = -kx$. The corresponding potential energy function is $U(x) = \frac{1}{2}kx^2$.

In studying physics, however, you'll encounter situations in which you are given an expression for the *potential energy* as a function of position and have to find the corresponding *force*. We'll see several examples of this kind when we study electric forces later in this book: It's often far easier to calculate the electric potential energy first and then determine the corresponding electric force afterward.

Here's how we find the force that corresponds to a given potential-energy expression. First let's consider motion along a straight line, with coordinate x. We denote the x-component of force, a function of x, by $F_x(x)$, and the potential energy as $U(x)$. This notation reminds us that both F_x and U are *functions* of x. Now we recall that in any displacement, the work W done by a conservative force equals the negative of the change ΔU in potential energy:

$$W = -\Delta U$$

Let's apply this to a small displacement Δx. The work done by the force $F_x(x)$ during this displacement is approximately equal to $F_x(x)\,\Delta x$. We have to say "approximately" because $F_x(x)$ may vary a little over the interval Δx. But it is at least approximately true that

$$F_x(x)\,\Delta x = -\Delta U \quad \text{and} \quad F_x(x) = -\frac{\Delta U}{\Delta x}$$

You can probably see what's coming. We take the limit as $\Delta x \to 0$; in this limit, the variation of F_x becomes negligible, and we have the exact relationship

$$F_x(x) = -\frac{dU(x)}{dx} \quad \text{(force from potential energy, one dimension)} \quad \text{(7.16)}$$

This result makes sense; in regions where $U(x)$ changes most rapidly with x (that is, where $dU(x)/dx$ is large), the greatest amount of work is done during a given displacement, and this corresponds to a large force magnitude. Also, when $F_x(x)$ is in the positive x-direction, $U(x)$ *decreases* with increasing x. So $F_x(x)$ and $dU(x)/dx$ should indeed have opposite signs. The physical meaning of Eq. (7.16) is that *a conservative force always acts to push the system toward lower potential energy.*

As a check, let's consider the function for elastic potential energy, $U(x) = \frac{1}{2}kx^2$. Substituting this into Eq. (7.16) yields

$$F_x(x) = -\frac{d}{dx}\left(\frac{1}{2}kx^2\right) = -kx$$

which is the correct expression for the force exerted by an ideal spring (Fig. 7.22a). Similarly, for gravitational potential energy we have $U(y) = mgy$; taking care to change x to y for the choice of axis, we get $F_y = -dU/dy = -d(mgy)/dy = -mg$, which is the correct expression for gravitational force (Fig. 7.22b).

7.22 A conservative force is the negative derivative of the corresponding potential energy.

(a) Spring potential energy and force as functions of x

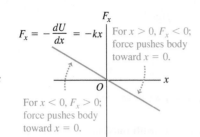

(b) Gravitational potential energy and force as functions of y

---

Example 7.13 | **An electric force and its potential energy**

An electrically charged particle is held at rest at the point $x = 0$; a second particle with equal charge is free to move along the positive x-axis. The potential energy of the system is $U(x) = C/x$, where C is a positive constant that depends on the magnitude of the charges. Derive an expression for the x-component of force acting on the movable particle as a function of its position.

SOLUTION

IDENTIFY and SET UP: We are given the potential-energy function $U(x)$. We'll find the corresponding force function using Eq. (7.16), $F_x(x) = -dU(x)/dx$.

EXECUTE: The derivative of $1/x$ with respect to x is $-1/x^2$. So for $x > 0$ the force on the movable charged particle $x > 0$ is

$$F_x(x) = -\frac{dU(x)}{dx} = -C\left(-\frac{1}{x^2}\right) = \frac{C}{x^2}$$

EVALUATE: The x-component of force is positive, corresponding to a repulsion between like electric charges. Both the potential energy and the force are very large when the particles are close together (small x), and both get smaller as the particles move farther apart (large x); the force pushes the movable particle toward large positive values of x, where the potential energy is lower. (We'll study electric forces in detail in Chapter 21.)

Force and Potential Energy in Three Dimensions

We can extend this analysis to three dimensions, where the particle may move in the x-, y-, or z-direction, or all at once, under the action of a conservative force that has components F_x, F_y, and F_z. Each component of force may be a function of the coordinates x, y, and z. The potential-energy function U is also a function of all three space coordinates. We can now use Eq. (7.16) to find each component of force. The potential-energy change ΔU when the particle moves a small distance Δx in the x-direction is again given by $-F_x \Delta x$; it doesn't depend on F_y and F_z, which represent force components that are perpendicular to the displacement and do no work. So we again have the approximate relationship

$$F_x = -\frac{\Delta U}{\Delta x}$$

The y- and z-components of force are determined in exactly the same way:

$$F_y = -\frac{\Delta U}{\Delta y} \qquad F_z = -\frac{\Delta U}{\Delta z}$$

To make these relationships exact, we take the limits $\Delta x \to 0$, $\Delta y \to 0$, and $\Delta z \to 0$ so that these ratios become derivatives. Because U may be a function of all three coordinates, we need to remember that when we calculate each of these derivatives, only one coordinate changes at a time. We compute the derivative of U with respect to x by assuming that y and z are constant and only x varies, and so on. Such a derivative is called a *partial derivative*. The usual notation for a partial derivative is $\partial U/\partial x$ and so on; the symbol ∂ is a modified d. So we write

$$F_x = -\frac{\partial U}{\partial x} \qquad F_y = -\frac{\partial U}{\partial y} \qquad F_z = -\frac{\partial U}{\partial z} \qquad \text{(force from potential energy)} \qquad (7.17)$$

We can use unit vectors to write a single compact vector expression for the force $\vec{F}$:

$$\vec{F} = -\left(\frac{\partial U}{\partial x}\hat{i} + \frac{\partial U}{\partial y}\hat{j} + \frac{\partial U}{\partial z}\hat{k}\right) \qquad \text{(force from potential energy)} \qquad (7.18)$$

The expression inside the parentheses represents a particular operation on the function U, in which we take the partial derivative of U with respect to each coordinate, multiply by the corresponding unit vector, and then take the vector sum. This operation is called the **gradient** of U and is often abbreviated as $\vec{\nabla}U$. Thus the force is the negative of the gradient of the potential-energy function:

$$\vec{F} = -\vec{\nabla}U \qquad (7.19)$$

As a check, let's substitute into Eq. (7.19) the function $U = mgy$ for gravitational potential energy:

$$\vec{F} = -\vec{\nabla}(mgy) = -\left(\frac{\partial(mgy)}{\partial x}\hat{i} + \frac{\partial(mgy)}{\partial y}\hat{j} + \frac{\partial(mgy)}{\partial z}\hat{k}\right) = (-mg)\hat{j}$$

This is just the familiar expression for the gravitational force.

Example 7.14 Force and potential energy in two dimensions

A puck with coordinates x and y slides on a level, frictionless air-hockey table. It is acted on by a conservative force described by the potential-energy function

$$U(x, y) = \tfrac{1}{2}k(x^2 + y^2)$$

Find a vector expression for the force acting on the puck, and find an expression for the magnitude of the force.

SOLUTION

IDENTIFY and SET UP: Starting with the function $U(x, y)$, we need to find the vector components and magnitude of the corresponding force $\vec{F}$. We'll find the components using Eq. (7.18). The function U doesn't depend on z, so the partial derivative of U with respect to z is $\partial U/\partial z = 0$ and the force has no z-component. We'll determine the magnitude F of the force using $F = \sqrt{F_x^2 + F_y^2}$.

EXECUTE: The x- and y-components of $\vec{F}$ are

$$F_x = -\frac{\partial U}{\partial x} = -kx \qquad F_y = -\frac{\partial U}{\partial y} = -ky$$

From Eq. (7.18), the vector expression for the force is

$$\vec{F} = (-kx)\hat{i} + (-ky)\hat{j} = -k(x\hat{i} + y\hat{j})$$

The magnitude of the force is

$$F = \sqrt{(-kx)^2 + (-ky)^2} = k\sqrt{x^2 + y^2} = kr$$

EVALUATE: Because $x\hat{i} + y\hat{j}$ is just the position vector $\vec{r}$ of the particle, we can rewrite our result as $\vec{F} = -k\vec{r}$. This represents a force that is opposite in direction to the particle's position vector—that is, a force directed toward the origin, $r = 0$. This is the force that would be exerted on the puck if it were attached to one end of a spring that obeys Hooke's law and has a negligibly small unstretched length compared to the other distances in the problem. (The other end is attached to the air-hockey table at $r = 0$.)

To check our result, note that $U = \tfrac{1}{2}kr^2$, where $r^2 = x^2 + y^2$. We can find the force from this expression using Eq. (7.16) with x replaced by r:

$$F_r = -\frac{dU}{dr} = -\frac{d}{dr}\left(\tfrac{1}{2}kr^2\right) = -kr$$

As we found above, the force has magnitude kr; the minus sign indicates that the force is toward the origin (at $r = 0$).

Application Topography and Potential Energy Gradient The greater the elevation of a hiker in Canada's Banff National Park, the greater is the gravitational potential energy U_{grav}. Think of an x-axis that runs horizontally from west to east and a y-axis that runs horizontally from south to north. Then the function $U_{grav}(x, y)$ tells us the elevation as a function of position in the park. Where the mountains have steep slopes, $\vec{F} = -\vec{\nabla}U_{grav}$ has a large magnitude and there's a strong force pushing you along the mountain's surface toward a region of lower elevation (and hence lower U_{grav}). There's zero force along the surface of the lake, which is all at the same elevation. Hence U_{grav} is constant at all points on the lake surface, and $\vec{F} = -\vec{\nabla}U_{grav} = 0$.

7.23 (a) A glider on an air track. The spring exerts a force $F_x = -kx$. (b) The potential-energy function.

(a)

The limits of the glider's motion are at $x = A$ and $x = -A$.

(b)

On the graph, the limits of motion are the points where the U curve intersects the horizontal line representing total mechanical energy E.

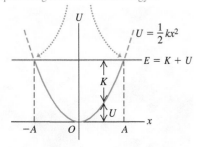

Application Acrobats in Equilibrium
Each of these acrobats is in *unstable* equilibrium. The gravitational potential energy is lower no matter which way an acrobat tips, so if she begins to fall she will keep on falling. Staying balanced requires the acrobats' constant attention.

Test Your Understanding of Section 7.4 A particle moving along the x-axis is acted on by a conservative force F_x. At a certain point, the force is zero. (a) Which of the following statements about the value of the potential-energy function $U(x)$ at that point is correct? (i) $U(x) = 0$; (ii) $U(x) > 0$; (iii) $U(x) < 0$; (iv) not enough information is given to decide. (b) Which of the following statements about the value of the derivative of $U(x)$ at that point is correct? (i) $dU(x)/dx = 0$; (ii) $dU(x)/dx > 0$; (iii) $dU(x)/dx < 0$; (iv) not enough information is given to decide.

7.5 Energy Diagrams

When a particle moves along a straight line under the action of a conservative force, we can get a lot of insight into its possible motions by looking at the graph of the potential-energy function $U(x)$. Figure 7.23a shows a glider with mass m that moves along the x-axis on an air track. The spring exerts on the glider a force with x-component $F_x = -kx$. Figure 7.23b is a graph of the corresponding potential-energy function $U(x) = \frac{1}{2}kx^2$. If the elastic force of the spring is the *only* horizontal force acting on the glider, the total mechanical energy $E = K + U$ is constant, independent of x. A graph of E as a function of x is thus a straight horizontal line. We use the term **energy diagram** for a graph like this, which shows both the potential-energy function $U(x)$ and the energy of the particle subjected to the force that corresponds to $U(x)$.

The vertical distance between the U and E graphs at each point represents the difference $E - U$, equal to the kinetic energy K at that point. We see that K is greatest at $x = 0$. It is zero at the values of x where the two graphs cross, labeled A and $-A$ in the diagram. Thus the speed v is greatest at $x = 0$, and it is zero at $x = \pm A$, the points of *maximum* possible displacement from $x = 0$ for a given value of the total energy E. The potential energy U can never be greater than the total energy E; if it were, K would be negative, and that's impossible. The motion is a back-and-forth oscillation between the points $x = A$ and $x = -A$.

At each point, the force F_x on the glider is equal to the negative of the slope of the $U(x)$ curve: $F_x = -dU/dx$ (see Fig. 7.22a). When the particle is at $x = 0$, the slope and the force are zero, so this is an *equilibrium* position. When x is positive, the slope of the $U(x)$ curve is positive and the force F_x is negative, directed toward the origin. When x is negative, the slope is negative and F_x is positive, again directed toward the origin. Such a force is called a *restoring force;* when the glider is displaced to either side of $x = 0$, the force tends to "restore" it back to $x = 0$. An analogous situation is a marble rolling around in a round-bottomed bowl. We say that $x = 0$ is a point of **stable equilibrium.** More generally, *any minimum in a potential-energy curve is a stable equilibrium position.*

Figure 7.24a shows a hypothetical but more general potential-energy function $U(x)$. Figure 7.24b shows the corresponding force $F_x = -dU/dx$. Points x_1 and x_3 are stable equilibrium points. At each of these points, F_x is zero because the slope of the $U(x)$ curve is zero. When the particle is displaced to either side, the force pushes back toward the equilibrium point. The slope of the $U(x)$ curve is also zero at points x_2 and x_4, and these are also equilibrium points. But when the particle is displaced a little to the right of either point, the slope of the $U(x)$ curve becomes negative, corresponding to a positive F_x that tends to push the particle still farther from the point. When the particle is displaced a little to the left, F_x is negative, again pushing away from equilibrium. This is analogous to a marble rolling on the top of a bowling ball. Points x_2 and x_4 are called **unstable equilibrium** points; *any maximum in a potential-energy curve is an unstable equilibrium position.*

7.24 The maxima and minima of a potential-energy function $U(x)$ correspond to points where $F_x = 0$.

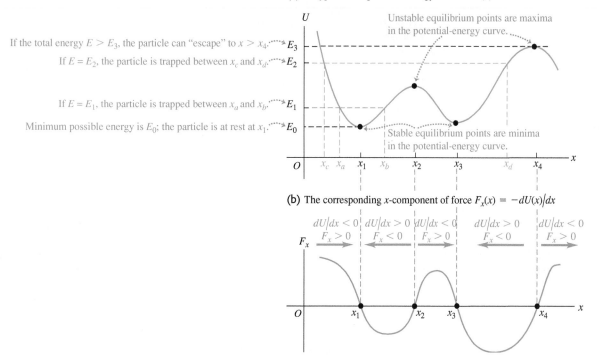

(a) A hypothetical potential-energy function $U(x)$

If the total energy $E > E_3$, the particle can "escape" to $x > x_4$. $\longrightarrow E_3$

If $E = E_2$, the particle is trapped between x_c and x_d. $\longrightarrow E_2$

Unstable equilibrium points are maxima in the potential-energy curve.

If $E = E_1$, the particle is trapped between x_a and x_b. $\longrightarrow E_1$

Minimum possible energy is E_0; the particle is at rest at x_1. $\longrightarrow E_0$

Stable equilibrium points are minima in the potential-energy curve.

O x_c x_a x_1 x_b x_2 x_3 x_d x_4 x

(b) The corresponding x-component of force $F_x(x) = -dU(x)/dx$

$dU/dx < 0$ $dU/dx > 0$ $dU/dx < 0$ $dU/dx > 0$ $dU/dx < 0$
$F_x > 0$ $F_x < 0$ $F_x > 0$ $F_x < 0$ $F_x > 0$

O x_1 x_2 x_3 x_4 x

CAUTION **Potential energy and the direction of a conservative force** The direction of the force on a body is *not* determined by the sign of the potential energy U. Rather, it's the sign of $F_x = -dU/dx$ that matters. As we discussed in Section 7.1, the physically significant quantity is the *difference* in the values of U between two points, which is just what the derivative $F_x = -dU/dx$ measures. This means that you can always add a constant to the potential-energy function without changing the physics of the situation.

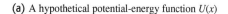

PhET: Energy Skate Park

If the total energy is E_1 and the particle is initially near x_1, it can move only in the region between x_a and x_b determined by the intersection of the E_1 and U graphs (Fig. 7.24a). Again, U cannot be greater than E_1 because K can't be negative. We speak of the particle as moving in a *potential well*, and x_a and x_b are the *turning points* of the particle's motion (since at these points, the particle stops and reverses direction). If we increase the total energy to the level E_2, the particle can move over a wider range, from x_c to x_d. If the total energy is greater than E_3, the particle can "escape" and move to indefinitely large values of x. At the other extreme, E_0 represents the least possible total energy the system can have.

Test Your Understanding of Section 7.5 The curve in Fig. 7.24b has a maximum at a point between x_2 and x_3. Which statement correctly describes what happens to the particle when it is at this point? (i) The particle's acceleration is zero. (ii) The particle accelerates in the positive x-direction; the magnitude of the acceleration is less than at any other point between x_2 and x_3. (iii) The particle accelerates in the positive x-direction; the magnitude of the acceleration is greater than at any other point between x_2 and x_3. (iv) The particle accelerates in the negative x-direction; the magnitude of the acceleration is less than at any other point between x_2 and x_3. (v) The particle accelerates in the negative x-direction; the magnitude of the acceleration is greater than at any other point between x_2 and x_3.

Gravitational potential energy and elastic energy: The work done on a particle by a constant gravitational force can be represented as a change in the gravitational potential energy $U_{grav} = mgy$. This energy is a shared property of the particle and the earth. A potential energy is also associated with the elastic force $F_x = -kx$ exerted by an ideal spring, where x is the amount of stretch or compression. The work done by this force can be represented as a change in the elastic potential energy of the spring, $U_{el} = \frac{1}{2}kx^2$.

$$W_{grav} = mgy_1 - mgy_2$$
$$= U_{grav,1} - U_{grav,2}$$
$$= -\Delta U_{grav} \qquad (7.1), (7.3)$$

$$W_{el} = \frac{1}{2}kx_1^2 - \frac{1}{2}kx_2^2$$
$$= U_{el,1} - U_{el,2} = -\Delta U_{el} \qquad (7.10)$$

When total mechanical energy is conserved: The total potential energy U is the sum of the gravitational and elastic potential energy: $U = U_{grav} + U_{el}$. If no forces other than the gravitational and elastic forces do work on a particle, the sum of kinetic and potential energy is conserved. This sum $E = K + U$ is called the total mechanical energy. (See Examples 7.1, 7.3, 7.4, and 7.7.)

$$K_1 + U_1 = K_2 + U_2 \qquad (7.4), (7.11)$$

When total mechanical energy is not conserved: When forces other than the gravitational and elastic forces do work on a particle, the work W_{other} done by these other forces equals the change in total mechanical energy (kinetic energy plus total potential energy). (See Examples 7.2, 7.5, 7.6, 7.8, and 7.9.)

$$K_1 + U_1 + W_{other} = K_2 + U_2 \qquad (7.14)$$

Conservative forces, nonconservative forces, and the law of conservation of energy: All forces are either conservative or nonconservative. A conservative force is one for which the work–kinetic energy relationship is completely reversible. The work of a conservative force can always be represented by a potential-energy function, but the work of a nonconservative force cannot. The work done by nonconservative forces manifests itself as changes in the internal energy of bodies. The sum of kinetic, potential, and internal energy is always conserved. (See Examples 7.10–7.12.)

$$\Delta K + \Delta U + \Delta U_{int} = 0 \qquad (7.15)$$

As friction slows block, mechanical energy is converted to internal energy of block and ramp.

Determining force from potential energy: For motion along a straight line, a conservative force $F_x(x)$ is the negative derivative of its associated potential-energy function U. In three dimensions, the components of a conservative force are negative partial derivatives of U. (See Examples 7.13 and 7.14.)

$$F_x(x) = -\frac{dU(x)}{dx} \qquad (7.16)$$

$$F_x = -\frac{\partial U}{\partial x} \qquad F_y = -\frac{\partial U}{\partial y} \qquad (7.17)$$

$$F_z = -\frac{\partial U}{\partial z}$$

$$\vec{F} = -\left(\frac{\partial U}{\partial x}\hat{i} + \frac{\partial U}{\partial y}\hat{j} + \frac{\partial U}{\partial z}\hat{k}\right) \qquad (7.18)$$

BRIDGING PROBLEM | **A Spring and Friction on an Incline**

A 2.00-kg package is released on a 53.1° incline, 4.00 m from a long spring with force constant $1.20 \times 10^2 \, \text{N/m}$ that is attached at the bottom of the incline (Fig. 7.25). The coefficients of friction between the package and incline are $\mu_s = 0.400$ and $\mu_k = 0.200$. The mass of the spring is negligible.

7.25 The initial situation.

$m = 2.00 \, \text{kg}$

$D = 4.00 \, \text{m}$

$\theta = 53.1°$

(a) What is the maximum compression of the spring? (b) The package rebounds up the incline. How close does it get to its original position? (c) What is the change in the internal energy of the package and incline from when the package is released to when it rebounds to its maximum height?

SOLUTION GUIDE

See MasteringPhysics® study area for a Video Tutor solution.

IDENTIFY and SET UP

1. This problem involves the gravitational force, a spring force, and the friction force, as well as the normal force that acts on the package. Since the spring force isn't constant, you'll have to use energy methods. Is mechanical energy conserved during any part of the motion? Why or why not?

2. Draw free-body diagrams for the package as it is sliding down the incline and sliding back up the incline. Include your choice of coordinate axis. (*Hint:* If you choose $x = 0$ to be at the end of the uncompressed spring, you'll be able to use $U_{el} = \frac{1}{2}kx^2$ for the elastic potential energy of the spring.)

3. Label the three critical points in the package's motion: its starting position, its position when it comes to rest with the spring maximally compressed, and its position when it's rebounded as far as possible up the incline. (*Hint:* You can assume that the

package is no longer in contact with the spring at the last of these positions. If this turns out to be incorrect, you'll calculate a value of x that tells you the spring is still partially compressed at this point.)

4. Make a list of the unknown quantities and decide which of these are the target variables.

EXECUTE

5. Find the magnitude of the friction force that acts on the package. Does the magnitude of this force depend on whether the package is moving up or down the incline, or on whether or not the package is in contact with the spring? Does the *direction* of the normal force depend on any of these?

6. Write the general energy equation for the motion of the package between the first two points you labeled in step 3. Use this equation to solve for the distance that the spring is compressed when the package is at its lowest point. (*Hint:* You'll have to solve a quadratic equation. To decide which of the two solutions of this equation is the correct one, remember that the distance the spring is compressed is positive.)

7. Write the general energy equation for the motion of the package between the second and third points you labeled in step 3. Use this equation to solve for how far the package rebounds.

8. Calculate the change in internal energy for the package's trip down and back up the incline. Remember that the amount the internal energy *increases* is equal to the amount the total mechanical energy *decreases*.

EVALUATE

9. Was it correct to assume in part (b) that the package is no longer in contact with the spring when it reaches it maximum rebound height?

10. Check your result for part (c) by finding the total work done by the force of friction over the entire trip. Is this in accordance with your result from step 8?

Problems

For instructor-assigned homework, go to MasteringPhysics®.

•, ••, •••: Problems of increasing difficulty. **CP**: Cumulative problems incorporating material from earlier chapters. **CALC**: Problems requiring calculus. **BIO**: Biosciences problems.

DISCUSSION QUESTIONS

Q7.1 A baseball is thrown straight up with initial speed v_0. If air resistance cannot be ignored, when the ball returns to its initial height its speed is less than v_0. Explain why, using energy concepts.

Q7.2 A projectile has the same initial kinetic energy no matter what the angle of projection. Why doesn't it rise to the same maximum height in each case?

Q7.3 An object is released from rest at the top of a ramp. If the ramp is frictionless, does the object's speed at the bottom of the ramp depend on the shape of the ramp or just on its height? Explain. What if the ramp is *not* frictionless?

Q7.4 An egg is released from rest from the roof of a building and falls to the ground. Its fall is observed by a student on the roof of the building, who uses coordinates with origin at the roof, and by a student on the ground, who uses coordinates with origin at the ground. Do the two students assign the same or different values to the initial gravitational potential energy, the final gravitational potential energy, the change in gravitational potential energy, and the kinetic energy of the egg just before it strikes the ground? Explain.

Q7.5 A physics teacher had a bowling ball suspended from a very long rope attached to the high ceiling of a large lecture hall. To illustrate his faith in conservation of energy, he would back up to one side of the stage, pull the ball far to one side until the taut rope brought it just to the end of his nose, and then release it. The massive ball would swing in a mighty arc across the stage and then return to stop momentarily just in front of the nose of the stationary, unflinching teacher. However, one day after the demonstration he looked up just in time to see a student at the other side of the stage *push* the ball away from his nose as he tried to duplicate the demonstration. Tell the rest of the story and explain the reason for the potentially tragic outcome.

Q7.6 Lost Energy? The principle of the conservation of energy tells us that energy is never lost, but only changes from one form to another. Yet in many ordinary situations, energy may appear to be lost. In each case, explain what happens to the "lost" energy. (a) A box sliding on the floor comes to a halt due to friction. How did friction take away its kinetic energy, and what happened to that energy? (b) A car stops when you apply the brakes. What happened to its kinetic energy? (c) Air resistance uses up some of the original gravitational potential energy of a falling object. What type of energy did the "lost" potential energy become? (d) When a returning space shuttle touches down on the runway, it has lost almost all its kinetic energy and gravitational potential energy. Where did all that energy go?

Q7.7 Is it possible for a frictional force to *increase* the mechanical energy of a system? If so, give examples.

Q7.8 A woman bounces on a trampoline, going a little higher with each bounce. Explain how she increases the total mechanical energy.

Q7.9 Fractured Physics. People often call their electric bill a *power* bill, yet the quantity on which the bill is based is expressed in *kilowatt-hours*. What are people really being billed for?

Q7.10 A rock of mass m and a rock of mass $2m$ are both released from rest at the same height and feel no air resistance as they fall. Which statements about these rocks are true? (There may be more than one correct choice.) (a) Both have the same initial gravitational potential energy. (b) Both have the same kinetic energy when they reach the ground. (c) Both reach the ground with the same speed. (d) When it reaches the ground, the heavier rock has twice the kinetic energy of the lighter one. (e) When it reaches the ground, the heavier rock has four times the kinetic energy of the lighter one.

Q7.11 On a friction-free ice pond, a hockey puck is pressed against (but not attached to) a fixed ideal spring, compressing the spring by a distance x_0. The maximum energy stored in the spring is U_0, the maximum speed the puck gains after being released is v_0, and its maximum kinetic energy is K_0. Now the puck is pressed so it compresses the spring twice as far as before. In this case, (a) what is the maximum potential energy stored in the spring (in terms of U_0), and (b) what are the puck's maximum kinetic energy and speed (in terms of K_0 and x_0)?

Q7.12 When people are cold, they often rub their hands together to warm them up. How does doing this produce heat? Where did the heat come from?

Q7.13 You often hear it said that most of our energy ultimately comes from the sun. Trace each of the following energies back to the sun: (a) the kinetic energy of a jet plane; (b) the potential energy gained by a mountain climber; (c) the electrical energy used to run a computer; (d) the electrical energy from a hydroelectric plant.

Q7.14 A box slides down a ramp and work is done on the box by the forces of gravity and friction. Can the work of each of these forces be expressed in terms of the change in a potential-energy function? For each force explain why or why not.

Q7.15 In physical terms, explain why friction is a nonconservative force. Does it store energy for future use?

Q7.16 A compressed spring is clamped in its compressed position and then is dissolved in acid. What becomes of its potential energy?

Q7.17 Since only changes in potential energy are important in any problem, a student decides to let the elastic potential energy of a spring be zero when the spring is stretched a distance x_1. The student decides, therefore, to let $U = \frac{1}{2}k(x - x_1)^2$. Is this correct? Explain.

Q7.18 Figure 7.22a shows the potential-energy function for the force $F_x = -kx$. Sketch the potential-energy function for the force $F_x = +kx$. For this force, is $x = 0$ a point of equilibrium? Is this equilibrium stable or unstable? Explain.

Q7.19 Figure 7.22b shows the potential-energy function associated with the gravitational force between an object and the earth. Use this graph to explain why objects always fall toward the earth when they are released.

Q7.20 For a system of two particles we often let the potential energy for the force between the particles approach zero as the separation of the particles approaches infinity. If this choice is made, explain why the potential energy at noninfinite separation is positive if the particles repel one another and negative if they attract.

Q7.21 Explain why the points $x = A$ and $x = -A$ in Fig. 7.23b are called *turning points*. How are the values of E and U related at a turning point?

Q7.22 A particle is in *neutral equilibrium* if the net force on it is zero and remains zero if the particle is displaced slightly in any direction. Sketch the potential-energy function near a point of neutral equilibrium for the case of one-dimensional motion. Give an example of an object in neutral equilibrium.

Q7.23 The net force on a particle of mass m has the potential-energy function graphed in Fig. 7.24a. If the total energy is E_1, graph the speed v of the particle versus its position x. At what value of x is the speed greatest? Sketch v versus x if the total energy is E_2.

Q7.24 The potential-energy function for a force $\vec{F}$ is $U = \alpha x^3$, where α is a positive constant. What is the direction of $\vec{F}$?

EXERCISES

Section 7.1 Gravitational Potential Energy

7.1 • In one day, a 75-kg mountain climber ascends from the 1500-m level on a vertical cliff to the top at 2400 m. The next day, she descends from the top to the base of the cliff, which is at an elevation of 1350 m. What is her change in gravitational potential energy (a) on the first day and (b) on the second day?

7.2 • **BIO How High Can We Jump?** The maximum height a typical human can jump from a crouched start is about 60 cm. By how much does the gravitational potential energy increase for a 72-kg person in such a jump? Where does this energy come from?

7.3 •• **CP** A 120-kg mail bag hangs by a vertical rope 3.5 m long. A postal worker then displaces the bag to a position 2.0 m sideways from its original position, always keeping the rope taut. (a) What horizontal force is necessary to hold the bag in the new position? (b) As the bag is moved to this position, how much work is done (i) by the rope and (ii) by the worker?

7.4 •• **BIO Food Calories.** The *food calorie*, equal to 4186 J, is a measure of how much energy is released when food is metabolized by the body. A certain brand of fruit-and-cereal bar contains

140 food calories per bar. (a) If a 65-kg hiker eats one of these bars, how high a mountain must he climb to "work off" the calories, assuming that all the food energy goes only into increasing gravitational potential energy? (b) If, as is typical, only 20% of the food calories go into mechanical energy, what would be the answer to part (a)? (*Note:* In this and all other problems, we are assuming that 100% of the food calories that are eaten are absorbed and used by the body. This is actually not true. A person's "metabolic efficiency" is the percentage of calories eaten that are actually used; the rest are eliminated by the body. Metabolic efficiency varies considerably from person to person.)

7.5 • A baseball is thrown from the roof of a 22.0-m-tall building with an initial velocity of magnitude 12.0 m/s and directed at an angle of 53.1° above the horizontal. (a) What is the speed of the ball just before it strikes the ground? Use energy methods and ignore air resistance. (b) What is the answer for part (a) if the initial velocity is at an angle of 53.1° *below* the horizontal? (c) If the effects of air resistance are included, will part (a) or (b) give the higher speed?

7.6 •• A crate of mass M starts from rest at the top of a frictionless ramp inclined at an angle α above the horizontal. Find its speed at the bottom of the ramp, a distance d from where it started. Do this in two ways: (a) Take the level at which the potential energy is zero to be at the bottom of the ramp with y positive upward. (b) Take the zero level for potential energy to be at the top of the ramp with y positive upward. (c) Why did the normal force not enter into your solution?

7.7 •• **BIO Human Energy vs. Insect Energy.** For its size, the common flea is one of the most accomplished jumpers in the animal world. A 2.0-mm-long, 0.50-mg critter can reach a height of 20 cm in a single leap. (a) Neglecting air drag, what is the takeoff speed of such a flea? (b) Calculate the kinetic energy of this flea at takeoff and its kinetic energy per kilogram of mass. (c) If a 65-kg, 2.0-m-tall human could jump to the same height compared with his length as the flea jumps compared with its length, how high could the human jump, and what takeoff speed would he need? (d) In fact, most humans can jump no more than 60 cm from a crouched start. What is the kinetic energy per kilogram of mass at takeoff for such a 65-kg person? (e) Where does the flea store the energy that allows it to make such a sudden leap?

7.8 •• An empty crate is given an initial push down a ramp, starting with speed v_0, and reaches the bottom with speed v and kinetic energy K. Some books are now placed in the crate, so that the total mass is quadrupled. The coefficient of kinetic friction is constant and air resistance is negligible. Starting again with v_0 at the top of the ramp, what are the speed and kinetic energy at the bottom? Explain the reasoning behind your answers.

7.9 •• **CP** A small rock with mass 0.20 kg is released from rest at point A, which is at the top edge of a large, hemispherical bowl with radius $R = 0.50$ m (Fig. E7.9). Assume that the size of the rock is small compared to R, so that the rock can be treated

Figure **E7.9**

as a particle, and assume that the rock slides rather than rolls. The work done by friction on the rock when it moves from point A to point B at the bottom of the bowl has magnitude 0.22 J. (a) Between points A and B, how much work is done on the rock by (i) the normal force and (ii) gravity? (b) What is the speed of the rock as it reaches point B? (c) Of the three forces acting on the rock as it slides down the bowl, which (if any) are constant and which

are not? Explain. (d) Just as the rock reaches point B, what is the normal force on it due to the bottom of the bowl?

7.10 •• **BIO Bone Fractures.** The maximum energy that a bone can absorb without breaking depends on its characteristics, such as its cross-sectional area and its elasticity. For healthy human leg bones of approximately 6.0 cm² cross-sectional area, this energy has been experimentally measured to be about 200 J. (a) From approximately what maximum height could a 60-kg person jump and land rigidly upright on both feet without breaking his legs? (b) You are probably surprised at how small the answer to part (a) is. People obviously jump from much greater heights without breaking their legs. How can that be? What else absorbs the energy when they jump from greater heights? (*Hint:* How did the person in part (a) land? How do people normally land when they jump from greater heights?) (c) In light of your answers to parts (a) and (b), what might be some of the reasons that older people are much more prone than younger ones to bone fractures from simple falls (such as a fall in the shower)?

7.11 •• You are testing a new amusement park roller coaster with an empty car of mass 120 kg. One part of the track is a vertical loop with radius 12.0 m. At the bottom of the loop (point A) the car has speed 25.0 m/s, and at the top of the loop (point B) it has speed 8.0 m/s. As the car rolls from point A to point B, how much work is done by friction?

7.12 • **Tarzan and Jane.** Tarzan, in one tree, sights Jane in another tree. He grabs the end of a vine with length 20 m that makes an angle of 45° with the vertical, steps off his tree limb, and swings down and then up to Jane's open arms. When he arrives, his vine makes an angle of 30° with the vertical. Determine whether he gives her a tender embrace or knocks her off her limb by calculating Tarzan's speed just before he reaches Jane. You can ignore air resistance and the mass of the vine.

7.13 •• **CP** A 10.0-kg microwave oven is pushed 8.00 m up the sloping surface of a loading ramp inclined at an angle of 36.9° above the horizontal, by a constant force $\vec{F}$ with a magnitude 110 N and acting parallel to the ramp. The coefficient of kinetic friction between the oven and the ramp is 0.250. (a) What is the work done on the oven by the force $\vec{F}$? (b) What is the work done on the oven by the friction force? (c) Compute the increase in potential energy for the oven. (d) Use your answers to parts (a), (b), and (c) to calculate the increase in the oven's kinetic energy. (e) Use $\Sigma\vec{F} = m\vec{a}$ to calculate the acceleration of the oven. Assuming that the oven is initially at rest, use the acceleration to calculate the oven's speed after traveling 8.00 m. From this, compute the increase in the oven's kinetic energy, and compare it to the answer you got in part (d).

Section 7.2 Elastic Potential Energy

7.14 •• An ideal spring of negligible mass is 12.00 cm long when nothing is attached to it. When you hang a 3.15-kg weight from it, you measure its length to be 13.40 cm. If you wanted to store 10.0 J of potential energy in this spring, what would be its *total* length? Assume that it continues to obey Hooke's law.

7.15 •• A force of 800 N stretches a certain spring a distance of 0.200 m. (a) What is the potential energy of the spring when it is stretched 0.200 m? (b) What is its potential energy when it is compressed 5.00 cm?

7.16 • **BIO Tendons.** Tendons are strong elastic fibers that attach muscles to bones. To a reasonable approximation, they obey Hooke's law. In laboratory tests on a particular tendon, it was found that, when a 250-g object was hung from it, the tendon stretched 1.23 cm. (a) Find the force constant of this tendon in N/m. (b) Because of its thickness, the maximum tension this tendon can support without rupturing is 138 N. By how much can the tendon stretch without rupturing, and how much energy is stored in it at that point?

7.17 • A spring stores potential energy U_0 when it is compressed a distance x_0 from its uncompressed length. (a) In terms of U_0, how much energy does it store when it is compressed (i) twice as much and (ii) half as much? (b) In terms of x_0, how much must it be compressed from its uncompressed length to store (i) twice as much energy and (ii) half as much energy?

7.18 • A slingshot will shoot a 10-g pebble 22.0 m straight up. (a) How much potential energy is stored in the slingshot's rubber band? (b) With the same potential energy stored in the rubber band, how high can the slingshot shoot a 25-g pebble? (c) What physical effects did you ignore in solving this problem?

7.19 •• A spring of negligible mass has force constant $k = 1600$ N/m. (a) How far must the spring be compressed for 3.20 J of potential energy to be stored in it? (b) You place the spring vertically with one end on the floor. You then drop a 1.20-kg book onto it from a height of 0.80 m above the top of the spring. Find the maximum distance the spring will be compressed.

7.20 • A 1.20-kg piece of cheese is placed on a vertical spring of negligible mass and force constant $k = 1800$ N/m that is compressed 15.0 cm. When the spring is released, how high does the cheese rise from this initial position? (The cheese and the spring are *not* attached.)

7.21 •• Consider the glider of Example 7.7 (Section 7.2) and Fig. 7.16. As in the example, the glider is released from rest with the spring stretched 0.100 m. What is the displacement x of the glider from its equilibrium position when its speed is 0.20 m/s? (You should get more than one answer. Explain why.)

7.22 •• Consider the glider of Example 7.7 (Section 7.2) and Fig. 7.16. (a) As in the example, the glider is released from rest with the spring stretched 0.100 m. What is the speed of the glider when it returns to $x = 0$? (b) What must the initial displacement of the glider be if its maximum speed in the subsequent motion is to be 2.50 m/s?

7.23 •• A 2.50-kg mass is pushed against a horizontal spring of force constant 25.0 N/cm on a frictionless air table. The spring is attached to the tabletop, and the mass is not attached to the spring in any way. When the spring has been compressed enough to store 11.5 J of potential energy in it, the mass is suddenly released from rest. (a) Find the greatest speed the mass reaches. When does this occur? (b) What is the greatest acceleration of the mass, and when does it occur?

7.24 •• (a) For the elevator of Example 7.9 (Section 7.2), what is the speed of the elevator after it has moved downward 1.00 m from point 1 in Fig. 7.17? (b) When the elevator is 1.00 m below point 1 in Fig. 7.17, what is its acceleration?

7.25 •• You are asked to design a spring that will give a 1160-kg satellite a speed of 2.50 m/s relative to an orbiting space shuttle. Your spring is to give the satellite a maximum acceleration of 5.00g. The spring's mass, the recoil kinetic energy of the shuttle, and changes in gravitational potential energy will all be negligible. (a) What must the force constant of the spring be? (b) What distance must the spring be compressed?

7.26 •• A 2.50-kg block on a horizontal floor is attached to a horizontal spring that is initially compressed 0.0300 m. The spring has force constant 840 N/m. The coefficient of kinetic friction between the floor and the block is $\mu_k = 0.40$. The block and spring are released from rest and the block slides along the floor. What is the speed of the block when it has moved a distance of 0.0200 m from its initial position? (At this point the spring is compressed 0.0100 m.)

Section 7.3 Conservative and Nonconservative Forces

7.27 • A 10.0-kg box is pulled by a horizontal wire in a circle on a rough horizontal surface for which the coefficient of kinetic friction is 0.250. Calculate the work done by friction during one complete circular trip if the radius is (a) 2.00 m and (b) 4.00 m. (c) On the basis of the results you just obtained, would you say that friction is a conservative or nonconservative force? Explain.

7.28 •• A 75-kg roofer climbs a vertical 7.0-m ladder to the flat roof of a house. He then walks 12 m on the roof, climbs down another vertical 7.0-m ladder, and finally walks on the ground back to his starting point. How much work is done on him by gravity (a) as he climbs up; (b) as he climbs down; (c) as he walks on the roof and on the ground? (d) What is the total work done on him by gravity during this round trip? (e) On the basis of your answer to part (d), would you say that gravity is a conservative or nonconservative force? Explain.

7.29 • A 0.60-kg book slides on a horizontal table. The kinetic friction force on the book has magnitude 1.2 N. (a) How much work is done on the book by friction during a displacement of 3.0 m to the left? (b) The book now slides 3.0 m to the right, returning to its starting point. During this second 3.0-m displacement, how much work is done on the book by friction? (c) What is the total work done on the book by friction during the complete round trip? (d) On the basis of your answer to part (c), would you say that the friction force is conservative or nonconservative? Explain.

7.30 •• **CALC** In an experiment, one of the forces exerted on a proton is $\vec{F} = -\alpha x^2 \hat{\imath}$, where $\alpha = 12$ N/m². (a) How much work does $\vec{F}$ do when the proton moves along the straight-line path from the point (0.10 m, 0) to the point (0.10 m, 0.40 m)? (b) Along the straight-line path from the point (0.10 m, 0) to the point (0.30 m, 0)? (c) Along the straight-line path from the point (0.30 m, 0) to the point (0.10 m, 0)? (d) Is the force $\vec{F}$ conservative? Explain. If $\vec{F}$ is conservative, what is the potential-energy function for it? Let $U = 0$ when $x = 0$.

7.31 • You and three friends stand at the corners of a square whose sides are 8.0 m long in the middle of the gym floor, as shown in Fig. E7.31. You take your physics book and push it from one person to the other. The book has a mass of 1.5 kg, and the coefficient of kinetic friction between the book and the floor is $\mu_k = 0.25$. (a) The book

Figure **E7.31**

slides from you to Beth and then from Beth to Carlos, along the lines connecting these people. What is the work done by friction during this displacement? (b) You slide the book from you to Carlos along the diagonal of the square. What is the work done by friction during this displacement? (c) You slide the book to Kim, who then slides it back to you. What is the total work done by friction during this motion of the book? (d) Is the friction force on the book conservative or nonconservative? Explain.

7.32 • While a roofer is working on a roof that slants at 36° above the horizontal, he accidentally nudges his 85.0-N toolbox, causing it to start sliding downward, starting from rest. If it starts 4.25 m from the lower edge of the roof, how fast will the toolbox be moving just as it reaches the edge of the roof if the kinetic friction force on it is 22.0 N?

7.33 •• A 62.0-kg skier is moving at 6.50 m/s on a frictionless, horizontal, snow-covered plateau when she encounters a rough patch 3.50 m long. The coefficient of kinetic friction between this patch and her skis is 0.300. After crossing the rough patch and returning to friction-free snow, she skis down an icy, frictionless hill 2.50 m high. (a) How fast is the skier moving when she gets to the bottom of the hill? (b) How much internal energy was generated in crossing the rough patch?

Section 7.4 Force and Potential Energy

7.34 •• CALC The potential energy of a pair of hydrogen atoms separated by a large distance x is given by $U(x) = -C_6/x^6$, where C_6 is a positive constant. What is the force that one atom exerts on the other? Is this force attractive or repulsive?

7.35 •• CALC A force parallel to the x-axis acts on a particle moving along the x-axis. This force produces potential energy $U(x)$ given by $U(x) = \alpha x^4$, where $\alpha = 1.20 \text{ J/m}^4$. What is the force (magnitude and direction) when the particle is at $x = -0.800$ m?

7.36 •• CALC An object moving in the xy-plane is acted on by a conservative force described by the potential-energy function $U(x, y) = \alpha(1/x^2 + 1/y^2)$, where α is a positive constant. Derive an expression for the force expressed in terms of the unit vectors $\hat{i}$ and $\hat{j}$.

7.37 •• CALC A small block with mass 0.0400 kg is moving in the xy-plane. The net force on the block is described by the potential-energy function $U(x, y) = (5.80 \text{ J/m}^2)x^2 - (3.60 \text{ J/m}^3)y^3$. What are the magnitude and direction of the acceleration of the block when it is at the point $x = 0.300$ m, $y = 0.600$ m?

Section 7.5 Energy Diagrams

7.38 • A marble moves along the x-axis. The potential-energy function is shown in Fig. E7.38. (a) At which of the labeled x-coordinates is the force on the marble zero? (b) Which of the labeled x-coordinates is a position of stable equilibrium? (c) Which of the labeled x-coordinates is a position of unstable equilibrium?

Figure **E7.38**

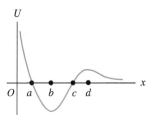

7.39 • CALC The potential energy of two atoms in a diatomic molecule is approximated by $U(r) = a/r^{12} - b/r^6$, where r is the spacing between atoms and a and b are positive constants. (a) Find the force $F(r)$ on one atom as a function of r. Draw two graphs: one of $U(r)$ versus r and one of $F(r)$ versus r. (b) Find the equilibrium distance between the two atoms. Is this equilibrium stable? (c) Suppose the distance between the two atoms is equal to the equilibrium distance found in part (b). What minimum energy must be added to the molecule to *dissociate* it—that is, to separate the two atoms to an infinite distance apart? This is called the *dissociation energy* of the molecule. (d) For the molecule CO, the equilibrium distance between the carbon and oxygen atoms is 1.13×10^{-10} m and the dissociation energy is 1.54×10^{-18} J per molecule. Find the values of the constants a and b.

PROBLEMS

7.40 •• Two blocks with different masses are attached to either end of a light rope that passes over a light, frictionless pulley suspended from the ceiling. The masses are released from rest, and the more massive one starts to descend. After this block has descended 1.20 m, its speed is 3.00 m/s. If the total mass of the two blocks is 15.0 kg, what is the mass of each block?

7.41 ••• At a construction site, a 65.0-kg bucket of concrete hangs from a light (but strong) cable that passes over a light, friction-free pulley and is connected to an 80.0-kg box on a horizontal roof (Fig. P7.41). The cable pulls horizontally on the box, and a 50.0-kg bag of gravel rests on top of the box. The coefficients of friction between the box and roof are shown. (a) Find the friction force on the bag of gravel and on the box. (b) Suddenly a worker picks up the bag of gravel. Use energy conservation to find the speed of the bucket after it has descended 2.00 m from rest. (You can check your answer by solving this problem using Newton's laws.)

Figure **P7.41**

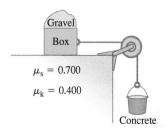

7.42 • A 2.00-kg block is pushed against a spring with negligible mass and force constant $k = 400$ N/m, compressing it 0.220 m. When the block is released, it moves along a frictionless, horizontal surface and then up a frictionless incline with slope 37.0° (Fig. P7.42). (a) What is the speed of the block as it slides along the horizontal surface after having left the spring? (b) How far does the block travel up the incline before starting to slide back down?

Figure **P7.42**

7.43 • A block with mass 0.50 kg is forced against a horizontal spring of negligible mass, compressing the spring a distance of 0.20 m (Fig. P7.43). When released, the block moves on a horizontal tabletop for 1.00 m before coming to rest. The spring constant k is 100 N/m. What is the coefficient of kinetic friction μ_k between the block and the tabletop?

Figure **P7.43**

7.44 • On a horizontal surface, a crate with mass 50.0 kg is placed against a spring that stores 360 J of energy. The spring is released, and the crate slides 5.60 m before coming to rest. What is the speed of the crate when it is 2.00 m from its initial position?

7.45 ·· A 350-kg roller coaster starts from rest at point A and slides down the frictionless loop-the-loop shown in Fig. P7.45. (a) How fast is this roller coaster moving at point B? (b) How hard does it press against the track at point B?

Figure **P7.45**

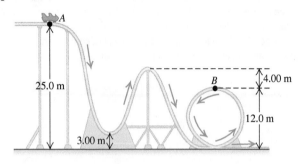

7.46 ·· CP **Riding a Loop-the-Loop.** A car in an amusement park ride rolls without friction around the track shown in Fig. P7.46. It starts from rest at point A at a height h above the bottom of the loop. Treat the car as a particle. (a) What is the minimum value of h (in terms of R) such that the car moves around the loop without falling off at the top (point B)? (b) If $h = 3.50R$ and $R = 20.0$ m, compute the speed, radial acceleration, and tangential acceleration of the passengers when the car is at point C, which is at the end of a horizontal diameter. Show these acceleration components in a diagram, approximately to scale.

Figure **P7.46**

7.47 ·· A 2.0-kg piece of wood slides on the surface shown in Fig. P7.47. The curved sides are perfectly smooth, but the rough horizontal bottom is 30 m long and has a kinetic friction coefficient of 0.20 with the wood. The piece of wood starts from rest 4.0 m above the rough bottom. (a) Where will this wood eventually come to rest? (b) For the motion from the initial release until the piece of wood comes to rest, what is the total amount of work done by friction?

Figure **P7.47**

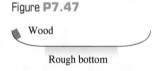

Rough bottom

7.48 ·· **Up and Down the Hill.** A 28-kg rock approaches the foot of a hill with a speed of 15 m/s. This hill slopes upward at a constant angle of 40.0° above the horizontal. The coefficients of static and kinetic friction between the hill and the rock are 0.75 and 0.20, respectively. (a) Use energy conservation to find the maximum height above the foot of the hill reached by the rock. (b) Will the rock remain at rest at its highest point, or will it slide back down the hill? (c) If the rock does slide back down, find its speed when it returns to the bottom of the hill.

7.49 ·· A 15.0-kg stone slides down a snow-covered hill (Fig. P7.49), leaving point A with a speed of 10.0 m/s. There is no friction on the hill between points A and B, but there is friction on the level ground at the bottom of the hill, between B and the wall. After entering the rough horizontal

Figure **P7.49**

region, the stone travels 100 m and then runs into a very long, light spring with force constant 2.00 N/m. The coefficients of kinetic and static friction between the stone and the horizontal ground are 0.20 and 0.80, respectively. (a) What is the speed of the stone when it reaches point B? (b) How far will the stone compress the spring? (c) Will the stone move again after it has been stopped by the spring?

7.50 ·· CP A 2.8-kg block slides over the smooth, icy hill shown in Fig. P7.50. The top of the hill is horizontal and 70 m higher than its base. What minimum speed must the block have at the base of the hill in order for it to pass over the pit at the far side of the hill?

Figure **P7.50**

7.51 ··· **Bungee Jump.** A bungee cord is 30.0 m long and, when stretched a distance x, it exerts a restoring force of magnitude kx. Your father-in-law (mass 95.0 kg) stands on a platform 45.0 m above the ground, and one end of the cord is tied securely to his ankle and the other end to the platform. You have promised him that when he steps off the platform he will fall a maximum distance of only 41.0 m before the cord stops him. You had several bungee cords to select from, and you tested them by stretching them out, tying one end to a tree, and pulling on the other end with a force of 380.0 N. When you do this, what distance will the bungee cord that you should select have stretched?

7.52 ·· **Ski Jump Ramp.** You are designing a ski jump ramp for the next Winter Olympics. You need to calculate the vertical height h from the starting gate to the bottom of the ramp. The skiers push off hard with their ski poles at the start, just above the starting gate, so they typically have a speed of 2.0 m/s as they reach the gate. For safety, the skiers should have a speed no higher than 30.0 m/s when they reach the bottom of the ramp. You determine that for a 85.0-kg skier with good form, friction and air resistance will do total work of magnitude 4000 J on him during his run down the ramp. What is the maximum height h for which the maximum safe speed will not be exceeded?

7.53 ··· The Great Sandini is a 60-kg circus performer who is shot from a cannon (actually a spring gun). You don't find many men of his caliber, so you help him design a new gun. This new gun has a very large spring with a very small mass and a force constant of 1100 N/m that he will compress with a force of 4400 N. The inside of the gun barrel is coated with Teflon, so the average friction force will be only 40 N during the 4.0 m he moves in the barrel. At what speed will he emerge from the end of the barrel, 2.5 m above his initial rest position?

7.54 ··· You are designing a delivery ramp for crates containing exercise equipment. The 1470-N crates will move at 1.8 m/s at the top of a ramp that slopes downward at 22.0°. The ramp exerts a 550-N kinetic friction force on each crate, and the maximum static friction force also has this value. Each crate will compress a spring at the bottom of the ramp and will come to rest after traveling a total distance of 8.0 m along the ramp. Once stopped, a crate must not rebound back up the ramp. Calculate the force constant of the spring that will be needed in order to meet the design criteria.

7.55 ·· A system of two paint buckets connected by a lightweight rope is released from rest with the 12.0-kg bucket 2.00 m above the floor (Fig. P7.55). Use the principle of conservation of energy to find the speed with which this bucket strikes the floor. You can ignore friction and the mass of the pulley.

Figure **P7.55**

t	x	y	v_x	v_y
0	0	0	30.0 m/s	40.0 m/s
3.05 s	70.2 m	53.6 m	18.6 m/s	0
6.59 s	124.4 m	0	11.9 m/s	−28.7 m/s

(a) How much work was done by the air on the baseball as it moved from its initial position to its maximum height? (b) How much work was done by the air on the baseball as it moved from its maximum height back to the starting elevation? (c) Explain why the magnitude of the answer in part (b) is smaller than the magnitude of the answer in part (a).

7.61 •• **Down the Pole.** A fireman of mass m slides a distance d down a pole. He starts from rest. He moves as fast at the bottom as if he had stepped off a platform a distance $h \leq d$ above the ground and descended with negligible air resistance. (a) What average friction force did the fireman exert on the pole? Does your answer make sense in the special cases of $h = d$ and $h = 0$? (b) Find a numerical value for the average friction force a 75-kg fireman exerts, for $d = 2.5$ m and $h = 1.0$ m. (c) In terms of g, h, and d, what is the speed of the fireman when he is a distance y above the bottom of the pole?

7.62 •• A 60.0-kg skier starts from rest at the top of a ski slope 65.0 m high. (a) If frictional forces do -10.5 kJ of work on her as she descends, how fast is she going at the bottom of the slope? (b) Now moving horizontally, the skier crosses a patch of soft snow, where $\mu_k = 0.20$. If the patch is 82.0 m wide and the average force of air resistance on the skier is 160 N, how fast is she going after crossing the patch? (c) The skier hits a snowdrift and penetrates 2.5 m into it before coming to a stop. What is the average force exerted on her by the snowdrift as it stops her?

7.56 •• A 1500-kg rocket is to be launched with an initial upward speed of 50.0 m/s. In order to assist its engines, the engineers will start it from rest on a ramp that rises 53° above the horizontal (Fig. P7.56). At the bottom, the ramp turns upward and launches the rocket vertically. The engines provide a constant forward thrust of 2000 N, and friction with

Figure **P7.56**

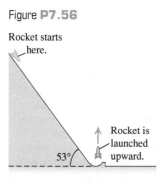

Rocket starts here.

Rocket is launched upward.

53°

the ramp surface is a constant 500 N. How far from the base of the ramp should the rocket start, as measured along the surface of the ramp?

7.57 • **Legal Physics.** In an auto accident, a car hit a pedestrian and the driver then slammed on the brakes to stop the car. During the subsequent trial, the driver's lawyer claimed that he was obeying the posted 35-mph speed limit, but that the legal speed was too high to allow him to see and react to the pedestrian in time. You have been called in as the state's expert witness. Your investigation of the accident found that the skid marks made while the brakes were applied were 280 ft long, and the tread on the tires produced a coefficient of kinetic friction of 0.30 with the road. (a) In your testimony in court, will you say that the driver was obeying the posted speed? You must be able to back up your conclusion with clear reasoning because one of the lawyers will surely cross-examine you. (b) If the driver's speeding ticket were $10 for each mile per hour he was driving above the posted speed limit, would he have to pay a fine? If so, how much would it be?

7.58 ••• A wooden rod of negligible mass and length 80.0 cm is pivoted about a horizontal axis through its center. A white rat with mass 0.500 kg clings to one end of the stick, and a mouse with mass 0.200 kg clings to the other end. The system is released from rest with the rod horizontal. If the animals can manage to hold on, what are their speeds as the rod swings through a vertical position?

7.59 •• **CP** A 0.300-kg potato is tied to a string with length 2.50 m, and the other end of the string is tied to a rigid support. The potato is held straight out horizontally from the point of support, with the string pulled taut, and is then released. (a) What is the speed of the potato at the lowest point of its motion? (b) What is the tension in the string at this point?

7.60 •• These data are from a computer simulation for a batted baseball with mass 0.145 kg, including air resistance:

7.63 • **CP** A skier starts at the top of a very large, frictionless snowball, with a very small initial speed, and skis straight down the side (Fig. P7.63). At what point does she lose contact with the snowball and fly off at a tangent? That is, at the instant she loses contact with the snowball, what angle α does a radial line from the center of the snowball to the skier make with the vertical?

Figure **P7.63**

α

7.64 •• A ball is thrown upward with an initial velocity of 15 m/s at an angle of 60.0° above the horizontal. Use energy conservation to find the ball's greatest height above the ground.

7.65 •• In a truck-loading station at a post office, a small 0.200-kg package is released from rest at point A on a track that is one-quarter of a circle with radius 1.60 m (Fig. P7.65). The size of the package is much less than 1.60 m, so the package can be treated as a particle. It slides down the track and reaches point B with a speed of 4.80 m/s. From point B, it slides on a level surface a distance of

Figure **P7.65**

A

$R = 1.60$ m

$m = 0.200$ kg

3.00 m

B C

3.00 m to point C, where it comes to rest. (a) What is the coefficient of kinetic friction on the horizontal surface? (b) How much work is done on the package by friction as it slides down the circular arc from A to B?

7.66 ••• A truck with mass m has a brake failure while going down an icy mountain road of constant downward slope angle α (Fig. P7.66). Initially the truck is moving downhill at speed v_0. After careening downhill a distance L with negligible friction, the truck driver steers the runaway vehicle onto a runaway truck ramp of constant upward slope angle β. The truck ramp has a soft sand surface for which the coefficient of rolling friction is μ_r. What is the distance that the truck moves up the ramp before coming to a halt? Solve using energy methods.

Figure **P7.66**

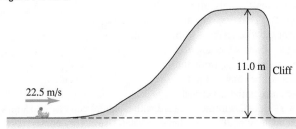

7.67 •• **CALC** A certain spring is found *not* to obey Hooke's law; it exerts a restoring force $F_x(x) = -\alpha x - \beta x^2$ if it is stretched or compressed, where $\alpha = 60.0 \text{ N/m}$ and $\beta = 18.0 \text{ N/m}^2$. The mass of the spring is negligible. (a) Calculate the potential-energy function $U(x)$ for this spring. Let $U = 0$ when $x = 0$. (b) An object with mass 0.900 kg on a frictionless, horizontal surface is attached to this spring, pulled a distance 1.00 m to the right (the $+x$-direction) to stretch the spring, and released. What is the speed of the object when it is 0.50 m to the right of the $x = 0$ equilibrium position?

7.68 •• **CP** A sled with rider having a combined mass of 125 kg travels over the perfectly smooth icy hill shown in Fig. 7.68. How far does the sled land from the foot of the cliff?

Figure **P7.68**

7.69 •• A 0.150-kg block of ice is placed against a horizontal, compressed spring mounted on a horizontal tabletop that is 1.20 m above the floor. The spring has force constant 1900 N/m and is initially compressed 0.045 m. The mass of the spring is negligible. The spring is released, and the block slides along the table, goes off the edge, and travels to the floor. If there is negligible friction between the block of ice and the tabletop, what is the speed of the block of ice when it reaches the floor?

7.70 •• A 3.00-kg block is connected to two ideal horizontal springs having force constants $k_1 = 25.0 \text{ N/cm}$ and $k_2 = 20.0 \text{ N/cm}$ (Fig. P7.70). The

Figure **P7.70**

system is initially in equilibrium on a horizontal, frictionless surface. The block is now pushed 15.0 cm to the right and released

from rest. (a) What is the maximum speed of the block? Where in the motion does the maximum speed occur? (b) What is the maximum compression of spring 1?

7.71 •• An experimental apparatus with mass m is placed on a vertical spring of negligible mass and pushed down until the spring is compressed a distance x. The apparatus is then released and reaches its maximum height at a distance h above the point where it is released. The apparatus is not attached to the spring, and at its maximum height it is no longer in contact with the spring. The maximum magnitude of acceleration the apparatus can have without being damaged is a, where $a > g$. (a) What should the force constant of the spring be? (b) What distance x must the spring be compressed initially?

7.72 •• If a fish is attached to a vertical spring and slowly lowered to its equilibrium position, it is found to stretch the spring by an amount d. If the same fish is attached to the end of the unstretched spring and then allowed to fall from rest, through what maximum distance does it stretch the spring? (*Hint:* Calculate the force constant of the spring in terms of the distance d and the mass m of the fish.)

7.73 ••• **CALC** A 3.00-kg fish is attached to the lower end of a vertical spring that has negligible mass and force constant 900 N/m. The spring initially is neither stretched nor compressed. The fish is released from rest. (a) What is its speed after it has descended 0.0500 m from its initial position? (b) What is the maximum speed of the fish as it descends?

7.74 •• A basket of negligible weight hangs from a vertical spring scale of force constant 1500 N/m. (a) If you suddenly put a 3.0-kg adobe brick in the basket, find the maximum distance that the spring will stretch. (b) If, instead, you release the brick from 1.0 m above the basket, by how much will the spring stretch at its maximum elongation?

7.75 • A 0.500-kg block, attached to a spring with length 0.60 m and force constant 40.0 N/m, is at rest with the back of the block at point A on a frictionless, horizontal air table (Fig. P7.75). The mass of the spring is negligible. You move the block to the right along the surface by pulling with a constant 20.0-N horizontal force. (a) What is the block's speed when the back of the block reaches point B, which is 0.25 m to the right of point A? (b) When the back of the block reaches point B, you let go of the block. In the subsequent motion, how close does the block get to the wall where the left end of the spring is attached?

Figure **P7.75**

7.76 •• **Fraternity Physics.** The brothers of Iota Eta Pi fraternity build a platform, supported at all four corners by vertical springs, in the basement of their frat house. A brave fraternity brother wearing a football helmet stands in the middle of the platform; his weight compresses the springs by 0.18 m. Then four of his fraternity brothers, pushing down at the corners of the platform, compress the springs another 0.53 m until the top of the brave brother's helmet is 0.90 m below the basement ceiling. They then simultaneously release the platform. You can ignore the masses of the springs and platform. (a) When the dust clears, the fraternity asks you to calculate their fraternity brother's speed just before his helmet hit the flimsy ceiling. (b) Without the ceiling, how high would he have gone? (c) In discussing their probation, the dean of students suggests that the next time they try this, they do it outdoors on another planet. Would the answer to part (b) be the same if this stunt were performed on a planet with a different value of g? Assume that the fraternity brothers push the platform down 0.53 m as before. Explain your reasoning.

7.77 ••• **CP** A small block with mass 0.0500 kg slides in a vertical circle of radius $R = 0.800$ m on the inside of a circular track. There is no friction between the track and the block. At the bottom of the block's path, the normal force the track exerts on the block has magnitude 3.40 N. What is the magnitude of the normal force that the track exerts on the block when it is at the top of its path?

7.78 ••• **CP** A small block with mass 0.0400 kg slides in a vertical circle of radius $R = 0.500$ m on the inside of a circular track. During one of the revolutions of the block, when the block is at the bottom of its path, point A, the magnitude of the normal force exerted on the block by the track has magnitude 3.95 N. In this same revolution, when the block reaches the top of its path, point B, the magnitude of the normal force exerted on the block has magnitude 0.680 N. How much work was done on the block by friction during the motion of the block from point A to point B?

7.79 •• A hydroelectric dam holds back a lake of surface area 3.0×10^6 m^2 that has vertical sides below the water level. The water level in the lake is 150 m above the base of the dam. When the water passes through turbines at the base of the dam, its mechanical energy is converted to electrical energy with 90% efficiency. (a) If gravitational potential energy is taken to be zero at the base of the dam, how much energy is stored in the top meter of the water in the lake? The density of water is 1000 kg/m^3. (b) What volume of water must pass through the dam to produce 1000 kilowatt-hours of electrical energy? What distance does the level of water in the lake fall when this much water passes through the dam?

7.80 •• **CALC** How much total energy is stored in the lake in Problem 7.79? As in that problem, take the gravitational potential energy to be zero at the base of the dam. Express your answer in joules and in kilowatt-hours. (*Hint:* Break the lake up into infinitesimal horizontal layers of thickness dy, and integrate to find the total potential energy.)

7.81 ••• A wooden block with mass 1.50 kg is placed against a compressed spring at the bottom of an incline of slope 30.0° (point A). When the spring is released, it projects the block up the incline. At point B, a distance of 6.00 m up the incline from A, the block is moving up the incline at 7.00 m/s and is no longer in contact with the spring. The coefficient of kinetic friction between the block and the incline is $\mu_k = 0.50$. The mass of the spring is negligible. Calculate the amount of potential energy that was initially stored in the spring.

7.82 •• **CP Pendulum.** A small rock with mass 0.12 kg is fastened to a massless string with length 0.80 m to form a pendulum. The pendulum is swinging so as to make a maximum angle of 45° with the vertical. Air resistance is negligible. (a) What is the speed of the rock when the string passes through the vertical position? (b) What is the tension in the string when it makes an angle of 45° with the vertical? (c) What is the tension in the string as it passes through the vertical?

7.83 ••• **CALC** A cutting tool under microprocessor control has several forces acting on it. One force is $\vec{F} = -\alpha xy^2\hat{\jmath}$, a force in the negative y-direction whose magnitude depends on the position of the tool. The constant is $\alpha = 2.50$ N/m^3. Consider the displacement of the tool from the origin to the point $x = 3.00$ m, $y = 3.00$ m. (a) Calculate the work done on the tool by $\vec{F}$ if this displacement is along the straight line $y = x$ that connects these two points. (b) Calculate the work done on the tool by $\vec{F}$ if the tool is first moved out along the x-axis to the point $x = 3.00$ m, $y = 0$ and then moved parallel to the y-axis to the point $x = 3.00$ m, $y = 3.00$ m. (c) Compare the work done by $\vec{F}$ along these two paths. Is $\vec{F}$ conservative or nonconservative? Explain.

7.84 • **CALC** (a) Is the force $\vec{F} = Cy^2\hat{\jmath}$, where C is a negative constant with units of N/m^2, conservative or nonconservative? Justify your answer. (b) Is the force $\vec{F} = Cy^2\hat{\imath}$, where C is a negative constant with units of N/m^2, conservative or nonconservative? Justify your answer.

7.85 •• **CALC** An object has several forces acting on it. One force is $\vec{F} = \alpha xy\hat{\imath}$, a force in the x-direction whose magnitude depends on the position of the object. (See Problem 6.98.) The constant is $\alpha = 2.00$ N/m^2. The object moves along the following path: (1) It starts at the origin and moves along the y-axis to the point $x = 0$, $y = 1.50$ m; (2) it moves parallel to the x-axis to the point $x = 1.50$ m, $y = 1.50$ m; (3) it moves parallel to the y-axis to the point $x = 1.50$ m, $y = 0$; (4) it moves parallel to the x-axis back to the origin. (a) Sketch this path in the xy-plane. (b) Calculate the work done on the object by $\vec{F}$ for each leg of the path and for the complete round trip. (c) Is $\vec{F}$ conservative or nonconservative? Explain.

7.86 • A particle moves along the x-axis while acted on by a single conservative force parallel to the x-axis. The force corresponds to the potential-energy function graphed in Fig. P7.86. The particle is released from rest at point A. (a) What is the direction of the force on the particle when it is at point A? (b) At point B? (c) At what value of x is the kinetic energy of the particle a maximum? (d) What is the force on the particle when it is at point C? (e) What is the largest value of x reached by the particle during its motion? (f) What value or values of x correspond to points of stable equilibrium? (g) Of unstable equilibrium?

Figure **P7.86**

CHALLENGE PROBLEM

7.87 ••• **CALC** A proton with mass m moves in one dimension. The potential-energy function is $U(x) = \alpha/x^2 - \beta/x$, where α and β are positive constants. The proton is released from rest at $x_0 = \alpha/\beta$. (a) Show that $U(x)$ can be written as

$$U(x) = \frac{\alpha}{x_0^2}\left[\left(\frac{x_0}{x}\right)^2 - \frac{x_0}{x}\right]$$

Graph $U(x)$. Calculate $U(x_0)$ and thereby locate the point x_0 on the graph. (b) Calculate $v(x)$, the speed of the proton as a function of position. Graph $v(x)$ and give a qualitative description of the motion. (c) For what value of x is the speed of the proton a maximum? What is the value of that maximum speed? (d) What is the force on the proton at the point in part (c)? (e) Let the proton be released instead at $x_1 = 3\alpha/\beta$. Locate the point x_1 on the graph of $U(x)$. Calculate $v(x)$ and give a qualitative description of the motion. (f) For each release point ($x = x_0$ and $x = x_1$), what are the maximum and minimum values of x reached during the motion?

Answers

Chapter Opening Question ?

The mallard's kinetic energy K remains constant because the speed remains the same, but the gravitational potential energy U_{grav} decreases as the mallard descends. Hence the total mechanical energy $E = K + U_{grav}$ decreases. The lost mechanical energy goes into warming the mallard's skin (that is, an increase in the mallard's internal energy) and stirring up the air through which the mallard passes (an increase in the internal energy of the air). See the discussion in Section 7.3.

Test Your Understanding Questions

7.1 Answer: (iii) The initial kinetic energy $K_1 = 0$, the initial potential energy $U_1 = mgy_1$, and the final potential energy $U_2 = mgy_2$ are the same for both blocks. Mechanical energy is conserved in both cases, so the final kinetic energy $K_2 = \frac{1}{2}mv_2^2$ is also the same for both blocks. Hence the speed at the right-hand end is the *same* in both cases!

7.2 Answer: (iii) The elevator is still moving downward, so the kinetic energy K is positive (remember that K can never be nega-

tive); the elevator is below point 1, so $y < 0$ and $U_{grav} < 0$; and the spring is compressed, so $U_{el} > 0$.

7.3 Answer: (iii) Because of friction in the turbines and between the water and turbines, some of the potential energy goes into raising the temperatures of the water and the mechanism.

7.4 Answers: (a) (iv), (b) (i) If $F_x = 0$ at a point, then the derivative of $U(x)$ must be zero at that point because $F_x = -dU(x)/dx$. However, this tells us absolutely nothing about the *value* of $U(x)$ at that point.

7.5 Answers: (iii) Figure 7.24b shows the x-component of force, F_x. Where this is maximum (most positive), the x-component of force and the x-acceleration have more positive values than at adjacent values of x.

Bridging Problem

Answers: (a) 1.06 m
(b) 1.32 m
(c) 20.7 J

11

EQUILIBRIUM AND ELASTICITY

LEARNING GOALS

By studying this chapter, you will learn:

• The conditions that must be satisfied for a body or structure to be in equilibrium.

• What is meant by the center of gravity of a body, and how it relates to the body's stability.

• How to solve problems that involve rigid bodies in equilibrium.

• How to analyze situations in which a body is deformed by tension, compression, pressure, or shear.

• What happens when a body is stretched so much that it deforms or breaks.

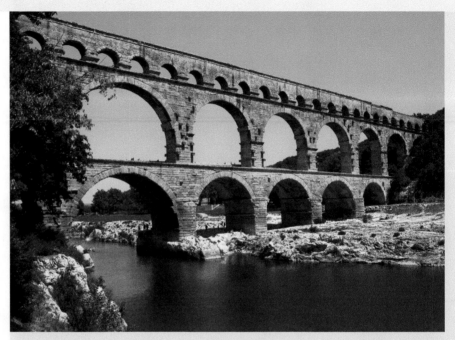

? This Roman aqueduct uses the principle of the arch to sustain the weight of the structure and the water it carries. Are the blocks that make up the arch being compressed, stretched, or a combination?

We've devoted a good deal of effort to understanding why and how bodies accelerate in response to the forces that act on them. But very often we're interested in making sure that bodies *don't* accelerate. Any building, from a multistory skyscraper to the humblest shed, must be designed so that it won't topple over. Similar concerns arise with a suspension bridge, a ladder leaning against a wall, or a crane hoisting a bucket full of concrete.

A body that can be modeled as a *particle* is in equilibrium whenever the vector sum of the forces acting on it is zero. But for the situations we've just described, that condition isn't enough. If forces act at different points on an extended body, an additional requirement must be satisfied to ensure that the body has no tendency to *rotate:* The sum of the *torques* about any point must be zero. This requirement is based on the principles of rotational dynamics developed in Chapter 10. We can compute the torque due to the weight of a body using the concept of center of gravity, which we introduce in this chapter.

Rigid bodies don't bend, stretch, or squash when forces act on them. But the rigid body is an idealization; all real materials are *elastic* and do deform to some extent. Elastic properties of materials are tremendously important. You want the wings of an airplane to be able to bend a little, but you'd rather not have them break off. The steel frame of an earthquake-resistant building has to be able to flex, but not too much. Many of the necessities of everyday life, from rubber bands to suspension bridges, depend on the elastic properties of materials. In this chapter we'll introduce the concepts of *stress, strain,* and *elastic modulus* and a simple principle called *Hooke's law* that helps us predict what deformations will occur when forces are applied to a real (not perfectly rigid) body.

11.1 Conditions for Equilibrium

We learned in Sections 4.2 and 5.1 that a particle is in *equilibrium*—that is, the particle does not accelerate—in an inertial frame of reference if the vector sum of all the forces acting on the particle is zero, $\sum \vec{F} = \mathbf{0}$. For an *extended* body, the equivalent statement is that the center of mass of the body has zero acceleration if the vector sum of all external forces acting on the body is zero, as discussed in Section 8.5. This is often called the **first condition for equilibrium.** In vector and component forms,

$$\sum \vec{F} = \mathbf{0}$$

$$\sum F_x = 0 \qquad \sum F_y = 0 \qquad \sum F_z = 0$$

(first condition for equilibrium)   (11.1)

A second condition for an extended body to be in equilibrium is that the body must have no tendency to *rotate*. This condition is based on the dynamics of rotational motion in exactly the same way that the first condition is based on Newton's first law. A rigid body that, in an inertial frame, is not rotating about a certain point has zero angular momentum about that point. If it is not to start rotating about that point, the rate of change of angular momentum must *also* be zero. From the discussion in Section 10.5, particularly Eq. (10.29), this means that the sum of torques due to all the external forces acting on the body must be zero. A rigid body in equilibrium can't have any tendency to start rotating about *any* point, so the sum of external torques must be zero about any point. This is the **second condition for equilibrium:**

$$\sum \vec{\tau} = \mathbf{0} \quad \text{about any point} \qquad \text{(second condition for equilibrium)} \quad (11.2)$$

The sum of the torques due to all external forces acting on the body, with respect to any specified point, must be zero.

In this chapter we will apply the first and second conditions for equilibrium to situations in which a rigid body is at rest (no translation or rotation). Such a body is said to be in **static equilibrium** (Fig. 11.1). But the same conditions apply to a rigid body in uniform *translational* motion (without rotation), such as an airplane in flight with constant speed, direction, and altitude. Such a body is in equilibrium but is not static.

Test Your Understanding of Section 11.1 Which situation satisfies both the first and second conditions for equilibrium? (i) a seagull gliding at a constant angle below the horizontal and at a constant speed; (ii) an automobile crankshaft turning at an increasing angular speed in the engine of a parked car; (iii) a thrown baseball that does not rotate as it sails through the air.

11.1 To be in static equilibrium, a body at rest must satisfy *both* conditions for equilibrium: It can have no tendency to accelerate as a whole or to start rotating.

(a) This body is in static equilibrium.

Equilibrium conditions:

First condition satisfied: Net force = 0, so body at rest has no tendency to start moving as a whole.

Second condition satisfied: Net torque about the axis = 0, so body at rest has no tendency to start rotating.

Axis of rotation (perpendicular to figure)

(b) This body has no tendency to accelerate as a whole, but it has a tendency to start rotating.

First condition satisfied: Net force = 0, so body at rest has no tendency to start moving as a whole.

Second condition NOT satisfied: There is a net clockwise torque about the axis, so body at rest will start rotating clockwise.

(c) This body has a tendency to accelerate as a whole but no tendency to start rotating.

First condition NOT satisfied: There is a net upward force, so body at rest will start moving upward.

Second condition satisfied: Net torque about the axis = 0, so body at rest has no tendency to start rotating.

11.2 Center of Gravity

In most equilibrium problems, one of the forces acting on the body is its weight. We need to be able to calculate the *torque* of this force. The weight doesn't act at a single point; it is distributed over the entire body. But we can always calculate the torque due to the body's weight by assuming that the entire force of gravity (weight) is concentrated at a point called the **center of gravity** (abbreviated "cg"). The acceleration due to gravity decreases with altitude; but if we can ignore this variation over the vertical dimension of the body, then the body's center of gravity is identical to its *center of mass* (abbreviated "cm"), which we defined in Section 8.5. We stated this result without proof in Section 10.2, and now we'll prove it.

First let's review the definition of the center of mass. For a collection of particles with masses m_1, m_2, ... and coordinates (x_1, y_1, z_1), (x_2, y_2, z_2), ..., the coordinates x_{cm}, y_{cm}, and z_{cm} of the center of mass are given by

$$x_{cm} = \frac{m_1 x_1 + m_2 x_2 + m_3 x_3 + \cdots}{m_1 + m_2 + m_3 + \cdots} = \frac{\sum_i m_i x_i}{\sum_i m_i}$$

$$y_{cm} = \frac{m_1 y_1 + m_2 y_2 + m_3 y_3 + \cdots}{m_1 + m_2 + m_3 + \cdots} = \frac{\sum_i m_i y_i}{\sum_i m_i} \quad \text{(center of mass)} \quad (11.3)$$

$$z_{cm} = \frac{m_1 z_1 + m_2 z_2 + m_3 z_3 + \cdots}{m_1 + m_2 + m_3 + \cdots} = \frac{\sum_i m_i z_i}{\sum_i m_i}$$

Also, x_{cm}, y_{cm}, and z_{cm} are the components of the position vector $\vec{r}_{cm}$ of the center of mass, so Eqs. (11.3) are equivalent to the vector equation

$$\vec{r}_{cm} = \frac{m_1 \vec{r}_1 + m_2 \vec{r}_2 + m_3 \vec{r}_3 + \cdots}{m_1 + m_2 + m_3 + \cdots} = \frac{\sum_i m_i \vec{r}_i}{\sum_i m_i} \quad (11.4)$$

11.2 The center of gravity (cg) and center of mass (cm) of an extended body.

The gravitational torque about O on a particle of mass m_i within the body is: $\vec{\tau}_i = \vec{r}_i \times \vec{w}_i$.

If $\vec{g}$ has the same value at all points on the body, the cg is identical to the cm.

The net gravitational torque about O on the entire body can be found by assuming that all the weight acts at the cg: $\vec{\tau} = \vec{r}_{cm} \times \vec{w}$.

Now consider the gravitational torque on a body of arbitrary shape (Fig. 11.2). We assume that the acceleration due to gravity $\vec{g}$ is the same at every point in the body. Every particle in the body experiences a gravitational force, and the total weight of the body is the vector sum of a large number of parallel forces. A typical particle has mass m_i and weight $\vec{w}_i = m_i \vec{g}$. If $\vec{r}_i$ is the position vector of this particle with respect to an arbitrary origin O, then the torque vector $\vec{\tau}_i$ of the weight $\vec{w}_i$ with respect to O is, from Eq. (10.3),

$$\vec{\tau}_i = \vec{r}_i \times \vec{w}_i = \vec{r}_i \times m_i \vec{g}$$

The *total* torque due to the gravitational forces on all the particles is

$$\vec{\tau} = \sum_i \vec{\tau}_i = \vec{r}_1 \times m_1 \vec{g} + \vec{r}_2 \times m_2 \vec{g} + \cdots$$

$$= (m_1 \vec{r}_1 + m_2 \vec{r}_2 + \cdots) \times \vec{g}$$

$$= \left(\sum_i m_i \vec{r}_i \right) \times \vec{g}$$

When we multiply and divide this by the total mass of the body,

$$M = m_1 + m_2 + \cdots = \sum_i m_i$$

we get

$$\vec{\tau} = \frac{m_1 \vec{r}_1 + m_2 \vec{r}_2 + \cdots}{m_1 + m_2 + \cdots} \times M\vec{g} = \frac{\sum_i m_i \vec{r}_i}{\sum_i m_i} \times M\vec{g}$$

The fraction in this equation is just the position vector $\vec{r}_{cm}$ of the center of mass, with components x_{cm}, y_{cm}, and z_{cm}, as given by Eq. (11.4), and $M\vec{g}$ is equal to the total weight $\vec{w}$ of the body. Thus

$$\vec{\tau} = \vec{r}_{cm} \times M\vec{g} = \vec{r}_{cm} \times \vec{w} \quad (11.5)$$

The total gravitational torque, given by Eq. (11.5), is the same as though the total weight $\vec{w}$ were acting on the position $\vec{r}_{cm}$ of the center of mass, which we also call the *center of gravity*. **If $\vec{g}$ has the same value at all points on a body, its center of gravity is identical to its center of mass.** Note, however, that the center of mass is defined independently of any gravitational effect.

While the value of $\vec{g}$ does vary somewhat with elevation, the variation is extremely slight (Fig. 11.3). Hence we will assume throughout this chapter that the center of gravity and center of mass are identical unless explicitly stated otherwise.

Finding and Using the Center of Gravity

We can often use symmetry considerations to locate the center of gravity of a body, just as we did for the center of mass. The center of gravity of a homogeneous sphere, cube, circular sheet, or rectangular plate is at its geometric center. The center of gravity of a right circular cylinder or cone is on its axis of symmetry.

For a body with a more complex shape, we can sometimes locate the center of gravity by thinking of the body as being made of symmetrical pieces. For example, we could approximate the human body as a collection of solid cylinders, with a sphere for the head. Then we can locate the center of gravity of the combination with Eqs. (11.3), letting $m_1, m_2, \ldots$ be the masses of the individual pieces and (x_1, y_1, z_1), $(x_2, y_2, z_2), \ldots$ be the coordinates of their centers of gravity.

When a body acted on by gravity is supported or suspended at a single point, the center of gravity is always at or directly above or below the point of suspension. If it were anywhere else, the weight would have a torque with respect to the point of suspension, and the body could not be in rotational equilibrium. Figure 11.4 shows how to use this fact to determine experimentally the location of the center of gravity of an irregular body.

Using the same reasoning, we can see that a body supported at several points must have its center of gravity somewhere within the area bounded by the supports. This explains why a car can drive on a straight but slanted road if the slant angle is relatively small (Fig. 11.5a) but will tip over if the angle is too steep (Fig. 11.5b). The truck in Fig. 11.5c has a higher center of gravity than the car and will tip over on a shallower incline. When a truck overturns on a highway and blocks traffic for hours, it's the high center of gravity that's to blame.

The lower the center of gravity and the larger the area of support, the more difficult it is to overturn a body. Four-legged animals such as deer and horses have a large area of support bounded by their legs; hence they are naturally stable and need only small feet or hooves. Animals that walk erect on two legs, such as humans and birds, need relatively large feet to give them a reasonable area of

11.3 The acceleration due to gravity at the bottom of the 452-m-tall Petronas Towers in Malaysia is only 0.014% greater than at the top. The center of gravity of the towers is only about 2 cm below the center of mass.

11.4 Finding the center of gravity of an irregularly shaped body—in this case, a coffee mug.

What is the center of gravity of this mug?

① Suspend the mug from any point. A vertical line extending down from the point of suspension passes through the center of gravity.

② Now suspend the mug from a different point. A vertical line extending down from this point intersects the first line at the center of gravity (which is inside the mug).

Center of gravity

11.5 In (a) the center of gravity is within the area bounded by the supports, and the car is in equilibrium. The car in (b) and the truck in (c) will tip over because their centers of gravity lie outside the area of support.

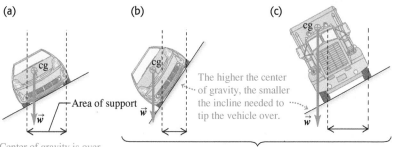

(a)

(b)

(c)

cg

Area of support

$\vec{w}$

cg

The higher the center of gravity, the smaller the incline needed to tip the vehicle over.

$\vec{w}$

cg

$\vec{w}$

Center of gravity is over the area of support: car is in equilibrium.

Center of gravity is outside the area of support: vehicle tips over.

Video Tutor Demo

support. If a two-legged animal holds its body approximately horizontal, like a chicken or the dinosaur *Tyrannosaurus rex,* it must perform a delicate balancing act as it walks to keep its center of gravity over the foot that is on the ground. A chicken does this by moving its head; *T. rex* probably did it by moving its massive tail.

Example 11.1 **Walking the plank**

A uniform plank of length $L = 6.0$ m and mass $M = 90$ kg rests on sawhorses separated by $D = 1.5$ m and equidistant from the center of the plank. Cousin Throckmorton wants to stand on the right-hand end of the plank. If the plank is to remain at rest, how massive can Throckmorton be?

SOLUTION

IDENTIFY and SET UP: To just balance, Throckmorton's mass m must be such that the center of gravity of the plank–Throcky system is directly over the right-hand sawhorse (Fig. 11.6). We take the origin at C, the geometric center and center of gravity of the plank, and take the positive x-axis horizontally to the right. Then the centers of gravity of the plank and Throcky are at $x_P = 0$ and $x_T = L/2 = 3.0$ m, respectively, and the right-hand sawhorse is at

11.6 Our sketch for this problem.

$x_S = D/2$. We'll use Eqs. (11.3) to locate the center of gravity x_{cg} of the plank–Throcky system.

EXECUTE: From the first of Eqs. (11.3),

$$x_{cg} = \frac{M(0) + m(L/2)}{M + m} = \frac{m}{M + m}\frac{L}{2}$$

We set $x_{cg} = x_S$ and solve for m:

$$\frac{m}{M + m}\frac{L}{2} = \frac{D}{2}$$

$$mL = (M + m)D$$

$$m = M\frac{D}{L - D} = (90 \text{ kg})\frac{1.5 \text{ m}}{6.0 \text{ m} - 1.5 \text{ m}} = 30 \text{ kg}$$

EVALUATE: As a check, let's repeat the calculation with the origin at the right-hand sawhorse. Now $x_S = 0$, $x_P = -D/2$, and $x_T = (L/2) - (D/2)$, and we require $x_{cg} = x_S = 0$:

$$x_{cg} = \frac{M(-D/2) + m[(L/2) - (D/2)]}{M + m} = 0$$

$$m = \frac{MD/2}{(L/2) - (D/2)} = M\frac{D}{L - D} = 30 \text{ kg}$$

The result doesn't depend on our choice of origin.

A 60-kg adult could stand only halfway between the right-hand sawhorse and the end of the plank. Can you see why?

11.7 At what point will the meter stick with rock attached be in balance?

Rock, mass m Meter stick, mass m

ActivPhysics 7.4: Two Painters on a Beam
ActivPhysics 7.5: Lecturing from a Beam

Test Your Understanding of Section 11.2 A rock is attached to the left end of a uniform meter stick that has the same mass as the rock. In order for the combination of rock and meter stick to balance atop the triangular object in Fig. 11.7, how far from the left end of the stick should the triangular object be placed? (i) less than 0.25 m; (ii) 0.25 m; (iii) between 0.25 m and 0.50 m; (iv) 0.50 m; (v) more than 0.50 m.

11.3 Solving Rigid-Body Equilibrium Problems

There are just two key conditions for rigid-body equilibrium: The vector sum of the forces on the body must be zero, and the sum of the torques about any point must be zero. To keep things simple, we'll restrict our attention to situations in which we can treat all forces as acting in a single plane, which we'll call the xy-plane. Then we can ignore the condition $\sum F_z = 0$ in Eqs. (11.1), and in Eq. (11.2) we need consider only the z-components of torque (perpendicular to the plane). The first and second conditions for equilibrium are then

$$\sum F_x = 0 \quad \text{and} \quad \sum F_y = 0 \qquad \text{(first condition for equilibrium, forces in } xy\text{-plane)}$$

$$\sum \tau_z = 0 \qquad \text{(second condition for equilibrium, forces in } xy\text{-plane)}$$

(11.6)

CAUTION **Choosing the reference point for calculating torques** In equilibrium problems, the choice of reference point for calculating torques in $\sum \tau_z$ is completely arbitrary. But once you make your choice, you must use the *same* point to calculate *all* the torques on a body. Choose the point so as to simplify the calculations as much as possible. ▮

The challenge is to apply these simple conditions to specific problems. Problem-Solving Strategy 11.1 is very similar to the suggestions given in Section 5.2 for the equilibrium of a particle. You should compare it with Problem-Solving Strategy 10.1 (Section 10.2) for rotational dynamics problems.

Problem-Solving Strategy 11.1 **Equilibrium of a Rigid Body**

IDENTIFY *the relevant concepts:* The first and second conditions for equilibrium ($\sum F_x = 0$, $\sum F_y = 0$, and $\sum \tau_z = 0$) are applicable to any rigid body that is not accelerating in space and not rotating.

SET UP *the problem* using the following steps:
1. Sketch the physical situation and identify the body in equilibrium to be analyzed. Sketch the body accurately; do *not* represent it as a point. Include dimensions.
2. Draw a free-body diagram showing all forces acting *on* the body. Show the point on the body at which each force acts.
3. Choose coordinate axes and specify their direction. Specify a positive direction of rotation for torques. Represent forces in terms of their components with respect to the chosen axes.
4. Choose a reference point about which to compute torques. Choose wisely; you can eliminate from your torque equation any force whose line of action goes through the point you

choose. The body doesn't actually have to be pivoted about an axis through the reference point.

EXECUTE *the solution* as follows:
1. Write equations expressing the equilibrium conditions. Remember that $\sum F_x = 0$, $\sum F_y = 0$, and $\sum \tau_z = 0$ are *separate* equations. You can compute the torque of a force by finding the torque of each of its components separately, each with its appropriate lever arm and sign, and adding the results.
2. To obtain as many equations as you have unknowns, you may need to compute torques with respect to two or more reference points; choose them wisely, too.

EVALUATE *your answer:* Check your results by writing $\sum \tau_z = 0$ with respect to a different reference point. You should get the same answers.

Example 11.2 **Weight distribution for a car**

An auto magazine reports that a certain sports car has 53% of its weight on the front wheels and 47% on its rear wheels. (That is, the total normal forces on the front and rear wheels are $0.53w$ and $0.47w$, respectively, where w is the car's weight.) The distance between the axles is 2.46 m. How far in front of the rear axle is the car's center of gravity?

11.8 Our sketches for this problem.

(a)

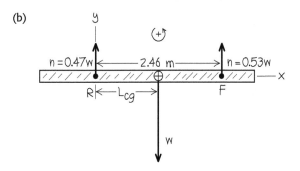

2.46 m

SOLUTION

IDENTIFY and SET UP: We can use the two conditions for equilibrium, Eqs. (11.6), for a car at rest (or traveling in a straight line at constant speed), since the net force and net torque on the car are zero. Figure 11.8 shows our sketch and a free-body diagram, including *x*- and *y*-axes and our convention that counterclockwise torques are positive. The weight w acts at the center of gravity. Our target variable is the distance L_{cg}, the lever arm of the weight with respect to the rear axle R, so it is wise to take torques with respect to R. The torque due to the weight is negative because it tends to cause a clockwise rotation about R. The torque due to the upward normal force at the front axle F is positive because it tends to cause a counterclockwise rotation about R.

EXECUTE: The first condition for equilibrium is satisfied (see Fig. 11.8b): $\sum F_x = 0$ because there are no *x*-components of force and $\sum F_y = 0$ because $0.47w + 0.53w + (-w) = 0$. We write the torque equation and solve for L_{cg}:

(b)

$$\sum \tau_R = 0.47w(0) - wL_{cg} + 0.53w(2.46 \text{ m}) = 0$$

$$L_{cg} = 1.30 \text{ m}$$

EVALUATE: The center of gravity is between the two supports, as it must be (see Section 11.2). You can check our result by writing the torque equation about the front axle F. You'll find that the center of gravity is 1.16 m behind the front axle, or (2.46 m) − (1.16 m) = 1.30 m in front of the rear axle.

Example 11.3 **Will the ladder slip?**

Sir Lancelot, who weighs 800 N, is assaulting a castle by climbing a uniform ladder that is 5.0 m long and weighs 180 N (Fig. 11.9a). The bottom of the ladder rests on a ledge and leans across the moat in equilibrium against a frictionless, vertical castle wall. The ladder makes an angle of 53.1° with the horizontal. Lancelot pauses one-third of the way up the ladder. (a) Find the normal and friction forces on the base of the ladder. (b) Find the minimum coefficient of static friction needed to prevent slipping at the base. (c) Find the magnitude and direction of the contact force on the base of the ladder.

SOLUTION

IDENTIFY and SET UP: The ladder–Lancelot system is stationary, so we can use the two conditions for equilibrium to solve part (a). In part (b), we need the relationship among the static friction force, the coefficient of static friction, and the normal force (see Section 5.3). In part (c), the contact force is the vector sum of the normal and friction forces acting at the base of the ladder, found in part (a). Figure 11.9b shows the free-body diagram, with x- and y-directions as shown and with counterclockwise torques taken to be positive. The ladder's center of gravity is at its geometric center. Lancelot's 800-N weight acts at a point one-third of the way up the ladder.

The wall exerts only a normal force n_1 on the top of the ladder. The forces on the base are an upward normal force n_2 and a static friction force f_s, which must point to the right to prevent slipping. The magnitudes n_2 and f_s are the target variables in part (a). From Eq. (5.6), these magnitudes are related by $f_s \leq \mu_s n_2$; the coefficient of static friction μ_s is the target variable in part (b).

EXECUTE: (a) From Eqs. (11.6), the first condition for equilibrium gives

$$\sum F_x = f_s + (-n_1) = 0$$
$$\sum F_y = n_2 + (-800\text{ N}) + (-180\text{ N}) = 0$$

These are two equations for the three unknowns n_1, n_2, and f_s. The second equation gives $n_2 = 980$ N. To obtain a third equation, we use the second condition for equilibrium. We take torques about point B, about which n_2 and f_s have no torque. The 53.1° angle creates a 3-4-5 right triangle, so from Fig. 11.9b the lever arm for the ladder's weight is 1.5 m, the lever arm for Lancelot's weight is 1.0 m, and the lever arm for n_1 is 4.0 m. The torque equation for point B is then

$$\sum \tau_B = n_1(4.0\text{ m}) - (180\text{ N})(1.5\text{ m})$$
$$- (800\text{ N})(1.0\text{ m}) + n_2(0) + f_s(0) = 0$$

Solving for n_1, we get $n_1 = 268$ N. We substitute this into the $\sum F_x = 0$ equation and get $f_s = 268$ N.

(b) The static friction force f_s cannot exceed $\mu_s n_2$, so the *minimum* coefficient of static friction to prevent slipping is

$$(\mu_s)_{\min} = \frac{f_s}{n_2} = \frac{268\text{ N}}{980\text{ N}} = 0.27$$

(c) The components of the contact force $\vec{F}_B$ at the base are the static friction force f_s and the normal force n_2, so

$$\vec{F}_B = f_s \hat{\imath} + n_2 \hat{\jmath} = (268\text{ N})\hat{\imath} + (980\text{ N})\hat{\jmath}$$

The magnitude and direction of $\vec{F}_B$ (Fig. 11.9c) are

$$F_B = \sqrt{(268\text{ N})^2 + (980\text{ N})^2} = 1020\text{ N}$$
$$\theta = \arctan\frac{980\text{ N}}{268\text{ N}} = 75°$$

EVALUATE: As Fig. 11.9c shows, the contact force $\vec{F}_B$ is *not* directed along the length of the ladder. Can you show that if $\vec{F}_B$ were directed along the ladder, there would be a net counterclockwise torque with respect to the top of the ladder, and equilibrium would be impossible?

As Lancelot climbs higher on the ladder, the lever arm and torque of his weight about B increase. This increases the values of n_1, f_s, and the required friction coefficient $(\mu_s)_{\min}$, so the ladder is more and more likely to slip as he climbs (see Problem 11.10). A simple way to make slipping less likely is to use a larger ladder angle (say, 75° rather than 53.1°). This decreases the lever arms with respect to B of the weights of the ladder and Lancelot and increases the lever arm of n_1, all of which decrease the required friction force.

If we had assumed friction on the wall as well as on the floor, the problem would be impossible to solve by using the equilibrium conditions alone. (Try it!) The difficulty is that it's no longer adequate to treat the body as being perfectly rigid. Another problem of this kind is a four-legged table; there's no way to use the equilibrium conditions alone to find the force on each separate leg.

11.9 (a) Sir Lancelot pauses a third of the way up the ladder, fearing it will slip. (b) Free-body diagram for the system of Sir Lancelot and the ladder. (c) The contact force at B is the superposition of the normal force and the static friction force.

Example 11.4 Equilibrium and pumping iron

Figure 11.10a shows a horizontal human arm lifting a dumbbell. The forearm is in equilibrium under the action of the weight $\vec{w}$ of the dumbbell, the tension $\vec{T}$ in the tendon connected to the biceps muscle, and the force $\vec{E}$ exerted on the forearm by the upper arm at the elbow joint. We neglect the weight of the forearm itself. (For clarity, the point A where the tendon is attached is drawn farther from the elbow than its actual position.) Given the weight w and the angle θ between the tension force and the horizontal, find T and the two components of $\vec{E}$ (three unknown scalar quantities in all).

SOLUTION

IDENTIFY and SET UP: The system is at rest, so we use the conditions for equilibrium. We represent $\vec{T}$ and $\vec{E}$ in terms of their components (Fig. 11.10b). We guess that the directions of E_x and E_y are as shown; the signs of E_x and E_y as given by our solution will tell us the actual directions. Our target variables are T, E_x, and E_y.

EXECUTE: To find T, we take torques about the elbow joint so that the torque equation does not contain E_x, E_y, or T_x:

$$\sum \tau_{\text{elbow}} = Lw - DT_y = 0$$

From this we find

$$T_y = \frac{Lw}{D} \quad \text{and} \quad T = \frac{Lw}{D\sin\theta}$$

To find E_x and E_y, we use the first conditions for equilibrium:

$$\sum F_x = T_x + (-E_x) = 0$$

$$E_x = T_x = T\cos\theta = \frac{Lw}{D\sin\theta}\cos\theta$$

$$= \frac{Lw}{D}\cot\theta = \frac{Lw}{D}\frac{D}{h} = \frac{Lw}{h}$$

$$\sum F_y = T_y + E_y + (-w) = 0$$

$$E_y = w - \frac{Lw}{D} = -\frac{(L-D)w}{D}$$

The negative sign for E_y tells us that it should actually point *down* in Fig. 11.10b.

EVALUATE: We can check our results for E_x and E_y by taking torques about points A and B, about both of which T has zero torque:

$$\sum \tau_A = (L-D)w + DE_y = 0 \quad \text{so} \quad E_y = -\frac{(L-D)w}{D}$$

$$\sum \tau_B = Lw - hE_x = 0 \quad \text{so} \quad E_x = \frac{Lw}{h}$$

As a realistic example, take $w = 200$ N, $D = 0.050$ m, $L = 0.30$ m, and $\theta = 80°$, so that $h = D\tan\theta = (0.050\text{ m})(5.67) = 0.28$ m. Using our results for T, E_x, and E_y, we find

$$T = \frac{Lw}{D\sin\theta} = \frac{(0.30\text{ m})(200\text{ N})}{(0.050\text{ m})(0.98)} = 1220\text{ N}$$

$$E_y = -\frac{(L-D)w}{D} = -\frac{(0.30\text{ m} - 0.050\text{ m})(200\text{ N})}{0.050\text{ m}}$$

$$= -1000\text{ N}$$

$$E_x = \frac{Lw}{h} = \frac{(0.30\text{ m})(200\text{ N})}{0.28\text{ m}} = 210\text{ N}$$

The magnitude of the force at the elbow is

$$E = \sqrt{E_x^2 + E_y^2} = 1020\text{ N}$$

The large values of T and E suggest that it was reasonable to neglect the weight of the forearm itself, which may be 20 N or so.

11.10 (a) The situation. (b) Our free-body diagram for the forearm. The weight of the forearm is neglected, and the distance D is greatly exaggerated for clarity.

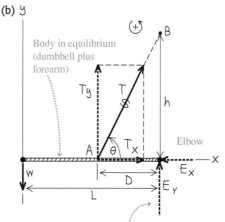

11.11 What are the tension in the diagonal cable and the force exerted by the hinge at P?

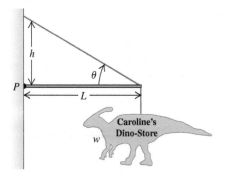

Test Your Understanding of Section 11.3 A metal advertising sign (weight w) for a specialty shop is suspended from the end of a horizontal rod of length L and negligible mass (Fig. 11.11). The rod is supported by a cable at an angle θ from the horizontal and by a hinge at point P. Rank the following force magnitudes in order from greatest to smallest: (i) the weight w of the sign; (ii) the tension in the cable; (iii) the vertical component of force exerted on the rod by the hinge at P.

11.4 Stress, Strain, and Elastic Moduli

The rigid body is a useful idealized model, but the stretching, squeezing, and twisting of real bodies when forces are applied are often too important to ignore. Figure 11.12 shows three examples. We want to study the relationship between the forces and deformations for each case.

For each kind of deformation we will introduce a quantity called **stress** that characterizes the strength of the forces causing the deformation, on a "force per unit area" basis. Another quantity, **strain,** describes the resulting deformation. When the stress and strain are small enough, we often find that the two are directly proportional, and we call the proportionality constant an **elastic modulus.** The harder you pull on something, the more it stretches; the more you squeeze it, the more it compresses. In equation form, this says

$$\frac{\text{Stress}}{\text{Strain}} = \text{Elastic modulus} \qquad \text{(Hooke's law)} \qquad (11.7)$$

The proportionality of stress and strain (under certain conditions) is called **Hooke's law,** after Robert Hooke (1635–1703), a contemporary of Newton. We used one form of Hooke's law in Sections 6.3 and 7.2: The elongation of an ideal spring is proportional to the stretching force. Remember that Hooke's "law" is not really a general law; it is valid over only a limited range. The last section of this chapter discusses what this limited range is.

Tensile and Compressive Stress and Strain

The simplest elastic behavior to understand is the stretching of a bar, rod, or wire when its ends are pulled (Fig. 11.12a). Figure 11.13 shows an object that initially has uniform cross-sectional area A and length l_0. We then apply forces of equal

11.12 Three types of stress. **(a)** Bridge cables under *tensile stress,* being stretched by forces acting at their ends. **(b)** A diver under *bulk stress,* being squeezed from all sides by forces due to water pressure. **(c)** A ribbon under *shear stress,* being deformed and eventually cut by forces exerted by the scissors.

magnitude $F_\perp$ but opposite directions at the ends (this ensures that the object has no tendency to move left or right). We say that the object is in **tension.** We've already talked a lot about tension in ropes and strings; it's the same concept here. The subscript $\perp$ is a reminder that the forces act perpendicular to the cross section.

We define the **tensile stress** at the cross section as the ratio of the force $F_\perp$ to the cross-sectional area A:

$$\text{Tensile stress} = \frac{F_\perp}{A} \qquad (11.8)$$

This is a *scalar* quantity because $F_\perp$ is the *magnitude* of the force. The SI unit of stress is the **pascal** (abbreviated Pa and named for the 17th-century French scientist and philosopher Blaise Pascal). Equation (11.8) shows that 1 pascal equals 1 newton per square meter (N/m^2):

$$1 \text{ pascal} = 1 \text{ Pa} = 1 \text{ N/m}^2$$

In the British system the logical unit of stress would be the pound per square foot, but the pound per square inch (lb/in.^{2} or psi) is more commonly used. The conversion factors are

$$1 \text{ psi} = 6895 \text{ Pa} \qquad \text{and} \qquad 1 \text{ Pa} = 1.450 \times 10^{-4} \text{ psi}$$

The units of stress are the same as those of *pressure,* which we will encounter often in later chapters. Air pressure in automobile tires is typically around $3 \times 10^5 \text{ Pa} = 300 \text{ kPa}$, and steel cables are commonly required to withstand tensile stresses of the order of 10^8 Pa.

The object shown in Fig. 11.13 stretches to a length $l = l_0 + \Delta l$ when under tension. The elongation Δl does not occur only at the ends; every part of the bar stretches in the same proportion. The **tensile strain** of the object is equal to the fractional change in length, which is the ratio of the elongation Δl to the original length l_0:

$$\text{Tensile strain} = \frac{l - l_0}{l_0} = \frac{\Delta l}{l_0} \qquad (11.9)$$

Tensile strain is stretch per unit length. It is a ratio of two lengths, always measured in the same units, and so is a pure (dimensionless) number with no units.

Experiment shows that for a sufficiently small tensile stress, stress and strain are proportional, as in Eq. (11.7). The corresponding elastic modulus is called **Young's modulus,** denoted by Y:

$$Y = \frac{\text{Tensile stress}}{\text{Tensile strain}} = \frac{F_\perp/A}{\Delta l/l_0} = \frac{F_\perp}{A}\frac{l_0}{\Delta l} \qquad \text{(Young's modulus)} \qquad (11.10)$$

Since strain is a pure number, the units of Young's modulus are the same as those of stress: force per unit area. Some typical values are listed in Table 11.1.

11.13 An object in tension. The net force on the object is zero, but the object deforms. The tensile stress (the ratio of the force to the cross-sectional area) produces a tensile strain (the elongation divided by the initial length). The elongation Δl is exaggerated for clarity.

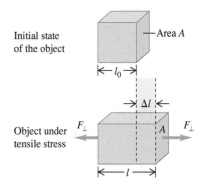

$$\text{Tensile stress} = \frac{F_\perp}{A} \qquad \text{Tensile strain} = \frac{\Delta l}{l_0}$$

Application Young's Modulus of a Tendon
The anterior tibial tendon connects your foot to the large muscle that runs along the side of your shinbone. (You can feel this tendon at the front of your ankle.) Measurements show that this tendon has a Young's modulus of 1.2×10^9 Pa, much less than for the solid materials listed in Table 11.1. Hence this tendon stretches substantially (up to 2.5% of its length) in response to the stresses experienced in walking and running.

Anterior tibial tendon ——

Table 11.1 Approximate Elastic Moduli

Material	Young's Modulus, Y (Pa)	Bulk Modulus, B (Pa)	Shear Modulus, S (Pa)
Aluminum	7.0×10^{10}	7.5×10^{10}	2.5×10^{10}
Brass	9.0×10^{10}	6.0×10^{10}	3.5×10^{10}
Copper	11×10^{10}	14×10^{10}	4.4×10^{10}
Crown glass	6.0×10^{10}	5.0×10^{10}	2.5×10^{10}
Iron	21×10^{10}	16×10^{10}	7.7×10^{10}
Lead	1.6×10^{10}	4.1×10^{10}	0.6×10^{10}
Nickel	21×10^{10}	17×10^{10}	7.8×10^{10}
Steel	20×10^{10}	16×10^{10}	7.5×10^{10}

11.14 An object in compression. The compressive stress and compressive strain are defined in the same way as tensile stress and strain (see Fig. 11.13), except that Δl now denotes the distance that the object contracts.

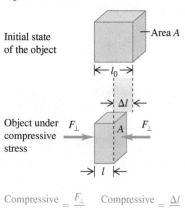

Initial state of the object

Area A

l_0

Δl

Object under compressive stress

$F_\perp$ A $F_\perp$

l

$$\text{Compressive stress} = \frac{F_\perp}{A} \qquad \text{Compressive strain} = \frac{\Delta l}{l_0}$$

(This table also gives values of two other elastic moduli that we will discuss later in this chapter.) A material with a large value of Y is relatively unstretchable; a large stress is required for a given strain. For example, the value of Y for cast steel (2×10^{11} Pa) is much larger than that for rubber (5×10^8 Pa).

When the forces on the ends of a bar are pushes rather than pulls (Fig. 11.14), the bar is in **compression** and the stress is a **compressive stress.** The **compressive strain** of an object in compression is defined in the same way as the tensile strain, but Δl has the opposite direction. Hooke's law and Eq. (11.10) are valid for compression as well as tension if the compressive stress is not too great. For many materials, Young's modulus has the same value for both tensile and compressive stresses. Composite materials such as concrete and stone are an exception; they can withstand compressive stresses but fail under comparable tensile stresses. Stone was the primary building material used by ancient civilizations such as the Babylonians, Assyrians, and Romans, so their structures had to be designed to avoid tensile stresses. Hence they used arches in doorways and bridges, where the weight of the overlying material compresses the stones of the arch together and does not place them under tension.

In many situations, bodies can experience both tensile and compressive stresses at the same time. As an example, a horizontal beam supported at each end sags under its own weight. As a result, the top of the beam is under compression, while the bottom of the beam is under tension (Fig. 11.15a). To minimize the stress and hence the bending strain, the top and bottom of the beam are given a large cross-sectional area. There is neither compression nor tension along the centerline of the beam, so this part can have a small cross section; this helps to keep the weight of the bar to a minimum and further helps to reduce the stress. The result is an I-beam of the familiar shape used in building construction (Fig. 11.15b).

11.15 (a) A beam supported at both ends is under both compression and tension. (b) The cross-sectional shape of an I-beam minimizes both stress and weight.

(a)

Top of beam is under compression.

Beam's centerline is under neither tension nor compression.

Bottom of beam is under tension.

(b)

The top and bottom of an I-beam are broad to minimize the compressive and tensile stresses.

The beam can be narrow near its centerline, which is under neither compression nor tension.

Example 11.5   **Tensile stress and strain**

A steel rod 2.0 m long has a cross-sectional area of 0.30 cm². It is hung by one end from a support, and a 550-kg milling machine is hung from its other end. Determine the stress on the rod and the resulting strain and elongation.

SOLUTION

IDENTIFY, SET UP, and EXECUTE: The rod is under tension, so we can use Eq. (11.8) to find the tensile stress; Eq. (11.9), with the value of Young's modulus Y for steel from Table 11.1, to find the corresponding strain; and Eq. (11.10) to find the elongation Δl:

$$\text{Tensile stress} = \frac{F_\perp}{A} = \frac{(550 \text{ kg})(9.8 \text{ m/s}^2)}{3.0 \times 10^{-5} \text{ m}^2} = 1.8 \times 10^8 \text{ Pa}$$

$$\text{Strain} = \frac{\Delta l}{l_0} = \frac{\text{Stress}}{Y} = \frac{1.8 \times 10^8 \text{ Pa}}{20 \times 10^{10} \text{ Pa}} = 9.0 \times 10^{-4}$$

$$\text{Elongation} = \Delta l = (\text{Strain}) \times l_0$$
$$= (9.0 \times 10^{-4})(2.0 \text{ m}) = 0.0018 \text{ m} = 1.8 \text{ mm}$$

EVALUATE: This small elongation, resulting from a load of over half a ton, is a testament to the stiffness of steel.

Bulk Stress and Strain

When a scuba diver plunges deep into the ocean, the water exerts nearly uniform pressure everywhere on his surface and squeezes him to a slightly smaller volume (see Fig. 11.12b). This is a different situation from the tensile and compressive stresses and strains we have discussed. The stress is now a uniform pressure on all sides, and the resulting deformation is a volume change. We use the terms **bulk stress** (or **volume stress**) and **bulk strain** (or **volume strain**) to describe these quantities.

If an object is immersed in a fluid (liquid or gas) at rest, the fluid exerts a force on any part of the object's surface; this force is *perpendicular* to the surface. (If we tried to make the fluid exert a force parallel to the surface, the fluid would slip sideways to counteract the effort.) The force $F_\perp$ per unit area that the fluid exerts on the surface of an immersed object is called the **pressure** p in the fluid:

$$p = \frac{F_\perp}{A} \quad \text{(pressure in a fluid)} \tag{11.11}$$

The pressure in a fluid increases with depth. For example, the pressure of the air is about 21% greater at sea level than in Denver (at an elevation of 1.6 km, or 1.0 mi). If an immersed object is relatively small, however, we can ignore pressure differences due to depth for the purpose of calculating bulk stress. Hence we will treat the pressure as having the same value at all points on an immersed object's surface.

Pressure has the same units as stress; commonly used units include 1 Pa ($=1 \text{ N/m}^2$) and 1 lb/in.^{2} (1 psi). Also in common use is the **atmosphere,** abbreviated atm. One atmosphere is the approximate average pressure of the earth's atmosphere at sea level:

$$1 \text{ atmosphere} = 1 \text{ atm} = 1.013 \times 10^5 \text{ Pa} = 14.7 \text{ lb/in.}^2$$

CAUTION **Pressure vs. force** Unlike force, pressure has no intrinsic direction: The pressure on the surface of an immersed object is the same no matter how the surface is oriented. Hence pressure is a *scalar* quantity, not a vector quantity.

Pressure plays the role of stress in a volume deformation. The corresponding strain is the fractional change in volume (Fig. 11.16)—that is, the ratio of the volume change ΔV to the original volume V_0:

$$\text{Bulk (volume) strain} = \frac{\Delta V}{V_0} \tag{11.12}$$

Volume strain is the change in volume per unit volume. Like tensile or compressive strain, it is a pure number, without units.

When Hooke's law is obeyed, an increase in pressure (bulk stress) produces a *proportional* bulk strain (fractional change in volume). The corresponding elastic modulus (ratio of stress to strain) is called the **bulk modulus,** denoted by B. When the pressure on a body changes by a small amount Δp, from p_0 to $p_0 + \Delta p$, and the resulting bulk strain is $\Delta V/V_0$, Hooke's law takes the form

$$B = \frac{\text{Bulk stress}}{\text{Bulk strain}} = -\frac{\Delta p}{\Delta V/V_0} \quad \text{(bulk modulus)} \tag{11.13}$$

We include a minus sign in this equation because an *increase* of pressure always causes a *decrease* in volume. In other words, if Δp is positive, ΔV is negative. The bulk modulus B itself is a positive quantity.

For small pressure changes in a solid or a liquid, we consider B to be constant. The bulk modulus of a *gas,* however, depends on the initial pressure p_0. Table 11.1 includes values of the bulk modulus for several solid materials. Its units, force per unit area, are the same as those of pressure (and of tensile or compressive stress).

Application **Bulk Stress on an Anglerfish**
The anglerfish (*Melanocetus johnsoni*) is found in oceans throughout the world at depths as great as 1000 m, where the pressure (that is, the bulk stress) is about 100 atmospheres. Anglerfish are able to withstand such stress because they have no internal air spaces, unlike fish found in the upper ocean where pressures are lower. The largest anglerfish are about 12 cm (5 in.) long.

11.16 An object under bulk stress. Without the stress, the cube has volume V_0; when the stress is applied, the cube has a smaller volume V. The volume change ΔV is exaggerated for clarity.

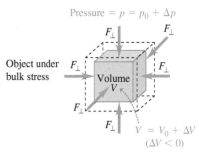

Table 11.2 Compressibilities of Liquids

Liquid	Compressibility, k	
	Pa^{-1}	atm^{-1}
Carbon disulfide	93×10^{-11}	94×10^{-6}
Ethyl alcohol	110×10^{-11}	111×10^{-6}
Glycerine	21×10^{-11}	21×10^{-6}
Mercury	3.7×10^{-11}	3.8×10^{-6}
Water	45.8×10^{-11}	46.4×10^{-6}

The reciprocal of the bulk modulus is called the **compressibility** and is denoted by k. From Eq. (11.13),

$$k = \frac{1}{B} = -\frac{\Delta V/V_0}{\Delta p} = -\frac{1}{V_0}\frac{\Delta V}{\Delta p} \quad \text{(compressibility)} \quad (11.14)$$

Compressibility is the fractional decrease in volume, $-\Delta V/V_0$, per unit increase Δp in pressure. The units of compressibility are those of *reciprocal pressure*, Pa^{-1} or atm^{-1}.

Table 11.2 lists the values of compressibility k for several liquids. For example, the compressibility of water is 46.4×10^{-6} atm^{-1}, which means that the volume of water decreases by 46.4 parts per million for each 1-atmosphere increase in pressure. Materials with small bulk modulus and large compressibility are easier to compress.

Example 11.6 Bulk stress and strain

A hydraulic press contains 0.25 m^3 (250 L) of oil. Find the decrease in the volume of the oil when it is subjected to a pressure increase $\Delta p = 1.6 \times 10^7$ Pa (about 160 atm or 2300 psi). The bulk modulus of the oil is $B = 5.0 \times 10^9$ Pa (about 5.0×10^4 atm) and its compressibility is $k = 1/B = 20 \times 10^{-6}$ atm^{-1}.

SOLUTION

IDENTIFY, SET UP, and EXECUTE: This example uses the ideas of bulk stress and strain. We are given both the bulk modulus and the compressibility, and our target variable is ΔV. Solving Eq. (11.13) for ΔV, we find

$$\Delta V = -\frac{V_0 \Delta p}{B} = -\frac{(0.25 \text{ m}^3)(1.6 \times 10^7 \text{ Pa})}{5.0 \times 10^9 \text{ Pa}}$$
$$= -8.0 \times 10^{-4} \text{ m}^3 = -0.80 \text{ L}$$

Alternatively, we can use Eq. (11.14) with the approximate unit conversions given above:

$$\Delta V = -kV_0 \Delta p = -(20 \times 10^{-6} \text{ atm}^{-1})(0.25 \text{ m}^3)(160 \text{ atm})$$
$$= -8.0 \times 10^{-4} \text{ m}^3$$

EVALUATE: The negative value of ΔV means that the volume decreases when the pressure increases. Even though the 160-atm pressure increase is large, the *fractional* change in volume is very small:

$$\frac{\Delta V}{V_0} = \frac{-8.0 \times 10^{-4} \text{ m}^3}{0.25 \text{ m}^3} = -0.0032 \quad \text{or} \quad -0.32\%$$

Shear Stress and Strain

The third kind of stress-strain situation is called *shear*. The ribbon in Fig. 11.12c is under **shear stress:** One part of the ribbon is being pushed up while an adjacent part is being pushed down, producing a deformation of the ribbon. Figure 11.17 shows a body being deformed by a shear stress. In the figure, forces of equal magnitude but opposite direction act *tangent* to the surfaces of opposite ends of the object. We define the shear stress as the force $F_\parallel$ acting tangent to the surface divided by the area A on which it acts:

$$\text{Shear stress} = \frac{F_\parallel}{A} \quad (11.15)$$

Shear stress, like the other two types of stress, is a force per unit area.

Figure 11.17 shows that one face of the object under shear stress is displaced by a distance x relative to the opposite face. We define **shear strain** as the ratio of the displacement x to the transverse dimension h:

$$\text{Shear strain} = \frac{x}{h} \quad (11.16)$$

In real-life situations, x is nearly always much smaller than h. Like all strains, shear strain is a dimensionless number; it is a ratio of two lengths.

11.17 An object under shear stress. Forces are applied tangent to opposite surfaces of the object (in contrast to the situation in Fig. 11.13, in which the forces act perpendicular to the surfaces). The deformation x is exaggerated for clarity.

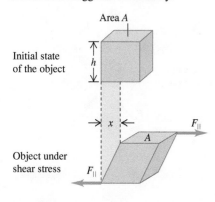

Shear stress $= \frac{F_\parallel}{A}$ Shear strain $= \frac{x}{h}$

If the forces are small enough that Hooke's law is obeyed, the shear strain is *proportional* to the shear stress. The corresponding elastic modulus (ratio of shear stress to shear strain) is called the **shear modulus,** denoted by S:

$$S = \frac{\text{Shear stress}}{\text{Shear strain}} = \frac{F_\parallel/A}{x/h} = \frac{F_\parallel}{A}\frac{h}{x} \qquad \text{(shear modulus)} \qquad (11.17)$$

with x and h defined as in Fig. 11.17.

Table 11.1 gives several values of shear modulus. For a given material, S is usually one-third to one-half as large as Young's modulus Y for tensile stress. Keep in mind that the concepts of shear stress, shear strain, and shear modulus apply to *solid* materials only. The reason is that *shear* refers to deforming an object that has a definite shape (see Fig. 11.17). This concept doesn't apply to gases and liquids, which do not have definite shapes.

| **Example 11.7** | **Shear stress and strain** |

Suppose the object in Fig. 11.17 is the brass base plate of an outdoor sculpture that experiences shear forces in an earthquake. The plate is 0.80 m square and 0.50 cm thick. What is the force exerted on each of its edges if the resulting displacement x is 0.16 mm?

SOLUTION

IDENTIFY and SET UP: This example uses the relationship among shear stress, shear strain, and shear modulus. Our target variable is the force $F_\parallel$ exerted parallel to each edge, as shown in Fig. 11.17. We'll find the shear strain using Eq. (11.16), the shear stress using Eq. (11.17), and $F_\parallel$ using Eq. (11.15). Table 11.1 gives the shear modulus of brass. In Fig. 11.17, h represents the 0.80-m length of each side of the plate. The area A in Eq. (11.15) is the product of the 0.80-m length and the 0.50-cm thickness.

EXECUTE: From Eq. (11.16),

$$\text{Shear strain} = \frac{x}{h} = \frac{1.6 \times 10^{-4} \text{ m}}{0.80 \text{ m}} = 2.0 \times 10^{-4}$$

From Eq. (11.17),

$$\text{Shear stress} = (\text{Shear strain}) \times S$$
$$= (2.0 \times 10^{-4})(3.5 \times 10^{10} \text{ Pa}) = 7.0 \times 10^{6} \text{ Pa}$$

Finally, from Eq. (11.15),

$$F_\parallel = (\text{Shear stress}) \times A$$
$$= (7.0 \times 10^{6} \text{ Pa})(0.80 \text{ m})(0.0050 \text{ m}) = 2.8 \times 10^{4} \text{ N}$$

EVALUATE: The shear force supplied by the earthquake is more than 3 tons! The large shear modulus of brass makes it hard to deform. Further, the plate is relatively thick (0.50 cm), so the area A is relatively large and a substantial force $F_\parallel$ is needed to provide the necessary stress $F_\parallel/A$.

Test Your Understanding of Section 11.4 A copper rod of cross-sectional area 0.500 cm^2 and length 1.00 m is elongated by 2.00×10^{-2} mm, and a steel rod of the same cross-sectional area but 0.100 m in length is elongated by 2.00×10^{-3} mm. (a) Which rod has greater tensile *strain*? (i) the copper rod; (ii) the steel rod; (iii) the strain is the same for both. (b) Which rod is under greater tensile *stress*? (i) the copper rod; (ii) the steel rod; (iii) the stress is the same for both.

11.5 Elasticity and Plasticity

Hooke's law—the proportionality of stress and strain in elastic deformations—has a limited range of validity. In the preceding section we used phrases such as "provided that the forces are small enough that Hooke's law is obeyed." Just what *are* the limitations of Hooke's law? We know that if you pull, squeeze, or twist *anything* hard enough, it will bend or break. Can we be more precise than that?

Let's look at tensile stress and strain again. Suppose we plot a graph of stress as a function of strain. If Hooke's law is obeyed, the graph is a straight line with a

11.18 Typical stress-strain diagram for a ductile metal under tension.

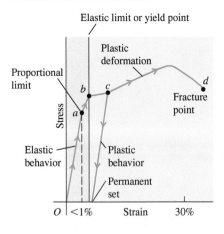

Elastic limit or yield point

Plastic deformation

Proportional limit

Fracture point

Elastic behavior

Plastic behavior

Permanent set

O | <1%   Strain   30%

11.19 Typical stress-strain diagram for vulcanized rubber. The curves are different for increasing and decreasing stress, a phenomenon called elastic hysteresis.

Stress-strain curve for increasing stress (stretching the object)

Stress-strain curve for decreasing stress (letting the object spring back)

O Strain   700%

Table 11.3 Approximate Breaking Stresses

Material	Breaking Stress (Pa or N/m^2)
Aluminum	2.2×10^8
Brass	4.7×10^8
Glass	10×10^8
Iron	3.0×10^8
Phosphor bronze	5.6×10^8
Steel	$5\text{–}20 \times 10^8$

slope equal to Young's modulus. Figure 11.18 shows a typical stress-strain graph for a metal such as copper or soft iron. The strain is shown as the *percent* elongation; the horizontal scale is not uniform beyond the first portion of the curve, up to a strain of less than 1%. The first portion is a straight line, indicating Hooke's law behavior with stress directly proportional to strain. This straight-line portion ends at point *a*; the stress at this point is called the *proportional limit.*

From *a* to *b*, stress and strain are no longer proportional, and Hooke's law is *not* obeyed. If the load is gradually removed, starting at any point between *O* and *b*, the curve is retraced until the material returns to its original length. The deformation is *reversible,* and the forces are conservative; the energy put into the material to cause the deformation is recovered when the stress is removed. In region *Ob* we say that the material shows *elastic behavior.* Point *b*, the end of this region, is called the *yield point;* the stress at the yield point is called the *elastic limit.*

When we increase the stress beyond point *b*, the strain continues to increase. But now when we remove the load at some point beyond *b*, say *c*, the material does not come back to its original length. Instead, it follows the red line in Fig. 11.18. The length at zero stress is now greater than the original length; the material has undergone an irreversible deformation and has acquired what we call a *permanent set.* Further increase of load beyond *c* produces a large increase in strain for a relatively small increase in stress, until a point *d* is reached at which *fracture* takes place. The behavior of the material from *b* to *d* is called *plastic flow* or *plastic deformation.* A plastic deformation is irreversible; when the stress is removed, the material does not return to its original state.

For some materials, such as the one whose properties are graphed in Fig. 11.18, a large amount of plastic deformation takes place between the elastic limit and the fracture point. Such a material is said to be *ductile.* But if fracture occurs soon after the elastic limit is passed, the material is said to be *brittle.* A soft iron wire that can have considerable permanent stretch without breaking is ductile, while a steel piano string that breaks soon after its elastic limit is reached is brittle.

Something very curious can happen when an object is stretched and then allowed to relax. An example is shown in Fig. 11.19, which is a stress-strain curve for vulcanized rubber that has been stretched by more than seven times its original length. The stress is not proportional to the strain, but the behavior is elastic because when the load is removed, the material returns to its original length. However, the material follows *different* curves for increasing and decreasing stress. This is called *elastic hysteresis.* The work done by the material when it returns to its original shape is less than the work required to deform it; there are nonconservative forces associated with internal friction. Rubber with large elastic hysteresis is very useful for absorbing vibrations, such as in engine mounts and shock-absorber bushings for cars.

The stress required to cause actual fracture of a material is called the *breaking stress,* the *ultimate strength,* or (for tensile stress) the *tensile strength.* Two materials, such as two types of steel, may have very similar elastic constants but vastly different breaking stresses. Table 11.3 gives typical values of breaking stress for several materials in tension. The conversion factor 6.9×10^8 Pa = 100,000 psi may help put these numbers in perspective. For example, if the breaking stress of a particular steel is 6.9×10^8 Pa, then a bar with a 1-in.^{2} cross section has a breaking strength of 100,000 lb.

Test Your Understanding of Section 11.5 While parking your car on a crowded street, you accidentally back into a steel post. You pull forward until the car no longer touches the post and then get out to inspect the damage. What does your rear bumper look like if the strain in the impact was (a) less than at the proportional limit; (b) greater than at the proportional limit, but less than at the yield point; (c) greater than at the yield point, but less than at the fracture point; and (d) greater than at the fracture point?

Conditions for equilibrium: For a rigid body to be in equilibrium, two conditions must be satisfied. First, the vector sum of forces must be zero. Second, the sum of torques about any point must be zero. The torque due to the weight of a body can be found by assuming the entire weight is concentrated at the center of gravity, which is at the same point as the center of mass if $\vec{g}$ has the same value at all points. (See Examples 11.1–11.4.)

$$\sum F_x = 0 \qquad \sum F_y = 0 \qquad \sum F_z = 0 \tag{11.1}$$

$$\sum \vec{\tau} = 0 \quad \text{about } any \text{ point} \tag{11.2}$$

$$\vec{r}_{cm} = \frac{m_1 \vec{r}_1 + m_2 \vec{r}_2 + m_3 \vec{r}_3 + \cdots}{m_1 + m_2 + m_3 + \cdots} \tag{11.4}$$

Stress, strain, and Hooke's law: Hooke's law states that in elastic deformations, stress (force per unit area) is proportional to strain (fractional deformation). The proportionality constant is called the elastic modulus.

$$\frac{\text{Stress}}{\text{Strain}} = \text{Elastic modulus} \tag{11.7}$$

Tensile and compressive stress: Tensile stress is tensile force per unit area, $F_\perp/A$. Tensile strain is fractional change in length, $\Delta l/l_0$. The elastic modulus is called Young's modulus Y. Compressive stress and strain are defined in the same way. (See Example 11.5.)

$$Y = \frac{\text{Tensile stress}}{\text{Tensile strain}} = \frac{F_\perp/A}{\Delta l/l_0} = \frac{F_\perp}{A}\frac{l_0}{\Delta l} \tag{11.10}$$

Bulk stress: Pressure in a fluid is force per unit area. Bulk stress is pressure change, Δp, and bulk strain is fractional volume change, $\Delta V/V_0$. The elastic modulus is called the bulk modulus, B. Compressibility, k, is the reciprocal of bulk modulus: $k = 1/B$. (See Example 11.6.)

$$p = \frac{F_\perp}{A} \tag{11.11}$$

$$B = \frac{\text{Bulk stress}}{\text{Bulk strain}} = -\frac{\Delta p}{\Delta V/V_0} \tag{11.13}$$

Shear stress: Shear stress is force per unit area, $F_\parallel/A$, for a force applied tangent to a surface. Shear strain is the displacement x of one side divided by the transverse dimension h. The elastic modulus is called the shear modulus, S. (See Example 11.7.)

$$S = \frac{\text{Shear stress}}{\text{Shear strain}} = \frac{F_\parallel/A}{x/h} = \frac{F_\parallel}{A}\frac{h}{x} \tag{11.17}$$

The limits of Hooke's law: The proportional limit is the maximum stress for which stress and strain are proportional. Beyond the proportional limit, Hooke's law is not valid. The elastic limit is the stress beyond which irreversible deformation occurs. The breaking stress, or ultimate strength, is the stress at which the material breaks.

BRIDGING PROBLEM **In Equilibrium and Under Stress**

A horizontal, uniform, solid copper rod has an original length l_0, cross-sectional area A, Young's modulus Y, bulk modulus B, shear modulus S, and mass m. It is supported by a frictionless pivot at its right end and by a cable a distance $l_0/4$ from its left end (Fig. 11.20). Both pivot and cable are attached so that they exert their forces uniformly over the rod's cross section. The cable makes an angle θ with the rod and compresses it. (a) Find the tension in the cable. (b) Find the magnitude and direction of the force exerted by the pivot on the right end of the rod. How does this magnitude compare to the cable tension? How does this angle compare to θ? (c) Find the change in length of the rod due to the stresses exerted by the cable and pivot on the rod. (d) By what factor would your answer in part (c) increase if the solid copper rod were twice as long but had the same cross-sectional area?

SOLUTION GUIDE

See MasteringPhysics® study area for a Video Tutor solution.

IDENTIFY and SET UP

1. Draw a free-body diagram for the rod. Be careful to place each force in the correct location.
2. Make a list of the unknown quantities, and decide which are the target variables.
3. What are the conditions that must be met so that the rod remains at rest? What kind of stress (and resulting strain) is involved? Use your answers to select the appropriate equations.

11.20 What are the forces on the rod? What are the stress and strain?

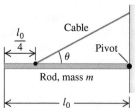

EXECUTE

4. Use your equations to solve for the target variables. (*Hint:* You can make the solution easier by carefully choosing the point around which you calculate torques.)
5. Use your knowledge of trigonometry to decide whether the pivot force or the cable tension has the greater magnitude, as well as to decide whether the angle of the pivot force is greater than, less than, or equal to θ.

EVALUATE

6. Check whether your answers are reasonable. Which force, the cable tension or the pivot force, holds up more of the weight of the rod? Does this make sense?

Problems

For instructor-assigned homework, go to MasteringPhysics®.

•, ••, •••: Problems of increasing difficulty. **CP**: Cumulative problems incorporating material from earlier chapters. **CALC**: Problems requiring calculus. **BIO**: Biosciences problems.

DISCUSSION QUESTIONS

Q11.1 Does a rigid object in uniform rotation about a fixed axis satisfy the first and second conditions for equilibrium? Why? Does it then follow that every particle in this object is in equilibrium? Explain.

Q11.2 (a) Is it possible for an object to be in translational equilibrium (the first condition) but *not* in rotational equilibrium (the second condition)? Illustrate your answer with a simple example. (b) Can an object be in rotational equilibrium yet *not* in translational equilibrium? Justify your answer with a simple example.

Q11.3 Car tires are sometimes "balanced" on a machine that pivots the tire and wheel about the center. Weights are placed around the wheel rim until it does not tip from the horizontal plane. Discuss this procedure in terms of the center of gravity.

Q11.4 Does the center of gravity of a solid body always lie within the material of the body? If not, give a counterexample.

Q11.5 In Section 11.2 we always assumed that the value of g was the same at all points on the body. This is *not* a good approximation if the dimensions of the body are great enough, because the value of g decreases with altitude. If this is taken into account, will the center of gravity of a long, vertical rod be above, below, or at its center of mass? Explain how this can be used to keep the long

axis of an orbiting spacecraft pointed toward the earth. (This would be useful for a weather satellite that must always keep its camera lens trained on the earth.) The moon is not exactly spherical but is somewhat elongated. Explain why this same effect is responsible for keeping the same face of the moon pointed toward the earth at all times.

Q11.6 You are balancing a wrench by suspending it at a single point. Is the equilibrium stable, unstable, or neutral if the point is above, at, or below the wrench's center of gravity? In each case give the reasoning behind your answer. (For rotation, a rigid body is in *stable* equilibrium if a small rotation of the body produces a torque that tends to return the body to equilibrium; it is in *unstable* equilibrium if a small rotation produces a torque that tends to take the body farther from equilibrium; and it is in *neutral* equilibrium if a small rotation produces no torque.)

Q11.7 You can probably stand flatfooted on the floor and then rise up and balance on your tiptoes. Why are you unable do it if your toes are touching the wall of your room? (Try it!)

Q11.8 You freely pivot a horseshoe from a horizontal nail through one of its nail holes. You then hang a long string with a weight at its bottom from the same nail, so that the string hangs vertically in front of the horseshoe without touching it. How do you know that the horseshoe's center of gravity is along the line behind the string? How can you locate the center of gravity by repeating the process at another nail hole? Will the center of gravity be within the solid material of the horseshoe?

Q11.9 An object consists of a ball of weight W glued to the end of a uniform bar also of weight W. If you release it from rest, with the bar horizontal, what will its behavior be as it falls if air resistance is negligible? Will it (a) remain horizontal; (b) rotate about its center of gravity; (c) rotate about the ball; or (d) rotate so that the ball swings downward? Explain your reasoning.

Q11.10 Suppose that the object in Question 11.9 is released from rest with the bar tilted at 60° above the horizontal with the ball at the upper end. As it is falling, will it (a) rotate about its center of gravity until it is horizontal; (b) rotate about its center of gravity until it is vertical with the ball at the bottom; (c) rotate about the ball until it is vertical with the ball at the bottom; or (d) remain at 60° above the horizontal?

Q11.11 Why must a water skier moving with constant velocity lean backward? What determines how far back she must lean? Draw a free-body diagram for the water skier to justify your answers.

Q11.12 In pioneer days, when a Conestoga wagon was stuck in the mud, people would grasp the wheel spokes and try to turn the wheels, rather than simply pushing the wagon. Why?

Q11.13 The mighty Zimbo claims to have leg muscles so strong that he can stand flat on his feet and lean forward to pick up an apple on the floor with his teeth. Should you pay to see him perform, or do you have any suspicions about his claim? Why?

Q11.14 Why is it easier to hold a 10-kg dumbbell in your hand at your side than it is to hold it with your arm extended horizontally?

Q11.15 Certain features of a person, such as height and mass, are fixed (at least over relatively long periods of time). Are the following features also fixed? (a) location of the center of gravity of the body; (b) moment of inertia of the body about an axis through the person's center of mass. Explain your reasoning.

Q11.16 During pregnancy, women often develop back pains from leaning backward while walking. Why do they have to walk this way?

Q11.17 Why is a tapered water glass with a narrow base easier to tip over than a glass with straight sides? Does it matter whether the glass is full or empty?

Q11.18 When a tall, heavy refrigerator is pushed across a rough floor, what factors determine whether it slides or tips?

Q11.19 If a metal wire has its length doubled and its diameter tripled, by what factor does its Young's modulus change?

Q11.20 Why is concrete with steel reinforcing rods embedded in it stronger than plain concrete?

Q11.21 A metal wire of diameter D stretches by 0.100 mm when supporting a weight W. If the same-length wire is used to support a weight three times as heavy, what would its diameter have to be (in terms of D) so it still stretches only 0.100 mm?

Q11.22 Compare the mechanical properties of a steel cable, made by twisting many thin wires together, with the properties of a solid steel rod of the same diameter. What advantages does each have?

Q11.23 The material in human bones and elephant bones is essentially the same, but an elephant has much thicker legs. Explain why, in terms of breaking stress.

Q11.24 There is a small but appreciable amount of elastic hysteresis in the large tendon at the back of a horse's leg. Explain how this can cause damage to the tendon if a horse runs too hard for too long a time.

Q11.25 When rubber mounting blocks are used to absorb machine vibrations through elastic hysteresis, as mentioned in Section 11.5, what becomes of the energy associated with the vibrations?

EXERCISES

Section 11.2 Center of Gravity

11.1 •• A 0.120-kg, 50.0-cm-long uniform bar has a small 0.055-kg mass glued to its left end and a small 0.110-kg mass glued to the other end. The two small masses can each be treated as point masses. You want to balance this system horizontally on a fulcrum placed just under its center of gravity. How far from the left end should the fulcrum be placed?

11.2 •• The center of gravity of a 5.00-kg irregular object is shown in Fig. E11.2. You need to move the center of gravity 2.20 cm to the left by gluing on a 1.50-kg mass, which will then be considered as part of the object. Where should the center of gravity of this additional mass be located?

Figure **E11.2**

11.3 • A uniform rod is 2.00 m long and has mass 1.80 kg. A 2.40-kg clamp is attached to the rod. How far should the center of gravity of the clamp be from the left-hand end of the rod in order for the center of gravity of the composite object to be 1.20 m from the left-hand end of the rod?

Section 11.3 Solving Rigid-Body Equilibrium Problems

11.4 • A uniform 300-N trapdoor in a floor is hinged at one side. Find the net upward force needed to begin to open it and the total force exerted on the door by the hinges (a) if the upward force is applied at the center and (b) if the upward force is applied at the center of the edge opposite the hinges.

11.5 •• **Raising a Ladder.** A ladder carried by a fire truck is 20.0 m long. The ladder weighs 2800 N and its center of gravity is at its center. The ladder is pivoted at one end (A) about a pin (Fig. E11.5); you can ignore the friction torque at the pin. The ladder is raised into position by a force applied by a hydraulic piston at C. Point C is 8.0 m from A, and the force $\vec{F}$ exerted by the piston makes an angle of 40° with the ladder. What magnitude must $\vec{F}$ have to just lift the ladder off the support bracket at B? Start with a free-body diagram of the ladder.

Figure **E11.5**

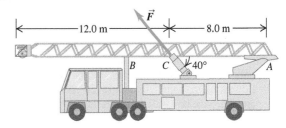

11.6 •• Two people are carrying a uniform wooden board that is 3.00 m long and weighs 160 N. If one person applies an upward force equal to 60 N at one end, at what point does the other person lift? Begin with a free-body diagram of the board.

11.7 •• Two people carry a heavy electric motor by placing it on a light board 2.00 m long. One person lifts at one end with a force of 400 N, and the other lifts the opposite end with a force of 600 N.

(a) What is the weight of the motor, and where along the board is its center of gravity located? (b) Suppose the board is not light but weighs 200 N, with its center of gravity at its center, and the two people each exert the same forces as before. What is the weight of the motor in this case, and where is its center of gravity located?

11.8 •• A 60.0-cm, uniform, 50.0-N shelf is supported horizontally by two vertical wires attached to the sloping ceiling (Fig. E11.8). A very small 25.0-N tool is placed on the shelf midway between the points where the wires are attached to it. Find the tension in each wire. Begin by making a free-body diagram of the shelf.

Figure **E11.8**

11.9 •• A 350-N, uniform, 1.50-m bar is suspended horizontally by two vertical cables at each end. Cable A can support a maximum tension of 500.0 N without breaking, and cable B can support up to 400.0 N. You want to place a small weight on this bar. (a) What is the heaviest weight you can put on without breaking either cable, and (b) where should you put this weight?

11.10 •• A uniform ladder 5.0 m long rests against a frictionless, vertical wall with its lower end 3.0 m from the wall. The ladder weighs 160 N. The coefficient of static friction between the foot of the ladder and the ground is 0.40. A man weighing 740 N climbs slowly up the ladder. Start by drawing a free-body diagram of the ladder. (a) What is the maximum frictional force that the ground can exert on the ladder at its lower end? (b) What is the actual frictional force when the man has climbed 1.0 m along the ladder? (c) How far along the ladder can the man climb before the ladder starts to slip?

11.11 • A diving board 3.00 m long is supported at a point 1.00 m from the end, and a diver weighing 500 N stands at the free end (Fig. E11.11). The diving board is of uniform cross section and weighs 280 N. Find (a) the force at the support point and (b) the force at the left-hand end.

Figure **E11.11**

11.12 • A uniform aluminum beam 9.00 m long, weighing 300 N, rests symmetrically on two supports 5.00 m apart (Fig. E11.12). A boy weighing 600 N starts at point A and walks toward the right. (a) In the same diagram construct two graphs showing the upward forces F_A and F_B exerted on the beam at points A and B, as functions of the coordinate x of the boy. Let 1 cm = 100 N vertically, and 1 cm = 1.00 m horizontally. (b) From your diagram, how far beyond point B can the boy walk before the beam tips? (c) How far

Figure **E11.12**

from the right end of the beam should support B be placed so that the boy can walk just to the end of the beam without causing it to tip?

11.13 • Find the tension T in each cable and the magnitude and direction of the force exerted on the strut by the pivot in each of the arrangements in Fig. E11.13. In each case let w be the weight of the suspended crate full of priceless art objects. The strut is uniform and also has weight w. Start each case with a free-body diagram of the strut.

Figure **E11.13**

(a)   (b)

11.14 • The horizontal beam in Fig. E11.14 weighs 150 N, and its center of gravity is at its center. Find (a) the tension in the cable and (b) the horizontal and vertical components of the force exerted on the beam at the wall.

Figure **E11.14**

11.15 •• **BIO** **Push-ups.** To strengthen his arm and chest muscles, an 82-kg athlete who is 2.0 m tall is doing push-ups as shown in Fig. E11.15. His center of mass is 1.15 m from the bottom of his feet, and the centers of

Figure **E11.15**

his palms are 30.0 cm from the top of his head. Find the force that the floor exerts on each of his feet and on each hand, assuming that both feet exert the same force and both palms do likewise. Begin with a free-body diagram of the athlete.

11.16 •• Suppose that you can lift no more than 650 N (around 150 lb) unaided. (a) How much can you lift using a 1.4-m-long wheelbarrow that weighs 80.0 N and whose center of gravity is 0.50 m from the center of the wheel (Fig. E11.16)? The center of gravity of the load carried in

Figure **E11.16**

the wheelbarrow is also 0.50 m from the center of the wheel. (b) Where does the force come from to enable you to lift more than 650 N using the wheelbarrow?

11.17 •• You take your dog Clea to the vet, and the doctor decides he must locate the little beast's center of gravity. It would be awkward to hang the pooch from the ceiling, so the vet must devise another method. He places Clea's front feet on one scale and her hind feet on another. The front scale reads 157 N, while the rear scale reads 89 N. The vet next measures Clea and finds that her rear feet are 0.95 m behind her front feet. How much does Clea weigh, and where is her center of gravity?

11.18 •• A 15,000-N crane pivots around a friction-free axle at its base and is supported by a cable making a 25° angle with the crane (Fig. E11.18). The crane is 16 m long and is not uniform, its center of gravity being 7.0 m from the axle as measured along the crane. The cable is attached 3.0 m from the upper end of the crane. When the crane is raised to 55° above the horizontal holding an 11,000-N pallet of bricks by a 2.2-m, very light cord, find (a) the tension in the cable and (b) the horizontal and vertical components of the force that the axle exerts on the crane. Start with a free-body diagram of the crane.

Figure **E11.18**

11.19 •• A 3.00-m-long, 240-N, uniform rod at the zoo is held in a horizontal position by two ropes at its ends (Fig. E11.19). The left rope makes an angle of 150° with the rod and the right rope makes an angle θ with the horizontal. A 90-N howler monkey (*Alouatta seniculus*) hangs motionless 0.50 m from the right end of the rod as he carefully studies you. Calculate the tensions in the two ropes and the angle θ. First make a free-body diagram of the rod.

Figure **E11.19**

11.20 •• A nonuniform beam 4.50 m long and weighing 1.00 kN makes an angle of 25.0° below the horizontal. It is held in position by a frictionless pivot at its upper right end and by a cable 3.00 m farther down the beam and perpendicular to it (Fig. E11.20). The center of gravity of the beam is 2.00 m down the beam from the pivot. Lighting equipment exerts a 5.00-kN downward force on the lower left end of the beam. Find the tension T in the cable and the horizontal and vertical components of the force exerted on the beam by the pivot. Start by sketching a free-body diagram of the beam.

Figure **E11.20**

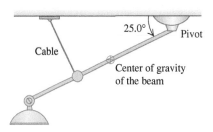

11.21 • **A Couple.** Two forces equal in magnitude and opposite in direction, acting on an object at two different points, form what is called a *couple.* Two antiparallel forces with equal magnitudes $F_1 = F_2 = 8.00$ *N* are applied to a rod as shown in Fig. E11.21. (a) What should the distance *l* between the forces be if they are to provide a net torque of 6.40 N·m about the left end of the rod? (b) Is the sense of this torque clockwise or counterclockwise? (c) Repeat parts (a) and (b) for a pivot at the point on the rod where $\vec{F}_2$ is applied.

Figure **E11.21**

11.22 •• **BIO A Good Workout.** You are doing exercises on a Nautilus machine in a gym to strengthen your deltoid (shoulder) muscles. Your arms are raised vertically and can pivot around the shoulder joint, and you grasp the cable of the machine in your hand 64.0 cm from your shoulder joint. The deltoid muscle is attached to the humerus 15.0 cm from the shoulder joint and makes a 12.0° angle with that bone (Fig. E11.22). If you have set the tension in the cable of the machine to 36.0 N on each arm, what is the tension in each deltoid muscle if you simply hold your outstretched arms in place? (*Hint:* Start by making a clear free-body diagram of your arm.)

Figure **E11.22**

11.23 •• **BIO Neck Muscles.** A student bends her head at 40.0° from the vertical while intently reading her physics book, pivoting the head around the upper vertebra (point P in Fig. E11.23). Her head has a mass of 4.50 kg (which is typical), and its center of mass is 11.0 cm from the pivot point P. Her neck muscles are 1.50 cm from point P, as measured *perpendicular* to these muscles. The neck itself and the vertebrae are held vertical. (a) Draw a free-body diagram of the student's head. (b) Find the tension in her neck muscles.

Figure **E11.23**

Section 11.4 Stress, Strain, and Elastic Moduli

11.24 · **BIO** **Biceps Muscle.** A relaxed biceps muscle requires a force of 25.0 N for an elongation of 3.0 cm; the same muscle under maximum tension requires a force of 500 N for the same elongation. Find Young's modulus for the muscle tissue under each of these conditions if the muscle is assumed to be a uniform cylinder with length 0.200 m and cross-sectional area 50.0 cm².

11.25 ·· A circular steel wire 2.00 m long must stretch no more than 0.25 cm when a tensile force of 400 N is applied to each end of the wire. What minimum diameter is required for the wire?

11.26 ·· Two circular rods, one steel and the other copper, are joined end to end. Each rod is 0.750 m long and 1.50 cm in diameter. The combination is subjected to a tensile force with magnitude 4000 N. For each rod, what are (a) the strain and (b) the elongation?

11.27 ·· A metal rod that is 4.00 m long and 0.50 cm² in cross-sectional area is found to stretch 0.20 cm under a tension of 5000 N. What is Young's modulus for this metal?

11.28 ·· **Stress on a Mountaineer's Rope.** A nylon rope used by mountaineers elongates 1.10 m under the weight of a 65.0-kg climber. If the rope is 45.0 m in length and 7.0 mm in diameter, what is Young's modulus for nylon?

11.29 ·· In constructing a large mobile, an artist hangs an aluminum sphere of mass 6.0 kg from a vertical steel wire 0.50 m long and 2.5×10^{-3} cm² in cross-sectional area. On the bottom of the sphere he attaches a similar steel wire, from which he hangs a brass cube of mass 10.0 kg. For each wire, compute (a) the tensile strain and (b) the elongation.

11.30 ·· A vertical, solid steel post 25 cm in diameter and 2.50 m long is required to support a load of 8000 kg. You can ignore the weight of the post. What are (a) the stress in the post; (b) the strain in the post; and (c) the change in the post's length when the load is applied?

11.31 ·· **BIO** **Compression of Human Bone.** The bulk modulus for bone is 15 GPa. (a) If a diver-in-training is put into a pressurized suit, by how much would the pressure have to be raised (in atmospheres) above atmospheric pressure to compress her bones by 0.10% of their original volume? (b) Given that the pressure in the ocean increases by 1.0×10^4 Pa for every meter of depth below the surface, how deep would this diver have to go for her bones to compress by 0.10%? Does it seem that bone compression is a problem she needs to be concerned with when diving?

11.32 · A solid gold bar is pulled up from the hold of the sunken RMS *Titanic*. (a) What happens to its volume as it goes from the pressure at the ship to the lower pressure at the ocean's surface? (b) The pressure difference is proportional to the depth. How many times greater would the volume change have been had the ship been twice as deep? (c) The bulk modulus of lead is one-fourth that of gold. Find the ratio of the volume change of a solid lead bar to that of a gold bar of equal volume for the same pressure change.

11.33 · **BIO** **Downhill Hiking.** During vigorous downhill hiking, the force on the knee cartilage (the medial and lateral meniscus) can be up to eight times body weight. Depending on the angle of descent, this force can cause a large shear force on the cartilage and deform it. The cartilage has an area of about 10 cm² and a shear modulus of 12 MPa. If the hiker plus his pack have a combined mass of 110 kg (not unreasonable), and if the maximum force at impact is 8 times his body weight (which, of course, includes the weight of his pack) at an angle of 12° with the cartilage (Fig. E11.33), through what angle (in degrees) will his knee cartilage be deformed? (Recall that the bone below the cartilage pushes upward with the same force as the downward force.)

Figure **E11.33**

11.34 ·· In the Challenger Deep of the Marianas Trench, the depth of seawater is 10.9 km and the pressure is 1.16×10^8 Pa (about 1.15×10^3 atm). (a) If a cubic meter of water is taken from the surface to this depth, what is the change in its volume? (Normal atmospheric pressure is about 1.0×10^5 Pa. Assume that k for seawater is the same as the freshwater value given in Table 11.2.) (b) What is the density of seawater at this depth? (At the surface, seawater has a density of 1.03×10^3 kg/m³.)

11.35 · A specimen of oil having an initial volume of 600 cm³ is subjected to a pressure increase of 3.6×10^6 Pa, and the volume is found to decrease by 0.45 cm³. What is the bulk modulus of the material? The compressibility?

11.36 ·· A square steel plate is 10.0 cm on a side and 0.500 cm thick. (a) Find the shear strain that results if a force of magnitude 9.0×10^5 N is applied to each of the four sides, parallel to the side. (b) Find the displacement x in centimeters.

11.37 ·· A copper cube measures 6.00 cm on each side. The bottom face is held in place by very strong glue to a flat horizontal surface, while a horizontal force F is applied to the upper face parallel to one of the edges. (Consult Table 11.1.) (a) Show that the glue exerts a force F on the bottom face that is equal but opposite to the force on the top face. (b) How large must F be to cause the cube to deform by 0.250 mm? (c) If the same experiment were performed on a lead cube of the same size as the copper one, by what distance would it deform for the same force as in part (b)?

11.38 · In lab tests on a 9.25-cm cube of a certain material, a force of 1375 N directed at 8.50° to the cube (Fig. E11.38) causes the cube to deform through an angle of 1.24°. What is the shear modulus of the material?

Figure **E11.38**

Section 11.5 Elasticity and Plasticity

11.39 ·· In a materials testing laboratory, a metal wire made from a new alloy is found to break when a tensile force of 90.8 N is applied perpendicular to each end. If the diameter of the wire is 1.84 mm, what is the breaking stress of the alloy?

11.40 · A 4.0-m-long steel wire has a cross-sectional area of 0.050 cm². Its proportional limit has a value of 0.0016 times its Young's modulus (see Table 11.1). Its breaking stress has a value of 0.0065 times its Young's modulus. The wire is fastened at its upper end and hangs vertically. (a) How great a weight can be hung from the wire without exceeding the proportional limit?

(b) How much will the wire stretch under this load? (c) What is the maximum weight that the wire can support?

11.41 •• **CP** A steel cable with cross-sectional area 3.00 cm² has an elastic limit of 2.40×10^8 Pa. Find the maximum upward acceleration that can be given a 1200-kg elevator supported by the cable if the stress is not to exceed one-third of the elastic limit.

11.42 •• A brass wire is to withstand a tensile force of 350 N without breaking. What minimum diameter must the wire have?

PROBLEMS

11.43 ••• A box of negligible mass rests at the left end of a 2.00-m, 25.0-kg plank (Fig. P11.43). The width of the box is 75.0 cm, and sand is to be distributed uniformly throughout it. The center of gravity of the nonuniform plank is 50.0 cm from the right end. What mass of sand should be put into the box so that the plank balances horizontally on a fulcrum placed just below its midpoint?

Figure **P11.43**

11.44 ••• A door 1.00 m wide and 2.00 m high weighs 280 N and is supported by two hinges, one 0.50 m from the top and the other 0.50 m from the bottom. Each hinge supports half the total weight of the door. Assuming that the door's center of gravity is at its center, find the horizontal components of force exerted on the door by each hinge.

11.45 ••• **Mountain Climbing.** Mountaineers often use a rope to lower themselves down the face of a cliff (this is called *rappelling*). They do this with their body nearly horizontal and their feet pushing against the cliff (Fig. P11.45). Suppose that an 82.0-kg climber, who is 1.90 m tall and has a center of gravity 1.1 m from his feet, rappels down a vertical cliff with his body raised 35.0° above the horizontal. He holds the rope 1.40 m from his feet, and it makes a 25.0° angle with the cliff face. (a) What tension does his rope need to support? (b) Find the horizontal and vertical components of the force that the cliff face exerts on the climber's feet. (c) What minimum coefficient of static friction is needed to prevent the climber's feet from slipping on the cliff face if he has one foot at a time against the cliff?

Figure **P11.45**

11.46 • Sir Lancelot rides slowly out of the castle at Camelot and onto the 12.0-m-long drawbridge that passes over the moat (Fig. P11.46). Unbeknownst to him, his enemies have partially severed the vertical cable holding up the front end of the bridge so that it will break under a tension of 5.80×10^3 N. The bridge has mass 200 kg and its center of gravity is at its center. Lancelot, his lance, his armor, and his horse together have a combined mass of 600 kg. Will the cable break before Lancelot reaches the end of the drawbridge? If so, how far from the castle end of the bridge will the center of gravity of the horse plus rider be when the cable breaks?

Figure **P11.46**

11.47 • Three vertical forces act on an airplane when it is flying at a constant altitude and with a constant velocity. These are the weight of the airplane, an aerodynamic force on the wing of the airplane, and an aerodynamic force on the airplane's horizontal tail. (The aerodynamic forces are exerted by the surrounding air and are reactions to the forces that the wing and tail exert on the air as the airplane flies through it.) For a particular light airplane with a weight of 6700 N, the center of gravity is 0.30 m in front of the point where the wing's vertical aerodynamic force acts and 3.66 m in front of the point where the tail's vertical aerodynamic force acts. Determine the magnitude and direction (upward or downward) of each of the two vertical aerodynamic forces.

11.48 •• A pickup truck has a wheelbase of 3.00 m. Ordinarily, 10,780 N rests on the front wheels and 8820 N on the rear wheels when the truck is parked on a level road. (a) A box weighing 3600 N is now placed on the tailgate, 1.00 m behind the rear axle. How much total weight now rests on the front wheels? On the rear wheels? (b) How much weight would need to be placed on the tailgate to make the front wheels come off the ground?

11.49 •• A uniform, 255-N rod that is 2.00 m long carries a 225-N weight at its right end and an unknown weight W toward the left end (Fig. P11.49). When W is placed 50.0 cm from the left end of the rod, the system just balances horizontally when the fulcrum is located 75.0 cm from the right end. (a) Find W. (b) If W is now moved 25.0 cm to the right, how far and in what direction must the fulcrum be moved to restore balance?

Figure **P11.49**

11.50 •• A uniform, 8.0-m, 1500-kg beam is hinged to a wall and supported by a thin cable attached 2.0 m from the free end of the beam, (Fig. P11.50). The beam is supported at an angle of 30.0° above the horizontal. (a) Draw a free-body diagram of the beam. (b) Find the tension in the cable. (c) How hard does the beam push inward on the wall?

Figure **P11.50**

11.51 •• You open a restaurant and hope to entice customers by hanging out a sign (Fig. P11.51). The uniform horizontal beam supporting the sign is 1.50 m long, has a mass of 12.0 kg, and is hinged to the wall. The sign itself is uniform with a mass of 28.0 kg and overall length of 1.20 m. The two wires supporting the sign are each 32.0 cm long, are 90.0 cm apart, and are equally spaced from the middle of the sign. The cable supporting the beam is 2.00 m long. (a) What minimum tension must your cable be able to support without having your sign come crashing down? (b) What minimum vertical force must the hinge be able to support without pulling out of the wall?

Figure **P11.51**

11.52 ••• A claw hammer is used to pull a nail out of a board (Fig. P11.52). The nail is at an angle of 60° to the board, and a force $\vec{F}_1$ of magnitude 400 N applied to the nail is required to pull it from the board. The hammer head contacts the board at point A, which is 0.080 m from where the nail enters the board. A horizontal force $\vec{F}_2$ is applied to the hammer handle at a distance of 0.300 m above the board. What magnitude of force $\vec{F}_2$ is required to apply the required 400-N force (F_1) to the nail? (You can ignore the weight of the hammer.)

Figure **P11.52**

11.53 • End A of the bar AB in Fig. P11.53 rests on a frictionless horizontal surface, and end B is hinged. A horizontal force $\vec{F}$ of magnitude 160 N is exerted on end A. You can ignore the weight of the bar. What are the horizontal and vertical components of the force exerted by the bar on the hinge at B?

Figure **P11.53**

11.54 • A museum of modern art is displaying an irregular 426-N sculpture by hanging it from two thin vertical wires, A and B, that are 1.25 m apart (Fig. P11.54). The center of gravity of this piece of art is located 48.0 cm from its extreme right tip. Find the tension in each wire.

Figure **P11.54**

11.55 •• **BIO** **Supporting a Broken Leg.** A therapist tells a 74-kg patient with a broken leg that he must have his leg in a cast suspended horizontally. For minimum discomfort, the leg should be supported by a vertical strap attached at the center of mass of the leg–cast system. (Fig. P11.55). In order to comply with these instructions, the patient consults a table of typical mass distributions and finds that both upper legs (thighs) together typically account for 21.5% of body weight and the center of mass of each thigh is 18.0 cm from the hip joint. The patient also reads that the two lower legs (including the feet) are 14.0% of body weight, with a center of mass 69.0 cm from the hip joint. The cast has a mass of 5.50 kg, and its center of mass is 78.0 cm from the hip joint. How far from the hip joint should the supporting strap be attached to the cast?

Figure **P11.55**

11.56 • **A Truck on a Drawbridge.** A loaded cement mixer drives onto an old drawbridge, where it stalls with its center of gravity three-quarters of the way across the span. The truck driver radios for help, sets the handbrake, and waits. Meanwhile, a boat approaches, so the drawbridge is raised by means of a cable attached to the end opposite the hinge (Fig. P11.56). The drawbridge is 40.0 m long and has a mass of 18,000 kg; its center of gravity is at its midpoint. The cement mixer, with driver, has mass 30,000 kg. When the drawbridge has been raised to an angle of 30° above the horizontal, the cable makes an angle of 70° with the surface of the bridge. (a) What is the tension T in the cable when the drawbridge is held in this position? (b) What are the horizontal and vertical components of the force the hinge exerts on the span?

Figure **P11.56**

11.57 •• **BIO** **Leg Raises.** In a simplified version of the musculature action in leg raises, the abdominal muscles pull on the femur (thigh bone) to raise the leg by pivoting it about one end (Fig. P11.57). When you are lying horizontally, these muscles make an angle of approximately 5° with the femur,

Figure **P11.57**

and if you raise your legs, the muscles remain approximately horizontal, so the angle θ increases. We shall assume for simplicity that these muscles attach to the femur in only one place, 10 cm from the hip joint (although, in reality, the situation is more complicated). For a certain 80-kg person having a leg 90 cm long, the mass of the leg is 15 kg and its center of mass is 44 cm from his hip joint as measured along the leg. If the person raises his leg to 60° above the horizontal, the angle between the abdominal muscles and his femur would also be about 60°. (a) With his leg raised to 60°, find the tension in the abdominal muscle on each leg. As usual, begin your solution with a free-body diagram. (b) When is the tension in this muscle greater: when the leg is raised to 60° or when the person just starts to raise it off the ground? Why? (Try this yourself to check your answer.) (c) If the abdominal muscles attached to the femur were perfectly horizontal when a person was lying down, could the person raise his leg? Why or why not?

11.58 • A nonuniform fire escape ladder is 6.0 m long when extended to the icy alley below. It is held at the top by a frictionless pivot, and there is negligible frictional force from the icy surface at the bottom. The ladder weighs 250 N, and its center of gravity is 2.0 m along the ladder from its bottom. A mother and child of total weight 750 N are on the ladder 1.5 m from the pivot. The ladder makes an angle θ with the horizontal. Find the magnitude and direction of (a) the force exerted by the icy alley on the ladder and (b) the force exerted by the ladder on the pivot. (c) Do your answers in parts (a) and (b) depend on the angle θ?

11.59 •• A uniform strut of mass m makes an angle θ with the horizontal. It is supported by a frictionless pivot located at one-third its length from its lower left end and a horizontal rope at its upper right end. A cable and package of total weight w hang from its upper right end. (a) Find the vertical and horizontal components V and H of the pivot's force on the strut as well as the tension T in the rope. (b) If the maximum safe tension in the rope is 700 N and the mass of the strut is 30.0 kg, find the maximum safe weight of the cable and package when the strut makes an angle of 55.0° with the horizontal. (c) For what angle θ can no weight be safely suspended from the right end of the strut?

11.60 • You are asked to design the decorative mobile shown in Fig. P11.60. The strings and rods have negligible weight, and the rods are to hang horizontally. (a) Draw a free-body diagram for each rod. (b) Find the weights of the balls A, B, and C. Find the tensions in the strings S_1, S_2, and S_3. (c) What can you say about the horizontal location of the mobile's center of gravity? Explain.

Figure **P11.60**

11.61 •• A uniform, 7.5-m-long beam weighing 5860 N is hinged to a wall and supported by a thin cable attached 1.5 m from the free end of the beam. The cable runs between the beam and the wall and makes a 40° angle with the beam. What is the tension in the cable when the beam is at an angle of 30° above the horizontal?

11.62 •• **CP** A uniform drawbridge must be held at a 37° angle above the horizontal to allow ships to pass underneath. The drawbridge weighs 45,000 N and is 14.0 m long. A cable is connected 3.5 m from the hinge where the bridge pivots (measured along the bridge) and pulls horizontally on the bridge to hold it in place. (a) What is the tension in the cable? (b) Find the magnitude and direction of the force the hinge exerts on the bridge. (c) If the cable suddenly breaks, what is the magnitude of the angular acceleration of the drawbridge just after the cable breaks? (d) What is the angular speed of the drawbridge as it becomes horizontal?

11.63 •• **BIO** **Tendon-Stretching Exercises.** As part of an exercise program, a 75-kg person does toe raises in which he raises his entire body weight on the ball of one foot (Fig. P11.63). The Achilles tendon pulls straight upward on the heel bone of his foot. This tendon is 25 cm long and has a cross-sectional area of 78 mm^2 and a Young's modulus of 1470 MPa. (a) Make a free-body diagram of the person's foot (everything below the ankle joint). You can neglect the weight of the foot. (b) What force does the Achilles tendon

Figure **P11.63**

exert on the heel during this exercise? Express your answer in newtons and in multiples of his weight. (c) By how many millimeters does the exercise stretch his Achilles tendon?

11.64 •• (a) In Fig. P11.64 a 6.00-m-long, uniform beam is hanging from a point 1.00 m to the right of its center. The beam weighs 140 N and makes an angle of 30.0° with the vertical. At the right-hand end of the beam a 100.0-N weight is hung; an unknown weight w hangs at the left end. If the system is in equilibrium, what is w? You can ignore the thickness of the beam. (b) If the beam makes, instead, an angle of 45.0° with the vertical, what is w?

11.65 ••• A uniform, horizontal flagpole 5.00 m long with a weight of 200 N is hinged to a vertical wall at one end. A 600-N stuntwoman hangs from its other end. The flagpole is supported by a guy wire running from its outer end to a point on the wall directly above the pole. (a) If the tension in this wire is not to exceed 1000 N, what is the minimum height above the pole at which it may be fastened to the wall? (b) If the flagpole remains horizontal, by how many newtons would the tension be increased if the wire were fastened 0.50 m below this point?

Figure **P11.64**

11.66 · A holiday decoration consists of two shiny glass spheres with masses 0.0240 kg and 0.0360 kg suspended from a uniform rod with mass 0.120 kg and length 1.00 m (Fig. P11.66). The rod is suspended from the ceiling by a vertical cord at each end, so that it is horizontal. Calculate the tension in each of the cords A through F.

Figure **P11.66**

11.67 ·· **BIO** Downward-Facing Dog. One yoga exercise, known as the "Downward-Facing Dog," requires stretching your hands straight out above your head and bending down to lean against the floor. This exercise is performed by a 750-N person, as shown in Fig. P11.67. When he bends his body at the hip to a 90° angle between his legs and trunk, his legs, trunk, head, and arms have the dimensions indicated. Furthermore, his legs and feet weigh a total of 277 N, and their center of mass is 41 cm from his hip, measured along his legs. The person's trunk, head, and arms weigh 473 N, and their center of gravity is 65 cm from his hip, measured along the upper body. (a) Find the normal force that the floor exerts on each foot and on each hand, assuming that the person does not favor either hand or either foot. (b) Find the friction force on each foot and on each hand, assuming that it is the same on both feet and on both hands (but not necessarily the same on the feet as on the hands). [*Hint:* First treat his entire body as a system; then isolate his legs (or his upper body).]

Figure **P11.67**

11.68 · When you stretch a wire, rope, or rubber band, it gets thinner as well as longer. When Hooke's law holds, the fractional decrease in width is proportional to the tensile strain. If w_0 is the original width and Δw is the change in width, then $\Delta w / w_0 = -\sigma \Delta l / l_0$, where the minus sign reminds us that width decreases when length increases. The dimensionless constant σ, different for different materials, is called *Poisson's ratio*. (a) If the steel rod of Example 11.5 (Section 11.4) has a circular cross section and a Poisson's ratio of 0.23, what is its change in diameter when the milling machine is hung from it? (b) A cylinder made of nickel (Poisson's ratio = 0.42) has radius 2.0 cm. What tensile force $F_\perp$ must be applied perpendicular to each end of the cylinder to cause its radius to decrease by 0.10 mm? Assume that the breaking stress and proportional limit for the metal are extremely large and are not exceeded.

11.69 · A worker wants to turn over a uniform, 1250-N, rectangular crate by pulling at 53.0° on one of its vertical sides (Fig. P11.69).

The floor is rough enough to prevent the crate from slipping. (a) What pull is needed to just start the crate to tip? (b) How hard does the floor push upward on the crate? (c) Find the friction force on the crate. (d) What is the minimum coefficient of static friction needed to prevent the crate from slipping on the floor?

Figure **P11.69**

11.70 ··· One end of a uniform meter stick is placed against a vertical wall (Fig. P11.70). The other end is held by a lightweight cord that makes an angle θ with the stick. The coefficient of static friction between the end of the meter stick and the wall is 0.40. (a) What is the maximum value the angle θ can have if the stick is to remain in equilibrium? (b) Let the angle θ be 15°. A block of the same weight as the meter stick is suspended from the stick, as shown, at a distance x from the wall. What is the minimum value of x for which the stick will remain in equilibrium? (c) When $\theta = 15°$, how large must the coefficient of static friction be so that the block can be attached 10 cm from the left end of the stick without causing it to slip?

Figure **P11.70**

11.71 ·· Two friends are carrying a 200-kg crate up a flight of stairs. The crate is 1.25 m long and 0.500 m high, and its center of gravity is at its center. The stairs make a 45.0° angle with respect to the floor. The crate also is carried at a 45.0° angle, so that its bottom side is parallel to the slope of the stairs (Fig. P11.71). If the force each person applies is vertical, what is the magnitude of each of these forces? Is it better to be the person above or below on the stairs?

Figure **P11.71**

11.72 ·· **BIO** Forearm. In the human arm, the forearm and hand pivot about the elbow joint. Consider a simplified model in which the biceps muscle is attached to the forearm 3.80 cm from the elbow joint. Assume that the person's hand and forearm together weigh 15.0 N and that their center of gravity is 15.0 cm from the elbow (not quite halfway to the hand). The forearm is held horizontally at a right angle to the upper arm, with the biceps muscle exerting its force perpendicular to the forearm. (a) Draw a free-body diagram for the forearm, and find the force exerted by the biceps when the hand is empty. (b) Now the person holds a 80.0-N weight in his hand, with the forearm still horizontal. Assume that the center of gravity of this weight is 33.0 cm from the elbow. Construct a free-body diagram for the forearm, and find the force now exerted by the biceps. Explain why the biceps muscle needs to be very strong. (c) Under the conditions of part (b), find the magnitude and direction of the force that the elbow joint exerts on the forearm. (d) While holding the 80.0-N weight, the person raises his forearm until it is at an angle of 53.0° above the horizontal. If the biceps muscle continues to exert its force perpendicular to the forearm, what is this force when the forearm is in this position? Has the force increased or decreased from its value in part (b)? Explain why this is so, and test your answer by actually doing this with your own arm.

11.73 •• **BIO CALC** Refer to the discussion of holding a dumbbell in Example 11.4 (Section 11.3). The maximum weight that can be held in this way is limited by the maximum allowable tendon tension T (determined by the strength of the tendons) and by the distance D from the elbow to where the tendon attaches to the forearm. (a) Let T_{max} represent the maximum value of the tendon tension. Use the results of Example 11.4 to express w_{max} (the maximum weight that can be held) in terms of T_{max}, L, D, and h. Your expression should *not* include the angle θ. (b) The tendons of different primates are attached to the forearm at different values of D. Calculate the derivative of w_{max} with respect to D, and determine whether the derivative is positive or negative. (c) A chimpanzee tendon is attached to the forearm at a point farther from the elbow than for humans. Use this to explain why chimpanzees have stronger arms than humans. (The disadvantage is that chimpanzees have less flexible arms than do humans.)

11.74 •• A uniform, 90.0-N table is 3.6 m long, 1.0 m high, and 1.2 m wide. A 1500-N weight is placed 0.50 m from one end of the table, a distance of 0.60 m from each side of the table. Draw a free-body diagram for the table and find the force that each of the four legs exerts on the floor.

11.75 ••• **Flying Buttress.** (a) A symmetric building has a roof sloping upward at 35.0° above the horizontal on each side. If each side of the uniform roof weighs 10,000 N, find the horizontal force that this roof exerts at the top of the wall, which tends to push out the walls. Which type of building would be more in danger of collapsing: one with tall walls or one with short walls? Explain. (b) As you saw in part (a), tall walls are in danger of collapsing from the weight of the roof. This problem plagued the ancient builders of large structures. A solution used in the great Gothic cathedrals during the 1200s was the flying buttress, a stone support running between the walls and the ground that helped to hold in the walls. A Gothic church has a uniform roof weighing a total of 20,000 N and rising at 40° above the horizontal at each wall. The walls are 40 m tall, and a flying buttress meets each wall 10 m below the base of the roof. What horizontal force must this flying buttress apply to the wall?

11.76 •• You are trying to raise a bicycle wheel of mass m and radius R up over a curb of height h. To do this, you apply a horizontal force $\vec{F}$ (Fig. P11.76). What is the smallest magnitude of the force $\vec{F}$ that will succeed in raising the wheel onto the curb when the force is applied (a) at the center of the wheel and (b) at the top of the wheel? (c) In which case is less force required?

Figure **P11.76**

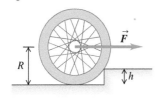

11.77 • **The Farmyard Gate.** A gate 4.00 m wide and 2.00 m high weighs 500 N. Its center of gravity is at its center, and it is hinged at A and B. To relieve the strain on the top hinge, a

Figure **P11.77**

wire CD is connected as shown in Fig. P11.77. The tension in CD is increased until the horizontal force at hinge A is zero. (a) What is the tension in the wire CD? (b) What is the magnitude of the horizontal component of the force at hinge B? (c) What is the combined vertical force exerted by hinges A and B?

11.78 • If you put a uniform block at the edge of a table, the center of the block must be over the table for the block not to fall off. (a) If you stack two identical blocks at the table edge, the center of the top block must be over the bottom block, and the center of gravity of the two blocks together must be over the table. In terms of the length L of each block, what is the maximum overhang possible (Fig. P11.78)? (b) Repeat part (a) for three identical blocks and for four identical blocks. (c) Is it possible to make a stack of blocks such that the uppermost block is not directly over the table at all? How many blocks would it take to do this? (Try this with your friends using copies of this book.)

Figure **P11.78**

11.79 ••• Two uniform, 75.0-g marbles 2.00 cm in diameter are stacked as shown in Fig. P11.79 in a container that is 3.00 cm wide. (a) Find the force that the container exerts on the marbles at the points of contact A, B, and C. (b) What force does each marble exert on the other?

Figure **P11.79**

11.80 •• Two identical, uniform beams weighing 260 N each are connected at one end by a frictionless hinge. A light horizontal crossbar attached at the midpoints of the beams maintains an angle of 53.0° between the beams. The beams are suspended from the ceiling by vertical wires such that they form a "V," as shown in Fig. P11.80. (a) What force does the crossbar exert on each beam? (b) Is the crossbar under tension or compression? (c) What force (magnitude and direction) does the hinge at point A exert on each beam?

Figure **P11.80**

11.81 • An engineer is designing a conveyor system for loading hay bales into a wagon (Fig. P11.81). Each bale is 0.25 m wide, 0.50 m high, and 0.80 m long (the dimension perpendicular to the plane of the figure), with mass 30.0 kg. The center of

Figure **P11.81**

gravity of each bale is at its geometrical center. The coefficient of static friction between a bale and the conveyor belt is 0.60, and the belt moves with constant speed. (a) The angle β of the conveyor is slowly increased. At some critical angle a bale will tip (if it doesn't slip first), and at some different critical angle it will slip (if it doesn't tip first). Find the two critical angles and determine which happens at the smaller angle. (b) Would the outcome of part (a) be different if the coefficient of friction were 0.40?

11.82 • A weight W is supported by attaching it to a vertical uniform metal pole by a thin cord passing over a pulley having negligible mass and friction. The cord is attached to the pole 40.0 cm below the top and pulls horizontally on it (Fig. P11.82). The pole is pivoted about a hinge at its base, is 1.75 m tall, and weighs 55.0 N. A thin wire connects the top of the pole to a vertical wall. The nail that holds this wire to the wall will pull out if an *outward* force greater than 22.0 N acts on it. (a) What is the greatest weight W that can be supported this way without pulling out the nail? (b) What is the *magnitude* of the force that the hinge exerts on the pole?

Figure **P11.82**

11.83 •• A garage door is mounted on an overhead rail (Fig. P11.83). The wheels at A and B have rusted so that they do not roll, but rather slide along the track. The coefficient of kinetic friction is 0.52. The distance between the wheels is 2.00 m, and each is 0.50 m from the vertical sides of the door. The door is uniform and weighs 950 N. It is pushed to the left at constant speed by a horizontal force $\vec{F}$. (a) If the distance h is 1.60 m, what is the vertical component of the force exerted on each wheel by the track? (b) Find the maximum value h can have without causing one wheel to leave the track.

Figure **P11.83**

11.84 •• A horizontal boom is supported at its left end by a frictionless pivot. It is held in place by a cable attached to the right-hand end of the boom. A chain and crate of total weight w hang from somewhere along the boom. The boom's weight w_b cannot be ignored and the boom may or may not be uniform. (a) Show that the tension in the cable is the same whether the cable makes an angle θ or an angle $180° - \theta$ with the horizontal, and that the horizontal force component exerted on the boom by the pivot has equal magnitude but opposite direction for the two angles. (b) Show that the cable cannot be horizontal. (c) Show that the tension in the cable is a minimum when the cable is vertical, pulling upward on the right end of the boom. (d) Show that when the cable is vertical, the force exerted by the pivot on the boom is vertical.

11.85 •• Prior to being placed in its hole, a 5700-N, 9.0-m-long, uniform utility pole makes some nonzero angle with the vertical. A vertical cable attached 2.0 m below its upper end holds it in place while its lower end rests on the ground. (a) Find the tension in the cable and the magnitude and direction of the force exerted by the ground on the pole. (b) Why don't we need to know the angle the pole makes with the vertical, as long as it is not zero?

11.86 ••• **Pyramid Builders.** Ancient pyramid builders are balancing a uniform rectangular slab of stone tipped at an angle θ above the horizontal using a rope (Fig. P11.86). The rope is held by five workers who share the force equally. (a) If $\theta = 20.0°$, what force does each worker exert on the rope? (b) As θ increases, does each worker have to exert more or less force than in part (a), assuming they do not change the angle of the rope? Why? (c) At what angle do the workers need to exert *no force* to balance the slab? What happens if θ exceeds this value?

Figure **P11.86**

11.87 • You hang a floodlamp from the end of a vertical steel wire. The floodlamp stretches the wire 0.18 mm and the stress is proportional to the strain. How much would it have stretched (a) if the wire were twice as long? (b) if the wire had the same length but twice the diameter? (c) for a copper wire of the original length and diameter?

11.88 •• **Hooke's Law for a Wire.** A wire of length l_0 and cross-sectional area A supports a hanging weight W. (a) Show that if the wire obeys Eq. (11.7), it behaves like a spring of force constant AY/l_0, where Y is Young's modulus for the material of which the wire is made. (b) What would the force constant be for a 75.0-cm length of 16-gauge (diameter = 1.291 mm) copper wire? See Table 11.1. (c) What would W have to be to stretch the wire in part (b) by 1.25 mm?

11.89 ••• **CP** A 12.0-kg mass, fastened to the end of an aluminum wire with an unstretched length of 0.50 m, is whirled in a vertical circle with a constant angular speed of 120 rev/min. The cross-sectional area of the wire is 0.014 cm². Calculate the elongation of the wire when the mass is (a) at the lowest point of the path and (b) at the highest point of its path.

11.90 • A metal wire 3.50 m long and 0.70 mm in diameter was given the following test. A load weighing 20 N was originally hung from the wire to keep it taut. The position of the lower end of the wire was read on a scale as load was added.

Added Load (N)	Scale Reading (cm)
0	3.02
10	3.07
20	3.12
30	3.17
40	3.22
50	3.27
60	3.32
70	4.27

(a) Graph these values, plotting the increase in length horizontally and the added load vertically. (b) Calculate the value of Young's modulus. (c) The proportional limit occurred at a scale reading of 3.34 cm. What was the stress at this point?

11.91 ••• A 1.05-m-long rod of negligible weight is supported at its ends by wires A and B of equal length (Fig. P11.91). The cross-sectional area of A is

Figure **P11.91**

2.00 mm^2 and that of B is 4.00 mm^2. Young's modulus for wire A is 1.80×10^{11} Pa; that for B is 1.20×10^{11} Pa. At what point along the rod should a weight w be suspended to produce (a) equal stresses in A and B and (b) equal strains in A and B?

11.92 ••• **CP** An amusement park ride consists of airplane-shaped cars attached to steel rods (Fig. P11.92). Each rod has a length of 15.0 m and a cross-sectional area of 8.00 cm^2. (a) How much is the rod stretched when the ride is at rest? (Assume that each car plus two people seated in it has a total weight of 1900 N.) (b) When operating, the ride has a maximum angular speed of 8.0 rev/min. How much is the rod stretched then?

Figure **P11.92**

11.93 • A brass rod with a length of 1.40 m and a cross-sectional area of 2.00 cm^2 is fastened end to end to a nickel rod with length L and cross-sectional area 1.00 cm^2. The compound rod is subjected to equal and opposite pulls of magnitude 4.00×10^4 N at its ends. (a) Find the length L of the nickel rod if the elongations of the two rods are equal. (b) What is the stress in each rod? (c) What is the strain in each rod?

11.94 ••• **CP BIO Stress on the Shin Bone.** The compressive strength of our bones is important in everyday life. Young's modulus for bone is about 1.4×10^{10} Pa. Bone can take only about a 1.0% change in its length before fracturing. (a) What is the maximum force that can be applied to a bone whose minimum cross-sectional area is 3.0 cm^2? (This is approximately the cross-sectional area of a tibia, or shin bone, at its narrowest point.) (b) Estimate the maximum height from which a 70-kg man could jump and not fracture the tibia. Take the time between when he first touches the floor and when he has stopped to be 0.030 s, and assume that the stress is distributed equally between his legs.

11.95 ••• A moonshiner produces pure ethanol (ethyl alcohol) late at night and stores it in a stainless steel tank in the form of a cylinder 0.300 m in diameter with a tight-fitting piston at the top. The total volume of the tank is 250 L (0.250 m^3). In an attempt to squeeze a little more into the tank, the moonshiner piles 1420 kg of lead bricks on top of the piston. What additional volume of ethanol can the moonshiner squeeze into the tank? (Assume that the wall of the tank is perfectly rigid.)

CHALLENGE PROBLEMS

11.96 ••• Two ladders, 4.00 m and 3.00 m long, are hinged at point A and tied together by a horizontal rope 0.90 m above the floor (Fig. P11.96). The ladders weigh 480 N and 360 N, respectively, and the center of gravity of each is at its center. Assume that

Figure **P11.96**

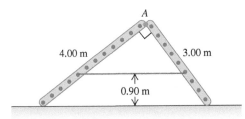

the floor is freshly waxed and frictionless. (a) Find the upward force at the bottom of each ladder. (b) Find the tension in the rope. (c) Find the magnitude of the force one ladder exerts on the other at point A. (d) If an 800-N painter stands at point A, find the tension in the horizontal rope.

11.97 ••• A bookcase weighing 1500 N rests on a horizontal surface for which the coefficient of static friction is $\mu_s = 0.40$. The bookcase is 1.80 m tall and 2.00 m wide; its center of gravity is at its geometrical center. The bookcase rests on four short legs that are each 0.10 m from the edge of the bookcase. A person pulls on a rope attached to an upper corner of the bookcase with a force $\vec{F}$ that makes an angle θ with the bookcase (Fig. P11.97). (a) If $\theta = 90°$, so $\vec{F}$ is horizontal, show that as F is increased from zero, the bookcase will start to slide before it tips, and calculate the magnitude of $\vec{F}$ that will start the bookcase sliding. (b) If $\theta = 0°$, so $\vec{F}$ is vertical, show that the bookcase will tip over rather than slide, and calculate the magnitude of $\vec{F}$ that will cause the bookcase to start to tip. (c) Calculate as a function of θ the magnitude of $\vec{F}$ that will cause the bookcase to start to slide and the magnitude that will cause it to start to tip. What is the smallest value that θ can have so that the bookcase will still start to slide before it starts to tip?

Figure **P11.97**

11.98 ••• **Knocking Over a Post.** One end of a post weighing 400 N and with height h rests on a rough horizontal surface with $\mu_s = 0.30$. The upper end is held by a rope fastened to the surface and making an angle of 36.9° with the post (Fig. P11.98). A horizontal force $\vec{F}$ is exerted on the post as shown. (a) If the force $\vec{F}$ is applied at the midpoint of the post, what is the largest value it can have without causing the post to slip? (b) How large can the force be without causing the post to slip if its point of application is $\frac{6}{10}$ of the way from the ground to the top of the post? (c) Show that if the point of application of the force is too high, the post cannot be made to slip, no matter how great the force. Find the critical height for the point of application.

Figure **P11.98**

11.99 ••• **CALC Minimizing the Tension.** A heavy horizontal girder of length L has several objects suspended from it. It is supported by a frictionless pivot at its left end and a cable of negligible weight that is attached to an I-beam at a point a distance h directly above the girder's center. Where should the other end of the cable be attached to the girder so that the cable's tension is a minimum? (*Hint:* In evaluating and presenting your answer, don't forget that the maximum distance of the point of attachment from the pivot is the length L of the beam.)

11.100 ••• **Bulk Modulus of an Ideal Gas.** The equation of state (the equation relating pressure, volume, and temperature) for an ideal gas is $pV = nRT$, where n and R are constants. (a) Show that if the gas is compressed while the temperature T is held constant, the bulk modulus is equal to the pressure. (b) When an ideal gas is compressed without the transfer of any heat into or out of it, the pressure and volume are related by $pV^\gamma = $ constant, where γ is a constant having different values for different gases. Show that, in this case, the bulk modulus is given by $B = \gamma p$.

11.101 ••• **CP** An angler hangs a 4.50-kg fish from a vertical steel wire 1.50 m long and 5.00×10^{-3} cm^2 in cross-sectional area. The upper end of the wire is securely fastened to a support. (a) Calculate the amount the wire is stretched by the hanging fish. The angler now applies a force $\vec{F}$ to the fish, pulling it very slowly downward by 0.500 mm from its equilibrium position. For this downward motion, calculate (b) the work done by gravity; (c) the work done by the force $\vec{F}$; (d) the work done by the force the wire exerts on the fish; and (e) the change in the elastic potential energy (the potential energy associated with the tensile stress in the wire). Compare the answers in parts (d) and (e).

Answers

Chapter Opening Question ?

Each stone in the arch is under compression, not tension. This is because the forces on the stones tend to push them inward toward the center of the arch and thus squeeze them together. Compared to a solid supporting wall, a wall with arches is just as strong yet much more economical to build.

Test Your Understanding Questions

11.1 Answer: (i) Situation (i) satisfies both equilibrium conditions because the seagull has zero acceleration (so $\Sigma \vec{F} = \mathbf{0}$) and no tendency to start rotating (so $\Sigma \vec{\tau} = \mathbf{0}$). Situation (ii) satisfies the first condition because the crankshaft as a whole does not accelerate through space, but it does not satisfy the second condition; the crankshaft has an angular acceleration, so $\Sigma \vec{\tau}$ is not zero. Situation (iii) satisfies the second condition (there is no tendency to rotate) but not the first one; the baseball accelerates in its flight (due to gravity), so $\Sigma \vec{F}$ is not zero.

11.2 Answer: (ii) In equilibrium, the center of gravity must be at the point of support. Since the rock and meter stick have the same mass and hence the same weight, the center of gravity of the system is midway between their respective centers. The center of gravity of the meter stick alone is 0.50 m from the left end (that is, at the middle of the meter stick), so the center of gravity of the combination of rock and meter stick is 0.25 m from the left end.

11.3 Answer: (ii), (i), (iii) This is the same situation described in Example 11.4, with the rod replacing the forearm, the hinge replacing the elbow, and the cable replacing the tendon. The only difference is that the cable attachment point is at the end of the rod, so the distances D and L are identical. From Example 11.4, the tension is

$$T = \frac{Lw}{L\sin\theta} = \frac{w}{\sin\theta}$$

Since $\sin\theta$ is less than 1, the tension T is greater than the weight w. The vertical component of the force exerted by the hinge is

$$E_y = -\frac{(L - L)w}{L} = 0$$

In this situation, the hinge exerts *no* vertical force. You can see this easily if you calculate torques around the right end of the horizontal rod: The only force that exerts a torque around this point is the vertical component of the hinge force, so this force component must be zero.

11.4 Answers: (a) (iii), (b) (ii) In (a), the copper rod has 10 times the elongation Δl of the steel rod, but it also has 10 times the original length l_0. Hence the tensile strain $\Delta l / l_0$ is the same for both rods. In (b), the stress is equal to Young's modulus Y multiplied by the strain. From Table 11.1, steel has a larger value of Y, so a greater stress is required to produce the same strain.

11.5 In (a) and (b), the bumper will have sprung back to its original shape (although the paint may be scratched). In (c), the bumper will have a permanent dent or deformation. In (d), the bumper will be torn or broken.

Bridging Problem

Answers:

(a) $T = \dfrac{2mg}{3\sin\theta}$

(b) $F = \dfrac{2mg}{3\sin\theta}\sqrt{\cos^2\theta + \tfrac{1}{4}\sin^2\theta}$, $\phi = \arctan\left(\tfrac{1}{2}\tan\theta\right)$

(c) $\Delta l = \dfrac{2mgl_0}{3AY\tan\theta}$ (d) 4

? Dogs walk with much quicker strides than do humans. Is this primarily because dogs' legs are shorter than human legs, less massive than human legs, or both?

LEARNING GOALS

By studying this chapter, you will learn:

- How to describe oscillations in terms of amplitude, period, frequency, and angular frequency.

- How to do calculations with simple harmonic motion, an important type of oscillation.

- How to use energy concepts to analyze simple harmonic motion.

- How to apply the ideas of simple harmonic motion to different physical situations.

- How to analyze the motions of a simple pendulum.

- What a physical pendulum is, and how to calculate the properties of its motion.

- What determines how rapidly an oscillation dies out.

- How a driving force applied to an oscillator at the right frequency can cause a very large response, or resonance.

Many kinds of motion repeat themselves over and over: the vibration of a quartz crystal in a watch, the swinging pendulum of a grandfather clock, the sound vibrations produced by a clarinet or an organ pipe, and the back-and-forth motion of the pistons in a car engine. This kind of motion, called **periodic motion** or **oscillation,** is the subject of this chapter. Understanding periodic motion will be essential for our later study of waves, sound, alternating electric currents, and light.

A body that undergoes periodic motion always has a stable equilibrium position. When it is moved away from this position and released, a force or torque comes into play to pull it back toward equilibrium. But by the time it gets there, it has picked up some kinetic energy, so it overshoots, stopping somewhere on the other side, and is again pulled back toward equilibrium. Picture a ball rolling back and forth in a round bowl or a pendulum that swings back and forth past its straight-down position.

In this chapter we will concentrate on two simple examples of systems that can undergo periodic motions: spring-mass systems and pendulums. We will also study why oscillations often tend to die out with time and why some oscillations can build up to greater and greater displacements from equilibrium when periodically varying forces act.

14.1 Describing Oscillation

Figure 14.1 shows one of the simplest systems that can have periodic motion. A body with mass *m* rests on a frictionless horizontal guide system, such as a linear air track, so it can move only along the *x*-axis. The body is attached to a spring of negligible mass that can be either stretched or compressed. The left end of the spring is held fixed and the right end is attached to the body. The spring force is the only horizontal force acting on the body; the vertical normal and gravitational forces always add to zero.

14.1 A system that can have periodic motion.

14.2 Model for periodic motion. When the body is displaced from its equilibrium position at $x = 0$, the spring exerts a restoring force back toward the equilibrium position.

(a)

$x > 0$: glider displaced to the right from the equilibrium position.

$F_x < 0$, so $a_x < 0$: stretched spring pulls glider toward equilibrium position.

(b)

$x = 0$: The relaxed spring exerts no force on the glider, so the glider has zero acceleration.

(c)

$x < 0$: glider displaced to the left from the equilibrium position.

$F_x > 0$, so $a_x > 0$: compressed spring pushes glider toward equilibrium position.

Application Wing Frequencies
The ruby-throated hummingbird (*Archilochus colubris*) normally flaps its wings at about 50 Hz, producing the characteristic sound that gives hummingbirds their name. Insects can flap their wings at even faster rates, from 330 Hz for a house fly and 600 Hz for a mosquito to an amazing 1040 Hz for the tiny biting midge.

It's simplest to define our coordinate system so that the origin O is at the equilibrium position, where the spring is neither stretched nor compressed. Then x is the x-component of the **displacement** of the body from equilibrium and is also the change in the length of the spring. The x-component of the force that the spring exerts on the body is F_x, and the x-component of acceleration a_x is given by $a_x = F_x/m$.

Figure 14.2 shows the body for three different displacements of the spring. Whenever the body is displaced from its equilibrium position, the spring force tends to restore it to the equilibrium position. We call a force with this character a **restoring force.** Oscillation can occur only when there is a restoring force tending to return the system to equilibrium.

Let's analyze how oscillation occurs in this system. If we displace the body to the right to $x = A$ and then let go, the net force and the acceleration are to the left (Fig. 14.2a). The speed increases as the body approaches the equilibrium position O. When the body is at O, the net force acting on it is zero (Fig. 14.2b), but because of its motion it *overshoots* the equilibrium position. On the other side of the equilibrium position the body is still moving to the left, but the net force and the acceleration are to the right (Fig. 14.2c); hence the speed decreases until the body comes to a stop. We will show later that with an ideal spring, the stopping point is at $x = -A$. The body then accelerates to the right, overshoots equilibrium again, and stops at the starting point $x = A$, ready to repeat the whole process. The body is oscillating! If there is no friction or other force to remove mechanical energy from the system, this motion repeats forever; the restoring force perpetually draws the body back toward the equilibrium position, only to have the body overshoot time after time.

In different situations the force may depend on the displacement x from equilibrium in different ways. But oscillation *always* occurs if the force is a *restoring* force that tends to return the system to equilibrium.

Amplitude, Period, Frequency, and Angular Frequency

Here are some terms that we'll use in discussing periodic motions of all kinds:

The **amplitude** of the motion, denoted by A, is the maximum magnitude of displacement from equilibrium—that is, the maximum value of $|x|$. It is always positive. If the spring in Fig. 14.2 is an ideal one, the total overall range of the motion is $2A$. The SI unit of A is the meter. A complete vibration, or **cycle,** is one complete round trip—say, from A to $-A$ and back to A, or from O to A, back through O to $-A$, and back to O. Note that motion from one side to the other (say, $-A$ to A) is a half-cycle, not a whole cycle.

The **period**, T, is the time for one cycle. It is always positive. The SI unit is the second, but it is sometimes expressed as "seconds per cycle."

The **frequency,** f, is the number of cycles in a unit of time. It is always positive. The SI unit of frequency is the hertz:

$$1 \text{ hertz} = 1 \text{ Hz} = 1 \text{ cycle/s} = 1 \text{ s}^{-1}$$

This unit is named in honor of the German physicist Heinrich Hertz (1857–1894), a pioneer in investigating electromagnetic waves.

The **angular frequency,** ω, is 2π times the frequency:

$$\omega = 2\pi f$$

We'll learn shortly why ω is a useful quantity. It represents the rate of change of an angular quantity (not necessarily related to a rotational motion) that is always measured in radians, so its units are rad/s. Since f is in cycle/s, we may regard the number 2π as having units rad/cycle.

From the definitions of period T and frequency f we see that each is the reciprocal of the other:

$$f = \frac{1}{T} \qquad T = \frac{1}{f} \qquad \text{(relationships between frequency and period)} \qquad (14.1)$$

Also, from the definition of ω,

$$\omega = 2\pi f = \frac{2\pi}{T} \quad \text{(angular frequency)} \quad (14.2)$$

Example 14.1 Period, frequency, and angular frequency

An ultrasonic transducer used for medical diagnosis oscillates at 6.7 MHz = 6.7×10^6 Hz. How long does each oscillation take, and what is the angular frequency?

SOLUTION

IDENTIFY and SET UP: The target variables are the period T and the angular frequency ω. We can find these using the given frequency f in Eqs. (14.1) and (14.2).

EXECUTE: From Eqs. (14.1) and (14.2),

$$T = \frac{1}{f} = \frac{1}{6.7 \times 10^6 \text{ Hz}} = 1.5 \times 10^{-7} \text{ s} = 0.15 \ \mu s$$

$$\omega = 2\pi f = 2\pi (6.7 \times 10^6 \text{ Hz})$$
$$= (2\pi \text{ rad/cycle})(6.7 \times 10^6 \text{ cycle/s})$$
$$= 4.2 \times 10^7 \text{ rad/s}$$

EVALUATE: This is a very rapid vibration, with large f and ω and small T. A slow vibration has small f and ω and large T.

Test Your Understanding of Section 14.1 A body like that shown in Fig. 14.2 oscillates back and forth. For each of the following values of the body's x-velocity v_x and x-acceleration a_x, state whether its displacement x is positive, negative, or zero. (a) $v_x > 0$ and $a_x > 0$; (b) $v_x > 0$ and $a_x < 0$; (c) $v_x < 0$ and $a_x > 0$; (d) $v_x < 0$ and $a_x < 0$; (e) $v_x = 0$ and $a_x < 0$; (f) $v_x > 0$ and $a_x = 0$.

14.2 Simple Harmonic Motion

The simplest kind of oscillation occurs when the restoring force F_x is *directly proportional* to the displacement from equilibrium x. This happens if the spring in Figs. 14.1 and 14.2 is an ideal one that obeys Hooke's law. The constant of proportionality between F_x and x is the force constant k. (You may want to review Hooke's law and the definition of the force constant in Section 6.3.) On either side of the equilibrium position, F_x and x always have opposite signs. In Section 6.3 we represented the force acting *on* a stretched ideal spring as $F_x = kx$. The x-component of force the spring exerts *on the body* is the negative of this, so the x-component of force F_x on the body is

$$F_x = -kx \quad \text{(restoring force exerted by an ideal spring)} \quad (14.3)$$

This equation gives the correct magnitude and sign of the force, whether x is positive, negative, or zero (Fig. 14.3). The force constant k is always positive and has units of N/m (a useful alternative set of units is kg/s^2). We are assuming that there is no friction, so Eq. (14.3) gives the *net* force on the body.

When the restoring force is directly proportional to the displacement from equilibrium, as given by Eq. (14.3), the oscillation is called **simple harmonic motion,** *abbreviated* **SHM.** The acceleration $a_x = d^2x/dt^2 = F_x/m$ of a body in SHM is given by

$$a_x = \frac{d^2x}{dt^2} = -\frac{k}{m}x \quad \text{(simple harmonic motion)} \quad (14.4)$$

The minus sign means the acceleration and displacement always have opposite signs. This acceleration is *not* constant, so don't even think of using the constant-acceleration equations from Chapter 2. We'll see shortly how to solve this equation to find the displacement x as a function of time. A body that undergoes simple harmonic motion is called a **harmonic oscillator.**

14.3 An idealized spring exerts a restoring force that obeys Hooke's law, $F_x = -kx$. Oscillation with such a restoring force is called simple harmonic motion.

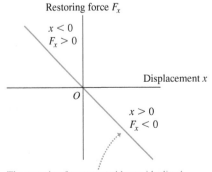

The restoring force exerted by an idealized spring is directly proportional to the displacement (Hooke's law, $F_x = -kx$): the graph of F_x versus x is a straight line.

14.4 In most real oscillations Hooke's law applies provided the body doesn't move too far from equilibrium. In such a case small-amplitude oscillations are approximately simple harmonic.

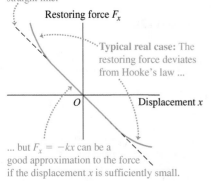

Ideal case: The restoring force obeys Hooke's law ($F_x = -kx$), so the graph of F_x versus x is a straight line.

Typical real case: The restoring force deviates from Hooke's law ...

... but $F_x = -kx$ can be a good approximation to the force if the displacement x is sufficiently small.

Why is simple harmonic motion important? Keep in mind that not all periodic motions are simple harmonic; in periodic motion in general, the restoring force depends on displacement in a more complicated way than in Eq. (14.3). But in many systems the restoring force is *approximately* proportional to displacement if the displacement is sufficiently small (Fig. 14.4). That is, if the amplitude is small enough, the oscillations of such systems are approximately simple harmonic and therefore approximately described by Eq. (14.4). Thus we can use SHM as an approximate model for many different periodic motions, such as the vibration of the quartz crystal in a watch, the motion of a tuning fork, the electric current in an alternating-current circuit, and the oscillations of atoms in molecules and solids.

Circular Motion and the Equations of SHM

To explore the properties of simple harmonic motion, we must express the displacement x of the oscillating body as a function of time, $x(t)$. The second derivative of this function, d^2x/dt^2, must be equal to $(-k/m)$ times the function itself, as required by Eq. (14.4). As we mentioned, the formulas for constant acceleration from Section 2.4 are no help because the acceleration changes constantly as the displacement x changes. Instead, we'll find $x(t)$ by noticing a striking similarity between SHM and another form of motion that we've already studied.

Figure 14.5a shows a top view of a horizontal disk of radius A with a ball attached to its rim at point Q. The disk rotates with constant angular speed ω (measured in rad/s), so the ball moves in uniform circular motion. A horizontal light beam shines on the rotating disk and casts a shadow of the ball on a screen. The shadow at point P oscillates back and forth as the ball moves in a circle. We then arrange a body attached to an ideal spring, like the combination shown in Figs. 14.1 and 14.2, so that the body oscillates parallel to the shadow. We will prove that the motion of the body and the motion of the ball's shadow are *identical* if the amplitude of the body's oscillation is equal to the disk radius A, and if the angular frequency $2\pi f$ of the oscillating body is equal to the angular speed ω of the rotating disk. That is, *simple harmonic motion is the projection of uniform circular motion onto a diameter.*

We can verify this remarkable statement by finding the acceleration of the shadow at P and comparing it to the acceleration of a body undergoing SHM, given by Eq. (14.4). The circle in which the ball moves so that its projection matches the motion of the oscillating body is called the **reference circle;** we will call the point Q the *reference point.* We take the reference circle to lie in the

14.5 (a) Relating uniform circular motion and simple harmonic motion. (b) The ball's shadow moves exactly like a body oscillating on an ideal spring.

(a) Apparatus for creating the reference circle

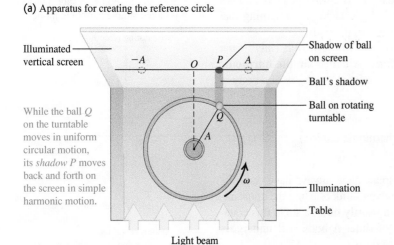

While the ball Q on the turntable moves in uniform circular motion, its *shadow* P moves back and forth on the screen in simple harmonic motion.

Illuminated vertical screen

Shadow of ball on screen

Ball's shadow

Ball on rotating turntable

Illumination

Table

Light beam

(b) An abstract representation of the motion in **(a)**

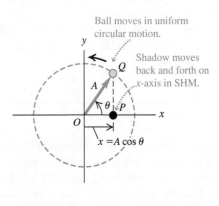

Ball moves in uniform circular motion.

Shadow moves back and forth on x-axis in SHM.

$x = A\cos\theta$

xy-plane, with the origin *O* at the center of the circle (Fig. 14.5b). At time *t* the vector *OQ* from the origin to the reference point *Q* makes an angle *θ* with the positive *x*-axis. As the point *Q* moves around the reference circle with constant angular speed *ω*, the vector *OQ* rotates with the same angular speed. Such a rotating vector is called a **phasor.** (This term was in use long before the invention of the Star Trek stun gun with a similar name. The phasor method for analyzing oscillations is useful in many areas of physics. We'll use phasors when we study alternating-current circuits in Chapter 31 and the interference of light in Chapters 35 and 36.)

The *x*-component of the phasor at time *t* is just the *x*-coordinate of the point *Q*:

$$x = A\cos\theta \qquad (14.5)$$

This is also the *x*-coordinate of the shadow *P*, which is the *projection* of *Q* onto the *x*-axis. Hence the *x*-velocity of the shadow *P* along the *x*-axis is equal to the *x*-component of the velocity vector of point *Q* (Fig. 14.6a), and the *x*-acceleration of *P* is equal to the *x*-component of the acceleration vector of *Q* (Fig. 14.6b). Since point *Q* is in uniform circular motion, its acceleration vector $\vec{a}_Q$ is always directed toward *O*. Furthermore, the magnitude of $\vec{a}_Q$ is constant and given by the angular speed squared times the radius of the circle (see Section 9.3):

$$a_Q = \omega^2 A \qquad (14.6)$$

Figure 14.6b shows that the *x*-component of $\vec{a}_Q$ is $a_x = -a_Q\cos\theta$. Combining this with Eqs. (14.5) and (14.6), we get that the acceleration of point *P* is

$$a_x = -a_Q\cos\theta = -\omega^2 A\cos\theta \qquad \text{or} \qquad (14.7)$$

$$a_x = -\omega^2 x \qquad (14.8)$$

The acceleration of point *P* is directly proportional to the displacement *x* and always has the opposite sign. These are precisely the hallmarks of simple harmonic motion.

Equation (14.8) is *exactly* the same as Eq. (14.4) for the acceleration of a harmonic oscillator, provided that the angular speed *ω* of the reference point *Q* is related to the force constant *k* and mass *m* of the oscillating body by

$$\omega^2 = \frac{k}{m} \qquad \text{or} \qquad \omega = \sqrt{\frac{k}{m}} \qquad (14.9)$$

We have been using the same symbol *ω* for the angular *speed* of the reference point *Q* and the angular *frequency* of the oscillating point *P*. The reason is that these quantities are equal! If point *Q* makes one complete revolution in time *T*, then point *P* goes through one complete cycle of oscillation in the same time; hence *T* is the period of the oscillation. During time *T* the point *Q* moves through 2π radians, so its angular speed is $\omega = 2\pi/T$. But this is just the same as Eq. (14.2) for the angular frequency of the point *P*, which verifies our statement about the two interpretations of *ω*. This is why we introduced angular frequency in Section 14.1; this quantity makes the connection between oscillation and circular motion. So we reinterpret Eq. (14.9) as an expression for the angular frequency of simple harmonic motion for a body of mass *m*, acted on by a restoring force with force constant *k*:

$$\omega = \sqrt{\frac{k}{m}} \qquad \text{(simple harmonic motion)} \qquad (14.10)$$

When you start a body oscillating in SHM, the value of *ω* is not yours to choose; it is predetermined by the values of *k* and *m*. The units of *k* are N/m or kg/s², so *k/m* is in (kg/s²)/kg = s⁻². When we take the square root in Eq. (14.10), we get s⁻¹, or more properly rad/s because this is an *angular* frequency (recall that a radian is not a true unit).

14.6 The (a) *x*-velocity and (b) *x*-acceleration of the ball's shadow *P* (see Fig. 14.5) are the *x*-components of the velocity and acceleration vectors, respectively, of the ball *Q*.

(a) Using the reference circle to determine the *x*-velocity of point *P*

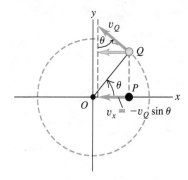

(b) Using the reference circle to determine the *x*-acceleration of point *P*

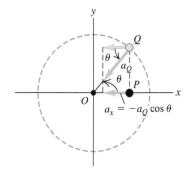

According to Eqs. (14.1) and (14.2), the frequency f and period T are

$$f = \frac{\omega}{2\pi} = \frac{1}{2\pi}\sqrt{\frac{k}{m}} \quad \text{(simple harmonic motion)} \quad \text{(14.11)}$$

$$T = \frac{1}{f} = \frac{2\pi}{\omega} = 2\pi\sqrt{\frac{m}{k}} \quad \text{(simple harmonic motion)} \quad \text{(14.12)}$$

14.7 The greater the mass m in a tuning fork's tines, the lower the frequency of oscillation $f = (1/2\pi)\sqrt{k/m}$ and the lower the pitch of the sound that the tuning fork produces.

Tines with large mass m:
low frequency f = 128 Hz

Tines with small mass m:
high frequency f = 4096 Hz

We see from Eq. (14.12) that a larger mass m, with its greater inertia, will have less acceleration, move more slowly, and take a longer time for a complete cycle (Fig. 14.7). In contrast, a stiffer spring (one with a larger force constant k) exerts a greater force at a given deformation x, causing greater acceleration, higher speeds, and a shorter time T per cycle.

CAUTION Don't confuse frequency and angular frequency You can run into trouble if you don't make the distinction between frequency f and angular frequency $\omega = 2\pi f$. Frequency tells you how many cycles of oscillation occur per second, while angular frequency tells you how many radians per second this corresponds to on the reference circle. In solving problems, pay careful attention to whether the goal is to find f or ω.

Period and Amplitude in SHM

Equations (14.11) and (14.12) show that the period and frequency of simple harmonic motion are completely determined by the mass m and the force constant k. *In simple harmonic motion the period and frequency do not depend on the amplitude A.* For given values of m and k, the time of one complete oscillation is the same whether the amplitude is large or small. Equation (14.3) shows why we should expect this. Larger A means that the body reaches larger values of $|x|$ and is subjected to larger restoring forces. This increases the average speed of the body over a complete cycle; this exactly compensates for having to travel a larger distance, so the same total time is involved.

The oscillations of a tuning fork are essentially simple harmonic motion, which means that it always vibrates with the same frequency, independent of amplitude. This is why a tuning fork can be used as a standard for musical pitch. If it were not for this characteristic of simple harmonic motion, it would be impossible to make familiar types of mechanical and electronic clocks run accurately or to play most musical instruments in tune. If you encounter an oscillating body with a period that *does* depend on the amplitude, the oscillation is *not* simple harmonic motion.

Example 14.2 **Angular frequency, frequency, and period in SHM**

A spring is mounted horizontally, with its left end fixed. A spring balance attached to the free end and pulled toward the right (Fig. 14.8a) indicates that the stretching force is proportional to the displacement, and a force of 6.0 N causes a displacement of 0.030 m. We replace the spring balance with a 0.50-kg glider, pull it 0.020 m to the right along a frictionless air track, and release it from rest (Fig. 14.8b). (a) Find the force constant k of the spring. (b) Find the angular frequency ω, frequency f, and period T of the resulting oscillation.

14.8 (a) The force exerted *on* the spring (shown by the vector F) has x-component $F_x = +6.0$ N. The force exerted *by* the spring has x-component $F_x = -6.0$ N. (b) A glider is attached to the same spring and allowed to oscillate.

(a)

(b)

SOLUTION

IDENTIFY and SET UP: Because the spring force (equal in magnitude to the stretching force) is proportional to the displacement, the motion is simple harmonic. We find k using Hooke's law, Eq. (14.3), and ω, f, and T using Eqs. (14.10), (14.11), and (14.12), respectively.

EXECUTE: (a) When $x = 0.030$ m, the force the spring exerts on the spring balance is $F_x = -6.0$ N. From Eq. (14.3),

$$k = -\frac{F_x}{x} = -\frac{-6.0 \text{ N}}{0.030 \text{ m}} = 200 \text{ N/m} = 200 \text{ kg/s}^2$$

(b) From Eq. (14.10), with $m = 0.50$ kg,

$$\omega = \sqrt{\frac{k}{m}} = \sqrt{\frac{200 \text{ kg/s}^2}{0.50 \text{ kg}}} = 20 \text{ rad/s}$$

$$f = \frac{\omega}{2\pi} = \frac{20 \text{ rad/s}}{2\pi \text{ rad/cycle}} = 3.2 \text{ cycle/s} = 3.2 \text{ Hz}$$

$$T = \frac{1}{f} = \frac{1}{3.2 \text{ cycle/s}} = 0.31 \text{ s}$$

EVALUATE: The amplitude of the oscillation is 0.020 m, the distance that we pulled the glider before releasing it. In SHM the angular frequency, frequency, and period are all independent of the amplitude. Note that a period is usually stated in "seconds" rather than "seconds per cycle."

Displacement, Velocity, and Acceleration in SHM

We still need to find the displacement x as a function of time for a harmonic oscillator. Equation (14.4) for a body in simple harmonic motion along the x-axis is identical to Eq. (14.8) for the x-coordinate of the reference point in uniform circular motion with constant angular speed $\omega = \sqrt{k/m}$. Hence Eq. (14.5), $x = A \cos \theta$, describes the x-coordinate for both of these situations. If at $t = 0$ the phasor OQ makes an angle ϕ (the Greek letter phi) with the positive x-axis, then at any later time t this angle is $\theta = \omega t + \phi$. We substitute this into Eq. (14.5) to obtain

$$x = A \cos(\omega t + \phi) \qquad \text{(displacement in SHM)} \qquad (14.13)$$

where $\omega = \sqrt{k/m}$. Figure 14.9 shows a graph of Eq. (14.13) for the particular case $\phi = 0$. The displacement x is a periodic function of time, as expected for SHM. We could also have written Eq. (14.13) in terms of a sine function rather than a cosine by using the identity $\cos \alpha = \sin(\alpha + \pi/2)$. *In simple harmonic motion the position is a periodic, sinusoidal function of time.* There are many other periodic functions, but none so simple as a sine or cosine function.

The value of the cosine function is always between -1 and 1, so in Eq. (14.13), x is always between $-A$ and A. This confirms that A is the amplitude of the motion.

The period T is the time for one complete cycle of oscillation, as Fig. 14.9 shows. The cosine function repeats itself whenever the quantity in parentheses in Eq. (14.13) increases by 2π radians. Thus, if we start at time $t = 0$, the time T to complete one cycle is given by

$$\omega T = \sqrt{\frac{k}{m}} T = 2\pi \qquad \text{or} \qquad T = 2\pi \sqrt{\frac{m}{k}}$$

which is just Eq. (14.12). Changing either m or k changes the period of oscillation, as shown in Figs. 14.10a and 14.10b. The period does not depend on the amplitude A (Fig. 14.10c).

(MP)

PhET: Motion in 2D
ActivPhysics 9.1: Position Graphs and Equations
ActivPhysics 9.2: Describing Vibrational Motion
ActivPhysics 9.5: Age Drops Tarzan

14.9 Graph of x versus t [see Eq. (14.13)] for simple harmonic motion. The case shown has $\phi = 0$.

14.10 Variations of simple harmonic motion. All cases shown have $\phi = 0$ [see Eq. (14.13)].

(MP)

(a) Increasing m; same A and k

Mass m increases from curve 1 to 2 to 3. Increasing m alone increases the period.

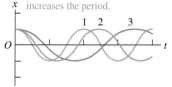

(b) Increasing k; same A and m

Force constant k increases from curve 1 to 2 to 3. Increasing k alone decreases the period.

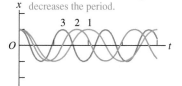

(c) Increasing A; same k and m

Amplitude A increases from curve 1 to 2 to 3. Changing A alone has no effect on the period.

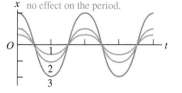

14.11 Variations of SHM: displacement versus time for the same harmonic oscillator with different phase angles ϕ.

These three curves show SHM with the same period T and amplitude A but with different phase angles ϕ.

The constant ϕ in Eq. (14.13) is called the **phase angle.** It tells us at what point in the cycle the motion was at $t = 0$ (equivalent to where around the circle the point Q was at $t = 0$). We denote the position at $t = 0$ by x_0. Putting $t = 0$ and $x = x_0$ in Eq. (14.13), we get

$$x_0 = A \cos \phi \qquad (14.14)$$

If $\phi = 0$, then $x_0 = A \cos 0 = A$, and the body starts at its maximum positive displacement. If $\phi = \pi$, then $x_0 = A \cos \pi = -A$, and the particle starts at its maximum *negative* displacement. If $\phi = \pi/2$, then $x_0 = A \cos(\pi/2) = 0$, and the particle is initially at the origin. Figure 14.11 shows the displacement x versus time for three different phase angles.

We find the velocity v_x and acceleration a_x as functions of time for a harmonic oscillator by taking derivatives of Eq. (14.13) with respect to time:

$$v_x = \frac{dx}{dt} = -\omega A \sin(\omega t + \phi) \qquad \text{(velocity in SHM)} \qquad (14.15)$$

$$a_x = \frac{dv_x}{dt} = \frac{d^2 x}{dt^2} = -\omega^2 A \cos(\omega t + \phi) \qquad \text{(acceleration in SHM)} \qquad (14.16)$$

14.12 Graphs of **(a)** x versus t, **(b)** v_x versus t, and **(c)** a_x versus t for a body in SHM. For the motion depicted in these graphs, $\phi = \pi/3$.

(a) Displacement x as a function of time t

$x = A \cos(\omega t + \phi)$

(b) Velocity v_x as a function of time t

$v_x = -\omega A \sin(\omega t + \phi)$

The v_x-t graph is shifted by $\frac{1}{4}$ cycle from the x-t graph.

(c) Acceleration a_x as a function of time t

$a_x = -\omega^2 A \cos(\omega t + \phi)$

The a_x-t graph is shifted by $\frac{1}{4}$ cycle from the v_x-t graph and by $\frac{1}{2}$ cycle from the x-t graph.

The velocity v_x oscillates between $v_{\max} = +\omega A$ and $-v_{\max} = -\omega A$, and the acceleration a_x oscillates between $a_{\max} = +\omega^2 A$ and $-a_{\max} = -\omega^2 A$ (Fig. 14.12). Comparing Eq. (14.16) with Eq. (14.13) and recalling that $\omega^2 = k/m$ from Eq. (14.9), we see that

$$a_x = -\omega^2 x = -\frac{k}{m} x$$

which is just Eq. (14.4) for simple harmonic motion. This confirms that Eq. (14.13) for x as a function of time is correct.

We actually derived Eq. (14.16) earlier in a geometrical way by taking the x-component of the acceleration vector of the reference point Q. This was done in Fig. 14.6b and Eq. (14.7) (recall that $\theta = \omega t + \phi$). In the same way, we could have derived Eq. (14.15) by taking the x-component of the velocity vector of Q, as shown in Fig. 14.6b. We'll leave the details for you to work out.

Note that the sinusoidal graph of displacement versus time (Fig. 14.12a) is shifted by one-quarter period from the graph of velocity versus time (Fig. 14.12b) and by one-half period from the graph of acceleration versus time (Fig. 14.12c). Figure 14.13 shows why this is so. When the body is passing through the equilibrium position so that the displacement is zero, the velocity equals either $v_{\max}$ or $-v_{\max}$ (depending on which way the body is moving) and the acceleration is zero. When the body is at either its maximum positive displacement, $x = +A$, or its maximum negative displacement, $x = -A$, the velocity is zero and the body is instantaneously at rest. At these points, the restoring force $F_x = -kx$ and the acceleration of the body have their maximum magnitudes. At $x = +A$ the acceleration is negative and equal to $-a_{\max}$. At $x = -A$ the acceleration is positive: $a_x = +a_{\max}$.

If we are given the initial position x_0 and initial velocity v_{0x} for the oscillating body, we can determine the amplitude A and the phase angle ϕ. Here's how to do it. The initial velocity v_{0x} is the velocity at time $t = 0$; putting $v_x = v_{0x}$ and $t = 0$ in Eq. (14.15), we find

$$v_{0x} = -\omega A \sin \phi \qquad (14.17)$$

To find ϕ, we divide Eq. (14.17) by Eq. (14.14). This eliminates A and gives an equation that we can solve for ϕ:

$$\frac{v_{0x}}{x_0} = \frac{-\omega A \sin\phi}{A \cos\phi} = -\omega \tan\phi$$

$$\phi = \arctan\left(-\frac{v_{0x}}{\omega x_0}\right) \quad \text{(phase angle in SHM)} \qquad (14.18)$$

It is also easy to find the amplitude A if we are given x_0 and v_{0x}. We'll sketch the derivation, and you can fill in the details. Square Eq. (14.14); then divide Eq. (14.17) by ω, square it, and add to the square of Eq. (14.14). The right side will be $A^2(\sin^2\phi + \cos^2\phi)$, which is equal to A^2. The final result is

$$A = \sqrt{x_0^2 + \frac{v_{0x}^2}{\omega^2}} \quad \text{(amplitude in SHM)} \qquad (14.19)$$

Note that when the body has both an initial displacement x_0 and a nonzero initial velocity v_{0x}, the amplitude A is *not* equal to the initial displacement. That's reasonable; if you start the body at a positive x_0 but give it a positive velocity v_{0x}, it will go *farther* than x_0 before it turns and comes back.

14.13 How x-velocity v_x and x-acceleration a_x vary during one cycle of SHM.

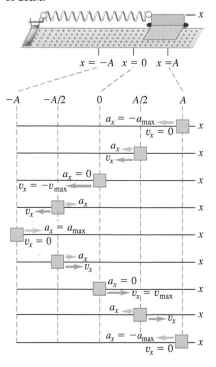

Problem-Solving Strategy 14.1 Simple Harmonic Motion I: Describing Motion

IDENTIFY *the relevant concepts:* An oscillating system undergoes simple harmonic motion (SHM) *only* if the restoring force is directly proportional to the displacement.

SET UP *the problem* using the following steps:
1. Identify the known and unknown quantities, and determine which are the target variables.
2. Distinguish between two kinds of quantities. *Properties of the system* include the mass m, the force constant k, and quantities derived from m and k, such as the period T, frequency f, and angular frequency ω. These are independent of *properties of the motion*, which describe how the system behaves when it is set into motion in a particular way; they include the amplitude A, maximum velocity v_{max}, and phase angle ϕ, and values of x, v_x, and a_x at particular times.
3. If necessary, define an x-axis as in Fig. 14.13, with the equilibrium position at $x = 0$.

EXECUTE *the solution* as follows:
1. Use the equations given in Sections 14.1 and 14.2 to solve for the target variables.
2. To find the values of x, v_x, and a_x at particular times, use Eqs. (14.13), (14.15), and (14.16), respectively. If the initial position x_0 and initial velocity v_{0x} are both given, determine ϕ and A from Eqs. (14.18) and (14.19). If the body has an initial positive displacement x_0 but zero initial velocity ($v_{0x} = 0$), then the amplitude is $A = x_0$ and the phase angle is $\phi = 0$. If it has an initial positive velocity v_{0x} but no initial displacement ($x_0 = 0$), the amplitude is $A = v_{0x}/\omega$ and the phase angle is $\phi = -\pi/2$. Express all phase angles in *radians*.

EVALUATE *your answer:* Make sure that your results are consistent. For example, suppose you used x_0 and v_{0x} to find general expressions for x and v_x at time t. If you substitute $t = 0$ into these expressions, you should get back the given values of x_0 and v_{0x}.

Example 14.3 Describing SHM

We give the glider of Example 14.2 an initial displacement $x_0 = +0.015$ m and an initial velocity $v_{0x} = +0.40$ m/s. (a) Find the period, amplitude, and phase angle of the resulting motion. (b) Write equations for the displacement, velocity, and acceleration as functions of time.

SOLUTION

IDENTIFY and SET UP: As in Example 14.2, the oscillations are SHM. We use equations from this section and the given values $k = 200$ N/m, $m = 0.50$ kg, x_0, and v_{0x} to calculate the target variables A and ϕ and to obtain expressions for x, v_x, and a_x.

Continued

EXECUTE: (a) In SHM the period and angular frequency are *properties of the system* that depend only on k and m, not on the amplitude, and so are the same as in Example 14.2 ($T = 0.31$ s and $\omega = 20$ rad/s). From Eq. (14.19), the amplitude is

$$A = \sqrt{x_0^2 + \frac{v_{0x}^2}{\omega^2}} = \sqrt{(0.015 \text{ m})^2 + \frac{(0.40 \text{ m/s})^2}{(20 \text{ rad/s})^2}} = 0.025 \text{ m}$$

We use Eq. (14.18) to find the phase angle:

$$\phi = \arctan\left(-\frac{v_{0x}}{\omega x_0}\right)$$

$$= \arctan\left(-\frac{0.40 \text{ m/s}}{(20 \text{ rad/s})(0.015 \text{ m})}\right) = -53° = -0.93 \text{ rad}$$

(b) The displacement, velocity, and acceleration at any time are given by Eqs. (14.13), (14.15), and (14.16), respectively. We substitute the values of A, ω, and ϕ into these equations:

$$x = (0.025 \text{ m})\cos[(20 \text{ rad/s})t - 0.93 \text{ rad}]$$
$$v_x = -(0.50 \text{ m/s})\sin[(20 \text{ rad/s})t - 0.93 \text{ rad}]$$
$$a_x = -(10 \text{ m/s}^2)\cos[(20 \text{ rad/s})t - 0.93 \text{ rad}]$$

EVALUATE: You can check the expressions for x and v_x by confirming that if you substitute $t = 0$, they yield $x = x_0 = 0.015$ m and $v_x = v_{0x} = 0.40$ m/s.

Test Your Understanding of Section 14.2   A glider is attached to a spring as shown in Fig. 14.13. If the glider is moved to $x = 0.10$ m and released from rest at time $t = 0$, it will oscillate with amplitude $A = 0.10$ m and phase angle $\phi = 0$. (a) Suppose instead that at $t = 0$ the glider is at $x = 0.10$ m and is moving to the right in Fig. 14.13. In this situation is the amplitude greater than, less than, or equal to 0.10 m? Is the phase angle greater than, less than, or equal to zero? (b) Suppose instead that at $t = 0$ the glider is at $x = 0.10$ m and is moving to the left in Fig. 14.13. In this situation is the amplitude greater than, less than, or equal to 0.10 m? Is the phase angle greater than, less than, or equal to zero?

PhET: Masses & Springs
ActivPhysics 9.3: Vibrational Energy
ActivPhysics 9.4: Two Ways to Weigh Young Tarzan
ActivPhysics 9.6: Releasing a Vibrating Skier I
ActivPhysics 9.7: Releasing a Vibrating Skier II
ActivPhysics 9.8: One- and Two-Spring Vibrating Systems
ActivPhysics 9.9: Vibro-Ride

14.3 Energy in Simple Harmonic Motion

We can learn even more about simple harmonic motion by using energy considerations. Take another look at the body oscillating on the end of a spring in Figs. 14.2 and 14.13. We've already noted that the spring force is the only horizontal force on the body. The force exerted by an ideal spring is a conservative force, and the vertical forces do no work, so the total mechanical energy of the system is *conserved*. We also assume that the mass of the spring itself is negligible.

The kinetic energy of the body is $K = \frac{1}{2}mv^2$ and the potential energy of the spring is $U = \frac{1}{2}kx^2$, just as in Section 7.2. (You'll find it helpful to review that section.) There are no nonconservative forces that do work, so the total mechanical energy $E = K + U$ is conserved:

$$E = \tfrac{1}{2}mv_x^2 + \tfrac{1}{2}kx^2 = \text{constant} \qquad (14.20)$$

(Since the motion is one-dimensional, $v^2 = v_x^2$.)

The total mechanical energy E is also directly related to the amplitude A of the motion. When the body reaches the point $x = A$, its maximum displacement from equilibrium, it momentarily stops as it turns back toward the equilibrium position. That is, when $x = A$ (or $-A$), $v_x = 0$. At this point the energy is entirely potential, and $E = \frac{1}{2}kA^2$. Because E is constant, it is equal to $\frac{1}{2}kA^2$ at any other point. Combining this expression with Eq. (14.20), we get

$$E = \tfrac{1}{2}mv_x^2 + \tfrac{1}{2}kx^2 = \tfrac{1}{2}kA^2 = \text{constant} \qquad \begin{array}{l}\text{(total mechanical} \\ \text{energy in SHM)}\end{array} \quad (14.21)$$

We can verify this equation by substituting x and v_x from Eqs. (14.13) and (14.15) and using $\omega^2 = k/m$ from Eq. (14.9):

$$E = \tfrac{1}{2}mv_x^2 + \tfrac{1}{2}kx^2 = \tfrac{1}{2}m[-\omega A\sin(\omega t + \phi)]^2 + \tfrac{1}{2}k[A\cos(\omega t + \phi)]^2$$
$$= \tfrac{1}{2}kA^2\sin^2(\omega t + \phi) + \tfrac{1}{2}kA^2\cos^2(\omega t + \phi)$$
$$= \tfrac{1}{2}kA^2$$

14.14 Graphs of E, K, and U versus displacement in SHM. The velocity of the body is *not* constant, so these images of the body at equally spaced positions are *not* equally spaced in time.

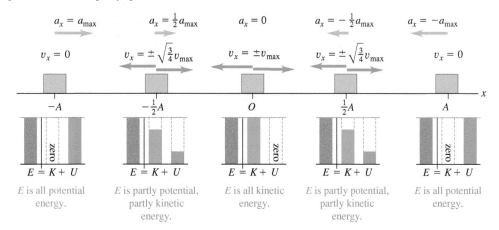

(Recall that $\sin^2\alpha + \cos^2\alpha = 1$.) Hence our expressions for displacement and velocity in SHM are consistent with energy conservation, as they must be.

We can use Eq. (14.21) to solve for the velocity v_x of the body at a given displacement x:

$$v_x = \pm\sqrt{\frac{k}{m}}\sqrt{A^2 - x^2} \qquad (14.22)$$

The $\pm$ sign means that at a given value of x the body can be moving in either direction. For example, when $x = \pm A/2$,

$$v_x = \pm\sqrt{\frac{k}{m}}\sqrt{A^2 - \left(\pm\frac{A}{2}\right)^2} = \pm\sqrt{\frac{3}{4}}\sqrt{\frac{k}{m}}A$$

Equation (14.22) also shows that the *maximum* speed v_{max} occurs at $x = 0$. Using Eq. (14.10), $\omega = \sqrt{k/m}$, we find that

$$v_{\text{max}} = \sqrt{\frac{k}{m}}A = \omega A \qquad (14.23)$$

This agrees with Eq. (14.15): v_x oscillates between $-\omega A$ and $+\omega A$.

Interpreting E, K, and U in SHM

Figure 14.14 shows the energy quantities E, K, and U at $x = 0$, $x = \pm A/2$, and $x = \pm A$. Figure 14.15 is a graphical display of Eq. (14.21); energy (kinetic, potential, and total) is plotted vertically and the coordinate x is plotted horizontally.

(a) The potential energy U and total mechanical energy E for a body in SHM as a function of displacement x

The total mechanical energy E is constant.

(b) The same graph as in (a), showing kinetic energy K as well

At $x = \pm A$ the energy is all potential; the kinetic energy is zero.

At $x = 0$ the energy is all kinetic; the potential energy is zero.

At these points the energy is half kinetic and half potential.

14.15 Kinetic energy K, potential energy U, and total mechanical energy E as functions of position for SHM. At each value of x the sum of the values of K and U equals the constant value of E. Can you show that the energy is half kinetic and half potential at $x = \pm\sqrt{\frac{1}{2}}A$?

The parabolic curve in Fig. 14.15a represents the potential energy $U = \frac{1}{2}kx^2$. The horizontal line represents the total mechanical energy E, which is constant and does not vary with x. At any value of x between $-A$ and A, the vertical distance from the x-axis to the parabola is U; since $E = K + U$, the remaining vertical distance up to the horizontal line is K. Figure 14.15b shows both K and U as functions of x. The horizontal line for E intersects the potential-energy curve at $x = -A$ and $x = A$, so at these points the energy is entirely potential, the kinetic energy is zero, and the body comes momentarily to rest before reversing direction. As the body oscillates between $-A$ and A, the energy is continuously transformed from potential to kinetic and back again.

Figure 14.15a shows the connection between the amplitude A and the corresponding total mechanical energy $E = \frac{1}{2}kA^2$. If we tried to make x greater than A (or less than $-A$), U would be greater than E, and K would have to be negative. But K can never be negative, so x can't be greater than A or less than $-A$.

Problem-Solving Strategy 14.2 | **Simple Harmonic Motion II: Energy**

The SHM energy equation, Eq. (14.21), is a useful relationship among velocity, position, and total mechanical energy. If the problem requires you to relate position, velocity, and acceleration without reference to time, consider using Eq. (14.4) (from Newton's second law) or Eq. (14.21) (from energy conservation). Because

Eq. (14.21) involves x^2 and v_x^2, you must infer the *signs* of x and v_x from the situation. For instance, if the body is moving from the equilibrium position toward the point of greatest positive displacement, then x is positive and v_x is positive.

Example 14.4 | **Velocity, acceleration, and energy in SHM**

(a) Find the maximum and minimum velocities attained by the oscillating glider of Example 14.2. (b) Find the maximum and minimum accelerations. (c) Find the velocity v_x and acceleration a_x when the glider is halfway from its initial position to the equilibrium position $x = 0$. (d) Find the total energy, potential energy, and kinetic energy at this position.

SOLUTION

IDENTIFY and SET UP: The problem concerns properties of the motion at specified *positions*, not at specified *times*, so we can use the energy relationships of this section. Figure 14.13 shows our choice of x-axis. The maximum displacement from equilibrium is $A = 0.020$ m. We use Eqs. (14.22) and (14.4) to find v_x and a_x for a given x. We then use Eq. (14.21) for given x and v_x to find the total, potential, and kinetic energies E, U, and K.

EXECUTE: (a) From Eq. (14.22), the velocity v_x at any displacement x is

$$v_x = \pm\sqrt{\frac{k}{m}}\sqrt{A^2 - x^2}$$

The glider's maximum *speed* occurs when it is moving through $x = 0$:

$$v_{max} = \sqrt{\frac{k}{m}}\,A = \sqrt{\frac{200\ \text{N/m}}{0.50\ \text{kg}}}(0.020\ \text{m}) = 0.40\ \text{m/s}$$

Its maximum and minimum (most negative) *velocities* are $+0.40$ m/s and -0.40 m/s, which occur when it is moving through $x = 0$ to the right and left, respectively.

(b) From Eq. (14.4), $a_x = -(k/m)x$. The glider's maximum (most positive) acceleration occurs at the most negative value of x, $x = -A$:

$$a_{max} = -\frac{k}{m}(-A) = -\frac{200\ \text{N/m}}{0.50\ \text{kg}}(-0.020\ \text{m}) = 8.0\ \text{m/s}^2$$

The minimum (most negative) acceleration is $a_{min} = -8.0$ m/s^2, which occurs at $x = +A = +0.020$ m.

(c) The point halfway from $x = x_0 = A$ to $x = 0$ is $x = A/2 = 0.010$ m. From Eq. (14.22), at this point

$$v_x = -\sqrt{\frac{200\ \text{N/m}}{0.50\ \text{kg}}}\sqrt{(0.020\ \text{m})^2 - (0.010\ \text{m})^2} = -0.35\ \text{m/s}$$

We choose the negative square root because the glider is moving from $x = A$ toward $x = 0$. From Eq. (14.4),

$$a_x = -\frac{200\ \text{N/m}}{0.50\ \text{kg}}(0.010\ \text{m}) = -4.0\ \text{m/s}^2$$

Figure 14.14 shows the conditions at $x = 0$, $\pm A/2$, and $\pm A$.

(d) The energies are

$$E = \tfrac{1}{2}kA^2 = \tfrac{1}{2}(200\ \text{N/m})(0.020\ \text{m})^2 = 0.040\ \text{J}$$

$$U = \tfrac{1}{2}kx^2 = \tfrac{1}{2}(200\ \text{N/m})(0.010\ \text{m})^2 = 0.010\ \text{J}$$

$$K = \tfrac{1}{2}mv_x^2 = \tfrac{1}{2}(0.50\ \text{kg})(-0.35\ \text{m/s})^2 = 0.030\ \text{J}$$

EVALUATE: At $x = A/2$, the total energy is one-fourth potential energy and three-fourths kinetic energy. You can confirm this by inspecting Fig. 14.15b.

Example 14.5 **Energy and momentum in SHM**

A block of mass M attached to a horizontal spring with force constant k is moving in SHM with amplitude A_1. As the block passes through its equilibrium position, a lump of putty of mass m is dropped from a small height and sticks to it. (a) Find the new amplitude and period of the motion. (b) Repeat part (a) if the putty is dropped onto the block when it is at one end of its path.

SOLUTION

IDENTIFY and SET UP: The problem involves the motion at a given position, not a given time, so we can use energy methods. Figure 14.16 shows our sketches. Before the putty falls, the mechanical energy of the block–spring system is constant. In part (a), the putty–block collision is completely inelastic: The horizontal component of momentum is conserved, kinetic energy decreases, and the amount of mass that's oscillating increases. After the collision, the mechanical energy remains constant at its new value. In part (b) the oscillating mass also increases, but the block isn't moving when the putty is added; there is effectively no collision at all, and no mechanical energy is lost. We find the amplitude A_2 after each collision from the final energy of the system using Eq. (14.21) and conservation of momentum. The period T_2 after the collision is a *property of the system*, so it is the same in both parts (a) and (b); we find it using Eq. (14.12).

EXECUTE: (a) Before the collision the total mechanical energy of the block and spring is $E_1 = \frac{1}{2}kA_1^2$. The block is at $x = 0$, so $U = 0$ and the energy is purely kinetic (Fig. 14.16a). If we let v_1 be the speed of the block at this point, then $E_1 = \frac{1}{2}kA_1^2 = \frac{1}{2}Mv_1^2$ and

$$v_1 = \sqrt{\frac{k}{M}}A_1$$

During the collision the x-component of momentum of the block–putty system is conserved. (Why?) Just before the collision this component is the sum of Mv_1 (for the block) and zero (for the putty). Just after the collision the block and putty move together with speed v_2, so their combined x-component of momentum is $(M + m)v_2$. From conservation of momentum,

$$Mv_1 + 0 = (M + m)v_2 \quad \text{so} \quad v_2 = \frac{M}{M + m}v_1$$

We assume that the collision lasts a very short time, so that the block and putty are still at the equilibrium position just after the collision. The energy is still purely kinetic but is *less* than before the collision:

$$E_2 = \frac{1}{2}(M + m)v_2^2 = \frac{1}{2}\frac{M^2}{M + m}v_1^2$$

$$= \frac{M}{M + m}\left(\frac{1}{2}Mv_1^2\right) = \left(\frac{M}{M + m}\right)E_1$$

14.16 Our sketches for this problem.

(a)

(b)

Since $E_2 = \frac{1}{2}kA_2^2$, where A_2 is the amplitude after the collision, we have

$$\frac{1}{2}kA_2^2 = \left(\frac{M}{M + m}\right)\frac{1}{2}kA_1^2$$

$$A_2 = A_1\sqrt{\frac{M}{M + m}}$$

From Eq. (14.12), the period of oscillation after the collision is

$$T_2 = 2\pi\sqrt{\frac{M + m}{k}}$$

(b) When the putty falls, the block is instantaneously at rest (Fig. 14.16b). The x-component of momentum is zero both before and after the collision. The block and putty have zero kinetic energy just before and just after the collision. The energy is all potential energy stored in the spring, so adding the putty has *no effect* on the mechanical energy. That is, $E_2 = E_1 = \frac{1}{2}kA_1^2$, and the amplitude is unchanged: $A_2 = A_1$. The period is again $T_2 = 2\pi\sqrt{(M + m)/k}$.

EVALUATE: Energy is lost in part (a) because the putty slides against the moving block during the collision, and energy is dissipated by kinetic friction. No energy is lost in part (b), because there is no sliding during the collision.

Test Your Understanding of Section 14.3 (a) To double the total energy for a mass-spring system oscillating in SHM, by what factor must the amplitude increase? (i) 4; (ii) 2; (iii) $\sqrt{2} = 1.414$; (iv) $\sqrt[4]{2} = 1.189$. (b) By what factor will the frequency change due to this amplitude increase? (i) 4; (ii) 2; (iii) $\sqrt{2} = 1.414$; (iv) $\sqrt[4]{2} = 1.189$; (v) it does not change.

14.4 Applications of Simple Harmonic Motion

So far, we've looked at a grand total of *one* situation in which simple harmonic motion (SHM) occurs: a body attached to an ideal horizontal spring. But SHM can occur in any system in which there is a restoring force that is directly proportional to the displacement from equilibrium, as given by Eq. (14.3), $F_x = -kx$. The restoring force will originate in different ways in different situations, so the force constant k has to be found for each case by examining the net force on the system. Once this is done, it's straightforward to find the angular frequency ω, frequency f, and period T; we just substitute the value of k into Eqs. (14.10), (14.11), and (14.12), respectively. Let's use these ideas to examine several examples of simple harmonic motion.

Vertical SHM

Suppose we hang a spring with force constant k (Fig. 14.17a) and suspend from it a body with mass m. Oscillations will now be vertical; will they still be SHM? In Fig. 14.17b the body hangs at rest, in equilibrium. In this position the spring is stretched an amount Δl just great enough that the spring's upward vertical force $k \, \Delta l$ on the body balances its weight mg:

$$k \, \Delta l = mg$$

Take $x = 0$ to be this equilibrium position and take the positive x-direction to be upward. When the body is a distance x *above* its equilibrium position (Fig. 14.17c), the extension of the spring is $\Delta l - x$. The upward force it exerts on the body is then $k(\Delta l - x)$, and the net x-component of force on the body is

$$F_{\text{net}} = k(\Delta l - x) + (-mg) = -kx$$

that is, a net downward force of magnitude kx. Similarly, when the body is *below* the equilibrium position, there is a net upward force with magnitude kx. In either case there is a restoring force with magnitude kx. If the body is set in vertical motion, it oscillates in SHM with the same angular frequency as though it were horizontal, $\omega = \sqrt{k/m}$. So vertical SHM doesn't differ in any essential way from horizontal SHM. The only real change is that the equilibrium position $x = 0$ no longer corresponds to the point at which the spring is unstretched. The same ideas hold if a body with weight mg is placed atop a compressible spring (Fig. 14.18) and compresses it a distance Δl.

14.17 A body attached to a hanging spring.

(a)

A hanging spring that obeys Hooke's law

(b) A body is suspended from the spring. It is in equilibrium when the upward force exerted by the stretched spring equals the body's weight.

$F = k\Delta l$

$x = 0$

mg

(c) If the body is displaced from equilibrium, the net force on the body is proportional to its displacement. The oscillations are SHM.

$\Delta l - x$

$F = k(\Delta l - x)$

x

mg

Example 14.6 | Vertical SHM in an old car

The shock absorbers in an old car with mass 1000 kg are completely worn out. When a 980-N person climbs slowly into the car at its center of gravity, the car sinks 2.8 cm. The car (with the person aboard) hits a bump, and the car starts oscillating up and down in SHM. Model the car and person as a single body on a single spring, and find the period and frequency of the oscillation.

SOLUTION

IDENTIFY and SET UP: The situation is like that shown in Fig. 14.18. The compression of the spring when the person's weight is added tells us the force constant, which we can use to find the period and frequency (the target variables).

EXECUTE: When the force increases by 980 N, the spring compresses an additional 0.028 m, and the x-coordinate of the car changes by -0.028 m. Hence the effective force constant (including the effect of the entire suspension) is

$$k = -\frac{F_x}{x} = -\frac{980 \text{ N}}{-0.028 \text{ m}} = 3.5 \times 10^4 \text{ kg/s}^2$$

The person's mass is $w/g = (980 \text{ N})/(9.8 \text{ m/s}^2) = 100$ kg. The *total* oscillating mass is $m = 1000 \text{ kg} + 100 \text{ kg} = 1100$ kg. The period T is

$$T = 2\pi\sqrt{\frac{m}{k}} = 2\pi\sqrt{\frac{1100 \text{ kg}}{3.5 \times 10^4 \text{ kg/s}^2}} = 1.11 \text{ s}$$

The frequency is $f = 1/T = 1/(1.11 \text{ s}) = 0.90$ Hz.

EVALUATE: A persistent oscillation with a period of about 1 second makes for a very unpleasant ride. The purpose of shock absorbers is to make such oscillations die out (see Section 14.7).

Angular SHM

A mechanical watch keeps time based on the oscillations of a balance wheel (Fig. 14.19). The wheel has a moment of inertia I about its axis. A coil spring exerts a restoring torque τ_z that is proportional to the angular displacement θ from the equilibrium position. We write $\tau_z = -\kappa\theta$, where κ (the Greek letter kappa) is a constant called the *torsion constant*. Using the rotational analog of Newton's second law for a rigid body, $\Sigma\tau_z = I\alpha_z = I \, d^2\theta/dt^2$, we can find the equation of motion:

$$-\kappa\theta = I\alpha \quad \text{or} \quad \frac{d^2\theta}{dt^2} = -\frac{\kappa}{I}\theta$$

The form of this equation is exactly the same as Eq. (14.4) for the acceleration in simple harmonic motion, with x replaced by θ and k/m replaced by κ/I. So we are dealing with a form of *angular* simple harmonic motion. The angular frequency ω and frequency f are given by Eqs. (14.10) and (14.11), respectively, with the same replacement:

$$\omega = \sqrt{\frac{\kappa}{I}} \quad \text{and} \quad f = \frac{1}{2\pi}\sqrt{\frac{\kappa}{I}} \quad \text{(angular SHM)} \quad \text{(14.24)}$$

The motion is described by the function

$$\theta = \Theta\cos(\omega t + \phi)$$

where Θ (the Greek letter theta) plays the role of an angular amplitude.

It's a good thing that the motion of a balance wheel *is* simple harmonic. If it weren't, the frequency might depend on the amplitude, and the watch would run too fast or too slow as the spring ran down.

Vibrations of Molecules

The following discussion of the vibrations of molecules uses the binomial theorem. If you aren't familiar with this theorem, you should read about it in the appropriate section of a math textbook.

When two atoms are separated from each other by a few atomic diameters, they can exert attractive forces on each other. But if the atoms are so close to each other that their electron shells overlap, the forces between the atoms are repulsive. Between these limits, there can be an equilibrium separation distance at which two atoms form a *molecule*. If these atoms are displaced slightly from equilibrium, they will oscillate.

14.18 If the weight mg compresses the spring a distance Δl, the force constant is $k = mg/\Delta l$ and the angular frequency for vertical SHM is $\omega = \sqrt{k/m}$—the same as if the body were suspended from the spring (see Fig. 14.17).

A body is placed atop the spring. It is in equilibrium when the upward force exerted by the compressed spring equals the body's weight.

A spring that obeys Hooke's law

14.19 The balance wheel of a mechanical watch. The spring exerts a restoring torque that is proportional to the angular displacement θ, so the motion is angular SHM.

Balance wheel   Spring

The spring torque τ_z opposes the angular displacement θ.

14.20 (a) Two atoms with centers separated by r. (b) Potential energy U in the van der Waals interaction as a function of r. (c) Force F_r on the right-hand atom as a function of r.

(a) Two-atom system

Distance between atom centers

r

Atoms

F_r = the force exerted by the left-hand atom on the right-hand atom

(b) Potential energy U of the two-atom system as a function of r

Near equilibrium, U can be approximated by a parabola.

The equilibrium point is at $r = R_0$ (where U is minimum).

(c) The force F_r as a function of r

Near equilibrium, F_r can be approximated by a straight line.

The equilibrium point is at $r = R_0$ (where F_r is zero).

As an example, we'll consider one type of interaction between atoms called the *van der Waals interaction.* Our immediate task here is to study oscillations, so we won't go into the details of how this interaction arises. Let the center of one atom be at the origin and let the center of the other atom be a distance r away (Fig. 14.20a); the equilibrium distance between centers is $r = R_0$. Experiment shows that the van der Waals interaction can be described by the potential-energy function

$$U = U_0 \left[\left(\frac{R_0}{r} \right)^{12} - 2 \left(\frac{R_0}{r} \right)^6 \right] \qquad (14.25)$$

where U_0 is a positive constant with units of joules. When the two atoms are very far apart, $U = 0$; when they are separated by the equilibrium distance $r = R_0$, $U = -U_0$. The force on the second atom is the negative derivative of Eq. (14.25):

$$F_r = -\frac{dU}{dr} = U_0 \left[\frac{12 R_0^{12}}{r^{13}} - 2 \frac{6 R_0^6}{r^7} \right] = 12 \frac{U_0}{R_0} \left[\left(\frac{R_0}{r} \right)^{13} - \left(\frac{R_0}{r} \right)^7 \right] \qquad (14.26)$$

Figures 14.20b and 14.20c plot the potential energy and force, respectively. The force is positive for $r < R_0$ and negative for $r > R_0$, so it is a *restoring* force.

Let's examine the restoring force F_r in Eq. (14.26). We let x represent the displacement from equilibrium:

$$x = r - R_0 \qquad \text{so} \qquad r = R_0 + x$$

In terms of x, the force F_r in Eq. (14.26) becomes

$$F_r = 12 \frac{U_0}{R_0} \left[\left(\frac{R_0}{R_0 + x} \right)^{13} - \left(\frac{R_0}{R_0 + x} \right)^7 \right]$$

$$= 12 \frac{U_0}{R_0} \left[\frac{1}{(1 + x/R_0)^{13}} - \frac{1}{(1 + x/R_0)^7} \right] \qquad (14.27)$$

This looks nothing like Hooke's law, $F_x = -kx$, so we might be tempted to conclude that molecular oscillations cannot be SHM. But let us restrict ourselves to *small-amplitude* oscillations so that the absolute value of the displacement x is small in comparison to R_0 and the absolute value of the ratio x/R_0 is much less than 1. We can then simplify Eq. (14.27) by using the *binomial theorem:*

$$(1 + u)^n = 1 + nu + \frac{n(n-1)}{2!} u^2 + \frac{n(n-1)(n-2)}{3!} u^3 + \cdots \qquad (14.28)$$

If $|u|$ is much less than 1, each successive term in Eq. (14.28) is much smaller than the one it follows, and we can safely approximate $(1 + u)^n$ by just the first two terms. In Eq. (14.27), u is replaced by x/R_0 and n equals -13 or -7, so

$$\frac{1}{(1 + x/R_0)^{13}} = (1 + x/R_0)^{-13} \approx 1 + (-13)\frac{x}{R_0}$$

$$\frac{1}{(1 + x/R_0)^7} = (1 + x/R_0)^{-7} \approx 1 + (-7)\frac{x}{R_0}$$

$$F_r \approx 12\frac{U_0}{R_0}\left[\left(1 + (-13)\frac{x}{R_0}\right) - \left(1 + (-7)\frac{x}{R_0}\right)\right] = -\left(\frac{72U_0}{R_0^2}\right)x \quad [14.29]$$

This is just Hooke's law, with force constant $k = 72U_0/R_0^2$. (Note that k has the correct units, J/m^2 or N/m.) So oscillations of molecules bound by the van der Waals interaction can be simple harmonic motion, provided that the amplitude is small in comparison to R_0 so that the approximation $|x/R_0| \ll 1$ used in the derivation of Eq. (14.29) is valid.

You can also use the binomial theorem to show that the potential energy U in Eq. (14.25) can be written as $U \approx \frac{1}{2}kx^2 + C$, where $C = -U_0$ and k is again equal to $72U_0/R_0^2$. Adding a constant to the potential energy has no effect on the physics, so the system of two atoms is fundamentally no different from a mass attached to a horizontal spring for which $U = \frac{1}{2}kx^2$.

Example 14.7 **Molecular vibration**

Two argon atoms form the molecule Ar_2 as a result of a van der Waals interaction with $U_0 = 1.68 \times 10^{-21}$ J and $R_0 = 3.82 \times 10^{-10}$ m. Find the frequency of small oscillations of one Ar atom about its equilibrium position.

SOLUTION

IDENTIFY and SET UP This is just the situation shown in Fig. 14.20. Because the oscillations are small, we can use Eq. (14.29) to find the force constant k and Eq. (14.11) to find the frequency f of SHM.

EXECUTE: From Eq. (14.29),

$$k = \frac{72U_0}{R_0^2} = \frac{72(1.68 \times 10^{-21}\text{ J})}{(3.82 \times 10^{-10}\text{ m})^2} = 0.829\text{ J/m}^2 = 0.829\text{ N/m}$$

(This force constant is comparable to that of a loose toy spring like a Slinky™.) From Appendix D, the average atomic mass of argon is $(39.948\text{ u})(1.66 \times 10^{-27}\text{ kg/1 u}) = 6.63 \times 10^{-26}$ kg.

From Eq. (14.11), if one atom is fixed and the other oscillates,

$$f = \frac{1}{2\pi}\sqrt{\frac{k}{m}} = \frac{1}{2\pi}\sqrt{\frac{0.829\text{ N/m}}{6.63 \times 10^{-26}\text{ kg}}} = 5.63 \times 10^{11}\text{ Hz}$$

EVALUATE: Our answer for f isn't quite right. If no net external force acts on the molecule, its center of mass (halfway between the atoms) doesn't accelerate, so *both* atoms must oscillate with the same amplitude in opposite directions. It turns out that we can account for this by replacing m with $m/2$ in our expression for f. This makes f larger by a factor of $\sqrt{2}$, so the correct frequency is $f = \sqrt{2}(5.63 \times 10^{11}\text{ Hz}) = 7.96 \times 10^{11}$ Hz. What's more, on the atomic scale we must use *quantum mechanics* rather than Newtonian mechanics to describe motion; happily, quantum mechanics also yields $f = 7.96 \times 10^{11}$ Hz.

Test Your Understanding of Section 14.4 A block attached to a hanging ideal spring oscillates up and down with a period of 10 s on earth. If you take the block and spring to Mars, where the acceleration due to gravity is only about 40% as large as on earth, what will be the new period of oscillation? (i) 10 s; (ii) more than 10 s; (iii) less than 10 s.

14.5 The Simple Pendulum

A **simple pendulum** is an idealized model consisting of a point mass suspended by a massless, unstretchable string. When the point mass is pulled to one side of its straight-down equilibrium position and released, it oscillates about the equilibrium position. Familiar situations such as a wrecking ball on a crane's cable or a person on a swing (Fig. 14.21a) can be modeled as simple pendulums.

PhET: Pendulum Lab
ActivPhysics 9.10: Pendulum Frequency
ActivPhysics 9.11: Risky Pendulum Walk
ActivPhysics 9.12: Physical Pendulum

14.21 The dynamics of a simple pendulum.

(a) A real pendulum

(b) An idealized simple pendulum

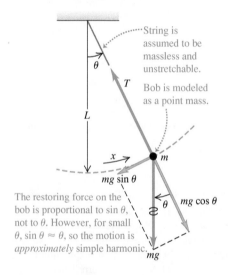

String is assumed to be massless and unstretchable.

Bob is modeled as a point mass.

The restoring force on the bob is proportional to sin θ, not to θ. However, for small θ, sin $\theta \approx \theta$, so the motion is *approximately* simple harmonic.

14.22 For small angular displacements θ, the restoring force $F_\theta = -mg \sin\theta$ on a simple pendulum is approximately equal to $-mg\theta$; that is, it is approximately proportional to the displacement θ. Hence for small angles the oscillations are simple harmonic.

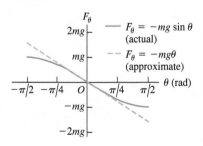

The path of the point mass (sometimes called a pendulum bob) is not a straight line but the arc of a circle with radius L equal to the length of the string (Fig. 14.21b). We use as our coordinate the distance x measured along the arc. If the motion is simple harmonic, the restoring force must be directly proportional to x or (because $x = L\theta$) to θ. Is it?

In Fig. 14.21b we represent the forces on the mass in terms of tangential and radial components. The restoring force F_θ is the tangential component of the net force:

$$F_\theta = -mg \sin\theta \qquad (14.30)$$

The restoring force is provided by gravity; the tension T merely acts to make the point mass move in an arc. The restoring force is proportional *not* to θ but to $\sin\theta$, so the motion is *not* simple harmonic. However, if the angle θ is *small*, $\sin\theta$ is very nearly equal to θ in radians (Fig. 14.22). For example, when $\theta = 0.1$ rad (about 6°), $\sin\theta = 0.0998$, a difference of only 0.2%. With this approximation, Eq. (14.30) becomes

$$F_\theta = -mg\theta = -mg\frac{x}{L} \qquad \text{or}$$

$$F_\theta = -\frac{mg}{L}x \qquad (14.31)$$

The restoring force is then proportional to the coordinate for small displacements, and the force constant is $k = mg/L$. From Eq. (14.10) the angular frequency ω of a simple pendulum with small amplitude is

$$\omega = \sqrt{\frac{k}{m}} = \sqrt{\frac{mg/L}{m}} = \sqrt{\frac{g}{L}} \qquad \begin{array}{l}\text{(simple pendulum,}\\ \text{small amplitude)}\end{array} \qquad (14.32)$$

The corresponding frequency and period relationships are

$$f = \frac{\omega}{2\pi} = \frac{1}{2\pi}\sqrt{\frac{g}{L}} \qquad \text{(simple pendulum, small amplitude)} \qquad (14.33)$$

$$T = \frac{2\pi}{\omega} = \frac{1}{f} = 2\pi\sqrt{\frac{L}{g}} \qquad \text{(simple pendulum, small amplitude)} \qquad (14.34)$$

Note that these expressions do not involve the *mass* of the particle. This is because the restoring force, a component of the particle's weight, is proportional to m. Thus the mass appears on *both* sides of $\Sigma\vec{F} = m\vec{a}$ and cancels out. (This is the same physics that explains why bodies of different masses fall with the same acceleration in a vacuum.) For small oscillations, the period of a pendulum for a given value of g is determined entirely by its length.

The dependence on L and g in Eqs. (14.32) through (14.34) is just what we should expect. A long pendulum has a longer period than a shorter one. Increasing g increases the restoring force, causing the frequency to increase and the period to decrease.

We emphasize again that the motion of a pendulum is only *approximately* simple harmonic. When the amplitude is not small, the departures from simple harmonic motion can be substantial. But how small is "small"? The period can be expressed by an infinite series; when the maximum angular displacement is Θ, the period T is given by

$$T = 2\pi\sqrt{\frac{L}{g}}\left(1 + \frac{1^2}{2^2}\sin^2\frac{\Theta}{2} + \frac{1^2\cdot3^2}{2^2\cdot4^2}\sin^4\frac{\Theta}{2} + \cdots\right) \qquad (14.35)$$

We can compute the period to any desired degree of precision by taking enough terms in the series. We invite you to check that when $\Theta = 15°$ (on either side of the central position), the true period is longer than that given by the approximate Eq. (14.34) by less than 0.5%.

The usefulness of the pendulum as a timekeeper depends on the period being *very nearly* independent of amplitude, provided that the amplitude is small. Thus, as a pendulum clock runs down and the amplitude of the swings decreases a little, the clock still keeps very nearly correct time.

Example 14.8 **A simple pendulum**

Find the period and frequency of a simple pendulum 1.000 m long at a location where $g = 9.800$ m/s^2.

SOLUTION

IDENTIFY and SET UP: This is a simple pendulum, so we can use the ideas of this section. We use Eq. (14.34) to determine the pendulum's period T from its length, and Eq. (14.1) to find the frequency f from T.

EXECUTE: From Eqs. (14.34) and (14.1),

$$T = 2\pi\sqrt{\frac{L}{g}} = 2\pi\sqrt{\frac{1.000 \text{ m}}{9.800 \text{ m/s}^2}} = 2.007 \text{ s}$$

$$f = \frac{1}{T} = \frac{1}{2.007 \text{ s}} = 0.4983 \text{ Hz}$$

EVALUATE: The period is almost exactly 2 s. When the metric system was established, the second was *defined* as half the period of a 1-m simple pendulum. This was a poor standard, however, because the value of g varies from place to place. We discussed more modern time standards in Section 1.3.

Test Your Understanding of Section 14.5 When a body oscillating on a horizontal spring passes through its equilibrium position, its acceleration is zero (see Fig. 14.2b). When the bob of an oscillating simple pendulum passes through its equilibrium position, is its acceleration zero?

14.6 The Physical Pendulum

A **physical pendulum** is any *real* pendulum that uses an extended body, as contrasted to the idealized model of the *simple* pendulum with all the mass concentrated at a single point. For small oscillations, analyzing the motion of a real, physical pendulum is almost as easy as for a simple pendulum. Figure 14.23 shows a body of irregular shape pivoted so that it can turn without friction about an axis through point O. In the equilibrium position the center of gravity is directly below the pivot; in the position shown in the figure, the body is displaced from equilibrium by an angle θ, which we use as a coordinate for the system. The distance from O to the center of gravity is d, the moment of inertia of the body about the axis of rotation through O is I, and the total mass is m. When the body is displaced as shown, the weight mg causes a restoring torque

$$\tau_z = -(mg)(d\sin\theta) \qquad (14.36)$$

The negative sign shows that the restoring torque is clockwise when the displacement is counterclockwise, and vice versa.

When the body is released, it oscillates about its equilibrium position. The motion is not simple harmonic because the torque τ_z is proportional to $\sin\theta$ rather than to θ itself. However, if θ is small, we can approximate $\sin\theta$ by θ in radians, just as we did in analyzing the simple pendulum. Then the motion is *approximately* simple harmonic. With this approximation,

$$\tau_z = -(mgd)\theta$$

The equation of motion is $\sum\tau_z = I\alpha_z$, so

$$-(mgd)\theta = I\alpha_z = I\frac{d^2\theta}{dt^2}$$

$$\frac{d^2\theta}{dt^2} = -\frac{mgd}{I}\theta \qquad (14.37)$$

14.23 Dynamics of a physical pendulum.

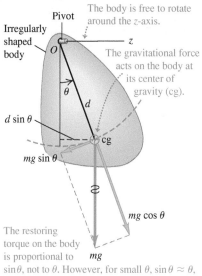

The body is free to rotate around the z-axis.

Pivot

Irregularly shaped body

O

z

The gravitational force acts on the body at its center of gravity (cg).

θ

d

$d\sin\theta$

cg

$mg\sin\theta$

$mg\cos\theta$

mg

The restoring torque on the body is proportional to $\sin\theta$, not to θ. However, for small θ, $\sin\theta \approx \theta$, so the motion is *approximately* simple harmonic.

Comparing this with Eq. (14.4), we see that the role of (k/m) for the spring-mass system is played here by the quantity (mgd/I). Thus the angular frequency is

$$\omega = \sqrt{\frac{mgd}{I}} \qquad \text{(physical pendulum, small amplitude)} \qquad (14.38)$$

The frequency f is $1/2\pi$ times this, and the period T is

$$T = 2\pi\sqrt{\frac{I}{mgd}} \qquad \text{(physical pendulum, small amplitude)} \qquad (14.39)$$

Equation (14.39) is the basis of a common method for experimentally determining the moment of inertia of a body with a complicated shape. First locate the center of gravity of the body by balancing. Then suspend the body so that it is free to oscillate about an axis, and measure the period T of small-amplitude oscillations. Finally, use Eq. (14.39) to calculate the moment of inertia I of the body about this axis from T, the body's mass m, and the distance d from the axis to the center of gravity (see Exercise 14.53). Biomechanics researchers use this method to find the moments of inertia of an animal's limbs. This information is important for analyzing how an animal walks, as we'll see in the second of the two following examples.

Example 14.9   Physical pendulum versus simple pendulum

If the body in Fig. 14.23 is a uniform rod with length L, pivoted at one end, what is the period of its motion as a pendulum?

SOLUTION

IDENTIFY and SET UP: Our target variable is the oscillation period T of a rod that acts as a physical pendulum. We find the rod's moment of inertia in Table 9.2, and then determine T using Eq. (14.39).

EXECUTE: The moment of inertia of a uniform rod about an axis through one end is $I = \frac{1}{3}ML^2$. The distance from the pivot to the rod's center of gravity is $d = L/2$. Then from Eq. (14.39),

$$T = 2\pi\sqrt{\frac{I}{mgd}} = 2\pi\sqrt{\frac{\frac{1}{3}ML^2}{MgL/2}} = 2\pi\sqrt{\frac{2L}{3g}}$$

EVALUATE: If the rod is a meter stick $(L = 1.00\ \text{m})$ and $g = 9.80\ \text{m/s}^2$, then

$$T = 2\pi\sqrt{\frac{2(1.00\ \text{m})}{3(9.80\ \text{m/s}^2)}} = 1.64\ \text{s}$$

The period is smaller by a factor of $\sqrt{\frac{2}{3}} = 0.816$ than that of a simple pendulum of the same length (see Example 14.8). The rod's moment of inertia around one end, $I = \frac{1}{3}ML^2$, is one-third that of the simple pendulum, and the rod's cg is half as far from the pivot as that of the simple pendulum. You can show that, taken together in Eq. (14.39), these two differences account for the factor $\sqrt{\frac{2}{3}}$ by which the periods differ.

Example 14.10   Tyrannosaurus rex and the physical pendulum

All walking animals, including humans, have a natural walking pace—a number of steps per minute that is more comfortable than a faster or slower pace. Suppose that this pace corresponds to the oscillation of the leg as a physical pendulum. (a) How does this pace depend on the length L of the leg from hip to foot? Treat the leg as a uniform rod pivoted at the hip joint. (b) Fossil evidence shows that *T. rex,* a two-legged dinosaur that lived about 65 million years ago, had a leg length $L = 3.1\ \text{m}$ and a stride length $S = 4.0\ \text{m}$ (the distance from one footprint to the next print of the same foot; see Fig. 14.24). Estimate the walking speed of *T. rex.*

SOLUTION

IDENTIFY and SET UP: Our target variables are (a) the relationship between walking pace and leg length L and (b) the walking speed of *T. rex.* We treat the leg as a physical pendulum, with a period of

14.24 The walking speed of *Tyrannosaurus rex* can be estimated from leg length L and stride length S.

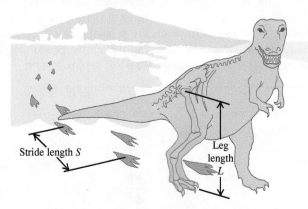

Stride length S

Leg length L

oscillation as found in Example 14.9. We can find the walking speed from the period and the stride length.

EXECUTE: (a) From Example 14.9 the period of oscillation of the leg is $T = 2\pi \sqrt{2L/3g}$, which is proportional to $\sqrt{L}$. Each step takes one-half a period, so the walking pace (in steps per second) is twice the oscillation frequency $f = 1/T$, which is proportional to $1/\sqrt{L}$. The greater the leg length L, the slower the walking pace.

(b) According to our model, T. rex traveled one stride length S in a time

$$T = 2\pi \sqrt{\frac{2L}{3g}} = 2\pi \sqrt{\frac{2(3.1 \text{ m})}{3(9.8 \text{ m/s}^2)}} = 2.9 \text{ s}$$

so its walking speed was

$$v = \frac{S}{T} = \frac{4.0 \text{ m}}{2.9 \text{ s}} = 1.4 \text{ m/s} = 5.0 \text{ km/h} = 3.1 \text{ mi/h}$$

This is roughly the walking speed of an adult human.

EVALUATE: A uniform rod isn't a very good model for a leg. The legs of many animals, including both *T. rex* and humans, are tapered; there is more mass between hip and knee than between knee and foot. The center of mass is therefore less than $L/2$ from the hip; a reasonable guess would be about $L/4$. The moment of inertia is therefore *considerably* less than $ML^2/3$—say, $ML^2/15$. Use the analysis of Example 14.9 with these corrections; you'll get a shorter oscillation period and an even greater walking speed for *T. rex*.

Test Your Understanding of Section 14.6 The center of gravity of a simple pendulum of mass m and length L is located at the position of the pendulum bob, a distance L from the pivot point. The center of gravity of a uniform rod of the same mass m and length $2L$ pivoted at one end is also a distance L from the pivot point. How does the period of this uniform rod compare to the period of the simple pendulum? (i) The rod has a longer period; (ii) the rod has a shorter period; (iii) the rod has the same period.

14.7 Damped Oscillations

The idealized oscillating systems we have discussed so far are frictionless. There are no nonconservative forces, the total mechanical energy is constant, and a system set into motion continues oscillating forever with no decrease in amplitude.

Real-world systems always have some dissipative forces, however, and oscillations die out with time unless we replace the dissipated mechanical energy (Fig. 14.25). A mechanical pendulum clock continues to run because potential energy stored in the spring or a hanging weight system replaces the mechanical energy lost due to friction in the pivot and the gears. But eventually the spring runs down or the weights reach the bottom of their travel. Then no more energy is available, and the pendulum swings decrease in amplitude and stop.

The decrease in amplitude caused by dissipative forces is called **damping,** and the corresponding motion is called **damped oscillation.** The simplest case to analyze in detail is a simple harmonic oscillator with a frictional damping force that is directly proportional to the *velocity* of the oscillating body. This behavior occurs in friction involving viscous fluid flow, such as in shock absorbers or sliding between oil-lubricated surfaces. We then have an additional force on the body due to friction, $F_x = -bv_x$, where $v_x = dx/dt$ is the velocity and b is a constant that describes the strength of the damping force. The negative sign shows that the force is always opposite in direction to the velocity. The *net* force on the body is then

$$\sum F_x = -kx - bv_x \tag{14.40}$$

and Newton's second law for the system is

$$-kx - bv_x = ma_x \quad \text{or} \quad -kx - b\frac{dx}{dt} = m\frac{d^2x}{dt^2} \tag{14.41}$$

Equation (14.41) is a differential equation for x; it would be the same as Eq. (14.4), the equation for the acceleration in SHM, except for the added term $-bdx/dt$. Solving this equation is a straightforward problem in differential equations, but we won't go into the details here. If the damping force is relatively small, the motion is described by

$$x = Ae^{-(b/2m)t}\cos(\omega't + \phi) \quad \text{(oscillator with little damping)} \tag{14.42}$$

14.25 A swinging bell left to itself will eventually stop oscillating due to damping forces (air resistance and friction at the point of suspension).

14.26 Graph of displacement versus time for an oscillator with little damping [see Eq. (14.42)] and with phase angle $\phi = 0$. The curves are for two values of the damping constant b.

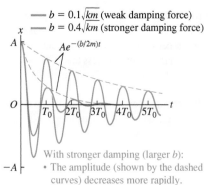

— $b = 0.1\sqrt{km}$ (weak damping force)
— $b = 0.4\sqrt{km}$ (stronger damping force)

With stronger damping (larger b):
• The amplitude (shown by the dashed curves) decreases more rapidly.
• The period T increases (T_0 = period with zero damping).

The angular frequency of oscillation ω' is given by

$$\omega' = \sqrt{\frac{k}{m} - \frac{b^2}{4m^2}} \quad \text{(oscillator with little damping)} \quad (14.43)$$

You can verify that Eq. (14.42) is a solution of Eq. (14.41) by calculating the first and second derivatives of x, substituting them into Eq. (14.41), and checking whether the left and right sides are equal. This is a straightforward but slightly tedious procedure.

The motion described by Eq. (14.42) differs from the undamped case in two ways. First, the amplitude $Ae^{-(b/2m)t}$ is not constant but decreases with time because of the decreasing exponential factor $e^{-(b/2m)t}$. Figure 14.26 is a graph of Eq. (14.42) for the case $\phi = 0$; it shows that the larger the value of b, the more quickly the amplitude decreases.

Second, the angular frequency ω', given by Eq. (14.43), is no longer equal to $\omega = \sqrt{k/m}$ but is somewhat smaller. It becomes zero when b becomes so large that

$$\frac{k}{m} - \frac{b^2}{4m^2} = 0 \quad \text{or} \quad b = 2\sqrt{km} \quad (14.44)$$

When Eq. (14.44) is satisfied, the condition is called **critical damping.** The system no longer oscillates but returns to its equilibrium position without oscillation when it is displaced and released.

If b is greater than $2\sqrt{km}$, the condition is called **overdamping.** Again there is no oscillation, but the system returns to equilibrium more slowly than with critical damping. For the overdamped case the solutions of Eq. (14.41) have the form

$$x = C_1 e^{-a_1 t} + C_2 e^{-a_2 t}$$

where C_1 and C_2 are constants that depend on the initial conditions and a_1 and a_2 are constants determined by m, k, and b.

When b is less than the critical value, as in Eq. (14.42), the condition is called **underdamping.** The system oscillates with steadily decreasing amplitude.

In a vibrating tuning fork or guitar string, it is usually desirable to have as little damping as possible. By contrast, damping plays a beneficial role in the oscillations of an automobile's suspension system. The shock absorbers provide a velocity-dependent damping force so that when the car goes over a bump, it doesn't continue bouncing forever (Fig. 14.27). For optimal passenger comfort, the system should be critically damped or slightly underdamped. Too much damping would be counterproductive; if the suspension is overdamped and the car hits a second bump just after the first one, the springs in the suspension will still be compressed somewhat from the first bump and will not be able to fully absorb the impact.

Energy in Damped Oscillations

In damped oscillations the damping force is nonconservative; the mechanical energy of the system is not constant but decreases continuously, approaching zero after a long time. To derive an expression for the rate of change of energy, we first write an expression for the total mechanical energy E at any instant:

$$E = \tfrac{1}{2}mv_x^2 + \tfrac{1}{2}kx^2$$

To find the rate of change of this quantity, we take its time derivative:

$$\frac{dE}{dt} = mv_x\frac{dv_x}{dt} + kx\frac{dx}{dt}$$

But $dv_x/dt = a_x$ and $dx/dt = v_x$, so

$$\frac{dE}{dt} = v_x(ma_x + kx)$$

14.27 An automobile shock absorber. The viscous fluid causes a damping force that depends on the relative velocity of the two ends of the unit.

Upper cylinder attached to car's frame; moves little.

Piston

Viscous fluid

Lower cylinder attached to axle; moves up and down.

Pushed up

Pushed down

From Eq. (14.41), $ma_x + kx = -bdx/dt = -bv_x$, so

$$\frac{dE}{dt} = v_x(-bv_x) = -bv_x^2 \quad \text{(damped oscillations)} \qquad (14.45)$$

The right side of Eq. (14.45) is **negative** whenever the oscillating body is in motion, whether the x-velocity v_x is positive or negative. This shows that as the body moves, the energy decreases, though not at a uniform rate. The term $-bv_x^2 = (-bv_x)v_x$ (force times velocity) is the rate at which the damping force does (negative) work on the system (that is, the damping *power*). This equals the rate of change of the total mechanical energy of the system.

Similar behavior occurs in electric circuits containing inductance, capacitance, and resistance. There is a natural frequency of oscillation, and the resistance plays the role of the damping constant b. We will study these circuits in detail in Chapters 30 and 31.

Test Your Understanding of Section 14.7 An airplane is flying in a straight line at a constant altitude. If a wind gust strikes and raises the nose of the airplane, the nose will bob up and down until the airplane eventually returns to its original attitude. Are these oscillations (i) undamped, (ii) underdamped, (iii) critically damped, or (iv) overdamped?

14.8 Forced Oscillations and Resonance

A damped oscillator left to itself will eventually stop moving altogether. But we can maintain a constant-amplitude oscillation by applying a force that varies with time in a periodic or cyclic way, with a definite period and frequency. As an example, consider your cousin Throckmorton on a playground swing. You can keep him swinging with constant amplitude by giving him a little push once each cycle. We call this additional force a **driving force.**

Damped Oscillation with a Periodic Driving Force

If we apply a periodically varying driving force with angular frequency ω_d to a damped harmonic oscillator, the motion that results is called a **forced oscillation** or a *driven oscillation.* It is different from the motion that occurs when the system is simply displaced from equilibrium and then left alone, in which case the system oscillates with a **natural angular frequency** ω' determined by m, k, and b, as in Eq. (14.43). In a forced oscillation, however, the angular frequency with which the mass oscillates is equal to the driving angular frequency ω_d. This does *not* have to be equal to the angular frequency ω' with which the system would oscillate without a driving force. If you grab the ropes of Throckmorton's swing, you can force the swing to oscillate with any frequency you like.

Suppose we force the oscillator to vibrate with an angular frequency ω_d that is nearly *equal* to the angular frequency ω' it would have with no driving force. What happens? The oscillator is naturally disposed to oscillate at $\omega = \omega'$, so we expect the amplitude of the resulting oscillation to be larger than when the two frequencies are very different. Detailed analysis and experiment show that this is just what happens. The easiest case to analyze is a *sinusoidally* varying force— say, $F(t) = F_{max} \cos \omega_d t$. If we vary the frequency ω_d of the driving force, the amplitude of the resulting forced oscillation varies in an interesting way (Fig. 14.28). When there is very little damping (small b), the amplitude goes through a sharp peak as the driving angular frequency ω_d nears the natural oscillation angular frequency ω'. When the damping is increased (larger b), the peak becomes broader and smaller in height and shifts toward lower frequencies.

We could work out an expression that shows how the amplitude A of the forced oscillation depends on the frequency of a sinusoidal driving force, with

14.28 Graph of the amplitude A of forced oscillation as a function of the angular frequency ω_d of the driving force. The horizontal axis shows the ratio of ω_d to the angular frequency $\omega = \sqrt{k/m}$ of an undamped oscillator. Each curve has a different value of the damping constant b.

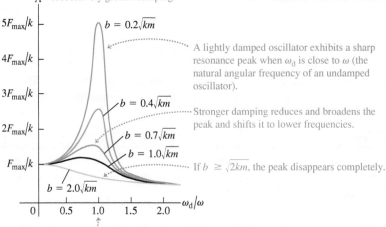

Each curve shows the amplitude A for an oscillator subjected to a driving force at various angular frequencies ω_d. Successive curves from blue to gold represent successively greater damping.

A lightly damped oscillator exhibits a sharp resonance peak when ω_d is close to ω (the natural angular frequency of an undamped oscillator).

Stronger damping reduces and broadens the peak and shifts it to lower frequencies.

If $b \geq \sqrt{2km}$, the peak disappears completely.

Driving frequency ω_d equals natural angular frequency ω of an undamped oscillator.

maximum value F_{max}. That would involve more differential equations than we're ready for, but here is the result:

Video Tutor Demo

$$A = \frac{F_{\text{max}}}{\sqrt{(k - m\omega_d^2)^2 + b^2\omega_d^2}} \quad \text{(amplitude of a driven oscillator)} \quad (14.46)$$

When $k - m\omega_d^2 = 0$, the first term under the radical is zero, so A has a maximum near $\omega_d = \sqrt{k/m}$. The height of the curve at this point is proportional to $1/b$; the less damping, the higher the peak. At the low-frequency extreme, when $\omega_d = 0$, we get $A = F_{\text{max}}/k$. This corresponds to a *constant* force F_{max} and a constant displacement $A = F_{\text{max}}/k$ from equilibrium, as we might expect.

Resonance and Its Consequences

The fact that there is an amplitude peak at driving frequencies close to the natural frequency of the system is called **resonance.** Physics is full of examples of resonance; building up the oscillations of a child on a swing by pushing with a frequency equal to the swing's natural frequency is one. A vibrating rattle in a car that occurs only at a certain engine speed or wheel-rotation speed is an all-too-familiar example. Inexpensive loudspeakers often have an annoying boom or buzz when a musical note happens to coincide with the resonant frequency of the speaker cone or the speaker housing. In Chapter 16 we will study other examples of resonance that involve sound. Resonance also occurs in electric circuits, as we will see in Chapter 31; a tuned circuit in a radio or television receiver responds strongly to waves having frequencies near its resonant frequency, and this fact is used to select a particular station and reject the others.

Resonance in mechanical systems can be destructive. A company of soldiers once destroyed a bridge by marching across it in step; the frequency of their steps was close to a natural vibration frequency of the bridge, and the resulting oscillation had large enough amplitude to tear the bridge apart. Ever since, marching soldiers have been ordered to break step before crossing a bridge. Some years ago, vibrations of the engines of a particular airplane had just the right frequency to resonate with the natural frequencies of its wings. Large oscillations built up, and occasionally the wings fell off.

Application Canine Resonance
Unlike humans, dogs have no sweat glands and so must pant in order to cool down. The frequency at which a dog pants is very close to the resonant frequency of its respiratory system. This causes the maximum amount of air to move in and out of the dog and so minimizes the effort that the dog must exert to cool itself.

Test Your Understanding of Section 14.8 When driven at a frequency near its natural frequency, an oscillator with very little damping has a much greater response than the same oscillator with more damping. When driven at a frequency that is much higher or lower than the natural frequency, which oscillator will have the greater response: (i) the one with very little damping or (ii) the one with more damping?

Periodic motion: Periodic motion is motion that repeats itself in a definite cycle. It occurs whenever a body has a stable equilibrium position and a restoring force that acts when it is displaced from equilibrium. Period T is the time for one cycle. Frequency f is the number of cycles per unit time. Angular frequency ω is 2π times the frequency. (See Example 14.1.)

$$f = \frac{1}{T} \qquad T = \frac{1}{f} \tag{14.1}$$

$$\omega = 2\pi f = \frac{2\pi}{T} \tag{14.2}$$

Simple harmonic motion: If the restoring force F_x in periodic motion is directly proportional to the displacement x, the motion is called simple harmonic motion (SHM). In many cases this condition is satisfied if the displacement from equilibrium is small. The angular frequency, frequency, and period in SHM do not depend on the amplitude, but only on the mass m and force constant k. The displacement, velocity, and acceleration in SHM are sinusoidal functions of time; the amplitude A and phase angle ϕ of the oscillation are determined by the initial position and velocity of the body. (See Examples 14.2, 14.3, 14.6, and 14.7.)

$$F_x = -kx \tag{14.3}$$

$$a_x = \frac{F_x}{m} = -\frac{k}{m}x \tag{14.4}$$

$$\omega = \sqrt{\frac{k}{m}} \tag{14.10}$$

$$f = \frac{\omega}{2\pi} = \frac{1}{2\pi}\sqrt{\frac{k}{m}} \tag{14.11}$$

$$T = \frac{1}{f} = 2\pi\sqrt{\frac{m}{k}} \tag{14.12}$$

$$x = A\cos(\omega t + \phi) \tag{14.13}$$

Energy in simple harmonic motion: Energy is conserved in SHM. The total energy can be expressed in terms of the force constant k and amplitude A. (See Examples 14.4 and 14.5.)

$$E = \tfrac{1}{2}mv_x^2 + \tfrac{1}{2}kx^2 = \tfrac{1}{2}kA^2 = \text{constant} \tag{14.21}$$

Angular simple harmonic motion: In angular SHM, the frequency and angular frequency are related to the moment of inertia I and the torsion constant κ.

$$\omega = \sqrt{\frac{\kappa}{I}} \quad \text{and} \quad f = \frac{1}{2\pi}\sqrt{\frac{\kappa}{I}} \tag{14.24}$$

Spring torque τ_z opposes angular displacement θ.

Simple pendulum: A simple pendulum consists of a point mass m at the end of a massless string of length L. Its motion is approximately simple harmonic for sufficiently small amplitude; the angular frequency, frequency, and period then depend only on g and L, not on the mass or amplitude. (See Example 14.8.)

$$\omega = \sqrt{\frac{g}{L}} \tag{14.32}$$

$$f = \frac{\omega}{2\pi} = \frac{1}{2\pi}\sqrt{\frac{g}{L}} \tag{14.33}$$

$$T = \frac{2\pi}{\omega} = \frac{1}{f} = 2\pi\sqrt{\frac{L}{g}} \tag{14.34}$$

Physical pendulum: A physical pendulum is any body suspended from an axis of rotation. The angular frequency and period for small-amplitude oscillations are independent of amplitude, but depend on the mass m, distance d from the axis of rotation to the center of gravity, and moment of inertia I about the axis. (See Examples 14.9 and 14.10.)

$$\omega = \sqrt{\frac{mgd}{I}} \tag{14.38}$$

$$T = 2\pi\sqrt{\frac{I}{mgd}} \tag{14.39}$$

Damped oscillations: When a force $F_x = -bv_x$ proportional to velocity is added to a simple harmonic oscillator, the motion is called a damped oscillation. If $b < 2\sqrt{km}$ (called underdamping), the system oscillates with a decaying amplitude and an angular frequency ω' that is lower than it would be without damping. If $b = 2\sqrt{km}$ (called critical damping) or $b > 2\sqrt{km}$ (called overdamping), when the system is displaced it returns to equilibrium without oscillating.

$$x = Ae^{-(b/2m)t}\cos(\omega't + \phi) \quad (14.42)$$

$$\omega' = \sqrt{\frac{k}{m} - \frac{b^2}{4m^2}} \quad (14.43)$$

Driven oscillations and resonance: When a sinusoidally varying driving force is added to a damped harmonic oscillator, the resulting motion is called a forced oscillation. The amplitude is a function of the driving frequency ω_d and reaches a peak at a driving frequency close to the natural frequency of the system. This behavior is called resonance.

$$A = \frac{F_{max}}{\sqrt{(k - m\omega_d^2)^2 + b^2\omega_d^2}} \quad (14.46)$$

BRIDGING PROBLEM | **Oscillating and Rolling**

14.29

Two uniform, solid cylinders of radius R and total mass M are connected along their common axis by a short, light rod and rest on a horizontal tabletop (Fig. 14.29). A frictionless ring at the center of the rod is attached to a spring with force constant k; the other end of the spring is fixed. The cylinders are pulled to the left a distance x, stretching the spring, and then released from rest. Due to friction between the tabletop and the cylinders, the cylinders roll without slipping as they oscillate. Show that the motion of the center of mass of the cylinders is simple harmonic, and find its period.

SOLUTION GUIDE

See MasteringPhysics® study area for a Video Tutor solution.

IDENTIFY and SET UP

1. What condition must be satisfied for the motion of the center of mass of the cylinders to be simple harmonic? (*Hint:* See Section 14.2.)
2. Which equations should you use to describe the translational and rotational motions of the cylinders? Which equation should you use to describe the condition that the cylinders roll without slipping? (*Hint:* See Section 10.3.)
3. Sketch the situation and choose a coordinate system. Make a list of the unknown quantities and decide which is the target variable.

EXECUTE

4. Draw a free-body diagram for the cylinders when they are displaced a distance x from equilibrium.
5. Solve the equations to find an expression for the acceleration of the center of mass of the cylinders. What does this expression tell you?
6. Use your result from step 5 to find the period of oscillation of the center of mass of the cylinders.

EVALUATE

7. What would be the period of oscillation if there were no friction and the cylinders didn't roll? Is this period larger or smaller than your result from step 6? Is this reasonable?

Problems

For instructor-assigned homework, go to MasteringPhysics®. (MP)

•, ••, •••: Problems of increasing difficulty. **CP**: Cumulative problems incorporating material from earlier chapters. **CALC**: Problems requiring calculus. **BIO**: Biosciences problems.

DISCUSSION QUESTIONS

Q14.1 An object is moving with SHM of amplitude A on the end of a spring. If the amplitude is doubled, what happens to the total distance the object travels in one period? What happens to the period? What happens to the maximum speed of the object? Discuss how these answers are related.

Q14.2 Think of several examples in everyday life of motions that are, at least approximately, simple harmonic. In what respects does each differ from SHM?

Q14.3 Does a tuning fork or similar tuning instrument undergo SHM? Why is this a crucial question for musicians?

Q14.4 A box containing a pebble is attached to an ideal horizontal spring and is oscillating on a friction-free air table. When the box has reached its maximum distance from the equilibrium point, the pebble is suddenly lifted out vertically without disturbing the box. Will the following characteristics of the motion increase, decrease, or remain the same in the subsequent motion of the box? Justify each answer. (a) frequency; (b) period; (c) amplitude; (d) the maximum kinetic energy of the box; (e) the maximum speed of the box.

Q14.5 If a uniform spring is cut in half, what is the force constant of each half? Justify your answer. How would the frequency of SHM using a half-spring differ from the frequency using the same mass and the entire spring?

Q14.6 The analysis of SHM in this chapter ignored the mass of the spring. How does the spring's mass change the characteristics of the motion?

Q14.7 Two identical gliders on an air track are connected by an ideal spring. Could such a system undergo SHM? Explain. How would the period compare with that of a single glider attached to a spring whose other end is rigidly attached to a stationary object? Explain.

Q14.8 You are captured by Martians, taken into their ship, and put to sleep. You awake some time later and find yourself locked in a small room with no windows. All the Martians have left you with is your digital watch, your school ring, and your long silver-chain necklace. Explain how you can determine whether you are still on earth or have been transported to Mars.

Q14.9 The system shown in Fig. 14.17 is mounted in an elevator. What happens to the period of the motion (does it increase, decrease, or remain the same) if the elevator (a) accelerates upward at 5.0 m/s^2; (b) moves upward at a steady 5.0 m/s; (c) accelerates downward at 5.0 m/s^2? Justify your answers.

Q14.10 If a pendulum has a period of 2.5 s on earth, what would be its period in a space station orbiting the earth? If a mass hung from a vertical spring has a period of 5.0 s on earth, what would its period be in the space station? Justify each of your answers.

Q14.11 A simple pendulum is mounted in an elevator. What happens to the period of the pendulum (does it increase, decrease, or remain the same) if the elevator (a) accelerates upward at 5.0 m/s^2; (b) moves upward at a steady 5.0 m/s; (c) accelerates downward at 5.0 m/s^2; (d) accelerates downward at 9.8 m/s^2? Justify your answers.

Q14.12 What should you do to the length of the string of a simple pendulum to (a) double its frequency; (b) double its period; (c) double its angular frequency?

Q14.13 If a pendulum clock is taken to a mountaintop, does it gain or lose time, assuming it is correct at a lower elevation? Explain your answer.

Q14.14 When the amplitude of a simple pendulum increases, should its period increase or decrease? Give a qualitative argument; do not rely on Eq. (14.35). Is your argument also valid for a physical pendulum?

Q14.15 Why do short dogs (like Chihuahuas) walk with quicker strides than do tall dogs (like Great Danes)?

Q14.16 At what point in the motion of a simple pendulum is the string tension greatest? Least? In each case give the reasoning behind your answer.

Q14.17 Could a standard of time be based on the period of a certain standard pendulum? What advantages and disadvantages would such a standard have compared to the actual present-day standard discussed in Section 1.3?

Q14.18 For a simple pendulum, clearly distinguish between ω (the angular velocity) and ω (the angular frequency). Which is constant and which is variable?

Q14.19 A glider is attached to a fixed ideal spring and oscillates on a horizontal, friction-free air track. A coin is atop the glider and oscillating with it. At what points in the motion is the friction force on the coin greatest? At what points is it least? Justify your answers.

Q14.20 In designing structures in an earthquake-prone region, how should the natural frequencies of oscillation of a structure relate to typical earthquake frequencies? Why? Should the structure have a large or small amount of damping?

EXERCISES

Section 14.1 Describing Oscillation

14.1 • **BIO** (a) **Music.** When a person sings, his or her vocal cords vibrate in a repetitive pattern that has the same frequency as the note that is sung. If someone sings the note B flat, which has a frequency of 466 Hz, how much time does it take the person's vocal cords to vibrate through one complete cycle, and what is the angular frequency of the cords? (b) **Hearing.** When sound waves strike the eardrum, this membrane vibrates with the same frequency as the sound. The highest pitch that typical humans can hear has a period of $50.0 \ \mu\text{s}$. What are the frequency and angular frequency of the vibrating eardrum for this sound? (c) **Vision.** When light having vibrations with angular frequency ranging from $2.7 \times 10^{15} \text{ rad/s}$ to $4.7 \times 10^{15} \text{ rad/s}$ strikes the retina of the eye, it stimulates the receptor cells there and is perceived as visible light. What are the limits of the period and frequency of this light? (d) **Ultrasound.** High-frequency sound waves (ultrasound) are used to probe the interior of the body, much as x rays do. To detect small objects such as tumors, a frequency of around 5.0 MHz is used. What are the period and angular frequency of the molecular vibrations caused by this pulse of sound?

14.2 • If an object on a horizontal, frictionless surface is attached to a spring, displaced, and then released, it will oscillate. If it is displaced 0.120 m from its equilibrium position and released with zero initial speed, then after 0.800 s its displacement is found to be

0.120 m on the opposite side, and it has passed the equilibrium position once during this interval. Find (a) the amplitude; (b) the period; (c) the frequency.

14.3 • The tip of a tuning fork goes through 440 complete vibrations in 0.500 s. Find the angular frequency and the period of the motion.

14.4 • The displacement of an oscillating object as a function of time is shown in Fig. E14.4. What are (a) the frequency; (b) the amplitude; (c) the period; (d) the angular frequency of this motion?

Figure **E14.4**

14.5 •• A machine part is undergoing SHM with a frequency of 5.00 Hz and amplitude 1.80 cm. How long does it take the part to go from $x = 0$ to $x = -1.80$ cm?

Section 14.2 Simple Harmonic Motion

14.6 •• In a physics lab, you attach a 0.200-kg air-track glider to the end of an ideal spring of negligible mass and start it oscillating. The elapsed time from when the glider first moves through the equilibrium point to the second time it moves through that point is 2.60 s. Find the spring's force constant.

14.7 • When a body of unknown mass is attached to an ideal spring with force constant 120 N/m, it is found to vibrate with a frequency of 6.00 Hz. Find (a) the period of the motion; (b) the angular frequency; (c) the mass of the body.

14.8 • When a 0.750-kg mass oscillates on an ideal spring, the frequency is 1.33 Hz. What will the frequency be if 0.220 kg are (a) added to the original mass and (b) subtracted from the original mass? Try to solve this problem *without* finding the force constant of the spring.

14.9 •• An object is undergoing SHM with period 0.900 s and amplitude 0.320 m. At $t = 0$ the object is at $x = 0.320$ m and is instantaneously at rest. Calculate the time it takes the object to go (a) from $x = 0.320$ m to $x = 0.160$ m and (b) from $x = 0.160$ m to $x = 0$.

14.10 • A small block is attached to an ideal spring and is moving in SHM on a horizontal, frictionless surface. When the block is at $x = 0.280$ m, the acceleration of the block is -5.30 m/s^2. What is the frequency of the motion?

14.11 • A 2.00-kg, frictionless block is attached to an ideal spring with force constant 300 N/m. At $t = 0$ the spring is neither stretched nor compressed and the block is moving in the negative direction at 12.0 m/s. Find (a) the amplitude and (b) the phase angle. (c) Write an equation for the position as a function of time.

14.12 •• Repeat Exercise 14.11, but assume that at $t = 0$ the block has velocity -4.00 m/s and displacement $+0.200$ m.

14.13 • The point of the needle of a sewing machine moves in SHM along the x-axis with a frequency of 2.5 Hz. At $t = 0$ its position and velocity components are $+1.1$ cm and -15 cm/s, respectively. (a) Find the acceleration component of the needle at $t = 0$. (b) Write equations giving the position, velocity, and acceleration components of the point as a function of time.

14.14 •• A small block is attached to an ideal spring and is moving in SHM on a horizontal, frictionless surface. When the ampli-

tude of the motion is 0.090 m, it takes the block 2.70 s to travel from $x = 0.090$ m to $x = -0.090$ m. If the amplitude is doubled, to 0.180 m, how long does it take the block to travel (a) from $x = 0.180$ m to $x = -0.180$ m and (b) from $x = 0.090$ m to $x = -0.090$ m?

14.15 • **BIO** **Weighing Astronauts.** This procedure has actually been used to "weigh" astronauts in space. A 42.5-kg chair is attached to a spring and allowed to oscillate. When it is empty, the chair takes 1.30 s to make one complete vibration. But with an astronaut sitting in it, with her feet off the floor, the chair takes 2.54 s for one cycle. What is the mass of the astronaut?

14.16 • A 0.400-kg object undergoing SHM has $a_x = -2.70$ m/s^2 when $x = 0.300$ m. What is the time for one oscillation?

14.17 • On a frictionless, horizontal air track, a glider oscillates at the end of an ideal spring of force constant 2.50 N/cm. The graph in Fig. E14.17 shows the acceleration of the glider as a function of time. Find (a) the mass of the glider; (b) the maximum displacement of the glider from the equilibrium point; (c) the maximum force the spring exerts on the glider.

Figure **E14.17**

14.18 • A 0.500-kg mass on a spring has velocity as a function of time given by $v_x(t) = -(3.60$ cm/s$) \sin[(4.71$ s$^{-1})t - \pi/2]$. What are (a) the period; (b) the amplitude; (c) the maximum acceleration of the mass; (d) the force constant of the spring?

14.19 • A 1.50-kg mass on a spring has displacement as a function of time given by the equation

$$x(t) = (7.40 \text{ cm}) \cos[(4.16 \text{ s}^{-1})t - 2.42]$$

Find (a) the time for one complete vibration; (b) the force constant of the spring; (c) the maximum speed of the mass; (d) the maximum force on the mass; (e) the position, speed, and acceleration of the mass at $t = 1.00$ s; (f) the force on the mass at that time.

14.20 • **BIO** **Weighing a Virus.** In February 2004, scientists at Purdue University used a highly sensitive technique to measure the mass of a vaccinia virus (the kind used in smallpox vaccine). The procedure involved measuring the frequency of oscillation of a tiny sliver of silicon (just 30 nm long) with a laser, first without the virus and then after the virus had attached itself to the silicon. The difference in mass caused a change in the frequency. We can model such a process as a mass on a spring. (a) Show that the ratio of the frequency with the virus attached (f_{S+V}) to the frequency without the virus (f_S) is given by the formula $\dfrac{f_{S+V}}{f_S} = \dfrac{1}{\sqrt{1 + (m_V/m_S)}}$, where m_V is the mass of the virus and m_S is the mass of the silicon sliver. Notice that it is *not* necessary to know or measure the force constant of the spring. (b) In some data, the silicon sliver has a mass of 2.10×10^{-16} g and a frequency of 2.00×10^{15} Hz without the virus and 2.87×10^{14} Hz with the virus. What is the mass of the virus, in grams and in femtograms?

14.21 •• **CALC** **Jerk.** A guitar string vibrates at a frequency of 440 Hz. A point at its center moves in SHM with an amplitude of

3.0 mm and a phase angle of zero. (a) Write an equation for the position of the center of the string as a function of time. (b) What are the maximum values of the magnitudes of the velocity and acceleration of the center of the string? (c) The derivative of the acceleration with respect to time is a quantity called the *jerk*. Write an equation for the jerk of the center of the string as a function of time, and find the maximum value of the magnitude of the jerk.

Section 14.3 Energy in Simple Harmonic Motion

14.22 •• For the oscillating object in Fig. E14.4, what are (a) its maximum speed and (b) its maximum acceleration?

14.23 • A small block is attached to an ideal spring and is moving in SHM on a horizontal, frictionless surface. The amplitude of the motion is 0.120 m. The maximum speed of the block is 3.90 m/s. What is the maximum magnitude of the acceleration of the block?

14.24 • A small block is attached to an ideal spring and is moving in SHM on a horizontal, frictionless surface. The amplitude of the motion is 0.250 m and the period is 3.20 s. What are the speed and acceleration of the block when $x = 0.160$ m?

14.25 •• A tuning fork labeled 392 Hz has the tip of each of its two prongs vibrating with an amplitude of 0.600 mm. (a) What is the maximum speed of the tip of a prong? (b) A housefly (*Musca domestica*) with mass 0.0270 g is holding onto the tip of one of the prongs. As the prong vibrates, what is the fly's maximum kinetic energy? Assume that the fly's mass has a negligible effect on the frequency of oscillation.

14.26 •• A harmonic oscillator has angular frequency ω and amplitude A. (a) What are the magnitudes of the displacement and velocity when the elastic potential energy is equal to the kinetic energy? (Assume that $U = 0$ at equilibrium.) (b) How often does this occur in each cycle? What is the time between occurrences? (c) At an instant when the displacement is equal to $A/2$, what fraction of the total energy of the system is kinetic and what fraction is potential?

14.27 • A 0.500-kg glider, attached to the end of an ideal spring with force constant $k = 450$ N/m, undergoes SHM with an amplitude of 0.040 m. Compute (a) the maximum speed of the glider; (b) the speed of the glider when it is at $x = -0.015$ m; (c) the magnitude of the maximum acceleration of the glider; (d) the acceleration of the glider at $x = -0.015$ m; (e) the total mechanical energy of the glider at any point in its motion.

14.28 •• A cheerleader waves her pom-pom in SHM with an amplitude of 18.0 cm and a frequency of 0.850 Hz. Find (a) the maximum magnitude of the acceleration and of the velocity; (b) the acceleration and speed when the pom-pom's coordinate is $x = +9.0$ cm; (c) the time required to move from the equilibrium position directly to a point 12.0 cm away. (d) Which of the quantities asked for in parts (a), (b), and (c) can be found using the energy approach used in Section 14.3, and which cannot? Explain.

14.29 • **CP** For the situation described in part (a) of Example 14.5, what should be the value of the putty mass m so that the amplitude after the collision is one-half the original amplitude? For this value of m, what fraction of the original mechanical energy is converted into heat?

14.30 • A 0.150-kg toy is undergoing SHM on the end of a horizontal spring with force constant $k = 300$ N/m. When the object is 0.0120 m from its equilibrium position, it is observed to have a speed of 0.300 m/s. What are (a) the total energy of the object at any point of its motion; (b) the amplitude of the motion; (c) the maximum speed attained by the object during its motion?

14.31 •• You are watching an object that is moving in SHM. When the object is displaced 0.600 m to the right of its equilibrium position, it has a velocity of 2.20 m/s to the right and an acceleration of 8.40 m/s² to the left. How much farther from this point will the object move before it stops momentarily and then starts to move back to the left?

14.32 •• On a horizontal, frictionless table, an open-topped 5.20-kg box is attached to an ideal horizontal spring having force constant 375 N/m. Inside the box is a 3.44-kg stone. The system is oscillating with an amplitude of 7.50 cm. When the box has reached its maximum speed, the stone is suddenly plucked vertically out of the box without touching the box. Find (a) the period and (b) the amplitude of the resulting motion of the box. (c) Without doing any calculations, is the new period greater or smaller than the original period? How do you know?

14.33 •• A mass is oscillating with amplitude A at the end of a spring. How far (in terms of A) is this mass from the equilibrium position of the spring when the elastic potential energy equals the kinetic energy?

14.34 •• A mass m is attached to a spring of force constant 75 N/m and allowed to oscillate. Figure E14.34 shows a graph of its velocity v_x as a function of time t. Find (a) the period, (b) the frequency, and (c) the angular frequency of this motion. (d) What is the amplitude (in cm), and at what times does the mass reach this position? (e) Find the maximum acceleration of the mass and the times at which it occurs. (f) What is the mass m?

Figure **E14.34**

14.35 • Inside a NASA test vehicle, a 3.50-kg ball is pulled along by a horizontal ideal spring fixed to a friction-free table. The force constant of the spring is 225 N/m. The vehicle has a steady acceleration of 5.00 m/s², and the ball is not oscillating. Suddenly, when the vehicle's speed has reached 45.0 m/s, its engines turn off, thus eliminating its acceleration but not its velocity. Find (a) the amplitude and (b) the frequency of the resulting oscillations of the ball. (c) What will be the ball's maximum speed relative to the vehicle?

Section 14.4 Applications of Simple Harmonic Motion

14.36 • A proud deep-sea fisherman hangs a 65.0-kg fish from an ideal spring having negligible mass. The fish stretches the spring 0.120 m. (a) Find the force constant of the spring. The fish is now pulled down 5.00 cm and released. (b) What is the period of oscillation of the fish? (c) What is the maximum speed it will reach?

14.37 • A 175-g glider on a horizontal, frictionless air track is attached to a fixed ideal spring with force constant 155 N/m. At the instant you make measurements on the glider, it is moving at 0.815 m/s and is 3.00 cm from its equilibrium point. Use *energy conservation* to find (a) the amplitude of the motion and (b) the maximum speed of the glider. (c) What is the angular frequency of the oscillations?

14.38 • A thrill-seeking cat with mass 4.00 kg is attached by a harness to an ideal spring of negligible mass and oscillates vertically in SHM. The amplitude is 0.050 m, and at the highest point of the motion the spring has its natural unstretched length. Calculate the elastic potential energy of the spring (take it to be zero for the unstretched spring), the kinetic energy of the cat, the gravitational potential energy of the system relative to the lowest point of the motion, and the sum of these three energies when the cat is (a) at its highest point; (b) at its lowest point; (c) at its equilibrium position.

14.39 •• A 1.50-kg ball and a 2.00-kg ball are glued together with the lighter one below the heavier one. The upper ball is attached to a vertical ideal spring of force constant 165 N/m, and the system is vibrating vertically with amplitude 15.0 cm. The glue connecting the balls is old and weak, and it suddenly comes loose when the balls are at the lowest position in their motion. (a) Why is the glue more likely to fail at the *lowest* point than at any other point in the motion? (b) Find the amplitude and frequency of the vibrations after the lower ball has come loose.

14.40 •• A uniform, solid metal disk of mass 6.50 kg and diameter 24.0 cm hangs in a horizontal plane, supported at its center by a vertical metal wire. You find that it requires a horizontal force of 4.23 N tangent to the rim of the disk to turn it by 3.34°, thus twisting the wire. You now remove this force and release the disk from rest. (a) What is the torsion constant for the metal wire? (b) What are the frequency and period of the torsional oscillations of the disk? (c) Write the equation of motion for $\theta(t)$ for the disk.

14.41 •• A certain alarm clock ticks four times each second, with each tick representing half a period. The balance wheel consists of a thin rim with radius 0.55 cm, connected to the balance staff by thin spokes of negligible mass. The total mass of the balance wheel is 0.90 g. (a) What is the moment of inertia of the balance wheel about its shaft? (b) What is the torsion constant of the coil spring (Fig. 14.19)?

14.42 • A thin metal disk with mass 2.00×10^{-3} kg and radius 2.20 cm is attached at its center to a long fiber (Fig. E14.42). The disk, when twisted and released, oscillates with a period of 1.00 s. Find the torsion constant of the fiber.

Figure **E14.42**

14.43 •• You want to find the moment of inertia of a complicated machine part about an axis through its center of mass. You suspend it from a wire along this axis. The wire has a torsion constant of 0.450 N·m/rad. You twist the part a small amount about this axis and let it go, timing 125 oscillations in 265 s. What is the moment of inertia you want to find?

14.44 •• **CALC** The balance wheel of a watch vibrates with an angular amplitude Θ, angular frequency ω, and phase angle $\phi = 0$. (a) Find expressions for the angular velocity $d\theta/dt$ and angular acceleration $d^2\theta/dt^2$ as functions of time. (b) Find the balance wheel's angular velocity and angular acceleration when its angular displacement is Θ, and when its angular displacement is $\Theta/2$ and θ is decreasing. (*Hint:* Sketch a graph of θ versus *t*.)

Section 14.5 The Simple Pendulum

14.45 •• You pull a simple pendulum 0.240 m long to the side through an angle of 3.50° and release it. (a) How much time does it take the pendulum bob to reach its highest speed? (b) How much time does it take if the pendulum is released at an angle of 1.75° instead of 3.50°?

14.46 • An 85.0-kg mountain climber plans to swing down, starting from rest, from a ledge using a light rope 6.50 m long. He holds one end of the rope, and the other end is tied higher up on a rock face. Since the ledge is not very far from the rock face, the rope makes a small angle with the vertical. At the lowest point of his swing, he plans to let go and drop a short distance to the ground. (a) How long after he begins his swing will the climber first reach his lowest point? (b) If he missed the first chance to drop off, how long after first beginning his swing will the climber reach his lowest point for the second time?

14.47 • A building in San Francisco has light fixtures consisting of small 2.35-kg bulbs with shades hanging from the ceiling at the end of light, thin cords 1.50 m long. If a minor earthquake occurs, how many swings per second will these fixtures make?

14.48 • **A Pendulum on Mars.** A certain simple pendulum has a period on the earth of 1.60 s. What is its period on the surface of Mars, where $g = 3.71$ m/s^2?

14.49 • After landing on an unfamiliar planet, a space explorer constructs a simple pendulum of length 50.0 cm. She finds that the pendulum makes 100 complete swings in 136 s. What is the value of g on this planet?

14.50 •• A small sphere with mass m is attached to a massless rod of length L that is pivoted at the top, forming a simple pendulum. The pendulum is pulled to one side so that the rod is at an angle Θ from the vertical, and released from rest. (a) In a diagram, show the pendulum just after it is released. Draw vectors representing the *forces* acting on the small sphere and the *acceleration* of the sphere. Accuracy counts! At this point, what is the linear acceleration of the sphere? (b) Repeat part (a) for the instant when the pendulum rod is at an angle $\Theta/2$ from the vertical. (c) Repeat part (a) for the instant when the pendulum rod is vertical. At this point, what is the linear speed of the sphere?

14.51 • A simple pendulum 2.00 m long swings through a maximum angle of 30.0° with the vertical. Calculate its period (a) assuming a small amplitude, and (b) using the first three terms of Eq. (14.35). (c) Which of the answers in parts (a) and (b) is more accurate? For the one that is less accurate, by what percent is it in error from the more accurate answer?

Section 14.6 The Physical Pendulum

14.52 •• We want to hang a thin hoop on a horizontal nail and have the hoop make one complete small-angle oscillation each 2.0 s. What must the hoop's radius be?

14.53 • A 1.80-kg connecting rod from a car engine is pivoted about a horizontal knife edge as shown in Fig. E14.53. The center of gravity of the rod was located by balancing and is 0.200 m from the pivot. When the rod is set into small-amplitude oscillation, it makes 100 complete swings in 120 s. Calculate the moment of inertia of the rod about the rotation axis through the pivot.

Figure **E14.53**

$d = 0.200$ m

cg

14.54 •• A 1.80-kg monkey wrench is pivoted 0.250 m from its center of mass and allowed to swing as a physical pendulum. The period for small-angle oscillations is 0.940 s. (a) What is the moment of inertia of the wrench about an axis through the pivot? (b) If the wrench is initially displaced 0.400 rad from its equilibrium position, what is the angular speed of the wrench as it passes through the equilibrium position?

14.55 • Two pendulums have the same dimensions (length L) and total mass (m). Pendulum A is a very small ball swinging at the end of a uniform massless bar. In pendulum B, half the mass is in the ball and half is in the uniform bar. Find the period of each pendulum for small oscillations. Which one takes longer for a swing?

14.56 •• CP A holiday ornament in the shape of a hollow sphere with mass $M = 0.015$ kg and radius $R = 0.050$ m is hung from a tree limb by a small loop of wire attached to the surface of the sphere. If the ornament is displaced a small distance and released, it swings back and forth as a physical pendulum with negligible friction. Calculate its period. (*Hint:* Use the parallel-axis theorem to find the moment of inertia of the sphere about the pivot at the tree limb.)

14.57 •• The two pendulums shown in Fig. E14.57 each consist of a uniform solid ball of mass M supported by a rigid massless rod, but the ball for pendulum A is very tiny while the ball for pendulum B is much larger. Find the period of each pendulum for small displacements. Which ball takes longer to complete a swing?

Figure **E14.57**

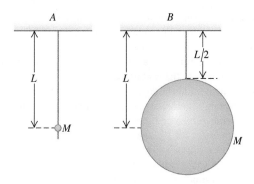

Section 14.7 Damped Oscillations

14.58 • A 2.50-kg rock is attached at the end of a thin, very light rope 1.45 m long. You start it swinging by releasing it when the rope makes an 11° angle with the vertical. You record the observation that it rises only to an angle of 4.5° with the vertical after $10\frac{1}{2}$ swings. (a) How much energy has this system lost during that time? (b) What happened to the "lost" energy? Explain *how* it could have been "lost."

14.59 • An unhappy 0.300-kg rodent, moving on the end of a spring with force constant $k = 2.50$ N/m, is acted on by a damping force $F_x = -bv_x$. (a) If the constant b has the value 0.900 kg/s, what is the frequency of oscillation of the rodent? (b) For what value of the constant b will the motion be critically damped?

14.60 •• A 50.0-g hard-boiled egg moves on the end of a spring with force constant $k = 25.0$ N/m. Its initial displacement is 0.300 m. A damping force $F_x = -bv_x$ acts on the egg, and the amplitude of the motion decreases to 0.100 m in 5.00 s. Calculate the magnitude of the damping constant b.

14.61 •• CALC The motion of an underdamped oscillator is described by Eq. (14.42). Let the phase angle ϕ be zero. (a) According to this equation, what is the value of x at $t = 0$? (b) What are the magnitude and direction of the velocity at $t = 0$? What does the result tell you about the slope of the graph of x versus t near $t = 0$? (c) Obtain an expression for the acceleration a_x at $t = 0$. For what value or range of values of the damping constant b (in terms of k and m) is the acceleration at $t = 0$ negative, zero, and positive? Discuss each case in terms of the shape of the graph of x versus t near $t = 0$.

14.62 •• A mass is vibrating at the end of a spring of force constant 225 N/m. Figure E14.62 shows a graph of its position x as a function of time t. (a) At what times is the mass not moving? (b) How much energy did this system originally contain? (c) How much energy did the system lose between $t = 1.0$ s and $t = 4.0$ s? Where did this energy go?

Figure **E14.62**

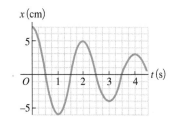

Section 14.8 Forced Oscillations and Resonance

14.63 • A sinusoidally varying driving force is applied to a damped harmonic oscillator. (a) What are the units of the damping constant b? (b) Show that the quantity $\sqrt{km}$ has the same units as b. (c) In terms of F_{max} and k, what is the amplitude for $\omega_d = \sqrt{k/m}$ when (i) $b = 0.2\sqrt{km}$ and (ii) $b = 0.4\sqrt{km}$? Compare your results to Fig. 14.28.

14.64 • A sinusoidally varying driving force is applied to a damped harmonic oscillator of force constant k and mass m. If the damping constant has a value b_1, the amplitude is A_1 when the driving angular frequency equals $\sqrt{k/m}$. In terms of A_1, what is the amplitude for the same driving frequency and the same driving force amplitude F_{max}, if the damping constant is (a) $3b_1$ and (b) $b_1/2$?

PROBLEMS

14.65 •• An object is undergoing SHM with period 1.200 s and amplitude 0.600 m. At $t = 0$ the object is at $x = 0$ and is moving in the negative x-direction. How far is the object from the equilibrium position when $t = 0.480$ s?

14.66 ••• An object is undergoing SHM with period 0.300 s and amplitude 6.00 cm. At $t = 0$ the object is instantaneously at rest at $x = 6.00$ cm. Calculate the time it takes the object to go from $x = 6.00$ cm to $x = -1.50$ cm.

14.67 • CP SHM in a Car Engine. The motion of the piston of an automobile engine is approximately simple harmonic. (a) If the stroke of an engine (twice the amplitude) is 0.100 m and the engine runs at 4500 rev/min, compute the acceleration of the piston at the endpoint of its stroke. (b) If the piston has mass 0.450 kg, what net force must be exerted on it at this point? (c) What are the speed and kinetic energy of the piston at the midpoint of its stroke? (d) What average power is required to accelerate the piston from rest to the speed found in part (c)? (e) If the engine runs at 7000 rev/min, what are the answers to parts (b), (c), and (d)?

14.68 • Four passengers with combined mass 250 kg compress the springs of a car with worn-out shock absorbers by 4.00 cm when they get in. Model the car and passengers as a single body on a single ideal spring. If the loaded car has a period of vibration of 1.92 s, what is the period of vibration of the empty car?

14.69 • A glider is oscillating in SHM on an air track with an amplitude A_1. You slow it so that its amplitude is halved. What happens to its (a) period, frequency, and angular frequency;

(b) total mechanical energy; (c) maximum speed; (d) speed at $x = \pm A_1/4$; (e) potential and kinetic energies at $x = \pm A_1/4$?

14.70 ••• CP A child with poor table manners is sliding his 250-g dinner plate back and forth in SHM with an amplitude of 0.100 m on a horizontal surface. At a point 0.060 m away from equilibrium, the speed of the plate is 0.400 m/s. (a) What is the period? (b) What is the displacement when the speed is 0.160 m/s? (c) In the center of the dinner plate is a 10.0-g carrot slice. If the carrot slice is just on the verge of slipping at the endpoint of the path, what is the coefficient of static friction between the carrot slice and the plate?

14.71 ••• A 1.50-kg, horizontal, uniform tray is attached to a vertical ideal spring of force constant 185 N/m and a 275-g metal ball is in the tray. The spring is below the tray, so it can oscillate up and down. The tray is then pushed down to point A, which is 15.0 cm below the equilibrium point, and released from rest. (a) How high above point A will the tray be when the metal ball leaves the tray? (*Hint:* This does *not* occur when the ball and tray reach their maximum speeds.) (b) How much time elapses between releasing the system at point A and the ball leaving the tray? (c) How fast is the ball moving just as it leaves the tray?

14.72 •• CP A block with mass M rests on a frictionless surface and is connected to a horizontal spring of force constant k. The other end of the spring is attached to a wall (Fig. P14.72). A second block with mass m rests on top of the first block. The coefficient of static friction between the blocks is μ_s. Find the *maximum* amplitude of oscillation such that the top block will not slip on the bottom block.

Figure **P14.72**

14.73 • CP A 10.0-kg mass is traveling to the right with a speed of 2.00 m/s on a smooth horizontal surface when it collides with and sticks to a second 10.0-kg mass that is initially at rest but is attached to a light spring with force constant 110.0 N/m. (a) Find the frequency, amplitude, and period of the subsequent oscillations. (b) How long does it take the system to return the first time to the position it had immediately after the collision?

14.74 • CP A rocket is accelerating upward at 4.00 m/s² from the launchpad on the earth. Inside a small, 1.50-kg ball hangs from the ceiling by a light, 1.10-m wire. If the ball is displaced 8.50° from the vertical and released, find the amplitude and period of the resulting swings of this pendulum.

14.75 ••• An apple weighs 1.00 N. When you hang it from the end of a long spring of force constant 1.50 N/m and negligible mass, it bounces up and down in SHM. If you stop the bouncing and let the apple swing from side to side through a small angle, the frequency of this simple pendulum is half the bounce frequency. (Because the angle is small, the back-and-forth swings do not cause any appreciable change in the length of the spring.) What is the unstretched length of the spring (with the apple removed)?

14.76 ••• CP **SHM of a Floating Object.** An object with height h, mass M, and a uniform cross-sectional area A floats upright in a liquid with density ρ. (a) Calculate the vertical distance from the surface of the liquid to the bottom of the floating object at equilibrium. (b) A downward force with magnitude F is applied to the top of the object. At the new equilibrium position, how much farther below the surface of the liquid is the bottom of the object than it was in part (a)? (Assume that some of the object remains above the surface of the liquid.) (c) Your result in part (b) shows that if the force is suddenly removed, the object will oscillate up and down in SHM. Calculate the period of this motion in terms of the density ρ of the liquid, the mass M, and the cross-sectional area A of the object. You can ignore the damping due to fluid friction (see Section 14.7).

14.77 •• CP A 950-kg, cylindrical can buoy floats vertically in salt water. The diameter of the buoy is 0.900 m. (a) Calculate the additional distance the buoy will sink when a 70.0-kg man stands on top of it. (Use the expression derived in part (b) of Problem 14.76.) (b) Calculate the period of the resulting vertical SHM when the man dives off. (Use the expression derived in part (c) of Problem 14.76, and as in that problem, you can ignore the damping due to fluid friction.)

14.78 ••• CP **Tarzan to the Rescue!** Tarzan spies a 35-kg chimpanzee in severe danger, so he swings to the rescue. He adjusts his strong, but very light, vine so that he will first come to rest 4.0 s after beginning his swing, at which time his vine makes a 12° angle with the vertical. (a) How long is Tarzan's vine, assuming that he swings at the bottom end of it? (b) What are the frequency and amplitude (in degrees) of Tarzan's swing? (c) Just as he passes through the lowest point in his swing, Tarzan nabs the chimp from the ground and sweeps him out of the jaws of danger. If Tarzan's mass is 65 kg, find the frequency and amplitude (in degrees) of the swing with Tarzan holding onto the grateful chimp.

14.79 •• CP A square object of mass m is constructed of four identical uniform thin sticks, each of length L, attached together. This object is hung on a hook at its upper corner (Fig. P14.79). If it is rotated slightly to the left and then released, at what frequency will it swing back and forth?

Figure **P14.79**

14.80 ••• An object with mass 0.200 kg is acted on by an elastic restoring force with force constant 10.0 N/m. (a) Graph elastic potential energy U as a function of displacement x over a range of x from -0.300 m to $+0.300$ m. On your graph, let 1 cm = 0.05 J vertically and 1 cm = 0.05 m horizontally. The object is set into oscillation with an initial potential energy of 0.140 J and an initial kinetic energy of 0.060 J. Answer the following questions by referring to the graph. (b) What is the amplitude of oscillation? (c) What is the potential energy when the displacement is one-half the amplitude? (d) At what displacement are the kinetic and potential energies equal? (e) What is the value of the phase angle ϕ if the initial velocity is positive and the initial displacement is negative?

14.81 • CALC A 2.00-kg bucket containing 10.0 kg of water is hanging from a vertical ideal spring of force constant 125 N/m and oscillating up and down with an amplitude of 3.00 cm. Suddenly the bucket springs a leak in the bottom such that water drops out at a steady rate of 2.00 g/s. When the bucket is half full, find

(a) the period of oscillation and (b) the rate at which the period is changing with respect to time. Is the period getting longer or shorter? (c) What is the shortest period this system can have?

14.82 ·· **CP** A hanging wire is 1.80 m long. When a 60.0-kg steel ball is suspended from the wire, the wire stretches by 2.00 mm. If the ball is pulled down a small additional distance and released, at what frequency will it vibrate? Assume that the stress on the wire is less than the proportional limit (see Section 11.5).

14.83 ·· A 5.00-kg partridge is suspended from a pear tree by an ideal spring of negligible mass. When the partridge is pulled down 0.100 m below its equilibrium position and released, it vibrates with a period of 4.20 s. (a) What is its speed as it passes through the equilibrium position? (b) What is its acceleration when it is 0.050 m above the equilibrium position? (c) When it is moving upward, how much time is required for it to move from a point 0.050 m below its equilibrium position to a point 0.050 m above it? (d) The motion of the partridge is stopped, and then it is removed from the spring. How much does the spring shorten?

14.84 ·· A 0.0200-kg bolt moves with SHM that has an amplitude of 0.240 m and a period of 1.500 s. The displacement of the bolt is +0.240 m when $t = 0$. Compute (a) the displacement of the bolt when $t = 0.500$ s; (b) the magnitude and direction of the force acting on the bolt when $t = 0.500$ s; (c) the minimum time required for the bolt to move from its initial position to the point where $x = -0.180$ m; (d) the speed of the bolt when $x = -0.180$ m.

14.85 ·· **CP SHM of a Butcher's Scale.** A spring of negligible mass and force constant $k = 400$ N/m is hung vertically, and a 0.200-kg pan is suspended from its lower end. A butcher drops a 2.2-kg steak onto the pan from a height of 0.40 m. The steak makes a totally inelastic collision with the pan and sets the system into vertical SHM. What are (a) the speed of the pan and steak immediately after the collision; (b) the amplitude of the subsequent motion; (c) the period of that motion?

14.86 ·· A uniform beam is suspended horizontally by two identical vertical springs that are attached between the ceiling and each end of the beam. The beam has mass 225 kg, and a 175-kg sack of gravel sits on the middle of it. The beam is oscillating in SHM, with an amplitude of 40.0 cm and a frequency of 0.600 cycle/s. (a) The sack of gravel falls off the beam when the beam has its maximum upward displacement. What are the frequency and amplitude of the subsequent SHM of the beam? (b) If the gravel instead falls off when the beam has its maximum speed, what are the frequency and amplitude of the subsequent SHM of the beam?

14.87 ··· **CP** On the planet Newtonia, a simple pendulum having a bob with mass 1.25 kg and a length of 185.0 cm takes 1.42 s, when released from rest, to swing through an angle of 12.5°, where it again has zero speed. The circumference of Newtonia is measured to be 51,400 km. What is the mass of the planet Newtonia?

14.88 ·· A 40.0-N force stretches a vertical spring 0.250 m. (a) What mass must be suspended from the spring so that the system will oscillate with a period of 1.00 s? (b) If the amplitude of the motion is 0.050 m and the period is that specified in part (a), where is the object and in what direction is it moving 0.35 s after it has passed the equilibrium position, moving downward? (c) What force (magnitude and direction) does the spring exert on the object when it is 0.030 m below the equilibrium position, moving upward?

14.89 ·· **Don't Miss the Boat.** While on a visit to Minnesota ("Land of 10,000 Lakes"), you sign up to take an excursion around one of the larger lakes. When you go to the dock where the 1500-kg boat is tied, you find that the boat is bobbing up and down in the waves, executing simple harmonic motion with amplitude 20 cm. The boat takes 3.5 s to make one complete up-and-down cycle.

When the boat is at its highest point, its deck is at the same height as the stationary dock. As you watch the boat bob up and down, you (mass 60 kg) begin to feel a bit woozy, due in part to the previous night's dinner of lutefisk. As a result, you refuse to board the boat unless the level of the boat's deck is within 10 cm of the dock level. How much time do you have to board the boat comfortably during each cycle of up-and-down motion?

14.90 · **CP** An interesting, though highly impractical example of oscillation is the motion of an object dropped down a hole that extends from one side of the earth, through its center, to the other side. With the assumption (not realistic) that the earth is a sphere of uniform density, prove that the motion is simple harmonic and find the period. [*Note:* The gravitational force on the object as a function of the object's distance r from the center of the earth was derived in Example 13.10 (Section 13.6). The motion is simple harmonic if the acceleration a_x and the displacement from equilibrium x are related by Eq. (14.8), and the period is then $T = 2\pi/\omega$.]

14.91 ··· **CP** A rifle bullet with mass 8.00 g and initial horizontal velocity 280 m/s strikes and embeds itself in a block with mass 0.992 kg that rests on a frictionless surface and is attached to one end of an ideal spring. The other end of the spring is attached to the wall. The impact compresses the spring a maximum distance of 18.0 cm. After the impact, the block moves in SHM. Calculate the period of this motion.

14.92 ·· **CP CALC** For a certain oscillator the net force on the body with mass m is given by $F_x = -cx^3$. (a) What is the potential energy function for this oscillator if we take $U = 0$ at $x = 0$? (b) One-quarter of a period is the time for the body to move from $x = 0$ to $x = A$. Calculate this time and hence the period. [*Hint:* Begin with Eq. (14.20), modified to include the potential-energy function you found in part (a), and solve for the velocity v_x as a function of x. Then replace v_x with dx/dt. Separate the variable by writing all factors containing x on one side and all factors containing t on the other side so that each side can be integrated. In the x-integral make the change of variable $u = x/A$. The resulting integral can be evaluated by numerical methods on a computer and has the value $\int_0^1 du/\sqrt{1 - u^4} = 1.31$.] (c) According to the result you obtained in part (b), does the period depend on the amplitude A of the motion? Are the oscillations simple harmonic?

14.93 · **CP CALC** An approximation for the potential energy of a KCl molecule is $U = A[(R_0^7/8r^8) - 1/r]$, where $R_0 = 2.67 \times 10^{-10}$ m, $A = 2.31 \times 10^{-28}$ J·m, and r is the distance between the two atoms. Using this approximation: (a) Show that the radial component of the force on each atom is $F_r = A[(R_0^7/r^9) - 1/r^2]$. (b) Show that R_0 is the equilibrium separation. (c) Find the minimum potential energy. (d) Use $r = R_0 + x$ and the first two terms of the binomial theorem (Eq. 14.28) to show that $F_r \approx -(7A/R_0^3)x$, so that the molecule's force constant is $k = 7A/R_0^3$. (e) With both the K and Cl atoms vibrating in opposite directions on opposite sides of the molecule's center of mass, $m_1m_2/(m_1 + m_2) = 3.06 \times 10^{-26}$ kg is the mass to use in calculating the frequency. Calculate the frequency of small-amplitude vibrations.

14.94 ··· **CP** Two uniform solid spheres, each with mass $M = 0.800$ kg and radius $R = 0.0800$ m, are connected by a short, light rod that is along a diameter of each sphere and are at rest on a horizontal tabletop. A spring with force constant $k = 160$ N/m has one end attached to the wall and the other end attached to a frictionless ring that passes over the rod at the center of mass of the spheres, which is midway between the centers of the two spheres. The spheres are each pulled the same distance from the wall, stretching the spring, and released. There is sufficient friction between the tabletop and the spheres for the spheres to roll without slipping as they move back and forth on the end of the spring. Show that the motion of the center of mass of the spheres is simple harmonic and calculate the period.

14.95 • **CP** In Fig. P14.95 the upper ball is released from rest, collides with the stationary lower ball, and sticks to it. The strings are both 50.0 cm long. The upper ball has mass 2.00 kg, and it is initially 10.0 cm higher than the lower ball, which has mass 3.00 kg. Find the frequency and maximum angular displacement of the motion after the collision.

Figure **P14.95**

10.0 cm

14.96 •• **CP BIO** *T. rex.* Model the leg of the *T. rex* in Example 14.10 (Section 14.6) as two uniform rods, each 1.55 m long, joined rigidly end to end. Let the lower rod have mass M and the upper rod mass $2M$. The composite object is pivoted about the top of the upper rod. Compute the oscillation period of this object for small-amplitude oscillations. Compare your result to that of Example 14.10.

14.97 •• **CALC** A slender, uniform, metal rod with mass M is pivoted without friction about an axis through its midpoint and perpendicular to the rod. A horizontal spring with force constant k is attached to the lower end of the rod, with the other end of the spring attached to a rigid support. If the rod is displaced by a small angle Θ from the vertical (Fig. P14.97) and released, show that it moves in angular SHM and calculate the period. (*Hint:* Assume that the angle Θ is small enough for the approximations $\sin \Theta \approx \Theta$ and $\cos \Theta \approx 1$ to be valid. The motion is simple harmonic if $d^2\theta/dt^2 = -\omega^2\theta$, and the period is then $T = 2\pi/\omega$.)

Figure **P14.97**

θ

14.98 •• **The Silently Ringing Bell Problem.** A large bell is hung from a wooden beam so it can swing back and forth with negligible friction. The center of mass of the bell is 0.60 m below the pivot, the bell has mass 34.0 kg, and the moment of inertia of the bell about an axis at the pivot is 18.0 kg·m². The clapper is a small, 1.8-kg mass attached to one end of a slender rod that has length L and negligible mass. The other end of the rod is attached to the inside of the bell so it can swing freely about the same axis as the bell. What should be the length L of the clapper rod for the bell to ring silently—that is, for the period of oscillation for the bell to equal that for the clapper?

14.99 ••• Two identical thin rods, each with mass m and length L, are joined at right angles to form an L-shaped object. This object is balanced on top of a sharp edge (Fig. P14.99). If the L-shaped object is deflected slightly, it oscillates. Find the frequency of oscillation.

Figure **P14.99**

L L

14.100 • **CP CALC** A uniform rod of length L oscillates through small angles about a point a distance x from its center. (a) Prove that its angular frequency is $\sqrt{gx/[(L^2/12) + x^2]}$. (b) Show that its maximum angular frequency occurs when $x = L/\sqrt{12}$. (c) What is the length of the rod if the maximum angular frequency is 2π rad/s?

CHALLENGE PROBLEMS

14.101 ••• **The Effective Force Constant of Two Springs.** Two springs with the same unstretched length but different force constants k_1 and k_2 are attached to a block with mass m on a level, frictionless surface. Calculate the effective force constant k_{eff} in each of the three cases (a), (b), and (c) depicted in Fig. P14.101. (The effective force constant is defined by $\Sigma F_x = -k_{\text{eff}}x$.) (d) An object with mass m, suspended from a uniform spring with a force constant k, vibrates with a frequency f_1. When the spring is cut in half and the same object is suspended from one of the halves, the frequency is f_2. What is the ratio f_2/f_1?

Figure **P14.101**

14.102 ••• Two springs, each with unstretched length 0.200 m but with different force constants k_1 and k_2, are attached to opposite ends of a block with mass m on a level, frictionless surface. The outer ends of the springs are now attached to two pins P_1 and P_2, 0.100 m from the original positions of the ends of the springs (Fig. P14.102). Let $k_1 = 2.00$ N/m, $k_2 = 6.00$ N/m, and $m = 0.100$ kg. (a) Find the length of each spring when the block is in its new equilibrium position after the springs have been attached to the pins. (b) Find the period of vibration of the block if it is slightly displaced from its new equilibrium position and released.

Figure **P14.102**

0.100 m 0.200 m   0.200 m 0.100 m

P_1 ⟋⟋⟋⟋⟋ m ⟋⟋⟋⟋⟋ P_2

14.103 ••• **CALC** **A Spring with Mass.** The preceding problems in this chapter have assumed that the springs had negligible mass. But of course no spring is completely massless. To find the effect of the spring's mass, consider a spring with mass M, equilibrium length L_0, and spring constant k. When stretched or compressed to a length L, the potential energy is $\frac{1}{2}kx^2$, where $x = L - L_0$. (a) Consider a spring, as described above, that has one end fixed and the other end moving with speed v. Assume that the speed of points along the length of the spring varies linearly with distance l from the fixed end. Assume also that the mass M of the spring is distributed uniformly along the length of the spring. Calculate the kinetic energy of the spring in terms of M and v. (*Hint:* Divide the spring into pieces of length dl; find the speed of each piece in terms of l, v, and L; find the mass of each piece in terms of dl, M, and L; and integrate from 0 to L. The result is *not* $\frac{1}{2}Mv^2$, since not all of the spring moves with the same speed.) (b) Take the time derivative of the conservation of energy equation, Eq. (14.21), for a mass m moving on the end of a *massless* spring. By comparing your results to Eq. (14.8), which defines ω, show that the angular frequency of oscillation is $\omega = \sqrt{k/m}$. (c) Apply the procedure of part (b) to obtain the angular frequency of oscillation ω of the spring considered in part (a). If the *effective mass M'* of the spring is defined by $\omega = \sqrt{k/M'}$, what is M' in terms of M?

Answers

Chapter Opening Question ?

The length of the leg is more important. The back-and-forth motion of a leg during walking is like a physical pendulum, for which the oscillation period is $T = 2\pi\sqrt{I/mgd}$ [see Eq. (14.39)]. In this expression I is the moment of inertia of the pendulum, m is its mass, and d is the distance from the rotation axis to the pendulum center of mass. The moment of inertia I is proportional to the mass m, so the mass cancels out of this expression for the period T. Hence only the dimensions of the leg matter. (See Examples 14.9 and 14.10.)

Test Your Understanding Questions

14.1 Answers: (a) $x < 0$, **(b)** $x > 0$, **(c)** $x < 0$, **(d)** $x > 0$, **(e)** $x > 0$, **(f)** $x = 0$ Figure 14.2 shows that the net x-component of force F_x and the x-acceleration a_x are both positive when $x < 0$ (so the body is displaced to the left and the spring is compressed), while F_x and a_x are both negative when $x > 0$ (so the body is displaced to the right and the spring is stretched). Hence x and a_x always have *opposite* signs. This is true whether the object is moving to the right ($v_x > 0$), to the left ($v_x < 0$), or not at all ($v_x = 0$), since the force exerted by the spring depends only on whether it is compressed or stretched and by what distance. This explains the answers to (a) through (e). If the acceleration is zero as in (f), the net force must also be zero and so the spring must be relaxed; hence $x = 0$.

14.2 Answers: (a) $A > 0.10$ m, $\phi < 0$; **(b)** $A > 0.10$ m, $\phi > 0$ In both situations the initial ($t = 0$) x-velocity v_{0x} is nonzero, so from Eq. (14.19) the amplitude $A = \sqrt{x_0^2 + (v_{0x}^2/\omega^2)}$ is greater than the initial x-coordinate $x_0 = 0.10$ m. From Eq. (14.18) the phase angle is $\phi = \arctan(-v_{0x}/\omega x_0)$, which is positive if the quantity $-v_{0x}/\omega x_0$ (the argument of the arctangent function) is positive and negative if $-v_{0x}/\omega x_0$ is negative. In part (a) x_0 and v_{0x} are both positive, so $-v_{0x}/\omega x_0 < 0$ and $\phi < 0$. In part (b) x_0 is positive and v_{0x} is negative, so $-v_{0x}/\omega x_0 > 0$ and $\phi > 0$.

14.3 Answers: (a) (iii), (b) (v) To increase the total energy $E = \frac{1}{2}kA^2$ by a factor of 2, the amplitude A must increase by a factor of $\sqrt{2}$. Because the motion is SHM, changing the amplitude has no effect on the frequency.

14.4 Answer: (i) The oscillation period of a body of mass m attached to a hanging spring of force constant k is given by $T = 2\pi\sqrt{m/k}$, the same expression as for a body attached to a horizontal spring. Neither m nor k changes when the apparatus is taken to Mars, so the period is unchanged. The only difference is that in equilibrium, the spring will stretch a shorter distance on Mars than on earth due to the weaker gravity.

14.5 Answer: no Just as for an object oscillating on a spring, at the equilibrium position the *speed* of the pendulum bob is instantaneously not changing (this is where the speed is maximum, so its derivative at this time is zero). But the *direction* of motion is changing because the pendulum bob follows a circular path. Hence the bob must have a component of acceleration perpendicular to the path and toward the center of the circle (see Section 3.4). To cause this acceleration at the equilibrium position when the string is vertical, the upward tension force at this position must be greater than the weight of the bob. This causes a net upward force on the bob and an upward acceleration toward the center of the circular path.

14.6 Answer: (i) The period of a physical pendulum is given by Eq. (14.39), $T = 2\pi\sqrt{I/mgd}$. The distance $d = L$ from the pivot to the center of gravity is the same for both the rod and the simple pendulum, as is the mass m. This means that for any displacement angle θ the same restoring torque acts on both the rod and the simple pendulum. However, the rod has a greater moment of inertia: $I_{rod} = \frac{1}{3}m(2L)^2 = \frac{4}{3}mL^2$ and $I_{simple} = mL^2$ (all the mass of the pendulum is a distance L from the pivot). Hence the rod has a longer period.

14.7 Answer: (ii) The oscillations are underdamped with a decreasing amplitude on each cycle of oscillation, like those graphed in Fig. 14.26. If the oscillations were undamped, they would continue indefinitely with the same amplitude. If they were critically damped or overdamped, the nose would not bob up and down but would return smoothly to the original equilibrium attitude without overshooting.

14.8 Answer: (i) Figure 14.28 shows that the curve of amplitude versus driving frequency moves upward at *all* frequencies as the value of the damping constant b is decreased. Hence for fixed values of k and m, the oscillator with the least damping (smallest value of b) will have the greatest response at any driving frequency.

Bridging Problem

Answer: $T = 2\pi\sqrt{3M/2k}$

15 MECHANICAL WAVES

LEARNING GOALS

By studying this chapter, you will learn:

- What is meant by a mechanical wave, and the different varieties of mechanical waves.

- How to use the relationship among speed, frequency, and wavelength for a periodic wave.

- How to interpret and use the mathematical expression for a sinusoidal periodic wave.

- How to calculate the speed of waves on a rope or string.

- How to calculate the rate at which a mechanical wave transports energy.

- What happens when mechanical waves overlap and interfere.

- The properties of standing waves on a string, and how to analyze these waves.

- How stringed instruments produce sounds of specific frequencies.

? When an earthquake strikes, the news of the event travels through the body of the earth in the form of seismic waves. Which aspects of a seismic wave determine how much power is carried by the wave?

Ripples on a pond, musical sounds, seismic tremors triggered by an earthquake—all these are *wave* phenomena. Waves can occur whenever a system is disturbed from equilibrium and when the disturbance can travel, or *propagate*, from one region of the system to another. As a wave propagates, it carries energy. The energy in light waves from the sun warms the surface of our planet; the energy in seismic waves can crack our planet's crust.

This chapter and the next are about mechanical waves—waves that travel within some material called a *medium*. (Chapter 16 is concerned with sound, an important type of mechanical wave.) We'll begin this chapter by deriving the basic equations for describing waves, including the important special case of *sinusoidal* waves in which the wave pattern is a repeating sine or cosine function. To help us understand waves in general, we'll look at the simple case of waves that travel on a stretched string or rope.

Waves on a string play an important role in music. When a musician strums a guitar or bows a violin, she makes waves that travel in opposite directions along the instrument's strings. What happens when these oppositely directed waves overlap is called *interference*. We'll discover that sinusoidal waves can occur on a guitar or violin string only for certain special frequencies, called *normal-mode frequencies*, determined by the properties of the string. The normal-mode frequencies of a stringed instrument determine the pitch of the musical sounds that the instrument produces. (In the next chapter we'll find that interference also helps explain the pitches of *wind* instruments such as flutes and pipe organs.)

Not all waves are mechanical in nature. *Electromagnetic* waves—including light, radio waves, infrared and ultraviolet radiation, and x rays—can propagate even in empty space, where there is *no* medium. We'll explore these and other nonmechanical waves in later chapters.

15.1 Types of Mechanical Waves

A **mechanical wave** is a disturbance that travels through some material or substance called the **medium** for the wave. As the wave travels through the medium, the particles that make up the medium undergo displacements of various kinds, depending on the nature of the wave.

Figure 15.1 shows three varieties of mechanical waves. In Fig. 15.1a the medium is a string or rope under tension. If we give the left end a small upward shake or wiggle, the wiggle travels along the length of the string. Successive sections of string go through the same motion that we gave to the end, but at successively later times. Because the displacements of the medium are perpendicular or *transverse* to the direction of travel of the wave along the medium, this is called a **transverse wave.**

In Fig. 15.1b the medium is a liquid or gas in a tube with a rigid wall at the right end and a movable piston at the left end. If we give the piston a single back-and-forth motion, displacement and pressure fluctuations travel down the length of the medium. This time the motions of the particles of the medium are back and forth along the *same* direction that the wave travels. We call this a **longitudinal wave.**

In Fig. 15.1c the medium is a liquid in a channel, such as water in an irrigation ditch or canal. When we move the flat board at the left end forward and back once, a wave disturbance travels down the length of the channel. In this case the displacements of the water have *both* longitudinal and transverse components.

Each of these systems has an equilibrium state. For the stretched string it is the state in which the system is at rest, stretched out along a straight line. For the fluid in a tube it is a state in which the fluid is at rest with uniform pressure. And for the liquid in a trough it is a smooth, level water surface. In each case the wave motion is a disturbance from the equilibrium state that travels from one region of the medium to another. And in each case there are forces that tend to restore the system to its equilibrium position when it is displaced, just as the force of gravity tends to pull a pendulum toward its straight-down equilibrium position when it is displaced.

Application Waves on a
Snake's Body
A snake moves itself along the ground by producing waves that travel backward along its body from its head to its tail. The waves remain stationary with respect to the ground as they push against the ground, so the snake moves forward.

ActivPhysics 10.1: Properties of Mechanical Waves

15.1 Three ways to make a wave that moves to the right. (a) The hand moves the string up and then returns, producing a transverse wave. (b) The piston moves to the right, compressing the gas or liquid, and then returns, producing a longitudinal wave. (c) The board moves to the right and then returns, producing a combination of longitudinal and transverse waves.

(a) Transverse wave on a string

As the wave passes, each particle of the string moves up and then down, *transversely* to the motion of the wave itself.

(b) Longitudinal wave in a fluid

As the wave passes, each particle of the fluid moves forward and then back, *parallel* to the motion of the wave itself.

(c) Waves on the surface of a liquid

As the wave passes, each particle of the liquid surface moves in a circle.

15.2 "Doing the wave" at a sports stadium is an example of a mechanical wave: The disturbance propagates through the crowd, but there is no transport of matter (none of the spectators moves from one seat to another).

These examples have three things in common. First, in each case the disturbance travels or *propagates* with a definite speed through the medium. This speed is called the speed of propagation, or simply the **wave speed.** Its value is determined in each case by the mechanical properties of the medium. We will use the symbol v for wave speed. (The wave speed is *not* the same as the speed with which particles move when they are disturbed by the wave. We'll return to this point in Section 15.3.) Second, the medium itself does not travel through space; its individual particles undergo back-and-forth or up-and-down motions around their equilibrium positions. The overall pattern of the wave disturbance is what travels. Third, to set any of these systems into motion, we have to put in energy by doing mechanical work on the system. The wave motion transports this energy from one region of the medium to another. *Waves transport energy, but not matter, from one region to another* (Fig. 15.2).

Test Your Understanding of Section 15.1 What type of wave is "the wave" shown in Fig. 15.2? (i) transverse; (ii) longitudinal; (iii) a combination of transverse and longitudinal.

15.2 Periodic Waves

The transverse wave on a stretched string in Fig. 15.1a is an example of a *wave pulse.* The hand shakes the string up and down just once, exerting a transverse force on it as it does so. The result is a single "wiggle," or pulse, that travels along the length of the string. The tension in the string restores its straight-line shape once the pulse has passed.

A more interesting situation develops when we give the free end of the string a repetitive, or *periodic,* motion. (You may want to review the discussion of periodic motion in Chapter 14 before going ahead.) Then each particle in the string also undergoes periodic motion as the wave propagates, and we have a **periodic wave.**

Periodic Transverse Waves

In particular, suppose we move the string up and down with *simple harmonic motion* (SHM) with amplitude A, frequency f, angular frequency $\omega = 2\pi f$, and period $T = 1/f = 2\pi/\omega$. Figure 15.3 shows one way to do this. The wave that results is a symmetrical sequence of *crests* and *troughs.* As we will see, periodic

15.3 A block of mass m attached to a spring undergoes simple harmonic motion, producing a sinusoidal wave that travels to the right on the string. (In a real-life system a driving force would have to be applied to the block to replace the energy carried away by the wave.)

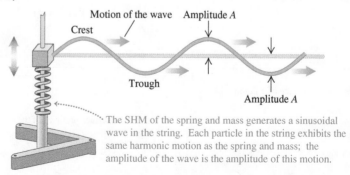

Motion of the wave   Amplitude A

Crest

Trough

Amplitude A

The SHM of the spring and mass generates a sinusoidal wave in the string. Each particle in the string exhibits the same harmonic motion as the spring and mass; the amplitude of the wave is the amplitude of this motion.

waves with simple harmonic motion are particularly easy to analyze; we call them **sinusoidal waves.** It also turns out that *any* periodic wave can be represented as a combination of sinusoidal waves. So this particular kind of wave motion is worth special attention.

In Fig. 15.3 the wave that advances along the string is a *continuous succession* of transverse sinusoidal disturbances. Figure 15.4 shows the shape of a part of the string near the left end at time intervals of $\frac{1}{8}$ of a period, for a total time of one period. The wave shape advances steadily toward the right, as indicated by the highlighted area. As the wave moves, any point on the string (any of the red dots, for example) oscillates up and down about its equilibrium position with simple harmonic motion. *When a sinusoidal wave passes through a medium, every particle in the medium undergoes simple harmonic motion with the same frequency.*

CAUTION **Wave motion vs. particle motion** Be very careful to distinguish between the motion of the *transverse wave* along the string and the motion of a *particle* of the string. The wave moves with constant speed v *along* the length of the string, while the motion of the particle is simple harmonic and *transverse* (perpendicular) to the length of the string. ▮

For a periodic wave, the shape of the string at any instant is a repeating pattern. The length of one complete wave pattern is the distance from one crest to the next, or from one trough to the next, or from any point to the corresponding point on the next repetition of the wave shape. We call this distance the **wavelength** of the wave, denoted by λ (the Greek letter lambda). The wave pattern travels with constant speed v and advances a distance of one wavelength λ in a time interval of one period T. So the wave speed v is given by $v = \lambda/T$ or, because $f = 1/T$,

$$v = \lambda f \qquad \text{(periodic wave)} \qquad (15.1)$$

The speed of propagation equals the product of wavelength and frequency. The frequency is a property of the *entire* periodic wave because all points on the string oscillate with the same frequency f.

Waves on a string propagate in just one dimension (in Fig. 15.4, along the *x*-axis). But the ideas of frequency, wavelength, and amplitude apply equally well to waves that propagate in two or three dimensions. Figure 15.5 shows a wave propagating in two dimensions on the surface of a tank of water. As with waves on a string, the wavelength is the distance from one crest to the next, and the amplitude is the height of a crest above the equilibrium level.

In many important situations including waves on a string, the wave speed v is determined entirely by the mechanical properties of the medium. In this case, increasing f causes λ to decrease so that the product $v = \lambda f$ remains the same, and waves of *all* frequencies propagate with the same wave speed. In this chapter we will consider *only* waves of this kind. (In later chapters we will study the propagation of light waves in matter for which the wave speed depends on frequency; this turns out to be the reason prisms break white light into a spectrum and raindrops create a rainbow.)

Periodic Longitudinal Waves

To understand the mechanics of a periodic *longitudinal* wave, we consider a long tube filled with a fluid, with a piston at the left end as in Fig. 15.1b. If we push the piston in, we compress the fluid near the piston, increasing the pressure in this

15.4 A sinusoidal transverse wave traveling to the right along a string. The vertical scale is exaggerated.

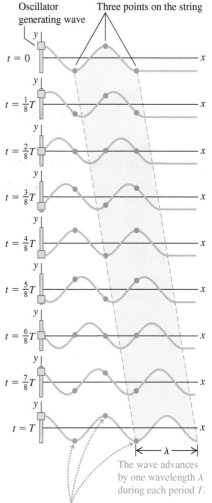

The string is shown at time intervals of $\frac{1}{8}$ period for a total of one period T. The highlighting shows the motion of one wavelength of the wave.

Oscillator generating wave

Three points on the string

$t = 0$

$t = \frac{1}{8}T$

$t = \frac{2}{8}T$

$t = \frac{3}{8}T$

$t = \frac{4}{8}T$

$t = \frac{5}{8}T$

$t = \frac{6}{8}T$

$t = \frac{7}{8}T$

$t = T$

λ

The wave advances by one wavelength λ during each period T.

Each point moves up and down in place. Particles one wavelength apart move in phase with each other.

15.5 A series of drops falling into water produces a periodic wave that spreads radially outward. The wave crests and troughs are concentric circles. The wavelength λ is the radial distance between adjacent crests or adjacent troughs.

15.6 Using an oscillating piston to make a sinusoidal longitudinal wave in a fluid.

Forward motion of the plunger creates a compression (a zone of high density); backward motion creates a rarefaction (a zone of low density).

Wavelength λ is the distance between corresponding points on successive cycles.

15.7 A sinusoidal longitudinal wave traveling to the right in a fluid. The wave has the same amplitude A and period T as the oscillation of the piston.

Longitudinal waves are shown at intervals of $\frac{1}{8}T$ for one period T.

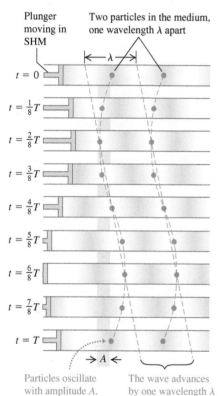

Particles oscillate with amplitude A.

The wave advances by one wavelength λ during each period T.

region. This region then pushes against the neighboring region of fluid, and so on, and a wave pulse moves along the tube.

Now suppose we move the piston back and forth with simple harmonic motion, along a line parallel to the axis of the tube (Fig. 15.6). This motion forms regions in the fluid where the pressure and density are greater or less than the equilibrium values. We call a region of increased density a *compression;* a region of reduced density is a *rarefaction.* Figure 15.6 shows compressions as darkly shaded areas and rarefactions as lightly shaded areas. The wavelength is the distance from one compression to the next or from one rarefaction to the next.

Figure 15.7 shows the wave propagating in the fluid-filled tube at time intervals of $\frac{1}{8}$ of a period, for a total time of one period. The pattern of compressions and rarefactions moves steadily to the right, just like the pattern of crests and troughs in a sinusoidal transverse wave (compare Fig. 15.4). Each particle in the fluid oscillates in SHM parallel to the direction of wave propagation (that is, left and right) with the same amplitude A and period T as the piston. The particles shown by the two red dots in Fig. 15.7 are one wavelength apart, and so oscillate in phase with each other.

Just like the sinusoidal transverse wave shown in Fig. 15.4, in one period T the longitudinal wave in Fig. 15.7 travels one wavelength λ to the right. Hence the fundamental equation $v = \lambda f$ holds for longitudinal waves as well as for transverse waves, and indeed for *all* types of periodic waves. Just as for transverse waves, in this chapter and the next we will consider only situations in which the speed of longitudinal waves does not depend on the frequency.

Example 15.1 **Wavelength of a musical sound**

Sound waves are longitudinal waves in air. The speed of sound depends on temperature; at 20°C it is 344 m/s (1130 ft/s). What is the wavelength of a sound wave in air at 20°C if the frequency is 262 Hz (the approximate frequency of middle C on a piano)?

SOLUTION

IDENTIFY and SET UP: This problem involves Eq. (15.1), $v = \lambda f$, which relates wave speed v, wavelength λ, and frequency f for a periodic wave. The target variable is the wavelength λ. We are given $v = 344$ m/s and $f = 262$ Hz $= 262$ s^{-1}.

EXECUTE: We solve Eq. (15.1) for λ:

$$\lambda = \frac{v}{f} = \frac{344 \text{ m/s}}{262 \text{ Hz}} = \frac{344 \text{ m/s}}{262 \text{ s}^{-1}} = 1.31 \text{ m}$$

EVALUATE: The speed v of sound waves does *not* depend on the frequency. Hence $\lambda = v/f$ says that wavelength changes in inverse proportion to frequency. As an example, high (soprano) C is two octaves above middle C. Each octave corresponds to a factor of 2 in frequency, so the frequency of high C is four times that of middle C: $f = 4(262 \text{ Hz}) = 1048$ Hz. Hence the *wavelength* of high C is *one-fourth* as large: $\lambda = (1.31 \text{ m})/4 = 0.328$ m.

Test Your Understanding of Section 15.2 If you double the wave-length of a wave on a particular string, what happens to the wave speed v and the frequency f? (i) v doubles and f is unchanged; (ii) v is unchanged and f doubles; (iii) v becomes one-half as great and f is unchanged; (iv) v is unchanged and f becomes one-half as great; (v) none of these. ┃

15.3 Mathematical Description of a Wave

Many characteristics of periodic waves can be described by using the concepts of wave speed, amplitude, period, frequency, and wavelength. Often, though, we need a more detailed description of the positions and motions of individual particles of the medium at particular times during wave propagation.

As a specific example, let's look at waves on a stretched string. If we ignore the sag of the string due to gravity, the equilibrium position of the string is along a straight line. We take this to be the x-axis of a coordinate system. Waves on a string are *transverse;* during wave motion a particle with equilibrium position x is displaced some distance y in the direction perpendicular to the x-axis. The value of y depends on which particle we are talking about (that is, y depends on x) and also on the time t when we look at it. Thus y is a *function* of both x and t; $y = y(x, t)$. We call $y(x, t)$ the **wave function** that describes the wave. If we know this function for a particular wave motion, we can use it to find the dis-placement (from equilibrium) of any particle at any time. From this we can find the velocity and acceleration of any particle, the shape of the string, and anything else we want to know about the behavior of the string at any time.

Wave Function for a Sinusoidal Wave

Let's see how to determine the form of the wave function for a sinusoidal wave. Suppose a sinusoidal wave travels from left to right (the direction of increasing x) along the string, as in Fig. 15.8. Every particle of the string oscillates with simple harmonic motion with the same amplitude and frequency. But the oscillations of particles at different points on the string are *not* all in step with each other. The particle at point B in Fig. 15.8 is at its maximum positive value of y at $t = 0$ and returns to $y = 0$ at $t = \frac{2}{8}T$; these same events occur for a particle at point A or point C at $t = \frac{4}{8}T$ and $t = \frac{6}{8}T$, exactly one half-period later. For any two particles of the string, the motion of the particle on the right (in terms of the wave, the "downstream" particle) lags behind the motion of the particle on the left by an amount proportional to the distance between the particles.

Hence the cyclic motions of various points on the string are out of step with each other by various fractions of a cycle. We call these differences *phase differences,* and we say that the *phase* of the motion is different for different points. For example, if one point has its maximum positive displacement at the same time that another has its maximum negative displacement, the two are a half-cycle out of phase. (This is the case for points A and B, or points B and C.)

Suppose that the displacement of a particle at the left end of the string $(x = 0)$, where the wave originates, is given by

$$y(x = 0, t) = A \cos \omega t = A \cos 2\pi f t \qquad (15.2)$$

That is, the particle oscillates in simple harmonic motion with amplitude A, fre-quency f, and angular frequency $\omega = 2\pi f$. The notation $y(x = 0, t)$ reminds us that the motion of this particle is a special case of the wave function $y(x, t)$ that describes the entire wave. At $t = 0$ the particle at $x = 0$ is at its maximum posi-tive displacement $(y = A)$ and is instantaneously at rest (because the value of y is a maximum).

The wave disturbance travels from $x = 0$ to some point x to the right of the origin in an amount of time given by x/v, where v is the wave speed. So the motion of point x at time t is the same as the motion of point $x = 0$ at the earlier time $t - x/v$. Hence we can find the displacement of point x at time t by simply

15.8 Tracking the oscillations of three points on a string as a sinusoidal wave propagates along it.

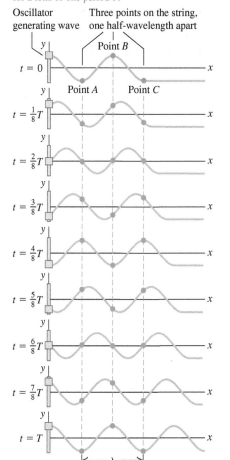

The string is shown at time intervals of $\frac{1}{8}$ period for a total of one period T.

replacing t in Eq. (15.2) by $(t - x/v)$. When we do that, we find the following expression for the wave function:

$$y(x, t) = A \cos\left[\omega\left(t - \frac{x}{v}\right)\right]$$

Because $\cos(-\theta) = \cos\theta$, we can rewrite the wave function as

$$y(x, t) = A \cos\left[\omega\left(\frac{x}{v} - t\right)\right] = A \cos\left[2\pi f\left(\frac{x}{v} - t\right)\right] \quad \begin{array}{l}\text{(sinusoidal wave} \\ \text{moving in} \\ \text{+}x\text{-direction)}\end{array} \quad (15.3)$$

The displacement $y(x, t)$ is a function of both the location x of the point and the time t. We could make Eq. (15.3) more general by allowing for different values of the phase angle, as we did for simple harmonic motion in Section 14.2, but for now we omit this.

We can rewrite the wave function given by Eq. (15.3) in several different but useful forms. We can express it in terms of the period $T = 1/f$ and the wavelength $\lambda = v/f$:

$$y(x, t) = A \cos\left[2\pi\left(\frac{x}{\lambda} - \frac{t}{T}\right)\right] \quad \begin{array}{l}\text{(sinusoidal wave moving} \\ \text{in +}x\text{-direction)}\end{array} \quad (15.4)$$

It's convenient to define a quantity k, called the **wave number:**

$$k = \frac{2\pi}{\lambda} \quad \text{(wave number)} \quad (15.5)$$

Substituting $\lambda = 2\pi/k$ and $f = \omega/2\pi$ into the wavelength–frequency relationship $v = \lambda f$ gives

$$\omega = vk \quad \text{(periodic wave)} \quad (15.6)$$

We can then rewrite Eq. (15.4) as

$$y(x, t) = A \cos(kx - \omega t) \quad \begin{array}{l}\text{(sinusoidal wave moving} \\ \text{in +}x\text{-direction)}\end{array} \quad (15.7)$$

Which of these various forms for the wave function $y(x, t)$ we use in any specific problem is a matter of convenience. Note that ω has units rad/s, so for unit consistency in Eqs. (15.6) and (15.7) the wave number k must have the units rad/m. (Some physicists define the wave number as $1/\lambda$ rather than $2\pi/\lambda$. When reading other texts, be sure to determine how this term is defined.)

Graphing the Wave Function

Figure 15.9a graphs the wave function $y(x, t)$ as a function of x for a specific time t. This graph gives the displacement y of a particle from its equilibrium position as a function of the coordinate x of the particle. If the wave is a transverse wave on a string, the graph in Fig. 15.9a represents the shape of the string at that instant, like a flash photograph of the string. In particular, at time $t = 0$,

$$y(x, t = 0) = A \cos kx = A \cos 2\pi\frac{x}{\lambda}$$

Figure 15.9b is a graph of the wave function versus time t for a specific coordinate x. This graph gives the displacement y of the particle at that coordinate as a function of time; that is, it describes the motion of that particle. In particular, at the position $x = 0$,

$$y(x = 0, t) = A \cos(-\omega t) = A \cos \omega t = A \cos 2\pi\frac{t}{T}$$

This is consistent with our original statement about the motion at $x = 0$, Eq. (15.2).

15.9 Two graphs of the wave function $y(x, t)$ in Eq. (15.7). **(a)** Graph of displacement y versus coordinate x at time $t = 0$. **(b)** Graph of displacement y versus time t at coordinate $x = 0$. The vertical scale is exaggerated in both (a) and (b).

(a) If we use Eq. (15.7) to plot y as a function of x for time $t = 0$, the curve shows the *shape* of the string at $t = 0$.

(b) If we use Eq. (15.7) to plot y as a function of t for position $x = 0$, the curve shows the *displacement* y of the particle at $x = 0$ as a function of time.

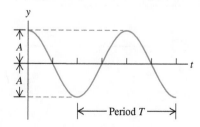

CAUTION **Wave graphs** Although they may look the same at first glance, Figs. 15.9a and 15.9b are *not* identical. Figure 15.9a is a picture of the shape of the string at $t = 0$, while Fig. 15.9b is a graph of the displacement y of a particle at $x = 0$ as a function of time.

More on the Wave Function

We can modify Eqs. (15.3) through (15.7) to represent a wave traveling in the *negative x*-direction. In this case the displacement of point x at time t is the same as the motion of point $x = 0$ at the *later* time $(t + x/v)$, so in Eq. (15.2) we replace t by $(t + x/v)$. For a wave traveling in the negative x-direction,

$$y(x, t) = A\cos\left[2\pi f\left(\frac{x}{v} + t\right)\right] = A\cos\left[2\pi\left(\frac{x}{\lambda} + \frac{t}{T}\right)\right] = A\cos(kx + \omega t) \quad (15.8)$$

(sinusoidal wave moving in $-x$-direction)

In the expression $y(x, t) = A\cos(kx \pm \omega t)$ for a wave traveling in the $-x$- or $+x$-direction, the quantity $(kx \pm \omega t)$ is called the **phase.** It plays the role of an angular quantity (always measured in radians) in Eq. (15.7) or (15.8), and its value for any values of x and t determines what part of the sinusoidal cycle is occurring at a particular point and time. For a crest (where $y = A$ and the cosine function has the value 1), the phase could be 0, 2π, 4π, and so on; for a trough (where $y = -A$ and the cosine has the value -1), it could be π, 3π, 5π, and so on.

The wave speed is the speed with which we have to move along with the wave to keep alongside a point of a given phase, such as a particular crest of a wave on a string. For a wave traveling in the $+x$-direction, that means $kx - \omega t = $ constant. Taking the derivative with respect to t, we find $k\, dx/dt = \omega$, or

$$\frac{dx}{dt} = \frac{\omega}{k}$$

Comparing this with Eq. (15.6), we see that dx/dt is equal to the speed v of the wave. Because of this relationship, v is sometimes called the *phase velocity* of the wave. (*Phase speed* would be a better term.)

Problem-Solving Strategy 15.1 **Mechanical Waves**

IDENTIFY *the relevant concepts:* As always, identify the target variables; these may include mathematical *expressions* (for example, the wave function for a given situation). Note that wave problems fall into two categories. *Kinematics* problems, concerned with describing wave motion, involve wave speed v, wavelength λ (or wave number k), frequency f (or angular frequency ω), and amplitude A. They may also involve the position, velocity, and acceleration of individual particles in the medium. *Dynamics* problems also use concepts from Newton's laws. Later in this chapter we'll encounter problems that involve the relationship of wave speed to the mechanical properties of the medium.

SET UP *the problem* using the following steps:
1. List the given quantities. Sketch graphs of y versus x (like Fig. 15.9a) and of y versus t (like Fig. 15.9b), and label them with known values.
2. Identify useful equations. These may include Eq. (15.1) ($v = \lambda f$), Eq. (15.6) ($\omega = vk$), and Eqs. (15.3), (15.4), and

(15.7), which express the wave function in various forms. From the wave function, you can find the value of y at any point (value of x) and at any time t.
3. If you need to determine the wave speed v and don't know both λ and f, you may be able to use a relationship between v and the mechanical properties of the system. (In the next section we'll develop this relationship for waves on a string.)

EXECUTE *the solution:* Solve for the unknown quantities using the equations you've identified. To determine the wave function from Eq. (15.3), (15.4), or (15.7), you must know A and any two of v, λ, and f (or v, k, and ω).

EVALUATE *your answer:* Confirm that the values of v, f, and λ (or v, ω, and k) agree with the relationships given in Eq. (15.1) or (15.6). If you've calculated the wave function, check one or more special cases for which you can predict the results.

Example 15.2 **Wave on a clothesline**

Cousin Throckmorton holds one end of the clothesline taut and wiggles it up and down sinusoidally with frequency 2.00 Hz and amplitude 0.075 m. The wave speed on the clothesline is $v = 12.0$ m/s. At $t = 0$ Throcky's end has maximum positive displacement and is instantaneously at rest. Assume that no wave bounces back from the far end. (a) Find the wave amplitude A, angular frequency ω, period T, wavelength λ, and wave number k. (b) Write a wave function describing the wave. (c) Write equations for the displacement, as a function of time, of Throcky's end of the clothesline and of a point 3.00 m from that end.

SOLUTION

IDENTIFY and SET UP: This is a kinematics problem about the clothesline's wave motion. Throcky produces a sinusoidal wave that propagates along the clothesline, so we can use all of the expressions of this section. In part (a) our target variables are A, ω, T, λ, and k. We use the relationships $\omega = 2\pi f$, $f = 1/T$, $v = \lambda f$, and $k = 2\pi/\lambda$. In parts (b) and (c) our target "variables" are expressions for displacement, which we'll obtain from an appropriate equation for the wave function. We take the positive x-direction to be the direction in which the wave propagates, so either Eq. (15.4) or (15.7) will yield the desired expression. A photograph of the clothesline at time $t = 0$ would look like Fig. 15.9a, with the maximum displacement at $x = 0$ (the end that Throcky holds).

EXECUTE: (a) The wave amplitude and frequency are the same as for the oscillations of Throcky's end of the clothesline, $A = 0.075$ m and $f = 2.00$ Hz. Hence

$$\omega = 2\pi f = \left(2\pi \frac{\text{rad}}{\text{cycle}}\right)\left(2.00 \frac{\text{cycles}}{\text{s}}\right)$$
$$= 4.00\pi \text{ rad/s} = 12.6 \text{ rad/s}$$

The period is $T = 1/f = 0.500$ s, and from Eq. (15.1),

$$\lambda = \frac{v}{f} = \frac{12.0 \text{ m/s}}{2.00 \text{ s}^{-1}} = 6.00 \text{ m}$$

We find the wave number from Eq. (15.5) or (15.6):

$$k = \frac{2\pi}{\lambda} = \frac{2\pi \text{ rad}}{6.00 \text{ m}} = 1.05 \text{ rad/m}$$

or

$$k = \frac{\omega}{v} = \frac{4.00\pi \text{ rad/s}}{12.0 \text{ m/s}} = 1.05 \text{ rad/m}$$

(b) We write the wave function using Eq. (15.4) and the values of A, T, and λ from part (a):

$$y(x,t) = A\cos 2\pi\left(\frac{x}{\lambda} - \frac{t}{T}\right)$$
$$= (0.075 \text{ m})\cos 2\pi\left(\frac{x}{6.00 \text{ m}} - \frac{t}{0.500 \text{ s}}\right)$$
$$= (0.075 \text{ m})\cos[(1.05 \text{ rad/m})x - (12.6 \text{ rad/s})t]$$

We can also get this same expression from Eq. (15.7) by using the values of ω and k from part (a).

(c) We can find the displacement as a function of time at $x = 0$ and $x = +3.00$ m by substituting these values into the wave function from part (b):

$$y(x = 0, t) = (0.075 \text{ m})\cos 2\pi\left(\frac{0}{6.00 \text{ m}} - \frac{t}{0.500 \text{ s}}\right)$$
$$= (0.075 \text{ m})\cos(12.6 \text{ rad/s})t$$

$$y(x = +3.00 \text{ m}, t) = (0.075 \text{ m})\cos 2\pi\left(\frac{3.00 \text{ m}}{6.00 \text{ m}} - \frac{t}{0.500 \text{ s}}\right)$$
$$= (0.075 \text{ m})\cos[\pi - (12.6 \text{ rad/s})t]$$
$$= -(0.075 \text{ m})\cos(12.6 \text{ rad/s})t$$

EVALUATE: In part (b), the quantity $(1.05 \text{ rad/m})x - (12.6 \text{ rad/s})t$ is the *phase* of a point x on the string at time t. The two points in part (c) oscillate in SHM with the same frequency and amplitude, but their oscillations differ in phase by $(1.05 \text{ rad/m})(3.00 \text{ m}) = 3.15$ rad $= \pi$ radians—that is, one-half cycle—because the points are separated by one half-wavelength: $\lambda/2 = (6.00 \text{ m})/2 = 3.00$ m. Thus, while a graph of y versus t for the point at $x = 0$ is a cosine curve (like Fig. 15.9b), a graph of y versus t for the point $x = 3.00$ m is a *negative* cosine curve (the same as a cosine curve shifted by one half-cycle).

Using the expression for $y(x = 0, t)$ in part (c), can you show that the end of the string at $x = 0$ is instantaneously at rest at $t = 0$, as stated at the beginning of this example? (*Hint:* Calculate the y-velocity at this point by taking the derivative of y with respect to t.)

Particle Velocity and Acceleration in a Sinusoidal Wave

From the wave function we can get an expression for the transverse velocity of any *particle* in a transverse wave. We call this v_y to distinguish it from the wave propagation speed v. To find the transverse velocity v_y at a particular point x, we take the derivative of the wave function $y(x, t)$ with respect to t, keeping x constant. If the wave function is

$$y(x, t) = A\cos(kx - \omega t)$$

then

$$v_y(x, t) = \frac{\partial y(x, t)}{\partial t} = \omega A\sin(kx - \omega t) \tag{15.9}$$

The ∂ in this expression is a modified d, used to remind us that $y(x, t)$ is a function of *two* variables and that we are allowing only one (t) to vary. The other (x) is constant because we are looking at a particular point on the string. This derivative is called a *partial derivative*. If you haven't reached this point yet in your study of calculus, don't fret; it's a simple idea.

Equation (15.9) shows that the transverse velocity of a particle varies with time, as we expect for simple harmonic motion. The maximum particle speed is ωA; this can be greater than, less than, or equal to the wave speed v, depending on the amplitude and frequency of the wave.

The *acceleration* of any particle is the *second* partial derivative of $y(x, t)$ with respect to t:

$$a_y(x, t) = \frac{\partial^2 y(x, t)}{\partial t^2} = -\omega^2 A \cos(kx - \omega t) = -\omega^2 y(x, t) \quad (15.10)$$

The acceleration of a particle equals $-\omega^2$ times its displacement, which is the result we obtained in Section 14.2 for simple harmonic motion.

We can also compute partial derivatives of $y(x, t)$ with respect to x, holding t constant. The first derivative $\partial y(x, t)/\partial x$ is the *slope* of the string at point x and at time t. The second partial derivative with respect to x is the *curvature* of the string:

$$\frac{\partial^2 y(x, t)}{\partial x^2} = -k^2 A \cos(kx - \omega t) = -k^2 y(x, t) \quad (15.11)$$

From Eqs. (15.10) and (15.11) and the relationship $\omega = vk$ we see that

$$\frac{\partial^2 y(x, t)/\partial t^2}{\partial^2 y(x, t)/\partial x^2} = \frac{\omega^2}{k^2} = v^2 \quad \text{and}$$

$$\frac{\partial^2 y(x, t)}{\partial x^2} = \frac{1}{v^2} \frac{\partial^2 y(x, t)}{\partial t^2} \quad \text{(wave equation)} \quad (15.12)$$

We've derived Eq. (15.12) for a wave traveling in the positive x-direction. You can use the same steps to show that the wave function for a sinusoidal wave propagating in the *negative* x-direction, $y(x, t) = A \cos(kx + \omega t)$, also satisfies this equation.

Equation (15.12), called the **wave equation,** is one of the most important equations in all of physics. Whenever it occurs, we know that a disturbance can propagate as a wave along the x-axis with wave speed v. The disturbance need not be a sinusoidal wave; we'll see in the next section that *any* wave on a string obeys Eq. (15.12), whether the wave is periodic or not (see also Problem 15.65). In Chapter 32 we will find that electric and magnetic fields satisfy the wave equation; the wave speed will turn out to be the speed of light, which will lead us to the conclusion that light is an electromagnetic wave.

Figure 15.10a shows the transverse velocity v_y and transverse acceleration a_y, given by Eqs. (15.9) and (15.10), for several points on a string as a sinusoidal wave passes along it. Note that at points where the string has an upward curvature $(\partial^2 y/\partial x^2 > 0)$, the acceleration of that point is positive $(a_y = \partial^2 y/\partial t^2 > 0)$; this follows from the wave equation, Eq. (15.12). For the same reason the acceleration is negative $(a_y = \partial^2 y/\partial t^2 < 0)$ at points where the string has a downward curvature $(\partial^2 y/\partial x^2 < 0)$, and the acceleration is zero $(a_y = \partial^2 y/\partial t^2 = 0)$ at points of inflection where the curvature is zero $(\partial^2 y/\partial x^2 = 0)$. We emphasize again that v_y and a_y are the *transverse* velocity and acceleration of points on the string; these points move along the y-direction, not along the propagation direction of the

15.10 (a) Another view of the wave at $t = 0$ in Fig. 15.9a. The vectors show the transverse velocity v_y and transverse acceleration a_y at several points on the string. (b) From $t = 0$ to $t = 0.05T$, a particle at point 1 is displaced to point 1′, a particle at point 2 is displaced to point 2′, and so on.

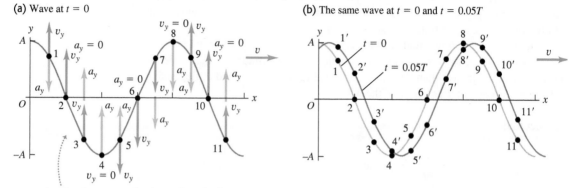

(a) Wave at $t = 0$

(b) The same wave at $t = 0$ and $t = 0.05T$

• Acceleration a_y at each point on the string is proportional to displacement y at that point.
• Acceleration is upward where string curves upward, downward where string curves downward.

wave. Figure 15.10b shows the transverse motions of several points on the string.

The concept of wave function is equally useful with *longitudinal* waves. The quantity y still measures the displacement of a particle of the medium from its equilibrium position; the difference is that for a longitudinal wave, this displacement is *parallel* to the x-axis instead of perpendicular to it. We'll discuss longitudinal waves in detail in Chapter 16.

Test Your Understanding of Section 15.3 Figure 15.8 shows a sinusoidal wave of period T on a string at times $0, \frac{1}{8}T, \frac{2}{8}T, \frac{3}{8}T, \frac{4}{8}T, \frac{5}{8}T, \frac{6}{8}T, \frac{7}{8}T$, and T. (a) At which time is point A on the string moving upward with maximum speed? (b) At which time does point B on the string have the greatest upward acceleration? (c) At which time does point C on the string have a downward acceleration but an upward velocity?

ActivPhysics 10.2: Speed of Waves on a String

15.4 Speed of a Transverse Wave

One of the key properties of any wave is the wave *speed*. Light waves in air have a much greater speed of propagation than do sound waves in air (3.00×10^8 m/s versus 344 m/s); that's why you see the flash from a bolt of lightning before you hear the clap of thunder. In this section we'll see what determines the speed of propagation of one particular kind of wave: transverse waves on a string. The speed of these waves is important to understand because it is an essential part of analyzing stringed musical instruments, as we'll discuss later in this chapter. Furthermore, the speeds of many kinds of mechanical waves turn out to have the same basic mathematical expression as does the speed of waves on a string.

The physical quantities that determine the speed of transverse waves on a string are the *tension* in the string and its *mass per unit length* (also called *linear mass density*). We might guess that increasing the tension should increase the restoring forces that tend to straighten the string when it is disturbed, thus increasing the wave speed. We might also guess that increasing the mass should make the motion more sluggish and decrease the speed. Both these guesses turn out to be right. We'll develop the exact relationship among wave speed, tension, and mass per unit length by two different methods. The first is simple in concept and considers a specific wave shape; the second is more general but also more formal. Choose whichever you like better.

15.11 Propagation of a transverse wave on a string.

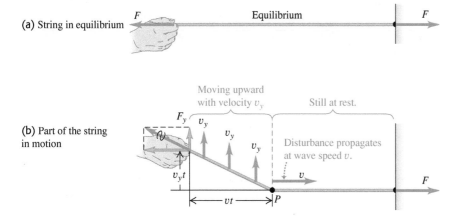

(a) String in equilibrium

(b) Part of the string in motion

Wave Speed on a String: First Method

We consider a perfectly flexible string (Fig. 15.11). In the equilibrium position the tension is F and the linear mass density (mass per unit length) is μ. (When portions of the string are displaced from equilibrium, the mass per unit length decreases a little, and the tension increases a little.) We ignore the weight of the string so that when the string is at rest in the equilibrium position, the string forms a perfectly straight line as in Fig. 15.11a.

Starting at time $t = 0$, we apply a constant upward force F_y at the left end of the string. We might expect that the end would move with constant acceleration; that would happen if the force were applied to a *point* mass. But here the effect of the force F_y is to set successively more and more mass in motion. The wave travels with constant speed v, so the division point P between moving and nonmoving portions moves with the same constant speed v (Fig. 15.11b).

Figure 15.11b shows that all particles in the moving portion of the string move upward with constant *velocity* v_y, not constant acceleration. To see why this is so, we note that the *impulse* of the force F_y up to time t is $F_y t$. According to the impulse–momentum theorem (see Section 8.1), the impulse is equal to the change in the total transverse component of momentum $(mv_y - 0)$ of the moving part of the string. Because the system started with *no* transverse momentum, this is equal to the total momentum at time t:

$$F_y t = mv_y$$

The total momentum thus must increase proportionately with time. But since the division point P moves with constant speed, the length of string that is in motion and hence the total mass m in motion are also proportional to the time t that the force has been acting. So the *change* of momentum must be associated entirely with the increasing amount of mass in motion, not with an increasing velocity of an individual mass element. That is, mv_y changes because m, not v_y, changes.

At time t, the left end of the string has moved up a distance $v_y t$, and the boundary point P has advanced a distance vt. The total force at the left end of the string has components F and F_y. Why F? There is no motion in the direction along the length of the string, so there is no unbalanced horizontal force. Therefore F, the magnitude of the horizontal component, does not change when the string is displaced. In the displaced position the tension is $(F^2 + F_y^2)^{1/2}$ (greater than F), and the string stretches somewhat.

To derive an expression for the wave speed v, we again apply the impulse–momentum theorem to the portion of the string in motion at time t—that is, the portion to the left of P in Fig. 15.11b. The transverse *impulse* (transverse force times time) is equal to the change of transverse *momentum* of the moving portion (mass times transverse component of velocity). The impulse of the transverse force F_y in time t is $F_y t$. In Fig. 15.11b the right triangle whose vertex is at P, with sides $v_y t$ and vt, is similar to the right triangle whose vertex is at the position of the hand, with sides F_y and F. Hence

$$\frac{F_y}{F} = \frac{v_y t}{vt} \qquad F_y = F\frac{v_y}{v}$$

and

$$\text{Transverse impulse} = F_y t = F\frac{v_y}{v}t$$

The mass of the moving portion of the string is the product of the mass per unit length μ and the length vt, or μvt. The transverse momentum is the product of this mass and the transverse velocity v_y:

$$\text{Transverse momentum} = (\mu vt)v_y$$

We note again that the momentum increases with time *not* because mass is moving faster, as was usually the case in Chapter 8, but because *more mass* is brought into motion. But the impulse of the force F_y is still equal to the total change in momentum of the system. Applying this relationship, we obtain

$$F\frac{v_y}{v}t = \mu vtv_y$$

Solving this for v, we find

$$v = \sqrt{\frac{F}{\mu}} \qquad \text{(speed of a transverse wave on a string)} \qquad (15.13)$$

Equation (15.13) confirms our prediction that the wave speed v should increase when the tension F increases but decrease when the mass per unit length μ increases (Fig. 15.12).

Note that v_y does not appear in Eq. (15.13); thus the wave speed doesn't depend on v_y. Our calculation considered only a very special kind of pulse, but we can consider *any* shape of wave disturbance as a series of pulses with different values of v_y. So even though we derived Eq. (15.13) for a special case, it is valid for *any* transverse wave motion on a string, including the sinusoidal and other periodic waves we discussed in Section 15.3. Note also that the wave speed doesn't depend on the amplitude or frequency of the wave, in accordance with our assumptions in Section 15.3.

Wave Speed on a String: Second Method

Here is an alternative derivation of Eq. (15.13). If you aren't comfortable with partial derivatives, it can be omitted. We apply Newton's second law, $\sum \vec{F} = m\vec{a}$, to a small segment of string whose length in the equilibrium position is Δx (Fig. 15.13). The mass of the segment is $m = \mu \, \Delta x$; the forces at the ends are represented in terms of their x- and y-components. The x-components have equal magnitude F and add to zero because the motion is transverse and there is no component of acceleration in the x-direction. To obtain F_{1y} and F_{2y}, we note that the ratio F_{1y}/F is equal in magnitude to the *slope* of the string at point x and that F_{2y}/F is equal to the slope at point $x + \Delta x$. Taking proper account of signs, we find

$$\frac{F_{1y}}{F} = -\left(\frac{\partial y}{\partial x}\right)_x \qquad \frac{F_{2y}}{F} = \left(\frac{\partial y}{\partial x}\right)_{x+\Delta x} \qquad (15.14)$$

15.12 These cables have a relatively large amount of mass per unit length (μ) and a low tension (F). If the cables are disturbed—say, by a bird landing on them—transverse waves will travel along them at a slow speed $v = \sqrt{F/\mu}$.

15.13 Free-body diagram for a segment of string. The force at each end of the string is tangent to the string at the point of application.

The string to the right of the segment (not shown) exerts a force $\vec{F}_2$ on the segment.

There can be a net vertical force on the segment, but the net horizontal force is zero (the motion is transverse).

F_2

F_{2y}

F

Equilibrium length of this segment of the string

F

F_{1y}

F_1

Δx

x $x + \Delta x$

The string to the left of the segment (not shown) exerts a force $\vec{F}_1$ on the segment.

The notation reminds us that the derivatives are evaluated at points x and $x + \Delta x$, respectively. From Eq. (15.14) we find that the net y-component of force is

$$F_y = F_{1y} + F_{2y} = F\left[\left(\frac{\partial y}{\partial x}\right)_{x+\Delta x} - \left(\frac{\partial y}{\partial x}\right)_x\right] \qquad (15.15)$$

We now equate F_y from Eq. (15.15) to the mass $\mu\, \Delta x$ times the y-component of acceleration $\partial^2 y / \partial t^2$. We obtain

$$F\left[\left(\frac{\partial y}{\partial x}\right)_{x+\Delta x} - \left(\frac{\partial y}{\partial x}\right)_x\right] = \mu\, \Delta x \frac{\partial^2 y}{\partial t^2} \qquad (15.16)$$

or, dividing by $F\Delta x$,

$$\frac{\left(\dfrac{\partial y}{\partial x}\right)_{x+\Delta x} - \left(\dfrac{\partial y}{\partial x}\right)_x}{\Delta x} = \frac{\mu}{F}\frac{\partial^2 y}{\partial t^2} \qquad (15.17)$$

We now take the limit as $\Delta x \to 0$. In this limit, the left side of Eq. (15.17) becomes the derivative of $\partial y / \partial x$ with respect to x (at constant t)—that is, the *second* (partial) derivative of y with respect to x:

$$\frac{\partial^2 y}{\partial x^2} = \frac{\mu}{F}\frac{\partial^2 y}{\partial t^2} \qquad (15.18)$$

Now, finally, comes the punch line of our story. Equation (15.18) has exactly the same form as the *wave equation,* Eq. (15.12), that we derived at the end of Section 15.3. That equation and Eq. (15.18) describe the very same wave motion, so they must be identical. Comparing the two equations, we see that for this to be so, we must have

$$v = \sqrt{\frac{F}{\mu}} \qquad (15.19)$$

which is the same expression as Eq. (15.13).

In going through this derivation, we didn't make any special assumptions about the shape of the wave. Since our derivation led us to rediscover Eq. (15.12), the wave equation, we conclude that the wave equation is valid for waves on a string that have *any* shape.

The Speed of Mechanical Waves

Equation (15.13) or (15.19) gives the wave speed for only the special case of mechanical waves on a stretched string or rope. Remarkably, it turns out that for many types of mechanical waves, including waves on a string, the expression for wave speed has the same general form:

$$v = \sqrt{\frac{\text{Restoring force returning the system to equilibrium}}{\text{Inertia resisting the return to equilibrium}}}$$

To interpret this expression, let's look at the now-familiar case of waves on a string. The tension F in the string plays the role of the restoring force; it tends to bring the string back to its undisturbed, equilibrium configuration. The mass of the string—or, more properly, the linear mass density μ—provides the inertia that prevents the string from returning instantaneously to equilibrium. Hence we have $v = \sqrt{F/\mu}$ for the speed of waves on a string.

In Chapter 16 we'll see a similar expression for the speed of sound waves in a gas. Roughly speaking, the gas pressure provides the force that tends to return the gas to its undisturbed state when a sound wave passes through. The inertia is provided by the density, or mass per unit volume, of the gas.

Example 15.3	Calculating wave speed

One end of a 2.00-kg rope is tied to a support at the top of a mine shaft 80.0 m deep (Fig. 15.14). The rope is stretched taut by a 20.0-kg box of rocks attached at the bottom. (a) The geologist at the bottom of the shaft signals to a colleague at the top by jerking the rope sideways. What is the speed of a transverse wave on the rope? (b) If a point on the rope is in transverse SHM with $f = 2.00$ Hz, how many cycles of the wave are there in the rope's length?

SOLUTION

IDENTIFY and SET UP: In part (a) we can find the wave speed (our target variable) using the *dynamic* relationship $v = \sqrt{F/\mu}$

15.14 Sending signals along a vertical rope using transverse waves.

$m_{rope} = 2.00$ kg

80.0 m

$m_{samples} = 20.0$ kg

[Eq. (15.13)]. In part (b) we find the wavelength from the *kinematic* relationship $v = f\lambda$; from that we can find the target variable, the number of wavelengths that fit into the rope's 80.0-m length. We'll assume that the rope is massless (even though its weight is 10% that of the box), so that the box alone provides the tension in the rope.

EXECUTE: (a) The tension in the rope due to the box is

$$F = m_{box}g = (20.0 \text{ kg})(9.80 \text{ m/s}^2) = 196 \text{ N}$$

and the rope's linear mass density is

$$\mu = \frac{m_{rope}}{L} = \frac{2.00 \text{ kg}}{80.0 \text{ m}} = 0.0250 \text{ kg/m}$$

Hence, from Eq. (15.13), the wave speed is

$$v = \sqrt{\frac{F}{\mu}} = \sqrt{\frac{196 \text{ N}}{0.0250 \text{ kg/m}}} = 88.5 \text{ m/s}$$

(b) From Eq. (15.1), the wavelength is

$$\lambda = \frac{v}{f} = \frac{88.5 \text{ m/s}}{2.00 \text{ s}^{-1}} = 44.3 \text{ m}$$

There are $(80.0 \text{ m})/(44.3 \text{ m}) = 1.81$ wavelengths (that is, cycles of the wave) in the rope.

EVALUATE: Because of the rope's weight, its tension is greater at the top than at the bottom. Hence both the wave speed and the wavelength increase as a wave travels up the rope. If you take account of this, can you verify that the wave speed at the top of the rope is 92.9 m/s?

Test Your Understanding of Section 15.4 The six strings of a guitar are the same length and under nearly the same tension, but they have different thicknesses. On which string do waves travel the fastest? (i) the thickest string; (ii) the thinnest string; (iii) the wave speed is the same on all strings.

15.5 Energy in Wave Motion

Application Surface Waves and the Swimming Speed of Ducks
When a duck swims, it necessarily produces waves on the surface of the water. The faster the duck swims, the larger the wave amplitude and the more power the duck must supply to produce these waves. The maximum power available from their leg muscles limits the maximum swimming speed of ducks to only about 0.7 m/s (2.5 km/h = 1.6 mi/h).

Every wave motion has *energy* associated with it. The energy we receive from sunlight and the destructive effects of ocean surf and earthquakes bear this out. To produce any of the wave motions we have discussed in this chapter, we have to apply a force to a portion of the wave medium; the point where the force is applied moves, so we do *work* on the system. As the wave propagates, each portion of the medium exerts a force and does work on the adjoining portion. In this way a wave can transport energy from one region of space to another.

As an example of energy considerations in wave motion, let's look again at transverse waves on a string. How is energy transferred from one portion of string to another? Picture a wave traveling from left to right (the positive *x*-direction) on the string, and consider a particular point *a* on the string (Fig. 15.15a). The string to the left of point *a* exerts a force on the string to the right of it, and vice versa. In Fig. 15.15b the string to the left of *a* has been removed, and the force it exerts at *a* is represented by the components F and F_y, as we did in Figs. 15.11 and

15.13. We note again that F_y/F is equal to the negative of the *slope* of the string at a, which is also given by $\partial y/\partial x$. Putting these together, we have

$$F_y(x, t) = -F\frac{\partial y(x, t)}{\partial x} \qquad (15.20)$$

We need the negative sign because F_y is negative when the slope is positive. We write the vertical force as $F_y(x, t)$ as a reminder that its value may be different at different points along the string and at different times.

When point a moves in the y-direction, the force F_y does *work* on this point and therefore transfers energy into the part of the string to the right of a. The corresponding power P (rate of doing work) at the point a is the transverse force $F_y(x, t)$ at a times the transverse velocity $v_y(x, t) = \partial y(x, t)/\partial t$ of that point:

$$P(x, t) = F_y(x, t)v_y(x, t) = -F\frac{\partial y(x, t)}{\partial x}\frac{\partial y(x, t)}{\partial t} \qquad (15.21)$$

This power is the *instantaneous* rate at which energy is transferred along the string. Its value depends on the position x on the string and on the time t. Note that energy is being transferred only at points where the string has a nonzero slope ($\partial y/\partial x$ is nonzero), so that there is a transverse component of the tension force, and where the string has a nonzero transverse velocity ($\partial y/\partial t$ is nonzero) so that the transverse force can do work.

Equation (15.21) is valid for *any* wave on a string, sinusoidal or not. For a sinusoidal wave with wave function given by Eq. (15.7), we have

$$y(x, t) = A\cos(kx - \omega t)$$
$$\frac{\partial y(x, t)}{\partial x} = -kA\sin(kx - \omega t)$$
$$\frac{\partial y(x, t)}{\partial t} = \omega A\sin(kx - \omega t)$$
$$P(x, t) = Fk\omega A^2\sin^2(kx - \omega t) \qquad (15.22)$$

By using the relationships $\omega = vk$ and $v^2 = F/\mu$, we can also express Eq. (15.22) in the alternative form

$$P(x, t) = \sqrt{\mu F}\,\omega^2 A^2\sin^2(kx - \omega t) \qquad (15.23)$$

The $\sin^2$ function is never negative, so the instantaneous power in a sinusoidal wave is either positive (so that energy flows in the positive x-direction) or zero (at points where there is no energy transfer). Energy is never transferred in the direction opposite to the direction of wave propagation (Fig. 15.16).

The maximum value of the instantaneous power $P(x, t)$ occurs when the $\sin^2$ function has the value unity:

$$P_{max} = \sqrt{\mu F}\,\omega^2 A^2 \qquad (15.24)$$

To obtain the *average* power from Eq. (15.23), we note that the *average* value of the $\sin^2$ function, averaged over any whole number of cycles, is $\frac{1}{2}$. Hence the average power is

$$P_{av} = \tfrac{1}{2}\sqrt{\mu F}\,\omega^2 A^2 \qquad \text{(average power, sinusoidal wave on a string)} \quad (15.25)$$

The average power is just one-half of the maximum instantaneous power (see Fig. 15.16).

The average rate of energy transfer is proportional to the square of the amplitude and to the square of the frequency. This proportionality is a general result for mechanical waves of all types, including seismic waves (see the photo that opens this chapter). For a mechanical wave, the rate of energy transfer

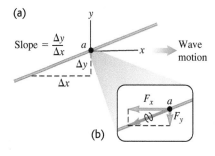

15.15 (a) Point a on a string carrying a wave from left to right. (b) The components of the force exerted on the part of the string to the right of point a by the part of the string to the left of point a.

15.16 The instantaneous power $P(x, t)$ in a sinusoidal wave as given by Eq. (15.23), shown as a function of time at coordinate $x = 0$. The power is never negative, which means that energy never flows opposite to the direction of wave propagation.

quadruples if the frequency is doubled (for the same amplitude) or if the amplitude is doubled (for the same frequency).

Electromagnetic waves turn out to be a bit different. While the average rate of energy transfer in an electromagnetic wave is proportional to the square of the amplitude, just as for mechanical waves, it is independent of the value of ω.

Example 15.4 Power in a wave

(a) In Example 15.2 (Section 15.3), at what maximum rate does Throcky put energy into the clothesline? That is, what is his maximum instantaneous power? The linear mass density of the clothesline is $\mu = 0.250$ kg/m, and Throcky applies tension $F = 36.0$ N. (b) What is his average power? (c) As Throcky tires, the amplitude decreases. What is the average power when the amplitude is 7.50 mm?

SOLUTION

IDENTIFY and SET UP: In part (a) our target variable is the *maximum instantaneous* power P_{max}, while in parts (b) and (c) it is the *average* power. For part (a) we'll use Eq. (15.24), and for parts (b) and (c) we'll use Eq. (15.25); Example 15.2 gives us all the needed quantities.

EXECUTE: (a) From Eq. (15.24),

$$P_{max} = \sqrt{\mu F \omega^2 A^2}$$
$$= \sqrt{(0.250 \text{ kg/m})(36.0 \text{ N})(4.00\pi \text{ rad/s})^2 (0.075 \text{ m})^2}$$
$$= 2.66 \text{ W}$$

(b) From Eqs. (15.24) and (15.25), the average power is one-half of the maximum instantaneous power, so

$$P_{av} = \tfrac{1}{2}P_{max} = \tfrac{1}{2}(2.66 \text{ W}) = 1.33 \text{ W}$$

(c) The new amplitude is $\frac{1}{10}$ of the value we used in parts (a) and (b). From Eq. (15.25), the average power is proportional to A^2, so the new average power is

$$P_{av} = \left(\tfrac{1}{10}\right)^2 (1.33 \text{ W}) = 0.0133 \text{ W} = 13.3 \text{ mW}$$

EVALUATE: Equation (15.23) shows that P_{max} occurs when $\sin^2(kx - \omega t) = 1$. At any given position x, this happens twice per period of the wave—once when the sine function is equal to $+1$, and once when it's equal to -1. The *minimum* instantaneous power is zero; this occurs when $\sin^2(kx - \omega t) = 0$, which also happens twice per period.

Can you confirm that the given values of μ and F give the wave speed mentioned in Example 15.2?

Wave Intensity

Waves on a string carry energy in just one dimension of space (along the direction of the string). But other types of waves, including sound waves in air and seismic waves in the body of the earth, carry energy across all three dimensions of space. For waves that travel in three dimensions, we define the **intensity** (denoted by I) to be *the time average rate at which energy is transported by the wave, per unit area,* across a surface perpendicular to the direction of propagation. That is, intensity I is average power per unit area. It is usually measured in watts per square meter (W/m^2).

If waves spread out equally in all directions from a source, the intensity at a distance r from the source is inversely proportional to r^2 (Fig. 15.17). This follows directly from energy conservation. If the power output of the source is P, then the average intensity I_1 through a sphere with radius r_1 and surface area $4\pi r_1^2$ is

$$I_1 = \frac{P}{4\pi r_1^2}$$

The average intensity I_2 through a sphere with a different radius r_2 is given by a similar expression. If no energy is absorbed between the two spheres, the power P must be the same for both, and

$$4\pi r_1^2 I_1 = 4\pi r_2^2 I_2$$

$$\frac{I_1}{I_2} = \frac{r_2^2}{r_1^2} \quad \text{(inverse-square law for intensity)} \tag{15.26}$$

15.17 The greater the distance from a wave source, the greater the area over which the wave power is distributed and the smaller the wave intensity.

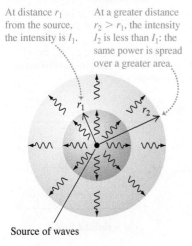

At distance r_1 from the source, the intensity is I_1.

At a greater distance $r_2 > r_1$, the intensity I_2 is less than I_1: the same power is spread over a greater area.

Source of waves

The intensity I at any distance r is therefore inversely proportional to r^2. This relationship is called the *inverse-square law* for intensity.

Example 15.5   **The inverse-square law**

A siren on a tall pole radiates sound waves uniformly in all directions. At a distance of 15.0 m from the siren, the sound intensity is 0.250 W/m². At what distance is the intensity 0.010 W/m²?

SOLUTION

IDENTIFY and SET UP: Because sound is radiated uniformly in all directions, we can use the inverse-square law, Eq. (15.26). At $r_1 = 15.0$ m the intensity is $I_1 = 0.250$ W/m², and the target variable is the distance r_2 at which the intensity is $I_2 = 0.010$ W/m².

EXECUTE: We solve Eq. (15.26) for r_2:

$$r_2 = r_1 \sqrt{\frac{I_1}{I_2}} = (15.0 \text{ m}) \sqrt{\frac{0.250 \text{ W/m}^2}{0.010 \text{ W/m}^2}} = 75.0 \text{ m}$$

EVALUATE: As a check on our answer, note that r_2 is five times greater than r_1. By the inverse-square law, the intensity I_2 should be $1/5^2 = 1/25$ as great as I_1, and indeed it is.

By using the inverse-square law, we've assumed that the sound waves travel in straight lines away from the siren. A more realistic solution, which is beyond our scope, would account for the reflection of sound waves from the ground.

Test Your Understanding of Section 15.5   Four identical strings each carry a sinusoidal wave of frequency 10 Hz. The string tension and wave amplitude are different for different strings. Rank the following strings in order from highest to lowest value of the average wave power: (i) tension 10 N, amplitude 1.0 mm; (ii) tension 40 N, amplitude 1.0 mm; (iii) tension 10 N, amplitude 4.0 mm; (iv) tension 20 N, amplitude 2.0 mm.

15.6 Wave Interference, Boundary Conditions, and Superposition

Up to this point we've been discussing waves that propagate continuously in the same direction. But when a wave strikes the boundaries of its medium, all or part of the wave is *reflected.* When you yell at a building wall or a cliff face some distance away, the sound wave is reflected from the rigid surface and you hear an echo. When you flip the end of a rope whose far end is tied to a rigid support, a pulse travels the length of the rope and is reflected back to you. In both cases, the initial and reflected waves overlap in the same region of the medium. This overlapping of waves is called **interference.** (In general, the term "interference" refers to what happens when two or more waves pass through the same region at the same time.)

As a simple example of wave reflections and the role of the boundary of a wave medium, let's look again at transverse waves on a stretched string. What happens when a wave pulse or a sinusoidal wave arrives at the *end* of the string?

If the end is fastened to a rigid support, it is a *fixed* end that cannot move. The arriving wave exerts a force on the support; the reaction to this force, exerted *by* the support *on* the string, "kicks back" on the string and sets up a *reflected* pulse or wave traveling in the reverse direction. Figure 15.18 is a series of photographs showing the reflection of a pulse at the fixed end of a long coiled spring. The reflected pulse moves in the opposite direction from the initial, or *incident,* pulse, and its displacement is also opposite. Figure 15.19a illustrates this situation for a wave pulse on a string.

The opposite situation from an end that is held stationary is a *free* end, one that is perfectly free to move in the direction perpendicular to the length of the string. For example, the string might be tied to a light ring that slides on a frictionless rod perpendicular to the string, as in Fig. 15.19b. The ring and rod maintain the tension but exert no transverse force. When a wave arrives at this free end, the ring slides along the rod. The ring reaches a maximum displacement, and both it and the string come momentarily to rest, as in drawing 4 in Fig. 15.19b. But the string is now stretched, giving increased tension, so the free end of the string is

15.18 A series of images of a wave pulse, equally spaced in time from top to bottom. The pulse starts at the left in the top image, travels to the right, and is reflected from the fixed end at the right.

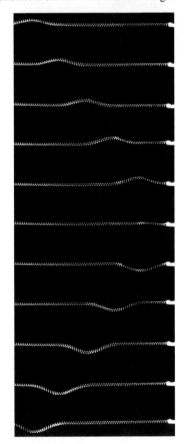

15.19 Reflection of a wave pulse **(a)** at a fixed end of a string and **(b)** at a free end. Time increases from top to bottom in each figure.

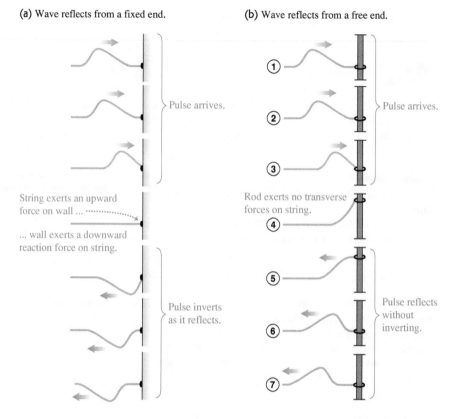

(a) Wave reflects from a fixed end.

Pulse arrives.

String exerts an upward force on wall ...

... wall exerts a downward reaction force on string.

Pulse inverts as it reflects.

(b) Wave reflects from a free end.

Pulse arrives.

Rod exerts no transverse forces on string.

Pulse reflects without inverting.

15.20 Overlap of two wave pulses—one right side up, one inverted—traveling in opposite directions. Time increases from top to bottom.

As the pulses overlap, the displacement of the string at any point is the algebraic sum of the displacements due to the individual pulses.

Shapes that each pulse would have on its own

O

pulled back down, and again a reflected pulse is produced (drawing 7). As for a fixed end, the reflected pulse moves in the opposite direction from the initial pulse, but now the direction of the displacement is the same as for the initial pulse. The conditions at the end of the string, such as a rigid support or the complete absence of transverse force, are called **boundary conditions.**

The formation of the reflected pulse is similar to the overlap of two pulses traveling in opposite directions. Figure 15.20 shows two pulses with the same shape, one inverted with respect to the other, traveling in opposite directions. As the pulses overlap and pass each other, the total displacement of the string is the *algebraic sum* of the displacements at that point in the individual pulses. Because these two pulses have the same shape, the total displacement at point O in the middle of the figure is zero at all times. Thus the motion of the left half of the string would be the same if we cut the string at point O, threw away the right side, and held the end at O fixed. The two pulses on the left side then correspond to the incident and reflected pulses, combining so that the total displacement at O is *always* zero. For this to occur, the reflected pulse must be inverted relative to the incident pulse.

Figure 15.21 shows two pulses with the same shape, traveling in opposite directions but *not* inverted relative to each other. The displacement at point O in the middle of the figure is not zero, but the slope of the string at this point is always zero. According to Eq. (15.20), this corresponds to the absence of any transverse force at this point. In this case the motion of the left half of the string would be the same as if we cut the string at point O and attached the end to a frictionless sliding ring (Fig. 15.19b) that maintains tension without exerting any transverse force. In other words, this situation corresponds to reflection of a pulse at a free end of a string at point O. In this case the reflected pulse is *not* inverted.

The Principle of Superposition

Combining the displacements of the separate pulses at each point to obtain the actual displacement is an example of the **principle of superposition:** When two waves overlap, the actual displacement of any point on the string at any time is obtained by adding the displacement the point would have if only the first wave were present and the displacement it would have if only the second wave were present. In other words, the wave function $y(x, t)$ that describes the resulting motion in this situation is obtained by *adding* the two wave functions for the two separate waves:

$$y(x, t) = y_1(x, t) + y_2(x, t) \quad \text{(principle of superposition)} \quad (15.27)$$

Mathematically, this additive property of wave functions follows from the form of the wave equation, Eq. (15.12) or (15.18), which every physically possible wave function must satisfy. Specifically, the wave equation is *linear;* that is, it contains the function $y(x, t)$ only to the first power (there are no terms involving $y(x, t)^2$, $y(x, t)^{1/2}$, etc.). As a result, if any two functions $y_1(x, t)$ and $y_2(x, t)$ satisfy the wave equation separately, their sum $y_1(x, t) + y_2(x, t)$ also satisfies it and is therefore a physically possible motion. Because this principle depends on the linearity of the wave equation and the corresponding linear-combination property of its solutions, it is also called the *principle of linear superposition.* For some physical systems, such as a medium that does not obey Hooke's law, the wave equation is *not* linear; this principle does not hold for such systems.

The principle of superposition is of central importance in all types of waves. When a friend talks to you while you are listening to music, you can distinguish the sound of speech and the sound of music from each other. This is precisely because the total sound wave reaching your ears is the algebraic sum of the wave produced by your friend's voice and the wave produced by the speakers of your stereo. If two sound waves did *not* combine in this simple linear way, the sound you would hear in this situation would be a hopeless jumble. Superposition also applies to electromagnetic waves (such as light) and many other types of waves.

Test Your Understanding of Section 15.6 Figure 15.22 shows two wave pulses with different shapes traveling in different directions along a string. Make a series of sketches like Fig. 15.21 showing the shape of the string as the two pulses approach, overlap, and then pass each other.

15.21 Overlap of two wave pulses—both right side up—traveling in opposite directions. Time increases from top to bottom. Compare to Fig. 15.20.

O

Video Tutor Demo

15.22 Two wave pulses with different shapes.

15.7 Standing Waves on a String

We have talked about the reflection of a wave *pulse* on a string when it arrives at a boundary point (either a fixed end or a free end). Now let's look at what happens when a *sinusoidal* wave is reflected by a fixed end of a string. We'll again approach the problem by considering the superposition of two waves propagating through the string, one representing the original or incident wave and the other representing the wave reflected at the fixed end.

Figure 15.23 shows a string that is fixed at its left end. Its right end is moved up and down in simple harmonic motion to produce a wave that travels to the left; the wave reflected from the fixed end travels to the right. The resulting motion when the two waves combine no longer looks like two waves traveling in opposite directions. The string appears to be subdivided into a number of segments, as in the time-exposure photographs of Figs. 15.23a, 15.23b, 15.23c, and 15.23d. Figure 15.23e shows two instantaneous shapes of the string in Fig. 15.23b. Let's compare this behavior with the waves we studied in Sections 15.1 through 15.5. In a wave that travels along the string, the amplitude is constant and the wave pattern moves with a speed equal to the wave speed. Here, instead, the wave pattern remains in the same position along the string and its amplitude

15.23 (a)–(d) Time exposures of standing waves in a stretched string. From (a) to (d), the frequency of oscillation of the right-hand end increases and the wavelength of the standing wave decreases. (e) The extremes of the motion of the standing wave in part (b), with nodes at the center and at the ends. The right-hand end of the string moves very little compared to the antinodes and so is essentially a node.

(a) String is one-half wavelength long.

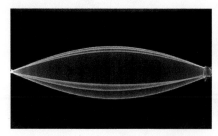

(b) String is one wavelength long.

(c) String is one and a half wavelengths long.

(d) String is two wavelengths long.

(e) The shape of the string in (b) at two different instants

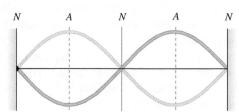

N = **nodes:** points at which the string never moves

A = **antinodes:** points at which the amplitude of string motion is greatest

fluctuates. There are particular points called **nodes** (labeled N in Fig. 15.23e) that never move at all. Midway between the nodes are points called **antinodes** (labeled A in Fig. 15.23e) where the amplitude of motion is greatest. Because the wave pattern doesn't appear to be moving in either direction along the string, it is called a **standing wave.** (To emphasize the difference, a wave that *does* move along the string is called a **traveling wave.**)

The principle of superposition explains how the incident and reflected waves combine to form a standing wave. In Fig. 15.24 the red curves show a wave traveling to the left. The blue curves show a wave traveling to the right with the same propagation speed, wavelength, and amplitude. The waves are shown at nine instants, $\frac{1}{16}$ of a period apart. At each point along the string, we add the displacements (the values of y) for the two separate waves; the result is the total wave on the string, shown in brown.

At certain instants, such as $t = \frac{1}{4}T$, the two wave patterns are exactly in phase with each other, and the shape of the string is a sine curve with twice the amplitude of either individual wave. At other instants, such as $t = \frac{1}{2}T$, the two waves are exactly out of phase with each other, and the total wave at that instant is zero. The resultant displacement is *always* zero at those places marked N at the bottom of Fig. 15.24. These are the *nodes.* At a node the displacements of the two waves in red and blue are always equal and opposite and cancel each other out. This cancellation is called **destructive interference.** Midway between the nodes are the points of *greatest* amplitude, or the *antinodes,* marked A. At the antinodes the displacements of the two waves in red and blue are always identical, giving a large resultant displacement; this phenomenon is called **constructive interference.** We can see from the figure that the distance between successive nodes or between successive antinodes is one half-wavelength, or $\lambda/2$.

We can derive a wave function for the standing wave of Fig. 15.24 by adding the wave functions $y_1(x, t)$ and $y_2(x, t)$ for two waves with equal amplitude, period, and wavelength traveling in opposite directions. Here $y_1(x, t)$ (the red curves in Fig. 15.24) represents an incoming, or *incident,* wave traveling to the

15.24 Formation of a standing wave. A wave traveling to the left (red curves) combines with a wave traveling to the right (blue curves) to form a standing wave (brown curves).

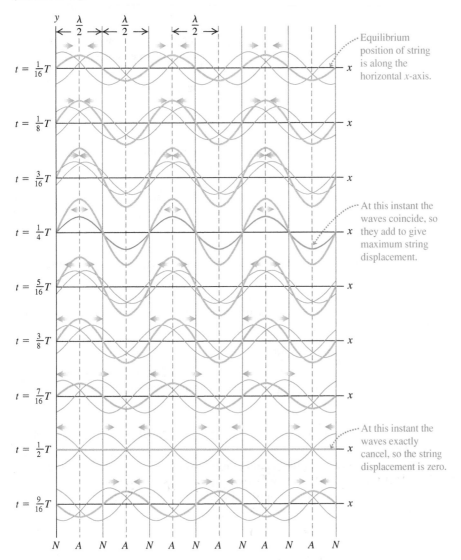

Equilibrium position of string is along the horizontal x-axis.

At this instant the waves coincide, so they add to give maximum string displacement.

At this instant the waves exactly cancel, so the string displacement is zero.

left along the $+x$-axis, arriving at the point $x = 0$ and being reflected; $y_2(x, t)$ (the blue curves in Fig. 15.24) represents the *reflected* wave traveling to the right from $x = 0$. We noted in Section 15.6 that the wave reflected from a fixed end of a string is inverted, so we give a negative sign to one of the waves:

$$y_1(x, t) = -A\cos(kx + \omega t) \quad \text{(incident wave traveling to the left)}$$
$$y_2(x, t) = A\cos(kx - \omega t) \quad \text{(reflected wave traveling to the right)}$$

Note also that the change in sign corresponds to a shift in *phase* of 180° or π radians. At $x = 0$ the motion from the reflected wave is $A\cos\omega t$ and the motion from the incident wave is $-A\cos\omega t$, which we can also write as $A\cos(\omega t + \pi)$. From Eq. (15.27), the wave function for the standing wave is the sum of the individual wave functions:

$$y(x, t) = y_1(x, t) + y_2(x, t) = A[-\cos(kx + \omega t) + \cos(kx - \omega t)]$$

We can rewrite each of the cosine terms by using the identities for the cosine of the sum and difference of two angles: $\cos(a \mp b) = \cos a \cos b \mp \sin a \sin b$.

Applying these and combining terms, we obtain the wave function for the standing wave:

$$y(x, t) = y_1(x, t) + y_2(x, t) = (2A \sin kx) \sin \omega t \quad \text{or}$$

$$y(x, t) = (A_{SW} \sin kx) \sin \omega t \quad \begin{pmatrix} \text{standing wave on a} \\ \text{string, fixed end at } x = 0 \end{pmatrix} \quad (15.28)$$

The standing-wave amplitude A_{SW} is twice the amplitude A of either of the original traveling waves:

$$A_{SW} = 2A$$

Equation (15.28) has two factors: a function of x and a function of t. The factor $A_{SW} \sin kx$ shows that at each instant the shape of the string is a sine curve. But unlike a wave traveling along a string, the wave shape stays in the same position, oscillating up and down as described by the $\sin \omega t$ factor. This behavior is shown graphically by the brown curves in Fig. 15.24. Each point in the string still undergoes simple harmonic motion, but all the points between any successive pair of nodes oscillate *in phase*. This is in contrast to the phase differences between oscillations of adjacent points that we see with a wave traveling in one direction.

We can use Eq. (15.28) to find the positions of the nodes; these are the points for which $\sin kx = 0$, so the displacement is *always* zero. This occurs when $kx = 0, \pi, 2\pi, 3\pi, \ldots$, or, using $k = 2\pi/\lambda$,

$$x = 0, \frac{\pi}{k}, \frac{2\pi}{k}, \frac{3\pi}{k}, \ldots$$
$$= 0, \frac{\lambda}{2}, \frac{2\lambda}{2}, \frac{3\lambda}{2}, \ldots \quad \begin{pmatrix} \text{nodes of a standing wave on} \\ \text{a string, fixed end at } x = 0 \end{pmatrix} \quad (15.29)$$

In particular, there is a node at $x = 0$, as there should be, since this point is a fixed end of the string.

A standing wave, unlike a traveling wave, *does not* transfer energy from one end to the other. The two waves that form it would individually carry equal amounts of power in opposite directions. There is a local flow of energy from each node to the adjacent antinodes and back, but the *average* rate of energy transfer is zero at every point. If you evaluate the wave power given by Eq. (15.21) using the wave function of Eq. (15.28), you will find that the average power is zero.

Problem-Solving Strategy 15.2   Standing Waves

IDENTIFY *the relevant concepts:* Identify the target variables. Then determine whether the problem is purely *kinematic* (involving only such quantities as wave speed v, wavelength λ, and frequency f) or whether *dynamic* properties of the medium (such as F and μ for transverse waves on a string) are also involved.

SET UP *the problem* using the following steps:
1. Sketch the shape of the standing wave at a particular instant. This will help you visualize the nodes (label them N) and antinodes (A). The distance between adjacent nodes (or antinodes) is $\lambda/2$; the distance between a node and the adjacent antinode is $\lambda/4$.
2. Choose the equations you'll use. The wave function for the standing wave, like Eq. (15.28), is often useful.

3. You can determine the wave speed if you know λ and f (or, equivalently, $k = 2\pi/\lambda$ and $\omega = 2\pi f$) or if you know the relevant properties of the medium (for a string, F and μ).

EXECUTE *the solution:* Solve for the target variables. Once you've found the wave function, you can find the displacement y at any point x and at any time t. You can find the velocity and acceleration of a particle in the medium by taking the first and second partial derivatives of y with respect to time.

EVALUATE *your answer:* Compare your numerical answers with your sketch. Check that the wave function satisfies the boundary conditions (for example, the displacement should be zero at a fixed end).

Example 15.6   Standing waves on a guitar string

A guitar string lies along the x-axis when in equilibrium. The end of the string at $x = 0$ (the bridge of the guitar) is fixed. A sinusoidal wave with amplitude $A = 0.750$ mm $= 7.50 \times 10^{-4}$ m and frequency $f = 440$ Hz, corresponding to the red curves in Fig. 15.24, travels along the string in the $-x$-direction at 143 m/s. It is reflected from the fixed end, and the superposition of the incident and reflected waves forms a standing wave. (a) Find the equation giving the displacement of a point on the string as a function of position and time. (b) Locate the nodes. (c) Find the amplitude of the standing wave and the maximum transverse velocity and acceleration.

SOLUTION

IDENTIFY and SET UP: This is a *kinematics* problem (see Problem-Solving Strategy 15.1 in Section 15.3). The target variables are: in part (a), the wave function of the standing wave; in part (b), the locations of the nodes; and in part (c), the maximum displacement y, transverse velocity v_y, and transverse acceleration a_y. Since there is a fixed end at $x = 0$, we can use Eqs. (15.28) and (15.29) to describe this standing wave. We will need the relationships $\omega = 2\pi f$, $v = \omega/k$, and $v = \lambda f$.

EXECUTE: (a) The standing-wave amplitude is $A_{SW} = 2A = 1.50 \times 10^{-3}$ m (twice the amplitude of either the incident or reflected wave). The angular frequency and wave number are

$$\omega = 2\pi f = (2\pi \text{ rad})(440 \text{ s}^{-1}) = 2760 \text{ rad/s}$$

$$k = \frac{\omega}{v} = \frac{2760 \text{ rad/s}}{143 \text{ m/s}} = 19.3 \text{ rad/m}$$

Equation (15.28) then gives

$$y(x, t) = (A_{SW} \sin kx) \sin \omega t$$
$$= [(1.50 \times 10^{-3} \text{ m}) \sin(19.3 \text{ rad/m})x] \sin(2760 \text{ rad/s})t$$

(b) From Eq. (15.29), the positions of the nodes are $x = 0$, $\lambda/2$, λ, $3\lambda/2, \ldots$. The wavelength is $\lambda = v/f = (143 \text{ m/s})/(440 \text{ Hz})$

$= 0.325$ m, so the nodes are at $x = 0$, 0.163 m, 0.325 m, 0.488 m, $\ldots$.

(c) From the expression for $y(x, t)$ in part (a), the maximum displacement from equilibrium is $A_{SW} = 1.50 \times 10^{-3}$ m $= 1.50$ mm. This occurs at the *antinodes,* which are midway between adjacent nodes (that is, at $x = 0.081$ m, 0.244 m, 0.406 m, $\ldots$).

For a particle on the string at any point x, the transverse (y-) velocity is

$$v_y(x, t) = \frac{\partial y(x, t)}{\partial t}$$
$$= [(1.50 \times 10^{-3} \text{ m}) \sin(19.3 \text{ rad/m})x]$$
$$\times [(2760 \text{ rad/s}) \cos(2760 \text{ rad/s})t]$$
$$= [(4.15 \text{ m/s}) \sin(19.3 \text{ rad/m})x] \cos(2760 \text{ rad/s})t$$

At an antinode, $\sin(19.3 \text{ rad/m})x = \pm 1$ and the transverse velocity varies between $+4.15$ m/s and -4.15 m/s. As is always the case in SHM, the maximum velocity occurs when the particle is passing through the equilibrium position ($y = 0$).

The transverse acceleration $a_y(x, t)$ is the *second* partial derivative of $y(x, t)$ with respect to time. You can show that

$$a_y(x, t) = \frac{\partial v_y(x, t)}{\partial t} = \frac{\partial^2 y(x, t)}{\partial t^2}$$
$$= [(-1.15 \times 10^4 \text{ m/s}^2) \sin(19.3 \text{ rad/m})x]$$
$$\times \sin(2760 \text{ rad/s})t$$

At the antinodes, the transverse acceleration varies between $+1.15 \times 10^4$ m/s^2 and -1.15×10^4 m/s^2.

EVALUATE: The maximum transverse velocity at an antinode is quite respectable (about 15 km/h, or 9.3 mi/h). But the maximum transverse acceleration is tremendous, 1170 times the acceleration due to gravity! Guitar strings are actually fixed at *both* ends; we'll see the consequences of this in the next section.

Test Your Understanding of Section 15.7   Suppose the frequency of the standing wave in Example 15.6 were doubled from 440 Hz to 880 Hz. Would all of the nodes for $f = 440$ Hz also be nodes for $f = 880$ Hz? If so, would there be additional nodes for $f = 880$ Hz? If not, which nodes are absent for $f = 880$ Hz?

15.8 Normal Modes of a String

When we described standing waves on a string rigidly held at one end, as in Fig. 15.23, we made no assumptions about the length of the string or about what was happening at the other end. Let's now consider a string of a definite length L, rigidly held at *both* ends. Such strings are found in many musical instruments, including pianos, violins, and guitars. When a guitar string is plucked, a wave is produced in the string; this wave is reflected and re-reflected from the ends of the string, making a standing wave. This standing wave on the string in turn produces a sound wave in the air, with a frequency determined by the properties of the string. This is what makes stringed instruments so useful in making music.

To understand these properties of standing waves on a string fixed at both ends, let's first examine what happens when we set up a sinusoidal wave on such a string. The standing wave that results must have a node at *both* ends of the string. We saw in the preceding section that adjacent nodes are one half-wavelength

PhET: Fourier: Making Waves
PhET: Waves on a String
ActivPhysics 10.4: Standing Waves on Strings
ActivPhysics 10.5: Tuning a Stringed Instrument: Standing Waves
ActivPhysics 10.6: String Mass and Standing Waves

$(\lambda/2)$ apart, so the length of the string must be $\lambda/2$, or $2(\lambda/2)$, or $3(\lambda/2)$, or in general some integer number of half-wavelengths:

$$L = n\frac{\lambda}{2} \quad (n = 1, 2, 3, \ldots) \qquad \text{(string fixed at both ends)} \quad (15.30)$$

That is, if a string with length L is fixed at both ends, a standing wave can exist only if its wavelength satisfies Eq. (15.30).

Solving this equation for λ and labeling the possible values of λ as λ_n, we find

$$\lambda_n = \frac{2L}{n} \quad (n = 1, 2, 3, \ldots) \qquad \text{(string fixed at both ends)} \quad (15.31)$$

Waves can exist on the string if the wavelength is *not* equal to one of these values, but there cannot be a steady wave pattern with nodes and antinodes, and the total wave cannot be a standing wave. Equation (15.31) is illustrated by the standing waves shown in Figs. 15.23a, 15.23b, 15.23c, and 15.23d; these represent $n = 1, 2, 3$, and 4, respectively.

Corresponding to the series of possible standing-wave wavelengths λ_n is a series of possible standing-wave frequencies f_n, each related to its corresponding wavelength by $f_n = v/\lambda_n$. The smallest frequency f_1 corresponds to the largest wavelength (the $n = 1$ case), $\lambda_1 = 2L$:

$$f_1 = \frac{v}{2L} \qquad \text{(string fixed at both ends)} \qquad (15.32)$$

This is called the **fundamental frequency.** The other standing-wave frequencies are $f_2 = 2v/2L$, $f_3 = 3v/2L$, and so on. These are all integer multiples of the fundamental frequency f_1, such as $2f_1$, $3f_1$, $4f_1$, and so on, and we can express *all* the frequencies as

$$f_n = n\frac{v}{2L} = nf_1 \quad (n = 1, 2, 3, \ldots) \qquad \text{(string fixed at both ends)} \quad (15.33)$$

These frequencies are called **harmonics,** and the series is called a **harmonic series.** Musicians sometimes call f_2, f_3, and so on **overtones;** f_2 is the second harmonic or the first overtone, f_3 is the third harmonic or the second overtone, and so on. The first harmonic is the same as the fundamental frequency (Fig. 15.25).

For a string with fixed ends at $x = 0$ and $x = L$, the wave function $y(x, t)$ of the nth standing wave is given by Eq. (15.28) (which satisfies the condition that there is a node at $x = 0$), with $\omega = \omega_n = 2\pi f_n$ and $k = k_n = 2\pi/\lambda_n$:

$$y_n(x, t) = A_{\text{SW}} \sin k_n x \sin \omega_n t \qquad (15.34)$$

You can easily show that this wave function has nodes at both $x = 0$ and $x = L$, as it must.

A **normal mode** of an oscillating system is a motion in which all particles of the system move sinusoidally with the same frequency. For a system made up of a string of length L fixed at both ends, each of the wavelengths given by Eq. (15.31) corresponds to a possible normal-mode pattern and frequency. There are infinitely many normal modes, each with its characteristic frequency and vibration pattern. Figure 15.26 shows the first four normal-mode patterns and their associated frequencies and wavelengths; these correspond to Eq. (15.34) with $n = 1, 2, 3$, and 4. By contrast, a harmonic oscillator, which has only one oscillating particle, has only one normal mode and one characteristic frequency. The string fixed at both ends has infinitely many normal modes because it is made up of a very large (effectively infinite) number of particles. More complicated oscillating systems also have infinite numbers of normal modes, though with more complex normal-mode patterns than a string (Fig. 15.27).

15.25 Each string of a violin naturally oscillates at one or more of its harmonic frequencies, producing sound waves in the air with the same frequencies.

15.26 The first four normal modes of a string fixed at both ends. (Compare these to the photographs in Fig. 15.23.)

(a) $n = 1$: fundamental frequency, f_1

N ——— A ——— N
$\frac{\lambda}{2} = L$

(b) $n = 2$: second harmonic, f_2 (first overtone)

N — A — N — A — N
$2\frac{\lambda}{2} = L$

(c) $n = 3$: third harmonic, f_3 (second overtone)

N — A — N — A — N — A — N
$3\frac{\lambda}{2} = L$

(d) $n = 4$: fourth harmonic, f_4 (third overtone)

N — A — N — A — N — A — N — A — N
$4\frac{\lambda}{2} = L$

Complex Standing Waves

If we could displace a string so that its shape is the same as one of the normal-mode patterns and then release it, it would vibrate with the frequency of that mode. Such a vibrating string would displace the surrounding air with the same frequency, producing a traveling sinusoidal sound wave that your ears would perceive as a pure tone. But when a string is struck (as in a piano) or plucked (as is done to guitar strings), the shape of the displaced string is *not* as simple as one of the patterns in Fig. 15.26. The fundamental as well as many overtones are present in the resulting vibration. This motion is therefore a combination or *superposition* of many normal modes. Several simple harmonic motions of different frequencies are present simultaneously, and the displacement of any point on the string is the sum (or superposition) of the displacements associated with the individual modes. The sound produced by the vibrating string is likewise a superposition of traveling sinusoidal sound waves, which you perceive as a rich, complex tone with the fundamental frequency f_1. The standing wave on the string and the traveling sound wave in the air have similar **harmonic content** (the extent to which frequencies higher than the fundamental are present). The harmonic content depends on how the string is initially set into motion. If you pluck the strings of an acoustic guitar in the normal location over the sound hole, the sound that you hear has a different harmonic content than if you pluck the strings next to the fixed end on the guitar body.

It is possible to represent every possible motion of the string as some superposition of normal-mode motions. Finding this representation for a given vibration pattern is called *harmonic analysis.* The sum of sinusoidal functions that represents a complex wave is called a *Fourier series.* Figure 15.28 shows how a standing wave that is produced by plucking a guitar string of length L at a point $L/4$ from one end can be represented as a combination of sinusoidal functions.

Standing Waves and String Instruments

As we have seen, the fundamental frequency of a vibrating string is $f_1 = v/2L$. The speed v of waves on the string is determined by Eq. (15.13), $v = \sqrt{F/\mu}$. Combining these equations, we find

$$f_1 = \frac{1}{2L}\sqrt{\frac{F}{\mu}} \qquad \text{(string fixed at both ends)} \qquad (15.35)$$

This is also the fundamental frequency of the sound wave created in the surrounding air by the vibrating string. Familiar musical instruments show how f_1 depends on the properties of the string. The inverse dependence of frequency on length L is illustrated by the long strings of the bass (low-frequency) section of the piano or the bass viol compared with the shorter strings of the treble section of the piano or the violin (Fig. 15.29). The pitch of a violin or guitar is usually

15.27 Astronomers have discovered that the sun oscillates in several different normal modes. This computer simulation shows one such mode.

Cross section of the sun's interior

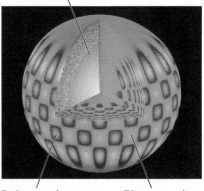

Red zones: where material is moving outward

Blue zones: where material is moving inward

ActivPhysics 10.10: Complex Waves: Fourier Analysis

15.28 When a guitar string is plucked (pulled into a triangular shape) and released, a standing wave results. The standing wave is well represented (except at the sharp maximum point) by the sum of just three sinusoidal functions. Including additional sinusoidal functions further improves the representation.

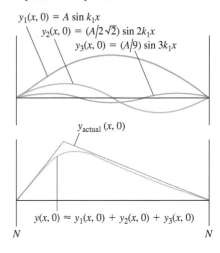

$y_1(x, 0) = A \sin k_1 x$

$y_2(x, 0) = (A/2\sqrt{2}) \sin 2k_1 x$

$y_3(x, 0) = (A/9) \sin 3k_1 x$

$y_{\text{actual}}(x, 0)$

$y(x, 0) \approx y_1(x, 0) + y_2(x, 0) + y_3(x, 0)$

15.29 Comparing the range of a concert grand piano to the ranges of a bass viol, a cello, a viola, and a violin. In all cases, longer strings produce bass notes and shorter strings produce treble notes.

varied by pressing a string against the fingerboard with the fingers to change the length L of the vibrating portion of the string. Increasing the tension F increases the wave speed v and thus increases the frequency (and the pitch). All string instruments are "tuned" to the correct frequencies by varying the tension; you tighten the string to raise the pitch. Finally, increasing the mass per unit length μ decreases the wave speed and thus the frequency. The lower notes on a steel guitar are produced by thicker strings, and one reason for winding the bass strings of a piano with wire is to obtain the desired low frequency from a relatively short string.

Wind instruments such as saxophones and trombones also have normal modes. As for stringed instruments, the frequencies of these normal modes determine the pitch of the musical tones that these instruments produce. We'll discuss these instruments and many other aspects of sound in Chapter 16.

Example 15.7   **A giant bass viol**

In an attempt to get your name in *Guinness World Records,* you build a bass viol with strings of length 5.00 m between fixed points. One string, with linear mass density 40.0 g/m, is tuned to a 20.0-Hz fundamental frequency (the lowest frequency that the human ear can hear). Calculate (a) the tension of this string, (b) the frequency and wavelength on the string of the second harmonic, and (c) the frequency and wavelength on the string of the second overtone.

SOLUTION

IDENTIFY and SET UP: In part (a) the target variable is the string tension F; we'll use Eq. (15.35), which relates F to the known values $f_1 = 20.0$ Hz, $L = 5.00$ m, and $\mu = 40.0$ g/m. In parts (b) and (c) the target variables are the frequency and wavelength of a given harmonic and a given overtone. We determine these from the given length of the string and the fundamental frequency, using Eqs. (15.31) and (15.33).

EXECUTE: (a) We solve Eq. (15.35) for F:

$$F = 4\mu L^2 f_1^2 = 4(40.0 \times 10^{-3}\ \text{kg/m})(5.00\ \text{m})^2(20.0\ \text{s}^{-1})^2$$
$$= 1600\ \text{N} = 360\ \text{lb}$$

(b) From Eqs. (15.33) and (15.31), the frequency and wavelength of the second harmonic $(n = 2)$ are

$$f_2 = 2f_1 = 2(20.0\ \text{Hz}) = 40.0\ \text{Hz}$$
$$\lambda_2 = \frac{2L}{2} = \frac{2(5.00\ \text{m})}{2} = 5.00\ \text{m}$$

(c) The second overtone is the "second tone over" (above) the fundamental—that is, $n = 3$. Its frequency and wavelength are

$$f_3 = 3f_1 = 3(20.0\ \text{Hz}) = 60.0\ \text{Hz}$$
$$\lambda_3 = \frac{2L}{3} = \frac{2(5.00\ \text{m})}{3} = 3.33\ \text{m}$$

EVALUATE: The string tension in a real bass viol is typically a few hundred newtons; the tension in part (a) is a bit higher than that. The wavelengths in parts (b) and (c) are equal to the length of the string and two-thirds the length of the string, respectively, which agrees with the drawings of standing waves in Fig. 15.26.

Example 15.8   **From waves on a string to sound waves in air**

What are the frequency and wavelength of the sound waves produced in the air when the string in Example 15.7 is vibrating at its fundamental frequency? The speed of sound in air at 20°C is 344 m/s.

SOLUTION

IDENTIFY and SET UP: Our target variables are the frequency and wavelength for the *sound wave* produced by the bass viol string. The frequency of the sound wave is the same as the fundamental frequency f_1 of the standing wave, because the string forces the surrounding air to vibrate at the same frequency. The wavelength of the sound wave is $\lambda_{1(\text{sound})} = v_{\text{sound}}/f_1$.

EXECUTE: We have $f = f_1 = 20.0$ Hz, so

$$\lambda_{1(\text{sound})} = \frac{v_{\text{sound}}}{f_1} = \frac{344\ \text{m/s}}{20.0\ \text{Hz}} = 17.2\ \text{m}$$

EVALUATE: In Example 15.7, the wavelength of the fundamental on the string was $\lambda_{1(\text{string})} = 2L = 2(5.00\ \text{m}) = 10.0$ m. Here $\lambda_{1(\text{sound})} = 17.2$ m is greater than that by the factor of $17.2/10.0 = 1.72$. This is as it should be: Because the frequencies of the sound wave and the standing wave are equal, $\lambda = v/f$ says that the wavelengths in air and on the string are in the same ratio as the corresponding wave speeds; here $v_{\text{sound}} = 344$ m/s is greater than $v_{\text{string}} = (10.0\ \text{m})(20.0\ \text{Hz}) = 200$ m/s by just the factor 1.72.

Test Your Understanding of Section 15.8   While a guitar string is vibrating, you gently touch the midpoint of the string to ensure that the string does not vibrate at that point. Which normal modes *cannot* be present on the string while you are touching it in this way?

Waves and their properties: A wave is any disturbance that propagates from one region to another. A mechanical wave travels within some material called the medium. The wave speed v depends on the type of wave and the properties of the medium.

In a periodic wave, the motion of each point of the medium is periodic with frequency f and period T. The wavelength λ is the distance over which the wave pattern repeats, and the amplitude A is the maximum displacement of a particle in the medium. The product of λ and f equals the wave speed. A sinusoidal wave is a special periodic wave in which each point moves in simple harmonic motion. (See Example 15.1.)

$$v = \lambda f \qquad (15.1)$$

Wave functions and wave dynamics: The wave function $y(x, t)$ describes the displacements of individual particles in the medium. Equations (15.3), (15.4), and (15.7) give the wave equation for a sinusoidal wave traveling in the $+x$-direction. If the wave is moving in the $-x$-direction, the minus signs in the cosine functions are replaced by plus signs. (See Example 15.2.)

The wave function obeys a partial differential equation called the wave equation, Eq. (15.12).

The speed of transverse waves on a string depends on the tension F and mass per unit length μ. (See Example 15.3.)

$$y(x, t) = A \cos\left[\omega\left(\frac{x}{v} - t\right)\right]$$
$$= A \cos 2\pi f\left(\frac{x}{v} - t\right) \qquad (15.3)$$
$$y(x, t) = A \cos 2\pi\left(\frac{x}{\lambda} - \frac{t}{T}\right) \qquad (15.4)$$
$$y(x, t) = A \cos(kx - \omega t) \qquad (15.7)$$
where $k = 2\pi/\lambda$ and $\omega = 2\pi f = vk$
$$\frac{\partial^2 y(x, t)}{\partial x^2} = \frac{1}{v^2}\frac{\partial^2 y(x, t)}{\partial t^2} \qquad (15.12)$$
$$v = \sqrt{\frac{F}{\mu}} \quad \text{(waves on a string)} \qquad (15.13)$$

Wave power: Wave motion conveys energy from one region to another. For a sinusoidal mechanical wave, the average power P_{av} is proportional to the square of the wave amplitude and the square of the frequency. For waves that spread out in three dimensions, the wave intensity I is inversely proportional to the square of the distance from the source. (See Examples 15.4 and 15.5.)

$$P_{av} = \tfrac{1}{2}\sqrt{\mu F}\,\omega^2 A^2 \qquad (15.25)$$
(average power, sinusoidal wave)
$$\frac{I_1}{I_2} = \frac{r_2^2}{r_1^2} \qquad (15.26)$$
(inverse-square law for intensity)

Wave superposition: A wave reflects when it reaches a boundary of its medium. At any point where two or more waves overlap, the total displacement is the sum of the displacements of the individual waves (principle of superposition).

$$y(x, t) = y_1(x, t) + y_2(x, t) \qquad (15.27)$$
(principle of superposition)

Standing waves on a string: When a sinusoidal wave is reflected from a fixed or free end of a stretched string, the incident and reflected waves combine to form a standing sinusoidal wave with nodes and antinodes. Adjacent nodes are spaced a distance $\lambda/2$ apart, as are adjacent antinodes. (See Example 15.6.)

When both ends of a string with length L are held fixed, standing waves can occur only when L is an integer multiple of $\lambda/2$. Each frequency with its associated vibration pattern is called a normal mode. (See Examples 15.7 and 15.8.)

$$y(x, t) = (A_{SW}\sin kx)\sin \omega t \qquad (15.28)$$
(standing wave on a string, fixed end at $x = 0$)
$$f_n = n\frac{v}{2L} = nf_1 \quad (n = 1, 2, 3, \dots) \qquad (15.33)$$
$$f_1 = \frac{1}{2L}\sqrt{\frac{F}{\mu}} \qquad (15.35)$$
(string fixed at both ends)

BRIDGING PROBLEM | **Waves on a Rotating Rope**

A uniform rope with length L and mass m is held at one end and whirled in a horizontal circle with angular velocity ω. You can ignore the force of gravity on the rope. (a) At a point on the rope a distance r from the end that is held, what is the tension F? (b) What is the speed of transverse waves at this point? (c) Find the time required for a transverse wave to travel from one end of the rope to the other.

SOLUTION GUIDE

See MasteringPhysics® Study Area for a Video Tutor solution.

IDENTIFY and SET UP

1. Draw a sketch of the situation and label the distances r and L. The tension in the rope will be different at different values of r. Do you see why? Where on the rope do you expect the tension to be greatest? Where do you expect it will be least?
2. Where on the rope do you expect the wave speed to be greatest? Where do you expect it will be least?
3. Think about the portion of the rope that is farther out than r from the end that is held. What forces act on this portion? (Remember that you can ignore gravity.) What is the mass of this portion? How far is its center of mass from the rotation axis?

4. Make a list of the unknown quantities and decide which are your target variables.

EXECUTE

5. Draw a free-body diagram for the portion of the rope that is farther out than r from the end that is held.
6. Use your free-body diagram to help you determine the tension in the rope at distance r.
7. Use your result from step 6 to find the wave speed at distance r.
8. Use your result from step 7 to find the time for a wave to travel from one end to the other. (*Hint:* The wave speed is $v = dr/dt$, so the time for the wave to travel a distance dr along the rope is $dt = dr/v$. Integrate this to find the total time. See Appendix B.)

EVALUATE

9. Do your results for parts (a) and (b) agree with your expectations from steps 1 and 2? Are the units correct?
10. Check your result for part (a) by considering the net force on a small segment of the rope at distance r with length dr and mass $dm = (m/L)dr$. [*Hint:* The tension forces on this segment are $F(r)$ on one side and $F(r + dr)$ on the other side. You will get an equation for dF/dr that you can integrate to find F as a function of r.]

Problems

For instructor-assigned homework, go to MasteringPhysics®.

•, ••, •••: Problems of increasing difficulty. **CP**: Cumulative problems incorporating material from earlier chapters. **CALC**: Problems requiring calculus. **BIO**: Biosciences problems.

DISCUSSION QUESTIONS

Q15.1 Two waves travel on the same string. Is it possible for them to have (a) different frequencies; (b) different wavelengths; (c) different speeds; (d) different amplitudes; (e) the same frequency but different wavelengths? Explain your reasoning.

Q15.2 Under a tension F, it takes 2.00 s for a pulse to travel the length of a taut wire. What tension is required (in terms of F) for the pulse to take 6.00 s instead?

Q15.3 What kinds of energy are associated with waves on a stretched string? How could you detect such energy experimentally?

Q15.4 The amplitude of a wave decreases gradually as the wave travels down a long, stretched string. What happens to the energy of the wave when this happens?

Q15.5 For the wave motions discussed in this chapter, does the speed of propagation depend on the amplitude? What makes you say this?

Q15.6 The speed of ocean waves depends on the depth of the water; the deeper the water, the faster the wave travels. Use this to explain why ocean waves crest and "break" as they near the shore.

Q15.7 Is it possible to have a longitudinal wave on a stretched string? Why or why not? Is it possible to have a transverse wave on a steel rod? Again, why or why not? If your answer is yes in either case, explain how you would create such a wave.

Q15.8 An echo is sound reflected from a distant object, such as a wall or a cliff. Explain how you can determine how far away the object is by timing the echo.

Q15.9 Why do you see lightning before you hear the thunder? A familiar rule of thumb is to start counting slowly, once per second, when you see the lightning; when you hear the thunder, divide the number you have reached by 3 to obtain your distance from the lightning in kilometers (or divide by 5 to obtain your distance in miles). Why does this work, or does it?

Q15.10 For transverse waves on a string, is the wave speed the same as the speed of any part of the string? Explain the difference between these two speeds. Which one is constant?

Q15.11 Children make toy telephones by sticking each end of a long string through a hole in the bottom of a paper cup and knotting it so it will not pull out. When the spring is pulled taut, sound can be transmitted from one cup to the other. How does this work? Why is the transmitted sound louder than the sound traveling through air for the same distance?

Q15.12 The four strings on a violin have different thicknesses, but are all under approximately the same tension. Do waves travel faster on the thick strings or the thin strings? Why? How does the fundamental vibration frequency compare for the thick versus the thin strings?

Q15.13 A sinusoidal wave can be described by a cosine function, which is negative just as often as positive. So why isn't the average power delivered by this wave zero?

Q15.14 Two strings of different mass per unit length μ_1 and μ_2 are tied together and stretched with a tension F. A wave travels along the string and passes the discontinuity in μ. Which of the following wave properties will be the same on both sides of the discontinuity, and which ones will change? speed of the wave; frequency; wavelength. Explain the physical reasoning behind each of your answers.

Q15.15 A long rope with mass m is suspended from the ceiling and hangs vertically. A wave pulse is produced at the lower end of the rope, and the pulse travels up the rope. Does the speed of the wave pulse change as it moves up the rope, and if so, does it increase or decrease?

Q15.16 In a transverse wave on a string, the motion of the string is perpendicular to the length of the string. How, then, is it possible for energy to move along the length of the string?

Q15.17 Both wave intensity and gravitation obey inverse-square laws. Do they do so for the same reason? Discuss the reason for each of these inverse-square laws as well as you can.

Q15.18 Energy can be transferred along a string by wave motion. However, in a standing wave on a string, no energy can ever be transferred past a node. Why not?

Q15.19 Can a standing wave be produced on a string by superposing two waves traveling in opposite directions with the same frequency but different amplitudes? Why or why not? Can a standing wave be produced by superposing two waves traveling in opposite directions with different frequencies but the same amplitude? Why or why not?

Q15.20 If you stretch a rubber band and pluck it, you hear a (somewhat) musical tone. How does the frequency of this tone change as you stretch the rubber band further? (Try it!) Does this agree with Eq. (15.35) for a string fixed at both ends? Explain.

Q15.21 A musical interval of an *octave* corresponds to a factor of 2 in frequency. By what factor must the tension in a guitar or violin string be increased to raise its pitch one octave? To raise it two octaves? Explain your reasoning. Is there any danger in attempting these changes in pitch?

Q15.22 By touching a string lightly at its center while bowing, a violinist can produce a note exactly one octave above the note to which the string is tuned—that is, a note with exactly twice the frequency. Why is this possible?

Q15.23 As we discussed in Section 15.1, water waves are a combination of longitudinal and transverse waves. Defend the following statement: "When water waves hit a vertical wall, the wall is a node of the longitudinal displacement but an antinode of the transverse displacement."

Q15.24 Violins are short instruments, while cellos and basses are long. In terms of the frequency of the waves they produce, explain why this is so.

Q15.25 What is the purpose of the frets on a guitar? In terms of frequency of the vibration of the strings, explain their use.

EXERCISES

Section 15.2 Periodic Waves

15.1 • The speed of sound in air at 20°C is 344 m/s. (a) What is the wavelength of a sound wave with a frequency of 784 Hz, corresponding to the note G_5 on a piano, and how many milliseconds does each vibration take? (b) What is the wavelength of a sound wave one octave higher than the note in part (a)?

15.2 • **BIO Audible Sound.** Provided the amplitude is sufficiently great, the human ear can respond to longitudinal waves over a range of frequencies from about 20.0 Hz to about 20.0 kHz. (a) If you were to mark the beginning of each complete wave pattern with a red dot for the long-wavelength sound and a blue dot for the short-wavelength sound, how far apart would the red dots be, and how far apart would the blue dots be? (b) In reality would adjacent dots in each set be far enough apart for you to easily measure their separation with a meter stick? (c) Suppose you repeated part (a) in water, where sound travels at 1480 m/s. How far apart would the dots be in each set? Could you readily measure their separation with a meter stick?

15.3 • **Tsunami!** On December 26, 2004, a great earthquake occurred off the coast of Sumatra and triggered immense waves (tsunami) that killed some 200,000 people. Satellites observing these waves from space measured 800 km from one wave crest to the next and a period between waves of 1.0 hour. What was the speed of these waves in m/s and in km/h? Does your answer help you understand why the waves caused such devastation?

15.4 • **BIO Ultrasound Imaging.** Sound having frequencies above the range of human hearing (about 20,000 Hz) is called *ultrasound*. Waves above this frequency can be used to penetrate the body and to produce images by reflecting from surfaces. In a typical ultrasound scan, the waves travel through body tissue with a speed of 1500 m/s. For a good, detailed image, the wavelength should be no more than 1.0 mm. What frequency sound is required for a good scan?

15.5 • **BIO** (a) **Audible wavelengths.** The range of audible frequencies is from about 20 Hz to 20,000 Hz. What is the range of the wavelengths of audible sound in air? (b) **Visible light.** The range of visible light extends from 400 nm to 700 nm. What is the range of visible frequencies of light? (c) **Brain surgery.** Surgeons can remove brain tumors by using a cavitron ultrasonic surgical aspirator, which produces sound waves of frequency 23 kHz. What is the wavelength of these waves in air? (d) **Sound in the body.** What would be the wavelength of the sound in part (c) in bodily fluids in which the speed of sound is 1480 m/s but the frequency is unchanged?

15.6 •• A fisherman notices that his boat is moving up and down periodically, owing to waves on the surface of the water. It takes 2.5 s for the boat to travel from its highest point to its lowest, a total distance of 0.62 m. The fisherman sees that the wave crests are spaced 6.0 m apart. (a) How fast are the waves traveling? (b) What is the amplitude of each wave? (c) If the total vertical distance traveled by the boat were 0.30 m but the other data remained the same, how would the answers to parts (a) and (b) be affected?

Section 15.3 Mathematical Description of a Wave

15.7 • Transverse waves on a string have wave speed 8.00 m/s, amplitude 0.0700 m, and wavelength 0.320 m. The waves travel in the $-x$-direction, and at $t = 0$ the $x = 0$ end of the string has its maximum upward displacement. (a) Find the frequency, period, and wave number of these waves. (b) Write a wave function describing the wave. (c) Find the transverse displacement of a particle at $x = 0.360$ m at time $t = 0.150$ s. (d) How much time must elapse from the instant in part (c) until the particle at $x = 0.360$ m next has maximum upward displacement?

15.8 • A certain transverse wave is described by

$$y(x, t) = (6.50 \text{ mm}) \cos 2\pi \left(\frac{x}{28.0 \text{ cm}} - \frac{t}{0.0360 \text{ s}} \right)$$

Determine the wave's (a) amplitude; (b) wavelength; (c) frequency; (d) speed of propagation; (e) direction of propagation.

15.9 • **CALC** Which of the following wave functions satisfies the wave equation, Eq. (15.12)? (a) $y(x, t) = A \cos(kx + \omega t)$; (b) $y(x, t) = A \sin(kx + \omega t)$; (c) $y(x, t) = A(\cos kx + \cos \omega t)$. (d) For the wave of part (b), write the equations for the transverse velocity and transverse acceleration of a particle at point x.

15.10 • A water wave traveling in a straight line on a lake is described by the equation

$$y(x, t) = (3.75 \text{ cm}) \cos(0.450 \text{ cm}^{-1} x + 5.40 \text{ s}^{-1} t)$$

where y is the displacement perpendicular to the undisturbed surface of the lake. (a) How much time does it take for one complete wave pattern to go past a fisherman in a boat at anchor, and what horizontal distance does the wave crest travel in that time? (b) What are the wave number and the number of waves per second that pass the fisherman? (c) How fast does a wave crest travel past the fisherman, and what is the maximum speed of his cork floater as the wave causes it to bob up and down?

15.11 • A sinusoidal wave is propagating along a stretched string that lies along the x-axis. The displacement of the string as a function of time is graphed in Fig. E15.11 for particles at $x = 0$ and at $x = 0.0900$ m. (a) What is the amplitude of the wave? (b) What is the period of the wave? (c) You are told that the two points $x = 0$ and $x = 0.0900$ m are within one wavelength of each other. If the wave is moving in the $+x$-direction, determine the wavelength and the wave speed. (d) If instead the wave is moving in the $-x$-direction, determine the wavelength and the wave speed. (e) Would it be possible to determine definitively the wavelength in parts (c) and (d) if you were not told that the two points were within one wavelength of each other? Why or why not?

Figure **E15.11**

15.12 •• **CALC** **Speed of Propagation vs. Particle Speed.** (a) Show that Eq. (15.3) may be written as

$$y(x, t) = A \cos\left[\frac{2\pi}{\lambda}(x - vt)\right]$$

(b) Use $y(x, t)$ to find an expression for the transverse velocity v_y of a particle in the string on which the wave travels. (c) Find the maximum speed of a particle of the string. Under what circumstances is this equal to the propagation speed v? Less than v? Greater than v?

15.13 •• A transverse wave on a string has amplitude 0.300 cm, wavelength 12.0 cm, and speed 6.00 cm/s. It is represented by $y(x, t)$ as given in Exercise 15.12. (a) At time $t = 0$, compute y at 1.5-cm intervals of x (that is, at $x = 0$, $x = 1.5$ cm, $x = 3.0$ cm, and so on) from $x = 0$ to $x = 12.0$ cm. Graph the results. This is the shape of the string at time $t = 0$. (b) Repeat the calculations for the same values of x at times $t = 0.400$ s and $t = 0.800$ s. Graph the shape of the string at these instants. In what direction is the wave traveling?

15.14 • A wave on a string is described by $y(x, t) = A \cos(kx - \omega t)$. (a) Graph y, v_y, and a_y as functions of x for time $t = 0$. (b) Consider the following points on the string: (i) $x = 0$; (ii) $x = \pi/4k$; (iii) $x = \pi/2k$; (iv) $x = 3\pi/4k$; (v) $x = \pi/k$; (vi) $x = 5\pi/4k$; (vii) $x = 3\pi/2k$; (viii) $x = 7\pi/4k$. For a particle at each of these points at $t = 0$, describe in words whether the particle is moving and in what direction, and whether the particle is speeding up, slowing down, or instantaneously not accelerating.

Section 15.4 Speed of a Transverse Wave

15.15 • One end of a horizontal rope is attached to a prong of an electrically driven tuning fork that vibrates the rope transversely at 120 Hz. The other end passes over a pulley and supports a 1.50-kg mass. The linear mass density of the rope is 0.0550 kg/m.

(a) What is the speed of a transverse wave on the rope? (b) What is the wavelength? (c) How would your answers to parts (a) and (b) change if the mass were increased to 3.00 kg?

15.16 • With what tension must a rope with length 2.50 m and mass 0.120 kg be stretched for transverse waves of frequency 40.0 Hz to have a wavelength of 0.750 m?

15.17 •• The upper end of a 3.80-m-long steel wire is fastened to the ceiling, and a 54.0-kg object is suspended from the lower end of the wire. You observe that it takes a transverse pulse 0.0492 s to travel from the bottom to the top of the wire. What is the mass of the wire?

15.18 •• A 1.50-m string of weight 0.0125 N is tied to the ceiling at its upper end, and the lower end supports a weight W. Neglect the very small variation in tension along the length of the string that is produced by the weight of the string. When you pluck the string slightly, the waves traveling up the string obey the equation

$$y(x, t) = (8.50 \text{ mm}) \cos(172 \text{ m}^{-1} x - 4830 \text{ s}^{-1} t)$$

Assume that the tension of the string is constant and equal to W. (a) How much time does it take a pulse to travel the full length of the string? (b) What is the weight W? (c) How many wavelengths are on the string at any instant of time? (d) What is the equation for waves traveling *down* the string?

15.19 • A thin, 75.0-cm wire has a mass of 16.5 g. One end is tied to a nail, and the other end is attached to a screw that can be adjusted to vary the tension in the wire. (a) To what tension (in newtons) must you adjust the screw so that a transverse wave of wavelength 3.33 cm makes 875 vibrations per second? (b) How fast would this wave travel?

15.20 • **Weighty Rope.** If in Example 15.3 (Section 15.4) we do *not* neglect the weight of the rope, what is the wave speed (a) at the bottom of the rope; (b) at the middle of the rope; (c) at the top of the rope?

15.21 • A simple harmonic oscillator at the point $x = 0$ generates a wave on a rope. The oscillator operates at a frequency of 40.0 Hz and with an amplitude of 3.00 cm. The rope has a linear mass density of 50.0 g/m and is stretched with a tension of 5.00 N. (a) Determine the speed of the wave. (b) Find the wavelength. (c) Write the wave function $y(x, t)$ for the wave. Assume that the oscillator has its maximum upward displacement at time $t = 0$. (d) Find the maximum transverse acceleration of points on the rope. (e) In the discussion of transverse waves in this chapter, the force of gravity was ignored. Is that a reasonable approximation for this wave? Explain.

Section 15.5 Energy in Wave Motion

15.22 •• A piano wire with mass 3.00 g and length 80.0 cm is stretched with a tension of 25.0 N. A wave with frequency 120.0 Hz and amplitude 1.6 mm travels along the wire. (a) Calculate the average power carried by the wave. (b) What happens to the average power if the wave amplitude is halved?

15.23 • A horizontal wire is stretched with a tension of 94.0 N, and the speed of transverse waves for the wire is 492 m/s. What must the amplitude of a traveling wave of frequency 69.0 Hz be in order for the average power carried by the wave to be 0.365 W?

15.24 •• A light wire is tightly stretched with tension F. Transverse traveling waves of amplitude A and wavelength λ_1 carry average power $P_{av,1} = 0.400$ W. If the wavelength of the waves is doubled, so $\lambda_2 = 2\lambda_1$, while the tension F and amplitude A are not altered, what then is the average power $P_{av,2}$ carried by the waves?

15.25 •• A jet plane at takeoff can produce sound of intensity 10.0 W/m^2 at 30.0 m away. But you prefer the tranquil sound of normal conversation, which is $1.0 \; \mu\text{W/m}^2$. Assume that the plane behaves like a point source of sound. (a) What is the closest distance you should live from the airport runway to preserve your peace of mind? (b) What intensity from the jet does your friend experience if she lives twice as far from the runway as you do? (c) What power of sound does the jet produce at takeoff?

15.26 •• **Threshold of Pain.** You are investigating the report of a UFO landing in an isolated portion of New Mexico, and you encounter a strange object that is radiating sound waves uniformly in all directions. Assume that the sound comes from a point source and that you can ignore reflections. You are slowly walking toward the source. When you are 7.5 m from it, you measure its intensity to be $0.11 \; \text{W/m}^2$. An intensity of $1.0 \; \text{W/m}^2$ is often used as the "threshold of pain." How much closer to the source can you move before the sound intensity reaches this threshold?

15.27 • **Energy Output.** By measurement you determine that sound waves are spreading out equally in all directions from a point source and that the intensity is $0.026 \; \text{W/m}^2$ at a distance of 4.3 m from the source. (a) What is the intensity at a distance of 3.1 m from the source? (b) How much sound energy does the source emit in one hour if its power output remains constant?

15.28 • A fellow student with a mathematical bent tells you that the wave function of a traveling wave on a thin rope is $y(x, t) = 2.30 \; \text{mm} \cos[(6.98 \; \text{rad/m})x + (742 \; \text{rad/s})t]$. Being more practical, you measure the rope to have a length of 1.35 m and a mass of 0.00338 kg. You are then asked to determine the following: (a) amplitude; (b) frequency; (c) wavelength; (d) wave speed; (e) direction the wave is traveling; (f) tension in the rope; (g) average power transmitted by the wave.

15.29 • At a distance of 7.00×10^{12} m from a star, the intensity of the radiation from the star is $15.4 \; \text{W/m}^2$. Assuming that the star radiates uniformly in all directions, what is the total power output of the star?

Section 15.6 Wave Interference, Boundary Conditions, and Superposition

15.30 • **Reflection.** A wave pulse on a string has the dimensions shown in Fig. E15.30 at $t = 0$. The wave speed is 40 cm/s. (a) If point O is a fixed end, draw the total wave on the string at $t = 15$ ms, 20 ms, 25 ms, 30 ms, 35 ms, 40 ms, and 45 ms. (b) Repeat part (a) for the case in which point O is a free end.

Figure **E15.30**

Figure **E15.31**

15.31 • **Reflection.** A wave pulse on a string has the dimensions shown in Fig. E15.31 at $t = 0$. The wave speed is 5.0 m/s. (a) If point O is a fixed end, draw the total wave on the string at $t = 1.0$ ms, 2.0 ms, 3.0 ms, 4.0 ms, 5.0 ms, 6.0 ms, and 7.0 ms. (b) Repeat part (a) for the case in which point O is a free end.

15.32 • **Interference of Triangular Pulses.** Two triangular wave pulses are traveling toward each other on a stretched string as shown in Fig. E15.32. Each pulse is identical to the other and travels at 2.00 cm/s. The leading edges of the pulses are 1.00 cm apart at $t = 0$. Sketch the shape of the string at $t = 0.250$ s, $t = 0.500$ s, $t = 0.750$ s, $t = 1.000$ s, and $t = 1.250$ s.

Figure **E15.32**

15.33 • Suppose that the left-traveling pulse in Exercise 15.32 is *below* the level of the unstretched string instead of above it. Make the same sketches that you did in that exercise.

15.34 •• Two pulses are moving in opposite directions at 1.0 cm/s on a taut string, as shown in Fig. E15.34. Each square is 1.0 cm. Sketch the shape of the string at the end of (a) 6.0 s; (b) 7.0 s; (c) 8.0 s.

Figure **E15.34**

15.35 •• **Interference of Rectangular Pulses.** Figure E15.35 shows two rectangular wave pulses on a stretched string traveling toward each other. Each pulse is traveling with a speed of 1.00 mm/s and has the height and width shown in the figure. If the leading edges of the pulses are 8.00 mm apart at $t = 0$, sketch the shape of the string at $t = 4.00$ s, $t = 6.00$ s, and $t = 10.0$ s.

Figure **E15.35**

Section 15.7 Standing Waves on a String
Section 15.8 Normal Modes of a String

15.36 •• **CALC** Adjacent antinodes of a standing wave on a string are 15.0 cm apart. A particle at an antinode oscillates in simple harmonic motion with amplitude 0.850 cm and period 0.0750 s. The string lies along the $+x$-axis and is fixed at $x = 0$. (a) How far apart are the adjacent nodes? (b) What are the wavelength, amplitude, and speed of the two traveling waves that form this pattern? (c) Find the maximum and minimum transverse speeds of a point at an antinode. (d) What is the shortest distance along the string between a node and an antinode?

15.37 • Standing waves on a wire are described by Eq. (15.28), with $A_{\text{SW}} = 2.50$ mm, $\omega = 942$ rad/s, and $k = 0.750\pi$ rad/m. The left end of the wire is at $x = 0$. At what distances from the left end are (a) the nodes of the standing wave and (b) the antinodes of the standing wave?

15.38 • **CALC** **Wave Equation and Standing Waves.** (a) Prove by direct substitution that $y(x, t) = (A_{\text{SW}} \sin kx) \sin \omega t$ is a solution of the wave equation, Eq. (15.12), for $v = \omega/k$. (b) Explain why the relationship $v = \omega/k$ for *traveling* waves also applies to *standing* waves.

15.39 • **CALC** Let $y_1(x, t) = A \cos(k_1 x - \omega_1 t)$ and $y_2(x, t) = A \cos(k_2 x - \omega_2 t)$ be two solutions to the wave equation, Eq. (15.12), for the same v. Show that $y(x, t) = y_1(x, t) + y_2(x, t)$ is also a solution to the wave equation.

15.40 • A 1.50-m-long rope is stretched between two supports with a tension that makes the speed of transverse waves 48.0 m/s. What are the wavelength and frequency of (a) the fundamental; (b) the second overtone; (c) the fourth harmonic?

15.41 • A wire with mass 40.0 g is stretched so that its ends are tied down at points 80.0 cm apart. The wire vibrates in its fundamental mode with frequency 60.0 Hz and with an amplitude at the antinodes of 0.300 cm. (a) What is the speed of propagation of transverse waves in the wire? (b) Compute the tension in the wire. (c) Find the maximum transverse velocity and acceleration of particles in the wire.

15.42 • A piano tuner stretches a steel piano wire with a tension of 800 N. The steel wire is 0.400 m long and has a mass of 3.00 g. (a) What is the frequency of its fundamental mode of vibration? (b) What is the number of the highest harmonic that could be heard by a person who is capable of hearing frequencies up to 10,000 Hz?

15.43 • **CALC** A thin, taut string tied at both ends and oscillating in its third harmonic has its shape described by the equation $y(x, t) = (5.60 \text{ cm}) \sin[(0.0340 \text{ rad/cm})x] \sin[(50.0 \text{ rad/s})t]$, where the origin is at the left end of the string, the x-axis is along the string, and the y-axis is perpendicular to the string. (a) Draw a sketch that shows the standing-wave pattern. (b) Find the amplitude of the two traveling waves that make up this standing wave. (c) What is the length of the string? (d) Find the wavelength, frequency, period, and speed of the traveling waves. (e) Find the maximum transverse speed of a point on the string. (f) What would be the equation $y(x, t)$ for this string if it were vibrating in its eighth harmonic?

15.44 • The wave function of a standing wave is $y(x, t) = 4.44 \text{ mm} \sin[(32.5 \text{ rad/m})x] \sin[(754 \text{ rad/s})t]$. For the two traveling waves that make up this standing wave, find the (a) amplitude; (b) wavelength; (c) frequency; (d) wave speed; (e) wave functions. (f) From the information given, can you determine which harmonic this is? Explain.

15.45 •• Consider again the rope and traveling wave of Exercise 15.28. Assume that the ends of the rope are held fixed and that this traveling wave and the reflected wave are traveling in the opposite direction. (a) What is the wave function $y(x, t)$ for the standing wave that is produced? (b) In which harmonic is the standing wave oscillating? (c) What is the frequency of the fundamental oscillation?

15.46 •• One string of a certain musical instrument is 75.0 cm long and has a mass of 8.75 g. It is being played in a room where the speed of sound is 344 m/s. (a) To what tension must you adjust the string so that, when vibrating in its second overtone, it produces sound of wavelength 0.765 m? (Assume that the breaking stress of the wire is very large and isn't exceeded.) (b) What frequency sound does this string produce in its fundamental mode of vibration?

15.47 • The portion of the string of a certain musical instrument between the bridge and upper end of the finger board (that part of the string that is free to vibrate) is 60.0 cm long, and this length of the string has mass 2.00 g. The string sounds an A_4 note (440 Hz) when played. (a) Where must the player put a finger (what distance x from the bridge) to play a D_5 note (587 Hz)? (See Fig. E15.47.)

For both the A_4 and D_5 notes, the string vibrates in its fundamental mode. (b) Without retuning, is it possible to play a G_4 note (392 Hz) on this string? Why or why not?

15.48 •• (a) A horizontal string tied at both ends is vibrating in its fundamental mode. The traveling waves have speed v, frequency f, amplitude A, and wavelength λ. Calculate the maximum transverse velocity and maximum transverse acceleration of points located at (i) $x = \lambda/2$, (ii) $x = \lambda/4$, and (iii) $x = \lambda/8$ from the left-hand end of the string. (b) At each of the points in part (a), what is the amplitude of the motion? (c) At each of the points in part (a), how much time does it take the string to go from its largest upward displacement to its largest downward displacement?

Figure **E15.47**

15.49 • **Guitar String.** One of the 63.5-cm-long strings of an ordinary guitar is tuned to produce the note B_3 (frequency 245 Hz) when vibrating in its fundamental mode. (a) Find the speed of transverse waves on this string. (b) If the tension in this string is increased by 1.0%, what will be the new fundamental frequency of the string? (c) If the speed of sound in the surrounding air is 344 m/s, find the frequency and wavelength of the sound wave produced in the air by the vibration of the B_3 string. How do these compare to the frequency and wavelength of the standing wave on the string?

15.50 • **Waves on a Stick.** A flexible stick 2.0 m long is not fixed in any way and is free to vibrate. Make clear drawings of this stick vibrating in its first three harmonics, and then use your drawings to find the wavelengths of each of these harmonics. (*Hint:* Should the ends be nodes or antinodes?)

PROBLEMS

15.51 • **CALC** A transverse sine wave with an amplitude of 2.50 mm and a wavelength of 1.80 m travels from left to right along a long, horizontal, stretched string with a speed of 36.0 m/s. Take the origin at the left end of the undisturbed string. At time $t = 0$ the left end of the string has its maximum upward displacement. (a) What are the frequency, angular frequency, and wave number of the wave? (b) What is the function $y(x, t)$ that describes the wave? (c) What is $y(t)$ for a particle at the left end of the string? (d) What is $y(t)$ for a particle 1.35 m to the right of the origin? (e) What is the maximum magnitude of transverse velocity of any particle of the string? (f) Find the transverse displacement and the transverse velocity of a particle 1.35 m to the right of the origin at time $t = 0.0625$ s.

15.52 • A transverse wave on a rope is given by

$$y(x, t) = (0.750 \text{ cm}) \cos \pi[(0.400 \text{ cm}^{-1})x + (250 \text{ s}^{-1})t]$$

(a) Find the amplitude, period, frequency, wavelength, and speed of propagation. (b) Sketch the shape of the rope at these values of t: 0, 0.0005 s, 0.0010 s. (c) Is the wave traveling in the $+x$- or $-x$-direction? (d) The mass per unit length of the rope is 0.0500 kg/m. Find the tension. (e) Find the average power of this wave.

15.53 •• Three pieces of string, each of length L, are joined together end to end, to make a combined string of length $3L$. The first piece of string has mass per unit length μ_1, the second piece has mass per unit length $\mu_2 = 4\mu_1$, and the third piece has mass per unit length $\mu_3 = \mu_1/4$. (a) If the combined string is under tension F, how much time does it take a transverse wave to travel the entire length $3L$? Give your answer in terms of L, F, and μ_1. (b) Does your answer to part (a) depend on the order in which the three pieces are joined together? Explain.

15.54 •• **CP** A 1750-N irregular beam is hanging horizontally by its ends from the ceiling by two vertical wires (A and B), each 1.25 m long and weighing 0.360 N. The center of gravity of this beam is one-third of the way along the beam from the end where wire A is attached. If you pluck both strings at the same time at the beam, what is the time delay between the arrival of the two pulses at the ceiling? Which pulse arrives first? (Neglect the effect of the weight of the wires on the tension in the wires.)

15.55 • **CALC** **Ant Joy Ride.** You place your pet ant Klyde (mass m) on top of a horizontal, stretched rope, where he holds on tightly. The rope has mass M and length L and is under tension F. You start a sinusoidal transverse wave of wavelength λ and amplitude A propagating along the rope. The motion of the rope is in a vertical plane. Klyde's mass is so small that his presence has no effect on the propagation of the wave. (a) What is Klyde's top speed as he oscillates up and down? (b) Klyde enjoys the ride and begs for more. You decide to double his top speed by changing the tension while keeping the wavelength and amplitude the same. Should the tension be increased or decreased, and by what factor?

15.56 •• **Weightless Ant.** An ant with mass m is standing peacefully on top of a horizontal, stretched rope. The rope has mass per unit length μ and is under tension F. Without warning, Cousin Throckmorton starts a sinusoidal transverse wave of wavelength λ propagating along the rope. The motion of the rope is in a vertical plane. What minimum wave amplitude will make the ant become momentarily weightless? Assume that m is so small that the presence of the ant has no effect on the propagation of the wave.

15.57 • **CP** When a transverse sinusoidal wave is present on a string, the particles of the string undergo SHM. This is the same motion as that of a mass m attached to an ideal spring of force constant k', for which the angular frequency of oscillation was found in Chapter 14 to be $\omega = \sqrt{k'/m}$. Consider a string with tension F and mass per unit length μ, along which is propagating a sinusoidal wave with amplitude A and wavelength λ. (a) Find the "force constant" k' of the restoring force that acts on a short segment of the string of length Δx (where $\Delta x \ll \lambda$). (b) How does the "force constant" calculated in part (b) depend on F, μ, A, and λ? Explain the physical reasons this should be so.

15.58 •• **Music.** You are designing a two-string instrument with metal strings 35.0 cm long, as shown in Fig. P15.58. Both strings are under the *same tension*. String S_1 has a mass of 8.00 g and produces the note middle C (frequency 262 Hz) in its fundamental mode. (a) What should be the tension in the string? (b) What should be the mass of string S_2 so that it will produce A-sharp (frequency 466 Hz) as its fundamental? (c) To extend the range of your instrument, you include a fret located just under the strings but not normally touching them.

Figure **P15.58**

How far from the upper end should you put this fret so that when you press S_1 tightly against it, this string will produce C-sharp (frequency 277 Hz) in its fundamental? That is, what is x in the figure?

(d) If you press S_2 against the fret, what frequency of sound will it produce in its fundamental?

15.59 ••• **CP** The lower end of a uniform bar of mass 45.0 kg is attached to a wall by a frictionless hinge. The bar is held by a horizontal wire attached at its upper end so that the bar makes an angle of 30.0° with the wall. The wire has length 0.330 m and mass 0.0920 kg. What is the frequency of the fundamental standing wave for transverse waves on the wire?

15.60 ••• **CP** You are exploring a newly discovered planet. The radius of the planet is 7.20×10^7 m. You suspend a lead weight from the lower end of a light string that is 4.00 m long and has mass 0.0280 kg. You measure that it takes 0.0600 s for a transverse pulse to travel from the lower end to the upper end of the string. On earth, for the same string and lead weight, it takes 0.0390 s for a transverse pulse to travel the length of the string. The weight of the string is small enough that its effect on the tension in the string can be neglected. Assuming that the mass of the planet is distributed with spherical symmetry, what is its mass?

15.61 •• For a string stretched between two supports, two successive standing-wave frequencies are 525 Hz and 630 Hz. There are other standing-wave frequencies lower than 525 Hz and higher than 630 Hz. If the speed of transverse waves on the string is 384 m/s, what is the length of the string? Assume that the mass of the wire is small enough for its effect on the tension in the wire to be neglected.

15.62 ••• **CP** A 5.00-m, 0.732-kg wire is used to support two uniform 235-N posts of equal length (Fig. P15.62). Assume that the wire is essentially horizontal and that the speed of sound is 344 m/s. A strong wind is blowing, causing the wire to vibrate in its 5th overtone. What are the frequency and wavelength of the sound this wire produces?

Figure **P15.62**

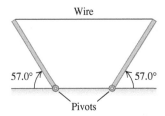

Wire

57.0°   57.0°

Pivots

15.63 ••• **CP** A 1.80-m-long uniform bar that weighs 536 N is suspended in a horizontal position by two vertical wires that are attached to the ceiling. One wire is aluminum and the other is copper. The aluminum wire is attached to the left-hand end of the bar, and the copper wire is attached 0.40 m to the left of the right-hand end. Each wire has length 0.600 m and a circular cross section with radius 0.280 mm. What is the fundamental frequency of transverse standing waves for each wire?

15.64 •• A continuous succession of sinusoidal wave pulses are produced at one end of a very long string and travel along the length of the string. The wave has frequency 70.0 Hz, amplitude 5.00 mm, and wavelength 0.600 m. (a) How long does it take the wave to travel a distance of 8.00 m along the length of the string? (b) How long does it take a point on the string to travel a distance of 8.00 m, once the wave train has reached the point and set it into motion? (c) In parts (a) and (b), how does the time change if the amplitude is doubled?

15.65 ••• **CALC** **Waves of Arbitrary Shape.** (a) Explain why *any* wave described by a function of the form $y(x, t) = f(x - vt)$ moves in the $+x$-direction with speed v. (b) Show that $y(x, t) = f(x - vt)$ satisfies the wave equation, no matter what the functional form of f. To do this, write $y(x, t) = f(u)$, where

$u = x - vt$. Then, to take partial derivatives of $y(x, t)$, use the chain rule:

$$\frac{\partial y(x, t)}{\partial t} = \frac{df(u)}{du} \frac{\partial u}{\partial t} = \frac{df(u)}{du}(-v)$$

$$\frac{\partial y(x, t)}{\partial t} = \frac{df(u)}{du} \frac{\partial u}{\partial x} = \frac{df(u)}{du}$$

(c) A wave pulse is described by the function $y(x, t) = De^{-(Bx - Ct)^2}$, where B, C, and D are all positive constants. What is the speed of this wave?

15.66 ••• **CP** A vertical, 1.20-m length of 18-gauge (diameter of 1.024 mm) copper wire has a 100.0-N ball hanging from it. (a) What is the wavelength of the third harmonic for this wire? (b) A 500.0-N ball now *replaces* the original ball. What is the change in the wavelength of the third harmonic caused by replacing the light ball with the heavy one? (*Hint:* See Table 11.1 for Young's modulus.)

15.67 • (a) Show that Eq. (15.25) can also be written as $P_{av} = \frac{1}{2}Fk\omega A^2$, where k is the wave number of the wave. (b) If the tension F in the string is quadrupled while the amplitude A is kept the same, how must k and ω each change to keep the average power constant? [*Hint:* Recall Eq. (15.6).]

15.68 ••• **CALC** Equation (15.7) for a sinusoidal wave can be made more general by including a phase angle ϕ, where $0 \leq \phi \leq 2\pi$ (in radians). Then the wave function $y(x, t)$ becomes

$$y(x, t) = A\cos(kx - \omega t + \phi)$$

(a) Sketch the wave as a function of x at $t = 0$ for $\phi = 0$, $\phi = \pi/4$, $\phi = \pi/2$, $\phi = 3\pi/4$, and $\phi = 3\pi/2$. (b) Calculate the transverse velocity $v_y = \partial y/\partial t$. (c) At $t = 0$, a particle on the string at $x = 0$ has displacement $y = A/\sqrt{2}$. Is this enough information to determine the value of ϕ? In addition, if you are told that a particle at $x = 0$ is moving toward $y = 0$ at $t = 0$, what is the value of ϕ? (d) Explain in general what you must know about the wave's behavior at a given instant to determine the value of ϕ.

15.69 ••• A sinusoidal transverse wave travels on a string. The string has length 8.00 m and mass 6.00 g. The wave speed is 30.0 m/s, and the wavelength is 0.200 m. (a) If the wave is to have an average power of 50.0 W, what must be the amplitude of the wave? (b) For this same string, if the amplitude and wavelength are the same as in part (a), what is the average power for the wave if the tension is increased such that the wave speed is doubled?

15.70 ••• **CALC** **Energy in a Triangular Pulse.** A triangular wave pulse on a taut string travels in the positive x-direction with speed v. The tension in the string is F, and the linear mass density of the string is μ. At $t = 0$, the shape of the pulse is given by

$$y(x, 0) = \begin{cases} 0 & \text{if } x < -L \\ h(L + x)/L & \text{for } -L < x < 0 \\ h(L - x)/L & \text{for } 0 < x < L \\ 0 & \text{for } x > L \end{cases}$$

(a) Draw the pulse at $t = 0$. (b) Determine the wave function $y(x, t)$ at all times t. (c) Find the instantaneous power in the wave. Show that the power is zero except for $-L < (x - vt) < L$ and that in this interval the power is constant. Find the value of this constant power.

15.71 ••• **CALC** **Instantaneous Power in a Wave.** (a) Graph $y(x, t)$ as given by Eq. (15.7) as a function of x for a given time t (say, $t = 0$). On the same axes, make a graph of the instantaneous power $P(x, t)$ as given by Eq. (15.23). (b) Explain the connection between the slope of the graph of $y(x, t)$ versus x and the value of $P(x, t)$. In particular, explain what is happening at points where $P = 0$, where there is no instantaneous energy transfer. (c) The quantity $P(x, t)$ always has the same sign. What does this imply about the direction of energy flow? (d) Consider a wave moving in the $-x$-direction, for which $y(x, t) = A\cos(kx + \omega t)$. Calculate $P(x, t)$ for this wave, and make a graph of $y(x, t)$ and $P(x, t)$ as functions of x for a given time t (say, $t = 0$). What differences arise from reversing the direction of the wave?

15.72 •• A vibrating string 50.0 cm long is under a tension of 1.00 N. The results from five successive stroboscopic pictures are shown in Fig. P15.72. The strobe rate is set at 5000 flashes per minute, and observations reveal that the maximum displacement occurred at flashes 1 and 5 with no other maxima in between. (a) Find the period, frequency, and wavelength for the traveling waves on this string. (b) In what normal mode (harmonic) is the string vibrating? (c) What is the speed of the traveling waves on the string? (d) How fast is point P moving when the string is in (i) position 1 and (ii) position 3? (e) What is the mass of this string? (See Section 15.3.)

Figure **P15.72**

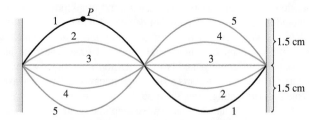

15.73 • **Clothesline Nodes.** Cousin Throckmorton is once again playing with the clothesline in Example 15.2 (Section 15.3). One end of the clothesline is attached to a vertical post. Throcky holds the other end loosely in his hand, so that the speed of waves on the clothesline is a relatively slow 0.720 m/s. He finds several frequencies at which he can oscillate his end of the clothesline so that a light clothespin 45.0 cm from the post doesn't move. What are these frequencies?

15.74 ••• **CALC** A guitar string is vibrating in its fundamental mode, with nodes at each end. The length of the segment of the string that is free to vibrate is 0.386 m. The maximum transverse acceleration of a point at the middle of the segment is 8.40×10^3 m/s^2 and the maximum transverse velocity is 3.80 m/s. (a) What is the amplitude of this standing wave? (b) What is the wave speed for the transverse traveling waves on this string?

15.75 •• **CALC** A string that lies along the $+x$-axis has a free end at $x = 0$. (a) By using steps similar to those used to derive Eq. (15.28), show that an incident traveling wave $y_1(x, t) = A\cos(kx + \omega t)$ gives rise to a standing wave $y(x, t) = 2A\cos\omega t\cos kx$. (b) Show that the standing wave has an antinode at its free end ($x = 0$). (c) Find the maximum displacement, maximum speed, and maximum acceleration of the free end of the string.

15.76 •• A string with both ends held fixed is vibrating in its third harmonic. The waves have a speed of 192 m/s and a frequency of 240 Hz. The amplitude of the standing wave at an antinode is 0.400 cm. (a) Calculate the amplitude at points on the string a distance of (i) 40.0 cm; (ii) 20.0 cm; and (iii) 10.0 cm from the left end of the string. (b) At each point in part (a), how much time does it take the string to go from its largest upward displacement to its largest downward displacement? (c) Calculate the maximum transverse velocity and the maximum transverse acceleration of the string at each of the points in part (a).

15.77 ••• A uniform cylindrical steel wire, 55.0 cm long and 1.14 mm in diameter, is fixed at both ends. To what tension must it be adjusted so that, when vibrating in its first overtone, it produces the note D-sharp of frequency 311 Hz? Assume that it stretches an insignificant amount. (*Hint:* See Table 12.1.)

15.78 • **Holding Up Under Stress.** A string or rope will break apart if it is placed under too much tensile stress [Eq. (11.8)]. Thicker ropes can withstand more tension without breaking because the thicker the rope, the greater the cross-sectional area and the smaller the stress. One type of steel has density 7800 kg/m³ and will break if the tensile stress exceeds 7.0×10^8 N/m². You want to make a guitar string from 4.0 g of this type of steel. In use, the guitar string must be able to withstand a tension of 900 N without breaking. Your job is the following: (a) Determine the maximum length and minimum radius the string can have. (b) Determine the highest possible fundamental frequency of standing waves on this string, if the entire length of the string is free to vibrate.

15.79 ••• **Combining Standing Waves.** A guitar string of length L is plucked in such a way that the total wave produced is the sum of the fundamental and the second harmonic. That is, the standing wave is given by

$$y(x, t) = y_1(x, t) + y_2(x, t)$$

where

$$y_1(x, t) = C \sin \omega_1 t \sin k_1 x$$
$$y_2(x, t) = C \sin \omega_2 t \sin k_2 x$$

with $\omega_1 = vk_1$ and $\omega_2 = vk_2$. (a) At what values of x are the nodes of y_1? (b) At what values of x are the nodes of y_2? (c) Graph the total wave at $t = 0$, $t = \frac{1}{8}f_1$, $t = \frac{1}{4}f_1$, $t = \frac{3}{8}f_1$, and $t = \frac{1}{2}f_1$. (d) Does the sum of the two standing waves y_1 and y_2 produce a standing wave? Explain.

15.80 •• **CP** When a massive aluminum sculpture is hung from a steel wire, the fundamental frequency for transverse standing waves on the wire is 250.0 Hz. The sculpture (but not the wire) is then completely submerged in water. (a) What is the new fundamental frequency? (*Hint:* See Table 12.1.) (b) Why is it a good approximation to treat the wire as being fixed at both ends?

15.81 ••• **CP** A large rock that weighs 164.0 N is suspended from the lower end of a thin wire that is 3.00 m long. The density of the rock is 3200 kg/m³. The mass of the wire is small enough that its effect on the tension in the wire can be neglected. The upper end of the wire is held fixed. When the rock is in air, the fundamental frequency for transverse standing waves on the wire is 42.0 Hz. When the rock is totally submerged in a liquid, with the top of the rock just below the surface, the fundamental frequency for the wire is 28.0 Hz. What is the density of the liquid?

15.82 •• **Tuning an Instrument.** A musician tunes the C-string of her instrument to a fundamental frequency of 65.4 Hz. The vibrating portion of the string is 0.600 m long and has a mass of 14.4 g. (a) With what tension must the musician stretch it? (b) What percent increase in tension is needed to increase the frequency from 65.4 Hz to 73.4 Hz, corresponding to a rise in pitch from C to D?

15.83 ••• One type of steel has a density of 7.8×10^3 kg/m³ and a breaking stress of 7.0×10^8 N/m². A cylindrical guitar string is to be made of 4.00 g of this steel. (a) What are the length and radius of the longest and thinnest string that can be placed under a tension of 900 N without breaking? (b) What is the highest fundamental frequency that this string could have?

CHALLENGE PROBLEMS

15.84 ••• **CP CALC** A deep-sea diver is suspended beneath the surface of Loch Ness by a 100-m-long cable that is attached to a boat on the surface (Fig. P15.84). The diver and his suit have a total mass of 120 kg and a volume of 0.0800 m³. The cable has a diameter of 2.00 cm and a linear mass density of $\mu = 1.10$ kg/m. The diver thinks he sees something moving in the murky depths and jerks the end of the cable back and forth to send transverse waves up the cable as a signal to his companions in the boat. (a) What is the tension in the cable at its lower end, where it is attached to the diver? Do not forget to include the buoyant force that the water (density 1000 kg/m³) exerts on him. (b) Calculate the tension in the cable a distance x above the diver. The buoyant force on the cable must be included in your calculation. (c) The speed of transverse waves on the cable is given by $v = \sqrt{F/\mu}$ (Eq. 15.13). The speed therefore varies along the cable, since the tension is not constant. (This expression neglects the damping force that the water exerts on the moving cable.) Integrate to find the time required for the first signal to reach the surface.

Figure **P15.84**

100 m

x

$m = 120$ kg

15.85 ••• **CALC** (a) Show that for a wave on a string, the kinetic energy *per unit length of string* is

$$u_k(x, t) = \tfrac{1}{2}\mu v_y^2(x, t) = \tfrac{1}{2}\mu\left(\frac{\partial y(x, t)}{\partial t}\right)^2$$

where μ is the mass per unit length. (b) Calculate $u_k(x, t)$ for a sinusoidal wave given by Eq. (15.7). (c) There is also elastic potential energy in the string, associated with the work required to deform and stretch the string. Consider a short segment of string at position x that has unstretched length Δx, as in Fig. 15.13. Ignoring the (small) curvature of the segment, its slope is $\partial y(x, t)/\partial x$. Assume that the displacement of the string from equilibrium is small, so that $\partial y/\partial x$ has a magnitude much less than unity. Show that the stretched length of the segment is approximately

$$\Delta x\left[1 + \tfrac{1}{2}\left(\frac{\partial y(x, t)}{\partial x}\right)^2\right]$$

(*Hint:* Use the relationship $\sqrt{1 + u} \approx 1 + \tfrac{1}{2}u$, valid for $|u| \ll 1$.) (d) The potential energy stored in the segment equals the work done by the string tension F (which acts along the string) to stretch the segment from its unstretched length Δx to the length calculated in part (c). Calculate this work and show that the potential energy *per unit length of string* is

$$u_p(x, t) = \tfrac{1}{2}F\left(\frac{\partial y(x, t)}{\partial x}\right)^2$$

(e) Calculate $u_p(x, t)$ for a sinusoidal wave given by Eq. (15.7). (f) Show that $u_k(x, t) = u_p(x, t)$, for all x and t. (g) Show $y(x, t)$, $u_k(x, t)$, and $u_p(x, t)$ as functions of x for $t = 0$ in one graph with all three functions on the same axes. Explain why u_k and u_p are maximum where y is zero, and vice versa. (h) Show that the instantaneous power in the wave, given by Eq. (15.22), is equal to the total energy per unit length multiplied by the wave speed v. Explain why this result is reasonable.

Answers

The power of a mechanical wave depends on its frequency and amplitude [see Eq. (15.25)].

Test Your Understanding Questions

15.1 Answer: (i) The "wave" travels horizontally from one spectator to the next along each row of the stadium, but the displacement of each spectator is vertically upward. Since the displacement is perpendicular to the direction in which the wave travels, the wave is transverse.

15.2 Answer: (iv) The speed of waves on a string, v, does not depend on the wavelength. We can rewrite the relationship $v = \lambda f$ as $f = v/\lambda$, which tells us that if the wavelength λ doubles, the frequency f becomes one-half as great.

15.3 Answers: (a) $\frac{2}{8}T$, **(b)** $\frac{4}{8}T$, **(c)** $\frac{5}{8}T$ Since the wave is sinusoidal, each point on the string oscillates in simple harmonic motion (SHM). Hence we can apply all of the ideas from Chapter 14 about SHM to the wave depicted in Fig. 15.8. (a) A particle in SHM has its maximum speed when it is passing through the equilibrium position ($y = 0$ in Fig. 15.8). The particle at point A is moving upward through this position at $t = \frac{2}{8}T$. (b) In vertical SHM the greatest *upward* acceleration occurs when a particle is at its maximum *downward* displacement. This occurs for the particle at point B at $t = \frac{4}{8}T$. (c) A particle in vertical SHM has a *downward* acceleration when its displacement is *upward*. The particle at C has an upward displacement and is moving downward at $t = \frac{5}{8}T$.

15.4 Answer: (ii) The relationship $v = \sqrt{F/\mu}$ [Eq. (15.13)] says that the wave speed is greatest on the string with the smallest linear mass density. This is the thinnest string, which has the smallest amount of mass m and hence the smallest linear mass density $\mu = m/L$ (all strings are the same length).

15.5 Answer: (iii), (iv), (ii), (i) Equation (15.25) says that the average power in a sinusoidal wave on a string is $P_{av} = \frac{1}{2}\sqrt{\mu F}\omega^2 A^2$. All four strings are identical, so all have the same mass, the same length, and the same linear mass density μ. The frequency f is the same for each wave, as is the angular frequency $\omega = 2\pi f$. Hence the average wave power for each string is proportional to the square root of the string tension F and the square of the amplitude A. Compared to string (i), the average power in each string is (ii) $\sqrt{4} = 2$ times greater; (iii) $4^2 = 16$ times greater; and (iv) $\sqrt{2}(2)^2 = 4\sqrt{2}$ times greater.

15.6 Answer:

15.7 Answers: yes, yes Doubling the frequency makes the wavelength half as large. Hence the spacing between nodes (equal to $\lambda/2$) is also half as large. There are nodes at all of the previous positions, but there is also a new node between every pair of old nodes.

15.8 Answers: $n = 1, 3, 5, \ldots$ When you touch the string at its center, you are demanding that there be a node at the center. Hence only standing waves with a node at $x = L/2$ are allowed. From Figure 15.26 you can see that the normal modes $n = 1, 3, 5, \ldots$ cannot be present.

Bridging Problem

Answers: (a) $F(r) = \dfrac{m\omega^2}{2L}(L^2 - r^2)$

(b) $v(r) = \omega\sqrt{\dfrac{L^2 - r^2}{2}}$

(c) $\dfrac{\pi}{\omega\sqrt{2}}$

SOUND AND HEARING

? Most people like to listen to music, but hardly anyone likes to listen to noise. What is the physical difference between musical sound and noise?

Of all the mechanical waves that occur in nature, the most important in our everyday lives are longitudinal waves in a medium—usually air—called *sound* waves. The reason is that the human ear is tremendously sensitive and can detect sound waves even of very low intensity. Besides their use in spoken communication, our ears allow us to pick up a myriad of cues about our environment, from the welcome sound of a meal being prepared to the warning sound of an approaching car. The ability to hear an unseen nocturnal predator was essential to the survival of our ancestors, so it is no exaggeration to say that we humans owe our existence to our highly evolved sense of hearing.

Up to this point we have described mechanical waves primarily in terms of displacement; however, a description of sound waves in terms of *pressure* fluctuations is often more appropriate, largely because the ear is primarily sensitive to changes in pressure. We'll study the relationships among displacement, pressure fluctuation, and intensity and the connections between these quantities and human sound perception.

When a source of sound or a listener moves through the air, the listener may hear a frequency different from the one emitted by the source. This is the Doppler effect, which has important applications in medicine and technology.

16.1 Sound Waves

The most general definition of **sound** is a longitudinal wave in a medium. Our main concern in this chapter is with sound waves in air, but sound can travel through any gas, liquid, or solid. You may be all too familiar with the propagation of sound through a solid if your neighbor's stereo speakers are right next to your wall.

The simplest sound waves are sinusoidal waves, which have definite frequency, amplitude, and wavelength. The human ear is sensitive to waves in the frequency range from about 20 to 20,000 Hz, called the **audible range,** but we also use the

16.1 A sinusoidal longitudinal wave traveling to the right in a fluid. (Compare to Fig. 15.7.)

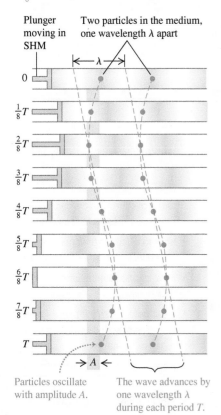

Longitudinal waves are shown at intervals of $\frac{1}{8}T$ for one period T.

Plunger moving in SHM

Two particles in the medium, one wavelength λ apart

Particles oscillate with amplitude A.

The wave advances by one wavelength λ during each period T.

term "sound" for similar waves with frequencies above (**ultrasonic**) and below (**infrasonic**) the range of human hearing.

Sound waves usually travel out in all directions from the source of sound, with an amplitude that depends on the direction and distance from the source. We'll return to this point in the next section. For now, we concentrate on the idealized case of a sound wave that propagates in the positive x-direction only. As we discussed in Section 15.3, such a wave is described by a wave function $y(x, t)$, which gives the instantaneous displacement y of a particle in the medium at position x at time t. If the wave is sinusoidal, we can express it using Eq. (15.7):

$$y(x, t) = A \cos(kx - \omega t) \quad \begin{array}{l}\text{(sound wave propagating}\\ \text{in the } +x\text{-direction)}\end{array} \quad (16.1)$$

Remember that in a longitudinal wave the displacements are *parallel* to the direction of travel of the wave, so distances x and y are measured parallel to each other, not perpendicular as in a transverse wave. The amplitude A is the maximum displacement of a particle in the medium from its equilibrium position (Fig. 16.1). Hence A is also called the **displacement amplitude.**

Sound Waves As Pressure Fluctuations

Sound waves may also be described in terms of variations of *pressure* at various points. In a sinusoidal sound wave in air, the pressure fluctuates above and below atmospheric pressure p_a in a sinusoidal variation with the same frequency as the motions of the air particles. The human ear operates by sensing such pressure variations. A sound wave entering the ear canal exerts a fluctuating pressure on one side of the eardrum; the air on the other side of the eardrum, vented to the outside by the Eustachian tube, is at atmospheric pressure. The pressure difference on the two sides of the eardrum sets it into motion. Microphones and similar devices also usually sense pressure differences, not displacements, so it is very useful to develop a relationship between these two descriptions.

Let $p(x, t)$ be the instantaneous pressure fluctuation in a sound wave at any point x at time t. That is, $p(x, t)$ is the amount by which the pressure *differs* from normal atmospheric pressure p_a. Think of $p(x, t)$ as the *gauge pressure* defined in Section 12.2; it can be either positive or negative. The *absolute* pressure at a point is then $p_a + p(x, t)$.

To see the connection between the pressure fluctuation $p(x, t)$ and the displacement $y(x, t)$ in a sound wave propagating in the $+x$-direction, consider an imaginary cylinder of a wave medium (gas, liquid, or solid) with cross-sectional area S and axis along the direction of propagation (Fig. 16.2). When no sound wave is present, the cylinder has length Δx and volume $V = S \Delta x$, as shown by the shaded volume in Fig. 16.2. When a wave is present, at time t the end of the cylinder that is initially at x is displaced by $y_1 = y(x, t)$, and the end that is initially at $x + \Delta x$ is displaced by $y_2 = y(x + \Delta x, t)$; this is shown by the red lines. If $y_2 > y_1$, as shown in Fig. 16.2, the cylinder's volume has increased, which causes a decrease in pressure. If $y_2 < y_1$, the cylinder's volume has decreased and the pressure has increased. If $y_2 = y_1$, the cylinder is simply shifted to the left or right; there is no volume change and no pressure fluctuation. The pressure fluctuation depends on the *difference* between the displacements at neighboring points in the medium.

Quantitatively, the change in volume ΔV of the cylinder is

$$\Delta V = S(y_2 - y_1) = S[y(x + \Delta x, t) - y(x, t)]$$

In the limit as $\Delta x \to 0$, the fractional change in volume dV/V (volume change divided by original volume) is

16.2 As a sound wave propagates along the x-axis, the left and right ends undergo different displacements y_1 and y_2.

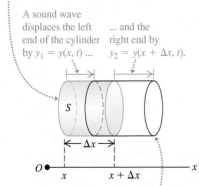

Undisturbed cylinder of fluid has cross-sectional area S, length Δx, and volume $S\Delta x$.

A sound wave displaces the left end of the cylinder by $y_1 = y(x, t)$ ...

... and the right end by $y_2 = y(x + \Delta x, t)$.

S

Δx

O x $x + \Delta x$ x

The change in volume of the disturbed cylinder of fluid is $S(y_2 - y_1)$.

$$\frac{dV}{V} = \lim_{\Delta x \to 0} \frac{S[y(x + \Delta x, t) - y(x, t)]}{S \Delta x} = \frac{\partial y(x, t)}{\partial x} \quad (16.2)$$

16.3 Three ways to describe a sound wave.

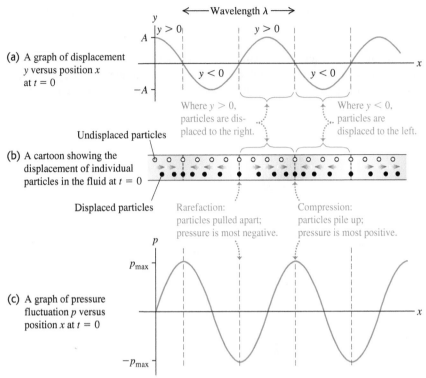

(a) A graph of displacement y versus position x at $t = 0$

←— Wavelength λ —→

$y > 0$

$y > 0$

A

$y < 0$

$y < 0$

$-A$

Where $y > 0$, particles are displaced to the right.

Where $y < 0$, particles are displaced to the left.

Undisplaced particles

(b) A cartoon showing the displacement of individual particles in the fluid at $t = 0$

Displaced particles

Rarefaction: particles pulled apart; pressure is most negative.

Compression: particles pile up; pressure is most positive.

(c) A graph of pressure fluctuation p versus position x at $t = 0$

p

p_{max}

$-p_{max}$

The fractional volume change is related to the pressure fluctuation by the bulk modulus B, which by definition [Eq. (11.13)] is $B = -p(x, t)/(dV/V)$ (see Section 11.4). Solving for $p(x, t)$, we have

$$p(x, t) = -B\frac{\partial y(x, t)}{\partial x}$$ (16.3)

The negative sign arises because when $\partial y(x, t)/\partial x$ is positive, the displacement is greater at $x + \Delta x$ than at x, corresponding to an increase in volume and a *decrease* in pressure.

When we evaluate $\partial y(x, t)/\partial x$ for the sinusoidal wave of Eq. (16.1), we find

$$p(x, t) = BkA \sin(kx - \omega t)$$ (16.4)

Figure 16.3 shows $y(x, t)$ and $p(x, t)$ for a sinusoidal sound wave at $t = 0$. It also shows how individual particles of the wave are displaced at this time. While $y(x, t)$ and $p(x, t)$ describe the same wave, these two functions are one-quarter cycle out of phase: At any time, the displacement is greatest where the pressure fluctuation is zero, and vice versa. In particular, note that the compressions (points of greatest pressure and density) and rarefactions (points of lowest pressure and density) are points of *zero* displacement.

CAUTION **Graphs of a sound wave** Keep in mind that the graphs in Fig. 16.3 show the wave at only *one* instant of time. Because the wave is propagating in the $+x$-direction, as time goes by the wave patterns in the functions $y(x, t)$ and $p(x, t)$ move to the right at the wave speed $v = \omega/k$. Hence the positions of the compressions and rarefactions also move to the right at this same speed. The particles, by contrast, simply oscillate back and forth in simple harmonic motion as shown in Fig. 16.1. ▮

Equation (16.4) shows that the quantity BkA represents the maximum pressure fluctuation. We call this the **pressure amplitude**, denoted by p_{max}:

$$p_{max} = BkA \qquad \text{(sinusoidal sound wave)}$$ (16.5)

The pressure amplitude is directly proportional to the displacement amplitude A, as we might expect, and it also depends on wavelength. Waves of shorter wavelength λ (larger wave number $k = 2\pi/\lambda$) have greater pressure variations for a given amplitude because the maxima and minima are squeezed closer together. A medium with a large value of bulk modulus B requires a relatively large pressure amplitude for a given displacement amplitude because large B means a less compressible medium; that is, greater pressure change is required for a given volume change.

Example 16.1   **Amplitude of a sound wave in air**

In a sinusoidal sound wave of moderate loudness, the maximum pressure variations are about 3.0×10^{-2} Pa above and below atmospheric pressure. Find the corresponding maximum displacement if the frequency is 1000 Hz. In air at normal atmospheric pressure and density, the speed of sound is 344 m/s and the bulk modulus is 1.42×10^5 Pa.

SOLUTION

IDENTIFY and SET UP: This problem involves the relationship between two ways of describing a sound wave: in terms of displacement and in terms of pressure. The target variable is the displacement amplitude A. We are given the pressure amplitude $p_{\max}$, wave speed v, frequency f, and bulk modulus B. Equation (16.5) relates the target variable A to $p_{\max}$. We use $\omega = vk$ [Eq. (15.6)] to

determine the wave number k from v and the angular frequency $\omega = 2\pi f$.

EXECUTE: From Eq. (15.6),

$$k = \frac{\omega}{v} = \frac{2\pi f}{v} = \frac{(2\pi \text{ rad})(1000 \text{ Hz})}{344 \text{ m/s}} = 18.3 \text{ rad/m}$$

Then from Eq. (16.5), the maximum displacement is

$$A = \frac{p_{\max}}{Bk} = \frac{3.0 \times 10^{-2} \text{ Pa}}{(1.42 \times 10^5 \text{ Pa})(18.3 \text{ rad/m})} = 1.2 \times 10^{-8} \text{ m}$$

EVALUATE: This displacement amplitude is only about $\frac{1}{100}$ the size of a human cell. The ear actually senses pressure fluctuations; it detects these minuscule displacements only indirectly.

Example 16.2   **Amplitude of a sound wave in the inner ear**

A sound wave that enters the human ear sets the eardrum into oscillation, which in turn causes oscillation of the *ossicles,* a chain of three tiny bones in the middle ear (Fig. 16.4). The ossicles transmit this oscillation to the fluid (mostly water) in the inner ear; there the fluid motion disturbs hair cells that send nerve impulses to the brain with information about the sound. The area of the moving part of the eardrum is about 43 mm^2, and that of the stapes (the smallest of the ossicles) where it connects to the inner ear is about 3.2 mm^2. For the sound in Example 16.1, determine (a) the pressure amplitude and (b) the displacement amplitude of the wave in the fluid of the inner ear, in which the speed of sound is 1500 m/s.

SOLUTION

IDENTIFY and SET UP: Although the sound wave here travels in liquid rather than air, the same principles and relationships among the properties of the wave apply. We can neglect the mass of the tiny ossicles (about 58 mg = 5.8×10^{-5} kg), so the force they exert on the inner-ear fluid is the same as that exerted on the eardrum and ossicles by the incident sound wave. (In Chapters 4 and 5 we used the same idea to say that the tension is the same at either end of a massless rope.) Hence the pressure amplitude in the inner ear, $p_{\max(\text{inner ear})}$, is greater than in the outside air, $p_{\max(\text{air})}$, because the same force is exerted on a smaller area (the area of the stapes versus the area of the eardrum). Given $p_{\max(\text{inner ear})}$, we find the displacement amplitude $A_{\text{inner ear}}$ using Eq. (16.5).

16.4 The anatomy of the human ear. The middle ear is the size of a small marble; the ossicles (incus, malleus, and stapes) are the smallest bones in the human body.

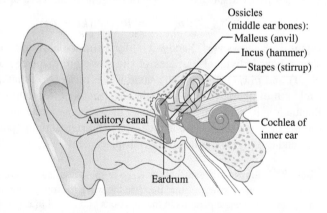

Ossicles
(middle ear bones):
— Malleus (anvil)
— Incus (hammer)
— Stapes (stirrup)

Auditory canal

Cochlea of inner ear

Eardrum

EXECUTE: (a) From the area of the eardrum and the pressure amplitude in air found in Example 16.1, the maximum force exerted by the sound wave in air on the eardrum is $F_{\max} = p_{\max(\text{air})}S_{\text{eardrum}}$. Then

$$p_{\max(\text{inner ear})} = \frac{F_{\max}}{S_{\text{stapes}}} = p_{\max(\text{air})}\frac{S_{\text{eardrum}}}{S_{\text{stapes}}}$$

$$= (3.0 \times 10^{-2} \text{ Pa})\frac{43 \text{ mm}^2}{3.2 \text{ mm}^2} = 0.40 \text{ Pa}$$

(b) To find the maximum displacement $A_{\text{inner ear}}$, we use $A = p_{\max}/Bk$ as in Example 16.1. The inner-ear fluid is mostly water, which has a much greater bulk modulus B than air. From Table 11.2 the compressibility of water (unfortunately also called k) is 45.8×10^{-11} Pa^{-1}, so $B_{\text{fluid}} = 1/(45.8 \times 10^{-11}$ Pa$^{-1}) = 2.18 \times 10^{9}$ Pa.

The wave in the inner ear has the same angular frequency ω as the wave in the air because the air, eardrum, ossicles, and inner-ear fluid all oscillate together (see Example 15.8 in Section 15.8). But because the wave speed v is greater in the inner ear than in the air (1500 m/s versus 344 m/s), the wave number $k = \omega/v$ is smaller. Using the value of ω from Example 16.1,

$$k_{\text{inner ear}} = \frac{\omega}{v_{\text{inner ear}}} = \frac{(2\pi \text{ rad})(1000 \text{ Hz})}{1500 \text{ m/s}} = 4.2 \text{ rad/m}$$

Putting everything together, we have

$$A_{\text{inner ear}} = \frac{p_{\max (\text{inner ear})}}{B_{\text{fluid}} k_{\text{inner ear}}} = \frac{0.40 \text{ Pa}}{(2.18 \times 10^{9} \text{ Pa})(4.2 \text{ rad/m})}$$
$$= 4.4 \times 10^{-11} \text{ m}$$

EVALUATE: In part (a) we see that the ossicles increase the pressure amplitude by a factor of $(43 \text{ mm}^2)/(3.2 \text{ mm}^2) = 13$. This amplification helps give the human ear its great sensitivity.

The displacement amplitude in the inner ear is even smaller than in the air. But *pressure* variations within the inner-ear fluid are what set the hair cells into motion, so what matters is that the pressure amplitude is larger in the inner ear than in the air.

Perception of Sound Waves

The physical characteristics of a sound wave are directly related to the perception of that sound by a listener. For a given frequency, the greater the pressure amplitude of a sinusoidal sound wave, the greater the perceived **loudness.** The relationship between pressure amplitude and loudness is not a simple one, and it varies from one person to another. One important factor is that the ear is not equally sensitive to all frequencies in the audible range. A sound at one frequency may seem louder than one of equal pressure amplitude at a different frequency. At 1000 Hz the minimum pressure amplitude that can be perceived with normal hearing is about 3×10^{-5} Pa; to produce the same loudness at 200 Hz or 15,000 Hz requires about 3×10^{-4} Pa. Perceived loudness also depends on the health of the ear. A loss of sensitivity at the high-frequency end usually happens naturally with age but can be further aggravated by excessive noise levels.

The frequency of a sound wave is the primary factor in determining the **pitch** of a sound, the quality that lets us classify the sound as "high" or "low." The higher the frequency of a sound (within the audible range), the higher the pitch that a listener will perceive. Pressure amplitude also plays a role in determining pitch. When a listener compares two sinusoidal sound waves with the same frequency but different pressure amplitudes, the one with the greater pressure amplitude is usually perceived as louder but also as slightly lower in pitch.

Musical sounds have wave functions that are more complicated than a simple sine function. The pressure fluctuation in the sound wave produced by a clarinet is shown in Fig. 16.5a. The pattern is so complex because the column of air in a wind instrument like a clarinet vibrates at a fundamental frequency and at many harmonics at the same time. (In Section 15.8, we described this same behavior for a string that has been plucked, bowed, or struck. We'll examine the physics of wind instruments in Section 16.5.) The sound wave produced in the surrounding air has a similar amount of each harmonic—that is, a similar *harmonic content.* Figure 16.5b shows the harmonic content of the sound of a clarinet. The mathematical process of translating a pressure–time graph like Fig. 16.5a into a graph of harmonic content like Fig. 16.5b is called *Fourier analysis.*

Two tones produced by different instruments might have the same fundamental frequency (and thus the same pitch) but sound different because of different harmonic content. The difference in sound is called *tone color, quality,* or **timbre** and is often described in subjective terms such as reedy, golden, round, mellow, and tinny. A tone that is rich in harmonics, like the clarinet tone in Figs. 16.5a and 16.5b, usually sounds thin and "stringy" or "reedy," while a tone containing mostly a fundamental, like the alto recorder tone in Figs. 16.5c and 16.5d, is more mellow and flutelike. The same principle applies to the human voice, which is another example of a wind instrument; the vowels "a" and "e" sound different because of differences in harmonic content.

Application Hearing Loss from Amplified Sound
Due to exposure to highly amplified music, many young popular musicians have suffered permanent ear damage and have hearing typical of persons 65 years of age. Headphones for personal music players used at high volume pose similar threats to hearing. Be careful!

16.5 Different representations of the sound of (a), (b) a clarinet and (c), (d) an alto recorder. (Graphs adapted from R.E. Berg and D.G. Stork, *The Physics of Sound,* Prentice-Hall, 1982.)

Pressure fluctuation versus time for a clarinet with fundamental frequency $f_1 = 233$ Hz

$T = 4.29$ ms

(a)

Harmonic content of the sound in (a)

(b)

$O \quad 5f_1 \ 10f_1 \quad 20f_1 \quad 30f_1 \quad 40f_1$

Pressure fluctuation versus time for an alto recorder with fundamental frequency $f_1 = 523$ Hz

$T = 1.91$ ms

(c)

Harmonic content of the sound in (c)

(d)

$O \quad 5f_1 \ 10f_1 \quad 20f_1 \quad 30f_1 \quad 40f_1$

Another factor in determining tone quality is the behavior at the beginning (*attack*) and end (*decay*) of a tone. A piano tone begins with a thump and then dies away gradually. A harpsichord tone, in addition to having different harmonic content, begins much more quickly with a click, and the higher harmonics begin before the lower ones. When the key is released, the sound also dies away much more rapidly with a harpsichord than with a piano. Similar effects are present in other musical instruments. With wind and string instruments the player has considerable control over the attack and decay of the tone, and these characteristics help to define the unique characteristics of each instrument.

Unlike the tones made by musical instruments or the vowels in human speech, **noise** is a combination of *all* frequencies, not just frequencies that are integer multiples of a fundamental frequency. (An extreme case is "white noise," which contains equal amounts of all frequencies across the audible range.) Examples include the sound of the wind and the hissing sound you make in saying the consonant "s."

Test Your Understanding of Section 16.1 You use an electronic signal generator to produce a sinusoidal sound wave in air. You then increase the frequency of the wave from 100 Hz to 400 Hz while keeping the pressure amplitude constant. What effect does this have on the displacement amplitude of the sound wave? (i) It becomes four times greater; (ii) it becomes twice as great; (iii) it is unchanged; (iv) it becomes $\frac{1}{2}$ as great; (v) it becomes $\frac{1}{4}$ as great.

16.2 Speed of Sound Waves

We found in Section 15.4 that the speed v of a transverse wave on a string depends on the string tension F and the linear mass density μ: $v = \sqrt{F/\mu}$. What, we may ask, is the corresponding expression for the speed of sound waves in a gas or liquid? On what properties of the medium does the speed depend?

We can make an educated guess about these questions by remembering a claim that we made in Section 15.4: For mechanical waves in general, the expression for the wave speed is of the form

$$v = \sqrt{\frac{\text{Restoring force returning the system to equilibrium}}{\text{Inertia resisting the return to equilibrium}}}$$

A sound wave in a bulk fluid causes compressions and rarefactions of the fluid, so the restoring-force term in the above expression must be related to how easy or difficult it is to compress the fluid. This is precisely what the bulk modulus B of the medium tells us. According to Newton's second law, inertia is related to mass. The "massiveness" of a bulk fluid is described by its density, or mass per unit volume, ρ. (The corresponding quantity for a string is the mass per unit length, μ.) Hence we expect that the speed of sound waves should be of the form $v = \sqrt{B/\rho}$.

To check our guess, we'll derive the speed of sound waves in a fluid in a pipe. This is a situation of some importance, since all musical wind instruments are fundamentally pipes in which a longitudinal wave (sound) propagates in a fluid (air) (Fig. 16.6). Human speech works on the same principle; sound waves propagate in your vocal tract, which is basically an air-filled pipe connected to the lungs at one end (your larynx) and to the outside air at the other end (your mouth). The steps in our derivation are completely parallel to those we used in Section 15.4 to find the speed of transverse waves, so you'll find it useful to review that section.

Speed of Sound in a Fluid

Figure 16.7 shows a fluid (either liquid or gas) with density ρ in a pipe with cross-sectional area A. In the equilibrium state, the fluid is under a uniform pressure p. In Fig. 16.7a the fluid is at rest. We take the x-axis along the length of the pipe. This is also the direction in which we make a longitudinal wave propagate, so the displacement y is also measured along the pipe, just as in Section 16.1 (see Fig. 16.2).

At time $t = 0$ we start the piston at the left end moving toward the right with constant speed v_y. This initiates a wave motion that travels to the right along the length of the pipe, in which successive sections of fluid begin to move and become compressed at successively later times.

Figure 16.7b shows the fluid at time t. All portions of fluid to the left of point P are moving to the right with speed v_y, and all portions to the right of P are still at rest. The boundary between the moving and stationary portions travels to the right with a speed equal to the speed of propagation or wave speed v. At time t the piston has moved a distance $v_y t$, and the boundary has advanced a distance vt. As with a transverse disturbance in a string, we can compute the speed of propagation from the impulse–momentum theorem.

The quantity of fluid set in motion in time t is the amount that originally occupied a section of the cylinder with length vt, cross-sectional area A, and volume vtA. The mass of this fluid is ρvtA, and its longitudinal momentum (that is, momentum along the length of the pipe) is

$$\text{Longitudinal momentum} = (\rho vtA)v_y$$

Next we compute the increase of pressure, Δp, in the moving fluid. The original volume of the moving fluid, Avt, has decreased by an amount $Av_y t$. From the definition of the bulk modulus B, Eq. (11.13) in Section 11.5,

$$B = \frac{-\text{Pressure change}}{\text{Fractional volume change}} = \frac{-\Delta p}{-Av_y t/Avt}$$

$$\Delta p = B\frac{v_y}{v}$$

The pressure in the moving fluid is $p + \Delta p$ and the force exerted on it by the piston is $(p + \Delta p)A$. The net force on the moving fluid (see Fig. 16.7b) is ΔpA, and the longitudinal impulse is

$$\text{Longitudinal impulse} = \Delta pAt = B\frac{v_y}{v}At$$

Because the fluid was at rest at time $t = 0$, the change in momentum up to time t is equal to the momentum at that time. Applying the impulse–momentum theorem (see Section 8.1), we find

$$B\frac{v_y}{v}At = \rho vtAv_y \qquad (16.6)$$

When we solve this expression for v, we get

$$v = \sqrt{\frac{B}{\rho}} \qquad \text{(speed of a longitudinal wave in a fluid)} \qquad (16.7)$$

which agrees with our educated guess. Thus the speed of propagation of a longitudinal pulse in a fluid depends only on the bulk modulus B and the density ρ of the medium.

While we derived Eq. (16.7) for waves in a pipe, it also applies to longitudinal waves in a bulk fluid. Thus the speed of sound waves traveling in air or water is determined by this equation.

Speed of Sound in a Solid

When a longitudinal wave propagates in a *solid* rod or bar, the situation is somewhat different. The rod expands sideways slightly when it is compressed

16.6 When a wind instrument like this French horn is played, sound waves propagate through the air within the instrument's pipes. The properties of the sound that emerges from the large bell depend on the speed of these waves.

16.7 A sound wave propagating in a fluid confined to a tube. (a) Fluid in equilibrium. (b) A time t after the piston begins moving to the right at speed v_y, the fluid between the piston and point P is in motion. The speed of sound waves is v.

longitudinally, while a fluid in a pipe with constant cross section cannot move sideways. Using the same kind of reasoning that led us to Eq. (16.7), we can show that the speed of a longitudinal pulse in the rod is given by

$$v = \sqrt{\frac{Y}{\rho}} \quad \text{(speed of a longitudinal wave in a solid rod)} \quad (16.8)$$

where Y is Young's modulus, defined in Section 11.4.

CAUTION **Solid rods vs. bulk solids** Equation (16.8) applies only to a rod or bar whose sides are free to bulge and shrink a little as the wave travels. It does not apply to longitudinal waves in a *bulk* solid, since in these materials, sideways motion in any element of material is prevented by the surrounding material. The speed of longitudinal waves in a bulk solid depends on the density, the bulk modulus, and the *shear* modulus; a full discussion is beyond the scope of this book.

As with the derivation for a transverse wave on a string, Eqs. (16.7) and (16.8) are valid for sinusoidal and other periodic waves, not just for the special case discussed here.

Table 16.1 lists the speed of sound in several bulk materials. Sound waves travel more slowly in lead than in aluminum or steel because lead has a lower bulk modulus and shear modulus and a higher density.

Table 16.1 Speed of Sound in Various Bulk Materials

Material	Speed of Sound (m/s)
Gases	
Air (20°C)	344
Helium (20°C)	999
Hydrogen (20°C)	1330
Liquids	
Liquid helium (4 K)	211
Mercury (20°C)	1451
Water (0°C)	1402
Water (20°C)	1482
Water (100°C)	1543
Solids	
Aluminum	6420
Lead	1960
Steel	5941

Example 16.3 Wavelength of sonar waves

A ship uses a sonar system (Fig. 16.8) to locate underwater objects. Find the speed of sound waves in water using Eq. (16.7), and find the wavelength of a 262-Hz wave.

SOLUTION

IDENTIFY and SET UP: Our target variables are the speed and wavelength of a sound wave in water. In Eq. (16.7), we use the density of water, $\rho = 1.00 \times 10^3 \text{ kg/m}^3$, and the bulk modulus of water, which we find from the compressibility (see Table 11.2). Given the speed and the frequency $f = 262$ Hz, we find the wavelength from $v = f\lambda$.

EXECUTE: In Example 16.2, we used Table 11.2 to find $B = 2.18 \times 10^9$ Pa. Then

$$v = \sqrt{\frac{B}{\rho}} = \sqrt{\frac{2.18 \times 10^9 \text{ Pa}}{1.00 \times 10^3 \text{ kg/m}^3}} = 1480 \text{ m/s}$$

and

$$\lambda = \frac{v}{f} = \frac{1480 \text{ m/s}}{262 \text{ s}^{-1}} = 5.65 \text{ m}$$

EVALUATE: The calculated value of v agrees well with the value in Table 16.1. Water is denser than air (ρ is larger) but is also much

16.8 A sonar system uses underwater sound waves to detect and locate submerged objects.

more incompressible (B is much larger), and so the speed $v = \sqrt{B/\rho}$ is greater than the 344-m/s speed of sound in air at ordinary temperatures. The relationship $\lambda = v/f$ then says that a sound wave in water must have a longer wavelength than a wave of the same frequency in air. Indeed, we found in Example 15.1 (Section 15.2) that a 262-Hz sound wave in air has a wavelength of only 1.31 m.

Dolphins emit high-frequency sound waves (typically 100,000 Hz) and use the echoes for guidance and for hunting. The corresponding wavelength in water is 1.48 cm. With this high-frequency "sonar" system they can sense objects that are roughly as small as the wavelength (but not much smaller). *Ultrasonic imaging* is a medical technique that uses exactly the same physical principle; sound waves of very high frequency and very short wavelength, called *ultrasound*, are scanned over the human body, and the "echoes" from interior organs are used to create an image. With ultrasound of frequency 5 MHz = 5×10^6 Hz, the wavelength in water (the primary constituent of the body) is 0.3 mm, and features as small as this can be discerned in the image. Ultrasound is used for the study of heart-valve action, detection of tumors, and prenatal examinations (Fig. 16.9). Ultrasound is more sensitive than x rays in distinguishing various kinds of tissues and does not have the radiation hazards associated with x rays.

Speed of Sound in a Gas

Most of the sound waves that we encounter on a daily basis propagate in air. To use Eq. (16.7) to find the speed of sound waves in air, we must keep in mind that the bulk modulus of a gas depends on the pressure of the gas: The greater the pressure applied to a gas to compress it, the more it resists further compression and hence the greater the bulk modulus. (That's why specific values of the bulk modulus for gases are not given in Table 11.1.) The expression for the bulk modulus of a gas for use in Eq. (16.7) is

$$B = \gamma p_0 \qquad (16.9)$$

where p_0 is the equilibrium pressure of the gas. The quantity γ (the Greek letter gamma) is called the *ratio of heat capacities*. It is a dimensionless number that characterizes the thermal properties of the gas. (We'll learn more about this quantity in Chapter 19.) As an example, the ratio of heat capacities for air is $\gamma = 1.40$. At normal atmospheric pressure $p_0 = 1.013 \times 10^5$ Pa, so $B = (1.40)(1.013 \times 10^5 \text{ Pa}) = 1.42 \times 10^5$ Pa. This value is minuscule compared to the bulk modulus of a typical solid (see Table 11.1), which is approximately 10^{10} to 10^{11} Pa. This shouldn't be surprising: It's simply a statement that air is far easier to compress than steel.

The density ρ of a gas also depends on the pressure, which in turn depends on the temperature. It turns out that the ratio B/ρ for a given type of ideal gas does *not* depend on the pressure at all, only the temperature. From Eq. (16.7), this means that the speed of sound in a gas is fundamentally a function of temperature T:

$$v = \sqrt{\frac{\gamma RT}{M}} \qquad \text{(speed of sound in an ideal gas)} \qquad (16.10)$$

This expression incorporates several quantities that you may recognize from your study of ideal gases in chemistry and that we will study in Chapters 17, 18, and 19. The temperature T is the *absolute* temperature in kelvins (K), equal to the Celsius temperature plus 273.15; thus 20.00°C corresponds to $T = 293.15$ K. The quantity M is the *molar mass*, or mass per mole of the substance of which the gas is composed. The *gas constant R* has the same value for all gases. The current best numerical value of R is

$$R = 8.314472(15) \text{ J/mol} \cdot \text{K}$$

which for practical calculations we can write as $8.314 \text{ J/mol} \cdot \text{K}$.

For any particular gas, γ, R, and M are constants, and the wave speed is proportional to the square root of the absolute temperature. We will see in Chapter 18 that Eq. (16.10) is almost identical to the expression for the average speed of molecules in an ideal gas. This shows that sound speeds and molecular speeds are closely related.

16.9 This three-dimensional image of a fetus in the womb was made using a sequence of ultrasound scans. Each individual scan reveals a two-dimensional "slice" through the fetus; many such slices were then combined digitally.

 Example 16.4 Speed of sound in air

Find the speed of sound in air at $T = 20$°C, and find the range of wavelengths in air to which the human ear (which can hear frequencies in the range of 20–20,000 Hz) is sensitive. The mean molar mass for air (a mixture of mostly nitrogen and oxygen) is $M = 28.8 \times 10^{-3}$ kg/mol and the ratio of heat capacities is $\gamma = 1.40$.

Continued

SOLUTION

IDENTIFY and SET UP: We use Eq. (16.10) to find the sound speed from γ, T, and M, and we use $v = f\lambda$ to find the wavelengths corresponding to the frequency limits. Note that in Eq. (16.10) temperature T *must* be expressed in kelvins, not Celsius degrees.

EXECUTE: At $T = 20°C = 293$ K, we find

$$v = \sqrt{\frac{\gamma RT}{M}} = \sqrt{\frac{(1.40)(8.314 \text{ J/mol} \cdot \text{K})(293 \text{ K})}{28.8 \times 10^{-3} \text{ kg/mol}}} = 344 \text{ m/s}$$

Using this value of v in $\lambda = v/f$, we find that at 20°C the frequency $f = 20$ Hz corresponds to $\lambda = 17$ m and $f = 20,000$ Hz to $\lambda = 1.7$ cm.

EVALUATE: Our calculated value of v agrees with the measured sound speed at $T = 20°C$ to within 0.3%.

In this discussion we have treated a gas as a continuous medium. A gas is actually composed of molecules in random motion, separated by distances that are large in comparison with their diameters. The vibrations that constitute a wave in a gas are superposed on the random thermal motion. At atmospheric pressure, a molecule travels an average distance of about 10^{-7} m between collisions, while the displacement amplitude of a faint sound may be only 10^{-9} m. We can think of a gas with a sound wave passing through as being comparable to a swarm of bees; the swarm as a whole oscillates slightly while individual insects move about through the swarm, apparently at random.

Test Your Understanding of Section 16.2   Mercury is 13.6 times denser than water. Based on Table 16.1, at 20°C which of these liquids has the greater bulk modulus? (i) mercury; (ii) water; (iii) both are about the same; (iv) not enough information is given to decide.

16.3 Sound Intensity

Traveling sound waves, like all other traveling waves, transfer energy from one region of space to another. We saw in Section 15.5 that a useful way to describe the energy carried by a sound wave is through the *wave intensity I*, equal to the time average rate at which energy is transported per unit area across a surface perpendicular to the direction of propagation. Let's see how to express the intensity of a sound wave in terms of the displacement amplitude A or pressure amplitude p_{max}.

Intensity and Displacement Amplitude

For simplicity, let us consider a sound wave propagating in the $+x$-direction so that we can use our expressions from Section 16.1 for the displacement $y(x, t)$ and pressure fluctuation $p(x, t)$—Eqs. (16.1) and (16.4), respectively. In Section 6.4 we saw that power equals the product of force and velocity [see Eq. (6.18)]. So the power per unit area in this sound wave equals the product of $p(x, t)$ (force per unit area) and the *particle* velocity $v_y(x, t)$. The particle velocity $v_y(x, t)$ is the velocity at time t of that portion of the wave medium at coordinate x. Using Eqs. (16.1) and (16.4), we find

$$v_y(x, t) = \frac{\partial y(x, t)}{\partial t} = \omega A \sin(kx - \omega t)$$

$$p(x, t)v_y(x, t) = [BkA \sin(kx - \omega t)][\omega A \sin(kx - \omega t)]$$

$$= B\omega k A^2 \sin^2(kx - \omega t)$$

CAUTION **Wave velocity vs. particle velocity** Remember that the velocity of the wave as a whole is *not* the same as the particle velocity. While the wave continues to move in the direction of propagation, individual particles in the wave medium merely slosh back and forth, as shown in Fig. 16.1. Furthermore, the maximum speed of a particle of the medium can be very different from the wave speed.

The intensity is, by definition, the time average value of $p(x, t)v_y(x, t)$. For any value of x the average value of the function $\sin^2(kx - \omega t)$ over one period $T = 2\pi/\omega$ is $\frac{1}{2}$, so

$$I = \tfrac{1}{2} B\omega k A^2 \qquad (16.11)$$

By using the relationships $\omega = vk$ and $v^2 = B/\rho$, we can transform Eq. (16.11) into the form

$$I = \tfrac{1}{2}\sqrt{\rho B}\,\omega^2 A^2 \qquad \text{(intensity of a sinusoidal sound wave)} \qquad (16.12)$$

This equation shows why in a stereo system, a low-frequency woofer has to vibrate with much larger amplitude than a high-frequency tweeter to produce the same sound intensity.

Intensity and Pressure Amplitude

It is usually more useful to express I in terms of the pressure amplitude p_{max}. Using Eq. (16.5) and the relationship $\omega = vk$, we find

$$I = \frac{\omega p_{max}^2}{2Bk} = \frac{v p_{max}^2}{2B} \qquad (16.13)$$

By using the wave speed relationship $v^2 = B/\rho$, we can also write Eq. (16.13) in the alternative forms

$$I = \frac{p_{max}^2}{2\rho v} = \frac{p_{max}^2}{2\sqrt{\rho B}} \qquad \text{(intensity of a sinusoidal sound wave)} \qquad (16.14)$$

You should verify these expressions. Comparison of Eqs. (16.12) and (16.14) shows that sinusoidal sound waves of the same intensity but different frequency have different displacement amplitudes A but the *same* pressure amplitude p_{max}. This is another reason it is usually more convenient to describe a sound wave in terms of pressure fluctuations, not displacement.

The *total* average power carried across a surface by a sound wave equals the product of the intensity at the surface and the surface area, if the intensity over the surface is uniform. The average total sound power emitted by a person speaking in an ordinary conversational tone is about 10^{-5} W, while a loud shout corresponds to about 3×10^{-2} W. If all the residents of New York City were to talk at the same time, the total sound power would be about 100 W, equivalent to the electric power requirement of a medium-sized light bulb. On the other hand, the power required to fill a large auditorium or stadium with loud sound is considerable (see Example 16.7.)

If the sound source emits waves in all directions equally, the intensity decreases with increasing distance r from the source according to the inverse-square law: The intensity is proportional to $1/r^2$. We discussed this law and its consequences in Section 15.5. If the sound goes predominantly in one direction, the inverse-square law does not apply and the intensity decreases with distance more slowly than $1/r^2$ (Fig. 16.10).

16.10 By cupping your hands like this, you direct the sound waves emerging from your mouth so that they don't propagate to the sides. Hence the intensity decreases with distance more slowly than the inverse-square law would predict, and you can be heard at greater distances.

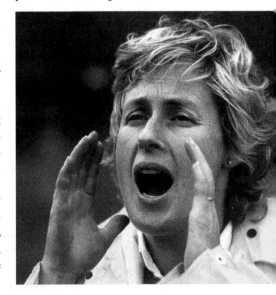

The inverse-square relationship also does not apply indoors because sound energy can reach a listener by reflection from the walls and ceiling. Indeed, part of the architect's job in designing an auditorium is to tailor these reflections so that the intensity is as nearly uniform as possible over the entire auditorium.

Problem-Solving Strategy 16.1   Sound Intensity

IDENTIFY *the relevant concepts:* The relationships between the intensity and amplitude of a sound wave are straightforward. Other quantities are involved in these relationships, however, so it's particularly important to decide which is your target variable.

SET UP *the problem* using the following steps:
1. Sort the physical quantities into categories. Wave properties include the displacement and pressure amplitudes A and p_{max} and the frequency f, which can be determined from the angular frequency ω, the wave number k, or the wavelength λ. These quantities are related through the wave speed v, which is determined by properties of the medium (B and ρ for a liquid, and γ, T, and M for a gas).

2. List the given quantities and identify the target variables. Find relationships that take you where you want to go.

EXECUTE *the solution*: Use your selected equations to solve for the target variables. Express the temperature in kelvins (Celsius temperature plus 273.15) to calculate the speed of sound in a gas.

EVALUATE *your answer:* If possible, use an alternative relationship to check your results.

Example 16.5   Intensity of a sound wave in air

Find the intensity of the sound wave in Example 16.1, with $p_{max} = 3.0 \times 10^{-2}$ Pa. Assume the temperature is 20°C so that the density of air is $\rho = 1.20$ kg/m^3 and the speed of sound is $v = 344$ m/s.

SOLUTION

IDENTIFY and SET UP: Our target variable is the intensity I of the sound wave. We are given the pressure amplitude p_{max} of the wave as well as the density ρ and wave speed v for the medium. We can determine I from p_{max}, ρ, and v using Eq. (16.14).

EXECUTE: From Eq. (16.14),

$$I = \frac{p_{max}^2}{2\rho v} = \frac{(3.0 \times 10^{-2}\text{ Pa})^2}{2(1.20\text{ kg/m}^3)(344\text{ m/s})}$$
$$= 1.1 \times 10^{-6}\text{ J/(s} \cdot \text{m}^2) = 1.1 \times 10^{-6}\text{ W/m}^2$$

EVALUATE: This seems like a very low intensity, but it is well within the range of sound intensities encountered on a daily basis. A very loud sound wave at the threshold of pain has a pressure amplitude of about 30 Pa and an intensity of about 1 W/m^2. The pressure amplitude of the faintest sound wave that can be heard is about 3×10^{-5} Pa, and the corresponding intensity is about 10^{-12} W/m^2. (Try these values of p_{max} in Eq. (16.14) to check that the corresponding intensities are as we have stated.)

Example 16.6   Same intensity, different frequencies

What are the pressure and displacement amplitudes of a 20-Hz sound wave with the same intensity as the 1000-Hz sound wave of Examples 16.1 and 16.5?

SOLUTION

IDENTIFY and SET UP: In Examples 16.1 and 16.5 we found that for a 1000-Hz sound wave with $p_{max} = 3.0 \times 10^{-2}$ Pa, $A = 1.2 \times 10^{-8}$ m and $I = 1.1 \times 10^{-6}$ W/m^2. Our target variables are p_{max} and A for a 20-Hz sound wave of the same intensity I. We can find these using Eqs. (16.14) and (16.12), respectively.

EXECUTE: We can rearrange Eqs. (16.14) and (16.12) as $p_{max}^2 = 2I\sqrt{\rho B}$ and $\omega^2 A^2 = 2I/\sqrt{\rho B}$, respectively. These tell us that for a given sound intensity I in a given medium (constant ρ and B), the

quantities p_{max} and ωA (or, equivalently, fA) are both *constants* that don't depend on frequency. From the first result we immediately have $p_{max} = 3.0 \times 10^{-2}$ Pa for $f = 20$ Hz, the same as for $f = 1000$ Hz. If write the second result as $f_{20}A_{20} = f_{1000}A_{1000}$, we have

$$A_{20} = \left(\frac{f_{1000}}{f_{20}}\right)A_{1000}$$
$$= \left(\frac{1000\text{ Hz}}{20\text{ Hz}}\right)(1.2 \times 10^{-8}\text{ m}) = 6.0 \times 10^{-7}\text{ m} = 0.60\ \mu\text{m}$$

EVALUATE: Our result reinforces the idea that pressure amplitude is a more convenient description of a sound wave and its intensity than displacement amplitude.

Example 16.7 **"Play it loud!"**

For an outdoor concert we want the sound intensity to be $1 \ \text{W/m}^2$ at a distance of 20 m from the speaker array. If the sound intensity is uniform in all directions, what is the required acoustic power output of the array?

SOLUTION

IDENTIFY, SET UP, and EXECUTE: This example uses the definition of sound intensity as power per unit area. The total power is the target variable; the area in question is a hemisphere centered on the speaker array. We assume that the speakers are on the ground and that none of the acoustic power is directed into the ground, so the acoustic power is uniform over a hemisphere 20 m in radius. The surface area of this hemisphere is $(\frac{1}{2})(4\pi)(20 \ \text{m})^2$, or about $2500 \ \text{m}^2$. The required power is the product of this area and the intensity: $(1 \ \text{W/m}^2)(2500 \ \text{m}^2) = 2500 \ \text{W} = 2.5 \ \text{kW}$.

EVALUATE: The electrical power input to the speaker would need to be considerably greater than 2.5 kW, because speaker efficiency is not very high (typically a few percent for ordinary speakers, and up to 25% for horn-type speakers).

The Decibel Scale

Because the ear is sensitive over a broad range of intensities, a *logarithmic* intensity scale is usually used. The **sound intensity level** β of a sound wave is defined by the equation

$$\beta = (10 \ \text{dB}) \log \frac{I}{I_0} \qquad \text{(definition of sound intensity level)} \qquad (16.15)$$

In this equation, I_0 is a reference intensity, chosen to be $10^{-12} \ \text{W/m}^2$, approximately the threshold of human hearing at 1000 Hz. Recall that "log" means the logarithm to base 10. Sound intensity levels are expressed in **decibels,** abbreviated dB. A decibel is $\frac{1}{10}$ of a *bel,* a unit named for Alexander Graham Bell (the inventor of the telephone). The bel is inconveniently large for most purposes, and the decibel is the usual unit of sound intensity level.

If the intensity of a sound wave equals I_0 or $10^{-12} \ \text{W/m}^2$, its sound intensity level is 0 dB. An intensity of $1 \ \text{W/m}^2$ corresponds to 120 dB. Table 16.2 gives the sound intensity levels in decibels of some familiar sounds. You can use Eq. (16.15) to check the value of sound intensity level β given for each intensity in the table.

Because the ear is not equally sensitive to all frequencies in the audible range, some sound-level meters weight the various frequencies unequally. One such scheme leads to the so-called dBA scale; this scale deemphasizes the low and very high frequencies, where the ear is less sensitive than at midrange frequencies.

Table 16.2 Sound Intensity Levels from Various Sources (Representative Values)

Source or Description of Sound	Sound Intensity Level, β (dB)	Intensity, $I \ (\text{W/m}^2)$
Military jet aircraft 30 m away	140	10^2
Threshold of pain	120	1
Riveter	95	3.2×10^{-3}
Elevated train	90	10^{-3}
Busy street traffic	70	10^{-5}
Ordinary conversation	65	3.2×10^{-6}
Quiet automobile	50	10^{-7}
Quiet radio in home	40	10^{-8}
Average whisper	20	10^{-10}
Rustle of leaves	10	10^{-11}
Threshold of hearing at 1000 Hz	0	10^{-12}

Example 16.8 **Temporary—or permanent—hearing loss**

A 10-min exposure to 120-dB sound will temporarily shift your threshold of hearing at 1000 Hz from 0 dB up to 28 dB. Ten years of exposure to 92-dB sound will cause a *permanent* shift to 28 dB. What sound intensities correspond to 28 dB and 92 dB?

SOLUTION

IDENTIFY and SET UP: We are given two sound intensity levels β; our target variables are the corresponding intensities. We can solve Eq. (16.15) to find the intensity I that corresponds to each value of β.

EXECUTE: We solve Eq. (16.15) for I by dividing both sides by 10 dB and using the relationship $10^{\log x} = x$:

$$I = I_0 10^{\beta/(10\ \text{dB})}$$

For $\beta = 28$ dB and $\beta = 92$ dB, the exponents are $\beta/(10\ \text{dB}) = 2.8$ and 9.2, respectively, so that

$$I_{28\ \text{dB}} = (10^{-12}\ \text{W/m}^2)10^{2.8} = 6.3 \times 10^{-10}\ \text{W/m}^2$$
$$I_{92\ \text{dB}} = (10^{-12}\ \text{W/m}^2)10^{9.2} = 1.6 \times 10^{-3}\ \text{W/m}^2$$

EVALUATE: If your answers are a factor of 10 too large, you may have entered 10×10^{-12} in your calculator instead of 1×10^{-12}. Be careful!

Example 16.9 **A bird sings in a meadow**

Consider an idealized bird (treated as a point source) that emits constant sound power, with intensity obeying the inverse-square law (Fig. 16.11). If you move twice the distance from the bird, by how many decibels does the sound intensity level drop?

SOLUTION

IDENTIFY and SET UP: The decibel scale is logarithmic, so the *difference* between two sound intensity levels (the target variable) corresponds to the *ratio* of the corresponding intensities, which is determined by the inverse-square law. We label the two points P_1 and P_2 (Fig. 16.11). We use Eq. (16.15), the definition of sound intensity level, at each point. We use Eq. (15.26), the inverse-square law, to relate the intensities at the two points.

EXECUTE: The difference $\beta_2 - \beta_1$ between any two sound intensity levels is related to the corresponding intensities by

$$\beta_2 - \beta_1 = (10\ \text{dB})\left(\log\frac{I_2}{I_0} - \log\frac{I_1}{I_0}\right)$$
$$= (10\ \text{dB})[(\log I_2 - \log I_0) - (\log I_1 - \log I_0)]$$
$$= (10\ \text{dB})\log\frac{I_2}{I_1}$$

For this inverse-square-law source, Eq. (15.26) yields $I_2/I_1 = r_1{}^2/r_2{}^2 = \frac{1}{4}$, so

$$\beta_2 - \beta_1 = (10\ \text{dB})\log\frac{I_1}{I_2} = (10\ \text{dB})\log\tfrac{1}{4} = -6.0\ \text{dB}$$

16.11 When you double your distance from a point source of sound, by how much does the sound intensity level decrease?

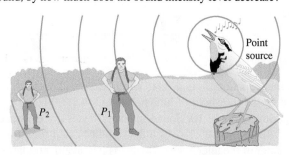

EVALUATE: Our result is negative, which tells us (correctly) that the sound intensity level is less at P_2 than at P_1. The 6-dB difference doesn't depend on the sound intensity level at P_1; *any* doubling of the distance from an inverse-square-law source reduces the sound intensity level by 6 dB.

Note that the perceived *loudness* of a sound is not directly proportional to its intensity. For example, most people interpret an increase of 8 dB to 10 dB in sound intensity level (corresponding to increasing intensity by a factor of 6 to 10) as a doubling of loudness.

Test Your Understanding of Section 16.3 You double the intensity of a sound wave in air while leaving the frequency unchanged. (The pressure, density, and temperature of the air remain unchanged as well.) What effect does this have on the displacement amplitude, pressure amplitude, bulk modulus, sound speed, and sound intensity level?

16.4 Standing Sound Waves and Normal Modes

When longitudinal (sound) waves propagate in a fluid in a pipe with finite length, the waves are reflected from the ends in the same way that transverse waves on a string are reflected at its ends. The superposition of the waves traveling in opposite directions again forms a standing wave. Just as for transverse standing waves on a string (see Section 15.7), standing sound waves (normal modes) in a pipe can

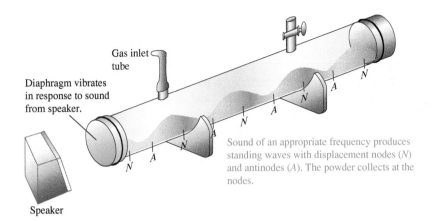

16.12 Demonstrating standing sound waves using a Kundt's tube. The blue shading represents the density of the gas at an instant when the gas pressure at the displacement nodes is a maximum or a minimum.

Gas inlet tube

Diaphragm vibrates in response to sound from speaker.

Speaker

Sound of an appropriate frequency produces standing waves with displacement nodes (*N*) and antinodes (*A*). The powder collects at the nodes.

be used to create sound waves in the surrounding air. This is the operating principle of the human voice as well as many musical instruments, including woodwinds, brasses, and pipe organs.

Transverse waves on a string, including standing waves, are usually described only in terms of the displacement of the string. But, as we have seen, sound waves in a fluid may be described either in terms of the displacement of the fluid or in terms of the pressure variation in the fluid. To avoid confusion, we'll use the terms **displacement node** and **displacement antinode** to refer to points where particles of the fluid have zero displacement and maximum displacement, respectively.

We can demonstrate standing sound waves in a column of gas using an apparatus called a Kundt's tube (Fig. 16.12). A horizontal glass tube a meter or so long is closed at one end and has a flexible diaphragm at the other end that can transmit vibrations. A nearby loudspeaker is driven by an audio oscillator and amplifier; this produces sound waves that force the diaphragm to vibrate sinusoidally with a frequency that we can vary. The sound waves within the tube are reflected at the other, closed end of the tube. We spread a small amount of light powder uniformly along the bottom of the tube. As we vary the frequency of the sound, we pass through frequencies at which the amplitude of the standing waves becomes large enough for the powder to be swept along the tube at those points where the gas is in motion. The powder therefore collects at the displacement nodes (where the gas is not moving). Adjacent nodes are separated by a distance equal to $\lambda/2$, and we can measure this distance. Given the wavelength, we can use this experiment to determine the wave speed: We read the frequency f from the oscillator dial, and we can then calculate the speed v of the waves from the relationship $v = \lambda f$.

Figure 16.13 shows the motions of nine different particles within a gas-filled tube in which there is a standing sound wave. A particle at a displacement node (*N*) does not move, while a particle at a displacement antinode (*A*) oscillates with maximum amplitude. Note that particles on opposite sides of a displacement node vibrate in opposite phase. When these particles approach each other, the gas between them is compressed and the pressure rises; when they recede from each other, there is an expansion and the pressure drops. Hence at a displacement *node* the gas undergoes the maximum amount of compression and expansion, and the variations in pressure and density above and below the average have their maximum value. By contrast, particles on opposite sides of a displacement *antinode* vibrate *in phase;* the distance between the particles is nearly constant, and there is *no* variation in pressure or density at a displacement antinode.

We use the term **pressure node** to describe a point in a standing sound wave at which the pressure and density do not vary and the term **pressure antinode** to describe a point at which the variations in pressure and density are greatest. Using these terms, we can summarize our observations about standing sound waves as follows:

A pressure node is always a displacement antinode, and a pressure antinode is always a displacement node.

16.13 In a standing sound wave, a displacement node *N* is a pressure antinode (a point where the pressure fluctuates the most) and a displacement antinode *A* is a pressure node (a point where the pressure does not fluctuate at all).

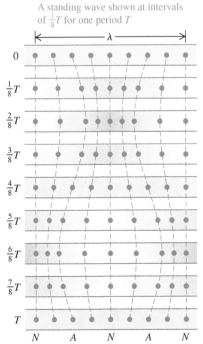

A standing wave shown at intervals of $\frac{1}{8}T$ for one period *T*

N = a displacement node = a pressure antinode
A = a displacement antinode = a pressure node

Figure 16.12 depicts a standing sound wave at an instant at which the pressure variations are greatest; the blue shading shows that the density and pressure of the gas have their maximum and minimum values at the displacement nodes.

When reflection takes place at a *closed* end of a pipe (an end with a rigid barrier or plug), the displacement of the particles at this end must always be zero, analogous to a fixed end of a string. Thus a closed end of a pipe is a displacement node and a pressure antinode; the particles do not move, but the pressure variations are maximum. An *open* end of a pipe is a pressure node because it is open to the atmosphere, where the pressure is constant. Because of this, an open end is always a displacement *antinode*, in analogy to a free end of a string; the particles oscillate with maximum amplitude, but the pressure does not vary. (Strictly speaking, the pressure node actually occurs somewhat beyond an open end of a pipe. But if the diameter of the pipe is small in comparison to the wavelength, which is true for most musical instruments, this effect can safely be neglected.) Thus longitudinal waves in a column of fluid are reflected at the closed and open ends of a pipe in the same way that transverse waves in a string are reflected at fixed and free ends, respectively.

Conceptual Example 16.10	The sound of silence

A directional loudspeaker directs a sound wave of wavelength λ at a wall (Fig. 16.14). At what distances from the wall could you stand and hear no sound at all?

SOLUTION

Your ear detects pressure variations in the air; you will therefore hear no sound if your ear is at a *pressure node*, which is a displacement antinode. The wall is at a displacement node; the distance from any node to an adjacent antinode is $\lambda/4$, and the distance from one antinode to the next is $\lambda/2$ (Fig. 16.14). Hence the displacement antinodes (pressure nodes), at which no sound will be heard, are at distances $d = \lambda/4$, $d = \lambda/4 + \lambda/2 = 3\lambda/4$, $d = 3\lambda/4 + \lambda/2 = 5\lambda/4$, . . . from the wall. If the loudspeaker is not highly directional, this effect is hard to notice because of reflections of sound waves from the floor, ceiling, and other walls.

16.14 When a sound wave is directed at a wall, it interferes with the reflected wave to create a standing wave. The N's and A's are *displacement* nodes and antinodes.

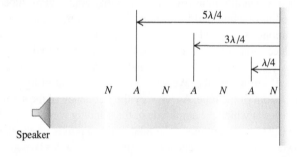

Organ Pipes and Wind Instruments

16.15 Organ pipes of different sizes produce tones with different frequencies.

The most important application of standing sound waves is the production of musical tones by wind instruments. Organ pipes are one of the simplest examples (Fig. 16.15). Air is supplied by a blower, at a gauge pressure typically of the order of 10^3 Pa (10^{-2} atm), to the bottom end of the pipe (Fig. 16.16). A stream of air emerges from the narrow opening at the edge of the horizontal surface and is directed against the top edge of the opening, which is called the *mouth* of the pipe. The column of air in the pipe is set into vibration, and there is a series of possible normal modes, just as with the stretched string. The mouth always acts as an open end; thus it is a pressure node and a displacement antinode. The other end of the pipe (at the top in Fig. 16.16) may be either open or closed.

In Fig. 16.17, both ends of the pipe are open, so both ends are pressure nodes and displacement antinodes. An organ pipe that is open at both ends is called an *open pipe*. The fundamental frequency f_1 corresponds to a standing-wave pattern with a displacement antinode at each end and a displacement node in the middle (Fig. 16.17a). The distance between adjacent antinodes is always equal to one half-wavelength, and in this case that is equal to the length L of the pipe; $\lambda/2 = L$. The corresponding frequency, obtained from the relationship $f = v/\lambda$, is

$$f_1 = \frac{v}{2L} \quad \text{(open pipe)} \tag{16.16}$$

Figures 16.17b and 16.17c show the second and third harmonics (first and second overtones); their vibration patterns have two and three displacement nodes, respectively. For these, a half-wavelength is equal to $L/2$ and $L/3$, respectively, and the frequencies are twice and three times the fundamental, respectively. That is, $f_2 = 2f_1$ and $f_3 = 3f_1$. For *every* normal mode of an open pipe the length L must be an integer number of half-wavelengths, and the possible wavelengths λ_n are given by

$$L = n\frac{\lambda_n}{2} \quad \text{or} \quad \lambda_n = \frac{2L}{n} \quad (n = 1, 2, 3, \ldots) \quad \text{(open pipe)} \tag{16.17}$$

The corresponding frequencies f_n are given by $f_n = v/\lambda_n$, so all the normal-mode frequencies for a pipe that is open at both ends are given by

$$f_n = \frac{nv}{2L} \quad (n = 1, 2, 3, \ldots) \quad \text{(open pipe)} \tag{16.18}$$

The value $n = 1$ corresponds to the fundamental frequency, $n = 2$ to the second harmonic (or first overtone), and so on. Alternatively, we can say

$$f_n = nf_1 \quad (n = 1, 2, 3, \ldots) \quad \text{(open pipe)} \tag{16.19}$$

with f_1 given by Eq. (16.16).

Figure 16.18 shows a pipe that is open at the left end but closed at the right end. This is called a *stopped pipe*. The left (open) end is a displacement antinode (pressure node), but the right (closed) end is a displacement node (pressure antinode). The distance between a node and the adjacent antinode is always one quarter-wavelength. Figure 16.18a shows the lowest-frequency mode; the length

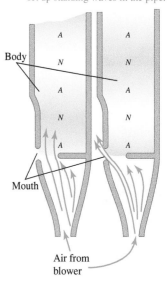

16.16 Cross sections of an organ pipe at two instants one half-period apart. The N's and A's are *displacement* nodes and antinodes; as the blue shading shows, these are points of maximum pressure variation and zero pressure variation, respectively.

16.17 A cross section of an open pipe showing the first three normal modes. The shading indicates the pressure variations. The red curves are graphs of the displacement along the pipe axis at two instants separated in time by one half-period. The N's and A's are the *displacement* nodes and antinodes; interchange these to show the *pressure* nodes and antinodes.

(a) Fundamental: $f_1 = \dfrac{v}{2L}$

(b) Second harmonic: $f_2 = 2\dfrac{v}{2L} = 2f_1$

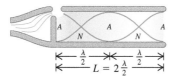

(c) Third harmonic: $f_3 = 3\dfrac{v}{2L} = 3f_1$

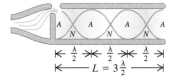

16.18 A cross section of a stopped pipe showing the first three normal modes as well as the *displacement* nodes and antinodes. Only odd harmonics are possible.

(a) Fundamental: $f_1 = \dfrac{v}{4L}$

(b) Third harmonic: $f_3 = 3\dfrac{v}{4L} = 3f_1$

(c) Fifth harmonic: $f_5 = 5\dfrac{v}{4L} = 5f_1$

of the pipe is a quarter-wavelength $(L = \lambda_1/4)$. The fundamental frequency is $f_1 = v/\lambda_1$, or

$$f_1 = \frac{v}{4L} \quad \text{(stopped pipe)} \tag{16.20}$$

This is one-half the fundamental frequency for an *open* pipe of the same length. In musical language, the *pitch* of a closed pipe is one octave lower (a factor of 2 in frequency) than that of an open pipe of the same length. Figure 16.18b shows the next mode, for which the length of the pipe is *three-quarters* of a wavelength, corresponding to a frequency $3f_1$. For Fig. 16.18c, $L = 5\lambda/4$ and the frequency is $5f_1$. The possible wavelengths are given by

$$L = n\frac{\lambda_n}{4} \quad \text{or} \quad \lambda_n = \frac{4L}{n} \quad (n = 1, 3, 5, \ldots) \quad \text{(stopped pipe)} \tag{16.21}$$

The normal-mode frequencies are given by $f_n = v/\lambda_n$, or

$$f_n = \frac{nv}{4L} \quad (n = 1, 3, 5, \ldots) \quad \text{(stopped pipe)} \tag{16.22}$$

or

$$f_n = nf_1 \quad (n = 1, 3, 5, \ldots) \quad \text{(stopped pipe)} \tag{16.23}$$

with f_1 given by Eq. (16.20). We see that the second, fourth, and all *even* harmonics are missing. In a pipe that is closed at one end, the fundamental frequency is $f_1 = v/4L$, and only the odd harmonics in the series $(3f_1, 5f_1, \ldots)$ are possible.

A final possibility is a pipe that is closed at *both* ends, with displacement nodes and pressure antinodes at both ends. This wouldn't be of much use as a musical instrument because there would be no way for the vibrations to get out of the pipe.

Example 16.11   A tale of two pipes

On a day when the speed of sound is 345 m/s, the fundamental frequency of a particular stopped organ pipe is 220 Hz. (a) How long is this pipe? (b) The second *overtone* of this pipe has the same wavelength as the third *harmonic* of an *open* pipe. How long is the open pipe?

SOLUTION

IDENTIFY and SET UP: This problem uses the relationship between the length and normal-mode frequencies of open pipes (Fig. 16.17) and stopped pipes (Fig. 16.18). In part (a), we determine the length of the stopped pipe from Eq. (16.22). In part (b), we must determine the length of an open pipe, for which Eq. (16.18) gives the frequencies.

EXECUTE: (a) For a stopped pipe $f_1 = v/4L$, so

$$L_{\text{stopped}} = \frac{v}{4f_1} = \frac{345 \text{ m/s}}{4(220 \text{ s}^{-1})} = 0.392 \text{ m}$$

(b) The frequency of the second overtone of a stopped pipe (the *third* possible frequency) is $f_5 = 5f_1 = 5(220 \text{ Hz}) = 1100 \text{ Hz}$. If the wavelengths for the two pipes are the same, the frequencies are also the same. Hence the frequency of the third harmonic of the open pipe, which is at $3f_1 = 3(v/2L)$, equals 1100 Hz. Then

$$1100 \text{ Hz} = 3\left(\frac{345 \text{ m/s}}{2L_{\text{open}}}\right) \quad \text{and} \quad L_{\text{open}} = 0.470 \text{ m}$$

EVALUATE: The 0.392-m stopped pipe has a fundamental frequency of 220 Hz; the *longer* (0.470-m) open pipe has a *higher* fundamental frequency, $(1100 \text{ Hz})/3 = 367 \text{ Hz}$. This is not a contradiction, as you can see if you compare Figs. 16.17a and 16.18a.

In an organ pipe in actual use, several modes are always present at once; the motion of the air is a superposition of these modes. This situation is analogous to a string that is struck or plucked, as in Fig. 15.28. Just as for a vibrating string, a complex standing wave in the pipe produces a traveling sound wave in the surrounding air with a harmonic content similar to that of the standing wave. A very narrow pipe produces a sound wave rich in higher harmonics, which we hear as a thin and "stringy" tone; a fatter pipe produces mostly the fundamental mode, heard as a softer, more flutelike tone. The harmonic content also depends on the shape of the pipe's mouth.

We have talked about organ pipes, but this discussion is also applicable to other wind instruments. The flute and the recorder are directly analogous. The most significant difference is that those instruments have holes along the pipe. Opening and closing the holes with the fingers changes the effective length L of the air column and thus changes the pitch. Any individual organ pipe, by comparison, can play only a single note. The flute and recorder behave as *open* pipes, while the clarinet acts as a *stopped* pipe (closed at the reed end, open at the bell).

Equations (16.18) and (16.22) show that the frequencies of any wind instrument are proportional to the speed of sound v in the air column inside the instrument. As Eq. (16.10) shows, v depends on temperature; it increases when temperature increases. Thus the pitch of all wind instruments rises with increasing temperature. An organ that has some of its pipes at one temperature and others at a different temperature is bound to sound out of tune.

Test Your Understanding of Section 16.4 If you connect a hose to one end of a metal pipe and blow compressed air into it, the pipe produces a musical tone. If instead you blow compressed helium into the pipe at the same pressure and temperature, will the pipe produce (i) the same tone, (ii) a higher-pitch tone, or (iii) a lower-pitch tone?

16.5 Resonance and Sound

Many mechanical systems have normal modes of oscillation. As we have seen, these include columns of air (as in an organ pipe) and stretched strings (as in a guitar; see Section 15.8). In each mode, every particle of the system oscillates with simple harmonic motion at the same frequency as the mode. Air columns and stretched strings have an infinite series of normal modes, but the basic concept is closely related to the simple harmonic oscillator, discussed in Chapter 14, which has only a single normal mode (that is, only one frequency at which it oscillates after being disturbed).

Suppose we apply a periodically varying force to a system that can oscillate. The system is then forced to oscillate with a frequency equal to the frequency of the applied force (called the *driving frequency*). This motion is called a *forced oscillation*. We talked about forced oscillations of the harmonic oscillator in Section 14.8, and we suggest that you review that discussion. In particular, we described the phenomenon of mechanical **resonance.** A simple example of resonance is pushing Cousin Throckmorton on a swing. The swing is a pendulum; it has only a single normal mode, with a frequency determined by its length. If we push the swing periodically with this frequency, we can build up the amplitude of the motion. But if we push with a very different frequency, the swing hardly moves at all.

Resonance also occurs when a periodically varying force is applied to a system with many normal modes. An example is shown in Fig. 16.19a. An open organ pipe is placed next to a loudspeaker that is driven by an amplifier and emits pure sinusoidal sound waves of frequency f, which can be varied by adjusting the amplifier. The air in the pipe is forced to vibrate with the same frequency f as the *driving force* provided by the loudspeaker. In general the amplitude of this motion is relatively small, and the air inside the pipe will not move in any of the normal-mode patterns shown in Fig. 16.17. But if the frequency f of the force is close to one of the normal-mode frequencies, the air in the pipe moves in the normal-mode pattern for that frequency, and the amplitude can become quite large. Figure 16.19b shows the amplitude of oscillation of the air

16.19 (a) The air in an open pipe is forced to oscillate at the same frequency as the sinusoidal sound waves coming from the loudspeaker. (b) The resonance curve of the open pipe graphs the amplitude of the standing sound wave in the pipe as a function of the driving frequency.

(a)

Speaker emits frequency f

Open organ pipe

• Air in pipe oscillates at the same frequency f emitted by the speaker.
• Wave amplitude A depends on frequency.

Amplifier

(b) Resonance curve: graph of amplitude A versus driving frequency f. Peaks occur at normal-mode frequencies of the pipe: f_1, $f_2 = 2f_1$, $f_3 = 3f_1$, ...

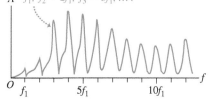

Application Resonance and the Sensitivity of the Ear
The auditory canal of the human ear (see Fig. 16.4) is an air-filled pipe open at one end and closed at the other (eardrum) end. The canal is about 2.5 cm = 0.025 m long, so it has a resonance at its fundamental frequency $f_1 = v/4L = (344 \text{ m/s})/[4(0.025 \text{ m})] = 3440$ Hz. The resonance means that a sound at this frequency produces a strong oscillation of the eardrum. That's why your ear is most sensitive to sounds near 3440 Hz.

in the pipe as a function of the driving frequency f. The shape of this graph is called the **resonance curve** of the pipe; it has peaks where f equals the normal-mode frequencies of the pipe. The detailed shape of the resonance curve depends on the geometry of the pipe.

If the frequency of the force is precisely *equal* to a normal-mode frequency, the system is in resonance, and the amplitude of the forced oscillation is maximum. If there were no friction or other energy-dissipating mechanism, a driving force at a normal-mode frequency would continue to add energy to the system, and the amplitude would increase indefinitely. In such an idealized case the peaks in the resonance curve of Fig. 16.19b would be infinitely high. But in any real system there is always some dissipation of energy, or damping, as we discussed in Section 14.8; the amplitude of oscillation in resonance may be large, but it cannot be infinite.

The "sound of the ocean" you hear when you put your ear next to a large seashell is due to resonance. The noise of the outside air moving past the seashell is a mixture of sound waves of almost all audible frequencies, which forces the air inside the seashell to oscillate. The seashell behaves like an organ pipe, with a set of normal-mode frequencies; hence the inside air oscillates most strongly at those frequencies, producing the seashell's characteristic sound. To hear a similar phenomenon, uncap a full bottle of your favorite beverage and blow across the open top. The noise is provided by your breath blowing across the top, and the "organ pipe" is the column of air inside the bottle above the surface of the liquid. If you take a drink and repeat the experiment, you will hear a lower tone because the "pipe" is longer and the normal-mode frequencies are lower.

Resonance also occurs when a stretched string is forced to oscillate (see Section 15.8). Suppose that one end of a stretched string is held fixed while the other is given a transverse sinusoidal motion with small amplitude, setting up standing waves. If the frequency of the driving mechanism is *not* equal to one of the normal-mode frequencies of the string, the amplitude at the antinodes is fairly small. However, if the frequency is equal to any one of the normal-mode frequencies, the string is in resonance, and the amplitude at the antinodes is very much larger than that at the driven end. The driven end is not precisely a node, but it lies much closer to a node than to an antinode when the string is in resonance. The photographs in Fig. 15.23 were made this way, with the left end of the string fixed and the right end oscillating vertically with small amplitude; large-amplitude standing waves resulted when the frequency of oscillation of the right end was equal to the fundamental frequency or to one of the first three overtones.

It is easy to demonstrate resonance with a piano. Push down the damper pedal (the right-hand pedal) so that the dampers are lifted and the strings are free to vibrate, and then sing a steady tone into the piano. When you stop singing, the piano seems to continue to sing the same note. The sound waves from your voice excite vibrations in the strings that have natural frequencies close to the frequencies (fundamental and harmonics) present in the note you sang.

A more spectacular example is a singer breaking a wine glass with her amplified voice. A good-quality wine glass has normal-mode frequencies that you can hear by tapping it. If the singer emits a loud note with a frequency corresponding exactly to one of these normal-mode frequencies, large-amplitude oscillations can build up and break the glass (Fig. 16.20).

16.20 The frequency of the sound from this trumpet exactly matches one of the normal-mode frequencies of the goblet. The resonant vibrations of the goblet have such large amplitude that the goblet tears itself apart.

Example 16.12 **An organ–guitar duet**

A stopped organ pipe is sounded near a guitar, causing one of the strings to vibrate with large amplitude. We vary the string tension until we find the maximum amplitude. The string is 80% as long as the pipe. If both pipe and string vibrate at their fundamental frequency, calculate the ratio of the wave speed on the string to the speed of sound in air.

SOLUTION

IDENTIFY and SET UP: The large response of the string is an example of resonance. It occurs because the organ pipe and the guitar string have the same fundamental frequency. Letting the subscripts a and s stand for the air in the pipe and the string, respectively, the condition for resonance is $f_{1a} = f_{1s}$. Equation (16.20) gives the fundamental frequency for a stopped pipe, and Eq. (15.32) gives the fundamental frequency for a guitar string held at both ends. These expressions involve the wave speed in air (v_a) and on the string (v_s) and the lengths of the pipe and string. We are given that $L_s = 0.80L_a$; our target variable is the ratio v_s/v_a.

EXECUTE: From Eqs. (16.20) and (15.32), $f_{1a} = v_a/4L_a$ and $f_{1s} = v_s/2L_s$. These frequencies are equal, so

$$\frac{v_a}{4L_a} = \frac{v_s}{2L_s}$$

Substituting $L_s = 0.80L_a$ and rearranging, we get $v_s/v_a = 0.40$.

EVALUATE: As an example, if the speed of sound in air is 345 m/s, the wave speed on the string is $(0.40)(345\ \text{m/s}) = 138\ \text{m/s}$. Note that while the standing waves in the pipe and on the string have the same frequency, they have different *wavelengths* $\lambda = v/f$ because the two media have different wave speeds v. Which standing wave has the greater wavelength?

Test Your Understanding of Section 16.5   A stopped organ pipe of length L has a fundamental frequency of 220 Hz. For which of the following organ pipes will there be a resonance if a tuning fork of frequency 660 Hz is sounded next to the pipe? (There may be more than one correct answer.) (i) a stopped organ pipe of length L; (ii) a stopped organ pipe of length $2L$; (iii) an open organ pipe of length L; (iii) an open organ pipe of length $2L$.

16.6 Interference of Waves

Wave phenomena that occur when two or more waves overlap in the same region of space are grouped under the heading *interference*. As we have seen, standing waves are a simple example of an interference effect: Two waves traveling in opposite directions in a medium combine to produce a standing wave pattern with nodes and antinodes that do not move.

Figure 16.21 shows an example of another type of interference that involves waves that spread out in space. Two speakers, driven in phase by the same amplifier, emit identical sinusoidal sound waves with the same constant frequency. We place a microphone at point P in the figure, equidistant from the speakers. Wave crests emitted from the two speakers at the same time travel equal distances and arrive at point P at the same time; hence the waves arrive in phase, and there is constructive interference. The total wave amplitude at P is twice the amplitude from each individual wave, and we can measure this combined amplitude with the microphone.

Now let's move the microphone to point Q, where the distances from the two speakers to the microphone differ by a half-wavelength. Then the two waves arrive a half-cycle out of step, or *out of phase;* a positive crest from one speaker arrives at the same time as a negative crest from the other. Destructive interference takes place, and the amplitude measured by the microphone is much *smaller* than when only one speaker is present. If the amplitudes from the two speakers are equal, the two waves cancel each other out completely at point Q, and the total amplitude there is zero.

CAUTION   **Interference and traveling waves**   Although this situation bears some resemblance to standing waves in a pipe, the total wave in Fig. 16.21 is a *traveling* wave, not a standing wave. To see why, recall that in a standing wave there is no net flow of energy in any direction. By contrast, in Fig. 16.21 there is an overall flow of energy from the speakers into the surrounding air; this is characteristic of a traveling wave. The interference between the waves from the two speakers simply causes the energy flow to be *channeled* into certain directions (for example, toward P) and away from other directions (for example, away from Q). You can see another difference between Fig. 16.21 and a standing wave by considering a point, such as Q, where destructive interference occurs. Such a point is *both* a displacement node *and* a pressure node because there is no wave at all at this point. Compare this to a standing wave, in which a pressure node is a displacement antinode, and vice versa.

PhET: Sound
PhET: Wave Interference

16.21 Two speakers driven by the same amplifier. Constructive interference occurs at point P, and destructive interference occurs at point Q.

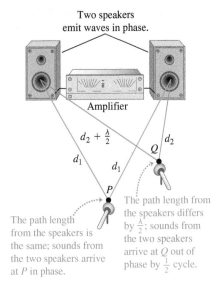

Two speakers emit waves in phase.

Amplifier

$d_2 + \frac{\lambda}{2}$ d_2

d_1 d_1

Q

P

The path length from the speakers is the same; sounds from the two speakers arrive at P in phase.

The path length from the speakers differs by $\frac{\lambda}{2}$; sounds from the two speakers arrive at Q out of phase by $\frac{1}{2}$ cycle.

Constructive interference occurs wherever the distances traveled by the two waves differ by a whole number of wavelengths, $0, \lambda, 2\lambda, 3\lambda, \ldots$; in all these cases the waves arrive at the microphone in phase (Fig. 16.22a). If the distances from the two speakers to the microphone differ by any half-integer number of wavelengths, $\lambda/2, 3\lambda/2, 5\lambda/2, \ldots$, the waves arrive at the microphone out of phase and there will be destructive interference (Fig. 16.22b). In this case, little or no sound energy flows toward the microphone directly in front of the speakers. The energy is instead directed to the sides, where constructive interference occurs.

16.22 Two speakers driven by the same amplifier, emitting waves in phase. Only the waves directed toward the microphone are shown, and they are separated for clarity. **(a)** Constructive interference occurs when the path difference is 0, $\lambda, 2\lambda, 3\lambda, \ldots$. **(b)** Destructive interference occurs when the path difference is $\lambda/2, 3\lambda/2, 5\lambda/2, \ldots$.

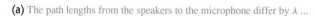

(a) The path lengths from the speakers to the microphone differ by λ ...

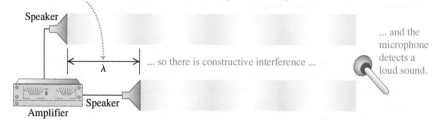

Speaker

... so there is constructive interference ...

λ

Amplifier

Speaker

... and the microphone detects a loud sound.

(b) The path lengths from the speakers to the microphone differ by $\frac{\lambda}{2}$ ...

Speaker

... so there is destructive interference ...

$\lambda/2$

Amplifier

Speaker

... and the microphone detects little or no sound.

Example 16.13 **Loudspeaker interference**

Two small loudspeakers, A and B (Fig. 16.23), are driven by the same amplifier and emit pure sinusoidal waves in phase. (a) For what frequencies does constructive interference occur at point P? (b) For what frequencies does destructive interference occur? The speed of sound is 350 m/s.

SOLUTION

IDENTIFY and SET UP: The nature of the interference at P depends on the difference d in path lengths from point A to P and from point B to P. We calculate the path lengths using the Pythagorean theorem. Constructive interference occurs when d equals a whole number of wavelengths, while destructive interference occurs

when d is a half-integer number of wavelengths. To find the corresponding frequencies, we use $v = f\lambda$.

EXECUTE: The distance from A to P is $[(2.00 \text{ m})^2 + (4.00 \text{ m})^2]^{1/2} = 4.47$ m, and the distance from B to P is $[(1.00 \text{ m})^2 + (4.00 \text{ m})^2]^{1/2} = 4.12$ m. The path difference is $d = 4.47 \text{ m} - 4.12 \text{ m} = 0.35$ m.

(a) Constructive interference occurs when $d = 0, \lambda, 2\lambda, \ldots$ or $d = 0, v/f, 2v/f, \ldots = nv/f$. So the possible frequencies are

$$f_n = \frac{nv}{d} = n\frac{350 \text{ m/s}}{0.35 \text{ m}} \qquad (n = 1, 2, 3, \ldots)$$

$$= 1000 \text{ Hz}, 2000 \text{ Hz}, 3000 \text{ Hz}, \ldots$$

(b) Destructive interference occurs when $d = \lambda/2, 3\lambda/2, 5\lambda/2, \ldots$ or $d = v/2f, 3v/2f, 5v/2f, \ldots$. The possible frequencies are

$$f_n = \frac{nv}{2d} = n\frac{350 \text{ m/s}}{2(0.35 \text{ m})} \qquad (n = 1, 3, 5, \ldots)$$

$$= 500 \text{ Hz}, 1500 \text{ Hz}, 2500 \text{ Hz}, \ldots$$

EVALUATE: As we increase the frequency, the sound at point P alternates between large and small (near zero) amplitudes, with maxima and minima at the frequencies given above. This effect may not be strong in an ordinary room because of reflections from the walls, floor, and ceiling. It is stronger outdoors and best in an anechoic chamber, which has walls that absorb almost all sound and thereby eliminate reflections.

16.23 What sort of interference occurs at P?

1.00 m

2.00 m

B

4.00 m

A

P

Interference effects are used to control noise from very loud sound sources such as gas-turbine power plants or jet engine test cells. The idea is to use additional sound sources that in some regions of space interfere destructively with the unwanted sound and cancel it out. Microphones in the controlled area feed signals back to the sound sources, which are continuously adjusted for optimum cancellation of noise in the controlled area.

Test Your Understanding of Section 16.6 Suppose that speaker *A* in Fig. 16.23 emits a sinusoidal sound wave of frequency 500 Hz and speaker *B* emits a sinusoidal sound wave of frequency 1000 Hz. What sort of interference will there be between these two waves? (i) constructive interference at various points, including point *P*, and destructive interference at various other points; (ii) destructive interference at various points, including point *P*, and constructive interference at various points; (iii) neither (i) nor (ii).

16.7 Beats

ActivPhysics 10.7: Beats and Beat Frequency

In Section 16.6 we talked about *interference* effects that occur when two different waves with the same frequency overlap in the same region of space. Now let's look at what happens when we have two waves with equal amplitude but slightly different frequencies. This occurs, for example, when two tuning forks with slightly different frequencies are sounded together, or when two organ pipes that are supposed to have exactly the same frequency are slightly "out of tune."

Consider a particular point in space where the two waves overlap. The displacements of the individual waves at this point are plotted as functions of time in Fig. 16.24a. The total length of the time axis represents 1 second, and the frequencies are 16 Hz (blue graph) and 18 Hz (red graph). Applying the principle of superposition, we add the two displacements at each instant of time to find the total displacement at that time. The result is the graph of Fig. 16.24b. At certain times the two waves are in phase; their maxima coincide and their amplitudes add. But because of their slightly different frequencies, the two waves cannot be in phase at all times. Indeed, at certain times (like *t* = 0.50 s in Fig. 16.24) the two waves are exactly *out* of phase. The two waves then cancel each other, and the total amplitude is zero.

The resultant wave in Fig. 16.24b looks like a single sinusoidal wave with a varying amplitude that goes from a maximum to zero and back. In this example the amplitude goes through two maxima and two minima in 1 second, so the frequency of this amplitude variation is 2 Hz. The amplitude variation causes variations of loudness called **beats**, and the frequency with which the loudness varies is called the **beat frequency.** In this example the beat frequency is the *difference*

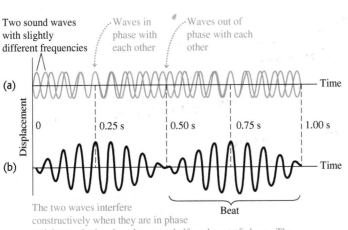

16.24 Beats are fluctuations in amplitude produced by two sound waves of slightly different frequency, here 16 Hz and 18 Hz. (a) Individual waves. (b) Resultant wave formed by superposition of the two waves. The beat frequency is 18 Hz − 16 Hz = 2 Hz.

Two sound waves with slightly different frequencies

Waves in phase with each other

Waves out of phase with each other

(a)

Displacement

0   0.25 s   0.50 s   0.75 s   1.00 s

Time

(b)

Time

The two waves interfere constructively when they are in phase and destructively when they are a half-cycle out of phase. The resultant wave rises and falls in intensity, forming beats.

Beat

of the two frequencies. If the beat frequency is a few hertz, we hear it as a waver or pulsation in the tone.

We can prove that the beat frequency is *always* the difference of the two frequencies f_a and f_b. Suppose f_a is larger than f_b; the corresponding periods are T_a and T_b, with $T_a < T_b$. If the two waves start out in phase at time $t = 0$, they are again in phase when the first wave has gone through exactly one more cycle than the second. This happens at a value of t equal to T_{beat}, the *period* of the beat. Let n be the number of cycles of the first wave in time T_{beat}; then the number of cycles of the second wave in the same time is $(n - 1)$, and we have the relationships

$$T_{\text{beat}} = nT_a \qquad \text{and} \qquad T_{\text{beat}} = (n - 1)T_b$$

Eliminating n between these two equations, we find

$$T_{\text{beat}} = \frac{T_a T_b}{T_b - T_a}$$

The reciprocal of the beat period is the beat *frequency*, $f_{\text{beat}} = 1/T_{\text{beat}}$, so

$$f_{\text{beat}} = \frac{T_b - T_a}{T_a T_b} = \frac{1}{T_a} - \frac{1}{T_b}$$

and finally

$$f_{\text{beat}} = f_a - f_b \qquad \text{(beat frequency)} \qquad (16.24)$$

As claimed, the beat frequency is the difference of the two frequencies. In using Eq. (16.24), remember that f_a is the higher frequency.

An alternative way to derive Eq. (16.24) is to write functions to describe the curves in Fig. 16.24a and then add them. Suppose that at a certain position the two waves are given by $y_a(t) = A \sin 2\pi f_a t$ and $y_b(t) = -A \sin 2\pi f_b t$. We use the trigonometric identity

$$\sin a - \sin b = 2 \sin \tfrac{1}{2}(a - b) \cos \tfrac{1}{2}(a + b)$$

We can then express the total wave $y(t) = y_a(t) + y_b(t)$ as

$$y_a(t) + y_b(t) = \left[2A \sin \tfrac{1}{2}(2\pi)(f_a - f_b)t \right] \cos \tfrac{1}{2}(2\pi)(f_a + f_b)t$$

The amplitude factor (the quantity in brackets) varies slowly with frequency $\tfrac{1}{2}(f_a - f_b)$. The cosine factor varies with a frequency equal to the *average* frequency $\tfrac{1}{2}(f_a + f_b)$. The *square* of the amplitude factor, which is proportional to the intensity that the ear hears, goes through two maxima and two minima per cycle. So the beat frequency f_{beat} that is heard is twice the quantity $\tfrac{1}{2}(f_a - f_b)$, or just $f_a - f_b$, in agreement with Eq. (16.24).

Beats between two tones can be heard up to a beat frequency of about 6 or 7 Hz. Two piano strings or two organ pipes differing in frequency by 2 or 3 Hz sound wavery and "out of tune," although some organ stops contain two sets of pipes deliberately tuned to beat frequencies of about 1 to 2 Hz for a gently undulating effect. Listening for beats is an important technique in tuning all musical instruments.

At frequency differences greater than about 6 or 7 Hz, we no longer hear individual beats, and the sensation merges into one of *consonance* or *dissonance*, depending on the frequency ratio of the two tones. In some cases the ear perceives a tone called a *difference tone,* with a pitch equal to the beat frequency of the two tones. For example, if you listen to a whistle that produces sounds at 1800 Hz and 1900 Hz when blown, you will hear not only these tones but also a much lower 100-Hz tone.

The engines on multiengine propeller aircraft have to be synchronized so that the propeller sounds don't cause annoying beats, which are heard as loud throbbing sounds (Fig. 16.25). On some planes this is done electronically; on others the pilot does it by ear, just like tuning a piano.

16.25 If the two propellers on this airplane are not precisely synchronized, the pilots, passengers, and listeners on the ground will hear beats.

Test Your Understanding of Section 16.7 One tuning fork vibrates at 440 Hz, while a second tuning fork vibrates at an unknown frequency. When both tuning forks are sounded simultaneously, you hear a tone that rises and falls in intensity three times per second. What is the frequency of the second tuning fork? (i) 434 Hz; (ii) 437 Hz; (iii) 443 Hz; (iv) 446 Hz; (v) either 434 Hz or 446 Hz; (vi) either 437 Hz or 443 Hz.   ❙

16.8 The Doppler Effect

ActivPhysics 10.8: Doppler Effect: Conceptual Introduction
ActivPhysics 10.9: Doppler Effect: Problems

You've probably noticed that when a car approaches you with its horn sounding, the pitch seems to drop as the car passes. This phenomenon, first described by the 19th-century Austrian scientist Christian Doppler, is called the **Doppler effect.** When a source of sound and a listener are in motion relative to each other, the frequency of the sound heard by the listener is not the same as the source frequency. A similar effect occurs for light and radio waves; we'll return to this later in this section.

To analyze the Doppler effect for sound, we'll work out a relationship between the frequency shift and the velocities of source and listener relative to the medium (usually air) through which the sound waves propagate. To keep things simple, we consider only the special case in which the velocities of both source and listener lie along the line joining them. Let v_S and v_L be the velocity components along this line for the source and the listener, respectively, relative to the medium. We choose the positive direction for both v_S and v_L to be the direction from the listener L to the source S. The speed of sound relative to the medium, v, is always considered positive.

Moving Listener and Stationary Source

Let's think first about a listener L moving with velocity v_L toward a stationary source S (Fig. 16.26). The source emits a sound wave with frequency f_S and wavelength $\lambda = v/f_S$. The figure shows four wave crests, separated by equal distances λ. The wave crests approaching the moving listener have a speed of propagation *relative to the listener* of $(v + v_L)$. So the frequency f_L with which the crests arrive at the listener's position (that is, the frequency the listener hears) is

$$f_L = \frac{v + v_L}{\lambda} = \frac{v + v_L}{v/f_S} \qquad (16.25)$$

or

$$f_L = \left(\frac{v + v_L}{v}\right)f_S = \left(1 + \frac{v_L}{v}\right)f_S \qquad \begin{array}{l}\text{(moving listener,}\\ \text{stationary source)}\end{array} \quad (16.26)$$

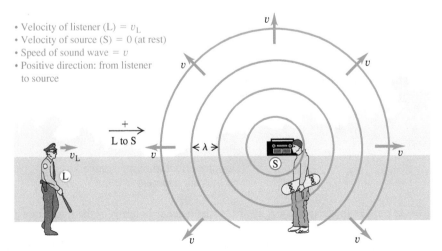

- Velocity of listener (L) $= v_L$
- Velocity of source (S) $= 0$ (at rest)
- Speed of sound wave $= v$
- Positive direction: from listener to source

$+$
L to S

v_L

L

$\langle \lambda \rangle$

S

16.26 A listener moving toward a stationary source hears a frequency that is higher than the source frequency. This is because the relative speed of listener and wave is greater than the wave speed v.

16.27 Wave crests emitted by a moving source are crowded together in front of the source (to the right of this source) and stretched out behind it (to the left of this source).

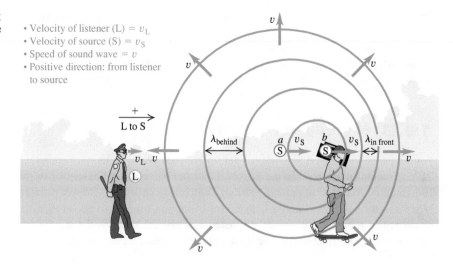

• Velocity of listener (L) = v_L
• Velocity of source (S) = v_S
• Speed of sound wave = v
• Positive direction: from listener to source

So a listener moving toward a source ($v_L > 0$), as in Fig. 16.26, hears a higher frequency (higher pitch) than does a stationary listener. A listener moving away from the source ($v_L < 0$) hears a lower frequency (lower pitch).

Moving Source and Moving Listener

Now suppose the source is also moving, with velocity v_S (Fig. 16.27). The wave speed relative to the wave medium (air) is still v; it is determined by the properties of the medium and is not changed by the motion of the source. But the wavelength is no longer equal to v/f_S. Here's why. The time for emission of one cycle of the wave is the period $T = 1/f_S$. During this time, the wave travels a distance $vT = v/f_S$ and the source moves a distance $v_S T = v_S/f_S$. The wavelength is the distance between successive wave crests, and this is determined by the *relative* displacement of source and wave. As Fig. 16.27 shows, this is different in front of and behind the source. In the region to the right of the source in Fig. 16.27 (that is, in front of the source), the wavelength is

$$\lambda_{\text{in front}} = \frac{v}{f_S} - \frac{v_S}{f_S} = \frac{v - v_S}{f_S} \qquad \text{(wavelength in front of a moving source)} \qquad \text{(16.27)}$$

In the region to the left of the source (that is, behind the source), it is

$$\lambda_{\text{behind}} = \frac{v + v_S}{f_S} \qquad \text{(wavelength behind a moving source)} \qquad \text{(16.28)}$$

The waves in front of and behind the source are compressed and stretched out, respectively, by the motion of the source.

To find the frequency heard by the listener behind the source, we substitute Eq. (16.28) into the first form of Eq. (16.25):

$$f_L = \frac{v + v_L}{\lambda_{\text{behind}}} = \frac{v + v_L}{(v + v_S)/f_S}$$

$$f_L = \frac{v + v_L}{v + v_S} f_S \qquad \text{(Doppler effect, moving source and moving listener)} \qquad \text{(16.29)}$$

This expresses the frequency f_L heard by the listener in terms of the frequency f_S of the source.

Although we derived it for the particular situation shown in Fig. 16.27, Eq. (16.29) includes *all* possibilities for motion of source and listener (relative to the medium) along the line joining them. If the listener happens to be at rest in the medium, v_L is zero. When both source and listener are at rest or have the same velocity relative to the medium, $v_L = v_S$ and $f_L = f_S$. Whenever the direction of the source or listener velocity is opposite to the direction from the listener toward the source (which we have defined as positive), the corresponding velocity to be used in Eq. (16.29) is negative.

As an example, the frequency heard by a listener at rest $(v_L = 0)$ is $f_L = [v/(v + v_S)]f_S$. If the source is moving toward the listener (in the negative direction), then $v_S < 0$, $f_L > f_S$, and the listener hears a higher frequency than that emitted by the source. If instead the source is moving away from the listener (in the positive direction), then $v_S > 0$, $f_L < f_S$, and the listener hears a lower frequency. This explains the change in pitch that you hear from the siren of an ambulance as it passes you (Fig. 16.28).

16.28 The Doppler effect explains why the siren on a fire engine or ambulance has a high pitch $(f_L > f_S)$ when it is approaching you $(v_S < 0)$ and a low pitch $(f_L < f_S)$ when it is moving away $(v_S > 0)$.

Problem-Solving Strategy 16.2   Doppler Effect

IDENTIFY *the relevant concepts:* The Doppler effect occurs whenever the source of waves, the wave detector (listener), or both are in motion.

SET UP *the problem* using the following steps:
1. Establish a coordinate system, with the positive direction from the listener toward the source. Carefully determine the signs of all relevant velocities. A velocity in the direction from the listener toward the source is positive; a velocity in the opposite direction is negative. All velocities must be measured relative to the air in which the sound travels.
2. Use consistent subscripts to identify the various quantities: S for source and L for listener.
3. Identify which unknown quantities are the target variables.

EXECUTE *the solution* as follows:
1. Use Eq. (16.29) to relate the frequencies at the source and the listener, the sound speed, and the velocities of the source and

the listener according to the sign convention of step 1. If the source is moving, you can find the wavelength measured by the listener using Eq. (16.27) or (16.28).
2. When a wave is reflected from a stationary or moving surface, solve the problem in two steps. In the first, the surface is the "listener"; the frequency with which the wave crests arrive at the surface is f_L. In the second, the surface is the "source," emitting waves with this same frequency f_L. Finally, determine the frequency heard by a listener detecting this new wave.

EVALUATE *your answer:* Is the *direction* of the frequency shift reasonable? If the source and the listener are moving toward each other, $f_L > f_S$; if they are moving apart, $f_L < f_S$. If the source and the listener have no relative motion, $f_L = f_S$.

Example 16.14   Doppler effect I: Wavelengths

A police car's siren emits a sinusoidal wave with frequency $f_S = 300$ Hz. The speed of sound is 340 m/s and the air is still. (a) Find the wavelength of the waves if the siren is at rest. (b) Find the wavelengths of the waves in front of and behind the siren if it is moving at 30 m/s.

SOLUTION

IDENTIFY and SET UP: In part (a) there is no Doppler effect because neither source nor listener is moving with respect to the air; $v = \lambda f$ gives the wavelength. Figure 16.29 shows the situation in part (b): The source is in motion, so we find the wavelengths using Eqs. (16.27) and (16.28) for the Doppler effect.

EXECUTE: (a) When the source is at rest,

$$\lambda = \frac{v}{f_S} = \frac{340 \text{ m/s}}{300 \text{ Hz}} = 1.13 \text{ m}$$

16.29 Our sketch for this problem.

Police car

$\lambda_{\text{behind}} = ?$ $v_S = 30$ m/s $\lambda_{\text{in front}} = ?$

(b) From Eq. (16.27), in front of the siren

$$\lambda_{\text{in front}} = \frac{v - v_S}{f_S} = \frac{340 \text{ m/s} - 30 \text{ m/s}}{300 \text{ Hz}} = 1.03 \text{ m}$$

From Eq. (16.28), behind the siren

$$\lambda_{\text{behind}} = \frac{v + v_S}{f_S} = \frac{340 \text{ m/s} + 30 \text{ m/s}}{300 \text{ Hz}} = 1.23 \text{ m}$$

EVALUATE: The wavelength is shorter in front of the siren and longer behind it, as we expect.

Example 16.15 Doppler effect II: Frequencies

If a listener L is at rest and the siren in Example 16.14 is moving away from L at 30 m/s, what frequency does the listener hear?

SOLUTION

IDENTIFY and SET UP: Our target variable is the frequency f_L heard by a listener behind the moving source. Figure 16.30 shows the situation. We have $v_L = 0$ and $v_S = +30$ m/s (positive, since the velocity of the source is in the direction from listener to source).

EXECUTE: From Eq. (16.29),

$$f_L = \frac{v}{v + v_S} f_S = \frac{340 \text{ m/s}}{340 \text{ m/s} + 30 \text{ m/s}} (300 \text{ Hz}) = 276 \text{ Hz}$$

EVALUATE: The source and listener are moving apart, so $f_L < f_S$. Here's a check on our numerical result. From Example 16.14, the

16.30 Our sketch for this problem.

wavelength behind the source (where the listener in Fig. 16.30 is located) is 1.23 m. The wave speed relative to the stationary listener is $v = 340$ m/s even though the source is moving, so

$$f_L = \frac{v}{\lambda} = \frac{340 \text{ m/s}}{1.23 \text{ m}} = 276 \text{ Hz}$$

Example 16.16 Doppler effect III: A moving listener

If the siren is at rest and the listener is moving away from it at 30 m/s, what frequency does the listener hear?

SOLUTION

IDENTIFY and SET UP: Again our target variable is f_L, but now L is in motion and S is at rest. Figure 16.31 shows the situation. The velocity of the listener is $v_L = -30$ m/s (negative, since the motion is in the direction from source to listener).

EXECUTE: From Eq. (16.29),

$$f_L = \frac{v + v_L}{v} f_S = \frac{340 \text{ m/s} + (-30 \text{ m/s})}{340 \text{ m/s}} (300 \text{ Hz}) = 274 \text{ Hz}$$

16.31 Our sketch for this problem.

EVALUATE: Again the source and listener are moving apart, so $f_L < f_S$. Note that the *relative velocity* of source and listener is the same as in Example 16.15, but the Doppler shift is different because v_S and v_L are different.

Example 16.17 Doppler effect IV: Moving source, moving listener

The siren is moving away from the listener with a speed of 45 m/s relative to the air, and the listener is moving toward the siren with a speed of 15 m/s relative to the air. What frequency does the listener hear?

SOLUTION

IDENTIFY and SET UP: Now *both* L and S are in motion. Again our target variable is f_L. Both the source velocity $v_S = +45$ m/s and the listener's velocity $v_L = +15$ m/s are positive because both velocities are in the direction from listener to source.

EXECUTE: From Eq. (16.29),

$$f_L = \frac{v + v_L}{v + v_S} f_S = \frac{340 \text{ m/s} + 15 \text{ m/s}}{340 \text{ m/s} + 45 \text{ m/s}} (300 \text{ Hz}) = 277 \text{ Hz}$$

16.32 Our sketch for this problem.

EVALUATE: As in Examples 16.15 and 16.16, the source and listener again move away from each other at 30 m/s, so again $f_L < f_S$. But f_L is different in all three cases because the Doppler effect for sound depends on how the source and listener are moving relative to the *air*, not simply on how they move relative to each other.

Example 16.18 Doppler effect V: A double Doppler shift

The police car is moving toward a warehouse at 30 m/s. What frequency does the driver hear reflected from the warehouse?

SOLUTION

IDENTIFY: In this situation there are *two* Doppler shifts (Fig. 16.33). In the first shift, the warehouse is the stationary "listener."

16.33 Two stages of the sound wave's motion from the police car to the warehouse and back to the police car.

(a) Sound travels from police car's siren (source S) to warehouse ("listener" L).

(b) Reflected sound travels from warehouse (source S) to police car (listener L).

The frequency of sound reaching the warehouse, which we call f_W, is greater than 300 Hz because the source is approaching. In the second shift, the warehouse acts as a source of sound with frequency f_W, and the listener is the driver of the police car; she hears a frequency greater than f_W because she is approaching the source.

SET UP: To determine f_W, we use Eq. (16.29) with f_L replaced by f_W. For this part of the problem, $v_L = v_W = 0$ (the warehouse is at rest) and $v_S = -30$ m/s (the siren is moving in the negative direction from source to listener).

To determine the frequency heard by the driver (our target variable), we again use Eq. (16.29) but now with f_S replaced by f_W. For this second part of the problem, $v_S = 0$ because the stationary warehouse is the source and the velocity of the listener (the driver) is $v_L = +30$ m/s. (The listener's velocity is positive because it is in the direction from listener to source.)

EXECUTE: The frequency reaching the warehouse is

$$f_W = \frac{v}{v + v_S} f_S = \frac{340 \text{ m/s}}{340 \text{ m/s} + (-30 \text{ m/s})}(300 \text{ Hz}) = 329 \text{ Hz}$$

Then the frequency heard by the driver is

$$f_L = \frac{v + v_L}{v} f_W = \frac{340 \text{ m/s} + 30 \text{ m/s}}{340 \text{ m/s}}(329 \text{ Hz}) = 358 \text{ Hz}$$

EVALUATE: Because there are two Doppler shifts, the reflected sound heard by the driver has an even higher frequency than the sound heard by a stationary listener in the warehouse.

Doppler Effect for Electromagnetic Waves

In the Doppler effect for sound, the velocities v_L and v_S are always measured relative to the *air* or whatever medium we are considering. There is also a Doppler effect for *electromagnetic* waves in empty space, such as light waves or radio waves. In this case there is no medium that we can use as a reference to measure velocities, and all that matters is the *relative* velocity of source and receiver. (By contrast, the Doppler effect for sound does not depend simply on this relative velocity, as discussed in Example 16.17.)

To derive the expression for the Doppler frequency shift for light, we have to use the special theory of relativity. We will discuss this in Chapter 37, but for now we quote the result without derivation. The wave speed is the speed of light, usually denoted by c, and it is the same for both source and receiver. In the frame of reference in which the receiver is at rest, the source is moving away from the receiver with velocity v. (If the source is *approaching* the receiver, v is negative.) The source frequency is again f_S. The frequency f_R measured by the receiver R (the frequency of arrival of the waves at the receiver) is then

$$f_R = \sqrt{\frac{c - v}{c + v}} f_S \qquad \text{(Doppler effect for light)} \qquad (16.30)$$

When v is positive, the source is moving directly *away* from the receiver and f_R is always *less* than f_S; when v is negative, the source is moving directly *toward* the receiver and f_R is *greater* than f_S. The qualitative effect is the same as for sound, but the quantitative relationship is different.

A familiar application of the Doppler effect for radio waves is the radar device mounted on the side window of a police car to check other cars' speeds. The electromagnetic wave emitted by the device is reflected from a moving car, which acts as a moving source, and the wave reflected back to the device is Doppler-shifted in frequency. The transmitted and reflected signals are combined to produce beats, and the speed can be computed from the frequency of the beats. Similar techniques ("Doppler radar") are used to measure wind velocities in the atmosphere.

16.34 Change of velocity component along the line of sight of a satellite passing a tracking station. The frequency received at the tracking station changes from high to low as the satellite passes overhead.

Earth

The Doppler effect is also used to track satellites and other space vehicles. In Fig. 16.34 a satellite emits a radio signal with constant frequency f_S. As the satellite orbits past, it first approaches and then moves away from the receiver; the frequency f_R of the signal received on earth changes from a value greater than f_S to a value less than f_S as the satellite passes overhead.

Test Your Understanding of Section 16.8 You are at an outdoor concert with a wind blowing at 10 m/s from the performers toward you. Is the sound you hear Doppler-shifted? If so, is it shifted to lower or higher frequencies? ▮

16.9 Shock Waves

You may have experienced "sonic booms" caused by an airplane flying overhead faster than the speed of sound. We can see qualitatively why this happens from Fig. 16.35. Let v_S denote the *speed* of the airplane relative to the air, so that it is always positive. The motion of the airplane through the air produces sound; if v_S is less than the speed of sound v, the waves in front of the airplane are crowded together with a wavelength given by Eq. (16.27):

$$\lambda_{\text{in front}} = \frac{v - v_S}{f_S}$$

As the speed v_S of the airplane approaches the speed of sound v, the wavelength approaches zero and the wave crests pile up on each other (Fig. 16.35a). The airplane must exert a large force to compress the air in front of it; by Newton's third law, the air exerts an equally large force back on the airplane. Hence there is a large increase in aerodynamic drag (air resistance) as the airplane approaches the speed of sound, a phenomenon known as the "sound barrier."

When v_S is greater in magnitude than v, the source of sound is **supersonic,** and Eqs. (16.27) and (16.29) for the Doppler effect no longer describe the sound wave in front of the source. Figure 16.35b shows a cross section of what happens. As the airplane moves, it displaces the surrounding air and produces sound. A series of wave crests is emitted from the nose of the airplane; each spreads out in a circle centered at the position of the airplane when it emitted the crest. After a time t the crest emitted from point S_1 has spread to a circle with radius vt, and the airplane has moved a greater distance v_St to position S_2. You can see that the circular crests interfere constructively at points along the blue line that makes an angle α with

16.35 Wave crests around a sound source S moving (a) slightly slower than the speed of sound v and (b) faster than the sound speed v. (c) This photograph shows a T-38 jet airplane moving at 1.1 times the speed of sound. Separate shock waves are produced by the nose, wings, and tail. The angles of these waves vary because the air speeds up and slows down as it moves around the airplane, so the relative speed v_S of the airplane and air is different for shock waves produced at different points.

(a) Sound source S (airplane) moving at nearly the speed of sound

(b) Sound source moving faster than the speed of sound

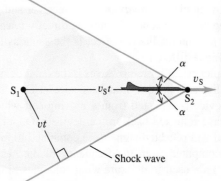

(c) Shock waves around a supersonic airplane

the direction of the airplane velocity, leading to a very-large-amplitude wave crest along this line. This large-amplitude crest is called a **shock wave** (Fig. 16.35c).

From the right triangle in Fig. 16.35b we can see that the angle α is given by

$$\sin\alpha = \frac{vt}{v_S t} = \frac{v}{v_S} \quad \text{(shock wave)} \qquad (16.31)$$

In this relationship, v_S is the *speed* of the source (the magnitude of its velocity) relative to the air and is always positive. The ratio v_S/v is called the **Mach number.** It is greater than unity for all supersonic speeds, and $\sin\alpha$ in Eq. (16.31) is the reciprocal of the Mach number. The first person to break the sound barrier was Capt. Chuck Yeager of the U.S. Air Force, flying the Bell X-1 at Mach 1.06 on October 14, 1947 (Fig. 16.36).

Shock waves are actually three-dimensional; a shock wave forms a *cone* around the direction of motion of the source. If the source (possibly a supersonic jet airplane or a rifle bullet) moves with constant velocity, the angle α is constant, and the shock-wave cone moves along with the source. It's the arrival of this shock wave that causes the sonic boom you hear after a supersonic airplane has passed by. The larger the airplane, the stronger the sonic boom; the shock wave produced at ground level by the (now retired) Concorde supersonic airliner flying at 12,000 m (40,000 ft) caused a sudden jump in air pressure of about 20 Pa. In front of the shock-wave cone, there is no sound. Inside the cone a stationary listener hears the Doppler-shifted sound of the airplane moving away.

CAUTION **Shock waves** We emphasize that a shock wave is produced *continuously* by any object that moves through the air at supersonic speed, not only at the instant that it "breaks the sound barrier." The sound waves that combine to form the shock wave, as in Fig. 16.35b, are created by the motion of the object itself, not by any sound source that the object may carry. The cracking noises of a bullet and of the tip of a circus whip are due to their supersonic motion. A supersonic jet airplane may have very loud engines, but these do not cause the shock wave. Indeed, a space shuttle makes a very loud sonic boom when coming in for a landing; its engines are out of fuel at this point, so it is a supersonic glider. |

Shock waves have applications outside of aviation. They are used to break up kidney stones and gallstones without invasive surgery, using a technique with the impressive name *extracorporeal shock-wave lithotripsy*. A shock wave produced outside the body is focused by a reflector or acoustic lens so that as much of it as possible converges on the stone. When the resulting stresses in the stone exceed its tensile strength, it breaks into small pieces and can be eliminated. This technique requires accurate determination of the location of the stone, which may be done using ultrasonic imaging techniques (see Fig. 16.9).

16.36 The first supersonic airplane, the Bell X-1, was shaped much like a 50-caliber bullet—which was known to be able to travel faster than sound.

Example 16.19 **Sonic boom from a supersonic airplane**

An airplane is flying at Mach 1.75 at an altitude of 8000 m, where the speed of sound is 320 m/s. How long after the plane passes directly overhead will you hear the sonic boom?

SOLUTION

IDENTIFY and SET UP: The shock wave forms a cone trailing backward from the airplane, so the problem is really asking for how much time elapses from when the airplane flies overhead to when the shock wave reaches you at point L (Fig. 16.37). During the time t (our target variable) since the airplane traveling at speed

v_S passed overhead, it has traveled a distance $v_S t$. Equation (16.31) gives the shock cone angle α; we use trigonometry to solve for t.

EXECUTE: From Eq. (16.31) the angle α of the shock cone is

$$\alpha = \arcsin\frac{1}{1.75} = 34.8°$$

The speed of the plane is the speed of sound multiplied by the Mach number:

$$v_S = (1.75)(320 \text{ m/s}) = 560 \text{ m/s}$$

Continued

16.37 You hear a sonic boom when the shock wave reaches you at L (*not* just when the plane breaks the sound barrier). A listener to the right of L has not yet heard the sonic boom but will shortly; a listener to the left of L has already heard the sonic boom.

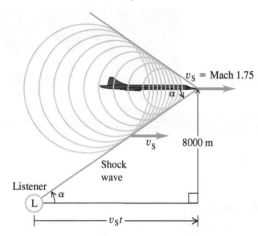

From Fig. 16.37 we have

$$\tan \alpha = \frac{8000 \text{ m}}{v_S t}$$

$$t = \frac{8000 \text{ m}}{(560 \text{ m/s})(\tan 34.8°)} = 20.5 \text{ s}$$

EVALUATE: You hear the boom 20.5 s after the airplane passes overhead, at which time it has traveled $(560 \text{ m/s})(20.5 \text{ s}) = 11.5$ km since it passed overhead. We have assumed that the speed of sound is the same at all altitudes, so that $\alpha = \arcsin v/v_S$ is constant and the shock wave forms a perfect cone. In fact, the speed of sound decreases with increasing altitude. How would this affect the value of t?

Test Your Understanding of Section 16.9 What would you hear if you were directly behind (to the left of) the supersonic airplane in Fig. 16.37? (i) a sonic boom; (ii) the sound of the airplane, Doppler-shifted to higher frequencies; (iii) the sound of the airplane, Doppler-shifted to lower frequencies; (iv) nothing.

❙

Sound waves: Sound consists of longitudinal waves in a medium. A sinusoidal sound wave is characterized by its frequency f and wavelength λ (or angular frequency ω and wave number k) and by its displacement amplitude A. The pressure amplitude p_{max} is directly proportional to the displacement amplitude, the wave number, and the bulk modulus B of the wave medium. (See Examples 16.1 and 16.2.)

The speed of a sound wave in a fluid depends on the bulk modulus B and density ρ. If the fluid is an ideal gas, the speed can be expressed in terms of the temperature T, molar mass M, and ratio of heat capacities γ of the gas. The speed of longitudinal waves in a solid rod depends on the density and Young's modulus Y. (See Examples 16.3 and 16.4.)

$$p_{max} = BkA \qquad (16.5)$$
(sinusoidal sound wave)

$$v = \sqrt{\frac{B}{\rho}} \qquad (16.7)$$
(longitudinal wave in a fluid)

$$v = \sqrt{\frac{\gamma RT}{M}} \qquad (16.10)$$
(sound wave in an ideal gas)

$$v = \sqrt{\frac{Y}{\rho}} \qquad (16.8)$$
(longitudinal wave in a solid rod)

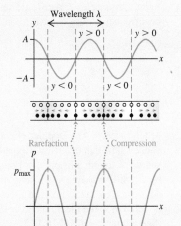

Intensity and sound intensity level: The intensity I of a sound wave is the time average rate at which energy is transported by the wave, per unit area. For a sinusoidal wave, the intensity can be expressed in terms of the displacement amplitude A or the pressure amplitude p_{max}. (See Examples 16.5–16.7.)

The sound intensity level β of a sound wave is a logarithmic measure of its intensity. It is measured relative to I_0, an arbitrary intensity defined to be 10^{-12} W/m^2. Sound intensity levels are expressed in decibels (dB). (See Examples 16.8 and 16.9.)

$$I = \frac{1}{2}\sqrt{\rho B}\,\omega^2 A^2 = \frac{p_{max}^2}{2\rho v}$$

$$= \frac{p_{max}^2}{2\sqrt{\rho B}} \qquad (16.12), (16.14)$$

(intensity of a sinusoidal sound wave)

$$\beta = (10\text{ dB})\log\frac{I}{I_0} \qquad (16.15)$$

(definition of sound intensity level)

Standing sound waves: Standing sound waves can be set up in a pipe or tube. A closed end is a displacement node and a pressure antinode; an open end is a displacement antinode and a pressure node. For a pipe of length L open at both ends, the normal-mode frequencies are integer multiples of the sound speed divided by $2L$. For a stopped pipe (one that is open at only one end), the normal-mode frequencies are the odd multiples of the sound speed divided by $4L$. (See Examples 16.10 and 16.11.)

A pipe or other system with normal-mode frequencies can be driven to oscillate at any frequency. A maximum response, or resonance, occurs if the driving frequency is close to one of the normal-mode frequencies of the system. (See Example 16.12.)

$$f_n = \frac{nv}{2L} \quad (n = 1, 2, 3, \ldots) \quad (16.18)$$
(open pipe)

$$f_n = \frac{nv}{4L} \quad (n = 1, 3, 5, \ldots) \quad (16.22)$$
(stopped pipe)

Interference: When two or more waves overlap in the same region of space, the resulting effects are called interference. The resulting amplitude can be either larger or smaller than the amplitude of each individual wave, depending on whether the waves are in phase (constructive interference) or out of phase (destructive interference). (See Example 16.13.)

Beats: Beats are heard when two tones with slightly different frequencies f_a and f_b are sounded together. The beat frequency f_{beat} is the difference between f_a and f_b.

$$f_{beat} = f_a - f_b \qquad (16.24)$$

(beat frequency)

Displacement

Beat

Doppler effect: The Doppler effect for sound is the frequency shift that occurs when there is motion of a source of sound, a listener, or both, relative to the medium. The source and listener frequencies f_S and f_L are related by the source and listener velocities v_S and v_L relative to the medium and to the speed of sound v. (See Examples 16.14–16.18.)

$$f_L = \frac{v + v_L}{v + v_S} f_S \qquad (16.29)$$

(Doppler effect, moving source and moving listener)

L to S

Shock waves: A sound source moving with a speed v_S greater than the speed of sound v creates a shock wave. The wave front is a cone with angle α. (See Example 16.19.)

$$\sin \alpha = \frac{v}{v_S} \qquad \text{(shock wave)} \qquad (16.31)$$

$v_S > v$

Shock wave

BRIDGING PROBLEM Loudspeaker Interference

Loudspeakers A and B are 7.00 m apart and vibrate in phase at 172 Hz. They radiate sound uniformly in all directions. Their acoustic power outputs are 8.00×10^{-4} W and 6.00×10^{-5} W, respectively. The air temperature is 20°C. (a) Determine the difference in phase of the two signals at a point C along the line joining A and B, 3.00 m from B and 4.00 m from A. (b) Determine the intensity and sound intensity level at C from speaker A alone (with B turned off) and from speaker B alone (with A turned off). (c) Determine the intensity and sound intensity level at C from both speakers together.

SOLUTION GUIDE

 See MasteringPhysics® study area for a Video Tutor solution.

IDENTIFY and SET UP

1. Sketch the situation and label the distances between A, B, and C.
2. Choose the equations that relate power, distance from the source, intensity, pressure amplitude, and sound intensity level.
3. Decide how you will determine the phase difference in part (a). Once you have found the phase difference, how can you use it to find the amplitude of the combined wave at C due to both sources?

4. List the unknown quantities for each part of the problem and identify your target variables.

EXECUTE

5. Determine the phase difference at point C.
6. Find the intensity, sound intensity level, and pressure amplitude at C due to each speaker alone.
7. Use your results from steps 5 and 6 to find the pressure amplitude at C due to both loudspeakers together.
8. Use your result from step 7 to find the intensity and sound intensity level at C due to both loudspeakers together.

EVALUATE

9. How do your results from part (c) for intensity and sound intensity level at C compare to those from part (b)? Does this make sense?
10. What result would you have gotten in part (c) if you had (incorrectly) combined the *intensities* from A and B directly, rather than (correctly) combining the *pressure amplitudes* as you did in step 7?

Problems

•, ••, •••: Problems of increasing difficulty. CP: Cumulative problems incorporating material from earlier chapters. CALC: Problems requiring calculus. BIO: Biosciences problems.

DISCUSSION QUESTIONS

Q16.1 When sound travels from air into water, does the frequency of the wave change? The speed? The wavelength? Explain your reasoning.

Q16.2 The hero of a western movie listens for an oncoming train by putting his ear to the track. Why does this method give an earlier warning of the approach of a train than just listening in the usual way?

Q16.3 Would you expect the pitch (or frequency) of an organ pipe to increase or decrease with increasing temperature? Explain.

Q16.4 In most modern wind instruments the pitch is changed by using keys or valves to change the length of the vibrating air column. The bugle, however, has no valves or keys, yet it can play many notes. How might this be possible? Are there restrictions on what notes a bugle can play?

Q16.5 Symphonic musicians always "warm up" their wind instruments by blowing into them before a performance. What purpose does this serve?

Q16.6 In a popular and amusing science demonstration, a person inhales helium and then his voice becomes high and squeaky. Why does this happen? (*Warning:* Inhaling too much helium can cause unconsciousness or death.)

Q16.7 Lane dividers on highways sometimes have regularly spaced ridges or ripples. When the tires of a moving car roll along such a divider, a musical note is produced. Why? Explain how this phenomenon could be used to measure the car's speed.

Q16.8 The tone quality of an acoustic guitar is different when the strings are plucked near the bridge (the lower end of the strings) than when they are plucked near the sound hole (close to the center of the strings). Why?

Q16.9 Which has a more direct influence on the loudness of a sound wave: the *displacement* amplitude or the *pressure* amplitude? Explain your reasoning.

Q16.10 If the pressure amplitude of a sound wave is halved, by what factor does the intensity of the wave decrease? By what factor must the pressure amplitude of a sound wave be increased in order to increase the intensity by a factor of 16? Explain.

Q16.11 Does the sound intensity level β obey the inverse-square law? Why?

Q16.12 A small fraction of the energy in a sound wave is absorbed by the air through which the sound passes. How does this modify the inverse-square relationship between intensity and distance from the source? Explain your reasoning.

Q16.13 A wire under tension and vibrating in its first overtone produces sound of wavelength λ. What is the new wavelength of the sound (in terms of λ) if the tension is doubled?

Q16.14 A small metal band is slipped onto one of the tines of a tuning fork. As this band is moved closer and closer to the end of the tine, what effect does this have on the wavelength and frequency of the sound the tine produces? Why?

Q16.15 An organist in a cathedral plays a loud chord and then releases the keys. The sound persists for a few seconds and gradually dies away. Why does it persist? What happens to the sound energy when the sound dies away?

Q16.16 Two vibrating tuning forks have identical frequencies, but one is stationary and the other is mounted at the rim of a rotating platform. What does a listener hear? Explain.

Q16.17 A large church has part of the organ in the front of the church and part in the back. A person walking rapidly down the aisle while both segments are playing at once reports that the two segments sound out of tune. Why?

Q16.18 A sound source and a listener are both at rest on the earth, but a strong wind is blowing from the source toward the listener. Is there a Doppler effect? Why or why not?

Q16.19 Can you think of circumstances in which a Doppler effect would be observed for surface waves in water? For elastic waves propagating in a body of water deep below the surface? If so, describe the circumstances and explain your reasoning. If not, explain why not.

Q16.20 Stars other than our sun normally appear featureless when viewed through telescopes. Yet astronomers can readily use the light from these stars to determine that they are rotating and even measure the speed of their surface. How do you think they can do this?

Q16.21 If you wait at a railroad crossing as a train approaches and passes, you hear a Doppler shift in its sound. But if you listen closely, you hear that the change in frequency is continuous; it does not suddenly go from one high frequency to another low frequency. Instead the frequency *smoothly* (but rather quickly) changes from high to low as the train passes. Why does this smooth change occur?

Q16.22 In case 1, a source of sound approaches a stationary observer at speed v. In case 2, the observer moves toward the stationary source at the same speed v. If the source is always producing the same frequency sound, will the observer hear the same frequency in both cases, since the relative speed is the same each time? Why or why not?

Q16.23 Does an aircraft make a sonic boom only at the instant its speed exceeds Mach 1? Explain your reasoning.

Q16.24 If you are riding in a supersonic aircraft, what do you hear? Explain your reasoning. In particular, do you hear a continuous sonic boom? Why or why not?

Q16.25 A jet airplane is flying at a constant altitude at a steady speed v_S greater than the speed of sound. Describe what observers at points A, B, and C hear at the instant shown in Fig. Q16.25, when the shock wave has just reached point B. Explain your reasoning.

Figure **Q16.25**

EXERCISES

Unless indicated otherwise, assume the speed of sound in air to be $v = 344 \text{ m/s}$.

Section 16.1 Sound Waves

16.1 • Example 16.1 (Section 16.1) showed that for sound waves in air with frequency 1000 Hz, a displacement amplitude of

1.2×10^{-8} m produces a pressure amplitude of 3.0×10^{-2} Pa. (a) What is the wavelength of these waves? (b) For 1000-Hz waves in air, what displacement amplitude would be needed for the pressure amplitude to be at the pain threshold, which is 30 Pa? (c) For what wavelength and frequency will waves with a displacement amplitude of 1.2×10^{-8} m produce a pressure amplitude of 1.5×10^{-3} Pa?

16.2 • Example 16.1 (Section 16.1) showed that for sound waves in air with frequency 1000 Hz, a displacement amplitude of 1.2×10^{-8} m produces a pressure amplitude of 3.0×10^{-2} Pa. Water at 20°C has a bulk modulus of 2.2×10^9 Pa, and the speed of sound in water at this temperature is 1480 m/s. For 1000-Hz sound waves in 20°C water, what displacement amplitude is produced if the pressure amplitude is 3.0×10^{-2} Pa? Explain why your answer is much less than 1.2×10^{-8} m.

16.3 • Consider a sound wave in air that has displacement amplitude 0.0200 mm. Calculate the pressure amplitude for frequencies of (a) 150 Hz; (b) 1500 Hz; (c) 15,000 Hz. In each case compare the result to the pain threshold, which is 30 Pa.

16.4 • A loud factory machine produces sound having a displacement amplitude of 1.00 μm, but the frequency of this sound can be adjusted. In order to prevent ear damage to the workers, the maximum pressure amplitude of the sound waves is limited to 10.0 Pa. Under the conditions of this factory, the bulk modulus of air is 1.42×10^5 Pa. What is the highest-frequency sound to which this machine can be adjusted without exceeding the prescribed limit? Is this frequency audible to the workers?

16.5 • **BIO** **Ultrasound and Infrasound.** (a) **Whale communication.** Blue whales apparently communicate with each other using sound of frequency 17 Hz, which can be heard nearly 1000 km away in the ocean. What is the wavelength of such a sound in seawater, where the speed of sound is 1531 m/s? (b) **Dolphin clicks.** One type of sound that dolphins emit is a sharp click of wavelength 1.5 cm in the ocean. What is the frequency of such clicks? (c) **Dog whistles.** One brand of dog whistles claims a frequency of 25 kHz for its product. What is the wavelength of this sound? (d) **Bats.** While bats emit a wide variety of sounds, one type emits pulses of sound having a frequency between 39 kHz and 78 kHz. What is the range of wavelengths of this sound? (e) **Sonograms.** Ultrasound is used to view the interior of the body, much as x rays are utilized. For sharp imagery, the wavelength of the sound should be around one-fourth (or less) the size of the objects to be viewed. Approximately what frequency of sound is needed to produce a clear image of a tumor that is 1.0 mm across if the speed of sound in the tissue is 1550 m/s?

Section 16.2 Speed of Sound Waves

16.6 • (a) In a liquid with density 1300 kg/m³, longitudinal waves with frequency 400 Hz are found to have wavelength 8.00 m. Calculate the bulk modulus of the liquid. (b) A metal bar with a length of 1.50 m has density 6400 kg/m³. Longitudinal sound waves take 3.90×10^{-4} s to travel from one end of the bar to the other. What is Young's modulus for this metal?

16.7 • A submerged scuba diver hears the sound of a boat horn directly above her on the surface of the lake. At the same time, a friend on dry land 22.0 m from the boat also hears the horn (Fig. E16.7). The horn is 1.2 m above the surface of the water.

Figure **E16.7**

What is the distance (labeled by "?" in Fig. E16.7) from the horn to the diver? Both air and water are at 20°C.

16.8 • At a temperature of 27.0°C, what is the speed of longitudinal waves in (a) hydrogen (molar mass 2.02 g/mol); (b) helium (molar mass 4.00 g/mol); (c) argon (molar mass 39.9 g/mol)? See Table 19.1 for values of γ. (d) Compare your answers for parts (a), (b), and (c) with the speed in air at the same temperature.

16.9 • An oscillator vibrating at 1250 Hz produces a sound wave that travels through an ideal gas at 325 m/s when the gas temperature is 22.0°C. For a certain experiment, you need to have the same oscillator produce sound of wavelength 28.5 cm in this gas. What should the gas temperature be to achieve this wavelength?

16.10 •• **CALC** (a) Show that the fractional change in the speed of sound (dv/v) due to a very small temperature change dT is given by $dv/v = \frac{1}{2} dT/T$. (*Hint:* Start with Eq. 16.10.) (b) The speed of sound in air at 20°C is found to be 344 m/s. Use the result in part (a) to find the change in the speed of sound for a 1.0°C change in air temperature.

16.11 •• An 80.0-m-long brass rod is struck at one end. A person at the other end hears two sounds as a result of two longitudinal waves, one traveling in the metal rod and the other traveling in the air. What is the time interval between the two sounds? (The speed of sound in air is 344 m/s; relevant information about brass can be found in Table 11.1 and Table 12.1.)

16.12 •• What must be the stress (F/A) in a stretched wire of a material whose Young's modulus is Y for the speed of longitudinal waves to equal 30 times the speed of transverse waves?

Section 16.3 Sound Intensity

16.13 •• **BIO** **Energy Delivered to the Ear.** Sound is detected when a sound wave causes the tympanic membrane (the eardrum) to vibrate. Typically, the diameter of this membrane is about 8.4 mm in humans. (a) How much energy is delivered to the eardrum each second when someone whispers (20 dB) a secret in your ear? (b) To comprehend how sensitive the ear is to very small amounts of energy, calculate how fast a typical 2.0-mg mosquito would have to fly (in mm/s) to have this amount of kinetic energy.

16.14 • Use information from Table 16.2 to answer the following questions about sound in air. At 20°C the bulk modulus for air is 1.42×10^5 Pa and its density is 1.20 kg/m³. At this temperature, what are the pressure amplitude (in Pa and atm) and the displacement amplitude (in m and nm) (a) for the softest sound a person can normally hear at 1000 Hz and (b) for the sound from a riveter at the same frequency? (c) How much energy per second does each wave deliver to a square 5.00 mm on a side?

16.15 •• **Longitudinal Waves in Different Fluids.** (a) A longitudinal wave propagating in a water-filled pipe has intensity 3.00×10^{-6} W/m² and frequency 3400 Hz. Find the amplitude A and wavelength λ of the wave. Water has density 1000 kg/m³ and bulk modulus 2.18×10^9 Pa. (b) If the pipe is filled with air at pressure 1.00×10^5 Pa and density 1.20 kg/m³, what will be the amplitude A and wavelength λ of a longitudinal wave with the same intensity and frequency as in part (a)? (c) In which fluid is the amplitude larger, water or air? What is the ratio of the two amplitudes? Why is this ratio so different from 1.00?

16.16 •• **BIO** **Human Hearing.** A fan at a rock concert is 30 m from the stage, and at this point the sound intensity level is 110 dB. (a) How much energy is transferred to her eardrums each second? (b) How fast would a 2.0-mg mosquito have to fly (in mm/s) to have this much kinetic energy? Compare the mosquito's speed with that found for the whisper in part (a) of Exercise 16.13.

16.17 · A sound wave in air at 20°C has a frequency of 150 Hz and a displacement amplitude of 5.00×10^{-3} mm. For this sound wave calculate the (a) pressure amplitude (in Pa); (b) intensity (in W/m²); (c) sound intensity level (in decibels).

16.18 ·· You live on a busy street, but as a music lover, you want to reduce the traffic noise. (a) If you install special sound-reflecting windows that reduce the sound intensity level (in dB) by 30 dB, by what fraction have you lowered the sound intensity (in W/m²)? (b) If, instead, you reduce the intensity by half, what change (in dB) do you make in the sound intensity level?

16.19 · BIO For a person with normal hearing, the faintest sound that can be heard at a frequency of 400 Hz has a pressure amplitude of about 6.0×10^{-5} Pa. Calculate the (a) intensity; (b) sound intensity level; (c) displacement amplitude of this sound wave at 20°C.

16.20 ·· The intensity due to a number of independent sound sources is the sum of the individual intensities. (a) When four quadruplets cry simultaneously, how many decibels greater is the sound intensity level than when a single one cries? (b) To increase the sound intensity level again by the same number of decibels as in part (a), how many more crying babies are required?

16.21 · CP A baby's mouth is 30 cm from her father's ear and 1.50 m from her mother's ear. What is the difference between the sound intensity levels heard by the father and by the mother?

16.22 ·· The Sacramento City Council adopted a law to reduce the allowed sound intensity level of the much-despised leaf blowers from their current level of about 95 dB to 70 dB. With the new law, what is the ratio of the new allowed intensity to the previously allowed intensity?

16.23 ·· CP At point A, 3.0 m from a small source of sound that is emitting uniformly in all directions, the sound intensity level is 53 dB. (a) What is the intensity of the sound at A? (b) How far from the source must you go so that the intensity is one-fourth of what it was at A? (c) How far must you go so that the sound intensity level is one-fourth of what it was at A? (d) Does intensity obey the inverse-square law? What about sound intensity level?

16.24 ·· (a) If two sounds differ by 5.00 dB, find the ratio of the intensity of the louder sound to that of the softer one. (b) If one sound is 100 times as intense as another, by how much do they differ in sound intensity level (in decibels)? (c) If you increase the volume of your stereo so that the intensity doubles, by how much does the sound intensity level increase?

Section 16.4 Standing Sound Waves and Normal Modes

16.25 · Standing sound waves are produced in a pipe that is 1.20 m long. For the fundamental and first two overtones, determine the locations along the pipe (measured from the left end) of the displacement nodes and the pressure nodes if (a) the pipe is open at both ends and (b) the pipe is closed at the left end and open at the right end.

16.26 · The fundamental frequency of a pipe that is open at both ends is 594 Hz. (a) How long is this pipe? If one end is now closed, find (b) the wavelength and (c) the frequency of the new fundamental.

16.27 · BIO **The Human Voice.** The human vocal tract is a pipe that extends about 17 cm from the lips to the vocal folds (also called "vocal cords") near the middle of your throat. The vocal folds behave rather like the reed of a clarinet, and the vocal tract acts like a stopped pipe. Estimate the first three standing-wave frequencies of the vocal tract. Use $v = 344$ m/s. (The answers are only an estimate, since the position of lips and tongue affects the motion of air in the vocal tract.)

16.28 ·· BIO **The Vocal Tract.** Many opera singers (and some pop singers) have a range of about $2\frac{1}{2}$ octaves or even greater. Suppose a soprano's range extends from A below middle C (frequency 220 Hz) up to E^b-flat above high C (frequency 1244 Hz). Although the vocal tract is quite complicated, we can model it as a resonating air column, like an organ pipe, that is open at the top and closed at the bottom. The column extends from the mouth down to the diaphragm in the chest cavity, and we can also assume that the lowest note is the fundamental. How long is this column of air if $v = 354$ m/s? Does your result seem reasonable, on the basis of observations of your own body?

16.29 ·· A certain pipe produces a fundamental frequency of 262 Hz in air. (a) If the pipe is filled with helium at the same temperature, what fundamental frequency does it produce? (The molar mass of air is 28.8 g/mol, and the molar mass of helium is 4.00 g/mol.) (b) Does your answer to part (a) depend on whether the pipe is open or stopped? Why or why not?

16.30 · **Singing in the Shower.** A pipe closed at both ends can have standing waves inside of it, but you normally don't hear them because little of the sound can get out. But you *can* hear them if you are *inside* the pipe, such as someone singing in the shower. (a) Show that the wavelengths of standing waves in a pipe of length L that is closed at both ends are $\lambda_n = 2L/n$ and the frequencies are given by $f_n = nv/2L = nf_1$, where $n = 1, 2, 3, \ldots$. (b) Modeling it as a pipe, find the frequency of the fundamental and the first two overtones for a shower 2.50 m tall. Are these frequencies audible?

Section 16.5 Resonance and Sound

16.31 · You blow across the open mouth of an empty test tube and produce the fundamental standing wave of the air column inside the test tube. The speed of sound in air is 344 m/s and the test tube acts as a stopped pipe. (a) If the length of the air column in the test tube is 14.0 cm, what is the frequency of this standing wave? (b) What is the frequency of the fundamental standing wave in the air column if the test tube is half filled with water?

16.32 ·· CP You have a stopped pipe of adjustable length close to a taut 85.0-cm, 7.25-g wire under a tension of 4110 N. You want to adjust the length of the pipe so that, when it produces sound at its fundamental frequency, this sound causes the wire to vibrate in its second *overtone* with very large amplitude. How long should the pipe be?

Section 16.6 Interference of Waves

16.33 · Two loudspeakers, A and B (Fig. E16.33), are driven by the same amplifier and emit sinusoidal waves in phase. Speaker B is 2.00 m to the right of speaker A. Consider point Q along the extension of the line connecting the speakers, 1.00 m to the right of speaker B. Both speakers emit sound waves that travel directly from the speaker to point Q. (a) What is the lowest frequency for which *constructive* interference occurs at point Q? (b) What is the lowest frequency for which *destructive* interference occurs at point Q?

Figure **E16.33**

16.34 •• Two loudspeakers, *A* and *B* (see Fig. E16.33), are driven by the same amplifier and emit sinusoidal waves in phase. Speaker *B* is 2.00 m to the right of speaker *A*. The frequency of the sound waves produced by the loudspeakers is 206 Hz. Consider point *P* between the speakers and along the line connecting them, a distance *x* to the right of speaker *A*. Both speakers emit sound waves that travel directly from the speaker to point *P*. (a) For what values of *x* will *destructive* interference occur at point *P*? (b) For what values of *x* will *constructive* interference occur at point *P*? (c) Interference effects like those in parts (a) and (b) are almost never a factor in listening to home stereo equipment. Why not?

16.35 •• Two loudspeakers, *A*, and *B*, are driven by the same amplifier and emit sinusoidal waves in phase. Speaker *B* is 12.0 m to the right of speaker *A*. The frequency of the waves emitted by each speaker is 688 Hz. You are standing between the speakers, along the line connecting them, and are at a point of constructive interference. How far must you walk toward speaker *B* to move to a point of destructive interference?

16.36 • Two loudspeakers, *A* and *B*, are driven by the same amplifier and emit sinusoidal waves in phase. The frequency of the waves emitted by each speaker is 172 Hz. You are 8.00 m from *A*. What is the closest you can be to *B* and be at a point of destructive interference?

16.37 • Two loudspeakers, *A* and *B*, are driven by the same amplifier and emit sinusoidal waves in phase. The frequency of the waves emitted by each speaker is 860 Hz. Point *P* is 12.0 m from *A* and 13.4 m from *B*. Is the interference at *P* constructive or destructive? Give the reasoning behind your answer.

16.38 •• Two small stereo speakers are driven in step by the same variable-frequency oscillator. Their sound is picked up by a microphone arranged as shown in Fig. E16.38. For what frequencies does their sound at the speakers produce (a) constructive interference and (b) destructive interference?

Figure **E16.38**

Section 16.7 Beats

16.39 •• **Tuning a Violin.** A violinist is tuning her instrument to concert A (440 Hz). She plays the note while listening to an electronically generated tone of exactly that frequency and hears a beat of frequency 3 Hz, which increases to 4 Hz when she tightens her violin string slightly. (a) What was the frequency of the note played by her violin when she heard the 3-Hz beat? (b) To get her violin perfectly tuned to concert A, should she tighten or loosen her string from what it was when she heard the 3-Hz beat?

16.40 •• Two guitarists attempt to play the same note of wavelength 6.50 cm at the same time, but one of the instruments is slightly out of tune and plays a note of wavelength 6.52 cm instead. What is the frequency of the beat these musicians hear when they play together?

16.41 •• Two organ pipes, open at one end but closed at the other, are each 1.14 m long. One is now lengthened by 2.00 cm. Find the frequency of the beat they produce when playing together in their fundamental.

16.42 •• **Adjusting Airplane Motors.** The motors that drive airplane propellers are, in some cases, tuned by using beats. The whirring motor produces a sound wave having the same frequency as the propeller. (a) If one single-bladed propeller is turning at 575 rpm and you hear a 2.0-Hz beat when you run the second propeller, what are the two possible frequencies (in rpm) of the second

propeller? (b) Suppose you increase the speed of the second propeller slightly and find that the beat frequency changes to 2.1 Hz. In part (a), which of the two answers was the correct one for the frequency of the second single-bladed propeller? How do you know?

Section 16.8 The Doppler Effect

16.43 •• On the planet Arrakis a male ornithoid is flying toward his mate at 25.0 m/s while singing at a frequency of 1200 Hz. If the stationary female hears a tone of 1240 Hz, what is the speed of sound in the atmosphere of Arrakis?

16.44 •• In Example 16.18 (Section 16.8), suppose the police car is moving away from the warehouse at 20 m/s. What frequency does the driver of the police car hear reflected from the warehouse?

16.45 • Two train whistles, *A* and *B*, each have a frequency of 392 Hz. *A* is stationary and *B* is moving toward the right (away from *A*) at a speed of 35.0 m/s. A listener is between the two whistles and is moving toward the right with a speed of 15.0 m/s (Fig. E16.45). No wind is blowing. (a) What is the frequency from *A* as heard by the listener? (b) What is the frequency from *B* as heard by the listener? (c) What is the beat frequency detected by the listener?

Figure **E16.45**

16.46 • A railroad train is traveling at 25.0 m/s in still air. The frequency of the note emitted by the locomotive whistle is 400 Hz. What is the wavelength of the sound waves (a) in front of the locomotive and (b) behind the locomotive? What is the frequency of the sound heard by a stationary listener (c) in front of the locomotive and (d) behind the locomotive?

16.47 • A swimming duck paddles the water with its feet once every 1.6 s, producing surface waves with this period. The duck is moving at constant speed in a pond where the speed of surface waves is 0.32 m/s, and the crests of the waves ahead of the duck are spaced 0.12 m apart. (a) What is the duck's speed? (b) How far apart are the crests behind the duck?

16.48 • **Moving Source vs. Moving Listener.** (a) A sound source producing 1.00-kHz waves moves toward a stationary listener at one-half the speed of sound. What frequency will the listener hear? (b) Suppose instead that the source is stationary and the listener moves toward the source at one-half the speed of sound. What frequency does the listener hear? How does your answer compare to that in part (a)? Explain on physical grounds why the two answers differ.

16.49 • A car alarm is emitting sound waves of frequency 520 Hz. You are on a motorcycle, traveling directly away from the car. How fast must you be traveling if you detect a frequency of 490 Hz?

16.50 • A railroad train is traveling at 30.0 m/s in still air. The frequency of the note emitted by the train whistle is 262 Hz. What frequency is heard by a passenger on a train moving in the opposite direction to the first at 18.0 m/s and (a) approaching the first and (b) receding from the first?

16.51 • Two swift canaries fly toward each other, each moving at 15.0 m/s relative to the ground, each warbling a note of frequency 1750 Hz. (a) What frequency note does each bird hear from the other one? (b) What wavelength will each canary measure for the note from the other one?

16.52 •• The siren of a fire engine that is driving northward at 30.0 m/s emits a sound of frequency 2000 Hz. A truck in front of this fire engine is moving northward at 20.0 m/s. (a) What is the frequency of the siren's sound that the fire engine's driver hears reflected from the back of the truck? (b) What wavelength would this driver measure for these reflected sound waves?

16.53 •• How fast (as a percentage of light speed) would a star have to be moving so that the frequency of the light we receive from it is 10.0% higher than the frequency of the light it is emitting? Would it be moving away from us or toward us? (Assume it is moving either directly away from us or directly toward us.)

16.54 • **Extrasolar Planets.** In the not-too-distant future, it should be possible to detect the presence of planets moving around other stars by measuring the Doppler shift in the infrared light they emit. If a planet is going around its star at 50.00 km/s while emitting infrared light of frequency 3.330×10^{14} Hz, what frequency light will be received from this planet when it is moving directly away from us? (*Note:* Infrared light is light having wavelengths longer than those of visible light.)

Section 16.9 Shock Waves

16.55 •• A jet plane flies overhead at Mach 1.70 and at a constant altitude of 950 m. (a) What is the angle α of the shock-wave cone? (b) How much time after the plane passes directly overhead do you hear the sonic boom? Neglect the variation of the speed of sound with altitude.

16.56 • The shock-wave cone created by the space shuttle at one instant during its reentry into the atmosphere makes an angle of 58.0° with its direction of motion. The speed of sound at this altitude is 331 m/s. (a) What is the Mach number of the shuttle at this instant, and (b) how fast (in m/s and in mi/h) is it traveling relative to the atmosphere? (c) What would be its Mach number and the angle of its shock-wave cone if it flew at the same speed but at low altitude where the speed of sound is 344 m/s?

PROBLEMS

16.57 ••• **CP** Two identical taut strings under the same tension F produce a note of the same fundamental frequency f_0. The tension in one of them is now increased by a very small amount ΔF. (a) If they are played together in their fundamental, show that the frequency of the beat produced is $f_{beat} = f_0(\Delta F/2F)$. (b) Two identical violin strings, when in tune and stretched with the same tension, have a fundamental frequency of 440.0 Hz. One of the strings is retuned by increasing its tension. When this is done, 1.5 beats per second are heard when both strings are plucked simultaneously at their centers. By what percentage was the string tension changed?

16.58 •• **CALC** (a) Defend the following statement: "In a sinusoidal sound wave, the pressure variation given by Eq. (16.4) is greatest where the displacement given by Eq. (16.1) is zero." (b) For a sinusoidal sound wave given by Eq. (16.1) with amplitude $A = 10.0 \ \mu$m and wavelength $\lambda = 0.250$ m, graph the displacement y and pressure fluctuation p as functions of x at time $t = 0$. Show at least two wavelengths of the wave on your graphs. (c) The displacement y in a *non*sinusoidal sound wave is shown in Fig. P16.58 as a function of x for $t = 0$. Draw a graph showing the pressure fluctuation p in this wave as a function of x at $t = 0$. This sound wave has the same 10.0-μm amplitude as the wave in part (b). Does it have the same pressure amplitude? Why or why not? (d) Is the statement in part (a) necessarily true if the sound wave is *not* sinusoidal? Explain your reasoning.

Figure **P16.58**

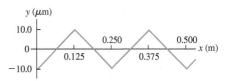

16.59 •• A soprano and a bass are singing a duet. While the soprano sings an A-sharp at 932 Hz, the bass sings an A-sharp but three octaves lower. In this concert hall, the density of air is 1.20 kg/m³ and its bulk modulus is 1.42×10^5 Pa. In order for their notes to have the same sound intensity level, what must be (a) the ratio of the pressure amplitude of the bass to that of the soprano and (b) the ratio of the displacement amplitude of the bass to that of the soprano? (c) What displacement amplitude (in m and in nm) does the soprano produce to sing her A-sharp at 72.0 dB?

16.60 •• **CP** The sound from a trumpet radiates uniformly in all directions in 20°C air. At a distance of 5.00 m from the trumpet the sound intensity level is 52.0 dB. The frequency is 587 Hz. (a) What is the pressure amplitude at this distance? (b) What is the displacement amplitude? (c) At what distance is the sound intensity level 30.0 dB?

16.61 ••• **A Thermometer.** Suppose you have a tube of length L containing a gas whose temperature you want to take, but you cannot get inside the tube. One end is closed, and the other end is open but a small speaker producing sound of variable frequency is at that end. You gradually increase the frequency of the speaker until the sound from the tube first becomes very loud. With further increase of the frequency, the loudness decreases but then gets very loud again at still higher frequencies. Call f_0 the lowest frequency at which the sound is very loud. (a) Show that the absolute temperature of this gas is given by $T = 16ML^2f_0^2/\gamma R$, where M is the molar mass of the gas, γ is the ratio of its heat capacities, and R is the ideal gas constant. (b) At what frequency above f_0 will the sound from the tube next reach a maximum in loudness? (c) How could you determine the speed of sound in this tube at temperature T?

16.62 •• **CP** A uniform 165-N bar is supported horizontally by two identical wires A and B (Fig. P16.62). A small 185-N cube of lead is placed three-fourths of the way from A to B. The wires are each 75.0 cm long and have a mass of 5.50 g.

Figure **P16.62**

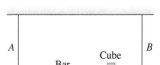

If both of them are simultaneously plucked at the center, what is the frequency of the beats that they will produce when vibrating in their fundamental?

16.63 • **CP** A person is playing a small flute 10.75 cm long, open at one end and closed at the other, near a taut string having a fundamental frequency of 600.0 Hz. If the speed of sound is 344.0 m/s, for which harmonics of the flute will the string resonate? In each case, which harmonic of the string is in resonance?

16.64 ••• **CP** **A New Musical Instrument.** You have designed a new musical instrument of very simple construction. Your design consists of a metal tube with length L and diameter $L/10$. You have stretched a string of mass per unit length μ across the open end of the tube. The other end of the tube is closed. To produce the musical effect you're looking for, you want the frequency of the third-harmonic standing wave on the string to be the same as the fundamental frequency for sound waves in the air column in the tube. The speed of sound waves in this air column is v_s. (a) What must be the tension of the string to produce the desired effect? (b) What happens to the sound produced by the instrument if the tension is changed to twice the value calculated in part (a)? (c) For the tension calculated in part (a), what other harmonics of the string, if any, are in resonance with standing waves in the air column?

16.65 • An organ pipe has two successive harmonics with frequencies 1372 and 1764 Hz. (a) Is this an open or a stopped pipe? Explain. (b) What two harmonics are these? (c) What is the length of the pipe?

16.66 • **Longitudinal Standing Waves in a Solid.** Longitudinal standing waves can be produced in a solid rod by holding it at some point between the fingers of one hand and stroking it with the other hand. The rod oscillates with antinodes at both ends. (a) Why are the ends antinodes and not nodes? (b) The fundamental frequency can be obtained by stroking the rod while it is held at its center. Explain why this is the *only* place to hold the rod to obtain the fundamental. (c) Calculate the fundamental frequency of a steel rod of length 1.50 m (see Table 16.1). (d) What is the next possible standing-wave frequency of this rod? Where should the rod be held to excite a standing wave of this frequency?

16.67 •• A long tube contains air at a pressure of 1.00 atm and a temperature of 77.0°C. The tube is open at one end and closed at the other by a movable piston. A tuning fork near the open end is vibrating with a frequency of 500 Hz. Resonance is produced when the piston is at distances 18.0, 55.5, and 93.0 cm from the open end. (a) From these measurements, what is the speed of sound in air at 77.0°C? (b) From the result of part (a), what is the value of γ? (c) These data show that a displacement antinode is slightly outside of the open end of the tube. How far outside is it?

16.68 ••• The frequency of the note F_4 is 349 Hz. (a) If an organ pipe is open at one end and closed at the other, what length must it have for its fundamental mode to produce this note at 20.0°C? (b) At what air temperature will the frequency be 370 Hz, corresponding to a rise in pitch from F to F-sharp? (Ignore the change in length of the pipe due to the temperature change.)

16.69 • A standing wave with a frequency of 1100 Hz in a column of methane (CH_4) at 20.0°C produces nodes that are 0.200 m apart. What is the value of γ for methane? (The molar mass of methane is 16.0 g/mol.)

16.70 •• Two identical loudspeakers are located at points A and B, 2.00 m apart. The loudspeakers are driven by the same amplifier and produce sound waves with a frequency of 784 Hz. Take the speed of sound in air to be 344 m/s. A small microphone is moved out from point B along a line perpendicular to the line connecting A and B (line BC in Fig. P16.70). (a) At what distances from B will there be *destructive* interference? (b) At what distances from B will there be *constructive* interference? (c) If the frequency is made low enough, there will be no positions along the line BC at which destructive interference occurs. How low must the frequency be for this to be the case?

Figure **P16.70**

16.71 • **Wagnerian Opera.** A man marries a great Wagnerian soprano but, alas, he discovers he cannot stand Wagnerian opera. In order to save his eardrums, the unhappy man decides he must silence his larklike wife for good. His plan is to tie her to the front of his car and send car and soprano speeding toward a brick wall. This soprano is quite shrewd, however, having studied physics in her student days at the music conservatory. She realizes that this wall has a resonant frequency of 600 Hz, which means that if a continuous sound wave of this frequency hits the wall, it will fall down, and she will be saved to sing more Isoldes. The car is heading toward the wall at a high speed of 30 m/s. (a) At what frequency must the soprano sing so that the wall will crumble? (b) What frequency will the soprano hear reflected from the wall just before it crumbles?

16.72 •• A bat flies toward a wall, emitting a steady sound of frequency 1.70 kHz. This bat hears its own sound plus the sound reflected by the wall. How fast should the bat fly in order to hear a beat frequency of 10.0 Hz?

16.73 •• **CP** A person leaning over a 125-m-deep well accidentally drops a siren emitting sound of frequency 2500 Hz. Just before this siren hits the bottom of the well, find the frequency and wavelength of the sound the person hears (a) coming directly from the siren and (b) reflected off the bottom of the well. (c) What beat frequency does this person perceive?

16.74 ••• **BIO** **Ultrasound in Medicine.** A 2.00-MHz sound wave travels through a pregnant woman's abdomen and is reflected from the fetal heart wall of her unborn baby. The heart wall is moving toward the sound receiver as the heart beats. The reflected sound is then mixed with the transmitted sound, and 72 beats per second are detected. The speed of sound in body tissue is 1500 m/s. Calculate the speed of the fetal heart wall at the instant this measurement is made.

16.75 •• The sound source of a ship's sonar system operates at a frequency of 22.0 kHz. The speed of sound in water (assumed to be at a uniform 20°C) is 1482 m/s. (a) What is the wavelength of the waves emitted by the source? (b) What is the difference in frequency between the directly radiated waves and the waves reflected from a whale traveling directly toward the ship at 4.95 m/s? The ship is at rest in the water.

16.76 • **CP** A police siren of frequency f_{siren} is attached to a vibrating platform. The platform and siren oscillate up and down in simple harmonic motion with amplitude A_p and frequency f_p. (a) Find the maximum and minimum sound frequencies that you would hear at a position directly above the siren. (b) At what point in the motion of the platform is the maximum frequency heard? The minimum frequency? Explain.

16.77 ••• **BIO** Horseshoe bats (genus *Rhinolophus*) emit sounds from their nostrils and then listen to the frequency of the sound reflected from their prey to determine the prey's speed. (The "horseshoe" that gives the bat its name is a depression around the nostrils that acts like a focusing mirror, so that the bat emits sound in a narrow beam like a flashlight.) A *Rhinolophus* flying at speed v_{bat} emits sound of frequency f_{bat}; the sound it hears reflected from an insect flying toward it has a higher frequency f_{refl}. (a) Show that the speed of the insect is

$$v_{insect} = v\left[\frac{f_{refl}(v - v_{bat}) - f_{bat}(v + v_{bat})}{f_{refl}(v - v_{bat}) + f_{bat}(v + v_{bat})}\right]$$

where v is the speed of sound. (b) If $f_{bat} = 80.7$ kHz, $f_{refl} = 83.5$ kHz, and $v_{bat} = 3.9$ m/s, calculate the speed of the insect.

16.78 •• (a) Show that Eq. (16.30) can be written as

$$f_R = f_S\left(1 - \frac{v}{c}\right)^{1/2}\left(1 + \frac{v}{c}\right)^{-1/2}$$

(b) Use the binomial theorem to show that if $v \ll c$, this is approximately equal to

$$f_R = f_S\left(1 - \frac{v}{c}\right)$$

(c) A pilotless reconnaissance aircraft emits a radio signal with a frequency of 243 MHz. It is flying directly toward a test engineer on the ground. The engineer detects beats between the received signal and a local signal also of frequency 243 MHz. The beat frequency is 46.0 Hz. What is the speed of the aircraft? (Radio waves travel at the speed of light, $c = 3.00 \times 10^8$ m/s.)

16.79 •• **Supernova!** The gas cloud known as the Crab Nebula can be seen with even a small telescope. It is the remnant of a *supernova,* a cataclysmic explosion of a star. The explosion was seen on the earth on July 4, 1054 C.E. The streamers glow with the characteristic red color of heated hydrogen gas. In a laboratory on the earth, heated hydrogen produces red light with frequency 4.568×10^{14} Hz; the red light received from streamers in the Crab Nebula pointed toward the earth has frequency 4.586×10^{14} Hz. (a) Estimate the speed with which the outer edges of the Crab Nebula are expanding. Assume that the speed of the center of the nebula relative to the earth is negligible. (You may use the formulas derived in Problem 16.78. The speed of light is 3.00×10^8 m/s.) (b) Assuming that the expansion speed has been constant since the supernova explosion, estimate the diameter of the Crab Nebula. Give your answer in meters and in light-years. (c) The angular diameter of the Crab Nebula as seen from earth is about 5 arc minutes (1 arc minute = $\frac{1}{60}$ degree). Estimate the distance (in light-years) to the Crab Nebula, and estimate the year in which the supernova explosion actually took place.

16.80 •• **CP** A turntable 1.50 m in diameter rotates at 75 rpm. Two speakers, each giving off sound of wavelength 31.3 cm, are attached to the rim of the table at opposite ends of a diameter. A listener stands in front of the turntable. (a) What is the greatest beat frequency the listener will receive from this system? (b) Will the listener be able to distinguish individual beats?

16.81 •• A woman stands at rest in front of a large, smooth wall. She holds a vibrating tuning fork of frequency f_0 directly in front of her (between her and the wall). (a) The woman now runs toward the wall with speed v_W. She detects beats due to the interference between the sound waves reaching her directly from the fork and those reaching her after being reflected from the wall. How many beats per second will she detect? (*Note:* If the beat frequency is too large, the woman may have to use some instrumentation other than

her ears to detect and count the beats.) (b) If the woman instead runs away from the wall, holding the tuning fork at her back so it is between her and the wall, how many beats per second will she detect?

16.82 •• On a clear day you see a jet plane flying overhead. From the apparent size of the plane, you determine that it is flying at a constant altitude h. You hear the sonic boom at time T after the plane passes directly overhead. Show that if the speed of sound v is the same at all altitudes, the speed of the plane is

$$v_S = \frac{hv}{\sqrt{h^2 - v^2T^2}}$$

(*Hint:* Trigonometric identities will be useful.)

CHALLENGE PROBLEMS

16.83 ••• **CALC** Figure P16.83 shows the pressure fluctuation p of a nonsinusoidal sound wave as a function of x for $t = 0$. The wave is traveling in the +x-direction. (a) Graph the pressure fluctuation p as a function of t for $x = 0$. Show at least two cycles of oscillation. (b) Graph the displacement y in this sound wave as a function of x at $t = 0$. At $x = 0$, the displacement at $t = 0$ is zero. Show at least two wavelengths of the wave. (c) Graph the displacement y as a function of t for $x = 0$. Show at least two cycles of oscillation. (d) Calculate the maximum velocity and the maximum acceleration of an element of the air through which this sound wave is traveling. (e) Describe how the cone of a loudspeaker must move as a function of time to produce the sound wave in this problem.

Figure **P16.83**

16.84 ••• **CP** **Longitudinal Waves on a Spring.** A long spring such as a Slinky™ is often used to demonstrate longitudinal waves. (a) Show that if a spring that obeys Hooke's law has mass m, length L, and force constant k', the speed of longitudinal waves on the spring is $v = L\sqrt{k'/m}$. (see Section 16.2). (b) Evaluate v for a spring with $m = 0.250$ kg, $L = 2.00$ m, and $k' = 1.50$ N/m.

Answers

Chapter Opening Question ?

Both musical sound and noise are made up of a combination of sinusoidal sound waves. The difference is that the frequencies of the sine waves in musical sound are all integer multiples of a fundamental frequency, while *all* frequencies are present in noise.

Test Your Understanding Questions

16.1 Answer: (v) From Eq. (16.5), the displacement amplitude is $A = p_{max}/Bk$. The pressure amplitude p_{max} and bulk modulus B remain the same, but the frequency f increases by a factor of 4. Hence the wave number $k = \omega/v = 2\pi f/v$ also increases by a factor of 4. Since A is inversely proportional to k, the displacement amplitude becomes $\frac{1}{4}$ as great. In other words, at higher frequency

a smaller maximum displacement is required to produce the same maximum pressure fluctuation.

16.2 Answer: (i) From Eq. (16.7), the speed of longitudinal waves (sound) in a fluid is $v = \sqrt{B/\rho}$. We can rewrite this to give an expression for the bulk modulus B in terms of the fluid density ρ and the sound speed v: $B = \rho v^2$. At 20°C the speed of sound in mercury is slightly less than in water (1451 m/s versus 1482 m/s), but the density of mercury is greater than that of water by a large factor (13.6). Hence the bulk modulus of mercury is greater than that of water by a factor of $(13.6)(1451/1482)^2 = 13.0$.

16.3 Answer: A and p_{max} increase by a factor of $\sqrt{2}$, B and v are unchanged, β increases by 3.0 dB Equations (16.9) and (16.10) show that the bulk modulus B and sound speed v remain the same because the physical properties of the air are unchanged. From Eqs. (16.12) and (16.14), the intensity is proportional to the square of the displacement amplitude or the square of the pressure amplitude. Hence doubling the intensity means that A and p_{max} both increase by a factor of $\sqrt{2}$. Example 16.9 shows that *multiplying* the intensity by a factor of $2(I_2/I_1 = 2)$ corresponds to *adding* to the sound intensity level by $(10\,\text{dB})\log(I_2/I_1) = (10\,\text{dB})\log 2 = 3.0\,\text{dB}$.

16.4 Answer: (ii) Helium is less dense and has a lower molar mass than air, so sound travels faster in helium than in air. The normal-mode frequencies for a pipe are proportional to the sound speed v, so the frequency and hence the pitch increase when the air in the pipe is replaced with helium.

16.5 Answer: (i) and (iv) There will be a resonance if 660 Hz is one of the pipe's normal-mode frequencies. A stopped organ pipe has normal-mode frequencies that are odd multiples of its fundamental frequency [see Eq. (16.22) and Fig. 16.18]. Hence pipe (i), which has fundamental frequency 220 Hz, also has a normal-mode frequency of $3(220\,\text{Hz}) = 660\,\text{Hz}$. Pipe (ii) has twice the length of pipe (i); from Eq. (16.20), the fundamental frequency of a stopped pipe is inversely proportional to the length, so pipe (ii) has a fundamental frequency of $\left(\frac{1}{2}\right)(220\,\text{Hz}) = 110\,\text{Hz}$. Its other normal-mode frequencies are 330 Hz, 550 Hz, 770 Hz, ..., so a 660-Hz tuning fork will not cause resonance. Pipe (iii) is an open pipe of the same length as pipe (i), so its fundamental frequency is twice as great as for pipe (i) [compare Eqs. (16.16) and (16.20)], or $2(220\,\text{Hz}) = 440\,\text{Hz}$. Its other normal-mode frequencies are integer multiples of the fundamental frequency [see Eq. (16.19)], or 880 Hz, 1320 Hz, ..., none of which match the 660-Hz frequency of the tuning fork. Pipe (iv) is also an open pipe but with twice the length of pipe (iii) [see Eq. (16.18)], so its normal-mode frequencies are one-half those of pipe (iii): 220 Hz, 440 Hz, 660 Hz, ..., so the third harmonic will resonate with the tuning fork.

16.6 Answer: (iii) Constructive and destructive interference between two waves can occur only if the two waves have the same frequency. In this case the frequencies are different, so there are no points where the two waves always reinforce each other (constructive interference) or always cancel each other (destructive interference).

16.7 Answer: (vi) The beat frequency is 3 Hz, so the difference between the two tuning fork frequencies is also 3 Hz. Hence the second tuning fork vibrates at a frequency of either 443 Hz or 437 Hz. You can distinguish between the two possibilities by comparing the pitches of the two tuning forks sounded one at a time: The frequency is 437 Hz if the second tuning fork has a lower pitch and 443 Hz if it has a higher pitch.

16.8 Answer: no The air (the medium for sound waves) is moving from the source toward the listener. Hence, relative to the air, both the source and the listener are moving in the direction from listener to source. So both velocities are positive and $v_S = v_L = +10\,\text{m/s}$. The equality of these two velocities means that the numerator and the denominator in Eq. (16.29) are the same, so $f_L = f_S$ and there is *no* Doppler shift.

16.9 Answer: (iii) Figure 16.37 shows that there are sound waves inside the cone of the shock wave. Behind the airplane the wave crests are spread apart, just as they are behind the moving source in Fig. 16.27. Hence the waves that reach you have an increased wavelength and a lower frequency.

Bridging Problem

Answers: (a) $180° = \pi\,\text{rad}$

     (b) *A* alone: $I = 3.98 \times 10^{-6}\,\text{W/m}^2$, $\beta = 66.0\,\text{dB}$; *B* alone: $I = 5.31 \times 10^{-7}\,\text{W/m}^2$, $\beta = 57.2\,\text{dB}$

     (c) $I = 1.60 \times 10^{-6}\,\text{W/m}^2$, $\beta = 62.1\,\text{dB}$

TEMPERATURE AND HEAT

? At a steelworks, molten iron is heated to 1500° Celsius to remove impurities. Is it accurate to say that the molten iron contains heat?

LEARNING GOALS

By studying this chapter, you will learn:

- The meaning of thermal equilibrium, and what thermometers really measure.

- How different types of thermometers function.

- The physics behind the absolute, or Kelvin, temperature scale.

- How the dimensions of an object change as a result of a temperature change.

- The meaning of heat, and how it differs from temperature.

- How to do calculations that involve heat flow, temperature changes, and changes of phase.

- How heat is transferred by conduction, convection, and radiation.

Whether it's a sweltering summer day or a frozen midwinter night, your body needs to be kept at a nearly constant temperature. It has effective temperature-control mechanisms, but sometimes it needs help. On a hot day you wear less clothing to improve heat transfer from your body to the air and for better cooling by evaporation of perspiration. You drink cold beverages and may sit near a fan or in an air-conditioned room. On a cold day you wear more clothes or stay indoors where it's warm. When you're outside, you keep active and drink hot liquids to stay warm. The concepts in this chapter will help you understand the basic physics of keeping warm or cool.

The terms "temperature" and "heat" are often used interchangeably in everyday language. In physics, however, these two terms have very different meanings. In this chapter we'll define temperature in terms of how it's measured and see how temperature changes affect the dimensions of objects. We'll see that heat refers to energy transfer caused by temperature differences and learn how to calculate and control such energy transfers.

Our emphasis in this chapter is on the concepts of temperature and heat as they relate to *macroscopic* objects such as cylinders of gas, ice cubes, and the human body. In Chapter 18 we'll look at these same concepts from a *microscopic* viewpoint in terms of the behavior of individual atoms and molecules. These two chapters lay the groundwork for the subject of **thermodynamics,** the study of energy transformations involving heat, mechanical work, and other aspects of energy and how these transformations relate to the properties of matter. Thermodynamics forms an indispensable part of the foundation of physics, chemistry, and the life sciences, and its applications turn up in such places as car engines, refrigerators, biochemical processes, and the structure of stars. We'll explore the key ideas of thermodynamics in Chapters 19 and 20.

17.1 Temperature and Thermal Equilibrium

The concept of **temperature** is rooted in qualitative ideas of "hot" and "cold" based on our sense of touch. A body that feels hot usually has a higher temperature than a similar body that feels cold. That's pretty vague, and the senses can be deceived. But many properties of matter that we can *measure* depend on temperature. The length of a metal rod, steam pressure in a boiler, the ability of a wire to conduct an electric current, and the color of a very hot glowing object—all these depend on temperature.

Temperature is also related to the kinetic energies of the molecules of a material. In general this relationship is fairly complex, so it's not a good place to start in *defining* temperature. In Chapter 18 we will look at the relationship between temperature and the energy of molecular motion for an ideal gas. It is important to understand, however, that temperature and heat can be defined independently of any detailed molecular picture. In this section we'll develop a *macroscopic* definition of temperature.

To use temperature as a measure of hotness or coldness, we need to construct a temperature scale. To do this, we can use any measurable property of a system that varies with its "hotness" or "coldness." Figure 17.1a shows a familiar system that is used to measure temperature. When the system becomes hotter, the colored liquid (usually mercury or ethanol) expands and rises in the tube, and the value of L increases. Another simple system is a quantity of gas in a constant-volume container (Fig. 17.1b). The pressure p, measured by the gauge, increases or decreases as the gas becomes hotter or colder. A third example is the electrical resistance R of a conducting wire, which also varies when the wire becomes hotter or colder. Each of these properties gives us a number (L, p, or R) that varies with hotness and coldness, so each property can be used to make a **thermometer.**

To measure the temperature of a body, you place the thermometer in contact with the body. If you want to know the temperature of a cup of hot coffee, you stick the thermometer in the coffee; as the two interact, the thermometer becomes hotter and the coffee cools off a little. After the thermometer settles down to a steady value, you read the temperature. The system has reached an *equilibrium* condition, in which the interaction between the thermometer and the coffee causes no further change in the system. We call this a state of **thermal equilibrium.**

If two systems are separated by an insulating material or **insulator** such as wood, plastic foam, or fiberglass, they influence each other more slowly. Camping coolers are made with insulating materials to delay the ice and cold food inside from warming up and attaining thermal equilibrium with the hot summer air outside. An *ideal insulator* is a material that permits no interaction at all between the two systems. It prevents the systems from attaining thermal equilibrium if they aren't in thermal equilibrium at the start. An ideal insulator is just that, an idealization; real insulators, like those in camping coolers, aren't ideal, so the contents of the cooler will warm up eventually.

The Zeroth Law of Thermodynamics

We can discover an important property of thermal equilibrium by considering three systems, A, B, and C, that initially are not in thermal equilibrium (Fig. 17.2). We surround them with an ideal insulating box so that they cannot interact with anything except each other. We separate systems A and B with an ideal insulating wall (the green slab in Fig. 17.2a), but we let system C interact with both systems A and B. This interaction is shown in the figure by a yellow slab representing a thermal **conductor,** a material that *permits* thermal interactions through it. We wait until thermal equilibrium is attained; then A and B are each in thermal equilibrium with C. But are they in thermal equilibrium *with each other?*

To find out, we separate system C from systems A and B with an ideal insulating wall (Fig. 17.2b), and then we replace the insulating wall between A and B

17.1 Two devices for measuring temperature.

(a) Changes in temperature cause the liquid's volume to change.

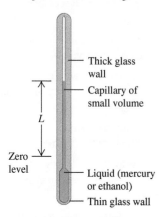

Thick glass wall

Capillary of small volume

L

Zero level

Liquid (mercury or ethanol)

Thin glass wall

(b) Changes in temperature cause the pressure of the gas to change.

p

Container of gas at constant volume

with a *conducting* wall that lets A and B interact. What happens? Experiment shows that *nothing* happens; there are no additional changes to A or B. We conclude:

> **If C is initially in thermal equilibrium with both A and B, then A and B are also in thermal equilibrium with each other. This result is called the zeroth law of thermodynamics.**

(The importance of this law was recognized only after the first, second, and third laws of thermodynamics had been named. Since it is fundamental to all of them, the name "zeroth" seemed appropriate.)

Now suppose system C is a thermometer, such as the liquid-in-tube system of Fig. 17.1a. In Fig. 17.2a the thermometer C is in contact with both A and B. In thermal equilibrium, when the thermometer reading reaches a stable value, the thermometer measures the temperature of both A and B; hence A and B both have the *same* temperature. Experiment shows that thermal equilibrium isn't affected by adding or removing insulators, so the reading of thermometer C wouldn't change if it were in contact only with A or only with B. We conclude:

> **Two systems are in thermal equilibrium if and only if they have the same temperature.**

This is what makes a thermometer useful; a thermometer actually measures *its own* temperature, but when a thermometer is in thermal equilibrium with another body, the temperatures must be equal. When the temperatures of two systems are different, they *cannot* be in thermal equilibrium.

Test Your Understanding of Section 17.1   You put a thermometer in a pot of hot water and record the reading. What temperature have you recorded? (i) the temperature of the water; (ii) the temperature of the thermometer; (iii) an equal average of the temperatures of the water and thermometer; (iv) a weighted average of the temperatures of the water and thermometer, with more emphasis on the temperature of the water; (v) a weighted average of the water and thermometer, with more emphasis on the temperature of the thermometer.

17.2 Thermometers and Temperature Scales

To make the liquid-in-tube device shown in Fig. 17.1a into a useful thermometer, we need to mark a scale on the tube wall with numbers on it. These numbers are arbitrary, and historically many different schemes have been used. Suppose we label the thermometer's liquid level at the freezing temperature of pure water "zero" and the level at the boiling temperature "100," and divide the distance between these two points into 100 equal intervals called *degrees*. The result is the **Celsius temperature scale** (formerly called the *centigrade* scale in English-speaking countries). The Celsius temperature for a state colder than freezing water is a negative number. The Celsius scale is used, both in everyday life and in science and industry, almost everywhere in the world.

Another common type of thermometer uses a *bimetallic strip,* made by bonding strips of two different metals together (Fig. 17.3a). When the temperature of the composite strip increases, one metal expands more than the other and the strip bends (Fig. 17.3b). This strip is usually formed into a spiral, with the outer end anchored to the thermometer case and the inner end attached to a pointer (Fig. 17.3c). The pointer rotates in response to temperature changes.

In a *resistance thermometer* the changing electrical resistance of a coil of fine wire, a carbon cylinder, or a germanium crystal is measured. Resistance thermometers are usually more precise than most other types.

17.2 The zeroth law of thermodynamics.

(a) If systems A and B are each in thermal equilibrium with system C …

(b) … then systems A and B are in thermal equilibrium with each other.

17.3 Use of a bimetallic strip as a thermometer.

(a) A bimetallic strip

(b) The strip bends when its temperature is raised.

When heated, metal 2 expands more than metal 1.

(c) A bimetallic strip used in a thermometer

17.4 A temporal artery thermometer measures infrared radiation from the skin that overlies one of the important arteries in the head. Although the thermometer cover touches the skin, the infrared detector inside the cover does not.

Some thermometers work by detecting the amount of infrared radiation emitted by an object. (We'll see in Section 17.7 that *all* objects emit electromagnetic radiation, including infrared, as a consequence of their temperature.) A modern example is a *temporal artery thermometer* (Fig. 17.4). A nurse runs this over a patient's forehead in the vicinity of the temporal artery, and an infrared sensor in the thermometer measures the radiation from the skin. Tests show that this device gives more accurate values of body temperature than do oral or ear thermometers.

In the **Fahrenheit temperature scale,** still used in everyday life in the United States, the freezing temperature of water is 32°F (thirty-two degrees Fahrenheit) and the boiling temperature is 212°F, both at standard atmospheric pressure. There are 180 degrees between freezing and boiling, compared to 100 on the Celsius scale, so one Fahrenheit degree represents only $\frac{100}{180}$, or $\frac{5}{9}$, as great a temperature change as one Celsius degree.

To convert temperatures from Celsius to Fahrenheit, note that a Celsius temperature T_C is the number of Celsius degrees above freezing; the number of Fahrenheit degrees above freezing is $\frac{9}{5}$ of this. But freezing on the Fahrenheit scale is at 32°F, so to obtain the actual Fahrenheit temperature T_F, multiply the Celsius value by $\frac{9}{5}$ and then add 32°. Symbolically,

$$T_F = \tfrac{9}{5}T_C + 32° \tag{17.1}$$

To convert Fahrenheit to Celsius, solve this equation for T_C:

$$T_C = \tfrac{5}{9}(T_F - 32°) \tag{17.2}$$

In words, subtract 32° to get the number of Fahrenheit degrees above freezing, and then multiply by $\frac{5}{9}$ to obtain the number of Celsius degrees above freezing—that is, the Celsius temperature.

We don't recommend memorizing Eqs. (17.1) and (17.2). Instead, try to understand the reasoning that led to them so that you can derive them on the spot when you need them, checking your reasoning with the relationship 100°C = 212°F.

It is useful to distinguish between an actual temperature and a temperature *interval* (a difference or change in temperature). An actual temperature of 20° is stated as 20°C (twenty degrees Celsius), and a temperature *interval* of 10° is 10 C° (ten Celsius degrees). A beaker of water heated from 20°C to 30°C undergoes a temperature change of 10 C°.

Application Mammalian Body Temperatures
Most mammals maintain body temperatures in the range from 36°C to 40°C (309 K to 313 K). A high metabolic rate warms the animal from within, and insulation (such as fur, feathers, and body fat) slows heat loss.

Test Your Understanding of Section 17.2 Which of the following types of thermometers have to be in thermal equilibrium with the object being measured in order to give accurate readings? (i) a bimetallic strip; (ii) a resistance thermometer; (iii) a temporal artery thermometer; (iv) both (i) and (ii); (v) all of (i), (ii), and (iii).

17.3 Gas Thermometers and the Kelvin Scale

When we calibrate two thermometers, such as a liquid-in-tube system and a resistance thermometer, so that they agree at 0°C and 100°C, they may not agree exactly at intermediate temperatures. Any temperature scale defined in this way always depends somewhat on the specific properties of the material used. Ideally, we would like to define a temperature scale that *doesn't* depend on the properties of a particular material. To establish a truly material-independent scale, we first need to develop some principles of thermodynamics. We'll return to this fundamental problem in Chapter 20. Here we'll discuss a thermometer that comes close to the ideal, the *gas thermometer.*

17.5 (a) Using a constant-volume gas thermometer to measure temperature. (b) The greater the amount of gas in the thermometer, the higher the graph of pressure p versus temperature T.

(a) A constant-volume gas thermometer

(b) Graphs of pressure versus temperature at constant volume for three different types and quantities of gas

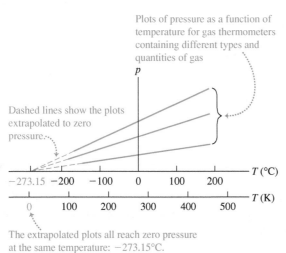

Plots of pressure as a function of temperature for gas thermometers containing different types and quantities of gas

Dashed lines show the plots extrapolated to zero pressure.

The extrapolated plots all reach zero pressure at the same temperature: $-273.15°C$.

The principle of a gas thermometer is that the pressure of a gas at constant volume increases with temperature. A quantity of gas is placed in a constant-volume container (Fig. 17.5a), and its pressure is measured by one of the devices described in Section 12.2. To calibrate a constant-volume gas thermometer, we measure the pressure at two temperatures, say 0°C and 100°C, plot these points on a graph, and draw a straight line between them. Then we can read from the graph the temperature corresponding to any other pressure. Figure 17.5b shows the results of three such experiments, each using a different type and quantity of gas.

By extrapolating this graph, we see that there is a hypothetical temperature, $-273.15°C$, at which the absolute pressure of the gas would become zero. We might expect that this temperature would be different for different gases, but it turns out to be the *same* for many different gases (at least in the limit of very low gas density). We can't actually observe this zero-pressure condition. Gases liquefy and solidify at very low temperatures, and the proportionality of pressure to temperature no longer holds.

We use this extrapolated zero-pressure temperature as the basis for a temperature scale with its zero at this temperature. This is the **Kelvin temperature scale,** named for the British physicist Lord Kelvin (1824–1907). The units are the same size as those on the Celsius scale, but the zero is shifted so that $0\text{ K} = -273.15°C$ and $273.15\text{ K} = 0°C$; that is,

$$T_K = T_C + 273.15 \qquad (17.3)$$

Figure 17.5b shows both the Celsius and Kelvin scales. A common room temperature, 20°C (= 68°F), is 20 + 273.15, or about 293 K.

CAUTION *Never say "degrees kelvin"* In SI nomenclature, "degree" is not used with the Kelvin scale; the temperature mentioned above is read "293 kelvins," not "degrees kelvin" (Fig. 17.6). We capitalize Kelvin when it refers to the temperature scale; however, the *unit* of temperature is the *kelvin,* which is not capitalized (but is nonetheless abbreviated as a capital K). ▌

17.6 Correct and incorrect uses of the Kelvin scale.

0.00°C

Ice and water

Kelvin temperatures are measured in kelvins ...

$T = 273.15$ K ◀ RIGHT!

... *not* "degrees" kelvin.

$T = 273.15$ °K ◀ WRONG

Example 17.1 **Body temperature**

You place a small piece of ice in your mouth. Eventually, the water all converts from ice at $T_1 = 32.00°F$ to body temperature, $T_2 = 98.60°F$. Express these temperatures in both Celsius degrees and kelvins, and find $\Delta T = T_2 - T_1$ in both cases.

SOLUTION

IDENTIFY and SET UP: Our target variables are stated above. We convert Fahrenheit temperatures to Celsius using Eq. (17.2), and Celsius temperatures to Kelvin using Eq. (17.3).

EXECUTE: From Eq. (17.2), $T_1 = 0.00°C$ and $T_2 = 37.00°C$; then $\Delta T = T_2 - T_1 = 37.00\ C°$. To get the Kelvin temperatures, just add 273.15 to each Celsius temperature: $T_1 = 273.15$ K and $T_2 = 310.15$ K. The temperature difference is $\Delta T = T_2 - T_1 = 37.00$ K.

EVALUATE: The Celsius and Kelvin scales have different zero points but the same size degrees. Therefore *any* temperature difference ΔT is the *same* on the Celsius and Kelvin scales. However, ΔT is *not* the same on the Fahrenheit scale; here, for example, $\Delta T = 66.60\ F°$.

The Kelvin Scale and Absolute Temperature

The Celsius scale has two fixed points: the normal freezing and boiling temperatures of water. But we can define the Kelvin scale using a gas thermometer with only a single reference temperature. We define the ratio of any two temperatures T_1 and T_2 on the Kelvin scale as the ratio of the corresponding gas-thermometer pressures p_1 and p_2:

$$\frac{T_2}{T_1} = \frac{p_2}{p_1} \qquad \text{(constant-volume gas thermometer, } T \text{ in kelvins)} \quad [17.4]$$

The pressure p is directly proportional to the Kelvin temperature, as shown in Fig. 17.5b. To complete the definition of T, we need only specify the Kelvin temperature of a single specific state. For reasons of precision and reproducibility, the state chosen is the *triple point* of water. This is the unique combination of temperature and pressure at which solid water (ice), liquid water, and water vapor can all coexist. It occurs at a temperature of 0.01°C and a water-vapor pressure of 610 Pa (about 0.006 atm). (This is the pressure of the *water;* it has nothing to do directly with the gas pressure in the *thermometer.*) The triple-point temperature T_{triple} of water is *defined* to have the value $T_{\text{triple}} = 273.16$ K, corresponding to 0.01°C. From Eq. (17.4), if p_{triple} is the pressure in a gas thermometer at temperature T_{triple} and p is the pressure at some other temperature T, then T is given on the Kelvin scale by

$$T = T_{\text{triple}} \frac{p}{p_{\text{triple}}} = (273.16\ \text{K}) \frac{p}{p_{\text{triple}}} \qquad [17.5]$$

Low-pressure gas thermometers using various gases are found to agree very closely, but they are large, bulky, and very slow to come to thermal equilibrium. They are used principally to establish high-precision standards and to calibrate other thermometers.

Figure 17.7 shows the relationships among the three temperature scales we have discussed. The Kelvin scale is called an **absolute temperature scale,** and its zero point ($T = 0\ \text{K} = -273.15°C$, the temperature at which $p = 0$ in Eq. (17.5)) is called **absolute zero.** At absolute zero a system of molecules (such as a quantity of a gas, a liquid, or a solid) has its *minimum* possible total energy (kinetic plus potential); because of quantum effects, however, it is *not* correct to say that all molecular motion ceases at absolute zero. To define more completely what we mean by absolute zero, we need to use the thermodynamic principles developed in the next several chapters. We will return to this concept in Chapter 20.

17.7 Relationships among Kelvin (K), Celsius (C), and Fahrenheit (F) temperature scales. Temperatures have been rounded off to the nearest degree.

Test Your Understanding of Section 17.3 Rank the following temperatures from highest to lowest: (i) 0.00°C; (ii) 0.00°F; (iii) 260.00 K; (iv) 77.00 K; (v) −180.00°C.

17.4 Thermal Expansion

Most materials expand when their temperatures increase. Rising temperatures make the liquid expand in a liquid-in-tube thermometer (Fig. 17.1a) and bend bimetallic strips (Fig. 17.3b). The decks of bridges need special joints and supports to allow for expansion. A completely filled and tightly capped bottle of water cracks when it is heated, but you can loosen a metal jar lid by running hot water over it. These are all examples of *thermal expansion.*

Linear Expansion

Suppose a rod of material has a length L_0 at some initial temperature T_0. When the temperature changes by ΔT, the length changes by ΔL. Experiments show that if ΔT is not too large (say, less than 100 C° or so), ΔL is *directly proportional* to ΔT (Fig. 17.8a). If two rods made of the same material have the same temperature change, but one is twice as long as the other, then the *change* in its length is also twice as great. Therefore ΔL must also be proportional to L_0 (Fig. 17.8b). Introducing a proportionality constant α (which is different for different materials), we may express these relationships in an equation:

$$\Delta L = \alpha L_0 \Delta T \quad \text{(linear thermal expansion)} \quad [17.6]$$

If a body has length L_0 at temperature T_0, then its length L at a temperature $T = T_0 + \Delta T$ is

$$L = L_0 + \Delta L = L_0 + \alpha L_0 \Delta T = L_0(1 + \alpha \Delta T) \quad [17.7]$$

The constant α, which describes the thermal expansion properties of a particular material, is called the **coefficient of linear expansion.** The units of α are K^{-1} or $(\text{C}°)^{-1}$. (Remember that a temperature *interval* is the same in the Kelvin and Celsius scales.) For many materials, every linear dimension changes according to Eq. (17.6) or (17.7). Thus L could be the thickness of a rod, the side length of a square sheet, or the diameter of a hole. Some materials, such as wood or single crystals, expand differently in different directions. We won't consider this complication.

We can understand thermal expansion qualitatively on a molecular basis. Picture the interatomic forces in a solid as springs, as in Fig. 17.9a. (We explored the analogy between spring forces and interatomic forces in Section 14.4.) Each atom vibrates about its equilibrium position. When the temperature increases, the energy and amplitude of the vibration also increase. The interatomic spring forces are not symmetrical about the equilibrium position; they usually behave like a spring that is easier to stretch than to compress. As a result, when the amplitude of vibration increases, the *average* distance between atoms also increases (Fig. 17.9b). As the atoms get farther apart, every dimension increases.

17.8 How the length of a rod changes with a change in temperature. (Length changes are exaggerated for clarity.)

(a) For moderate temperature changes, ΔL is directly proportional to ΔT.

(b) ΔL is also directly proportional to L_0.

(a) A model of the forces between neighboring atoms in a solid

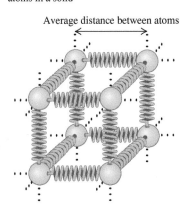

Average distance between atoms

(b) A graph of the "spring" potential energy $U(x)$

$U(x)$ x = distance between atoms
● = average distance between atoms

E_3
E_2
E_1

As energy increases from E_1 to E_2 to E_3, average distance between atoms increases.

17.9 **(a)** We can model atoms in a solid as being held together by "springs" that are easier to stretch than to compress. **(b)** A graph of the "spring" potential energy $U(x)$ versus distance x between neighboring atoms is *not* symmetrical (compare Fig. 14.20b). As the energy increases and the atoms oscillate with greater amplitude, the average distance increases.

17.10 When an object undergoes thermal expansion, any holes in the object expand as well. (The expansion is exaggerated.)

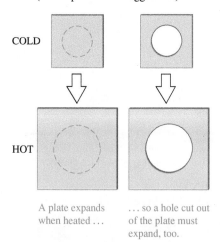

COLD

HOT

A plate expands when heated ...

... so a hole cut out of the plate must expand, too.

17.11 When this SR-71 aircraft is sitting on the ground, its wing panels fit together so loosely that fuel leaks out of the wings onto the ground. But once it is in flight at over three times the speed of sound, air friction heats the panels so much that they expand to make a perfect fit. (In-flight refueling makes up for the lost fuel.)

CAUTION **Heating an object with a hole** If a solid object has a hole in it, what happens to the size of the hole when the temperature of the object increases? A common misconception is that if the object expands, the hole will shrink because material expands into the hole. But the truth of the matter is that if the object expands, the hole will expand too (Fig. 17.10); as we stated above, *every* linear dimension of an object changes in the same way when the temperature changes. If you're not convinced, think of the atoms in Fig. 17.9a as outlining a cubical hole. When the object expands, the atoms move apart and the hole increases in size. The only situation in which a "hole" will fill in due to thermal expansion is when two separate objects expand and close the gap between them (Fig. 17.11).

The direct proportionality expressed by Eq. (17.6) is not exact; it is *approximately* correct only for sufficiently small temperature changes. For a given material, α varies somewhat with the initial temperature T_0 and the size of the temperature interval. We'll ignore this complication here, however. Average values of α for several materials are listed in Table 17.1. Within the precision of these values we don't need to worry whether T_0 is 0°C or 20°C or some other temperature. Note that typical values of α are very small; even for a temperature change of 100 C°, the fractional length change $\Delta L/L_0$ is only of the order of $\frac{1}{1000}$ for the metals in the table.

Volume Expansion

Increasing temperature usually causes increases in *volume* for both solid and liquid materials. Just as with linear expansion, experiments show that if the temperature change ΔT is not too great (less than 100 C° or so), the increase in volume ΔV is approximately proportional to both the temperature change ΔT and the initial volume V_0:

$$\Delta V = \beta V_0 \Delta T \qquad \text{(volume thermal expansion)} \qquad (17.8)$$

The constant β characterizes the volume expansion properties of a particular material; it is called the **coefficient of volume expansion.** The units of β are K^{-1} or $(C°)^{-1}$. As with linear expansion, β varies somewhat with temperature, and Eq. (17.8) is an approximate relationship that is valid only for small temperature changes. For many substances, β decreases at low temperatures. Several values of β in the neighborhood of room temperature are listed in Table 17.2. Note that the values for liquids are generally much larger than those for solids.

For solid materials there is a simple relationship between the volume expansion coefficient β and the linear expansion coefficient α. To derive this relationship, we consider a cube of material with side length L and volume $V = L^3$. At the initial temperature the values are L_0 and V_0. When the temperature increases by dT, the side length increases by dL and the volume increases by an amount dV given by

$$dV = \frac{dV}{dL} dL = 3L^2 dL$$

Table 17.1 Coefficients of Linear Expansion

Material	$\alpha \, [K^{-1} \text{ or } (C°)^{-1}]$
Aluminum	2.4×10^{-5}
Brass	2.0×10^{-5}
Copper	1.7×10^{-5}
Glass	$0.4 – 0.9 \times 10^{-5}$
Invar (nickel–iron alloy)	0.09×10^{-5}
Quartz (fused)	0.04×10^{-5}
Steel	1.2×10^{-5}

Table 17.2 Coefficients of Volume Expansion

Solids	$\beta \, [K^{-1} \text{ or } (C°)^{-1}]$	Liquids	$\beta \, [K^{-1} \text{ or } (C°)^{-1}]$
Aluminum	7.2×10^{-5}	Ethanol	75×10^{-5}
Brass	6.0×10^{-5}	Carbon disulfide	115×10^{-5}
Copper	5.1×10^{-5}	Glycerin	49×10^{-5}
Glass	$1.2 – 2.7 \times 10^{-5}$	Mercury	18×10^{-5}
Invar	0.27×10^{-5}		
Quartz (fused)	0.12×10^{-5}		
Steel	3.6×10^{-5}		

Now we replace L and V by the initial values L_0 and V_0. From Eq. (17.6), dL is

$$dL = \alpha L_0 \, dT$$

Since $V_0 = L_0^3$, this means that dV can also be expressed as

$$dV = 3L_0^2 \alpha L_0 \, dT = 3\alpha V_0 \, dT$$

This is consistent with the infinitesimal form of Eq. (17.8), $dV = \beta V_0 \, dT$, only if

$$\beta = 3\alpha \qquad (17.9)$$

You should check this relationship for some of the materials listed in Tables 17.1 and 17.2.

Problem-Solving Strategy 17.1 **Thermal Expansion**

IDENTIFY *the relevant concepts:* Decide whether the problem involves changes in length (linear thermal expansion) or in volume (volume thermal expansion).

SET UP *the problem* using the following steps:
1. List the known and unknown quantities and identify the target variables.
2. Choose Eq. (17.6) for linear expansion and Eq. (17.8) for volume expansion.

EXECUTE *the solution* as follows:
1. Solve for the target variables. If you are given an initial temperature T_0 and must find a final temperature T corresponding to a given length or volume change, find ΔT and calculate $T = T_0 + \Delta T$. Remember that the size of a hole in a material varies with temperature just as any other linear dimension, and that the volume of a hole (such as the interior of a container) varies just as that of the corresponding solid shape.
2. Maintain unit consistency. Both L_0 and ΔL (or V_0 and ΔV) must have the same units. If you use a value of α or β in K^{-1} or $(C°)^{-1}$, then ΔT must be in either kelvins or Celsius degrees; from Example 17.1, the two scales are equivalent *for temperature differences.*

EVALUATE *your answer:* Check whether your results make sense.

Example 17.2 **Length change due to temperature change**

A surveyor uses a steel measuring tape that is exactly 50.000 m long at a temperature of 20°C. The markings on the tape are calibrated for this temperature. (a) What is the length of the tape when the temperature is 35°C? (b) When it is 35°C, the surveyor uses the tape to measure a distance. The value that she reads off the tape is 35.794 m. What is the actual distance?

SOLUTION

IDENTIFY and SET UP: This problem concerns the linear expansion of a measuring tape. We are given the tape's initial length $L_0 = 50.000$ m at $T_0 = 20°C$. In part (a) we use Eq. (17.6) to find the change ΔL in the tape's length at $T = 35°C$, and use Eq. (17.7) to find L. (Table 17.1 gives the value of α for steel.) Since the tape expands, at 35°C the distance between two successive meter marks is greater than 1 m. Hence the actual distance in part (b) is *larger* than the distance read off the tape by a factor equal to the ratio of the tape's length L at 35°C to its length L_0 at 20°C.

EXECUTE: (a) The temperature change is $\Delta T = T - T_0 = 15$ C°; from Eqs. (17.6) and (17.7),

$\Delta L = \alpha L_0 \, \Delta T = (1.2 \times 10^{-5} \, K^{-1})(50 \, m)(15 \, K)$
$= 9.0 \times 10^{-3} \, m = 9.0 \, mm$

$L = L_0 + \Delta L = 50.000 \, m + 0.009 \, m = 50.009 \, m$

(b) Our result from part (a) shows that at 35°C, the slightly expanded tape reads a distance of 50.000 m when the true distance is 50.009 m. We can rewrite the algebra of part (a) as $L = L_0(1 + \alpha \, \Delta T)$; at 35°C, *any* true distance will be greater than the reading by the factor $50.009/50.000 = 1 + \alpha \, \Delta T = 1 + 1.8 \times 10^{-4}$. The true distance is therefore

$$(1 + 1.8 \times 10^{-4})(35.794 \, m) = 35.800 \, m$$

EVALUATE: Note that in part (a) we needed only two of the five significant figures of L_0 to compute ΔL to the same number of decimal places as L_0. Our result shows that metals expand very little under moderate temperature changes. However, even the small difference 0.009 m = 9 mm found in part (b) between the scale reading and the true distance can be important in precision work.

Example 17.3 **Volume change due to temperature change**

A 200-cm³ glass flask is filled to the brim with mercury at 20°C. How much mercury overflows when the temperature of the system is raised to 100°C? The coefficient of *linear* expansion of the glass is $0.40 \times 10^{-5} \, K^{-1}$.

Continued

SOLUTION

IDENTIFY and SET UP: This problem involves the volume expansion of the glass and of the mercury. The amount of overflow depends on the *difference* between the volume changes ΔV for these two materials, both given by Eq. (17.8). The mercury will overflow if its coefficient of volume expansion β (given in Table 17.2) is greater than that of glass, which we find from Eq. (17.9) using the given value of α.

EXECUTE: From Table 17.2, $\beta_{Hg} = 18 \times 10^{-5}\,\text{K}^{-1}$. That is indeed greater than β_{glass}: From Eq. (17.9), $\beta_{glass} = 3\alpha_{glass} = 3(0.40 \times 10^{-5}\,\text{K}^{-1}) = 1.2 \times 10^{-5}\,\text{K}^{-1}$. The volume overflow is then

$$\Delta V_{Hg} - \Delta V_{glass} = \beta_{Hg} V_0 \Delta T - \beta_{glass} V_0 \Delta T$$
$$= V_0 \Delta T (\beta_{Hg} - \beta_{glass})$$
$$= (200\ \text{cm}^3)(80\ \text{C}°)(18 \times 10^{-5} - 1.2 \times 10^{-5})$$
$$= 2.7\ \text{cm}^3$$

EVALUATE: This is basically how a mercury-in-glass thermometer works; the column of mercury inside a sealed tube rises as T increases because mercury expands faster than glass.

As Tables 17.1 and 17.2 show, glass has smaller coefficients of expansion α and β than do most metals. This is why you can use hot water to loosen a metal lid on a glass jar; the metal expands more than the glass does.

Thermal Expansion of Water

Water, in the temperature range from 0°C to 4°C, *decreases* in volume with increasing temperature. In this range its coefficient of volume expansion is *negative*. Above 4°C, water expands when heated (Fig. 17.12). Hence water has its greatest density at 4°C. Water also expands when it freezes, which is why ice humps up in the middle of the compartments in an ice cube tray. By contrast, most materials contract when they freeze.

This anomalous behavior of water has an important effect on plant and animal life in lakes. A lake cools from the surface down; above 4°C, the cooled water at the surface flows to the bottom because of its greater density. But when the surface temperature drops below 4°C, the water near the surface is less dense than the warmer water below. Hence the downward flow ceases, and the water near the surface remains colder than that at the bottom. As the surface freezes, the ice floats because it is less dense than water. The water at the bottom remains at 4°C until nearly the entire lake is frozen. If water behaved like most substances, contracting continuously on cooling and freezing, lakes would freeze from the bottom up. Circulation due to density differences would continuously carry warmer water to the surface for efficient cooling, and lakes would freeze solid much more easily. This would destroy all plant and animal life that cannot withstand freezing. If water did not have this special property, the evolution of life would have taken a very different course.

17.12 The volume of 1 gram of water in the temperature range from 0°C to 100°C. By 100°C the volume has increased to 1.034 cm³. If the coefficient of volume expansion were constant, the curve would be a straight line.

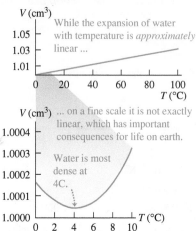

Thermal Stress

If we clamp the ends of a rod rigidly to prevent expansion or contraction and then change the temperature, **thermal stresses** develop. The rod would like to expand or contract, but the clamps won't let it. The resulting stresses may become large enough to strain the rod irreversibly or even break it. (You may want to review the discussion of stress and strain in Section 11.4).

Engineers must account for thermal stress when designing structures. Concrete highways and bridge decks usually have gaps between sections, filled with a flexible material or bridged by interlocking teeth (Fig. 17.13), to permit expansion and contraction of the concrete. Long steam pipes have expansion joints or U-shaped sections to prevent buckling or stretching with temperature changes. If one end of a steel bridge is rigidly fastened to its abutment, the other end usually rests on rollers.

To calculate the thermal stress in a clamped rod, we compute the amount the rod *would* expand (or contract) if not held and then find the stress needed to compress (or stretch) it back to its original length. Suppose that a rod with length L_0 and cross-sectional area A is held at constant length while the temperature is reduced (negative ΔT), causing a tensile stress. The fractional change in length if the rod were free to contract would be

$$\left(\frac{\Delta L}{L_0}\right)_{\text{thermal}} = \alpha\,\Delta T \qquad (17.10)$$

17.13 Expansion joints on bridges are needed to accommodate changes in length that result from thermal expansion.

Both ΔL and ΔT are negative. The tension must increase by an amount F that is just enough to produce an equal and opposite fractional change in length $(\Delta L/L_0)_{tension}$. From the definition of Young's modulus, Eq. (11.10),

$$Y = \frac{F/A}{\Delta L/L_0} \quad \text{so} \quad \left(\frac{\Delta L}{L_0}\right)_{tension} = \frac{F}{AY} \qquad (17.11)$$

If the length is to be constant, the *total* fractional change in length must be zero. From Eqs. (17.10) and (17.11), this means that

$$\left(\frac{\Delta L}{L_0}\right)_{thermal} + \left(\frac{\Delta L}{L_0}\right)_{tension} = \alpha \, \Delta T + \frac{F}{AY} = 0$$

Solving for the tensile stress F/A required to keep the rod's length constant, we find

$$\frac{F}{A} = -Y\alpha \, \Delta T \qquad \text{(thermal stress)} \qquad (17.12)$$

For a decrease in temperature, ΔT is negative, so F and F/A are positive; this means that a *tensile* force and stress are needed to maintain the length. If ΔT is positive, F and F/A are negative, and the required force and stress are *compressive*.

If there are temperature differences within a body, nonuniform expansion or contraction will result and thermal stresses can be induced. You can break a glass bowl by pouring very hot water into it; the thermal stress between the hot and cold parts of the bowl exceeds the breaking stress of the glass, causing cracks. The same phenomenon makes ice cubes crack when dropped into warm water. Heat-resistant glasses such as Pyrex™ have exceptionally low expansion coefficients and high strength.

Example 17.4 **Thermal stress**

An aluminum cylinder 10 cm long, with a cross-sectional area of 20 cm², is used as a spacer between two steel walls. At 17.2°C it just slips between the walls. Calculate the stress in the cylinder and the total force it exerts on each wall when it warms to 22.3°C, assuming that the walls are perfectly rigid and a constant distance apart.

SOLUTION

IDENTIFY and SET UP: Figure 17.14 shows our sketch of the situation. Our target variables are the thermal stress F/A in the cylinder, whose cross-sectional area A is given, and the associated force F it

exerts on the walls. We use Eq. (17.12) to relate F/A to the temperature change ΔT, and from that calculate F. (The length of the cylinder is irrelevant.) We find Young's modulus Y_{Al} and the coefficient of linear expansion α_{Al} from Tables 11.1 and 17.1, respectively.

EXECUTE: We have $Y_{Al} = 7.0 \times 10^{10}$ Pa and $\alpha_{Al} = 2.4 \times 10^{-5}\,\text{K}^{-1}$, and $\Delta T = 22.3°C - 17.2°C = 5.1\,\text{C}° = 5.1$ K. From Eq. (17.12), the stress is

$$\frac{F}{A} = -Y_{Al}\alpha_{Al}\Delta T$$
$$= -(7.0 \times 10^{10}\,\text{Pa})(2.4 \times 10^{-5}\,\text{K}^{-1})(5.1\,\text{K})$$
$$= -8.6 \times 10^6\,\text{Pa} = -1200\,\text{lb/in.}^2$$

The total force is the cross-sectional area times the stress:

$$F = A\left(\frac{F}{A}\right) = (20 \times 10^{-4}\,\text{m}^2)(-8.6 \times 10^6\,\text{Pa})$$
$$= -1.7 \times 10^4\,\text{N} = 1.9\,\text{tons}$$

EVALUATE: The stress on the cylinder and the force it exerts on each wall are immense. Such thermal stresses must be accounted for in engineering.

17.14 Our sketch for this problem.

$A = 20\,\text{cm}^2$

10 cm

Test Your Understanding of Section 17.4 In the bimetallic strip shown in Fig. 17.3a, metal 1 is copper. Which of the following materials could be used for metal 2? (There may be more than one correct answer). (i) steel; (ii) brass; (iii) aluminum.

17.5 Quantity of Heat

17.15 The same temperature change of the same system may be accomplished by (a) doing work on it or (b) adding heat to it.

(a) Raising the temperature of water by doing work on it

The water warms as the paddle does work on it; the temperature rise is proportional to the amount of work done.

(b) Raising the temperature of water by direct heating

Direct heating can produce the same temperature change as doing work on the water.

When you put a cold spoon into a cup of hot coffee, the spoon warms up and the coffee cools down as they approach thermal equilibrium. The interaction that causes these temperature changes is fundamentally a transfer of *energy* from one substance to another. Energy transfer that takes place solely because of a temperature difference is called *heat flow* or *heat transfer,* and energy transferred in this way is called **heat.**

An understanding of the relationship between heat and other forms of energy emerged during the 18th and 19th centuries. Sir James Joule (1818–1889) studied how water can be warmed by vigorous stirring with a paddle wheel (Fig. 17.15a). The paddle wheel adds energy to the water by doing *work* on it, and Joule found that *the temperature rise is directly proportional to the amount of work done.* The same temperature change can also be caused by putting the water in contact with some hotter body (Fig. 17.15b); hence this interaction must also involve an energy exchange. We will explore the relationship between heat and mechanical energy in Chapters 19 and 20.

CAUTION **Temperature vs. heat** It is absolutely essential for you to distinguish between *temperature* and *heat.* Temperature depends on the physical state of a material and is a quantitative description of its hotness or coldness. In physics the term "heat" always refers to energy in transit from one body or system to another because of a temperature difference, never to the amount of energy contained within a particular system. We can change the temperature of a body by adding heat to it or taking heat away, or by adding or subtracting energy in other ways, such as mechanical work (Fig. 17.15a). If we cut a body in half, each half has the same temperature as the whole; but to raise the temperature of each half by a given interval, we add *half* as much heat as for the whole.

We can define a *unit* of quantity of heat based on temperature changes of some specific material. The **calorie** (abbreviated cal) is defined as *the amount of heat required to raise the temperature of 1 gram of water from 14.5°C to 15.5°C.* The kilocalorie (kcal), equal to 1000 cal, is also used; a food-value calorie is actually a kilocalorie (Fig. 17.16). A corresponding unit of heat using Fahrenheit degrees and British units is the **British thermal unit,** or Btu. One Btu is the quantity of heat required to raise the temperature of 1 pound (weight) of water 1 F° from 63°F to 64°F.

Because heat is energy in transit, there must be a definite relationship between these units and the familiar mechanical energy units such as the joule. Experiments similar in concept to Joule's have shown that

$$1 \text{ cal} = 4.186 \text{ J}$$
$$1 \text{ kcal} = 1000 \text{ cal} = 4186 \text{ J}$$
$$1 \text{ Btu} = 778 \text{ ft} \cdot \text{lb} = 252 \text{ cal} = 1055 \text{ J}$$

The calorie is not a fundamental SI unit. The International Committee on Weights and Measures recommends using the joule as the basic unit of energy in all forms, including heat. We will follow that recommendation in this book.

Specific Heat

We use the symbol Q for quantity of heat. When it is associated with an infinitesimal temperature change dT, we call it dQ. The quantity of heat Q required to increase the temperature of a mass m of a certain material from T_1 to T_2 is found to be approximately proportional to the temperature change $\Delta T = T_2 - T_1$. It is also proportional to the mass m of material. When you're heating water to make tea, you need twice as much heat for two cups as for one if the temperature change is the same. The quantity of heat needed also depends on the nature of the material; raising the temperature of 1 kilogram of water by 1 C° requires 4190 J of heat, but only 910 J is needed to raise the temperature of 1 kilogram of aluminum by 1 C°.

17.16 The word "energy" is of Greek origin. This label on a can of Greek coffee shows that 100 milliliters of prepared coffee have an energy content (ενέργεια) of 9.6 kilojoules or 2.3 kilocalories.

Putting all these relationships together, we have

$$Q = mc\,\Delta T \quad \text{(heat required for temperature change } \Delta T \text{ of mass } m)} \quad (17.13)$$

where c is a quantity, different for different materials, called the **specific heat** of the material. For an infinitesimal temperature change dT and corresponding quantity of heat dQ,

$$dQ = mc\,dT \qquad (17.14)$$

$$c = \frac{1}{m}\frac{dQ}{dT} \qquad \text{(specific heat)} \qquad (17.15)$$

In Eqs. (17.13), (17.14), and (17.15), Q (or dQ) and ΔT (or dT) can be either positive or negative. When they are positive, heat enters the body and its temperature increases; when they are negative, heat leaves the body and its temperature decreases.

CAUTION **The definition of heat** Remember that dQ does not represent a change in the amount of heat *contained* in a body; this is a meaningless concept. Heat is always energy *in transit* as a result of a temperature difference. There is no such thing as "the amount of heat in a body."

The specific heat of water is approximately

$$4190 \text{ J/kg} \cdot \text{K} \qquad 1 \text{ cal/g} \cdot \text{C}° \qquad \text{or} \qquad 1 \text{ Btu/lb} \cdot \text{F}°$$

The specific heat of a material always depends somewhat on the initial temperature and the temperature interval. Figure 17.17 shows this dependence for water. In the problems and examples in this chapter we will usually ignore this small variation.

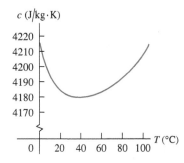

17.17 Specific heat of water as a function of temperature. The value of c varies by less than 1% between 0°C and 100°C.

Example 17.5 Feed a cold, starve a fever

During a bout with the flu an 80-kg man ran a fever of 39.0°C (102.2°F) instead of the normal body temperature of 37.0°C (98.6°F). Assuming that the human body is mostly water, how much heat is required to raise his temperature by that amount?

SOLUTION

IDENTIFY and SET UP: This problem uses the relationship among heat (the target variable), mass, specific heat, and temperature change. We use Eq. (17.13) to determine the required heat Q, with $m = 80$ kg, $c = 4190$ J/kg·K (for water), and $\Delta T = 39.0°C - 37.0°C = 2.0$ C° = 2.0 K.

EXECUTE: From Eq. (17.13),

$$Q = mc\,\Delta T = (80 \text{ kg})(4190 \text{ J/kg} \cdot \text{K})(2.0 \text{ K}) = 6.7 \times 10^5 \text{ J}$$

EVALUATE: This corresponds to 160 kcal. In fact, the specific heat of the human body is about 3480 J/kg·K, 83% that of water, because protein, fat, and minerals have lower specific heats. Hence a more accurate answer is $Q = 5.6 \times 10^5$ J = 133 kcal. Either result shows us that were it not for the body's temperature-regulating systems, taking in energy in the form of food would produce measurable changes in body temperature. (The elevated temperature of a person with the flu results from the body's extra activity in response to infection.)

Example 17.6 Overheating electronics

You are designing an electronic circuit element made of 23 mg of silicon. The electric current through it adds energy at the rate of 7.4 mW = 7.4×10^{-3} J/s. If your design doesn't allow any heat transfer out of the element, at what rate does its temperature increase? The specific heat of silicon is 705 J/kg·K.

SOLUTION

IDENTIFY and SET UP: The energy added to the circuit element gives rise to a temperature increase, just as if heat were flowing into the element at the rate $dQ/dt = 7.4 \times 10^{-3}$ J/s. Our target variable is the rate of temperature change dT/dt. We can use Eq. (17.14), which relates infinitesimal temperature changes dT to the corresponding heat dQ, to obtain an expression for dQ/dt in terms of dT/dt.

EXECUTE: We divide both sides of Eq. (17.14) by dt and rearrange:

$$\frac{dT}{dt} = \frac{dQ/dt}{mc} = \frac{7.4 \times 10^{-3} \text{ J/s}}{(23 \times 10^{-6} \text{ kg})(705 \text{ J/kg} \cdot \text{K})} = 0.46 \text{ K/s}$$

EVALUATE: At this rate of temperature rise (27 K/min), the circuit element would soon self-destruct. Heat transfer is an important design consideration in electronic circuit elements.

Molar Heat Capacity

Sometimes it's more convenient to describe a quantity of substance in terms of the number of *moles n* rather than the *mass m* of material. Recall from your study of chemistry that a mole of any pure substance always contains the same number of molecules. (We will discuss this point in more detail in Chapter 18.) The *molar mass* of any substance, denoted by M, is the mass per mole. (The quantity M is sometimes called *molecular weight,* but *molar mass* is preferable; the quantity depends on the mass of a molecule, not its weight.) For example, the molar mass of water is $18.0 \text{ g/mol} = 18.0 \times 10^{-3} \text{ kg/mol}$; 1 mole of water has a mass of $18.0 \text{ g} = 0.0180 \text{ kg}$. The total mass m of material is equal to the mass per mole M times the number of moles n:

$$m = nM \qquad (17.16)$$

Replacing the mass m in Eq. (17.13) by the product nM, we find

$$Q = nMc \, \Delta T \qquad (17.17)$$

The product Mc is called the **molar heat capacity** (or *molar specific heat*) and is denoted by C (capitalized). With this notation we rewrite Eq. (17.17) as

$$Q = nC \, \Delta T \qquad \text{(heat required for temperature change of } n \text{ moles)} \qquad (17.18)$$

Comparing to Eq. (17.15), we can express the molar heat capacity C (heat per mole per temperature change) in terms of the specific heat c (heat per mass per temperature change) and the molar mass M (mass per mole):

$$C = \frac{1}{n}\frac{dQ}{dT} = Mc \qquad \text{(molar heat capacity)} \qquad (17.19)$$

For example, the molar heat capacity of water is

$$C = Mc = (0.0180 \text{ kg/mol})(4190 \text{ J/kg} \cdot \text{K}) = 75.4 \text{ J/mol} \cdot \text{K}$$

Values of specific heat and molar heat capacity for several substances are given in Table 17.3. Note the remarkably large specific heat for water (Fig. 17.18).

CAUTION **The meaning of "heat capacity"** The term "heat capacity" is unfortunate because it gives the erroneous impression that a body *contains* a certain amount of heat. Remember, heat is energy in transit to or from a body, not the energy residing in the body. ∎

Video Tutor Demo   **Video Tutor Demo**

17.18 Water has a much higher specific heat than the glass or metals used to make cookware. This helps explain why it takes several minutes to boil water on a stove, even though the pot or kettle reaches a high temperature very quickly.

Table 17.3 Approximate Specific Heats and Molar Heat Capacities (Constant Pressure)

Substance	Specific Heat, c (J/kg · K)	Molar Mass, M (kg/mol)	Molar Heat Capacity, C (J/mol · K)
Aluminum	910	0.0270	24.6
Beryllium	1970	0.00901	17.7
Copper	390	0.0635	24.8
Ethanol	2428	0.0461	111.9
Ethylene glycol	2386	0.0620	148.0
Ice (near 0°C)	2100	0.0180	37.8
Iron	470	0.0559	26.3
Lead	130	0.207	26.9
Marble ($CaCO_3$)	879	0.100	87.9
Mercury	138	0.201	27.7
Salt (NaCl)	879	0.0585	51.4
Silver	234	0.108	25.3
Water (liquid)	4190	0.0180	75.4

Precise measurements of specific heats and molar heat capacities require great experimental skill. Usually, a measured quantity of energy is supplied by an electric current in a heater wire wound around the specimen. The temperature change ΔT is measured with a resistance thermometer or thermocouple embedded in the specimen. This sounds simple, but great care is needed to avoid or compensate for unwanted heat transfer between the sample and its surroundings. Measurements for solid materials are usually made at constant atmospheric pressure; the corresponding values are called the *specific heat* and *molar heat capacity at constant pressure,* denoted by c_p and C_p. For a gas it is usually easier to keep the substance in a container with constant *volume;* the corresponding values are called the *specific heat* and *molar heat capacity at constant volume,* denoted by c_V and C_V. For a given substance, C_V and C_p are different. If the system can expand while heat is added, there is additional energy exchange through the performance of *work* by the system on its surroundings. If the volume is constant, the system does no work. For gases the difference between C_p and C_V is substantial. We will study heat capacities of gases in detail in Section 19.7.

The last column of Table 17.3 shows something interesting. The molar heat capacities for most elemental solids are about the same: about 25 J/mol $\cdot$ K. This correlation, named the *rule of Dulong and Petit* (for its discoverers), forms the basis for a very important idea. The number of atoms in 1 mole is the same for all elemental substances. This means that on a *per atom* basis, about the same amount of heat is required to raise the temperature of each of these elements by a given amount, even though the *masses* of the atoms are very different. The heat required for a given temperature increase depends only on *how many* atoms the sample contains, not on the mass of an individual atom. We will see the reason the rule of Dulong and Petit works so well when we study the molecular basis of heat capacities in greater detail in Chapter 18.

Test Your Understanding of Section 17.5 You wish to raise the temperature of each of the following samples from 20°C to 21°C. Rank these in order of the amount of heat needed to do this, from highest to lowest. (i) 1 kilogram of mercury; (ii) 1 kilogram of ethanol; (iii) 1 mole of mercury; (iv) 1 mole of ethanol.

17.6 Calorimetry and Phase Changes

Calorimetry means "measuring heat." We have discussed the energy transfer (heat) involved in temperature changes. Heat is also involved in *phase changes,* such as the melting of ice or boiling of water. Once we understand these additional heat relationships, we can analyze a variety of problems involving quantity of heat.

Phase Changes

We use the term **phase** to describe a specific state of matter, such as a solid, liquid, or gas. The compound H_2O exists in the *solid phase* as ice, in the *liquid phase* as water, and in the *gaseous phase* as steam. (These are also referred to as **states of matter:** the solid state, the liquid state, and the gaseous state.) A transition from one phase to another is called a **phase change** or *phase transition.* For any given pressure a phase change takes place at a definite temperature, usually accompanied by absorption or emission of heat and a change of volume and density.

A familiar example of a phase change is the melting of ice. When we add heat to ice at 0°C and normal atmospheric pressure, the temperature of the ice *does not* increase. Instead, some of it melts to form liquid water. If we add the heat slowly, to maintain the system very close to thermal equilibrium, the temperature remains at 0°C until all the ice is melted (Fig. 17.19). The effect of adding heat to this system is not to raise its temperature but to change its *phase* from solid to liquid.

To change 1 kg of ice at 0°C to 1 kg of liquid water at 0°C and normal atmospheric pressure requires 3.34×10^5 J of heat. The heat required per unit mass is

17.19 The surrounding air is at room temperature, but this ice–water mixture remains at 0°C until all of the ice has melted and the phase change is complete.

PhET: States of Matter

called the **heat of fusion** (or sometimes *latent heat of fusion*), denoted by L_f. For water at normal atmospheric pressure the heat of fusion is

$$L_f = 3.34 \times 10^5 \text{ J/kg} = 79.6 \text{ cal/g} = 143 \text{ Btu/lb}$$

More generally, to melt a mass m of material that has a heat of fusion L_f requires a quantity of heat Q given by

$$Q = mL_f$$

This process is *reversible*. To freeze liquid water to ice at 0°C, we have to *remove* heat; the magnitude is the same, but in this case, Q is negative because heat is removed rather than added. To cover both possibilities and to include other kinds of phase changes, we write

$$Q = \pm mL \qquad \text{(heat transfer in a phase change)} \qquad (17.20)$$

The plus sign (heat entering) is used when the material melts; the minus sign (heat leaving) is used when it freezes. The heat of fusion is different for different materials, and it also varies somewhat with pressure.

For any given material at any given pressure, the freezing temperature is the same as the melting temperature. At this unique temperature the liquid and solid phases (liquid water and ice, for example) can coexist in a condition called **phase equilibrium.**

We can go through this whole story again for *boiling* or *evaporation,* a phase transition between liquid and gaseous phases. The corresponding heat (per unit mass) is called the **heat of vaporization** L_v. At normal atmospheric pressure the heat of vaporization L_v for water is

$$L_v = 2.256 \times 10^6 \text{ J/kg} = 539 \text{ cal/g} = 970 \text{ Btu/lb}$$

That is, it takes 2.256×10^6 J to change 1 kg of liquid water at 100°C to 1 kg of water vapor at 100°C. By comparison, to raise the temperature of 1 kg of water from 0°C to 100°C requires $Q = mc \, \Delta T = (1.00 \text{ kg})(4190 \text{ J/kg} \cdot \text{C}°) \times (100 \text{ C}°) = 4.19 \times 10^5$ J, less than one-fifth as much heat as is required for vaporization at 100°C. This agrees with everyday kitchen experience; a pot of water may reach boiling temperature in a few minutes, but it takes a much longer time to completely evaporate all the water away.

Like melting, boiling is a reversible transition. When heat is removed from a gas at the boiling temperature, the gas returns to the liquid phase, or *condenses,* giving up to its surroundings the same quantity of heat (heat of vaporization) that was needed to vaporize it. At a given pressure the boiling and condensation temperatures are always the same; at this temperature the liquid and gaseous phases can coexist in phase equilibrium.

Both L_v and the boiling temperature of a material depend on pressure. Water boils at a lower temperature (about 95°C) in Denver than in Pittsburgh because Denver is at higher elevation and the average atmospheric pressure is lower. The heat of vaporization is somewhat greater at this lower pressure, about 2.27×10^6 J/kg.

Table 17.4 lists heats of fusion and vaporization for some materials and their melting and boiling temperatures at normal atmospheric pressure. Very few *elements* have melting temperatures in the vicinity of ordinary room temperatures; one of the few is the metal gallium, shown in Fig. 17.20.

Figure 17.21 shows how the temperature varies when we add heat continuously to a specimen of ice with an initial temperature below 0°C (point *a*). The temperature rises until we reach the melting point (point *b*). As more heat is added, the temperature remains constant until all the ice has melted (point *c*). Then the temperature rises again until the boiling temperature is reached (point *d*). At that point the temperature again is constant until all the water is transformed into the vapor phase (point *e*). If the rate of heat input is constant, the line for the solid phase (ice) has a steeper slope than does the line for the liquid phase (water). Do you see why? (See Table 17.3.)

17.20 The metal gallium, shown here melting in a person's hand, is one of the few elements that melt in the vicinity of room temperature. Its melting temperature is 29.8°C, and its heat of fusion is 8.04×10^4 J/kg.

Table **17.4** **Heats of Fusion and Vaporization**

Substance	Normal Melting Point K	Normal Melting Point °C	Heat of Fusion, L_f (J/kg)	Normal Boiling Point K	Normal Boiling Point °C	Heat of Vaporization, L_v (J/kg)
Helium	*	*	*	4.216	−268.93	20.9×10^3
Hydrogen	13.84	−259.31	58.6×10^3	20.26	−252.89	452×10^3
Nitrogen	63.18	−209.97	25.5×10^3	77.34	−195.8	201×10^3
Oxygen	54.36	−218.79	13.8×10^3	90.18	−183.0	213×10^3
Ethanol	159	−114	104.2×10^3	351	78	854×10^3
Mercury	234	−39	11.8×10^3	630	357	272×10^3
Water	273.15	0.00	334×10^3	373.15	100.00	2256×10^3
Sulfur	392	119	38.1×10^3	717.75	444.60	326×10^3
Lead	600.5	327.3	24.5×10^3	2023	1750	871×10^3
Antimony	903.65	630.50	165×10^3	1713	1440	561×10^3
Silver	1233.95	960.80	88.3×10^3	2466	2193	2336×10^3
Gold	1336.15	1063.00	64.5×10^3	2933	2660	1578×10^3
Copper	1356	1083	134×10^3	1460	1187	5069×10^3

*A pressure in excess of 25 atmospheres is required to make helium solidify. At 1 atmosphere pressure, helium remains a liquid down to absolute zero.

A substance can sometimes change directly from the solid to the gaseous phase. This process is called *sublimation,* and the solid is said to *sublime.* The corresponding heat is called the *heat of sublimation, L_s.* Liquid carbon dioxide cannot exist at a pressure lower than about 5×10^5 Pa (about 5 atm), and "dry ice" (solid carbon dioxide) sublimes at atmospheric pressure. Sublimation of water from frozen food causes freezer burn. The reverse process, a phase change from gas to solid, occurs when frost forms on cold bodies such as refrigerator cooling coils.

Very pure water can be cooled several degrees below the freezing temperature without freezing; the resulting unstable state is described as *supercooled.* When a small ice crystal is dropped in or the water is agitated, it crystallizes within a second or less. Supercooled water *vapor* condenses quickly into fog droplets when a disturbance, such as dust particles or ionizing radiation, is introduced. This principle is used in "seeding" clouds, which often contain supercooled water vapor, to cause condensation and rain.

A liquid can sometimes be *superheated* above its normal boiling temperature. Any small disturbance such as agitation causes local boiling with bubble formation.

Steam heating systems for buildings use a boiling–condensing process to transfer heat from the furnace to the radiators. Each kilogram of water that is

Phase of water changes. During these periods, temperature stays constant and the phase change proceeds as heat is added: $Q = +mL$.

Ice melts to liquid water at 0°C.

Liquid water vaporizes to steam at 100°C.

Boiling point

Melting point

Ice warms.   Liquid water warms.   Steam warms.

Temperature of water changes. During these periods, temperature rises as heat is added: $Q = mc\,\Delta T.$

17.21 Graph of temperature versus time for a specimen of water initially in the solid phase (ice). Heat is added to the specimen at a constant rate. The temperature remains constant during each change of phase, provided that the pressure remains constant.

17.22 The water may be warm and it may be a hot day, but these children will feel cold when they first step out of the swimming pool. That's because as water evaporates from their skin, it removes the heat of vaporization from their bodies. To stay warm, they will need to dry off immediately.

turned to steam in the boiler absorbs over 2×10^6 J (the heat of vaporization L_v of water) from the boiler and gives it up when it condenses in the radiators. Boiling–condensing processes are also used in refrigerators, air conditioners, and heat pumps. We will discuss these systems in Chapter 20.

The temperature-control mechanisms of many warm-blooded animals make use of heat of vaporization, removing heat from the body by using it to evaporate water from the tongue (panting) or from the skin (sweating). Evaporative cooling enables humans to maintain normal body temperature in hot, dry desert climates where the air temperature may reach 55°C (about 130°F). The skin temperature may be as much as 30°C cooler than the surrounding air. Under these conditions a normal person may perspire several liters per day, and this lost water must be replaced. Old-time desert rats (such as one of the authors) state that in the desert, any canteen that holds less than a gallon should be viewed as a toy! Evaporative cooling also explains why you feel cold when you first step out of a swimming pool (Fig. 17.22).

Evaporative cooling is also used to cool buildings in hot, dry climates and to condense and recirculate "used" steam in coal-fired or nuclear-powered electric-generating plants. That's what goes on in the large, tapered concrete towers that you see at such plants.

Chemical reactions such as combustion are analogous to phase changes in that they involve definite quantities of heat. Complete combustion of 1 gram of gasoline produces about 46,000 J or about 11,000 cal, so the **heat of combustion** L_c of gasoline is

$$L_c = 46{,}000 \text{ J/g} = 4.6 \times 10^7 \text{ J/kg}$$

Energy values of foods are defined similarly. When we say that a gram of peanut butter "contains 6 calories," we mean that 6 kcal of heat (6000 cal or 25,000 J) is released when the carbon and hydrogen atoms in the peanut butter react with oxygen (with the help of enzymes) and are completely converted to CO_2 and H_2O. Not all of this energy is directly useful for mechanical work. We will study the *efficiency* of energy utilization in Chapter 20.

Heat Calculations

Let's look at some examples of calorimetry calculations (calculations with heat). The basic principle is very simple: When heat flow occurs between two bodies that are isolated from their surroundings, the amount of heat lost by one body must equal the amount gained by the other. Heat is energy in transit, so this principle is really just conservation of energy. Calorimetry, dealing entirely with one conserved quantity, is in many ways the simplest of all physical theories!

Problem-Solving Strategy 17.2 **Calorimetry Problems**

IDENTIFY *the relevant concepts:* When heat flow occurs between two or more bodies that are isolated from their surroundings, the *algebraic sum* of the quantities of heat transferred to all the bodies is zero. We take a quantity of heat *added* to a body as *positive* and a quantity *leaving* a body as *negative*.

SET UP *the problem* using the following steps:
1. Identify the objects that exchange heat.
2. Each object may undergo a temperature change only, a phase change at constant temperature, or both. Use Eq. (17.13) for the heat transferred in a temperature change and Eq. (17.20) for the heat transferred in a phase change.
3. Consult Table 17.3 for values of specific heat or molar heat capacity and Table 17.4 for heats of fusion or vaporization.
4. List the known and unknown quantities and identify the target variables.

EXECUTE *the solution* as follows:
1. Use Eq. (17.13) and/or Eq. (17.20) and the energy-conservation relation $\Sigma Q = 0$ to solve for the target variables. Ensure that you use the correct algebraic signs for Q and ΔT terms, and that you correctly write $\Delta T = T_{\text{final}} - T_{\text{initial}}$ and not the reverse.
2. If a phase change occurs, you may not know in advance whether all, or only part, of the material undergoes a phase change. Make a reasonable guess; if that leads to an unreasonable result (such as a final temperature higher or lower than any initial temperature), the guess was wrong. Try again!

EVALUATE *your answer:* Double-check your calculations, and ensure that the results are physically sensible.

Example 17.7 **A temperature change with no phase change**

A camper pours 0.300 kg of coffee, initially in a pot at 70.0°C, into a 0.120-kg aluminum cup initially at 20.0°C. What is the equilibrium temperature? Assume that coffee has the same specific heat as water and that no heat is exchanged with the surroundings.

SOLUTION

IDENTIFY and SET UP: The target variable is the common final temperature T of the cup and coffee. No phase changes occur, so we need only Eq. (17.13). With subscripts C for coffee, W for water, and Al for aluminum, we have $T_{0C} = 70.0°$ and $T_{0Al} = 20.0°$; Table 17.3 gives $c_W = 4190$ J/kg·K and $c_{Al} = 910$ J/kg·K.

EXECUTE: The (negative) heat gained by the coffee is $Q_C = m_C c_W \Delta T_C$. The (positive) heat gained by the cup is $Q_{Al} = m_{Al} c_{Al} \Delta T_{Al}$. We set $Q_C + Q_{Al} = 0$ (see Problem-Solving Strategy 17.2) and substitute $\Delta T_C = T - T_{0C}$ and $\Delta T_{Al} = T - T_{0Al}$:

$$Q_C + Q_{Al} = m_C c_W \Delta T_C + m_{Al} c_{Al} \Delta T_{Al} = 0$$
$$m_C c_W (T - T_{0C}) + m_{Al} c_{Al} (T - T_{0Al}) = 0$$

Then we solve this expression for the final temperature T. A little algebra gives

$$T = \frac{m_C c_W T_{0C} + m_{Al} c_{Al} T_{0Al}}{m_C c_W + m_{Al} c_{Al}} = 66.0°C$$

EVALUATE: The final temperature is much closer to the initial temperature of the coffee than to that of the cup; water has a much higher specific heat than aluminum, and we have more than twice as much mass of water. We can also find the quantities of heat by substituting the value $T = 66.0°C$ back into the original equations. We find $Q_C = -5.0 \times 10^3$ J and $Q_{Al} = +5.0 \times 10^3$ J. As expected, Q_C is negative: The coffee loses heat to the cup.

Example 17.8 **Changes in both temperature and phase**

A glass contains 0.25 kg of Omni-Cola (mostly water) initially at 25°C. How much ice, initially at −20°C, must you add to obtain a final temperature of 0°C with all the ice melted? Neglect the heat capacity of the glass.

SOLUTION

IDENTIFY and SET UP: The Omni-Cola and ice exchange heat. The cola undergoes a temperature change; the ice undergoes both a temperature change and a phase change from solid to liquid. We use subscripts C for cola, I for ice, and W for water. The target variable is the mass of ice, m_I. We use Eq. (17.13) to obtain an expression for the amount of heat involved in cooling the drink to $T = 0°C$ and warming the ice to $T = 0°C$, and Eq. (17.20) to obtain an expression for the heat required to melt the ice at 0°C. We have $T_{0C} = 25°C$ and $T_{0I} = −20°C$, Table 17.3 gives $c_W = 4190$ J/kg·K and $c_I = 2100$ J/kg·K, and Table 17.4 gives $L_f = 3.34 \times 10^5$ J/kg.

EXECUTE: From Eq. (17.13), the (negative) heat gained by the Omni-Cola is $Q_C = m_C c_W \Delta T_C$. The (positive) heat gained by the ice in warming is $Q_I = m_I c_I \Delta T_I$. The (positive) heat required to melt the ice is $Q_2 = m_I L_f$. We set $Q_C + Q_I + Q_2 = 0$, insert $\Delta T_C = T - T_{0C}$ and $\Delta T_I = T - T_{0I}$, and solve for m_I:

$$m_C c_W \Delta T_C + m_I c_I \Delta T_I + m_I L_f = 0$$
$$m_C c_W (T - T_{0C}) + m_I c_I (T - T_{0I}) + m_I L_f = 0$$
$$m_I [c_I (T - T_{0I}) + L_f] = -m_C c_W (T - T_{0C})$$
$$m_I = m_C \frac{c_W (T_{0C} - T)}{c_I (T - T_{0I}) + L_f}$$

Substituting numerical values, we find that $m_I = 0.070$ kg = 70 g.

EVALUATE: Three or four medium-size ice cubes would make about 70 g, which seems reasonable given the 250 g of Omni-Cola to be cooled.

Example 17.9 **What's cooking?**

A hot copper pot of mass 2.0 kg (including its copper lid) is at a temperature of 150°C. You pour 0.10 kg of cool water at 25°C into the pot, then quickly replace the lid so no steam can escape. Find the final temperature of the pot and its contents, and determine the phase of the water (liquid, gas, or a mixture). Assume that no heat is lost to the surroundings.

SOLUTION

IDENTIFY and SET UP: The water and the pot exchange heat. Three outcomes are possible: (1) No water boils, and the final temperature T is less than 100°C; (2) some water boils, giving a mixture of water and steam at 100°C; or (3) all the water boils, giving 0.10 kg of steam at 100°C or greater. We use Eq. (17.13) for the heat transferred in a temperature change and Eq. (17.20) for the heat transferred in a phase change.

EXECUTE: First consider case (1), which parallels Example 17.8 exactly. The equation that states that the heat flow into the water equals the heat flow out of the pot is

$$Q_W + Q_{Cu} = m_W c_W (T - T_{0W}) + m_{Cu} c_{Cu} (T - T_{0Cu}) = 0$$

Here we use subscripts W for water and Cu for copper, with $m_W = 0.10$ kg, $m_{Cu} = 2.0$ kg, $T_{0W} = 25°C$, and $T_{0Cu} = 150°C$. From Table 17.3, $c_W = 4190$ J/kg·K and $c_{Cu} = 390$ J/kg·K. Solving for the final temperature T and substituting these values, we get

$$T = \frac{m_W c_W T_{0W} + m_{Cu} c_{Cu} T_{0Cu}}{m_W c_W + m_{Cu} c_{Cu}} = 106°C$$

But this is above the boiling point of water, which contradicts our assumption that no water boils! So at least some of the water boils.

Continued

So consider case (2), in which the final temperature is $T = 100°C$ and some unknown fraction x of the water boils, where (if this case is correct) x is greater than zero and less than or equal to 1. The (positive) amount of heat needed to vaporize this water is $xm_W L_v$. The energy-conservation condition $Q_W + Q_{Cu} = 0$ is then

$$m_W c_W(100°C - T_{0W}) + xm_W L_v + m_{Cu} c_{Cu}(100°C - T_{0Cu}) = 0$$

We solve for the target variable x:

$$x = \frac{-m_{Cu} c_{Cu}(100°C - T_{0Cu}) - m_W c_W(100°C - T_{0W})}{m_W L_v}$$

With $L_v = 2.256 \times 10^6$ J from Table 17.4, this yields $x = 0.034$. We conclude that the final temperature of the water and copper is $100°C$ and that $0.034(0.10$ kg$) = 0.0034$ kg $= 3.4$ g of the water is converted to steam at $100°C$.

EVALUATE: Had x turned out to be greater than 1, case (3) would have held; all the water would have vaporized, and the final temperature would have been greater than $100°C$. Can you show that this would have been the case if we had originally poured less than 15 g of $25°C$ water into the pot?

Example 17.10 Combustion, temperature change, and phase change

In a particular camp stove, only 30% of the energy released in burning gasoline goes to heating the water in a pot on the stove. How much gasoline must we burn to heat 1.00 L (1.00 kg) of water from 20°C to 100°C and boil away 0.25 kg of it?

SOLUTION

IDENTIFY and SET UP: All of the water undergoes a temperature change and part of it undergoes a phase change, from liquid to gas. We determine the heat required to cause both of these changes, and then use the 30% combustion efficiency to determine the amount of gasoline that must be burned (the target variable). We use Eqs. (17.13) and (17.20) and the idea of heat of combustion.

EXECUTE: To raise the temperature of the water from 20°C to 100°C requires

$$Q_1 = mc\,\Delta T = (1.00 \text{ kg})(4190 \text{ J/kg} \cdot \text{K})(80 \text{ K})$$
$$= 3.35 \times 10^5 \text{ J}$$

To boil 0.25 kg of water at 100°C requires

$$Q_2 = mL_v = (0.25 \text{ kg})(2.256 \times 10^6 \text{ J/kg}) = 5.64 \times 10^5 \text{ J}$$

The total energy needed is $Q_1 + Q_2 = 8.99 \times 10^5$ J. This is 30% $= 0.30$ of the total heat of combustion, which is therefore $(8.99 \times 10^5 \text{ J})/0.30 = 3.00 \times 10^6$ J. As we mentioned earlier, the combustion of 1 g of gasoline releases 46,000 J, so the mass of gasoline required is $(3.00 \times 10^6 \text{ J})/(46,000 \text{ J/g}) = 65$ g, or a volume of about 0.09 L of gasoline.

EVALUATE: This result suggests the tremendous amount of energy released in burning even a small quantity of gasoline. Another 123 g of gasoline would be required to boil away the remaining water; can you prove this?

Test Your Understanding of Section 17.6 You take a block of ice at 0°C and add heat to it at a steady rate. It takes a time t to completely convert the block of ice to steam at 100°C. What do you have at time $t/2$? (i) all ice at 0°C; (ii) a mixture of ice and water at 0°C; (iii) water at a temperature between 0°C and 100°C; (iv) a mixture of water and steam at 100°C.

PhET: The Greenhouse Effect

17.7 Mechanisms of Heat Transfer

We have talked about *conductors* and *insulators,* materials that permit or prevent heat transfer between bodies. Now let's look in more detail at *rates* of energy transfer. In the kitchen you use a metal or glass pot for good heat transfer from the stove to whatever you're cooking, but your refrigerator is insulated with a material that *prevents* heat from flowing into the food inside the refrigerator. How do we describe the difference between these two materials?

The three mechanisms of heat transfer are conduction, convection, and radiation. *Conduction* occurs within a body or between two bodies in contact. *Convection* depends on motion of mass from one region of space to another. *Radiation* is heat transfer by electromagnetic radiation, such as sunshine, with no need for matter to be present in the space between bodies.

Conduction

If you hold one end of a copper rod and place the other end in a flame, the end you are holding gets hotter and hotter, even though it is not in direct contact with the flame. Heat reaches the cooler end by **conduction** through the material.

On the atomic level, the atoms in the hotter regions have more kinetic energy, on the average, than their cooler neighbors. They jostle their neighbors, giving them some of their energy. The neighbors jostle *their* neighbors, and so on through the material. The atoms themselves do not move from one region of material to another, but their energy does.

Most metals also use another, more effective mechanism to conduct heat. Within the metal, some electrons can leave their parent atoms and wander through the crystal lattice. These "free" electrons can rapidly carry energy from the hotter to the cooler regions of the metal, so metals are generally good conductors of heat. A metal rod at 20°C feels colder than a piece of wood at 20°C because heat can flow more easily from your hand into the metal. The presence of "free" electrons also causes most metals to be good electrical conductors.

Heat transfer occurs only between regions that are at different temperatures, and the direction of heat flow is always from higher to lower temperature. Figure 17.23a shows a rod of conducting material with cross-sectional area A and length L. The left end of the rod is kept at a temperature T_H and the right end at a lower temperature T_C, so heat flows from left to right. The sides of the rod are covered by an ideal insulator, so no heat transfer occurs at the sides.

When a quantity of heat dQ is transferred through the rod in a time dt, the rate of heat flow is dQ/dt. We call this rate the **heat current,** denoted by H. That is, $H = dQ/dt$. Experiments show that the heat current is proportional to the cross-sectional area A of the rod (Fig. 17.23b) and to the temperature difference $(T_H - T_C)$ and is inversely proportional to the rod length L (Fig. 17.23c). Introducing a proportionality constant k called the **thermal conductivity** of the material, we have

$$H = \frac{dQ}{dt} = kA\frac{T_H - T_C}{L} \quad \text{(heat current in conduction)} \quad (17.21)$$

The quantity $(T_H - T_C)/L$ is the temperature difference *per unit length;* it is called the magnitude of the **temperature gradient.** The numerical value of k depends on the material of the rod. Materials with large k are good conductors of heat; materials with small k are poor conductors, or insulators. Equation (17.21) also gives the heat current through a slab or through *any* homogeneous body with uniform cross section A perpendicular to the direction of flow; L is the length of the heat-flow path.

The units of heat current H are units of energy per time, or power; the SI unit of heat current is the watt (1 W = 1 J/s). We can find the units of k by solving Eq. (17.21) for k; you can show that the SI units are W/m · K. Some numerical values of k are given in Table 17.5.

The thermal conductivity of "dead" (that is, nonmoving) air is very small. A wool sweater keeps you warm because it traps air between the fibers. In fact, many insulating materials such as Styrofoam and fiberglass are mostly dead air.

If the temperature varies in a nonuniform way along the length of the conducting rod, we introduce a coordinate x along the length and generalize the temperature gradient to be dT/dx. The corresponding generalization of Eq. (17.21) is

$$H = \frac{dQ}{dt} = -kA\frac{dT}{dx} \quad (17.22)$$

The negative sign shows that heat always flows in the direction of *decreasing* temperature.

17.23 Steady-state heat flow due to conduction in a uniform rod.

(a) Heat current H

(b) Doubling the cross-sectional area of the conductor doubles the heat current (H is proportional to A).

(c) Doubling the length of the conductor halves the heat current (H is inversely proportional to L).

Table 17.5 Thermal Conductivities

Substance	k (W/m · K)
Metals	
Aluminum	205.0
Brass	109.0
Copper	385.0
Lead	34.7
Mercury	8.3
Silver	406.0
Steel	50.2
Solids (representative values)	
Brick, insulating	0.15
Brick, red	0.6
Concrete	0.8
Cork	0.04
Felt	0.04
Fiberglass	0.04
Glass	0.8
Ice	1.6
Rock wool	0.04
Styrofoam	0.027
Wood	0.12–0.04
Gases	
Air	0.024
Argon	0.016
Helium	0.14
Hydrogen	0.14
Oxygen	0.023

Application Fur Versus Blubber
The fur of an arctic fox is a good thermal insulator because it traps air, which has a low thermal conductivity k. (The value $k = 0.04$ W/m·K for fur is higher than for air, $k = 0.024$ W/m·K, because fur also includes solid hairs.) The layer of fat beneath a bowhead whale's skin, called blubber, has six times the thermal conductivity of fur ($k = 0.24$ W/m·K). So a 6-cm thickness of blubber ($L = 6$ cm) is required to give the same insulation as 1 cm of fur.

For thermal insulation in buildings, engineers use the concept of **thermal resistance,** denoted by R. The thermal resistance R of a slab of material with area A is defined so that the heat current H through the slab is

$$H = \frac{A(T_H - T_C)}{R} \tag{17.23}$$

where T_H and T_C are the temperatures on the two sides of the slab. Comparing this with Eq. (17.21), we see that R is given by

$$R = \frac{L}{k} \tag{17.24}$$

where L is the thickness of the slab. The SI unit of R is 1 m²·K/W. In the units used for commercial insulating materials in the United States, H is expressed in Btu/h, A is in ft², and $T_H - T_C$ in F°. (1 Btu/h = 0.293 W.) The units of R are then ft²·F°·h/Btu, though values of R are usually quoted without units; a 6-inch-thick layer of fiberglass has an R value of 19 (that is, $R = 19$ ft²·F°·h/Btu), a 2-inch-thick slab of polyurethane foam has an R value of 12, and so on. Doubling the thickness doubles the R value. Common practice in new construction in severe northern climates is to specify R values of around 30 for exterior walls and ceilings. When the insulating material is in layers, such as a plastered wall, fiberglass insulation, and wood exterior siding, the R values are additive. Do you see why? (See Problem 17.108.)

Problem-Solving Strategy 17.3 | **Heat Conduction**

IDENTIFY *the relevant concepts:* Heat conduction occurs whenever two objects at different temperatures are placed in contact.

SET UP *the problem* using the following steps:
1. Identify the direction of heat flow (from hot to cold). In Eq. (17.21), L is measured along this direction, and A is an area perpendicular to this direction. You can often approximate an irregular-shaped container with uniform wall thickness as a flat slab with the same thickness and total wall area.

2. List the known and unknown quantities and identify the target variable.

EXECUTE *the solution* as follows:
1. If heat flows through a single object, use Eq. (17.21) to solve for the target variable.
2. If the heat flows through two different materials in succession (in *series*), the temperature T at the interface between them is

intermediate between T_H and T_C, so that the temperature differences across the two materials are $(T_H - T)$ and $(T - T_C)$. In steady-state heat flow, the same heat must pass through both materials, so the heat current H must be the *same* in both materials.

3. If heat flows through two or more *parallel* paths, then the total heat current H is the sum of the currents $H_1, H_2, \ldots$ for the separate paths. An example is heat flow from inside a room to outside, both through the glass in a window and through the surrounding wall. In parallel heat flow the temperature difference is the same for each path, but L, A, and k may be different for each path.

4. Use consistent units. If k is expressed in W/m·K, for example, use distances in meters, heat in joules, and T in kelvins.

EVALUATE *your answer:* Are the results physically reasonable?

Example 17.11 | **Conduction into a picnic cooler**

A Styrofoam cooler (Fig. 17.24a) has total wall area (including the lid) of 0.80 m² and wall thickness 2.0 cm. It is filled with ice, water, and cans of Omni-Cola, all at 0°C. What is the rate of heat flow into the cooler if the temperature of the outside wall is 30°C? How much ice melts in 3 hours?

SOLUTION

IDENTIFY and SET UP: The target variables are the heat current H and the mass m of ice melted. We use Eq. (17.21) to determine H and Eq. (17.20) to determine m.

EXECUTE: We assume that the total heat flow is the same as it would be through a flat Styrofoam slab of area 0.80 m² and thickness 2.0 cm = 0.020 m (Fig. 17.24b). We find k from Table 17.5. From Eq. (17.21),

$$H = kA\frac{T_H - T_C}{L} = (0.027 \text{ W/m·K})(0.80 \text{ m}^2)\frac{30°C - 0°C}{0.020 \text{ m}}$$
$$= 32.4 \text{ W} = 32.4 \text{ J/s}$$

The total heat flow is $Q = Ht$, with $t = 3$ h $= 10,800$ s. From Table 17.4, the heat of fusion of ice is $L_f = 3.34 \times 10^5$ J/kg, so from Eq. (17.20) the mass of ice that melts is

$$m = \frac{Q}{L_f} = \frac{(32.4 \text{ J/s})(10,800 \text{ s})}{3.34 \times 10^5 \text{ J/kg}} = 1.0 \text{ kg}$$

EVALUATE: The low heat current is a result of the low thermal conductivity of Styrofoam.

17.24 Conduction of heat across the walls of a Styrofoam cooler.

(a) A cooler at the beach

(b) Our sketch for this problem

Example 17.12 **Conduction through two bars I**

A steel bar 10.0 cm long is welded end to end to a copper bar 20.0 cm long. Each bar has a square cross section, 2.00 cm on a side. The free end of the steel bar is kept at 100°C by placing it in contact with steam, and the free end of the copper bar is kept at 0°C by placing it in contact with ice. Both bars are perfectly insulated on their sides. Find the steady-state temperature at the junction of the two bars and the total rate of heat flow through the bars.

SOLUTION

IDENTIFY and SET UP: Figure 17.25 shows the situation. The heat currents in these end-to-end bars must be the same (see Problem-Solving Strategy 17.3). We are given "hot" and "cold" temperatures $T_H = 100°C$ and $T_C = 0°C$. With subscripts S for steel and Cu for copper, we write Eq. (17.21) separately for the heat currents H_S and H_{Cu} and set the resulting expressions equal to each other.

EXECUTE: Setting $H_S = H_{Cu}$, we have from Eq. (17.21)

$$H_S = k_S A \frac{T_H - T}{L_S} = H_{Cu} = k_{Cu} A \frac{T - T_C}{L_{Cu}}$$

We divide out the equal cross-sectional areas A and solve for T:

$$T = \frac{\dfrac{k_S}{L_S}T_H + \dfrac{k_{Cu}}{L_{Cu}}T_C}{\left(\dfrac{k_S}{L_S} + \dfrac{k_{Cu}}{L_{Cu}}\right)}$$

17.25 Our sketch for this problem.

Substituting $L_S = 10.0$ cm and $L_{Cu} = 20.0$ cm, the given values of T_H and T_C, and the values of k_S and k_{Cu} from Table 17.5, we find $T = 20.7°C$.

We can find the total heat current by substituting this value of T into either the expression for H_S or the one for H_{Cu}:

$$H_S = (50.2 \text{ W/m} \cdot \text{K})(0.0200 \text{ m})^2 \frac{100°C - 20.7°C}{0.100 \text{ m}}$$
$$= 15.9 \text{ W}$$

$$H_{Cu} = (385 \text{ W/m} \cdot \text{K})(0.0200 \text{ m})^2 \frac{20.7°C}{0.200 \text{ m}} = 15.9 \text{ W}$$

EVALUATE: Even though the steel bar is shorter, the temperature drop across it is much greater (from 100°C to 20.7°C) than across the copper bar (from 20.7°C to 0°C). That's because steel is a much poorer conductor than copper.

Example 17.13 **Conduction through two bars II**

Suppose the two bars of Example 17.12 are separated. One end of each bar is kept at 100°C and the other end of each bar is kept at 0°C. What is the *total* heat current in the two bars?

SOLUTION

IDENTIFY and SET UP: Figure 17.26 shows the situation. For each bar, $T_H - T_C = 100°C - 0°C = 100$ K. The total heat current is the sum of the currents in the two bars, $H_S + H_{Cu}$.

17.26 Our sketch for this problem.

Continued

EXECUTE: We write the heat currents for the two rods individually, and then add them to get the total heat current:

$$H = H_S + H_{Cu} = k_S A \frac{T_H - T_C}{L_S} + k_{Cu} A \frac{T_H - T_C}{L_{Cu}}$$

$$= (50.2 \text{ W/m} \cdot \text{K})(0.0200 \text{ m})^2 \frac{100 \text{ K}}{0.100 \text{ m}}$$

$$+ (385 \text{ W/m} \cdot \text{K})(0.0200 \text{ m})^2 \frac{100 \text{ K}}{0.200 \text{ m}}$$

$$= 20.1 \text{ W} + 77.0 \text{ W} = 97.1 \text{ W}$$

EVALUATE: The heat flow in the copper bar is much greater than that in the steel bar, even though it is longer, because the thermal conductivity of copper is much larger. The total heat flow is greater than in Example 17.12 because the total cross section for heat flow is greater and because the full 100-K temperature difference appears across each bar.

**Video Tutor
Demo**

17.27 A heating element in the tip of this submerged tube warms the surrounding water, producing a complex pattern of free convection.

17.28 This false-color infrared photograph reveals radiation emitted by various parts of the man's body. The strongest emission (colored red) comes from the warmest areas, while there is very little emission from the bottle of cold beverage.

Convection

Convection is the transfer of heat by mass motion of a fluid from one region of space to another. Familiar examples include hot-air and hot-water home heating systems, the cooling system of an automobile engine, and the flow of blood in the body. If the fluid is circulated by a blower or pump, the process is called *forced convection;* if the flow is caused by differences in density due to thermal expansion, such as hot air rising, the process is called *natural convection* or *free convection* (Fig. 17.27).

Free convection in the atmosphere plays a dominant role in determining the daily weather, and convection in the oceans is an important global heat-transfer mechanism. On a smaller scale, soaring hawks and glider pilots make use of thermal updrafts from the warm earth. The most important mechanism for heat transfer within the human body (needed to maintain nearly constant temperature in various environments) is *forced* convection of blood, with the heart serving as the pump.

Convective heat transfer is a very complex process, and there is no simple equation to describe it. Here are a few experimental facts:

1. The heat current due to convection is directly proportional to the surface area. This is the reason for the large surface areas of radiators and cooling fins.
2. The viscosity of fluids slows natural convection near a stationary surface, giving a surface film that on a vertical surface typically has about the same insulating value as 1.3 cm of plywood (*R* value = 0.7). Forced convection decreases the thickness of this film, increasing the rate of heat transfer. This is the reason for the "wind-chill factor"; you get cold faster in a cold wind than in still air with the same temperature.
3. The heat current due to convection is found to be approximately proportional to the $\frac{5}{4}$ power of the temperature difference between the surface and the main body of fluid.

Radiation

Radiation is the transfer of heat by electromagnetic waves such as visible light, infrared, and ultraviolet radiation. Everyone has felt the warmth of the sun's radiation and the intense heat from a charcoal grill or the glowing coals in a fireplace. Most of the heat from these very hot bodies reaches you not by conduction or convection in the intervening air but by *radiation.* This heat transfer would occur even if there were nothing but vacuum between you and the source of heat.

Every body, even at ordinary temperatures, emits energy in the form of electromagnetic radiation. Around 20°C, nearly all the energy is carried by infrared waves with wavelengths much longer than those of visible light (see Figs. 17.4 and 17.28). As the temperature rises, the wavelengths shift to shorter values. At 800°C, a body emits enough visible radiation to appear "red-hot," although even at this temperature most of the energy is carried by infrared waves. At 3000°C, the temperature of an incandescent lamp filament, the radiation contains enough visible light that the body appears "white-hot."

The rate of energy radiation from a surface is proportional to the surface area A and to the fourth power of the absolute (Kelvin) temperature T. The rate also depends on the nature of the surface; this dependence is described by a quantity e called the **emissivity.** A dimensionless number between 0 and 1, e represents the ratio of the rate of radiation from a particular surface to the rate of radiation from an equal area of an ideal radiating surface at the same temperature. Emissivity also depends somewhat on temperature. Thus the heat current $H = dQ/dt$ due to radiation from a surface area A with emissivity e at absolute temperature T can be expressed as

$$H = Ae\sigma T^4 \qquad \text{(heat current in radiation)} \qquad (17.25)$$

where σ is a fundamental physical constant called the **Stefan–Boltzmann constant.** This relationship is called the **Stefan–Boltzmann law** in honor of its late-19th-century discoverers. The current best numerical value of σ is

$$\sigma = 5.670400(40) \times 10^{-8} \text{ W/m}^2 \cdot \text{K}^4$$

We invite you to check unit consistency in Eq. (17.25). Emissivity (e) is often larger for dark surfaces than for light ones. The emissivity of a smooth copper surface is about 0.3, but e for a dull black surface can be close to unity.

Example 17.14 **Heat transfer by radiation**

A thin, square steel plate, 10 cm on a side, is heated in a black-smith's forge to 800°C. If the emissivity is 0.60, what is the total rate of radiation of energy from the plate?

SOLUTION

IDENTIFY and SET UP: The target variable is H, the rate of emission of energy from the plate's two surfaces. We use Eq. (17.25) to calculate H.

EXECUTE: The total surface area is $2(0.10 \text{ m})^2 = 0.020 \text{ m}^2$, and $T = 800°\text{C} = 1073 \text{ K}$. Then Eq. (17.25) gives

$$H = Ae\sigma T^4$$
$$= (0.020 \text{ m}^2)(0.60)(5.67 \times 10^{-8} \text{ W/m}^2 \cdot \text{K}^4)(1073 \text{ K})^4$$
$$= 900 \text{ W}$$

EVALUATE: The nearby blacksmith will easily feel the heat radiated from this plate.

Radiation and Absorption

While a body at absolute temperature T is radiating, its surroundings at temperature T_s are also radiating, and the body *absorbs* some of this radiation. If it is in thermal equilibrium with its surroundings, $T = T_s$ and the rates of radiation and absorption must be equal. For this to be true, the rate of absorption must be given in general by $H = Ae\sigma T_s^4$. Then the *net* rate of radiation from a body at temperature T with surroundings at temperature T_s is

$$H_{\text{net}} = Ae\sigma T^4 - Ae\sigma T_s^4 = Ae\sigma(T^4 - T_s^4) \qquad (17.26)$$

In this equation a positive value of H means a net heat flow *out of* the body. Equation (17.26) shows that for radiation, as for conduction and convection, the heat current depends on the temperature *difference* between two bodies.

Example 17.15 **Radiation from the human body**

What is the total rate of radiation of energy from a human body with surface area 1.20 m^2 and surface temperature 30°C = 303 K? If the surroundings are at a temperature of 20°C, what is the *net* rate of radiative heat loss from the body? The emissivity of the human body is very close to unity, irrespective of skin pigmentation.

SOLUTION

IDENTIFY and SET UP: We must consider both the radiation that the body emits and the radiation that it absorbs from its surroundings. Equation (17.25) gives the rate of radiation of energy from the body, and Eq. (17.26) gives the net rate of heat loss.

Continued

EXECUTE: Taking $e = 1$ in Eq. (17.25), we find that the body radiates at a rate

$$H = Ae\sigma T^4$$
$$= (1.20 \ \text{m}^2)(1)(5.67 \times 10^{-8} \ \text{W/m}^2 \cdot \text{K}^4)(303 \ \text{K})^4 = 574 \ \text{W}$$

This loss is partly offset by absorption of radiation, which depends on the temperature of the surroundings. From Eq. (17.26), the *net* rate of radiative energy transfer is

$$H_{\text{net}} = Ae\sigma(T^4 - T_{\text{s}}^4)$$
$$= (1.20 \ \text{m}^2)(1)(5.67 \times 10^{-8} \ \text{W/m}^2 \cdot \text{K}^4)[(303 \ \text{K})^4$$
$$- (293 \ \text{K})^4] = 72 \ \text{W}$$

EVALUATE: The value of H_{net} is positive because the body is losing heat to its colder surroundings.

Applications of Radiation

Heat transfer by radiation is important in some surprising places. A premature baby in an incubator can be cooled dangerously by radiation if the walls of the incubator happen to be cold, even when the *air* in the incubator is warm. Some incubators regulate the air temperature by measuring the baby's skin temperature.

A body that is a good absorber must also be a good emitter. An ideal radiator, with an emissivity of unity, is also an ideal absorber, absorbing *all* of the radiation that strikes it. Such an ideal surface is called an ideal black body or simply a **blackbody.** Conversely, an ideal *reflector,* which absorbs *no* radiation at all, is also a very ineffective radiator.

This is the reason for the silver coatings on vacuum ("Thermos") bottles, invented by Sir James Dewar (1842–1923). A vacuum bottle has double glass walls. The air is pumped out of the spaces between the walls; this eliminates nearly all heat transfer by conduction and convection. The silver coating on the walls reflects most of the radiation from the contents back into the container, and the wall itself is a very poor emitter. Thus a vacuum bottle can keep coffee or soup hot for several hours. The Dewar flask, used to store very cold liquefied gases, is exactly the same in principle.

Radiation, Climate, and Climate Change

Our planet constantly absorbs radiation coming from the sun. In thermal equilibrium, the rate at which our planet absorbs solar radiation must equal the rate at which it emits radiation into space. The presence of an atmosphere on our planet has a significant effect on this equilibrium.

Most of the radiation emitted by the sun (which has a surface temperature of 5800 K) is in the visible part of the spectrum, to which our atmosphere is transparent. But the average surface temperature of the earth is only 287 K (14°C). Hence most of the radiation that our planet emits into space is infrared radiation, just like the radiation from the person shown in Fig. 17.28. However, our atmosphere is *not* completely transparent to infrared radiation. This is because our atmosphere contains carbon dioxide (CO_2), which is its fourth most abundant constituent (after nitrogen, oxygen, and argon). Molecules of CO_2 in the atmosphere have the property that they *absorb* some of the infrared radiation coming upward from the surface. They then re-radiate the absorbed energy, but some of the re-radiated energy is directed back down toward the surface instead of escaping into space. In order to maintain thermal equilibrium, the earth's surface must compensate for this by increasing its temperature T and hence its total rate of radiating energy (which is proportional to T^4). This phenomenon, called the **greenhouse effect,** makes our planet's surface temperature about 33°C higher than it would be if there were no atmospheric CO_2. If CO_2 were absent, the earth's average surface temperature would be below the freezing point of water, and life as we know it would be impossible.

While atmospheric CO_2 has a beneficial effect, too much of it can have extremely negative consequences. Measurements of air trapped in ancient Antarctic ice show that over the past 650,000 years CO_2 has constituted less than 300 parts per million of our atmosphere. Since the beginning of the industrial age, however, the burning of fossil fuels such as coal and petroleum has elevated the atmospheric CO_2 concentration to unprecedented levels (Fig. 17.29a). As a consequence, since the 1950s the global average surface temperature has increased by 0.6°C and the earth has experienced the hottest years ever recorded (Fig. 17.29b). If we continue to consume fossil fuels at the same rate, by 2050 the atmospheric CO_2 concentration will reach 600 parts per million, well off the scale of Fig. 17.29a. The resulting temperature increase will have dramatic effects on climate around the world. In the polar regions massive quantities of ice will melt and run from solid land to the sea, thus raising ocean levels worldwide and threatening the homes and lives of hundreds of millions of people who live near the coast. Coping with these threats is one of the greatest challenges facing 21st-century civilization.

17.29 (a) The concentration of atmospheric CO_2 has increased by 22% since continuous measurements began in 1958. (The yearly variations are due to increased intake of CO_2 by plants in spring and summer.) (b) The increase in global average temperature since the beginning of the industrial era is a result of the increase in CO_2 concentration.

(a) (b)

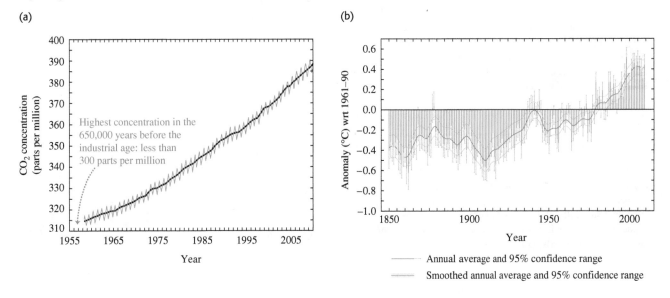

Test Your Understanding of Section 17.7 A room has one wall made of concrete, one wall made of copper, and one wall made of steel. All of the walls are the same size and at the same temperature of 20°C. Which wall feels coldest to the touch? (i) the concrete wall; (ii) the copper wall; (iii) the steel wall; (iv) all three walls feel equally cold.

Video Tutor Solutions

Temperature and temperature scales: Two bodies in thermal equilibrium must have the same temperature. A conducting material between two bodies permits them to interact and come to thermal equilibrium; an insulating material impedes this interaction.

The Celsius and Fahrenheit temperature scales are based on the freezing ($0°C = 32°F$) and boiling ($100°C = 212°F$) temperatures of water. One Celsius degree equals $\frac{9}{5}$ Fahrenheit degrees. (See Example 17.1.)

The Kelvin scale has its zero at the extrapolated zero-pressure temperature for a gas thermometer, $-273.15°C = 0$ K. In the gas-thermometer scale, the ratio of two temperatures T_1 and T_2 is defined to be equal to the ratio of the two corresponding gas-thermometer pressures p_1 and p_2.

$$T_F = \tfrac{9}{5}T_C + 32° \quad (17.1)$$

$$T_C = \tfrac{5}{9}(T_F - 32°) \quad (17.2)$$

$$T_K = T_C + 273.15 \quad (17.3)$$

$$\frac{T_2}{T_1} = \frac{p_2}{p_1} \quad (17.4)$$

If systems A and B are each in thermal equilibrium with system C ...

... then systems A and B are in thermal equilibrium with each other.

Thermal expansion and thermal stress: A temperature change ΔT causes a change in any linear dimension L_0 of a solid body. The change ΔL is approximately proportional to L_0 and ΔT. Similarly, a temperature change causes a change ΔV in the volume V_0 of any solid or liquid; ΔV is approximately proportional to V_0 and ΔT. The quantities α and β are the coefficients of linear expansion and volume expansion, respectively. For solids, $\beta = 3\alpha$. (See Examples 17.2 and 17.3.)

When a material is cooled or heated and held so it cannot contract or expand, it is under a tensile stress F/A. (See Example 17.4.)

$$\Delta L = \alpha L_0 \Delta T \quad (17.6)$$

$$\Delta V = \beta V_0 \Delta T \quad (17.8)$$

$$\frac{F}{A} = -Y\alpha \Delta T \quad (17.12)$$

$$L = L_0 + \Delta L = L_0(1 + \alpha \Delta T)$$

Heat, phase changes, and calorimetry: Heat is energy in transit from one body to another as a result of a temperature difference. Equations (17.13) and (17.18) give the quantity of heat Q required to cause a temperature change ΔT in a quantity of material with mass m and specific heat c (alternatively, with number of moles n and molar heat capacity $C = Mc$, where M is the molar mass and $m = nM$). When heat is added to a body, Q is positive; when it is removed, Q is negative. (See Examples 17.5 and 16.6.)

To change a mass m of a material to a different phase at the same temperature (such as liquid to vapor), a quantity of heat given by Eq. (17.20) must be added or subtracted. Here L is the heat of fusion, vaporization, or sublimation.

In an isolated system whose parts interact by heat exchange, the algebraic sum of the Q's for all parts of the system must be zero. (See Examples 17.7–17.10.)

$$Q = mc \Delta T \quad (17.13)$$

$$Q = nC \Delta T \quad (17.18)$$

$$Q = \pm mL \quad (17.20)$$

Phase changes, temperature is constant: $Q = +mL$

Temperature rises, phase does not change: $Q = mc\Delta T$

Conduction, convection, and radiation: Conduction is the transfer of heat within materials without bulk motion of the materials. The heat current H depends on the area A through which the heat flows, the length L of the heat-flow path, the temperature difference $(T_H - T_C)$, and the thermal conductivity k of the material. (See Examples 17.11–17.13.)

Convection is a complex heat-transfer process that involves mass motion from one region to another.

Radiation is energy transfer through electromagnetic radiation. The radiation heat current H depends on the surface area A, the emissivity e of the surface (a pure number between 0 and 1), and the Kelvin temperature T. Here σ is the Stefan–Boltzmann constant. The *net* radiation heat current H_{net} from a body at temperature T to its surroundings at temperature T_s depends on both T and T_s. (See Examples 17.14 and 17.15.)

$$H = \frac{dQ}{dt} = kA\frac{T_H - T_C}{L} \quad (17.21)$$

$$H = Ae\sigma T^4 \quad (17.25)$$

$$H_{net} = Ae\sigma(T^4 - T_s^4) \quad (17.26)$$

Heat current H

Heat current $H = kA\dfrac{T_H - T_C}{L}$

BRIDGING PROBLEM *Steady-State Heat Flow: Radiation and Conduction*

One end of a solid cylindrical copper rod 0.200 m long and 0.0250 m in radius is inserted into a large block of solid hydrogen at its melting temperature, 13.84 K. The other end is blackened and exposed to thermal radiation from surrounding walls at 500.0 K. The sides of the rod are insulated, so no energy is lost or gained except at the ends of the rod. (a) When equilibrium is reached, what is the temperature of the blackened end? The thermal conductivity of copper at temperatures near 20 K is 1670 Wm · K. (b) At what rate (in kg/h) does the solid hydrogen melt?

SOLUTION GUIDE

See MasteringPhysics® study area for a Video Tutor solution.

IDENTIFY and SET UP

1. Draw a sketch of the situation, showing all relevant dimensions.
2. List the known and unknown quantities, and identify the target variables.
3. In order for the rod to be in equilibrium, how must the radiation heat current from the walls into the blackened end of the rod compare to the conduction heat current from this end to the

other end and into the solid hydrogen? Use your answers to select the appropriate equations for part (a).

4. How does the heat current from the rod into the hydrogen determine the rate at which the hydrogen melts? (*Hint:* See Table 17.4.) Use your answer to select the appropriate equations for part (b).

EXECUTE

5. Solve for the temperature of the blackened end of the rod. (*Hint:* Since copper is an excellent conductor of heat at low temperature, you can assume that the temperature of the blackened end is only slightly higher than 13.84 K.)
6. Use your result from step 5 to find the rate at which the hydrogen melts.

EVALUATE

7. Is your result from step 5 consistent with the hint given in that step?
8. How would your results from steps 5 and 6 be affected if the rod had twice the radius?

Problems

For instructor-assigned homework, go to MasteringPhysics®.

•, ••, •••: Problems of increasing difficulty. **CP**: Cumulative problems incorporating material from earlier chapters. **CALC**: Problems requiring calculus. **BIO**: Biosciences problems.

DISCUSSION QUESTIONS

Q17.1 Explain why it would not make sense to use a full-size glass thermometer to measure the temperature of a thimbleful of hot water.

Q17.2 If you heat the air inside a rigid, sealed container until its Kelvin temperature doubles, the air pressure in the container will also double. Is the same thing true if you double the Celsius temperature of the air in the container? Explain.

Q17.3 Many automobile engines have cast-iron cylinders and aluminum pistons. What kinds of problems could occur if the engine gets too hot? (The coefficient of volume expansion of cast iron is approximately the same as that of steel.)

Q17.4 Why do frozen water pipes burst? Would a mercury thermometer break if the temperature went below the freezing temperature of mercury? Why or why not?

Q17.5 Two bodies made of the same material have the same external dimensions and appearance, but one is solid and the other is hollow. When their temperature is increased, is the overall volume expansion the same or different? Why?

Q17.6 The inside of an oven is at a temperature of 200°C (392°F). You can put your hand in the oven without injury as long as you don't touch anything. But since the air inside the oven is also at 200°C, why isn't your hand burned just the same?

Q17.7 A newspaper article about the weather states that "the temperature of a body measures how much heat the body contains." Is this description correct? Why or why not?

Q17.8 To raise the temperature of an object, must you add heat to it? If you add heat to an object, must you raise its temperature? Explain.

Q17.9 A student asserts that a suitable unit for specific heat is 1 $m^2/s^2 \cdot C°$. Is she correct? Why or why not?

Q17.10 In some household air conditioners used in dry climates, air is cooled by blowing it through a water-soaked filter, evaporating some of the water. How does this cool the air? Would such a system work well in a high-humidity climate? Why or why not?

Q17.11 The units of specific heat c are J/kg · K, but the units of heat of fusion L_f or heat of vaporization L_v are simply J/kg. Why do the units of L_f and L_v not include a factor of $(K)^{-1}$ to account for a temperature change?

Q17.12 Why is a hot, humid day in the tropics generally more uncomfortable for human beings than a hot, dry day in the desert?

Q17.13 A piece of aluminum foil used to wrap a potato for baking in a hot oven can usually be handled safely within a few seconds after the potato is removed from the oven. The same is not true of the potato, however! Give two reasons for this difference.

Q17.14 Desert travelers sometimes keep water in a canvas bag. Some water seeps through the bag and evaporates. How does this cool the water inside the bag?

Q17.15 When you first step out of the shower, you feel cold. But as soon as you are dry you feel warmer, even though the room temperature does not change. Why?

Q17.16 The climate of regions adjacent to large bodies of water (like the Pacific and Atlantic coasts) usually features a narrower range of temperature than the climate of regions far from large bodies of water (like the prairies). Why?

Q17.17 When water is placed in ice-cube trays in a freezer, why doesn't the water freeze all at once when the temperature has reached 0°C? In fact, the water freezes first in a layer adjacent to the sides of the tray. Why?

Q17.18 Before giving you an injection, a physician swabs your arm with isopropyl alcohol at room temperature. Why does this make your arm feel cold? (*Hint:* The reason is *not* the fear of the injection! The boiling point of isopropyl alcohol is 82.4°C.)

Q17.19 A cold block of metal feels colder than a block of wood at the same temperature. Why? A *hot* block of metal feels hotter than a block of wood at the same temperature. Again, why? Is there any temperature at which the two blocks feel equally hot or cold? What temperature is this?

Q17.20 A person pours a cup of hot coffee, intending to drink it five minutes later. To keep the coffee as hot as possible, should she put cream in it now or wait until just before she drinks it? Explain.

Q17.21 When a freshly baked apple pie has just been removed from the oven, the crust and filling are both at the same temperature. Yet if you sample the pie, the filling will burn your tongue but the crust will not. Why is there a difference? (*Hint:* The filling is moist while the crust is dry.)

Q17.22 Old-time kitchen lore suggests that things cook better (evenly and without burning) in heavy cast-iron pots. What desirable characteristics do such pots have?

Q17.23 In coastal regions in the winter, the temperature over the land is generally colder than the temperature over the nearby ocean; in the summer, the reverse is usually true. Explain. (*Hint:* The specific heat of soil is only 0.2–0.8 times as great as that of water.)

Q17.24 It is well known that a potato bakes faster if a large nail is stuck through it. Why? Does an aluminum nail work better than a steel one? Why or why not? (*Note:* Don't try this in a microwave oven!) There is also a gadget on the market to hasten the roasting of meat; it consists of a hollow metal tube containing a wick and some water. This is claimed to work much better than a solid metal rod. How does it work?

Q17.25 Glider pilots in the Midwest know that thermal updrafts are likely to occur in the vicinity of freshly plowed fields. Why?

Q17.26 Some folks claim that ice cubes freeze faster if the trays are filled with hot water, because hot water cools off faster than cold water. What do you think?

Q17.27 We're lucky that the earth isn't in thermal equilibrium with the sun (which has a surface temperature of 5800 K). But why aren't the two bodies in thermal equilibrium?

Q17.28 When energy shortages occur, magazine articles sometimes urge us to keep our homes at a constant temperature day and night to conserve fuel. They argue that when we turn down the heat at night, the walls, ceilings, and other areas cool off and must be reheated in the morning. So if we keep the temperature constant, these parts of the house will not cool off and will not have to be reheated. Does this argument make sense? Would we really save energy by following this advice?

EXERCISES

Section 17.2 Thermometers and Temperature Scales

17.1 • Convert the following Celsius temperatures to Fahrenheit: (a) −62.8°C, the lowest temperature ever recorded in North America (February 3, 1947, Snag, Yukon); (b) 56.7°C, the highest temperature ever recorded in the United States (July 10, 1913, Death Valley, California); (c) 31.1°C, the world's highest average annual temperature (Lugh Ferrandi, Somalia).

17.2 • **BIO Temperatures in Biomedicine.** (a) **Normal body temperature.** The average normal body temperature measured in the mouth is 310 K. What would Celsius and Fahrenheit thermometers read for this temperature? (b) **Elevated body temperature.** During very vigorous exercise, the body's temperature can go as high as 40°C. What would Kelvin and Fahrenheit thermometers read for this temperature? (c) **Temperature difference in the body.** The surface temperature of the body is normally about 7 C° lower than the internal temperature. Express this temperature difference in kelvins and in Fahrenheit degrees. (d) **Blood storage.** Blood stored at 4.0°C lasts safely for about 3 weeks, whereas blood stored at −160°C lasts for 5 years. Express both temperatures on the Fahrenheit and Kelvin scales. (e) **Heat stroke.** If the body's temperature is above 105°F for a prolonged period, heat stroke can result. Express this temperature on the Celsius and Kelvin scales.

17.3 • (a) On January 22, 1943, the temperature in Spearfish, South Dakota, rose from −4.0°F to 45.0°F in just 2 minutes. What was the temperature change in Celsius degrees? (b) The temperature in Browning, Montana, was 44.0°F on January 23, 1916. The next day the temperature plummeted to −56°F. What was the temperature change in Celsius degrees?

Section 17.3 Gas Thermometers and the Kelvin Scale

17.4 • (a) Calculate the one temperature at which Fahrenheit and Celsius thermometers agree with each other. (b) Calculate the one temperature at which Fahrenheit and Kelvin thermometers agree with each other.

17.5 •• You put a bottle of soft drink in a refrigerator and leave it until its temperature has dropped 10.0 K. What is its temperature change in (a) F° and (b) C°?

17.6 • Convert the following Kelvin temperatures to the Celsius and Fahrenheit scales: (a) the midday temperature at the surface of the moon (400 K); (b) the temperature at the tops of the clouds in the atmosphere of Saturn (95 K); (c) the temperature at the center of the sun (1.55×10^7 K).

17.7 • The pressure of a gas at the triple point of water is 1.35 atm. If its volume remains unchanged, what will its pressure be at the temperature at which CO_2 solidifies?

17.8 •• A gas thermometer registers an absolute pressure corresponding to 325 mm of mercury when in contact with water at the triple point. What pressure does it read when in contact with water at the normal boiling point?

17.9 •• **A Constant-Volume Gas Thermometer.** An experimenter using a gas thermometer found the pressure at the triple point of water (0.01°C) to be 4.80×10^4 Pa and the pressure at the normal boiling point (100°C) to be 6.50×10^4 Pa. (a) Assuming that the pressure varies linearly with temperature, use these two data points to find the Celsius temperature at which the gas pressure would be zero (that is, find the Celsius temperature of absolute zero). (b) Does the gas in this thermometer obey Eq. (17.4) precisely? If that equation were precisely obeyed and the pressure at 100°C were 6.50×10^4 Pa, what pressure would the experimenter have measured at 0.01°C? (As we will learn in Section 18.1, Eq. (17.4) is accurate only for gases at very low density.)

17.10 • Like the Kelvin scale, the *Rankine scale* is an absolute temperature scale: Absolute zero is zero degrees Rankine (0°R). However, the units of this scale are the same size as those of the Fahrenheit scale rather than the Celsius scale. What is the numerical value of the triple-point temperature of water on the Rankine scale?

Section 17.4 Thermal Expansion

17.11 • The Humber Bridge in England has the world's longest single span, 1410 m. Calculate the change in length of the steel deck of the span when the temperature increases from −5.0°C to 18.0°C.

17.12 • One of the tallest buildings in the world is the Taipei 101 in Taiwan, at a height of 1671 feet. Assume that this height was measured on a cool spring day when the temperature was 15.5°C. You could use the building as a sort of giant thermometer on a hot summer day by carefully measuring its height. Suppose you do this and discover that the Taipei 101 is 0.471 foot taller than its official height. What is the temperature, assuming that the building is in thermal equilibrium with the air and that its entire frame is made of steel?

17.13 • A U.S. penny has a diameter of 1.9000 cm at 20.0°C. The coin is made of a metal alloy (mostly zinc) for which the coefficient of linear expansion is 2.6×10^{-5} K^{-1}. What would its diameter be on a hot day in Death Valley (48.0°C)? On a cold night in the mountains of Greenland (−53°C)?

17.14 • **Ensuring a Tight Fit.** Aluminum rivets used in airplane construction are made slightly larger than the rivet holes and cooled by "dry ice" (solid CO_2) before being driven. If the diameter of a hole is 4.500 mm, what should be the diameter of a rivet at 23.0°C if its diameter is to equal that of the hole when the rivet is cooled to −78.0°C, the temperature of dry ice? Assume that the expansion coefficient remains constant at the value given in Table 17.1.

17.15 •• The outer diameter of a glass jar and the inner diameter of its iron lid are both 725 mm at room temperature (20.0°C). What will be the size of the difference in these diameters if the lid is briefly held under hot water until its temperature rises to 50.0°C, without changing the temperature of the glass?

17.16 •• A geodesic dome constructed with an aluminum framework is a nearly perfect hemisphere; its diameter measures 55.0 m on a winter day at a temperature of −15°C. How much more interior space does the dome have in the summer, when the temperature is 35°C?

17.17 •• A copper cylinder is initially at 20.0°C. At what temperature will its volume be 0.150% larger than it is at 20.0°C?

17.18 •• A steel tank is completely filled with 2.80 m³ of ethanol when both the tank and the ethanol are at a temperature of 32.0°C. When the tank and its contents have cooled to 18.0°C, what additional volume of ethanol can be put into the tank?

17.19 •• A glass flask whose volume is 1000.00 cm³ at 0.0°C is completely filled with mercury at this temperature. When flask and mercury are warmed to 55.0°C, 8.95 cm³ of mercury overflow. If the coefficient of volume expansion of mercury is 18.0×10^{-5} K^{-1}, compute the coefficient of volume expansion of the glass.

17.20 •• (a) If an area measured on the surface of a solid body is A_0 at some initial temperature and then changes by ΔA when the temperature changes by ΔT, show that

$$\Delta A = (2\alpha)A_0 \Delta T$$

where α is the coefficient of linear expansion. (b) A circular sheet of aluminum is 55.0 cm in diameter at 15.0°C. By how much does the area of one side of the sheet change when the temperature increases to 27.5°C?

17.21 •• A machinist bores a hole of diameter 1.35 cm in a steel plate at a temperature of 25.0°C. What is the cross-sectional area of the hole (a) at 25.0°C and (b) when the temperature of the plate is increased to 175°C? Assume that the coefficient of linear expansion remains constant over this temperature range. (*Hint:* See Exercise 17.20.)

17.22 •• As a new mechanical engineer for Engines Inc., you have been assigned to design brass pistons to slide inside steel cylinders. The engines in which these pistons will be used will operate between 20.0°C and 150.0°C. Assume that the coefficients of expansion are constant over this temperature range. (a) If the piston just fits inside the chamber at 20.0°C, will the engines be able to run at higher temperatures? Explain. (b) If the cylindrical pistons are 25.000 cm in diameter at 20.0°C, what should be the minimum diameter of the cylinders at that temperature so the pistons will operate at 150.0°C?

17.23 • (a) A wire that is 1.50 m long at 20.0°C is found to increase in length by 1.90 cm when warmed to 420.0°C. Compute its average coefficient of linear expansion for this temperature range. (b) The wire is stretched just taut (zero tension) at 420.0°C. Find the stress in the wire if it is cooled to 20.0°C without being allowed to contract. Young's modulus for the wire is 2.0×10^{11} Pa.

17.24 •• A brass rod is 185 cm long and 1.60 cm in diameter. What force must be applied to each end of the rod to prevent it from contracting when it is cooled from 120.0°C to 10.0°C?

17.25 •• Steel train rails are laid in 12.0-m-long segments placed end to end. The rails are laid on a winter day when their temperature is −2.0°C. (a) How much space must be left between adjacent rails if they are just to touch on a summer day when their temperature is 33.0°C? (b) If the rails are originally laid in contact, what is the stress in them on a summer day when their temperature is 33.0°C?

Section 17.5 Quantity of Heat

17.26 • In an effort to stay awake for an all-night study session, a student makes a cup of coffee by first placing a 200-W electric immersion heater in 0.320 kg of water. (a) How much heat must be added to the water to raise its temperature from 20.0°C to 80.0°C? (b) How much time is required? Assume that all of the heater's power goes into heating the water.

17.27 •• An aluminum tea kettle with mass 1.50 kg and containing 1.80 kg of water is placed on a stove. If no heat is lost to the surroundings, how much heat must be added to raise the temperature from 20.0°C to 85.0°C?

17.28 • **BIO Heat Loss During Breathing.** In very cold weather a significant mechanism for heat loss by the human body is energy expended in warming the air taken into the lungs with each breath. (a) On a cold winter day when the temperature is −20°C, what amount of heat is needed to warm to body temperature (37°C) the 0.50 L of air exchanged with each breath? Assume that the specific heat of air is 1020 J/kg·K and that 1.0 L of air has mass 1.3×10^{-3} kg. (b) How much heat is lost per hour if the respiration rate is 20 breaths per minute?

17.29 • You are given a sample of metal and asked to determine its specific heat. You weigh the sample and find that its weight is 28.4 N. You carefully add 1.25×10^4 J of heat energy to the sample and find that its temperature rises 18.0 C°. What is the sample's specific heat?

17.30 •• **On-Demand Water Heaters.** Conventional hot-water heaters consist of a tank of water maintained at a fixed temperature. The hot water is to be used when needed. The drawbacks are that energy is wasted because the tank loses heat when it is not in use and that you can run out of hot water if you use too much. Some utility companies are encouraging the use of *on-demand* water heaters (also known as *flash heaters*), which consist of heating units to heat the water as you use it. No water tank is involved, so no heat is wasted. A typical household shower flow rate is 2.5 gal/min

(9.46 L/min) with the tap water being heated from 50°F (10°C) to 120°F (49°C) by the on-demand heater. What rate of heat input (either electrical or from gas) is required to operate such a unit, assuming that all the heat goes into the water?

17.31 • **BIO** While running, a 70-kg student generates thermal energy at a rate of 1200 W. For the runner to maintain a constant body temperature of 37°C, this energy must be removed by perspiration or other mechanisms. If these mechanisms failed and the heat could not flow out of the student's body, for what amount of time could a student run before irreversible body damage occurred? (*Note:* Protein structures in the body are irreversibly damaged if body temperature rises to 44°C or higher. The specific heat of a typical human body is 3480 J/kg·K, slightly less than that of water. The difference is due to the presence of protein, fat, and minerals, which have lower specific heats.)

17.32 • **CP** While painting the top of an antenna 225 m in height, a worker accidentally lets a 1.00-L water bottle fall from his lunchbox. The bottle lands in some bushes at ground level and does not break. If a quantity of heat equal to the magnitude of the change in mechanical energy of the water goes into the water, what is its increase in temperature?

17.33 •• **CP** A crate of fruit with mass 35.0 kg and specific heat 3650 J/kg·K slides down a ramp inclined at 36.9° below the horizontal. The ramp is 8.00 m long. (a) If the crate was at rest at the top of the incline and has a speed of 2.50 m/s at the bottom, how much work was done on the crate by friction? (b) If an amount of heat equal to the magnitude of the work done by friction goes into the crate of fruit and the fruit reaches a uniform final temperature, what is its temperature change?

17.34 • **CP** A 25,000-kg subway train initially traveling at 15.5 m/s slows to a stop in a station and then stays there long enough for its brakes to cool. The station's dimensions are 65.0 m long by 20.0 m wide by 12.0 m high. Assuming all the work done by the brakes in stopping the train is transferred as heat uniformly to all the air in the station, by how much does the air temperature in the station rise? Take the density of the air to be 1.20 kg/m³ and its specific heat to be 1020 J/kg·K.

17.35 • **CP** A nail driven into a board increases in temperature. If we assume that 60% of the kinetic energy delivered by a 1.80-kg hammer with a speed of 7.80 m/s is transformed into heat that flows into the nail and does not flow out, what is the temperature increase of an 8.00-g aluminum nail after it is struck ten times?

17.36 • A technician measures the specific heat of an unidentified liquid by immersing an electrical resistor in it. Electrical energy is converted to heat transferred to the liquid for 120 s at a constant rate of 65.0 W. The mass of the liquid is 0.780 kg, and its temperature increases from 18.55°C to 22.54°C. (a) Find the average specific heat of the liquid in this temperature range. Assume that negligible heat is transferred to the container that holds the liquid and that no heat is lost to the surroundings. (b) Suppose that in this experiment heat transfer from the liquid to the container or surroundings cannot be ignored. Is the result calculated in part (a) an *overestimate* or an *underestimate* of the average specific heat? Explain.

17.37 •• **CP** A 15.0-g bullet traveling horizontally at 865 m/s passes through a tank containing 13.5 kg of water and emerges with a speed of 534 m/s. What is the maximum temperature increase that the water could have as a result of this event?

Section 17.6 Calorimetry and Phase Changes

17.38 •• As a physicist, you put heat into a 500.0-g solid sample at the rate of 10.0 kJ/min, while recording its temperature as a function of time. You plot your data and obtain the graph shown in Fig. E17.38. (a) What is the latent heat of fusion for this solid? (b) What are the specific heats of the liquid and solid states of the material?

Figure **E17.38**

17.39 •• A 500.0-g chunk of an unknown metal, which has been in boiling water for several minutes, is quickly dropped into an insulating Styrofoam beaker containing 1.00 kg of water at room temperature (20.0°C). After waiting and gently stirring for 5.00 minutes, you observe that the water's temperature has reached a constant value of 22.0°C. (a) Assuming that the Styrofoam absorbs a negligibly small amount of heat and that no heat was lost to the surroundings, what is the specific heat of the metal? (b) Which is more useful for storing thermal energy: this metal or an equal weight of water? Explain. (c) What if the heat absorbed by the Styrofoam actually is not negligible. How would the specific heat you calculated in part (a) be in error? Would it be too large, too small, or still correct? Explain.

17.40 • **BIO** **Treatment for a Stroke.** One suggested treatment for a person who has suffered a stroke is immersion in an ice-water bath at 0°C to lower the body temperature, which prevents damage to the brain. In one set of tests, patients were cooled until their internal temperature reached 32.0°C. To treat a 70.0-kg patient, what is the minimum amount of ice (at 0°C) you need in the bath so that its temperature remains at 0°C? The specific heat of the human body is 3480 J/kg·C°, and recall that normal body temperature is 37.0°C.

17.41 •• A copper pot with a mass of 0.500 kg contains 0.170 kg of water, and both are at a temperature of 20.0°C. A 0.250-kg block of iron at 85.0°C is dropped into the pot. Find the final temperature of the system, assuming no heat loss to the surroundings.

17.42 •• **BIO** **Bicycling on a Warm Day.** If the air temperature is the same as the temperature of your skin (about 30°C), your body cannot get rid of heat by transferring it to the air. In that case, it gets rid of the heat by evaporating water (sweat). During bicycling, a typical 70-kg person's body produces energy at a rate of about 500 W due to metabolism, 80% of which is converted into heat. (a) How many kilograms of water must the person's body evaporate in an hour to get rid of this heat? The heat of vaporization of water at body temperature is 2.42×10^6 J/kg. (b) The evaporated water must, of course, be replenished, or the person will dehydrate. How many 750-mL bottles of water must the bicyclist drink per hour to replenish the lost water? (Recall that the mass of a liter of water is 1.0 kg.)

17.43 •• **BIO** **Overheating.** (a) By how much would the body temperature of the bicyclist in the preceeding problem increase in an hour if he were unable to get rid of the excess heat? (b) Is this temperature increase large enough to be serious? To find out, how high a fever would it be equivalent to, in °F? (Recall that the normal internal body temperature is 98.6°F and the specific heat of the body is 3480 J/kg · C°.)

17.44 · In a container of negligible mass, 0.200 kg of ice at an initial temperature of −40.0°C is mixed with a mass m of water that has an initial temperature of 80.0°C. No heat is lost to the surroundings. If the final temperature of the system is 20.0°C, what is the mass m of the water that was initially at 80.0°C?

17.45 · A 6.00-kg piece of solid copper metal at an initial temperature T is placed with 2.00 kg of ice that is initially at −20.0°C. The ice is in an insulated container of negligible mass and no heat is exchanged with the surroundings. After thermal equilibrium is reached, there is 1.20 kg of ice and 0.80 kg of liquid water. What was the initial temperature of the piece of copper?

17.46 · **BIO** Before going in for his annual physical, a 70.0-kg man whose body temperature is 37.0°C consumes an entire 0.355-L can of a soft drink (mostly water) at 12.0°C. (a) What will his body temperature be after equilibrium is attained? Ignore any heating by the man's metabolism. The specific heat of the man's body is 3480 J/kg · K. (b) Is the change in his body temperature great enough to be measured by a medical thermometer?

17.47 ·· **BIO** In the situation described in Exercise 17.46, the man's metabolism will eventually return the temperature of his body (and of the soft drink that he consumed) to 37.0°C. If his body releases energy at a rate of 7.00×10^3 kJ/day (the *basal metabolic rate,* or BMR), how long does this take? Assume that all of the released energy goes into raising the temperature.

17.48 ·· An ice-cube tray of negligible mass contains 0.350 kg of water at 18.0°C. How much heat must be removed to cool the water to 0.00°C and freeze it? Express your answer in joules, calories, and Btu.

17.49 · How much heat is required to convert 12.0 g of ice at −10.0°C to steam at 100.0°C? Express your answer in joules, calories, and Btu.

17.50 ·· An open container holds 0.550 kg of ice at −15.0°C. The mass of the container can be ignored. Heat is supplied to the container at the constant rate of 800.0 J/min for 500.0 min. (a) After how many minutes does the ice *start* to melt? (b) After how many minutes, from the time when the heating is first started, does the temperature begin to rise above 0.0°C? (c) Plot a curve showing the temperature as a function of the elapsed time.

17.51 · **CP** What must the initial speed of a lead bullet be at a temperature of 25.0°C so that the heat developed when it is brought to rest will be just sufficient to melt it? Assume that all the initial mechanical energy of the bullet is converted to heat and that no heat flows from the bullet to its surroundings. (Typical rifles have muzzle speeds that exceed the speed of sound in air, which is 347 m/s at 25.0°C.)

17.52 ·· **BIO** **Steam Burns Versus Water Burns.** What is the amount of heat input to your skin when it receives the heat released (a) by 25.0 g of steam initially at 100.0°C, when it is cooled to skin temperature (34.0°C)? (b) By 25.0 g of water initially at 100.0°C, when it is cooled to 34.0°C? (c) What does this tell you about the relative severity of steam and hot water burns?

17.53 · **BIO** **"The Ship of the Desert."** Camels require very little water because they are able to tolerate relatively large changes in their body temperature. While humans keep their body temperatures constant to within one or two Celsius degrees, a dehydrated camel permits its body temperature to drop to 34.0°C overnight and rise to 40.0°C during the day. To see how effective this mechanism is for saving water, calculate how many liters of water a 400-kg camel would have to drink if it attempted to keep its body temperature at a constant 34.0°C by evaporation of sweat during the day (12 hours) instead of letting it rise to 40.0°C. (*Note:* The specific heat of a camel or other mammal is about the same as that of a typical human, 3480 J/kg · K. The heat of vaporization of water at 34°C is 2.42×10^6 J/kg.)

17.54 · **BIO** Evaporation of sweat is an important mechanism for temperature control in some warm-blooded animals. (a) What mass of water must evaporate from the skin of a 70.0-kg man to cool his body 1.00 C°? The heat of vaporization of water at body temperature (37°C) is 2.42×10^6 J/kg. The specific heat of a typical human body is 3480 J/kg · K (see Exercise 17.31). (b) What volume of water must the man drink to replenish the evaporated water? Compare to the volume of a soft-drink can (355 cm^3).

17.55 ·· **CP** An asteroid with a diameter of 10 km and a mass of 2.60×10^{15} kg impacts the earth at a speed of 32.0 km/s, landing in the Pacific Ocean. If 1.00% of the asteroid's kinetic energy goes to boiling the ocean water (assume an initial water temperature of 10.0°C), what mass of water will be boiled away by the collision? (For comparison, the mass of water contained in Lake Superior is about 2×10^{15} kg.)

17.56 · A laboratory technician drops a 0.0850-kg sample of unknown solid material, at a temperature of 100.0°C, into a calorimeter. The calorimeter can, initially at 19.0°C, is made of 0.150 kg of copper and contains 0.200 kg of water. The final temperature of the calorimeter can and contents is 26.1°C. Compute the specific heat of the sample.

17.57 ·· An insulated beaker with negligible mass contains 0.250 kg of water at a temperature of 75.0°C. How many kilograms of ice at a temperature of −20.0°C must be dropped into the water to make the final temperature of the system 40.0°C?

17.58 ·· A glass vial containing a 16.0-g sample of an enzyme is cooled in an ice bath. The bath contains water and 0.120 kg of ice. The sample has specific heat 2250 J/kg · K; the glass vial has mass 6.00 g and specific heat 2800 J/kg · K. How much ice melts in cooling the enzyme sample from room temperature (19.5°C) to the temperature of the ice bath?

17.59 · A 4.00-kg silver ingot is taken from a furnace, where its temperature is 750.0°C, and placed on a large block of ice at 0.0°C. Assuming that all the heat given up by the silver is used to melt the ice, how much ice is melted?

17.60 ·· A copper calorimeter can with mass 0.100 kg contains 0.160 kg of water and 0.0180 kg of ice in thermal equilibrium at atmospheric pressure. If 0.750 kg of lead at a temperature of 255°C is dropped into the calorimeter can, what is the final temperature? Assume that no heat is lost to the surroundings.

17.61 ·· A vessel whose walls are thermally insulated contains 2.40 kg of water and 0.450 kg of ice, all at a temperature of 0.0°C. The outlet of a tube leading from a boiler in which water is boiling at atmospheric pressure is inserted into the water. How many grams of steam must condense inside the vessel (also at atmospheric pressure) to raise the temperature of the system to 28.0°C? You can ignore the heat transferred to the container.

Section 17.7 Mechanisms of Heat Transfer

17.62 ·· Two rods, one made of brass and the other made of copper, are joined end to end. The length of the brass section is 0.200 m and the length of the copper section is 0.800 m. Each segment has cross-sectional area 0.00500 m^2. The free end of the brass segment is in boiling water and the free end of the copper segment is in an ice and water mixture, in both cases under normal atmospheric pressure. The sides of the rods are insulated so there is no heat loss to the surroundings. (a) What is the temperature of the point where the brass and copper segments are joined? (b) What mass of ice is melted in 5.00 min by the heat conducted by the composite rod?

17.63 • Suppose that the rod in Fig. 17.23a is made of copper, is 45.0 cm long, and has a cross-sectional area of 1.25 cm^2. Let $T_H = 100.0°C$ and $T_C = 0.0°C$. (a) What is the final steady-state temperature gradient along the rod? (b) What is the heat current in the rod in the final steady state? (c) What is the final steady-state temperature at a point in the rod 12.0 cm from its left end?

17.64 •• One end of an insulated metal rod is maintained at 100.0°C, and the other end is maintained at 0.00°C by an ice–water mixture. The rod is 60.0 cm long and has a cross-sectional area of 1.25 cm^2. The heat conducted by the rod melts 8.50 g of ice in 10.0 min. Find the thermal conductivity k of the metal.

17.65 •• A carpenter builds an exterior house wall with a layer of wood 3.0 cm thick on the outside and a layer of Styrofoam insulation 2.2 cm thick on the inside wall surface. The wood has $k = 0.080$ W/m·K, and the Styrofoam has $k = 0.010$ W/m·K. The interior surface temperature is 19.0°C, and the exterior surface temperature is −10.0°C. (a) What is the temperature at the plane where the wood meets the Styrofoam? (b) What is the rate of heat flow per square meter through this wall?

17.66 • An electric kitchen range has a total wall area of 1.40 m^2 and is insulated with a layer of fiberglass 4.00 cm thick. The inside surface of the fiberglass has a temperature of 175°C, and its outside surface is at 35.0°C. The fiberglass has a thermal conductivity of 0.040 W/m·K. (a) What is the heat current through the insulation, assuming it may be treated as a flat slab with an area of 1.40 m^2? (b) What electric-power input to the heating element is required to maintain this temperature?

17.67 • BIO **Conduction Through the Skin.** The blood plays an important role in removing heat from the body by bringing this heat directly to the surface where it can radiate away. Nevertheless, this heat must still travel through the skin before it can radiate away. We shall assume that the blood is brought to the bottom layer of skin at a temperature of 37.0°C and that the outer surface of the skin is at 30.0°C. Skin varies in thickness from 0.50 mm to a few millimeters on the palms and soles, so we shall assume an average thickness of 0.75 mm. A 165-lb, 6-ft-tall person has a surface area of about 2.0 m^2 and loses heat at a net rate of 75 W while resting. On the basis of our assumptions, what is the thermal conductivity of this person's skin?

17.68 • A long rod, insulated to prevent heat loss along its sides, is in perfect thermal contact with boiling water (at atmospheric pressure) at one end and with an ice–water mixture at the other (Fig. E17.68). The rod consists of a 1.00-m section of copper (one end in boiling water) joined end to end to a length L_2 of steel (one end in the ice–water mixture). Both sections of the rod have cross-sectional areas of 4.00 cm^2. The temperature of the copper–steel junction is 65.0°C after a steady state has been set up. (a) How much heat per second flows from the boiling water to the ice–water mixture? (b) What is the length L_2 of the steel section?

Figure **E17.68**

17.69 • A pot with a steel bottom 8.50 mm thick rests on a hot stove. The area of the bottom of the pot is 0.150 m^2. The water inside the pot is at 100.0°C, and 0.390 kg are evaporated every 3.00 min. Find the temperature of the lower surface of the pot, which is in contact with the stove.

17.70 •• You are asked to design a cylindrical steel rod 50.0 cm long, with a circular cross section, that will conduct 150.0 J/s from a furnace at 400.0°C to a container of boiling water under 1 atmosphere. What must the rod's diameter be?

17.71 •• A picture window has dimensions of 1.40 m × 2.50 m and is made of glass 5.20 mm thick. On a winter day, the outside temperature is −20.0°C, while the inside temperature is a comfortable 19.5°C. (a) At what rate is heat being lost through the window by conduction? (b) At what rate would heat be lost through the window if you covered it with a 0.750-mm-thick layer of paper (thermal conductivity 0.0500 W/m·K)?

17.72 • What is the rate of energy radiation per unit area of a blackbody at a temperature of (a) 273 K and (b) 2730 K?

17.73 • **Size of a Light-Bulb Filament.** The operating temperature of a tungsten filament in an incandescent light bulb is 2450 K, and its emissivity is 0.350. Find the surface area of the filament of a 150-W bulb if all the electrical energy consumed by the bulb is radiated by the filament as electromagnetic waves. (Only a fraction of the radiation appears as visible light.)

17.74 •• The emissivity of tungsten is 0.350. A tungsten sphere with radius 1.50 cm is suspended within a large evacuated enclosure whose walls are at 290.0 K. What power input is required to maintain the sphere at a temperature of 3000.0 K if heat conduction along the supports is neglected?

17.75 • **The Sizes of Stars.** The hot glowing surfaces of stars emit energy in the form of electromagnetic radiation. It is a good approximation to assume $e = 1$ for these surfaces. Find the radii of the following stars (assumed to be spherical): (a) Rigel, the bright blue star in the constellation Orion, which radiates energy at a rate of $2.7 × 10^{32}$ W and has surface temperature 11,000 K; (b) Procyon B (visible only using a telescope), which radiates energy at a rate of $2.1 × 10^{23}$ W and has surface temperature 10,000 K. (c) Compare your answers to the radius of the earth, the radius of the sun, and the distance between the earth and the sun. (Rigel is an example of a *supergiant* star, and Procyon B is an example of a *white dwarf* star.)

PROBLEMS

17.76 •• Suppose that a steel hoop could be constructed to fit just around the earth's equator at a temperature of 20.0°C. What would be the thickness of space between the hoop and the earth if the temperature of the hoop were increased by 0.500 C°?

17.77 ••• You propose a new temperature scale with temperatures given in °M. You define 0.0°M to be the normal melting point of mercury and 100.0° to be the normal boiling point of mercury. (a) What is the normal boiling point of water in °M? (b) A temperature change of 10.0 M° corresponds to how many C°?

17.78 • CP, CALC A 250-kg weight is hanging from the ceiling by a thin copper wire. In its fundamental mode, this wire vibrates at the frequency of concert A (440 Hz). You then increase the temperature of the wire by 40 C°. (a) By how much will the fundamental frequency change? Will it increase or decrease? (b) By what percentage will the speed of a wave on the wire change? (c) By what percentage will the wavelength of the fundamental standing wave change? Will it increase or decrease?

17.79 ••• You are making pesto for your pasta and have a cylindrical measuring cup 10.0 cm high made of ordinary glass $[\beta = 2.7 \times 10^{-5} \ (\text{C}°)^{-1}]$ that is filled with olive oil $[\beta = 6.8 \times 10^{-4} \ (\text{C}°)^{-1}]$ to a height of 2.00 mm below the top of the cup. Initially, the cup and oil are at room temperature (22.0°C). You get a phone call and forget about the olive oil, which you inadvertently leave on the hot stove. The cup and oil heat up slowly and have a common temperature. At what temperature will the olive oil start to spill out of the cup?

17.80 •• A surveyor's 30.0-m steel tape is correct at a temperature of 20.0°C. The distance between two points, as measured by this tape on a day when its temperature is 5.00°C, is 25.970 m. What is the true distance between the points?

17.81 •• CP A Foucault pendulum consists of a brass sphere with a diameter of 35.0 cm suspended from a steel cable 10.5 m long (both measurements made at 20.0°C). Due to a design oversight, the swinging sphere clears the floor by a distance of only 2.00 mm when the temperature is 20.0°C. At what temperature will the sphere begin to brush the floor?

17.82 •• You pour 108 cm³ of ethanol, at a temperature of −10.0°C, into a graduated cylinder initially at 20.0°C, filling it to the very top. The cylinder is made of glass with a specific heat of 840 J/kg·K and a coefficient of volume expansion of $1.2 \times 10^{-5} \ \text{K}^{-1}$; its mass is 0.110 kg. The mass of the ethanol is 0.0873 kg. (a) What will be the final temperature of the ethanol, once thermal equilibrium is reached? (b) How much ethanol will overflow the cylinder before thermal equilibrium is reached?

17.83 •• A metal rod that is 30.0 cm long expands by 0.0650 cm when its temperature is raised from 0.0°C to 100.0°C. A rod of a different metal and of the same length expands by 0.0350 cm for the same rise in temperature. A third rod, also 30.0 cm long, is made up of pieces of each of the above metals placed end to end and expands 0.0580 cm between 0.0°C and 100.0°C. Find the length of each portion of the composite rod.

17.84 •• On a cool (4.0°C) Saturday morning, a pilot fills the fuel tanks of her Pitts S-2C (a two-seat aerobatic airplane) to their full capacity of 106.0 L. Before flying on Sunday morning, when the temperature is again 4.0°C, she checks the fuel level and finds only 103.4 L of gasoline in the tanks. She realizes that it was hot on Saturday afternoon, and that thermal expansion of the gasoline caused the missing fuel to empty out of the tank's vent. (a) What was the maximum temperature (in °C) reached by the fuel and the tank on Saturday afternoon? The coefficient of volume expansion of gasoline is $9.5 \times 10^{-4} \ \text{K}^{-1}$, and the tank is made of aluminum. (b) In order to have the maximum amount of fuel available for flight, when should the pilot have filled the fuel tanks?

17.85 ••• (a) Equation (17.12) gives the stress required to keep the length of a rod constant as its temperature changes. Show that if the length is permitted to change by an amount ΔL when its temperature changes by ΔT, the stress is equal to

$$\frac{F}{A} = Y\left(\frac{\Delta L}{L_0} - \alpha \Delta T\right)$$

where F is the tension on the rod, L_0 is the original length of the rod, A its cross-sectional area, α its coefficient of linear expansion, and Y its Young's modulus. (b) A heavy brass bar has projections at its ends, as in Fig. P17.85. Two fine steel wires, fastened between the pro-

Figure **P17.85**

Steel wires Brass

jections, are just taut (zero tension) when the whole system is at 20°C. What is the tensile stress in the steel wires when the temperature of the system is raised to 140°C? Make any simplifying assumptions you think are justified, but state what they are.

17.86 •• CP A metal wire, with density ρ and Young's modulus Y, is stretched between rigid supports. At temperature T, the speed of a transverse wave is found to be v_1. When the temperature is increased to $T + \Delta T$, the speed decreases to $v_2 < v_1$. Determine the coefficient of linear expansion of the wire.

17.87 •• CP **Out of Tune.** The B-string of a guitar is made of steel (density 7800 kg/m³), is 63.5 cm long, and has diameter 0.406 mm. The fundamental frequency is $f = 247.0$ Hz. (a) Find the string tension. (b) If the tension F is changed by a small amount ΔF, the frequency f changes by a small amount Δf. Show that

$$\frac{\Delta f}{f} = \frac{\Delta F}{2F}$$

(c) The string is tuned to a fundamental frequency of 247.0 Hz when its temperature is 18.5°C. Strenuous playing can make the temperature of the string rise, changing its vibration frequency. Find Δf if the temperature of the string rises to 29.5°C. The steel string has a Young's modulus of 2.00×10^{11} Pa and a coefficient of linear expansion of $1.20 \times 10^{-5} \ (\text{C}°)^{-1}$. Assume that the temperature of the body of the guitar remains constant. Will the vibration frequency rise or fall?

17.88 ••• A steel rod 0.450 m long and an aluminum rod 0.250 m long, both with the same diameter, are placed end to end between rigid supports with no initial stress in the rods. The temperature of the rods is now raised by 60.0 C°. What is the stress in each rod? (*Hint:* The length of the combined rod remains the same, but the lengths of the individual rods do not. See Problem 17.85.)

17.89 •• A steel ring with a 2.5000-in. inside diameter at 20.0°C is to be warmed and slipped over a brass shaft with a 2.5020-in. outside diameter at 20.0°C. (a) To what temperature should the ring be warmed? (b) If the ring and the shaft together are cooled by some means such as liquid air, at what temperature will the ring just slip off the shaft?

17.90 •• **Bulk Stress Due to a Temperature Increase.** (a) Prove that, if an object under pressure has its temperature raised but is not allowed to expand, the increase in pressure is

$$\Delta p = B\beta \Delta T$$

where the bulk modulus B and the average coefficient of volume expansion β are both assumed positive and constant. (b) What pressure is necessary to prevent a steel block from expanding when its temperature is increased from 20.0°C to 35.0°C?

17.91 •• A liquid is enclosed in a metal cylinder that is provided with a piston of the same metal. The system is originally at a pressure of 1.00 atm (1.013×10^5 Pa) and at a temperature of 30.0°C. The piston is forced down until the pressure on the liquid is increased by 50.0 atm, and then clamped in this position. Find the new temperature at which the pressure of the liquid is again 1.00 atm. Assume that the cylinder is sufficiently strong so that its volume is not altered by changes in pressure, but only by changes in temperature. Use the result derived in Problem 17.90. (*Hint:* See Section 11.4.)
Compressibility of liquid: $k = 8.50 \times 10^{-10} \ \text{Pa}^{-1}$
Coefficient of volume expansion of liquid: $\beta = 4.80 \times 10^{-4} \ \text{K}^{-1}$
Coefficient of volume expansion of metal: $\beta = 3.90 \times 10^{-5} \ \text{K}^{-1}$

17.92 •• You cool a 100.0-g slug of red-hot iron (temperature 745°C) by dropping it into an insulated cup of negligible mass containing 85.0 g of water at 20.0°C. Assuming no heat exchange with the surroundings, (a) what is the final temperature of the water and (b) what is the final mass of the iron and the remaining water?

17.93 • **CP Spacecraft Reentry.** A spacecraft made of aluminum circles the earth at a speed of 7700 m/s. (a) Find the ratio of its kinetic energy to the energy required to raise its temperature from 0°C to 600°C. (The melting point of aluminum is 660°C. Assume a constant specific heat of 910 J/kg·K.) (b) Discuss the bearing of your answer on the problem of the reentry of a manned space vehicle into the earth's atmosphere.

17.94 • **CP** A capstan is a rotating drum or cylinder over which a rope or cord slides in order to provide a great amplification of the rope's tension while keeping both ends free (Fig. P17.94). Since the added tension in the rope is due to friction, the capstan generates thermal energy. (a) If the difference in tension between the two ends of the rope is 520.0 N and the capstan has a diameter of 10.0 cm and turns once in 0.900 s, find the rate at which thermal energy is generated. Why does the number of turns not matter? (b) If the capstan is made of iron and has mass 6.00 kg, at what rate does its temperature rise? Assume that the temperature in the capstan is uniform and that all the thermal energy generated flows into it.

Figure **P17.94**

17.95 • • **CALC Debye's T^3 Law.** At very low temperatures the molar heat capacity of rock salt varies with temperature according to Debye's T^3 law:

$$C = k\frac{T^3}{\Theta^3}$$

where $k = 1940$ J/mol·K and $\Theta = 281$ K. (a) How much heat is required to raise the temperature of 1.50 mol of rock salt from 10.0 K to 40.0 K? (*Hint:* Use Eq. (17.18) in the form $dQ = nC\,dT$ and integrate.) (b) What is the average molar heat capacity in this range? (c) What is the true molar heat capacity at 40.0 K?

17.96 • • **CP** A person of mass 70.0 kg is sitting in the bathtub. The bathtub is 190.0 cm by 80.0 cm; before the person got in, the water was 16.0 cm deep. The water is at a temperature of 37.0°C. Suppose that the water were to cool down spontaneously to form ice at 0.0°C, and that all the energy released was used to launch the hapless bather vertically into the air. How high would the bather go? (As you will see in Chapter 20, this event is allowed by energy conservation but is prohibited by the second law of thermodynamics.)

17.97 • **Hot Air in a Physics Lecture.** (a) A typical student listening attentively to a physics lecture has a heat output of 100 W. How much heat energy does a class of 90 physics students release into a lecture hall over the course of a 50-min lecture? (b) Assume that all the heat energy in part (a) is transferred to the 3200 m³ of air in the room. The air has specific heat 1020 J/kg·K and density 1.20 kg/m³. If none of the heat escapes and the air conditioning system is off, how much will the temperature of the air in the room rise during the 50-min lecture? (c) If the class is taking an exam, the heat output per student rises to 280 W. What is the temperature rise during 50 min in this case?

17.98 • • • **CALC** The molar heat capacity of a certain substance varies with temperature according to the empirical equation

$$C = 29.5 \text{ J/mol·K} + (8.20 \times 10^{-3} \text{ J/mol·K}^2)T$$

How much heat is necessary to change the temperature of 3.00 mol of this substance from 27°C to 227°C? (*Hint:* Use Eq. (17.18) in the form $dQ = nC\,dT$ and integrate.)

17.99 • • • For your cabin in the wilderness, you decide to build a primitive refrigerator out of Styrofoam, planning to keep the interior cool with a block of ice that has an initial mass of 24.0 kg. The box has dimensions of 0.500 m × 0.800 m × 0.500 m. Water from melting ice collects in the bottom of the box. Suppose the ice block is at 0.00°C and the outside temperature is 21.0°C. If the top of the empty box is never opened and you want the interior of the box to remain at 5.00°C for exactly one week, until all the ice melts, what must be the thickness of the Styrofoam?

17.100 • • **Hot Water Versus Steam Heating.** In a household hot-water heating system, water is delivered to the radiators at 70.0°C (158.0°F) and leaves at 28.0°C (82.4°F). The system is to be replaced by a steam system in which steam at atmospheric pressure condenses in the radiators and the condensed steam leaves the radiators at 35.0°C (95.0°F). How many kilograms of steam will supply the same heat as was supplied by 1.00 kg of hot water in the first system?

17.101 • • • A copper calorimeter can with mass 0.446 kg contains 0.0950 kg of ice. The system is initially at 0.0°C. (a) If 0.0350 kg of steam at 100.0°C and 1.00 atm pressure is added to the can, what is the final temperature of the calorimeter can and its contents? (b) At the final temperature, how many kilograms are there of ice, how many of liquid water, and how many of steam?

17.102 • A Styrofoam bucket of negligible mass contains 1.75 kg of water and 0.450 kg of ice. More ice, from a refrigerator at −15.0°C, is added to the mixture in the bucket, and when thermal equilibrium has been reached, the total mass of ice in the bucket is 0.868 kg. Assuming no heat exchange with the surroundings, what mass of ice was added?

17.103 • • • In a container of negligible mass, 0.0400 kg of steam at 100°C and atmospheric pressure is added to 0.200 kg of water at 50.0°C. (a) If no heat is lost to the surroundings, what is the final temperature of the system? (b) At the final temperature, how many kilograms are there of steam and how many of liquid water?

17.104 • • **BIO Mammal Insulation.** Animals in cold climates often depend on *two* layers of insulation: a layer of body fat (of thermal conductivity 0.20 W/m·K) surrounded by a layer of air trapped inside fur or down. We can model a black bear (*Ursus americanus*) as a sphere 1.5 m in diameter having a layer of fat 4.0 cm thick. (Actually, the thickness varies with the season, but we are interested in hibernation, when the fat layer is thickest.) In studies of bear hibernation, it was found that the outer surface layer of the fur is at 2.7°C during hibernation, while the inner surface of the fat layer is at 31.0°C. (a) What is the temperature at the fat–inner fur boundary? (b) How thick should the air layer (contained within the fur) be so that the bear loses heat at a rate of 50.0 W?

17.105 • • • A worker pours 1.250 kg of molten lead at a temperature of 327.3°C into 0.5000 kg of water at a temperature of 75.00°C in an insulated bucket of negligible mass. Assuming no heat loss to the surroundings, calculate the mass of lead and water remaining in the bucket when the materials have reached thermal equilibrium.

17.106 ·· One experimental method of measuring an insulating material's thermal conductivity is to construct a box of the material and measure the power input to an electric heater inside the box that maintains the interior at a measured temperature above the outside surface. Suppose that in such an apparatus a power input of 180 W is required to keep the interior surface of the box 65.0 C° (about 120 F°) above the temperature of the outer surface. The total area of the box is 2.18 m², and the wall thickness is 3.90 cm. Find the thermal conductivity of the material in SI units.

17.107 ·· **Effect of a Window in a Door.** A carpenter builds a solid wood door with dimensions 2.00 m × 0.95 m × 5.0 cm. Its thermal conductivity is $k = 0.120$ W/m·K. The air films on the inner and outer surfaces of the door have the same combined thermal resistance as an additional 1.8-cm thickness of solid wood. The inside air temperature is 20.0°C, and the outside air temperature is −8.0°C. (a) What is the rate of heat flow through the door? (b) By what factor is the heat flow increased if a window 0.500 m on a side is inserted in the door? The glass is 0.450 cm thick, and the glass has a thermal conductivity of 0.80 W/m·K. The air films on the two sides of the glass have a total thermal resistance that is the same as an additional 12.0 cm of glass.

17.108 · A wood ceiling with thermal resistance R_1 is covered with a layer of insulation with thermal resistance R_2. Prove that the effective thermal resistance of the combination is $R = R_1 + R_2$.

17.109 ·· Compute the ratio of the rate of heat loss through a single-pane window with area 0.15 m² to that for a double-pane window with the same area. The glass of a single pane is 4.2 mm thick, and the air space between the two panes of the double-pane window is 7.0 mm thick. The glass has thermal conductivity 0.80 W/m·K. The air films on the room and outdoor surfaces of either window have a combined thermal resistance of 0.15 m²·K/W.

17.110 · Rods of copper, brass, and steel are welded together to form a Y-shaped figure. The cross-sectional area of each rod is 2.00 cm². The free end of the copper rod is maintained at 100.0°C, and the free ends of the brass and steel rods at 0.0°C. Assume there is no heat loss from the surfaces of the rods. The lengths of the rods are: copper, 13.0 cm; brass, 18.0 cm; steel, 24.0 cm. (a) What is the temperature of the junction point? (b) What is the heat current in each of the three rods?

17.111 ··· **CALC** **Time Needed for a Lake to Freeze Over.** (a) When the air temperature is below 0°C, the water at the surface of a lake freezes to form an ice sheet. Why doesn't freezing occur throughout the entire volume of the lake? (b) Show that the thickness of the ice sheet formed on the surface of a lake is proportional to the square root of the time if the heat of fusion of the water freezing on the underside of the ice sheet is conducted through the sheet. (c) Assuming that the upper surface of the ice sheet is at −10°C and the bottom surface is at 0°C, calculate the time it will take to form an ice sheet 25 cm thick. (d) If the lake in part (c) is uniformly 40 m deep, how long would it take to freeze all the water in the lake? Is this likely to occur?

17.112 ·· A rod is initially at a uniform temperature of 0°C throughout. One end is kept at 0°C, and the other is brought into contact with a steam bath at 100°C. The surface of the rod is insulated so that heat can flow only lengthwise along the rod. The cross-sectional area of the rod is 2.50 cm², its length is 120 cm, its thermal conductivity is 380 W/m·K, its density is 1.00×10^4 kg/m³, and its specific heat is 520 J/kg·K. Consider a short cylindrical element of the rod 1.00 cm in length. (a) If the temperature gradient at the cooler end of this element is 140 C°/m, how many joules of heat energy flow across this end per second? (b) If the average temperature of the element is

increasing at the rate of what is the temperature gradient at the other end of the element?

17.113 ·· A rustic cabin has a floor area of 3.50 m × 3.00 m. Its walls, which are 2.50 m tall, are made of wood (thermal conductivity 0.0600 W/m·K) 1.80 cm thick and are further insulated with 1.50 cm of a synthetic material. When the outside temperature is 2.00°C, it is found necessary to heat the room at a rate of 1.25 kW to maintain its temperature at 19.0°C. Calculate the thermal conductivity of the insulating material. Neglect the heat lost through the ceiling and floor. Assume the inner and outer surfaces of the wall have the same termperature as the air inside and outside the cabin.

17.114 · The rate at which radiant energy from the sun reaches the earth's upper atmosphere is about 1.50 kW/m². The distance from the earth to the sun is 1.50×10^{11} m, and the radius of the sun is 6.96×10^8 m. (a) What is the rate of radiation of energy per unit area from the sun's surface? (b) If the sun radiates as an ideal blackbody, what is the temperature of its surface?

17.115 ··· **A Thermos for Liquid Helium.** A physicist uses a cylindrical metal can 0.250 m high and 0.090 m in diameter to store liquid helium at 4.22 K; at that temperature the heat of vaporization of helium is 2.09×10^4 J/kg. Completely surrounding the metal can are walls maintained at the temperature of liquid nitrogen, 77.3 K, with vacuum between the can and the surrounding walls. How much helium is lost per hour? The emissivity of the metal can is 0.200. The only heat transfer between the metal can and the surrounding walls is by radiation.

17.116 ·· **BIO** **Basal Metabolic Rate.** The basal metabolic rate is the rate at which energy is produced in the body when a person is at rest. A 75-kg (165-lb) person of height 1.83 m (6 ft) has a body surface area of approximately 2.0 m². (a) What is the net amount of heat this person could radiate per second into a room at 18°C (about 65°F) if his skin's surface temperature is 30°C? (At such temperatures, nearly all the heat is infrared radiation, for which the body's emissivity is 1.0, regardless of the amount of pigment.) (b) Normally, 80% of the energy produced by metabolism goes into heat, while the rest goes into things like pumping blood and repairing cells. Also normally, a person at rest can get rid of this excess heat just through radiation. Use your answer to part (a) to find this person's basal metabolic rate.

17.117 ·· **BIO** **Jogging in the Heat of the Day.** You have probably seen people jogging in extremely hot weather and wondered Why? As we shall see, there are good reasons not to do this! When jogging strenuously, an average runner of mass 68 kg and surface area 1.85 m² produces energy at a rate of up to 1300 W, 80% of which is converted to heat. The jogger radiates heat, but actually absorbs more from the hot air than he radiates away. At such high levels of activity, the skin's temperature can be elevated to around 33°C instead of the usual 30°C. (We shall neglect conduction, which would bring even more heat into his body.) The only way for the body to get rid of this extra heat is by evaporating water (sweating). (a) How much heat per second is produced just by the act of jogging? (b) How much *net* heat per second does the runner gain just from radiation if the air temperature is 40.0°C (104°F)? (Remember that he radiates out, but the environment radiates back in.) (c) What is the *total* amount of excess heat this runner's body must get rid of per second? (d) How much water must the jogger's body evaporate every minute due to his activity? The heat of vaporization of water at body temperature is 2.42×10^6 J/kg. (e) How many 750-mL bottles of water must he drink after (or preferably before!) jogging for a half hour? Recall that a liter of water has a mass of 1.0 kg.

17.118 ·· **BIO Overheating While Jogging.**   (a) If the jogger in the preceding problem were not able to get rid of the excess heat, by how much would his body temperature increase above the normal 37°C in a half hour of jogging? The specific heat for a human is about 3500 J/kg·K. (b) How high a fever (in °F) would this temperature increase be equivalent to? Is the increase large enough to be of concern? (Recall that normal body temperature is 98.6°F.)

17.119 ·· An engineer is developing an electric water heater to provide a continuous supply of hot water. One trial design is shown in Fig. P17.119. Water is flowing at the rate of 0.500 kg/min, the inlet thermometer registers 18.0°C, the voltmeter reads 120 V, and the ammeter reads 15.0 A [corresponding to a power input of (120 V) × (15.0 A) = 1800 W]. (a) When a steady state is finally reached, what is the reading of the outlet thermometer? (b) Why is it unnecessary to take into account the heat capacity *mc* of the apparatus itself?

Figure **P17.119**

17.120 · **Food Intake of a Hamster.**   The energy output of an animal engaged in an activity is called the basal metabolic rate (BMR) and is a measure of the conversion of food energy into other forms of energy. A simple calorimeter to measure the BMR consists of an insulated box with a thermometer to measure the temperature of the air. The air has density 1.20 kg/m³ and specific heat 1020 J/kg·K. A 50.0-g hamster is placed in a calorimeter that contains 0.0500 m³ of air at room temperature. (a) When the hamster is running in a wheel, the temperature of the air in the calorimeter rises 1.60 C° per hour. How much heat does the running hamster generate in an hour? Assume that all this heat goes into the air in the calorimeter. You can ignore the heat that goes into the walls of the box and into the thermometer, and assume that no heat is lost to the surroundings. (b) Assuming that the hamster converts seed into heat with an efficiency of 10% and that hamster seed has a food energy value of 24 J/g, how many grams of seed must the hamster eat per hour to supply this energy?

17.121 ·· The icecaps of Greenland and Antarctica contain about 1.75% of the total water (by mass) on the earth's surface; the oceans contain about 97.5%, and the other 0.75% is mainly groundwater. Suppose the icecaps, currently at an average temperature of about −30°C, somehow slid into the ocean and melted. What would be the resulting temperature decrease of the ocean? Assume that the average temperature of ocean water is currently 5.00°C.

17.122 ·· **Why Do the Seasons Lag?**   In the northern hemisphere, June 21 (the summer solstice) is both the longest day of the year and the day on which the sun's rays strike the earth most vertically, hence delivering the greatest amount of heat to the surface. Yet the hottest summer weather usually occurs about a month or so later. Let us see why this is the case. Because of the large specific heat of water, the oceans are slower to warm up than the land (and also slower to cool off in winter). In addition to perusing pertinent information in the tables included in this book, it is useful to know

that approximately two-thirds of the earth's surface is ocean composed of salt water having a specific heat of 3890 J/kg·K and that the oceans, on the average, are 4000 m deep. Typically, an average of 1050 W/m² of solar energy falls on the earth's surface, and the oceans absorb essentially all of the light that strikes them. However, most of that light is absorbed in the upper 100 m of the surface. Depths below that do not change temperature seasonally. Assume that the sunlight falls on the surface for only 12 hours per day and that the ocean retains all the heat it absorbs. What will be the rise in temperature of the upper 100 m of the oceans during the month following the summer solstice? Does this seem to be large enough to be perceptible?

CHALLENGE PROBLEMS

17.123 ··· **CALC** Suppose that both ends of the rod in Fig. 17.23a are kept at a temperature of 0°C, and that the initial temperature distribution along the rod is given by $T = (100°C) \sin \pi x/L$, where x is measured from the left end of the rod. Let the rod be copper, with length $L = 0.100$ m and cross-sectional area 1.00 cm². (a) Show the initial temperature distribution in a diagram. (b) What is the final temperature distribution after a very long time has elapsed? (c) Sketch curves that you think would represent the temperature distribution at intermediate times. (d) What is the initial temperature gradient at the ends of the rod? (e) What is the initial heat current from the ends of the rod into the bodies making contact with its ends? (f) What is the initial heat current at the center of the rod? Explain. What is the heat current at this point at any later time? (g) What is the value of the *thermal diffusivity* $k/\rho c$ for copper, and in what unit is it expressed? (Here k is the thermal conductivity, $\rho = 8.9 \times 10^3$ kg/m³ is the density, and c is the specific heat.) (h) What is the initial time rate of change of temperature at the center of the rod? (i) How much time would be required for the center of the rod to reach its final temperature if the temperature continued to decrease at this rate? (This time is called the *relaxation time* of the rod.) (j) From the graphs in part (c), would you expect the magnitude of the rate of temperature change at the midpoint to remain constant, increase, or decrease as a function of time? (k) What is the initial rate of change of temperature at a point in the rod 2.5 cm from its left end?

17.124 ··· **CALC** (a) A spherical shell has inner and outer radii a and b, respectively, and the temperatures at the inner and outer surfaces are T_2 and T_1. The thermal conductivity of the material of which the shell is made is k. Derive an equation for the total heat current through the shell. (b) Derive an equation for the temperature variation within the shell in part (a); that is, calculate T as a function of r, the distance from the center of the shell. (c) A hollow cylinder has length L, inner radius a, and outer radius b, and the temperatures at the inner and outer surfaces are T_2 and T_1. (The cylinder could represent an insulated hot-water pipe, for example.) The thermal conductivity of the material of which the cylinder is made is k. Derive an equation for the total heat current through the walls of the cylinder. (d) For the cylinder of part (c), derive an equation for the temperature variation inside the cylinder walls. (e) For the spherical shell of part (a) and the hollow cylinder of part (c), show that the equation for the total heat current in each case reduces to Eq. (17.21) for linear heat flow when the shell or cylinder is very thin.

17.125 ··· A steam pipe with a radius of 2.00 cm, carrying steam at 140°C, is surrounded by a cylindrical jacket with inner and outer radii 2.00 cm and 4.00 cm and made of a type of cork with thermal conductivity 4.00×10^{-2} W/m·K. This in turn is surrounded by a cylindrical jacket made of a brand of Styrofoam with thermal conductivity 1.00×10^{-2} W/m·K and having inner and outer radii 4.00 cm and 6.00 cm (Fig. P17.125). The outer surface of the Styrofoam is in contact with air at 15°C. Assume that this outer surface has a temperature of 15°C. (a) What is the temperature at a radius of 4.00 cm, where the two insulating layers meet? (b) What is the total rate of transfer of heat out of a 2.00-m length of pipe? (*Hint:* Use the expression derived in part (c) of Challenge Problem 17.124.)

Figure **P17.125**

17.126 ••• **CP Temperature Change in a Clock.** A pendulum clock is designed to tick off one second on each side-to-side swing of the pendulum (two ticks per complete period). (a) Will a pendulum clock gain time in hot weather and lose it in cold, or the reverse? Explain your reasoning. (b) A particular pendulum clock keeps correct time at 20.0°C. The pendulum shaft is steel, and its mass can be ignored compared with that of the bob. What is the fractional change in the length of the shaft when it is cooled to 10.0°C? (c) How many seconds per day will the clock gain or lose at 10.0°C? (d) How closely must the temperature be controlled if the clock is not to gain or lose more than 1.00 s a day? Does the answer depend on the period of the pendulum?

17.127 ••• **BIO A Walk in the Sun.** Consider a poor lost soul walking at 5 km/h on a hot day in the desert, wearing only a bathing suit. This person's skin temperature tends to rise due to four mechanisms: (i) energy is generated by metabolic reactions in the body at a rate of 280 W, and almost all of this energy is converted to heat that flows to the skin; (ii) heat is delivered to the skin by convection from the outside air at a rate equal to $k'A_{skin}(T_{air} - T_{skin})$, where k' is 54 J/h·C°·m², the exposed skin area A_{skin} is 1.5 m², the air temperature T_{air} is 47°C, and the skin temperature T_{skin} is 36°C; (iii) the skin absorbs radiant energy from the sun at a rate of 1400 W/m²; (iv) the skin absorbs radiant energy from the environment, which has temperature 47°C. (a) Calculate the net rate (in watts) at which the person's skin is heated by all four of these mechanisms. Assume that the emissivity of the skin is $e = 1$ and that the skin temperature is initially 36°C. Which mechanism is the most important? (b) At what rate (in L/h) must perspiration evaporate from this person's skin to maintain a constant skin temperature? (The heat of vaporization of water at 36°C is 2.42×10^6 J/kg.) (c) Suppose instead the person is protected by light-colored clothing ($e \approx 0$) so that the exposed skin area is only 0.45 m². What rate of perspiration is required now? Discuss the usefulness of the traditional clothing worn by desert peoples.

Answers

Chapter Opening Question

No. By "heat" we mean energy that is in transit from one body to another as a result of temperature difference between the bodies. Bodies do not *contain* heat.

Test Your Understanding Questions

17.1 Answer: (ii) A liquid-in-tube thermometer actually measures its own temperature. If the thermometer stays in the hot water long enough, it will come to thermal equilibrium with the water and its temperature will be the same as that of the water.

17.2 Answer: (iv) Both a bimetallic strip and a resistance thermometer measure their own temperature. For this to be equal to the temperature of the object being measured, the thermometer and object must be in contact and in thermal equilibrium. A temporal artery thermometer detects the infrared radiation from a person's skin, so there is no need for the detector and skin to be at the same temperature.

17.3 Answer: (i), (iii), (ii), (v), (iv) To compare these temperatures, convert them all to the Kelvin scale. For (i), the Kelvin temperature is $T_K = T_C + 273.15 = 0.00 + 273.15 = 273.15$ K; for (ii), $T_C = \frac{5}{9}(T_F - 32°) = \frac{5}{9}(0.00° - 32°) = -17.78°C$ and $T_K = T_C + 273.15 = -17.78 + 273.15 = 255.37$ K; for (iii), $T_K = 260.00$ K; for (iv), $T_K = 77.00$ K; and for (v), $T_K = T_C + 273.15 = -180.00 + 273.15 = 93.15$ K.

17.4 Answer: (ii) and (iii) Metal 2 must expand more than metal 1 when heated and so must have a larger coefficient of linear expansion

α. From Table 17.1, brass and aluminum have larger values of α than copper, but steel does not.

17.5 Answer: (ii), (i), (iv), (iii) For (i) and (ii), the relevant quantity is the specific heat c of the substance, which is the amount of heat required to raise the temperature of 1 *kilogram* of that substance by 1 K (1 C°). From Table 17.3, these values are (i) 138 J for mercury and (ii) 2428 J for ethanol. For (iii) and (iv) we need the molar heat capacity C, which is the amount of heat required to raise the temperature of 1 *mole* of that substance by 1 C°. Again from Table 17.3, these values are (iii) 27.7 J for mercury and (iv) 111.9 J for ethanol. (The ratio of molar heat capacities is different from the ratio of the specific heats because a mole of mercury and a mole of ethanol have different masses.)

17.6 Answer: (iv) In time t the system goes from point b to point e in Fig. 17.21. According to this figure, at time $t/2$ (halfway along the horizontal axis from b to e), the system is at 100°C and is still boiling; that is, it is a mixture of liquid and gas. This says that most of the heat added goes into boiling the water.

17.7 Answer: (ii) When you touch one of the walls, heat flows from your hand to the lower-temperature wall. The more rapidly heat flows from your hand, the colder you will feel. Equation (17.21) shows that the rate of heat flow is proportional to the thermal conductivity k. From Table 17.5, copper has a much higher thermal conductivity (385.0 W/m·K) than steel (50.2 W/m·K) or concrete (0.8 W/m·K), and so the copper wall feels the coldest.

Bridging Problem

Answers: (a) 14.26 K **(b)** 0.427 kg/h

18 THERMAL PROPERTIES OF MATTER

LEARNING GOALS

By studying this chapter, you will learn:

- How to relate the pressure, volume, and temperature of a gas.

- How the interactions between the molecules of a substance determine the properties of the substance.

- How the pressure and temperature of a gas are related to the kinetic energy of its molecules.

- How the heat capacities of a gas reveal whether its molecules are rotating or vibrating.

- What determines whether a substance is a gas, a liquid, or a solid.

? The higher the temperature of a gas, the greater the average kinetic energy of its molecules. How much faster are molecules moving in the air above a frying pan (100°C) than in the surrounding kitchen air (25°C)?

The kitchen is a great place to learn about how the properties of matter depend on temperature. When you boil water in a tea kettle, the increase in temperature produces steam that whistles out of the spout at high pressure. If you forget to poke holes in a potato before baking it, the high-pressure steam produced inside the potato can cause it to explode messily. Water vapor in the air can condense into droplets of liquid on the sides of a glass of ice water; if the glass is just out of the freezer, frost will form on the sides as water vapor changes to a solid.

These examples show the relationships among the large-scale or *macroscopic* properties of a substance, such as pressure, volume, temperature, and mass. But we can also describe a substance using a *microscopic* perspective. This means investigating small-scale quantities such as the masses, speeds, kinetic energies, and momenta of the individual molecules that make up a substance.

The macroscopic and microscopic descriptions are intimately related. For example, the (microscopic) forces that occur when air molecules strike a solid surface (such as your skin) cause (macroscopic) atmospheric pressure. To produce standard atmospheric pressure of 1.01×10^5 Pa, 10^{32} molecules strike your skin every day with an average speed of over 1700 km/h (1000 mi/h)!

In this chapter we'll begin our study of the thermal properties of matter by looking at some macroscopic aspects of matter in general. We'll pay special attention to the *ideal gas,* one of the simplest types of matter to understand. Using our knowledge of momentum and kinetic energy, we'll relate the macroscopic properties of an ideal gas to the microscopic behavior of its individual molecules. We'll also use microscopic ideas to understand the heat capacities of both gases and solids. Finally, we'll take a look at the various phases of matter—gas, liquid, and solid—and the conditions under which each occurs.

18.1 Equations of State

The conditions in which a particular material exists are described by physical quantities such as pressure, volume, temperature, and amount of substance. For example, a tank of oxygen in a welding outfit has a pressure gauge and a label stating its volume. We could add a thermometer and place the tank on a scale to determine its mass. These variables describe the *state* of the material and are called **state variables.**

The volume V of a substance is usually determined by its pressure p, temperature T, and amount of substance, described by the mass m_{total} or number of moles n. (We are calling the total mass of a substance m_{total} because later in the chapter we will use m for the mass of one molecule.) Ordinarily, we can't change one of these variables without causing a change in another. When the tank of oxygen gets hotter, the pressure increases. If the tank gets too hot, it explodes.

In a few cases the relationship among p, V, T, and m (or n) is simple enough that we can express it as an equation called the **equation of state.** When it's too complicated for that, we can use graphs or numerical tables. Even then, the relationship among the variables still exists; we call it an equation of state even when we don't know the actual equation.

Here's a simple (though approximate) equation of state for a solid material. The temperature coefficient of volume expansion β (see Section 17.4) is the fractional volume change $\Delta V/V_0$ per unit temperature change, and the compressibility k (see Section 11.4) is the negative of the fractional volume change $\Delta V/V_0$ per unit pressure change. If a certain amount of material has volume V_0 when the pressure is p_0 and the temperature is T_0, the volume V at slightly differing pressure p and temperature T is approximately

$$V = V_0[1 + \beta(T - T_0) - k(p - p_0)] \qquad (18.1)$$

(There is a negative sign in front of the term $k(p - p_0)$ because an *increase* in pressure causes a *decrease* in volume.)

The Ideal-Gas Equation

Another simple equation of state is the one for an *ideal gas*. Figure 18.1 shows an experimental setup to study the behavior of a gas. The cylinder has a movable piston to vary the volume, the temperature can be varied by heating, and we can pump any desired amount of any gas into the cylinder. We then measure the pressure, volume, temperature, and amount of gas. Note that *pressure* refers both to the force per unit area exerted by the cylinder on the gas and to the force per unit area exerted by the gas on the cylinder; by Newton's third law, these must be equal.

It is usually easiest to describe the amount of gas in terms of the number of moles n, rather than the mass. (We did this when we defined molar heat capacity in Section 17.5.) The **molar mass** M of a compound (sometimes called *molecular weight*) is the mass per mole, and the total mass m_{total} of a given quantity of that compound is the number of moles n times the mass per mole M:

$$m_{\text{total}} = nM \qquad \text{(total mass, number of moles, and molar mass)} \quad (18.2)$$

Hence if we know the number of moles of gas in the cylinder, we can determine the mass of gas using Eq. (18.2).

Measurements of the behavior of various gases lead to three conclusions:

1. The volume V is proportional to the number of moles n. If we double the number of moles, keeping pressure and temperature constant, the volume doubles.

ActivPhysics 8.4: State Variables and Ideal Gas Law

18.1 A hypothetical setup for studying the behavior of gases. By heating the gas, varying the volume with a movable piston, and adding more gas, we can control the gas pressure p, volume V, temperature T, and number of moles n.

2. The volume varies *inversely* with the absolute pressure p. If we double the pressure while holding the temperature T and number of moles n constant, the gas compresses to one-half of its initial volume. In other words, $pV =$ constant when n and T are constant.

3. The pressure is proportional to the *absolute* temperature. If we double the absolute temperature, keeping the volume and number of moles constant, the pressure doubles. In other words, $p =$ (constant)T when n and V are constant.

18.2 The ideal-gas equation $pV = nRT$ gives a good description of the air inside an inflated vehicle tire, where the pressure is about 3 atmospheres and the temperature is much too high for nitrogen or oxygen to liquefy. As the tire warms (T increases), the volume V changes only slightly but the pressure p increases.

These three relationships can be combined neatly into a single equation, called the **ideal-gas equation:**

$$pV = nRT \quad \text{(ideal-gas equation)} \tag{18.3}$$

where R is a proportionality constant. An **ideal gas** is one for which Eq. (18.3) holds precisely for *all* pressures and temperatures. This is an idealized model; it works best at very low pressures and high temperatures, when the gas molecules are far apart and in rapid motion. It is reasonably good (within a few percent) at moderate pressures (such as a few atmospheres) and at temperatures well above those at which the gas liquefies (Fig. 18.2).

We might expect that the constant R in the ideal-gas equation would have different values for different gases, but it turns out to have the same value for *all* gases, at least at sufficiently high temperature and low pressure. It is called the **gas constant** (or *ideal-gas constant*). The numerical value of R depends on the units of p, V, and T. In SI units, in which the unit of p is Pa (1 Pa $= 1$ N/m^2) and the unit of V is m^3, the current best numerical value of R is

$$R = 8.314472(15) \text{ J/mol} \cdot \text{K}$$

or $R = 8.314$ J/mol $\cdot$ K to four significant figures. Note that the units of pressure times volume are the same as the units of work or energy (for example, N/m^2 times m^3); that's why R has units of energy per mole per unit of absolute temperature. In chemical calculations, volumes are often expressed in liters (L) and pressures in atmospheres (atm). In this system, to four significant figures,

$$R = 0.08206 \frac{\text{L} \cdot \text{atm}}{\text{mol} \cdot \text{K}}$$

Application Respiration and the Ideal-Gas Equation
To breathe, you rely on the ideal-gas equation $pV = nRT$. Contraction of the dome-shaped diaphragm muscle increases the volume V of the thoracic cavity (which encloses the lungs), decreasing its pressure p. The lowered pressure causes the lungs to expand and fill with air. (The temperature T is kept constant.) When you exhale, the diaphragm relaxes, allowing the lungs to contract and expel the air.

We can express the ideal-gas equation, Eq. (18.3), in terms of the mass m_{total} of gas, using $m_{\text{total}} = nM$ from Eq. (18.2):

$$pV = \frac{m_{\text{total}}}{M} RT \tag{18.4}$$

From this we can get an expression for the density $\rho = m_{\text{total}}/V$ of the gas:

$$\rho = \frac{pM}{RT} \tag{18.5}$$

CAUTION Density vs. pressure When using Eq. (18.5), be certain that you distinguish between the Greek letter ρ (rho) for density and the letter p for pressure.

Inhalation:
Diaphragm contracts; lungs expand

Exhalation:
Diaphragm relaxes; lungs contract

For a *constant mass* (or constant number of moles) of an ideal gas the product nR is constant, so the quantity pV/T is also constant. If the subscripts 1 and 2 refer to any two states of the same mass of a gas, then

$$\frac{p_1 V_1}{T_1} = \frac{p_2 V_2}{T_2} = \text{constant} \quad \text{(ideal gas, constant mass)} \tag{18.6}$$

Notice that you don't need the value of R to use this equation.

We used the proportionality of pressure to absolute temperature in Chapter 17 to define a temperature scale in terms of pressure in a constant-volume gas thermometer. That may make it seem that the pressure–temperature relationship in the ideal-gas equation, Eq. (18.3), is just a result of the way we define temperature. But the equation also tells us what happens when we change the volume or the amount of substance. Also, we'll see in Chapter 20 that the gas-thermometer scale corresponds closely to a temperature scale that does *not* depend on the properties of any particular material. For now, consider Eq. (18.6) as being based on this genuinely material-independent temperature scale.

Problem-Solving Strategy 18.1 Ideal Gases

IDENTIFY *the relevant concepts:* Unless the problem states otherwise, you can use the ideal-gas equation to find quantities related to the state of a gas, such as pressure p, volume V, temperature T, and/or number of moles n.

SET UP *the problem* using the following steps:
1. List the known and unknown quantities. Identify the target variables.
2. If the problem concerns only one state of the system, use Eq. (18.3), $pV = nRT$.
3. Use Eq. (18.5), $\rho = pM/RT$, as an alternative to Eq. (18.3) if the problem involves the density ρ rather than n and V.
4. In problems that concern two states (call them 1 and 2) of the same amount of gas, if all but one of the six quantities p_1, p_2, V_1, V_2, T_1, and T_2 are known, use Eq. (18.6), $p_1V_1/T_1 = p_2V_2/T_2 = \text{constant}$. Otherwise, use Eq. (18.3) or Eq. (18.5) as appropriate.

EXECUTE *the solution* as follows:
1. Use consistent units. (SI units are entirely consistent.) The problem statement may make one system of units more con-

venient than others. Make appropriate unit conversions, such as from atmospheres to pascals or from liters to cubic meters.
2. You may have to convert between mass m_{total} and number of moles n, using $m_{total} = Mn$, where M is the molar mass. If you use Eq. (18.4), you *must* use the same mass units for m_{total} and M. So if M is in grams per mole (the usual units for molar mass), then m_{total} must also be in grams. To use m_{total} in kilograms, you must convert M to kg/mol. For example, the molar mass of oxygen is 32 g/mol or 32×10^{-3} kg/mol.
3. Remember that in the ideal-gas equations, T is always an *absolute* (Kelvin) temperature and p is always an absolute (not gauge) pressure.
4. Solve for the target variables.

EVALUATE *your answer:* Do your results make physical sense? Use benchmarks, such as the result of Example 18.1 below that a mole of an ideal gas at 1 atmosphere pressure occupies a volume of 22.4 liters.

Example 18.1 Volume of an ideal gas at STP

What is the volume of a container that holds exactly 1 mole of an ideal gas at *standard temperature and pressure* (STP), defined as $T = 0°C = 273.15$ K and $p = 1$ atm $= 1.013 \times 10^5$ Pa?

SOLUTION

IDENTIFY and SET UP: This problem involves the properties of a single state of an ideal gas, so we use Eq. (18.3). We are given the pressure p, temperature T, and number of moles n; our target variable is the corresponding volume V.

EXECUTE: From Eq. (18.3), using R in J/mol · K,

$$V = \frac{nRT}{p} = \frac{(1\ \text{mol})(8.314\ \text{J/mol} \cdot \text{K})(273.15\ \text{K})}{1.013 \times 10^5\ \text{Pa}}$$

$$= 0.0224\ \text{m}^3 = 22.4\ \text{L}$$

EVALUATE: At STP, 1 mole of an ideal gas occupies 22.4 L. This is the volume of a cube 0.282 m (11.1 in.) on a side, or of a sphere 0.350 m (13.8 in.) in diameter.

Example 18.2 Compressing gas in an automobile engine

In an automobile engine, a mixture of air and vaporized gasoline is compressed in the cylinders before being ignited. A typical engine has a compression ratio of 9.00 to 1; that is, the gas in the cylinders is compressed to $\frac{1}{9.00}$ of its original volume (Fig. 18.3). The intake

and exhaust valves are closed during the compression, so the quantity of gas is constant. What is the final temperature of the compressed gas if its initial temperature is 27°C and the initial and final pressures are 1.00 atm and 21.7 atm, respectively?

Continued

SOLUTION

IDENTIFY and SET UP: We must compare two states of the same quantity of ideal gas, so we use Eq. (18.6). In the uncompressed state, $p_1 = 1.00$ atm and $T_1 = 27°C = 300$ K. In the compressed state 2, $p_2 = 21.7$ atm. The cylinder volumes are not given, but we have $V_1 = 9.00V_2$. The temperature T_2 of the compressed gas is the target variable.

EXECUTE: We solve Eq. (18.6) for T_2:

$$T_2 = T_1\frac{p_2V_2}{p_1V_1} = (300 \text{ K})\frac{(21.7 \text{ atm})V_2}{(1.00 \text{ atm})(9.00V_2)} = 723 \text{ K} = 450°C$$

EVALUATE: This is the temperature of the air–gasoline mixture *before* the mixture is ignited; when burning starts, the temperature becomes higher still.

18.3 Cutaway of an automobile engine. While the air–gasoline mixture is being compressed prior to ignition, the intake and exhaust valves are both in the closed (up) position.

Intake valve
Exhaust valve
Fuel injector
Combustion chamber
Fuel pump

Example 18.3 Mass of air in a scuba tank

An "empty" aluminum scuba tank contains 11.0 L of air at 21°C and 1 atm. When the tank is filled rapidly from a compressor, the air temperature is 42°C and the gauge pressure is 2.10×10^7 Pa. What mass of air was added? (Air is about 78% nitrogen, 21% oxygen, and 1% miscellaneous; its average molar mass is 28.8 g/mol = 28.8×10^{-3} kg/mol.)

SOLUTION

IDENTIFY and SET UP: Our target variable is the difference $m_2 - m_1$ between the masses present at the end (state 2) and at the beginning (state 1). We are given the molar mass M of air, so we can use Eq. (18.2) to find the target variable if we know the number of moles present in states 1 and 2. We determine n_1 and n_2 by applying Eq. (18.3) to each state individually.

EXECUTE: We convert temperatures to the Kelvin scale by adding 273 and convert the pressure to absolute by adding 1.013×10^5 Pa.

The tank's volume is hardly affected by the increased temperature and pressure, so $V_2 = V_1$. From Eq. (18.3), the numbers of moles in the empty tank (n_1) and the full tank (n_2) are

$$n_1 = \frac{p_1V_1}{RT_1} = \frac{(1.013 \times 10^5 \text{ Pa})(11.0 \times 10^{-3} \text{ m}^3)}{(8.314 \text{ J/mol}\cdot\text{K})(294 \text{ K})} = 0.46 \text{ mol}$$

$$n_2 = \frac{p_2V_2}{RT_2} = \frac{(2.11 \times 10^7 \text{ Pa})(11.0 \times 10^{-3} \text{ m}^3)}{(8.314 \text{ J/mol}\cdot\text{K})(315 \text{ K})} = 88.6 \text{ mol}$$

We added $n_2 - n_1 = 88.6$ mol $- 0.46$ mol $= 88.1$ mol to the tank. From Eq. (18.2), the added mass is $M(n_2 - n_1) = (28.8 \times 10^{-3}$ kg/mol$)(88.1$ mol$) = 2.54$ kg.

EVALUATE: The added mass is not insubstantial: You could certainly use a scale to determine whether the tank was empty or full.

Example 18.4 Variation of atmospheric pressure with elevation

Find the variation of atmospheric pressure with elevation in the earth's atmosphere. Assume that at all elevations, $T = 0°C$ and $g = 9.80 \text{ m/s}^2$.

SOLUTION

IDENTIFY and SET UP: As the elevation y increases, both the atmospheric pressure p and the density ρ decrease. Hence we have *two* unknown functions of y; to solve for them, we need two independent equations. One is the ideal-gas equation, Eq. (18.5), which is expressed in terms of p and ρ. The other is Eq. (12.4), the relationship that we found in Section 12.2 among p, ρ, and y in a fluid in equilibrium: $dp/dy = -\rho g$. We are told to assume that g and T are the same at all elevations; we also assume that the atmosphere has the same chemical composition, and hence the same molar mass M, at all heights. We combine the two equations and solve for $p(y)$.

EXECUTE: We substitute $\rho = pM/RT$ into $dp/dy = -\rho g$, separate variables, and integrate, letting p_1 be the pressure at elevation y_1 and p_2 be the pressure at y_2:

$$\frac{dp}{dy} = -\frac{pM}{RT}g$$

$$\int_{p_1}^{p_2}\frac{dp}{p} = -\frac{Mg}{RT}\int_{y_1}^{y_2}dy$$

$$\ln\frac{p_2}{p_1} = -\frac{Mg}{RT}(y_2 - y_1)$$

$$\frac{p_2}{p_1} = e^{-Mg(y_2-y_1)/RT}$$

Now let $y_1 = 0$ be at sea level and let the pressure at that point be $p_0 = 1.013 \times 10^5$ Pa. Then the pressure p at any height y is

$$p = p_0e^{-Mgy/RT}$$

EVALUATE: According to our calculation, the pressure decreases exponentially with elevation. The graph in Fig. 18.4 shows that the slope dp/dy becomes less negative with greater elevation. That result makes sense, since $dp/dy = -\rho g$ and the density also

18.4 The variation of atmospheric pressure p with elevation y, assuming a constant temperature T.

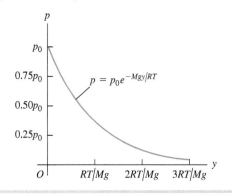

decreases with elevation. At the summit of Mount Everest, where $y = 8863$ m,

$$\frac{Mgy}{RT} = \frac{(28.8 \times 10^{-3} \text{ kg/mol})(9.80 \text{ m/s}^2)(8863 \text{ m})}{(8.314 \text{ J/mol} \cdot \text{K})(273 \text{ K})} = 1.10$$

$$p = (1.013 \times 10^5 \text{ Pa})e^{-1.10} = 0.337 \times 10^5 \text{ Pa} = 0.33 \text{ atm}$$

The assumption of constant temperature isn't realistic, and g decreases a little with increasing elevation (see Challenge Problem 18.92). Even so, this example shows why mountaineers need to carry oxygen on Mount Everest. It also shows why jet airliners, which typically fly at altitudes of 8000 to 12,000 m, *must* have pressurized cabins for passenger comfort and health.

The van der Waals Equation

The ideal-gas equation, Eq. (18.3), can be obtained from a simple molecular model that ignores the volumes of the molecules themselves and the attractive forces between them (Fig. 18.5a). We'll examine that model in Section 18.3. Meanwhile, we mention another equation of state, the **van der Waals equation,** that makes approximate corrections for these two omissions (Fig. 18.5b). This equation was developed by the 19th-century Dutch physicist J. D. van der Waals; the interaction between atoms that we discussed in Section 14.4 was named the *van der Waals interaction* after him. The van der Waals equation is

$$\left(p + \frac{an^2}{V^2}\right)(V - nb) = nRT \tag{18.7}$$

The constants a and b are empirical constants, different for different gases. Roughly speaking, b represents the volume of a mole of molecules; the total volume of the molecules is then nb, and the volume remaining in which the molecules can move is $V - nb$. The constant a depends on the attractive intermolecular forces, which reduce the pressure of the gas for given values of n, V, and T by *pulling* the molecules together as they *push* on the walls of the container. The decrease in pressure is proportional to the number of molecules per unit volume in a layer near the wall (which are exerting the pressure on the wall) and is also proportional to the number per unit volume in the next layer beyond the wall (which are doing the attracting). Hence the decrease in pressure due to intermolecular forces is proportional to n^2/V^2.

When n/V is small (that is, when the gas is *dilute*), the average distance between molecules is large, the corrections in the van der Waals equation become insignificant, and Eq. (18.7) reduces to the ideal-gas equation. As an example, for carbon dioxide gas (CO_2) the constants in the van der Waals equation are $a = 0.364 \text{ J} \cdot \text{m}^3/\text{mol}^2$ and $b = 4.27 \times 10^{-5} \text{ m}^3/\text{mol}$. We found in Example 18.1 that 1 mole of an ideal gas at $T = 0°\text{C} = 273.15$ K and $p = 1$ atm $= 1.013 \times 10^5$ Pa occupies a volume $V = 0.0224 \text{ m}^3$; according to Eq. (18.7),

(a) An idealized model of a gas

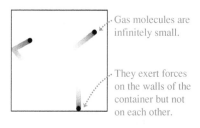

Gas molecules are infinitely small.

They exert forces on the walls of the container but not on each other.

(b) A more realistic model of a gas

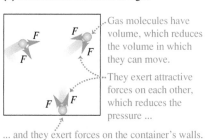

Gas molecules have volume, which reduces the volume in which they can move.

They exert attractive forces on each other, which reduces the pressure ...

... and they exert forces on the container's walls.

18.5 A gas as modeled by **(a)** the ideal-gas equation and **(b)** the van der Waals equation.

1 mole of CO_2 occupying this volume at this temperature would be at a pressure 532 Pa less than 1 atm, a difference of only 0.5% from the ideal-gas value.

pV-Diagrams

We could in principle represent the p-V-T relationship graphically as a *surface* in a three-dimensional space with coordinates p, V, and T. This representation sometimes helps us grasp the overall behavior of the substance, but ordinary two-dimensional graphs are usually more convenient. One of the most useful of these is a set of graphs of pressure as a function of volume, each for a particular constant temperature. Such a diagram is called a *pV-diagram.* Each curve, representing behavior at a specific temperature, is called an **isotherm,** or a *pV-isotherm.*

Figure 18.6 shows pV-isotherms for a constant amount of an ideal gas. Since $p = nRT/V$ from Eq. (18.3), along an isotherm (constant T) the pressure p is inversely proportional to the volume V and the isotherms are hyperbolic curves.

Figure 18.7 shows a pV-diagram for a material that *does not* obey the ideal-gas equation. At temperatures below T_c the isotherms develop flat regions in which we can compress the material (that is, reduce the volume V) without increasing the pressure p. Observation shows that the gas is *condensing* from the vapor (gas) to the liquid phase. The flat parts of the isotherms in the shaded area of Fig. 18.7 represent conditions of liquid-vapor *phase equilibrium.* As the volume decreases, more and more material goes from vapor to liquid, but the pressure does not change. (To keep the temperature constant during condensation, we have to remove the heat of vaporization, discussed in Section 17.6.)

When we compress such a gas at a constant temperature T_2 in Fig. 18.7, it is vapor until point *a* is reached. Then it begins to liquefy; as the volume decreases further, more material liquefies, and *both* the pressure and the temperature remain constant. At point *b*, all the material is in the liquid state. After this, any further compression requires a very rapid rise of pressure, because liquids are in general much less compressible than gases. At a lower constant temperature T_1, similar behavior occurs, but the condensation begins at lower pressure and greater volume than at the constant temperature T_2. At temperatures greater than T_c, *no* phase transition occurs as the material is compressed; at the highest temperatures, such as T_4, the curves resemble the ideal-gas curves of Fig. 18.6. We call T_c the *critical temperature* for this material. In Section 18.6 we'll discuss what happens to the phase of the gas above the critical temperature.

We will use pV-diagrams often in the next two chapters. We will show that the *area* under a pV-curve (whether or not it is an isotherm) represents the *work* done by the system during a volume change. This work, in turn, is directly related to heat transfer and changes in the *internal energy* of the system.

18.6 Isotherms, or constant-temperature curves, for a constant amount of an ideal gas. The highest temperature is T_4; the lowest is T_1. This is a graphical representation of the ideal-gas equation of state.

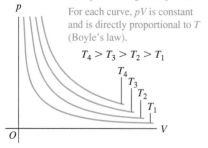

Each curve represents pressure as a function of volume for an ideal gas at a single temperature.

For each curve, pV is constant and is directly proportional to T (Boyle's law).

$T_4 > T_3 > T_2 > T_1$

18.7 A pV-diagram for a nonideal gas, showing isotherms for temperatures above and below the critical temperature T_c. The liquid–vapor equilibrium region is shown as a green shaded area. At still lower temperatures the material might undergo phase transitions from liquid to solid or from gas to solid; these are not shown in this diagram.

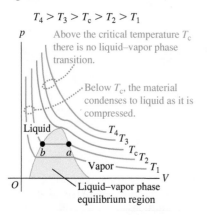

$T_4 > T_3 > T_c > T_2 > T_1$

Above the critical temperature T_c there is no liquid–vapor phase transition.

Below T_c, the material condenses to liquid as it is compressed.

Liquid–vapor phase equilibrium region

Test Your Understanding of Section 18.1 Rank the following ideal gases in order from highest to lowest number of moles: (i) pressure 1 atm, volume 1 L, and temperature 300 K; (ii) pressure 2 atm, volume 1 L, and temperature 300 K; (iii) pressure 1 atm, volume 2 L, and temperature 300 K; (iv) pressure 1 atm, volume 1 L, and temperature 600 K; (v) pressure 2 atm, volume 1 L, and temperature 600 K.

18.2 Molecular Properties of Matter

We have studied several properties of matter in bulk, including elasticity, density, surface tension, heat capacities, and equations of state. Now we want to look in more detail at the relationship of bulk behavior to *molecular* structure. We begin with a general discussion of the molecular structure of matter. Then in the next two sections we develop the kinetic-molecular model of an ideal gas, obtaining from this molecular model the equation of state and an expression for heat capacity.

Molecules and Intermolecular Forces

Any specific chemical compound is made up of identical **molecules.** The smallest molecules contain one atom each and are of the order of 10^{-10} m in size; the largest contain many atoms and are at least 10,000 times larger. In gases the molecules move nearly independently; in liquids and solids they are held together by intermolecular forces. These forces arise from interactions among the electrically charged particles that make up the molecules. Gravitational forces between molecules are negligible in comparison with electrical forces.

The interaction of two *point* electric charges is described by a force (repulsive for like charges, attractive for unlike charges) with a magnitude proportional to $1/r^2$, where r is the distance between the points. We will study this relationship, called *Coulomb's law,* in Chapter 21. Molecules are *not* point charges but complex structures containing both positive and negative charge, and their interactions are more complex. The force between molecules in a gas varies with the distance r between molecules somewhat as shown in Fig. 18.8, where a positive F_r corresponds to a repulsive force and a negative F_r to an attractive force. When molecules are far apart, the intermolecular forces are very small and usually attractive. As a gas is compressed and its molecules are brought closer together, the attractive forces increase. The intermolecular force becomes zero at an equilibrium spacing r_0, corresponding roughly to the spacing between molecules in the liquid and solid states. In liquids and solids, relatively large pressures are needed to compress the substance appreciably. This shows that at molecular distances slightly *less* than the equilibrium spacing, the forces become *repulsive* and relatively large.

Figure 18.8 also shows the potential energy as a function of r. This function has a *minimum* at r_0, where the force is zero. The two curves are related by $F_r(r) = -dU/dr$, as we showed in Section 7.4. Such a potential-energy function is often called a **potential well.** A molecule at rest at a distance r_0 from a second molecule would need an additional energy $|U_0|$, the "depth" of the potential well, to "escape" to an indefinitely large value of r.

Molecules are always in motion; their kinetic energies usually increase with temperature. At very low temperatures the average kinetic energy of a molecule may be much *less* than the depth of the potential well. The molecules then condense into the liquid or solid phase with average intermolecular spacings of about r_0. But at higher temperatures the average kinetic energy becomes larger than the depth $|U_0|$ of the potential well. Molecules can then escape the intermolecular force and become free to move independently, as in the gaseous phase of matter.

In *solids,* molecules vibrate about more or less fixed points. In a crystalline solid these points are arranged in a *crystal lattice.* Figure 18.9 shows the cubic crystal structure of sodium chloride, and Fig. 18.10 shows a scanning tunneling microscope image of individual silicon atoms on the surface of a crystal.

The vibration of molecules in a solid about their equilibrium positions may be nearly simple harmonic if the potential well is approximately parabolic in shape at distances close to r_0. (We discussed this kind of simple harmonic motion in Section 14.4.) But if the potential-energy curve rises more gradually for $r > r_0$ than for $r < r_0$, as in Fig. 18.8, the average position shifts to larger r with increasing amplitude. As we pointed out in Section 17.4, this is the basis of thermal expansion.

In a *liquid,* the intermolecular distances are usually only slightly greater than in the solid phase of the same substance, but the molecules have much greater freedom of movement. Liquids show regularity of structure only in the immediate neighborhood of a few molecules.

The molecules of a *gas* are usually widely separated and so have only very small attractive forces. A gas molecule moves in a straight line until it collides with another molecule or with a wall of the container. In molecular terms, an *ideal gas* is a gas whose molecules exert *no* attractive forces on each other (see Fig. 18.5a) and therefore have no *potential* energy.

18.8 How the force between molecules and their potential energy of interaction depend on their separation r.

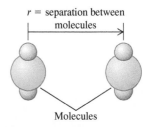

r = separation between molecules

Molecules

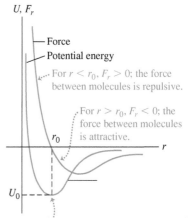

U, F_r

— Force
— Potential energy

For $r < r_0$, $F_r > 0$; the force between molecules is repulsive.

For $r > r_0$, $F_r < 0$; the force between molecules is attractive.

r_0

r

U_0

At a separation $r = r_0$, the potential energy of the two molecules is minimum and the force between the molecules is zero.

18.9 Schematic representation of the cubic crystal structure of sodium chloride (ordinary salt).

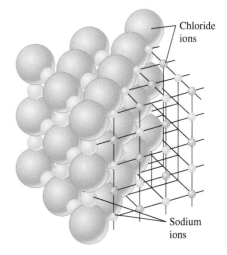

Chloride ions

Sodium ions

18.10 A scanning tunneling microscope image of the surface of a silicon crystal. The area shown is only 9.0 nm (9.0×10^{-9} m) across. Each blue "bead" is an individual silicon atom; you can clearly see how these atoms are arranged in a (nearly) perfect array of hexagons.

At low temperatures, most common substances are in the solid phase. As the temperature rises, a substance melts and then vaporizes. From a molecular point of view, these transitions are in the direction of increasing molecular kinetic energy. Thus temperature and molecular kinetic energy are closely related.

Moles and Avogadro's Number

We have used the mole as a measure of quantity of substance. One **mole** of any pure chemical element or compound contains a definite number of molecules, the same number for all elements and compounds. The official SI definition is:

> **One mole is the amount of substance that contains as many elementary entities as there are atoms in 0.012 kilogram of carbon-12.**

In our discussion, the "elementary entities" are molecules. (In a monatomic substance such as carbon or helium, each molecule is a single atom.) Atoms of a given element may occur in any of several isotopes, which are chemically identical but have different atomic masses; "carbon-12" is a specific isotope of carbon.

The number of molecules in a mole is called **Avogadro's number,** denoted by N_A. The current best numerical value of N_A is

$$N_A = 6.02214179(30) \times 10^{23} \text{ molecules/mol (Avogadro's number)}$$

The *molar mass M* of a compound is the mass of 1 mole. It is equal to the mass m of a single molecule multiplied by Avogadro's number:

$$M = N_A m \qquad \text{(molar mass, Avogadro's number, and mass of a molecule)} \qquad (18.8)$$

When the molecule consists of a single atom, the term *atomic mass* is often used instead of molar mass or molecular weight.

Example 18.5 Atomic and molecular mass

Find the mass of a single hydrogen atom and of a single oxygen molecule.

SOLUTION

IDENTIFY and SET UP: This problem involves the relationship between the mass of a molecule or atom (our target variable) and the corresponding molar mass M. We use Eq. (18.8) in the form $m = M/N_A$ and the values of the atomic masses from the periodic table of the elements (see Appendix D).

EXECUTE: For atomic hydrogen the atomic mass (molar mass) is $M_H = 1.008$ g/mol, so the mass m_H of a single hydrogen atom is

$$m_H = \frac{1.008 \text{ g/mol}}{6.022 \times 10^{23} \text{ atoms/mol}} = 1.674 \times 10^{-24} \text{ g/atom}$$

For oxygen the atomic mass is 16.0 g/mol, so for the diatomic (two-atom) oxygen molecule the molar mass is 32.0 g/mol. Then the mass of a single oxygen molecule is

$$m_{O_2} = \frac{32.0 \text{ g/mol}}{6.022 \times 10^{23} \text{ molecules/mol}} = 53.1 \times 10^{-24} \text{ g/molecule}$$

EVALUATE: We note that the values in Appendix D are for the *average* atomic masses of a natural sample of each element. Such a sample may contain several *isotopes* of the element, each with a different atomic mass. Natural samples of hydrogen and oxygen are almost entirely made up of just one isotope.

Test Your Understanding of Section 18.2 Suppose you could adjust the value of r_0 for the molecules of a certain chemical compound (Fig. 18.8) by turning a dial. If you doubled the value of r_0, the density of the solid form of this compound would become (i) twice as great; (ii) four times as great; (iii) eight times as great; (iv) $\frac{1}{2}$ as great; (v) $\frac{1}{4}$ as great; (vi) $\frac{1}{8}$ as great.

18.3 Kinetic-Molecular Model of an Ideal Gas

PhET: Balloons & Buoyancy
PhET: Friction
PhET: Gas Properties
ActivPhysics 8.1: Characteristics of a Gas

The goal of any molecular theory of matter is to understand the *macroscopic* properties of matter in terms of its atomic or molecular structure and behavior. Once we have this understanding, we can design materials to have specific desired properties. Theories have led to the development of high-strength steels, semiconductor materials for electronic devices, and countless other materials essential to contemporary technology.

In this and the following sections we will consider a simple molecular model of an ideal gas. This *kinetic-molecular model* represents the gas as a large number of particles bouncing around in a closed container. In this section we use the kinetic-molecular model to understand how the ideal-gas equation of state, Eq. (18.3), is related to Newton's laws. In the following section we use the kinetic-molecular model to predict the molar heat capacity of an ideal gas. We'll go on to elaborate the model to include "particles" that are not points but have a finite size.

Our discussion of the kinetic-molecular model has several steps, and you may need to go over them several times. Don't get discouraged!

Here are the assumptions of our model:

1. A container with volume V contains a very large number N of identical molecules, each with mass m.
2. The molecules behave as point particles that are small compared to the size of the container and to the average distance between molecules.
3. The molecules are in constant motion. Each molecule collides occasionally with a wall of the container. These collisions are perfectly elastic.
4. The container walls are rigid and infinitely massive and do not move.

CAUTION **Molecules vs. moles** Make sure you don't confuse N, the number of *molecules* in the gas, with n, the number of *moles*. The number of molecules is equal to the number of moles multiplied by Avogadro's number: $N = nN_A$. ∎

Collisions and Gas Pressure

During collisions the molecules exert *forces* on the walls of the container; this is the origin of the *pressure* that the gas exerts. In a typical collision (Fig. 18.11) the velocity component parallel to the wall is unchanged, and the component perpendicular to the wall reverses direction but does not change in magnitude.

Our program is first to determine the *number* of collisions that occur per unit time for a certain area A of wall. Then we find the total momentum change associated with these collisions and the force needed to cause this momentum change. From this we can determine the pressure, which is force per unit area, and compare the result to the ideal-gas equation. We'll find a direct connection between the temperature of the gas and the kinetic energy of the gas molecules.

To begin, we will assume that all molecules in the gas have the same *magnitude* of x-velocity, $|v_x|$. This isn't right, but making this temporary assumption helps to clarify the basic ideas. We will show later that this assumption isn't really necessary.

As shown in Fig. 18.11, for each collision the x-component of velocity changes from $-|v_x|$ to $+|v_x|$. So the x-component of momentum changes from $-m|v_x|$ to $+m|v_x|$, and the *change* in the x-component of momentum is $m|v_x| - (-m|v_x|) = 2m|v_x|$.

If a molecule is going to collide with a given wall area A during a small time interval dt, then at the beginning of dt it must be within a distance $|v_x|\, dt$ from the wall (Fig. 18.12) and it must be headed toward the wall. So the number of molecules that collide with A during dt is equal to the number of molecules within a cylinder with base area A and length $|v_x|\, dt$ that have their x-velocity aimed

18.11 Elastic collision of a molecule with an idealized container wall.

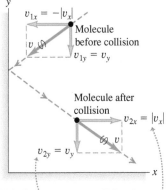

• Velocity component parallel to the wall (y-component) does not change.
• Velocity component perpendicular to the wall (x-component) reverses direction.
• Speed v does not change.

18.12 For a molecule to strike the wall in area A during a time interval dt, the molecule must be headed for the wall and be within the shaded cylinder of length $|v_x|\, dt$ at the beginning of the interval.

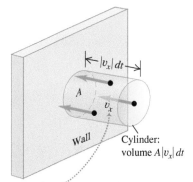

All molecules are assumed to have the same magnitude $|v_x|$ of x-velocity.

toward the wall. The volume of such a cylinder is $A|v_x|\,dt$. Assuming that the number of molecules per unit volume (N/V) is uniform, the *number* of molecules in this cylinder is $(N/V)(A|v_x|\,dt)$. On the average, half of these molecules are moving toward the wall and half are moving away from it. So the number of collisions with A during dt is

$$\tfrac{1}{2}\left(\frac{N}{V}\right)(A|v_x|\,dt)$$

For the system of all molecules in the gas, the total momentum change dP_x during dt is the *number* of collisions multiplied by $2m|v_x|$:

$$dP_x = \tfrac{1}{2}\left(\frac{N}{V}\right)(A|v_x|\,dt)(2m|v_x|) = \frac{NAmv_x^2\,dt}{V} \tag{18.9}$$

(We are using capital P for total momentum and small p for pressure. Be careful!) We wrote v_x^2 rather than $|v_x|^2$ in the final expression because the square of the absolute value of a number is equal to the square of that number. The *rate* of change of momentum component P_x is

$$\frac{dP_x}{dt} = \frac{NAmv_x^2}{V} \tag{18.10}$$

According to Newton's second law, this rate of change of momentum equals the force exerted by the wall area A on the gas molecules. From Newton's *third* law this is equal and opposite to the force exerted *on* the wall *by* the molecules. Pressure p is the magnitude of the force exerted on the wall per unit area, and we obtain

$$p = \frac{F}{A} = \frac{Nmv_x^2}{V} \tag{18.11}$$

The pressure exerted by the gas depends on the number of molecules per volume (N/V), the mass m per molecule, and the speed of the molecules.

Pressure and Molecular Kinetic Energies

We mentioned that $|v_x|$ is really *not* the same for all the molecules. But we could have sorted the molecules into groups having the same $|v_x|$ within each group, then added up the resulting contributions to the pressure. The net effect of all this is just to replace v_x^2 in Eq. (18.11) by the *average* value of v_x^2, which we denote by $(v_x^2)_{av}$. We can relate $(v_x^2)_{av}$ to the *speeds* of the molecules. The speed v of a molecule is related to the velocity components v_x, v_y, and v_z by

$$v^2 = v_x^2 + v_y^2 + v_z^2$$

We can average this relation over all molecules:

$$(v^2)_{av} = (v_x^2)_{av} + (v_y^2)_{av} + (v_z^2)_{av}$$

But there is no real difference in our model between the x-, y-, and z-directions. (Molecular speeds are very fast in a typical gas, so the effects of gravity are negligibly small.) It follows that $(v_x^2)_{av}$, $(v_y^2)_{av}$, and $(v_z^2)_{av}$ must all be *equal*. Hence $(v^2)_{av}$ is equal to $3(v_x^2)_{av}$ and

$$(v_x^2)_{av} = \tfrac{1}{3}(v^2)_{av}$$

so Eq. (18.11) becomes

$$pV = \tfrac{1}{3}Nm(v^2)_{av} = \tfrac{2}{3}N\left[\tfrac{1}{2}m(v^2)_{av}\right] \tag{18.12}$$

We notice that $\tfrac{1}{2}m(v^2)_{av}$ is the average translational kinetic energy of a single molecule. The product of this and the total number of molecules N equals the total random kinetic energy K_{tr} of translational motion of all the molecules. (The notation K_{tr} reminds us that this is the energy of *translational* motion. There may also be energies associated with molecular rotation and vibration.) The product pV equals two-thirds of the total translational kinetic energy:

$$pV = \tfrac{2}{3}K_{tr} \qquad (18.13)$$

Now we compare this with the ideal-gas equation,

$$pV = nRT$$

which is based on experimental studies of gas behavior. For the two equations to agree, we must have

$$K_{tr} = \tfrac{3}{2}nRT \qquad \text{(average translational kinetic energy of } n \text{ moles of ideal gas)} \qquad (18.14)$$

This remarkably simple result shows that K_{tr} is *directly proportional* to the absolute temperature T (Fig. 18.13).

The average translational kinetic energy of a single molecule is the total translational kinetic energy K_{tr} of all molecules divided by the number of molecules, N:

$$\frac{K_{tr}}{N} = \tfrac{1}{2}m(v^2)_{av} = \frac{3nRT}{2N}$$

Also, the total number of molecules N is the number of moles n multiplied by Avogadro's number N_A, so

$$N = nN_A \qquad \frac{n}{N} = \frac{1}{N_A}$$

and

$$\frac{K_{tr}}{N} = \tfrac{1}{2}m(v^2)_{av} = \tfrac{3}{2}\left(\frac{R}{N_A}\right)T \qquad (18.15)$$

The ratio R/N_A occurs frequently in molecular theory. It is called the **Boltzmann constant**, k:

$$k = \frac{R}{N_A} = \frac{8.314 \text{ J/mol} \cdot \text{K}}{6.022 \times 10^{23} \text{ molecules/mol}}$$

$$= 1.381 \times 10^{-23} \text{ J/molecule} \cdot \text{K}$$

(The current best numerical value of k is $1.3806504(24) \times 10^{-23}$ J/molecule $\cdot$ K). In terms of k we can rewrite Eq. (18.15) as

$$\tfrac{1}{2}m(v^2)_{av} = \tfrac{3}{2}kT \qquad \text{(average translational kinetic energy of a gas molecule)} \qquad (18.16)$$

This shows that the average translational kinetic energy *per molecule* depends only on the temperature, not on the pressure, volume, or kind of molecule. We can obtain the average translational kinetic energy *per mole* by multiplying Eq. (18.16) by Avogadro's number and using the relation $M = N_Am$:

$$N_A\tfrac{1}{2}m(v^2)_{av} = \tfrac{1}{2}M(v^2)_{av} = \tfrac{3}{2}RT \qquad \text{(average translational kinetic energy per mole of gas)} \qquad (18.17)$$

The translational kinetic energy of a mole of an ideal gas depends only on T.

18.13 Summer air (top) is warmer than winter air (bottom); that is, the average translational kinetic energy of air molecules is greater in summer.

Finally, it is sometimes convenient to rewrite the ideal-gas equation on a molecular basis. We use $N = N_A n$ and $R = N_A k$ to obtain this alternative form:

$$pV = NkT \qquad (18.18)$$

This shows that we can think of the Boltzmann constant k as a gas constant on a "per-molecule" basis instead of the usual "per-mole" basis for R.

Molecular Speeds

From Eqs. (18.16) and (18.17) we can obtain expressions for the square root of $(v^2)_{av}$, called the **root-mean-square speed** (or **rms speed**) v_{rms}:

$$v_{rms} = \sqrt{(v^2)_{av}} = \sqrt{\frac{3kT}{m}} = \sqrt{\frac{3RT}{M}} \quad \begin{array}{l}\text{(root-mean-square speed}\\\text{of a gas molecule)}\end{array} \qquad (18.19)$$

It might seem more natural to characterize molecular speeds by their *average* value rather than by v_{rms}, but we see that v_{rms} follows more directly from Eqs. (18.16) and (18.17). To compute the rms speed, we square each molecular speed, add, divide by the number of molecules, and take the square root; v_{rms} is the *root* of the *mean* of the *squares*. Example 18.7 illustrates this procedure.

Equations (18.16) and (18.19) show that at a given temperature T, gas molecules of different mass m have the same average kinetic energy but different root-mean-square speeds. On average, the nitrogen molecules ($M = 28$ g/mol) in the air around you are moving faster than are the oxygen molecules ($M = 32$ g/mol). Hydrogen molecules ($M = 2$ g/mol) are fastest of all; this is why there is hardly any hydrogen in the earth's atmosphere, despite its being the most common element in the universe (Fig. 18.14). A sizable fraction of any H_2 molecules in the atmosphere would have speeds greater than the earth's escape speed of 1.12×10^4 m/s (calculated in Example 13.5 in Section 13.3) and would escape into space. The heavier, slower-moving gases cannot escape so easily, which is why they predominate in our atmosphere.

The assumption that individual molecules undergo perfectly elastic collisions with the container wall is actually a little too simple. More detailed investigation has shown that in most cases, molecules actually adhere to the wall for a short time and then leave again with speeds that are characteristic of the temperature *of the wall*. However, the gas and the wall are ordinarily in thermal equilibrium and have the same temperature. So there is no net energy transfer between gas and wall, and this discovery does not alter the validity of our conclusions.

18.14 While hydrogen is a desirable fuel for vehicles, it is only a trace constituent of our atmosphere (0.00005% by volume). Hence hydrogen fuel has to be generated by electrolysis of water, which is itself an energy-intensive process.

Problem-Solving Strategy 18.2 **Kinetic-Molecular Theory**

IDENTIFY *the relevant concepts:* Use the results of the kinetic-molecular model to relate the macroscopic properties of a gas, such as temperature and pressure, to microscopic properties, such as molecular speeds.

SET UP *the problem* using the following steps:
1. List knowns and unknowns; identify the target variables.
2. Choose appropriate equation(s) from among Eqs. (18.14), (18.16), and (18.19).

EXECUTE *the solution* as follows: Maintain consistency in units. Note especially the following:
1. The usual units for molar mass M are grams per mole; these units are often omitted in tables. In equations such as Eq. (18.19), when you use SI units you must express M in kilograms per

mole. For example, for oxygen $M_{O_2} = 32$ g/mol $= 32 \times 10^{-3}$ kg/mol.
2. Are you working on a "per-molecule" basis (with m, N, and k) or a "per-mole" basis (with M, n, and R)? To check units, think of N as having units of "molecules"; then m has units of mass per molecule, and k has units of joules per molecule per kelvin. Similarly, n has units of moles; then M has units of mass per mole and R has units of joules per mole per kelvin.
3. Remember that T is always *absolute* (Kelvin) temperature.

EVALUATE *your answer:* Are your answers reasonable? Here's a benchmark: Typical molecular speeds at room temperature are several hundred meters per second.

Example 18.6 **Molecular kinetic energy and v_{rms}**

(a) What is the average translational kinetic energy of an ideal-gas molecule at 27°C? (b) What is the total random translational kinetic energy of the molecules in 1 mole of this gas? (c) What is the root-mean-square speed of oxygen molecules at this temperature?

SOLUTION

IDENTIFY and SET UP: This problem involves the translational kinetic energy of an ideal gas on a per-molecule and per-mole basis, as well as the root-mean-square molecular speed v_{rms}. We are given $T = 27°C = 300$ K and $n = 1$ mol; we use the molecular mass m for oxygen. We use Eq. (18.16) to determine the average kinetic energy of a molecule, Eq. (18.14) to find the total molecular kinetic energy K_{tr} of 1 mole, and Eq. (18.19) to find v_{rms}.

EXECUTE: (a) From Eq. (18.16),

$$\tfrac{1}{2}m(v^2)_{av} = \tfrac{3}{2}\,kT = \tfrac{3}{2}(1.38 \times \ 10^{-23}\ \text{J/K})(300\ \text{K})$$
$$= 6.21 \times \ 10^{-21}\ \text{J}$$

(b) From Eq. (18.14), the kinetic energy of one mole is

$$K_{tr} = \tfrac{3}{2}nRT = \tfrac{3}{2}(1\ \text{mol})(8.314\ \text{J/mol}\cdot\text{K})(300\ \text{K}) = 3740\ \text{J}$$

(c) We found the mass per molecule m and molar mass M of molecular oxygen in Example 18.5. Using Eq. (18.19), we can calculate v_{rms} in two ways:

$$v_{rms} = \sqrt{\frac{3kT}{m}} = \sqrt{\frac{3(1.38 \times \ 10^{-23}\ \text{J/K})(300\ \text{K})}{5.31 \times 10^{-26}\ \text{kg}}}$$
$$= 484\ \text{m/s} = 1740\ \text{km/h} = 1080\ \text{mi/h}$$

$$v_{rms} = \sqrt{\frac{3RT}{M}} = \sqrt{\frac{3(8.314\ \text{J/mol}\cdot\text{K})(300\ \text{K})}{32.0 \times \ 10^{-3}\ \text{kg/mol}}} = 484\ \text{m/s}$$

EVALUATE: The answer in part (a) does not depend on the mass of the molecule. We can check our result in part (b) by noting that the translational kinetic energy per mole must be equal to the product of the average translational kinetic energy per molecule from part (a) and Avogadro's number N_A: $K_{tr} = (6.022 \times 10^{23}\ \text{molecules})$ $(6.21 \times 10^{-21}\ \text{J/molecule}) = 3740\ \text{J}$.

Example 18.7 **Calculating rms and average speeds**

Five gas molecules chosen at random are found to have speeds of 500, 600, 700, 800, and 900 m/s. What is the rms speed? What is the *average* speed?

SOLUTION

IDENTIFY and SET UP: We use the definitions of the root mean square and the average of a collection of numbers. To find v_{rms}, we square each speed, find the average (mean) of the squares, and take the square root of the result. We find v_{av} as usual.

EXECUTE: The average value of v^2 and the resulting v_{rms} for the five molecules are

$$(v^2)_{av} = \frac{500^2 + 600^2 + 700^2 + 800^2 + 900^2}{5}\ \text{m}^2/\text{s}^2$$
$$= 5.10 \times 10^5\ \text{m}^2/\text{s}^2$$

$$v_{rms} = \sqrt{(v^2)_{av}} = 714\ \text{m/s}$$

The average speed v_{av} is

$$v_{av} = \frac{500 + 600 + 700 + 800 + 900}{5}\ \text{m/s} = 700\ \text{m/s}$$

EVALUATE: In general v_{rms} and v_{av} are *not* the same. Roughly speaking, v_{rms} gives greater weight to the higher speeds than does v_{av}.

Collisions Between Molecules

We have ignored the possibility that two gas molecules might collide. If they are really points, they *never* collide. But consider a more realistic model in which the molecules are rigid spheres with radius r. How often do they collide with other molecules? How far do they travel, on average, between collisions? We can get approximate answers from the following rather primitive model.

Consider N spherical molecules with radius r in a volume V. Suppose only one molecule is moving. When it collides with another molecule, the distance between centers is $2r$. Suppose we draw a cylinder with radius $2r$, with its axis parallel to the velocity of the molecule (Fig. 18.15). The moving molecule collides with any other molecule whose center is inside this cylinder. In a short time dt a molecule with speed v travels a distance $v\,dt$; during this time it collides with any molecule that is in the cylindrical volume of radius $2r$ and length $v\,dt$. The volume of the cylinder is $4\pi r^2 v\,dt$. There are N/V molecules per unit volume, so the number dN with centers in this cylinder is

$$dN = 4\pi r^2 v\,dt\,N/V$$

18.15 In a time dt a molecule with radius r will collide with any other molecule within a cylindrical volume of radius $2r$ and length $v\,dt$.

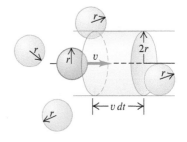

Thus the number of collisions *per unit time* is

$$\frac{dN}{dt} = \frac{4\pi r^2 vN}{V}$$

This result assumes that only one molecule is moving. The analysis is quite a bit more involved when all the molecules move at once. It turns out that in this case the collisions are more frequent, and the above equation has to be multiplied by a factor of $\sqrt{2}$:

$$\frac{dN}{dt} = \frac{4\pi \sqrt{2}\, r^2 vN}{V}$$

The average time t_{mean} between collisions, called the *mean free time*, is the reciprocal of this expression:

$$t_{\text{mean}} = \frac{V}{4\pi \sqrt{2}\, r^2 vN} \tag{18.20}$$

The average distance traveled between collisions is called the **mean free path**, denoted by λ (the Greek letter lambda). In our simple model, this is just the molecule's speed v multiplied by t_{mean}:

$$\lambda = vt_{\text{mean}} = \frac{V}{4\pi \sqrt{2}\, r^2 N} \quad \text{(mean free path of a gas molecule)} \tag{18.21}$$

The mean free path is inversely proportional to the number of molecules per unit volume (N/V) and inversely proportional to the cross-sectional area πr^2 of a molecule; the more molecules there are and the larger the molecule, the shorter the mean distance between collisions (Fig. 18.16). Note that the mean free path *does not* depend on the speed of the molecule.

We can express Eq. (18.21) in terms of macroscopic properties of the gas, using the ideal-gas equation in the form of Eq. (18.18), $pV = NkT$. We find

$$\lambda = \frac{kT}{4\pi \sqrt{2}\, r^2 p} \tag{18.22}$$

If the temperature is increased at constant pressure, the gas expands, the average distance between molecules increases, and λ increases. If the pressure is increased at constant temperature, the gas compresses and λ decreases.

18.16 If you try to walk through a crowd, your mean free path—the distance you can travel on average without running into another person—depends on how large the people are and how closely they are spaced.

Example 18.8 **Calculating mean free path**

(a) Estimate the mean free path of a molecule of air at 27°C and 1 atm. Model the molecules as spheres with radius $r = 2.0 \times 10^{-10}$ m. (b) Estimate the mean free time of an oxygen molecule with $v = v_{\text{rms}}$ at 27°C and 1 atm.

SOLUTION

IDENTIFY and SET UP: This problem uses the concepts of mean free path and mean free time (our target variables). We use Eq. (18.22) to determine the mean free path λ. We then use the basic relationship $\lambda = vt_{\text{mean}}$ in Eq. (18.21), with $v = v_{\text{rms}}$, to find the mean free time t_{mean}.

EXECUTE: (a) From Eq. (18.22),

$$\lambda = \frac{kT}{4\pi \sqrt{2} r^2 p} = \frac{(1.38 \times 10^{-23} \text{ J/K})(300 \text{ K})}{4\pi \sqrt{2}(2.0 \times 10^{-10} \text{ m})^2 (1.01 \times 10^5 \text{ Pa})}$$

$$= 5.8 \times 10^{-8} \text{ m}$$

(b) From Example 18.6, for oxygen at 27°C the root-mean-square speed is $v_{\text{rms}} = 484$ m/s, so the mean free time for a molecule with this speed is

$$t_{\text{mean}} = \frac{\lambda}{v} = \frac{5.8 \times 10^{-8} \text{ m}}{484 \text{ m/s}} = 1.2 \times 10^{-10} \text{ s}$$

This molecule undergoes about 10^{10} collisions per second!

EVALUATE: Note that from Eqs. (18.21) and (18.22) the mean free *path* doesn't depend on the molecule's speed, but the mean free *time* does. Slower molecules have a longer average time interval t_{mean} between collisions than do fast ones, but the average *distance* λ between collisions is the same no matter what the molecule's speed. Our answer to part (a) says that the molecule doesn't go far between collisions, but the mean free path is still several hundred times the molecular radius r.

Test Your Understanding of Section 18.3 Rank the following gases in order from (a) highest to lowest rms speed of molecules and (b) highest to lowest average translational kinetic energy of a molecule: (i) oxygen ($M = 32.0$ g/mol) at 300 K; (ii) nitrogen ($M = 28.0$ g/mol) at 300 K; (iii) oxygen at 330 K; (iv) nitrogen at 330 K.

18.4 Heat Capacities

When we introduced the concept of heat capacity in Section 17.5, we talked about ways to *measure* the specific heat or molar heat capacity of a particular material. Now we'll see how to *predict* these on theoretical grounds.

Heat Capacities of Gases

The basis of our analysis is that heat is *energy* in transit. When we add heat to a substance, we are increasing its molecular energy. In this discussion the volume of the gas will remain constant so that we don't have to worry about energy transfer through mechanical work. If we were to let the gas expand, it would do work by pushing on moving walls of its container, and this additional energy transfer would have to be included in our calculations. We'll return to this more general case in Chapter 19. For now, with the volume held constant, we are concerned with C_V, the molar heat capacity *at constant volume*.

In the simple kinetic-molecular model of Section 18.3 the molecular energy consists only of the translational kinetic energy K_{tr} of the pointlike molecules. This energy is directly proportional to the absolute temperature T, as shown by Eq. (18.14), $K_{tr} = \frac{3}{2}nRT$. When the temperature changes by a small amount dT, the corresponding change in kinetic energy is

$$dK_{tr} = \tfrac{3}{2} nR \, dT \qquad (18.23)$$

From the definition of molar heat capacity at constant volume, C_V (see Section 17.5), we also have

$$dQ = nC_V \, dT \qquad (18.24)$$

where dQ is the heat input needed for a temperature change dT. Now if K_{tr} represents the total molecular energy, as we have assumed, then dQ and dK_{tr} must be *equal* (Fig. 18.17). From Eqs. (18.23) and (18.24), this says

$$nC_V \, dT = \tfrac{3}{2} nR \, dT$$

$$C_V = \tfrac{3}{2}R \qquad \text{(ideal gas of point particles)} \qquad (18.25)$$

This surprisingly simple result says that the molar heat capacity at constant volume is $3R/2$ for *any* gas whose molecules can be represented as points.

Does Eq. (18.25) agree with measured values of molar heat capacities? In SI units, Eq. (18.25) gives

$$C_V = \tfrac{3}{2}(8.314 \text{ J/mol} \cdot \text{K}) = 12.47 \text{ J/mol} \cdot \text{K}$$

For comparison, Table 18.1 gives measured values of C_V for several gases. We see that for *monatomic* gases our prediction is right on the money, but that it is way off for diatomic and polyatomic gases.

This comparison tells us that our point-molecule model is good enough for monatomic gases but that for diatomic and polyatomic molecules we need something more sophisticated. For example, we can picture a diatomic molecule as

18.17 (a) A fixed volume V of a monatomic ideal gas. (b) When an amount of heat dQ is added to the gas, the total translational kinetic energy increases by $dK_{tr} = dQ$ and the temperature increases by $dT = dQ/nC_V$.

(a)

(b)

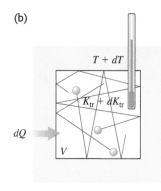

Table 18.1 Molar Heat Capacities of Gases

Type of Gas	Gas	C_V (J/mol · K)
Monatomic	He	12.47
	Ar	12.47
Diatomic	H_2	20.42
	N_2	20.76
	O_2	20.85
	CO	20.85
Polyatomic	CO_2	28.46
	SO_2	31.39
	H_2S	25.95

18.18 Motions of a diatomic molecule.

(a) **Translational motion.** The molecule moves as a whole; its velocity may be described as the x-, y-, and z-velocity components of its center of mass.

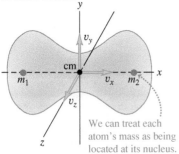

We can treat each atom's mass as being located at its nucleus.

(b) **Rotational motion.** The molecule rotates about its center of mass. This molecule has two independent axes of rotation.

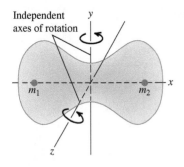

Independent axes of rotation

(c) **Vibrational motion.** The molecule oscillates as though the nuclei were connected by a spring.

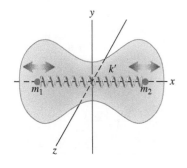

two point masses, like a little elastic dumbbell, with an interaction force between the atoms of the kind shown in Fig. 18.8. Such a molecule can have additional kinetic energy associated with *rotation* about axes through its center of mass. The atoms may also have *vibrating* motion along the line joining them, with additional kinetic and potential energies. Figure 18.18 shows these possibilities.

When heat flows into a *monatomic* gas at constant volume, *all* of the added energy goes into an increase in random *translational* molecular kinetic energy. Equation (18.23) shows that this gives rise to an increase in temperature. But when the temperature is increased by the same amount in a *diatomic* or *polyatomic* gas, additional heat is needed to supply the increased rotational and vibrational energies. Thus polyatomic gases have *larger* molar heat capacities than monatomic gases, as Table 18.1 shows.

But how do we know how much energy is associated with each additional kind of motion of a complex molecule, compared to the translational kinetic energy? The new principle that we need is called the principle of **equipartition of energy.** It can be derived from sophisticated statistical-mechanics considerations; that derivation is beyond our scope, and we will treat the principle as an axiom.

The principle of equipartition of energy states that each velocity component (either linear or angular) has, on average, an associated kinetic energy per molecule of $\frac{1}{2}kT$, or one-half the product of the Boltzmann constant and the absolute temperature. The number of velocity components needed to describe the motion of a molecule completely is called the number of **degrees of freedom.** For a monatomic gas, there are three degrees of freedom (for the velocity components v_x, v_y, and v_z); this gives a total average kinetic energy per molecule of $3(\frac{1}{2}kT)$, consistent with Eq. (18.16).

For a *diatomic* molecule there are two possible axes of rotation, perpendicular to each other and to the molecule's axis. (We don't include rotation about the molecule's own axis because in ordinary collisions there is no way for this rotational motion to change.) If we assign five degrees of freedom to a diatomic molecule, the average total kinetic energy per molecule is $\frac{5}{2}kT$ instead of $\frac{3}{2}kT$. The total kinetic energy of n moles is $K_{\text{total}} = nN_A(\frac{5}{2}kT) = \frac{5}{2}n(kN_A)T = \frac{5}{2}nRT$, and the molar heat capacity (at constant volume) is

$$C_V = \tfrac{5}{2}R \qquad \text{(diatomic gas, including rotation)} \qquad (18.26)$$

In SI units,

$$C_V = \tfrac{5}{2}(8.314 \text{ J/mol} \cdot \text{K}) = 20.79 \text{ J/mol} \cdot \text{K}$$

This agrees within a few percent with the measured values for diatomic gases given in Table 18.1.

Vibrational motion can also contribute to the heat capacities of gases. Molecular bonds are not rigid; they can stretch and bend, and the resulting vibrations lead to additional degrees of freedom and additional energies. For most diatomic gases, however, vibrational motion does *not* contribute appreciably to heat capacity. The reason for this is a little subtle and involves some concepts of quantum mechanics. Briefly, vibrational energy can change only in finite steps. If the energy change of the first step is much larger than the energy possessed by most molecules, then nearly all the molecules remain in the minimum-energy state of motion. In that case, changing the temperature does not change their average vibrational energy appreciably, and the vibrational degrees of freedom are said to be "frozen out." In more complex molecules the gaps between permitted energy levels are sometimes much smaller, and then vibration *does* contribute to heat capacity. The rotational energy of a molecule also changes by finite steps, but they are usually much

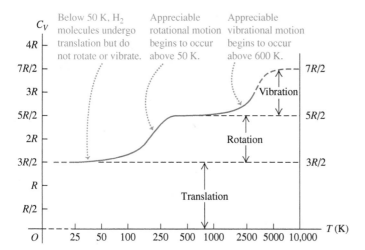

smaller; the "freezing out" of rotational degrees of freedom occurs only in rare instances, such as for the hydrogen molecule below about 100 K.

In Table 18.1 the large values of C_V for some polyatomic molecules show the contributions of vibrational energy. In addition, a molecule with three or more atoms that are not in a straight line has three, not two, rotational degrees of freedom.

From this discussion we expect heat capacities to be temperature-dependent, generally increasing with increasing temperature. Figure 18.19 is a graph of the temperature dependence of C_V for hydrogen gas (H_2), showing the temperatures at which the rotational and vibrational energies begin to contribute.

Heat Capacities of Solids

We can carry out a similar heat-capacity analysis for a crystalline solid. Consider a crystal consisting of N identical atoms (a *monatomic solid*). Each atom is bound to an equilibrium position by interatomic forces. The elasticity of solid materials shows us that these forces must permit stretching and bending of the bonds. We can think of a crystal as an array of atoms connected by little springs (Fig. 18.20). Each atom can *vibrate* about its equilibrium position.

Each atom has three degrees of freedom, corresponding to its three components of velocity. According to the equipartition principle, each atom has an average kinetic energy of $\frac{1}{2}kT$ for each degree of freedom. In addition, each atom has *potential* energy associated with the elastic deformation. For a simple harmonic oscillator (discussed in Chapter 14) it is not hard to show that the average kinetic energy of an atom is *equal* to its average potential energy. In our model of a crystal, each atom is essentially a three-dimensional harmonic oscillator; it can be shown that the equality of average kinetic and potential energies also holds here, provided that the "spring" forces obey Hooke's law.

Thus we expect each atom to have an average kinetic energy $\frac{3}{2}kT$ and an average potential energy $\frac{3}{2}kT$, or an average total energy $3kT$ per atom. If the crystal contains N atoms or n moles, its total energy is

$$E_{\text{total}} = 3NkT = 3nRT \qquad (18.27)$$

From this we conclude that the molar heat capacity of a crystal should be

$$C_V = 3R \qquad \text{(ideal monatomic solid)} \qquad (18.28)$$

In SI units,

$$C_V = (3)(8.314 \text{ J/mol} \cdot \text{K}) = 24.9 \text{ J/mol} \cdot \text{K}$$

18.20 To visualize the forces between neighboring atoms in a crystal, envision every atom as being attached to its neighbors by springs.

This is the **rule of Dulong and Petit,** which we encountered as an *empirical* finding in Section 17.5: Elemental solids all have molar heat capacities of about 25 J/mol · K. Now we have *derived* this rule from kinetic theory. The agreement is only approximate, to be sure, but considering the very simple nature of our model, it is quite significant.

At low temperatures, the heat capacities of most solids *decrease* with decreasing temperature (Fig. 18.21) for the same reason that vibrational degrees of freedom of molecules are frozen out at low temperatures. At very low temperatures the quantity kT is much *smaller* than the smallest energy step the vibrating atoms can take. Hence most of the atoms remain in their lowest energy states because the next higher energy level is out of reach. The average vibrational energy per atom is then *less* than $3kT$, and the heat capacity per molecule is *less* than $3k$. At higher temperatures when kT is *large* in comparison to the minimum energy step, the equipartition principle holds, and the total heat capacity is $3k$ per molecule or $3R$ per mole as the Dulong and Petit rule predicts. Quantitative understanding of the temperature variation of heat capacities was one of the triumphs of quantum mechanics during its initial development in the 1920s.

Test Your Understanding of Section 18.4 A cylinder with a fixed volume contains hydrogen gas (H_2) at 25 K. You then add heat to the gas at a constant rate until its temperature reaches 500 K. Does the temperature of the gas increase at a constant rate? Why or why not? If not, does the temperature increase most rapidly near the beginning or near the end of this process? ▌

18.21 Experimental values of C_V for lead, aluminum, silicon, and diamond. At high temperatures, C_V for each solid approaches about $3R$, in agreement with the rule of Dulong and Petit. At low temperatures, C_V is much less than $3R$.

18.5 Molecular Speeds

As we mentioned in Section 18.3, the molecules in a gas don't all have the same speed. Figure 18.22 shows one experimental scheme for measuring the distribution of molecular speeds. A substance is vaporized in a hot oven; molecules of the vapor escape through an aperture in the oven wall and into a vacuum chamber. A series of slits blocks all molecules except those in a narrow beam, which is aimed at a pair of rotating disks. A molecule passing through the slit in the first disk is blocked by the second disk unless it arrives just as the slit in the second disk is lined up with the beam. The disks function as a speed selector that passes only molecules within a certain narrow speed range. This range can be varied by changing the disk rotation speed, and we can measure how many molecules lie within each of various speed ranges.

To describe the results of such measurements, we define a function $f(v)$ called a *distribution function.* If we observe a total of N molecules, the number dN having speeds in the range between v and $v + dv$ is given by

$$dN = Nf(v)\, dv \tag{18.29}$$

18.22 A molecule with a speed v passes through the slit in the first rotating disk. When the molecule reaches the second rotating disk, the disks have rotated through the offset angle θ. If $v = \omega x/\theta$, the molecule passes through the slit in the second rotating disk and reaches the detector.

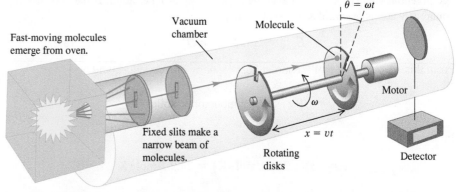

We can also say that the *probability* that a randomly chosen molecule will have a speed in the interval v to $v + dv$ is $f(v)\,dv$. Hence $f(v)$ is the probability per unit speed *interval;* it is *not* equal to the probability that a molecule has speed exactly equal to v. Since a probability is a pure number, $f(v)$ has units of reciprocal speed (s/m).

Figure 18.23a shows distribution functions for three different temperatures. At each temperature the height of the curve for any value of v is proportional to the number of molecules with speeds near v. The peak of the curve represents the *most probable speed* v_{mp} for the corresponding temperature. As the temperature increases, the average molecular kinetic energy increases, and so the peak of $f(v)$ shifts to higher and higher speeds.

Figure 18.23b shows that the area under a curve between any two values of v represents the fraction of all the molecules having speeds in that range. Every molecule must have *some* value of v, so the integral of $f(v)$ over all v must be unity for any T.

If we know $f(v)$, we can calculate the most probable speed v_{mp}, the average speed v_{av}, and the rms speed v_{rms}. To find v_{mp}, we simply find the point where $df/dv = 0$; this gives the value of the speed where the curve has its peak. To find v_{av}, we take the number $Nf(v)\,dv$ having speeds in each interval dv, multiply each number by the corresponding speed v, add all these products (by integrating over all v from zero to infinity), and finally divide by N. That is,

$$v_{\text{av}} = \int_0^\infty v f(v)\,dv \tag{18.30}$$

The rms speed is obtained similarly; the average of v^2 is given by

$$(v^2)_{\text{av}} = \int_0^\infty v^2 f(v)\,dv \tag{18.31}$$

and v_{rms} is the square root of this.

The Maxwell–Boltzmann Distribution

The function $f(v)$ describing the actual distribution of molecular speeds is called the **Maxwell–Boltzmann distribution.** It can be derived from statistical-mechanics considerations, but that derivation is beyond our scope. Here is the result:

$$f(v) = 4\pi\left(\frac{m}{2\pi kT}\right)^{3/2} v^2 e^{-mv^2/2kT} \qquad \text{(Maxwell–Boltzmann distribution)} \tag{18.32}$$

We can also express this function in terms of the translational kinetic energy of a molecule, which we denote by ϵ; that is, $\epsilon = \frac{1}{2}mv^2$. We invite you to verify that when this is substituted into Eq. (18.32), the result is

$$f(v) = \frac{8\pi}{m}\left(\frac{m}{2\pi kT}\right)^{3/2} \epsilon e^{-\epsilon/kT} \tag{18.33}$$

This form shows that the exponent in the Maxwell–Boltzmann distribution function is $-\epsilon/kT$ and that the shape of the curve is determined by the relative magnitude of ϵ and kT at any point. We leave it to you (see Exercise 18.48) to prove that the *peak* of each curve occurs where $\epsilon = kT$, corresponding to a most probable speed v_{mp} given by

$$v_{\text{mp}} = \sqrt{\frac{2kT}{m}} \tag{18.34}$$

To find the average speed, we substitute Eq. (18.32) into Eq. (18.30) and carry out the integration, making a change of variable $v^2 = x$ and then integrating by parts. The result is

$$v_{\text{av}} = \sqrt{\frac{8kT}{\pi m}} \tag{18.35}$$

18.23 (a) Curves of the Maxwell–Boltzmann distribution function $f(v)$ for three temperatures. (b) The shaded areas under the curve represent the fractions of molecules within certain speed ranges. The most probable speed v_{mp} for a given temperature is at the peak of the curve.

(a)

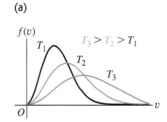

As temperature increases:
• the curve flattens.
• the maximum shifts to higher speeds.

(b)

ActivPhysics 8.2: Maxwell-Boltzmann Distribution—Conceptual Analysis
ActivPhysics 8.3: Maxwell-Boltzmann Distribution—Quantitative Analysis

Finally, to find the rms speed, we substitute Eq. (18.32) into Eq. (18.31). Evaluating the resulting integral takes some mathematical acrobatics, but we can find it in a table of integrals. The result is

$$v_{rms} = \sqrt{\frac{3kT}{m}} \qquad (18.36)$$

This result agrees with Eq. (18.19); it *must* agree if the Maxwell–Boltzmann distribution is to be consistent with the equipartition principle and our other kinetic-theory calculations.

Table 18.2 shows the fraction of all the molecules in an ideal gas that have speeds *less than* various multiples of v_{rms}. These numbers were obtained by numerical integration; they are the same for all ideal gases.

The distribution of molecular speeds in liquids is similar, although not identical, to that for gases. We can understand the vapor pressure of a liquid and the phenomenon of boiling on this basis. Suppose a molecule must have a speed at least as great as v_A in Fig. 18.23b to escape from the surface of a liquid into the adjacent vapor. The number of such molecules, represented by the area under the "tail" of each curve (to the right of v_A), increases rapidly with temperature. Thus the rate at which molecules can escape is strongly temperature-dependent. This process is balanced by another one in which molecules in the vapor phase collide inelastically with the surface and are trapped back into the liquid phase. The number of molecules suffering this fate per unit time is proportional to the pressure in the vapor phase. Phase equilibrium between liquid and vapor occurs when these two competing processes proceed at exactly the same rate. So if the molecular speed distributions are known for various temperatures, we can make a theoretical prediction of vapor pressure as a function of temperature. When liquid evaporates, it's the high-speed molecules that escape from the surface. The ones that are left have less energy on average; this gives us a molecular view of evaporative cooling.

Rates of chemical reactions are often strongly temperature-dependent, and the reason is contained in the Maxwell–Boltzmann distribution. When two reacting molecules collide, the reaction can occur only when the molecules are close enough for the electric-charge distributions of their electrons to interact strongly. This requires a minimum energy, called the *activation energy,* and thus a certain minimum molecular speed. Figure 18.23a shows that the number of molecules in the high-speed tail of the curve increases rapidly with temperature. Thus we expect the rate of any reaction that depends on an activation energy to increase rapidly with temperature.

Table 18.2 Fractions of Molecules in an Ideal Gas with Speeds Less than Various Multiples of v/v_{rms}

v/v_{rms}	Fraction
0.20	0.011
0.40	0.077
0.60	0.218
0.80	0.411
1.00	0.608
1.20	0.771
1.40	0.882
1.60	0.947
1.80	0.979
2.00	0.993

Application Activation Energy and Moth Activity

This hawkmoth of genus *Manduca* cannot fly if the temperature of its muscles is below 29°C. The reason is that the enzyme-catalyzed reactions that power aerobic metabolism and enable muscle action require a minimum molecular energy (activation energy). Just like the molecules in an ideal gas, at low temperatures very few of the molecules involved in these reactions have high energy. As the temperature increases, more molecules have the required minimum energy and the reactions take place at a greater rate. Above 29°C, enough power is generated to allow the hawkmoth to fly.

Test Your Understanding of Section 18.5 A quantity of gas containing N molecules has a speed distribution function $f(v)$. How many molecules have speeds between v_1 and $v_2 > v_1$? (i) $\int_0^{v_2} f(v)\, dv - \int_0^{v_1} f(v)\, dv$; (ii) $N[\int_0^{v_2} f(v)\, dv - \int_0^{v_1} f(v)\, dv]$; (iii) $\int_0^{v_1} f(v)\, dv - \int_0^{v_2} f(v)\, dv$; (iv) $N[\int_0^{v_1} f(v)\, dv - \int_0^{v_2} f(v)\, dv]$; (v) none of these.

18.6 Phases of Matter

An ideal gas is the simplest system to analyze from a molecular viewpoint because we ignore the interactions between molecules. But those interactions are the very thing that makes matter condense into the liquid and solid phases under some conditions. So it's not surprising that theoretical analysis of liquid and solid structure and behavior is a lot more complicated than that for gases. We won't try to go far here with a microscopic picture, but we can talk in general about phases of matter, phase equilibrium, and phase transitions.

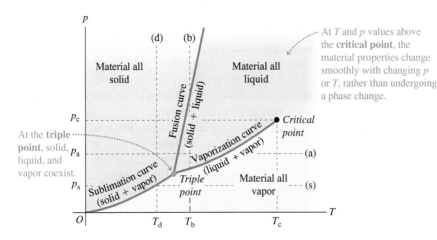

18.24 A typical pT phase diagram, showing regions of temperature and pressure at which the various phases exist and where phase changes occur.

In Section 17.6 we learned that each phase is stable only in certain ranges of temperature and pressure. A transition from one phase to another ordinarily requires **phase equilibrium** between the two phases, and for a given pressure this occurs at only one specific temperature. We can represent these conditions on a graph with axes p and T, called a **phase diagram;** Fig. 18.24 shows an example. Each point on the diagram represents a pair of values of p and T.

Only a single phase can exist at each point in Fig. 18.24, except for points on the solid lines, where two phases can coexist in phase equilibrium. The fusion curve separates the solid and liquid areas and represents possible conditions of solid-liquid phase equilibrium. The vaporization curve separates the liquid and vapor areas, and the sublimation curve separates the solid and vapor areas. All three curves meet at the **triple point,** the only condition under which all three phases can coexist (Fig. 18.25). In Section 17.3 we used the triple-point temperature of water to define the Kelvin temperature scale. Table 18.3 gives triple-point data for several substances.

If we add heat to a substance at a constant pressure p_a, it goes through a series of states represented by the horizontal line (a) in Fig. 18.24. The melting and boiling temperatures at this pressure are the temperatures at which the line intersects the fusion and vaporization curves, respectively. When the pressure is p_s, constant-pressure heating transforms a substance from solid directly to vapor. This process is called *sublimation;* the intersection of line (s) with the sublimation curve gives the temperature T_s at which it occurs for a pressure p_s. At any pressure less than the triple-point pressure, no liquid phase is possible. The triple-point pressure for carbon dioxide is 5.1 atm. At normal atmospheric pressure, solid carbon dioxide ("dry ice") undergoes sublimation; there is no liquid phase at this pressure.

Line (b) in Fig. 18.24 represents compression at a constant temperature T_b. The material passes from vapor to liquid and then to solid at the points where line (b) crosses the vaporization curve and fusion curve, respectively. Line (d) shows constant-temperature compression at a lower temperature T_d; the material passes from vapor to solid at the point where line (d) crosses the sublimation curve.

We saw in the pV-diagram of Fig. 18.7 that a liquid-vapor phase transition occurs only when the temperature and pressure are less than those at the point lying at the top of the green shaded area labeled "Liquid-vapor phase equilibrium region." This point corresponds to the endpoint at the top of the vaporization curve in Fig. 18.24. It is called the **critical point,** and the corresponding values of p and T are called the critical pressure and temperature, p_c and T_c. A gas at a pressure *above* the critical pressure does not separate into two phases when it is cooled at constant pressure (along a horizontal line above the critical point in Fig. 18.24). Instead, its properties change gradually and continuously from those we ordinarily associate with a gas (low density, large compressibility) to those of a liquid (high density, small compressibility) *without a phase transition.*

18.25 Atmospheric pressure on earth is higher than the triple-point pressure of water (see line (a) in Fig. 18.24). Depending on the temperature, water can exist as a vapor (in the atmosphere), as a liquid (in the ocean), or as a solid (like the iceberg shown here).

Table **18.3** **Triple-Point Data**

Substance	Temperature (K)	Pressure (Pa)
Hydrogen	13.80	0.0704×10^5
Deuterium	18.63	0.171×10^5
Neon	24.56	0.432×10^5
Nitrogen	63.18	0.125×10^5
Oxygen	54.36	0.00152×10^5
Ammonia	195.40	0.0607×10^5
Carbon dioxide	216.55	5.17×10^5
Sulfur dioxide	197.68	0.00167×10^5
Water	273.16	0.00610×10^5

PhET: States of Matter

You can understand this by thinking about liquid-phase transitions at successively higher points on the vaporization curve. As we approach the critical point, the *differences* in physical properties (such as density and compressibility) between the liquid and vapor phases become smaller. Exactly *at* the critical point they all become zero, and at this point the distinction between liquid and vapor disappears. The heat of vaporization also grows smaller as we approach the critical point, and it too becomes zero at the critical point.

For nearly all familiar materials the critical pressures are much greater than atmospheric pressure, so we don't observe this behavior in everyday life. For example, the critical point for water is at 647.4 K and 221.2×10^5 Pa (about 218 atm or 3210 psi). But high-pressure steam boilers in electric generating plants regularly run at pressures and temperatures well above the critical point.

Many substances can exist in more than one solid phase. A familiar example is carbon, which exists as noncrystalline soot and crystalline graphite and diamond. Water is another example; at least eight types of ice, differing in crystal structure and physical properties, have been observed at very high pressures.

pVT-Surfaces

We remarked in Section 18.1 that the equation of state of any material can be represented graphically as a surface in a three-dimensional space with coordinates p, V, and T. Visualizing such a surface can add to our understanding of the behavior of materials at various temperatures and pressures. Figure 18.26 shows a typical *pVT*-surface. The light lines represent *pV*-isotherms; projecting them onto the *pV*-plane gives a diagram similar to Fig. 18.7. The *pV*-isotherms represent contour lines on the *pVT*-surface, just as contour lines on a topographic map represent the elevation (the third dimension) at each point. The projections of the edges of the surface onto the *pT*-plane give the *pT* phase diagram of Fig. 18.24.

Line *abcdef* in Fig. 18.26 represents constant-pressure heating, with melting along *bc* and vaporization along *de*. Note the volume changes that occur as T increases along this line. Line *ghjklm* corresponds to an isothermal (constant temperature) compression, with liquefaction along *hj* and solidification along *kl*. Between these, segments *gh* and *jk* represent isothermal compression with increase in pressure; the pressure increases are much greater in the liquid region

18.26 A *pVT*-surface for a substance that expands on melting. Projections of the boundaries on the surface onto the *pT*- and *pV*-planes are also shown.

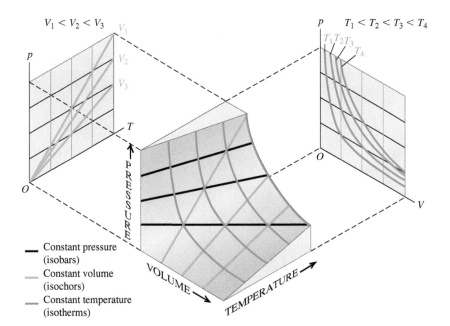

18.27 A pVT-surface for an ideal gas. At the left, each red line corresponds to a certain constant volume; at the right, each green line corresponds to a certain constant temperature.

$V_1 < V_2 < V_3$

$T_1 < T_2 < T_3 < T_4$

— Constant pressure (isobars)
— Constant volume (isochors)
— Constant temperature (isotherms)

PRESSURE

VOLUME

TEMPERATURE

jk and the solid region *lm* than in the vapor region *gh*. Finally, line *nopq* represents isothermal solidification directly from vapor, as in the formation of snowflakes or frost.

Figure 18.27 shows the much simpler pVT-surface for a substance that obeys the ideal-gas equation of state under all conditions. The projections of the constant-temperature curves onto the pV-plane correspond to the curves of Fig. 18.6, and the projections of the constant-volume curves onto the pT-plane show that pressure is directly proportional to absolute temperature.

Test Your Understanding of Section 18.6 The average atmospheric pressure on Mars is 6.0×10^2 Pa. Could there be lakes or rivers of liquid water on Mars today? What about in the past, when the atmospheric pressure is thought to have been substantially greater than today?

Video Tutor Solutions

Equations of state: The pressure p, volume V, and absolute temperature T of a given quantity of a substance are related by an equation of state. This relationship applies only for equilibrium states, in which p and T are uniform throughout the system. The ideal-gas equation of state, Eq. (18.3), involves the number of moles n and a constant R that is the same for all gases. (See Examples 18.1–18.4.)

$$pV = nRT \qquad (18.3)$$

Molecular properties of matter: The molar mass M of a pure substance is the mass per mole. The mass m_{total} of a quantity of substance equals M multiplied by the number of moles n. Avogadro's number N_A is the number of molecules in a mole. The mass m of an individual molecule is M divided by N_A. (See Example 18.5.)

$$m_{\text{total}} = nM \qquad (18.2)$$

$$M = N_A m \qquad (18.8)$$

Chloride ions

Sodium ions

Kinetic-molecular model of an ideal gas: In an ideal gas, the total translational kinetic energy of the gas as a whole (K_{tr}) and the average translational kinetic energy per molecule $[\frac{1}{2}m(v^2)_{\text{av}}]$ are proportional to the absolute temperature T, and the root-mean-square speed of molecules is proportional to the square root of T. These expressions involve the Boltzmann constant $k = R/N_A$. (See Examples 18.6 and 18.7.) The mean free path λ of molecules in an ideal gas depends on the number of molecules per volume (N/V) and the molecular radius r. (See Example 18.8.)

$$K_{\text{tr}} = \tfrac{3}{2}nRT \qquad (18.14)$$

$$\tfrac{1}{2}m(v^2)_{\text{av}} = \tfrac{3}{2}kT \qquad (18.16)$$

$$v_{\text{rms}} = \sqrt{(v^2)_{\text{av}}} = \sqrt{\frac{3kT}{m}} \qquad (18.19)$$

$$\lambda = vt_{\text{mean}} = \frac{V}{4\pi\sqrt{2}\,r^2 N} \qquad (18.21)$$

Heat capacities: The molar heat capacity at constant volume C_V is a simple multiple of the gas constant R for certain idealized cases: an ideal monatomic gas [Eq. (18.25)]; an ideal diatomic gas including rotational energy [Eq. (18.26)]; and an ideal monatomic solid [Eq. (18.28)]. Many real systems are approximated well by these idealizations.

$$C_V = \tfrac{3}{2}R \quad \text{(monatomic gas)} \qquad (18.25)$$

$$C_V = \tfrac{5}{2}R \quad \text{(diatomic gas)} \qquad (18.26)$$

$$C_V = 3R \quad \text{(monatomic solid)} \qquad (18.28)$$

Molecular speeds: The speeds of molecules in an ideal gas are distributed according to the Maxwell–Boltzmann distribution $f(v)$. The quantity $f(v)\,dv$ describes what fraction of the molecules have speeds between v and $v + dv$.

$$f(v) = 4\pi\left(\frac{m}{2\pi kT}\right)^{3/2} v^2 e^{-mv^2/2kT} \qquad (18.32)$$

Phases of matter: Ordinary matter exists in the solid, liquid, and gas phases. A phase diagram shows conditions under which two phases can coexist in phase equilibrium. All three phases can coexist at the triple point. The vaporization curve ends at the critical point, above which the distinction between the liquid and gas phases disappears.

BRIDGING PROBLEM | **Gas on Jupiter's Moon Europa**

An astronaut visiting Jupiter's satellite Europa leaves a canister of 1.20 mol of nitrogen gas (28.0 g/mol) at 25.0°C on the satellite's surface. Europa has no significant atmosphere, and the acceleration due to gravity at its surface is 1.30 m/s². The canister springs a leak, allowing molecules to escape from a small hole. (a) What is the maximum height (in km) above Europa's surface that is reached by a nitrogen molecule whose speed equals the rms speed? Assume that the molecule is shot straight up out of the hole in the canister, and ignore the variation in *g* with altitude. (b) The escape speed from Europa is 2025 m/s. Can any of the nitrogen molecules escape from Europa and into space?

SOLUTION GUIDE

See MasteringPhysics® study area for a Video Tutor solution.

IDENTIFY and SET UP

1. Draw a sketch of the situation, showing all relevant dimensions.
2. Make a list of the unknown quantities, and decide which are the target variables.

3. How will you find the rms speed of the nitrogen molecules? What principle will you use to find the maximum height that a molecule with this speed can reach?
4. Does the rms speed of molecules in an ideal gas represent the maximum speed of the molecules? If not, what is the maximum speed?

EXECUTE

5. Solve for the rms speed. Use this to calculate the maximum height that a molecule with this speed can reach.
6. Use your result from step 5 to answer the question in part (b).

EVALUATE

7. Do your results depend on the amount of gas in the container? Why or why not?
8. How would your results from steps 5 and 6 be affected if the gas cylinder were instead left on Jupiter's satellite Ganymede, which has higher surface gravity than Europa and a higher escape speed? Like Europa, Ganymede has no significant atmosphere.

Problems

For instructor-assigned homework, go to MasteringPhysics®.

•, ••, •••: Problems of increasing difficulty. **CP**: Cumulative problems incorporating material from earlier chapters. **CALC**: Problems requiring calculus. **BIO**: Biosciences problems.

DISCUSSION QUESTIONS

Q18.1 Section 18.1 states that ordinarily, pressure, volume, and temperature cannot change individually without one affecting the others. Yet when a liquid evaporates, its volume changes, even though its pressure and temperature are constant. Is this inconsistent? Why or why not?

Q18.2 In the ideal-gas equation, could an equivalent Celsius temperature be used instead of the Kelvin one if an appropriate numerical value of the constant *R* is used? Why or why not?

Q18.3 On a chilly morning you can "see your breath." Can you really? What are you actually seeing? Does this phenomenon depend on the temperature of the air, the humidity, or both? Explain.

Q18.4 When a car is driven some distance, the air pressure in the tires increases. Why? Should you let out some air to reduce the pressure? Why or why not?

Q18.5 The coolant in an automobile radiator is kept at a pressure higher than atmospheric pressure. Why is this desirable? The radiator cap will release coolant when the gauge pressure of the coolant reaches a certain value, typically 15 lb/in.² or so. Why not just seal the system completely?

Q18.6 Unwrapped food placed in a freezer experiences dehydration, known as "freezer burn." Why?

Q18.7 "Freeze-drying" food involves the same process as "freezer burn," referred to in Discussion Question Q18.6. For freeze-drying, the food is usually frozen first, and then placed in a vacuum chamber and irradiated with infrared radiation. What is the purpose of the vacuum? The radiation? What advantages might freeze-drying have in comparison to ordinary drying?

Q18.8 A group of students drove from their university (near sea level) up into the mountains for a skiing weekend. Upon arriving at the slopes, they discovered that the bags of potato chips they had brought for snacks had all burst open. What caused this to happen?

Q18.9 How does evaporation of perspiration from your skin cool your body?

Q18.10 A rigid, perfectly insulated container has a membrane dividing its volume in half. One side contains a gas at an absolute temperature T_0 and pressure p_0, while the other half is completely empty. Suddenly a small hole develops in the membrane, allowing the gas to leak out into the other half until it eventually occupies twice its original volume. In terms of T_0 and p_0, what will be the new temperature and pressure of the gas when it is distributed equally in both halves of the container? Explain your reasoning.

Q18.11 (a) Which has more atoms: a kilogram of hydrogen or a kilogram of lead? Which has more mass? (b) Which has more atoms: a mole of hydrogen or a mole of lead? Which has more mass? Explain your reasoning.

Q18.12 Use the concepts of the kinetic-molecular model to explain: (a) why the pressure of a gas in a rigid container increases as heat is added to the gas and (b) why the pressure of a gas increases as we compress it, even if we do not change its temperature.

Q18.13 The proportions of various gases in the earth's atmosphere change somewhat with altitude. Would you expect the proportion of oxygen at high altitude to be greater or less than at sea level compared to the proportion of nitrogen? Why?

Q18.14 Comment on the following statement: *When two gases are mixed, if they are to be in thermal equilibrium, they must have the* *same average molecular speed.* Is the statement correct? Why or why not?

Q18.15 The kinetic-molecular model contains a hidden assumption about the temperature of the container walls. What is this assumption? What would happen if this assumption were not valid?

Q18.16 The temperature of an ideal gas is directly proportional to the average kinetic energy of its molecules. If a container of ideal gas is moving past you at 2000 m/s, is the temperature of the gas higher than if the container was at rest? Explain your reasoning.

Q18.17 If the pressure of an ideal monatomic gas is increased while the number of moles is kept constant, what happens to the average translational kinetic energy of one atom of the gas? Is it possible to change *both* the volume and the pressure of an ideal gas and keep the average translational kinetic energy of the atoms constant? Explain.

Q18.18 In deriving the ideal-gas equation from the kinetic-molecular model, we ignored potential energy due to the earth's gravity. Is this omission justified? Why or why not?

Q18.19 The derivation of the ideal-gas equation included the assumption that the number of molecules is very large, so that we could compute the average force due to many collisions. However, the ideal-gas equation holds accurately only at low pressures, where the molecules are few and far between. Is this inconsistent? Why or why not?

Q18.20 A gas storage tank has a small leak. The pressure in the tank drops more quickly if the gas is hydrogen or helium than if it is oxygen. Why?

Q18.21 Consider two specimens of ideal gas at the same temperature. Specimen A has the same total mass as specimen B, but the molecules in specimen A have greater molar mass than they do in specimen B. In which specimen is the total kinetic energy of the gas greater? Does your answer depend on the molecular structure of the gases? Why or why not?

Q18.22 The temperature of an ideal monatomic gas is increased from 25°C to 50°C. Does the average translational kinetic energy of each gas atom double? Explain. If your answer is no, what would the final temperature be if the average translational kinetic energy was doubled?

Q18.23 If the root-mean-square speed of the atoms of an ideal gas is to be doubled, by what factor must the Kelvin temperature of the gas be increased? Explain.

Q18.24 (a) If you apply the same amount of heat to 1.00 mol of an ideal monatomic gas and 1.00 mol of an ideal diatomic gas, which one (if any) will increase more in temperature? (b) Physically, *why* do diatomic gases have a greater molar heat capacity than monatomic gases?

Q18.25 The discussion in Section 18.4 concluded that all ideal diatomic gases have the same heat capacity C_V. Does this mean that it takes the same amount of heat to raise the temperature of 1.0 g of each one by 1.0 K? Explain your reasoning.

Q18.26 In a gas that contains N molecules, is it accurate to say that the number of molecules with speed v is equal to $f(v)$? Is it accurate to say that this number is given by $Nf(v)$? Explain your answers.

Q18.27 Imagine a special air filter placed in a window of a house. The tiny holes in the filter allow only air molecules moving faster than a certain speed to exit the house, and allow only air molecules moving slower than that speed to enter the house from outside. What effect would this filter have on the temperature inside the house? (It turns out that the second law of thermodynamics—which we will discuss in Chapter 20—tells us that such a wonderful air filter would be impossible to make.)

Q18.28 A beaker of water at room temperature is placed in an enclosure, and the air pressure in the enclosure is slowly reduced. When the air pressure is reduced sufficiently, the water begins to boil. The temperature of the water does not rise when it boils; in fact, the temperature *drops* slightly. Explain these phenomena.

Q18.29 Ice is slippery to walk on, and especially slippery if you wear ice skates. What does this tell you about how the melting temperature of ice depends on pressure? Explain.

Q18.30 Hydrothermal vents are openings in the ocean floor that discharge very hot water. The water emerging from one such vent off the Oregon coast, 2400 m below the surface, has a temperature of 279°C. Despite its high temperature, the water doesn't boil. Why not?

Q18.31 The dark areas on the moon's surface are called *maria*, Latin for "seas," and were once thought to be bodies of water. In fact, the maria are not "seas" at all, but plains of solidified lava. Given that there is no atmosphere on the moon, how can you explain the absence of liquid water on the moon's surface?

Q18.32 In addition to the normal cooking directions printed on the back of a box of rice, there are also "high-altitude directions." The only difference is that the "high-altitude directions" suggest increasing the cooking time and using a greater volume of boiling water in which to cook the rice. Why should the directions depend on the altitude in this way?

EXERCISES

Section 18.1 Equations of State

18.1 • A 20.0-L tank contains 4.86×10^{-4} kg of helium at 18.0°C. The molar mass of helium is 4.00 g/mol. (a) How many moles of helium are in the tank? (b) What is the pressure in the tank, in pascals and in atmospheres?

18.2 •• Helium gas with a volume of 2.60 L, under a pressure of 0.180 atm and at a temperature of 41.0°C, is warmed until both pressure and volume are doubled. (a) What is the final temperature? (b) How many grams of helium are there? The molar mass of helium is 4.00 g/mol.

18.3 • A cylindrical tank has a tight-fitting piston that allows the volume of the tank to be changed. The tank originally contains 0.110 m³ of air at a pressure of 0.355 atm. The piston is slowly pulled out until the volume of the gas is increased to 0.390 m³. If the temperature remains constant, what is the final value of the pressure?

18.4 • A 3.00-L tank contains air at 3.00 atm and 20.0°C. The tank is sealed and cooled until the pressure is 1.00 atm. (a) What is the temperature then in degrees Celsius? Assume that the volume of the tank is constant. (b) If the temperature is kept at the value found in part (a) and the gas is compressed, what is the volume when the pressure again becomes 3.00 atm?

18.5 • **Planetary Atmospheres.** (a) Calculate the density of the atmosphere at the surface of Mars (where the pressure is 650 Pa and the temperature is typically 253 K, with a CO_2 atmosphere), Venus (with an average temperature of 730 K and pressure of 92 atm, with a CO_2 atmosphere), and Saturn's moon Titan (where the pressure is 1.5 atm and the temperature is −178°C, with a N_2 atmosphere). (b) Compare each of these densities with that of the earth's atmosphere, which is 1.20 kg/m³. Consult the periodic chart in Appendix D to determine molar masses.

18.6 •• You have several identical balloons. You experimentally determine that a balloon will break if its volume exceeds 0.900 L. The pressure of the gas inside the balloon equals air pressure (1.00 atm). (a) If the air inside the balloon is at a constant temperature of

22.0°C and behaves as an ideal gas, what mass of air can you blow into one of the balloons before it bursts? (b) Repeat part (a) if the gas is helium rather than air.

18.7 •• A Jaguar XK8 convertible has an eight-cylinder engine. At the beginning of its compression stroke, one of the cylinders contains 499 cm^3 of air at atmospheric pressure $(1.01 \times 10^5$ Pa) and a temperature of 27.0°C. At the end of the stroke, the air has been compressed to a volume of 46.2 cm^3 and the gauge pressure has increased to 2.72×10^6 Pa. Compute the final temperature.

18.8 •• A welder using a tank of volume 0.0750 m^3 fills it with oxygen (molar mass 32.0 g/mol) at a gauge pressure of 3.00×10^5 Pa and temperature of 37.0°C. The tank has a small leak, and in time some of the oxygen leaks out. On a day when the temperature is 22.0°C, the gauge pressure of the oxygen in the tank is 1.80×10^5 Pa. Find (a) the initial mass of oxygen and (b) the mass of oxygen that has leaked out.

18.9 •• A large cylindrical tank contains 0.750 m^3 of nitrogen gas at 27°C and 7.50×10^3 Pa (absolute pressure). The tank has a tight-fitting piston that allows the volume to be changed. What will be the pressure if the volume is decreased to 0.480 m^3 and the temperature is increased to 157°C?

18.10 • An empty cylindrical canister 1.50 m long and 90.0 cm in diameter is to be filled with pure oxygen at 22.0°C to store in a space station. To hold as much gas as possible, the absolute pressure of the oxygen will be 21.0 atm. The molar mass of oxygen is 32.0 g/mol. (a) How many moles of oxygen does this canister hold? (b) For someone lifting this canister, by how many kilograms does this gas increase the mass to be lifted?

18.11 • The gas inside a balloon will always have a pressure nearly equal to atmospheric pressure, since that is the pressure applied to the outside of the balloon. You fill a balloon with helium (a nearly ideal gas) to a volume of 0.600 L at a temperature of 19.0°C. What is the volume of the balloon if you cool it to the boiling point of liquid nitrogen (77.3 K)?

18.12 • **Deviations from the Ideal-Gas Equation.** For carbon dioxide gas (CO_2), the constants in the van der Waals equation are $a = 0.364$ J·m^3/mol^2 and $b = 4.27 \times 10^{-5}$ m^3/mol. (a) If 1.00 mol of CO_2 gas at 350 K is confined to a volume of 400 cm^3, find the pressure of the gas using the ideal-gas equation and the van der Waals equation. (b) Which equation gives a lower pressure? Why? What is the percentage difference of the van der Waals equation result from the ideal-gas equation result? (c) The gas is kept at the same temperature as it expands to a volume of 4000 cm^3. Repeat the calculations of parts (a) and (b). (d) Explain how your calculations show that the van der Waals equation is equivalent to the ideal-gas equation if n/V is small.

18.13 •• If a certain amount of ideal gas occupies a volume V at STP on earth, what would be its volume (in terms of V) on Venus, where the temperature is 1003°C and the pressure is 92 atm?

18.14 • A diver observes a bubble of air rising from the bottom of a lake (where the absolute pressure is 3.50 atm) to the surface (where the pressure is 1.00 atm). The temperature at the bottom is 4.0°C, and the temperature at the surface is 23.0°C. (a) What is the ratio of the volume of the bubble as it reaches the surface to its volume at the bottom? (b) Would it be safe for the diver to hold his breath while ascending from the bottom of the lake to the surface? Why or why not?

18.15 • A metal tank with volume 3.10 L will burst if the absolute pressure of the gas it contains exceeds 100 atm. (a) If 11.0 mol of an ideal gas is put into the tank at a temperature of 23.0°C, to what temperature can the gas be warmed before the tank ruptures? You can ignore the thermal expansion of the tank. (b) Based on your answer to part (a), is it reasonable to ignore the thermal expansion of the tank? Explain.

18.16 • Three moles of an ideal gas are in a rigid cubical box with sides of length 0.200 m. (a) What is the force that the gas exerts on each of the six sides of the box when the gas temperature is 20.0°C? (b) What is the force when the temperature of the gas is increased to 100.0°C?

18.17 • With the assumptions of Example 18.4 (Section 18.1), at what altitude above sea level is air pressure 90% of the pressure at sea level?

18.18 • Make the same assumptions as in Example 18.4 (Section 18.1). How does the percentage decrease in air pressure in going from sea level to an altitude of 100 m compare to that when going from sea level to an altitude of 1000 m? If your second answer is not 10 times your first answer, explain why.

18.19 •• (a) Calculate the mass of nitrogen present in a volume of 3000 cm^3 if the temperature of the gas is 22.0°C and the absolute pressure of 2.00×10^{-13} atm is a partial vacuum easily obtained in laboratories. (b) What is the density (in kg/m^3) of the N_2?

18.20 •• With the assumption that the air temperature is a uniform 0.0°C (as in Example 18.4), what is the density of the air at an altitude of 1.00 km as a percentage of the density at the surface?

18.21 • At an altitude of 11,000 m (a typical cruising altitude for a jet airliner), the air temperature is −56.5°C and the air density is 0.364 kg/m^3. What is the pressure of the atmosphere at that altitude? (*Note:* The temperature at this altitude is not the same as at the surface of the earth, so the calculation of Example 18.4 in Section 18.1 doesn't apply.)

Section 18.2 Molecular Properties of Matter

18.22 • A large organic molecule has a mass of 1.41×10^{-21} kg. What is the molar mass of this compound?

18.23 •• Suppose you inherit 3.00 mol of gold from your uncle (an eccentric chemist) at a time when this metal is selling for $14.75 per gram. Consult the periodic table in Appendix D and Table 12.1. (a) To the nearest dollar, what is this gold worth? (b) If you have your gold formed into a spherical nugget, what is its diameter?

18.24 •• Modern vacuum pumps make it easy to attain pressures of the order of 10^{-13} atm in the laboratory. Consider a volume of air and treat the air as an ideal gas. (a) At a pressure of 9.00×10^{-14} atm and an ordinary temperature of 300.0 K, how many molecules are present in a volume of 1.00 cm^3? (b) How many molecules would be present at the same temperature but at 1.00 atm instead?

18.25 •• The Lagoon Nebula (Fig. E18.25) is a cloud of hydrogen gas located 3900 light-years from the earth. The cloud is about 45 light-years in diameter and glows because of its high temperature of 7500 K. (The gas is raised to this temperature by the stars that

Figure **E18.25**

lie within the nebula.) The cloud is also very thin; there are only 80 molecules per cubic centimeter. (a) Find the gas pressure (in atmospheres) in the Lagoon Nebula. Compare it to the laboratory pressure referred to in Exercise 18.24. (b) Science-fiction films sometimes show starships being buffeted by turbulence as they fly through gas clouds such as the Lagoon Nebula. Does this seem realistic? Why or why not?

18.26 •• In a gas at standard conditions, what is the length of the side of a cube that contains a number of molecules equal to the population of the earth (about 6×10^9 people)?

18.27 • How many moles are in a 1.00-kg bottle of water? How many molecules? The molar mass of water is 18.0 g/mol.

18.28 •• **How Close Together Are Gas Molecules?** Consider an ideal gas at 27°C and 1.00 atm pressure. To get some idea how close these molecules are to each other, on the average, imagine them to be uniformly spaced, with each molecule at the center of a small cube. (a) What is the length of an edge of each cube if adjacent cubes touch but do not overlap? (b) How does this distance compare with the diameter of a typical molecule? (c) How does their separation compare with the spacing of atoms in solids, which typically are about 0.3 nm apart?

18.29 •• Consider 5.00 mol of liquid water. (a) What volume is occupied by this amount of water? The molar mass of water is 18.0 g/mol. (b) Imagine the molecules to be, on average, uniformly spaced, with each molecule at the center of a small cube. What is the length of an edge of each small cube if adjacent cubes touch but don't overlap? (c) How does this distance compare with the diameter of a molecule?

Section 18.3 Kinetic-Molecular Model of an Ideal Gas

18.30 • A flask contains a mixture of neon (Ne), krypton (Kr), and radon (Rn) gases. Compare (a) the average kinetic energies of the three types of atoms and (b) the root-mean-square speeds. (*Hint:* The periodic table in Appendix D shows the molar mass (in g/mol) of each element under the chemical symbol for that element.)

18.31 • **Gaseous Diffusion of Uranium.** (a) A process called *gaseous diffusion* is often used to separate isotopes of uranium— that is, atoms of the elements that have different masses, such as ^{235}U and ^{238}U. The only gaseous compound of uranium at ordinary temperatures is uranium hexafluoride, UF_6. Speculate on how $^{235}UF_6$ and $^{238}UF_6$ molecules might be separated by diffusion. (b) The molar masses for $^{235}UF_6$ and $^{238}UF_6$ molecules are 0.349 kg/mol and 0.352 kg/mol, respectively. If uranium hexafluoride acts as an ideal gas, what is the ratio of the root-mean-square speed of $^{235}UF_6$ molecules to that of $^{238}UF_6$ molecules if the temperature is uniform?

18.32 • The ideas of average and root-mean-square value can be applied to any distribution. A class of 150 students had the following scores on a 100-point quiz:

Score	Number of Students
10	11
20	12
30	24
40	15
50	19
60	10
70	12
80	20
90	17
100	10

(a) Find the average score for the class. (b) Find the root-mean-square score for the class.

18.33 • We have two equal-size boxes, A and B. Each box contains gas that behaves as an ideal gas. We insert a thermometer into each box and find that the gas in box A is at a temperature of 50°C while the gas in box B is at 10°C. This is all we know about the gas in the boxes. Which of the following statements *must* be true? Which *could* be true? (a) The pressure in A is higher than in B. (b) There are more molecules in A than in B. (c) A and B do not contain the same type of gas. (d) The molecules in A have more average kinetic energy per molecule than those in B. (e) The molecules in A are moving faster than those in B. Explain the reasoning behind your answers.

18.34 • A container with volume 1.48 L is initially evacuated. Then it is filled with 0.226 g of N_2. Assume that the pressure of the gas is low enough for the gas to obey the ideal-gas law to a high degree of accuracy. If the root-mean-square speed of the gas molecules is 182 m/s, what is the pressure of the gas?

18.35 •• (a) A deuteron, ^2_1H, is the nucleus of a hydrogen isotope and consists of one proton and one neutron. The plasma of deuterons in a nuclear fusion reactor must be heated to about 300 million K. What is the rms speed of the deuterons? Is this a significant fraction of the speed of light ($c = 3.0 \times 10^8$ m/s)? (b) What would the temperature of the plasma be if the deuterons had an rms speed equal to $0.10c$?

18.36 • **Martian Climate.** The atmosphere of Mars is mostly CO_2 (molar mass 44.0 g/mol) under a pressure of 650 Pa, which we shall assume remains constant. In many places the temperature varies from 0.0°C in summer to −100°C in winter. Over the course of a Martian year, what are the ranges of (a) the rms speeds of the CO_2 molecules and (b) the density (in mol/m³) of the atmosphere?

18.37 •• (a) Oxygen (O_2) has a molar mass of 32.0 g/mol. What is the average translational kinetic energy of an oxygen molecule at a temperature of 300 K? (b) What is the average value of the square of its speed? (c) What is the root-mean-square speed? (d) What is the momentum of an oxygen molecule traveling at this speed? (e) Suppose an oxygen molecule traveling at this speed bounces back and forth between opposite sides of a cubical vessel 0.10 m on a side. What is the average force the molecule exerts on one of the walls of the container? (Assume that the molecule's velocity is perpendicular to the two sides that it strikes.) (f) What is the average force per unit area? (g) How many oxygen molecules traveling at this speed are necessary to produce an average pressure of 1 atm? (h) Compute the number of oxygen molecules that are actually contained in a vessel of this size at 300 K and atmospheric pressure. (i) Your answer for part (h) should be three times as large as the answer for part (g). Where does this discrepancy arise?

18.38 •• Calculate the mean free path of air molecules at a pressure of 3.50×10^{-13} atm and a temperature of 300 K. (This pressure is readily attainable in the laboratory; see Exercise 18.24.) As in Example 18.8, model the air molecules as spheres of radius 2.0×10^{-10} m.

18.39 •• At what temperature is the root-mean-square speed of nitrogen molecules equal to the root-mean-square speed of hydrogen molecules at 20.0°C? (*Hint:* The periodic table in Appendix D shows the molar mass (in g/mol) of each element under the chemical symbol for that element. The molar mass of H_2 is twice the molar mass of hydrogen atoms, and similarly for N_2.)

18.40 • Smoke particles in the air typically have masses of the order of 10^{-16} kg. The Brownian motion (rapid, irregular movement) of these particles, resulting from collisions with air molecules, can be observed with a microscope. (a) Find the root-mean-square speed of Brownian motion for a particle with a mass of 3.00×10^{-16} kg in air at 300 K. (b) Would the root-mean-square speed be different if the particle were in hydrogen gas at the same temperature? Explain.

Section 18.4 Heat Capacities

18.41 • (a) How much heat does it take to increase the temperature of 2.50 mol of a diatomic ideal gas by 50.0 K near room temperature if the gas is held at constant volume? (b) What is the answer to the question in part (a) if the gas is monatomic rather than diatomic?

18.42 •• Perfectly rigid containers each hold n moles of ideal gas, one being hydrogen (H_2) and other being neon (Ne). If it takes 300 J of heat to increase the temperature of the hydrogen by $2.50°C$, by how many degrees will the same amount of heat raise the temperature of the neon?

18.43 •• (a) Compute the specific heat at constant volume of nitrogen (N_2) gas, and compare it with the specific heat of liquid water. The molar mass of N_2 is 28.0 g/mol. (b) You warm 1.00 kg of water at a constant volume of 1.00 L from $20.0°C$ to $30.0°C$ in a kettle. For the same amount of heat, how many kilograms of $20.0°C$ air would you be able to warm to $30.0°C$? What volume (in liters) would this air occupy at $20.0°C$ and a pressure of 1.00 atm? Make the simplifying assumption that air is 100% N_2.

18.44 •• (a) Calculate the specific heat at constant volume of water vapor, assuming the nonlinear triatomic molecule has three translational and three rotational degrees of freedom and that vibrational motion does not contribute. The molar mass of water is 18.0 g/mol. (b) The actual specific heat of water vapor at low pressures is about 2000 J/kg·K. Compare this with your calculation and comment on the actual role of vibrational motion.

18.45 •• (a) Use Eq. 18.28 to calculate the specific heat at constant volume of aluminum in units of J/kg·K. Consult the periodic table in Appendix D. (b) Compare the answer in part (a) with the value given in Table 17.3. Try to explain any disagreement between these two values.

Section 18.5 Molecular Speeds

18.46 • For a gas of nitrogen molecules (N_2), what must the temperature be if 94.7% of all the molecules have speeds less than (a) 1500 m/s; (b) 1000 m/s; (c) 500 m/s? Use Table 18.2. The molar mass of N_2 is 28.0 g/mol.

18.47 • For diatomic carbon dioxide gas (CO_2, molar mass 44.0 g/mol) at $T = 300$ K, calculate (a) the most probable speed v_{mp}; (b) the average speed v_{av}; (c) the root-mean-square speed v_{rms}.

18.48 • CALC Prove that $f(v)$ as given by Eq. (18.33) is maximum for $\epsilon = kT$. Use this result to obtain Eq. (18.34).

Section 18.6 Phases of Matter

18.49 • Solid water (ice) is slowly warmed from a very low temperature. (a) What minimum external pressure p_1 must be applied to the solid if a melting phase transition is to be observed? Describe the sequence of phase transitions that occur if the applied pressure p is such that $p < p_1$. (b) Above a certain maximum pressure p_2, no boiling transition is observed. What is this pressure? Describe the sequence of phase transitions that occur if $p_1 < p < p_2$.

18.50 • Puffy cumulus clouds, which are made of water droplets, occur at lower altitudes in the atmosphere. Wispy cirrus clouds, which are made of ice crystals, occur only at higher altitudes. Find the altitude y (measured from sea level) above which only cirrus clouds can occur. On a typical day and at altitudes less than 11 km, the temperature at an altitude y is given by $T = T_0 - \alpha y$, where $T_0 = 15.0°C$ and $\alpha = 6.0$ C°/1000 m.

18.51 • The atmosphere of the planet Mars is 95.3% carbon dioxide (CO_2) and about 0.03% water vapor. The atmospheric pressure is only about 600 Pa, and the surface temperature varies from $-30°C$ to $-100°C$. The polar ice caps contain both CO_2 ice and water ice. Could there be *liquid* CO_2 on the surface of Mars? Could there be liquid water? Why or why not?

18.52 • A physics lecture room has a volume of 216 m^3. (a) For a pressure of 1.00 atm and a temperature of $27.0°C$, use the ideal-gas law to estimate the number of air molecules in the room. Assume all the air is N_2. (b) Calculate the particle density—that is, the number of N_2 molecules per cubic centimeter. (c) Calculate the mass of the air in the room.

PROBLEMS

18.53 •• CP BIO **The Effect of Altitude on the Lungs.** (a) Calculate the *change* in air pressure you will experience if you climb a 1000-m mountain, assuming that the temperature and air density do not change over this distance and that they were 22°C and 1.2 kg/m^3, respectively, at the bottom of the mountain. (Note that the result of Example 18.4 doesn't apply, since the expression derived in that example accounts for the variation of air density with altitude and we are told to ignore that in this problem.) (b) If you took a 0.50-L breath at the foot of the mountain and managed to hold it until you reached the top, what would be the volume of this breath when you exhaled it there?

18.54 •• CP BIO **The Bends.** If deep-sea divers rise to the surface too quickly, nitrogen bubbles in their blood can expand and prove fatal. This phenomenon is known as the *bends*. If a scuba diver rises quickly from a depth of 25 m in Lake Michigan (which is fresh water), what will be the volume at the surface of an N_2 bubble that occupied 1.0 mm^3 in his blood at the lower depth? Does it seem that this difference is large enough to be a problem? (Assume that the pressure difference is due only to the changing water pressure, not to any temperature difference, an assumption that is reasonable, since we are warm-blooded creatures.)

18.55 ••• CP A hot-air balloon stays aloft because hot air at atmospheric pressure is less dense than cooler air at the same pressure. If the volume of the balloon is 500.0 m^3 and the surrounding air is at 15.0°C, what must the temperature of the air in the balloon be for it to lift a total load of 290 kg (in addition to the mass of the hot air)? The density of air at 15.0°C and atmospheric pressure is 1.23 kg/m^3.

18.56 •• (a) Use Eq. (18.1) to estimate the change in the volume of a solid steel sphere of volume 11 L when the temperature and pressure increase from 21°C and 1.013×10^5 Pa to 42°C and 2.10×10^7 Pa. (*Hint:* Consult Chapters 11 and 17 to determine the values of β and k.) (b) In Example 18.3 the change in volume of an 11-L steel scuba tank was ignored. Was this a good approximation? Explain.

18.57 ••• A cylinder 1.00 m tall with inside diameter 0.120 m is used to hold propane gas (molar mass 44.1 g/mol) for use in a barbecue. It is initially filled with gas until the gauge pressure is 1.30×10^6 Pa and the temperature is 22.0°C. The temperature of the gas remains constant as it is partially emptied out of the tank, until the gauge pressure is 2.50×10^5 Pa. Calculate the mass of propane that has been used.

18.58 • CP During a test dive in 1939, prior to being accepted by the U.S. Navy, the submarine *Squalus* sank at a point where the depth of water was 73.0 m. The temperature at the surface was 27.0°C, and at the bottom it was 7.0°C. The density of seawater is 1030 kg/m³. (a) A diving bell was used to rescue 33 trapped crewmen from the *Squalus*. The diving bell was in the form of a circular cylinder 2.30 m high, open at the bottom and closed at the top. When the diving bell was lowered to the bottom of the sea, to what height did water rise within the diving bell? (*Hint:* You may ignore the relatively small variation in water pressure between the bottom of the bell and the surface of the water within the bell.) (b) At what gauge pressure must compressed air have been supplied to the bell while on the bottom to expel all the water from it?

18.59 • **Atmosphere of Titan.** Titan, the largest satellite of Saturn, has a thick nitrogen atmosphere. At its surface, the pressure is 1.5 earth-atmospheres and the temperature is 94 K. (a) What is the surface temperature in °C? (b) Calculate the surface density in Titan's atmosphere in molecules per cubic meter. (c) Compare the density of Titan's surface atmosphere to the density of earth's atmosphere at 22°C. Which body has denser atmosphere?

18.60 • **Pressure on Venus.** At the surface of Venus the average temperature is a balmy 460°C due to the greenhouse effect (global warming!), the pressure is 92 earth-atmospheres, and the acceleration due to gravity is $0.894g_{earth}$. The atmosphere is nearly all CO_2 (molar mass 44.0 g/mol) and the temperature remains remarkably constant. We shall assume that the temperature does not change at all with altitude. (a) What is the atmospheric pressure 1.00 km above the surface of Venus? Express your answer in Venus-atmospheres and earth-atmospheres. (b) What is the root-mean-square speed of the CO_2 molecules at the surface of Venus and at an altitude of 1.00 km?

18.61 •• An automobile tire has a volume of 0.0150 m³ on a cold day when the temperature of the air in the tire is 5.0°C and atmospheric pressure is 1.02 atm. Under these conditions the gauge pressure is measured to be 1.70 atm (about 25 lb/in.²). After the car is driven on the highway for 30 min, the temperature of the air in the tires has risen to 45.0°C and the volume has risen to 0.0159 m³. What then is the gauge pressure?

18.62 •• A flask with a volume of 1.50 L, provided with a stopcock, contains ethane gas (C_2H_6) at 300 K and atmospheric pressure (1.013×10^5 Pa). The molar mass of ethane is 30.1 g/mol. The system is warmed to a temperature of 490 K, with the stopcock open to the atmosphere. The stopcock is then closed, and the flask is cooled to its original temperature. (a) What is the final pressure of the ethane in the flask? (b) How many grams of ethane remain in the flask?

18.63 •• CP A balloon whose volume is 750 m³ is to be filled with hydrogen at atmospheric pressure (1.01×10^5 Pa). (a) If the hydrogen is stored in cylinders with volumes of 1.90 m³ at a gauge pressure of 1.20×10^6 Pa, how many cylinders are required? Assume that the temperature of the hydrogen remains constant. (b) What is the total weight (in addition to the weight of the gas) that can be supported by the balloon if the gas in the balloon and the surrounding air are both at 15.0°C? The molar mass of hydrogen (H_2) is 2.02 g/mol. The density of air at 15.0°C and atmospheric pressure is 1.23 kg/m³. See Chapter 12 for a discussion of buoyancy. (c) What weight could be supported if the balloon were filled with helium (molar mass 4.00 g/mol) instead of hydrogen, again at 15.0°C?

18.64 •• A vertical cylindrical tank contains 1.80 mol of an ideal gas under a pressure of 0.500 atm at 20.0°C. The round part of the tank has a radius of 10.0 cm, and the gas is supporting a piston that

can move up and down in the cylinder without friction. There is a vacuum above the piston. (a) What is the mass of this piston? (b) How tall is the column of gas that is supporting the piston?

18.65 •• CP A large tank of water has a hose connected to it, as shown in Fig. P18.65. The tank is sealed at the top and has compressed air between the water surface and the top. When the water height h has the value 3.50 m, the absolute pressure p of the compressed air is 4.20×10^5 Pa. Assume that the air above the water expands at constant temperature, and take the atmospheric pressure to be 1.00×10^5 Pa. (a) What is the speed with which water flows out of the hose when $h = 3.50$ m? (b) As water flows out of the tank, h decreases. Calculate the speed of flow for $h = 3.00$ m and for $h = 2.00$ m. (c) At what value of h does the flow stop?

Figure **P18.65**

18.66 •• BIO A person at rest inhales 0.50 L of air with each breath at a pressure of 1.00 atm and a temperature of 20.0°C. The inhaled air is 21.0% oxygen. (a) How many oxygen molecules does this person inhale with each breath? (b) Suppose this person is now resting at an elevation of 2000 m but the temperature is still 20.0°C. Assuming that the oxygen percentage and volume per inhalation are the same as stated above, how many oxygen molecules does this person now inhale with each breath? (c) Given that the body still requires the same number of oxygen molecules per second as at sea level to maintain its functions, explain why some people report "shortness of breath" at high elevations.

18.67 •• BIO **How Many Atoms Are You?** Estimate the number of atoms in the body of a 50-kg physics student. Note that the human body is mostly water, which has molar mass 18.0 g/mol, and that each water molecule contains three atoms.

18.68 • The size of an oxygen molecule is about 2.0×10^{-10} m. Make a rough estimate of the pressure at which the finite volume of the molecules should cause noticeable deviations from ideal-gas behavior at ordinary temperatures ($T = 300$ K).

18.69 •• You have two identical containers, one containing gas A and the other gas B. The masses of these molecules are $m_A = 3.34 \times 10^{-27}$ kg and $m_B = 5.34 \times 10^{-26}$ kg. Both gases are under the same pressure and are at 10.0°C. (a) Which molecules (A or B) have greater translational kinetic energy per molecule and rms speeds? (b) Now you want to raise the temperature of only one of these containers so that both gases will have the same rms speed. For which gas should you raise the temperature? (c) At what temperature will you accomplish your goal? (d) Once you have accomplished your goal, which molecules (A or B) now have greater average translational kinetic energy per molecule?

18.70 • **Insect Collisions.** A cubical cage 1.25 m on each side contains 2500 angry bees, each flying randomly at 1.10 m/s. We can model these insects as spheres 1.50 cm in diameter. On the average, (a) how far does a typical bee travel between collisions, (b) what is the average time between collisions, and (c) how many collisions per second does a bee make?

18.71 •• You blow up a spherical balloon to a diameter of 50.0 cm until the absolute pressure inside is 1.25 atm and the temperature is 22.0°C. Assume that all the gas is N_2, of molar mass 28.0 g/mol. (a) Find the mass of a single N_2 molecule. (b) How much translational kinetic energy does an average N_2 molecule have? (c) How many N_2 molecules are in this balloon? (d) What is the *total* translational kinetic energy of all the molecules in the balloon?

18.72 · CP (a) Compute the increase in gravitational potential energy for a nitrogen molecule (molar mass 28.0 g/mol) for an increase in elevation of 400 m near the earth's surface. (b) At what temperature is this equal to the average kinetic energy of a nitrogen molecule? (c) Is it possible that a nitrogen molecule near sea level where $T = 15.0°C$ could rise to an altitude of 400 m? Is it likely that it could do so without hitting any other molecules along the way? Explain.

18.73 ·· CP, CALC **The Lennard-Jones Potential.** A commonly used potential-energy function for the interaction of two molecules (see Fig. 18.8) is the Lennard-Jones 6-12 potential:

$$U(r) = U_0\left[\left(\frac{R_0}{r}\right)^{12} - 2\left(\frac{R_0}{r}\right)^6\right]$$

where r is the distance between the centers of the molecules and U_0 and R_0 are positive constants. The corresponding force $F(r)$ is given in Eq. (14.26). (a) Graph $U(r)$ and $F(r)$ versus r. (b) Let r_1 be the value of r at which $U(r) = 0$, and let r_2 be the value of r at which $F(r) = 0$. Show the locations of r_1 and r_2 on your graphs of $U(r)$ and $F(r)$. Which of these values represents the equilibrium separation between the molecules? (c) Find the values of r_1 and r_2 in terms of R_0, and find the ratio r_1/r_2. (d) If the molecules are located a distance r_2 apart [as calculated in part (c)], how much work must be done to pull them apart so that $r \to \infty$?

18.74 · (a) What is the total random translational kinetic energy of 5.00 L of hydrogen gas (molar mass 2.016 g/mol) with pressure 1.01×10^5 Pa and temperature 300 K? (*Hint:* Use the procedure of Problem 18.71 as a guide.) (b) If the tank containing the gas is placed on a swift jet moving at 300.0 m/s, by what percentage is the *total* kinetic energy of the gas increased? (c) Since the kinetic energy of the gas molecules is greater when it is on the jet, does this mean that its temperature has gone up? Explain.

18.75 · The speed of propagation of a sound wave in air at 27°C is about 350 m/s. Calculate, for comparison, (a) v_{rms} for nitrogen molecules and (b) the rms value of v_x at this temperature. The molar mass of nitrogen (N_2) is 28.0 g/mol.

18.76 · **Hydrogen on the Sun.** The surface of the sun has a temperature of about 5800 K and consists largely of hydrogen atoms. (a) Find the rms speed of a hydrogen atom at this temperature. (The mass of a single hydrogen atom is 1.67×10^{-27} kg.) (b) The escape speed for a particle to leave the gravitational influence of the sun is given by $(2GM/R)^{1/2}$, where M is the sun's mass, R its radius, and G the gravitational constant (see Example 13.5 of Section 13.3). Use the data in Appendix F to calculate this escape speed. (c) Can appreciable quantities of hydrogen escape from the sun? Can *any* hydrogen escape? Explain.

18.77 ·· CP (a) Show that a projectile with mass m can "escape" from the surface of a planet if it is launched vertically upward with a kinetic energy greater than mgR_p, where g is the acceleration due to gravity at the planet's surface and R_p is the planet's radius. Ignore air resistance. (See Problem 18.76.) (b) If the planet in question is the earth, at what temperature does the average translational kinetic energy of a nitrogen molecule (molar mass 28.0 g/mol) equal that required to escape? What about a hydrogen molecule (molar mass 2.02 g/mol)? (c) Repeat part (b) for the moon, for which $g = 1.63$ m/s^2 and $R_p = 1740$ km. (d) While the earth and the moon have similar average surface temperatures, the moon has essentially no atmosphere. Use your results from parts (b) and (c) to explain why.

18.78 · **Planetary Atmospheres.** (a) The temperature near the top of Jupiter's multicolored cloud layer is about 140 K. The temperature at the top of the earth's troposphere, at an altitude of about 20 km, is about 220 K. Calculate the rms speed of hydrogen molecules in both these environments. Give your answers in m/s and as a fraction of the escape speed from the respective planet (see Problem 18.76). (b) Hydrogen gas (H_2) is a rare element in the earth's atmosphere. In the atmosphere of Jupiter, by contrast, 89% of all molecules are H_2. Explain why, using your results from part (a). (c) Suppose an astronomer claims to have discovered an oxygen (O_2) atmosphere on the asteroid Ceres. How likely is this? Ceres has a mass equal to 0.014 times the mass of the moon, a density of 2400 kg/m^3, and a surface temperature of about 200 K.

18.79 ·· (a) For what mass of molecule or particle is v_{rms} equal to 1.00 mm/s at 300 K? (b) If the particle is an ice crystal, how many molecules does it contain? The molar mass of water is 18.0 g/mol. (c) Calculate the diameter of the particle if it is a spherical piece of ice. Would it be visible to the naked eye?

18.80 ·· In describing the heat capacities of solids in Section 18.4, we stated that the potential energy $U = \frac{1}{2}kx^2$ of a harmonic oscillator averaged over one period of the motion is equal to the kinetic energy $K = \frac{1}{2}mv^2$ averaged over one period. Prove this result using Eqs. (14.13) and (14.15) for the position and velocity of a simple harmonic oscillator. For simplicity, assume that the initial position and velocity make the phase angle ϕ equal to zero. (*Hint:* Use the trigonometric identities $\cos^2(\theta) = [1 + \cos(2\theta)]/2$ and $\sin^2(\theta) = [1 - \cos(2\theta)]/2$. What is the average value of $\cos(2\omega t)$ over one period?)

18.81 ·· It is possible to make crystalline solids that are only one layer of atoms thick. Such "two-dimensional" crystals can be created by depositing atoms on a very flat surface. (a) If the atoms in such a two-dimensional crystal can move only within the plane of the crystal, what will be its molar heat capacity near room temperature? Give your answer as a multiple of R and in J/mol·K. (b) At very low temperatures, will the molar heat capacity of a two-dimensional crystal be greater than, less than, or equal to the result you found in part (a)? Explain why.

18.82 ·· (a) Calculate the total *rotational* kinetic energy of the molecules in 1.00 mol of a diatomic gas at 300 K. (b) Calculate the moment of inertia of an oxygen molecule (O_2) for rotation about either the y- or z-axis shown in Fig. 18.18b. Treat the molecule as two massive points (representing the oxygen atoms) separated by a distance of 1.21×10^{-10} m. The molar mass of oxygen *atoms* is 16.0 g/mol. (c) Find the rms angular velocity of rotation of an oxygen molecule about either the y- or z-axis shown in Fig. 18.18b. How does your answer compare to the angular velocity of a typical piece of rapidly rotating machinery (10,000 rev/min)?

18.83 · For each polyatomic gas in Table 18.1, compute the value of the molar heat capacity at constant volume, C_V, on the assumption that there is no vibrational energy. Compare with the measured values in the table, and compute the fraction of the total heat capacity that is due to vibration for each of the three gases. (*Note:* CO_2 is linear; SO_2 and H_2S are not. Recall that a linear polyatomic molecule has two rotational degrees of freedom, and a nonlinear molecule has three.)

18.84 ·· CALC (a) Show that $\int_0^\infty f(v)\,dv = 1$, where $f(v)$ is the Maxwell–Boltzmann distribution of Eq. (18.32). (b) In terms of the physical definition of $f(v)$, explain why the integral in part (a) *must* have this value.

18.85 ·· CALC Calculate the integral in Eq. (18.31), $\int_0^\infty v^2 f(v)\,dv$, and compare this result to $(v^2)_{av}$ as given by Eq. (18.16). (*Hint:* You may use the tabulated integral

$$\int_0^\infty x^{2n} e^{-\alpha x^2}\,dx = \frac{1 \cdot 3 \cdot 5 \cdots (2n - 1)}{2^{n+1}\alpha^n}\sqrt{\frac{\pi}{\alpha}}$$

where n is a positive integer and α is a positive constant.)

18.86 ·· **CALC** Calculate the integral in Eq. (18.30), $\int_0^\infty vf(v)\,dv$, and compare this result to v_{av} as given by Eq. (18.35). (*Hint:* Make the change of variable $v^2 = x$ and use the tabulated integral

$$\int_0^\infty x^n e^{-\alpha x}\,dx = \frac{n!}{\alpha^{n+1}}$$

where n is a positive integer and α is a positive constant.)

18.87 ·· **CALC** (a) Explain why in a gas of N molecules, the number of molecules having speeds in the *finite* interval v to $v + \Delta v$ is $\Delta N = N\int_v^{v+\Delta v} f(v)\,dv$. (b) If Δv is small, then $f(v)$ is approximately constant over the interval and $\Delta N \approx Nf(v)\Delta v$. For oxygen gas ($O_2$, molar mass 32.0 g/mol) at $T = 300$ K, use this approximation to calculate the number of molecules with speeds within $\Delta v = 20$ m/s of v_{mp}. Express your answer as a multiple of N. (c) Repeat part (b) for speeds within $\Delta v = 20$ m/s of $7v_{mp}$. (d) Repeat parts (b) and (c) for a temperature of 600 K. (e) Repeat parts (b) and (c) for a temperature of 150 K. (f) What do your results tell you about the shape of the distribution as a function of temperature? Do your conclusions agree with what is shown in Fig. 18.23?

18.88 · **Meteorology.** The *vapor pressure* is the pressure of the vapor phase of a substance when it is in equilibrium with the solid or liquid phase of the substance. The *relative humidity* is the partial pressure of water vapor in the air divided by the vapor pressure of water at that same temperature, expressed as a percentage. The air is saturated when the humidity is 100%. (a) The vapor pressure of water at 20.0°C is 2.34×10^3 Pa. If the air temperature is 20.0°C and the relative humidity is 60%, what is the partial pressure of water vapor in the atmosphere (that is, the pressure due to water vapor alone)? (b) Under the conditions of part (a), what is the mass of water in 1.00 m³ of air? (The molar mass of water is 18.0 g/mol. Assume that water vapor can be treated as an ideal gas.)

18.89 · **The Dew Point.** The vapor pressure of water (see Problem 18.88) decreases as the temperature decreases. If the amount of water vapor in the air is kept constant as the air is cooled, a temperature is reached, called the *dew point,* at which the partial pressure and vapor pressure coincide and the vapor is saturated. If the air is cooled further, vapor condenses to liquid until the partial pressure again equals the vapor pressure at that temperature. The temperature in a room is 30.0°C. A meteorologist cools a metal can by gradually adding cold water. When the can temperature reaches 16.0°C, water droplets form on its outside surface. What is the relative humidity of the 30.0°C air in the room? The table lists the vapor pressure of water at various temperatures:

Temperature (°C)	Vapor Pressure (Pa)
10.0	1.23×10^3
12.0	1.40×10^3
14.0	1.60×10^3
16.0	1.81×10^3
18.0	2.06×10^3
20.0	2.34×10^3
22.0	2.65×10^3
24.0	2.99×10^3
26.0	3.36×10^3
28.0	3.78×10^3
30.0	4.25×10^3

18.90 ··· **Altitude at Which Clouds Form.** On a spring day in the midwestern United States, the air temperature at the surface is 28.0°C. Puffy cumulus clouds form at an altitude where the air temperature equals the dew point (see Problem 18.89). If the air temperature decreases with altitude at a rate of 0.6 C°/100 m, at approximately what height above the ground will clouds form if the relative humidity at the surface is 35% and 80%? (*Hint:* Use the table in Problem 18.89.)

CHALLENGE PROBLEMS

18.91 ··· **CP Dark Nebulae and the Interstellar Medium.** The dark area in Fig. P18.91 that appears devoid of stars is a *dark nebula,* a cold gas cloud in interstellar space that contains enough material to block out light from the stars behind it. A typical dark nebula is about 20 light-years in diameter and contains about 50 hydrogen atoms per cubic centimeter (monatomic hydrogen, *not* H_2) at a temperature of about 20 K. (A light-year is the distance light travels in vacuum in one year and is equal to 9.46×10^{15} m.) (a) Estimate the mean free path for a hydrogen atom in a dark nebula. The radius of a hydrogen atom is 5.0×10^{-11} m. (b) Estimate the rms speed of a hydrogen atom and the mean free time (the average time between collisions for a given atom). Based on this result, do you think that atomic collisions, such as those leading to H_2 molecule formation, are very important in determining the composition of the nebula? (c) Estimate the pressure inside a dark nebula. (d) Compare the rms speed of a hydrogen atom to the escape speed at the surface of the nebula (assumed spherical). If the space around the nebula were a vacuum, would such a cloud be stable or would it tend to evaporate? (e) The stability of dark nebulae is explained by the presence of the *interstellar medium* (ISM), an even thinner gas that permeates space and in which the dark nebulae are embedded. Show that for dark nebulae to be in equilibrium with the ISM, the numbers of atoms per volume (N/V) and the temperatures (T) of dark nebulae and the ISM must be related by

$$\frac{(N/V)_{nebula}}{(N/V)_{ISM}} = \frac{T_{ISM}}{T_{nebula}}$$

(f) In the vicinity of the sun, the ISM contains about 1 hydrogen atom per 200 cm³. Estimate the temperature of the ISM in the vicinity of the sun. Compare to the temperature of the sun's surface, about 5800 K. Would a spacecraft coasting through interstellar space burn up? Why or why not?

Figure **P18.91**

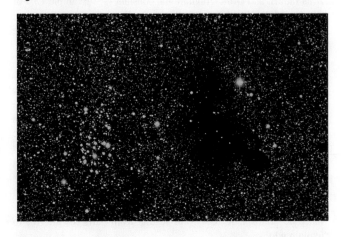

18.92 ··· **CALC Earth's Atmosphere.** In the *troposphere,* the part of the atmosphere that extends from earth's surface to an altitude of about 11 km, the temperature is not uniform but decreases with increasing elevation. (a) Show that if the temperature variation is approximated by the linear relationship

$$T = T_0 - \alpha y$$

where T_0 is the temperature at the earth's surface and T is the temperature at height y, the pressure p at height y is given by

$$\ln\left(\frac{p}{p_0}\right) = \frac{Mg}{R\alpha}\ln\left(\frac{T_0 - \alpha y}{T_0}\right)$$

where p_0 is the pressure at the earth's surface and M is the molar mass for air. The coefficient α is called the lapse rate of temperature. It varies with atmospheric conditions, but an average value is about 0.6 C°/100 m. (b) Show that the above result reduces to the result of Example 18.4 (Section 18.1) in the limit that $\alpha \to 0$. (c) With $\alpha = 0.6$ C°/100 m, calculate p for $y = 8863$ m and compare your answer to the result of Example 18.4. Take $T_0 = 288$ K and $p_0 = 1.00$ atm.

18.93 ••• In Example 18.7 (Section 18.3) we saw that $v_{\text{rms}} > v_{\text{av}}$. It is not difficult to show that this is *always* the case. (The only exception is when the particles have the same speed, in which case $v_{\text{rms}} = v_{\text{av}}$.) (a) For two particles with speeds v_1 and v_2, show that $v_{\text{rms}} \geq v_{\text{av}}$, regardless of the numerical values of v_1 and v_2. Then show that $v_{\text{rms}} > v_{\text{av}}$ if $v_1 \neq v_2$. (b) Suppose that for a collection of N particles you know that $v_{\text{rms}} > v_{\text{av}}$. Another particle, with speed u, is added to the collection of particles. If the new rms and average speeds are denoted as v'_{rms} and v'_{av}, show that

$$v'_{\text{rms}} = \sqrt{\frac{Nv_{\text{rms}}^2 + u^2}{N+1}} \quad \text{and} \quad v'_{\text{av}} = \frac{Nv_{\text{av}} + u}{N+1}$$

(c) Use the expressions in part (b) to show that $v'_{\text{rms}} > v'_{\text{av}}$ regardless of the numerical value of u. (d) Explain why your results for (a) and (c) together show that $v_{\text{rms}} > v_{\text{av}}$ for any collection of particles if the particles do not all have the same speed.

Answers

Chapter Opening Question ?

From Eq. (18.19), the root-mean-square speed of a gas molecule is proportional to the square root of the absolute temperature T. The temperature range we're considering is from $(25 + 273.15)$ K = 298 K to $(100 + 273.15)$ K = 373 K. Hence the speeds increase by a factor of $\sqrt{(373\text{ K})/(298\text{ K})} = 1.12$; that is, there is a 12% increase. While 100°C feels far warmer than 25°C, the difference in molecular speeds is relatively small.

Test Your Understanding Questions

18.1 Answer: (ii) and (iii) (tie), (i) and (v) (tie), (iv) We can rewrite the ideal-gas equation, Eq. (18.3), as $n = pV/RT$. This tells us that the number of moles n is proportional to the pressure and volume and inversely proportional to the absolute temperature. Hence, compared to (i), the number of moles in each case is (ii) $(2)(1)/(1) = 2$ times as much, (iii) $(1)(2)/(1) = 2$ times as much, (iv) $(1)(1)/(2) = \frac{1}{2}$ as much, and (v) $(2)(1)/(2) = 1$ time as much (that is, equal).

18.2 Answer: (vi) The value of r_0 determines the equilibrium separation of the molecules in the solid phase, so doubling r_0 means that the separation doubles as well. Hence a solid cube of this compound might grow from 1 cm on a side to 2 cm on a side. The volume would then be $2^3 = 8$ times larger, and the density (mass divided by volume) would be $\frac{1}{8}$ as great.

18.3 Answers: (a) (iv), (ii), (iii), (i); (b) (iii) and (iv) (tie), (i) and (ii) (tie) (a) Equation (18.19) tells us that $v_{\text{rms}} = \sqrt{3RT/M}$, so the rms speed is proportional to the square root of the ratio of absolute temperature T to molar mass M. Compared to (i) oxygen at 300 K, v_{rms} in the other cases is (ii) $\sqrt{(32.0\text{ g/mol})/(28.0\text{ g/mol})} = 1.07$ times faster, (iii) $\sqrt{(330\text{ K})/(300\text{ K})} = 1.05$ times faster, and (iv) $\sqrt{(330\text{ K})(32.0\text{ g/mol})/(300\text{ K})(28.0\text{ g/mol})} = 1.12$ times faster. (b) From Eq. (18.16), the average translational kinetic energy per molecule is $\frac{1}{2}m(v^2)_{\text{av}} = \frac{3}{2}kT$, which is directly proportional to T and independent of M. We have $T = 300$ K for cases (i) and (ii) and $T = 330$ K for cases (iii) and (iv), so $\frac{1}{2}m(v^2)_{\text{av}}$ has equal values for cases (iii) and (iv) and equal (but smaller) values for cases (i) and (ii).

18.4 Answers: no, near the beginning Adding a small amount of heat dQ to the gas changes the temperature by dT, where $dQ = nC_V dT$ from Eq. (18.24). Figure 18.19 shows that C_V for H_2 varies with temperature between 25 K and 500 K, so a given amount of heat gives rise to different amounts of temperature change during the process. Hence the temperature will *not* increase at a constant rate. The temperature change $dT = dQ/nC_V$ is inversely proportional to C_V, so the temperature increases most rapidly at the beginning of the process when the temperature is lowest and C_V is smallest (see Fig. 18.19).

18.5 Answer: (ii) Figure 18.23b shows that the *fraction* of molecules with speeds between v_1 and v_2 equals the area under the curve of $f(v)$ versus v from $v = v_1$ to $v = v_2$. This is equal to the integral $\int_{v_1}^{v_2} f(v)\,dv$, which in turn is equal to the difference between the integrals $\int_0^{v_2} f(v)\,dv$ (the fraction of molecules with speeds from 0 to v_2) and $\int_0^{v_1} f(v)\,dv$ (the fraction of molecules with speeds from 0 to the slower speed v_1). The *number* of molecules with speeds from v_1 to v_2 equals the fraction of molecules in this speed range multiplied by N, the total number of molecules.

18.6 Answers: no, yes The triple-point pressure of water from Table 18.3 is 6.10×10^2 Pa. The present-day pressure on Mars is just less than this value, corresponding to the line labeled p_s in Fig. 18.24. Hence liquid water cannot exist on the present-day Martian surface, and there are no rivers or lakes. Planetary scientists conclude that liquid water could have and almost certainly did exist on Mars in the past, when the atmosphere was thicker.

Bridging Problem

Answers: **(a)** 102 km **(b)** yes

19 THE FIRST LAW OF THERMODYNAMICS

? A steam locomotive operates using the first law of thermodynamics: Water is heated and boils, and the expanding steam does work to propel the locomotive. Would it be possible for the steam to propel the locomotive by doing work as it *condenses*?

Every time you drive a car, turn on an air conditioner, or cook a meal, you reap the practical benefits of *thermodynamics,* the study of relationships involving heat, mechanical work, and other aspects of energy and energy transfer. For example, in a car engine heat is generated by the chemical reaction of oxygen and vaporized gasoline in the engine's cylinders. The heated gas pushes on the pistons within the cylinders, doing mechanical work that is used to propel the car. This is an example of a *thermodynamic process.*

The first law of thermodynamics, central to the understanding of such processes, is an extension of the principle of conservation of energy. It broadens this principle to include energy exchange by both heat transfer and mechanical work and introduces the concept of the *internal energy* of a system. Conservation of energy plays a vital role in every area of physical science, and the first law has extremely broad usefulness. To state energy relationships precisely, we need the concept of a *thermodynamic system.* We'll discuss *heat* and *work* as two means of transferring energy into or out of such a system.

19.1 Thermodynamic Systems

We have studied energy transfer through mechanical work (Chapter 6) and through heat transfer (Chapters 17 and 18). Now we are ready to combine and generalize these principles.

We always talk about energy transfer to or from some specific *system.* The system might be a mechanical device, a biological organism, or a specified quantity of material, such as the refrigerant in an air conditioner or steam expanding in a turbine. In general, a **thermodynamic system** is any collection of objects that is convenient to regard as a unit, and that may have the potential to exchange energy with its surroundings. A familiar example is a quantity of popcorn kernels in a pot with a lid. When the pot is placed on a stove, energy is added to the popcorn

19.1 The popcorn in the pot is a thermodynamic system. In the thermodynamic process shown here, heat is added to the system, and the system does work on its surroundings to lift the lid of the pot.

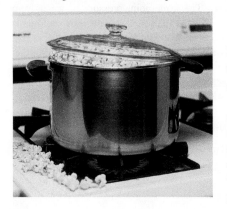

by conduction of heat. As the popcorn pops and expands, it does work as it exerts an upward force on the lid and moves it through a displacement (Fig. 19.1). The *state* of the popcorn changes in this process, since the volume, temperature, and pressure of the popcorn all change as it pops. A process such as this one, in which there are changes in the state of a thermodynamic system, is called a **thermodynamic process.**

In mechanics we used the concept of *system* with free-body diagrams and with conservation of energy and momentum. For *thermodynamic* systems, as for all others, it is essential to define clearly at the start exactly what is and is not included in the system. Only then can we describe unambiguously the energy transfers into and out of that system. For instance, in our popcorn example we defined the system to include the popcorn but not the pot, lid, or stove.

Thermodynamics has its roots in many practical problems other than popping popcorn (Fig. 19.2). The gasoline engine in an automobile, the jet engines in an airplane, and the rocket engines in a launch vehicle use the heat of combustion of their fuel to perform mechanical work in propelling the vehicle. Muscle tissue in living organisms metabolizes chemical energy in food and performs mechanical work on the organism's surroundings. A steam engine or steam turbine uses the heat of combustion of coal or other fuel to perform mechanical work such as driving an electric generator or pulling a train.

19.2 (a) A rocket engine uses the heat of combustion of its fuel to do work propelling the launch vehicle. (b) Humans and other biological organisms are more complicated systems than we can analyze fully in this book, but the same basic principles of thermodynamics apply to them.

(a)   (b)

Signs for Heat and Work in Thermodynamics

We describe the energy relationships in any thermodynamic process in terms of the quantity of heat Q added *to* the system and the work W done *by* the system. Both Q and W may be positive, negative, or zero (Fig. 19.3). A positive value of Q represents heat flow *into* the system, with a corresponding input of energy to it; negative Q represents heat flow *out of* the system. A positive value of W represents work done *by* the system against its surroundings, such as work done by an expanding gas, and hence corresponds to energy *leaving* the system. Negative W, such as work done during compression of a gas in which work is done *on the gas* by its surroundings, represents energy *entering* the system. We will use these conventions consistently in the examples in this chapter and the next.

CAUTION **Be careful with the sign of work** W Note that our sign rule for work is *opposite* to the one we used in mechanics, in which we always spoke of the work done by the forces acting *on* a body. In thermodynamics it is usually more convenient to call W the work done *by* the system so that when a system expands, the pressure, volume change, and work are all positive. Take care to use the sign rules for work and heat consistently!

19.3 A thermodynamic system may exchange energy with its surroundings (environment) by means of heat, work, or both. Note the sign conventions for Q and W.

Test Your Understanding of Section 19.1 In Example 17.8 (Section 17.6), what is the sign of Q for the coffee? For the aluminum cup? If a block slides along a horizontal surface with friction, what is the sign of W for the block?   ∣

19.2 Work Done During Volume Changes

A simple but common example of a thermodynamic system is a quantity of gas enclosed in a cylinder with a movable piston. Internal-combustion engines, steam engines, and compressors in refrigerators and air conditioners all use some version of such a system. In the next several sections we will use the gas-in-cylinder system to explore several kinds of processes involving energy transformations.

We'll use a microscopic viewpoint, based on the kinetic and potential energies of individual molecules in a material, to develop intuition about thermodynamic quantities. But it is important to understand that the central principles of thermodynamics can be treated in a completely *macroscopic* way, without reference to microscopic models. Indeed, part of the great power and generality of thermodynamics is that it does *not* depend on details of the structure of matter.

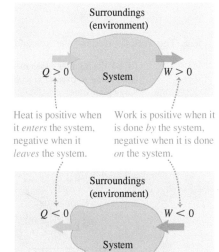

Surroundings (environment)

$Q > 0$ System $W > 0$

Heat is positive when it *enters* the system, negative when it *leaves* the system.

Work is positive when it is done *by* the system, negative when it is done *on* the system.

Surroundings (environment)

$Q < 0$ $W < 0$

System

19.4 A molecule striking a piston **(a)** does positive work if the piston is moving away from the molecule and **(b)** does negative work if the piston is moving toward the molecule. Hence a gas does positive work when it expands as in **(a)** but does negative work when it compresses as in **(b)**.

(a)

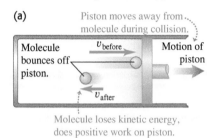

Piston moves away from molecule during collision.

Molecule bounces off piston.

v_{before}

Motion of piston

v_{after}

Molecule loses kinetic energy, does positive work on piston.

(b)

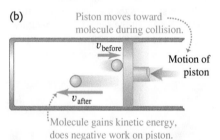

Piston moves toward molecule during collision.

v_{before}

Motion of piston

v_{after}

Molecule gains kinetic energy, does negative work on piston.

19.5 The infinitesimal work done by the system during the small expansion dx is $dW = pA\,dx$.

System

dx

pA

A

Force that system exerts on piston

First we consider the *work* done by the system during a volume change. When a gas expands, it pushes outward on its boundary surfaces as they move outward. Hence an expanding gas always does positive work. The same thing is true of any solid or fluid material that expands under pressure, such as the popcorn in Fig. 19.1.

We can understand the work done by a gas in a volume change by considering the molecules that make up the gas. When one such molecule collides with a stationary surface, it exerts a momentary force on the wall but does no work because the wall does not move. But if the surface is moving, like a piston in a gasoline engine, the molecule *does* do work on the surface during the collision. If the piston in Fig. 19.4a moves to the right, so that the volume of the gas increases, the molecules that strike the piston exert a force through a distance and do *positive* work on the piston. If the piston moves toward the left as in Fig. 19.4b, so the volume of the gas decreases, then positive work is done *on* the molecule during the collision. Hence the gas molecules do *negative* work on the piston.

Figure 19.5 shows a system whose volume can change (a gas, liquid, or solid) in a cylinder with a movable piston. Suppose that the cylinder has cross-sectional area A and that the pressure exerted by the system at the piston face is p. The total force F exerted by the system on the piston is $F = pA$. When the piston moves out an infinitesimal distance dx, the work dW done by this force is

$$dW = F\,dx = pA\,dx$$

But

$$A\,dx = dV$$

where dV is the infinitesimal change of volume of the system. Thus we can express the work done by the system in this infinitesimal volume change as

$$dW = p\,dV \qquad (19.1)$$

In a finite change of volume from V_1 to V_2,

$$W = \int_{V_1}^{V_2} p\,dV \qquad \text{(work done in a volume change)} \qquad (19.2)$$

In general, the pressure of the system may vary during the volume change. For example, this is the case in the cylinders of an automobile engine as the pistons move back and forth. To evaluate the integral in Eq. (19.2), we have to know how the pressure varies as a function of volume. We can represent this relationship as a graph of p as a function of V (a pV-diagram, described at the end of Section 18.1). Figure 19.6 a shows a simple example. In this figure, Eq. (19.2) is represented

19.6 The work done equals the area under the curve on a pV-diagram.

(a) pV-diagram for a system undergoing an expansion with varying pressure

p

p_1 · · 1

p_2 · · · · · · · · · 2

Work = Area
$= \int_{V_1}^{V_2} p\,dV > 0$

O V_1 V_2 V

(b) pV-diagram for a system undergoing a compression with varying pressure

p

p_2 · · 2

Cross-hatching indicates negative work.

p_1 · · · · · · · · · 1

Work = Area
$= \int_{V_1}^{V_2} p\,dV < 0$

O V_2 V_1 V

(c) pV-diagram for a system undergoing an expansion with constant pressure

p

p · · 1 ————→ 2

Work = Area =
$p(V_2 - V_1) > 0$

O V_1 V_2 V

graphically as the *area* under the curve of p versus V between the limits V_1 and V_2. (In Section 6.3 we used a similar interpretation of the work done by a force F as the area under the curve of F versus x between the limits x_1 and x_2.)

According to the rule we stated in Section 19.1, work is *positive* when a system *expands*. In an expansion from state 1 to state 2 in Fig. 19.6a, the area under the curve and the work are positive. A *compression* from 1 to 2 in Fig. 19.6b gives a *negative* area; when a system is compressed, its volume decreases and it does *negative* work on its surroundings (see also Fig. 19.4b).

CAUTION **Be careful with subscripts 1 and 2** When using Eq. (19.2), always remember that V_1 is the *initial* volume and V_2 is the *final* volume. That's why the labels 1 and 2 are reversed in Fig. 19.6b compared to Fig. 19.6a, even though both processes move between the same two thermodynamic states.

If the pressure p remains constant while the volume changes from V_1 to V_2 (Fig. 19.6c), the work done by the system is

$$W = p(V_2 - V_1) \qquad \text{(work done in a volume change at constant pressure)} \qquad (19.3)$$

MP
ActivPhysics 8.5: Work Done By a Gas

In any process in which the volume is *constant*, the system does no work because there is no displacement.

Example 19.1 **Isothermal expansion of an ideal gas**

As an ideal gas undergoes an *isothermal* (constant-temperature) expansion at temperature T, its volume changes from V_1 to V_2. How much work does the gas do?

SOLUTION

IDENTIFY and SET UP: The ideal-gas equation, Eq. (18.3), tells us that if the temperature T of n moles of an ideal gas is constant, the quantity $pV = nRT$ is also constant: p and V are inversely related. If V changes, p changes as well, so we *cannot* use Eq. (19.3) to calculate the work done. Instead we must use Eq. (19.2). To evaluate the integral in Eq. (19.2) we must know p as a function of V; for this we use Eq. (18.3).

EXECUTE: From Eq. (18.3),

$$p = \frac{nRT}{V}$$

We substitute this into the integral of Eq. (19.2), take the constant factor nRT outside, and evaluate the integral:

$$W = \int_{V_1}^{V_2} p \, dV$$

$$= nRT \int_{V_1}^{V_2} \frac{dV}{V} = nRT \ln\frac{V_2}{V_1} \quad \text{(ideal gas, isothermal process)}$$

We can rewrite this expression for W in terms of p_1 and p_2. Because $pV = nRT$ is constant,

$$p_1 V_1 = p_2 V_2 \qquad \text{or} \qquad \frac{V_2}{V_1} = \frac{p_1}{p_2}$$

so

$$W = nRT \ln\frac{p_1}{p_2} \quad \text{(ideal gas, isothermal process)}$$

EVALUATE: We check our result by noting that in an expansion $V_2 > V_1$ and the ratio V_2/V_1 is greater than 1. The logarithm of a number greater than 1 is positive, so $W > 0$, as it should be. As an additional check, look at our second expression for W: In an isothermal expansion the volume increases and the pressure drops, so $p_2 < p_1$, the ratio $p_1/p_2 > 1$, and $W = nRT \ln(p_1/p_2)$ is again positive.

These results also apply to an isothermal *compression* of a gas, for which $V_2 < V_1$ and $p_2 > p_1$.

Test Your Understanding of Section 19.2 A quantity of ideal gas undergoes an expansion that increases its volume from V_1 to $V_2 = 2V_1$. The final pressure of the gas is p_2. Does the gas do more work on its surroundings if the expansion is at constant *pressure* or at constant *temperature*? (i) constant pressure; (ii) constant temperature; (iii) the same amount of work is done in both cases; (iv) not enough information is given to decide.

MP

19.3 Paths Between Thermodynamic States

We've seen that if a thermodynamic process involves a change in volume, the system undergoing the process does work (either positive or negative) on its surroundings. Heat also flows into or out of the system during the process if there is a temperature difference between the system and its surroundings. Let's now examine how the work done by and the heat added to the system during a thermodynamic process depend on the details of how the process takes place.

Work Done in a Thermodynamic Process

When a thermodynamic system changes from an initial state to a final state, it passes through a series of intermediate states. We call this series of states a **path.** There are always infinitely many different possibilities for these intermediate states. When they are all equilibrium states, the path can be plotted on a pV-diagram (Fig. 19.7a). Point 1 represents an initial state with pressure p_1 and volume V_1, and point 2 represents a final state with pressure p_2 and volume V_2. To pass from state 1 to state 2, we could keep the pressure constant at p_1 while the system expands to volume V_2 (point 3 in Fig. 19.7b), then reduce the pressure to p_2 (probably by decreasing the temperature) while keeping the volume constant at V_2 (to point 2 on the diagram). The work done by the system during this process is the area under the line $1 \rightarrow 3$; no work is done during the constant-volume process $3 \rightarrow 2$. Or the system might traverse the path $1 \rightarrow 4 \rightarrow 2$ (Fig. 19.7c); in that case the work is the area under the line $4 \rightarrow 2$, since no work is done during the constant-volume process $1 \rightarrow 4$. The smooth curve from 1 to 2 is another possibility (Fig. 19.7d), and the work for this path is different from that for either of the other paths.

We conclude that *the work done by the system depends not only on the initial and final states, but also on the intermediate states—that is, on the path.* Furthermore, we can take the system through a series of states forming a closed loop, such as $1 \rightarrow 3 \rightarrow 2 \rightarrow 4 \rightarrow 1$. In this case the final state is the same as the initial state, but the total work done by the system is *not* zero. (In fact, it is represented on the graph by the area enclosed by the loop; can you prove that? See Exercise 19.7.) It follows that it doesn't make sense to talk about the amount of work *contained in* a system. In a particular state, a system may have definite values of the state coordinates p, V, and T, but it wouldn't make sense to say that it has a definite value of W.

Heat Added in a Thermodynamic Process

Like work, the *heat* added to a thermodynamic system when it undergoes a change of state depends on the path from the initial state to the final state. Here's an example. Suppose we want to change the volume of a certain quantity of an ideal gas from 2.0 L to 5.0 L while keeping the temperature constant at $T = 300$ K. Figure 19.8 shows two different ways in which we can do this. In Fig. 19.8a the gas is contained in a cylinder with a piston, with an initial volume of 2.0 L. We let the gas expand slowly, supplying heat from the electric heater to keep the temperature at 300 K. After expanding in this slow, controlled, isothermal manner, the gas reaches its final volume of 5.0 L; it absorbs a definite amount of heat in the process.

Figure 19.8b shows a different process leading to the same final state. The container is surrounded by insulating walls and is divided by a thin, breakable partition into two compartments. The lower part has volume 2.0 L and the upper part has volume 3.0 L. In the lower compartment we place the same amount of the same gas as in Fig. 19.8a, again at $T = 300$ K. The initial state is the same as before. Now we break the partition; the gas undergoes a rapid, uncontrolled expansion, with no heat passing through the insulating walls. The final volume is 5.0 L, the same as in Fig. 19.8a. The gas does no work during this expansion

19.7 The work done by a system during a transition between two states depends on the path chosen.

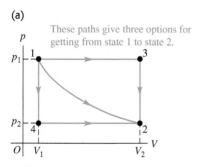

(a)

These paths give three options for getting from state 1 to state 2.

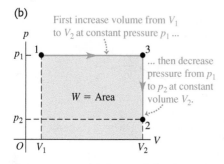

(b)

First increase volume from V_1 to V_2 at constant pressure p_1 ...

... then decrease pressure from p_1 to p_2 at constant volume V_2.

$W = $ Area

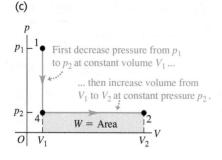

(c)

First decrease pressure from p_1 to p_2 at constant volume V_1 ...

... then increase volume from V_1 to V_2 at constant pressure p_2.

$W = $ Area

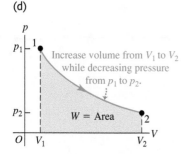

(d)

Increase volume from V_1 to V_2 while decreasing pressure from p_1 to p_2.

$W = $ Area

because it doesn't push against anything that moves. This uncontrolled expansion of a gas into vacuum is called a **free expansion;** we will discuss it further in Section 19.6.

Experiments have shown that when an ideal gas undergoes a free expansion, there is no temperature change. Therefore the final state of the gas is the same as in Fig. 19.8a. The intermediate states (pressures and volumes) during the transition from state 1 to state 2 are entirely different in the two cases; Figs. 19.8a and 19.8b represent *two different paths* connecting the *same states* 1 and 2. For the path in Fig. 19.8b, *no* heat is transferred into the system, and the system does no work. Like work, *heat depends not only on the initial and final states but also on the path.*

Because of this path dependence, it would not make sense to say that a system "contains" a certain quantity of heat. To see this, suppose we assign an arbitrary value to the "heat in a body" in some reference state. Then presumably the "heat in the body" in some other state would equal the heat in the reference state plus the heat added when the body goes to the second state. But that's ambiguous, as we have just seen; the heat added depends on the *path* we take from the reference state to the second state. We are forced to conclude that there is *no* consistent way to define "heat in a body"; it is not a useful concept.

While it doesn't make sense to talk about "work in a body" or "heat in a body," it *does* make sense to speak of the amount of *internal energy* in a body. This important concept is our next topic.

Test Your Understanding of Section 19.3 The system described in Fig. 19.7a undergoes four different thermodynamic processes. Each process is represented in a *pV*-diagram as a straight line from the initial state to the final state. (These processes are different from those shown in the *pV*-diagrams of Fig. 19.7.) Rank the processes in order of the amount of work done by the system, from the most positive to the most negative. (i) 1 → 2; (ii) 2 → 1; (iii) 3 → 4; (iv) 4 → 3.

19.4 Internal Energy and the First Law of Thermodynamics

Internal energy is one of the most important concepts in thermodynamics. In Section 7.3, when we discussed energy changes for a body sliding with friction, we stated that warming a body increased its internal energy and that cooling the body decreased its internal energy. But what *is* internal energy? We can look at it in various ways; let's start with one based on the ideas of mechanics. Matter consists of atoms and molecules, and these are made up of particles having kinetic and potential energies. We *tentatively* define the **internal energy** of a system as the sum of the kinetic energies of all of its constituent particles, plus the sum of all the potential energies of interaction among these particles.

CAUTION **Is it internal?** Note that internal energy does *not* include potential energy arising from the interaction between the system and its surroundings. If the system is a glass of water, placing it on a high shelf increases the gravitational potential energy arising from the interaction between the glass and the earth. But this has no effect on the interaction between the molecules of the water, and so the internal energy of the water does not change.

We use the symbol U for internal energy. (We used this same symbol in our study of mechanics to represent potential energy. You may have to remind yourself occasionally that U has a different meaning in thermodynamics.) During a change of state of the system, the internal energy may change from an initial value U_1 to a final value U_2. We denote the change in internal energy as $\Delta U = U_2 - U_1$.

19.8 (a) Slow, controlled isothermal expansion of a gas from an initial state 1 to a final state 2 with the same temperature but lower pressure. (b) Rapid, uncontrolled expansion of the same gas starting at the same state 1 and ending at the same state 2.

(a) System does work on piston; hot plate adds heat to system ($W > 0$ and $Q > 0$).

(b) System does no work; no heat enters or leaves system ($W = 0$ and $Q = 0$).

ActivPhysics 8.6: Heat, Internal Energy, and First Law of Thermodynamics

19.9 In a thermodynamic process, the internal energy U of a system may (a) increase ($\Delta U > 0$), (b) decrease ($\Delta U < 0$), or (c) remain the same ($\Delta U = 0$).

(a) More heat is added to system than system does work: Internal energy of system increases.

Surroundings (environment)

$Q = 150\,\text{J}$ $W = 100\,\text{J}$

System

$\Delta U = Q - W = +50\,\text{J}$

(b) More heat flows out of system than work is done: Internal energy of system decreases.

Surroundings (environment)

$Q = -150\,\text{J}$ $W = -100\,\text{J}$

System

$\Delta U = Q - W = -50\,\text{J}$

(c) Heat added to system equals work done by system: Internal energy of system unchanged.

Surroundings (environment)

$Q = 150\,\text{J}$ $W = 150\,\text{J}$

System

$\Delta U = Q - W = 0$

Application The First Law of Exercise Thermodynamics
Your body is a thermodynamic system. When you exercise, your body does work (such as the work done to lift your body as a whole in a push-up). Hence $W > 0$. Your body also warms up during exercise; by perspiration and other means the body rids itself of this heat, so $Q < 0$. Since Q is negative and W is positive, $\Delta U = Q - W < 0$ and the body's internal energy decreases. That's why exercise helps you lose weight: It uses up some of the internal energy stored in your body in the form of fat.

When we add a quantity of heat Q to a system and the system does no work during the process (so $W = 0$), the internal energy increases by an amount equal to Q; that is, $\Delta U = Q$. When a system does work W by expanding against its surroundings and no heat is added during the process, energy leaves the system and the internal energy decreases: W is positive, Q is zero, and $\Delta U = -W$. When *both* heat transfer and work occur, the *total* change in internal energy is

$$U_2 - U_1 = \Delta U = Q - W \quad \text{(first law of thermodynamics)} \quad (19.4)$$

We can rearrange this to the form

$$Q = \Delta U + W \quad (19.5)$$

The message of Eq. (19.5) is that in general, when heat Q is added to a system, some of this added energy remains within the system, changing its internal energy by an amount ΔU; the remainder leaves the system again as the system does work W against its surroundings. Because W and Q may be positive, negative, or zero, ΔU can be positive, negative, or zero for different processes (Fig. 19.9).

Equation (19.4) or (19.5) is the **first law of thermodynamics.** It is a generalization of the principle of conservation of energy to include energy transfer through heat as well as mechanical work. As you will see in later chapters, this principle can be extended to ever-broader classes of phenomena by identifying additional forms of energy and energy transfer. In every situation in which it seems that the total energy in all known forms is not conserved, it has been possible to identify a new form of energy such that the total energy, including the new form, *is* conserved. There is energy associated with electric fields, with magnetic fields, and, according to the theory of relativity, even with mass itself.

Understanding the First Law of Thermodynamics

At the beginning of this discussion we tentatively defined internal energy in terms of microscopic kinetic and potential energies. This has drawbacks, however. Actually *calculating* internal energy in this way for any real system would be hopelessly complicated. Furthermore, this definition isn't an *operational* one because it doesn't describe how to determine internal energy from physical quantities that we can measure directly.

So let's look at internal energy in another way. Starting over, we define the *change* in internal energy ΔU during any change of a system as the quantity given by Eq. (19.4), $\Delta U = Q - W$. This *is* an operational definition because we can measure Q and W. It does not define U itself, only ΔU. This is not a shortcoming because we can *define* the internal energy of a system to have a specified value in some reference state, and then use Eq. (19.4) to define the internal energy in any other state. This is analogous to our treatment of potential energy in Chapter 7, in which we arbitrarily defined the potential energy of a mechanical system to be zero at a certain position.

This new definition trades one difficulty for another. If we define ΔU by Eq. (19.4), then when the system goes from state 1 to state 2 by two different paths, how do we know that ΔU is the same for the two paths? We have already seen that Q and W are, in general, *not* the same for different paths. If ΔU, which equals $Q - W$, is also path dependent, then ΔU is ambiguous. If so, the concept of internal energy of a system is subject to the same criticism as the erroneous concept of quantity of heat in a system, as we discussed at the end of Section 19.3.

The only way to answer this question is through *experiment*. For various materials we measure Q and W for various changes of state and various paths to learn whether ΔU is or is not path dependent. The results of many such investigations are clear and unambiguous: While Q and W depend on the path, $\Delta U = Q - W$ *is independent of path. The change in internal energy of a system during any thermodynamic process depends only on the initial and final states, not on the path leading from one to the other.*

Experiment, then, is the ultimate justification for believing that a thermodynamic system in a specific state has a unique internal energy that depends only on that state. An equivalent statement is that the internal energy U of a system is a function of the state coordinates p, V, and T (actually, any two of these, since the three variables are related by the equation of state).

To say that the first law of thermodynamics, given by Eq. (19.4) or (19.5), represents conservation of energy for thermodynamic processes is correct, as far as it goes. But an important *additional* aspect of the first law is the fact that internal energy depends only on the state of a system (Fig. 19.10). In changes of state, the change in internal energy is independent of the path.

All this may seem a little abstract if you are satisfied to think of internal energy as microscopic mechanical energy. There's nothing wrong with that view, and we will make use of it at various times during our discussion. But in the interest of precise *operational* definitions, internal energy, like heat, can and must be defined in a way that is independent of the detailed microscopic structure of the material.

Cyclic Processes and Isolated Systems

Two special cases of the first law of thermodynamics are worth mentioning. A process that eventually returns a system to its initial state is called a *cyclic process*. For such a process, the final state is the same as the initial state, and so the *total* internal energy change must be zero. Then

$$U_2 = U_1 \quad \text{and} \quad Q = W$$

If a net quantity of work W is done by the system during this process, an equal amount of energy must have flowed into the system as heat Q. But there is no reason either Q or W individually has to be zero (Fig. 19.11).

Another special case occurs in an *isolated system*, one that does no work on its surroundings and has no heat flow to or from its surroundings. For any process taking place in an isolated system,

$$W = Q = 0$$

and therefore

$$U_2 = U_1 = \Delta U = 0$$

In other words, *the internal energy of an isolated system is constant.*

19.10 The internal energy of a cup of coffee depends on just its thermodynamic state—how much water and ground coffee it contains, and what its temperature is. It does not depend on the history of how the coffee was prepared—that is, the thermodynamic path that led to its current state.

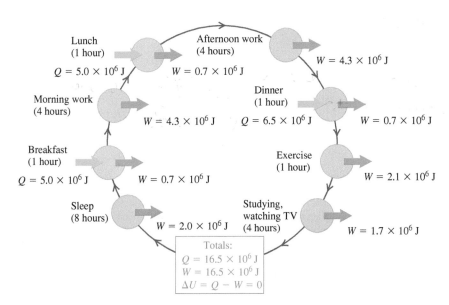

Lunch
(1 hour)

Afternoon work
(4 hours)

$Q = 5.0 \times 10^6$ J

$W = 0.7 \times 10^6$ J

$W = 4.3 \times 10^6$ J

Morning work
(4 hours)

Dinner
(1 hour)

$W = 4.3 \times 10^6$ J

$Q = 6.5 \times 10^6$ J

$W = 0.7 \times 10^6$ J

Breakfast
(1 hour)

Exercise
(1 hour)

$Q = 5.0 \times 10^6$ J

$W = 0.7 \times 10^6$ J

$W = 2.1 \times 10^6$ J

Sleep
(8 hours)

Studying,
watching TV
(4 hours)

$W = 2.0 \times 10^6$ J

$W = 1.7 \times 10^6$ J

Totals:
$Q = 16.5 \times 10^6$ J
$W = 16.5 \times 10^6$ J
$\Delta U = Q - W = 0$

19.11 Every day, your body (a thermodynamic system) goes through a cyclic thermodynamic process like this one. Heat Q is added by metabolizing food, and your body does work W in breathing, walking, and other activities. If you return to the same state at the end of the day, $Q = W$ and the net change in your internal energy is zero.

Problem-Solving Strategy 19.1 The First Law of Thermodynamics

IDENTIFY *the relevant concepts:* The first law of thermodynamics is the statement of the law of conservation of energy in its most general form. You can apply it to *any* thermodynamic process in which the internal energy of a system changes, heat flows into or out of the system, and/or work is done by or on the system.

SET UP *the problem* using the following steps:
1. Define the thermodynamic system to be considered.
2. If the thermodynamic process has more than one step, identify the initial and final states for each step.
3. List the known and unknown quantities and identify the target variables.
4. Confirm that you have enough equations. You can apply the first law, $\Delta U = Q - W$, just once to each step in a thermodynamic process, so you will often need additional equations. These may include Eq. (19.2), $W = \int_{V_1}^{V_2} p \, dV$, which gives the work W done in a volume change, and the equation of state of the material that makes up the thermodynamic system (for an ideal gas, $pV = nRT$).

EXECUTE *the solution* as follows:
1. Be sure to use consistent units. If p is in Pa and V in m³, then W is in joules. If a heat capacity is given in terms of calories,

convert it to joules. When you use $n = m_{total}/M$ to relate total mass m_{total} to number of moles n, remember that if m_{total} is in kilograms, M must be in *kilograms* per mole; M is usually tabulated in *grams* per mole.
2. The internal energy change ΔU in any thermodynamic process or series of processes is independent of the path, whether the substance is an ideal gas or not. If you can calculate ΔU for *any* path between given initial and final states, you know ΔU for *every possible path* between those states; you can then relate the various energy quantities for any of those other paths.
3. In a process comprising several steps, tabulate Q, W, and ΔU for each step, with one line per step and with the Q's, W's, and ΔU's forming columns (see Example 19.4). You can apply the first law to each line, and you can add each column and apply the first law to the sums. Do you see why?
4. Using steps 1–3, solve for the target variables.

EVALUATE *your answer:* Check your results for reasonableness. Ensure that each of your answers has the correct algebraic sign. A positive Q means that heat flows *into* the system; a negative Q means that heat flows *out of* the system. A positive W means that work is done *by* the system on its environment; a negative W means that work is done *on* the system by its environment.

Example 19.2 Working off your dessert

You propose to climb several flights of stairs to work off the energy you took in by eating a 900-calorie hot fudge sundae. How high must you climb? Assume that your mass is 60.0 kg.

SOLUTION

IDENTIFY and SET UP: The thermodynamic system is your body. You climb the stairs to make the final state of the system the same as the initial state (no fatter, no leaner). There is therefore no net change in internal energy: $\Delta U = 0$. Eating the hot fudge sundae corresponds to a heat flow into your body, and you do work climbing the stairs. We can relate these quantities using the first law of thermodynamics. We are given that $Q = 900$ food calories (900 kcal) of heat flow into your body. The work you must do to raise your mass m a height h is $W = mgh$; our target variable is h.

EXECUTE: From the first law of thermodynamics, $\Delta U = 0 = Q - W$, so $W = mgh = Q$. Hence you must climb to height $h = Q/mg$. First convert units: $Q = (900 \text{ kcal})(4186 \text{ J}/1 \text{ kcal}) = 3.77 \times 10^6$ J. Then

$$h = \frac{Q}{mg} = \frac{3.77 \times 10^6 \text{ J}}{(60.0 \text{ kg})(9.80 \text{ m/s}^2)} = 6410 \text{ m}$$

EVALUATE: We have unrealistically assumed 100% efficiency in the conversion of food energy into mechanical work. You would in fact have to climb considerably *less* than 6140 m (about 21,000 ft).

Example 19.3 A cyclic process

Figure 19.12 shows a pV-diagram for a *cyclic* process in which the initial and final states of some thermodynamic system are the same. As shown, the state of the system starts at point a and proceeds counterclockwise in the pV-diagram to point b, then back to a; the total work is $W = -500$ J. (a) Why is the work negative? (b) Find the change in internal energy and the heat added during this process.

SOLUTION

IDENTIFY and SET UP: We must relate the change in internal energy, the heat added, and the work done in a thermodynamic process. Hence we can apply the first law of thermodynamics. The process is cyclic, and it has two steps: $a \rightarrow b$ via the lower curve in Fig. 19.12 and $b \rightarrow a$ via the upper curve. We are asked only about the *entire* cyclic process $a \rightarrow b \rightarrow a$.

19.12 The net work done by the system in the process *aba* is −500 J. What would it have been if the process had proceeded clockwise in this *pV*-diagram?

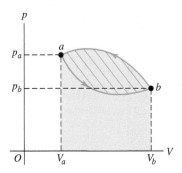

EXECUTE: (a) The work done in any step equals the area under the curve in the *pV*-diagram, with the area taken as positive if $V_2 > V_1$

and negative if $V_2 < V_1$; this rule yields the signs that result from the actual integrations in Eq. (19.2), $W = \int_{V_1}^{V_2} p\,dV$. The area under the lower curve $a \rightarrow b$ is therefore positive, but it is smaller than the absolute value of the (negative) area under the upper curve $b \rightarrow a$. Therefore the net area (the area enclosed by the path, shown with red stripes) and the net work W are negative. In other words, 500 J more work is done *on* the system than *by* the system in the complete process.

(b) In any cyclic process, $\Delta U = 0$, so $Q = W$. Here, that means $Q = -500$ J; that is, 500 J of heat flows *out of* the system.

EVALUATE:

In cyclic processes, the total work is positive if the process goes clockwise around the *pV*-diagram representing the cycle, and negative if the process goes counterclockwise (as here).

Example 19.4   **Comparing thermodynamic processes**

The *pV*-diagram of Fig. 19.13 shows a series of thermodynamic processes. In process *ab*, 150 J of heat is added to the system; in process *bd*, 600 J of heat is added. Find (a) the internal energy change in process *ab*; (b) the internal energy change in process *abd* (shown in light blue); and (c) the total heat added in process *acd* (shown in dark blue).

SOLUTION

IDENTIFY and SET UP: In each process we use $\Delta U = Q - W$ to determine the desired quantity. We are given $Q_{ab} = +150$ J and $Q_{bd} = +600$ J (both values are positive because heat is *added* to the system). Our target variables are (a) ΔU_{ab}, (b) ΔU_{abd}, and (c) Q_{acd}.

EXECUTE: (a) No volume change occurs during process *ab*, so the system does no work: $W_{ab} = 0$ and so $\Delta U_{ab} = Q_{ab} = 150$ J.

(b) Process *bd* is an expansion at constant pressure, so from Eq. (19.3),

$$W_{bd} = p(V_2 - V_1)$$
$$= (8.0 \times 10^4 \text{ Pa})(5.0 \times 10^{-3} \text{ m}^3 - 2.0 \times 10^{-3} \text{ m}^3)$$
$$= 240 \text{ J}$$

The total work for the two-step process *abd* is then

$$W_{abd} = W_{ab} + W_{bd} = 0 + 240 \text{ J} = 240 \text{ J}$$

and the total heat is

$$Q_{abd} = Q_{ab} + Q_{bd} = 150 \text{ J} + 600 \text{ J} = 750 \text{ J}$$

Applying Eq. (19.4) to *abd*, we then have

$$\Delta U_{abd} = Q_{abd} - W_{abd} = 750 \text{ J} - 240 \text{ J} = 510 \text{ J}$$

(c) Because ΔU is *independent of the path* from a to d, the internal energy change is the same for path *acd* as for path *abd*:

$$\Delta U_{acd} = \Delta U_{abd} = 510 \text{ J}$$

19.13 A *pV*-diagram showing the various thermodynamic processes.

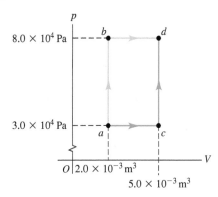

The total work for path *acd* is

$$W_{acd} = W_{ac} + W_{cd} = p(V_2 - V_1) + 0$$
$$= (3.0 \times 10^4 \text{ Pa})(5.0 \times 10^{-3} \text{ m}^3 - 2.0 \times 10^{-3} \text{ m}^3)$$
$$= 90 \text{ J}$$

Now we apply Eq. (19.5) to process *acd*:

$$Q_{acd} = \Delta U_{acd} + W_{acd} = 510 \text{ J} + 90 \text{ J} = 600 \text{ J}$$

We tabulate the quantities above:

Step	Q	W	$\Delta U = Q - W$	Step	Q	W	$\Delta U = Q - W$
ab	150 J	0 J	150 J	*ac*	?	90 J	?
bd	600 J	240 J	360 J	*cd*	?	0 J	?
abd	750 J	240 J	510 J	*acd*	600 J	90 J	510 J

EVALUATE: Be sure that you understand how each entry in the table above was determined. Although ΔU is the same (510 J) for *abd* and *acd*, W (240 J versus 90 J) and Q (750 J versus 600 J) are quite different. Although we couldn't find Q or ΔU for processes *ac* and *cd*, we could analyze the composite process *acd* by comparing it with process *abd*, which has the same initial and final states and for which we have more information.

Example 19.5 **Thermodynamics of boiling water**

One gram of water (1 cm^3) becomes 1671 cm^3 of steam when boiled at a constant pressure of 1 atm (1.013 × 10^5 Pa). The heat of vaporization at this pressure is L_v = 2.256 × 10^6 J/kg. Compute (a) the work done by the water when it vaporizes and (b) its increase in internal energy.

SOLUTION

IDENTIFY and SET UP: The heat added causes the system (water) to change phase from liquid to vapor. We can analyze this process using the first law of thermodynamics, which holds for thermodynamic processes of *all* kinds. The water is boiled at constant pressure, so we can use Eq. (19.3) to calculate the work W done by the vaporizing water as it expands. We are given the mass of water and the heat of vaporization, so we can use Eq. (17.20), $Q = mL_v$, to calculate the heat Q added to the water. We can then find the internal energy change using Eq. (19.4), $\Delta U = Q - W$.

EXECUTE: (a) From Eq. (19.3), the water does work

$$W = p(V_2 - V_1)$$
$$= (1.013 × 10^5 \text{ Pa})(1671 × 10^{-6} \text{ m}^3 - 1 × 10^{-6} \text{ m}^3)$$
$$= 169 \text{ J}$$

(b) From Eq. (17.20), the heat added to the water is

$$Q = mL_v = (10^{-3} \text{ kg})(2.256 × 10^6 \text{ J/kg}) = 2256 \text{ J}$$

Then from Eq. (19.4),

$$\Delta U = Q - W = 2256 \text{ J} - 169 \text{ J} = 2087 \text{ J}$$

EVALUATE: To vaporize 1 g of water, we must add 2256 J of heat, most of which (2087 J) remains in the system as an increase in internal energy. The remaining 169 J leaves the system as the system expands from liquid to vapor and does work against the surroundings. (The increase in internal energy is associated mostly with the attractive intermolecular forces that hold the molecules together in the liquid state. The associated potential energies are greater after work has been done to pull the molecules apart, forming the vapor state. It's like increasing gravitational potential energy by pulling an elevator farther from the center of the earth.)

Infinitesimal Changes of State

In the preceding examples the initial and final states differ by a finite amount. Later we will consider *infinitesimal* changes of state in which a small amount of heat dQ is added to the system, the system does a small amount of work dW, and its internal energy changes by an amount dU. For such a process we state the first law in differential form as

$$dU = dQ - dW \qquad \text{(first law of thermodynamics, infinitesimal process)} \qquad \text{(19.6)}$$

For the systems we will discuss, the work dW is given by $dW = p\,dV$, so we can also state the first law as

$$dU = dQ - p\,dV \qquad \text{(19.7)}$$

Test Your Understanding of Section 19.4 Rank the following thermodynamic processes according to the change in internal energy in each process, from most positive to most negative. (i) As you do 250 J of work on a system, it transfers 250 J of heat to its surroundings; (ii) as you do 250 J of work on a system, it absorbs 250 J of heat from its surroundings; (iii) as a system does 250 J of work on you, it transfers 250 J of heat to its surroundings; (iv) as a system does 250 J of work on you, it absorbs 250 J of heat from its surroundings.

ActivPhysics 8.4: State Variables and Ideal Gas Law

19.5 Kinds of Thermodynamic Processes

In this section we describe four specific kinds of thermodynamic processes that occur often in practical situations. These can be summarized briefly as "no heat transfer" or *adiabatic,* "constant volume" or *isochoric,* "constant pressure" or *isobaric,* and "constant temperature" or *isothermal.* For some of these processes we can use a simplified form of the first law of thermodynamics.

Adiabatic Process

An **adiabatic process** (pronounced "ay-dee-ah-*bat*-ic") is defined as one with no heat transfer into or out of a system; $Q = 0$. We can prevent heat flow either by surrounding the system with thermally insulating material or by carrying out the process so quickly that there is not enough time for appreciable heat flow. From the first law we find that for every adiabatic process,

$$U_2 - U_1 = \Delta U = -W \quad \text{(adiabatic process)} \quad \text{(19.8)}$$

When a system expands adiabatically, W is positive (the system does work on its surroundings), so ΔU is negative and the internal energy decreases. When a system is *compressed* adiabatically, W is negative (work is done on the system by its surroundings) and U increases. In many (but not all) systems an increase of internal energy is accompanied by a rise in temperature, and a decrease in internal energy by a drop in temperature (Fig. 19.14).

The compression stroke in an internal-combustion engine is an approximately adiabatic process. The temperature rises as the air–fuel mixture in the cylinder is compressed. The expansion of the burned fuel during the power stroke is also an approximately adiabatic expansion with a drop in temperature. In Section 19.8 we'll consider adiabatic processes in an ideal gas.

Isochoric Process

An **isochoric process** (pronounced "eye-so-*kor*-ic") is a *constant-volume* process. When the volume of a thermodynamic system is constant, it does no work on its surroundings. Then $W = 0$ and

$$U_2 - U_1 = \Delta U = Q \quad \text{(isochoric process)} \quad \text{(19.9)}$$

In an isochoric process, all the energy added as heat remains in the system as an increase in internal energy. Heating a gas in a closed constant-volume container is an example of an isochoric process. The processes *ab* and *cd* in Example 19.4 are also examples of isochoric processes. (Note that there are types of work that do not involve a volume change. For example, we can do work on a fluid by stirring it. In some literature, "isochoric" is used to mean that no work of any kind is done.)

Isobaric Process

An **isobaric process** (pronounced "eye-so-*bear*-ic") is a *constant-pressure* process. In general, none of the three quantities ΔU, Q, and W is zero in an isobaric process, but calculating W is easy nonetheless. From Eq. (19.3),

$$W = p(V_2 - V_1) \quad \text{(isobaric process)} \quad \text{(19.10)}$$

Example 19.5 concerns an isobaric process, boiling water at constant pressure (Fig. 19.15).

Isothermal Process

An **isothermal process** is a *constant-temperature* process. For a process to be isothermal, any heat flow into or out of the system must occur slowly enough that thermal equilibrium is maintained. In general, none of the quantities ΔU, Q, or W is zero in an isothermal process.

In some special cases the internal energy of a system depends *only* on its temperature, not on its pressure or volume. The most familiar system having this special property is an ideal gas, as we'll discuss in the next section. For such systems, if the temperature is constant, the internal energy is also constant; $\Delta U = 0$ and $Q = W$. That is, any energy entering the system as heat Q must leave it again as work W done by the system. Example 19.1, involving an ideal gas, is an example of an isothermal process in which U is also constant. For most systems other than ideal gases, the internal energy depends on pressure as well as temperature, so U may vary even when T is constant.

19.14 When the cork is popped on a bottle of champagne, the pressurized gases inside the bottle expand rapidly and do work on the outside air ($W > 0$). There is no time for the gases to exchange heat with their surroundings, so the expansion is adiabatic ($Q = 0$). Hence the internal energy of the expanding gases decreases ($\Delta U = -W < 0$) and their temperature drops. This makes water vapor condense and form a miniature cloud.

19.15 Most cooking involves isobaric processes. That's because the air pressure above a saucepan or frying pan, or inside a microwave oven, remains essentially constant while the food is being heated.

19.16 Four different processes for a constant amount of an ideal gas, all starting at state a. For the adiabatic process, $Q = 0$; for the isochoric process, $W = 0$; and for the isothermal process, $\Delta U = 0$. The temperature increases only during the isobaric expansion.

19.17 The partition is broken (or removed) to start the free expansion of gas into the vacuum region.

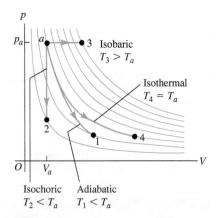

Figure 19.16 shows a pV-diagram for these four processes for a constant amount of an ideal gas. The path followed in an adiabatic process (a to 1) is called an **adiabat.** A vertical line (constant volume) is an **isochor,** a horizontal line (constant pressure) is an **isobar,** and a curve of constant temperature (shown as light blue lines in Fig. 19.16) is an **isotherm.**

Test Your Understanding of Section 19.5 Which of the processes in Fig. 19.7 are isochoric? Which are isobaric? Is it possible to tell if any of the processes are isothermal or adiabatic?

19.6 Internal Energy of an Ideal Gas

We now show that for an ideal gas, the internal energy U depends only on temperature, not on pressure or volume. Let's think again about the free-expansion experiment described in Section 19.3. A thermally insulated container with rigid walls is divided into two compartments by a partition (Fig. 19.17). One compartment has a quantity of an ideal gas and the other is evacuated.

When the partition is removed or broken, the gas expands to fill both parts of the container. The gas does no work on its surroundings because the walls of the container don't move, and there is no heat flow through the insulation. So both Q and W are zero and the internal energy U is constant. This is true of any substance, whether it is an ideal gas or not.

Does the *temperature* change during a free expansion? Suppose it *does* change, while the internal energy stays the same. In that case we have to conclude that the internal energy depends on both the temperature and the volume or on both the temperature and the pressure, but certainly not on the temperature alone. But if T is constant during a free expansion, for which we know that U is constant even though both p and V change, then we have to conclude that U depends only on T, not on p or V.

Many experiments have shown that when a low-density gas undergoes a free expansion, its temperature *does not* change. Such a gas is essentially an ideal gas. The conclusion is:

> **The internal energy of an ideal gas depends only on its temperature, not on its pressure or volume.**

This property, in addition to the ideal-gas equation of state, is part of the ideal-gas model. Make sure you understand that U depends only on T for an ideal gas, for we will make frequent use of this fact.

For nonideal gases, some temperature change occurs during free expansions, even though the internal energy is constant. This shows that the internal energy cannot depend *only* on temperature; it must depend on pressure as well. From the microscopic viewpoint, in which internal energy U is the sum of the kinetic and potential energies for all the particles that make up the system, this is not surprising. Nonideal gases usually have attractive intermolecular forces, and when molecules move farther apart, the associated potential energies increase. If the total internal energy is constant, the kinetic energies must decrease. Temperature is directly related to molecular *kinetic* energy, and for such a gas a free expansion is usually accompanied by a *drop* in temperature.

Test Your Understanding of Section 19.6 Is the internal energy of a solid likely to be independent of its volume, as is the case for an ideal gas? Explain your reasoning. (*Hint:* See Fig. 18.20.)

19.7 Heat Capacities of an Ideal Gas

We defined specific heat and molar heat capacity in Section 17.5. We also remarked at the end of that section that the specific heat or molar heat capacity of a substance depends on the conditions under which the heat is added. It is usually easiest to measure the heat capacity of a gas in a closed container under constant-volume conditions. The corresponding heat capacity is the **molar heat capacity at constant volume,** denoted by C_V. Heat capacity measurements for solids and liquids are usually carried out in the atmosphere under constant atmospheric pressure, and we call the corresponding heat capacity the **molar heat capacity at constant pressure,** C_p. If neither p nor V is constant, we have an infinite number of possible heat capacities.

Let's consider C_V and C_p for an ideal gas. To measure C_V, we raise the temperature of an ideal gas in a rigid container with constant volume, neglecting its thermal expansion (Fig. 19.18a). To measure C_p, we let the gas expand just enough to keep the pressure constant as the temperature rises (Fig. 19.18b).

Why should these two molar heat capacities be different? The answer lies in the first law of thermodynamics. In a constant-volume temperature increase, the system does no work, and the change in internal energy ΔU equals the heat added Q. In a constant-pressure temperature increase, on the other hand, the volume *must* increase; otherwise, the pressure (given by the ideal-gas equation of state, $p = nRT/V$) could not remain constant. As the material expands, it does an amount of work W. According to the first law,

$$Q = \Delta U + W \qquad (19.11)$$

For a given temperature increase, the internal energy change ΔU of an ideal gas has the same value no matter what the process (remember that the internal energy of an ideal gas depends only on temperature, not on pressure or volume). Equation (19.11) then shows that the heat input for a constant-pressure process must be *greater* than that for a constant-volume process because additional energy must be supplied to account for the work W done during the expansion. So C_p is greater than C_V for an ideal gas. The pV-diagram in Fig. 19.19 shows this relationship. For air, C_p is 40% greater than C_V.

For a very few substances (one of which is water between 0°C and 4°C) the volume *decreases* during heating. In this case, W is negative, the heat input is *less* than in the constant-volume case, and C_p is *less* than C_V.

Relating C_p and C_V for an Ideal Gas

We can derive a simple relationship between C_p and C_V for an ideal gas. First consider the constant-*volume* process. We place n moles of an ideal gas at temperature T in a constant-volume container. We place it in thermal contact with a hotter body; an infinitesimal quantity of heat dQ flows into the gas, and its temperature increases by an infinitesimal amount dT. By the definition of C_V, the molar heat capacity at constant volume,

$$dQ = nC_V\,dT \qquad (19.12)$$

The pressure increases during this process, but the gas does no work ($dW = 0$) because the volume is constant. The first law in differential form, Eq. (19.6), is $dQ = dU + dW$. Since $dW = 0$, $dQ = dU$ and Eq. (19.12) can also be written as

$$dU = nC_V\,dT \qquad (19.13)$$

Now consider a constant-*pressure* process with the same temperature change dT. We place the same gas in a cylinder with a piston that we can allow to move just enough to maintain constant pressure, as shown in Fig. 19.18b. Again we bring the system into contact with a hotter body. As heat flows into

19.18 Measuring the molar heat capacity of an ideal gas **(a)** at constant volume and **(b)** at constant pressure.

(a) Constant volume: $dQ = nC_V\,dT$

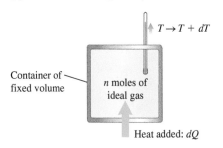

(b) Constant pressure: $dQ = nC_p\,dT$

19.19 Raising the temperature of an ideal gas from T_1 to T_2 by a constant-volume or a constant-pressure process. For an ideal gas, U depends only on T, so ΔU is the same for both processes. But for the constant-pressure process, more heat Q must be added to both increase U and do work W. Hence $C_p > C_V$.

ActivPhysics 8.7: Heat Capacity
ActivPhysics 8.8: Isochoric Process
ActivPhysics 8.9: Isobaric Process
ActivPhysics 8.10: Isothermal Process

the gas, it expands at constant pressure and does work. By the definition of C_p, the molar heat capacity at constant pressure, the amount of heat dQ entering the gas is

$$dQ = nC_p \, dT \qquad (19.14)$$

The work dW done by the gas in this constant-pressure process is

$$dW = p \, dV$$

We can also express dW in terms of the temperature change dT by using the ideal-gas equation of state, $pV = nRT$. Because p is constant, the change in V is proportional to the change in T:

$$dW = p \, dV = nR \, dT \qquad (19.15)$$

Now we substitute Eqs. (19.14) and (19.15) into the first law, $dQ = dU + dW$. We obtain

$$nC_p \, dT = dU + nR \, dT \qquad (19.16)$$

Now here comes the crux of the calculation. The internal energy change dU for the constant-pressure process is again given by Eq. (19.13), $dU = nC_V \, dT$, *even though now the volume is not constant.* Why is this so? Recall the discussion of Section 19.6; one of the special properties of an ideal gas is that its internal energy depends *only* on temperature. Thus the *change* in internal energy during any process must be determined only by the temperature change. If Eq. (19.13) is valid for an ideal gas for one particular kind of process, it must be valid for an ideal gas for *every* kind of process with the same dT. So we may replace dU in Eq. (19.16) by $nC_V \, dT$:

$$nC_p \, dT = nC_V \, dT + nR \, dT$$

When we divide each term by the common factor $n \, dT$, we get

$$C_p = C_V + R \qquad \text{(molar heat capacities of an ideal gas)} \qquad (19.17)$$

As we predicted, the molar heat capacity of an ideal gas at constant pressure is *greater* than the molar heat capacity at constant volume; the difference is the gas constant R. (Of course, R must be expressed in the same units as C_p and C_V, such as J/mol·K.)

We have used the ideal-gas model to derive Eq. (19.17), but it turns out to be obeyed to within a few percent by many real gases at moderate pressures. Measured values of C_p and C_V are given in Table 19.1 for several real gases at low pressures; the difference in most cases is approximately $R = 8.314$ J/mol·K.

The table also shows that the molar heat capacity of a gas is related to its molecular structure, as we discussed in Section 18.4. In fact, the first two columns of Table 19.1 are the same as Table 18.1.

Table 19.1 Molar Heat Capacities of Gases at Low Pressure

Type of Gas	Gas	C_V (J/mol·K)	C_p (J/mol·K)	$C_p - C_V$ (J/mol·K)	$\gamma = C_p/C_V$
Monatomic	He	12.47	20.78	8.31	1.67
	Ar	12.47	20.78	8.31	1.67
Diatomic	H_2	20.42	28.74	8.32	1.41
	N_2	20.76	29.07	8.31	1.40
	O_2	20.85	29.17	8.31	1.40
	CO	20.85	29.16	8.31	1.40
Polyatomic	CO_2	28.46	36.94	8.48	1.30
	SO_2	31.39	40.37	8.98	1.29
	H_2S	25.95	34.60	8.65	1.33

The Ratio of Heat Capacities

The last column of Table 19.1 lists the values of the dimensionless **ratio of heat capacities,** C_p/C_V, denoted by γ (the Greek letter gamma):

$$\gamma = \frac{C_p}{C_V} \qquad \text{(ratio of heat capacities)} \qquad (19.18)$$

(This is sometimes called the "ratio of specific heats.") For gases, C_p is always greater than C_V and γ is always greater than unity. This quantity plays an important role in *adiabatic* processes for an ideal gas, which we will study in the next section.

We can use our kinetic-theory discussion of the molar heat capacity of an ideal gas (see Section 18.4) to predict values of γ. As an example, an ideal monatomic gas has $C_V = \frac{3}{2}R$. From Eq. (19.17),

$$C_p = C_V + R = \tfrac{3}{2}R + R = \tfrac{5}{2}R$$

so

$$\gamma = \frac{C_p}{C_V} = \frac{\frac{5}{2}R}{\frac{3}{2}R} = \tfrac{5}{3} = 1.67$$

As Table 19.1 shows, this agrees well with values of γ computed from measured heat capacities. For most diatomic gases near room temperature, $C_V = \frac{5}{2}R$, $C_p = C_V + R = \frac{7}{2}R$, and

$$\gamma = \frac{C_p}{C_V} = \frac{\frac{7}{2}R}{\frac{5}{2}R} = \tfrac{7}{5} = 1.40$$

also in good agreement with measured values.

Here's a final reminder: For an ideal gas the internal energy change in *any* process is given by $\Delta U = nC_V \Delta T$, *whether the volume is constant or not.* This relationship, which comes in handy in the following example, holds for other substances *only* when the volume is constant.

Example 19.6   **Cooling your room**

A typical dorm room or bedroom contains about 2500 moles of air. Find the change in the internal energy of this much air when it is cooled from 35.0°C to 26.0°C at a constant pressure of 1.00 atm. Treat the air as an ideal gas with $\gamma = 1.400$.

SOLUTION

IDENTIFY and SET UP: Our target variable is the change in the internal energy ΔU of an ideal gas in a constant-pressure process. We are given the number of moles, the temperature change, and the value of γ for air. We use Eq. (19.13), $\Delta U = nC_V \Delta T$, which gives the internal energy change for an ideal gas in *any* process, *whether the volume is constant or not.* [See the discussion following Eq. (19.16).] We use Eqs. (19.17) and (19.18) to find C_V.

EXECUTE: From Eqs. (19.17) and (19.18),

$$\gamma = \frac{C_p}{C_V} = \frac{C_V + R}{C_V} = 1 + \frac{R}{C_V}$$

$$C_V = \frac{R}{\gamma - 1} = \frac{8.314 \text{ J/mol} \cdot \text{K}}{1.400 - 1} = 20.79 \text{ J/mol} \cdot \text{K}$$

Then from Eq. (19.13),

$$\Delta U = nC_V \Delta T$$
$$= (2500 \text{ mol})(20.79 \text{ J/mol} \cdot \text{K})(26.0°\text{C} - 35.0°\text{C})$$
$$= -4.68 \times 10^5 \text{ J}$$

EVALUATE: To cool 2500 moles of air from 35.0°C to 26.0°C, a room air conditioner must extract this much internal energy from the air and transfer it to the air outside. In Chapter 20 we'll discuss how this is done.

Test Your Understanding of Section 19.7 You want to cool a storage cylinder containing 10 moles of compressed gas from 30°C to 20°C. For which kind of gas would this be easiest? (i) a monatomic gas; (ii) a diatomic gas; (iii) a polyatomic gas; (iv) it would be equally easy for all of these.

19.8 Adiabatic Processes for an Ideal Gas

An adiabatic process, defined in Section 19.5, is a process in which no heat transfer takes place between a system and its surroundings. Zero heat transfer is an idealization, but a process is approximately adiabatic if the system is well insulated or if the process takes place so quickly that there is not enough time for appreciable heat flow to occur.

In an adiabatic process, $Q = 0$, so from the first law, $\Delta U = -W$. An adiabatic process for an ideal gas is shown in the pV-diagram of Fig. 19.20. As the gas expands from volume V_a to V_b, it does positive work, so its internal energy decreases and its temperature drops. If point a, representing the initial state, lies on an isotherm at temperature $T + dT$, then point b for the final state is on a different isotherm at a lower temperature T. For an ideal gas an adiabatic curve (adiabat) at any point is always *steeper* than the isotherm passing through the same point. For an adiabatic *compression* from V_b to V_a the situation is reversed and the temperature rises.

The air in the output hoses of air compressors used in gasoline stations, in paint-spraying equipment, and to fill scuba tanks is always warmer than the air entering the compressor; this is because the compression is rapid and hence approximately adiabatic. Adiabatic *cooling* occurs when you open a bottle of your favorite carbonated beverage. The gas just above the beverage surface expands rapidly in a nearly adiabatic process; the temperature of the gas drops so much that water vapor in the gas condenses, forming a miniature cloud (see Fig. 19.14).

CAUTION *"Heating" and "cooling" without heat* Keep in mind that when we talk about "adiabatic heating" and "adiabatic cooling," we really mean "raising the temperature" and "lowering the temperature," respectively. In an adiabatic process, the temperature change is due to work done by or on the system; there is *no* heat flow at all.

Adiabatic Ideal Gas: Relating V, T, and p

We can derive a relationship between volume and temperature changes for an infinitesimal adiabatic process in an ideal gas. Equation (19.13) gives the internal energy change dU for *any* process for an ideal gas, adiabatic or not, so we have $dU = nC_V \, dT$. Also, the work done by the gas during the process is given by $dW = p \, dV$. Then, since $dU = -dW$ for an adiabatic process, we have

$$nC_V \, dT = -p \, dV \qquad (19.19)$$

To obtain a relationship containing only the volume V and temperature T, we eliminate p using the ideal-gas equation in the form $p = nRT/V$. Substituting this into Eq. (19.19) and rearranging, we get

$$nC_V \, dT = -\frac{nRT}{V} \, dV$$

$$\frac{dT}{T} + \frac{R}{C_V} \frac{dV}{V} = 0$$

The coefficient R/C_V can be expressed in terms of $\gamma = C_p/C_V$. We have

$$\frac{R}{C_V} = \frac{C_p - C_V}{C_V} = \frac{C_p}{C_V} - 1 = \gamma - 1$$

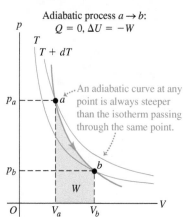

19.20 A pV-diagram of an adiabatic ($Q = 0$) process for an ideal gas. As the gas expands from V_a to V_b, it does positive work W on its environment, its internal energy decreases ($\Delta U = -W < 0$), and its temperature drops from $T + dT$ to T. (An adiabatic process is also shown in Fig. 19.16.)

ActivPhysics 8.11: Adiabatic Process

$$\frac{dT}{T} + (\gamma - 1)\frac{dV}{V} = 0 \qquad (19.20)$$

Because γ is always greater than unity for a gas, $(\gamma - 1)$ is always positive. This means that in Eq. (19.20), dV and dT always have opposite signs. An adiabatic *expansion* of an ideal gas $(dV > 0)$ always occurs with a *drop* in temperature $(dT < 0)$, and an adiabatic *compression* $(dV < 0)$ always occurs with a *rise* in temperature $(dT > 0)$; this confirms our earlier prediction.

For finite changes in temperature and volume we integrate Eq. (19.20), obtaining

$$\ln T + (\gamma - 1)\ln V = \text{constant}$$

$$\ln T + \ln V^{\gamma-1} = \text{constant}$$

$$\ln (TV^{\gamma-1}) = \text{constant}$$

and finally,

$$TV^{\gamma-1} = \text{constant} \qquad (19.21)$$

Thus for an initial state (T_1, V_1) and a final state (T_2, V_2),

$$T_1 V_1^{\gamma-1} = T_2 V_2^{\gamma-1} \quad \text{(adiabatic process, ideal gas)} \qquad (19.22)$$

Because we have used the ideal-gas equation in our derivation of Eqs. (19.21) and (19.22), the T's must always be *absolute* (Kelvin) temperatures.

We can also convert Eq. (19.21) into a relationship between pressure and volume by eliminating T, using the ideal-gas equation in the form $T = pV/nR$. Substituting this into Eq. (19.21), we find

$$\frac{pV}{nR}V^{\gamma-1} = \text{constant}$$

or, because n and R are constant,

$$pV^\gamma = \text{constant} \qquad (19.23)$$

For an initial state (p_1, V_1) and a final state (p_2, V_2), Eq. (19.23) becomes

$$p_1 V_1^\gamma = p_2 V_2^\gamma \quad \text{(adiabatic process, ideal gas)} \qquad (19.24)$$

We can also calculate the *work* done by an ideal gas during an adiabatic process. We know that $Q = 0$ and $W = -\Delta U$ for *any* adiabatic process. For an ideal gas, $\Delta U = nC_V(T_2 - T_1)$. If the number of moles n and the initial and final temperatures T_1 and T_2 are known, we have simply

$$W = nC_V(T_1 - T_2) \quad \text{(adiabatic process, ideal gas)} \qquad (19.25)$$

We may also use $pV = nRT$ in this equation to obtain

$$W = \frac{C_V}{R}(p_1 V_1 - p_2 V_2) = \frac{1}{\gamma - 1}(p_1 V_1 - p_2 V_2) \quad \begin{array}{l}\text{(adiabatic process,}\\ \text{ideal gas)}\end{array} \qquad (19.26)$$

(We used the result $C_V = R/(\gamma - 1)$ from Example 19.6.) If the process is an expansion, the temperature drops, T_1 is greater than T_2, $p_1 V_1$ is greater than $p_2 V_2$, and the work is *positive*, as we should expect. If the process is a compression, the work is negative.

Throughout this analysis of adiabatic processes we have used the ideal-gas equation of state, which is valid only for *equilibrium* states. Strictly speaking, our results are valid only for a process that is fast enough to prevent appreciable heat exchange with the surroundings (so that $Q = 0$ and the process is adiabatic), yet slow enough that the system does not depart very much from thermal and mechanical equilibrium. Even when these conditions are not strictly satisfied, though, Eqs. (19.22), (19.24), and (19.26) give useful approximate results.

Example 19.7 **Adiabatic compression in a diesel engine**

The compression ratio of a diesel engine is 15.0 to 1; that is, air in a cylinder is compressed to $\frac{1}{(15.0)}$ of its initial volume (Fig. 19.21). (a) If the initial pressure is 1.01×10^5 Pa and the initial temperature is 27°C (300 K), find the final pressure and the temperature after adiabatic compression. (b) How much work does the gas do during the compression if the initial volume of the cylinder is $1.00 \text{ L} = 1.00 \times 10^{-3} \text{ m}^3$? Use the values $C_V = 20.8 \text{ J/mol} \cdot \text{K}$ and $\gamma = 1.400$ for air.

SOLUTION

IDENTIFY and SET UP: This problem involves the adiabatic compression of an ideal gas, so we can use the ideas of this section. In part (a) we are given the initial pressure and temperature $p_1 = 1.01 \times 10^5$ Pa and $T_1 = 300$ K; the ratio of initial and final volumes is $V_1/V_2 = 15.0$. We use Eq. (19.22) to find the final temperature T_2 and Eq. (19.24) to find the final pressure p_2. In part (b) our target variable is W, the work done *by* the gas during the adiabatic compression. We use Eq. (19.26) to calculate W.

19.21 Adiabatic compression of air in a cylinder of a diesel engine.

Initial volume

Maximum compression

$V_2 = \dfrac{1}{(15.0)} V_1$

V_1

EXECUTE: (a) From Eqs. (19.22) and (19.24),

$$T_2 = T_1 \left(\frac{V_1}{V_2}\right)^{\gamma - 1} = (300 \text{ K})(15.0)^{0.40} = 886 \text{ K} = 613°C$$

$$p_2 = p_1 \left(\frac{V_1}{V_2}\right)^{\gamma} = (1.01 \times 10^5 \text{ Pa})(15.0)^{1.40}$$

$$= 44.8 \times 10^5 \text{ Pa} = 44 \text{ atm}$$

(b) From Eq. (19.26), the work done is

$$W = \frac{1}{\gamma - 1}(p_1 V_1 - p_2 V_2)$$

Using $V_1/V_2 = 15.0$, this becomes

$$W = \frac{1}{1.400 - 1}\left[\begin{array}{l} (1.01 \times 10^5 \text{ Pa})(1.00 \times 10^{-3} \text{ m}^3) \\ - (44.8 \times 10^5 \text{ Pa})\left(\dfrac{1.00 \times 10^{-3} \text{ m}^3}{15.0}\right) \end{array} \right]$$

$$= -494 \text{ J}$$

EVALUATE: If the compression had been isothermal, the final pressure would have been 15.0 atm. Because the temperature also increases during an adiabatic compression, the final pressure is much greater. When fuel is injected into the cylinders near the end of the compression stroke, the high temperature of the air attained during compression causes the fuel to ignite spontaneously without the need for spark plugs.

We can check our result in part (b) using Eq. (19.25). The number of moles of gas in the cylinder is

$$n = \frac{p_1 V_1}{RT_1} = \frac{(1.01 \times 10^5 \text{ Pa})(1.00 \times 10^{-3} \text{ m}^3)}{(8.314 \text{ J/mol} \cdot \text{K})(300 \text{ K})} = 0.0405 \text{ mol}$$

Then Eq. (19.25) gives

$$W = nC_V(T_1 - T_2)$$

$$= (0.0405 \text{ mol})(20.8 \text{ J/mol} \cdot \text{K})(300 \text{ K} - 886 \text{ K})$$

$$= -494 \text{ J}$$

The work is negative because the gas is compressed.

Test Your Understanding of Section 19.8 You have four samples of ideal gas, each of which contains the same number of moles of gas and has the same initial temperature, volume, and pressure. You compress each sample to one-half of its initial volume. Rank the four samples in order from highest to lowest value of the final pressure. (i) a monatomic gas compressed isothermally; (ii) a monatomic gas compressed adiabatically; (iii) a diatomic gas compressed isothermally; (iv) a diatomic gas compressed adiabatically.

Heat and work in thermodynamic processes: A thermodynamic system has the potential to exchange energy with its surroundings by heat transfer or by mechanical work. When a system at pressure p changes volume from V_1 to V_2, it does an amount of work W given by the integral of p with respect to volume. If the pressure is constant, the work done is equal to p times the change in volume. A negative value of W means that work is done on the system. (See Example 19.1.)

In any thermodynamic process, the heat added to the system and the work done by the system depend not only on the initial and final states, but also on the path (the series of intermediate states through which the system passes).

$$W = \int_{V_1}^{V_2} p\, dV \qquad (19.2)$$

$$W = p(V_2 - V_1) \qquad (19.3)$$
(constant pressure only)

The first law of thermodynamics: The first law of thermodynamics states that when heat Q is added to a system while the system does work W, the internal energy U changes by an amount equal to $Q - W$. This law can also be expressed for an infinitesimal process. (See Examples 19.2, 19.3, and 19.5.)

The internal energy of any thermodynamic system depends only on its state. The change in internal energy in any process depends only on the initial and final states, not on the path. The internal energy of an isolated system is constant. (See Example 19.4.)

$$\Delta U = Q - W \qquad (19.4)$$

$$dU = dQ - dW \qquad (19.6)$$
(infinitesimal process)

Important kinds of thermodynamic processes:

- Adiabatic process: No heat transfer into or out of a system; $Q = 0$.
- Isochoric process: Constant volume; $W = 0$.
- Isobaric process: Constant pressure; $W = p(V_2 - V_1)$.
- Isothermal process: Constant temperature.

Thermodynamics of ideal gases: The internal energy of an ideal gas depends only on its temperature, not on its pressure or volume. For other substances the internal energy generally depends on both pressure and temperature.

The molar heat capacities C_V and C_p of an ideal gas differ by R, the ideal-gas constant. The dimensionless ratio of heat capacities, C_p/C_V, is denoted by γ. (See Example 19.6.)

$$C_p = C_V + R \qquad (19.17)$$

$$\gamma = \frac{C_p}{C_V} \qquad (19.18)$$

Adiabatic processes in ideal gases: For an adiabatic process for an ideal gas, the quantities $TV^{\gamma-1}$ and pV^γ are constant. The work done by an ideal gas during an adiabatic expansion can be expressed in terms of the initial and final values of temperature, or in terms of the initial and final values of pressure and volume. (See Example 19.7.)

$$W = nC_V(T_1 - T_2)$$

$$= \frac{C_V}{R}(p_1V_1 - p_2V_2) \qquad (19.25)$$

$$= \frac{1}{\gamma - 1}(p_1V_1 - p_2V_2) \qquad (19.26)$$

BRIDGING PROBLEM | **Work Done by a Van Der Waals Gas**

The van der Waals equation of state, an approximate representation of the behavior of gases at high pressure, is given by Eq. (18.7): $[p + (an^2/V^2)](V - nb) = nRT$, where a and b are constants having different values for different gases. (In the special case of $a = b = 0$, this is the ideal-gas equation.) (a) Calculate the work done by a gas with this equation of state in an isothermal expansion from V_1 to V_2. (b) For ethane gas (C_2H_6), $a = 0.554$ J·m³/mol² and $b = 6.38 \times 10^{-5}$ m³/mol. Calculate the work W done by 1.80 mol of ethane when it expands from 2.00×10^{-3} m³ to 4.00×10^{-3} m³ at a constant temperature of 300 K. Do the calculation using (i) the van der Waals equation of state and (ii) the ideal-gas equation of state. (c) For which equation of state is W larger? Why should this be so?

SOLUTION GUIDE

See MasteringPhysics® study area for a Video Tutor solution.

IDENTIFY and SET UP

1. Review the discussion of the van der Waals equation of state in Section 18.1. What is the significance of the quantities a and b?
2. Decide how to find the work done by an expanding gas whose pressure p does not depend on V in the same way as for an ideal gas. (*Hint:* See Section 19.2.)
3. How will you find the work done by an expanding ideal gas?

EXECUTE

4. Find the general expression for the work done by a van der Waals gas as it expands from volume V_1 to volume V_2. (*Hint:* If you set $a = b = 0$ in your result, it should reduce to the expression for the work done by an expanding ideal gas.)
5. Use your result from step 4 to solve part (b) for ethane treated as a van der Waals gas.
6. Use the formula you chose in step 3 to solve part (b) for ethane treated as an ideal gas.

EVALUATE

7. Is the difference between W for the two equations of state large enough to be significant?
8. Does the term with a in the van der Waals equation of state increase or decrease the amount of work done? What about the term with b? Which one is more important for the ethane in this problem?

Problems

For instructor-assigned homework, go to MasteringPhysics®.

•, ••, •••: Problems of increasing difficulty. **CP**: Cumulative problems incorporating material from earlier chapters. **CALC**: Problems requiring calculus. **BIO**: Biosciences problems.

DISCUSSION QUESTIONS

Q19.1 For the following processes, is the work done by the system (defined as the expanding or contracting gas) on the environment positive or negative? (a) expansion of the burned gasoline–air mixture in the cylinder of an automobile engine; (b) opening a bottle of champagne; (c) filling a scuba tank with compressed air; (d) partial crumpling of a sealed, empty water bottle, as you drive from the mountains down to sea level.

Q19.2 It is not correct to say that a body contains a certain amount of heat, yet a body can transfer heat to another body. How can a body give away something it does not have in the first place?

Q19.3 In which situation must you do more work: inflating a balloon at sea level or inflating the same balloon to the same volume at the summit of Mt. McKinley? Explain in terms of pressure and volume change.

Q19.4 If you are told the initial and final states of a system and the associated change in internal energy, can you determine whether the internal energy change was due to work or to heat transfer? Explain.

Q19.5 Discuss the application of the first law of thermodynamics to a mountaineer who eats food, gets warm and perspires a lot during a climb, and does a lot of mechanical work in raising herself to the summit. The mountaineer also gets warm during the descent. Is the source of this energy the same as the source during the ascent?

Q19.6 When ice melts at 0°C, its volume decreases. Is the internal energy change greater than, less than, or equal to the heat added? How can you tell?

Q19.7 You hold an inflated balloon over a hot-air vent in your house and watch it slowly expand. You then remove it and let it cool back to room temperature. During the expansion, which was larger: the heat added to the balloon or the work done by the air inside it? Explain. (Assume that air is an ideal gas.) Once the balloon has returned to room temperature, how does the net heat gained or lost by the air inside it compare to the net work done on or by the surrounding air?

Q19.8 You bake chocolate chip cookies and put them, still warm, in a container with a loose (not airtight) lid. What kind of process does the air inside the container undergo as the cookies gradually cool to room temperature (isothermal, isochoric, adiabatic, isobaric, or some combination)? Explain your answer.

Q19.9 Imagine a gas made up entirely of negatively charged electrons. Like charges repel, so the electrons exert repulsive forces on each other. Would you expect that the temperature of such a gas would rise, fall, or stay the same in a free expansion? Why?

Q19.10 There are a few materials that contract when their temperature is increased, such as water between 0°C and 4°C. Would you expect C_p for such materials to be greater or less than C_V? Explain?

Q19.11 When you blow on the back of your hand with your mouth wide open, your breath feels warm. But if you partially close your mouth to form an "o" and then blow on your hand, your breath feels cool. Why?

Q19.12 An ideal gas expands while the pressure is kept constant. During this process, does heat flow into the gas or out of the gas? Justify your answer.

Q19.13 A liquid is irregularly stirred in a well-insulated container and thereby undergoes a rise in temperature. Regard the liquid as the system. Has heat been transferred? How can you tell? Has work been done? How can you tell? Why is it important that the stirring is irregular? What is the sign of ΔU? How can you tell?

Q19.14 When you use a hand pump to inflate the tires of your bicycle, the pump gets warm after a while. Why? What happens to the temperature of the air in the pump as you compress it? Why does this happen? When you raise the pump handle to draw outside air into the pump, what happens to the temperature of the air taken in? Again, why does this happen?

Q19.15 In the carburetor of an aircraft or automobile engine, air flows through a relatively small aperture and then expands. In cool, foggy weather, ice sometimes forms in this aperture even though the outside air temperature is above freezing. Why?

Q19.16 On a sunny day, large "bubbles" of air form on the sun-warmed earth, gradually expand, and finally break free to rise through the atmosphere. Soaring birds and glider pilots are fond of using these "thermals" to gain altitude easily. This expansion is essentially an adiabatic process. Why?

Q19.17 The prevailing winds on the Hawaiian island of Kauai blow from the northeast. The winds cool as they go up the slope of Mt. Waialeale (elevation 1523 m), causing water vapor to condense and rain to fall. There is much more precipitation at the summit than at the base of the mountain. In fact, Mt. Waialeale is the rainiest spot on earth, averaging 11.7 m of rainfall a year. But what makes the winds cool?

Q19.18 Applying the same considerations as in Question Q19.17, explain why the island of Niihau, a few kilometers to the southwest of Kauai, is almost a desert and farms there need to be irrigated.

Q19.19 In a constant-volume process, $dU = nC_V\,dT$. But in a constant-pressure process, it is *not* true that $dU = nC_p\,dT$. Why not?

Q19.20 When a gas surrounded by air is compressed adiabatically, its temperature rises even though there is no heat input to the gas. Where does the energy come from to raise the temperature?

Q19.21 When a gas expands adiabatically, it does work on its surroundings. But if there is no heat input to the gas, where does the energy come from to do the work?

Q19.22 The gas used in separating the two uranium isotopes ^{235}U and ^{238}U has the formula UF_6. If you added heat at equal rates to a mole of UF_6 gas and a mole of H_2 gas, which one's temperature would you expect to rise faster? Explain.

EXERCISES

Section 19.2 Work Done During Volume Changes and Section 19.3 Paths Between Thermodynamic States

19.1 •• Two moles of an ideal gas are heated at constant pressure from $T = 27°C$ to $T = 107°C$. (a) Draw a pV-diagram for this process. (b) Calculate the work done by the gas.

19.2 • Six moles of an ideal gas are in a cylinder fitted at one end with a movable piston. The initial temperature of the gas is 27.0°C and the pressure is constant. As part of a machine design project, calculate the final temperature of the gas after it has done 2.40×10^3 J of work.

19.3 •• CALC Two moles of an ideal gas are compressed in a cylinder at a constant temperature of 65.0°C until the original pressure has tripled. (a) Sketch a pV-diagram for this process. (b) Calculate the amount of work done.

19.4 •• BIO **Work Done by the Lungs.** The graph in Fig. E19.4 shows a pV-diagram of the air in a human lung when a person is inhaling and then exhaling a deep breath. Such graphs, obtained in clinical practice, are normally somewhat curved, but we have modeled one as a set of straight lines of the same general shape. (*Important:* The

Figure **E19.4**

pressure shown is the *gauge* pressure, *not* the absolute pressure.) (a) How many joules of *net* work does this person's lung do during one complete breath? (b) The process illustrated here is somewhat different from those we have been studying, because the pressure change is due to changes in the amount of gas in the lung, not to temperature changes. (Think of your own breathing. Your lungs do not expand because they've gotten hot.) If the temperature of the air in the lung remains a reasonable 20°C, what is the maximum number of moles in this person's lung during a breath?

19.5 •• CALC During the time 0.305 mol of an ideal gas undergoes an isothermal compression at 22.0°C, 468 J of work is done on it by the surroundings. (a) If the final pressure is 1.76 atm, what was the initial pressure? (b) Sketch a pV-diagram for the process.

19.6 •• A gas undergoes two processes. In the first, the volume remains constant at 0.200 m³ and the pressure increases from 2.00×10^5 Pa to 5.00×10^5 Pa. The second process is a compression to a volume of 0.120 m³ at a constant pressure of 5.00×10^5 Pa. (a) In a pV-diagram, show both processes. (b) Find the total work done by the gas during both processes.

19.7 • **Work Done in a Cyclic Process.** (a) In Fig. 19.7a, consider the closed loop $1 \rightarrow 3 \rightarrow 2 \rightarrow 4 \rightarrow 1$. This is a *cyclic* process in which the initial and final states are the same. Find the total work done by the system in this cyclic process, and show that it is equal to the area enclosed by the loop. (b) How is the work done for the process in part (a) related to the work done if the loop is traversed in the opposite direction, $1 \rightarrow 4 \rightarrow 2 \rightarrow 3 \rightarrow 1$? Explain.

Section 19.4 Internal Energy and the First Law of Thermodynamics

19.8 •• Figure E19.8 shows a pV-diagram for an ideal gas in which its absolute temperature at b is one-fourth of its absolute temperature at a. (a) What volume does this gas occupy at point b? (b) How many joules of work was done by or on the gas in this process?

Figure **E19.8**

Was it done by or on the gas? (c) Did the internal energy of the gas increase or decrease from a to b? How do you know? (d) Did heat enter or leave the gas from a to b? How do you know?

19.9 • A gas in a cylinder expands from a volume of 0.110 m³ to 0.320 m³. Heat flows into the gas just rapidly enough to keep the pressure constant at 1.65×10^5 Pa during the expansion. The total heat added is 1.15×10^5 J. (a) Find the work done by the gas. (b) Find the change in internal energy of the gas. (c) Does it matter whether the gas is ideal? Why or why not?

19.10 •• Five moles of an ideal monatomic gas with an initial temperature of 127°C expand and, in the process, absorb 1200 J of heat and do 2100 J of work. What is the final temperature of the gas?

19.11 •• The process *abc* shown in the *pV*-diagram in Fig. E19.11 involves 0.0175 mole of an ideal gas. (a) What was the lowest temperature the gas reached in this process? Where did it occur? (b) How much work was done by or on the gas from *a* to *b*? From *b* to *c*? (c) If 215 J of heat was put into the gas during *abc*, how many of those joules went into internal energy?

Figure **E19.11**

19.12 • A gas in a cylinder is held at a constant pressure of 1.80×10^5 Pa and is cooled and compressed from 1.70 m³ to 1.20 m³. The internal energy of the gas decreases by 1.40×10^5 J. (a) Find the work done by the gas. (b) Find the absolute value $|Q|$ of the heat flow into or out of the gas, and state the direction of the heat flow. (c) Does it matter whether the gas is ideal? Why or why not?

19.13 • **BIO Doughnuts: Breakfast of Champions!** A typical doughnut contains 2.0 g of protein, 17.0 g of carbohydrates, and 7.0 g of fat. The average food energy values of these substances are 4.0 kcal/g for protein and carbohydrates and 9.0 kcal/g for fat. (a) During heavy exercise, an average person uses energy at a rate of 510 kcal/h. How long would you have to exercise to "work off" one doughnut? (b) If the energy in the doughnut could somehow be converted into the kinetic energy of your body as a whole, how fast could you move after eating the doughnut? Take your mass to be 60 kg, and express your answer in m/s and in km/h.

19.14 • **Boiling Water at High Pressure.** When water is boiled at a pressure of 2.00 atm, the heat of vaporization is 2.20×10^6 J/kg and the boiling point is 120°C. At this pressure, 1.00 kg of water has a volume of 1.00×10^{-3} m³, and 1.00 kg of steam has a volume of 0.824 m³. (a) Compute the work done when 1.00 kg of steam is formed at this temperature. (b) Compute the increase in internal energy of the water.

19.15 • An ideal gas is taken from *a* to *b* on the *pV*-diagram shown in Fig. E19.15. During this process, 700 J of heat is added and the pressure doubles. (a) How much work is done by or on the gas? Explain. (b) How does the temperature of the gas at *a* compare to its temperature at *b*? Be specific. (c) How does the internal energy of the gas at *a* compare to the internal energy at *b*? Again, be specific and explain.

Figure **E19.15**

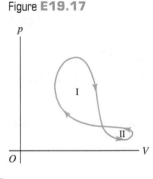

19.16 • A system is taken from state *a* to state *b* along the three paths shown in Fig. E19.16. (a) Along which path is the work done by the system the greatest? The least? (b) If $U_b > U_a$, along which path is

Figure **E19.16**

the absolute value $|Q|$ of the heat transfer the greatest? For this path, is heat absorbed or liberated by the system?

19.17 • A thermodynamic system undergoes a cyclic process as shown in Fig. E19.17. The cycle consists of two closed loops: I and II. (a) Over one complete cycle, does the system do positive or negative work? (b) In each of loops I and II, is the net work done by the system positive or negative? (c) Over one complete cycle, does heat flow into or out of the system? (d) In each of loops I and II, does heat flow into or out of the system?

Figure **E19.17**

Section 19.5 Kinds of Thermodynamic Processes, Section 19.6 Internal Energy of an Ideal Gas, and Section 19.7 Heat Capacities of an Ideal Gas

19.18 • During an isothermal compression of an ideal gas, 335 J of heat must be removed from the gas to maintain constant temperature. How much work is done by the gas during the process?

19.19 • A cylinder contains 0.250 mol of carbon dioxide (CO_2) gas at a temperature of 27.0°C. The cylinder is provided with a frictionless piston, which maintains a constant pressure of 1.00 atm on the gas. The gas is heated until its temperature increases to 127.0°C. Assume that the CO_2 may be treated as an ideal gas. (a) Draw a *pV*-diagram for this process. (b) How much work is done by the gas in this process? (c) On what is this work done? (d) What is the change in internal energy of the gas? (e) How much heat was supplied to the gas? (f) How much work would have been done if the pressure had been 0.50 atm?

19.20 • A cylinder contains 0.0100 mol of helium at $T = 27.0$°C. (a) How much heat is needed to raise the temperature to 67.0°C while keeping the volume constant? Draw a *pV*-diagram for this process. (b) If instead the pressure of the helium is kept constant, how much heat is needed to raise the temperature from 27.0°C to 67.0°C? Draw a *pV*-diagram for this process. (c) What accounts for the difference between your answers to parts (a) and (b)? In which case is more heat required? What becomes of the additional heat? (d) If the gas is ideal, what is the change in its internal energy in part (a)? In part (b)? How do the two answers compare? Why?

19.21 • In an experiment to simulate conditions inside an automobile engine, 0.185 mol of air at a temperature of 780 K and a pressure of 3.00×10^6 Pa is contained in a cylinder of volume 40.0 cm³. Then 645 J of heat is transferred to the cylinder. (a) If the volume of the cylinder is constant while the heat is added, what is the final temperature of the air? Assume that the air is essentially nitrogen gas, and use the data in Table 19.1 even though the pressure is not low. Draw a *pV*-diagram for this process. (b) If instead the volume of the cylinder is allowed to increase while the pressure remains constant, find the final temperature of the air. Draw a *pV*-diagram for this process.

19.22 •• When a quantity of monatomic ideal gas expands at a constant pressure of 4.00×10^4 Pa, the volume of the gas increases from 2.00×10^{-3} m³ to 8.00×10^{-3} m³. What is the change in the internal energy of the gas?

19.23 • Heat *Q* flows into a monatomic ideal gas, and the volume increases while the pressure is kept constant. What fraction of the heat energy is used to do the expansion work of the gas?

19.24 • Three moles of an ideal monatomic gas expands at a constant pressure of 2.50 atm; the volume of the gas changes from 3.20×10^{-2} m³ to 4.50×10^{-2} m³. (a) Calculate the initial and final temperatures of the gas. (b) Calculate the amount of work the gas does in expanding. (c) Calculate the amount of heat added to the gas. (d) Calculate the change in internal energy of the gas.

19.25 • A cylinder with a movable piston contains 3.00 mol of N_2 gas (assumed to behave like an ideal gas). (a) The N_2 is heated at constant volume until 1557 J of heat have been added. Calculate the change in temperature. (b) Suppose the same amount of heat is added to the N_2, but this time the gas is allowed to expand while remaining at constant pressure. Calculate the temperature change. (c) In which case, (a) or (b), is the final internal energy of the N_2 higher? How do you know? What accounts for the difference between the two cases?

19.26 • Propane gas (C_3H_8) behaves like an ideal gas with $\gamma = 1.127$. Determine the molar heat capacity at constant volume and the molar heat capacity at constant pressure.

19.27 • **CALC** The temperature of 0.150 mol of an ideal gas is held constant at 77.0°C while its volume is reduced to 25.0% of its initial volume. The initial pressure of the gas is 1.25 atm. (a) Determine the work done by the gas. (b) What is the change in its internal energy? (c) Does the gas exchange heat with its surroundings? If so, how much? Does the gas absorb or liberate heat?

19.28 • An experimenter adds 970 J of heat to 1.75 mol of an ideal gas to heat it from 10.0°C to 25.0°C at constant pressure. The gas does +223 J of work during the expansion. (a) Calculate the change in internal energy of the gas. (b) Calculate γ for the gas.

Section 19.8 Adiabatic Processes for an Ideal Gas

19.29 • A monatomic ideal gas that is initially at a pressure of 1.50×10^5 Pa and has a volume of 0.0800 m³ is compressed adiabatically to a volume of 0.0400 m³. (a) What is the final pressure? (b) How much work is done by the gas? (c) What is the ratio of the final temperature of the gas to its initial temperature? Is the gas heated or cooled by this compression?

19.30 • In an adiabatic process for an ideal gas, the pressure decreases. In this process does the internal energy of the gas increase or decrease? Explain your reasoning.

19.31 •• Two moles of carbon monoxide (CO) start at a pressure of 1.2 atm and a volume of 30 liters. The gas is then compressed adiabatically to $\frac{1}{3}$ this volume. Assume that the gas may be treated as ideal. What is the change in the internal energy of the gas? Does the internal energy increase or decrease? Does the temperature of the gas increase or decrease during this process? Explain.

19.32 • The engine of a Ferrari F355 F1 sports car takes in air at 20.0°C and 1.00 atm and compresses it adiabatically to 0.0900 times the original volume. The air may be treated as an ideal gas with $\gamma = 1.40$. (a) Draw a pV-diagram for this process. (b) Find the final temperature and pressure.

19.33 • During an adiabatic expansion the temperature of 0.450 mol of argon (Ar) drops from 50.0°C to 10.0°C. The argon may be treated as an ideal gas. (a) Draw a pV-diagram for this process. (b) How much work does the gas do? (c) What is the change in internal energy of the gas?

19.34 •• A player bounces a basketball on the floor, compressing it to 80.0% of its original volume. The air (assume it is essentially N_2 gas) inside the ball is originally at a temperature of 20.0°C and a pressure of 2.00 atm. The ball's inside diameter is 23.9 cm. (a) What temperature does the air in the ball reach at its maximum compression? Assume the compression is adiabatic and treat the gas as ideal. (b) By how much does the internal energy of the air change between the ball's original state and its maximum compression?

19.35 •• On a warm summer day, a large mass of air (atmospheric pressure 1.01×10^5 Pa) is heated by the ground to a temperature of 26.0°C and then begins to rise through the cooler surrounding air. (This can be treated approximately as an adiabatic process; why?) Calculate the temperature of the air mass when it has risen to a level at which atmospheric pressure is only 0.850×10^5 Pa. Assume that air is an ideal gas, with $\gamma = 1.40$. (This rate of cooling for dry, rising air, corresponding to roughly 1°C per 100 m of altitude, is called the *dry adiabatic lapse rate*.)

19.36 • A cylinder contains 0.100 mol of an ideal monatomic gas. Initially the gas is at a pressure of 1.00×10^5 Pa and occupies a volume of 2.50×10^{-3} m³. (a) Find the initial temperature of the gas in kelvins. (b) If the gas is allowed to expand to twice the initial volume, find the final temperature (in kelvins) and pressure of the gas if the expansion is (i) isothermal; (ii) isobaric; (iii) adiabatic.

PROBLEMS

19.37 •• One mole of ideal gas is slowly compressed to one-third of its original volume. In this compression, the work done on the gas has magnitude 600 J. For the gas, $C_p = 7R/2$. (a) If the process is isothermal, what is the heat flow Q for the gas? Does heat flow into or out of the gas? (b) If the process is isobaric, what is the change in internal energy of the gas? Does the internal energy increase or decrease?

19.38 •• **CALC** Figure P19.38 shows the pV-diagram for an isothermal expansion of 1.50 mol of an ideal gas, at a temperature of 15.0°C. (a) What is the change in internal energy of the gas? Explain. (b) Calculate the work done by (or on) the gas and the heat absorbed (or released) by the gas during the expansion.

Figure **P19.38**

19.39 •• A quantity of air is taken from state a to state b along a path that is a straight line in the pV-diagram (Fig. P19.39). (a) In this process, does the temperature of the gas increase, decrease, or stay the same? Explain. (b) If $V_a = 0.0700$ m³, $V_b = 0.1100$ m³, $p_a = 1.00 \times 10^5$ Pa, and $p_b = 1.40 \times 10^5$ Pa, what is the work W done by the gas in this process? Assume that the gas may be treated as ideal.

Figure **P19.39**

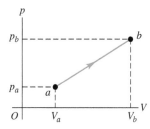

19.40 • One-half mole of an ideal gas is taken from state a to state c, as shown in Fig. P19.40. (a) Calculate the final temperature of the gas. (b) Calculate the work done on (or by) the gas as it moves from state a to state c. (c) Does heat leave the system or enter the system during this process? How much heat? Explain.

Figure **P19.40**

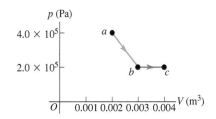

19.41 •• When a system is taken from state a to state b in Fig. P19.41 along the path acb, 90.0 J of heat flows into the system and 60.0 J of work is done by the system. (a) How much heat flows into the system along path adb if the work done by the system is 15.0 J? (b) When the system is returned from b to a along the curved path, the

Figure **P19.41**

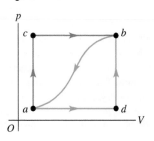

absolute value of the work done by the system is 35.0 J. Does the system absorb or liberate heat? How much heat? (c) If $U_a = 0$ and $U_d = 8.0$ J, find the heat absorbed in the processes ad and db.

19.42 • A thermodynamic system is taken from state a to state c in Fig. P19.42 along either path abc or path adc. Along path abc, the work W done by the system is 450 J. Along path adc, W is 120 J. The internal energies of each of the four states shown in the figure are $U_a = 150$ J, $U_b = 240$ J, $U_c = 680$ J, and $U_d = 330$ J. Calculate the heat

Figure **P19.42**

flow Q for each of the four processes ab, bc, ad, and dc. In each process, does the system absorb or liberate heat?

19.43 • A volume of air (assumed to be an ideal gas) is first cooled without changing its volume and then expanded without changing its pressure, as shown by the path abc in Fig. P19.43. (a) How does the final temperature of the gas compare with its initial temperature? (b) How much heat does the air exchange with its surroundings during the process

Figure **P19.43**

abc? Does the air absorb heat or release heat during this process? Explain. (c) If the air instead expands from state a to state c by the straight-line path shown, how much heat does it exchange with its surroundings?

19.44 • Three moles of argon gas (assumed to be an ideal gas) originally at a pressure of 1.50×10^4 Pa and a volume of 0.0280 m^3 are first heated and expanded at constant pressure to a volume of 0.0435 m^3, then heated at constant volume until the pressure reaches 3.50×10^4 Pa, then cooled and compressed at constant pressure until the volume is again 0.0280 m^3, and finally cooled at constant volume until the pressure drops to its original value of 1.50×10^4 Pa. (a) Draw the pV-diagram for this cycle. (b) Calculate the total work done by (or on) the gas during the cycle. (c) Calculate the net heat exchanged with the surroundings. Does the gas gain or lose heat overall?

19.45 •• Two moles of an ideal monatomic gas go through the cycle abc. For the complete cycle, 800 J of heat flows out of the gas. Process ab is at constant pressure, and process bc is at constant volume. States a and b have temperatures $T_a = 200$ K and $T_b = 300$ K. (a) Sketch the pV-diagram for the cycle. (b) What is the work W for the process ca?

19.46 •• Three moles of an ideal gas are taken around the cycle acb shown in Fig. P19.46. For this gas, $C_p = 29.1$ J/mol · K. Process ac is at constant pressure, process ba is at constant volume,

and process cb is adiabatic. The temperatures of the gas in states a, c, and b are $T_a = 300$ K, $T_c = 492$ K, and $T_b = 600$ K. Calculate the total work W for the cycle.

Figure **P19.46**

Figure **P19.47**

19.47 •• Figure P19.47 shows a pV-diagram for 0.0040 mole of ideal H$_2$ gas. The temperature of the gas does not change during segment bc. (a) What volume does this gas occupy at point c? (b) Find the temperature of the gas at points a, b, and c. (c) How much heat went into or out of the gas during segments ab, ca, and bc? Indicate whether the heat has gone into or out of the gas. (d) Find the change in the internal energy of this hydrogen during segments ab, bc, and ca. Indicate whether the internal energy increased or decreased during each of these segments.

19.48 •• The graph in Fig. P19.48 shows a pV-diagram for 3.25 moles of ideal helium (He) gas. Part ca of this process is isothermal. (a) Find the pressure of the He at point a. (b) Find the temperature of the He at points a, b, and c. (c) How much heat entered or left the He during segments ab, bc, and ca? In each segment, did

Figure **P19.48**

the heat enter or leave? (d) By how much did the internal energy of the He change from a to b, from b to c, and from c to a? Indicate whether this energy increased or decreased.

19.49 •• (a) One-third of a mole of He gas is taken along the path abc shown as the solid line in Fig. P19.49. Assume that the gas may be treated as ideal. How much heat is transferred into or out of the gas? (b) If the gas instead went from state a to state c along the horizontal dashed line in Fig. P19.49, how much heat would be transferred into or out of the gas? (c) How does Q in part (b) compare with Q in part (a)? Explain.

Figure **P19.49**

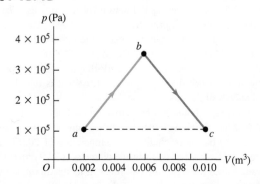

19.50 •• Two moles of helium are initially at a temperature of 27.0°C and occupy a volume of 0.0300 m^3. The helium first expands at constant pressure until its volume has doubled. Then it expands adiabatically until the temperature returns to its initial value. Assume that the helium can be treated as an ideal gas. (a) Draw a diagram of the process in the pV-plane. (b) What is the total heat supplied to the helium in the process? (c) What is the total change in internal energy of the helium? (d) What is the total work done by the helium? (e) What is the final volume of the helium?

19.51 ••• Starting with 2.50 mol of N_2 gas (assumed to be ideal) in a cylinder at 1.00 atm and 20.0°C, a chemist first heats the gas at constant volume, adding 1.52×10^4 J of heat, then continues heating and allows the gas to expand at constant pressure to twice its original volume. (a) Calculate the final temperature of the gas. (b) Calculate the amount of work done by the gas. (c) Calculate the amount of heat added to the gas while it was expanding. (d) Calculate the change in internal energy of the gas for the whole process.

19.52 •• Nitrogen gas in an expandable container is cooled from 50.0°C to 10.0°C with the pressure held constant at 3.00×10^5 Pa. The total heat liberated by the gas is 2.50×10^4 J. Assume that the gas may be treated as ideal. (a) Find the number of moles of gas. (b) Find the change in internal energy of the gas. (c) Find the work done by the gas. (d) How much heat would be liberated by the gas for the same temperature change if the volume were constant?

19.53 • In a certain process, 2.15×10^5 J of heat is liberated by a system, and at the same time the system contracts under a constant external pressure of 9.50×10^5 Pa. The internal energy of the system is the same at the beginning and end of the process. Find the change in volume of the system. (The system is *not* an ideal gas.)

19.54 • CALC A cylinder with a frictionless, movable piston like that shown in Fig. 19.5 contains a quantity of helium gas. Initially the gas is at a pressure of 1.00×10^5 Pa, has a temperature of 300 K, and occupies a volume of 1.50 L. The gas then undergoes two processes. In the first, the gas is heated and the piston is allowed to move to keep the temperature equal to 300 K. This continues until the pressure reaches 2.50×10^4 Pa. In the second process, the gas is compressed at constant pressure until it returns to its original volume of 1.50 L. Assume that the gas may be treated as ideal. (a) In a pV-diagram, show both processes. (b) Find the volume of the gas at the end of the first process, and find the pressure and temperature at the end of the second process. (c) Find the total work done by the gas during both processes. (d) What would you have to do to the gas to return it to its original pressure and temperature?

19.55 •• CP **A Thermodynamic Process in a Liquid.** A chemical engineer is studying the properties of liquid methanol (CH_3OH). She uses a steel cylinder with a cross-sectional area of 0.0200 m^2 and containing 1.20×10^{-2} m^3 of methanol. The cylinder is equipped with a tightly fitting piston that supports a load of 3.00×10^4 N. The temperature of the system is increased from 20.0°C to 50.0°C. For methanol, the coefficient of volume expansion is 1.20×10^{-3} K^{-1}, the density is 791 kg/m^3, and the specific heat at constant pressure is $c_p = 2.51 \times 10^3$ J/kg $\cdot$ K. You can ignore the expansion of the steel cylinder. Find (a) the increase in volume of the methanol; (b) the mechanical work done by the methanol against the 3.00×10^4 N force; (c) the amount of heat added to the methanol; (d) the change in internal energy of the methanol. (e) Based on your results, explain whether there is any substantial difference between the specific heats c_p (at constant pressure) and c_V (at constant volume) for methanol under these conditions.

19.56 • CP **A Thermodynamic Process in a Solid.** A cube of copper 2.00 cm on a side is suspended by a string. (The physical properties of copper are given in Tables 14.1, 17.2, and 17.3.) The cube is heated with a burner from 20.0°C to 90.0°C. The air surrounding the cube is at atmospheric pressure (1.01×10^5 Pa). Find (a) the increase in volume of the cube; (b) the mechanical work done by the cube to expand against the pressure of the surrounding air; (c) the amount of heat added to the cube; (d) the change in internal energy of the cube. (e) Based on your results, explain whether there is any substantial difference between the specific heats c_p (at constant pressure) and c_V (at constant volume) for copper under these conditions.

19.57 • BIO **A Thermodynamic Process in an Insect.** The African bombardier beetle (*Stenaptinus insignis*) can emit a jet of defensive spray from the movable tip of its abdomen (Fig. P19.57). The beetle's body has reservoirs of two different chemicals; when the beetle is disturbed, these chemicals are combined in a reaction chamber, producing a compound that is warmed from 20°C to 100°C by the heat of reaction. The high

Figure **P19.57**

pressure produced allows the compound to be sprayed out at speeds up to 19 m/s (68 km/h), scaring away predators of all kinds. (The beetle shown in the figure is 2 cm long.) Calculate the heat of reaction of the two chemicals (in J/kg). Assume that the specific heat of the two chemicals and the spray is the same as that of water, 4.19×10^3 J/kg $\cdot$ K, and that the initial temperature of the chemicals is 20°C.

19.58 ••• **High-Altitude Research.** A large research balloon containing 2.00×10^3 m^3 of helium gas at 1.00 atm and a temperature of 15.0°C rises rapidly from ground level to an altitude at which the atmospheric pressure is only 0.900 atm (Fig. P19.58). Assume the helium behaves like an ideal gas and the balloon's ascent is too rapid to permit much heat exchange with the surrounding air. (a) Calculate the volume of the gas at the higher altitude. (b) Calculate the temperature of the gas at the higher altitude. (c) What is the change in internal energy of the helium as the balloon rises to the higher altitude?

Figure **P19.58**

19.59 ••• **Chinook.** During certain seasons strong winds called chinooks blow from the west across the eastern slopes of the Rockies and downhill into Denver and nearby areas. Although the mountains are cool, the wind in Denver is very hot; within a few minutes after the chinook wind arrives, the temperature can climb 20 C° ("chinook" is a Native American word meaning "snow eater"). Similar winds occur in the Alps (called foehns) and in southern California (called Santa Anas). (a) Explain why the temperature of the chinook wind rises as it descends the slopes. Why is it important that the wind be fast moving? (b) Suppose a strong wind is blowing toward Denver (elevation 1630 m) from Grays Peak (80 km west of Denver, at an elevation of 4350 m), where the air pressure is

5.60 × 10^4 Pa and the air temperature is −15.0°C. The temperature and pressure in Denver before the wind arrives are 2.0°C and 8.12 × 10^4 Pa. By how many Celsius degrees will the temperature in Denver rise when the chinook arrives?

19.60 •• A certain ideal gas has molar heat capacity at constant volume C_V. A sample of this gas initially occupies a volume V_0 at pressure p_0 and absolute temperature T_0. The gas expands isobarically to a volume $2V_0$ and then expands further adiabatically to a final volume $4V_0$. (a) Draw a pV-diagram for this sequence of processes. (b) Compute the total work done by the gas for this sequence of processes. (c) Find the final temperature of the gas. (d) Find the absolute value $|Q|$ of the total heat flow into or out of the gas for this sequence of processes, and state the direction of heat flow.

19.61 ••• An air pump has a cylinder 0.250 m long with a movable piston. The pump is used to compress air from the atmosphere (at absolute pressure 1.01 × 10^5 Pa) into a very large tank at 4.20 × 10^5 Pa gauge pressure. (For air, C_V = 20.8 J/mol·K.) (a) The piston begins the compression stroke at the open end of the cylinder. How far down the length of the cylinder has the piston moved when air first begins to flow from the cylinder into the tank? Assume that the compression is adiabatic. (b) If the air is taken into the pump at 27.0°C, what is the temperature of the compressed air? (c) How much work does the pump do in putting 20.0 mol of air into the tank?

19.62 •• **Engine Turbochargers and Intercoolers.** The power output of an automobile engine is directly proportional to the mass of air that can be forced into the volume of the engine's cylinders to react chemically with gasoline. Many cars have a *turbocharger*, which compresses the air before it enters the engine, giving a greater mass of air per volume. This rapid, essentially adiabatic compression also heats the air. To compress it further, the air then passes through an *intercooler* in which the air exchanges heat with its surroundings at essentially constant pressure. The air is then drawn into the cylinders. In a typical installation, air is taken into the turbocharger at atmospheric pressure (1.01 × 10^5 Pa), density ρ = 1.23 kg/m^3, and temperature 15.0°C. It is compressed adiabatically to 1.45 × 10^5 Pa. In the intercooler, the air is cooled to the original temperature of 15.0°C at a constant pressure of 1.45 × 10^5 Pa. (a) Draw a pV-diagram for this sequence of processes. (b) If the volume of one of the engine's cylinders is 575 cm^3, what mass of air exiting from the intercooler will fill the cylinder at 1.45 × 10^5 Pa? Compared to the power output of an engine that takes in air at 1.01 × 10^5 Pa at 15.0°C, what percentage increase in power is obtained by using the turbocharger and intercooler? (c) If the intercooler is not used, what mass of air exiting from the turbocharger will fill the cylinder at 1.45 × 10^5 Pa? Compared to the power output of an engine that takes in air at 1.01 × 10^5 Pa at 15.0°C, what percentage increase in power is obtained by using the turbocharger alone?

19.63 • A monatomic ideal gas expands slowly to twice its original volume, doing 300 J of work in the process. Find the heat added to the gas and the change in internal energy of the gas if the process is (a) isothermal; (b) adiabatic; (c) isobaric.

19.64 •• **CALC** A cylinder with a piston contains 0.250 mol of oxygen at 2.40 × 10^5 Pa and 355 K. The oxygen may be treated as an ideal gas. The gas first expands isobarically to twice its original volume. It is then compressed isothermally back to its original volume, and finally it is cooled isochorically to its original pressure. (a) Show the series of processes on a pV-diagram. (b) Compute the temperature during the isothermal compression. (c) Compute the maximum pressure. (d) Compute the total work done by the piston on the gas during the series of processes.

19.65 • Use the conditions and processes of Problem 19.64 to compute (a) the work done by the gas, the heat added to it, and its internal energy change during the initial expansion; (b) the work done, the heat added, and the internal energy change during the final cooling; (c) the internal energy change during the isothermal compression.

19.66 •• **CALC** A cylinder with a piston contains 0.150 mol of nitrogen at 1.80 × 10^5 Pa and 300 K. The nitrogen may be treated as an ideal gas. The gas is first compressed isobarically to half its original volume. It then expands adiabatically back to its original volume, and finally it is heated isochorically to its original pressure. (a) Show the series of processes in a pV-diagram. (b) Compute the temperatures at the beginning and end of the adiabatic expansion. (c) Compute the minimum pressure.

19.67 • Use the conditions and processes of Problem 19.66 to compute (a) the work done by the gas, the heat added to it, and its internal energy change during the initial compression; (b) the work done by the gas, the heat added to it, and its internal energy change during the adiabatic expansion; (c) the work done, the heat added, and the internal energy change during the final heating.

19.68 • **Comparing Thermodynamic Processes.** In a cylinder, 1.20 mol of an ideal monatomic gas, initially at 3.60 × 10^5 Pa and 300 K, expands until its volume triples. Compute the work done by the gas if the expansion is (a) isothermal; (b) adiabatic; (c) isobaric. (d) Show each process in a pV-diagram. In which case is the absolute value of the work done by the gas greatest? Least? (e) In which case is the absolute value of the heat transfer greatest? Least? (f) In which case is the absolute value of the change in internal energy of the gas greatest? Least?

CHALLENGE PROBLEMS

19.69 ••• **CP** **Oscillations of a Piston.** A vertical cylinder of radius r contains a quantity of ideal gas and is fitted with a piston with mass m that is free to move (Fig. P19.69). The piston and the walls of the cylinder are frictionless, and the entire cylinder is placed in a constant-temperature bath. The outside air pressure is p_0. In equilibrium, the piston sits at a height h above the bottom of the cylinder. (a) Find the absolute pressure of the gas trapped below the piston when in equilibrium. (b) The piston is pulled up by a small distance and released. Find the net force acting on the piston when its base is a distance $h + y$ above the bottom of the cylinder, where y is much less than h. (c) After the piston is displaced from equilibrium and released, it oscillates up and down. Find the frequency of these small oscillations. If the displacement is not small, are the oscillations simple harmonic? How can you tell?

Figure **P19.69**

Open to outside air, pressure p_0

Piston, mass m

Ideal gas

r

h

Answers

Chapter Opening Question ?

No. The work done by a gas as its volume changes from V_1 to V_2 is equal to the integral $\int p\,dV$ between those two volume limits. If the volume of the gas contracts, the final volume V_2 is less than the initial volume V_1 and the gas does negative work. Propelling the locomotive requires that the gas do positive work, so the gas doesn't contribute to propulsion while contracting.

Test Your Understanding Questions

19.1 Answers: negative, positive, positive Heat flows out of the coffee, so $Q_{coffee} < 0$; heat flows into the aluminum cup, so $Q_{aluminum} > 0$. In mechanics, we would say that negative work is done *on* the block, since the surface exerts a force on the block that opposes the block's motion. But in thermodynamics we use the opposite convention and say that $W > 0$, which means that positive work is done *by* the block on the surface.

19.2 Answer: (ii) The work done in an expansion is represented by the area under the curve of pressure p versus volume V. In an isothermal expansion the pressure decreases as the volume increases, so the pV-diagram looks like Fig. 19.6a and the work done equals the shaded area under the blue curve from point 1 to point 2. If, however, the expansion is at constant pressure, the curve of p versus V would be the same as the dashed horizontal line at pressure p_2 in Fig. 19.6a. The area under this dashed line is smaller than the area under the blue curve for an isothermal expansion, so less work is done in the constant-pressure expansion than in the isothermal expansion.

19.3 Answer: (i) and (iv) (tie), (ii) and (iii) (tie) The accompanying figure shows the pV-diagrams for each of the four processes. The trapezoidal area under the curve, and hence the absolute value of the work, is the same in all four cases. In cases (i) and (iv) the volume increases, so the system does positive work as it expands against its surroundings. In cases (ii) and (iii) the volume decreases, so the system does negative work (shown by cross-hatching) as the surroundings push inward on it.

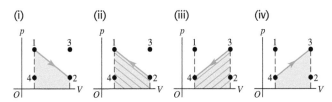

19.4 Answer: (ii), (i) and (iv) (tie), (iii) In the expression $\Delta U = Q - W$, Q is the heat *added* to the system and W is the work done *by* the system. If heat is transferred from the system to its surroundings, Q is negative; if work is done on the system, W is negative. Hence we have (i) $Q = -250$ J, $W = -250$ J, $\Delta U = -250$ J $-(-250$ J$) = 0$; (ii) $Q = 250$ J, $W = -250$ J, $\Delta U = 250$ J $-(-250$ J$) = 500$ J; (iii) $Q = -250$ J, $W = 250$ J, $\Delta U = -250$ J $- 250$ J $= -500$ J; and (iv) $Q = 250$ J, $W = 250$ J, $\Delta U = 250$ J $- 250$ J $= 0$.

19.5 Answers: $1 \to 4$ and $3 \to 2$ are isochoric; $1 \to 3$ and $4 \to 2$ are isobaric; no In a pV-diagram like those shown in Fig. 19.7, isochoric processes are represented by vertical lines (lines of constant volume) and isobaric processes are represented by horizontal lines (lines of constant pressure). The process $1 \to 2$ in Fig. 19.7 is shown as a curved line, which superficially resembles the adiabatic and isothermal processes for an ideal gas in Fig. 19.16. Without more information we can't tell whether process $1 \to 2$ is isothermal, adiabatic, or neither.

19.6 Answer: no Using the model of a solid in Fig. 18.20, we can see that the internal energy of a solid *does* depend on its volume. Compressing the solid means compressing the "springs" between the atoms, thereby increasing their stored potential energy and hence the internal energy of the solid.

19.7 Answer: (i) For a given number of moles n and a given temperature change ΔT, the amount of heat that must be transferred out of a fixed volume of air is $Q = nC_V\Delta T$. Hence the amount of heat transfer required is least for the gas with the smallest value of C_V. From Table 19.1, C_V is smallest for monatomic gases.

19.8 Answer: (ii), (iv), (i) and (iii) (tie) Samples (i) and (iii) are compressed isothermally, so pV = constant. The volume of each sample decreases to one-half of its initial value, so the final pressure is twice the initial pressure. Samples (ii) and (iv) are compressed adiabatically, so pV^γ = constant and the pressure increases by a factor of 2^γ. Sample (ii) is a monatomic gas for which $\gamma = \frac{5}{3}$, so its final pressure is $2^{5/3} = 3.17$ times greater than the initial pressure. Sample (iv) is a diatomic gas for which $\gamma = \frac{7}{5}$, so its final pressure is greater than the initial pressure by a factor of $2^{7/5} = 2.64$.

Bridging Problem

Answers: (a) $W = nRT \ln\left[\dfrac{V_2 - nb}{V_1 - nb}\right] + an^2\left[\dfrac{1}{V_2} - \dfrac{1}{V_1}\right]$

(b) (i) $W = 2.80 \times 10^3$ J, (ii) $W = 3.11 \times 10^3$ J

(c) Ideal gas, for which there is no attraction between molecules

20 THE SECOND LAW OF THERMODYNAMICS

LEARNING GOALS

By studying this chapter, you will learn:

- What determines whether a thermodynamic process is reversible or irreversible.

- What a heat engine is, and how to calculate its efficiency.

- The physics of internal-combustion engines.

- How refrigerators and heat engines are related, and how to analyze the performance of a refrigerator.

- How the second law of thermodynamics sets limits on the efficiency of engines and the performance of refrigerators.

- How to do calculations involving the idealized Carnot cycle for engines and refrigerators.

- What is meant by entropy, and how to use this concept to analyze thermodynamic processes.

? The second law of thermodynamics tells us that heat naturally flows from a hot body (such as molten lava, shown here flowing into the ocean in Hawaii) to a cold one (such as ocean water, which is heated to make steam). Is it *ever* possible for heat to flow from a cold body to a hot one?

Many thermodynamic processes proceed naturally in one direction but not the opposite. For example, heat by itself always flows from a hot body to a cooler body, never the reverse. Heat flow from a cool body to a hot body would not violate the first law of thermodynamics; energy would be conserved. But it doesn't happen in nature. Why not? As another example, note that it is easy to convert mechanical energy completely into heat; this happens every time we use a car's brakes to stop it. In the reverse direction, there are plenty of devices that convert heat *partially* into mechanical energy. (An automobile engine is an example.) But no one has ever managed to build a machine that converts heat *completely* into mechanical energy. Again, why not?

The answer to both of these questions has to do with the *directions* of thermodynamic processes and is called the *second law of thermodynamics*. This law places fundamental limitations on the efficiency of an engine or a power plant. It also places limitations on the minimum energy input needed to operate a refrigerator. So the second law is directly relevant for many important practical problems.

We can also state the second law in terms of the concept of *entropy*, a quantitative measure of the degree of disorder or randomness of a system. The idea of entropy helps explain why ink mixed with water never spontaneously unmixes and why we never observe a host of other seemingly possible processes.

20.1 Directions of Thermodynamic Processes

Thermodynamic processes that occur in nature are all **irreversible processes.** These are processes that proceed spontaneously in one direction but not the other (Fig. 20.1a). The flow of heat from a hot body to a cooler body is irreversible, as is the free expansion of a gas discussed in Sections 19.3 and 19.6. Sliding a book across a table converts mechanical energy into heat by friction;

(a) A block of ice melts *irreversibly* when we place it in a hot (70°C) metal box.

Heat flows from the box into the ice and water, never the reverse.

(b) A block of ice at 0°C can be melted *reversibly* if we put it in a 0°C metal box.

By infinitesimally raising or lowering the temperature of the box, we can make heat flow into the ice to melt it or make heat flow out of the water to refreeze it.

20.1 Reversible and irreversible processes.

this process is irreversible, for no one has ever observed the reverse process (in which a book initially at rest on the table would spontaneously start moving and the table and book would cool down). Our main topic for this chapter is the *second law of thermodynamics,* which determines the preferred direction for such processes.

Despite this preferred direction for every natural process, we can think of a class of idealized processes that *would* be reversible. A system that undergoes such an idealized **reversible process** is always very close to being in thermodynamic equilibrium within itself and with its surroundings. Any change of state that takes place can then be reversed by making only an infinitesimal change in the conditions of the system. For example, we can reverse heat flow between two bodies whose temperatures differ only infinitesimally by making only a very small change in one temperature or the other (Fig. 20.1b).

Reversible processes are thus **equilibrium processes,** with the system always in thermodynamic equilibrium. Of course, if a system were *truly* in thermodynamic equilibrium, no change of state would take place. Heat would not flow into or out of a system with truly uniform temperature throughout, and a system that is truly in mechanical equilibrium would not expand and do work against its surroundings. A reversible process is an idealization that can never be precisely attained in the real world. But by making the temperature gradients and the pressure differences in the substance very small, we can keep the system very close to equilibrium states and make the process nearly reversible.

By contrast, heat flow with finite temperature difference, free expansion of a gas, and conversion of work to heat by friction are all *irreversible* processes; no small change in conditions could make any of them go the other way. They are also all *nonequilibrium* processes, in that the system is not in thermodynamic equilibrium at any point until the end of the process.

Disorder and Thermodynamic Processes

There is a relationship between the direction of a process and the *disorder* or *randomness* of the resulting state. For example, imagine a thousand names written on file cards and arranged in alphabetical order. Throw the alphabetized stack of cards into the air, and they will likely come down in a random, disordered state. In the free expansion of a gas discussed in Sections 19.3 and 19.6, the air is more disordered after it has expanded into the entire box than when it was confined in one side, just as your clothes are more disordered when scattered all over your floor than when confined to your closet.

Similarly, macroscopic kinetic energy is energy associated with organized, coordinated motions of many molecules, but heat transfer involves changes in energy of random, disordered molecular motion. Therefore conversion of mechanical energy into heat involves an increase of randomness or disorder.

In the following sections we will introduce the second law of thermodynamics by considering two broad classes of devices: *heat engines,* which are partly successful in converting heat into work, and *refrigerators,* which are partly successful in transporting heat from cooler to hotter bodies.

Test Your Understanding of Section 20.1   Your left and right hands are normally at the same temperature, just like the metal box and ice in Fig. 20.1b. Is rubbing your hands together to warm them (i) a reversible process or (ii) an irreversible process? ∎

ActivPhysics 8.12: Cyclic Process—Strategies
ActivPhysics 8.13: Cyclic Process—Problems

20.2 All motorized vehicles other than purely electric vehicles use heat engines for propulsion. (Hybrid vehicles use their internal-combustion engine to help charge the batteries for the electric motor.)

20.2 Heat Engines

The essence of our technological society is the ability to use sources of energy other than muscle power. Sometimes, mechanical energy is directly available; water power and wind power are examples. But most of our energy comes from the burning of fossil fuels (coal, oil, and gas) and from nuclear reactions. They supply energy that is transferred as *heat.* This is directly useful for heating buildings, for cooking, and for chemical processing, but to operate a machine or propel a vehicle, we need *mechanical* energy.

Thus it's important to know how to take heat from a source and convert as much of it as possible into mechanical energy or work. This is what happens in gasoline engines in automobiles, jet engines in airplanes, steam turbines in electric power plants, and many other systems. Closely related processes occur in the animal kingdom; food energy is "burned" (that is, carbohydrates combine with oxygen to yield water, carbon dioxide, and energy) and partly converted to mechanical energy as an animal's muscles do work on its surroundings.

Any device that transforms heat partly into work or mechanical energy is called a **heat engine** (Fig. 20.2). Usually, a quantity of matter inside the engine undergoes inflow and outflow of heat, expansion and compression, and sometimes change of phase. We call this matter the **working substance** of the engine. In internal-combustion engines, such as those used in automobiles, the working substance is a mixture of air and fuel; in a steam turbine it is water.

The simplest kind of engine to analyze is one in which the working substance undergoes a **cyclic process,** a sequence of processes that eventually leaves the substance in the same state in which it started. In a steam turbine the water is recycled and used over and over. Internal-combustion engines do not use the same air over and over, but we can still analyze them in terms of cyclic processes that approximate their actual operation.

Hot and Cold Reservoirs

All heat engines *absorb* heat from a source at a relatively high temperature, perform some mechanical work, and *discard* or *reject* some heat at a lower temperature. As far as the engine is concerned, the discarded heat is wasted. In internal-combustion engines the waste heat is that discarded in the hot exhaust gases and the cooling system; in a steam turbine it is the heat that must flow out of the used steam to condense and recycle the water.

When a system is carried through a cyclic process, its initial and final internal energies are equal. For any cyclic process, the first law of thermodynamics requires that

$$U_2 - U_1 = 0 = Q - W \qquad \text{so} \qquad Q = W$$

That is, the net heat flowing into the engine in a cyclic process equals the net work done by the engine.

When we analyze heat engines, it helps to think of two bodies with which the working substance of the engine can interact. One of these, called the *hot reservoir,* represents the heat source; it can give the working substance large amounts of heat at a constant temperature T_H without appreciably changing its own temperature. The other body, called the *cold reservoir,* can absorb large amounts of discarded heat from the engine at a constant lower temperature T_C. In a steam-turbine system the flames and hot gases in the boiler are the hot reservoir, and the cold water and air used to condense and cool the used steam are the cold reservoir.

We denote the quantities of heat transferred from the hot and cold reservoirs as Q_H and Q_C, respectively. A quantity of heat Q is positive when heat is transferred *into* the working substance and is negative when heat leaves the working substance. Thus in a heat engine, Q_H is positive but Q_C is negative, representing heat *leaving* the working substance. This sign convention is consistent with the rules we stated in Section 19.1; we will continue to use those rules here. For clarity, we'll often state the relationships in terms of the absolute values of the Q's and W's because absolute values are always positive.

Energy-Flow Diagrams and Efficiency

We can represent the energy transformations in a heat engine by the *energy-flow diagram* of Fig. 20.3. The engine itself is represented by the circle. The amount of heat Q_H supplied to the engine by the hot reservoir is proportional to the width of the incoming "pipeline" at the top of the diagram. The width of the outgoing pipeline at the bottom is proportional to the magnitude $|Q_C|$ of the heat rejected in the exhaust. The branch line to the right represents the portion of the heat supplied that the engine converts to mechanical work, W.

When an engine repeats the same cycle over and over, Q_H and Q_C represent the quantities of heat absorbed and rejected by the engine *during one cycle;* Q_H is positive, and Q_C is negative. The *net* heat Q absorbed per cycle is

$$Q = Q_H + Q_C = |Q_H| - |Q_C| \qquad (20.1)$$

The useful output of the engine is the net work W done by the working substance. From the first law,

$$W = Q = Q_H + Q_C = |Q_H| - |Q_C| \qquad (20.2)$$

Ideally, we would like to convert *all* the heat Q_H into work; in that case we would have $Q_H = W$ and $Q_C = 0$. Experience shows that this is impossible; there is always some heat wasted, and Q_C *is never zero.* We define the **thermal efficiency** of an engine, denoted by e, as the quotient

$$e = \frac{W}{Q_H} \qquad (20.3)$$

The thermal efficiency e represents the fraction of Q_H that *is* converted to work. To put it another way, e is what you get divided by what you pay for. This is always less than unity, an all-too-familiar experience! In terms of the flow diagram of Fig. 20.3, the most efficient engine is one for which the branch pipeline representing the work output is as wide as possible and the exhaust pipeline representing the heat thrown away is as narrow as possible.

When we substitute the two expressions for W given by Eq. (20.2) into Eq. (20.3), we get the following equivalent expressions for e:

$$e = \frac{W}{Q_H} = 1 + \frac{Q_C}{Q_H} = 1 - \left| \frac{Q_C}{Q_H} \right| \quad \text{(thermal efficiency of an engine)} \quad (20.4)$$

Note that e is a quotient of two energy quantities and thus is a pure number, without units. Of course, we must always express W, Q_H, and Q_C in the same units.

20.3 Schematic energy-flow diagram for a heat engine.

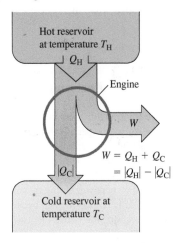

$$W = Q_H + Q_C$$
$$= |Q_H| - |Q_C|$$

Application Biological Efficiency
Although a biological organism is not a heat engine, the concept of efficiency still applies: Here e is the ratio of the work done to the energy that was used to do that work. To exercise on a stationary bike, your body must first convert the chemical-bond energy in glucose to chemical-bond energy in ATP (adenosine triphosphate), then convert energy from ATP into motion of your leg muscles, and finally convert muscular motion into motion of the pedals. The overall efficiency of this entire process is only about 25%. The remaining 75% of the energy liberated from glucose goes into heating your body.

Problems involving heat engines are, fundamentally, problems in the first law of thermodynamics. You should review Problem-Solving Strategy 19.1 (Section 19.4).

IDENTIFY *the relevant concepts:* A heat engine is any device that converts heat partially to work, as shown schematically in Fig. 20.3. We will see in Section 20.4 that a refrigerator is essentially a heat engine running in reverse, so many of the same concepts apply.

SET UP *the problem* as suggested in Problem-Solving Strategy 19.1. Use Eq. (20.4) if the thermal efficiency of the engine is relevant. Sketch an energy-flow diagram like Fig. 20.3.

EXECUTE *the solution* as follows:
1. Be careful with the sign conventions for W and the various Q's. W is positive when the system expands and does work; W is

negative when the system is compressed and work is done on it. Each Q is positive if it represents heat entering the system and is negative if it represents heat leaving the system. When you know that a quantity is negative, such as Q_C in the above discussion, it sometimes helps to write it as $Q_C = -|Q_C|$.
2. Power is work per unit time ($P = W/t$), and rate of heat transfer (heat current) H is heat transfer per unit time ($H = Q/t$). In problems involving these concepts it helps to ask, "What is W or Q in one second (or one hour)?"
3. Keeping steps 1 and 2 in mind, solve for the target variables.

EVALUATE *your answer:* Use the first law of thermodynamics to check your results. Pay particular attention to algebraic signs.

Example 20.1 | **Analyzing a heat engine**

A gasoline truck engine takes in 10,000 J of heat and delivers 2000 J of mechanical work per cycle. The heat is obtained by burning gasoline with heat of combustion $L_c = 5.0 \times 10^4$ J/g. (a) What is the thermal efficiency of this engine? (b) How much heat is discarded in each cycle? (c) If the engine goes through 25 cycles per second, what is its power output in watts? In horsepower? (d) How much gasoline is burned in each cycle? (e) How much gasoline is burned per second? Per hour?

SOLUTION

IDENTIFY and SET UP: This problem concerns a heat engine, so we can use the ideas of this section. Figure 20.4 is our energy-flow diagram for one cycle. In each cycle the engine does $W = 2000$ J of work and takes in heat $Q_H = 10,000$ J. We use Eq. (20.4), in the form $e = W/Q_H$, to find the thermal efficiency. We use Eq. (20.2) to find the amount of heat Q_C rejected per cycle. The heat of combustion tells us how much gasoline must be burned per cycle and hence per unit time. The power output is the time rate at which the work W is done.

20.4 Our sketch for this problem.

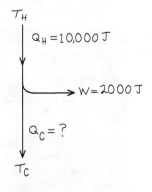

EXECUTE: (a) From Eq. (20.4), the thermal efficiency is

$$e = \frac{W}{Q_H} = \frac{2000 \text{ J}}{10,000 \text{ J}} = 0.20 = 20\%$$

(b) From Eq. (20.2), $W = Q_H + Q_C$, so

$$Q_C = W - Q_H = 2000 \text{ J} - 10,000 \text{ J} = -8000 \text{ J}$$

That is, 8000 J of heat leaves the engine during each cycle.

(c) The power P equals the work per cycle multiplied by the number of cycles per second:

$$P = (2000 \text{ J/cycle})(25 \text{ cycles/s}) = 50,000 \text{ W} = 50 \text{ kW}$$

$$= (50,000 \text{ W})\frac{1 \text{ hp}}{746 \text{ W}} = 67 \text{ hp}$$

(d) Let m be the mass of gasoline burned during each cycle. Then $Q_H = mL_c$ and

$$m = \frac{Q_H}{L_c} = \frac{10,000 \text{ J}}{5.0 \times 10^4 \text{ J/g}} = 0.20 \text{ g}$$

(e) The mass of gasoline burned per second equals the mass per cycle multiplied by the number of cycles per second:

$$(0.20 \text{ g/cycle})(25 \text{ cycles/s}) = 5.0 \text{ g/s}$$

The mass burned per hour is

$$(5.0 \text{ g/s})\frac{3600 \text{ s}}{1 \text{ h}} = 18,000 \text{ g/h} = 18 \text{ kg/h}$$

EVALUATE: An efficiency of 20% is fairly typical for cars and trucks if W includes only the work delivered to the wheels. We can check the mass burned per hour by expressing it in miles per gallon ("mileage"). The density of gasoline is about 0.70 g/cm³, so this is about 25,700 cm³, 25.7 L, or 6.8 gallons of gasoline per hour. If the truck is traveling at 55 mi/h (88 km/h), this represents fuel consumption of 8.1 miles/gallon (3.4 km/L). This is a fairly typical mileage for large trucks.

Test Your Understanding of Section 20.2 Rank the following heat engines in order from highest to lowest thermal efficiency. (i) an engine that in one cycle absorbs 5000 J of heat and rejects 4500 J of heat; (ii) an engine that in one cycle absorbs 25,000 J of heat and does 2000 J of work; (iii) an engine that in one cycle does 400 J of work and rejects 2800 J of heat.

20.3 Internal-Combustion Engines

The gasoline engine, used in automobiles and many other types of machinery, is a familiar example of a heat engine. Let's look at its thermal efficiency. Figure 20.5 shows the operation of one type of gasoline engine. First a mixture of air and gasoline vapor flows into a cylinder through an open intake valve while the piston descends, increasing the volume of the cylinder from a minimum of V (when the piston is all the way up) to a maximum of rV (when it is all the way down). The quantity r is called the **compression ratio;** for present-day automobile engines its value is typically 8 to 10. At the end of this *intake stroke,* the intake valve closes and the mixture is compressed, approximately adiabatically, to volume V during the *compression stroke.* The mixture is then ignited by the spark plug, and the heated gas expands, approximately adiabatically, back to volume rV, pushing on the piston and doing work; this is the *power stroke.* Finally, the exhaust valve opens, and the combustion products are pushed out (during the *exhaust stroke*), leaving the cylinder ready for the next intake stroke.

The Otto Cycle

Figure 20.6 is a pV-diagram for an idealized model of the thermodynamic processes in a gasoline engine. This model is called the **Otto cycle.** At point a the gasoline–air mixture has entered the cylinder. The mixture is compressed adiabatically to point b and is then ignited. Heat Q_H is added to the system by the burning gasoline along line bc, and the power stroke is the adiabatic expansion to d. The gas is cooled to the temperature of the outside air along line da; during this process, heat $|Q_C|$ is rejected. This gas leaves the engine as exhaust and does not enter the engine again. But since an equivalent amount of gasoline and air enters, we may consider the process to be cyclic.

20.5 Cycle of a four-stroke internal-combustion engine.

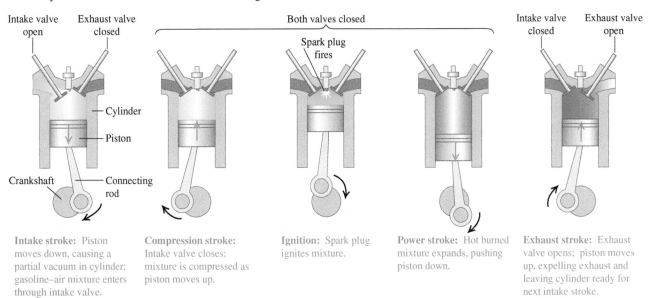

Intake stroke: Piston moves down, causing a partial vacuum in cylinder; gasoline–air mixture enters through intake valve.

Compression stroke: Intake valve closes; mixture is compressed as piston moves up.

Ignition: Spark plug ignites mixture.

Power stroke: Hot burned mixture expands, pushing piston down.

Exhaust stroke: Exhaust valve opens; piston moves up, expelling exhaust and leaving cylinder ready for next intake stroke.

20.6 The pV-diagram for the Otto cycle, an idealized model of the thermodynamic processes in a gasoline engine.

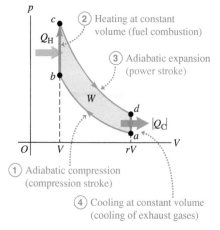

Otto cycle

② Heating at constant volume (fuel combustion)

③ Adiabatic expansion (power stroke)

① Adiabatic compression (compression stroke)

④ Cooling at constant volume (cooling of exhaust gases)

We can calculate the efficiency of this idealized cycle. Processes bc and da are constant-volume, so the heats Q_H and Q_C are related simply to the temperatures:

$$Q_H = nC_V(T_c - T_b) > 0$$
$$Q_C = nC_V(T_a - T_d) < 0$$

The thermal efficiency is given by Eq. (20.4). Inserting the above expressions and cancelling out the common factor nC_V, we find

$$e = \frac{Q_H + Q_C}{Q_H} = \frac{T_c - T_b + T_a - T_d}{T_c - T_b} \qquad (20.5)$$

To simplify this further, we use the temperature–volume relationship for adiabatic processes for an ideal gas, Eq. (19.22). For the two adiabatic processes ab and cd,

$$T_a(rV)^{\gamma-1} = T_bV^{\gamma-1} \qquad \text{and} \qquad T_d(rV)^{\gamma-1} = T_cV^{\gamma-1}$$

We divide each of these equations by the common factor $V^{\gamma-1}$ and substitute the resulting expressions for T_b and T_c back into Eq. (20.5). The result is

$$e = \frac{T_dr^{\gamma-1} - T_ar^{\gamma-1} + T_a - T_d}{T_dr^{\gamma-1} - T_ar^{\gamma-1}} = \frac{(T_d - T_a)(r^{\gamma-1} - 1)}{(T_d - T_a)r^{\gamma-1}}$$

Dividing out the common factor $(T_d - T_a)$, we get

$$e = 1 - \frac{1}{r^{\gamma-1}} \qquad \text{(thermal efficiency in Otto cycle)} \qquad (20.6)$$

The thermal efficiency given by Eq. (20.6) is always less than unity, even for this idealized model. With $r = 8$ and $\gamma = 1.4$ (the value for air) the theoretical efficiency is $e = 0.56$, or 56%. The efficiency can be increased by increasing r. However, this also increases the temperature at the end of the adiabatic compression of the air–fuel mixture. If the temperature is too high, the mixture explodes spontaneously during compression instead of burning evenly after the spark plug ignites it. This is called *pre-ignition* or *detonation;* it causes a knocking sound and can damage the engine. The octane rating of a gasoline is a measure of its antiknock qualities. The maximum practical compression ratio for high-octane, or "premium," gasoline is about 10 to 13.

The Otto cycle is a highly idealized model. It assumes that the mixture behaves as an ideal gas; it neglects friction, turbulence, loss of heat to cylinder walls, and many other effects that reduce the efficiency of an engine. Efficiencies of real gasoline engines are typically around 35%.

The Diesel Cycle

The Diesel engine is similar in operation to the gasoline engine. The most important difference is that there is no fuel in the cylinder at the beginning of the compression stroke. A little before the beginning of the power stroke, the injectors start to inject fuel directly into the cylinder, just fast enough to keep the pressure approximately constant during the first part of the power stroke. Because of the high temperature developed during the adiabatic compression, the fuel ignites spontaneously as it is injected; no spark plugs are needed.

Figure 20.7 shows the idealized **Diesel cycle.** Starting at point a, air is compressed adiabatically to point b, heated at constant pressure to point c, expanded adiabatically to point d, and cooled at constant volume to point a. Because there is no fuel in the cylinder during most of the compression stroke, pre-ignition cannot occur, and the compression ratio r can be much higher than for a gasoline engine. This improves efficiency and ensures reliable ignition when the fuel is injected (because of the high temperature reached during the

20.7 The pV-diagram for the idealized Diesel cycle.

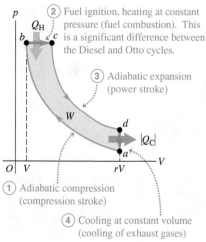

Diesel cycle

② Fuel ignition, heating at constant pressure (fuel combustion). This is a significant difference between the Diesel and Otto cycles.

③ Adiabatic expansion (power stroke)

① Adiabatic compression (compression stroke)

④ Cooling at constant volume (cooling of exhaust gases)

adiabatic compression). Values of r of 15 to 20 are typical; with these values and $\gamma = 1.4$, the theoretical efficiency of the idealized Diesel cycle is about 0.65 to 0.70. As with the Otto cycle, the efficiency of any actual engine is substantially less than this. While Diesel engines are very efficient, they must be built to much tighter tolerances than gasoline engines and the fuel-injection system requires careful maintenance.

Test Your Understanding of Section 20.3 For an Otto-cycle engine with cylinders of a fixed size and a fixed compression ratio, which of the following aspects of the pV-diagram in Fig. 20.6 would change if you doubled the amount of fuel burned per cycle? (There may be more than one correct answer.) (i) the vertical distance between points b and c; (ii) the vertical distance between points a and d; (iii) the horizontal distance between points b and a. ❚

20.4 Refrigerators

We can think of a **refrigerator** as a heat engine operating in reverse. A heat engine takes heat from a hot place and gives off heat to a colder place. A refrigerator does the opposite; it takes heat from a cold place (the inside of the refrigerator) and gives it off to a warmer place (usually the air in the room where the refrigerator is located). A heat engine has a net *output* of mechanical work; the refrigerator requires a net *input* of mechanical work. Using the sign conventions from Section 20.2, for a refrigerator Q_C is positive but both W and Q_H are negative; hence $|W| = -W$ and $|Q_H| = -Q_H$.

Figure 20.8 shows an energy-flow diagram for a refrigerator. From the first law for a cyclic process,

$$Q_H + Q_C - W = 0 \quad \text{or} \quad -Q_H = Q_C - W$$

or, because both Q_H and W are negative,

$$|Q_H| = Q_C + |W| \tag{20.7}$$

Thus, as the diagram shows, the heat $|Q_H|$ leaving the working substance and given to the hot reservoir is always *greater* than the heat Q_C taken from the cold reservoir. Note that the absolute-value relationship

$$|Q_H| = |Q_C| + |W| \tag{20.8}$$

is valid for both heat engines and refrigerators.

From an economic point of view, the best refrigeration cycle is one that removes the greatest amount of heat $|Q_C|$ from the inside of the refrigerator for the least expenditure of mechanical work, $|W|$. The relevant ratio is therefore $|Q_C|/|W|$; the larger this ratio, the better the refrigerator. We call this ratio the **coefficient of performance**, denoted by K. From Eq. (20.8), $|W| = |Q_H| - |Q_C|$, so

$$K = \frac{|Q_C|}{|W|} = \frac{|Q_C|}{|Q_H| - |Q_C|} \qquad \text{(coefficient of performance of a refrigerator)} \tag{20.9}$$

As always, we measure Q_H, Q_C, and W all in the same energy units; K is then a dimensionless number.

Practical Refrigerators

The principles of the common refrigeration cycle are shown schematically in Fig. 20.9a. The fluid "circuit" contains a refrigerant fluid (the working substance). The left side of the circuit (including the cooling coils inside the refrigerator) is at low temperature and low pressure; the right side (including the condenser coils outside the refrigerator) is at high temperature and high pressure. Ordinarily, both sides contain liquid and vapor in phase equilibrium.

20.8 Schematic energy-flow diagram of a refrigerator.

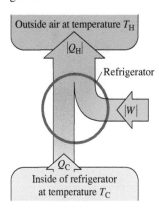

20.9 (a) Principle of the mechanical refrigeration cycle. (b) How the key elements are arranged in a practical refrigerator.

(a)

(b)

The compressor takes in fluid, compresses it adiabatically, and delivers it to the condenser coil at high pressure. The fluid temperature is then higher than that of the air surrounding the condenser, so the refrigerant gives off heat $|Q_H|$ and partially condenses to liquid. The fluid then expands adiabatically into the evaporator at a rate controlled by the expansion valve. As the fluid expands, it cools considerably, enough that the fluid in the evaporator coil is colder than its surroundings. It absorbs heat $|Q_C|$ from its surroundings, cooling them and partially vaporizing. The fluid then enters the compressor to begin another cycle. The compressor, usually driven by an electric motor (Fig. 20.9b), requires energy input and does work $|W|$ *on* the working substance during each cycle.

An air conditioner operates on exactly the same principle. In this case the refrigerator box becomes a room or an entire building. The evaporator coils are inside, the condenser is outside, and fans circulate air through these (Fig. 20.10). In large installations the condenser coils are often cooled by water. For air conditioners the quantities of greatest practical importance are the *rate* of heat removal (the heat current H from the region being cooled) and the *power* input $P = W/t$

20.10 An air conditioner works on the same principle as a refrigerator.

to the compressor. If heat $|Q_C|$ is removed in time t, then $H = |Q_C|/t$. Then we can express the coefficient of performance as

$$K = \frac{|Q_C|}{|W|} = \frac{Ht}{Pt} = \frac{H}{P}$$

Typical room air conditioners have heat removal rates H of 5000 to 10,000 Btu/h, or about 1500–3000 W, and require electric power input of about 600 to 1200 W. Typical coefficients of performance are about 3; the actual values depend on the inside and outside temperatures.

A variation on this theme is the **heat pump,** used to heat buildings by cooling the outside air. It functions like a refrigerator turned inside out. The evaporator coils are outside, where they take heat from cold air, and the condenser coils are inside, where they give off heat to the warmer air. With proper design, the heat $|Q_H|$ delivered to the inside per cycle can be considerably greater than the work $|W|$ required to get it there.

Work is *always* needed to transfer heat from a colder to a hotter body. Heat flows spontaneously from hotter to colder, and to reverse this flow requires the addition of work from the outside. Experience shows that it is impossible to make a refrigerator that transports heat from a colder body to a hotter body without the addition of work. If no work were needed, the coefficient of performance would be infinite. We call such a device a *workless refrigerator;* it is a mythical beast, like the unicorn and the free lunch.

Test Your Understanding of Section 20.4   Can you cool your house by leaving the refrigerator door open?   ❚

20.5 The Second Law of Thermodynamics

Experimental evidence suggests strongly that it is *impossible* to build a heat engine that converts heat completely to work—that is, an engine with 100% thermal efficiency. This impossibility is the basis of one statement of the **second law of thermodynamics,** as follows:

> **It is impossible for any system to undergo a process in which it absorbs heat from a reservoir at a single temperature and converts the heat completely into mechanical work, with the system ending in the same state in which it began.**

We will call this the "engine" statement of the second law. (It is also known to physicists as the *Kelvin–Planck statement* of this law.)

The basis of the second law of thermodynamics is the difference between the nature of internal energy and that of macroscopic mechanical energy. In a moving body the molecules have random motion, but superimposed on this is a coordinated motion of every molecule in the direction of the body's velocity. The kinetic energy associated with this *coordinated* macroscopic motion is what we call the kinetic energy of the moving body. The kinetic and potential energies associated with the *random* motion constitute the internal energy.

When a body sliding on a surface comes to rest as a result of friction, the organized motion of the body is converted to random motion of molecules in the body and in the surface. Since we cannot control the motions of individual molecules, we cannot convert this random motion completely back to organized motion. We can convert *part* of it, and this is what a heat engine does.

If the second law were *not* true, we could power an automobile or run a power plant by cooling the surrounding air. Neither of these impossibilities violates the *first* law of thermodynamics. The second law, therefore, is not a deduction from the first but stands by itself as a separate law of nature. The first law denies the possibility of creating or destroying energy; the second law limits the *availability* of energy and the ways in which it can be used and converted.

Restating the Second Law

Our analysis of refrigerators in Section 20.4 forms the basis for an alternative statement of the second law of thermodynamics. Heat flows spontaneously from hotter to colder bodies, never the reverse. A refrigerator does take heat from a colder to a hotter body, but its operation requires an input of mechanical energy or work. Generalizing this observation, we state:

> **It is impossible for any process to have as its sole result the transfer of heat from a cooler to a hotter body.**

We'll call this the "refrigerator" statement of the second law. (It is also known as the *Clausius statement.*) It may not seem to be very closely related to the "engine" statement. In fact, though, the two statements are completely equivalent. For example, if we could build a workless refrigerator, violating the second or "refrigerator" statement of the second law, we could use it in conjunction with a heat engine, pumping the heat rejected by the engine back to the hot reservoir to be reused. This composite machine (Fig. 20.11a) would violate the "engine" statement of the second law because its net effect would be to take a net quantity of heat $Q_H - |Q_C|$ from the hot reservoir and convert it completely to work W.

Alternatively, if we could make an engine with 100% thermal efficiency, in violation of the first statement, we could run it using heat from the hot reservoir and use the work output to drive a refrigerator that pumps heat from the cold reservoir to the hot (Fig. 20.11b). This composite device would violate the "refrigerator" statement because its net effect would be to take heat Q_C from the

20.11 Energy-flow diagrams showing that the two forms of the second law are equivalent.

(a) The "engine" statement of the second law of thermodynamics

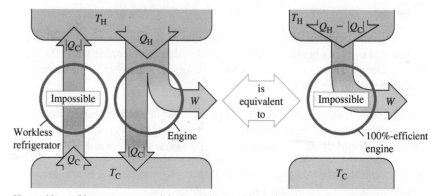

If a workless refrigerator were possible, it could be used in conjunction with an ordinary heat engine to form a 100%-efficient engine, converting heat $Q_H - |Q_C|$ completely to work.

(b) The "refrigerator" statement of the second law of thermodynamics

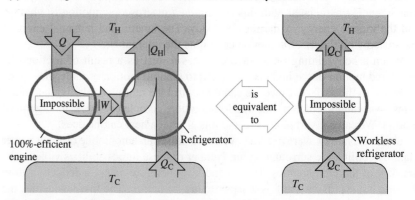

If a 100%-efficient engine were possible, it could be used in conjunction with an ordinary refrigerator to form a workless refrigerator, transferring heat Q_C from the cold to the hot reservoir with no input of work.

cold reservoir and deliver it to the hot reservoir without requiring any input of work. Thus any device that violates one form of the second law can be used to make a device that violates the other form. If violations of the first form are impossible, so are violations of the second!

The conversion of work to heat and the heat flow from hot to cold across a finite temperature gradient are *irreversible* processes. The "engine" and "refrigerator" statements of the second law state that these processes can be only partially reversed. We could cite other examples. Gases naturally flow from a region of high pressure to a region of low pressure; gases and miscible liquids left by themselves always tend to mix, not to unmix. The second law of thermodynamics is an expression of the inherent one-way aspect of these and many other irreversible processes. Energy conversion is an essential aspect of all plant and animal life and of human technology, so the second law of thermodynamics is of fundamental importance.

Test Your Understanding of Section 20.5 Would a 100%-efficient engine (Fig. 20.11a) violate the *first* law of thermodynamics? What about a workless refrigerator (Fig. 20.11b)? ❚

20.6 The Carnot Cycle

According to the second law, no heat engine can have 100% efficiency. How great an efficiency *can* an engine have, given two heat reservoirs at temperatures T_H and T_C? This question was answered in 1824 by the French engineer Sadi Carnot (1796–1832), who developed a hypothetical, idealized heat engine that has the maximum possible efficiency consistent with the second law. The cycle of this engine is called the **Carnot cycle.**

To understand the rationale of the Carnot cycle, we return to *reversibility* and its relationship to directions of thermodynamic processes. Conversion of work to heat is an irreversible process; the purpose of a heat engine is a *partial* reversal of this process, the conversion of heat to work with as great an efficiency as possible. For maximum heat-engine efficiency, therefore, *we must avoid all irreversible processes* (Fig. 20.12).

Heat flow through a finite temperature drop is an irreversible process. Therefore, during heat transfer in the Carnot cycle there must be *no* finite temperature difference. When the engine takes heat from the hot reservoir at temperature T_H, the working substance of the engine must also be at T_H; otherwise, irreversible heat flow would occur. Similarly, when the engine discards heat to the cold reservoir at T_C, the engine itself must be at T_C. That is, every process that involves heat transfer must be *isothermal* at either T_H or T_C.

Conversely, in any process in which the temperature of the working substance of the engine is intermediate between T_H and T_C, there must be *no* heat transfer between the engine and either reservoir because such heat transfer could not be reversible. Therefore any process in which the temperature T of the working substance changes must be *adiabatic*.

The bottom line is that every process in our idealized cycle must be either isothermal or adiabatic. In addition, thermal and mechanical equilibrium must be maintained at all times so that each process is completely reversible.

20.12 The temperature of the firebox of a steam engine is much higher than the temperature of water in the boiler, so heat flows irreversibly from firebox to water. Carnot's quest to understand the efficiency of steam engines led him to the idea that an ideal engine would involve only *reversible* processes.

ActivPhysics 8.14: Carnot Cycle

Steps of the Carnot Cycle

The Carnot cycle consists of two reversible isothermal and two reversible adiabatic processes. Figure 20.13 shows a Carnot cycle using as its working substance an ideal gas in a cylinder with a piston. It consists of the following steps:

1. The gas expands isothermally at temperature T_H, absorbing heat Q_H (*ab*).
2. It expands adiabatically until its temperature drops to T_C (*bc*).
3. It is compressed isothermally at T_C, rejecting heat $|Q_C|$ (*cd*).
4. It is compressed adiabatically back to its initial state at temperature T_H (*da*).

20.13 The Carnot cycle for an ideal gas. The light blue lines in the *pV*-diagram are isotherms (curves of constant temperature) and the dark blue lines are adiabats (curves of zero heat flow).

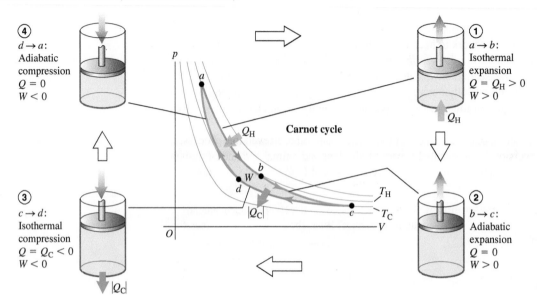

We can calculate the thermal efficiency *e* of a Carnot engine in the special case shown in Fig. 20.13 in which the working substance is an *ideal gas*. To carry out this calculation, we will first find the ratio Q_C/Q_H of the quantities of heat transferred in the two isothermal processes and then use Eq. (20.4) to find *e*.

For an ideal gas the internal energy *U* depends only on temperature and is thus constant in any isothermal process. For the isothermal expansion *ab*, $\Delta U_{ab} = 0$ and Q_H is equal to the work W_{ab} done by the gas during its isothermal expansion at temperature T_H. We calculated this work in Example 19.1 (Section 19.2); using that result, we have

$$Q_H = W_{ab} = nRT_H \ln \frac{V_b}{V_a} \tag{20.10}$$

Similarly,

$$Q_C = W_{cd} = nRT_C \ln \frac{V_d}{V_c} = -nRT_C \ln \frac{V_c}{V_d} \tag{20.11}$$

Because V_d is less than V_c, Q_C is negative ($Q_C = -|Q_C|$); heat flows out of the gas during the isothermal compression at temperature T_C.

The ratio of the two quantities of heat is thus

$$\frac{Q_C}{Q_H} = -\left(\frac{T_C}{T_H}\right) \frac{\ln (V_c/V_d)}{\ln (V_b/V_a)} \tag{20.12}$$

This can be simplified further by use of the temperature–volume relationship for an adiabatic process, Eq. (19.22). We find for the two adiabatic processes:

$$T_H V_b{}^{\gamma-1} = T_C V_c{}^{\gamma-1} \quad \text{and} \quad T_H V_a{}^{\gamma-1} = T_C V_d{}^{\gamma-1}$$

Dividing the first of these by the second, we find

$$\frac{V_b{}^{\gamma-1}}{V_a{}^{\gamma-1}} = \frac{V_c{}^{\gamma-1}}{V_d{}^{\gamma-1}} \quad \text{and} \quad \frac{V_b}{V_a} = \frac{V_c}{V_d}$$

Thus the two logarithms in Eq. (20.12) are equal, and that equation reduces to

$$\frac{Q_C}{Q_H} = -\frac{T_C}{T_H} \quad \text{or} \quad \frac{|Q_C|}{|Q_H|} = \frac{T_C}{T_H} \qquad \text{(heat transfer in a Carnot engine)} \quad \text{(20.13)}$$

The ratio of the heat rejected at T_C to the heat absorbed at T_H is just equal to the ratio T_C/T_H. Then from Eq. (20.4) the efficiency of the Carnot engine is

$$e_{Carnot} = 1 - \frac{T_C}{T_H} = \frac{T_H - T_C}{T_H} \qquad \text{(efficiency of a Carnot engine)} \quad \text{(20.14)}$$

This simple result says that the efficiency of a Carnot engine depends only on the temperatures of the two heat reservoirs. The efficiency is large when the temperature *difference* is large, and it is very small when the temperatures are nearly equal. The efficiency can never be exactly unity unless $T_C = 0$; we'll see later that this, too, is impossible.

CAUTION **Use Kelvin temperature in Carnot calculations** In all calculations involving the Carnot cycle, you must make sure that you use *absolute* (Kelvin) temperatures only. That's because Eqs. (20.10) through (20.14) come from the ideal-gas equation $pV = nRT$, in which T is absolute temperature.

Example 20.2 **Analyzing a Carnot engine I**

A Carnot engine takes 2000 J of heat from a reservoir at 500 K, does some work, and discards some heat to a reservoir at 350 K. How much work does it do, how much heat is discarded, and what is its efficiency?

SOLUTION

IDENTIFY and SET UP: This problem involves a Carnot engine, so we can use the ideas of this section and those of Section 20.2 (which apply to heat engines of all kinds). Figure 20.14 shows the energy-flow diagram. We have $Q_H = 2000$ J, $T_H = 500$ K, and $T_C = 350$ K. We use Eq. (20.13) to find Q_C, and then use the first law of thermodynamics as given by Eq. (20.2) to find W. We find the efficiency e from T_C and T_H using Eq. (20.14).

EXECUTE: From Eq. (20.13),

$$Q_C = -Q_H \frac{T_C}{T_H} = -(2000 \text{ J})\frac{350 \text{ K}}{500 \text{ K}} = -1400 \text{ J}$$

Then from Eq. (20.2), the work done is

$$W = Q_H + Q_C = 2000 \text{ J} + (-1400 \text{ J}) = 600 \text{ J}$$

From Eq. (20.14), the thermal efficiency is

$$e = 1 - \frac{T_C}{T_H} = 1 - \frac{350 \text{ K}}{500 \text{ K}} = 0.30 = 30\%$$

EVALUATE: The negative sign of Q_C is correct: It shows that 1400 J of heat flows *out* of the engine and into the cold reservoir. We can check our result for e by using the basic definition of thermal efficiency, Eq. (20.3):

$$e = \frac{W}{Q_H} = \frac{600 \text{ J}}{2000 \text{ J}} = 0.30 = 30\%$$

20.14 Our sketch for this problem.

$T_H = 500 \text{ K}$

$Q_H = 2000 \text{ J}$

$W = ?$

$e = ?$

$Q_C = ?$

$T_C = 350 \text{ K}$

Example 20.3 **Analyzing a Carnot engine II**

Suppose 0.200 mol of an ideal diatomic gas ($\gamma = 1.40$) undergoes a Carnot cycle between 227°C and 27°C, starting at $p_a = 10.0 \times 10^5$ Pa at point a in the pV-diagram of Fig. 20.13. The volume doubles during the isothermal expansion step $a \rightarrow b$. (a) Find the pressure and volume at points a, b, c, and d. (b) Find Q, W, and ΔU for each step and for the entire cycle. (c) Find the efficiency directly from the results of part (b), and compare with the value calculated from Eq. (20.14).

Continued

SOLUTION

IDENTIFY and SET UP: This problem involves the properties of the Carnot cycle and those of an ideal gas. We are given the number of moles n and the pressure and temperature at point a (which is at the higher of the two reservoir temperatures); we can find the volume at a using the ideal-gas equation $pV = nRT$. We then find the pressure and volume at points b, c, and d from the known doubling of volume in step $a \rightarrow b$, from equations given in this section, and from $pV = nRT$. In each step we use Eqs. (20.10) and (20.11) to find the heat flow and work done and Eq. (19.13) to find the internal energy change.

EXECUTE: (a) With $T_H = (227 + 273.15)$ K = 500 K and $T_C =$ $(27 + 273.15)$ K = 300 K, $pV = nRT$ yields

$$V_a = \frac{nRT_H}{p_a} = \frac{(0.200 \text{ mol})(8.314 \text{ J/mol} \cdot \text{K})(500 \text{ K})}{10.0 \times 10^5 \text{ Pa}}$$

$$= 8.31 \times 10^{-4} \text{ m}^3$$

The volume doubles during the isothermal expansion $a \rightarrow b$:

$$V_b = 2V_a = 2(8.31 \times 10^{-4} \text{ m}^3) = 16.6 \times 10^{-4} \text{ m}^3$$

Because the expansion $a \rightarrow b$ is isothermal, $p_a V_a = p_b V_b$, so

$$p_b = \frac{p_a V_a}{V_b} = 5.00 \times 10^5 \text{ Pa}$$

For the adiabatic expansion $b \rightarrow c$, we use the equation $T_H V_b^{\gamma-1} = T_C V_c^{\gamma-1}$ that follows Eq. (20.12) as well as the ideal-gas equation:

$$V_c = V_b \left(\frac{T_H}{T_C}\right)^{1/(\gamma-1)} = (16.6 \times 10^{-4} \text{ m}^3)\left(\frac{500 \text{ K}}{300 \text{ K}}\right)^{2.5}$$

$$= 59.6 \times 10^{-4} \text{ m}^3$$

$$p_c = \frac{nRT_C}{V_c} = \frac{(0.200 \text{ mol})(8.314 \text{ J/mol} \cdot \text{K})(300 \text{ K})}{59.6 \times 10^{-4} \text{ m}^3}$$

$$= 0.837 \times 10^5 \text{ Pa}$$

For the adiabatic compression $d \rightarrow a$ we have $T_C V_d^{\gamma-1} = T_H V_a^{\gamma-1}$ and so

$$V_d = V_a \left(\frac{T_H}{T_C}\right)^{1/(\gamma-1)} = (8.31 \times 10^{-4} \text{ m}^3)\left(\frac{500 \text{ K}}{300 \text{ K}}\right)^{2.5}$$

$$= 29.8 \times 10^{-4} \text{ m}^3$$

$$p_d = \frac{nRT_C}{V_d} = \frac{(0.200 \text{ mol})(8.314 \text{ J/mol} \cdot \text{K})(300 \text{ K})}{29.8 \times 10^{-4} \text{ m}^3}$$

$$= 1.67 \times 10^5 \text{ Pa}$$

(b) For the isothermal expansion $a \rightarrow b$, $\Delta U_{ab} = 0$. From Eq. (20.10),

$$W_{ab} = Q_H = nRT_H \ln \frac{V_b}{V_a}$$

$$= (0.200 \text{ mol})(8.314 \text{ J/mol} \cdot \text{K})(500 \text{ K})(\ln 2) = 576 \text{ J}$$

For the adiabatic expansion $b \rightarrow c$, $Q_{bc} = 0$. From the first law of thermodynamics, $\Delta U_{bc} = Q_{bc} - W_{bc} = -W_{bc}$; the work W_{bc} done by the gas in this adiabatic expansion equals the negative of the change in internal energy of the gas. From Eq. (19.13) we have $\Delta U = nC_V \Delta T$, where $\Delta T = T_C - T_H$. Using $C_V = 20.8$ J/mol · K for an ideal diatomic gas, we find

$$W_{bc} = -\Delta U_{bc} = -nC_V(T_C - T_H) = nC_V(T_H - T_C)$$

$$= (0.200 \text{ mol})(20.8 \text{ J/mol} \cdot \text{K})(500 \text{ K} - 300 \text{ K}) = 832 \text{ J}$$

For the isothermal compression $c \rightarrow d$, $\Delta U_{cd} = 0$; Eq. (20.11) gives

$$W_{cd} = Q_C = nRT_C \ln \frac{V_d}{V_c}$$

$$= (0.200 \text{ mol})(8.314 \text{ J/mol} \cdot \text{K})(300 \text{ K})\left(\ln \frac{29.8 \times 10^{-4} \text{ m}^3}{59.6 \times 10^{-4} \text{ m}^3}\right)$$

$$= -346 \text{ J}$$

For the adiabatic compression $d \rightarrow a$, $Q_{da} = 0$ and

$$W_{da} = -\Delta U_{da} = -nC_V(T_H - T_C) = nC_V(T_C - T_H)$$

$$= (0.200 \text{ mol})(20.8 \text{ J/mol} \cdot \text{K})(300 \text{ K} - 500 \text{ K}) = -832 \text{ J}$$

We can tabulate these results as follows:

Process	Q	W	ΔU
$a \rightarrow b$	576 J	576 J	0
$b \rightarrow c$	0	832 J	−832 J
$c \rightarrow d$	−346 J	−346 J	0
$d \rightarrow a$	0	−832 J	832 J
Total	230 J	230 J	0

(c) From the above table, $Q_H = 576$ J and the total work is 230 J. Thus

$$e = \frac{W}{Q_H} = \frac{230 \text{ J}}{576 \text{ J}} = 0.40 = 40\%$$

We can compare this to the result from Eq. (20.14),

$$e = \frac{T_H - T_C}{T_H} = \frac{500 \text{ K} - 300 \text{ K}}{500 \text{ K}} = 0.40 = 40\%$$

EVALUATE: The table in part (b) shows that for the entire cycle $Q = W$ and $\Delta U = 0$, just as we would expect: In a complete cycle, the *net* heat input is used to do work, and there is zero net change in the internal energy of the system. Note also that the quantities of work in the two adiabatic processes are negatives of each other. Can you show from the analysis leading to Eq. (20.13) that this must *always* be the case in a Carnot cycle?

The Carnot Refrigerator

Because each step in the Carnot cycle is reversible, the *entire cycle* may be reversed, converting the engine into a refrigerator. The coefficient of performance of the Carnot refrigerator is obtained by combining the general definition of K, Eq. (20.9), with Eq. (20.13) for the Carnot cycle. We first rewrite Eq. (20.9) as

$$K = \frac{|Q_C|}{|Q_H| - |Q_C|} = \frac{|Q_C|/|Q_H|}{1 - |Q_C|/|Q_H|}$$

Then we substitute Eq. (20.13), $|Q_C|/|Q_H| = T_C/T_H$, into this expression. The result is

$$K_{\text{Carnot}} = \frac{T_C}{T_H - T_C} \qquad \begin{array}{l}\text{(coefficient of performance}\\ \text{of a Carnot refrigerator)}\end{array} \qquad (20.15)$$

When the temperature difference $T_H - T_C$ is small, K is much larger than unity; in this case a lot of heat can be "pumped" from the lower to the higher temperature with only a little expenditure of work. But the greater the temperature difference, the smaller the value of K and the more work is required to transfer a given quantity of heat.

Example 20.4 Analyzing a Carnot refrigerator

If the cycle described in Example 20.3 is run backward as a refrigerator, what is its coefficient of performance?

SOLUTION

IDENTIFY and SET UP: This problem uses the ideas of Section 20.3 (for refrigerators in general) and the above discussion of Carnot refrigerators. Equation (20.9) gives the coefficient of performance K of *any* refrigerator in terms of the heat Q_C extracted from the cold reservoir per cycle and the work W that must be done per cycle.

EXECUTE: In Example 20.3 we found that in one cycle the Carnot engine rejects heat $Q_C = -346$ J to the cold reservoir and does work $W = 230$ J. When run in reverse as a refrigerator, the system

extracts heat $Q_C = +346$ J from the cold reservoir while requiring a work input of $W = -230$ J. From Eq. (20.9),

$$K = \frac{|Q_C|}{|W|} = \frac{346 \text{ J}}{230 \text{ J}} = 1.50$$

Because this is a Carnot cycle, we can also use Eq. (20.15):

$$K = \frac{T_C}{T_H - T_C} = \frac{300 \text{ K}}{500 \text{ K} - 300 \text{ K}} = 1.50$$

EVALUATE: Equations (20.14) and (20.15) show that e and K for a Carnot cycle depend only on T_H and T_C, and we don't need to calculate Q and W. For cycles containing irreversible processes, however, these two equations are not valid, and more detailed calculations are necessary.

The Carnot Cycle and the Second Law

We can prove that **no engine can be more efficient than a Carnot engine operating between the same two temperatures.** The key to the proof is the above observation that since each step in the Carnot cycle is reversible, the *entire cycle* may be reversed. Run backward, the engine becomes a refrigerator. Suppose we have an engine that is more efficient than a Carnot engine (Fig. 20.15). Let the Carnot engine, run backward as a refrigerator by negative work $-|W|$, take

20.15 Proving that the Carnot engine has the highest possible efficiency. A "superefficient" engine (more efficient than a Carnot engine) combined with a Carnot refrigerator could convert heat completely into work with no net heat transfer to the cold reservoir. This would violate the second law of thermodynamics.

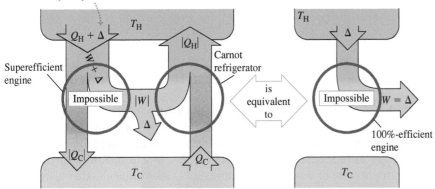

If a superefficient engine were possible, it could be used in conjunction with a Carnot refrigerator to convert the heat Δ completely to work, with no net transfer to the cold reservoir.

in heat Q_C from the cold reservoir and expel heat $|Q_H|$ to the hot reservoir. The superefficient engine expels heat $|Q_C|$, but to do this, it takes in a greater amount of heat $Q_H + \Delta$. Its work output is then $W + \Delta$, and the net effect of the two machines together is to take a quantity of heat Δ and convert it completely into work. This violates the engine statement of the second law. We could construct a similar argument that a superefficient engine could be used to violate the refrigerator statement of the second law. Note that we don't have to assume that the superefficient engine is reversible. In a similar way we can show that *no refrigerator can have a greater coefficient of performance than a Carnot refrigerator operating between the same two temperatures.*

Thus the statement that no engine can be more efficient than a Carnot engine is yet another equivalent statement of the second law of thermodynamics. It also follows directly that **all Carnot engines operating between the same two temperatures have the same efficiency, irrespective of the nature of the working substance.** Although we derived Eq. (20.14) for a Carnot engine using an ideal gas as its working substance, it is in fact valid for *any* Carnot engine, no matter what its working substance.

Equation (20.14), the expression for the efficiency of a Carnot engine, sets an upper limit to the efficiency of a real engine such as a steam turbine. To maximize this upper limit and the actual efficiency of the real engine, the designer must make the intake temperature T_H as high as possible and the exhaust temperature T_C as low as possible (Fig. 20.16).

The exhaust temperature cannot be lower than the lowest temperature available for cooling the exhaust. For a steam turbine at an electric power plant, T_C may be the temperature of river or lake water; then we want the boiler temperature T_H to be as high as possible. The vapor pressures of all liquids increase rapidly with temperature, so we are limited by the mechanical strength of the boiler. At 500°C the vapor pressure of water is about 240×10^5 Pa (235 atm); this is about the maximum practical pressure in large present-day steam boilers.

20.16 To maximize efficiency, the temperatures inside a jet engine are made as high as possible. Exotic ceramic materials are used that can withstand temperatures in excess of 1000°C without melting or becoming soft.

The Kelvin Temperature Scale

In Chapter 17 we expressed the need for a temperature scale that doesn't depend on the properties of any particular material. We can now use the Carnot cycle to define such a scale. The thermal efficiency of a Carnot engine operating between two heat reservoirs at temperatures T_H and T_C is independent of the nature of the working substance and depends only on the temperatures. From Eq. (20.4), this thermal efficiency is

$$e = \frac{Q_H + Q_C}{Q_H} = 1 + \frac{Q_C}{Q_H}$$

Therefore the ratio Q_C/Q_H is the same for *all* Carnot engines operating between two given temperatures T_H and T_C.

Kelvin proposed that we *define* the ratio of the temperatures, T_C/T_H, to be equal to the magnitude of the ratio Q_C/Q_H of the quantities of heat absorbed and rejected:

$$\frac{T_C}{T_H} = \frac{|Q_C|}{|Q_H|} = -\frac{Q_C}{Q_H} \qquad \text{(definition of Kelvin temperature)} \quad (20.16)$$

Equation (20.16) looks identical to Eq. (20.13), but there is a subtle and crucial difference. The temperatures in Eq. (20.13) are based on an ideal-gas thermometer, as defined in Section 17.3, while Eq. (20.16) *defines* a temperature scale based on the Carnot cycle and the second law of thermodynamics and is independent of the behavior of any particular substance. Thus the **Kelvin temperature scale** is truly *absolute*. To complete the definition of the Kelvin scale, we assign, as in Section 17.3, the arbitrary value of 273.16 K to the temperature of the triple point of water. When a substance is taken around a Carnot cycle, the ratio of the heats absorbed and rejected, $|Q_H|/|Q_C|$, is equal to the ratio of the temperatures of the reservoirs *as expressed on the gas-thermometer scale* defined in Section 17.3. Since the triple point of water is chosen to be 273.16 K in both scales, it follows that *the Kelvin and ideal-gas scales are identical.*

The zero point on the Kelvin scale is called **absolute zero.** At absolute zero a system has its *minimum* possible total internal energy (kinetic plus potential). Because of quantum effects, however, it is *not* true that at $T = 0$, all molecular motion ceases. There are theoretical reasons for believing that absolute zero cannot be attained experimentally, although temperatures below 10^{-7} K have been achieved. The more closely we approach absolute zero, the more difficult it is to get closer. One statement of the *third law of thermodynamics* is that it is impossible to reach absolute zero in a finite number of thermodynamic steps.

Test Your Understanding of Section 20.6   An inventor looking for financial support comes to you with an idea for a gasoline engine that runs on a novel type of thermodynamic cycle. His design is made entirely of copper and is air-cooled. He claims that the engine will be 85% efficient. Should you invest in this marvelous new engine? (*Hint:* See Table 17.4.)   ❙

20.7 Entropy

The second law of thermodynamics, as we have stated it, is not an equation or a quantitative relationship but rather a statement of *impossibility*. However, the second law *can* be stated as a quantitative relationship with the concept of *entropy,* the subject of this section.

We have talked about several processes that proceed naturally in the direction of increasing disorder. Irreversible heat flow increases disorder because the molecules are initially sorted into hotter and cooler regions; this sorting is lost when the system comes to thermal equilibrium. Adding heat to a body increases its disorder because it increases average molecular speeds and therefore the randomness of molecular motion. Free expansion of a gas increases its disorder because the molecules have greater randomness of position after the expansion than before. Figure 20.17 shows another process in which disorder increases.

Entropy and Disorder

Entropy provides a *quantitative* measure of disorder. To introduce this concept, let's consider an infinitesimal isothermal expansion of an ideal gas. We add heat dQ and let the gas expand just enough to keep the temperature constant. Because the internal energy of an ideal gas depends only on its temperature, the internal energy is also constant; thus from the first law, the work dW done by the gas is equal to the heat dQ added. That is,

$$dQ = dW = p\,dV = \frac{nRT}{V}\,dV \quad \text{so} \quad \frac{dV}{V} = \frac{dQ}{nRT}$$

The gas is more disordered after the expansion than before: The molecules are moving in a larger volume and have more randomness of position. Thus the fractional volume change dV/V is a measure of the increase in disorder, and the above equation shows that it is proportional to the quantity dQ/T. We introduce the symbol S for the entropy of the system, and we define the infinitesimal entropy change dS during an infinitesimal reversible process at absolute temperature T as

$$dS = \frac{dQ}{T} \quad \text{(infinitesimal reversible process)} \qquad (20.17)$$

If a total amount of heat Q is added during a reversible isothermal process at absolute temperature T, the total entropy change $\Delta S = S_2 - S_1$ is given by

$$\Delta S = S_2 - S_1 = \frac{Q}{T} \quad \text{(reversible isothermal process)} \qquad (20.18)$$

20.17 When firecrackers explode, disorder increases: The neatly packaged chemicals within each firecracker are dispersed in all directions, and the stored chemical energy is converted to random kinetic energy of the fragments.

Entropy has units of energy divided by temperature; the SI unit of entropy is 1 J/K.

We can see how the quotient Q/T is related to the increase in disorder. Higher temperature means greater randomness of motion. If the substance is initially cold, with little molecular motion, adding heat Q causes a substantial fractional increase in molecular motion and randomness. But if the substance is already hot, the same quantity of heat adds relatively little to the greater molecular motion already present. So Q/T is an appropriate characterization of the increase in randomness or disorder when heat flows into a system.

Example 20.5 Entropy change in melting

What is the change of entropy of 1 kg of ice that is melted reversibly at 0°C and converted to water at 0°C? The heat of fusion of water is $L_f = 3.34 \times 10^5$ J/kg.

SOLUTION

IDENTIFY and SET UP: The melting occurs at a constant temperature $T = 0°C = 273$ K, so this is an *isothermal* reversible process. We can calculate the added heat Q required to melt the ice, then calculate the entropy change ΔS using Eq. (20.18).

EXECUTE: The heat needed to melt the ice is $Q = mL_f = 3.34 \times 10^5$ J. Then from Eq. (20.18),

$$\Delta S = S_2 - S_1 = \frac{Q}{T} = \frac{3.34 \times 10^5 \text{ J}}{273 \text{ K}} = 1.22 \times 10^3 \text{ J/K}$$

EVALUATE: This entropy increase corresponds to the increase in disorder when the water molecules go from the highly ordered state of a crystalline solid to the much more disordered state of a liquid. In *any* isothermal reversible process, the entropy change equals the heat transferred divided by the absolute temperature. When we refreeze the water, Q has the opposite sign, and the entropy change is $\Delta S = -1.22 \times 10^3$ J/K. The water molecules rearrange themselves into a crystal to form ice, so disorder and entropy both decrease.

Entropy in Reversible Processes

We can generalize the definition of entropy change to include *any* reversible process leading from one state to another, whether it is isothermal or not. We represent the process as a series of infinitesimal reversible steps. During a typical step, an infinitesimal quantity of heat dQ is added to the system at absolute temperature T. Then we sum (integrate) the quotients dQ/T for the entire process; that is,

$$\Delta S = \int_1^2 \frac{dQ}{T} \qquad \text{(entropy change in a reversible process)} \quad (20.19)$$

The limits 1 and 2 refer to the initial and final states.

Because entropy is a measure of the disorder of a system in any specific state, it must depend only on the current state of the system, not on its past history. (We will verify this later.) When a system proceeds from an initial state with entropy S_1 to a final state with entropy S_2, the change in entropy $\Delta S = S_2 - S_1$ defined by Eq. (20.19) does not depend on the path leading from the initial to the final state but is the same for *all possible* processes leading from state 1 to state 2. Thus the entropy of a system must also have a definite value for any given state of the system. *Internal energy*, introduced in Chapter 19, also has this property, although entropy and internal energy are very different quantities.

Since entropy is a function only of the state of a system, we can also compute entropy changes in *irreversible* (nonequilibrium) processes for which Eqs. (20.17) and (20.19) are not applicable. We simply invent a path connecting the given initial and final states that *does* consist entirely of reversible equilibrium processes and compute the total entropy change for that path. It is not the actual path, but the entropy change must be the same as for the actual path.

As with internal energy, the above discussion does not tell us how to calculate entropy itself, but only the change in entropy in any given process. Just as with internal energy, we may arbitrarily assign a value to the entropy of a system in a specified reference state and then calculate the entropy of any other state with reference to this.

Example 20.6 Entropy change in a temperature change

One kilogram of water at 0°C is heated to 100°C. Compute its change in entropy. Assume that the specific heat of water is constant at 4190 J/kg·K over this temperature range.

SOLUTION

IDENTIFY and SET UP: The entropy change of the water depends only on the initial and final states of the system, no matter whether the process is reversible or irreversible. We can imagine a reversible process in which the water temperature is increased in a sequence of infinitesimal steps dT. We can use Eq. (20.19) to integrate over all these steps and calculate the entropy change for such a reversible process. (Heating the water on a stove whose cooking surface is maintained at 100°C would be an irreversible process. The entropy change would be the same, however.)

EXECUTE: From Eq. (17.14) the heat required to carry out each infinitesimal step is $dQ = mc\,dT$. Substituting this into Eq. (20.19) and integrating, we find

$$\Delta S = S_2 - S_1 = \int_1^2 \frac{dQ}{T} = \int_{T_1}^{T_2} mc\,\frac{dT}{T} = mc\,\ln\frac{T_2}{T_1}$$

$$= (1.00\text{ kg})(4190\text{ J/kg·K})\left(\ln\frac{373\text{ K}}{273\text{ K}}\right)$$

$$= 1.31 \times 10^3\text{ J/K}$$

EVALUATE: The entropy change is positive, as it must be for a process in which the system absorbs heat. Our assumption about the specific heat is a pretty good one, since c for water increases by only 1% between 0°C and 100°C.

CAUTION **When $\Delta S = Q/T$ can (and cannot) be used** In solving this problem you might be tempted to avoid doing an integral by using the simpler expression in Eq. (20.18), $\Delta S = Q/T$. This would be incorrect, however, because Eq. (20.18) is applicable only to *isothermal* processes, and the initial and final temperatures in our example are *not* the same. The *only* correct way to find the entropy change in a process with different initial and final temperatures is to use Eq. (20.19). ▮

Conceptual Example 20.7 Entropy change in a reversible adiabatic process

A gas expands adiabatically and reversibly. What is its change in entropy?

SOLUTION

In an adiabatic process, no heat enters or leaves the system. Hence $dQ = 0$ and there is *no* change in entropy in this reversible

process: $\Delta S = 0$. Every *reversible* adiabatic process is a constant-entropy process. (That's why such processes are also called *isentropic* processes.) The increase in disorder resulting from the gas occupying a greater volume is exactly balanced by the decrease in disorder associated with the lowered temperature and reduced molecular speeds.

Example 20.8 Entropy change in a free expansion

A partition divides a thermally insulated box into two compartments, each of volume V (Fig. 20.18). Initially, one compartment contains n moles of an ideal gas at temperature T, and the other compartment is evacuated. We break the partition and the gas expands, filling both compartments. What is the entropy change in this free-expansion process?

SOLUTION

IDENTIFY and SET UP: For this process, $Q = 0$, $W = 0$, $\Delta U = 0$, and therefore (because the system is an ideal gas) $\Delta T = 0$. We might think that the entropy change is zero because there is no heat exchange. But Eq. (20.19) can be used to calculate entropy changes for *reversible* processes only; this free expansion is *not* reversible, and there *is* an entropy change. As we mentioned at the beginning of this section, entropy increases in a free expansion because the positions of the molecules are more random than before the expansion. To calculate ΔS, we recall that the entropy change depends only on the initial and final states. We can devise a

20.18 (a, b) Free expansion of an insulated ideal gas. (c) The free-expansion process doesn't pass through equilibrium states from a to b. However, the entropy change $S_b - S_a$ can be calculated by using the isothermal path shown or *any* reversible path from a to b.

(a)　　　　　(b)　　　　　(c)

  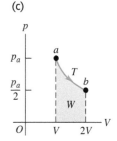

reversible process having the same endpoints as this free expansion, and in general we can then use Eq. (20.19) to calculate its entropy change, which will be the same as for the free expansion.

Continued

An appropriate reversible process is an *isothermal* expansion from V to $2V$ at temperature T, which allows us to use the simpler Eq. (20.18) to calculate ΔS. The gas does work W during this expansion, so an equal amount of heat Q must be supplied to keep the internal energy constant.

EXECUTE: We saw in Example 19.1 that the work done by n moles of ideal gas in an isothermal expansion from V_1 to V_2 is $W = nRT \ln(V_2/V_1)$. With $V_1 = V$ and $V_2 = 2V$, we have

$$Q = W = nRT \ln\frac{2V}{V} = nRT \ln 2$$

From Eq. (20.18), the entropy change is

$$\Delta S = \frac{Q}{T} = nR \ln 2$$

EVALUATE: For 1 mole, $\Delta S = (1\ \text{mol})(8.314\ \text{J/mol}\cdot\text{K})(\ln 2) = 5.76\ \text{J/K}$. The entropy change is positive, as we predicted. The factor $(\ln 2)$ in our answer is a result of the volume having increased by a factor of 2, from V to $2V$. Can you show that if the volume increases in a free expansion from V to xV, where x is an arbitrary number, the entropy change is $\Delta S = nR \ln x$?

Example 20.9   **Entropy and the Carnot cycle**

For the Carnot engine in Example 20.2 (Section 20.6), what is the total entropy change during one cycle?

SOLUTION

IDENTIFY and SET UP: All four steps in the Carnot cycle (see Fig. 20.13) are reversible, so we can use our expressions for the entropy change ΔS in a reversible process. We find ΔS for each step and add them to get ΔS for the complete cycle.

EXECUTE: There is no entropy change during the adiabatic expansion $b \to c$ or the adiabatic compression $d \to a$. During the isothermal expansion $a \to b$ at $T_H = 500$ K, the engine takes in 2000 J of heat, and from Eq. (20.18),

$$\Delta S_H = \frac{Q_H}{T_H} = \frac{2000\ \text{J}}{500\ \text{K}} = 4.0\ \text{J/K}$$

During the isothermal compression $c \to d$ at $T_C = 350$ K, the engine gives off 1400 J of heat, and

$$\Delta S_C = \frac{Q_C}{T_C} = \frac{-1400\ \text{J}}{350\ \text{K}} = -4.0\ \text{J/K}$$

The total entropy change in the engine during one cycle is $\Delta S_\text{tot} = \Delta S_H + \Delta S_C = 4.0\ \text{J/K} + (-4.0\ \text{J/K}) = 0$.

EVALUATE: The result $\Delta S_\text{total} = 0$ tells us that when the Carnot engine completes a cycle, it has the same entropy as it did at the beginning of the cycle. We'll explore this result in the next subsection.

What is the total entropy change of the engine's *environment* during this cycle? During the reversible isothermal expansion $a \to b$, the hot (500 K) reservoir gives off 2000 J of heat, so its entropy change is $(-2000\ \text{J})/(500\ \text{K}) = -4.0\ \text{J/K}$. During the reversible isothermal compression $c \to d$, the cold (350 K) reservoir absorbs 1400 J of heat, so its entropy change is $(+1400\ \text{J})/(350\ \text{K}) = +4.0\ \text{J/K}$. Thus the hot and cold reservoirs each have an entropy change, but the sum of these changes—that is, the total entropy change of the system's environment—is zero.

These results apply to the special case of the Carnot cycle, for which *all* of the processes are reversible. In this case we find that the total entropy change of the system and the environment together is zero. We will see that if the cycle includes irreversible processes (as is the case for the Otto and Diesel cycles of Section 20.3), the total entropy change of the system and the environment *cannot* be zero, but rather must be positive.

Entropy in Cyclic Processes

Example 20.9 showed that the total entropy change for a cycle of a particular Carnot engine, which uses an ideal gas as its working substance, is zero. This result follows directly from Eq. (20.13), which we can rewrite as

$$\frac{Q_H}{T_H} + \frac{Q_C}{T_C} = 0 \qquad (20.20)$$

The quotient Q_H/T_H equals ΔS_H, the entropy change of the engine that occurs at $T = T_H$. Likewise, Q_C/T_C equals ΔS_C, the (negative) entropy change of the engine that occurs at $T = T_C$. Hence Eq. (20.20) says that $\Delta S_H + \Delta S_C = 0$; that is, there is zero net entropy change in one cycle.

What about Carnot engines that use a different working substance? According to the second law, *any* Carnot engine operating between given temperatures T_H and T_C has the same efficiency $e = 1 - T_C/T_H$ [Eq. (20.14)]. Combining this expression for e with Eq. (20.4), $e = 1 + Q_C/Q_H$, just reproduces Eq. (20.20). So Eq. (20.20) is valid for any Carnot engine working between these temperatures, whether its working substance is an ideal gas or not. We conclude that *the total entropy change in one cycle of any Carnot engine is zero.*

20.19 (a) A reversible cyclic process for an ideal gas is shown as a red closed path on a pV-diagram. Several ideal-gas isotherms are shown in blue. (b) We can approximate the path in (a) by a series of long, thin Carnot cycles; one of these is highlighted in gold. The total entropy change is zero for each Carnot cycle and for the actual cyclic process. (c) The entropy change between points a and b is independent of the path.

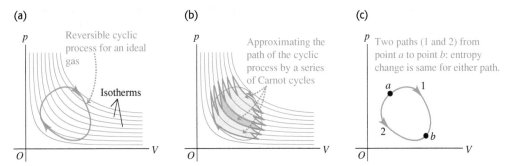

This result can be generalized to show that the total entropy change during *any* reversible cyclic process is zero. A reversible cyclic process appears on a pV-diagram as a closed path (Fig. 20.19a). We can approximate such a path as closely as we like by a sequence of isothermal and adiabatic processes forming parts of many long, thin Carnot cycles (Fig. 20.19b). The total entropy change for the full cycle is the sum of the entropy changes for each small Carnot cycle, each of which is zero. So **the total entropy change during *any* reversible cycle is zero:**

$$\oint \frac{dQ}{T} = 0 \qquad \text{(reversible cyclic process)} \qquad \text{(20.21)}$$

It follows that when a system undergoes a reversible process leading from any state a to any other state b, *the entropy change of the system is independent of the path* (Fig. 20.19c). If the entropy change for path 1 were different from the change for path 2, the system could be taken along path 1 and then backward along path 2 to the starting point, with a nonzero net change in entropy. This would violate the conclusion that the total entropy change in such a cyclic process must be zero. Because the entropy change in such processes is independent of path, we conclude that in any given state, the system has a definite value of entropy that depends only on the state, not on the processes that led to that state.

Entropy in Irreversible Processes

In an idealized, reversible process involving only equilibrium states, the total entropy change of the system and its surroundings is zero. But all *irreversible* processes involve an increase in entropy. Unlike energy, *entropy is not a conserved quantity.* The entropy of an isolated system *can* change, but as we shall see, it can never decrease. The free expansion of a gas, described in Example 20.8, is an irreversible process in an isolated system in which there is an entropy increase.

Application Entropy Changes in a Living Organism
When a kitten or other growing animal eats, it takes ordered chemical energy from the food and uses it to make new cells that are even more highly ordered. This process alone lowers entropy. But most of the energy in the food is either excreted in the animal's feces or used to generate heat, processes that lead to a large increase in entropy. So while the entropy of the animal alone decreases, the *total* entropy of animal plus food *increases*.

Example 20.10   **Entropy change in an irreversible process**

Suppose 1.00 kg of water at 100°C is placed in thermal contact with 1.00 kg of water at 0°C. What is the total change in entropy? Assume that the specific heat of water is constant at 4190 J/kg·K over this temperature range.

SOLUTION

IDENTIFY and SET UP: This process involves irreversible heat flow because of the temperature differences. There are equal masses of 0°C water and 100°C water, so the final temperature is the average of these two temperatures: 50°C = 323 K. Although the processes are irreversible, we can calculate the entropy changes for the (initially) hot water and the (initially) cold water by assuming that the process occurs reversibly. As in Example 20.6, we must use Eq. (20.19) to calculate ΔS for each substance because the temperatures are not constant.

Continued

EXECUTE: The entropy changes of the hot water (subscript H) and the cold water (subscript C) are

$$\Delta S_H = mc \int_{T_1}^{T_2} \frac{dT}{T} = (1.00 \text{ kg})(4190 \text{ J/kg} \cdot \text{K}) \int_{373 \text{ K}}^{323 \text{ K}} \frac{dT}{T}$$

$$= (4190 \text{ J/K})\left(\ln\frac{323 \text{ K}}{373 \text{ K}}\right) = -603 \text{ J/K}$$

$$\Delta S_C = (4190 \text{ J/K})\left(\ln\frac{323 \text{ K}}{273 \text{ K}}\right) = +705 \text{ J/K}$$

The *total* entropy change of the system is

$$\Delta S_{tot} = \Delta S_H + \Delta S_C = (-603 \text{ J/K}) + 705 \text{ J/K} = +102 \text{ J/K}$$

EVALUATE: An irreversible heat flow in an isolated system is accompanied by an increase in entropy. We could reach the same end state by mixing the hot and cold water, which is also an irreversible process; the total entropy change, which depends only on the initial and final states of the system, would again be 102 J/K.

Note that the entropy of the system increases *continuously* as the two quantities of water come to equilibrium. For example, the first 4190 J of heat transferred cools the hot water to 99°C and warms the cold water to 1°C. The net change in entropy for this step is approximately

$$\Delta S = \frac{-4190 \text{ J}}{373 \text{ K}} + \frac{4190 \text{ J}}{273 \text{ K}} = +4.1 \text{ J/K}$$

Can you show in a similar way that the net entropy change is positive for *any* one-degree temperature change leading to the equilibrium condition?

Entropy and the Second Law

The results of Example 20.10 about the flow of heat from a higher to a lower temperature are characteristic of *all* natural (that is, irreversible) processes. When we include the entropy changes of all the systems taking part in the process, the increases in entropy are always greater than the decreases. In the special case of a *reversible* process, the increases and decreases are equal. Hence we can state the general principle: **When all systems taking part in a process are included, the entropy either remains constant or increases.** In other words: **No process is possible in which the total entropy decreases, when all systems taking part in the process are included.** This is an alternative statement of the second law of thermodynamics in terms of entropy. Thus it is equivalent to the "engine" and "refrigerator" statements discussed earlier. Figure 20.20 shows a specific example of this general principle.

The increase of entropy in every natural, irreversible process measures the increase of disorder or randomness in the universe associated with that process. Consider again the example of mixing hot and cold water (Example 20.10). We *might* have used the hot and cold water as the high- and low-temperature reservoirs of a heat engine. While removing heat from the hot water and giving heat to the cold water, we could have obtained some mechanical work. But once the hot and cold water have been mixed and have come to a uniform temperature, this opportunity to convert heat to mechanical work is lost irretrievably. The lukewarm water will never *unmix* itself and separate into hotter and colder portions. No decrease in *energy* occurs when the hot and cold water are mixed. What has been lost is the *opportunity* to convert part of the heat from the hot water into mechanical work. Hence when entropy increases, energy becomes less *available*, and the universe becomes more random or "run down."

20.20 The mixing of colored ink and water starts from a state of relative order (low entropy) in which each fluid is separate and distinct from the other. The final state after mixing is more disordered (has greater entropy). Spontaneous unmixing of the ink and water, a process in which there would be a net decrease in entropy, is never observed.

Test Your Understanding of Section 20.7 Suppose 2.00 kg of water at 50°C spontaneously changes temperature, so that half of the water cools to 0°C while the other half spontaneously warms to 100°C. (All of the water remains liquid, so it doesn't freeze or boil.) What would be the entropy change of the water? Is this process possible? (*Hint: See Example 20.10.*)

20.8 Microscopic Interpretation of Entropy

We described in Section 19.4 how the internal energy of a system could be calculated, at least in principle, by adding up all the kinetic energies of its constituent particles and all the potential energies of interaction among the particles. This is called a *microscopic* calculation of the internal energy. We can also make a microscopic calculation of the entropy S of a system. Unlike energy, however, entropy is not something that belongs to each individual particle or pair of particles in the system. Rather, entropy is a measure of the disorder of the system as a whole. To see how to calculate entropy microscopically, we first have to introduce the idea of *macroscopic* and *microscopic states*.

Suppose you toss N identical coins on the floor, and half of them show heads and half show tails. This is a description of the large-scale or **macroscopic state** of the system of N coins. A description of the **microscopic state** of the system includes information about each individual coin: Coin 1 was heads, coin 2 was tails, coin 3 was tails, and so on. There can be many microscopic states that correspond to the same macroscopic description. For instance, with $N = 4$ coins there are six possible states in which half are heads and half are tails (Fig. 20.21). The number of microscopic states grows rapidly with increasing N; for $N = 100$ there are $2^{100} = 1.27 \times 10^{30}$ microscopic states, of which 1.01×10^{29} are half heads and half tails.

The least probable outcomes of the coin toss are the states that are either all heads or all tails. It is certainly possible that you could throw 100 heads in a row, but don't bet on it; the probability of doing this is only 1 in 1.27×10^{30}. The most probable outcome of tossing N coins is that half are heads and half are tails. The reason is that this *macroscopic* state has the greatest number of corresponding *microscopic* states, as Fig. 20.21 shows.

To make the connection to the concept of entropy, note that N coins that are all heads constitute a completely ordered macroscopic state; the description "all heads" completely specifies the state of each one of the N coins. The same is true if the coins are all tails. But the macroscopic description "half heads, half tails" by itself tells you very little about the state (heads or tails) of each individual coin. We say that the system is *disordered* because we know so little about its microscopic state. Compared to the state "all heads" or "all tails," the state "half heads, half tails" has a much greater number of possible microscopic states, much greater disorder, and hence much greater entropy (which is a quantitative measure of disorder).

Now instead of N coins, consider a mole of an ideal gas containing Avogadro's number of molecules. The macroscopic state of this gas is given by its pressure p, volume V, and temperature T; a description of the microscopic state involves stating the position and velocity for each molecule in the gas. At a given pressure, volume, and temperature, the gas may be in any one of an astronomically large number of microscopic states, depending on the positions and velocities of its 6.02×10^{23} molecules. If the gas undergoes a free expansion into a greater volume, the range of possible positions increases, as does the number of possible microscopic states. The system becomes more disordered, and the entropy increases as calculated in Example 20.8 (Section 20.7).

We can draw the following general conclusion: **For any system, the most probable macroscopic state is the one with the greatest number of corresponding microscopic states, which is also the macroscopic state with the greatest disorder and the greatest entropy.**

20.21 All possible microscopic states of four coins. There can be several possible microscopic states for each macroscopic state.

Calculating Entropy: Microscopic States

Let w represent the number of possible microscopic states for a given macroscopic state. (For the four coins shown in Fig. 20.21 the state of four heads has $w = 1$, the state of three heads and one tails has $w = 4$, and so on.) Then the entropy S of a macroscopic state can be shown to be given by

$$S = k \ln w \quad \text{(microscopic expression for entropy)} \quad (20.22)$$

where $k = R/N_A$ is the Boltzmann constant (gas constant per molecule) introduced in Section 18.3. As Eq. (20.22) shows, increasing the number of possible microscopic states w increases the entropy S.

What matters in a thermodynamic process is not the absolute entropy S but the *difference* in entropy between the initial and final states. Hence an equally valid and useful definition would be $S = k \ln w + C$, where C is a constant, since C cancels in any calculation of an entropy difference between two states. But it's convenient to set this constant equal to zero and use Eq. (20.22). With this choice, since the smallest possible value of w is unity, the smallest possible value of S for any system is $k \ln 1 = 0$. Entropy can *never* be negative.

In practice, calculating w is a difficult task, so Eq. (20.22) is typically used only to calculate the absolute entropy S of certain special systems. But we can use this relationship to calculate *differences* in entropy between one state and another. Consider a system that undergoes a thermodynamic process that takes it from macroscopic state 1, for which there are w_1 possible microscopic states, to macroscopic state 2, with w_2 associated microscopic states. The change in entropy in this process is

$$\Delta S = S_2 - S_1 = k \ln w_2 - k \ln w_1 = k \ln \frac{w_2}{w_1} \quad (20.23)$$

The *difference* in entropy between the two macroscopic states depends on the *ratio* of the numbers of possible microscopic states.

As the following example shows, using Eq. (20.23) to calculate a change in entropy from one macroscopic state to another gives the same results as considering a reversible process connecting those two states and using Eq. (20.19).

Example 20.11 | **A microscopic calculation of entropy change**

Use Eq. (20.23) to calculate the entropy change in the free expansion of n moles of gas at temperature T described in Example 20.8 (Fig. 20.22).

SOLUTION

IDENTIFY and SET UP: We are asked to calculate the entropy change using the number of microstates in the initial and final macroscopic states (Figs. 20.22a and b). When the partition is broken, no work is done, so the velocities of the molecules are unaffected. But each molecule now has twice as much volume in which it can move and hence has twice the number of possible positions. This is all we need to calculate the entropy change using Eq. (20.23).

EXECUTE: Let w_1 be the number of microscopic states of the system as a whole when the gas occupies volume V (Fig. 20.22a). The number of molecules is $N = n N_A$, and each of these N molecules has twice as many possible states after the partition is broken. Hence the number w_2 of microscopic states when the gas occupies volume $2V$ (Fig. 20.22b) is greater by a factor of 2^N; that is, $w_2 = 2^N w_1$. The change in entropy in this process is

$$\Delta S = k \ln \frac{w_2}{w_1} = k \ln \frac{2^N w_1}{w_1} = k \ln 2^N = Nk \ln 2$$

Since $N = n N_A$ and $k = R/N_A$, this becomes

$$\Delta S = (n N_A)(R/N_A) \ln 2 = n R \ln 2$$

EVALUATE: We found the same result as in Example 20.8, but without any reference to the thermodynamic path taken.

20.22 In a free expansion of N molecules in which the volume doubles, the number of possible microscopic states increases by 2^N.

(a) Gas occupies volume V; number of microstates = w_1.

(b) Gas occupies volume $2V$; number of microstates = $w_2 = 2^N w_1$.

Microscopic States and the Second Law

The relationship between entropy and the number of microscopic states gives us new insight into the entropy statement of the second law of thermodynamics: that the entropy of a closed system can never decrease. From Eq. (20.22) this means that a closed system can never spontaneously undergo a process that decreases the number of possible microscopic states.

An example of such a forbidden process would be if all of the air in your room spontaneously moved to one half of the room, leaving a vacuum in the other half. Such a "free compression" would be the reverse of the free expansion of Examples 20.8 and 20.11. This would decrease the number of possible microscopic states by a factor of 2^N. Strictly speaking, this process is not impossible! The probability of finding a given molecule in one half of the room is $\frac{1}{2}$, so the probability of finding all of the molecules in one half of the room at once is $\left(\frac{1}{2}\right)^N$. (This is exactly the same as the probability of having a tossed coin come up heads N times in a row.) This probability is *not* zero. But lest you worry about suddenly finding yourself gasping for breath in the evacuated half of your room, consider that a typical room might hold 1000 moles of air, and so $N = 1000N_A = 6.02 \times 10^{26}$ molecules. The probability of all the molecules being in the same half of the room is therefore $\left(\frac{1}{2}\right)^{6.02 \times 10^{26}}$. Expressed as a decimal, this number has more than 10^{26} zeros to the right of the decimal point!

Because the probability of such a "free compression" taking place is so vanishingly small, it has almost certainly never occurred anywhere in the universe since the beginning of time. We conclude that for all practical purposes the second law of thermodynamics is never violated.

Test Your Understanding of Section 20.8 A quantity of N molecules of an ideal gas initially occupies volume V. The gas then expands to volume $2V$. The number of microscopic states of the gas increases in this expansion. Under which of the following circumstances will this number increase the most? (i) if the expansion is reversible and isothermal; (ii) if the expansion is reversible and adiabatic; (iii) the number will change by the same amount for both circumstances.

Reversible and irreversible processes: A reversible process is one whose direction can be reversed by an infinitesimal change in the conditions of the process, and in which the system is always in or very close to thermal equilibrium. All other thermodynamic processes are irreversible.

Heat engines: A heat engine takes heat Q_H from a source, converts part of it to work W, and discards the remainder $|Q_C|$ at a lower temperature. The thermal efficiency e of a heat engine measures how much of the absorbed heat is converted to work. (See Example 20.1.)

$$e = \frac{W}{Q_H} = 1 + \frac{Q_C}{Q_H} = 1 - \left|\frac{Q_C}{Q_H}\right| \quad (20.4)$$

The Otto cycle: A gasoline engine operating on the Otto cycle has a theoretical maximum thermal efficiency e that depends on the compression ratio r and the ratio of heat capacities γ of the working substance.

$$e = 1 - \frac{1}{r^{\gamma - 1}} \quad (20.6)$$

Refrigerators: A refrigerator takes heat Q_C from a colder place, has a work input $|W|$, and discards heat $|Q_H|$ at a warmer place. The effectiveness of the refrigerator is given by its coefficient of performance K.

$$K = \frac{|Q_C|}{|W|} = \frac{|Q_C|}{|Q_H| - |Q_C|} \quad (20.9)$$

The second law of thermodynamics: The second law of thermodynamics describes the directionality of natural thermodynamic processes. It can be stated in several equivalent forms. The *engine* statement is that no cyclic process can convert heat completely into work. The *refrigerator* statement is that no cyclic process can transfer heat from a colder place to a hotter place with no input of mechanical work.

The Carnot cycle: The Carnot cycle operates between two heat reservoirs at temperatures T_H and T_C and uses only reversible processes. Its thermal efficiency depends only on T_H and T_C. An additional equivalent statement of the second law is that no engine operating between the same two temperatures can be more efficient than a Carnot engine. (See Examples 20.2 and 20.3.)

$$e_{Carnot} = 1 - \frac{T_C}{T_H} = \frac{T_H - T_C}{T_H} \quad (20.14)$$

A Carnot engine run backward is a Carnot refrigerator. Its coefficient of performance depends only on T_H and T_C. Another form of the second law states that no refrigerator operating between the same two temperatures can have a larger coefficient of performance than a Carnot refrigerator. (See Example 20.4.)

$$K_{Carnot} = \frac{T_C}{T_H - T_C} \quad (20.15)$$

Entropy: Entropy is a quantitative measure of the disorder of a system. The entropy change in any reversible process depends on the amount of heat flow and the absolute temperature T. Entropy depends only on the state of the system, and the change in entropy between given initial and final states is the same for all processes leading from one state to the other. This fact can be used to find the entropy change in an irreversible process. (See Examples 20.5–20.10.)

$$\Delta S = \int_1^2 \frac{dQ}{T} \quad (20.19)$$
(reversible process)

An important statement of the second law of thermo-dynamics is that the entropy of an isolated system may increase but can never decrease. When a system interacts with its surroundings, the total entropy change of system and surroundings can never decrease. When the interaction involves only reversible processes, the total entropy is constant and $\Delta S = 0$; when there is any irreversible process, the total entropy increases and $\Delta S > 0$.

Entropy and microscopic states: When a system is in a particular macroscopic state, the particles that make up the system may be in any of w possible microscopic states. The greater the number w, the greater the entropy. (See Example 20.11.)

$$S = k \ln w \qquad (20.22)$$

w microstates $\qquad$ $2^N w$ microstates

BRIDGING PROBLEM   Entropy Changes: Cold Ice in Hot Water

An insulated container of negligible mass holds 0.600 kg of water at 45.0°C. You put a 0.0500-kg ice cube at −15.0°C in the water. (a) Calculate the final temperature of the water once the ice has melted. (b) Calculate the change in entropy of the system.

SOLUTION GUIDE

See MasteringPhysics® study area for a Video Tutor solution.

IDENTIFY and SET UP

1. Make a list of the known and unknown quantities, and identify the target variables.
2. How will you find the final temperature of the ice–water mixture? How will you decide whether or not all the ice melts?
3. Once you find the final temperature of the mixture, how will you determine the changes in entropy of (i) the ice initially at −15.0°C and (ii) the water initially at 45.0°C?

EXECUTE

4. Use the methods of Chapter 17 to calculate the final temperature T. (*Hint:* First assume that all of the ice melts, then write

an equation which says that the heat that flows into the ice equals the heat that flows out of the water. If your assumption is correct, the final temperature that you calculate will be greater than 0°C. If your assumption is incorrect, the final temperature will be 0°C or less, which means that some ice remains. You'll then need to redo the calculation to account for this.)

5. Use your result from step 4 to calculate the entropy changes of the ice and the water. (*Hint:* You must include the heat flow associated with temperature changes, as in Example 20.6, as well as the heat flow associated with the change of phase.)
6. Find the total change in entropy of the system.

EVALUATE

7. Do the signs of the entropy changes make sense? Why or why not?

Problems

For instructor-assigned homework, go to MasteringPhysics®.

•, ••, •••: Problems of increasing difficulty. **CP**: Cumulative problems incorporating material from earlier chapters. **CALC**: Problems requiring calculus. **BIO**: Biosciences problems.

DISCUSSION QUESTIONS

Q20.1 A pot is half-filled with water, and a lid is placed on it, forming a tight seal so that no water vapor can escape. The pot is heated on a stove, forming water vapor inside the pot. The heat is then turned off and the water vapor condenses back to liquid. Is this cycle reversible or irreversible? Why?

Q20.2 Give two examples of reversible processes and two examples of irreversible processes in purely mechanical systems, such as blocks sliding on planes, springs, pulleys, and strings. Explain what makes each process reversible or irreversible.

Q20.3 What irreversible processes occur in a gasoline engine? Why are they irreversible?

Q20.4 Suppose you try to cool the kitchen of your house by leaving the refrigerator door open. What happens? Why? Would the result be the same if you left open a picnic cooler full of ice? Explain the reason for any differences.

Q20.5 A member of the U.S. Congress proposed a scheme to produce energy as follows. Water molecules (H_2O) are to be broken apart to produce hydrogen and oxygen. The hydrogen is then burned (that is, combined with oxygen), releasing energy in the process. The only product of this combustion is water, so there is no pollution. In light of the second law of thermodynamics, what do you think of this energy-producing scheme?

Q20.6 Is it a violation of the second law of thermodynamics to convert mechanical energy completely into heat? To convert heat completely into work? Explain your answers.

Q20.7 Imagine a special air filter placed in a window of a house. The tiny holes in the filter allow only air molecules moving faster than a certain speed to exit the house, and allow only air molecules moving slower than that speed to enter the house from outside. Explain why such an air filter would cool the house, and why the second law of thermodynamics makes building such a filter an impossible task.

Q20.8 An electric motor has its shaft coupled to that of an electric generator. The motor drives the generator, and some current from the generator is used to run the motor. The excess current is used to light a home. What is wrong with this scheme?

Q20.9 When a wet cloth is hung up in a hot wind in the desert, it is cooled by evaporation to a temperature that may be 20 C° or so below that of the air. Discuss this process in light of the second law of thermodynamics.

Q20.10 Compare the pV-diagram for the Otto cycle in Fig. 20.6 with the diagram for the Carnot heat engine in Fig. 20.13. Explain some of the important differences between the two cycles.

Q20.11 If no real engine can be as efficient as a Carnot engine operating between the same two temperatures, what is the point of developing and using Eq. (20.14)?

Q20.12 The efficiency of heat engines is high when the temperature difference between the hot and cold reservoirs is large. Refrigerators, on the other hand, work better when the temperature difference is small. Thinking of the mechanical refrigeration cycle shown in Fig. 20.9, explain in physical terms why it takes less work to remove heat from the working substance if the two reservoirs (the inside of the refrigerator and the outside air) are at nearly the same temperature, than if the outside air is much warmer than the interior of the refrigerator.

Q20.13 What would be the efficiency of a Carnot engine operating with $T_H = T_C$? What would be the efficiency if $T_C = 0$ K and T_H were any temperature above 0 K? Interpret your answers.

Q20.14 Real heat engines, like the gasoline engine in a car, always have some friction between their moving parts, although lubricants keep the friction to a minimum. Would a heat engine with completely frictionless parts be 100% efficient? Why or why not? Does the answer depend on whether or not the engine runs on the Carnot cycle? Again, why or why not?

Q20.15 Does a refrigerator full of food consume more power if the room temperature is 20°C than if it is 15°C? Or is the power consumption the same? Explain your reasoning.

Q20.16 In Example 20.4, a Carnot refrigerator requires a work input of only 230 J to extract 346 J of heat from the cold reservoir. Doesn't this discrepancy imply a violation of the law of conservation of energy? Explain why or why not.

Q20.17 Explain why each of the following processes is an example of increasing disorder or randomness: mixing hot and cold water; free expansion of a gas; irreversible heat flow; developing heat by mechanical friction. Are entropy increases involved in all of these? Why or why not?

Q20.18 The free expansion of a gas is an adiabatic process and so no heat is transferred. No work is done, so the internal energy does not change. Thus, $Q/T = 0$, yet the disorder of the system and thus its entropy have increased after the expansion. Why does Eq. (20.19) not apply to this situation?

Q20.19 Are the earth and sun in thermal equilibrium? Are there entropy changes associated with the transmission of energy from the sun to the earth? Does radiation differ from other modes of heat transfer with respect to entropy changes? Explain your reasoning.

Q20.20 Discuss the entropy changes involved in the preparation and consumption of a hot fudge sundae.

Q20.21 If you run a movie film backward, it is as if the direction of time were reversed. In the time-reversed movie, would you see processes that violate conservation of energy? Conservation of linear momentum? Would you see processes that violate the second law of thermodynamics? In each case, if law-breaking processes could occur, give some examples.

Q20.22 BIO Some critics of biological evolution claim that it violates the second law of thermodynamics, since evolution involves simple life forms developing into more complex and more highly ordered organisms. Explain why this is not a valid argument against evolution.

Q20.23 BIO A growing plant creates a highly complex and organized structure out of simple materials such as air, water, and trace minerals. Does this violate the second law of thermodynamics? Why or why not? What is the plant's ultimate source of energy? Explain your reasoning.

EXERCISES

Section 20.2 Heat Engines

20.1 · A diesel engine performs 2200 J of mechanical work and discards 4300 J of heat each cycle. (a) How much heat must be supplied to the engine in each cycle? (b) What is the thermal efficiency of the engine?

20.2 · An aircraft engine takes in 9000 J of heat and discards 6400 J each cycle. (a) What is the mechanical work output of the engine during one cycle? (b) What is the thermal efficiency of the engine?

20.3 · **A Gasoline Engine.** A gasoline engine takes in 1.61×10^4 J of heat and delivers 3700 J of work per cycle. The heat is obtained by burning gasoline with a heat of combustion of 4.60×10^4 J/g. (a) What is the thermal efficiency? (b) How much heat is discarded in each cycle? (c) What mass of fuel is burned in each cycle? (d) If the engine goes through 60.0 cycles per second, what is its power output in kilowatts? In horsepower?

20.4 · A gasoline engine has a power output of 180 kW (about 241 hp). Its thermal efficiency is 28.0%. (a) How much heat must be supplied to the engine per second? (b) How much heat is discarded by the engine per second?

20.5 ·· The pV-diagram in Fig. E20.5 shows a cycle of a heat engine that uses 0.250 mole of an ideal gas having $\gamma = 1.40$. The curved part ab

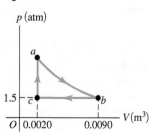

Figure **E20.5**

of the cycle is adiabatic. (a) Find the pressure of the gas at point *a*. (b) How much heat enters this gas per cycle, and where does it happen? (c) How much heat leaves this gas in a cycle, and where does it occur? (d) How much work does this engine do in a cycle? (e) What is the thermal efficiency of the engine?

Section 20.3 Internal-Combustion Engines

20.6 • (a) Calculate the theoretical efficiency for an Otto-cycle engine with $\gamma = 1.40$ and $r = 9.50$. (b) If this engine takes in 10,000 J of heat from burning its fuel, how much heat does it discard to the outside air?

20.7 •• The Otto-cycle engine in a Mercedes-Benz SLK230 has a compression ratio of 8.8. (a) What is the ideal efficiency of the engine? Use $\gamma = 1.40$. (b) The engine in a Dodge Viper GT2 has a slightly higher compression ratio of 9.6. How much increase in the ideal efficiency results from this increase in the compression ratio?

Section 20.4 Refrigerators

20.8 • The coefficient of performance $K = H/P$ is a dimensionless quantity. Its value is independent of the units used for H and P, as long as the same units, such as watts, are used for both quantities. However, it is common practice to express H in Btu/h and P in watts. When these mixed units are used, the ratio H/P is called the energy efficiency rating (EER). If a room air conditioner has a coefficient of performance $K = 3.0$, what is its EER?

20.9 • A refrigerator has a coefficient of performance of 2.10. In each cycle it absorbs 3.40×10^4 J of heat from the cold reservoir. (a) How much mechanical energy is required each cycle to operate the refrigerator? (b) During each cycle, how much heat is discarded to the high-temperature reservoir?

20.10 • A room air conditioner has a coefficient of performance of 2.9 on a hot day and uses 850 W of electrical power. (a) How many joules of heat does the air conditioner remove from the room in one minute? (b) How many joules of heat does the air conditioner deliver to the hot outside air in one minute? (c) Explain why your answers to parts (a) and (b) are not the same.

20.11 •• A refrigerator has a coefficient of performance of 2.25, runs on an input of 95 W of electrical power, and keeps its inside compartment at 5°C. If you put a dozen 1.0-L plastic bottles of water at 31°C into this refrigerator, how long will it take for them to be cooled down to 5°C? (Ignore any heat that leaves the plastic.)

20.12 •• A freezer has a coefficient of performance of 2.40. The freezer is to convert 1.80 kg of water at 25.0°C to 1.80 kg of ice at −5.0°C in one hour. (a) What amount of heat must be removed from the water at 25.0°C to convert it to ice at −5.0°C? (b) How much electrical energy is consumed by the freezer during this hour? (c) How much wasted heat is delivered to the room in which the freezer sits?

Section 20.6 The Carnot Cycle

20.13 • A Carnot engine whose high-temperature reservoir is at 620 K takes in 550 J of heat at this temperature in each cycle and gives up 335 J to the low-temperature reservoir. (a) How much mechanical work does the engine perform during each cycle? (b) What is the temperature of the low-temperature reservoir? (c) What is the thermal efficiency of the cycle?

20.14 • A Carnot engine is operated between two heat reservoirs at temperatures of 520 K and 300 K. (a) If the engine receives 6.45 kJ of heat energy from the reservoir at 520 K in each cycle, how many joules per cycle does it discard to the reservoir at 300 K? (b) How much mechanical work is performed by the engine during each cycle? (c) What is the thermal efficiency of the engine?

20.15 • A Carnot engine has an efficiency of 59% and performs 2.5×10^4 J of work in each cycle. (a) How much heat does the engine extract from its heat source in each cycle? (b) Suppose the engine exhausts heat at room temperature (20.0°C). What is the temperature of its heat source?

20.16 •• An ice-making machine operates in a Carnot cycle. It takes heat from water at 0.0°C and rejects heat to a room at 24.0°C. Suppose that 85.0 kg of water at 0.0°C are converted to ice at 0.0°C. (a) How much heat is discharged into the room? (b) How much energy must be supplied to the device?

20.17 • A Carnot refrigerator is operated between two heat reservoirs at temperatures of 320 K and 270 K. (a) If in each cycle the refrigerator receives 415 J of heat energy from the reservoir at 270 K, how many joules of heat energy does it deliver to the reservoir at 320 K? (b) If the refrigerator completes 165 cycles each minute, what power input is required to operate it? (c) What is the coefficient of performance of the refrigerator?

20.18 •• A certain brand of freezer is advertised to use 730 kW · h of energy per year. (a) Assuming the freezer operates for 5 hours each day, how much power does it require while operating? (b) If the freezer keeps its interior at a temperature of −5.0°C in a 20.0°C room, what is its theoretical maximum performance coefficient? (c) What is the theoretical maximum amount of ice this freezer could make in an hour, starting with water at 20.0°C?

20.19 •• A Carnot heat engine has a thermal efficiency of 0.600, and the temperature of its hot reservoir is 800 K. If 3000 J of heat is rejected to the cold reservoir in one cycle, what is the work output of the engine during one cycle?

20.20 •• A Carnot heat engine uses a hot reservoir consisting of a large amount of boiling water and a cold reservoir consisting of a large tub of ice and water. In 5 minutes of operation, the heat rejected by the engine melts 0.0400 kg of ice. During this time, how much work W is performed by the engine?

20.21 •• You design an engine that takes in 1.50×10^4 J of heat at 650 K in each cycle and rejects heat at a temperature of 350 K. The engine completes 240 cycles in 1 minute. What is the theoretical maximum power output of your engine, in horsepower?

Section 20.7 Entropy

20.22 • A 4.50-kg block of ice at 0.00°C falls into the ocean and melts. The average temperature of the ocean is 3.50°C, including all the deep water. By how much does the melting of this ice change the entropy of the world? Does it make it larger or smaller? (*Hint:* Do you think that the ocean will change temperature appreciably as the ice melts?)

20.23 • A sophomore with nothing better to do adds heat to 0.350 kg of ice at 0.0°C until it is all melted. (a) What is the change in entropy of the water? (b) The source of heat is a very massive body at a temperature of 25.0°C. What is the change in entropy of this body? (c) What is the total change in entropy of the water and the heat source?

20.24 • CALC You decide to take a nice hot bath but discover that your thoughtless roommate has used up most of the hot water. You fill the tub with 270 kg of 30.0°C water and attempt to warm it further by pouring in 5.00 kg of boiling water from the stove. (a) Is this a reversible or an irreversible process? Use physical reasoning to explain. (b) Calculate the final temperature of the bath water. (c) Calculate the net change in entropy of the system (bath water + boiling water), assuming no heat exchange with the air or the tub itself.

20.25 •• A 15.0-kg block of ice at 0.0°C melts to liquid water at 0.0°C inside a large room that has a temperature of 20.0°C. Treat the ice and the room as an isolated system, and assume that the room is large enough for its temperature change to be ignored. (a) Is the melting of the ice reversible or irreversible? Explain, using simple physical reasoning without resorting to any equations. (b) Calculate the net entropy change of the system during this process. Explain whether or not this result is consistent with your answer to part (a).

20.26 •• **CALC** You make tea with 0.250 kg of 85.0°C water and let it cool to room temperature (20.0°C) before drinking it. (a) Calculate the entropy change of the water while it cools. (b) The cooling process is essentially isothermal for the air in your kitchen. Calculate the change in entropy of the air while the tea cools, assuming that all the heat lost by the water goes into the air. What is the total entropy change of the system tea + air?

20.27 • Three moles of an ideal gas undergo a reversible isothermal compression at 20.0°C. During this compression, 1850 J of work is done on the gas. What is the change of entropy of the gas?

20.28 •• What is the change in entropy of 0.130 kg of helium gas at the normal boiling point of helium when it all condenses isothermally to 1.00 L of liquid helium? (*Hint:* See Table 17.4 in Section 17.6.)

20.29 • (a) Calculate the change in entropy when 1.00 kg of water at 100°C is vaporized and converted to steam at 100°C (see Table 17.4). (b) Compare your answer to the change in entropy when 1.00 kg of ice is melted at 0°C, calculated in Example 20.5 (Section 20.7). Is the change in entropy greater for melting or for vaporization? Interpret your answer using the idea that entropy is a measure of the randomness of a system.

20.30 • (a) Calculate the change in entropy when 1.00 mol of water (molecular mass 18.0 g/mol) at 100°C evaporates to form water vapor at 100°C. (b) Repeat the calculation of part (a) for 1.00 mol of liquid nitrogen, 1.00 mol of silver, and 1.00 mol of mercury when each is vaporized at its normal boiling point. (See Table 17.4 for the heats of vaporization, and Appendix D for the molar masses. Note that the nitrogen molecule is N_2.) (c) Your results in parts (a) and (b) should be in relatively close agreement. (This is called the *rule of Drepez and Trouton.*) Explain why this should be so, using the idea that entropy is a measure of the randomness of a system.

20.31 •• A 10.0-L gas tank containing 3.20 moles of ideal He gas at 20.0°C is placed inside a completely evacuated, insulated bell jar of volume 35.0 L. A small hole in the tank allows the He to leak out into the jar until the gas reaches a final equilibrium state with no more leakage. (a) What is the change in entropy of this system due to the leaking of the gas? (b) Is the process reversible or irreversible? How do you know?

Section 20.8 Microscopic Interpretation of Entropy

20.32 • A box is separated by a partition into two parts of equal volume. The left side of the box contains 500 molecules of nitrogen gas; the right side contains 100 molecules of oxygen gas. The two gases are at the same temperature. The partition is punctured, and equilibrium is eventually attained. Assume that the volume of the box is large enough for each gas to undergo a free expansion and not change temperature. (a) On average, how many molecules of each type will there be in either half of the box? (b) What is the change in entropy of the system when the partition is punctured? (c) What is the probability that the molecules will be found in the same distribution as they were before the partition was punctured— that is, 500 nitrogen molecules in the left half and 100 oxygen molecules in the right half?

20.33 • **CALC** Two moles of an ideal gas occupy a volume *V*. The gas expands isothermally and reversibly to a volume 3*V*. (a) Is the velocity distribution changed by the isothermal expansion? Explain. (b) Use Eq. (20.23) to calculate the change in entropy of the gas. (c) Use Eq. (20.18) to calculate the change in entropy of the gas. Compare this result to that obtained in part (b).

20.34 • **CALC** A lonely party balloon with a volume of 2.40 L and containing 0.100 mol of air is left behind to drift in the temporarily uninhabited and depressurized International Space Station. Sunlight coming through a porthole heats and explodes the balloon, causing the air in it to undergo a free expansion into the empty station, whose total volume is 425 m^3. Calculate the entropy change of the air during the expansion.

PROBLEMS

20.35 •• **CP** An ideal Carnot engine operates between 500°C and 100°C with a heat input of 250 J per cycle. (a) How much heat is delivered to the cold reservoir in each cycle? (b) What minimum number of cycles is necessary for the engine to lift a 500-kg rock through a height of 100 m?

20.36 • You are designing a Carnot engine that has 2 mol of CO_2 as its working substance; the gas may be treated as ideal. The gas is to have a maximum temperature of 527°C and a maximum pressure of 5.00 atm. With a heat input of 400 J per cycle, you want 300 J of useful work. (a) Find the temperature of the cold reservoir. (b) For how many cycles must this engine run to melt completely a 10.0-kg block of ice originally at 0.0°C, using only the heat rejected by the engine?

20.37 •• **CP** A certain heat engine operating on a Carnot cycle absorbs 150 J of heat per cycle at its hot reservoir at 135°C and has a thermal efficiency of 22.0%. (a) How much work does this engine do per cycle? (b) How much heat does the engine waste each cycle? (c) What is the temperature of the cold reservoir? (d) By how much does the engine change the entropy of the world each cycle? (e) What mass of water could this engine pump per cycle from a well 35.0 m deep?

20.38 •• **BIO Entropy of Metabolism.** An average sleeping person metabolizes at a rate of about 80 W by digesting food or burning fat. Typically, 20% of this energy goes into bodily functions, such as cell repair, pumping blood, and other uses of mechanical energy, while the rest goes to heat. Most people get rid of all this excess heat by transferring it (by conduction and the flow of blood) to the surface of the body, where it is radiated away. The normal internal temperature of the body (where the metabolism takes place) is 37°C, and the skin is typically 7 C° cooler. By how much does the person's entropy change per second due to this heat transfer?

20.39 •• **BIO Entropy Change from Digesting Fat.** Digesting fat produces 9.3 food calories per gram of fat, and typically 80% of this energy goes to heat when metabolized. (One food calorie is 1000 calories and therefore equals 4186 J.) The body then moves all this heat to the surface by a combination of thermal conductivity and motion of the blood. The internal temperature of the body (where digestion occurs) is normally 37°C, and the surface is usually about 30°C. By how much do the digestion and metabolism of a 2.50-g pat of butter change your body's entropy? Does it increase or decrease?

20.40 • A heat engine takes 0.350 mol of a diatomic ideal gas around the cycle shown in the *pV*-diagram of Fig. P20.40. Process $1 \rightarrow 2$ is at constant volume, process $2 \rightarrow 3$ is adiabatic, and process 3 → 1 is at a constant pressure of 1.00 atm. The value of γ for this gas is 1.40. (a) Find the pressure and volume at points 1, 2, and 3. (b) Calculate Q, W, and ΔU for each of the three processes. (c) Find the net work done by the gas in the cycle. (d) Find the net heat flow into the engine in one cycle. (e) What is the

Figure **P20.40**

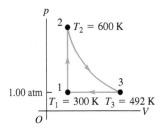

thermal efficiency of the engine? How does this compare to the efficiency of a Carnot-cycle engine operating between the same minimum and maximum temperatures T_1 and T_2?

20.41 ·· **CALC** You build a heat engine that takes 1.00 mol of an ideal diatomic gas through the cycle shown in Fig. P20.41. (a) Show that segment ab is an isothermal compression. (b) During which segment(s) of the cycle is heat absorbed by the gas? During which segment(s) is heat rejected?

Figure **P20.41**

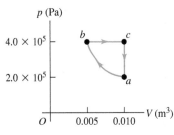

How do you know? (c) Calculate the temperature at points a, b, and c. (d) Calculate the net heat exchanged with the surroundings and the net work done by the engine in one cycle. (e) Calculate the thermal efficiency of the engine.

20.42 · **Heat Pump.** A heat pump is a heat engine run in reverse. In winter it pumps heat from the cold air outside into the warmer air inside the building, maintaining the building at a comfortable temperature. In summer it pumps heat from the cooler air inside the building to the warmer air outside, acting as an air conditioner. (a) If the outside temperature in winter is $-5.0°C$ and the inside temperature is $17.0°C$, how many joules of heat will the heat pump deliver to the inside for each joule of electrical energy used to run the unit, assuming an ideal Carnot cycle? (b) Suppose you have the option of using electrical resistance heating rather than a heat pump. How much electrical energy would you need in order to deliver the same amount of heat to the inside of the house as in part (a)? Consider a Carnot heat pump delivering heat to the inside of a house to maintain it at $68°F$. Show that the heat pump delivers less heat for each joule of electrical energy used to operate the unit as the outside temperature decreases. Notice that this behavior is opposite to the dependence of the efficiency of a Carnot heat engine on the difference in the reservoir temperatures. Explain why this is so.

20.43 · **CALC** A heat engine operates using the cycle shown in Fig. P20.43. The working substance is 2.00 mol of helium gas, which reaches a maximum temperature of $327°C$. Assume the helium can be treated as an ideal gas. Process bc is isothermal. The pressure in states a and c is 1.00×10^5 Pa, and the pressure in state b is 3.00×10^5 Pa. (a) How much heat enters the gas and how much

Figure **P20.43**

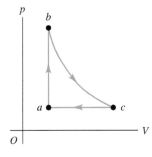

leaves the gas each cycle? (b) How much work does the engine do each cycle, and what is its efficiency? (c) Compare this engine's efficiency with the maximum possible efficiency attainable with the hot and cold reservoirs used by this cycle.

20.44 · **CP** As a budding mechanical engineer, you are called upon to design a Carnot engine that has 2.00 mol of a monatomic ideal gas as its working substance and operates from a high-temperature reservoir at $500°C$. The engine is to lift a 15.0-kg weight 2.00 m per cycle, using 500 J of heat input. The gas in the engine chamber can have a minimum volume of 5.00 L during the cycle. (a) Draw a pV-diagram for this cycle. Show in your diagram where heat enters and leaves the gas. (b) What must be the temperature of the cold reservoir? (c) What is the thermal efficiency of the engine? (d) How much heat energy does this engine waste per cycle? (e) What is the maximum pressure that the gas chamber will have to withstand?

20.45 ··· An experimental power plant at the Natural Energy Laboratory of Hawaii generates electricity from the temperature gradient of the ocean. The surface and deep-water temperatures are $27°C$ and $6°C$, respectively. (a) What is the maximum theoretical efficiency of this power plant? (b) If the power plant is to produce 210 kW of power, at what rate must heat be extracted from the warm water? At what rate must heat be absorbed by the cold water? Assume the maximum theoretical efficiency. (c) The cold water that enters the plant leaves it at a temperature of $10°C$. What must be the flow rate of cold water through the system? Give your answer in kg/h and in L/h.

20.46 ·· What is the thermal efficiency of an engine that operates by taking n moles of diatomic ideal gas through the cycle $1 \rightarrow 2 \rightarrow 3 \rightarrow 4 \rightarrow 1$ shown in Fig. P20.46?

Figure **P20.46**

20.47 · **CALC** A cylinder contains oxygen at a pressure of 2.00 atm. The volume is 4.00 L, and the temperature is 300 K. Assume that the oxygen may be treated as an ideal gas. The oxygen is carried through the following processes:

(i) Heated at constant pressure from the initial state (state 1) to state 2, which has $T = 450$ K.
(ii) Cooled at constant volume to 250 K (state 3).
(iii) Compressed at constant temperature to a volume of 4.00 L (state 4).
(iv) Heated at constant volume to 300 K, which takes the system back to state 1.

(a) Show these four processes in a pV-diagram, giving the numerical values of p and V in each of the four states. (b) Calculate Q and W for each of the four processes. (c) Calculate the net work done by the oxygen in the complete cycle. (d) What is the efficiency of this device as a heat engine? How does this compare to the efficiency of a Carnot-cycle engine operating between the same minimum and maximum temperatures of 250 K and 450 K?

20.48 ·· **CP BIO Human Entropy.** A person who has skin of surface area 1.85 m² and temperature $30.0°C$ is resting in an insulated room where the ambient air temperature is $20.0°C$. In this state, a person gets rid of excess heat by radiation. By how much does the person change the entropy of the air in this room each second?

(Recall that the room radiates back into the person and that the emissivity of the skin is 1.00.)

20.49 •• **CP BIO** **A Human Engine.** You decide to use your body as a Carnot heat engine. The operating gas is in a tube with one end in your mouth (where the temperature is 37.0°C) and the other end at the surface of your skin, at 30.0°C. (a) What is the maximum efficiency of such a heat engine? Would it be a very useful engine? (b) Suppose you want to use this human engine to lift a 2.50-kg box from the floor to a tabletop 1.20 m above the floor. How much must you increase the gravitational potential energy, and how much heat input is needed to accomplish this? (c) If your favorite candy bar has 350 food calories (1 food calorie = 4186 J) and 80% of the food energy goes into heat, how many of these candy bars must you eat to lift the box in this way?

20.50 •• **CP** **Entropy Change Due to the Sun.** Our sun radiates from a surface at 5800 K (with an emissivity of 1.0) into the near-vacuum of space, which is at a temperature of 3 K. (a) By how much does our sun change the entropy of the universe every second? (Consult Appendix F.) (b) Is the process reversible or irreversible? Is your answer to part (a) consistent with this conclusion? Explain.

20.51 • A monatomic ideal gas is taken around the cycle shown in Fig. P20.51 in the direction shown in the figure. The path for process $c \rightarrow a$ is a straight line in the pV-diagram. (a) Calculate Q, W, and ΔU for each process $a \rightarrow b$, $b \rightarrow c$, and $c \rightarrow a$. (b) What are Q, W, and ΔU for one complete cycle? (c) What is the efficiency of the cycle?

Figure **P20.51**

20.52 •• **CALC** **A Stirling-Cycle Engine.** The *Stirling cycle* is similar to the Otto cycle, except that the compression and expansion of the gas are done at constant temperature, not adiabatically as in the Otto cycle. The Stirling cycle is used in *external* combustion engines (in fact, burning fuel is not necessary; *any* way of producing a temperature difference will do—solar, geothermal, ocean temperature gradient, etc.), which means that the gas inside the cylinder is not used in the combustion process. Heat is supplied by burning fuel steadily outside the cylinder, instead of explosively inside the cylinder as in the Otto cycle. For this reason Stirling-cycle engines are quieter than Otto-cycle engines, since there are no intake and exhaust valves (a major source of engine noise). While small Stirling engines are used for a variety of purposes, Stirling engines for automobiles have not been successful because they are larger, heavier, and more expensive than conventional automobile engines. In the cycle, the working fluid goes through the following sequence of steps (Fig. P20.52):

Figure **P20.52**

(i) Compressed isothermally at temperature T_1 from the initial state a to state b, with a compression ratio r.
(ii) Heated at constant volume to state c at temperature T_2.
(iii) Expanded isothermally at T_2 to state d.
(iv) Cooled at constant volume back to the initial state a.

Assume that the working fluid is n moles of an ideal gas (for which C_V is independent of temperature). (a) Calculate Q, W, and ΔU for each of the processes $a \rightarrow b$, $b \rightarrow c$, $c \rightarrow d$, and $d \rightarrow a$. (b) In the Stirling cycle, the heat transfers in the processes $b \rightarrow c$ and $d \rightarrow a$ do not involve external heat sources but rather use *regeneration*: The same substance that transfers heat to the gas inside the cylinder in the process $b \rightarrow c$ also absorbs heat back from the gas in the process $d \rightarrow a$. Hence the heat transfers $Q_{b \rightarrow c}$ and $Q_{d \rightarrow a}$ do not play a role in determining the efficiency of the engine. Explain this last statement by comparing the expressions for $Q_{b \rightarrow c}$ and $Q_{d \rightarrow a}$ calculated in part (a). (c) Calculate the efficiency of a Stirling-cycle engine in terms of the temperatures T_1 and T_2. How does this compare to the efficiency of a Carnot-cycle engine operating between these same two temperatures? (Historically, the Stirling cycle was devised before the Carnot cycle.) Does this result violate the second law of thermodynamics? Explain. Unfortunately, actual Stirling-cycle engines cannot achieve this efficiency due to problems with the heat-transfer processes and pressure losses in the engine.

20.53 •• A Carnot engine operates between two heat reservoirs at temperatures T_H and T_C. An inventor proposes to increase the efficiency by running one engine between T_H and an intermediate temperature T' and a second engine between T' and T_C, using as input the heat expelled by the first engine. Compute the efficiency of this composite system, and compare it to that of the original engine.

20.54 ••• A typical coal-fired power plant generates 1000 MW of usable power at an overall thermal efficiency of 40%. (a) What is the rate of heat input to the plant? (b) The plant burns anthracite coal, which has a heat of combustion of 2.65×10^7 J/kg. How much coal does the plant use per day, if it operates continuously? (c) At what rate is heat ejected into the cool reservoir, which is the nearby river? (d) The river's temperature is 18.0°C before it reaches the power plant and 18.5°C after it has received the plant's waste heat. Calculate the river's flow rate, in cubic meters per second. (e) By how much does the river's entropy increase each second?

20.55 • **Automotive Thermodynamics.** A Volkswagen Passat has a six-cylinder Otto-cycle engine with compression ratio $r = 10.6$. The diameter of each cylinder, called the *bore* of the engine, is 82.5 mm. The distance that the piston moves during the compression in Fig. 20.5, called the *stroke* of the engine, is 86.4 mm. The initial pressure of the air–fuel mixture (at point a in Fig. 20.6) is 8.50×10^4 Pa, and the initial temperature is 300 K (the same as the outside air). Assume that 200 J of heat is added to each cylinder in each cycle by the burning gasoline, and that the gas has $C_V = 20.5$ J/mol·K and $\gamma = 1.40$. (a) Calculate the total work done in one cycle in each cylinder of the engine, and the heat released when the gas is cooled to the temperature of the outside air. (b) Calculate the volume of the air–fuel mixture at point a in the cycle. (c) Calculate the pressure, volume, and temperature of the gas at points b, c, and d in the cycle. In a pV-diagram, show the numerical values of p, V, and T for each of the four states. (d) Compare the efficiency of this engine with the efficiency of a Carnot-cycle engine operating between the same maximum and minimum temperatures.

20.56 • An air conditioner operates on 800 W of power and has a performance coefficient of 2.80 with a room temperature of 21.0°C and an outside temperature of 35.0°C. (a) Calculate the rate of heat removal for this unit. (b) Calculate the rate at which heat is discharged to the outside air. (c) Calculate the total entropy change in the room if the air conditioner runs for 1 hour. Calculate the total entropy change in the outside air for the same time period. (d) What is the net change in entropy for the system (room + outside air)?

20.57 •• CALC **Unavailable Energy.** The discussion of entropy and the second law that follows Example 20.10 (Section 20.7) says that the increase in entropy in an irreversible process is associated with energy becoming less available. Consider a Carnot cycle that uses a low-temperature reservoir with Kelvin temperature T_c. This is a true reservoir—that is, large enough not to change temperature when it accepts heat from the engine. Let the engine accept heat from an object of temperature T', where $T' > T_c$. The object is of finite size, so it cools as heat is extracted from it. The engine continues to operate until $T' = T_c$. (a) Show that the total magnitude of heat rejected to the low-temperature reservoir is $T_c |\Delta S_h|$, where ΔS_h is the change in entropy of the high-temperature reservoir. (b) Apply the result of part (a) to 1.00 kg of water initially at a temperature of 373 K as the heat source for the engine and $T_c = 273$ K. How much total mechanical work can be performed by the engine until it stops? (c) Repeat part (b) for 2.00 kg of water at 323 K. (d) Compare the amount of work that can be obtained from the energy in the water of Example 20.10 before and after it is mixed. Discuss whether your result shows that energy has become less available.

20.58 ••• CP The maximum power that can be extracted by a wind turbine from an air stream is approximately

$$P = kd^2v^3$$

where d is the blade diameter, v is the wind speed, and the constant $k = 0.5$ W·s^3/m^5. (a) Explain the dependence of P on d and on v by considering a cylinder of air that passes over the turbine blades in time t (Fig. P20.58). This cylinder has diameter d, length $L = vt$, and density ρ. (b) The Mod-5B wind turbine at Kahaku on the Hawaiian island of Oahu has a blade diameter of 97 m (slightly longer than a football field) and sits atop a 58-m tower. It can produce 3.2 MW of electric power. Assuming 25% efficiency, what wind speed is required to produce this amount of power? Give your answer in m/s and in km/h. (c) Commercial wind turbines are commonly located in or downwind of mountain passes. Why?

Figure **P20.58**

20.59 •• CALC (a) For the Otto cycle shown in Fig. 20.6, calculate the changes in entropy of the gas in each of the constant-volume processes $b \rightarrow c$ and $d \rightarrow a$ in terms of the temperatures T_a, T_b, T_c, and T_d and the number of moles n and the heat capacity C_V of the

gas. (b) What is the total entropy change in the engine during one cycle? (*Hint:* Use the relationships between T_a and T_b and between T_d and T_c.) (c) The processes $b \rightarrow c$ and $d \rightarrow a$ occur irreversibly in a real Otto engine. Explain how can this be reconciled with your result in part (b).

20.60 •• CALC **A TS-Diagram.** (a) Graph a Carnot cycle, plotting Kelvin temperature vertically and entropy horizontally. This is called a temperature–entropy diagram, or *TS*-diagram. (b) Show that the area under any curve representing a reversible path in a temperature–entropy diagram represents the heat absorbed by the system. (c) Derive from your diagram the expression for the thermal efficiency of a Carnot cycle. (d) Draw a temperature–entropy diagram for the Stirling cycle described in Problem 20.52. Use this diagram to relate the efficiencies of the Carnot and Stirling cycles.

20.61 • A physics student immerses one end of a copper rod in boiling water at 100°C and the other end in an ice–water mixture at 0°C. The sides of the rod are insulated. After steady-state conditions have been achieved in the rod, 0.120 kg of ice melts in a certain time interval. For this time interval, find (a) the entropy change of the boiling water; (b) the entropy change of the ice–water mixture; (c) the entropy change of the copper rod; (d) the total entropy change of the entire system.

20.62 •• CALC To heat 1 cup of water (250 cm^3) to make coffee, you place an electric heating element in the cup. As the water temperature increases from 20°C to 78°C, the temperature of the heating element remains at a constant 120°C. Calculate the change in entropy of (a) the water; (b) the heating element; (c) the system of water and heating element. (Make the same assumption about the specific heat of water as in Example 20.10 in Section 20.7, and ignore the heat that flows into the ceramic coffee cup itself.) (d) Is this process reversible or irreversible? Explain.

20.63 •• CALC An object of mass m_1, specific heat c_1, and temperature T_1 is placed in contact with a second object of mass m_2, specific heat c_2, and temperature $T_2 > T_1$. As a result, the temperature of the first object increases to T and the temperature of the second object decreases to T'. (a) Show that the entropy increase of the system is

$$\Delta S = m_1 c_1 \ln\frac{T}{T_1} + m_2 c_2 \ln\frac{T'}{T_2}$$

and show that energy conservation requires that

$$m_1 c_1 (T - T_1) = m_2 c_2 (T_2 - T')$$

(b) Show that the entropy change ΔS, considered as a function of T, is a *maximum* if $T = T'$, which is just the condition of thermodynamic equilibrium. (c) Discuss the result of part (b) in terms of the idea of entropy as a measure of disorder.

CHALLENGE PROBLEM

20.64 ••• Consider a Diesel cycle that starts (at point a in Fig. 20.7) with air at temperature T_a. The air may be treated as an ideal gas. (a) If the temperature at point c is T_c, derive an expression for the efficiency of the cycle in terms of the compression ratio r. (b) What is the efficiency if $T_a = 300$ K, $T_c = 950$ K, $\gamma = 1.40$, and $r = 21.0$?

Answers

Chapter Opening Question ?

Yes. That's what a refrigerator does: It makes heat flow from the cold interior of the refrigerator to the warm outside. The second law of thermodynamics says that heat cannot *spontaneously* flow from a cold body to a hot one. A refrigerator has a motor that does work on the system to *force* the heat to flow in that way.

Test Your Understanding Questions

20.1 Answer: (ii) Like sliding a book across a table, rubbing your hands together uses friction to convert mechanical energy into heat. The (impossible) reverse process would involve your hands spontaneously getting colder, with the released energy forcing your hands to move rhythmically back and forth!

20.2 Answer: (iii), (i), (ii) From Eq. (20.4) the efficiency is $e = W/Q_H$, and from Eq. (20.2) $W = Q_H + Q_C = |Q_H| - |Q_C|$. For engine (i) $Q_H = 5000\,J$ and $Q_C = -4500\,J$, so $W = 5000\,J + (-4500\,J) = 500\,J$ and $e = (500\,J)/(5000\,H) = 0.100$. For engine (ii) $Q_H = 25{,}000\,J$ and $W = 2000\,J$, so $e = (2000\,J)/(25{,}000\,J) = 0.080$. For engine (iii) $W = 400\,J$ and $Q_C = -2800\,J$, so $Q_H = W - Q_C = 400\,J - (-2800\,J) = 3200\,J$ and $e = (400\,J)/(3200\,J) = 0.125$.

20.3 Answers: (i), (ii) Doubling the amount of fuel burned per cycle means that Q_H is doubled, so the resulting pressure increase from b to c in Fig. 20.6 is greater. The compression ratio and hence the efficiency remain the same, so $|Q_C|$ (the amount of heat rejected to the environment) must increase by the same factor as Q_H. Hence the pressure drop from d to a in Fig. 20.6 is also greater. The volume V and the compression ratio r don't change, so the horizontal dimensions of the pV-diagram don't change.

20.4 Answer: no A refrigerator uses an input of work to transfer heat from one system (the refrigerator's interior) to another system (its exterior, which includes the house in which the refrigerator is installed). If the door is open, these two systems are really the *same* system and will eventually come to the same temperature. By the first law of thermodynamics, all of the work input to the refrigerator motor will be converted into heat and the temperature in your house will actually *increase*. To cool the house you need a system that will transfer heat from it to the outside world, such as an air conditioner or heat pump.

20.5 Answers: no, no Both the 100%-efficient engine of Fig. 20.11a and the workless refrigerator of Fig. 20.11b return to the same state at the end of a cycle as at the beginning, so the net change in internal energy of each system is zero ($\Delta U = 0$). For the 100%-efficient engine, the net heat flow into the engine equals the net work done, so $Q = W$, $Q - W = 0$, and the first law ($\Delta U = Q - W$) is obeyed. For the workless refrigerator, no net work is done (so $W = 0$) and as much heat flows into it as out (so $Q = 0$), so again $Q - W = 0$ and $\Delta U = Q - W$ in accordance with the first law. It is the *second* law of thermodynamics that tells us that both the 100%-efficient engine and the workless refrigerator are impossible.

20.6 Answer: no The efficiency can be no better than that of a Carnot engine running between the same two temperature limits, $e_{Carnot} = 1 - (T_C/T_H)$ [Eq. (20.14)]. The temperature T_C of the cold reservoir for this air-cooled engine is about 300 K (ambient temperature), and the temperature T_H of the hot reservoir cannot exceed the melting point of copper, 1356 K (see Table 17.4). Hence the maximum possible Carnot efficiency is $e = 1 - (300\,K)/(1356\,K) = 0.78$, or 78%. The temperature of any real engine would be less than this, so it would be impossible for the inventor's engine to attain 85% efficiency. You should invest your money elsewhere.

20.7 Answers: $-102\,J/K$, no The process described is exactly the opposite of the process used in Example 20.10. The result violates the second law of thermodynamics, which states that the entropy of an isolated system cannot decrease.

20.8 Answer: (i) For case (i), we saw in Example 20.8 (Section 20.7) that for an ideal gas, the entropy change in a free expansion is the same as in an isothermal expansion. From Eq. (20.23), this implies that the ratio of the number of microscopic states after and before the expansion, w_2/w_1, is also the same for these two cases. From Example 20.11, $w_2/w_1 = 2^N$, so the number of microscopic states increases by a factor 2^N. For case (ii), in a reversible expansion the entropy change is $\Delta S = \int dQ/T = 0$; if the expansion is adiabatic there is no heat flow, so $\Delta S = 0$. From Eq. (20.23), $w_2/w_1 = 1$ and there is *no* change in the number of microscopic states. The difference is that in an adiabatic expansion the temperature drops and the molecules move more slowly, so they have fewer microscopic states available to them than in an isothermal expansion.

Bridging Problem

Answers: (a) 34.83°C **(b)** +12.1 J/K

33

THE NATURE AND PROPAGATION OF LIGHT

LEARNING GOALS

By studying this chapter, you will learn:

- What light rays are, and how they are related to wave fronts.

- The laws that govern the reflection and refraction of light.

- The circumstances under which light is totally reflected at an interface.

- How to make polarized light out of ordinary light.

- How Huygens's principle helps us analyze reflection and refraction.

? These drafting tools are made of clear plastic, but a rainbow of colors appears when they are placed between two special filters called polarizers. How does this cause the colors?

Blue lakes, ochre deserts, green forests, and multicolored rainbows can be enjoyed by anyone who has eyes with which to see them. But by studying the branch of physics called **optics,** which deals with the behavior of light and other electromagnetic waves, we can reach a deeper appreciation of the visible world. A knowledge of the properties of light allows us to understand the blue color of the sky and the design of optical devices such as telescopes, microscopes, cameras, eyeglasses, and the human eye. The same basic principles of optics also lie at the heart of modern developments such as the laser, optical fibers, holograms, optical computers, and new techniques in medical imaging.

The importance of optics to physics, and to science and engineering in general, is so great that we will devote the next four chapters to its study. In this chapter we begin with a study of the laws of reflection and refraction and the concepts of dispersion, polarization, and scattering of light. Along the way we compare the various possible descriptions of light in terms of particles, rays, or waves, and we introduce Huygens's principle, an important link that connects the ray and wave viewpoints. In Chapter 34 we'll use the ray description of light to understand how mirrors and lenses work, and we'll see how mirrors and lenses are used in optical instruments such as cameras, microscopes, and telescopes. We'll explore the wave characteristics of light further in Chapters 35 and 36.

33.1 The Nature of Light

Until the time of Isaac Newton (1642–1727), most scientists thought that light consisted of streams of particles (called *corpuscles*) emitted by light sources. Galileo and others tried (unsuccessfully) to measure the speed of light. Around 1665, evidence of *wave* properties of light began to be discovered. By the early 19th century, evidence that light is a wave had grown very persuasive.

In 1873, James Clerk Maxwell predicted the existence of electromagnetic waves and calculated their speed of propagation, as we learned in Chapter 32. This development, along with the experimental work of Heinrich Hertz starting in 1887, showed conclusively that light is indeed an electromagnetic wave.

The Two Personalities of Light

The wave picture of light is not the whole story, however. Several effects associated with emission and absorption of light reveal a particle aspect, in that the energy carried by light waves is packaged in discrete bundles called *photons* or *quanta*. These apparently contradictory wave and particle properties have been reconciled since 1930 with the development of quantum electrodynamics, a comprehensive theory that includes *both* wave and particle properties. The *propagation* of light is best described by a wave model, but understanding emission and absorption requires a particle approach.

The fundamental sources of all electromagnetic radiation are electric charges in accelerated motion. All bodies emit electromagnetic radiation as a result of thermal motion of their molecules; this radiation, called *thermal radiation,* is a mixture of different wavelengths. At sufficiently high temperatures, all matter emits enough visible light to be self-luminous; a very hot body appears "red-hot" (Fig. 33.1) or "white-hot." Thus hot matter in any form is a light source. Familiar examples are a candle flame, hot coals in a campfire, the coils in an electric room heater, and an incandescent lamp filament (which usually operates at a temperature of about 3000°C).

Light is also produced during electrical discharges through ionized gases. The bluish light of mercury-arc lamps, the orange-yellow of sodium-vapor lamps, and the various colors of "neon" signs are familiar. A variation of the mercury-arc lamp is the *fluorescent* lamp (see Fig. 30.7). This light source uses a material called a *phosphor* to convert the ultraviolet radiation from a mercury arc into visible light. This conversion makes fluorescent lamps more efficient than incandescent lamps in transforming electrical energy into light.

In most light sources, light is emitted independently by different atoms within the source; in a *laser,* by contrast, atoms are induced to emit light in a cooperative, coherent fashion. The result is a very narrow beam of radiation that can be enormously intense and that is much more nearly *monochromatic*, or single-frequency, than light from any other source. Lasers are used by physicians for microsurgery, in a DVD or Blu-ray player to scan the information recorded on a video disc, in industry to cut through steel and to fuse high-melting-point materials, and in many other applications (Fig. 33.2).

No matter what its source, electromagnetic radiation travels in vacuum at the same speed. As we saw in Sections 1.3 and 32.1, the speed of light in vacuum is defined to be

$$c = 2.99792458 \times 10^8 \text{ m/s}$$

or 3.00×10^8 m/s to three significant figures. The duration of one second is defined by the cesium clock (see Section 1.3), so one meter is defined to be the distance that light travels in $1/299{,}792{,}458$ s.

Waves, Wave Fronts, and Rays

We often use the concept of a **wave front** to describe wave propagation. We introduced this concept in Section 32.2 to describe the leading edge of a wave. More generally, we define a wave front as *the locus of all adjacent points at which the phase of vibration of a physical quantity associated with the wave is the same.* That is, at any instant, all points on a wave front are at the same part of the cycle of their variation.

When we drop a pebble into a calm pool, the expanding circles formed by the wave crests, as well as the circles formed by the wave troughs between

33.1 An electric heating element emits primarily infrared radiation. But if its temperature is high enough, it also emits a discernible amount of visible light.

33.2 Ophthalmic surgeons use lasers for repairing detached retinas and for cauterizing blood vessels in retinopathy. Pulses of blue-green light from an argon laser are ideal for this purpose, since they pass harmlessly through the transparent part of the eye but are absorbed by red pigments in the retina.

33.3 Spherical wave fronts of sound spread out uniformly in all directions from a point source in a motionless medium, such as still air, that has the same properties in all regions and in all directions. Electromagnetic waves in vacuum also spread out as shown here.

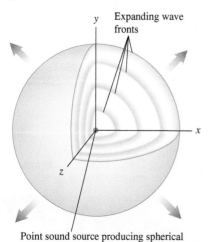

Point sound source producing spherical sound waves (alternating compressions and rarefactions of air)

33.4 Wave fronts (blue) and rays (purple).

(a)

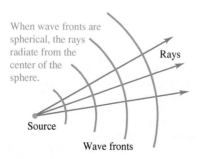

When wave fronts are spherical, the rays radiate from the center of the sphere.

Rays

Source

Wave fronts

(b)

When wave fronts are planar, the rays are perpendicular to the wave fronts and parallel to each other.

Rays

Wave fronts

ActivPhysics 15.1: Reflection and Refraction
ActivPhysics 15.3: Refraction Applications

them, are wave fronts. Similarly, when sound waves spread out in still air from a pointlike source, or when electromagnetic radiation spreads out from a pointlike emitter, any spherical surface that is concentric with the source is a wave front, as shown in Fig. 33.3. In diagrams of wave motion we usually draw only parts of a few wave fronts, often choosing consecutive wave fronts that have the same phase and thus are one wavelength apart, such as crests of water waves. Similarly, a diagram for sound waves might show only the "pressure crests," the surfaces over which the pressure is maximum, and a diagram for electromagnetic waves might show only the "crests" on which the electric or magnetic field is maximum.

We will often use diagrams that show the shapes of the wave fronts or their cross sections in some reference plane. For example, when electromagnetic waves are radiated by a small light source, we can represent the wave fronts as spherical surfaces concentric with the source or, as in Fig. 33.4a, by the circular intersections of these surfaces with the plane of the diagram. Far away from the source, where the radii of the spheres have become very large, a section of a spherical surface can be considered as a plane, and we have a *plane* wave like those discussed in Sections 32.2 and 32.3 (Fig, 33.4b).

To describe the directions in which light propagates, it's often convenient to represent a light wave by **rays** rather than by wave fronts. Rays were used to describe light long before its wave nature was firmly established. In a particle theory of light, rays are the paths of the particles. From the wave viewpoint *a ray is an imaginary line along the direction of travel of the wave.* In Fig. 33.4a the rays are the radii of the spherical wave fronts, and in Fig. 33.4b they are straight lines perpendicular to the wave fronts. When waves travel in a homogeneous isotropic material (a material with the same properties in all regions and in all directions), the rays are always straight lines normal to the wave fronts. At a boundary surface between two materials, such as the surface of a glass plate in air, the wave speed and the direction of a ray may change, but the ray segments in the air and in the glass are straight lines.

The next several chapters will give you many opportunities to see the interplay of the ray, wave, and particle descriptions of light. The branch of optics for which the ray description is adequate is called **geometric optics;** the branch dealing specifically with wave behavior is called **physical optics.** This chapter and the following one are concerned mostly with geometric optics. In Chapters 35 and 36 we will study wave phenomena and physical optics.

Test Your Understanding of Section 33.1 Some crystals are *not* isotropic: Light travels through the crystal at a higher speed in some directions than in others. In a crystal in which light travels at the same speed in the x- and z-directions but at a faster speed in the y-direction, what would be the shape of the wave fronts produced by a light source at the origin? (i) spherical, like those shown in Fig. 33.3; (ii) ellipsoidal, flattened along the y-axis; (iii) ellipsoidal, stretched out along the y-axis.

33.2 Reflection and Refraction

In this section we'll use the *ray* model of light to explore two of the most important aspects of light propagation: **reflection** and **refraction.** When a light wave strikes a smooth interface separating two transparent materials (such as air and glass or water and glass), the wave is in general partly *reflected* and partly *refracted* (transmitted) into the second material, as shown in Fig. 33.5a. For example, when you look into a restaurant window from the street, you see a reflection of the street scene, but a person inside the restaurant can look out through the window at the same scene as light reaches him by refraction.

33.5 (a) A plane wave is in part reflected and in part refracted at the boundary between two media (in this case, air and glass). The light that reaches the inside of the coffee shop is refracted twice, once entering the glass and once exiting the glass. (b), (c) How light behaves at the interface between the air outside the coffee shop (material *a*) and the glass (material *b*). For the case shown here, material *b* has a larger index of refraction than material $a(n_b > n_a)$ and the angle θ_b is smaller than θ_a.

(a) Plane waves reflected and refracted from a window

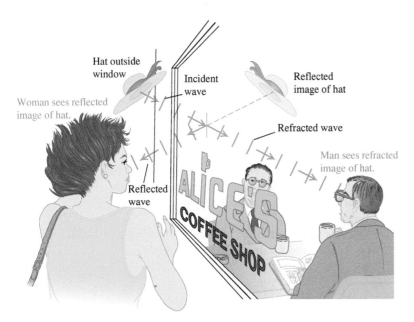

(b) The waves in the outside air and glass represented by rays

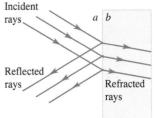

(c) The representation simplified to show just one set of rays

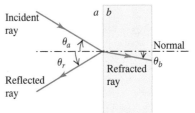

The segments of plane waves shown in Fig. 33.5a can be represented by bundles of rays forming *beams* of light (Fig. 33.5b). For simplicity we often draw only one ray in each beam (Fig. 33.5c). Representing these waves in terms of rays is the basis of geometric optics. We begin our study with the behavior of an individual ray.

We describe the directions of the incident, reflected, and refracted (transmitted) rays at a smooth interface between two optical materials in terms of the angles they make with the *normal* (perpendicular) to the surface at the point of incidence, as shown in Fig. 33.5c. If the interface is rough, both the transmitted light and the reflected light are scattered in various directions, and there is no single angle of transmission or reflection. Reflection at a definite angle from a very smooth surface is called **specular reflection** (from the Latin word for "mirror"); scattered reflection from a rough surface is called **diffuse reflection.** This distinction is shown in Fig. 33.6. Both kinds of reflection can occur with either transparent materials or *opaque* materials that do not transmit light. The vast majority of objects in your environment (including plants, other people, and this book) are visible to you because they reflect light in a diffuse manner from their surfaces. Our primary concern, however, will be with specular reflection from a very smooth surface such as highly polished glass or metal. Unless stated otherwise, when referring to "reflection" we will always mean *specular* reflection.

The **index of refraction** of an optical material (also called the **refractive index**), denoted by *n*, plays a central role in geometric optics. It is the ratio of the speed of light *c* in vacuum to the speed *v* in the material:

$$n = \frac{c}{v} \quad \text{(index of refraction)} \quad (33.1)$$

Light always travels *more slowly* in a material than in vacuum, so the value of *n* in anything other than vacuum is always greater than unity. For vacuum, $n = 1$.

33.6 Two types of reflection.

(a) Specular reflection

(b) Diffuse reflection

Since n is a ratio of two speeds, it is a pure number without units. (The relationship of the value of n to the electric and magnetic properties of a material is described in Section 32.3.)

CAUTION **Wave speed and index of refraction** Keep in mind that the wave speed v is *inversely* proportional to the index of refraction n. The greater the index of refraction in a material, the *slower* the wave speed in that material. Failure to remember this point can lead to serious confusion! ▮

33.7 The laws of reflection and refraction.

1. The incident, reflected, and refracted rays and the normal to the surface all lie in the same plane.

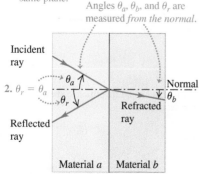

Angles θ_a, θ_b, and θ_r are measured *from the normal*.

2. $\theta_r = \theta_a$

3. When a monochromatic light ray crosses the interface between two given materials a and b, the angles θ_a and θ_b are related to the indexes of refraction of a and b by
$$\frac{\sin\theta_a}{\sin\theta_b} = \frac{n_b}{n_a}.$$

The Laws of Reflection and Refraction

Experimental studies of the directions of the incident, reflected, and refracted rays at a smooth interface between two optical materials lead to the following conclusions (Fig. 33.7):

1. **The incident, reflected, and refracted rays and the normal to the surface all lie in the same plane.** The plane of the three rays and the normal, called the **plane of incidence,** is perpendicular to the plane of the boundary surface between the two materials. We always draw ray diagrams so that the incident, reflected, and refracted rays are in the plane of the diagram.

2. **The angle of reflection θ_r is equal to the angle of incidence θ_a for all wavelengths and for any pair of materials.** That is, in Fig. 33.5c,

$$\theta_r = \theta_a \quad \text{(law of reflection)} \tag{33.2}$$

This relationship, together with the observation that the incident and reflected rays and the normal all lie in the same plane, is called the **law of reflection.**

3. For monochromatic light and for a given pair of materials, a and b, on opposite sides of the interface, **the ratio of the sines of the angles θ_a and θ_b, where both angles are measured from the normal to the surface, is equal to the inverse ratio of the two indexes of refraction:**

$$\frac{\sin\theta_a}{\sin\theta_b} = \frac{n_b}{n_a} \tag{33.3}$$

or

$$n_a\sin\theta_a = n_b\sin\theta_b \quad \text{(law of refraction)} \tag{33.4}$$

This experimental result, together with the observation that the incident and refracted rays and the normal all lie in the same plane, is called the **law of refraction** or **Snell's law,** after the Dutch scientist Willebrord Snell (1591–1626). There is some doubt that Snell actually discovered it. The discovery that $n = c/v$ came much later.

While these results were first observed experimentally, they can be derived theoretically from a wave description of light. We do this in Section 33.7.

Equations (33.3) and (33.4) show that when a ray passes from one material (a) into another material (b) having a larger index of refraction ($n_b > n_a$) and hence a slower wave speed, the angle θ_b with the normal is *smaller* in the second material than the angle θ_a in the first; hence the ray is bent *toward* the normal (Fig. 33.8a). When the second material has a *smaller* index of refraction than the first material ($n_b < n_a$) and hence a faster wave speed, the ray is bent *away from* the normal (Fig. 33.8b).

No matter what the materials on either side of the interface, in the case of *normal* incidence the transmitted ray is not bent at all (Fig. 33.8c). In this case

33.8 Refraction and reflection in three cases. (a) Material b has a larger index of refraction than material a. (b) Material b has a smaller index of refraction than material a. (c) The incident light ray is normal to the interface between the materials.

(a) A ray entering a material of *larger* index of refraction bends *toward* the normal.

(b) A ray entering a material of *smaller* index of refraction bends *away from* the normal.

(c) A ray oriented along the normal does not bend, regardless of the materials.

33.9 (a) This ruler is actually straight, but it appears to bend at the surface of the water. (b) Light rays from any submerged object bend away from the normal when they emerge into the air. As seen by an observer above the surface of the water, the object appears to be much closer to the surface than it actually is.

(a) A straight ruler half-immersed in water

(b) Why the ruler appears bent

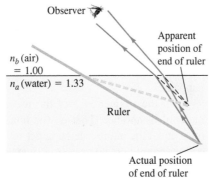

Observer

Apparent position of end of ruler

n_b (air) = 1.00

n_a (water) = 1.33

Ruler

Actual position of end of ruler

33.10 (a) The index of refraction of air is slightly greater than 1, so light rays from the setting sun bend downward when they enter our atmosphere. (The effect is exaggerated in this figure.) (b) Stronger refraction occurs for light coming from the lower limb of the sun (the part that appears closest to the horizon), which passes through denser air in the lower atmosphere. As a result, the setting sun appears flattened vertically. (See Problem 33.55.)

(a) Atmosphere (not to scale)

Light ray from the sun

Earth

(b)

$\theta_a = 0$ and $\sin\theta_a = 0$, so from Eq. (33.4) θ_b is also equal to zero, so the transmitted ray is also normal to the interface. Equation (33.2) shows that θ_r, too, is equal to zero, so the reflected ray travels back along the same path as the incident ray.

The law of refraction explains why a partially submerged ruler or drinking straw appears bent; light rays coming from below the surface change in direction at the air–water interface, so the rays appear to be coming from a position above their actual point of origin (Fig. 33.9). A similar effect explains the appearance of the setting sun (Fig. 33.10).

An important special case is refraction that occurs at an interface between vacuum, for which the index of refraction is unity by definition, and a material. When a ray passes from vacuum into a material (b), so that $n_a = 1$ and $n_b > 1$, the ray is always bent *toward* the normal. When a ray passes from a material into vacuum, so that $n_a > 1$ and $n_b = 1$, the ray is always bent *away from* the normal.

The laws of reflection and refraction apply regardless of which side of the interface the incident ray comes from. If a ray of light approaches the interface in Fig. 33.8a or 33.8b from the right rather than from the left, there are again reflected and refracted rays; these two rays, the incident ray, and the normal to the surface again lie in the same plane. Furthermore, the path of a refracted ray is *reversible;* it follows the same path when going from b to a as when going from a to b. [You can verify this using Eq. (33.4).] Since reflected and incident rays make the same angle with the normal, the path of a reflected ray is also reversible. That's why when you see someone's eyes in a mirror, they can also see you.

The *intensities* of the reflected and refracted rays depend on the angle of incidence, the two indexes of refraction, and the polarization (that is, the direction of the electric-field vector) of the incident ray. The fraction reflected is smallest at normal incidence ($\theta_a = 0°$), where it is about 4% for an air–glass interface. This fraction increases with increasing angle of incidence to 100% at grazing incidence, when $\theta_a = 90°$.

It's possible to use Maxwell's equations to predict the amplitude, intensity, phase, and polarization states of the reflected and refracted waves. Such an analysis is beyond our scope, however.

The index of refraction depends not only on the substance but also on the wavelength of the light. The dependence on wavelength is called *dispersion;* we will consider it in Section 33.4. Indexes of refraction for several solids and liquids are given in Table 33.1 for a particular wavelength of yellow light.

Application Transparency and Index of Refraction

An eel in its larval stage is nearly as transparent as the seawater in which it swims. The larva in this photo is nonetheless easy to see because its index of refraction is higher than that of seawater, so that some of the light striking it is reflected instead of transmitted. The larva appears particularly shiny around its edges because the light reaching the camera from those points struck the larva at near-grazing incidence ($\theta_a = 90°$), resulting in almost 100% reflection.

Table 33.1 Index of Refraction for Yellow Sodium Light, $\lambda_0 = 589$ nm

Substance	Index of Refraction, n
Solids	
Ice (H_2O)	1.309
Fluorite (CaF_2)	1.434
Polystyrene	1.49
Rock salt (NaCl)	1.544
Quartz (SiO_2)	1.544
Zircon ($ZrO_2 \cdot SiO_2$)	1.923
Diamond (C)	2.417
Fabulite ($SrTiO_3$)	2.409
Rutile (TiO_2)	2.62
Glasses (typical values)	
Crown	1.52
Light flint	1.58
Medium flint	1.62
Dense flint	1.66
Lanthanum flint	1.80
Liquids at 20°C	
Methanol (CH_3OH)	1.329
Water (H_2O)	1.333
Ethanol (C_2H_5OH)	1.36
Carbon tetrachloride (CCl_4)	1.460
Turpentine	1.472
Glycerine	1.473
Benzene	1.501
Carbon disulfide (CS_2)	1.628

The index of refraction of air at standard temperature and pressure is about 1.0003, and we will usually take it to be exactly unity. The index of refraction of a gas increases as its density increases. Most glasses used in optical instruments have indexes of refraction between about 1.5 and 2.0. A few substances have larger indexes; one example is diamond, with 2.417.

Index of Refraction and the Wave Aspects of Light

We have discussed how the direction of a light ray changes when it passes from one material to another material with a different index of refraction. It's also important to see what happens to the *wave* characteristics of the light when this happens.

First, the frequency f of the wave does not change when passing from one material to another. That is, the number of wave cycles arriving per unit time must equal the number leaving per unit time; this is a statement that the boundary surface cannot create or destroy waves.

Second, the wavelength λ of the wave *is* different in general in different materials. This is because in any material, $v = \lambda f$; since f is the same in any material as in vacuum and v is always less than the wave speed c in vacuum, λ is also correspondingly reduced. Thus the wavelength λ of light in a material is *less than* the wavelength λ_0 of the same light in vacuum. From the above discussion, $f = c/\lambda_0 = v/\lambda$. Combining this with Eq. (33.1), $n = c/v$, we find

$$\lambda = \frac{\lambda_0}{n} \qquad \text{(wavelength of light in a material)} \qquad (33.5)$$

When a wave passes from one material into a second material with larger index of refraction, so that $n_b > n_a$, the wave speed decreases. The wavelength $\lambda_b = \lambda_0/n_b$ in the second material is then shorter than the wavelength $\lambda_a = \lambda_0/n_a$ in the first material. If instead the second material has a smaller index of refraction than the first material, so that $n_b < n_a$, then the wave speed increases. Then the wavelength λ_b in the second material is longer than the wavelength λ_a in the first material. This makes intuitive sense; the waves get "squeezed" (the wavelength gets shorter) if the wave speed decreases and get "stretched" (the wavelength gets longer) if the wave speed increases.

Problem-Solving Strategy 33.1 **Reflection and Refraction**

IDENTIFY *the relevant concepts:* Use geometric optics, discussed in this section, whenever light (or electromagnetic radiation of *any* frequency and wavelength) encounters a boundary between materials. In general, part of the light is reflected back into the first material and part is refracted into the second material.

SET UP *the problem* using the following steps:
1. In problems involving rays and angles, start by drawing a large, neat diagram. Label all known angles and indexes of refraction.
2. Identify the target variables.

EXECUTE *the solution* as follows:
1. Apply the laws of reflection, Eq. (33.2), and refraction, Eq. (33.4). Measure angles of incidence, reflection, and refraction with respect to the *normal* to the surface, *never* from the surface itself.

2. Apply geometry or trigonometry in working out angular relationships. Remember that the sum of the acute angles of a right triangle is 90° (they are *complementary*) and the sum of the interior angles in any triangle is 180°.
3. The frequency of the electromagnetic radiation does not change when it moves from one material to another; the wavelength changes in accordance with Eq. (33.5), $\lambda = \lambda_0/n$.

EVALUATE *your answer:* In problems that involve refraction, check that your results are consistent with Snell's law ($n_a \sin\theta_a = n_b \sin\theta_b$). If the second material has a higher index of refraction than the first, the angle of refraction must be *smaller* than the angle of incidence: The refracted ray bends toward the normal. If the first material has the higher index of refraction, the refracted angle must be larger than the incident angle: The refracted ray bends away from the normal.

Example 33.1   **Reflection and refraction**

In Fig. 33.11, material a is water and material b is glass with index of refraction 1.52. The incident ray makes an angle of 60.0° with the normal; find the directions of the reflected and refracted rays.

SOLUTION

IDENTIFY and SET UP: This is a problem in geometric optics. We are given the angle of incidence $\theta_a = 60.0°$ and the indexes of

33.11 Reflection and refraction of light passing from water to glass.

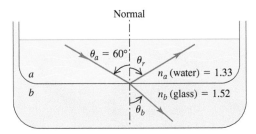

refraction $n_a = 1.33$ and $n_b = 1.52$. We must find the angles of reflection and refraction θ_r and θ_b; to do this we use Eqs. (33.2) and (33.4), respectively. Figure 33.11 shows the rays and angles; n_b is slightly greater than n_a, so by Snell's law [Eq. (33.4)] θ_b is slightly smaller than θ_a, as the figure shows.

EXECUTE: According to Eq. (33.2), the angle the reflected ray makes with the normal is the same as that of the incident ray, so $\theta_r = \theta_a = 60.0°$.

To find the direction of the refracted ray we use Snell's law, Eq. (33.4):

$$n_a \sin\theta_a = n_b \sin\theta_b$$
$$\sin\theta_b = \frac{n_a}{n_b}\sin\theta_a = \frac{1.33}{1.52}\sin 60.0° = 0.758$$
$$\theta_b = \arcsin(0.758) = 49.3°$$

EVALUATE: The second material has a larger refractive index than the first, as in Fig. 33.8a. Hence the refracted ray is bent toward the normal and $\theta_b < \theta_a$.

Example 33.2   **Index of refraction in the eye**

The wavelength of the red light from a helium-neon laser is 633 nm in air but 474 nm in the aqueous humor inside your eyeball. Calculate the index of refraction of the aqueous humor and the speed and frequency of the light in it.

SOLUTION

IDENTIFY and SET UP: The key ideas here are (i) the definition of index of refraction n in terms of the wave speed v in a medium and the speed c in vacuum, and (ii) the relationship between wavelength λ_0 in vacuum and wavelength λ in a medium of index n. We use Eq. (33.1), $n = c/v$; Eq. (33.5), $\lambda = \lambda_0/n$; and $v = \lambda f$.

EXECUTE: The index of refraction of air is very close to unity, so we assume that the wavelength λ_0 in vacuum is the same as that in air, 633 nm. Then from Eq. (33.5),

$$\lambda = \frac{\lambda_0}{n} \qquad n = \frac{\lambda_0}{\lambda} = \frac{633 \text{ nm}}{474 \text{ nm}} = 1.34$$

This is about the same index of refraction as for water. Then, using $n = c/v$ and $v = \lambda f$, we find

$$v = \frac{c}{n} = \frac{3.00 \times 10^8 \text{ m/s}}{1.34} = 2.25 \times 10^8 \text{ m/s}$$
$$f = \frac{v}{\lambda} = \frac{2.25 \times 10^8 \text{ m/s}}{474 \times 10^{-9} \text{ m}} = 4.74 \times 10^{14} \text{ Hz}$$

EVALUATE: Note that while the speed and wavelength have different values in air and in the aqueous humor, the *frequency* in air, f_0, is the same as the frequency f in the aqueous humor:

$$f_0 = \frac{c}{\lambda_0} = \frac{3.00 \times 10^8 \text{ m/s}}{633 \times 10^{-9} \text{ m}} = 4.74 \times 10^{14} \text{ Hz}$$

When a light wave passes from one material into another, the wave speed and wavelength both change but the wave frequency is unchanged.

Example 33.3   **A twice-reflected ray**

Two mirrors are perpendicular to each other. A ray traveling in a plane perpendicular to both mirrors is reflected from one mirror, then the other, as shown in Fig. 33.12. What is the ray's final direction relative to its original direction?

SOLUTION

IDENTIFY and SET UP: This problem involves the law of reflection, which we must apply twice (once for each mirror).

EXECUTE: For mirror 1 the angle of incidence is θ_1, and this equals the angle of reflection. The sum of interior angles in the triangle shown in the figure is 180°, so we see that the angles of incidence and reflection for mirror 2 are both $90° - \theta_1$. The total change in direction of the ray after both reflections is therefore $2(90° - \theta_1) + 2\theta_1 = 180°$. That is, the ray's final direction is opposite to its original direction.

Continued

33.12 A ray moving in the *xy*-plane. The first reflection changes the sign of the *y*-component of its velocity, and the second reflection changes the sign of the *x*-component. For a different ray with a *z*-component of velocity, a third mirror (perpendicular to the two shown) could be used to change the sign of that component.

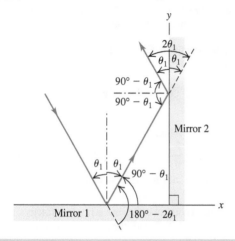

EVALUATE: An alternative viewpoint is that reflection reverses the sign of the component of light velocity perpendicular to the surface but leaves the other components unchanged. We invite you to verify this in detail. You should also be able to use this result to show that when a ray of light is successively reflected by three mirrors forming a corner of a cube (a "corner reflector"), its final direction is again opposite to its original direction. This principle is widely used in tail-light lenses and bicycle reflectors to improve their night-time visibility. Apollo astronauts placed arrays of corner reflectors on the moon. By use of laser beams reflected from these arrays, the earth–moon distance has been measured to within 0.15 m.

Test Your Understanding of Section 33.2 You are standing on the shore of a lake. You spot a tasty fish swimming some distance below the lake surface. (a) If you want to spear the fish, should you aim the spear (i) above, (ii) below, or (iii) directly at the apparent position of the fish? (b) If instead you use a high-power laser to simultaneously kill and cook the fish, should you aim the laser (i) above, (ii) below, or (iii) directly at the apparent position of the fish? ∎

ActivPhysics 15.2: Total Internal Reflection

33.3 Total Internal Reflection

We have described how light is partially reflected and partially transmitted at an interface between two materials with different indexes of refraction. Under certain circumstances, however, *all* of the light can be reflected back from the interface, with none of it being transmitted, even though the second material is transparent. Figure 33.13a shows how this can occur. Several rays are shown radiating from a point source in material *a* with index of refraction n_a. The rays

33.13 (a) Total internal reflection. The angle of incidence for which the angle of refraction is 90° is called the critical angle: This is the case for ray 3. The reflected portions of rays 1, 2, and 3 are omitted for clarity. (b) Rays of laser light enter the water in the fishbowl from above; they are reflected at the bottom by mirrors tilted at slightly different angles. One ray undergoes total internal reflection at the air–water interface.

(a) Total internal reflection

(b) Total internal reflection demonstrated with a laser, mirrors, and water in a fishbowl strike the surface of a second material b with index n_b, where $n_a > n_b$. (Materials a and b could be water and air, respectively.) From Snell's law of refraction,

$$\sin\theta_b = \frac{n_a}{n_b}\sin\theta_a$$

Because n_a/n_b is greater than unity, $\sin\theta_b$ is larger than $\sin\theta_a$; the ray is bent *away from* the normal. Thus there must be some value of θ_a *less than* 90° for which $\sin\theta_b = 1$ and $\theta_b = 90°$. This is shown by ray 3 in the diagram, which emerges just grazing the surface at an angle of refraction of 90°. Compare Fig. 33.13a to the photograph of light rays in Fig. 33.13b.

The angle of incidence for which the refracted ray emerges tangent to the surface is called the **critical angle,** denoted by θ_{crit}. (A more detailed analysis using Maxwell's equations shows that as the incident angle approaches the critical angle, the transmitted intensity approaches zero.) If the angle of incidence is *larger* than the critical angle, the sine of the angle of refraction, as computed by Snell's law, would have to be greater than unity, which is impossible. Beyond the critical angle, the ray *cannot* pass into the upper material; it is trapped in the lower material and is completely reflected at the boundary surface. This situation, called **total internal reflection,** occurs only when a ray in material a is incident on a second material b whose index of refraction is *smaller* than that of material a (that is, $n_b < n_a$).

We can find the critical angle for two given materials a and b by setting $\theta_b = 90°(\sin\theta_b = 1)$ in Snell's law. We then have

$$\sin\theta_{\text{crit}} = \frac{n_b}{n_a} \quad \text{(critical angle for total internal reflection)} \quad [33.6]$$

Total internal reflection will occur if the angle of incidence θ_a is larger than or equal to θ_{crit}.

Applications of Total Internal Reflection

Total internal reflection finds numerous uses in optical technology. As an example, consider glass with index of refraction $n = 1.52$. If light propagating within this glass encounters a glass–air interface, the critical angle is

$$\sin\theta_{\text{crit}} = \frac{1}{1.52} = 0.658 \qquad \theta_{\text{crit}} = 41.1°$$

The light will be *totally reflected* if it strikes the glass–air surface at an angle of 41.1° or larger. Because the critical angle is slightly smaller than 45°, it is possible to use a prism with angles of 45°−45°−90° as a totally reflecting surface. As reflectors, totally reflecting prisms have some advantages over metallic surfaces such as ordinary coated-glass mirrors. While no metallic surface reflects 100% of the light incident on it, light can be *totally* reflected by a prism. These reflecting properties of a prism are permanent and unaffected by tarnishing.

A 45°−45°−90° prism, used as in Fig. 33.14a, is called a *Porro* prism. Light enters and leaves at right angles to the hypotenuse and is totally reflected at each of the shorter faces. The total change of direction of the rays is 180°. Binoculars often use combinations of two Porro prisms, as in Fig. 33.14b.

When a beam of light enters at one end of a transparent rod (Fig. 33.15), the light can be totally reflected internally if the index of refraction of the rod is greater than that of the surrounding material. The light is "trapped" within the rod even if the rod is curved, provided that the curvature is not too great. Such a

33.14 (a) Total internal reflection in a Porro prism. (b) A combination of two Porro prisms in binoculars.

(a) Total internal reflection in a Porro prism

If the incident beam is oriented as shown, total internal reflection occurs on the 45° faces (because, for a glass–air interface, $\theta_{\text{crit}} = 41.1$).

(b) Binoculars use Porro prisms to reflect the light to each eyepiece.

Porro prisms

33.15 A transparent rod with refractive index greater than that of the surrounding material.

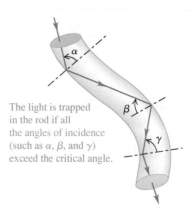

The light is trapped in the rod if all the angles of incidence (such as α, β, and γ) exceed the critical angle.

33.16 This colored x-ray image of a patient's abdomen shows an endoscope winding through the colon.

33.17 To maximize their brilliance, diamonds are cut so that there is total internal reflection on their back surfaces.

rod is sometimes called a *light pipe*. A bundle of fine glass or plastic fibers behaves in the same way and has the advantage of being flexible. A bundle may consist of thousands of individual fibers, each of the order of 0.002 to 0.01 mm in diameter. If the fibers are assembled in the bundle so that the relative positions of the ends are the same (or mirror images) at both ends, the bundle can transmit an image.

Fiber-optic devices have found a wide range of medical applications in instruments called *endoscopes*, which can be inserted directly into the bronchial tubes, the bladder, the colon, and other organs for direct visual examination (Fig. 33.16). A bundle of fibers can even be enclosed in a hypodermic needle for studying tissues and blood vessels far beneath the skin.

Fiber optics also have applications in communication systems, in which they are used to transmit a modulated laser beam. The rate at which information can be transmitted by a wave (light, radio, or whatever) is proportional to the frequency. To see qualitatively why this is so, consider modulating (modifying) the wave by chopping off some of the wave crests. Suppose each crest represents a binary digit, with a chopped-off crest representing a zero and an unmodified crest representing a one. The number of binary digits we can transmit per unit time is thus proportional to the frequency of the wave. Infrared and visible-light waves have much higher frequency than do radio waves, so a modulated laser beam can transmit an enormous amount of information through a single fiber-optic cable.

Another advantage of optical fibers is that they can be made thinner than conventional copper wire, so more fibers can be bundled together in a cable of a given diameter. Hence more distinct signals (for instance, different phone lines) can be sent over the same cable. Because fiber-optic cables are electrical insulators, they are immune to electrical interference from lightning and other sources, and they don't allow unwanted currents between source and receiver. For these and other reasons, fiber-optic cables play an important role in long-distance telephone, television, and Internet communication.

Total internal reflection also plays an important role in the design of jewelry. The brilliance of diamond is due in large measure to its very high index of refraction ($n = 2.417$) and correspondingly small critical angle. Light entering a cut diamond is totally internally reflected from facets on its back surface, and then emerges from its front surface (Fig. 33.17). "Imitation diamond" gems, such as cubic zirconia, are made from less expensive crystalline materials with comparable indexes of refraction.

Conceptual Example 33.4   **A leaky periscope**

A submarine periscope uses two totally reflecting $45°-45°-90°$ prisms with total internal reflection on the sides adjacent to the 45° angles. Explain why the periscope will no longer work if it springs a leak and the bottom prism is covered with water.

SOLUTION

The critical angle for water ($n_b = 1.33$) on glass ($n_a = 1.52$) is

$$\theta_{\text{crit}} = \arcsin\frac{1.33}{1.52} = 61.0°$$

The 45° angle of incidence for a totally reflecting prism is *smaller* than this new 61° critical angle, so total internal reflection does not occur at the glass–water interface. Most of the light is transmitted into the water, and very little is reflected back into the prism.

Test Your Understanding of Section 33.3   In which of the following situations is there total internal reflection? (i) Light propagating in water ($n = 1.33$) strikes a water–air interface at an incident angle of 70°; (ii) light propagating in glass ($n = 1.52$) strikes a glass–water interface at an incident angle of 70°; (iii) light propagating in water strikes a water–glass interface at an incident angle of 70°.

33.4 Dispersion

Ordinary white light is a superposition of waves with wavelengths extending throughout the visible spectrum. The speed of light *in vacuum* is the same for all wavelengths, but the speed in a material substance is different for different wavelengths. Therefore the index of refraction of a material depends on wavelength. The dependence of wave speed and index of refraction on wavelength is called **dispersion.**

Figure 33.18 shows the variation of index of refraction n with wavelength for some common optical materials. Note that the horizontal axis of this figure is the wavelength of the light *in vacuum*, λ_0; the wavelength in the material is given by Eq. (33.5), $\lambda = \lambda_0/n$. In most materials the value of n *decreases* with increasing wavelength and decreasing frequency, and thus n *increases* with decreasing wavelength and increasing frequency. In such a material, light of longer wavelength has greater speed than light of shorter wavelength.

Figure 33.19 shows a ray of white light incident on a prism. The deviation (change of direction) produced by the prism increases with increasing index of refraction and frequency and decreasing wavelength. Violet light is deviated most, and red is deviated least; other colors are in intermediate positions. When it comes out of the prism, the light is spread out into a fan-shaped beam, as shown. The light is said to be *dispersed* into a spectrum. The amount of dispersion depends on the *difference* between the refractive indexes for violet light and for red light. From Fig. 33.18 we can see that for a substance such as fluorite, the difference between the indexes for red and violet is small, and the dispersion will also be small. A better choice of material for a prism whose purpose is to produce a spectrum would be silicate flint glass, for which there is a larger difference in the value of n between red and violet.

33.18 Variation of index of refraction n with wavelength for different transparent materials. The horizontal axis shows the wavelength λ_0 of the light *in vacuum;* the wavelength in the material is equal to $\lambda = \lambda_0/n$.

33.19 Dispersion of light by a prism. The band of colors is called a spectrum.

As we mentioned in Section 33.3, the brilliance of diamond is due in part to its unusually large refractive index; another important factor is its large dispersion, which causes white light entering a diamond to emerge as a multicolored spectrum. Crystals of rutile and of strontium titanate, which can be produced synthetically, have about eight times the dispersion of diamond.

Rainbows

When you experience the beauty of a rainbow, as in Fig. 33.20a, you are seeing the combined effects of dispersion, refraction, and reflection. Sunlight comes from behind you, enters a water droplet, is (partially) reflected from the back surface of the droplet, and is refracted again upon exiting the droplet (Fig. 33.20b). A light ray that enters the middle of the raindrop is reflected straight back. All other rays

33.20 How rainbows form.

(a) A double rainbow

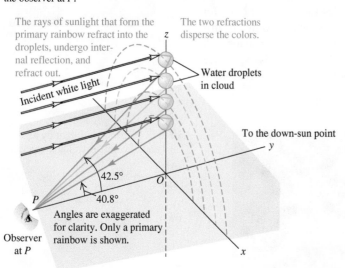

(b) The paths of light rays entering the upper half of a raindrop

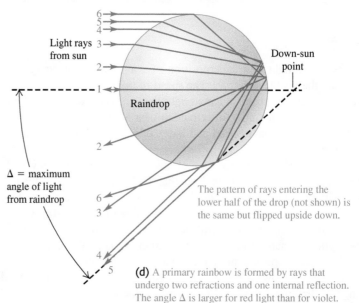

(c) Forming a rainbow. The sun in this illustration is directly behind the observer at *P*.

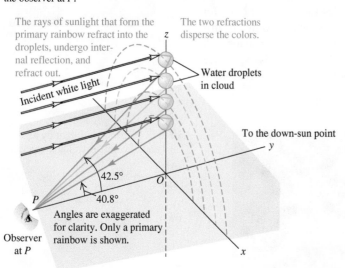

(d) A primary rainbow is formed by rays that undergo two refractions and one internal reflection. The angle Δ is larger for red light than for violet.

(e) A secondary rainbow is formed by rays that undergo two refractions and *two* internal reflections. The angle Δ is larger for violet light than for red.

exit the raindrop within an angle Δ of that middle ray, with many rays "piling up" at the angle Δ. What you see is a disk of light of angular radius Δ centered on the down-sun point (the point in the sky opposite the sun); due to the "piling up" of light rays, the disk is brightest around its rim, which we see as a rainbow (Fig. 33.20c). Because no light reaches your eye from angles larger than Δ, the sky looks dark outside the rainbow (see Fig. 33.20a). The value of the angle Δ depends on the index of refraction of the water that makes up the raindrops, which in turn depends on the wavelength (Fig. 33.20d). The bright disk of red light is slightly larger than that for orange light, which in turn is slightly larger than that for yellow light, and so on. As a result, you see the rainbow as a band of colors.

In many cases you can see a second, larger rainbow. It is the result of dispersion, refraction, and *two* reflections from the back surface of the droplet (Fig. 33.20e). Each time a light ray hits the back surface, part of the light is refracted out of the drop (not shown in Fig. 33.20); after two such hits, relatively little light is left inside the drop, which is why the secondary rainbow is noticeably fainter than the primary rainbow. Just as a mirror held up to a book reverses the printed letters, so the second reflection reverses the sequence of colors in the secondary rainbow. You can see this effect in Fig. 33.20a.

33.5 Polarization

Polarization is a characteristic of all transverse waves. This chapter is about light, but to introduce some basic polarization concepts, let's go back to the transverse waves on a string that we studied in Chapter 15. For a string that in equilibrium lies along the x-axis, the displacements may be along the y-direction, as in Fig. 33.21a. In this case the string always lies in the xy-plane. But the displacements might instead be along the z-axis, as in Fig. 33.21b; then the string always lies in the xz-plane.

When a wave has only y-displacements, we say that it is **linearly polarized** in the y-direction; a wave with only z-displacements is linearly polarized in the z-direction. For mechanical waves we can build a **polarizing filter,** or **polarizer,** that permits only waves with a certain polarization direction to pass. In Fig. 33.21c the string can slide vertically in the slot without friction, but no horizontal motion is possible. This filter passes waves that are polarized in the y-direction but blocks those that are polarized in the z-direction.

This same language can be applied to electromagnetic waves, which also have polarization. As we learned in Chapter 32, an electromagnetic wave is a *transverse* wave; the fluctuating electric and magnetic fields are perpendicular to each other and to the direction of propagation. We always define the direction of polarization of an electromagnetic wave to be the direction of the *electric*-field vector $\vec{E}$, not the magnetic field, because many common electromagnetic-wave detectors respond to the electric forces on electrons in materials, not the magnetic forces. Thus the electromagnetic wave described by Eq. (32.17),

$$\vec{E}(x, t) = \hat{\jmath} E_{\max} \cos(kx - \omega t)$$
$$\vec{B}(x, t) = \hat{k} B_{\max} \cos(kx - \omega t)$$

(MP) **ActivPhysics 16.9:** Physical Optics: Polarization

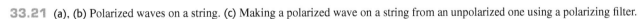

33.21 (a), (b) Polarized waves on a string. (c) Making a polarized wave on a string from an unpolarized one using a polarizing filter.

(a) Transverse wave linearly polarized in the y-direction

(b) Transverse wave linearly polarized in the z-direction

(c) The slot functions as a polarizing filter, passing only components polarized in the y-direction.

33.22 (a) Electrons in the red and white broadcast antenna oscillate vertically, producing vertically polarized electromagnetic waves that propagate away from the antenna in the horizontal direction. (The small gray antennas are for relaying cellular phone signals.) (b) No matter how this light bulb is oriented, the random motion of electrons in the filament produces unpolarized light waves.

(a)

(b)

is said to be polarized in the *y*-direction because the electric field has only a *y*-component.

CAUTION **The meaning of "polarization"** It's unfortunate that the same word "polarization" that is used to describe the direction of $\vec{E}$ in an electromagnetic wave is also used to describe the shifting of electric charge within a body, such as in response to a nearby charged body; we described this latter kind of polarization in Section 21.2 (see Fig. 21.7). You should remember that while these two concepts have the same name, they do not describe the same phenomenon.

Polarizing Filters

Waves emitted by a radio transmitter are usually linearly polarized. The vertical antennas that are used for radio broadcasting emit waves that, in a horizontal plane around the antenna, are polarized in the vertical direction (parallel to the antenna) (Fig. 33.22a).

The situation is different for visible light. Light from incandescent light bulbs and fluorescent light fixtures is *not* polarized (Fig. 33.22b). The "antennas" that radiate light waves are the molecules that make up the sources. The waves emitted by any one molecule may be linearly polarized, like those from a radio antenna. But any actual light source contains a tremendous number of molecules with random orientations, so the emitted light is a random mixture of waves linearly polarized in all possible transverse directions. Such light is called **unpolarized light** or **natural light.** To create polarized light from unpolarized natural light requires a filter that is analogous to the slot for mechanical waves in Fig. 33.21c.

Polarizing filters for electromagnetic waves have different details of construction, depending on the wavelength. For microwaves with a wavelength of a few centimeters, a good polarizer is an array of closely spaced, parallel conducting wires that are insulated from each other. (Think of a barbecue grill with the outer metal ring replaced by an insulating one.) Electrons are free to move along the length of the conducting wires and will do so in response to a wave whose $\vec{E}$ field is parallel to the wires. The resulting currents in the wires dissipate energy by I^2R heating; the dissipated energy comes from the wave, so whatever wave passes through the grid is greatly reduced in amplitude. Waves with $\vec{E}$ oriented perpendicular to the wires pass through almost unaffected, since electrons cannot move through the air between the wires. Hence a wave that passes through such a filter will be predominantly polarized in the direction perpendicular to the wires.

The most common polarizing filter for visible light is a material known by the trade name Polaroid, widely used for sunglasses and polarizing filters for camera lenses. Developed originally by the American scientist Edwin H. Land, this material incorporates substances that have **dichroism,** a selective absorption in which one of the polarized components is absorbed much more strongly than the other (Fig. 33.23). A Polaroid filter transmits 80% or more of the intensity of a wave that is polarized parallel to a certain axis in the material, called the **polarizing**

33.23 A Polaroid filter is illuminated by unpolarized natural light (shown by $\vec{E}$ vectors that point in all directions perpendicular to the direction of propagation). The transmitted light is linearly polarized along the polarizing axis (shown by $\vec{E}$ vectors along the polarization direction only).

Filter only partially absorbs vertically polarized component of light.

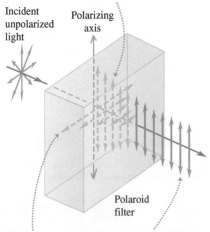

Incident unpolarized light

Polarizing axis

Polaroid filter

Filter almost completely absorbs horizontally polarized component of light.

Transmitted light is linearly polarized in the vertical direction.

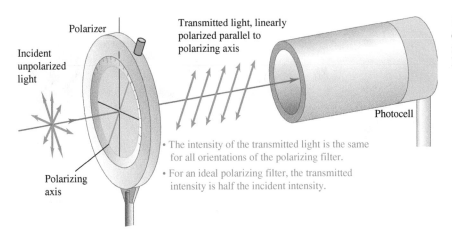

Polarizer

Incident
unpolarized
light

Polarizing
axis

Transmitted light, linearly
polarized parallel to
polarizing axis

Photocell

• The intensity of the transmitted light is the same
for all orientations of the polarizing filter.
• For an ideal polarizing filter, the transmitted
intensity is half the incident intensity.

33.24 Unpolarized natural light is incident on the polarizing filter. The photocell measures the intensity of the transmitted linearly polarized light.

axis, but only 1% or less for waves that are polarized perpendicular to this axis. In one type of Polaroid filter, long-chain molecules within the filter are oriented with their axis perpendicular to the polarizing axis; these molecules preferentially absorb light that is polarized along their length, much like the conducting wires in a polarizing filter for microwaves.

Using Polarizing Filters

An *ideal* polarizing filter (polarizer) passes 100% of the incident light that is polarized parallel to the filter's polarizing axis but completely blocks all light that is polarized perpendicular to this axis. Such a device is an unattainable idealization, but the concept is useful in clarifying the basic ideas. In the following discussion we will assume that all polarizing filters are ideal. In Fig. 33.24 unpolarized light is incident on a flat polarizing filter. The $\vec{E}$ vector of the incident wave can be represented in terms of components parallel and perpendicular to the polarizer axis (shown in blue); only the component of $\vec{E}$ parallel to the polarizing axis is transmitted. Hence the light emerging from the polarizer is linearly polarized parallel to the polarizing axis.

When unpolarized light is incident on an ideal polarizer as in Fig. 33.24, the intensity of the transmitted light is *exactly half* that of the incident unpolarized light, no matter how the polarizing axis is oriented. Here's why: We can resolve the $\vec{E}$ field of the incident wave into a component parallel to the polarizing axis and a component perpendicular to it. Because the incident light is a random mixture of all states of polarization, these two components are, on average, equal. The ideal polarizer transmits only the component that is parallel to the polarizing axis, so half the incident intensity is transmitted.

What happens when the linearly polarized light emerging from a polarizer passes through a second polarizer, or *analyzer*, as in Fig. 33.25? Suppose the polarizing axis of the analyzer makes an angle ϕ with the polarizing axis of the

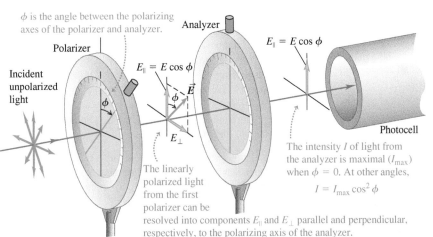

ϕ is the angle between the polarizing
axes of the polarizer and analyzer.

Analyzer

Polarizer

Incident
unpolarized
light

$E_\parallel = E \cos\phi$

$\vec{E}$

ϕ

$E_\perp$

$E_\parallel = E \cos\phi$

Photocell

The linearly
polarized light
from the first
polarizer can be
resolved into components $E_\parallel$ and $E_\perp$ parallel and perpendicular,
respectively, to the polarizing axis of the analyzer.

The intensity I of light from
the analyzer is maximal (I_{max})
when $\phi = 0$. At other angles,

$$I = I_{max} \cos^2\phi$$

33.25 An ideal analyzer transmits only the electric field component parallel to its transmission direction (that is, its polarizing axis).

33.26 These photos show the view through Polaroid sunglasses whose polarizing axes are (left) aligned ($\phi = 0$) and (right) perpendicular ($\phi = 90°$). The transmitted intensity is greatest when the axes are aligned; it is zero when the axes are perpendicular.

Video Tutor Demo

first polarizer. We can resolve the linearly polarized light that is transmitted by the first polarizer into two components, as shown in Fig. 33.25, one parallel and the other perpendicular to the axis of the analyzer. Only the parallel component, with amplitude $E\cos\phi$, is transmitted by the analyzer. The transmitted intensity is greatest when $\phi = 0$, and it is zero when the polarizer and analyzer are *crossed* so that $\phi = 90°$ (Fig. 33.26). To determine the direction of polarization of the light transmitted by the first polarizer, rotate the analyzer until the photocell in Fig. 33.25 measures zero intensity; the polarization axis of the first polarizer is then perpendicular to that of the analyzer.

To find the transmitted intensity at intermediate values of the angle ϕ, we recall from our energy discussion in Section 32.4 that the intensity of an electromagnetic wave is proportional to the *square* of the amplitude of the wave [see Eq. (32.29)]. The ratio of transmitted to incident *amplitude* is $\cos\phi$, so the ratio of transmitted to incident *intensity* is $\cos^2\phi$. Thus the intensity of the light transmitted through the analyzer is

$$I = I_{\max}\cos^2\phi \qquad \text{(Malus's law, polarized light passing through an analyzer)} \qquad (33.7)$$

where $I_{\max}$ is the maximum intensity of light transmitted (at $\phi = 0$) and I is the amount transmitted at angle ϕ. This relationship, discovered experimentally by Etienne Louis Malus in 1809, is called **Malus's law.** Malus's law applies *only* if the incident light passing through the analyzer is already linearly polarized.

Problem-Solving Strategy 33.2 **Linear Polarization**

IDENTIFY *the relevant concepts:* In all electromagnetic waves, including light waves, the direction of polarization is the direction of the $\vec{E}$ field and is perpendicular to the propagation direction. Problems about polarizers are therefore about the components of $\vec{E}$ parallel and perpendicular to the polarizing axis.

SET UP *the problem* using the following steps:
1. Start by drawing a large, neat diagram. Label all known angles, including the angles of all polarizing axes.
2. Identify the target variables.

EXECUTE *the solution* as follows:
1. Remember that a polarizer lets pass only electric-field components parallel to its polarizing axis.
2. If the incident light is linearly polarized and has amplitude E and intensity $I_{\max}$, the light that passes through an ideal polarizer has amplitude $E\cos\phi$ and intensity $I_{\max}\cos^2\phi$, where ϕ is

the angle between the incident polarization direction and the filter's polarizing axis.
3. Unpolarized light is a random mixture of all possible polarization states, so on the average it has equal components in any two perpendicular directions. When passed through an ideal polarizer, unpolarized light becomes linearly polarized light with half the incident intensity. Partially linearly polarized light is a superposition of linearly polarized and unpolarized light.
4. The intensity (average power per unit area) of a wave is proportional to the *square* of its amplitude. If you find that two waves differ in amplitude by a certain factor, their intensities differ by the square of that factor.

EVALUATE *your answer:* Check your answer for any obvious errors. If your results say that light emerging from a polarizer has greater intensity than the incident light, something's wrong: A polarizer can't add energy to a light wave.

Example 33.5 **Two polarizers in combination**

In Fig. 33.25 the incident unpolarized light has intensity I_0. Find the intensities transmitted by the first and second polarizers if the angle between the axes of the two filters is 30°.

SOLUTION

IDENTIFY and SET UP: This problem involves a polarizer (a polarizing filter on which unpolarized light shines, producing polarized light) and an analyzer (a second polarizing filter on which the polarized light shines). We are given the intensity I_0 of the incident light and the angle $\phi = 30°$ between the axes of the polarizers. We use Malus's law, Eq. (33.7), to solve for the intensities of the light emerging from each polarizer.

EXECUTE: The incident light is unpolarized, so the intensity of the linearly polarized light transmitted by the first polarizer is $I_0/2$. From Eq. (33.7) with $\phi = 30°$, the second polarizer reduces the intensity by a further factor of $\cos^2 30° = \frac{3}{4}$. Thus the intensity transmitted by the second polarizer is

$$\left(\frac{I_0}{2}\right)\left(\tfrac{3}{4}\right) = \tfrac{3}{8}I_0$$

EVALUATE: Note that the intensity decreases after each passage through a polarizer. The only situation in which the transmitted intensity does *not* decrease is if the polarizer is ideal (so it absorbs none of the light that passes through it) and if the incident light is linearly polarized along the polarizing axis, so $\phi = 0$.

33.27 When light is incident on a reflecting surface at the polarizing angle, the reflected light is linearly polarized.

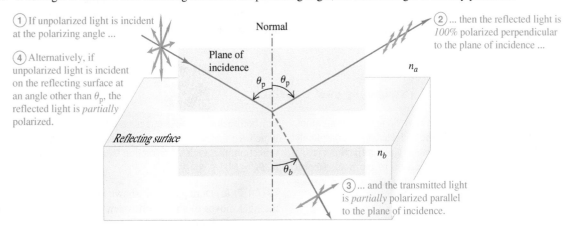

Polarization by Reflection

Unpolarized light can be polarized, either partially or totally, by *reflection*. In Fig. 33.27, unpolarized natural light is incident on a reflecting surface between two transparent optical materials. For most angles of incidence, waves for which the electric-field vector $\vec{E}$ is perpendicular to the plane of incidence (that is, parallel to the reflecting surface) are reflected more strongly than those for which $\vec{E}$ lies in this plane. In this case the reflected light is *partially polarized* in the direction perpendicular to the plane of incidence.

But at one particular angle of incidence, called the **polarizing angle** θ_p, the light for which $\vec{E}$ lies in the plane of incidence is *not reflected at all* but is completely refracted. At this same angle of incidence the light for which $\vec{E}$ is perpendicular to the plane of incidence is partially reflected and partially refracted. The *reflected* light is therefore *completely* polarized perpendicular to the plane of incidence, as shown in Fig. 33.27. The *refracted* (transmitted) light is *partially* polarized parallel to this plane; the refracted light is a mixture of the component parallel to the plane of incidence, all of which is refracted, and the remainder of the perpendicular component.

In 1812 the British scientist Sir David Brewster discovered that when the angle of incidence is equal to the polarizing angle θ_p, the reflected ray and the refracted ray are perpendicular to each other (Fig. 33.28). In this case the angle of refraction θ_b equals $90° - \theta_p$. From the law of refraction,

$$n_a \sin\theta_p = n_b \sin\theta_b$$

33.28 The significance of the polarizing angle. The open circles represent a component of $\vec{E}$ that is perpendicular to the plane of the figure (the plane of incidence) and parallel to the surface between the two materials.

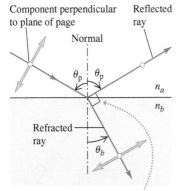

Note: This is a side view of the situation shown in Fig. 33.27.

When light strikes a surface at the polarizing angle, the reflected and refracted rays are perpendicular to each other and
$$\tan\theta_p = \frac{n_b}{n_a}$$

so we find

$$n_a \sin\theta_p = n_b \sin(90° - \theta_p) = n_b \cos\theta_p$$

$$\tan\theta_p = \frac{n_b}{n_a} \quad \text{(Brewster's law for the polarizing angle)} \quad (33.8)$$

This relationship is known as **Brewster's law.** Although discovered experimentally, it can also be *derived* from a wave model using Maxwell's equations.

Polarization by reflection is the reason polarizing filters are widely used in sunglasses (Fig. 33.26). When sunlight is reflected from a horizontal surface, the plane of incidence is vertical, and the reflected light contains a preponderance of light that is polarized in the horizontal direction. When the reflection occurs at a smooth asphalt road surface or the surface of a lake, it causes unwanted glare. Vision can be improved by eliminating this glare. The manufacturer makes the polarizing axis of the lens material vertical, so very little of the horizontally polarized light reflected from the road is transmitted to the eyes. The glasses also reduce the overall intensity of the transmitted light to somewhat less than 50% of the intensity of the unpolarized incident light.

Example 33.6 Reflection from a swimming pool's surface

Sunlight reflects off the smooth surface of a swimming pool. (a) For what angle of reflection is the reflected light completely polarized? (b) What is the corresponding angle of refraction? (c) At night, an underwater floodlight is turned on in the pool. Repeat parts (a) and (b) for rays from the floodlight that strike the surface from below.

SOLUTION

IDENTIFY and SET UP: This problem involves polarization by reflection at an air–water interface in parts (a) and (b) and at a water–air interface in part (c). Figure 33.29 shows our sketches.

33.29 Our sketches for this problem.

For both cases our first target variable is the polarizing angle θ_p, which we find using Brewster's law, Eq. (33.8). For this angle of reflection, the angle of refraction θ_b is the complement of θ_p (that is, $\theta_b = 90° - \theta_p$).

EXECUTE: (a) During the day (shown in the upper part of Fig. 33.29) the light moves in air toward water, so $n_a = 1.00$ (air) and $n_b = 1.33$ (water). From Eq. (33.8),

$$\theta_p = \arctan\frac{n_b}{n_a} = \arctan\frac{1.33}{1.00} = 53.1°$$

(b) The incident light is at the polarizing angle, so the reflected and refracted rays are perpendicular; hence

$$\theta_b = 90° - \theta_p = 90° - 53.1° = 36.9°$$

(c) At night (shown in the lower part of Fig. 33.29) the light moves in water toward air, so now $n_a = 1.33$ and $n_b = 1.00$. Again using Eq. (33.8), we have

$$\theta_p = \arctan\frac{1.00}{1.33} = 36.9°$$
$$\theta_b = 90° - 36.9° = 53.1°$$

EVALUATE: We check our answer in part (b) by using Snell's law, $n_a \sin\theta_a = n_b \sin\theta_b$, to solve for θ_b:

$$\sin\theta_b = \frac{n_a \sin\theta_p}{n_b} = \frac{1.00\sin 53.1°}{1.33} = 0.600$$
$$\theta_b = \arcsin(0.600) = 36.9°$$

Note that the two polarizing angles found in parts (a) and (c) add to 90°. This is *not* an accident; can you see why?

Circular and Elliptical Polarization

Light and other electromagnetic radiation can also have *circular* or *elliptical* polarization. To introduce these concepts, let's return once more to mechanical waves on a stretched string. In Fig. 33.21, suppose the two linearly polarized waves in parts (a) and (b) are in phase and have equal amplitude. When they are superposed, each point in the string has simultaneous *y*- and *z*-displacements of equal magnitude. A little thought shows that the resultant wave lies in a plane oriented at 45° to the *y*- and *z*-axes (i.e., in a plane making a 45° angle with the *xy*- and *xz*-planes). The amplitude of the resultant wave is larger by a factor of $\sqrt{2}$ than that of either component wave, and the resultant wave is linearly polarized.

But now suppose the two equal-amplitude waves differ in phase by a quarter-cycle. Then the resultant motion of each point corresponds to a superposition of two simple harmonic motions at right angles, with a quarter-cycle phase difference. The *y*-displacement at a point is greatest at times when the *z*-displacement is zero, and vice versa. The motion of the string as a whole then no longer takes place in a single plane. It can be shown that each point on the rope moves in a *circle* in a plane parallel to the *yz*-plane. Successive points on the rope have successive phase differences, and the overall motion of the string has the appearance of a rotating helix. This is shown to the left of the polarizing filter in Fig. 33.21c. This particular superposition of two linearly polarized waves is called **circular polarization.**

Figure 33.30 shows the analogous situation for an electromagnetic wave. Two sinusoidal waves of equal amplitude, polarized in the *y*- and *z*-directions and with a quarter-cycle phase difference, are superposed. The result is a wave in which the $\vec{E}$ vector at each point has a constant magnitude but *rotates* around the direction of propagation. The wave in Fig. 33.30 is propagating toward you and the $\vec{E}$ vector appears to be rotating clockwise, so it is called a *right circularly polarized* electromagnetic wave. If instead the $\vec{E}$ vector of a wave coming toward you appears to be rotating counterclockwise, it is called a *left circularly polarized* electromagnetic wave.

If the phase difference between the two component waves is something other than a quarter-cycle, or if the two component waves have different amplitudes, then each point on the string traces out not a circle but an *ellipse*. The resulting wave is said to be **elliptically polarized.**

For electromagnetic waves with radio frequencies, circular or elliptical polarization can be produced by using two antennas at right angles, fed from the same

33.30 Circular polarization of an electromagnetic wave moving toward you parallel to the *x*-axis. The *y*-component of $\vec{E}$ lags the *z*-component by a quarter-cycle. This phase difference results in right circular polarization.

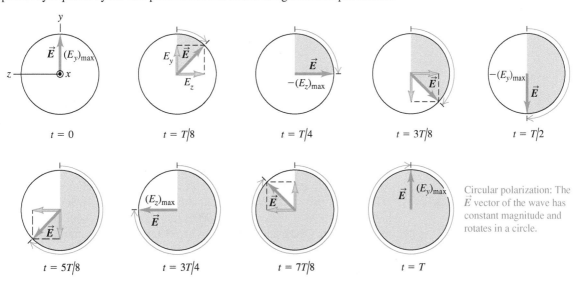

transmitter but with a phase-shifting network that introduces the appropriate phase difference. For light, the phase shift can be introduced by use of a material that exhibits *birefringence*—that is, has different indexes of refraction for different directions of polarization. A common example is calcite ($CaCO_3$). When a calcite crystal is oriented appropriately in a beam of unpolarized light, its refractive index (for a wavelength in vacuum of 589 nm) is 1.658 for one direction of polarization and 1.486 for the perpendicular direction. When two waves with equal amplitude and with perpendicular directions of polarization enter such a material, they travel with different speeds. If they are in phase when they enter the material, then in general they are no longer in phase when they emerge. If the crystal is just thick enough to introduce a quarter-cycle phase difference, then the crystal converts linearly polarized light to circularly polarized light. Such a crystal is called a *quarter-wave plate*. Such a plate also converts circularly polarized light to linearly polarized light. Can you prove this?

Photoelasticity

33.31 This plastic model of an artificial hip joint was photographed between two polarizing filters (a polarizer and an analyzer) with perpendicular polarizing axes. The colored interference pattern reveals the direction and magnitude of stresses in the model. Engineers use these results to help design the metal artificial hip joint used in medicine.

Some optical materials that are not normally birefringent become so when they are subjected to mechanical stress. This is the basis of the science of *photoelasticity*. Stresses in girders, boiler plates, gear teeth, and cathedral pillars can be analyzed by constructing a transparent model of the object, usually of a plastic material, subjecting it to stress, and examining it between a polarizer and an analyzer in the crossed position. Very complicated stress distributions can be studied by these optical methods.

Figure 33.31 is a photograph of a photoelastic model under stress. The polarized light that enters the model can be thought of as having a component along each of the two directions of the birefringent plastic. Since these two components travel through the plastic at different speeds, the light that emerges from the other side of the model can have a different overall direction of polarization. Hence some of this transmitted light will be able to pass through the analyzer even though its polarization axis is at a 90° angle to the polarizer's axis, and the stressed areas in the plastic will appear as bright spots. The amount of birefringence is different for different wavelengths and hence different colors of light; the color that appears at each location in Fig. 33.31 is that for which the transmitted light is most nearly polarized along the analyzer's polarization axis.

Test Your Understanding of Section 33.5   You are taking a photograph of a sunlit high-rise office building. In order to minimize the reflections from the building's windows, you place a polarizing filter on the camera lens. How should you orient the filter? (i) with the polarizing axis vertical; (ii) with the polarizing axis horizontal; (iii) either orientation will minimize the reflections just as well; (iv) neither orientation will have any effect.

33.6 Scattering of Light

The sky is blue. Sunsets are red. Skylight is partially polarized; that's why the sky looks darker from some angles than from others when it is viewed through Polaroid sunglasses. As we will see, a single phenomenon is responsible for all of these effects.

When you look at the daytime sky, the light that you see is sunlight that has been absorbed and then re-radiated in a variety of directions. This process is called **scattering.** (If the earth had no atmosphere, the sky would appear as black in the daytime as it does at night, just as it does to an astronaut in space or on the moon.) Figure 33.32 shows some of the details of the scattering process. Sunlight, which is unpolarized, comes from the left along the *x*-axis and passes over an observer looking vertically upward along the *y*-axis. (We are viewing the situation

33.32 When the sunbathing observer on the left looks up, he sees blue, polarized sunlight that has been scattered by air molecules. The observer on the right sees reddened, unpolarized light when he looks at the sun.

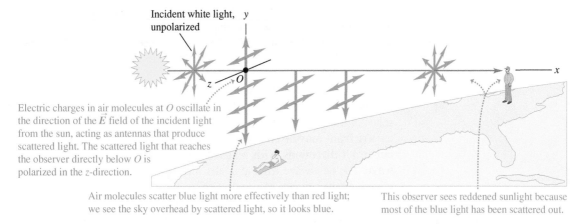

Incident white light, unpolarized

Electric charges in air molecules at O oscillate in the direction of the $\vec{E}$ field of the incident light from the sun, acting as antennas that produce scattered light. The scattered light that reaches the observer directly below O is polarized in the z-direction.

Air molecules scatter blue light more effectively than red light; we see the sky overhead by scattered light, so it looks blue.

This observer sees reddened sunlight because most of the blue light has been scattered out.

from the side.) Consider the molecules of the earth's atmosphere located at point O. The electric field in the beam of sunlight sets the electric charges in these molecules into vibration. Since light is a transverse wave, the direction of the electric field in any component of the sunlight lies in the yz-plane, and the motion of the charges takes place in this plane. There is no field, and hence no motion of charges, in the direction of the x-axis.

An incident light wave sets the electric charges in the molecules at point O vibrating along the line of $\vec{E}$. We can resolve this vibration into two components, one along the y-axis and the other along the z-axis. Each component in the incident light produces the equivalent of two molecular "antennas," oscillating with the same frequency as the incident light and lying along the y- and z-axes.

We mentioned in Chapter 32 that an oscillating charge, like those in an antenna, does not radiate in the direction of its oscillation. (See Fig. 32.3 in Section 32.1.) Thus the "antenna" along the y-axis does not send any light to the observer directly below it, although it does emit light in other directions. Therefore the only light reaching this observer comes from the other molecular "antenna," corresponding to the oscillation of charge along the z-axis. This light is linearly polarized, with its electric field along the z-axis (parallel to the "antenna"). The red vectors on the y-axis below point O in Fig. 33.32 show the direction of polarization of the light reaching the observer.

As the original beam of sunlight passes though the atmosphere, its intensity decreases as its energy goes into the scattered light. Detailed analysis of the scattering process shows that the intensity of the light scattered from air molecules increases in proportion to the fourth power of the frequency (inversely to the fourth power of the wavelength). Thus the intensity ratio for the two ends of the visible spectrum is $(750 \text{ nm}/380 \text{ nm})^4 = 15$. Roughly speaking, scattered light contains 15 times as much blue light as red, and that's why the sky is blue.

Clouds contain a high concentration of water droplets or ice crystals, which also scatter light. Because of this high concentration, light passing through the cloud has many more opportunities for scattering than does light passing through a clear sky. Thus light of *all* wavelengths is eventually scattered out of the cloud, so the cloud looks white (Fig. 33.33). Milk looks white for the same reason; the scattering is due to fat globules in the milk.

Near sunset, when sunlight has to travel a long distance through the earth's atmosphere, a substantial fraction of the blue light is removed by scattering. White light minus blue light looks yellow or red. This explains the yellow or red hue that we so often see from the setting sun (and that is seen by the observer at the far right of Fig. 33.32).

Application Bee Vision and Polarized Light from the Sky
The eyes of a bee can detect the polarization of light. Bees use this to help them navigate between the hive and food sources. As Fig. 33.32 shows, a bee sees unpolarized light if it looks directly toward the sun and sees completely polarized light if it looks 90° away from the sun. These polarizations are unaffected by the presence of clouds, so a bee can navigate relative to the sun even on an overcast day.

Eyes

33.33 Clouds are white because they efficiently scatter sunlight of all wavelengths.

33.7 Huygens's Principle

The laws of reflection and refraction of light rays that we introduced in Section 33.2 were discovered experimentally long before the wave nature of light was firmly established. However, we can *derive* these laws from wave considerations and show that they are consistent with the wave nature of light.

We begin with a principle called **Huygens's principle.** This principle, stated originally by the Dutch scientist Christiaan Huygens in 1678, is a geometrical method for finding, from the known shape of a wave front at some instant, the shape of the wave front at some later time. Huygens assumed that **every point of a wave front may be considered the source of secondary wavelets that spread out in all directions with a speed equal to the speed of propagation of the wave.** The new wave front at a later time is then found by constructing a surface *tangent* to the secondary wavelets or, as it is called, the *envelope* of the wavelets. All the results that we obtain from Huygens's principle can also be obtained from Maxwell's equations. Thus it is not an independent principle, but it is often very convenient for calculations with wave phenomena.

Huygens's principle is shown in Fig. 33.34. The original wave front AA' is traveling outward from a source, as indicated by the arrows. We want to find the shape of the wave front after a time interval t. We assume that v, the speed of propagation of the wave, is the same at all points. Then in time t the wave front travels a distance vt. We construct several circles (traces of spherical wavelets) with radius $r = vt$, centered at points along AA'. The trace of the envelope of these wavelets, which is the new wave front, is the curve BB'.

Reflection and Huygens's Principle

To derive the law of reflection from Huygens's principle, we consider a plane wave approaching a plane reflecting surface. In Fig. 33.35a the lines AA', OB', and NC' represent successive positions of a wave front approaching the surface MM'. Point A on the wave front AA' has just arrived at the reflecting surface. We can use Huygens's principle to find the position of the wave front after a time interval t. With points on AA' as centers, we draw several secondary wavelets with radius vt. The wavelets that originate near the upper end of AA' spread out unhindered, and their envelope gives the portion OB' of the new wave front. If the reflecting surface were not there, the wavelets originating near the lower end of AA' would similarly reach the positions shown by the broken circular arcs. Instead, these wavelets strike the reflecting surface.

The effect of the reflecting surface is to *change the direction* of travel of those wavelets that strike it, so the part of a wavelet that would have penetrated the surface actually lies to the left of it, as shown by the full lines. The first such wavelet is centered at point A; the envelope of all such reflected wavelets is the portion OB of the wave front. The trace of the entire wave front at this instant is the bent line BOB'. A similar construction gives the line CNC' for the wave front after another interval t.

From plane geometry the angle θ_a between the incident *wave front* and the *surface* is the same as that between the incident *ray* and the *normal* to the surface and is therefore the angle of incidence. Similarly, θ_r is the angle of reflection. To find the relationship between these angles, we consider Fig. 33.35b. From O we draw $OP = vt$, perpendicular to AA'. Now OB, by construction, is tangent to a circle of radius vt with center at A. If we draw AQ from A to the point of tangency, the triangles APO and OQA are congruent because they are right triangles with the side AO in common and with $AQ = OP = vt$. The angle θ_a therefore equals the angle θ_r, and we have the law of reflection.

Refraction and Huygens's Principle

We can derive the law of *refraction* by a similar procedure. In Fig. 33.36a we consider a wave front, represented by line AA', for which point A has just

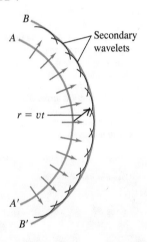

33.34 Applying Huygens's principle to wave front AA' to construct a new wave front BB'.

33.35 Using Huygens's principle to derive the law of reflection.

(a) Successive positions of a plane wave AA' as it is reflected from a plane surface

(b) Magnified portion of **(a)**

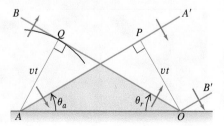

arrived at the boundary surface SS' between two transparent materials a and b, with indexes of refraction n_a and n_b and wave speeds v_a and v_b. (The *reflected* waves are not shown in the figure; they proceed as in Fig. 33.35.) We can apply Huygens's principle to find the position of the refracted wave fronts after a time t.

With points on AA' as centers, we draw several secondary wavelets. Those originating near the upper end of AA' travel with speed v_a and, after a time interval t, are spherical surfaces of radius $v_a t$. The wavelet originating at point A, however, is traveling in the second material b with speed v_b and at time t is a spherical surface of radius $v_b t$. The envelope of the wavelets from the original wave front is the plane whose trace is the bent line BOB'. A similar construction leads to the trace CPC' after a second interval t.

The angles θ_a and θ_b between the surface and the incident and refracted wave fronts are the angle of incidence and the angle of refraction, respectively. To find the relationship between these angles, refer to Fig. 33.36b. We draw $OQ = v_a t$, perpendicular to AQ, and we draw $AB = v_b t$, perpendicular to BO. From the right triangle AOQ,

$$\sin\theta_a = \frac{v_a t}{AO}$$

and from the right triangle AOB,

$$\sin\theta_b = \frac{v_b t}{AO}$$

Combining these, we find

$$\frac{\sin\theta_a}{\sin\theta_b} = \frac{v_a}{v_b} \tag{33.9}$$

We have defined the index of refraction n of a material as the ratio of the speed of light c in vacuum to its speed v in the material: $n_a = c/v_a$ and $n_b = c/v_b$. Thus

$$\frac{n_b}{n_a} = \frac{c/v_b}{c/v_a} = \frac{v_a}{v_b}$$

and we can rewrite Eq. (33.9) as

$$\frac{\sin\theta_a}{\sin\theta_b} = \frac{n_b}{n_a} \quad \text{or}$$

$$n_a \sin\theta_a = n_b \sin\theta_b$$

which we recognize as Snell's law, Eq. (33.4). So we have derived Snell's law from a wave theory. Alternatively, we may choose to regard Snell's law as an experimental result that defines the index of refraction of a material; in that case this analysis helps to confirm the relationship $v = c/n$ for the speed of light in a material.

Mirages offer an interesting example of Huygens's principle in action. When the surface of pavement or desert sand is heated intensely by the sun, a hot, less dense, smaller-n layer of air forms near the surface. The speed of light is slightly greater in the hotter air near the ground, the Huygens wavelets have slightly larger radii, the wave fronts tilt slightly, and rays that were headed toward the surface with a large angle of incidence (near 90°) can be bent up as shown in Fig. 33.37. Light farther from the ground is bent less and travels nearly in a straight line. The observer sees the object in its natural position, with an inverted image below it, as though seen in a horizontal reflecting surface. The mind of a thirsty traveler can interpret the apparent reflecting surface as a sheet of water.

33.36 Using Huygens's principle to derive the law of refraction. The case $v_b < v_a$ ($n_b > n_a$) is shown.

(a) Successive positions of a plane wave AA' as it is refracted by a plane surface

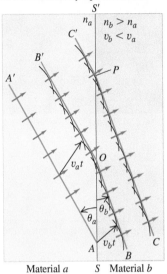

(b) Magnified portion of (a)

33.37 How mirages are formed.

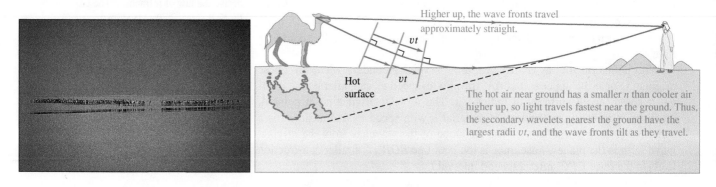

Higher up, the wave fronts travel approximately straight.

vt

Hot surface

vt

The hot air near ground has a smaller n than cooler air higher up, so light travels fastest near the ground. Thus, the secondary wavelets nearest the ground have the largest radii vt, and the wave fronts tilt as they travel.

It is important to keep in mind that Maxwell's equations are the fundamental relationships for electromagnetic wave propagation. But Huygens's principle provides a convenient way to visualize this propagation.

Test Your Understanding of Section 33.7   Sound travels faster in warm air than in cold air. Imagine a weather front that runs north-south, with warm air to the west of the front and cold air to the east. A sound wave traveling in a northeast direction in the warm air encounters this front. How will the direction of this sound wave change when it passes into the cold air? (i) The wave direction will deflect toward the north; (ii) the wave direction will deflect toward the east; (iii) the wave direction will be unchanged.

Video Tutor Solutions

Light and its properties: Light is an electromagnetic wave. When emitted or absorbed, it also shows particle properties. It is emitted by accelerated electric charges.

A wave front is a surface of constant phase; wave fronts move with a speed equal to the propagation speed of the wave. A ray is a line along the direction of propagation, perpendicular to the wave fronts.

When light is transmitted from one material to another, the frequency of the light is unchanged, but the wavelength and wave speed can change. The index of refraction n of a material is the ratio of the speed of light in vacuum c to the speed v in the material. If λ_0 is the wavelength in vacuum, the same wave has a shorter wavelength λ in a medium with index of refraction n. (See Example 33.2.)

$$n = \frac{c}{v} \quad (33.1)$$

$$\lambda = \frac{\lambda_0}{n} \quad (33.5)$$

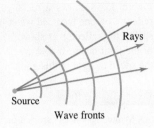

Reflection and refraction: At a smooth interface between two optical materials, the incident, reflected, and refracted rays and the normal to the interface all lie in a single plane called the plane of incidence. The law of reflection states that the angles of incidence and reflection are equal. The law of refraction relates the angles of incidence and refraction to the indexes of refraction of the materials. (See Examples 33.1 and 33.3.)

$$\theta_r = \theta_a \quad (33.2)$$
(law of reflection)

$$n_a \sin\theta_a = n_b \sin\theta_b \quad (33.4)$$
(law of refraction)

Total internal reflection: When a ray travels in a material of greater index of refraction n_a toward a material of smaller index n_b, total internal reflection occurs at the interface when the angle of incidence exceeds a critical angle θ_{crit}. (See Example 33.4.)

$$\sin\theta_{crit} = \frac{n_b}{n_a} \quad (33.6)$$

Polarization of light: The direction of polarization of a linearly polarized electromagnetic wave is the direction of the $\vec{E}$ field. A polarizing filter passes waves that are linearly polarized along its polarizing axis and blocks waves polarized perpendicularly to that axis. When polarized light of intensity I_{max} is incident on a polarizing filter used as an analyzer, the intensity I of the light transmitted through the analyzer depends on the angle ϕ between the polarization direction of the incident light and the polarizing axis of the analyzer. (See Example 33.5.)

$$I = I_{max}\cos^2\phi \quad (33.7)$$
(Malus's law)

Polarization by reflection: When unpolarized light strikes an interface between two materials, Brewster's law states that the reflected light is completely polarized perpendicular to the plane of incidence (parallel to the interface) if the angle of incidence equals the polarizing angle θ_p. (See Example 33.6.)

$$\tan\theta_p = \frac{n_b}{n_a} \quad (33.8)$$
(Brewster's law)

Huygens's principle: Huygens's principle states that if the position of a wave front at one instant is known, then the position of the front at a later time can be constructed by imagining the front as a source of secondary wavelets. Huygens's principle can be used to derive the laws of reflection and refraction.

BRIDGING PROBLEM	Reflection and Refraction

Figure 33.38 shows a rectangular glass block that has a metal reflector on one face and water on an adjoining face. A light beam strikes the reflector as shown. You gradually increase the angle θ of the light beam. If $\theta \geq 59.2°$, no light enters the water. What is the speed of light in this glass?

33.38

SOLUTION GUIDE

See MasteringPhysics® study area for a Video Tutor solution. **(MP)**

IDENTIFY and SET UP

1. Specular reflection occurs where the light ray in the glass strikes the reflector. If no light is to enter the water, we require that there be reflection only and no refraction where this ray strikes the glass–water interface—that is, there must be total internal reflection.
2. The target variable is the speed of light v in the glass, which you can determine from the index of refraction n of the glass. (Table 33.1 gives the index of refraction of water.) Write down the equations you will use to find n and v.

EXECUTE

3. Use the figure to find the angle of incidence of the ray at the glass–water interface.
4. Use the result of step 3 to find n.
5. Use the result of step 4 to find v.

EVALUATE

6. How does the speed of light in the glass compare to the speed in water? Does this make sense?

Problems

For instructor-assigned homework, go to MasteringPhysics®.

•, ••, •••: Problems of increasing difficulty. **CP**: Cumulative problems incorporating material from earlier chapters. **CALC**: Problems requiring calculus. **BIO**: Biosciences problems.

DISCUSSION QUESTIONS

Q33.1 Light requires about 8 minutes to travel from the sun to the earth. Is it delayed appreciably by the earth's atmosphere? Explain.

Q33.2 Sunlight or starlight passing through the earth's atmosphere is always bent toward the vertical. Why? Does this mean that a star is not really where it appears to be? Explain.

Q33.3 A beam of light goes from one material into another. On *physical* grounds, explain *why* the wavelength changes but the frequency and period do not.

Q33.4 A student claimed that, because of atmospheric refraction (see Discussion Question Q33.2), the sun can be seen after it has set and that the day is therefore longer than it would be if the earth had no atmosphere. First, what does she mean by saying that the sun can be seen after it has set? Second, comment on the validity of her conclusion.

Q33.5 When hot air rises from a radiator or heating duct, objects behind it appear to shimmer or waver. What causes this?

Q33.6 Devise straightforward experiments to measure the speed of light in a given glass using (a) Snell's law; (b) total internal reflection; (c) Brewster's law.

Q33.7 Sometimes when looking at a window, you see two reflected images slightly displaced from each other. What causes this?

Q33.8 If you look up from underneath toward the surface of the water in your aquarium, you may see an upside-down reflection of your pet fish in the surface of the water. Explain how this can happen.

Q33.9 A ray of light in air strikes a glass surface. Is there a range of angles for which total reflection occurs? Explain.

Q33.10 When light is incident on an interface between two materials, the angle of the refracted ray depends on the wavelength, but the angle of the reflected ray does not. Why should this be?

Q33.11 A salesperson at a bargain counter claims that a certain pair of sunglasses has Polaroid filters; you suspect that the glasses are just tinted plastic. How could you find out for sure?

Q33.12 Does it make sense to talk about the polarization of a *longitudinal* wave, such as a sound wave? Why or why not?

Q33.13 How can you determine the direction of the polarizing axis of a single polarizer?

Q33.14 It has been proposed that automobile windshields and headlights should have polarizing filters to reduce the glare of oncoming lights during night driving. Would this work? How should the polarizing axes be arranged? What advantages would this scheme have? What disadvantages?

Q33.15 When a sheet of plastic food wrap is placed between two crossed polarizers, no light is transmitted. When the sheet is stretched in one direction, some light passes through the crossed polarizers. What is happening?

Q33.16 If you sit on the beach and look at the ocean through Polaroid sunglasses, the glasses help to reduce the glare from sunlight reflecting off the water. But if you lie on your side on the beach, there is little reduction in the glare. Explain why there is a difference.

Q33.17 When unpolarized light is incident on two crossed polarizers, no light is transmitted. A student asserted that if a third polarizer is inserted between the other two, some transmission will occur. Does this make sense? How can adding a third filter *increase* transmission?

Q33.18 For the old "rabbit-ear" style TV antennas, it's possible to alter the quality of reception considerably simply by changing the orientation of the antenna. Why?

Q33.19 In Fig. 33.32, since the light that is scattered out of the incident beam is polarized, why is the transmitted beam not also partially polarized?

Q33.20 You are sunbathing in the late afternoon when the sun is relatively low in the western sky. You are lying flat on your back, looking straight up through Polaroid sunglasses. To minimize the amount of sky light reaching your eyes, how should you lie: with your feet pointing north, east, south, west, or in some other direction? Explain your reasoning.

Q33.21 Light scattered from blue sky is strongly polarized because of the nature of the scattering process described in Section 33.6. But light scattered from white clouds is usually *not* polarized. Why not?

Q33.22 Atmospheric haze is due to water droplets or smoke particles ("smog"). Such haze reduces visibility by scattering light, so that the light from distant objects becomes randomized and images become indistinct. Explain why visibility through haze can be improved by wearing red-tinted sunglasses, which filter out blue light.

Q33.23 The explanation given in Section 33.6 for the color of the setting sun should apply equally well to the *rising* sun, since sunlight travels the same distance through the atmosphere to reach your eyes at either sunrise or sunset. Typically, however, sunsets are redder than sunrises. Why? (*Hint:* Particles of all kinds in the atmosphere contribute to scattering.)

Q33.24 Huygens's principle also applies to sound waves. During the day, the temperature of the atmosphere decreases with increasing altitude above the ground. But at night, when the ground cools, there is a layer of air just above the surface in which the temperature *increases* with altitude. Use this to explain why sound waves from distant sources can be heard more clearly at night than in the daytime. (*Hint:* The speed of sound increases with increasing temperature. Use the ideas displayed in Fig. 33.37 for light.)

Q33.25 Can water waves be reflected and refracted? Give examples. Does Huygens's principle apply to water waves? Explain.

EXERCISES

Section 33.2 Reflection and Refraction

33.1 • Two plane mirrors intersect at right angles. A laser beam strikes the first of them at a point 11.5 cm from their point of intersection, as shown in Fig. E33.1 For what angle of incidence at the first mirror will this ray strike the midpoint of the second mirror (which is 28.0 cm long) after reflecting from the first mirror?

Figure **E33.1**

33.2 • **BIO Light Inside the Eye.** The vitreous humor, a transparent, gelatinous fluid that fills most of the eyeball, has an index of refraction of 1.34. Visible light ranges in wavelength from 380 nm (violet) to 750 nm (red), as measured in air. This light travels through the vitreous humor and strikes the rods and cones at the surface of the retina. What are the ranges of (a) the wavelength, (b) the frequency, and (c) the speed of the light just as it approaches the retina within the vitreous humor?

33.3 • A beam of light has a wavelength of 650 nm in vacuum. (a) What is the speed of this light in a liquid whose index of refraction at this wavelength is 1.47? (b) What is the wavelength of these waves in the liquid?

33.4 • Light with a frequency of 5.80×10^{14} Hz travels in a block of glass that has an index of refraction of 1.52. What is the wavelength of the light (a) in vacuum and (b) in the glass?

33.5 • A light beam travels at 1.94×10^8 m/s in quartz. The wavelength of the light in quartz is 355 nm. (a) What is the index of refraction of quartz at this wavelength? (b) If this same light travels through air, what is its wavelength there?

33.6 •• Light of a certain frequency has a wavelength of 438 nm in water. What is the wavelength of this light in benzene?

33.7 •• A parallel beam of light in air makes an angle of 47.5° with the surface of a glass plate having a refractive index of 1.66. (a) What is the angle between the reflected part of the beam and the surface of the glass? (b) What is the angle between the refracted beam and the surface of the glass?

33.8 •• A laser beam shines along the surface of a block of transparent material (see Fig. E33.8.). Half of the beam goes straight to a detector, while the other half travels through the block and then hits the detector. The time delay between the arrival of the two light beams at the detector is 6.25 ns. What is the index of refraction of this material?

Figure **E33.8**

33.9 • Light traveling in air is incident on the surface of a block of plastic at an angle of 62.7° to the normal and is bent so that it makes a 48.1° angle with the normal in the plastic. Find the speed of light in the plastic.

33.10 • (a) A tank containing methanol has walls 2.50 cm thick made of glass of refractive index 1.550. Light from the outside air strikes the glass at a 41.3° angle with the normal to the glass. Find the angle the light makes with the normal in the methanol. (b) The tank is emptied and refilled with an unknown liquid. If light incident at the same angle as in part (a) enters the liquid in the tank at an angle of 20.2° from the normal, what is the refractive index of the unknown liquid?

33.11 •• As shown in Fig. E33.11, a layer of water covers a slab of material X in a beaker. A ray of light traveling upward follows the path indicated. Using the information on the figure, find (a) the index of refraction of material X and (b) the angle the light makes with the normal in the *air*.

Figure **E33.11**

33.12 •• A horizontal, parallel-sided plate of glass having a refractive index of 1.52 is in contact with the surface of water in a tank. A ray coming from above in air makes an angle of incidence of 35.0° with the normal to the top surface of the glass. (a) What angle does the ray refracted into the water make with the normal to the surface? (b) What is the dependence of this angle on the refractive index of the glass?

33.13 •• In a material having an index of refraction n, a light ray has frequency f, wavelength λ, and speed v. What are the frequency, wavelength, and speed of this light (a) in vacuum and

(b) in a material having refractive index n'? In each case, express your answers in terms of only f, λ, v, n, and n'.

33.14 • A ray of light traveling in water is incident on an interface with a flat piece of glass. The wavelength of the light in the water is 726 nm and its wavelength in the glass is 544 nm. If the ray in water makes an angle of 42.0° with respect to the normal to the interface, what angle does the refracted ray in the glass make with respect to the normal?

33.15 • A ray of light is incident on a plane surface separating two sheets of glass with refractive indexes 1.70 and 1.58. The angle of incidence is 62.0°, and the ray originates in the glass with $n = 1.70$. Compute the angle of refraction.

Section 33.3 Total Internal Reflection

33.16 • A flat piece of glass covers the top of a vertical cylinder that is completely filled with water. If a ray of light traveling in the glass is incident on the interface with the water at an angle of $\theta_a = 36.2°$, the ray refracted into the water makes an angle of 49.8° with the normal to the interface. What is the smallest value of the incident angle θ_a for which none of the ray refracts into the water?

33.17 • **Light Pipe.** Light enters a solid pipe made of plastic having an index of refraction of 1.60. The light travels parallel to the upper part of the pipe (Fig. E33.17). You want to cut the face AB so that all the light will reflect back into the pipe after it first strikes that face. (a) What is the largest that θ can be if the pipe is in air? (b) If the pipe is immersed in water of refractive index 1.33, what is the largest that θ can be?

Figure **E33.17**

33.18 • A beam of light is traveling inside a solid glass cube having index of refraction 1.53. It strikes the surface of the cube from the inside. (a) If the cube is in air, at what minimum angle with the normal inside the glass will this light *not* enter the air at this surface? (b) What would be the minimum angle in part (a) if the cube were immersed in water?

33.19 •• The critical angle for total internal reflection at a liquid–air interface is 42.5°. (a) If a ray of light traveling in the liquid has an angle of incidence at the interface of 35.0°, what angle does the refracted ray in the air make with the normal? (b) If a ray of light traveling in air has an angle of incidence at the interface of 35.0°, what angle does the refracted ray in the liquid make with the normal?

33.20 • At the very end of Wagner's series of operas *Ring of the Nibelung*, Brünnhilde takes the golden ring from the finger of the dead Siegfried and throws it into the Rhine, where it sinks to the bottom of the river. Assuming that the ring is small enough compared to the depth of the river to be treated as a point and that the Rhine is 10.0 m deep where the ring goes in, what is the area of the largest circle at the surface of the water over which light from the ring could escape from the water?

33.21 • A ray of light is traveling in a glass cube that is totally immersed in water. You find that if the ray is incident on the glass–water interface at an angle to the normal larger than 48.7°, no light is refracted into the water. What is the refractive index of the glass?

33.22 • Light is incident along the normal on face AB of a glass prism of refractive index 1.52, as shown in Fig. E33.22. Find the largest value the angle α can have without any light refracted out of the prism at face AC if (a) the prism is immersed in air and (b) the prism is immersed in water.

Figure **E33.22**

33.23 • A piece of glass with a flat surface is at the bottom of a tank of water. If a ray of light traveling in the glass is incident on the interface with the water at an angle with respect to the normal that is greater than 62.0°, no light is refracted into the water. For smaller angles of incidence, part of the ray is refracted into the water. If the light has wavelength 408 nm in the glass, what is the wavelength of the light in the water?

33.24 •• We define the index of refraction of a material for sound waves to be the ratio of the speed of sound in air to the speed of sound in the material. Snell's law then applies to the refraction of sound waves. The speed of a sound wave is 344 m/s in air and 1320 m/s in water. (a) Which medium has the higher index of refraction for sound? (b) What is the critical angle for a sound wave incident on the surface between air and water? (c) For total internal reflection to occur, must the sound wave be traveling in the air or in the water? (d) Use your results to explain why it is possible to hear people on the opposite shore of a river or small lake extremely clearly.

Section 33.4 Dispersion

33.25 •• A narrow beam of white light strikes one face of a slab of silicate flint glass. The light is traveling parallel to the two adjoining faces, as shown in Fig. E33.25. For the transmitted light inside the glass, through what angle $\Delta\theta$ is the portion of the visible spectrum between 400 nm and 700 nm dispersed? (Consult the graph in Fig. 33.18.)

Figure **E33.25**

33.26 • A beam of light strikes a sheet of glass at an angle of 57.0° with the normal in air. You observe that red light makes an angle of 38.1° with the normal in the glass, while violet light makes a 36.7° angle. (a) What are the indexes of refraction of this glass for these colors of light? (b) What are the speeds of red and violet light in the glass?

Section 33.5 Polarization

33.27 • Unpolarized light with intensity I_0 is incident on two polarizing filters. The axis of the first filter makes an angle of 60.0° with the vertical, and the axis of the second filter is horizontal. What is the intensity of the light after it has passed through the second filter?

33.28 •• (a) At what angle above the horizontal is the sun if sunlight reflected from the surface of a calm lake is completely polarized? (b) What is the plane of the electric-field vector in the reflected light?

33.29 •• A beam of unpolarized light of intensity I_0 passes through a series of ideal polarizing filters with their polarizing directions turned to various angles as shown in Fig. E33.29. (a) What is the light intensity (in terms of I_0) at points A, B, and C? (b) If we remove the middle filter, what will be the light intensity at point C?

Figure **E33.29**

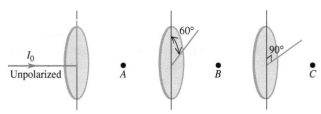

33.30 • Light traveling in water strikes a glass plate at an angle of incidence of 53.0°; part of the beam is reflected and part is refracted. If the reflected and refracted portions make an angle of 90.0° with each other, what is the index of refraction of the glass?

33.31 • A parallel beam of unpolarized light in air is incident at an angle of 54.5° (with respect to the normal) on a plane glass surface. The reflected beam is completely linearly polarized. (a) What is the refractive index of the glass? (b) What is the angle of refraction of the transmitted beam?

33.32 •• Light of original intensity I_0 passes through two ideal polarizing filters having their polarizing axes oriented as shown in Fig. E33.32. You want to adjust the angle ϕ so that the intensity at point P is equal to $I_0/10$. (a) If the original light is unpolarized, what should ϕ be? (b) If the original light is linearly polarized in the same direction as the polarizing axis of the first polarizer the light reaches, what should ϕ be?

Figure **E33.32**

33.33 •• A beam of polarized light passes through a polarizing filter. When the angle between the polarizing axis of the filter and the direction of polarization of the light is θ, the intensity of the emerging beam is I. If you now want the intensity to be $I/2$, what should be the angle (in terms of θ) between the polarizing angle of the filter and the original direction of polarization of the light?

33.34 • The refractive index of a certain glass is 1.66. For what incident angle is light reflected from the surface of this glass completely polarized if the glass is immersed in (a) air and (b) water?

33.35 •• Unpolarized light of intensity 20.0 W/cm² is incident on two polarizing filters. The axis of the first filter is at an angle of 25.0° counterclockwise from the vertical (viewed in the direction the light is traveling), and the axis of the second filter is at 62.0° counterclockwise from the vertical. What is the intensity of the light after it has passed through the second polarizer?

33.36 ••• Three polarizing filters are stacked, with the polarizing axis of the second and third filters at 23.0° and 62.0°, respectively, to that of the first. If unpolarized light is incident on the stack, the light has intensity 75.0 W/cm² after it passes through the stack. If the incident intensity is kept constant, what is the intensity of the light after it has passed through the stack if the second polarizer is removed?

33.37 • **Three Polarizing Filters.** Three polarizing filters are stacked with the polarizing axes of the second and third at 45.0° and 90.0°, respectively, with that of the first. (a) If unpolarized light of intensity I_0 is incident on the stack, find the intensity and

state of polarization of light emerging from each filter. (b) If the second filter is removed, what is the intensity of the light emerging from each remaining filter?

33.38 • A beam of white light passes through a uniform thickness of air. If the intensity of the scattered light in the middle of the green part of the visible spectrum is I, find the intensity (in terms of I) of scattered light in the middle of (a) the red part of the spectrum and (b) the violet part of the spectrum. Consult Table 32.1.

PROBLEMS

33.39 •• **The Corner Reflector.** An inside corner of a cube is lined with mirrors to make a corner reflector (see Example 33.3 in Section 33.2). A ray of light is reflected successively from each of three mutually perpendicular mirrors; show that its final direction is always exactly opposite to its initial direction.

33.40 • A light beam is directed parallel to the axis of a hollow cylindrical tube. When the tube contains only air, it takes the light 8.72 ns to travel the length of the tube, but when the tube is filled with a transparent jelly, it takes the light 2.04 ns longer to travel its length. What is the refractive index of this jelly?

33.41 •• **BIO Heart Sonogram.** Physicians use high-frequency ($f = 1-5$ MHz) sound waves, called ultrasound, to image internal organs. The speed of these ultrasound waves is 1480 m/s in muscle and 344 m/s in air. We define the index of refraction of a material for sound waves to be the ratio of the speed of sound in air to the speed of sound in the material. Snell's law then applies to the refraction of sound waves. (a) At what angle from the normal does an ultrasound beam enter the heart if it leaves the lungs at an angle of 9.73° from the normal to the heart wall? (Assume that the speed of sound in the lungs is 344 m/s.) (b) What is the critical angle for sound waves in air incident on muscle?

33.42 ••• In a physics lab, light with wavelength 490 nm travels in air from a laser to a photocell in 17.0 ns. When a slab of glass 0.840 m thick is placed in the light beam, with the beam incident along the normal to the parallel faces of the slab, it takes the light 21.2 ns to travel from the laser to the photocell. What is the wavelength of the light in the glass?

33.43 •• A ray of light is incident in air on a block of a transparent solid whose index of refraction is n. If $n = 1.38$, what is the largest angle of incidence θ_a for which total internal reflection will occur at the vertical face (point A shown in Fig. P33.43)?

Figure **P33.43**

33.44 • A light ray in air strikes the right-angle prism shown in Fig. P33.44. The prism angle at B is 30.0°. This ray consists of two different wavelengths. When it emerges at face AB, it has been split into two different rays that diverge from each other by 8.50°. Find the index of refraction of the prism for each of the two wavelengths.

33.45 •• A ray of light traveling *in* a block of glass ($n = 1.52$) is incident on the top surface at an angle of 57.2° with respect to the normal in the glass. If a layer of oil is placed on the top surface

Figure **P33.44**

of the glass, the ray is totally reflected. What is the maximum possible index of refraction of the oil?

33.46 ••• A glass plate 2.50 mm thick, with an index of refraction of 1.40, is placed between a point source of light with wavelength 540 nm (in vacuum) and a screen. The distance from source to screen is 1.80 cm. How many wavelengths are there between the source and the screen?

33.47 •• Old photographic plates were made of glass with a light-sensitive emulsion on the front surface. This emulsion was somewhat transparent. When a bright point source is focused on the front of the plate, the developed photograph will show a halo around the image of the spot. If the glass plate is 3.10 mm thick and the halos have an inner radius of 5.34 mm, what is the index of refraction of the glass? (*Hint:* Light from the spot on the front surface is scattered in all directions by the emulsion. Some of it is then totally reflected at the back surface of the plate and returns to the front surface.)

33.48 • After a long day of driving you take a late-night swim in a motel swimming pool. When you go to your room, you realize that you have lost your room key in the pool. You borrow a powerful flashlight and walk around the pool, shining the light into it. The light shines on the key, which is lying on the bottom of the pool, when the flashlight is held 1.2 m above the water surface and is directed at the surface a horizontal distance of 1.5 m from the edge (Fig. P33.48). If the water here is 4.0 m deep, how far is the key from the edge of the pool?

Figure **P33.48**

33.49 • You sight along the rim of a glass with vertical sides so that the top rim is lined up with the opposite edge of the bottom (Fig. P33.49a). The glass is a thin-walled, hollow cylinder 16.0 cm high. The diameter of the top and bottom of the glass is 8.0 cm. While you keep your eye in the same position, a friend fills the glass with a transparent liquid, and you then see a dime that is lying at the center of the bottom of the glass (Fig. P33.49b). What is the index of refraction of the liquid?

Figure **P33.49**

(a)   (b)

33.50 •• A 45°–45°–90° prism is immersed in water. A ray of light is incident normally on one of its shorter faces. What is the minimum index of refraction that the prism must have if this ray is to be totally reflected within the glass at the long face of the prism?

33.51 • A thin layer of ice ($n = 1.309$) floats on the surface of water ($n = 1.333$) in a bucket. A ray of light from the bottom of the bucket travels upward through the water. (a) What is the largest angle with respect to the normal that the ray can make at the ice–water interface and still pass out into the air above the ice? (b) What is this angle after the ice melts?

33.52 •• Light is incident normally on the short face of a 30°–60°–90° prism (Fig. P33.52). A drop of liquid is placed on the hypotenuse of the prism. If the index of refraction of the prism is 1.62, find the maximum index that the liquid may have if the light is to be totally reflected.

Figure **P33.52**

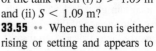

33.53 •• The prism shown in Fig. P33.53 has a refractive index of 1.66, and the angles A are 25.0°. Two light rays m and n are parallel as they enter the prism. What is the angle between them after they emerge?

Figure **P33.53**

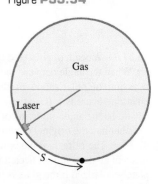

33.54 •• A horizontal cylindrical tank 2.20 m in diameter is half full of water. The space above the water is filled with a pressurized gas of unknown refractive index. A small laser can move along the curved bottom of the water and aims a light beam toward the center of the water surface (Fig. P33.54). You observe that when the laser has moved a distance $S = 1.09$ m or more (measured along the curved surface) from the lowest point in the water, no light enters the gas. (a) What is the index of refraction of the gas? (b) What minimum time does it take the light beam to travel from the laser to the rim of the tank when (i) $S > 1.09$ m and (ii) $S < 1.09$ m?

Figure **P33.54**

33.55 •• When the sun is either rising or setting and appears to be just on the horizon, it is in fact *below* the horizon. The explanation for this seeming paradox is that light from the sun bends slightly when entering the earth's atmosphere, as shown in Fig. P33.55. Since our perception is based on the idea that light travels in straight lines, we perceive the light to be coming from an apparent position that is an angle δ above the sun's true position. (a) Make the simplifying assumptions that the atmosphere has uniform density, and hence uniform index of refraction n, and extends to a height h above the earth's surface, at which point it abruptly stops. Show that the angle δ is given by

$$\delta = \arcsin\left(\frac{nR}{R + h}\right) - \arcsin\left(\frac{R}{R + h}\right)$$

where $R = 6378$ km is the radius of the earth. (b) Calculate δ using $n = 1.0003$ and $h = 20$ km. How does this compare to the angular radius of the sun, which is about one quarter of a degree?

(In actuality a light ray from the sun bends gradually, not abruptly, since the density and refractive index of the atmosphere change gradually with altitude.)

Figure **P33.55**

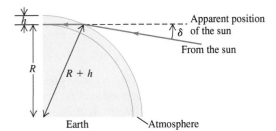

33.56 ·· **CALC** **Fermat's Principle of Least Time.** A ray of light traveling with speed c leaves point 1 shown in Fig. P33.56 and is reflected to point 2. The ray strikes the reflecting surface a horizontal distance x from point 1. (a) Show that the time t required for the light to travel from 1 to 2 is

$$t = \frac{\sqrt{y_1^2 + x^2} + \sqrt{y_2^2 + (l - x)^2}}{c}$$

(b) Take the derivative of t with respect to x. Set the derivative equal to zero to show that this time reaches its *minimum* value when $\theta_1 = \theta_2$, which is the law of reflection and corresponds to the actual path taken by the light. This is an example of Fermat's *principle of least time,* which states that among all possible paths between two points, the one actually taken by a ray of light is that for which the time of travel is a *minimum.* (In fact, there are some cases in which the time is a maximum rather than a minimum.)

Figure **P33.56**

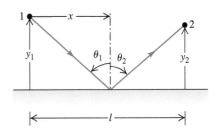

33.57 ·· **CALC** A ray of light goes from point A in a medium in which the speed of light is v_1 to point B in a medium in which the speed is v_2 (Fig. P33.57). The ray strikes the interface a horizontal distance x to the right of point A. (a) Show that the time required for the light to go from A to B is

Figure **P33.57**

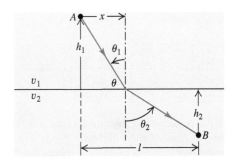

$$t = \frac{\sqrt{h_1^2 + x^2}}{v_1} + \frac{\sqrt{h_2^2 + (l - x)^2}}{v_2}$$

(b) Take the derivative of t with respect to x. Set this derivative equal to zero to show that this time reaches its *minimum* value when $n_1 \sin\theta_1 = n_2 \sin\theta_2$. This is Snell's law and corresponds to the actual path taken by the light. This is another example of Fermat's principle of least time (see Problem 33.56).

33.58 ·· Light is incident in air at an angle θ_a (Fig. P33.58) on the upper surface of a transparent plate, the surfaces of the plate being plane and parallel to each other. (a) Prove that $\theta_a = \theta_a'$. (b) Show that this is true for any number of different parallel plates. (c) Prove that the lateral displacement d of the emergent beam is given by the relationship

$$d = t \frac{\sin(\theta_a - \theta_b')}{\cos \theta_b'}$$

where t is the thickness of the plate. (d) A ray of light is incident at an angle of 66.0° on one surface of a glass plate 2.40 cm thick with an index of refraction of 1.80. The medium on either side of the plate is air. Find the lateral displacement between the incident and emergent rays.

Figure **P33.58**

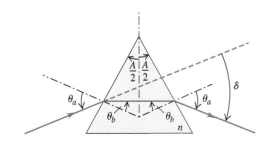

33.59 ·· **Angle of Deviation.** The incident angle θ_a shown in Fig. P33.59 is chosen so that the light passes symmetrically through the prism, which has refractive index n and apex angle A. (a) Show that the angle of deviation δ (the angle between the initial and final directions of the ray) is given by

$$\sin \frac{A + \delta}{2} = n \sin \frac{A}{2}$$

(When the light passes through symmetrically, as shown, the angle of deviation is a minimum.) (b) Use the result of part (a) to find the angle of deviation for a ray of light passing symmetrically through a prism having three equal angles ($A = 60.0°$) and $n = 1.52$. (c) A certain glass has a refractive index of 1.61 for red light (700 nm) and 1.66 for violet light (400 nm). If both colors pass through symmetrically, as described in part (a), and if $A = 60.0°$, find the difference between the angles of deviation for the two colors.

Figure **P33.59**

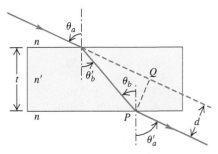

33.60 · A thin beam of white light is directed at a flat sheet of silicate flint glass at an angle of 20.0° to the surface of the sheet. Due to dispersion in the glass, the beam is spread out in a spectrum as shown in Fig. P33.60. The refractive index of silicate flint glass versus wavelength is graphed in Fig. 33.18. (a) The rays a and b shown in Fig. P33.60 correspond to the extreme wavelengths shown in Fig. 33.18. Which corresponds to red and which to violet? Explain your reasoning. (b) For what thickness d of the glass sheet will the spectrum be 1.0 mm wide, as shown (see Problem 33.58)?

Figure **P33.60**

33.61 · A beam of light traveling horizontally is made of an unpolarized component with intensity I_0 and a polarized component with intensity I_p. The plane of polarization of the polarized component is oriented at an angle of θ with respect to the vertical. The data in the table give the intensity measured through a polarizer with an orientation of ϕ with respect to the vertical. (a) What is the orientation of the polarized component? (That is, what is the angle θ?) (b) What are the values of I_0 and I_p?

$\phi\,(°)$	$I_{total}\,(W/m^2)$	$\phi\,(°)$	$I_{total}\,(W/m^2)$
0	18.4	100	8.6
10	21.4	110	6.3
20	23.7	120	5.2
30	24.8	130	5.2
40	24.8	140	6.3
50	23.7	150	8.6
60	21.4	160	11.6
70	18.4	170	15.0
80	15.0	180	18.4
90	11.6		

33.62 ·· **BIO** **Optical Activity of Biological Molecules.** Many biologically important molecules are optically active. When linearly polarized light traverses a solution of compounds containing these molecules, its plane of polarization is rotated. Some compounds rotate the polarization clockwise; others rotate the polarization counterclockwise. The amount of rotation depends on the amount of material in the path of the light. The following data give the amount of rotation through two amino acids over a path length of 100 cm:

	Rotation (°)	
	d-glutamic	Concentration
l-leucine	acid	(g/100 mL)
−0.11	0.124	1.0
−0.22	0.248	2.0
−0.55	0.620	5.0
−1.10	1.24	10.0
−2.20	2.48	20.0
−5.50	6.20	50.0
−11.0	12.4	100.0

From these data, find the relationship between the concentration C (in grams per 100 mL) and the rotation of the polarization (in degrees) of each amino acid. (*Hint:* Graph the concentration as a function of the rotation angle for each amino acid.)

33.63 ·· A beam of unpolarized sunlight strikes the vertical plastic wall of a water tank at an unknown angle. Some of the light reflects from the wall and enters the water (Fig. P33.63). The refractive index of the plastic wall is 1.61. If the light that has been reflected from the wall into the water is observed to be completely polarized, what angle does this beam make with the normal inside the water?

Figure **P33.63**

33.64 ·· A certain birefringent material has indexes of refraction n_1 and n_2 for the two perpendicular components of linearly polarized light passing through it. The corresponding wavelengths are $\lambda_1 = \lambda_0/n_1$ and λ_0/n_2, where λ_0 is the wavelength in vacuum. (a) If the crystal is to function as a quarter-wave plate, the number of wavelengths of each component within the material must differ by $\frac{1}{4}$. Show that the minimum thickness for a quarter-wave plate is

$$d = \frac{\lambda_0}{4(n_1 - n_2)}$$

(b) Find the minimum thickness of a quarter-wave plate made of siderite ($FeO \cdot CO_2$) if the indexes of refraction are $n_1 = 1.875$ and $n_2 = 1.635$ and the wavelength in vacuum is $\lambda_0 = 589$ nm.

CHALLENGE PROBLEMS

33.65 ··· Consider two vibrations of equal amplitude and frequency but differing in phase, one along the x-axis,

$$x = a \sin(\omega t - \alpha)$$

and the other along the y-axis,

$$y = a \sin(\omega t - \beta)$$

These can be written as follows:

$$\frac{x}{a} = \sin \omega t \cos \alpha - \cos \omega t \sin \alpha \qquad (1)$$

$$\frac{y}{a} = \sin \omega t \cos \beta - \cos \omega t \sin \beta \qquad (2)$$

(a) Multiply Eq. (1) by $\sin \beta$ and Eq. (2) by $\sin \alpha$, and then subtract the resulting equations. (b) Multiply Eq. (1) by $\cos \beta$ and Eq. (2) by $\cos \alpha$, and then subtract the resulting equations. (c) Square and add the results of parts (a) and (b). (d) Derive the equation $x^2 + y^2 - 2xy \cos \delta = a^2 \sin^2 \delta$, where $\delta = \alpha - \beta$. (e) Use the above result to justify each of the diagrams in Fig. P33.65. In the figure, the angle given is the phase difference between two simple harmonic motions of the same frequency and amplitude, one horizontal (along the x-axis) and the other vertical (along the y-axis). The figure thus shows the resultant motion from the superposition of the two perpendicular harmonic motions.

Figure **P33.65**

| 0 | $\frac{\pi}{4}$ | $\frac{\pi}{2}$ | $\frac{3\pi}{4}$ | π | $\frac{5\pi}{4}$ | $\frac{3\pi}{2}$ | $\frac{7\pi}{4}$ | 2π |

33.66 ··· **CALC** A rainbow is produced by the reflection of sunlight by spherical drops of water in the air. Figure P33.66 shows a ray that refracts into a drop at point A, is reflected from the back surface of the drop at point B, and refracts back into the air at point C. The angles of incidence and refraction, θ_a and θ_b, are shown at points A and C, and the angles of incidence and reflection, θ_a and θ_r, are shown at point B. (a) Show that $\theta_a{}^B = \theta_b{}^A$, $\theta_a{}^C = \theta_b{}^A$, and $\theta_b{}^C = \theta_a{}^A$. (b) Show that the angle in radians between the ray before it enters the drop at A and after it exits at C (the total angular deflection of the ray) is $\Delta = 2\theta_a{}^A - 4\theta_b{}^A + \pi$. (*Hint:* Find the angular deflections that occur at A, B, and C, and add them to get Δ.) (c) Use Snell's law to write Δ in terms of $\theta_a{}^A$ and n, the

Figure **P33.66**

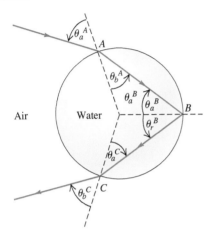

refractive index of the water in the drop. (d) A rainbow will form when the angular deflection Δ is *stationary* in the incident angle $\theta_a{}^A$—that is, when $d\Delta/d\theta_a{}^A = 0$. If this condition is satisfied, all the rays with incident angles close to $\theta_a{}^A$ will be sent back in the same direction, producing a bright zone in the sky. Let θ_1 be the value of $\theta_a{}^A$ for which this occurs. Show that $\cos^2\theta_1 = \frac{1}{3}(n^2 - 1)$. (*Hint:* You may find the derivative formula $d(\arcsin u(x))/dx = (1 - u^2)^{-1/2}(du/dx)$ helpful.) (e) The index of refraction in water is 1.342 for violet light and 1.330 for red light. Use the results of parts (c) and (d) to find θ_1 and Δ for violet and red light. Do your results agree with the angles shown in Fig. 33.20d? When you view the rainbow, which color, red or violet, is higher above the horizon?

33.67 ••• **CALC** A *secondary rainbow* is formed when the incident light undergoes two internal reflections in a spherical drop of water as shown in Fig. 33.20e. (See Challenge Problem 33.66.) (a) In terms of the incident angle $\theta_a{}^A$ and the refractive index n of the drop, what is the angular deflection Δ of the ray? That is, what is the angle between the ray before it enters the drop and after it exits? (b) What is the incident angle θ_2 for which the derivative of Δ with respect to the incident angle $\theta_a{}^A$ is zero? (c) The indexes of refraction for red and violet light in water are given in part (e) of Challenge Problem 33.66. Use the results of parts (a) and (b) to find θ_2 and Δ for violet and red light. Do your results agree with the angles shown in Fig. 33.20e? When you view a secondary rainbow, is red or violet higher above the horizon? Explain.

Answers

Chapter Opening Question ?

This is the same effect as shown in Fig. 33.31. The drafting tools are placed between two polarizing filters whose polarizing axes are perpendicular. In places where the clear plastic is under stress, the plastic becomes birefringent; that is, light travels through it at a speed that depends on its polarization. The result is that the light that emerges from the plastic has a different polarization than the light that enters. A spot on the plastic appears bright if the emerging light has the same polarization as the second polarizing filter. The amount of birefringence depends on the wavelength of the light as well as the amount of stress on the plastic, so different colors are seen at different locations on the plastic.

Test Your Understanding Questions

33.1 Answer: (iii) The waves go farther in the y-direction in a given amount of time than in the other directions, so the wave fronts are elongated in the y-direction.

33.2 Answers: (a) (ii), (b) (iii) As shown in the figure, light rays coming from the fish bend away from the normal when they pass from the water ($n = 1.33$) into the air ($n = 1.00$). As a result, the

fish appears to be higher in the water than it actually is. Hence you should aim a spear *below* the apparent position of the fish. If you use a laser beam, you should aim *at* the apparent position of the fish: The beam of laser light takes the same path from you to the fish as ordinary light takes from the fish to you (though in the opposite direction).

33.3 Answers: (i), (ii) Total internal reflection can occur only if two conditions are met: n_b must be less than n_a, and the critical angle θ_{crit} (where $\sin\theta_{crit} = n_b/n_a$) must be smaller than the angle of incidence θ_a. In the first two cases both conditions are met: The critical angles are (i) $\theta_{crit} = \sin^{-1}(1/1.33) = 48.8°$ and (ii) $\theta_{crit} = \sin^{-1}(1.33/1.52) = 61.0°$, both of which are smaller than $\theta_a = 70°$. In the third case $n_b = 1.52$ is greater than $n_a = 1.33$, so total internal reflection cannot occur for any incident angle.

33.5 Answer: (ii) The sunlight reflected from the windows of the high-rise building is partially polarized in the vertical direction, since each window lies in a vertical plane. The Polaroid filter in front of the lens is oriented with its polarizing axis perpendicular to the dominant direction of polarization of the reflected light.

33.7 Answer: (ii) Huygens's principle applies to waves of all kinds, including sound waves. Hence this situation is exactly like that shown in Fig. 33.36, with material a representing the warm air, material b representing the cold air in which the waves travel more slowly, and the interface between the materials representing the weather front. North is toward the top of the figure and east is toward the right, so Fig. 33.36 shows that the rays (which indicate the direction of propagation) deflect toward the east.

Bridging Problem

Answer: 1.93×10^8 m/s

INTERFERENCE

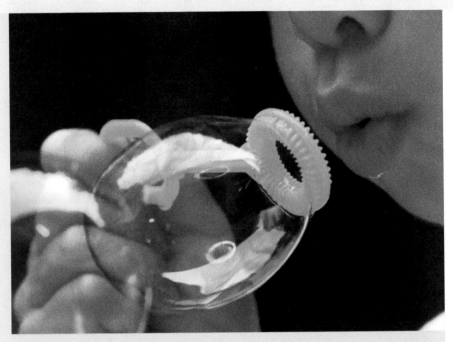

LEARNING GOALS

By studying this chapter, you will learn:

- What happens when two waves combine, or interfere, in space.

- How to understand the interference pattern formed by the interference of two coherent light waves.

- How to calculate the intensity at various points in an interference pattern.

- How interference occurs when light reflects from the two surfaces of a thin film.

- How interference makes it possible to measure extremely small distances.

? Soapy water is colorless, but when blown into bubbles it shows vibrant colors. How does the thickness of the bubble walls determine the particular colors that appear?

An ugly black oil spot on the pavement can become a thing of beauty after a rain, when the oil reflects a rainbow of colors. Multicolored reflections can also be seen from the surfaces of soap bubbles and DVDs. How is it possible for colorless objects to produce these remarkable colors?

In our discussion of lenses, mirrors, and optical instruments we used the model of *geometric optics,* in which we represent light as *rays,* straight lines that are bent at a reflecting or refracting surface. But many aspects of the behavior of light *can't* be understood on the basis of rays. We have already learned that light is fundamentally a *wave,* and in some situations we have to consider its wave properties explicitly. If two or more light waves of the same frequency overlap at a point, the total effect depends on the *phases* of the waves as well as their amplitudes. The resulting patterns of light are a result of the *wave* nature of light and cannot be understood on the basis of rays. Optical effects that depend on the wave nature of light are grouped under the heading **physical optics.**

In this chapter we'll look at *interference* phenomena that occur when two waves combine. The colors seen in oil films and soap bubbles are a result of interference between light reflected from the front and back surfaces of a thin film of oil or soap solution. Effects that occur when *many* sources of waves are present are called *diffraction* phenomena; we'll study these in Chapter 36. In that chapter we'll see that diffraction effects occur whenever a wave passes through an aperture or around an obstacle. They are important in practical applications of physical optics such as diffraction gratings, x-ray diffraction, and holography.

While our primary concern is with light, interference and diffraction can occur with waves of *any* kind. As we go along, we'll point out applications to other types of waves such as sound and water waves.

35.1 Interference and Coherent Sources

As we discussed in Chapter 15, the term **interference** refers to any situation in which two or more waves overlap in space. When this occurs, the total wave at any point at any instant of time is governed by the **principle of superposition,** which we introduced in Section 15.6 in the context of waves on a string. This principle also applies to electromagnetic waves and is the most important principle in all of physical optics. The principle of superposition states:

> **When two or more waves overlap, the resultant displacement at any point and at any instant is found by adding the instantaneous displacements that would be produced at the point by the individual waves if each were present alone.**

(In some special situations, such as electromagnetic waves propagating in a crystal, this principle may not apply. A discussion of these is beyond our scope.)

We use the term "displacement" in a general sense. With waves on the surface of a liquid, we mean the actual displacement of the surface above or below its normal level. With sound waves, the term refers to the excess or deficiency of pressure. For electromagnetic waves, we usually mean a specific component of electric or magnetic field.

Interference in Two or Three Dimensions

We have already discussed one important case of interference, in which two identical waves propagating in opposite directions combine to produce a *standing wave.* We saw this in Chapters 15 and 16 for transverse waves on a string and for longitudinal waves in a fluid filling a pipe; we described the same phenomenon for electromagnetic waves in Section 32.5. In all of these cases the waves propagated along only a single axis: along a string, along the length of a fluid-filled pipe, or along the propagation direction of an electromagnetic plane wave. But light waves can (and do) travel in *two* or *three* dimensions, as can any kind of wave that propagates in a two- or three-dimensional medium. In this section we'll see what happens when we combine waves that spread out in two or three dimensions from a pair of identical wave sources.

Interference effects are most easily seen when we combine *sinusoidal* waves with a single frequency f and wavelength λ. Figure 35.1 shows a "snapshot" of a *single* source S_1 of sinusoidal waves and some of the wave fronts produced by this source. The figure shows only the wave fronts corresponding to wave *crests,* so the spacing between successive wave fronts is one wavelength. The material surrounding S_1 is uniform, so the wave speed is the same in all directions, and there is no refraction (and hence no bending of the wave fronts). If the waves are two-dimensional, like waves on the surface of a liquid, the circles in Fig. 35.1 represent circular wave fronts; if the waves propagate in three dimensions, the circles represent spherical wave fronts spreading away from S_1.

In optics, sinusoidal waves are characteristic of **monochromatic light** (light of a single color). While it's fairly easy to make water waves or sound waves of a single frequency, common sources of light *do not* emit monochromatic (single-frequency) light. For example, incandescent light bulbs and flames emit a continuous distribution of wavelengths. By far the most nearly monochromatic source that is available at present is the *laser.* An example is the helium–neon laser, which emits red light at 632.8 nm with a wavelength range of the order of ± 0.000001 nm, or about one part in 10^9. As we analyze interference and diffraction effects in this chapter and the next, we will assume that we are working with monochromatic waves (unless we explicitly state otherwise).

Constructive and Destructive Interference

Two identical sources of monochromatic waves, S_1 and S_2, are shown in Fig. 35.2a. The two sources produce waves of the same amplitude and the same wavelength λ.

35.1 A "snapshot" of sinusoidal waves of frequency f and wavelength λ spreading out from source S_1 in all directions.

Wave fronts: crests of the wave (frequency f) separated by one wavelength λ

The wave fronts move outward from source S_1 at the wave speed $v = f\lambda$.

In addition, the two sources are permanently *in phase;* they vibrate in unison. They might be two loudspeakers driven by the same amplifier, two radio antennas powered by the same transmitter, or two small slits in an opaque screen, illuminated by the same monochromatic light source. We will see that if there were not a constant phase relationship between the two sources, the phenomena we are about to discuss would not occur. Two monochromatic sources of the same frequency and with a constant phase relationship (not necessarily in phase) are said to be **coherent.** We also use the term *coherent waves* (or, for light waves, *coherent light*) to refer to the waves emitted by two such sources.

If the waves emitted by the two coherent sources are *transverse,* like electromagnetic waves, then we will also assume that the wave disturbances produced by both sources have the same *polarization* (that is, they lie along the same line). For example, the sources S_1 and S_2 in Fig. 35.2a could be two radio antennas in the form of long rods oriented parallel to the z-axis (perpendicular to the plane of the figure); at any point in the xy-plane the waves produced by both antennas have $\vec{E}$ fields with only a z-component. Then we need only a single scalar function to describe each wave; this makes the analysis much easier.

We position the two sources of equal amplitude, equal wavelength, and (if the waves are transverse) the same polarization along the y-axis in Fig. 35.2a, equidistant from the origin. Consider a point a on the x-axis. From symmetry the two distances from S_1 to a and from S_2 to a are *equal;* waves from the two sources thus require equal times to travel to a. Hence waves that leave S_1 and S_2 in phase arrive at a in phase. The two waves add, and the total amplitude at a is *twice* the amplitude of each individual wave. This is true for *any* point on the x-axis.

Similarly, the distance from S_2 to point b is exactly two wavelengths *greater* than the distance from S_1 to b. A wave crest from S_1 arrives at b exactly two cycles earlier than a crest emitted at the same time from S_2, and again the two waves arrive in phase. As at point a, the total amplitude is the sum of the amplitudes of the waves from S_1 and S_2.

In general, when waves from two or more sources arrive at a point *in phase,* they reinforce each other: The amplitude of the resultant wave is the *sum* of the amplitudes of the individual waves. This is called **constructive interference** (Fig. 35.2b). Let the distance from S_1 to any point P be r_1, and let the distance from S_2 to P be r_2. For constructive interference to occur at P, the path difference $r_2 - r_1$ for the two sources must be an integral multiple of the wavelength λ:

$$r_2 - r_1 = m\lambda \quad (m = 0, \pm 1, \pm 2, \pm 3, \dots)$$

(constructive interference, sources in phase) [35.1]

In Fig. 35.2a, points a and b satisfy Eq. (35.1) with $m = 0$ and $m = +2$, respectively.

Something different occurs at point c in Fig. 35.2a. At this point, the path difference $r_2 - r_1 = -2.50\lambda$, which is a *half-integral* number of wavelengths. Waves from the two sources arrive at point c exactly a half-cycle out of phase. A crest of one wave arrives at the same time as a crest in the opposite direction (a "trough") of the other wave (Fig. 35.2c). The resultant amplitude is the *difference* between the two individual amplitudes. If the individual amplitudes are equal, then the total amplitude is *zero!* This cancellation or partial cancellation of the individual waves is called **destructive interference.** The condition for destructive interference in the situation shown in Fig. 35.2a is

$$r_2 - r_1 = \left(m + \tfrac{1}{2}\right)\lambda \quad (m = 0, \pm 1, \pm 2, \pm 3, \dots)$$

(destructive interference, sources in phase) [35.2]

The path difference at point c in Fig. 35.2a satisfies Eq. (35.2) with $m = -3$.

35.2 (a) A "snapshot" of sinusoidal waves spreading out from two coherent sources S_1 and S_2. Constructive interference occurs at point a (equidistant from the two sources) and (b) at point b. (c) Destructive interference occurs at point c.

(a) Two coherent wave sources separated by a distance 4λ

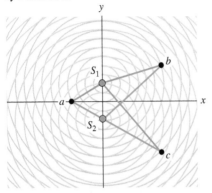

(b) Conditions for constructive interference: Waves interfere constructively if their path lengths differ by an integral number of wavelengths: $r_2 - r_1 = m\lambda$.

(c) Conditions for destructive interference: Waves interfere destructively if their path lengths differ by a half-integral number of wavelengths: $r_2 - r_1 = (m + \tfrac{1}{2})\lambda$.

35.3 The same as Fig. 35.2a, but with red antinodal curves (curves of maximum amplitude) superimposed. All points on each curve satisfy Eq. (35.1) with the value of *m* shown. The nodal curves (not shown) lie between each adjacent pair of antinodal curves.

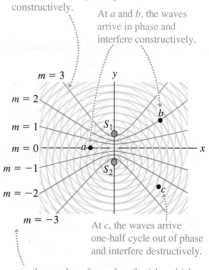

Antinodal curves (red) mark positions where the waves from S_1 and S_2 interfere constructively.

At *a* and *b*, the waves arrive in phase and interfere constructively.

At *c*, the waves arrive one-half cycle out of phase and interfere destructively.

m = the number of wavelengths λ by which the path lengths from S_1 and S_2 differ.

Figure 35.3 shows the same situation as in Fig. 35.2a, but with red curves that show all positions where *constructive* interference occurs. On each curve, the path difference $r_2 - r_1$ is equal to an integer *m* times the wavelength, as in Eq. (35.1). These curves are called **antinodal curves.** They are directly analogous to *antinodes* in the standing-wave patterns described in Chapters 15 and 16 and Section 32.5. In a standing wave formed by interference between waves propagating in opposite directions, the antinodes are points at which the amplitude is maximum; likewise, the wave amplitude in the situation of Fig. 35.3 is maximum along the antinodal curves. Not shown in Fig. 35.3 are the **nodal curves,** which are the curves that show where *destructive* interference occurs in accordance with Eq. (35.2); these are analogous to the *nodes* in a standing-wave pattern. A nodal curve lies between each two adjacent antinodal curves in Fig. 35.3; one such curve, corresponding to $r_2 - r_1 = -2.50\lambda$, passes through point *c*.

In some cases, such as two loudspeakers or two radio-transmitter antennas, the interference pattern is three-dimensional. Think of rotating the color curves of Fig. 35.3 around the *y*-axis; then maximum constructive interference occurs at all points on the resulting surfaces of revolution.

CAUTION **Interference patterns are not standing waves** The interference patterns in Figs. 35.2a and 35.3 are *not* standing waves, though they have some similarities to the standing-wave patterns described in Chapters 15 and 16 and Section 32.5. In a standing wave, the interference is between two waves propagating in opposite directions; there is *no* net energy flow in either direction (the energy in the wave is left "standing"). In the situations shown in Figs. 35.2a and 35.3, there is likewise a stationary pattern of antinodal and nodal curves, but there is a net flow of energy *outward* from the two sources. All that interference does is to "channel" the energy flow so that it is greatest along the antinodal curves and least along the nodal curves.

For Eqs. (35.1) and (35.2) to hold, the two sources must have the same wavelength and must *always* be in phase. These conditions are rather easy to satisfy for sound waves. But with *light* waves there is no practical way to achieve a constant phase relationship (coherence) with two independent sources. This is because of the way light is emitted. In ordinary light sources, atoms gain excess energy by thermal agitation or by impact with accelerated electrons. Such an "excited" atom begins to radiate energy and continues until it has lost all the energy it can, typically in a time of the order of 10^{-8} s. The many atoms in a source ordinarily radiate in an unsynchronized and random phase relationship, and the light that is emitted from *two* such sources has no definite phase relationship.

However, the light from a single source can be split so that parts of it emerge from two or more regions of space, forming two or more *secondary sources.* Then any random phase change in the source affects these secondary sources equally and does not change their *relative* phase.

The distinguishing feature of light from a *laser* is that the emission of light from many atoms is synchronized in frequency and phase. As a result, the random phase changes mentioned above occur much less frequently. Definite phase relationships are preserved over correspondingly much greater lengths in the beam, and laser light is much more coherent than ordinary light.

Test Your Understanding of Section 35.1 Consider a point in Fig. 35.3 on the positive *y*-axis above S_1. Does this point lie on (i) an antinodal curve; (ii) a nodal curve; or (iii) neither? (*Hint:* The distance between S_1 and S_2 is 4λ.)

35.2 Two-Source Interference of Light

The interference pattern produced by two coherent sources of *water* waves of the same wavelength can be readily seen in a ripple tank with a shallow layer of water (Fig. 35.4). This pattern is not directly visible when the interference is between *light* waves, since light traveling in a uniform medium cannot be seen. (A shaft of afternoon sunlight in a room is made visible by scattering from airborne dust particles.)

One of the earliest quantitative experiments to reveal the interference of light from two sources was performed in 1800 by the English scientist Thomas Young. We will refer back to this experiment several times in this and later chapters, so it's important to understand it in detail. Young's apparatus is shown in perspective in Fig. 35.5a. A light source (not shown) emits monochromatic light; however, this light is not suitable for use in an interference experiment because emissions from different parts of an ordinary source are not synchronized. To remedy this, the light is directed at a screen with a narrow slit S_0, 1 μm or so wide. The light emerging from the slit originated from only a small region of the light source; thus slit S_0 behaves more nearly like the idealized source shown in Fig. 35.1. (In modern versions of the experiment, a laser is used as a source of coherent light, and the slit S_0 isn't needed.) The light from slit S_0 falls on a screen with two other narrow slits S_1 and S_2, each 1 μm or so wide and a few tens or hundreds of micrometers apart. Cylindrical wave fronts spread out from slit S_0 and reach slits S_1 and S_2 *in phase* because they travel equal distances from S_0. The waves *emerging* from slits S_1 and S_2 are therefore also always in phase, so S_1 and S_2 are *coherent* sources. The interference of waves from S_1 and S_2 produces a pattern in space like that to the right of the sources in Figs. 35.2a and 35.3.

To visualize the interference pattern, a screen is placed so that the light from S_1 and S_2 falls on it (Fig. 35.5b). The screen will be most brightly illuminated at points P, where the light waves from the slits interfere constructively, and will be darkest at points where the interference is destructive.

To simplify the analysis of Young's experiment, we assume that the distance R from the slits to the screen is so large in comparison to the distance d between the slits that the lines from S_1 and S_2 to P are very nearly parallel, as in Fig. 35.5c. This is usually the case for experiments with light; the slit separation is typically a few millimeters, while the screen may be a meter or more away. The difference in path length is then given by

35.4 The concepts of constructive interference and destructive interference apply to these water waves as well as to light waves and sound waves.

35.5 (a) Young's experiment to show interference of light passing through two slits. A pattern of bright and dark areas appears on the screen (see Fig. 35.6). (b) Geometrical analysis of Young's experiment. For the case shown, $r_2 > r_1$ and both y and θ are positive. If point P is on the other side of the screen's center, $r_2 < r_1$ and both y and θ are negative. (c) Approximate geometry when the distance R to the screen is much greater than the distance d between the slits.

(a) Interference of light waves passing through two slits

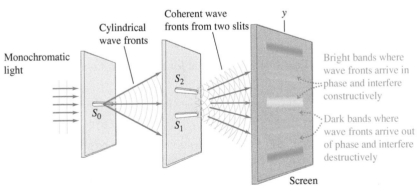

Coherent wave fronts from two slits

Cylindrical wave fronts

y

Monochromatic light

S_2

S_0

S_1

Bright bands where wave fronts arrive in phase and interfere constructively

Dark bands where wave fronts arrive out of phase and interfere destructively

Screen

(b) Actual geometry (seen from the side)

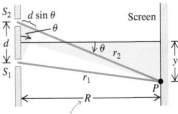

S_2
$d \sin \theta$
Screen
θ
d
θ r_2
S_1
r_1
P
y
R

In real situations, the distance R to the screen is usually very much greater than the distance d between the slits ...

(c) Approximate geometry

S_2
$d \sin \theta$
d
r_2
θ
S_1
r_1
To screen

... so we can treat the rays as parallel, in which case the path-length difference is simply $r_2 - r_1 = d \sin \theta$.

PhET: Wave Interference
ActivPhysics 16.1: Two-Source Interference: Introduction
ActivPhysics 16.2: Two-Source Interference: Qualitative Questions
ActivPhysics 16.3: Two-Source Interference: Problems

$$r_2 - r_1 = d \sin\theta \qquad (35.3)$$

where θ is the angle between a line from slits to screen (shown in blue in Fig. 35.5c) and the normal to the plane of the slits (shown as a thin black line).

Constructive and Destructive Two-Slit Interference

We found in Section 35.1 that constructive interference (reinforcement) occurs at points where the path difference is an integral number of wavelengths, $m\lambda$, where $m = 0, \pm1, \pm2, \pm3, \ldots$. So the bright regions on the screen in Fig. 35.5a occur at angles θ for which

$$d\sin\theta = m\lambda \qquad (m = 0, \pm1, \pm2, \ldots) \qquad \text{(constructive interference, two slits)} \qquad (35.4)$$

Similarly, destructive interference (cancellation) occurs, forming dark regions on the screen, at points for which the path difference is a half-integral number of wavelengths, $\left(m + \frac{1}{2}\right)\lambda$:

$$d\sin\theta = \left(m + \tfrac{1}{2}\right)\lambda \qquad (m = 0, \pm1, \pm2, \ldots) \qquad \text{(destructive interference, two slits)} \qquad (35.5)$$

Thus the pattern on the screen of Figs. 35.5a and 35.5b is a succession of bright and dark bands, or **interference fringes,** parallel to the slits S_1 and S_2. A photograph of such a pattern is shown in Fig. 35.6. The center of the pattern is a bright band corresponding to $m = 0$ in Eq. (35.4); this point on the screen is equidistant from the two slits.

We can derive an expression for the positions of the centers of the bright bands on the screen. In Fig. 35.5b, y is measured from the center of the pattern, corresponding to the distance from the center of Fig. 35.6. Let y_m be the distance from the center of the pattern ($\theta = 0$) to the center of the mth bright band. Let θ_m be the corresponding value of θ; then

$$y_m = R \tan\theta_m$$

In experiments such as this, the distances y_m are often much smaller than the distance R from the slits to the screen. Hence θ_m is very small, $\tan\theta_m$ is very nearly equal to $\sin\theta_m$, and

$$y_m = R\sin\theta_m$$

Combining this with Eq. (35.4), we find that *for small angles only,*

$$y_m = R\frac{m\lambda}{d} \qquad \text{(constructive interference in Young's experiment)} \qquad (35.6)$$

We can measure R and d, as well as the positions y_m of the bright fringes, so this experiment provides a direct measurement of the wavelength λ. Young's experiment was in fact the first direct measurement of wavelengths of light.

35.6 Photograph of interference fringes produced on a screen in Young's double-slit experiment.

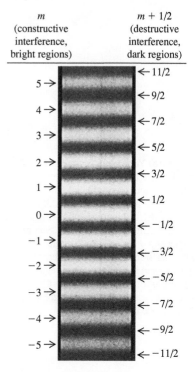

m (constructive interference, bright regions)	$m + 1/2$ (destructive interference, dark regions)
5 →	← 11/2
4 →	← 9/2
3 →	← 7/2
2 →	← 5/2
1 →	← 3/2
0 →	← 1/2
−1 →	← −1/2
−2 →	← −3/2
−3 →	← −5/2
−4 →	← −7/2
−5 →	← −9/2
	← −11/2

CAUTION **Equation (35.6) is for small angles only** While Eqs. (35.4) and (35.5) are valid for any angle, Eq. (35.6) is valid only for *small* angles. It can be used *only* if the distance R from slits to screen is much greater than the slit separation d and if R is much greater than the distance y_m from the center of the interference pattern to the mth bright fringe.

The distance between adjacent bright bands in the pattern is *inversely* proportional to the distance d between the slits. The closer together the slits are, the more the pattern spreads out. When the slits are far apart, the bands in the pattern are closer together.

While we have described the experiment that Young performed with visible light, the results given in Eqs. (35.4) and (35.5) are valid for *any* type of wave, provided that the resultant wave from two coherent sources is detected at a point that is far away in comparison to the separation *d*.

Example 35.1 Two-slit interference

Figure 35.7 shows a two-slit interference experiment in which the slits are 0.200 mm apart and the screen is 1.00 m from the slits. The *m* = 3 bright fringe in the figure is 9.49 mm from the central fringe. Find the wavelength of the light.

35.7 Using a two-slit interference experiment to measure the wavelength of light.

SOLUTION

IDENTIFY and SET UP: Our target variable in this two-slit interference problem is the wavelength λ. We are given the slit separation $d = 0.200$ mm, the distance from slits to screen $R = 1.00$ m, and the distance $y_3 = 9.49$ mm on the screen from the center of the interference pattern to the $m = 3$ bright fringe. We may use Eq. (35.6) to find λ, since the value of R is so much greater than the values of d or y_3.

EXECUTE: We solve Eq. (35.6) for λ for the case $m = 3$:

$$\lambda = \frac{y_m d}{mR} = \frac{(9.49 \times 10^{-3}\ \text{m})(0.200 \times 10^{-3}\ \text{m})}{(3)(1.00\ \text{m})}$$

$$= 633 \times 10^{-9}\ \text{m} = 633\ \text{nm}$$

EVALUATE: This bright fringe could also correspond to $m = -3$. Can you show that this gives the same result for λ?

Example 35.2 Broadcast pattern of a radio station

It is often desirable to radiate most of the energy from a radio transmitter in particular directions rather than uniformly in all directions. Pairs or rows of antennas are often used to produce the desired radiation pattern. As an example, consider two identical vertical antennas 400 m apart, operating at 1500 kHz = 1.5×10^6 Hz (near the top end of the AM broadcast band) and oscillating in phase. At distances much greater than 400 m, in what directions is the intensity from the two antennas greatest?

SOLUTION

IDENTIFY and SET UP: The antennas, shown in Fig. 35.8, correspond to sources S_1 and S_2 in Fig. 35.5. Hence we can apply

the ideas of two-slit interference to this problem. Since the resultant wave is detected at distances much greater than $d = 400$ m, we may use Eq. (35.4) to give the directions of the intensity maxima, the values of θ for which the path difference is zero or a whole number of wavelengths.

EXECUTE: The wavelength is $\lambda = c/f = 200$ m. From Eq. (35.4) with $m = 0, \pm 1$, and ± 2, the intensity maxima are given by

$$\sin \theta = \frac{m\lambda}{d} = \frac{m(200\ \text{m})}{400\ \text{m}} = \frac{m}{2} \qquad \theta = 0, \pm 30°, \pm 90°$$

In this example, values of *m* greater than 2 or less than −2 give values of $\sin \theta$ greater than 1 or less than −1, which is impossible. There is *no* direction for which the path difference is three or more wavelengths, so values of *m* of ±3 or beyond have no meaning in this example.

EVALUATE: We can check our result by calculating the angles for *minimum* intensity, using Eq. (35.5). There should be one intensity minimum between each pair of intensity maxima, just as in Fig. 35.6. From Eq. (35.5), with $m = -2, -1, 0$, and 1,

$$\sin \theta = \frac{(m + \frac{1}{2})\lambda}{d} = \frac{m + \frac{1}{2}}{2} \qquad \theta = \pm 14.5°, \pm 48.6°$$

These angles fall between the angles for intensity maxima, as they should. The angles are not small, so the angles for the minima are *not* exactly halfway between the angles for the maxima.

35.8 Two radio antennas broadcasting in phase. The purple arrows indicate the directions of maximum intensity. The waves that are emitted toward the lower half of the figure are not shown.

Test Your Understanding of Section 35.2 You shine a tunable laser (whose wavelength can be adjusted by turning a knob) on a pair of closely spaced slits. The light emerging from the two slits produces an interference pattern on a screen like that shown in Fig. 35.6. If you adjust the wavelength so that the laser light changes from red to blue, how will the spacing between bright fringes change? (i) The spacing increases; (ii) the spacing decreases; (iii) the spacing is unchanged; (iv) not enough information is given to decide.

35.3 Intensity in Interference Patterns

In Section 35.2 we found the positions of maximum and minimum intensity in a two-source interference pattern. Let's now see how to find the intensity at *any* point in the pattern. To do this, we have to combine the two sinusoidally varying fields (from the two sources) at a point P in the radiation pattern, taking proper account of the phase difference of the two waves at point P, which results from the path difference. The intensity is then proportional to the square of the resultant electric-field amplitude, as we learned in Chapter 32.

To calculate the intensity, we will assume that the two sinusoidal functions (corresponding to waves from the two sources) have equal amplitude E and that the $\vec{E}$ fields lie along the same line (have the same polarization). This assumes that the sources are identical and neglects the slight amplitude difference caused by the unequal path lengths (the amplitude decreases with increasing distance from the source). From Eq. (32.29), each source by itself would give an intensity $\frac{1}{2}\epsilon_0 cE^2$ at point P. If the two sources are in phase, then the waves that arrive at P differ in phase by an amount proportional to the difference in their path lengths, $(r_2 - r_1)$. If the phase angle between these arriving waves is ϕ, then we can use the following expressions for the two electric fields superposed at P:

$$E_1(t) = E\cos(\omega t + \phi)$$
$$E_2(t) = E\cos \omega t$$

The superposition of the two fields at P is a sinusoidal function with some amplitude E_P that depends on E and the phase difference ϕ. First we'll work on finding the amplitude E_P if E and ϕ are known. Then we'll find the intensity I of the resultant wave, which is proportional to E_P^2. Finally, we'll relate the phase difference ϕ to the path difference, which is determined by the geometry of the situation.

Amplitude in Two-Source Interference

To add the two sinusoidal functions with a phase difference, we use the same *phasor* representation that we used for simple harmonic motion (see Section 14.2) and for voltages and currents in ac circuits (see Section 31.1). We suggest that you review these sections now. Each sinusoidal function is represented by a rotating vector (phasor) whose projection on the horizontal axis at any instant represents the instantaneous value of the sinusoidal function.

In Fig. 35.9, E_1 is the horizontal component of the phasor representing the wave from source S_1, and E_2 is the horizontal component of the phasor for the wave from S_2. As shown in the diagram, both phasors have the same magnitude E, but E_1 is *ahead* of E_2 in phase by an angle ϕ. Both phasors rotate counterclockwise with constant angular speed ω, and the sum of the projections on the horizontal axis at any time gives the instantaneous value of the total E field at point P. Thus the amplitude E_P of the resultant sinusoidal wave at P is the magnitude of the dark red phasor in the diagram (labeled E_P); this is the *vector sum* of the other two phasors. To find E_P, we use the law of cosines and the trigonometric identity $\cos(\pi - \phi) = -\cos\phi$:

$$E_P^2 = E^2 + E^2 - 2E^2\cos(\pi - \phi)$$
$$= E^2 + E^2 + 2E^2\cos\phi$$

35.9 Phasor diagram for the superposition at a point P of two waves of equal amplitude E with a phase difference ϕ.

All phasors rotate counterclockwise with angular speed ω.

The resultant wave has amplitude E_P.

$E_P = 2E\left|\cos\dfrac{\phi}{2}\right|$.

$E_2 = E\cos \omega t$

$E_1 = E\cos(\omega t + \phi)$

Then, using the identity $1 + \cos\phi = 2\cos^2(\phi/2)$, we obtain

$$E_P^2 = 2E^2(1 + \cos\phi) = 4E^2\cos^2\left(\frac{\phi}{2}\right)$$

$$E_P = 2E\left|\cos\frac{\phi}{2}\right| \qquad \text{(amplitude in two-source interference)} \qquad (35.7)$$

You can also obtain this result without using phasors (see Problem 35.50).

When the two waves are in phase, $\phi = 0$ and $E_P = 2E$. When they are exactly a half-cycle out of phase, $\phi = \pi \text{ rad} = 180°$, $\cos(\phi/2) = \cos(\pi/2) = 0$, and $E_P = 0$. Thus the superposition of two sinusoidal waves with the same frequency and amplitude but with a phase difference yields a sinusoidal wave with the same frequency and an amplitude between zero and twice the individual amplitudes, depending on the phase difference.

Intensity in Two-Source Interference

To obtain the intensity I at point P, we recall from Section 32.4 that I is equal to the average magnitude of the Poynting vector, S_{av}. For a sinusoidal wave with electric-field amplitude E_P, this is given by Eq. (32.29) with E_{max} replaced by E_P. Thus we can express the intensity in several equivalent forms:

$$I = S_{av} = \frac{E_P^2}{2\mu_0 c} = \frac{1}{2}\sqrt{\frac{\epsilon_0}{\mu_0}}E_P^2 = \frac{1}{2}\epsilon_0 c E_P^2 \qquad (35.8)$$

The essential content of these expressions is that I is proportional to E_P^2. When we substitute Eq. (35.7) into the last expression in Eq. (35.8), we get

$$I = \frac{1}{2}\epsilon_0 c E_P^2 = 2\epsilon_0 c E^2 \cos^2\frac{\phi}{2} \qquad (35.9)$$

In particular, the *maximum* intensity I_0, which occurs at points where the phase difference is zero ($\phi = 0$), is

$$I_0 = 2\epsilon_0 c E^2$$

Note that the maximum intensity I_0 is *four times* (not twice) as great as the intensity $\frac{1}{2}\epsilon_0 c E^2$ from each individual source.

Substituting the expression for I_0 into Eq. (35.9), we can express the intensity I at any point very simply in terms of the maximum intensity I_0:

$$I = I_0\cos^2\frac{\phi}{2} \qquad \text{(intensity in two-source interference)} \qquad (35.10)$$

For some phase angles ϕ the intensity is I_0, four times as great as for an individual wave source, but for other phase angles the intensity is zero. If we average Eq. (35.10) over all possible phase differences, the result is $I_0/2 = \epsilon_0 c E^2$ (the average of $\cos^2(\phi/2)$ is $\frac{1}{2}$). This is just twice the intensity from each individual source, as we should expect. The total energy output from the two sources isn't changed by the interference effects, but the energy is redistributed (as we mentioned in Section 35.1).

Phase Difference and Path Difference

Our next task is to find the phase difference ϕ between the two fields at any point P. We know that ϕ is proportional to the difference in path length from the two sources to point P. When the path difference is one wavelength, the phase difference is one cycle, and $\phi = 2\pi \text{ rad} = 360°$. When the path difference is

$\lambda/2$, $\phi = \pi$ rad $= 180°$, and so on. That is, the ratio of the phase difference ϕ to 2π is equal to the ratio of the path difference $r_2 - r_1$ to λ:

$$\frac{\phi}{2\pi} = \frac{r_2 - r_1}{\lambda}$$

Thus a path difference $(r_2 - r_1)$ causes a phase difference given by

$$\phi = \frac{2\pi}{\lambda}(r_2 - r_1) = k(r_2 - r_1) \qquad \text{(phase difference related to path difference)} \qquad (35.11)$$

where $k = 2\pi/\lambda$ is the *wave number* introduced in Section 15.3.

If the material in the space between the sources and P is anything other than vacuum, we must use the wavelength *in the material* in Eq. (35.11). If the material has index of refraction n, then

$$\lambda = \frac{\lambda_0}{n} \qquad \text{and} \qquad k = nk_0 \qquad (35.12)$$

where λ_0 and k_0 are the wavelength and the wave number, respectively, in vacuum.

Finally, if the point P is far away from the sources in comparison to their separation d, the path difference is given by Eq. (35.3):

$$r_2 - r_1 = d\sin\theta$$

Combining this with Eq. (35.11), we find

$$\phi = k(r_2 - r_1) = kd\sin\theta = \frac{2\pi d}{\lambda}\sin\theta \qquad (35.13)$$

When we substitute this into Eq. (35.10), we find

$$I = I_0\cos^2\left(\tfrac{1}{2}kd\sin\theta\right) = I_0\cos^2\left(\frac{\pi d}{\lambda}\sin\theta\right) \qquad \text{(intensity far from two sources)} \qquad (35.14)$$

The directions of *maximum* intensity occur when the cosine has the values ± 1—that is, when

$$\frac{\pi d}{\lambda}\sin\theta = m\pi \qquad (m = 0, \pm 1, \pm 2, \ldots)$$

or

$$d\sin\theta = m\lambda$$

in agreement with Eq. (35.4). You can also derive Eq. (35.5) for the zero-intensity directions from Eq. (35.14).

As we noted in Section 35.2, in experiments with light we visualize the interference pattern due to two slits by using a screen placed at a distance R from the slits. We can describe positions on the screen with the coordinate y; the positions of the bright fringes are given by Eq. (35.6), where ordinarily $y \ll R$. In that case, $\sin\theta$ is approximately equal to y/R, and we obtain the following expressions for the intensity at *any* point on the screen as a function of y:

$$I = I_0\cos^2\left(\frac{kdy}{2R}\right) = I_0\cos^2\left(\frac{\pi dy}{\lambda R}\right) \quad \text{(intensity in two-slit interference)} \quad (35.15)$$

Figure 35.10 shows a graph of Eq. (35.15); we can compare this with the photographically recorded pattern of Fig. 35.6. The peaks in Fig. 35.10 all have the same intensity, while those in Fig. 35.6 fade off as we go away from the center. We'll explore the reasons for this variation in peak intensity in Chapter 36.

35.10 Intensity distribution in the interference pattern from two identical slits.

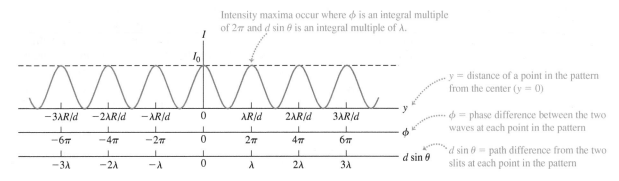

Intensity maxima occur where ϕ is an integral multiple of 2π and $d \sin\theta$ is an integral multiple of λ.

y = distance of a point in the pattern from the center ($y = 0$)

ϕ = phase difference between the two waves at each point in the pattern

$d \sin\theta$ = path difference from the two slits at each point in the pattern

---

Example 35.3 **A directional transmitting antenna array**

Suppose the two identical radio antennas of Fig. 35.8 are moved to be only 10.0 m apart and the broadcast frequency is increased to $f = 60.0$ MHz. At a distance of 700 m from the point midway between the antennas and in the direction $\theta = 0$ (see Fig. 35.8), the intensity is $I_0 = 0.020$ W/m^2. At this same distance, find (a) the intensity in the direction $\theta = 4.0°$; (b) the direction near $\theta = 0$ for which the intensity is $I_0/2$; and (c) the directions in which the intensity is zero.

SOLUTION

IDENTIFY and SET UP: This problem involves the intensity distribution as a function of angle. Because the 700-m distance from the antennas to the point at which the intensity is measured is much greater than the distance $d = 10.0$ m between the antennas, the amplitudes of the waves from the two antennas are very nearly equal. Hence we can use Eq. (35.14) to relate intensity I and angle θ.

EXECUTE: The wavelength is $\lambda = c/f = 5.00$ m. The spacing $d = 10.0$ m between the antennas is just twice the wavelength (as was the case in Example 35.2), so $d/\lambda = 2.00$ and Eq. (35.14) becomes

$$I = I_0 \cos^2\left(\frac{\pi d}{\lambda} \sin\theta\right) = I_0 \cos^2[(2.00\pi \text{ rad})\sin\theta]$$

(a) When $\theta = 4.0°$,

$$I = I_0 \cos^2[(2.00\pi \text{ rad}) \sin 4.0°] = 0.82 I_0$$
$$= (0.82)(0.020 \text{ W/m}^2) = 0.016 \text{ W/m}^2$$

(b) The intensity I equals $I_0/2$ when the cosine in Eq. (35.14) has the value $\pm 1/\sqrt{2}$. The smallest angles at which this occurs correspond to $2.00\pi \sin\theta = \pm\pi/4$ rad, so that $\sin\theta = \pm(1/8.00) = \pm 0.125$ and $\theta = \pm 7.2°$.

(c) The intensity is zero when $\cos[(2.00\pi \text{ rad})\sin\theta] = 0$. This occurs for $2.00\pi \sin\theta = \pm\pi/2, \pm 3\pi/2, \pm 5\pi/2, \ldots$, or $\sin\theta = \pm 0.250, \pm 0.750, \pm 1.25, \ldots$. Values of $\sin\theta$ greater than 1 have no meaning, so the answers are

$$\theta = \pm 14.5°, \pm 48.6°$$

EVALUATE: The condition in part (b) that $I = I_0/2$, so that $(2.00\pi \text{ rad})\sin\theta = \pm\pi/4$ rad, is also satisfied when $\sin\theta = \pm 0.375, \pm 0.625$, or ± 0.875 so that $\theta = \pm 22.0°, \pm 38.7°$, or $\pm 61.0°$. (Can you verify this?) It would be incorrect to include these angles in the solution, however, because the problem asked for the angle *near* $\theta = 0$ at which $I = I_0/2$. These additional values of θ aren't the ones we're looking for.

Test Your Understanding of Section 35.3 A two-slit interference experiment uses coherent light of wavelength 5.00×10^{-7} m. Rank the following points in the interference pattern according to the intensity at each point, from highest to lowest. (i) a point that is closer to one slit than the other by 4.00×10^{-7} m; (ii) a point where the light waves received from the two slits are out of phase by 4.00 rad; (iii) a point that is closer to one slit than the other by 7.50×10^{-7} m; (iv) a point where the light waves received by the two slits are out of phase by 2.00 rad. ❚

35.4 Interference in Thin Films

You often see bright bands of color when light reflects from a thin layer of oil floating on water or from a soap bubble (see the photograph that opens this chapter). These are the results of interference. Light waves are reflected from the front and back surfaces of such thin films, and constructive interference between the two reflected waves (with different path lengths) occurs in different

35.11 (a) A diagram and (b) a photograph showing interference of light reflected from a thin film.

(a) Interference between rays reflected from the two surfaces of a thin film

Light reflected from the upper and lower surfaces of the film comes together in the eye at P and undergoes interference.

Some colors interfere constructively and others destructively, creating the color bands we see.

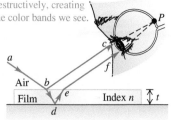

(b) The rainbow fringes of an oil slick on water

35.12 Interference between light waves reflected from the two sides of an air wedge separating two glass plates. The angles and the thickness of the air wedge have been exaggerated for clarity; in the text we assume that the light strikes the upper plate at normal incidence and that the distances h and t are much less than l.

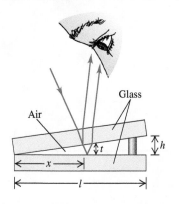

places for different wavelengths. Figure 35.11a shows the situation. Light shining on the upper surface of a thin film with thickness t is partly reflected at the upper surface (path abc). Light *transmitted* through the upper surface is partly reflected at the lower surface (path $abdef$). The two reflected waves come together at point P on the retina of the eye. Depending on the phase relationship, they may interfere constructively or destructively. Different colors have different wavelengths, so the interference may be constructive for some colors and destructive for others. That's why we see colored rings or fringes in Fig. 35.11b (which shows a thin film of oil floating on water) and in the photograph that opens this chapter (which shows thin films of soap solution that make up the bubble walls). The complex shapes of the colored rings in each photograph result from variations in the thickness of the film.

Thin-Film Interference and Phase Shifts During Reflection

Let's look at a simplified situation in which *monochromatic* light reflects from two nearly parallel surfaces at nearly normal incidence. Figure 35.12 shows two plates of glass separated by a thin wedge, or film, of air. We want to consider interference between the two light waves reflected from the surfaces adjacent to the air wedge, as shown. (Reflections also occur at the top surface of the upper plate and the bottom surface of the lower plate; to keep our discussion simple, we won't include these.) The situation is the same as in Fig. 35.11a except that the film (wedge) thickness is not uniform. The path difference between the two waves is just twice the thickness t of the air wedge at each point. At points where $2t$ is an integer number of wavelengths, we expect to see constructive interference and a bright area; where it is a half-integer number of wavelengths, we expect to see destructive interference and a dark area. Along the line where the plates are in contact, there is practically *no* path difference, and we expect a bright area.

When we carry out the experiment, the bright and dark fringes appear, but they are interchanged! Along the line where the plates are in contact, we find a *dark* fringe, not a bright one. This suggests that one or the other of the reflected waves has undergone a half-cycle phase shift during its reflection. In that case the two waves that are reflected at the line of contact are a half-cycle out of phase even though they have the same path length.

In fact, this phase shift can be predicted from Maxwell's equations and the electromagnetic nature of light. The details of the derivation are beyond our scope, but here is the result. Suppose a light wave with electric-field amplitude E_i is traveling in an optical material with index of refraction n_a. It strikes, at normal incidence, an interface with another optical material with index n_b. The amplitude E_r of the wave reflected from the interface is proportional to the amplitude E_i of the incident wave and is given by

$$E_r = \frac{n_a - n_b}{n_a + n_b} E_i \quad \text{(normal incidence)} \tag{35.16}$$

This result shows that the incident and reflected amplitudes have the same sign when n_a is larger than n_b and opposite sign when n_b is larger than n_a. We can distinguish three cases, as shown in Fig. 35.13:

Figure 35.13a: When $n_a > n_b$, light travels more slowly in the first material than in the second. In this case, E_r and E_i have the same sign, and the phase shift of the reflected wave relative to the incident wave is zero. This is analogous to reflection of a transverse mechanical wave on a heavy rope at a point where it is tied to a lighter rope or a ring that can move vertically without friction.

Figure 35.13b: When $n_a = n_b$, the amplitude E_r of the reflected wave is zero. The incident light wave can't "see" the interface, and there is *no* reflected wave.

35.13 Upper figures: electromagnetic waves striking an interface between optical materials at normal incidence (shown as a small angle for clarity). Lower figures: mechanical wave pulses on ropes.

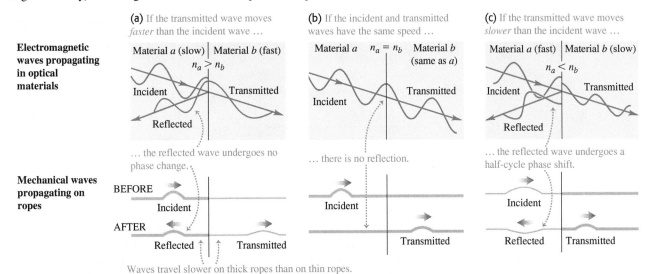

Figure 35.13c: When $n_a < n_b$, light travels more slowly in the second material than in the first. In this case, E_r and E_i have opposite signs, and the phase shift of the reflected wave relative to the incident wave is π rad (180° or a half-cycle). This is analogous to reflection (with inversion) of a transverse mechanical wave on a light rope at a point where it is tied to a heavier rope or a rigid support.

Let's compare with the situation of Fig. 35.12. For the wave reflected from the upper surface of the air wedge, n_a (glass) is greater than n_b, so this wave has zero phase shift. For the wave reflected from the lower surface, n_a (air) is less than n_b (glass), so this wave has a half-cycle phase shift. Waves that are reflected from the line of contact have no path difference to give additional phase shifts, and they interfere destructively; this is what we observe. You can use the above principle to show that for normal incidence, the wave reflected at point b in Fig. 35.11a is shifted by a half-cycle, while the wave reflected at d is not (if there is air below the film).

We can summarize this discussion mathematically. If the film has thickness t, the light is at normal incidence and has wavelength λ in the film; if neither or both of the reflected waves from the two surfaces have a half-cycle reflection phase shift, the conditions for constructive and destructive interference are

$$2t = m\lambda \qquad (m = 0, 1, 2, \dots)$$

(constructive reflection from thin film, no relative phase shift)   (35.17a)

$$2t = \left(m + \tfrac{1}{2}\right)\lambda \qquad (m = 0, 1, 2, \dots)$$

(destructive reflection from thin film, no relative phase shift)   (35.17b)

If *one* of the two waves has a half-cycle reflection phase shift, the conditions for constructive and destructive interference are reversed:

$$2t = \left(m + \tfrac{1}{2}\right)\lambda \qquad (m = 0, 1, 2, \dots)$$

(constructive reflection from thin film, half-cycle relative phase shift)   (35.18a)

$$2t = m\lambda \qquad (m = 0, 1, 2, \dots)$$

(destructive reflection from thin film, half-cycle relative phase shift)   (35.18b)

35.14 (a) Light reflecting from a thin film produces a steady interference pattern, but (b) light reflecting from a thick film does not.

(a) Light reflecting from a thin film

Bursts of light a few μm long

The waves reflected from the two surfaces are part of the same burst and are coherent.

Thin film

(b) Light reflecting from a thick film

The waves reflected from the two surfaces are from different bursts and are *not* coherent.

Thick film

Thin and Thick Films

We have emphasized *thin* films in our discussion because of a principle we introduced in Section 35.1: In order for two waves to cause a steady interference pattern, the waves must be *coherent*, with a definite and constant phase relationship. The sun and light bulbs emit light in a stream of short bursts, each of which is only a few micrometers long (1 micrometer = 1 μm = 10^{-6} m). If light reflects from the two surfaces of a thin film, the two reflected waves are part of the same burst (Fig. 35.14a). Hence these waves are coherent and interference occurs as we have described. If the film is too thick, however, the two reflected waves will belong to different bursts (Fig. 35.14b). There is no definite phase relationship between different light bursts, so the two waves are incoherent and there is no fixed interference pattern. That's why you see interference colors in light reflected from an oil slick a few micrometers thick (see Fig. 35.11b), but you do *not* see such colors in the light reflected from a pane of window glass with a thickness of a few millimeters (a thousand times greater).

Problem-Solving Strategy 35.1 | **Interference in Thin Films**

IDENTIFY *the relevant concepts:* Problems with thin films involve interference of two waves, one reflected from the film's front surface and one reflected from the back surface. Typically you will be asked to relate the wavelength, the film thickness, and the index of refraction of the film.

SET UP *the problem* using the following steps:
1. Make a drawing showing the geometry of the film. Identify the materials that adjoin the film; their properties determine whether one or both of the reflected waves have a half-cycle phase shift.
2. Identify the target variable.

EXECUTE *the solution* as follows:
1. Apply the rule for phase changes to each reflected wave: There is a half-cycle phase shift when $n_b > n_a$ and none when $n_b < n_a$.

2. If *neither* reflected wave undergoes a phase shift, or if *both* do, use Eqs. (35.17). If only one reflected wave undergoes a phase shift, use Eqs. (35.18).
3. Solve the resulting equation for the target variable. Use the wavelength $\lambda = \lambda_0/n$ of light *in the film* in your calculations, where n is the index of refraction of the film. (For air, $n = 1.000$ to four-figure precision.)
4. If you are asked about the wave that is transmitted through the film, remember that minimum intensity in the reflected wave corresponds to maximum *transmitted* intensity, and vice versa.

EVALUATE *your answer:* Interpret your results by examining what would happen if the wavelength were changed or if the film had a different thickness.

Example 35.4 | **Thin-film interference I**

Suppose the two glass plates in Fig. 35.12 are two microscope slides 10.0 cm long. At one end they are in contact; at the other end they are separated by a piece of paper 0.0200 mm thick. What is the spacing of the interference fringes seen by reflection? Is the fringe at the line of contact bright or dark? Assume monochromatic light with a wavelength in air of $\lambda = \lambda_0 = 500$ nm.

SOLUTION

IDENTIFY and SET UP: Figure 35.15 depicts the situation. We'll consider only interference between the light reflected from the upper and lower surfaces of the air wedge between the microscope slides. [The top slide has a relatively great thickness, about 1 mm,

35.15 Our sketch for this problem.

$\lambda_0 = 500$ nm

$h = 0.0200$ mm

$\ell = 10.0$ cm

so we can ignore interference between the light reflected from its upper and lower surfaces (see Fig. 35.14b).] Light travels more slowly in the glass of the slides than it does in air. Hence the wave reflected from the upper surface of the air wedge has no phase shift (see Fig. 35.13a), while the wave reflected from the lower surface has a half-cycle phase shift (see Fig. 35.13c).

EXECUTE: Since only one of the reflected waves undergoes a phase shift, the condition for *destructive* interference (a dark fringe) is Eq. (35.18b):

$$2t = m\lambda_0 \quad (m = 0, 1, 2, \dots)$$

From similar triangles in Fig. 35.15 the thickness t of the air wedge at each point is proportional to the distance x from the line of contact:

$$\frac{t}{x} = \frac{h}{l}$$

Combining this with Eq. (35.18b), we find

$$\frac{2xh}{l} = m\lambda_0$$

$$x = m\frac{l\lambda_0}{2h} = m\frac{(0.100 \text{ m})(500 \times 10^{-9} \text{ m})}{(2)(0.0200 \times 10^{-3} \text{ m})} = m(1.25 \text{ mm})$$

Successive dark fringes, corresponding to $m = 1, 2, 3, \dots$, are spaced 1.25 mm apart. Substituting $m = 0$ into this equation gives $x = 0$, which is where the two slides touch (at the left-hand side of Fig. 35.15). Hence there is a dark fringe at the line of contact.

EVALUATE: Our result shows that the fringe spacing is proportional to the wavelength of the light used; the fringes would be farther apart with red light (larger λ_0) than with blue light (smaller λ_0). If we use white light, the reflected light at any point is a mixture of wavelengths for which constructive interference occurs; the wavelengths that interfere destructively are weak or absent in the reflected light. (This same effect explains the colors seen when an oil film on water is illuminated by white light, as in Fig. 35.11b).

Example 35.5   **Thin-film interference II**

Suppose the glass plates of Example 35.4 have $n = 1.52$ and the space between plates contains water ($n = 1.33$) instead of air. What happens now?

SOLUTION

IDENTIFY and SET UP: The index of refraction of the water wedge is still less than that of the glass on either side of it, so the phase shifts are the same as in Example 35.4. Once again we use Eq. (35.18b) to find the positions of the dark fringes; the only difference is that the wavelength λ in this equation is now the wavelength in water instead of in air.

EXECUTE: In the film of water ($n = 1.33$), the wavelength is $\lambda = \lambda_0/n = (500 \text{ nm})/(1.33) = 376$ nm. When we replace λ_0 by λ in the expression from Example 35.4 for the position x of the mth dark fringe, we find that the fringe spacing is reduced by the same factor of 1.33 and is equal to 0.940 mm. There is still a dark fringe at the line of contact.

EVALUATE: Can you see that to obtain the same fringe spacing as in Example 35.4, the dimension h in Fig. 35.15 would have to be reduced to $(0.0200 \text{ mm})/1.33 = 0.0150$ mm? This shows that what matters in thin-film interference is the *ratio* t/λ between film thickness and wavelength. [You can see this by considering Eqs. (35.17) and (35.18).]

Example 35.6   **Thin-film interference III**

Suppose the upper of the two plates of Example 35.4 is a plastic with $n = 1.40$, the wedge is filled with a silicone grease with $n = 1.50$, and the bottom plate is a dense flint glass with $n = 1.60$. What happens now?

SOLUTION

IDENTIFY and SET UP: The geometry is again the same as shown in Fig. 35.15, but now half-cycle phase shifts occur at *both* surfaces of the grease wedge (see Fig. 35.13c). Hence there is no *relative* phase shift and we must use Eq. (35.17b) to find the positions of the dark fringes.

EXECUTE: The value of λ to use in Eq. (35.17b) is the wavelength in the silicone grease, $\lambda = \lambda_0/n = (500 \text{ nm})/1.50 = 333$ nm. You can readily show that the fringe spacing is 0.833 mm. Note that the two reflected waves from the line of contact are in phase (they both undergo the same phase shift), so the line of contact is at a *bright* fringe.

EVALUATE: What would happen if you carefully removed the upper microscope slide so that the grease wedge retained its shape? There would still be half-cycle phase changes at the upper and lower surfaces of the wedge, so the pattern of fringes would be the same as with the upper slide present.

35.16 (a) Air film between a convex lens and a plane surface. The thickness of the film t increases from zero as we move out from the center, giving (b) a series of alternating dark and bright rings for monochromatic light.

(a) A convex lens in contact with a glass plane

(b) Newton's rings: circular interference fringes

Newton's Rings

Figure 35.16a shows the convex surface of a lens in contact with a plane glass plate. A thin film of air is formed between the two surfaces. When you view the setup with monochromatic light, you see circular interference fringes (Fig. 35.16b). These were studied by Newton and are called **Newton's rings.**

We can use interference fringes to compare the surfaces of two optical parts by placing the two in contact and observing the interference fringes. Figure 35.17 is a photograph made during the grinding of a telescope objective lens. The lower, larger-diameter, thicker disk is the correctly shaped master, and the smaller, upper disk is the lens under test. The "contour lines" are Newton's interference fringes; each one indicates an additional distance between the specimen and the master of one half-wavelength. At 10 lines from the center spot the distance between the two surfaces is five wavelengths, or about 0.003 mm. This isn't very good; high-quality lenses are routinely ground with a precision of less than one wavelength. The surface of the primary mirror of the Hubble Space Telescope was ground to a precision of better than $\frac{1}{50}$ wavelength. Unfortunately, it was ground to incorrect specifications, creating one of the most precise errors in the history of optical technology (see Section 34.2).

35.17 The surface of a telescope objective lens under inspection during manufacture.

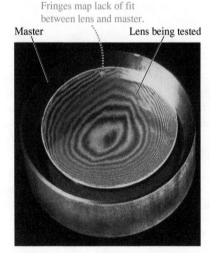

Fringes map lack of fit between lens and master.
Master   Lens being tested

Nonreflective and Reflective Coatings

Nonreflective coatings for lens surfaces make use of thin-film interference. A thin layer or film of hard transparent material with an index of refraction smaller than that of the glass is deposited on the lens surface, as in Fig. 35.18. Light is reflected from both surfaces of the layer. In both reflections the light is reflected from a medium of greater index than that in which it is traveling, so the same phase change occurs in both reflections. If the film thickness is a quarter (one-fourth) of the wavelength *in the film* (assuming normal incidence), the total path difference is a half-wavelength. Light reflected from the first surface is then a half-cycle out of phase with light reflected from the second, and there is destructive interference.

The thickness of the nonreflective coating can be a quarter-wavelength for only one particular wavelength. This is usually chosen in the central yellow-green portion of the spectrum ($\lambda = 550$ nm), where the eye is most sensitive. Then there is somewhat more reflection at both longer (red) and shorter (blue) wavelengths, and the reflected light has a purple hue. The overall reflection from a lens or prism surface can be reduced in this way from 4–5% to less than 1%. This also increases the net amount of light that is *transmitted* through the lens, since light that is not reflected will be transmitted. The same principle is used to minimize reflection from silicon photovoltaic solar cells ($n = 3.5$) by use of a thin surface layer of silicon monoxide (SiO, $n = 1.45$); this helps to increase the amount of light that actually reaches the solar cells.

35.18 A nonreflective coating has an index of refraction intermediate between those of glass and air.

Destructive interference occurs when
• the film is about $\frac{1}{4}\lambda$ thick and
• the light undergoes a phase change at both reflecting surfaces,

so that the two reflected waves emerge from the film about $\frac{1}{2}$ cycle out of phase.

$n_{\text{glass}} > n_{\text{film}} > n_{\text{air}}$

"Nonreflecting" film

Air
Film
Glass

$t = \frac{1}{4}\lambda$

If a quarter-wavelength thickness of a material with an index of refraction *greater* than that of glass is deposited on glass, then the reflectivity is *increased,* and the deposited material is called a **reflective coating.** In this case there is a half-cycle phase shift at the air–film interface but none at the film–glass interface, and reflections from the two sides of the film interfere constructively. For example, a coating with refractive index 2.5 causes 38% of the incident energy to be reflected, compared with 4% or so with no coating. By use of multiple-layer coatings, it is possible to achieve nearly 100% transmission or reflection for particular wavelengths. Some practical applications of these coatings are for color separation in television cameras and for infrared "heat reflectors" in motion-picture projectors, solar cells, and astronauts' visors.

Example 35.7 A nonreflective coating

A common lens coating material is magnesium fluoride (MgF_2), with $n = 1.38$. What thickness should a nonreflective coating have for 550-nm light if it is applied to glass with $n = 1.52$?

SOLUTION

IDENTIFY and SET UP: This coating is of the sort shown in Fig. 35.18. The thickness must be one-quarter of the wavelength of this light *in the coating.*

EXECUTE: The wavelength in air is $\lambda_0 = 550$ nm, so its wavelength in the MgF_2 coating is $\lambda = \lambda_0/n = (550 \text{ nm})/1.38 = 400$ nm. The coating thickness should be one-quarter of this, or $\lambda/4 = 100$ nm.

EVALUATE: This is a very thin film, no more than a few hundred molecules thick. Note that this coating is *reflective* for light whose wavelength is *twice* the coating thickness; light of that wavelength reflected from the coating's lower surface travels one wavelength farther than light reflected from the upper surface, so the two waves are in phase and interfere constructively. This occurs for light with a wavelength in MgF_2 of 200 nm and a wavelength in air of $(200 \text{ nm})(1.38) = 276$ nm. This is an ultraviolet wavelength (see Section 32.1), so designers of optical lenses with nonreflective coatings need not worry about such enhanced reflection.

Test Your Understanding of Section 35.4 A thin layer of benzene ($n = 1.501$) ties on top of a sheet of fluorite ($n = 1.434$). It is illuminated from above with light whose wavelength in benzene is 400 nm. Which of the following possible thicknesses of the benzene layer will maximize the brightness of the reflected light? (i) 100 nm; (ii) 200 nm; (iii) 300 nm; (iv) 400 nm.

35.5 The Michelson Interferometer

An important experimental device that uses interference is the **Michelson interferometer.** Michelson interferometers are used to make precise measurements of wavelengths and of very small distances, such as the minute changes in thickness of an axon when a nerve impulse propagates along its length. Like the Young two-slit experiment, a Michelson interferometer takes monochromatic light from a single source and divides it into two waves that follow different paths. In Young's experiment, this is done by sending part of the light through one slit and part through another; in a Michelson interferometer a device called a *beam splitter* is used. Interference occurs in both experiments when the two light waves are recombined.

How a Michelson Interferometer Works

Figure 35.19 shows the principal components of a Michelson interferometer. A ray of light from a monochromatic source A strikes the beam splitter C, which is a glass plate with a thin coating of silver on its right side. Part of the light (ray 1) passes through the silvered surface and the compensator plate D and is reflected from mirror M_1. It then returns through D and is reflected from the silvered surface of C to the observer. The remainder of the light (ray 2) is reflected from the silvered surface at point P to the mirror M_2 and back through C to the observer's eye.

Application Interference and Butterfly Wings

Many of the most brilliant colors in the animal world are created by *interference* rather than by pigments. These photos show the butterfly *Morpho rhetenor* and the microscopic scales that cover the upper surfaces of its wings. The scales have a profusion of tiny ridges (middle photo); these carry regularly spaced flanges (bottom photo) that function as reflectors. These are spaced so that the reflections interfere constructively for blue light. The multilayered structure reflects 70% of the blue light that strikes it, giving the wings a mirror-like brilliance. (The undersides of the wings do not have these structures and are a dull brown.)

35.19 A schematic Michelson interferometer. The observer sees an interference pattern that results from the difference in path lengths for rays 1 and 2.

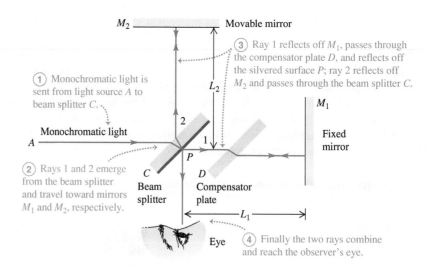

① Monochromatic light is sent from light source A to beam splitter C.

③ Ray 1 reflects off M_1, passes through the compensator plate D, and reflects off the silvered surface P; ray 2 reflects off M_2 and passes through the beam splitter C.

② Rays 1 and 2 emerge from the beam splitter and travel toward mirrors M_1 and M_2, respectively.

④ Finally the two rays combine and reach the observer's eye.

Application Imaging Cells with a Michelson Interferometer

This false-color image of a human colon cancer cell was made using a microscope that was mated to a Michelson interferometer. The cell is in one arm of the interferometer, and light passing through the cell undergoes a phase shift that depends on the cell thickness and the organelles within the cell. The fringe pattern can then be used to construct a three-dimensional view of the cell. Scientists have used this technique to observe how different types of cells behave when prodded by microscopic probes. Cancer cells turn out to be "softer" than normal cells, a distinction that may make cancer stem cells easier to identify.

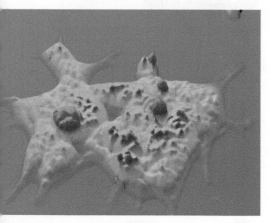

The purpose of the compensator plate D is to ensure that rays 1 and 2 pass through the same thickness of glass; plate D is cut from the same piece of glass as plate C, so their thicknesses are identical to within a fraction of a wavelength.

The whole apparatus in Fig. 35.19 is mounted on a very rigid frame, and the position of mirror M_2 can be adjusted with a fine, very accurate micrometer screw. If the distances L_1 and L_2 are exactly equal and the mirrors M_1 and M_2 are exactly at right angles, the virtual image of M_1 formed by reflection at the silvered surface of plate C coincides with mirror M_2. If L_1 and L_2 are *not* exactly equal, the image of M_1 is displaced slightly from M_2; and if the mirrors are not exactly perpendicular, the image of M_1 makes a slight angle with M_2. Then the mirror M_2 and the virtual image of M_1 play the same roles as the two surfaces of a wedge-shaped thin film (see Section 35.4), and light reflected from these surfaces forms the same sort of interference fringes.

Suppose the angle between mirror M_2 and the virtual image of M_1 is just large enough that five or six vertical fringes are present in the field of view. If we now move the mirror M_2 slowly either backward or forward a distance $\lambda/2$, the difference in path length between rays 1 and 2 changes by λ, and each fringe moves to the left or right a distance equal to the fringe spacing. If we observe the fringe positions through a telescope with a crosshair eyepiece and m fringes cross the crosshairs when we move the mirror a distance y, then

$$y = m\frac{\lambda}{2} \quad \text{or} \quad \lambda = \frac{2y}{m} \qquad (35.19)$$

If m is several thousand, the distance y is large enough that it can be measured with good accuracy, and we can obtain an accurate value for the wavelength λ. Alternatively, if the wavelength is known, a distance y can be measured by simply counting fringes when M_2 is moved by this distance. In this way, distances that are comparable to a wavelength of light can be measured with relative ease.

The Michelson-Morley Experiment

The original application of the Michelson interferometer was to the historic **Michelson-Morley experiment.** Before the electromagnetic theory of light became established, most physicists thought that the propagation of light waves occurred in a medium called the **ether,** which was believed to permeate all space. In 1887 the American scientists Albert Michelson and Edward Morley used the Michelson interferometer in an attempt to detect the motion of the earth through the ether. Suppose the interferometer in Fig. 35.19 is moving from left to right relative to the ether. According to the ether theory, this would lead to changes in the speed of light in the portions of the path shown as horizontal lines in the figure. There would be fringe shifts relative to the positions that the fringes would have if the instrument were at rest in the ether. Then when the entire instrument was rotated 90°, the other portions of the paths would be similarly affected, giving a fringe shift in the opposite direction.

Michelson and Morley expected that the motion of the earth through the ether would cause a shift of about four-tenths of a fringe when the instrument was rotated. The shift that was actually observed was less than a hundredth of a fringe and, within the limits of experimental uncertainty, appeared to be exactly zero. Despite its orbital motion around the sun, the earth appeared to be *at rest* relative to the ether. This negative result baffled physicists until 1905, when Albert Einstein developed the special theory of relativity (which we will study in detail in Chapter 37). Einstein postulated that the speed of a light wave in vacuum has the same magnitude c relative to *all* inertial reference frames, no matter what their velocity may be relative to each other. The presumed ether then plays no role, and the concept of an ether has been abandoned.

Test Your Understanding of Section 35.5   You are observing the pattern of fringes in a Michelson interferometer like that shown in Fig. 35.19. If you change the index of refraction (but not the thickness) of the compensator plate, will the pattern change?

Video Tutor Solutions

Interference and coherent sources: Monochromatic light is light with a single frequency. Coherence is a definite, unchanging phase relationship between two waves. The overlap of waves from two coherent sources of monochromatic light forms an interference pattern. The principle of superposition states that the total wave disturbance at any point is the sum of the disturbances from the separate waves.

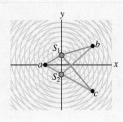

Two-source interference of light: When two sources are in phase, constructive interference occurs where the difference in path length from the two sources is zero or an integer number of wavelengths; destructive interference occurs where the path difference is a half-integer number of wavelengths. If two sources separated by a distance d are both very far from a point P, and the line from the sources to P makes an angle θ with the line perpendicular to the line of the sources, then the condition for constructive interference at P is Eq. (35.4). The condition for destructive interference is Eq. (35.5). When θ is very small, the position y_m of the mth bright fringe on a screen located a distance R from the sources is given by Eq. (35.6). (See Examples 35.1 and 35.2.)

$$d\sin\theta = m\lambda \quad (m = 0, \pm 1, \pm 2, \dots)$$
(constructive interference) (35.4)

$$d\sin\theta = \left(m + \tfrac{1}{2}\right)\lambda$$
$$(m = 0, \pm 1, \pm 2, \dots)$$ (35.5)
(destructive interference)

$$y_m = R\frac{m\lambda}{d}$$ (35.6)
(bright fringes)

Intensity in interference patterns: When two sinusoidal waves with equal amplitude E and phase difference ϕ are superimposed, the resultant amplitude E_P and intensity I are given by Eqs. (35.7) and (35.10), respectively. If the two sources emit in phase, the phase difference ϕ at a point P (located a distance r_1 from source 1 and a distance r_2 from source 2) is directly proportional to the difference in path length $r_2 - r_1$. (See Example 35.3.)

$$E_P = 2E\left|\cos\frac{\phi}{2}\right|$$ (35.7)

$$I = I_0\cos^2\frac{\phi}{2}$$ (35.10)

$$\phi = \frac{2\pi}{\lambda}(r_2 - r_1) = k(r_2 - r_1)$$ (35.11)

Interference in thin films: When light is reflected from both sides of a thin film of thickness t and no phase shift occurs at either surface, constructive interference between the reflected waves occurs when $2t$ is equal to an integral number of wavelengths. If a half-cycle phase shift occurs at one surface, this is the condition for destructive interference. A half-cycle phase shift occurs during reflection whenever the index of refraction in the second material is greater than that in the first. (See Examples 35.4–35.7.)

$$2t = m\lambda \quad (m = 0, 1, 2, \dots)$$
(constructive reflection from thin film, no relative phase shift) (35.17a)

$$2t = \left(m + \tfrac{1}{2}\right)\lambda \quad (m = 0, 1, 2, \dots)$$
(destructive reflection from thin film, no relative phase shift) (35.17b)

$$2t = \left(m + \tfrac{1}{2}\right)\lambda \quad (m = 0, 1, 2, \dots)$$
(constructive reflection from thin film, half-cycle relative phase shift) (35.18a)

$$2t = m\lambda \quad (m = 0, 1, 2, \dots)$$
(destructive reflection from thin film, half-cycle relative phase shift) (35.18b)

Michelson interferometer: The Michelson interferometer uses a monochromatic light source and can be used for high-precision measurements of wavelengths. Its original purpose was to detect motion of the earth relative to a hypothetical ether, the supposed medium for electromagnetic waves. The ether has never been detected, and the concept has been abandoned; the speed of light is the same relative to all observers. This is part of the foundation of the special theory of relativity.

BRIDGING PROBLEM   Modifying a Two-Slit Experiment

An oil tanker spills a large amount of oil ($n = 1.45$) into the sea ($n = 1.33$). (a) If you look down onto the oil spill from overhead, what predominant wavelength of light do you see at a point where the oil is 380 nm thick? What color is the light? (*Hint:* See Table 32.1.) (b) In the water under the slick, what visible wavelength (as measured in air) is predominant in the transmitted light at the same place in the slick as in part (a)?

SOLUTION GUIDE

See MasteringPhysics® study area for a Video Tutor solution.

IDENTIFY and SET UP

1. The oil layer acts as a thin film, so we must consider interference between light that reflects from the top and bottom surfaces of the oil. If a wavelength is prominent in the *transmitted* light, there is destructive interference for that wavelength in the *reflected* light.

2. Choose the appropriate interference equations that relate the thickness of the oil film and the wavelength of light. Take account of the indexes of refraction of the air, oil, and water.

EXECUTE

3. For part (a), find the wavelengths for which there is constructive interference as seen from above the oil film. Which of these are in the visible spectrum?

4. For part (b), find the visible wavelength for which there is destructive interference as seen from above the film. (This will ensure that there is substantial transmitted light at the wavelength.)

EVALUATE

5. If a diver below the water's surface shines a light up at the bottom of the oil film, at what wavelengths would there be constructive interference in the light that reflects back downward?

Problems

For instructor-assigned homework, go to MasteringPhysics®.

•, ••, •••: Problems of increasing difficulty. **CP**: Cumulative problems incorporating material from earlier chapters. **CALC**: Problems requiring calculus. **BIO**: Biosciences problems.

DISCUSSION QUESTIONS

Q35.1 A two-slit interference experiment is set up, and the fringes are displayed on a screen. Then the whole apparatus is immersed in the nearest swimming pool. How does the fringe pattern change?

Q35.2 Could an experiment similar to Young's two-slit experiment be performed with sound? How might this be carried out? Does it matter that sound waves are longitudinal and electromagnetic waves are transverse? Explain.

Q35.3 Monochromatic coherent light passing through two thin slits is viewed on a distant screen. Are the bright fringes equally spaced on the screen? If so, why? If not, which ones are closest to being equally spaced?

Q35.4 In a two-slit interference pattern on a distant screen, are the bright fringes midway between the dark fringes? Is this ever a good approximation?

Q35.5 Would the headlights of a distant car form a two-source interference pattern? If so, how might it be observed? If not, why not?

Q35.6 The two sources S_1 and S_2 shown in Fig. 35.3 emit waves of the same wavelength λ and are in phase with each other. Suppose S_1 is a weaker source, so that the waves emitted by S_1 have half the amplitude of the waves emitted by S_2. How would this affect the positions of the antinodal lines and nodal lines? Would there be total reinforcement at points on the antinodal curves? Would there be total cancellation at points on the nodal curves? Explain your answers.

Q35.7 Could the Young two-slit interference experiment be performed with gamma rays? If not, why not? If so, discuss differences in the experimental design compared to the experiment with visible light.

Q35.8 Coherent red light illuminates two narrow slits that are 25 cm apart. Will a two-slit interference pattern be observed when the light from the slits falls on a screen? Explain.

Q35.9 Coherent light with wavelength λ falls on two narrow slits separated by a distance d. If d is less than some minimum value, no dark fringes are observed. Explain. In terms of λ, what is this minimum value of d?

Q35.10 A fellow student, who values memorizing equations above understanding them, combines Eqs. (35.4) and (35.13) to "prove" that ϕ can *only* equal $2\pi m$. How would you explain to this student that ϕ can have values other than $2\pi m$?

Q35.11 If the monochromatic light shown in Fig. 35.5a were replaced by white light, would a two-slit interference pattern be seen on the screen? Explain.

Q35.12 In using the superposition principle to calculate intensities in interference patterns, could you add the intensities of the waves instead of their amplitudes? Explain.

Q35.13 A glass windowpane with a thin film of water on it reflects less than when it is perfectly dry. Why?

Q35.14 A *very* thin soap film ($n = 1.33$), whose thickness is much less than a wavelength of visible light, looks black; it appears to reflect no light at all. Why? By contrast, an equally thin layer of soapy water ($n = 1.33$) on glass ($n = 1.50$) appears quite shiny. Why is there a difference?

Q35.15 Interference can occur in thin films. Why is it important that the films be *thin*? Why don't you get these effects with a relatively *thick* film? Where should you put the dividing line between "thin" and "thick"? Explain your reasoning.

Q35.16 If we shine white light on an air wedge like that shown in Fig. 35.12, the colors that are weak in the light *reflected* from any point along the wedge are strong in the light *transmitted* through the wedge. Explain why this should be so.

Q35.17 Monochromatic light is directed at normal incidence on a thin film. There is destructive interference for the reflected light, so the intensity of the reflected light is very low. What happened to the energy of the incident light?

Q35.18 When a thin oil film spreads out on a puddle of water, the thinnest part of the film looks dark in the resulting interference pattern. What does this tell you about the relative magnitudes of the refractive indexes of oil and water?

EXERCISES

Section 35.1 Interference and Coherent Sources

35.1 • Two small stereo speakers A and B that are 1.40 m apart are sending out sound of wavelength 34 cm in all directions and all in phase. A person at point P starts out equidistant from both speakers and walks so that he is always 1.50 m from speaker B (Fig. E35.1). For what values of x will the sound this person hears be (a) maximally reinforced, (b) cancelled? Limit your solution to the cases where $x \leq 1.50$ m.

Figure **E35.1**

35.2 •• Two speakers that are 15.0 m apart produce in-phase sound waves of frequency 250.0 Hz in a room where the speed of sound is 340.0 m/s. A woman starts out at the midpoint between the two speakers. The room's walls and ceiling are covered with absorbers to eliminate reflections, and she listens with only one ear for best precision. (a) What does she hear: constructive or destructive interference? Why? (b) She now walks slowly toward one of the speakers. How far from the center must she walk before she first hears the sound reach a minimum intensity? (c) How far from the center must she walk before she first hears the sound maximally enhanced?

35.3 •• Two identical audio speakers connected to the same amplifier produce in-phase sound waves with a single frequency that can be varied between 300 and 600 Hz. The speed of sound is 340 m/s. You find that where you are standing, you hear minimum-intensity sound. (a) Explain why you hear minimum-intensity sound. (b) If one of the speakers is moved 39.8 cm toward you, the sound you hear has maximum intensity. What is the frequency of the sound? (c) How much closer to you from the position in part (b) must the speaker be moved to the next position where you hear maximum intensity?

35.4 • **Radio Interference.** Two radio antennas A and B radiate in phase. Antenna B is 120 m to the right of antenna A. Consider point Q along the extension of the line connecting the antennas, a horizontal distance of 40 m to the right of antenna B. The frequency, and hence the wavelength, of the emitted waves can be varied. (a) What is the longest wavelength for which there will be destructive interference at point Q? (b) What is the longest wavelength for which there will be constructive interference at point Q?

35.5 •• A radio transmitting station operating at a frequency of 120 MHz has two identical antennas that radiate in phase. Antenna B is 9.00 m to the right of antenna A. Consider point P between the antennas and along the line connecting them, a horizontal distance x to the right of antenna A. For what values of x will constructive interference occur at point P?

35.6 • Two light sources can be adjusted to emit monochromatic light of any visible wavelength. The two sources are coherent, 2.04 μm apart, and in line with an observer, so that one source is 2.04 μm farther from the observer than the other. (a) For what visible wavelengths (380 to 750 nm) will the observer see the brightest light, owing to constructive interference? (b) How would your answers to part (a) be affected if the two sources were not in line with the observer, but were still arranged so that one source is 2.04 μm farther away from the observer than the other? (c) For what visible wavelengths will there be *destructive* interference at the location of the observer?

35.7 • Two speakers, emitting identical sound waves of wavelength 2.0 m in phase with each other, and an observer are located as shown in Fig. E35.7. (a) At the observer's location, what is the path difference for waves from the two speakers? (b) Will the sound waves interfere constructively or destructively at the observer's location—or something in between constructive and destructive? (c) Suppose the observer now increases her distance from the closest speaker to 17.0 m, staying directly in front of the same speaker as initially. Answer the questions of parts (a) and (b) for this new situation.

Figure **E35.7**

Observer

8.0 m

6.0 m

35.8 •• Figure 35.3 shows the wave pattern produced by two identical, coherent sources emitting waves with wavelength λ and separated by a distance $d = 4\lambda$. (a) Explain why the positive y-axis above S_1 constitutes an antinodal curve with $m = +4$ and why the negative y-axis below S_2 constitutes an antinodal curve with $m = -4$. (b) Draw the wave pattern produced when the separation between the sources is reduced to 3λ. In your drawing, sketch all antinodal curves—that is, the curves on which $r_2 - r_1 = m\lambda$. Label each curve by its value of m. (c) In general, what determines the maximum (most positive) and minimum (most negative) values of the integer m that labels the antinodal lines? (d) Suppose the separation between the sources is increased to $7\frac{1}{2}\lambda$. How many antinodal curves will there be? To what values of m do they correspond? Explain your reasoning. (You should not have to make a drawing to answer these questions.)

Section 35.2 Two-Source Interference of Light

35.9 • Young's experiment is performed with light from excited helium atoms ($\lambda = 502$ nm). Fringes are measured carefully on a screen 1.20 m away from the double slit, and the center of the 20th fringe (not counting the central bright fringe) is found to be 10.6 mm from the center of the central bright fringe. What is the separation of the two slits?

35.10 •• Coherent light with wavelength 450 nm falls on a double slit. On a screen 1.80 m away, the distance between dark fringes is 4.20 mm. What is the separation of the slits?

35.11 •• Two slits spaced 0.450 mm apart are placed 75.0 cm from a screen. What is the distance between the second and third dark lines of the interference pattern on the screen when the slits are illuminated with coherent light with a wavelength of 500 nm?

35.12 •• If the entire apparatus of Exercise 35.11 (slits, screen, and space in between) is immersed in water, what then is the distance between the second and third dark lines?

35.13 •• Two thin parallel slits that are 0.0116 mm apart are illuminated by a laser beam of wavelength 585 nm. (a) On a very large distant screen, what is the *total* number of bright fringes (those indicating complete constructive interference), including the central fringe and those on both sides of it? Solve this problem without calculating all the angles! (*Hint:* What is the largest that $\sin\theta$ can be? What does this tell you is the largest value of m?) (b) At what angle, relative to the original direction of the beam, will the fringe that is most distant from the central bright fringe occur?

35.14 • Coherent light with wavelength 400 nm passes through two very narrow slits that are separated by 0.200 mm, and the interference pattern is observed on a screen 4.00 m from the slits. (a) What is the width (in mm) of the central interference maximum? (b) What is the width of the first-order bright fringe?

35.15 •• Two very narrow slits are spaced 1.80 μm apart and are placed 35.0 cm from a screen. What is the distance between the first and second dark lines of the interference pattern when the slits are illuminated with coherent light with $\lambda = 550$ nm? (*Hint:* The angle θ in Eq. (35.5) is *not* small.)

35.16 •• Coherent light that contains two wavelengths, 660 nm (red) and 470 nm (blue), passes through two narrow slits separated by 0.300 mm, and the interference pattern is observed on a screen 5.00 m from the slits. What is the distance on the screen between the first-order bright fringes for the two wavelengths?

35.17 •• Coherent light with wavelength 600 nm passes through two very narrow slits and the interference pattern is observed on a screen 3.00 m from the slits. The first-order bright fringe is at 4.84 mm from the center of the central bright fringe. For what wavelength of light will the first-order dark fringe be observed at this same point on the screen?

35.18 •• Coherent light of frequency 6.32×10^{14} Hz passes through two thin slits and falls on a screen 85.0 cm away. You observe that the third bright fringe occurs at ± 3.11 cm on either side of the central bright fringe. (a) How far apart are the two slits? (b) At what distance from the central bright fringe will the third dark fringe occur?

Section 35.3 Intensity in Interference Patterns

35.19 •• In a two-slit interference pattern, the intensity at the peak of the central maximum is I_0. (a) At a point in the pattern where the phase difference between the waves from the two slits is 60.0°, what is the intensity? (b) What is the path difference for 480-nm light from the two slits at a point where the phase angle is 60.0°?

35.20 • Coherent sources A and B emit electromagnetic waves with wavelength 2.00 cm. Point P is 4.86 m from A and 5.24 m from B. What is the phase difference at P between these two waves?

35.21 • Coherent light with wavelength 500 nm passes through narrow slits separated by 0.340 mm. At a distance from the slits large compared to their separation, what is the phase difference (in radians) in the light from the two slits at an angle of 23.0° from the centerline?

35.22 • Two slits spaced 0.260 mm apart are placed 0.700 m from a screen and illuminated by coherent light with a wavelength of 660 nm. The intensity at the center of the central maximum ($\theta = 0°$) is I_0. (a) What is the distance on the screen from the center of the central maximum to the first minimum? (b) What is the distance on the screen from the center of the central maximum to the point where the intensity has fallen to $I_0/2$?

35.23 •• Points A and B are 56.0 m apart along an east-west line. At each of these points, a radio transmitter is emitting a 12.5-MHz signal horizontally. These transmitters are in phase with each other and emit their beams uniformly in a horizontal plane. A receiver is taken 0.500 km north of the AB line and initially placed at point C, directly opposite the midpoint of AB. The receiver can be moved only along an east-west direction but, due to its limited sensitivity, it must always remain within a range so that the intensity of the signal it receives from the transmitter is no less than $\frac{1}{4}$ of its maximum value. How far from point C (along an east-west line) can the receiver be moved and always be able to pick up the signal?

35.24 • Consider two antennas separated by 9.00 m that radiate in phase at 120 MHz, as described in Exercise 35.5. A receiver placed 150 m from both antennas measures an intensity I_0. The receiver is moved so that it is 1.8 m closer to one antenna than to the other. (a) What is the phase difference ϕ between the two radio waves produced by this path difference? (b) In terms of I_0, what is the intensity measured by the receiver at its new position?

Section 35.4 Interference in Thin Films

35.25 • What is the thinnest film of a coating with $n = 1.42$ on glass ($n = 1.52$) for which destructive interference of the red component (650 nm) of an incident white light beam in air can take place by reflection?

35.26 •• **Nonglare Glass.** When viewing a piece of art that is behind glass, one often is affected by the light that is reflected off the front of the glass (called *glare*), which can make it difficult to see the art clearly. One solution is to coat the outer surface of the glass with a film to cancel part of the glare. (a) If the glass has a refractive index of 1.62 and you use TiO_2, which has an index of refraction of 2.62, as the coating, what is the minimum film thickness that will cancel light of wavelength 505 nm? (b) If this coating is too thin to stand up to wear, what other thickness would also work? Find only the three thinnest ones.

35.27 •• Two rectangular pieces of plane glass are laid one upon the other on a table. A thin strip of paper is placed between them at one edge so that a very thin wedge of air is formed. The plates are illuminated at normal incidence by 546-nm light from a mercury-vapor lamp. Interference fringes are formed, with 15.0 fringes per centimeter. Find the angle of the wedge.

35.28 •• A plate of glass 9.00 cm long is placed in contact with a second plate and is held at a small angle with it by a metal strip

0.0800 mm thick placed under one end. The space between the plates is filled with air. The glass is illuminated from above with light having a wavelength in air of 656 nm. How many interference fringes are observed per centimeter in the reflected light?

35.29 •• A uniform film of TiO_2, 1036 nm thick and having index of refraction 2.62, is spread uniformly over the surface of crown glass of refractive index 1.52. Light of wavelength 520.0 nm falls at normal incidence onto the film from air. You want to increase the thickness of this film so that the reflected light cancels. (a) What is the *minimum* thickness of TiO_2 that you must *add* so the reflected light cancels as desired? (b) After you make the adjustment in part (a), what is the path difference between the light reflected off the top of the film and the light that cancels it after traveling through the film? Express your answer in (i) nanometers and (ii) wavelengths of the light in the TiO_2 film.

35.30 • A plastic film with index of refraction 1.85 is put on the surface of a car window to increase the reflectivity and thus to keep the interior of the car cooler. The window glass has index of refraction 1.52. (a) What minimum thickness is required if light with wavelength 550 nm in air reflected from the two sides of the film is to interfere constructively? (b) It is found to be difficult to manufacture and install coatings as thin as calculated in part (a). What is the next greatest thickness for which there will also be constructive interference?

35.31 • The walls of a soap bubble have about the same index of refraction as that of plain water, $n = 1.33$. There is air both inside and outside the bubble. (a) What wavelength (in air) of visible light is most strongly reflected from a point on a soap bubble where its wall is 290 nm thick? To what color does this correspond (see Fig. 32.4 and Table 32.1)? (b) Repeat part (a) for a wall thickness of 340 nm.

35.32 •• Light with wavelength 648 nm in air is incident perpendicularly from air on a film 8.76 μm thick and with refractive index 1.35. Part of the light is reflected from the first surface of the film, and part enters the film and is reflected back at the second surface, where the film is again in contact with air. (a) How many waves are contained along the path of this second part of the light in its round trip through the film? (b) What is the phase difference between these two parts of the light as they leave the film?

35.33 •• **Compact Disc Player.** A compact disc (CD) is read from the bottom by a semiconductor laser with wavelength 790 nm passing through a plastic substrate of refractive index 1.8. When the beam encounters a pit, part of the beam is reflected from the pit and part from the flat region between the pits, so these two beams interfere with each other (Fig. E35.33). What must the minimum pit depth be so that the part of the beam reflected from a pit cancels the part of the beam reflected from the flat region? (It is this cancellation that allows the player to recognize the beginning and end of a pit.)

Figure **E35.33**

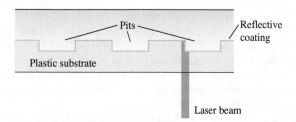

Pits — Reflective coating

Plastic substrate

Laser beam

35.34 • What is the thinnest soap film (excluding the case of zero thickness) that appears black when illuminated with light with

wavelength 480 nm? The index of refraction of the film is 1.33, and there is air on both sides of the film.

Section 35.5 The Michelson Interferometer

35.35 • How far must the mirror M_2 (see Fig. 35.19) of the Michelson interferometer be moved so that 1800 fringes of He-Ne laser light ($\lambda = 633$ nm) move across a line in the field of view?

35.36 • Jan first uses a Michelson interferometer with the 606-nm light from a krypton-86 lamp. He displaces the movable mirror away from him, counting 818 fringes moving across a line in his field of view. Then Linda replaces the krypton lamp with filtered 502-nm light from a helium lamp and displaces the movable mirror toward her. She also counts 818 fringes, but they move across the line in her field of view opposite to the direction they moved for Jan. Assume that both Jan and Linda counted to 818 correctly. (a) What distance did each person move the mirror? (b) What is the resultant displacement of the mirror?

PROBLEMS

35.37 ••• The radius of curvature of the convex surface of a planoconvex lens is 68.4 cm. The lens is placed convex side down on a perfectly flat glass plate that is illuminated from above with red light having a wavelength of 580 nm. Find the diameter of the second bright ring in the interference pattern.

35.38 •• Newton's rings can be seen when a planoconvex lens is placed on a flat glass surface. For a particular lens with an index of refraction of $n = 1.50$ and a glass plate with an index of $n = 1.80$, the diameter of the third bright ring is 0.720 mm. If water ($n = 1.33$) now fills the space between the lens and the plate, what is the new diameter of this ring?

35.39 • **BIO** **Coating Eyeglass Lenses.** Eyeglass lenses can be coated on the *inner* surfaces to reduce the reflection of stray light to the eye. If the lenses are medium flint glass of refractive index 1.62 and the coating is fluorite of refractive index 1.432, (a) what minimum thickness of film is needed on the lenses to cancel light of wavelength 550 nm reflected toward the eye at normal incidence? (b) Will any other wavelengths of visible light be cancelled or enhanced in the reflected light?

35.40 •• **BIO** **Sensitive Eyes.** After an eye examination, you put some eyedrops on your sensitive eyes. The cornea (the front part of the eye) has an index of refraction of 1.38, while the eyedrops have a refractive index of 1.45. After you put in the drops, your friends notice that your eyes look red, because red light of wavelength 600 nm has been reinforced in the reflected light. (a) What is the minimum thickness of the film of eyedrops on your cornea? (b) Will any other wavelengths of visible light be reinforced in the reflected light? Will any be cancelled? (c) Suppose you had contact lenses, so that the eyedrops went on them instead of on your corneas. If the refractive index of the lens material is 1.50 and the layer of eyedrops has the same thickness as in part (a), what wavelengths of visible light will be reinforced? What wavelengths will be cancelled?

35.41 •• Two flat plates of glass with parallel faces are on a table, one plate on the other. Each plate is 11.0 cm long and has a refractive index of 1.55. A very thin sheet of metal foil is inserted under the end of the upper plate to raise it slightly at that end, in a manner similar to that discussed in Example 35.4. When you view the glass plates from above with reflected white light, you observe that, at 1.15 mm from the line where the sheets are in contact, the violet light of wavelength 400.0 nm is enhanced in this reflected light, but no visible light is enhanced closer to the line of contact.

(a) How far from the line of contact will green light (of wavelength 550 nm) and orange light (of wavelength 600.0 nm) first be enhanced? (b) How far from the line of contact will the violet, green, and orange light again be enhanced in the reflected light? (c) How thick is the metal foil holding the ends of the plates apart?

35.42 •• In a setup similar to that of Problem 35.41, the glass has an index of refraction of 1.53, the plates are each 8.00 cm long, and the metal foil is 0.015 mm thick. The space between the plates is filled with a jelly whose refractive index is not known precisely, but is known to be greater than that of the glass. When you illuminate these plates from above with light of wavelength 525 nm, you observe a series of equally spaced dark fringes in the reflected light. You measure the spacing of these fringes and find that there are 10 of them every 6.33 mm. What is the index of refraction of the jelly?

35.43 ••• Suppose you illuminate two thin slits by monochromatic coherent light in air and find that they produce their first interference *minima* at ±35.20° on either side of the central bright spot. You then immerse these slits in a transparent liquid and illuminate them with the same light. Now you find that the first minima occur at ±19.46° instead. What is the index of refraction of this liquid?

35.44 •• CP CALC A very thin sheet of brass contains two thin parallel slits. When a laser beam shines on these slits at normal incidence and room temperature (20.0°C), the first interference dark fringes occur at ±32.5° from the original direction of the laser beam when viewed from some distance. If this sheet is now slowly heated up to 135°C, by how many degrees do these dark fringes change position? Do they move closer together or get farther apart? See Table 17.1 for pertinent information, and ignore any effects that might occur due to change in the thickness of the slits. (*Hint:* Since thermal expansion normally produces very small changes in length, you can use differentials to find the change in the angle.)

35.45 •• Two speakers, 2.50 m apart, are driven by the same audio oscillator so that each one produces a sound consisting of *two* distinct frequencies, 0.900 kHz and 1.20 kHz. The speed of sound in the room is 344 m/s. Find all the angles relative to the usual centerline in front of (and far from) the speakers at which *both* frequencies interfere constructively.

35.46 •• Two radio antennas radiating in phase are located at points A and B, 200 m apart (Fig. P35.46). The radio waves have a frequency of 5.80 MHz. A radio receiver is moved out from point B along a line perpendicular to the line connecting A and B (line BC shown in Fig. P35.46). At what distances from B will there be *destructive* interference? (*Note:* The distance of the receiver from the sources is not large in comparison to the separation of the sources, so Eq. (35.5) does not apply.)

Figure **P35.46**

35.47 •• One round face of a 3.25-m, solid, cylindrical plastic pipe is covered with a thin black coating that completely blocks light. The opposite face is covered with a fluorescent coating that glows when it is struck by light. Two straight, thin, parallel scratches, 0.225 mm apart, are made in the center of the black face. When laser light of wavelength 632.8 nm shines through the slits perpendicular to the black face, you find that the central bright fringe on the opposite face is 5.82 mm wide, measured between the dark fringes that border it on either side. What is the index of refraction of the plastic?

35.48 • A uniform thin film of material of refractive index 1.40 coats a glass plate of refractive index 1.55. This film has the proper thickness to cancel normally incident light of wavelength 525 nm that strikes the film surface from air, but it is somewhat greater than the minimum thickness to achieve this cancellation. As time goes by, the film wears away at a steady rate of 4.20 nm per year. What is the minimum number of years before the reflected light of this wavelength is now enhanced instead of cancelled?

35.49 •• Two speakers A and B are 3.50 m apart, and each one is emitting a frequency of 444 Hz. However, because of signal delays in the cables, speaker A is one-fourth of a period *ahead* of speaker B. For points far from the speakers, find all the angles relative to the centerline (Fig. P35.49) at which the sound from these speakers cancels. Include angles on *both* sides of the centerline. The speed of sound is 340 m/s.

Figure **P35.49**

35.50 ••• CP The electric fields received at point P from two identical, coherent wave sources are $E_1(t) = E\cos(\omega t + \phi)$ and $E_2(t) = E\cos\omega t$. (a) Use the trigonometric identities in Appendix B to show that the resultant wave is $E_P(t) = 2E\cos(\phi/2)\cos(\omega t + \phi/2)$. (b) Show that the amplitude of this resultant wave is given by Eq. (35.7). (c) Use the result of part (a) to show that at an interference maximum, the amplitude of the resultant wave is in phase with the original waves $E_1(t)$ and $E_2(t)$. (d) Use the result of part (a) to show that near an interference minimum, the resultant wave is approximately $\frac{1}{4}$ cycle out of phase with either of the original waves. (e) Show that the *instantaneous* Poynting vector at point P has magnitude $S = 4\epsilon_0 c E^2\cos^2(\phi/2)\cos^2(\omega t + \phi/2)$ and that the *time-averaged* Poynting vector is given by Eq. (35.9).

35.51 •• CP A thin uniform film of refractive index 1.750 is placed on a sheet of glass of refractive index 1.50. At room temperature (20.0°C), this film is just thick enough for light with wavelength 582.4 nm reflected off the top of the film to be cancelled by light reflected from the top of the glass. After the glass is placed in an oven and slowly heated to 170°C, you find that the film cancels reflected light with wavelength 588.5 nm. What is the coefficient of linear expansion of the film? (Ignore any changes in the refractive index of the film due to the temperature change.)

35.52 ••• **GPS Transmission.** The GPS (Global Positioning System) satellites are approximately 5.18 m across and transmit two low-power signals, one of which is at 1575.42 MHz (in the UHF band). In a series of laboratory tests on the satellite, you put two 1575.42-MHz UHF transmitters at opposite ends of the satellite. These broadcast in phase uniformly in all directions. You measure the intensity at points on a circle that is several hundred meters in radius and centered on the satellite. You measure angles on this circle relative to a point that lies along the centerline of the satellite (that is, the perpendicular bisector of a line that extends from one transmitter to the other). At this point on the circle, the measured intensity is 2.00 W/m². (a) At how many other angles in the range 0° < θ < 90° is the intensity also 2.00 W/m²? (b) Find the four smallest angles in the range 0° < θ < 90° for which the intensity is 2.00 W/m². (c) What is the intensity at a point on the circle at an angle of 4.65° from the centerline?

35.53 •• Consider a two-slit interference pattern, for which the intensity distribution is given by Eq. (35.14). Let θ_m be the angular position of the mth bright fringe, where the intensity is I_0. Assume that θ_m is small, so that $\sin \theta_m \cong \theta_m$. Let $\theta_m{}^+$ and $\theta_m{}^-$ be the two angles on either side of θ_m for which $I = \frac{1}{2}I_0$. The quantity $\Delta \theta_m = |\theta_m{}^+ - \theta_m{}^-|$ is the half-width of the mth fringe. Calculate $\Delta \theta_m$. How does $\Delta \theta_m$ depend on m?

35.54 •• White light reflects at normal incidence from the top and bottom surfaces of a glass plate ($n = 1.52$). There is air above and below the plate. Constructive interference is observed for light whose wavelength in air is 477.0 nm. What is the thickness of the plate if the next longer wavelength for which there is constructive interference is 540.6 nm?

35.55 ••• A source S of monochromatic light and a detector D are both located in air a distance h above a horizontal plane sheet of glass and are separated by a horizontal distance x. Waves reaching D directly from S interfere with waves that reflect off the glass. The distance x is small compared to h so that the reflection is at close to normal incidence. (a) Show that the condition for constructive interference is $\sqrt{x^2 + 4h^2} - x = \left(m + \frac{1}{2}\right)\lambda$, and the condition for destructive interference is $\sqrt{x^2 + 4h^2} - x = m\lambda$. (*Hint:* Take into account the phase change on reflection.) (b) Let $h = 24$ cm and $x = 14$ cm. What is the longest wavelength for which there will be constructive interference?

35.56 •• **BIO** **Reflective Coatings and Herring.** Herring and related fish have a brilliant silvery appearance that camouflages them while they are swimming in a sunlit ocean. The silveriness is due to *platelets* attached to the surfaces of these fish. Each platelet is made up of several alternating layers of crystalline guanine ($n = 1.80$) and of cytoplasm ($n = 1.333$, the same as water), with a guanine layer on the outside in contact with the surrounding water (Fig. P35.56). In one typical platelet, the guanine layers are 74 nm thick and the cytoplasm layers are 100 nm thick. (a) For light striking the platelet surface at normal incidence, for which vacuum wavelengths of visible light will all of the reflections R_1, R_2, R_3, R_4, and R_5, shown in Fig. P35.56, be approximately in phase? If white light is shone on this platelet, what color will be most strongly reflected (see Fig. 32.4)? The surface of a herring has very many platelets side by side with layers of different thickness, so that *all* visible wavelengths are reflected. (b) Explain why such a "stack" of layers is more reflective than a single layer of guanine with cytoplasm underneath. (A stack of five guanine layers separated by cytoplasm layers reflects more than 80% of incident light at the wavelength for which it is "tuned.") (c) The color that is most strongly reflected from a platelet depends on the angle at which it is viewed. Explain why this should be so. (You can see these changes in color by examining a herring from different

Figure **P35.56**

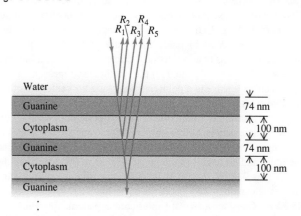

angles. Most of the platelets on these fish are oriented in the same way, so that they are vertical when the fish is swimming.)

35.57 • Two thin parallel slits are made in an opaque sheet of film. When a monochromatic beam of light is shone through them at normal incidence, the first bright fringes in the transmitted light occur in air at $\pm 18.0°$ with the original direction of the light beam on a distant screen when the apparatus is in air. When the apparatus is immersed in a liquid, the same bright fringes now occur at $\pm 12.6°$. Find the index of refraction of the liquid.

35.58 •• Red light with wavelength 700 nm is passed through a two-slit apparatus. At the same time, monochromatic visible light with another wavelength passes through the same apparatus. As a result, most of the pattern that appears on the screen is a mixture of two colors; however, the center of the third bright fringe ($m = 3$) of the red light appears pure red, with none of the other color. What are the possible wavelengths of the second type of visible light? Do you need to know the slit spacing to answer this question? Why or why not?

35.59 ••• In a Young's two-slit experiment a piece of glass with an index of refraction n and a thickness L is placed in front of the upper slit. (a) Describe qualitatively what happens to the interference pattern. (b) Derive an expression for the intensity I of the light at points on a screen as a function of n, L, and θ. Here θ is the usual angle measured from the center of the two slits. That is, determine the equation analogous to Eq. (35.14) but that also involves L and n for the glass plate. (c) From your result in part (b) derive an expression for the values of θ that locate the maxima in the interference pattern [that is, derive an equation analogous to Eq. (35.4)].

35.60 •• After a laser beam passes through two thin parallel slits, the first completely dark fringes occur at $\pm 19.0°$ with the original direction of the beam, as viewed on a screen far from the slits. (a) What is the ratio of the distance between the slits to the wavelength of the light illuminating the slits? (b) What is the smallest angle, relative to the original direction of the laser beam, at which the intensity of the light is $\frac{1}{10}$ the maximum intensity on the screen?

CHALLENGE PROBLEMS

35.61 ••• **CP** The index of refraction of a glass rod is 1.48 at $T = 20.0°$C and varies linearly with temperature, with a coefficient of $2.50 \times 10^{-5}/$C°. The coefficient of linear expansion of the glass is $5.00 \times 10^{-6}/$C°. At 20.0°C the length of the rod is 3.00 cm. A Michelson interferometer has this glass rod in one arm, and the rod is being heated so that its temperature increases at a rate of 5.00 C°/min. The light source has wavelength $\lambda = 589$ nm, and the rod initially is at $T = 20.0°$C. How many fringes cross the field of view each minute?

35.62 ••• **CP** Figure P35.62 shows an interferometer known as *Fresnel's biprism.* The magnitude of the prism angle A is

Figure **P35.62**

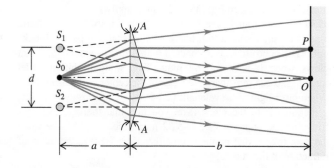

extremely small. (a) If S_0 is a very narrow source slit, show that the separation of the two virtual coherent sources S_1 and S_2 is given by $d = 2aA(n - 1)$, where n is the index of refraction of the material of the prism. (b) Calculate the spacing of the fringes of green light with wavelength 500 nm on a screen 2.00 m from the biprism. Take $a = 0.200$ m, $A = 3.50$ mrad, and $n = 1.50$.

Answers

Chapter Opening Question ?

The colors appear due to constructive interference between light waves reflected from the outer and inner surfaces of the soap bubble. The thickness of the bubble walls at each point determines the wavelength of light for which the most constructive interference occurs and hence the color that appears the brightest at that point (see Example 35.4 in Section 35.4).

Test Your Understanding Questions

35.1 Answer: (i) At any point P on the positive y-axis above S_1, the distance r_2 from S_2 to P is greater than the distance r_1 from S_1 to P by 4λ. This corresponds to $m = 4$ in Eq. (35.1), the equation for constructive interference. Hence all such points make up an antinodal curve.

35.2 Answer: (ii) Blue light has a shorter wavelength than red light (see Section 32.1). Equation (35.6) tells us that the distance y_m from the center of the pattern to the mth bright fringe is proportional to the wavelength λ. Hence all of the fringes will move toward the center of the pattern as the wavelength decreases, and the spacing between fringes will decrease.

35.3 Answer: (i), (iv), (ii), (iii) In cases (i) and (iii) we are given the wavelength λ and path difference $d\sin\theta$. Hence we use Eq. (35.14), $I = I_0\cos^2[(\pi d\sin\theta)/\lambda]$. In parts (ii) and (iii) we are given the phase difference ϕ and we use Eq. (35.10), $I = I_0\cos^2(\phi/2)$. We find:

(i) $I = I_0\cos^2[\pi(4.00 \times 10^{-7}$ m$)/(5.00 \times 10^{-7}$ m$)] = I_0\cos^2(0.800\pi$ rad$) = 0.655I_0$;

(ii) $I = I_0\cos^2[(4.00$ rad$)/2] = I_0\cos^2(2.00$ rad$) = 0.173I_0$;

(iii) $I = I_0\cos^2[\pi(7.50 \times 10^{-7}$ m$)/(5.00 \times 10^{-7}$ m$)] = I_0\cos^2(1.50\pi$ rad$) = 0$;

(iv) $I = I_0\cos^2[(2.00$ rad$)/2] = I_0\cos^2(1.00$ rad$) = 0.292I_0$.

35.4 Answers: (i) and (iii) Benzene has a larger index of refraction than air, so light that reflects off the upper surface of the benzene undergoes a half-cycle phase shift. Fluorite has a *smaller* index of refraction than benzene, so light that reflects off the benzene–fluorite interface does not undergo a phase shift. Hence the equation for constructive reflection is Eq. (35.18a), $2t = \left(m + \frac{1}{2}\right)\lambda$, which we can rewrite as $t = \left(m + \frac{1}{2}\right)\lambda/2 = \left(m + \frac{1}{2}\right)(400$ mm$)/2 = 100$ nm, 300 nm, 500 nm, ...

35.5 Answer: yes Changing the index of refraction changes the wavelength of the light inside the compensator plate, and so changes the number of wavelengths within the thickness of the plate. Hence this has the same effect as changing the distance L_1 from the beam splitter to mirror M_1, which would change the interference pattern.

Bridging Problem

Answers: (a) 441 nm **(b)** 551 nm

39 PARTICLES BEHAVING AS WAVES

LEARNING GOALS

By studying this chapter, you will learn:

- De Broglie's proposal that electrons, protons, and other particles can behave like waves.

- How electron diffraction experiments provided evidence for de Broglie's ideas.

- How electron microscopes can provide much higher magnification than visible-light microscopes.

- How physicists discovered the atomic nucleus.

- How Bohr's model of electron orbits explained the spectra of hydrogen and hydrogenlike atoms.

- How a laser operates.

- How the idea of energy levels, coupled with the photon model of light, explains the spectrum of light emitted by a hot, opaque object.

- What the uncertainty principle tells us about the nature of the atom.

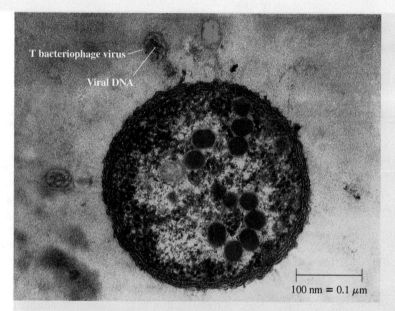

T bacteriophage virus

Viral DNA

100 nm = 0.1 μm

? Viruses (shown in blue) have landed on an *E. coli* bacterium and injected their DNA, converting the bacterium into a virus factory. This false-color image was made using a beam of electrons rather than a light beam. What properties of electrons make them useful for imaging such fine details?

I n Chapter 38 we discovered one aspect of nature's wave–particle duality: Light and other electromagnetic radiation act sometimes like waves and sometimes like particles. Interference and diffraction demonstrate wave behavior, while emission and absorption of photons demonstrate particle behavior.

If light waves can behave like particles, can the particles of matter behave like waves? As we will discover, the answer is a resounding yes. Electrons can be made to interfere and diffract just like other kinds of waves. We will see that the wave nature of electrons is not merely a laboratory curiosity: It is the fundamental reason why atoms, which according to classical physics should be profoundly unstable, are able to exist. In this chapter we'll use the wave nature of matter to help us understand the structure of atoms, the operating principles of a laser, and the curious properties of the light emitted by a heated, glowing object. Without the wave picture of matter, there would be no way to explain these phenomena.

In Chapter 40 we'll introduce an even more complete wave picture of matter called *quantum mechanics*. Through the remainder of this book we'll use the ideas of quantum mechanics to understand the nature of molecules, solids, atomic nuclei, and the fundamental particles that are the building blocks of our universe.

39.4 The Laser

PhET: Lasers

The **laser** is a light source that produces a beam of highly coherent and very nearly monochromatic light as a result of cooperative emission from many atoms. The name "laser" is an acronym for "light amplification by stimulated emission of radiation." We can understand the principles of laser operation from what we have learned about atomic energy levels and photons. To do this we'll have to introduce two new concepts: *stimulated emission* and *population inversion.*

Spontaneous and Stimulated Emission

Consider a gas of atoms in a transparent container. Each atom is initially in its ground level of energy E_g and also has an excited level of energy E_{ex}. If we shine light of frequency f on the container, an atom can absorb one of the photons provided the photon energy $E = hf$ equals the energy difference $E_{ex} - E_g$ between the levels. Figure 39.28a shows this process, in which three atoms A each absorb a photon and go into the excited level. Some time later, the excited atoms (which we denote as A*) return to the ground level by each emitting a photon with the same frequency as the one originally absorbed (Fig. 39.28b). This process is called **spontaneous emission.** The direction and phase of the spontaneously emitted photons are random.

In **stimulated emission** (Fig. 39.28c), each incident photon encounters a previously excited atom. A kind of resonance effect induces each atom to emit a second photon with the same frequency, direction, phase, and polarization as the incident photon, which is not changed by the process. For each atom there is one photon before a stimulated emission and two photons after—thus the name *light amplification.* Because the two photons have the same phase, they emerge together as *coherent* radiation. The laser makes use of stimulated emission to produce a beam consisting of a large number of such coherent photons.

To discuss stimulated emission from atoms in excited levels, we need to know something about how many atoms are in each of the various energy levels. First, we need to make the distinction between the terms *energy level* and *state*. A system may have more than one way to attain a given energy level; each different way is a different **state.** For instance, there are two ways of putting an ideal unstretched spring in a given energy level. Remembering that the spring potential energy is $U = \frac{1}{2}kx^2$, we could compress the spring by $x = -b$ or we could stretch it by $x = +b$ to get the same $U = \frac{1}{2}kb^2$. The Bohr model had only one state in each energy level, but we will find in Chapter 41 that the hydrogen atom (Fig. 39.24b) actually has two states in its -13.60-eV ground level, eight states in its -3.40-eV first exited level, and so on.

The Maxwell–Boltzmann distribution function (see Section 18.5) determines the number of atoms in a given state in a gas. The function tells us that when the gas is in thermal equilibrium at absolute temperature T, the number n_i of atoms in a state with energy E_i equals $Ae^{-E_i/kT}$, where k is Boltzmann's constant and A is another constant determined by the total number of atoms in the gas. (In Section 18.5, E was the kinetic energy $\frac{1}{2}mv^2$ of a gas molecule; here we're talking about the internal energy of an atom.) Because of the negative exponent, fewer atoms are in higher-energy states, as we should expect. If E_g is a ground-state energy and E_{ex} is the energy of an excited state, then the ratio of numbers of atoms in the two states is

$$\frac{n_{ex}}{n_g} = \frac{Ae^{-E_{ex}/kT}}{Ae^{-E_g/kT}} = e^{-(E_{ex}-E_g)/kT} \tag{39.18}$$

39.28 Three processes in which atoms interact with light.

(a) Absorption

Atom in its ground level

(b) Spontaneous emission

Atom in an excited level

(c) Stimulated emission

For example, suppose $E_{ex} - E_g = 2.0\,\text{eV} = 3.2 \times 10^{-19}\,\text{J}$, the energy of a 620-nm visible-light photon. At $T = 3000\,\text{K}$ (the temperature of the filament in an incandescent light bulb),

$$\frac{E_{ex} - E_g}{kT} = \frac{3.2 \times 10^{-19}\,\text{J}}{(1.38 \times 10^{-23}\,\text{J/K})(3000\,\text{K})} = 7.73$$

and

$$e^{-(E_{ex}-E_g)/kT} = e^{-7.73} = 0.00044$$

That is, the fraction of atoms in a state 2.0 eV above a ground state is extremely small, even at this high temperature. The point is that at any reasonable temperature there aren't enough atoms in excited states for any appreciable amount of stimulated emission from these states to occur. Rather, a photon emitted by one of the rare excited atoms will almost certainly be absorbed by an atom in the ground state rather than encountering another excited atom.

Enhancing Stimulated Emission: Population Inversions

To make a laser, we need to promote stimulated emission by increasing the number of atoms in excited states. Can we do that simply by illuminating the container with radiation of frequency $f = E/h$ corresponding to the energy difference $E = E_{ex} - E_g$, as in Fig. 39.28a? Some of the atoms absorb photons of energy E and are raised to the excited state, and the population ratio n_{ex}/n_g momentarily increases. But because n_g is originally so much larger than n_{ex}, an enormously intense beam of light would be required to momentarily increase n_{ex} to a value comparable to n_g. The rate at which energy is *absorbed* from the beam by the n_g ground-state atoms far exceeds the rate at which energy is added to the beam by stimulated emission from the relatively rare (n_{ex}) excited atoms.

We need to create a *nonequilibrium* situation in which the number of atoms in a higher-energy state is greater than the number in a lower-energy state. Such a situation is called a **population inversion.** Then the rate of energy radiation by stimulated emission can *exceed* the rate of absorption, and the system will act as a net *source* of radiation with photon energy E. It turns out that we can achieve a population inversion by starting with atoms that have the right kinds of excited states. Figure 39.29a shows an energy-level diagram for such an atom with a ground state and *three* excited states of energies E_1, E_2, and E_3. A laser that uses a material with energy levels like these is called a *four-level laser*. For the laser action to work, the states of energies E_1 and E_3 must have ordinary short lifetimes of about 10^{-8} s, while the state of energy E_2 must have an unusually long lifetime of 10^{-3} s or so. Such a long-lived **metastable state** can occur if, for instance, there are restrictions imposed by conservation of angular momentum that hinder photon emission from this state. (We'll discuss these restrictions in Chapter 41.) The metastable state is the one that we want to populate.

To produce a population inversion, we *pump* the material to excite the atoms out of the ground state into the states of energies E_1, E_2, and E_3 (Fig. 39.29b). If the atoms are in a gas, this pumping can be done by inserting two electrodes into the gas container. When a burst of sufficiently high voltage is applied to the electrodes, an electric discharge occurs. Collisions between ionized atoms and electrons carrying the discharge current then excite the atoms to various energy states. Within about 10^{-8} s the atoms that are excited to states E_1 and E_3 undergo spontaneous photon emission, so these states end up depopulated. But atoms "pile up" in the metastable state with energy E_2. The number of atoms in the metastable state is *less* than the number in the ground state, but is *much greater* than in the nearly unoccupied state of energy E_1. Hence there is a population inversion of state E_2 relative to state E_1 (Fig. 39.29c). You can see why we need

39.29 (a), (b), (c) Stages in the operation of a four-level laser. (d) The light emitted by atoms making spontaneous transitions from state E_2 to state E_1 is reflected between mirrors, so it continues to stimulate emission and gives rise to coherent light. One mirror is partially transmitting and allows the high-intensity light beam to escape.

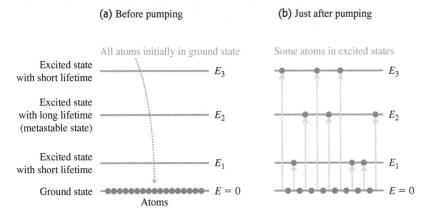

(a) Before pumping

(b) Just after pumping

(c) About 10^{-8} s after pumping

(d) Schematic of gas laser

the two levels E_1 and E_3: atoms that undergo spontaneous emission from the E_3 level help to populate the E_2 level, and the presence of the E_1 level makes a population inversion possible.

Over the next 10^{-3} s, some of the atoms in the long-lived metastable state E_2 transition to state E_1 by spontaneous emission. The emitted photons of energy $hf = E_2 - E_1$ are sent back and forth through the gas many times by a pair of parallel mirrors (Fig. 39.29d), so that they can *stimulate* emission from as many of the atoms in state E_2 as possible. The net result of all these processes is a beam of light of frequency f that can be quite intense, has parallel rays, is highly monochromatic, and is spatially *coherent* at all points within a given cross section—that is, a laser beam. One of the mirrors is partially transparent, so a portion of the beam emerges.

What we've described is a *pulsed* laser that produces a burst of coherent light every time the atoms are pumped. Pulsed lasers are used in LASIK eye surgery (an acronym for *laser-assisted in situ keratomileusis*) to reshape the cornea and correct for nearsightedness, farsightedness, or astigmatism. In a *continuous* laser, such as those found in the barcode scanners used at retail checkout counters, energy is supplied to the atoms continuously (for instance, by having the power supply in Fig. 39.29d provide a steady voltage to the electrodes) and a steady beam of light emerges from the laser. For such a laser the pumping must be intense enough to sustain the population inversion, so that the rate at which atoms are added to level E_2 through pumping equals the rate at which atoms in this level emit a photon and transition to level E_1.

Since a special arrangement of energy levels is needed for laser action, it's not surprising that only certain materials can be used to make a laser. Some types of laser use a solid, transparent material such as neodymium glass rather than a gas. The most common kind of laser—used in laser printers (Section 21.2), laser pointers, and to read the data on the disc in a DVD player or Blu-ray player—is a *semiconductor laser,* which doesn't use atomic energy levels at all. As we'll discuss in Chapter 42, these lasers instead use the energy levels of electrons that are free to roam throughout the volume of the semiconductors.

Test Your Understanding of Section 39.4 An ordinary neon light fixture like those used in advertising signs emits red light of wavelength 632.8 nm. Neon atoms are also used in a helium–neon laser (a type of gas laser). The light emitted by a neon light fixture is (i) spontaneous emission; (ii) stimulated emission; (iii) both spontaneous and stimulated emission.

PhET: Blackbody Spectrum
PhET: The Greenhouse Effect

39.30 A hollow box with a small aperture behaves like a blackbody. When the box is heated, the electromagnetic radiation that emerges from the aperture has a blackbody spectrum.

Hollow box with small aperture
(cross section)

Light that enters box is eventually absorbed. Hence box approximates a perfect blackbody.

39.31 This close-up view of the sun's surface shows two dark sunspots. Their temperature is about 4000 K, while the surrounding solar material is at $T = 5800$ K. From the Stefan–Boltzmann law, the intensity from a given area of sunspot is only $(4000 \text{ K}/5800 \text{ K})^4 = 0.23$ as great as the intensity from the same area of the surrounding material—which is why sunspots appear dark.

39.5 Continuous Spectra

Emission line spectra come from matter in the gaseous state, in which the atoms are so far apart that interactions between them are negligible and each atom behaves as an isolated system. By contrast, a heated solid or liquid (in which atoms are close to each other) nearly always emits radiation with a *continuous* distribution of wavelengths rather than a line spectrum.

Here's an analogy that suggests why there is a difference. A tuning fork emits sound waves of a single definite frequency (a pure tone) when struck. But if you tightly pack a suitcase full of tuning forks and then shake the suitcase, the proximity of the tuning forks to each other affects the sound that they produce. What you hear is mostly noise, which is sound with a continuous distribution of all frequencies. In the same manner, isolated atoms in a gas emit light of certain distinct frequencies when excited, but if the same atoms are crowded together in a solid or liquid they produce a continuous spectrum of light.

In this section we'll study an idealized case of continuous-spectrum radiation from a hot, dense object. Just as was the case for the emission line spectrum of light from an atom, we'll find that we can understand the continuous spectrum only if we use the ideas of energy levels and photons.

In the same way that an atom's emission spectrum has the same lines as its absorption spectrum, the ideal surface for *emitting* light with a continuous spectrum is one that also *absorbs* all wavelengths of electromagnetic radiation. Such an ideal surface is called a *blackbody* because it would appear perfectly black when illuminated; it would reflect no light at all. The continuous-spectrum radiation that a blackbody emits is called **blackbody radiation.** Like a perfectly frictionless incline or a massless rope, a perfect blackbody does not exist but is nonetheless a useful idealization.

A good approximation to a blackbody is a hollow box with a small aperture in one wall (Fig. 39.30). Light that enters the aperture will eventually be absorbed by the walls of the box, so the box is a nearly perfect absorber. Conversely, when we heat the box, the light that emanates from the aperture is nearly ideal blackbody radiation with a continuous spectrum.

By 1900 blackbody radiation had been studied extensively, and three characteristics had been established. First, the total intensity I (the average rate of radiation of energy per unit surface area or average power per area) emitted from the surface of an ideal radiator is proportional to the fourth power of the absolute temperature (Fig. 39.31). We studied this relationship in Section 17.7 during our study of heat-transfer mechanisms. This total intensity I emitted at absolute temperature T is given by the **Stefan–Boltzmann law:**

$$I = \sigma T^4 \qquad \text{(Stefan–Boltzmann law for a blackbody)} \qquad (39.19)$$

where σ is a fundamental physical constant called the *Stefan–Boltzmann constant.* In SI units,

$$\sigma = 5.670400(40) \times 10^{-8} \frac{\text{W}}{\text{m}^2 \cdot \text{K}^4}$$

Second, the intensity is not uniformly distributed over all wavelengths. Its distribution can be measured and described by the intensity per wavelength interval $I(\lambda)$, called the *spectral emittance.* Thus $I(\lambda)\,d\lambda$ is the intensity corresponding to wavelengths in the interval from λ to $\lambda + d\lambda$. The *total* intensity I, given by Eq. (39.19), is the *integral* of the distribution function $I(\lambda)$ over all wavelengths, which equals the area under the $I(\lambda)$ versus λ curve:

$$I = \int_0^\infty I(\lambda)\,d\lambda \qquad (39.20)$$

CAUTION **Spectral emittance vs. intensity** Although we use the symbol $I(\lambda)$ for spectral emittance, keep in mind that spectral emittance is *not* the same thing as intensity I. Intensity is power per unit area, with units W/m^2. Spectral emittance is power per unit area *per unit wavelength interval*, with units W/m^3. ▮

Figure 39.32 shows the measured spectral emittances $I(\lambda)$ for blackbody radiation at three different temperatures. Each has a peak wavelength λ_m at which the emitted intensity per wavelength interval is largest. Experiment shows that λ_m is inversely proportional to T, so their product is constant. This observation is called the **Wien displacement law.** The experimental value of the constant is 2.90×10^{-3} m $\cdot$ K:

$$\lambda_m T = 2.90 \times 10^{-3} \text{ m} \cdot \text{K} \qquad \text{(Wien displacement law)} \qquad (39.21)$$

As the temperature rises, the peak of $I(\lambda)$ becomes higher and shifts to shorter wavelengths. Yellow light has shorter wavelengths than red light, so a body that glows yellow is hotter and brighter than one of the same size that glows red.

Third, experiments show that the *shape* of the distribution function is the same for all temperatures. We can make a curve for one temperature fit any other temperature by simply changing the scales on the graph.

Rayleigh and the "Ultraviolet Catastrophe"

During the last decade of the 19th century, many attempts were made to derive these empirical results about blackbody radiation from basic principles. In one attempt, the English physicist Lord Rayleigh considered the light enclosed within a rectangular box like that shown in Fig. 39.30. Such a box, he reasoned, has a series of possible *normal modes* for electromagnetic waves, as we discussed in Section 32.5. It also seemed reasonable to assume that the distribution of energy among the various modes would be given by the equipartition principle (see Section 18.4), which had been used successfully in the analysis of heat capacities.

Including both the electric- and magnetic-field energies, Rayleigh assumed that the total energy of each normal mode was equal to kT. Then by computing the *number* of normal modes corresponding to a wavelength interval $d\lambda$, Rayleigh calculated the expected distribution of wavelengths in the radiation within the box. Finally, he computed the predicted intensity distribution $I(\lambda)$ for the radiation emerging from the hole. His result was quite simple:

$$I(\lambda) = \frac{2\pi ckT}{\lambda^4} \qquad \text{(Rayleigh's calculation)} \qquad (39.22)$$

At large wavelengths this formula agrees quite well with the experimental results shown in Fig. 39.32, but there is serious disagreement at small wavelengths. The experimental curves in Fig. 39.32 fall toward zero at small λ. By contrast, Rayleigh's prediction in Eq. (39.22) goes in the opposite direction, approaching infinity at $1/\lambda^4$, a result that was called in Rayleigh's time the "ultraviolet catastrophe." Even worse, the integral of Eq. (39.22) over all λ is infinite, indicating an infinitely large *total* radiated intensity. Clearly, something is wrong.

Planck and the Quantum Hypothesis

Finally, in 1900, the German physicist Max Planck succeeded in deriving a function, now called the **Planck radiation law,** that agreed very well with experimental intensity distribution curves. In his derivation he made what seemed at the time to be a crazy assumption. Planck assumed that electromagnetic oscillators (electrons) in the walls of Rayleigh's box vibrating at a frequency f could have only certain values of energy equal to nhf, where $n = 0, 1, 2, 3, \ldots$ and h turned

39.32 These graphs show the spectral emittance $I(\lambda)$ for radiation from a blackbody at three different temperatures.

As the temperature increases, the peak of the spectral emittance curve becomes higher and shifts to shorter wavelengths.

Dashed blue lines are values of λ_m in Eq. (39.21) for each temperature.

out to be the constant that now bears Planck's name. These oscillators were in equilibrium with the electromagnetic waves in the box, so they both emitted and absorbed light. His assumption gave quantized energy levels and said that the energy in each normal mode was also a multiple of hf. This was in sharp contrast to Rayleigh's point of view that each normal mode could have any amount of energy.

Planck was not comfortable with this quantum hypothesis; he regarded it as a calculational trick rather than a fundamental principle. In a letter to a friend, he called it "an act of desperation" into which he was forced because "a theoretical explanation had to be found at any cost, whatever the price." But five years later, Einstein identified the energy change hf between levels as the energy of a photon to explain the photoelectric effect (see Section 38.1), and other evidence quickly mounted. By 1915 there was little doubt about the validity of the quantum concept and the existence of photons. By discussing atomic spectra *before* continuous spectra, we have departed from the historical order of things. The credit for inventing the concept of quantization of energy levels goes to Planck, even though he didn't believe it at first. He received the 1918 Nobel Prize in physics for his achievements.

Figure 39.33 shows energy-level diagrams for two of the oscillators that Planck envisioned in the walls of the rectangular box, one with a low frequency and the other with a high frequency. The spacing in energy between adjacent levels is hf. This spacing is small for the low-frequency oscillator that emits and absorbs photons of low frequency f and long wavelength $\lambda = c/f$. The energy spacing is greater for the high-frequency oscillator, which emits high-frequency photons of short wavelength.

According to Rayleigh's picture, both of these oscillators have the same amount of energy kT and are equally effective at emitting radiation. In Planck's model, however, the high-frequency oscillator is very ineffective as a source of light. To see why, we can use the ideas from Section 39.4 about the populations of various energy states. If we consider all the oscillators of a given frequency f in a box at temperature T, the number of oscillators that have energy nhf is $Ae^{-nhf/kT}$. The ratio of the number of oscillators in the first excited state ($n = 1$, energy hf) to the number of oscillators in the ground state ($n = 0$, energy zero) is

$$\frac{n_1}{n_0} = \frac{Ae^{-hf/kT}}{Ae^{-(0)/kT}} = e^{-hf/kT} \tag{39.23}$$

Let's evaluate Eq. (39.23) for $T = 2000$ K, one of the temperatures shown in Fig. 39.32. At this temperature $kT = 2.76 \times 10^{-20}$ J $= 0.172$ eV. For an oscillator that emits photons of wavelength $\lambda = 3.00\ \mu$m, we can show that $hf = hc/\lambda = 0.413$ eV; for a higher-frequency oscillator that emits photons of wavelength $\lambda = 0.500\ \mu$m, $hf = hc/\lambda = 2.48$ eV. For these two cases Eq. (39.23) gives

$$\frac{n_1}{n_0} = e^{-hf/kT} = 0.0909 \text{ for } \lambda = 3.00\ \mu\text{m}$$

$$\frac{n_1}{n_0} = e^{-hf/kT} = 5.64 \times 10^{-7} \text{ for } \lambda = 0.500\ \mu\text{m}$$

The value for $\lambda = 3.00\ \mu$m means that of all the oscillators that can emit light at this wavelength, 0.0909 of them—about one in 11—are in the first excited state. These excited oscillators can each emit a 3.00-μm photon and contribute it to the radiation inside the box. Hence we would expect that this radiation would be rather plentiful in the spectrum of radiation from a 2000 K blackbody. By contrast, the value for $\lambda = 0.500\ \mu$m means that only 5.64×10^{-7} (about one in two million) of the oscillators that can emit this wavelength are in the first excited

39.33 Energy levels for two of the oscillators that Planck envisioned in the walls of a blackbody like that shown in Fig. 39.30. The spacing between adjacent energy levels for each oscillator is hf, which is smaller for the low-frequency oscillator.

Low-frequency oscillator	High-frequency oscillator
$12hf$ ———	$2hf$ ———
$11hf$ ———	
$10hf$ ———	
$9hf$ ———	
$8hf$ ———	
$7hf$ ———	
$6hf$ ———	hf ———
$5hf$ ———	
$4hf$ ———	
$3hf$ ———	
$2hf$ ———	
$1hf$ ———	
hf ———	
0 ———	0 ———

state. An oscillator can't emit if it's in the ground state, so the amount of radiation in the box at this wavelength is *tremendously* suppressed compared to Rayleigh's prediction. That's why the spectral emittance curve for 2000 K in Fig. 39.32 has such a low value at $\lambda = 0.500$ μm and shorter wavelengths. So Planck's quantum hypothesis provided a natural way to suppress the spectral emittance of a blackbody at short wavelengths, and hence averted the ultraviolet catastrophe that plagued Rayleigh's calculations.

We won't go into all the details of Planck's derivation of the spectral emittance. Here is his result:

$$I(\lambda) = \frac{2\pi hc^2}{\lambda^5 (e^{hc/\lambda kT} - 1)} \qquad \text{(Planck radiation law)} \qquad (39.24)$$

where h is Planck's constant, c is the speed of light, k is Boltzmann's constant, T is the absolute temperature, and λ is the wavelength. This function turns out to agree well with experimental emittance curves such as those in Fig. 39.32.

The Planck radiation law also contains the Wien displacement law and the Stefan–Boltzmann law as consequences. To derive the Wien law, we find the value of λ at which $I(\lambda)$ is maximum by taking the derivative of Eq. (39.24) and setting it equal to zero. We leave it to you to fill in the details; the result is

$$\lambda_m = \frac{hc}{4.965kT} \qquad (39.25)$$

To obtain this result, you have to solve the equation

$$5 - x = 5e^{-x} \qquad (39.26)$$

The root of this equation, found by trial and error or more sophisticated means, is 4.965 to four significant figures. You should evaluate the constant $hc/4.965k$ and show that it agrees with the experimental value of 2.90×10^{-3} m · K given in Eq. (39.21).

We can obtain the Stefan–Boltzmann law for a blackbody by integrating Eq. (39.24) over all λ to find the *total* radiated intensity (see Problem 39.67). This is not a simple integral; the result is

$$I = \int_0^\infty I(\lambda)\, d\lambda = \frac{2\pi^5 k^4}{15c^2 h^3}T^4 = \sigma T^4 \qquad (39.27)$$

in agreement with Eq. (39.19). Our result in Eq. (39.27) also shows that the constant σ in that law can be expressed as a combination of other fundamental constants:

$$\sigma = \frac{2\pi^5 k^4}{15c^2 h^3} \qquad (39.28)$$

You should substitute the values of k, c, and h from Appendix F and verify that you obtain the value $\sigma = 5.6704 \times 10^{-8}$ W/m^2 · K^4 for the Stefan–Boltzmann constant.

The Planck radiation law, Eq. (39.24), looks so different from the unsuccessful Rayleigh expression, Eq. (39.22), that it may seem unlikely that they would agree at large values of λ. But when λ is large, the exponent in the denominator of Eq. (39.24) is very small. We can then use the approximation $e^x \approx 1 + x$ (for $x = 1$). You should verify that when this is done, the result approaches Eq. (39.22), showing that the two expressions do agree in the limit of very large λ. We also note that the Rayleigh expression does not contain h. At very long wavelengths (very small photon energies), quantum effects become unimportant.

Example 39.7 | **Light from the sun**

To a good approximation, the sun's surface is a blackbody with a surface temperature of 5800 K. (We are ignoring the absorption produced by the sun's atmosphere, shown in Fig. 39.9.) (a) At what wavelength does the sun emit most strongly? (b) What is the total radiated power per unit surface area?

SOLUTION

IDENTIFY and SET UP: Our target variables are the peak-intensity wavelength λ_m and the radiated power per area I. Hence we'll use the Wien displacement law, Eq. (39.21) (which relates λ_m to the blackbody temperature T), and the Stefan–Boltzmann law, Eq. (39.19) (which relates I to T).

EXECUTE: (a) From Eq. (39.21),

$$\lambda_m = \frac{2.90 \times 10^{-3} \text{ m} \cdot \text{K}}{T} = \frac{2.90 \times 10^{-3} \text{ m} \cdot \text{K}}{5800 \text{ K}}$$

$$= 0.500 \times 10^{-6} \text{ m} = 500 \text{ nm}$$

(b) From Eq. (39.19),

$$I = \sigma T^4 = (5.67 \times 10^{-8} \text{ W/m}^2 \cdot \text{K}^4)(5800 \text{ K})^4$$

$$= 6.42 \times 10^7 \text{ W/m}^2 = 64.2 \text{ MW/m}^2$$

EVALUATE: The 500-nm wavelength found in part (a) is near the middle of the visible spectrum. This should not be a surprise: The human eye evolved to take maximum advantage of natural light.

The enormous value $I = 64.2 \text{ MW/m}^2$ found in part (b) is the intensity at the *surface* of the sun, a sphere of radius 6.96×10^8 m. When this radiated energy reaches the earth, 1.50×10^{11} m away, the intensity has decreased by the factor $[(6.96 \times 10^8 \text{ m})/(1.50 \times 10^{11} \text{ m})]^2 = 2.15 \times 10^{-5}$ to the still-impressive 1.4 kW/m^2.

Example 39.8 | **A slice of sunlight**

Find the power per unit area radiated from the sun's surface in the wavelength range 600.0 to 605.0 nm.

SOLUTION

IDENTIFY and SET UP: This question concerns the power emitted by a blackbody over a narrow range of wavelengths, and so involves the spectral emittance $I(\lambda)$ given by the Planck radiation law, Eq. (39.24). This requires that we find the area under the $I(\lambda)$ curve between 600.0 and 605.0 nm. We'll *approximate* this area as the product of the height of the curve at the median wavelength $\lambda = 602.5$ nm and the width of the interval, $\Delta\lambda = 5.0$ nm. From Example 39.7, $T = 5800$ K.

EXECUTE: To obtain the height of the $I(\lambda)$ curve at $\lambda = 602.5$ nm $= 6.025 \times 10^{-7}$ m, we first evaluate the quantity $hc/\lambda kT$ in Eq. (39.24) and then substitute the result into Eq. (39.24):

$$\frac{hc}{\lambda kT} = \frac{(6.626 \times 10^{-34} \text{ J} \cdot \text{s})(2.998 \times 10^8 \text{ m/s})}{(6.025 \times 10^{-7} \text{ m})(1.381 \times 10^{-23} \text{ J/K})(5800 \text{ K})} = 4.116$$

$$I(\lambda) = \frac{2\pi(6.626 \times 10^{-34} \text{ J} \cdot \text{s})(2.998 \times 10^8 \text{ m/s})^2}{(6.025 \times 10^{-7} \text{ m})^5(e^{4.116} - 1)}$$

$$= 7.81 \times 10^{13} \text{ W/m}^3$$

The intensity in the 5.0-nm range from 600.0 to 605.0 nm is then approximately

$$I(\lambda)\Delta\lambda = (7.81 \times 10^{13} \text{ W/m}^3)(5.0 \times 10^{-9} \text{ m})$$

$$= 3.9 \times 10^5 \text{ W/m}^2 = 0.39 \text{ MW/m}^2$$

EVALUATE: In part (b) of Example 39.7, we found the power radiated per unit area by the sun at *all* wavelengths to be $I = 64.2 \text{ MW/m}^2$; here we have found that the power radiated per unit area in the wavelength range from 600 to 605 nm is $I(\lambda)\Delta\lambda = 0.39 \text{ MW/m}^2$, about 0.6% of the total.

Test Your Understanding of Section 39.5 (a) Does a blackbody at 2000 K emit x rays? (b) Does it emit radio waves?

APPENDIX A

The Système International d'Unités, abbreviated SI, is the system developed by the General Conference on Weights and Measures and adopted by nearly all the industrial nations of the world. The following material is adapted from the National Institute of Standards and Technology (**http://physics.nist.gov/cuu**).

Quantity	Name of unit	Symbol	
SI base units			
length	meter	m	
mass	kilogram	kg	
time	second	s	
electric current	ampere	A	
thermodynamic temperature	kelvin	K	
amount of substance	mole	mol	
luminous intensity	candela	cd	
SI derived units			**Equivalent units**
area	square meter	m^2	
volume	cubic meter	m^3	
frequency	hertz	Hz	s^{-1}
mass density (density)	kilogram per cubic meter	kg/m^3	
speed, velocity	meter per second	m/s	
angular velocity	radian per second	rad/s	
acceleration	meter per second squared	m/s^2	
angular acceleration	radian per second squared	rad/s^2	
force	newton	N	$kg \cdot m/s^2$
pressure (mechanical stress)	pascal	Pa	N/m^2
kinematic viscosity	square meter per second	m^2/s	
dynamic viscosity	newton-second per square meter	$N \cdot s/m^2$	
work, energy, quantity of heat	joule	J	$N \cdot m$
power	watt	W	J/s
quantity of electricity	coulomb	C	$A \cdot s$
potential difference, electromotive force	volt	V	J/C, W/A
electric field strength	volt per meter	V/m	N/C
electric resistance	ohm	Ω	V/A
capacitance	farad	F	$A \cdot s/V$
magnetic flux	weber	Wb	$V \cdot s$
inductance	henry	H	$V \cdot s/A$
magnetic flux density	tesla	T	Wb/m^2
magnetic field strength	ampere per meter	A/m	
magnetomotive force	ampere	A	
luminous flux	lumen	lm	$cd \cdot sr$
luminance	candela per square meter	cd/m^2	
illuminance	lux	lx	lm/m^2
wave number	1 per meter	m^{-1}	
entropy	joule per kelvin	J/K	
specific heat capacity	joule per kilogram-kelvin	$J/kg \cdot K$	
thermal conductivity	watt per meter-kelvin	$W/m \cdot K$	

Quantity	Name of unit	Symbol	Equivalent units
radiant intensity	watt per steradian	W/sr	
activity (of a radioactive source)	becquerel	Bq	s^{-1}
radiation dose	gray	Gy	J/kg
radiation dose equivalent	sievert	Sv	J/kg
SI supplementary units			
plane angle	radian	rad	
solid angle	steradian	sr	

Definitions of SI Units

meter (m)   The *meter* is the length equal to the distance traveled by light, in vacuum, in a time of 1/299,792,458 second.

kilogram (kg)   The *kilogram* is the unit of mass; it is equal to the mass of the international prototype of the kilogram. (The international prototype of the kilogram is a particular cylinder of platinum-iridium alloy that is preserved in a vault at Sévres, France, by the International Bureau of Weights and Measures.)

second (s)   The *second* is the duration of 9,192,631,770 periods of the radiation corresponding to the transition between the two hyperfine levels of the ground state of the cesium-133 atom.

ampere (A)   The *ampere* is that constant current that, if maintained in two straight parallel conductors of infinite length, of negligible circular cross section, and placed 1 meter apart in vacuum, would produce between these conductors a force equal to 2×10^{-7} newton per meter of length.

kelvin (K)   The *kelvin,* unit of thermodynamic temperature, is the fraction 1/273.16 of the thermodynamic temperature of the triple point of water.

ohm (Ω)   The *ohm* is the electric resistance between two points of a conductor when a constant difference of potential of 1 volt, applied between these two points, produces in this conductor a current of 1 ampere, this conductor not being the source of any electromotive force.

coulomb (C)   The *coulomb* is the quantity of electricity transported in 1 second by a current of 1 ampere.

candela (cd)   The *candela* is the luminous intensity, in a given direction, of a source that emits monochromatic radiation of frequency 540×10^{12} hertz and that has a radiant intensity in that direction of 1/683 watt per steradian.

mole (mol)   The *mole* is the amount of substance of a system that contains as many elementary entities as there are carbon atoms in 0.012 kg of carbon 12. The elementary entities must be specified and may be atoms, molecules, ions, electrons, other particles, or specified groups of such particles.

newton (N)   The *newton* is that force that gives to a mass of 1 kilogram an acceleration of 1 meter per second per second.

joule (J)   The *joule* is the work done when the point of application of a constant force of 1 newton is displaced a distance of 1 meter in the direction of the force.

watt (W)   The *watt* is the power that gives rise to the production of energy at the rate of 1 joule per second.

volt (V)   The *volt* is the difference of electric potential between two points of a conducting wire carrying a constant current of 1 ampere, when the power dissipated between these points is equal to 1 watt.

weber (Wb)   The *weber* is the magnetic flux that, linking a circuit of one turn, produces in it an electromotive force of 1 volt as it is reduced to zero at a uniform rate in 1 second.

lumen (lm)   The *lumen* is the luminous flux emitted in a solid angle of 1 steradian by a uniform point source having an intensity of 1 candela.

farad (F)   The *farad* is the capacitance of a capacitor between the plates of which there appears a difference of potential of 1 volt when it is charged by a quantity of electricity equal to 1 coulomb.

henry (H)   The *henry* is the inductance of a closed circuit in which an electromotive force of 1 volt is produced when the electric current in the circuit varies uniformly at a rate of 1 ampere per second.

radian (rad)   The *radian* is the plane angle between two radii of a circle that cut off on the circumference an arc equal in length to the radius.

steradian (sr)   The *steradian* is the solid angle that, having its vertex in the center of a sphere, cuts off an area of the surface of the sphere equal to that of a square with sides of length equal to the radius of the sphere.

SI Prefixes   To form the names of multiples and submultiples of SI units, apply the prefixes listed in Appendix F.

APPENDIX B

USEFUL MATHEMATICAL RELATIONS

Algebra

$$a^{-x} = \frac{1}{a^x} \qquad a^{(x+y)} = a^x a^y \qquad a^{(x-y)} = \frac{a^x}{a^y}$$

Logarithms: If $\log a = x$, then $a = 10^x$. $\log a + \log b = \log(ab)$ $\log a - \log b = \log(a/b)$ $\log(a^n) = n\log a$

If $\ln a = x$, then $a = e^x$. $\ln a + \ln b = \ln(ab)$ $\ln a - \ln b = \ln(a/b)$ $\ln(a^n) = n\ln a$

Quadratic formula: If $ax^2 + bx + c = 0$, $x = \dfrac{-b \pm \sqrt{b^2 - 4ac}}{2a}$.

Binomial Theorem

$$(a + b)^n = a^n + na^{n-1}b + \frac{n(n-1)a^{n-2}b^2}{2!} + \frac{n(n-1)(n-2)a^{n-3}b^3}{3!} + \cdots$$

Trigonometry
In the right triangle ABC, $x^2 + y^2 = r^2$.

Definitions of the trigonometric functions:
$\sin\alpha = y/r \qquad \cos\alpha = x/r \qquad \tan\alpha = y/x$

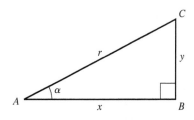

Identities: $\sin^2\alpha + \cos^2\alpha = 1 \qquad\qquad \tan\alpha = \dfrac{\sin\alpha}{\cos\alpha}$

$\sin 2\alpha = 2\sin\alpha\cos\alpha \qquad\qquad \cos 2\alpha = \cos^2\alpha - \sin^2\alpha = 2\cos^2\alpha - 1$
$$= 1 - 2\sin^2\alpha$$

$\sin\frac{1}{2}\alpha = \sqrt{\dfrac{1 - \cos\alpha}{2}} \qquad\qquad \cos\frac{1}{2}\alpha = \sqrt{\dfrac{1 + \cos\alpha}{2}}$

$\sin(-\alpha) = -\sin\alpha \qquad\qquad \sin(\alpha \pm \beta) = \sin\alpha\cos\beta \pm \cos\alpha\sin\beta$
$\cos(-\alpha) = \cos\alpha \qquad\qquad \cos(\alpha \pm \beta) = \cos\alpha\cos\beta \mp \sin\alpha\sin\beta$
$\sin(\alpha \pm \pi/2) = \pm\cos\alpha \qquad\quad \sin\alpha + \sin\beta = 2\sin\frac{1}{2}(\alpha + \beta)\cos\frac{1}{2}(\alpha - \beta)$
$\cos(\alpha \pm \pi/2) = \mp\sin\alpha \qquad\quad \cos\alpha + \cos\beta = 2\cos\frac{1}{2}(\alpha + \beta)\cos\frac{1}{2}(\alpha - \beta)$

For _any_ triangle $A'B'C'$ (not necessarily a right triangle) with sides a, b, and c and angles α, β, and γ:

Law of sines: $\dfrac{\sin\alpha}{a} = \dfrac{\sin\beta}{b} = \dfrac{\sin\gamma}{c}$

Law of cosines: $c^2 = a^2 + b^2 - 2ab\cos\gamma$

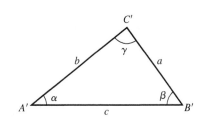

Geometry

Circumference of circle of radius r:	$C = 2\pi r$	Surface area of sphere of radius r:	$A = 4\pi r^2$
Area of circle of radius r:	$A = \pi r^2$	Volume of cylinder of radius r and height h:	$V = \pi r^2 h$
Volume of sphere of radius r:	$V = 4\pi r^3/3$		

Derivatives:

$$\frac{d}{dx}x^n = nx^{n-1}$$

$$\frac{d}{dx}\ln ax = \frac{1}{x}$$

$$\frac{d}{dx}e^{ax} = ae^{ax}$$

$$\frac{d}{dx}\sin ax = a\cos ax$$

$$\frac{d}{dx}\cos ax = -a\sin ax$$

Integrals:

$$\int x^n\,dx = \frac{x^{n+1}}{n+1} \quad (n \neq -1)$$

$$\int \frac{dx}{x} = \ln x$$

$$\int e^{ax}\,dx = \frac{1}{a}e^{ax}$$

$$\int \sin ax\,dx = -\frac{1}{a}\cos ax$$

$$\int \cos ax\,dx = \frac{1}{a}\sin ax$$

$$\int \frac{dx}{\sqrt{a^2 - x^2}} = \arcsin\frac{x}{a}$$

$$\int \frac{dx}{\sqrt{x^2 + a^2}} = \ln\left(x + \sqrt{x^2 + a^2}\right)$$

$$\int \frac{dx}{x^2 + a^2} = \frac{1}{a}\arctan\frac{x}{a}$$

$$\int \frac{dx}{(x^2 + a^2)^{3/2}} = \frac{1}{a^2}\frac{x}{\sqrt{x^2 + a^2}}$$

$$\int \frac{x\,dx}{(x^2 + a^2)^{3/2}} = -\frac{1}{\sqrt{x^2 + a^2}}$$

Power series (convergent for range of x shown):

$$(1 + x)^n = 1 + nx + \frac{n(n-1)x^2}{2!} + \frac{n(n-1)(n-2)}{3!}x^3 + \cdots \quad (|x| < 1)$$

$$\sin x = x - \frac{x^3}{3!} + \frac{x^5}{5!} - \frac{x^7}{7!} + \cdots \quad (\text{all } x)$$

$$\cos x = 1 - \frac{x^2}{2!} + \frac{x^4}{4!} - \frac{x^6}{6!} + \cdots \quad (\text{all } x)$$

$$\tan x = x + \frac{x^3}{3} + \frac{2x^2}{15} + \frac{17x^7}{315} + \cdots \quad (|x| < \pi/2)$$

$$e^x = 1 + x + \frac{x^2}{2!} + \frac{x^3}{3!} + \cdots \quad (\text{all } x)$$

$$\ln(1 + x) = x - \frac{x^2}{2} + \frac{x^3}{3} - \frac{x^4}{4} + \cdots \quad (|x| < 1)$$

APPENDIX C

THE GREEK ALPHABET

Name	Capital	Lowercase	Name	Capital	Lowercase	Name	Capital	Lowercase
Alpha	A	α	Iota	I	ι	Rho	P	ρ
Beta	B	β	Kappa	K	κ	Sigma	Σ	σ
Gamma	Γ	γ	Lambda	Λ	λ	Tau	T	τ
Delta	Δ	δ	Mu	M	μ	Upsilon	Y	υ
Epsilon	E	ϵ	Nu	N	ν	Phi	Φ	ϕ
Zeta	Z	ζ	Xi	Ξ	ξ	Chi	X	χ
Eta	H	η	Omicron	O	o	Psi	Ψ	ψ
Theta	Θ	θ	Pi	Π	π	Omega	Ω	ω

APPENDIX D

PERIODIC TABLE OF THE ELEMENTS

Group	1	2	3	4	5	6	7	8	9	10	11	12	13	14	15	16	17	18
Period																		
1	1 **H** 1.008																	2 **He** 4.003
2	3 **Li** 6.941	4 **Be** 9.012											5 **B** 10.811	6 **C** 12.011	7 **N** 14.007	8 **O** 15.999	9 **F** 18.998	10 **Ne** 20.180
3	11 **Na** 22.990	12 **Mg** 24.305											13 **Al** 26.982	14 **Si** 28.086	15 **P** 30.974	16 **S** 32.065	17 **Cl** 35.453	18 **Ar** 39.948
4	19 **K** 39.098	20 **Ca** 40.078	21 **Sc** 44.956	22 **Ti** 47.867	23 **V** 50.942	24 **Cr** 51.996	25 **Mn** 54.938	26 **Fe** 55.845	27 **Co** 58.933	28 **Ni** 58.693	29 **Cu** 63.546	30 **Zn** 65.409	31 **Ga** 69.723	32 **Ge** 72.64	33 **As** 74.922	34 **Se** 78.96	35 **Br** 79.904	36 **Kr** 83.798
5	37 **Rb** 85.468	38 **Sr** 87.62	39 **Y** 88.906	40 **Zr** 91.224	41 **Nb** 92.906	42 **Mo** 95.94	43 **Tc** (98)	44 **Ru** 101.07	45 **Rh** 102.906	46 **Pd** 106.42	47 **Ag** 107.868	48 **Cd** 112.411	49 **In** 114.818	50 **Sn** 118.710	51 **Sb** 121.760	52 **Te** 127.60	53 **I** 126.904	54 **Xe** 131.293
6	55 **Cs** 132.905	56 **Ba** 137.327	71 **Lu** 174.967	72 **Hf** 178.49	73 **Ta** 180.948	74 **W** 183.84	75 **Re** 186.207	76 **Os** 190.23	77 **Ir** 192.217	78 **Pt** 195.078	79 **Au** 196.967	80 **Hg** 200.59	81 **Tl** 204.383	82 **Pb** 207.2	83 **Bi** 208.980	84 **Po** (209)	85 **At** (210)	86 **Rn** (222)
7	87 **Fr** (223)	88 **Ra** (226)	103 **Lr** (262)	104 **Rf** (261)	105 **Db** (262)	106 **Sg** (266)	107 **Bh** (264)	108 **Hs** (269)	109 **Mt** (268)	110 **Ds** (271)	111 **Rg** (272)	112 **Uub** (285)	113 **Uut** (284)	114 **Uuq** (289)	115 **Uup** (288)	116 **Uuh** (292)	117 **Uus** (294)	118 **Uuo**

Lanthanoids

57 **La** 138.905	58 **Ce** 140.116	59 **Pr** 140.908	60 **Nd** 144.24	61 **Pm** (145)	62 **Sm** 150.36	63 **Eu** 151.964	64 **Gd** 157.25	65 **Tb** 158.925	66 **Dy** 162.500	67 **Ho** 164.930	68 **Er** 167.259	69 **Tm** 168.934	70 **Yb** 173.04

Actinoids

89 **Ac** (227)	90 **Th** (232)	91 **Pa** (231)	92 **U** (238)	93 **Np** (237)	94 **Pu** (244)	95 **Am** (243)	96 **Cm** (247)	97 **Bk** (247)	98 **Cf** (251)	99 **Es** (252)	100 **Fm** (257)	101 **Md** (258)	102 **No** (259)

For each element the average atomic mass of the mixture of isotopes occurring in nature is shown. For elements having no stable isotope, the approximate atomic mass of the longest-lived isotope is shown in parentheses. For elements that have been predicted but not yet confirmed, no atomic mass is given. All atomic masses are expressed in atomic mass units (1 u = 1.660538782(83) × 10^{-27} kg), equivalent to grams per mole (g/mol).

APPENDIX E

UNIT CONVERSION FACTORS

Length

$1 \text{ m} = 100 \text{ cm} = 1000 \text{ mm} = 10^6 \, \mu\text{m} = 10^9 \text{ nm}$

$1 \text{ km} = 1000 \text{ m} = 0.6214 \text{ mi}$

$1 \text{ m} = 3.281 \text{ ft} = 39.37 \text{ in.}$

$1 \text{ cm} = 0.3937 \text{ in.}$

$1 \text{ in.} = 2.540 \text{ cm}$

$1 \text{ ft} = 30.48 \text{ cm}$

$1 \text{ yd} = 91.44 \text{ cm}$

$1 \text{ mi} = 5280 \text{ ft} = 1.609 \text{ km}$

$1 \text{ Å} = 10^{-10} \text{ m} = 10^{-8} \text{ cm} = 10^{-1} \text{ nm}$

$1 \text{ nautical mile} = 6080 \text{ ft}$

$1 \text{ light year} = 9.461 \times 10^{15} \text{ m}$

Area

$1 \text{ cm}^2 = 0.155 \text{ in.}^2$

$1 \text{ m}^2 = 10^4 \text{ cm}^2 = 10.76 \text{ ft}^2$

$1 \text{ in.}^2 = 6.452 \text{ cm}^2$

$1 \text{ ft}^2 = 144 \text{ in.}^2 = 0.0929 \text{ m}^2$

Volume

$1 \text{ liter} = 1000 \text{ cm}^3 = 10^{-3} \text{ m}^3 = 0.03531 \text{ ft}^3 = 61.02 \text{ in.}^3$

$1 \text{ ft}^3 = 0.02832 \text{ m}^3 = 28.32 \text{ liters} = 7.477 \text{ gallons}$

$1 \text{ gallon} = 3.788 \text{ liters}$

Time

$1 \text{ min} = 60 \text{ s}$

$1 \text{ h} = 3600 \text{ s}$

$1 \text{ d} = 86{,}400 \text{ s}$

$1 \text{ y} = 365.24 \text{ d} = 3.156 \times 10^7 \text{ s}$

Angle

$1 \text{ rad} = 57.30° = 180°/\pi$

$1° = 0.01745 \text{ rad} = \pi/180 \text{ rad}$

$1 \text{ revolution} = 360° = 2\pi \text{ rad}$

$1 \text{ rev/min (rpm)} = 0.1047 \text{ rad/s}$

Speed

$1 \text{ m/s} = 3.281 \text{ ft/s}$

$1 \text{ ft/s} = 0.3048 \text{ m/s}$

$1 \text{ mi/min} = 60 \text{ mi/h} = 88 \text{ ft/s}$

$1 \text{ km/h} = 0.2778 \text{ m/s} = 0.6214 \text{ mi/h}$

$1 \text{ mi/h} = 1.466 \text{ ft/s} = 0.4470 \text{ m/s} = 1.609 \text{ km/h}$

$1 \text{ furlong/fortnight} = 1.662 \times 10^{-4} \text{ m/s}$

Acceleration

$1 \text{ m/s}^2 = 100 \text{ cm/s}^2 = 3.281 \text{ ft/s}^2$

$1 \text{ cm/s}^2 = 0.01 \text{ m/s}^2 = 0.03281 \text{ ft/s}^2$

$1 \text{ ft/s}^2 = 0.3048 \text{ m/s}^2 = 30.48 \text{ cm/s}^2$

$1 \text{ mi/h} \cdot \text{s} = 1.467 \text{ ft/s}^2$

Mass

$1 \text{ kg} = 10^3 \text{ g} = 0.0685 \text{ slug}$

$1 \text{ g} = 6.85 \times 10^{-5} \text{ slug}$

$1 \text{ slug} = 14.59 \text{ kg}$

$1 \text{ u} = 1.661 \times 10^{-27} \text{ kg}$

$1 \text{ kg has a weight of } 2.205 \text{ lb when } g = 9.80 \text{ m/s}^2$

Force

$1 \text{ N} = 10^5 \text{ dyn} = 0.2248 \text{ lb}$

$1 \text{ lb} = 4.448 \text{ N} = 4.448 \times 10^5 \text{ dyn}$

Pressure

$1 \text{ Pa} = 1 \text{ N/m}^2 = 1.450 \times 10^{-4} \text{ lb/in.}^2 = 0.209 \text{ lb/ft}^2$

$1 \text{ bar} = 10^5 \text{ Pa}$

$1 \text{ lb/in.}^2 = 6895 \text{ Pa}$

$1 \text{ lb/ft}^2 = 47.88 \text{ Pa}$

$1 \text{ atm} = 1.013 \times 10^5 \text{ Pa} = 1.013 \text{ bar}$
$= 14.7 \text{ lb/in.}^2 = 2117 \text{ lb/ft}^2$

$1 \text{ mm Hg} = 1 \text{ torr} = 133.3 \text{ Pa}$

Energy

$1 \text{ J} = 10^7 \text{ ergs} = 0.239 \text{ cal}$

$1 \text{ cal} = 4.186 \text{ J (based on 15° calorie)}$

$1 \text{ ft} \cdot \text{lb} = 1.356 \text{ J}$

$1 \text{ Btu} = 1055 \text{ J} = 252 \text{ cal} = 778 \text{ ft} \cdot \text{lb}$

$1 \text{ eV} = 1.602 \times 10^{-19} \text{ J}$

$1 \text{ kWh} = 3.600 \times 10^6 \text{ J}$

Mass–Energy Equivalence

$1 \text{ kg} \leftrightarrow 8.988 \times 10^{16} \text{ J}$

$1 \text{ u} \leftrightarrow 931.5 \text{ MeV}$

$1 \text{ eV} \leftrightarrow 1.074 \times 10^{-9} \text{ u}$

Power

$1 \text{ W} = 1 \text{ J/s}$

$1 \text{ hp} = 746 \text{ W} = 550 \text{ ft} \cdot \text{lb/s}$

$1 \text{ Btu/h} = 0.293 \text{ W}$

APPENDIX F

NUMERICAL CONSTANTS

Fundamental Physical Constants*

Name	Symbol	Value
Speed of light in vacuum	c	2.99792458×10^8 m/s
Magnitude of charge of electron	e	$1.602176487(40) \times 10^{-19}$ C
Gravitational constant	G	$6.67428(67) \times 10^{-11}$ N$\cdot$m^2/kg^2
Planck's constant	h	$6.62606896(33) \times 10^{-34}$ J$\cdot$s
Boltzmann constant	k	$1.3806504(24) \times 10^{-23}$ J/K
Avogadro's number	N_A	$6.02214179(30) \times 10^{23}$ molecules/mol
Gas constant	R	$8.314472(15)$ J/mol$\cdot$K
Mass of electron	m_e	$9.10938215(45) \times 10^{-31}$ kg
Mass of proton	m_p	$1.672621637(83) \times 10^{-27}$ kg
Mass of neutron	m_n	$1.674927211(84) \times 10^{-27}$ kg
Permeability of free space	μ_0	$4\pi \times 10^{-7}$ Wb/A$\cdot$m
Permittivity of free space	$\epsilon_0 = 1/\mu_0 c^2$	$8.854187817\ldots \times 10^{-12}$ C^2/N$\cdot$m^2
	$1/4\pi\epsilon_0$	$8.987551787\ldots \times 10^9$ N$\cdot$m^2/C^2

Other Useful Constants*

Mechanical equivalent of heat		4.186 J/cal ($15°$ calorie)
Standard atmospheric pressure	1 atm	1.01325×10^5 Pa
Absolute zero	0 K	$-273.15°$C
Electron volt	1 eV	$1.602176487(40) \times 10^{-19}$ J
Atomic mass unit	1 u	$1.660538782(83) \times 10^{-27}$ kg
Electron rest energy	$m_e c^2$	$0.510998910(13)$ MeV
Volume of ideal gas ($0°$C and 1 atm)		$22.413996(39)$ liter/mol
Acceleration due to gravity (standard)	g	9.80665 m/s^2

*Source: National Institute of Standards and Technology (**http://physics.nist.gov/cuu**). Numbers in parentheses show the uncertainty in the final digits of the main number; for example, the number 1.6454(21) means 1.6454 ± 0.0021. Values shown without uncertainties are exact.

Astronomical Data[†]

Body	Mass (kg)	Radius (m)	Orbit radius (m)	Orbit period
Sun	1.99×10^{30}	6.96×10^8	—	—
Moon	7.35×10^{22}	1.74×10^6	3.84×10^8	27.3 d
Mercury	3.30×10^{23}	2.44×10^6	5.79×10^{10}	88.0 d
Venus	4.87×10^{24}	6.05×10^6	1.08×10^{11}	224.7 d
Earth	5.97×10^{24}	6.38×10^6	1.50×10^{11}	365.3 d
Mars	6.42×10^{23}	3.40×10^6	2.28×10^{11}	687.0 d
Jupiter	1.90×10^{27}	6.91×10^7	7.78×10^{11}	11.86 y
Saturn	5.68×10^{26}	6.03×10^7	1.43×10^{12}	29.45 y
Uranus	8.68×10^{25}	2.56×10^7	2.87×10^{12}	84.02 y
Neptune	1.02×10^{26}	2.48×10^7	4.50×10^{12}	164.8 y
Pluto[‡]	1.31×10^{22}	1.15×10^6	5.91×10^{12}	247.9 y

[†]Source: NASA Jet Propulsion Laboratory Solar System Dynamics Group (**http://ssd.jpl.nasa.gov**), and P. Kenneth Seidelmann, ed., ***Explanatory Supplement to the Astronomical Almanac*** (University Science Books, Mill Valley, CA, 1992), pp. 704–706. For each body, "radius" is its radius at its equator and "orbit radius" is its average distance from the sun or (for the moon) from the earth.

[‡]In August 2006, the International Astronomical Union reclassified Pluto and other small objects that orbit the sun as "dwarf planets."

Prefixes for Powers of 10

Power of ten	Prefix	Abbreviation	Pronunciation
10^{-24}	yocto-	y	*yoc*-toe
10^{-21}	zepto-	z	*zep*-toe
10^{-18}	atto-	a	*at*-toe
10^{-15}	femto-	f	*fem*-toe
10^{-12}	pico-	p	*pee*-koe
10^{-9}	nano-	n	*nan*-oe
10^{-6}	micro-	μ	*my*-crow
10^{-3}	milli-	m	*mil*-i
10^{-2}	centi-	c	*cen*-ti
10^{3}	kilo-	k	*kil*-oe
10^{6}	mega-	M	*meg*-a
10^{9}	giga-	G	*jig*-a or *gig*-a
10^{12}	tera-	T	*ter*-a
10^{15}	peta-	P	*pet*-a
10^{18}	exa-	E	*ex*-a
10^{21}	zetta-	Z	*zet*-a
10^{24}	yotta-	Y	*yot*-a

Examples:

1 femtometer = 1 fm = 10^{-15} m

1 picosecond = 1 ps = 10^{-12} s

1 nanocoulomb = 1 nC = 10^{-9} C

1 microkelvin = 1μK = 10^{-6} K

1 millivolt = 1 mV = 10^{-3} V

1 kilopascal = 1 kPa = 10^3 Pa

1 megawatt = 1 MW = 10^6 W

1 gigahertz = 1 GHz = 10^9 Hz

ANSWERS TO ODD-NUMBERED PROBLEMS

Chapter 6

6.1 a) 3.60 J b) −0.900 J
  c) 0 d) 0
  e) 2.70 J
6.3 a) 74 N b) 333 J
  c) −330 J d) 0, 0
  e) 0
6.5 a) −1750 J b) no
6.7 a) (i) 9.00 J (ii) −9.00 J
  b) (i) 0 (ii) 9.00 J (iii) −9.00 J (iv) 0
  c) zero for each block
6.9 a) (i) 0 (ii) 0
  b) (i) 0 (ii) −25.1 J
6.11 a) 324 J b) −324 J
  c) 0
6.13 a) 36,000 J b) 4
6.15 a) 1.0×10^{16} J b) 2.4
6.17 a) 7.50 N b) (i) 9.00 J (ii) 5.40 J
  c) 14.4 J, same d) 2.97 m/s
6.19 a) 43.2 m/s b) 101 m/s
  c) 5.80 m d) 3.53 m/s
  e) 7.35 m
6.21 $\sqrt{2gh(1 + \mu_k/\tan\alpha)}$
6.23 32.0 N
6.25 a) 4.48 m/s b) 3.61 m/s
6.27 a) 4.96 m/s b) 1.43 m/s², 4.96 m/s
6.29 a) $\dfrac{v_0^2}{2\mu_k g}$ b) (i) $^1/_2$ (ii) 4 (iii) 2
6.31 a) 40.0 N/m b) 0.456 N
6.33 b) 14.4 cm, 13.6 cm, 12.8 cm
6.35 a) 2.83 m/s b) 3.46 m/s
6.37 8.5 cm
6.39 a) 1.76 b) 0.666 m/s
6.41 a) 4.0 J b) 0
  c) −1.0 J d) 3.0 J
  e) −1.0 J
6.43 a) 2.83 m/s b) 2.40 m/s
6.45 a) 0.0565 m b) 0.57 J, no
6.47 8.17 m/s
6.49 a) 360,000 J b) 100 m/s
6.51 $3.9 \times 10^{13} P$
6.53 745 W ≈ 1 hp
6.55 a) 84.6/min b) 22.7/min
6.57 29.6 kW
6.59 0.20 W
6.61 877 J
6.63 a) 532 J b) −315 J
  c) 0 d) −202 J
  e) 15 J f) 1.2 m/s
6.65 a) 987 J b) 3.02 s
6.67 a) 2.59×10^{12} J b) 4800 J
6.69 a) 1.8 m/s = 4.0 mph
  b) 180 m/s² ≈ 18g, 900 N
6.71 a) $k\left(\dfrac{1}{x_2} - \dfrac{1}{x_1}\right)$, negative
  b) $k\left(\dfrac{1}{x_1} - \dfrac{1}{x_2}\right)$, positive
  c) same magnitude but opposite signs because the net work is zero
6.73 a) 5.11 m b) 0.304
  c) 10.3 m
6.75 a) 0.11 N b) 7.1 N c) 0.33 J
6.77 a) 2.56 m/s b) 3.52 N c) 13.1 J
6.79 6.3×10^4 N/m
6.81 1.1 m
6.83 a) 1.02×10^4 N/m, 8.16 m
6.85 a) 0.600 m b) 1.50 m/s
6.87 0.786
6.89 1.3 m
6.91 a) 1.10×10^5 J b) 1.30×10^5 J
  c) 3.99 kW
6.93 3.6 h
6.95 a) 1.26×10^5 J b) 1.46 W
6.97 a) 2.4 MW b) 61 MW c) 6.0 MW
6.99 a) 513 W b) 354 W c) 52.1 W
6.101 a) 358 N b) 47.1 hp c) 4.06 hp
  d) 2.03%
6.103 a) $\dfrac{Mv^2}{6}$ b) 6.1 m/s
  c) 3.9 m/s d) 0.40 J, 0.60 J

Chapter 7

7.1 a) 6.6×10^5 J b) -7.7×10^5 J
7.3 a) 820 N b) (i) 0 (ii) 740 J
7.5 a) 24.0 m/s b) 24.0 m/s c) part (b)
7.7 a) 2.0 m/s b) 9.8×10^{-7} J, 2.0 J/kg
  c) 200 m, 63 m/s d) 5.9 J/kg
7.9 a) (i) 0 (ii) 0.98 J b) 2.8 m/s
  c) only gravity is constant d) 5.1 N
7.11 −5400 J
7.13 a) 880 J b) −157 J c) 470 J d) 253 J
  e) 3.16 m/s², 7.11 m/s, 253 J
7.15 a) 80.0 J b) 5.0 J
7.17 a) (i) $4U_0$ (ii) $U_0/4$
  b) (i) $x_0\sqrt{2}$ (ii) $x_0/\sqrt{2}$
7.19 a) 6.32 cm b) 12 cm
7.21 ±0.092 m
7.23 a) 3.03 m/s, as it leaves the spring
  b) 95.9 m/s², when the spring has its maximum compression
7.25 a) 4.46×10^5 N/m b) 0.128 m
7.27 a) −308 J b) −616 J
  c) nonconservative
7.29 a) −3.6 J b) −3.6 J
  c) −7.2 J d) nonconservative
7.31 a) −59 J b) −42 J
  c) −59 J d) nonconservative
7.33 a) 8.41 m/s b) 638 J
7.35 2.46 N, +x-direction
7.37 130 m/s², 132° counterclockwise from the +x-axis
7.39 a) $F(r) = (12a/r^{13}) - (6b/r^7)$
  b) $(2a/b)^{1/6}$, stable c) $b^2/4a$
  d) $a = 6.67 \times 10^{-138}$ J·m¹², $b = 6.41 \times 10^{-78}$ J·m⁶
7.41 a) zero, 637 N b) 2.99 m/s
7.43 0.41
7.45 a) 16.0 m/s b) 11,500 N
7.47 a) 20.0 m along the rough bottom
  b) −78.4 J
7.49 a) 22.2 m/s b) 16.4 m c) no
7.51 0.602 m
7.53 15.5 m/s
7.55 4.4 m/s
7.57 a) no b) yes, $150
7.59 a) 7.00 m/s b) 8.82 N
7.61 a) $mg(1 - h/d)$ b) 441 N
  c) $\sqrt{2gh(1 - y/d)}$
7.63 48.2°
7.65 a) 0.392 b) −0.83 J
7.67 a) $U(x) = \frac{1}{2}\alpha x^2 + \frac{1}{3}\beta x^3$ b) 7.85 m/s
7.69 7.01 m/s
7.71 a) $\dfrac{m(g + a)^2}{2gh}$ b) $\dfrac{2gh}{g + a}$
7.73 a) 0.480 m/s b) 0.566 m/s
7.75 a) 3.87 m/s b) 0.10 m
7.77 0.456 N
7.79 a) 4.4×10^{12} J
  b) 2.7×10^3 m³, 9.0×10^{-4} m
7.81 119 J
7.83 a) −50.6 J b) −67.5 J c) nonconservative
7.85 b) 0, 3.38 J, 0, 0; 3.38 J c) nonconservative
7.87 b) $v(x) = \sqrt{\dfrac{2\alpha}{mx_0^2}\left[\dfrac{x_0}{x} - \left(\dfrac{x_0}{x}\right)^2\right]}$
  c) $x = 2x_0, v = \sqrt{\dfrac{\alpha}{2mx_0^2}}$ d) 0
  e) $v(x) = \sqrt{\dfrac{2\alpha}{mx_0^2}\left[\dfrac{x_0}{x} - \left(\dfrac{x_0}{x}\right)^2 - \dfrac{2}{9}\right]}$
  f) first case: x_0, ∞; second case: $3x_0/2, 3x_0$

Chapter 11

11.1 29.8 cm
11.3 1.35 m
11.5 5.45 kN

11.7 a) 1000 N, 0.800 m from the end where the 600-N force is applied
  b) 800 N, 0.75 m from the end where the 600-N force is applied
11.9 a) 550 N
  b) 0.614 m from A
11.11 a) 1920 N b) 1140 N
11.13 a) T = 2.60w; 3.28w, 37.6°
  b) T = 4.10w; 5.39w, 48.8°
11.15 272 N on each hand, 130 N on each foot
11.17 246 N, 0.34 m from the front feet
11.19 270 N, 303 N, 40°
11.21 a) 0.800 m b) clockwise
  c) 0.800 m, clockwise
11.23 b) 208 N
11.25 1.4 mm
11.27 2.0×10^{11} Pa
11.29 a) 3.1×10^{-3}(upper), 2.0×10^{-3} (lower)
  b) 1.6 mm (upper), 1.0 mm (lower)
11.31 a) 150 atm b) 1.5 km, no
11.33 8.6°
11.35 4.8×10^9 Pa, 2.1×10^{-10} Pa⁻¹
11.37 b) 6.6×10^5 N c) 1.8 mm
11.39 3.41×10^7 Pa
11.41 10.2 m/s²
11.43 20.0 kg
11.45 a) 525 N b) 222 N, 328 N c) 1.48
11.47 tail: 600 N down, wing: 7300 N up
11.49 a) 140 N b) 6 cm to the right
11.51 a) 379 N b) 141 N
11.53 160 N to the right, 213 N upward
11.55 49.9 cm
11.57 a) 370 N b) when he starts to raise his leg c) no
11.59 a) $V = mg + w, H = T = \left(w + \dfrac{mg}{4}\right)\cot\theta$
  b) 926 N c) 6.00°
11.61 4900 N
11.63 b) 2000 N = 2.72mg c) 4.4 mm
11.65 a) 4.90 m b) 60 N
11.67 a) 175 N at each hand, 200 N at each foot
  b) 91 N at each hand and at each foot
11.69 a) 1150 N b) 1940 N
  c) 918 N d) 0.473
11.71 590 N (person above), 1370 N (person below); person above
11.73 a) $\dfrac{T_{\max} hD}{L\sqrt{h^2 + D^2}}$
  b) positive, $\dfrac{T_{\max} h}{L\sqrt{h^2 + D^2}}\left(1 - \dfrac{D^2}{h^2 + D^2}\right)$
11.75 a) 7140 N, tall walls b) 7900 N
11.77 a) 268 N b) 232 N
  c) 366 N
11.79 a) 0.424 N (A), 1.47 N (B), 0.424 N (C)
  b) 0.848 N
11.81 a) 27° to tip, 31° to slip, tips first
  b) 27° to tip, 22° to slip, slips first
11.83 a) 80 N (A), 870 N (B) b) 1.92 m
11.85 a) T = 3700 N, 2000 N upward
11.87 a) 0.36 mm b) 0.045 mm
  c) 0.33 mm
11.89 a) 0.54 cm b) 0.42 cm
11.91 a) 0.70 m from A b) 0.60 m from A
11.93 a) 1.63 m
  b) brass: 2.00×10^8 Pa, nickel: 4.00×10^8 Pa
  c) brass: 2.22×10^{-3}, nickel: 1.90×10^{-3}
11.95 0.0542 L
11.97 a) 600 N b) 13.5 kN
  c) $F = \dfrac{\mu_s w}{\sin\theta - \mu_s \cos\theta}$ (to slide),
  $F = \dfrac{w}{(1/9)\cos\theta + 2\sin\theta}$ (to tip), 66°
11.99 $h^2/L + L/2$; L if $h > L/\sqrt{2}$
11.101 a) 0.66 mm b) 0.022 J c) 8.35×10^{-3} J
  d) -3.04×10^{-2} J e) 3.04×10^{-2} J

Chapter 14

14.1 a) 2.15 ms, 2930 rad/s
b) 2.00×10^4 Hz, 1.26×10^5 rad/s
c) 4.3×10^{14} Hz $\le f \le 7.5 \times 10^{14}$ Hz;
1.3×10^{-15} s $\le T \le 2.3 \times 10^{-15}$ s
d) 2.0×10^{-7} s, 3.1×10^7 rad/s

14.3 5530 rad/s, 1.14 ms
14.5 0.0500 s
14.7 a) 0.167 s   b) 37.7 rad/s   c) 0.0844 kg
14.9 a) 0.150 s   b) 0.0750 s
14.11 a) 0.98 m   b) $\pi/2$ rad
c) $x = (-0.98 \text{ m}) \sin{[(12.2 \text{ rad/s})t]}$

14.13 a) -2.71 m/s^2
b) $x = (1.46 \text{ cm}) \cos{[(15.7 \text{ rad/s})t}$
$+ 0.715 \text{ rad}]$,
$v_x = (-22.9 \text{ cm/s}) \sin{[(15.7 \text{ rad/s})t}$
$+ 0.715 \text{ rad}]$,
$a_x = (-359 \text{ cm/s}^2) \cos{[(15.7 \text{ rad/s})t}$
$+ 0.715 \text{ rad}]$

14.15 120 kg
14.17 a) 0.253 kg   b) 1.21 cm
c) 3.03 N
14.19 a) 1.51 s   b) 26.0 N/m
c) 30.8 cm/s   d) 1.92 N
e) -0.0125 m, 30.4 cm/s, 0.216 m/s^2
f) 0.324 N
14.21 a) $x = (0.0030 \text{ m}) \cos{[(2760 \text{ rad/s})t]}$
b) 8.3 m/s, 2.3×10^4 m/s^2
c) $da_x/dt = (6.3 \times 10^7 \text{ m/s}^3)$
$\times \sin{[(2760 \text{ rad/s})t]}$, 6.3×10^7 m/s^3
14.23 127 m/s^2
14.25 a) 1.48 m/s   b) 2.96×10^{-5} J
14.27 a) 1.20 m/s   b) 1.11 m/s
c) 36 m/s^2 d) 13.5 m/s^2 e) 0.36 J
14.29 $3M, \sqrt[3]{4}$
14.31 0.240 m
14.33 $A/2\sqrt{2}$
14.35 a) 0.0778 m   b) 1.28 Hz   c) 0.624 m/s
14.37 a) 4.06 cm   b) 1.21 m/s   c) 29.8 rad/s
14.39 b) 23.9 cm, 1.45 Hz
14.41 a) 2.7×10^{-8} kg · m^2
b) 4.3×10^{-6} N · m/rad
14.43 0.0512 kg · m^2
14.45 a) 0.25 s   b) 0.25 s
14.47 0.407 swings per second
14.49 10.7 m/s^2
14.51 a) 2.84 s   b) 2.89 s
c) 2.89 s, -2%
14.53 0.129 kg · m^2
14.55 $A: 2\pi\sqrt{\dfrac{L}{g}}, B: \dfrac{2\sqrt{2}}{3}\left(2\pi\sqrt{\dfrac{L}{g}}\right)$, pendulum A
14.57 $A: 2\pi\sqrt{\dfrac{L}{g}}, B: \sqrt{\dfrac{11}{10}}\left(2\pi\sqrt{\dfrac{L}{g}}\right)$, pendulum B
14.59 a) 0.393 Hz   b) 1.73 kg/s
14.61 a) A b) $-Ab/2m$
c) $A\left(\dfrac{b^2}{2m^2} - \dfrac{k}{m}\right)$; negative if $b < \sqrt{2km}$,
zero if $b = \sqrt{2km}$, positive if $b > \sqrt{2km}$
14.63 a) kg/s
c) (i) $5.0\dfrac{F_{\max}}{k}$ (ii) $2.5\dfrac{F_{\max}}{k}$
14.65 0.353 m
14.67 a) 1.11×10^4 m/s^2 b) 5.00×10^3 N
c) 23.6 m/s, 125 J   d) 37.5 kW
e) 1.21×10^4 N, 36.7 m/s, 302 J, 141 kW
14.69 a) none of them change
b) $^1/_4$ as great   c) $^1/_2$ as great
d) $1/2\sqrt{5}$ as great
e) potential energy is the same, kinetic energy
is 1/5 as great
14.71 a) 24.4 cm   b) 0.221 s   c) 1.19 m/s
14.73 a) 0.373 Hz, 0.426 m, 2.68 s   b) 1.34 s
14.75 2.00 m

14.77 a) 0.107 m   b) 2.42 s
14.79 $(0.921)\left(\dfrac{1}{2\pi}\sqrt{\dfrac{g}{L}}\right)$
14.81 a) 1.49 s   b) -2.12×10^{-4} s per s, shorter
c) 0.795 s
14.83 a) 0.150 m/s   b) 0.112 m/s^2 downward
c) 0.700 s   d) 4.38 m
14.85 a) 2.6 m/s   b) 0.21 m   c) 0.49 s
14.87 9.08×10^{24} kg
14.89 1.17 s
14.91 0.505 s
14.93 c) -7.57×10^{-19} J   e) 8.39×10^{12} Hz
14.95 0.705 Hz, 14.5°
14.97 $2\pi\sqrt{\dfrac{M}{3k}}$
14.99 $\dfrac{1}{4\pi}\sqrt{\dfrac{6g}{\sqrt{2}L}}$
14.101 a) $k_1 + k_2$ b) $k_1 + k_2$
c) $\dfrac{k_1 k_2}{k_1 + k_2}$ d) $\sqrt{2}$
14.103 a) $Mv^2/6$ c) $\omega = \sqrt{\dfrac{3k}{M}}, M' = M/3$

Chapter 15

15.1 a) 0.439 m, 1.28 ms
b) 0.219 m
15.3 220 m/s = 800 km/h
15.5 a) 1.7 cm to 17 m
b) 4.3×10^{14} Hz to 7.5×10^{14} Hz
c) 1.5 cm   d) 6.4 cm
15.7 a) 25.0 Hz, 0.0400 s, 19.6 rad/m
b) $y(x, t) = (0.0700 \text{ m}) \cos{[(19.6 \text{ m}^{-1})x +}$
$(157 \text{ rad/s})t]$ c) 4.95 cm
d) 0.0050 s
15.9 a) yes   b) yes   c) no
d) $v_y = \omega A \cos{(kx + \omega t)}$,
$a_y = -\omega^2 A \sin{(kx + \omega t)}$
15.11 a) 4 mm   b) 0.040 s   c) 0.14 m, 3.5 m/s
d) 0.24 m, 6.0 m/s   e) no
15.13 b) $+x$-direction
15.15 a) 16.3 m/s   b) 0.136 m
c) both increase by a factor of $2\sqrt{2}$
15.17 0.337 kg
15.19 a) 18.6 N   b) 29.1 m/s
15.21 a) 10.0 m/s   b) 0.250 m
c) $y(x, t) = (3.00 \text{ cm}) \cos{[\pi(8.00 \text{ rad/m})x -}$
$(80.0\pi \text{ rad/s})t]$ d) 1890 m/s^2 e) yes
15.23 4.51 mm
15.25 a) 95 km   b) 0.25 μW/m^2
c) 110 kW
15.27 a) 0.050 W/m^2 b) 22 kJ
15.29 9.48×10^{27} W
15.37 a) $(1.33 \text{ m})n, n = 0, 1, 2, \ldots$
b) $(1.33 \text{ m})(n + ^1/_2), n = 0, 1, 2, \ldots$
15.41 a) 96.0 m/s   b) 461 N
c) 1.13 m/s, 426 m/s^2
15.43 b) 2.80 cm   c) 277 cm
d) 185 cm, 7.96 Hz, 0.126 s, 1470 cm/s
e) 280 cm/s
f) $y(x, t) = (5.60 \text{ cm}) \times$
$\sin{[(0.0906 \text{ rad/cm})x]} \sin{[(133 \text{ rad/s})t]}$
15.45 a) $y(x, t) = (4.60 \text{ mm}) \times$
$\sin{[(6.98 \text{ rad/m})x]} \sin{[(742 \text{ rad/s})t]}$
b) 3rd harmonic   c) 39.4 Hz
15.47 a) 45.0 cm   b) no
15.49 a) 311 m/s   b) 246 Hz
c) 245 Hz, 1.40 m
15.51 a) 20.0 Hz, 126 rad/s, 3.49 rad/m
b) $y(x, t) = (2.50 \times 10^{-3} \text{ m}) \times$
$\cos{[(3.49 \text{ rad/m})x - (126 \text{ rad/s})t]}$
c) $y(0, t) = (2.50 \times 10^{-3} \text{ m}) \times$
$\cos{[(126 \text{ rad/s})t]}$
d) $y(1.35 \text{ m}, t) = (2.50 \times 10^{-3} \text{ m}) \times$
$\cos{[(126 \text{ rad/s})t - 3\pi/2 \text{ rad}]}$
e) 0.315 m/s
f) -2.50×10^{-3} m, 0
15.53 a) $\dfrac{7L}{2}\sqrt{\dfrac{\mu_1}{F}}$ b) no

15.55 a) $\dfrac{2\pi A}{\lambda}\sqrt{\dfrac{FL}{M}}$ b) increase F by a factor of 4
15.57 a) $\dfrac{4\pi^2 F \Delta x}{\lambda^2}$
15.59 32.4 Hz
15.61 1.83 m
15.63 330 Hz (copper), 447 Hz (aluminum)
15.65 c) C/B
15.67 b) ω must be decreased by a
factor of $1/\sqrt{2}$, k must be decreased by a
factor of $1/\sqrt{8}$
15.69 a) 7.07 cm   b) 0.400 kW
15.71 d) $P(x, t) = -Fk\omega A^2 \sin^2(kx + \omega t)$
15.73 $(0.800 \text{ Hz})n, n = 1, 2, 3, \ldots$
15.75 c) $2A, 2A\omega, 2A\omega^2$
15.77 233 N
15.79 a) $0, L$ b) $0, L/2, L$ d) no
15.81 1780 kg/m^3
15.83 a) $r = 0.640$ mm, $L = 0.40$ m
b) 380 Hz
15.85 b) $u_k = \dfrac{1}{2}\mu\omega^2 A^2 \sin^2(kx - \omega t)$
e) $u_p = \dfrac{1}{2}Fk^2 A^2 \sin^2(kx - \omega t)$

Chapter 16

16.1 a) 0.344 m   b) 1.2×10^{-5} m
c) 6.9 m, 50 Hz
16.3 a) 7.78 Pa   b) 77.8 Pa   c) 778 Pa
16.5 a) 90 m   b) 102 kHz   c) 1.4 cm
d) 4.4 mm to 8.8 mm   e) 6.2 MHz
16.7 90.8 m
16.9 81.4°C
16.11 0.208 s
16.13 a) 5.5×10^{-15} J   b) 0.074 mm/s
16.15 a) 9.44×10^{-11} m, 0.434 m
b) 5.66×10^{-9} m, 0.100 m
16.17 a) 1.95 Pa   b) 4.58×10^{-3} W/m^2
c) 96.6 dB
16.19 a) 4.4×10^{-12} W/m^2 b) 6.4 dB
c) 5.8×10^{-11} m
16.21 14.0 dB
16.23 a) 2.0×10^{-7} W/m^2 b) 6.0 m   c) 290 m
16.25 a) *fundamental:* displacement node at 0.60 m,
pressure nodes at 0 and 1.20 m; *first overtone:*
displacement nodes at 0.30 m and 0.90 m,
pressure nodes at 0, 0.60 m, 1.20 m; *second
overtone:* displacement nodes at 0.20 m,
0.60 m, 1.00 m, pressure nodes at 0, 0.40 m,
0.80 m, 1.20 m
b) *fundamental:* displacement node at 0,
pressure node at 1.20 m; *first overtone:*
displacement nodes at 0 and 0.80 m, pressure
nodes at 0.40 m and 1.20 m; *second overtone:*
displacement nodes at 0, 0.48 m, 0.96 m,
pressure nodes at 0.24 m, 0.72 m, 1.20 m
16.27 506 Hz, 1517 Hz, 2529 Hz
16.29 a) 767 Hz   b) no
16.31 a) 614 Hz   b) 1230 Hz
16.33 a) 172 Hz   b) 86 Hz
16.35 0.125 m
16.37 destructive
16.39 a) 433 Hz   b) loosen
16.41 1.3 Hz
16.43 780 m/s
16.45 a) 375 Hz   b) 371 Hz   c) 4 Hz
16.47 a) 0.25 m/s   b) 0.91 m
16.49 19.8 m/s
16.51 a) 1910 Hz   b) 0.188 m
16.53 $0.0950c$, toward us
16.55 a) 36.0°   b) 2.23 s
16.57 b) 0.68%
16.59 a) 1.00   b) 8.00
c) 4.73×10^{-8} m = 47.3 nm
16.61 b) $3f_0$
16.63 flute harmonic $3N$ resonates with string
harmonic $4N, N = 1, 3, 5, \ldots$
16.65 a) stopped   b) 7th and 9th   c) 0.439 m
16.67 a) 375 m/s   b) 1.39   c) 0.8 cm

16.69 1.27
16.71 a) 548 Hz b) 652 Hz
16.73 a) 2186 Hz, 0.157 m b) 2920 Hz, 0.118 m
       c) 734 Hz
16.75 a) 0.0674 m b) 147 Hz
16.77 b) 2.0 m/s
16.79 a) 1.2×10^6 m/s
       b) 3.6×10^{16} m = 3.8 ly
       c) 5200 y, about 4100 BCE

16.81 a) $f_0\left(\dfrac{2v_w}{v - v_w}\right)$ b) $f_0\left(\dfrac{2v_w}{v + v_w}\right)$

16.83 a) 9.69 cm/s, 667 m/s^2

Chapter 17

17.1 a) $-81.0°$F b) $134.1°$F c) $88.0°$F
17.3 a) 27.2 C° b) -55.6 C°
17.5 a) -18.0 F° b) -10.0 C°
17.7 0.964 atm
17.9 a) $-282°$C b) 47,600 Pa, no
17.11 0.39 m
17.13 Death Valley: 1.9014 cm, Greenland: 1.8964 cm
17.15 0.26 mm
17.17 49.4°C
17.19 1.7×10^{-5} (C°)$^{-1}$
17.21 a) 1.431 cm^2 b) 1.436 cm^2
17.23 a) 3.2×10^{-5} (C°)$^{-1}$ b) 2.6×10^9 Pa
17.25 a) 5.0 mm b) -8.4×10^7 Pa
17.27 5.79×10^5 J
17.29 240 J/kg·K
17.31 23 min
17.33 a) -1.54 kJ b) 0.0121 C°
17.35 45.2 C°
17.37 0.0613 C°
17.39 a) 215 J/kg·K b) water c) too small
17.41 27.5°C
17.43 a) 5.9 C° b) yes; 109°F
17.45 150°C
17.47 7.6 min
17.49 36.4 kJ, 8.70 kcal, 34.5 Btu
17.51 357 m/s
17.53 3.45 L
17.55 5.05×10^{15} kg
17.57 0.0674 kg
17.59 2.10 kg
17.61 190 g
17.63 a) 222 K/m b) 10.7 W c) 73.3°C
17.65 a) $-5.8°$C b) 11 W/m^2
17.67 4.0×10^{-3} W/m·C°
17.69 105.5°C
17.71 a) 21 kW b) 6.4 kW
17.73 2.1 cm^2
17.75 a) 1.61×10^{11} m b) 5.43×10^6 m
17.77 a) 35.1°M b) 39.6 C°
17.79 53.3°C
17.81 35.0°C
17.83 23.0 cm, 7.0 cm
17.85 b) 1.9×10^8 Pa
17.87 a) 99.4 N c) -4.2 Hz, falls
17.89 a) 87°C b) $-80°$C
17.91 20.2°C
17.93 54.3
17.95 a) 83.6 J b) 1.86 J/mol·K
       c) 5.60 J/mol·K
17.97 a) 2.70×10^7 J b) 6.89 C° c) 19.3 C°
17.99 2.5 cm
17.101 a) 86.1°C b) no ice, no steam, 0.130 kg
        liquid water
17.103 a) 100°C b) 0.0214 kg steam, 0.219 kg
        liquid water
17.105 1.743 kg
17.107 a) 93.9 W b) 1.35
17.109 2.9
17.111 c) 170 h d) 1.5×10^{10} s $\approx$ 500 y, no
17.113 0.106 W/m·K
17.115 5.82 g
17.117 a) 1.04 kW b) 87.1 W c) 1.13 kW
        d) 28 g e) 1.1 bottles
17.119 a) 69.6°C
17.121 1.76 C°
17.123 b) 0°C d) 3140 C°/m e) 121 W f) zero

g) 1.1×10^{-4} m^2/s h) -11 C°/s
i) 9.17 s j) decrease k) -7.71 C°/s
17.125 a) 103°C b) 27 W
17.127 a) (i) 280 W (ii) 0.248 W (iii) 2.10 kW
        (iv) 116 W; radiation from the sun
        b) 3.72 L/h c) 1.4 L/h

Chapter 18

18.1 a) 0.122 mol b) 14,700 Pa, 0.145 atm
18.3 0.100 atm
18.5 a) 0.0136 kg/m^3 (Mars), 67.6 kg/m^3 (Venus),
      5.39 kg/m^3 (Titan)
18.7 503°C
18.9 16.8 kPa
18.11 0.159 L
18.13 0.0508V
18.15 a) 70.2°C b) yes
18.17 850 m
18.19 a) 6.95×10^{-16} kg b) 2.32×10^{-13} kg/m^3
18.21 22.8 kPa
18.23 a) \$8720 b) 3.88 cm
18.25 a) 8.2×10^{-17} atm b) no
18.27 55.6 mol, 3.35×10^{25} molecules
18.29 a) 9.00×10^{-5} m^3 b) 3.1×10^{-10} m
        c) about the same
18.31 b) 1.004
18.33 (d) must be true, the others could be true
18.35 a) 1.93×10^6 m/s, no b) 7.3×10^{10} K
18.37 a) 6.21×10^{-21} J b) 2.34×10^5 m^2/s^2
        c) 484 m/s d) 2.57×10^{-23} kg·m/s
        e) 1.24×10^{-19} N f) 1.24×10^{-17} Pa
        g) 8.17×10^{21} molecules
        h) 2.45×10^{22} molecules
18.39 3800°C
18.41 a) 2600 J b) 1560 J
18.43 a) 741 J/kg·K, $c_w = 5.65c_{N_2}$
        b) 5.65 kg; 4.85 m^3
18.45 a) 923 J/kg·K
        b) The value calculated is too large by
        about 1.4%.
18.47 a) 337 m/s b) 380 m/s c) 412 m/s
18.49 a) 610 Pa b) 22.12 MPa
18.51 no, no
18.53 a) 11.8 kPa b) 0.566 L
18.55 272°C
18.57 0.213 kg
18.59 a) $-179°$C b) 1.2×10^{26} molecules/m^3
        c) The atmosphere of Titan is 4.8 times denser
        than that of the earth.
18.61 1.92 atm
18.63 a) 30.7 cylinders b) 8420 N c) 7800 N
18.65 a) 26.2 m/s b) 16.1 m/s, 5.44 m/s
        c) 1.74 m
18.67 $\approx 5 \times 10^{27}$ atoms
18.69 a) A b) B c) 4250°C d) B
18.71 a) 4.65×10^{-26} kg b) 6.11×10^{-21} J
        c) 2.04×10^{24} molecules d) 12.5 kJ

18.73 b) r_2 c) $r_1 = \dfrac{R_0}{2^{1/6}}, r_2 = R_0, 2^{-1/6}$ d) U_0

18.75 a) 517 m/s b) 298 m/s
18.77 b) 1.40×10^5 K (N), 1.01×10^4 K (H)
        c) 6370 K (N), 459 K (H)
18.79 a) 1.24×10^{-14} kg
        b) 4.16×10^{11} molecules
        c) 2.95 μm, no
18.81 a) $2R = 16.6$ J/mol·K b) less
18.83 CO$_2$: 20.79 J/mol·K, 27%; SO$_2$: 24.94
        J/mol·K, 21%; H$_2$S: 24.94 J/mol·K, 3.9%
18.85 $3kT/m$
18.87 b) 0.0421N c) $2.94 \times 10^{-21}N$
        d) 0.0297N, $2.08 \times 10^{-21}N$
        e) 0.0595N, $4.15 \times 10^{-21}N$
18.89 42.6%
18.91 a) 4.5×10^{11} m
        b) 703 m/s, 6.4×10^8 s ($\approx$20 y)
        c) 1.4×10^{-14} Pa d) 650 m/s, evaporate
        f) 2×10^5 K, >3 times the temperature of the
        sun, no

Chapter 19

19.1 b) 1330 J
19.3 b) -6180 J
19.5 a) 0.942 atm
19.7 a) $(p_1 - p_2)(V_2 - V_1)$ b) Negative of work
      done in reverse direction
19.9 a) 34.7 kJ b) 80.4 kJ c) no
19.11 a) 278 K b) 0, 162 J c) 53 J
19.13 a) 16.4 min b) 139 m/s = 501 km/h
19.15 a) 0 b) $T_b = 2T_a$ c) $U_b = U_a + 700$ J
19.17 a) positive b) $W_{\rm I} > 0, W_{\rm II} < 0$
        c) into the system d) into the system for
        loop I, out of the system for loop II
19.19 b) 208 J c) on the piston d) 712 J
        e) 920 J f) 208 J
19.21 a) 948 K b) 900 K
19.23 2/5
19.25 a) 25.0 K b) 17.9 K c) higher for (a)
19.27 a) -605 J b) 0 c) liberates 605 J
19.29 a) 476 kPa b) -10.6 kJ c) 1.59, heated
19.31 5.05 kJ, internal energy and temperature both
        increase
19.33 b) 224 J c) -224 J
19.35 11.6°C
19.37 a) 600 J out of the gas
        b) -1500 J, decreases
19.39 a) increases b) 4800 J
19.41 a) 45.0 J b) liberates 65.0 J
        c) 23.0 J, 22.0 J
19.43 a) the same b) absorbs 4.0 kJ c) 8.0 kJ
19.45 b) -2460 J
19.47 a) 0.80 L b) 305 K, 1220 K, 1220 K
        c) ab: 76 J, into the gas;
           ca: -107 J, out of the gas
           bc: 56 J, into the gas
        d) ab: 76 J, increase
           bc: 0, no change
           ca: -76 J, decrease
19.49 a) 3.00 kJ, into the gas
        b) 2.00 kJ, into the gas c) $Q_a > Q_b$
19.51 a) 899°C b) 12.2 kJ
        c) 42.6 kJ d) 45.6 kJ
19.53 -0.226 m^3
19.55 a) 4.32×10^{-4} m^3 b) 648 J c) 715 kJ
        d) 715 kJ e) no substantial difference
19.57 3.4×10^5 J/kg
19.59 b) 11.9 C°
19.61 a) 0.173 m b) 207°C c) 74.7 kJ
19.63 a) $Q = 300$ J, $\Delta U = 0$
        b) $Q = 0$, $\Delta U = -300$ J
        c) $Q = 750$ J, $\Delta U = 450$ J
19.65 a) $W = 738$ J, $Q = 2590$ J, $\Delta U = 1850$ J
        b) $W = 0$, $Q = -1850$ J, $\Delta U = -1850$ J
        c) $\Delta U = 0$
19.67 a) $W = -187$ J, $Q = -654$ J, $\Delta U = -467$ J
        b) $W = 113$ J, $Q = 0$, $\Delta U = -113$ J
        c) $W = 0$, $Q = 580$ J, $\Delta U = 580$ J

19.69 a) $p_0 + \dfrac{mg}{\pi r^2}$

       b) $-\left(\dfrac{y}{h}\right)(p_0\pi r^2 + mg)$

       c) $\dfrac{1}{2\pi}\sqrt{\dfrac{g}{h}\left(1 + \dfrac{p_0\pi r^2}{mg}\right)}$, no

Chapter 20

20.1 a) 6500 J b) 34%
20.3 a) 23% b) 12,400 J
      c) 0.350 g d) 222 kW = 298 hp
20.5 a) 12.3 atm b) 5470 J (ca) c) 3723 J (bc)
      d) 1747 J e) 31.9%
20.7 a) 58% b) 1.4%
20.9 a) 16.2 kJ b) 50.2 kJ
20.11 1.7 h
20.13 a) 215 J b) 378 K c) 39.0%
20.15 a) 42.4 kJ b) 441°C
20.17 a) 492 J b) 212 W c) 5.4
20.19 4.5 kJ
20.21 37.1 hp

20.23 a) 429 J/K   b) −393 J/k   c) 36 J/K
20.25 a) irreversible   b) 1250 J/K
20.27 −6.31 J/K
20.29 a) 6.05 kJ/K
    b) about five times greater for vaporization
20.31 a) 33.3 J/K   b) irreversible
20.33 a) no   b) 18.3 J/K   c) 18.3 J/K
20.35 a) 121 J   b) 3800 cycles
20.37 a) 33 J   b) 117 J   c) 45°C   d) 0   e) 96.2 g
20.39 −5.8 J/K, decrease
20.41 b) absorbed during bc, rejected during ab
    and ca c) $T_a = T_b = 241$ K, $T_c = 481$ K
    d) 610 J, 610 J   e) 8.7%
20.43 a) 21.0 kJ (enters), 16.6 kJ (leaves)
    b) 4.4 kJ, 21%   c) 67%
20.45 a) 7.0%   b) 3.0 MW, 2.8 MW
    c) 6×10^5 kg/h = 6×10^5 L/h
20.47 a) 2.00 atm, 4.00 L; 2.00 atm, 6.00 L; 1.11 atm,
    6.00 L; 1.67 atm, 4.00 L
    b) $1 \rightarrow 2$: 1422 J, 405 J; $2 \rightarrow 3$: −1355 J, 0;
    $3 \rightarrow 4$: −274 J, −274 J; $4 \rightarrow 1$: 339 J, 0
    c) 131 J   d) 7.44%, 44.4%
20.49 a) 2.26%   b) 29.4 J (gravitational), 1.30 kJ
    c) 1.11×10^{-3} candy bars
20.51 a) ab: 225 kJ, 90 kJ, 135 kJ;
    bc: −240 kJ, 0, −240 kJ;
    ca: 45 kJ, −60 kJ, 105 kJ
    b) 30 kJ, 30 kJ, 0   c) 11.1%
20.53 $1 - T_C/T_H$
20.55 a) 122 J, −78 J   b) 5.10×10^{-4} m^3
    c) at b: 2.32 MPa, 4.81×10^{-5} m^3, 771 K;
    at c: 4.01 MPa, 4.81×10^{-5} m^3, 1332 K;
    at d: 0.147 MPa, 5.10×10^{-4} m^3, 518 K
    d) 61.1%, 77.5%
20.57 b) 357 kJ, 62 kJ   c) 385 kJ, 34 kJ
20.59 a) $nC_V \ln(T_c/T_b), nC_V \ln(T_a/T_d)$ b) zero
20.61 a) −107 J/K   b) 147 J/K   c) 0
    d) 39.4 J/K

Chapter 33

33.1   39.4°
33.3   a) 2.04×10^8 m/s
    b) 442 nm
33.5   a) 1.55   b) 550 nm

33.7   a) 47.5°   b) 66.0°
33.9 2.51×10^8 m/s
33.11 a) 2.34   b) 82°
33.13 a) $f, n\lambda, nv$
    b) $f, (n/n')\lambda, (n/n')v$
33.15 71.8°
33.17 a) 51.3°   b) 33.6°
33.19 a) 58.1°   b) 22.8°
33.21 1.77
33.23 462 nm
33.25 0.6°
33.27 $0.375I_0$
33.29 a) $I_0/2, 0.125I_0, 0.0938I_0$ b) 0
33.31 a) 1.40   b) 35.5°
33.33 $\arccos\left(\dfrac{\cos\theta}{\sqrt{2}}\right)$

33.35 6.38 W/m^2
33.37 a) $I_0/2, 0.250I_0, 0.125I_0$, linearly polarized
    along the axis of each filter   b) $I_0/2$ linearly
    polarized along the axis of the filter; 0
33.41 a) 46.7°   b) 13.4°
33.43 72.1°
33.45 1.28
33.47 1.53
33.49 1.84
33.51 a) 48.6°   b) 48.6°
33.53 39.1°
33.55 0.23°, about the same
33.59 a) 38.9°   c) 5.0°
33.61 a) 35°   b) $I_p = 19.9$ W/m^2, $I_0 = 10.1$ W/m^2
33.63 23.3°

33.67 a) $\Delta = 2\theta_a^A - 6\arcsin\left(\dfrac{\sin\theta_a^A}{n}\right) + 2\pi$

    b) $\cos^2\theta_2 = \dfrac{n^2 - 1}{8}$

    c) violet: $\theta_2 = 71.55°$, $\Delta = 233.2°$;
    red: $\theta_2 = 71.94°$, $\Delta = 230.1°$

Chapter 35

35.1   a) 14 cm, 48 cm, 82 cm, 116 cm, 150 cm
    b) 31 cm, 65 cm, 99 cm, 133 cm
35.3   b) 427 Hz   b) 0.796 m
35.5   0.75 m, 2.00 m, 3.25 m, 4.50 m, 5.75 m,
    7.00 m, 8.25 m

35.7   a) 2.0 m   b) constructively
    c) 1.0 m, destructively
35.9   1.14 mm
35.11 0.83 mm
35.13 a) 39   b) ±73.3°
35.15 12.6 cm
35.17 1200 nm
35.19 a) $0.750I_0$ b) 80 nm
35.21 1670 rad
35.23 71.4 m
35.25 114 nm
35.27 0.0234°
35.29 a) 55.6 nm   b) (i) 2180 nm   (ii) 11.0
    wavelengths
35.31 a) 514 nm, green   b) 603 nm, orange
35.33 0.11 μm
35.35 0.570 mm
35.37 1.54 mm
35.39 a) 96.0 nm   b) no, no
35.41 a) 1.58 mm (green), 1.72 mm (orange)
    b) 3.45 mm (violet), 4.74 mm (green),
    5.16 mm (orange)   c) 9.57 μm
35.43 1.730
35.45 0°, 27.3°, 66.5°
35.47 1.57
35.49 above centerline: 3.14°, 15.9°, 29.5°, 45.4°,
    68.6°; below centerline: 9.45°, 22.5°, 37.0°, 55.2°
35.51 6.8×10^{-5} (C°)$^{-1}$
35.53 $\lambda/2d$, independent of m
35.55 b) 0.72 m
35.57 1.42

35.59 b) $I = I_0\cos^2\left\{\dfrac{\pi[d\sin\theta + L(n-1)]}{\lambda_0}\right\}$

    c) $\sin\theta = \dfrac{m\lambda_0 - L(n-1)}{d}$

35.61 14.0

PHOTO CREDITS

Chapter 6 Opener: Flickr RM/Getty Images; 6.1: Allison Michael Orenstein/Getty Images; App. 6.1: Steve Gschmeissner/Photo Researchers, Inc.; 6.13: Bojan Fatur/iStockphoto; App. 6.2: Steve Gschmeissner/Photo Researchers, Inc.; 6.26: Hulton Archive/Getty Images; 6.27a: Keystone/Getty Images; 6.27b: Adrian Pingstone; 6.28: Shutterstock

Chapter 7 Opener: Geoff de Feu/Getty Images; 7.1: Shutterstock; App. 7.1: Yuji Sakai/Getty Images; 7.3: Robert F. Bukaty/AP; 7.5: Joggie Botma/iStockphoto; 7.12: Jupiterimages/Brand X/Corbis; App. 7.2: iStockphoto; 7.15: William Loy/iStockphoto; 7.21: Bill Grove/iStockphoto; App. 7.3: Matt Naylor/iStockphoto; App. 7.4: Peter Menzel/Photo Researchers, Inc.

Chapter 11 Opener: iStockphoto; 11.3: Jeremy Woodhouse/Getty Images; 11.12a: Shutterstock; 11.12b: Jonathan Blair/Corbis; 11.12c: Photodisc Green/Getty Images; App. 11.2: Dante Fenolio/Photo Researchers, Inc.

Chapter 14 Opener: Tim McCaig/iStockphoto; App. 14.1: Nigel Cattlin/Photo Researchers, Inc.; 14.7: American Diagnostic Corporation; 14.21: Frank Herholdt/Getty Images; 14.25: Christopher Griffin/Alamy; App. 14.2: Shutterstock

Chapter 15 Opener: REUTERS/Nicky Loh; App. 15.1: MARCO POLO COLLECTION/Alamy; 15.2: REUTERS/Charles Platiau; 15.5: David Parker/Photo Researchers, Inc.; 15.12: iStockphoto; App. 15.2: iStockphoto; 15.18: Reproduced from *PSSC Physics*, 2nd ed. (1965), D.C. Heath & Company with Educational Development Center, Inc., Newton Massachusets; 15.23: Richard Megna/Fundamental Photographs; 15.25: iStockphoto; 15.27: National Optical Astronomy Observatories

Chapter 16 Opener: iStockphoto; App. 16.1: Steve Thorne/Getty Images; 16.5a: Lisa Pines/Getty Images; 16.5c: David Young-Wolff/PhotoEdit Inc.; 16.6: Dorling Kindersley; 16.9: Kretztechnik/Photo Researchers, Inc.; 16.10: Eastcott-Momatiuk/The Image Works; 16.15: Dorothy Y Riess/The Image Works; App. 16.2: iStockphoto; 16.20: Martin Bough/Fundamental Photographs; 16.25: Shutterstock; 16.28: Mark Reinstein/The Image Works; 16.35c: NASA/Langley Research Center; 16.36: NASA/Robert A. Hoover, Dryden Flight Research Center

Chapter 17 Opener: Shutterstock; 17.4: Exergen Corporation; App.17.1: Shutterstock; 17.5: Sargent-Welch/VWR International, Courtesy of Cenco Physics; 17.11: NASA/Jim Ross, Dryden Flight Research Center; 17.13: Eric Schrader - Pearson Science; 17.16: Roger Freedman; 17.18: Paul Seheult/

Corbis; 17.19: Adam Hart-Davis/Photo Researchers, Inc.; 17.20: Richard Megna/Fundamental Photographs; 17.22: Shutterstock; App. 17.2a: iStockphoto; App. 17.2b: Paul Nicklen/National Geographic Creative/Getty Image; 17.27: Hugh D. Young; 17.28: Dr. Arthur Tucker/Photo Researchers, Inc.

Chapter 18 Opener: iStockphoto; 18.2: John Powell/The Image Works; 18.10: ThermoMicroscopes/Park Scientific Instruments; 18.13: Stone/Getty Images; 18.14: ARCTIC IMAGES/Alamy; 18.16: David Grossman/The Image Works; App. 18.2: Ray Coleman/Photo Researchers, Inc.; 18.25: PhotoDisc/Getty Images; E18.25: David Malin, Royal Observatory, Edinburgh and Anglo-Australian Telescope Board; P18.91: David Malin, Royal Observatory, Edinburgh and Anglo-Australian Telescope Board

Chapter 19 Opener: Richard A. Cooke III/Getty Images; 19.1: John P. Surey; 19.2a: PhotoDisc/StockTrek/Getty Images; 19.2b: iStockphoto; App. 19.1: iStockphoto; 19.10: Shutterstock; 19.14: Tom Branch/Photo Researchers, Inc.; 19.15: Shutterstock; P19.57: Photolibrary

Chapter 20 Opener: G. Brad Lewis/Getty Images; 20.2: Shutterstock; App. 20.1: Shutterstock; 20.12: Bill Bachman/Photo Researchers, Inc.; 20.16: U.S. Air Force photo by Staff Sgt. Robert Zoellner; 20.17: Erich Schrempp/Photo Researchers, Inc.; App. 20.2: iStockphoto; 20.20: Eric Schrader - Pearson Science

Chapter 33 Opener: Peter Aprahamian/Photo Researchers, Inc.; 33.1: iStockphoto; 33.2: National Institutes of Health/Photo Researchers, Inc.; 33.9: Roger A. Freedman; 33.10a: NASA/John F. Kennedy Space Center; 33.10b: iStockphoto; App. 33.1: Peter Herring/imagequestmarine.com; 33.13b: Susan Schwartzenberg, The Exploratorium; 33.16: VEM / Photo Researchers, Inc.; 33.17: iStockphoto; 33.20a: Randy O'Rourke/Corbis; 33.22a: Dougal Walters/Getty Images; 33.22b: Pixtal/AGE Fotostock; 33.26: Diane Hirsch/

Fundamental Photographs; 33.31: Peter Aprahamian/Sharples Stress Engineers/Photo Researchers, Inc.; App. 33.2: iStockphoto; 33.33: Roger Freedman; 33.37a: K. Nomachi/Photo Researchers, Inc.

Chapter 35 Opener: iStockphoto; 35.4: Roger Freedman; 35.6: Pearson Education; 35.11b: Shutterstock; 35.16b: Bausch & Lomb Incorporated; 35.17: Bausch & Lomb Incorporated; App. 35.1, top: iStockphoto; App. 35.1, right and bottom: Peter Vukusic; App. 35.2: J. Reed and J.K.Gimzewski, UCLA California Nanosystems Institute, 2007

Chapter 39 Opener: Lee D. Simon/Photo Researchers, Inc.; 39.31: Royal Swedish Academy of Sciences

INDEX